SIXTH EDITION

LITERATURE
THE HUMAN EXPERIENCE

SIXTH EDITION

LITERATURE
THE HUMAN EXPERIENCE

RICHARD ABCARIAN AND MARVIN KLOTZ, EDITORS

California State University, Northridge

ST. MARTIN'S PRESS

New York

Senior editor: Catherine Pusateri
Associate editor: Melissa Cook Candela
Managing editor: Patricia Mansfield-Phelan
Project editor: Suzanne Holt/Erica Appel
Production supervisor: Alan Fischer
Art director: Sheree Goodman
Art research: Elnora Bode
Cover design: Jeanette Jacobs Design
Cover art: Rene Magritte, *The False Mirror*, 1935. Private collection. © 1993
    C. Herscovici/ARS, NY.

For information, write:
St. Martin's Press, Inc.
175 Fifth Avenue
New York, NY 10010

ISBN: 0-312-08408-0

ACKNOWLEDGMENTS

Woody Allen, "Death Knocks." From *Getting Even* by Woody Allen. Copyright © 1968 by Woody Allen. Reprinted by permission of Random House, Inc.

Anonymous, "The Ruin." From *The Earliest English Poems* translated by Michael Alexander. (Penguin Classics, Second edition, 1977). Copyright © Michael Alexander, 1966, 1977. Reprinted by permission of Penguin Books Ltd.

W. H. Auden, "Five Songs," "In Memory of W.B. Yeats," "Musee des Beaux Arts," "The Unknown Citizen." From *W. H. Auden: Collected Poems* by W. H. Auden, ed. by Edward Mendelson. Copyright 1940 and renewed 1968 by W. H. Auden. Reprinted by permission of Random House, Inc., and Faber and Faber.

Donald W. Baker, "Formal Application." Reprinted by permission of the author.

Toni Cade Bambara, "The Lesson." From *Gorilla, My Love* by Toni Cade Bambara. Reprinted by permission of Random House, Inc.

Elizabeth Brewster, "Disqualification." Reprinted by permission of the author.

Amiri Baraka (LeRoi Jones), *The Dutchman.* From *The Dutchman and The Slave* published by William Morrow & Co., 1964. Reprinted by permission of Sterling Lord Literistic, Inc. Copyright © 1964 by Amiri Baraka.

Donald Barthelme, "The Sandman." From *Sadness* by Donald Barthelme copyright 1972 by Donald Barthelme, reprinted with the permission of Wylie, Aitken & Stone, Inc.

Elizabeth Bishop, "One Art." From *The Complete Poems 1927–1979* by Elizabeth Bishop. Copyright © 1979, 1983 by Alice Helen Methfessel. Reprinted with permission of Farrar, Straus & Giroux, Inc.

Louise Bogan, "The Dream." From *The Blue Estuaries* by Louise Bogan. Copyright © 1968 by Louise Bogan. Reprinted with permission of Farrar, Straus & Giroux.

Acknowledgments and copyrights are continued at the back of the book on pages 1383–1390, which constitute an extension of the copyright page.

To Joan and Debra

Love: a word properly applied to our delight in particular kinds of food; sometimes metaphorically spoken of the favorite objects of all our appetites.

Henry Fielding

PREFACE

And wisdom is a butterfly
And not a gloomy bird of prey.

W. B. Yeats

The short stories, poems, and plays in this sixth edition of *Literature: The Human Experience* represent literary traditions ranging from 400 B.C. to the present and reflect diverse cultural and ethnic experiences. We have arranged the works into four thematic groups—Innocence and Experience, Conformity and Rebellion, Love and Hate, and The Presence of Death. Each section is introduced by a short essay of general observations on the theme. Within each thematic section, the works are grouped by genre—fiction, poetry, drama—and arranged chronologically by the author's birth date. Each work is dated to indicate the date of composition or earliest appearance. We have not attempted to date traditional ballads.

Study questions and writing topics follow about half the stories and poems, all the plays, and each thematic section. These questions are designed to help students focus on the works' thematic and stylistic elements, and often invite the students to find, in the work they read, connections to their own lives.

The first of several appendices, "Poems about Poetry," offers some verse meditations by poets on what poetry is and why it is written. These poems reveal diverse motives and aims, as well as the difficulty even poets have in describing exactly what it is they do.

The next three appendices, "Reading Fiction," "Reading Poetry," and "Reading Drama," acquaint students with some formal concepts and historical considerations basic to the study of literature. These are general introductions that instructors will no doubt want to augment as they discuss the formal sources of readers' pleasure or, for that matter, boredom.

A "Glossary of Critical Approaches" is new to this edition. Since the publication of the first edition of this anthology some twenty years ago, the so-called New Criticism, with its unyielding emphasis on formalism, has been dethroned by a wide variety of competing critical approaches. Whatever else one might say about this development, it has certainly had the important and salutary effect of broadening and deepening the range of discourse about literature. For example, feminist criticism, like Marxism before it, has insisted on the connections between literature and the larger world of power and politics. Deconstructionism, by calling our attention to the instability and contradictoriness of language, has challenged the view that great literary works embody a consciously designed seamless web of interrelated parts. Reader-response criticism celebrates the reader by arguing that, in any meaningful sense, a literary text only comes into being when a particular reader confronts a particular work. Finally, the new historical criticism contends that knowledge of historical context is as important as any other kind of knowledge in understanding a literary work. The "Glossary of Critical Approaches" attempts to explain the basic assumptions of these various schools of critical practice. We hope that from what may seem a bewildering and even confusing array of approaches, students will at least learn that there is not some "correct" way to approach a literary work and, further, that many of the approaches complement one another.

"Writing about Literature" outlines a number of writing strategies ranging from the free writing of a student's journal through discussions of more formal explication, analysis, and comparison-and-contrast essay assignments. We provide several samples of student writing to guide students in the preparation of their own papers. "Suggested Topics for Writing" offers instructors over eighty focused writing assignments. The appendix concludes with a section illustrating manuscript mechanics based on the *MLA Handbook*.

The appendix "Biographical Notes on the Authors" provides students with information about some of the major events, biographical and literary, in the career of each author. We hope these notes will not only satisfy students' natural curiosity about writers' lives but will also, from time to time, stimulate them enough to want to learn more.

A "Glossary of Literary Terms," with brief excerpts to illustrate the definitions, concludes the text.

We preserve, of course, the major writers in the Western dramatic tradition—Sophocles, Shakespeare, Ibsen—and retain Susan Glaspell, Bruce Jay Friedman, Imamu Amiri Baraka, and Woody Allen. As well, we are restoring George Bernard Shaw's pungent examination of conventional morality, *Major Barbara*. In each thematic section, however, we have added a new play. Since the feminist perspective is represented in many other works in the anthology, we have replaced Ibsen's *A Doll's House* with the same author's *An Enemy of the People*, a play strikingly modern in its examination of the political corruption and moral cowardice that occur when the public health and private gain conflict. In *M. Butterfly*, David Henry Hwang draws on an actual historical event to create an extraordinary drama of sexual intrigue in the context of power politics and cross-cultural confusion. Pam Gems's *Loving Women* examines the conflict in male/female relationships between modern, liberal enlightenment and traditional roles while Harvey Fierstein's *Widows and Children First!* examines the sorrows and triumphs of a gay protagonist who wants, essentially, what everyone wants—a nurturing and loving family. We have also added *No Exit*, Jean-Paul Sartre's classic play about three people who review their lives from a room in hell, condemned to eternally torment one another. Finally, we have added Art Spiegelman's powerful comic strip on the tragic suicide of his mother, who killed herself more than twenty years after she was freed from a Nazi concentration camp.

Among the other new selections are works by Robert Olen Butler, Elizabeth Brewster, Marianne Burke, Raymond Carver, Kate Daniels, Louise Erdrich, James Fenton, Tess Gallagher, Molly Giles, Dana Gioia, Nadine Gordimer, Barry Hannah, Amy Hempel, William Heyen, Edward Hirsch, Linda Hogan, Pam Houston, David Leavitt, Duane Locke, Felix Mnthali, Bharati Mukherjee, Kathleen Norris, Molly Peacock, Alberto Ríos, Gjertrud Schnackenberg, and Kathleen Weigner.

ACKNOWLEDGMENTS

Among the great many people who have helped us, we should like especially to acknowledge our colleagues Meredith Bilson, Joel W. Athey, Dick Lid, and Susanne Collier (and her husband David Lakeman), whose literary taste and knowledge we profited from immensely. Dianne Armstrong (University of Southern California) gave us invaluable criticism and advice about the appendices.

We are also grateful to the following colleagues across the country who have sent us helpful reactions and suggestions for this sixth edition: Martha Ackmann (Mount Holyoke College), Cheryl Allen-Pfitzner (Fullerton College), Iska Alter (Hofstra University), Nancy Topping Bazin (Old Dominion University), D. S. Berlotti (General Motors Institute), George Blecher (Lehman College—CUNY), Annette Briscoe (Indiana University Southeast), Shulamith W. Caine (Drexel University), Michael Castro (Lindenwood College), Patricia Clark (Grand Valley State University), Michael Cleary (Broward Community College—Central), J. Rocky Colavito (University of Arizona), Therese Coyne (Carlow College), John Darling (Sacramento City College), Carl H. DeVasto (Framingham State College), Lorraine Eitel (Bethel College), Mary Finelli (Florida Atlantic University), John Freeman (University of Detroit, Mercy), Anthony R. Grasso (King's College), Carol Peterson Haviland (California State University—San Bernardino), Susanna Hoeness-Krupsaw (University of Southern Indiana), Barbara Horwitz (C.W. Post Campus of Long Island University), Thomas L. Kinney (Bowling Green State University), Michele Frucht Levy (Xavier College), Joseph Lolavito (University of Arizona), James J. Massey (Immaculata College), Ann V. Miller (Baylor University), James J. Mooney (Immaculata College), William Murphy (University of Akron), Barbara Reese (Casper College), Victoria Shannon (DePaul University), Walter Shear (Pittsburg State University), Louise Simons (Boston University), Loretta W. Smith (Widener University), Cara Snyder (Dallas Christian College), Phillip Stambovsky (Albertus Magnus College), Gerald K. Strawmatt (Inver Hills Community College), Joan Sussman (Garrett Community College), Peter Ulisse (Housatonic Community Technical College), Nathaniel Wallace (South Carolina State College), Laura H. Weaver (University of Evansville), Dede Yow (Kennesaw State College), and Ruth Zielke (Concordia College, Ann Arbor).

Finally, we wish to thank the many people at St. Martin's Press for the care they took in the preparation of this edition, and for their good humor, particularly our editor, the indispensable Melissa Cook Candela. Our thanks as well to senior editor Cathy Pusateri, project editors Suzanne Holt and Erica Appel, and production supervisor Alan Fischer.

Richard Abcarian
Marvin Klotz

CONTENTS

Innocence and Experience   2

For Thinking and Writing   5

Conformity and Rebellion   320

POETRY   458

DRAMA   778

The Presence of Death   970

FICTION   976

POETRY   1092

Appendices   1232

POEMS ABOUT POETRY   1233

ALTERNATE TABLE OF CONTENTS

arranged by genre*

---

* Within each genre, authors are listed chronologically by date of birth.

DRAMA

SIXTH EDITION

LITERATURE

THE HUMAN EXPERIENCE

Innocence
and
Experience

The Garden of the Peaceful Arts (Allegory of the Court of Isabelle d'Este), ca. 1530 by Lorenzo Costa

Humans strive to give order and meaning to their lives, to reduce the mystery and unpredictability that constantly threaten them. Life is infinitely more complex and surprising than we imagine, and the categories we establish to give it order and meaning are, for the most part, "momentary stays against confusion." At any time, the equilibrium of our lives, the comfortable image of ourselves and the world around us, may be disrupted suddenly by something new, forcing us into painful reevaluation. These disruptions create pain, anxiety, and terror but also wisdom and awareness.

The works in this section deal generally with the movement of a central character from moral simplicities and certainties into a more complex and problematic world. Though these works frequently issue in awareness, even wisdom, their central figures rarely act decisively; the protagonist is more often a passive figure who learns the difference between the ideal world he or she imagines and the injurious real world. If the protagonist survives the ordeal (and he or she doesn't always, emotionally or physically), the protagonist will doubtless be a better human—better able to wrest some satisfaction from a bleak and threatening world. It is no accident that so many of the works here deal with the passage from childhood to adulthood, for childhood is a time of simplicities and certainties that must give way to the complexities and uncertainties of adult life.

Almost universally, innocence is associated with childhood and youth, as experience is with age. We teach the young about an ideal world, without explaining that it has not yet been and may never be achieved. As innocents, they are terribly vulnerable to falsehood, to intrusive sexuality, and to the machinations of the wicked, who, despite all the moral tales, often do triumph.

But the terms *innocence* and *experience* range widely in meaning, and that range is reflected here. Innocence may be defined almost biologically, as illustrated by the sexual innocence of the young boy in Frank O'Connor's "My Oedipus Complex." Innocence may be social—the innocence of Brown in Nathaniel Hawthorne's "Young Goodman Brown." Or innocence may be seen as the child's ignorance of his or her own mortality, as in Gerard Manley Hopkins's "Spring and Fall" and Dylan Thomas's "Fern Hill." In such works as Sophocles' *Oedipus Rex* and Robert Browning's "My Last Duchess," one discovers the tragic and violent consequences of an innocence that is blind.

And in Imamu Amiri Baraka's *Dutchman*, the black man Clay loses not only his innocence but also his life at the hands of the disdainful, racist Lula.

The contrast between what we thought in our youth and what we have come to know, painfully, as adults stands as an emblem of the passage from innocence to experience. Yet, all of us remain, to one degree or another, innocent throughout life, since we never, except with death, stop learning from experience. Looked at in this way, experience is the ceaseless assault life makes upon our innocence, moving us to a greater wisdom about ourselves and the world around us.

FOR THINKING AND WRITING

As you read the selections in this section, consider the following questions. You may want to write out your thoughts informally in a journal or notebook as a way of preparing to respond to the selections, or you may wish to make one of these questions the basis for a formal essay.

1. Innocence is often associated with childhood and responsibility with adulthood. Were you happier or more contented as a pre-teen than you are now? Why? Which particular aspects of your childhood do you remember with pleasure? Which with pain? Do you look forward to the future with pleasurable anticipation or with dread? Why?

2. Do you know any adults who seem to be innocents? On what do you base your judgment? Do you know any pre-teens who seem to be particularly "adult" in their behavior (beyond politeness and good manners—they may, for example, have to cope with severe family difficulties)? On what do you base your judgment?

3. Most of you have spent your lives under the authority of others, such as parents, teachers, and employers. How do you deal with authorities you resent? Do you look forward to exercising authority over others (your own children, your own students, employees under your supervision)? How will your experiences affect your behavior as an authority?

4. How does the growth from innocence to experience affect one's sexual behavior? Social behavior? Political behavior?

INNOCENCE
AND
EXPERIENCE

Woman and Child on a Beach, ca. 1901 by Pablo Picasso

FICTION

Young Goodman Brown 1846

NATHANIEL HAWTHORNE [1804–1864]

Young Goodman[1] Brown came forth at sunset into the street at Salem village; but put his head back, after crossing the threshold, to exchange a parting kiss with his young wife. And Faith, as the wife was aptly named, thrust her own pretty head into the street, letting the wind play with the pink ribbons of her cap while she called to Goodman Brown.

"Dearest heart," whispered she, softly and rather sadly, when her lips were close to his ear, "prithee put off your journey until sunrise and sleep in your own bed to-night. A lone woman is troubled with such dreams and such thoughts that she's afeared of herself sometimes. Pray tarry with me this night, dear husband, of all nights in the year."

"My love and my Faith," replied young Goodman Brown, "of all nights in the year, this one night must I tarry away from thee. My journey, as thou callest it, forth and back again, must needs be done 'twixt now and sunrise. What, my sweet, pretty wife, dost thou doubt me already, and we but three months married?"

"Then God bless you!" said Faith, with the pink ribbons; "and may you find all well when you come back."

"Amen!" cried Goodman Brown. "Say thy prayers, dear Faith, and go to bed at dusk, and no harm will come to thee."

So they parted; and the young man pursued his way until, being about to turn the corner by the meeting-house, he looked back and saw the head of Faith still peeping after him with a melancholy air, in spite of her pink ribbons.

"Poor little Faith!" thought he, for his heart smote him. "What a wretch am I to leave her on such an errand! She talks of dreams, too. Methought as she spoke there was trouble in her face, as if a dream had warned her what work is to be done to-night. But no, no; 'twould kill her to think it. Well, she's a blessed

---

[1] Equivalent to *Mr.*, a title given to a man below the rank of gentleman.

angel on earth; and after this one night I'll cling to her skirts and follow her to heaven."

With this excellent resolve for the future, Goodman Brown felt himself justified in making more haste on his present evil purpose. He had taken a dreary road, darkened by all the gloomiest trees of the forest, which barely stood aside to let the narrow path creep through, and closed immediately behind. It was all as lonely as could be; and there is this peculiarity in such a solitude, that the traveller knows not who may be concealed by the innumerable trunks and the thick boughs overhead; so that with lonely footsteps he may yet be passing through an unseen multitude.

"There may be a devilish Indian behind every tree," said Goodman Brown to himself; and he glanced fearfully behind him as he added, "What if the devil himself should be at my very elbow!"

His head being turned back, he passed a crook of the road, and, looking forward again, beheld the figure of a man, in grave and decent attire, seated at the foot of an old tree. He arose at Goodman Brown's approach and walked onward side by side with him.

"You are late, Goodman Brown," said he. "The clock of the Old South[2] was striking as I came through Boston, and that is full fifteen minutes agone."

"Faith kept me back a while," replied the young man, with a tremor in his voice, caused by the sudden appearance of his companion, though not wholly unexpected.

It was now deep dusk in the forest, and deepest in that part of it where these two were journeying. As nearly as could be discerned, the second traveller was about fifty years old, apparently in the same rank of life as Goodman Brown, and bearing a considerable resemblance to him, though perhaps more in expression than features. Still they might have been taken for father and son. And yet, though the elder person was as simply clad as the younger, and as simple in manner too, he had an indescribable air of one who knew the world, and who would not have felt abashed at the governor's dinner table or in King William's[3] court, were it possible that his affairs should call him thither. But the only thing about him that could be fixed upon as remarkable was his staff, which bore the likeness of a great black snake, so curiously wrought that it might almost be seen to twist and wriggle itself like a living serpent. This, of course, must have been an ocular deception, assisted by the uncertain light.

"Come, Goodman Brown," cried his fellow-traveller, "this is a dull pace for the beginning of a journey. Take my staff, if you are so soon weary."

"Friend," said the other, exchanging his slow pace for a full stop, "having kept covenant by meeting thee here, it is my purpose now to return whence I came. I have scruples touching the matter thou wot'st of."

"Sayest thou so?" replied he of the serpent, smiling apart. "Let us walk on,

---

[2] A church in Boston.
[3] Ruler of England from 1689–1702.

nevertheless, reasoning as we go; and if I convince thee not thou shalt turn back. We are but a little way in the forest yet."

"Too far! too far!" exclaimed the goodman, unconsciously resuming his walk. "My father never went into the woods on such an errand, nor his father before him. We have been a race of honest men and good Christians since the days of the martyrs;[4] and shall I be the first of the name of Brown that ever took this path and kept—"

"Such company, thou wouldst say," observed the elder person, interpreting his pause. "Well said, Goodman Brown! I have been as well acquainted with your family as with ever a one among the Puritans; and that's no trifle to say. I helped your grandfather, the constable, when he lashed the Quaker woman so smartly through the streets of Salem; and it was I that brought your father a pitch-pine knot, kindled at my own hearth, to set fire to an Indian village, in King Philip's war.[5] They were my good friends, both; and many a pleasant walk have we had along this path, and returned merrily after midnight. I would fain be friends with you for their sake."

"If it be as thou sayest," replied Goodman Brown, "I marvel they never spoke of these matters; or, verily, I marvel not, seeing that the least rumor of the sort would have driven them from New England. We are a people of prayer, and good works to boot, and abide no such wickedness."

"Wickedness or not," said the traveller, with the twisted staff, "I have a very general acquaintance here in New England. The deacons of many a church have drunk the communion wine with me; the selectmen of divers towns make me their chairman; and a majority of the Great and General Court[6] are firm supporters of my interest. The governor and I, too—But these are state secrets."

"Can this be so?" cried Goodman Brown, with a stare of amazement at his undisturbed companion. "Howbeit, I have nothing to do with the governor and council; they have their own ways, and are no rule for a simple husbandman[7] like me. But, were I to go on with thee, how should I meet the eye of that good old man, our minister, at Salem village? Oh, his voice would make me tremble both Sabbath day and lecture day."

Thus far the elder traveller had listened with due gravity; but now burst into a fit of irrepressible mirth, shaking himself so violently that his snake-like staff actually seemed to wriggle in sympathy.

"Ha! ha! ha!" shouted he again and again; then composing himself, "Well, go on, Goodman Brown, go on; but, prithee, don't kill me with laughing."

"Well, then, to end the matter at once," said Goodman Brown, considerably nettled, "there is my wife, Faith. It would break her dear little heart; and I'd rather break my own."

---

[4] A reference to the persecution of Protestants in England by the Catholic monarch Mary Tudor (1553–1558).

[5] War waged (1675–1676) against the colonists of New England by the Indian chief Metacomset, also known as "King Philip."

[6] The Puritan legislature.

[7] An ordinary person.

"Nay, if that be the case," answered the other, "e'en go thy ways, Goodman Brown. I would not for twenty old women like the one hobbling before us that Faith should come to any harm."

As he spoke he pointed his staff at a female figure on the path, in whom Goodman Brown recognized a very pious and exemplary dame, who had taught him his catechism in youth, and was still his moral and spiritual adviser, jointly with the minister and Deacon Gookin.

"A marvel, truly, that Goody[8] Cloyse should be so far in the wilderness at nightfall," said he. "But with your leave, friend, I shall take a cut through the woods until we have left this Christian woman behind. Being a stranger to you, she might ask whom I was consorting with and whither I was going."

"Be it so," said his fellow-traveller. "Betake you to the woods, and let me keep the path."

Accordingly the young man turned aside, but took care to watch his companion, who advanced softly along the road until he had come within a staff's length of the old dame. She, meanwhile, was making the best of her way, with singular speed for so aged a woman, and mumbling some indistinct words—a prayer, doubtless—as she went. The traveller put forth his staff and touched her withered neck with what seemed the serpent's tail.

"The devil!" screamed the pious old lady.

"Then Goody Cloyse knows her old friend?" observed the traveller, confronting her and leaning on his writhing stick.

"Ah, forsooth, and is it your worship indeed?" cried the good dame. "Yea, truly is it, and in the very image of my old gossip, Goodman Brown, the grandfather of the silly fellow that now is. But—would your worship believe it?—my broomstick hath strangely disappeared, stolen, as I suspect, by that unhanged witch, Goody Cory, and that, too, when I was all anointed with the juice of smallage and cinquefoil and wolf's bane"[9]—

"Mingled with fine wheat and the fat of a new-born babe," said the shape of old Goodman Brown.

"Ah, your worship knows the recipe," cried the old lady, cackling aloud. "So, as I was saying, being all ready for the meeting, and no horse to ride on, I made up my mind to foot it; for they tell me there is a nice young man to be taken into communion to-night. But now your good worship will lend me your arm, and we shall be there in a twinkling."

"That can hardly be," answered her friend. "I may not spare you my arm, Goody Cloyse; but here is my staff, if you will."

So saying, he threw it down at her feet, where, perhaps, it assumed life, being one of the rods which its owner had formerly lent to the Egyptian magi.[10] Of this fact, however, Goodman Brown could not take cognizance. He had cast

---

[8] A polite title for a wife of humble rank.

[9] All these plants were associated with magic and witchcraft.

[10] Allusion to the biblical magicians who turned their rods into serpents (Exodus 7:11–12).

up his eyes in astonishment, and, looking down again, beheld neither Goody Cloyse nor the serpentine staff, but his fellow-traveller alone, who waited for him as calmly as if nothing had happened.

"That old woman taught me my catechism," said the young man; and there was a world of meaning in this simple comment.

They continued to walk onward, while the elder traveller exhorted his companion to make good speed and persevere in the path, discoursing so aptly that his arguments seemed rather to spring up in the bosom of his auditor than to be suggested by himself. As they went, he plucked a branch of maple to serve for a walking stick, and began to strip it of the twigs and little boughs, which were wet with evening dew. The moment his fingers touched them they became strangely withered and dried up as with a week's sunshine. Thus the pair proceeded, at a good free pace, until suddenly, in a gloomy hollow of the road, Goodman Brown sat himself down on the stump of a tree and refused to go any farther.

"Friend," said he, stubbornly, "my mind is made up. Not another step will I budge on this errand. What if a wretched old woman do choose to go to the devil when I thought she was going to heaven: is that any reason why I should quit my dear Faith and go after her?"

"You will think better of this by and by," said his acquaintance, composedly. "Sit here and rest yourself a while; and when you feel like moving again, there is my staff to help you along."

Without more words, he threw his companion the maple stick, and was as speedily out of sight as if he had vanished into the deepening gloom. The young man sat a few moments by the roadside, applauding himself greatly, and thinking with how clear a conscience he should meet the minister in his morning walk, nor shrink from the eye of good old Deacon Gookin. And what calm sleep would be his that very night, which was to have been spent so wickedly, but so purely and sweetly now, in the arms of Faith! Amidst these pleasant and praiseworthy meditations, Goodman Brown heard the tramp of horses along the road, and deemed it advisable to conceal himself within the verge of the forest, conscious of the guilty purpose that had brought him thither, though now so happily turned from it.

On came the hoof tramps and the voices of the riders, two grave old voices, conversing soberly as they drew near. These mingled sounds appeared to pass along the road, within a few yards of the young man's hiding-place; but, owing doubtless to the depth of the gloom at that particular spot, neither the travellers nor their steeds were visible. Though their figures brushed the small boughs by the wayside, it could not be seen that they intercepted, even for a moment, the faint gleam from the strip of bright sky athwart which they must have passed. Goodman Brown alternately crouched and stood on tiptoe, pulling aside the branches and thrusting forth his head as far as he durst without discerning so much as a shadow. It vexed him the more, because he could have sworn, were such a thing possible, that he recognized the voices of the minister and Deacon

Gookin, jogging along quietly, as they were wont to do, when bound to some ordination or ecclesiastical council. While yet within hearing, one of the riders stopped to pluck a switch.

"Of the two, reverend sir," said the voice like the deacon's, "I had rather miss an ordination dinner than to-night's meeting. They tell me that some of our community are to be here from Falmouth[11] and beyond, and others from Connecticut and Rhode Island, besides several of the Indian powwows,[12] who, after their fashion, know almost as much deviltry as the best of us. Moreover, there is a goodly young woman to be taken into communion."

"Mighty well, Deacon Gookin!" replied the solemn old tones of the minister. "Spur up, or we shall be late. Nothing can be done, you know, until I get on the ground."

The hoofs clattered again; and the voices, talking so strangely in the empty air, passed on through the forest, where no church had ever been gathered, nor solitary Christian prayed. Whither, then, could these holy men be journeying so deep into the heathen wilderness? Young Goodman Brown caught hold of a tree for support, being ready to sink down on the ground, faint and overburdened with the heavy sickness of his heart. He looked up to the sky, doubting whether there really was a heaven above him. Yet there was the blue arch, and the stars brightening in it.

"With heaven above and Faith below, I will yet stand firm against the devil!" cried Goodman Brown.

While he still gazed upward into the deep arch of the firmament and had lifted his hands to pray, a cloud, though no wind was stirring, hurried across the zenith and hid the brightening stars. The blue sky was still visible, except directly overhead, where this black mass of cloud was sweeping swiftly northward. Aloft in the air, as if from the depths of the cloud, came a confused and doubtful sound of voices. Once the listener fancied that he could distinguish the accents of towns-people of his own, men and women, both pious and ungodly, many of whom he had met at the communion table, and had seen others rioting at the tavern. The next moment, so indistinct were the sounds, he doubted whether he had heard aught but the murmur of the old forest, whispering without a wind. Then came a stronger swell of those familiar tones, heard daily in the sunshine at Salem village, but never until now from a cloud of night. There was one voice, of a young woman, uttering lamentations, yet with an uncertain sorrow, and entreating for some favor, which, perhaps, it would grieve her to obtain; and all the unseen multitude, both saints and sinners, seemed to encourage her onward.

"Faith!" shouted Goodman Brown, in a voice of agony and desperation; and the echoes of the forest mocked him, crying, "Faith! Faith!" as if bewildered wretches were seeking her all through the wilderness.

---

[11] A town near Salem, Massachusetts.
[12] Medicine men.

The cry of grief, rage, and terror was yet piercing the night, when the unhappy husband held his breath for a response. There was a scream, drowned immediately in a louder murmur of voices, fading into far-off laughter, as the dark cloud swept away, leaving the clear and silent sky above Goodman Brown. But something fluttered lightly down through the air and caught on the branch of a tree. The young man seized it, and beheld a pink ribbon.

"My Faith is gone!" cried he, after one stupefied moment. "There is no good on earth; and sin is but a name. Come, devil; for to thee is this world given."

And, maddened with despair, so that he laughed loud and long, did Goodman Brown grasp his staff and set forth again, at such a rate that he seemed to fly along the forest path rather than to walk or run. The road grew wilder and drearier and more faintly traced, and vanished at length, leaving him in the heart of the dark wilderness, still rushing onward with the instinct that guides mortal man to evil. The whole forest was peopled with frightful sounds—the creaking of the trees, the howling of wild beasts, and the yell of Indians; while sometimes the wind tolled like a distant church bell, and sometimes gave a broad roar around the traveller, as if all Nature were laughing him to scorn. But he was himself the chief horror of the scene, and shrank not from its other horrors.

"Ha! ha! ha!" roared Goodman Brown when the wind laughed at him. "Let us hear which will laugh loudest. Think not to frighten me with your deviltry. Come witch, come wizard, come Indian powwow, come devil himself, and here comes Goodman Brown. You may as well fear him as he fear you."

In truth, all through the haunted forest there could be nothing more frightful than the figure of Goodman Brown. On he flew among the black pines, brandishing his staff with frenzied gestures, now giving vent to an inspiration of horrid blasphemy, and now shouting forth such laughter as set all the echoes of the forest laughing like demons around him. The fiend in his own shape is less hideous than when he rages in the breast of man. Thus sped the demoniac on his course, until, quivering among the trees, he saw a red light before him, as when the felled trunks and branches of a clearing have been set on fire, and throw up their lurid blaze against the sky, at the hour of midnight. He paused, in a lull of the tempest that had driven him onward, and heard the swell of what seemed a hymn, rolling solemnly from a distance with the weight of many voices. He knew the tune; it was a familiar one in the choir of the village meetinghouse. The verse died heavily away, and was lengthened by a chorus, not of human voices, but of all the sounds of the benighted wilderness pealing in awful harmony together. Goodman Brown cried out, and his cry was lost to his own ear by its unison with the cry of the desert.

In the interval of silence he stole forward until the light glared full upon his eyes. At one extremity of an open space, hemmed in by the dark wall of the forest, arose a rock, bearing some rude, natural resemblance either to an altar or a pulpit, and surrounded by four blazing pines, their tops aflame, their stems untouched, like candles at an evening meeting. The mass of foliage that had overgrown the summit of the rock was all on fire, blazing high into the night and fitfully illuminating the whole field. Each pendent twig and leafy festoon was in a blaze. As the red light arose and fell, a numerous congregation alternately shone forth, then disappeared in shadow, and again grew, as it were, out of the darkness, peopling the heart of the solitary woods at once.

"A grave and dark-clad company," quoth Goodman Brown.

In truth they were such. Among them, quivering to and fro between gloom and splendor, appeared faces that would be seen next day at the council board of the province, and others which, Sabbath after Sabbath, looked devoutly heavenward, and benignantly over the crowded pews, from the holiest pulpits in the land. Some affirm that the lady of the governor was there. At least there were high dames well known to her, and wives of honored husbands, and widows, a great multitude, and ancient maidens, all of excellent repute, and fair young girls, who trembled lest their mothers should espy them. Either the sudden gleams of light flashing over the obscure field bedazzled Goodman Brown, or he recognized a score of the church members of Salem village famous for their especial sanctity. Good old Deacon Gookin had arrived, and waited at the skirts of that venerable saint, his revered pastor. But, irreverently consorting with these grave, reputable, and pious people, these elders of the church, these chaste dames and dewy virgins, there were men of dissolute lives and women of spotted fame, wretches given over to all mean and filthy vice, and suspected even of horrid crimes. It was strange to see that the good shrank not from the wicked, nor were the sinners abashed by the saints. Scattered also among their pale-faced enemies were the Indian priests, or powwows, who had often scared their native forest with more hideous incantations than any known to English witchcraft.

"But where is Faith?" thought Goodman Brown; and, as hope came into his heart, he trembled.

Another verse of the hymn arose, a slow and mournful strain, such as the pious love, but joined to words which expressed all that our nature can conceive of sin, and darkly hinted at far more. Unfathomable to mere mortals is the lore of fiends. Verse after verse was sung; and still the chorus of the desert swelled between like the deepest tone of a mighty organ; and with the final peal of that dreadful anthem there came a sound, as if the roaring wind, the rushing streams, the howling beasts, and every other voice of the unconcerted wilderness were mingling and according with the voice of guilty man in homage to the prince of all. The four blazing pines threw up a loftier flame, and obscurely discovered shapes and visages of horror on the smoke wreaths above the impious assembly. At the same moment the fire on the rock shot redly forth and formed a glowing arch above its base, where now appeared a figure. With reverence be it spoken, the figure bore no slight similitude, both in garb and manner, to some grave divine of the New England churches.

"Bring forth the converts!" cried a voice that echoed through the field and rolled into the forest.

At the word, Goodman Brown stepped forth from the shadow of the trees and approached the congregation, with whom he felt a loathful brotherhood by the sympathy of all that was wicked in his heart. He could have well-nigh sworn that the shape of his own dead father beckoned him to advance, looking downward from a smoke wreath, while a woman, with dim features of despair, threw out her hand to warn him back. Was it his mother? But he had no power to retreat one step, nor to resist, even in thought, when the minister and good old Deacon Gookin seized his arms and led him to the blazing rock. Thither came also the slender form of a veiled female, led between Goody Cloyse, that pious teacher of the catechism, and Martha Carrier,[13] who had received the devil's promise to be queen of hell. A rampant hag was she. And there stood the proselytes beneath the canopy of fire.

"Welcome, my children," said the dark figure, "to the communion of your race. Ye have found thus young your nature and your destiny. My children, look behind you!"

They turned; and flashing forth, as it were, in a sheet of flame, the fiend worshippers were seen; the smile of welcome gleamed darkly on every visage.

"There," resumed the sable form, "are all whom ye have reverenced from youth. Ye deemed them holier than yourselves, and shrank from your own sin, contrasting it with their lives of righteousness and prayerful aspirations heavenward. Yet here are they all in my worshipping assembly. This night it shall be granted you to know their secret deeds: how hoary-bearded elders of the church have whispered wanton words to the young maids of their households; how many a woman, eager for widows' weeds, has given her husband a drink at bedtime and let him sleep his last sleep in her bosom; how beardless youths have made haste to inherit their fathers' wealth; and how fair damsels—blush not, sweet ones—have dug little graves in the garden, and bidden me, the sole guest, to an infant's funeral. By the sympathy of your human hearts for sin ye shall scent out all the places—whether in church, bed-chamber, street, field, or forest—where crime has been committed, and shall exult to behold the whole earth one stain of guilt, one mighty blood spot. Far more than this. It shall be yours to penetrate, in every bosom, the deep mystery of sin, the fountain of all wicked arts, and which inexhaustibly supplies more evil impulses than human power—than my power at its utmost—can make manifest in deeds. And now, my children, look upon each other."

They did so; and, by the blaze of the hell-kindled torches, the wretched man beheld his Faith, and the wife her husband, trembling before that unhallowed altar.

"Lo, there ye stand, my children," said the figure, in a deep and solemn tone, almost sad with its despairing awfulness, as if his once angelic nature could yet mourn for our miserable race. "Depending upon one another's hearts, ye had still hoped that virtue were not all a dream. Now are ye undeceived. Evil is the nature of mankind. Evil must be your only happiness. Welcome again, my children, to the communion of your race."

---

[13] One of the women hanged in Salem in 1697 for witchcraft.

"Welcome," repeated the fiend worshippers, in one cry of despair and triumph.

And there they stood, the only pair, as it seemed, who were yet hesitating on the verge of wickedness in this dark world. A basin was hollowed, naturally, in the rock. Did it contain water, reddened by the lurid light? or was it blood? or, perchance, a liquid flame? Herein did the shape of evil dip his hand and prepare to lay the mark of baptism upon their foreheads, that they might be partakers of the mystery of sin, more conscious of the secret guilt of others, both in deed and thought, than they could now be of their own. The husband cast one look at his pale wife, and Faith at him. What polluted wretches would the next glance show them to each other, shuddering alike at what they disclosed and what they saw!

"Faith! Faith!" cried the husband, "look up to heaven, and resist the wicked one."

Whether Faith obeyed he knew not. Hardly had he spoken when he found himself amid calm night and solitude, listening to a roar of the wind which died heavily away through the forest. He staggered against the rock, and felt it chill and damp; while a hanging twig, that had been all on fire, besprinkled his cheek with the coldest dew.

The next morning young Goodman Brown came slowly into the street of Salem village, staring around him like a bewildered man. The good old minister was taking a walk along the graveyard to get an appetite for breakfast and meditate his sermon, and bestowed a blessing, as he passed, on Goodman Brown. He shrank from the venerable saint as if to avoid an anathema. Old Deacon Gookin was at domestic worship, and the holy words of his prayer were heard through the open window. "What God doth the wizard pray to?" quoth Goodman Brown. Goody Cloyse, that excellent old Christian, stood in the early sunshine at her own lattice, catechizing a little girl who had brought her a pint of morning's milk. Goodman Brown snatched away the child as from the grasp of the fiend himself. Turning the corner by the meeting-house, he spied the head of Faith, with the pink ribbons, gazing anxiously forth, and bursting into such joy at sight of him that she skipped along the street and almost kissed her husband before the whole village. But Goodman Brown looked sternly and sadly into her face, and passed on without a greeting.

Had Goodman Brown fallen asleep in the forest and only dreamed a wild dream of a witch-meeting?

Be it so if you will; but, alas! it was a dream of evil omen for young Goodman Brown. A stern, a sad, a darkly meditative, a distrustful, if not a desperate man did he become from the night of that fearful dream. On the Sabbath day, when the congregation were singing a holy psalm, he could not listen because an anthem of sin rushed loudly upon his ear and drowned all the blessed strain. When the minister spoke from the pulpit with power and fervid eloquence, and, with his hand on the open Bible, of the sacred truths of our religion, and of saint-like lives and triumphant deaths, and of future bliss or misery unutterable, then did Goodman Brown turn pale, dreading lest the roof should thunder down upon the gray blasphemer and his hearers. Often, awakening suddenly at midnight, he shrank from the bosom of Faith; and at morning or eventide, when the family knelt down at prayer, he scowled and muttered to himself, and gazed sternly at his wife, and turned away. And when he had lived long, and was borne to his grave a hoary corpse, followed by Faith, an aged woman, and children and grandchildren, a goodly procession, besides neighbors not a few, they carved no hopeful verse upon his tombstone, for his dying hour was gloom.

QUESTIONS

1. At the end of the story, Hawthorne asks, "Had Goodman Brown fallen asleep in the forest and only dreamed a wild dream of a witch-meeting?" Why does he not answer the question?   **2.** How would you characterize the setting of this story?   **3.** What elements of the story can be described as allegoric or symbolic? Explain.   **4.** Write out a paraphrase of Satan's sermon.

WRITING TOPIC

Does the final paragraph of the story tell us that Brown's lifelong gloom is justified? Or does it express disapproval of Brown?

The Bride Comes to Yellow Sky

1898

STEPHEN CRANE [1871–1900]

I

The great Pullman was whirling onward with such dignity of motion that a glance from the window seemed simply to prove that the plains of Texas were pouring eastward. Vast flats of green grass, dull-hued space of mesquit and cactus, little groups of frame houses, woods of light and tender trees, all were sweeping into the east, sweeping over the horizon, a precipice.

A newly married pair had boarded this coach at San Antonio. The man's face was reddened from many days in the wind and sun, and a direct result of his new black clothes was that his brick-colored hands were constantly performing in a most conscious fashion. From time to time he looked down respectfully at his attire. He sat with a hand on each knee, like a man waiting in a barber's shop. The glances he devoted to other passengers were furtive and shy.

The bride was not pretty, nor was she very young. She wore a dress of blue cashmere, with small reservations of velvet here and there, and with steel buttons abounding. She continually twisted her head to regard her puff sleeves, very stiff, straight, and high. They embarrassed her. It was quite apparent that she had cooked, and that she expected to cook, dutifully. The blushes caused by the careless scrutiny of some passengers as she had entered the car were strange to see upon this plain, under-class countenance, which was drawn in placid, almost emotionless lines.

They were evidently very happy. "Ever been in a parlour-car before?" he asked, smiling with delight.

"No," she answered; "I never was. It's fine, ain't it?"

"Great! And then after a while we'll go forward to the diner, and get a big lay-out. Finest meal in the world. Charge a dollar."

"Oh, do they?" cried the bride. "Charge a dollar? Why, that's too much—for us—ain't it, Jack?"

"Not this trip, anyhow," he answered bravely. "We're going to go the whole thing."

Later he explained to her about the trains. "You see, it's a thousand miles from one end of Texas to the other; and this train runs right across it, and never stops but four times." He had the pride of an owner. He pointed out to her the dazzling fittings of the coach; and in truth her eyes opened wider as she contemplated the sea-green figured velvet, the shining brass, silver, and glass, the wood that gleamed as darkly brilliant as the surface of a pool of oil. At one end a bronze figure sturdily held a support for a separated chamber, and at convenient places on the ceiling were frescos in olive and silver.

To the minds of the pair, their surroundings reflected the glory of their marriage that morning in San Antonio; this was the environment of their new estate; and the man's face in particular beamed with an elation that made him appear ridiculous to the negro porter. This individual at times surveyed them from afar with an amused and superior grin. On other occasions he bullied them with skill in ways that did not make it exactly plain to them that they were being bullied. He subtly used all the manners of the most unconquerable kind of snobbery. He oppressed them; but of this oppression they had small knowledge, and they speedily forgot that infrequently a number of travellers covered them with stares of derisive enjoyment. Historically there was supposed to be something infinitely humorous in their situation.

"We are due in Yellow Sky at 3:42," he said, looking tenderly into her eyes.

"Oh, are we?" she said, as if she had not been aware of it. To evince surprise at her husband's statement was part of her wifely amiability. She took from a pocket a little silver watch; and as she held it before her, and stared at it with a frown of attention, the new husband's face shone.

"I bought it in San Anton' from a friend of mine," he told her gleefully.

"It's seventeen minutes past twelve," she said, looking up at him with a kind of shy and clumsy coquetry. A passenger, noting this play, grew excessively sardonic, and winked at himself in one of the numerous mirrors.

At last they went to the dining-car. Two rows of negro waiters, in glowing white suits, surveyed their entrance with the interest, and also the equanimity, of men who had been forewarned. The pair fell to the lot of a waiter who happened to feel pleasure in steering them through their meal. He viewed them with the manner of a fatherly pilot, his countenance radiant with benevolence. The patronage, entwined with the ordinary deference, was not plain to them. And yet, as they returned to their coach, they showed in their faces a sense of escape.

To the left, miles down a long purple slope, was a little ribbon of mist where moved the keening Rio Grande. The train was approaching it at an angle, and the apex was Yellow Sky. Presently it was apparent that, as the distance from Yellow Sky grew shorter, the husband became commensurately restless. His brick-red hands were more insistent in their prominence. Occasionally he was even rather absent-minded and far-away when the bride leaned forward and addressed him.

As a matter of truth, Jack Potter was beginning to find the shadow of a deed weigh upon him like a leaden slab. He, the town marshal of Yellow Sky, a man known, liked, and feared in his corner, a prominent person, had gone to San Antonio to meet a girl he believed he loved, and there, after the usual prayers, had actually induced her to marry him, without consulting Yellow Sky for any part of the transaction. He was now bringing his bride before an innocent and unsuspecting community.

Of course people in Yellow Sky married as it pleased them, in accordance with a general custom; but such was Potter's thought of his duty to his friends, or of their idea of his duty, or of an unspoken form which does not control men in these matters, that he felt he was heinous. He had committed an extraordinary crime. Face to face with this girl in San Antonio, and spurred by his sharp impulse, he had gone headlong over all the social hedges. At San Antonio he was like a man hidden in the dark. A knife to sever any friendly duty, any form, was easy to his hand in that remote city. But the hour of Yellow Sky—the hour of daylight—was approaching.

He knew full well that his marriage was an important thing to his town. It could only be exceeded by the burning of the new hotel. His friends could not forgive him. Frequently he had reflected on the advisability of telling them by telegraph, but a new cowardice had been upon him. He feared to do it. And now the train was hurrying him toward a scene of amazement, glee, and reproach. He glanced out of the window at the line of haze swinging slowly in toward the train.

Yellow Sky had a kind of brass band, which played painfully, to the delight of the populace. He laughed without heart as he thought of it. If the citizens could dream of his prospective arrival with his bride, they would parade the band at the station and escort them, amid cheers and laughing congratulations, to his adobe home.

He resolved that he would use all the devices of speed and plainscraft in making the journey from the station to his house. Once within that safe citadel, he could issue some sort of vocal bulletin, and then not go among the citizens until they had time to wear off a little of their enthusiasm.

The bride looked anxiously at him. "What's worrying you, Jack?"

He laughed again. "I'm not worrying, girl; I'm only thinking of Yellow Sky."

She flushed in comprehension.

A sense of mutual guilt invaded their minds and developed a finer tenderness. They looked at each other with eyes softly aglow. But Potter often laughed the same nervous laugh; the flush upon the bride's face seemed quite permanent.

The traitor to the feelings of Yellow Sky narrowly watched the speeding landscape. "We're nearly there," he said.

Presently the porter came and announced the proximity of Potter's home. He held a brush in his hand, and, with all his airy superiority gone, he brushed Potter's new clothes as the latter slowly turned this way and that way. Potter fumbled out a coin and gave it to the porter, as he had seen others do. It was a heavy and muscle-bound business, as that of a man shoeing his first horse.

The porter took their bag, and as the train began to slow they moved forward to the hooded platform of the car. Presently the two engines and their string of coaches rushed into the station of Yellow Sky.

"They have to take water here," said Potter, from a constricted throat and in mournful cadence, as one announcing death. Before the train stopped his eye had swept the length of the platform, and he was glad and astonished to see there was none upon it but the station-agent, who, with a slightly hurried and anxious air, was walking toward the water-tanks. When the train had halted, the porter alighted first, and placed in position a little temporary step.

"Come on, girl," said Potter, hoarsely. As he helped her down they each laughed on a false note. He took the bag from the negro, and bade his wife cling to his arm. As they slunk rapidly away, his hang-dog glance perceived that they were unloading the two trunks, and also that the station-agent, far ahead near the baggage-car, had turned and was running toward him, making gestures. He laughed, and groaned as he laughed, when he noted the first effect of his marital bliss upon Yellow Sky. He gripped his wife's arm firmly to his side, and they fled. Behind them the porter stood, chuckling fatuously.

II

The California express on the Southern Railway was due at Yellow Sky in twenty-one minutes. There were six men at the bar of the Weary Gentleman saloon. One was a drummer who talked a great deal and rapidly; three were Texans who did not care to talk at that time; and two were Mexican sheep-herders, who did not talk as a general practice in the Weary Gentleman saloon. The barkeeper's dog lay on the board walk that crossed in front of the door. His head was on his paws, and he glanced drowsily here and there with the constant vigilance of a dog that is kicked on occasion. Across the sandy street were some vivid green grass-plots, so wonderful in appearance, amid the sands that burned near them in a blazing sun, that they caused a doubt in the mind. They exactly resembled the grass mats used to represent lawns on the stage. At the cooler end of the railway station, a man without a coat sat in a tilted chair and smoked his pipe. The fresh-cut bank of the Rio Grande circled near the town, and there could be seen beyond it a great plum-coloured plain of mesquit.

Save for the busy drummer and his companions in the saloon, Yellow Sky was dozing. The new-comer leaned gracefully upon the bar, and recited many tales with the confidence of a bard who has come upon a new field.

"—and at the moment that the old man fell downstairs with the bureau in his arms, the old woman was coming up with two scuttles of coal, and of course—"

The drummer's tale was interrupted by a young man who suddenly appeared in the open door. He cried: "Scratchy Wilson's drunk, and has turned loose with both hands." The two Mexicans at once set down their glasses and faded out of the rear entrance of the saloon.

The drummer, innocent and jocular, answered: "All right, old man. S'pose he has? Come in and have a drink, anyhow."

But the information had made such an obvious cleft in every skull in the room that the drummer was obliged to see its importance. All had become instantly solemn. "Say," said he, mystified, "what is this?" His three companions made the introductory gesture of eloquent speech; but the young man at the door forestalled them.

"It means, my friend," he answered, as he came into the saloon, "that for the next two hours this town won't be a health resort."

The barkeeper went to the door, and locked and barred it; reaching out of the window, he pulled in heavy wooden shutters, and barred them. Immediately a solemn, chapel-like gloom was upon the place. The drummer was looking from one to another.

"But, say," he cried, "what is this, anyhow? You don't mean there is going to be a gun-fight?"

"Don't know whether there'll be a fight or not," answered one man, grimly; "but there'll be some shootin'—some good shootin'."

The young man who had warned them waved his hand. "Oh, there'll be a fight fast enough, if any one wants it. Anybody can get a fight out there in the street. There's a fight just waiting."

The drummer seemed to be swayed between the interest of a foreigner and a perception of personal danger.

"What did you say his name was?" he asked.

"Scratchy Wilson," they answered in chorus.

"And will he kill anybody? What are you going to do? Does this happen often? Does he rampage around like this once a week or so? Can he break in that door?"

"No; he can't break down that door," replied the barkeeper. "He's tried it three times. But when he comes you'd better lay down on the floor, stranger. He's dead sure to shoot at it, and a bullet may come through."

Thereafter the drummer kept a strict eye upon the door. The time had not yet called for him to hug the floor, but, as a minor precaution, he sidled near the wall. "Will he kill anybody?" he said again.

The men laughed low and scornfully at the question.

"He's out to shoot, and he's out for trouble. Don't see any good in experimentin' with him."

"But what do you do in a case like this? What do you do?"

A man responded: "Why, he and Jack Potter—"

"But," in chorus the other men interrupted, "Jack Potter's in San Anton'."

"Well, who is he? What's he got to do with it?"

"Oh, he's the town marshal. He goes out and fights Scratchy when he gets on one of these tears."

"Wow!" said the drummer, mopping his brow. "Nice job he's got."

The voices had toned away to mere whisperings. The drummer wished to ask further questions, which were born of an increasing anxiety and bewilderment; but when he attempted them, the men merely looked at him in irritation and motioned him to remain silent. A tense waiting hush was upon them. In the deep shadows of the room their eyes shone as they listened for sounds from the street. One man made three gestures at the barkeeper; and the latter, moving like a ghost, handed him a glass and a bottle. The man poured a full glass of whisky, and set down the bottle noiselessly. He gulped the whisky in a swallow, and turned again toward the door in immovable silence. The drummer saw that the barkeeper, without a sound, had taken a Winchester from beneath the bar. Later he saw this individual beckoning to him, so he tiptoed across the room.

"You better come with me back of the bar."

"No thanks," said the drummer, perspiring; "I'd rather be where I can make a break for the back door."

Whereupon the man of bottles made a kindly but peremptory gesture. The drummer obeyed it, and, finding himself seated on a box with his head below the level of the bar, balm was laid upon his soul at sight of various zinc and copper fittings that bore a resemblance to armour-plate. The barkeeper took a seat comfortably upon an adjacent box.

"You see," he whispered, "this here Scratchy Wilson is a wonder with a gun—a perfect wonder; and when he goes on the war-trail, we hunt our holes—naturally. He's about the last one of the old gang that used to hang out along the river here. He's a terror when he's drunk. When he's sober he's all right—kind of simple—wouldn't hurt a fly—nicest fellow in town. But when he's drunk—whoo!"

There were periods of stillness. "I wish Jack Potter was back from San Anton'," said the barkeeper. "He shot Wilson up once—in the leg—and he would sail in and pull out the kinks in this thing."

Presently they heard from a distance the sound of a shot, followed by three wild yowls. It instantly removed a bond from the men in the darkened saloon. There was a shuffling of feet. They looked at each other. "Here he comes," they said.

III

A man in a maroon-coloured flannel shirt, which had been purchased for purposes of decoration, and made principally by some Jewish women on the East Side of New York, rounded a corner and walked into the middle of the main street of Yellow Sky. In either hand the man held a long, heavy, blue-black revolver. Often he yelled, and these cries rang through a semblance of a deserted village, shrilly flying over the roofs in a volume that seemed to have no relation to the ordinary vocal strength of a man. It was as if the surrounding stillness formed the arch of a tomb over him. These cries of ferocious challenge rang against walls of silence. And his boots had red tops with gilded imprints, of the kind beloved in winter by little sledding boys on the hillsides of New England.

The man's face flamed in a rage begot of whisky. His eyes, rolling, and yet keen for ambush, hunted the still doorways and windows. He walked with the creeping movement of the midnight cat. As it occurred to him, he roared menacing information. The long revolvers in his hands were as easy as straws; they were moved with an electric swiftness. The little fingers of each hand played sometimes in a musician's way. Plain from the low collar of the shirt, the cords of his neck straightened and sank, straightened and sank, as passion moved him. The only sounds were his terrible invitations. The calm adobes preserved their demeanor at the passing of this small thing in the middle of the street.

There was no offer of fight—no offer of fight. The man called to the sky. There were no attractions. He bellowed and fumed and swayed his revolvers here and everywhere.

The dog of the barkeeper of the Weary Gentleman saloon had not appreciated the advance of events. He yet lay dozing in front of his master's door. At sight of the dog, the man paused and raised his revolver humorously. At sight of the man, the dog sprang up and walked diagonally away, with a sullen head, and growling. The man yelled, and the dog broke into a gallop. As it was about to enter an alley, there was a loud noise, a whistling, and something spat the ground directly before it. The dog screamed, and, wheeling in terror, galloped headlong in a new direction. Again there was a noise, a whistling, and sand was kicked viciously before it. Fear-stricken, the dog turned and flurried like an animal in a pen. The man stood laughing, his weapons at his hips.

Ultimately the man was attracted by the closed door of the Weary Gentleman saloon. He went to it and, hammering with a revolver, demanded drink.

The door remaining imperturbable, he picked a bit of paper from the walk, and nailed it to the framework with a knife. He then turned his back contemptuously upon this popular resort and, walking to the opposite side of the street and spinning there on his heel quickly and lithely, fired at the bit of paper. He missed it by a half-inch. He swore at himself, and went away. Later he comfortably fusilladed the windows of his most intimate friend. The man was playing with this town; it was a toy for him.

But still there was no offer of fight. The name of Jack Potter, his ancient antagonist, entered his mind, and he concluded that it would be a glad thing if he should go to Potter's house and by bombardment induce him to come out and fight. He moved in the direction of his desire, chanting Apache scalp-music.

When he arrived at it, Potter's house presented the same still front as had the other adobes. Taking up a strategic position, the man howled a challenge. But this house regarded him as might a great stone god. It gave no sign. After a decent wait, the man howled further challenges, mingling with them wonderful epithets.

Presently there came the spectacle of a man churning himself into deepest rage over the immobility of a house. He fumed at it as the winter wind attacks a prairie cabin in the North. To the distance there should have gone the sound of a tumult like the fighting of two hundred Mexicans. As necessity bade him, he paused for breath or to reload his revolvers.

IV

Potter and his bride walked sheepishly and with speed. Sometimes they laughed together shamefacedly and low.

"Next corner, dear," he said finally.

They put forth the efforts of a pair walking bowed against a strong wind. Potter was about to raise a finger to point the first appearance of the new home when, as they circled the corner, they came face to face with a man in a maroon-colored shirt, who was feverishly pushing cartridges into a large revolver. Upon the instant the man dropped his revolver to the ground and, like lightning, whipped another from its holster. The second weapon was aimed at the bride-groom's chest.

There was a silence. Potter's mouth seemed to be merely a grave for his tongue. He exhibited an instinct to at once loosen his arm from the woman's grip, and he dropped the bag to the sand. As for the bride, her face had gone as yellow as old cloth. She was a slave to hideous rites, gazing at the apparitional snake.

The two men faced each other at a distance of three paces. He of the revolver smiled with a new and quiet ferocity.

"Tried to sneak up on me," he said. "Tried to sneak up on me!" His eyes grew more baleful. As Potter made a slight movement, the man thrust his revolver venomously forward. "No, don't you do it, Jack Potter. Don't you move a finger toward a gun just yet. Don't you move an eyelash. The time has come for me to settle with you, and I'm goin' to do it my own way, and loaf along with no interferin'. So if you don't want a gun bent on you, just mind what I tell you."

Potter looked at his enemy. "I ain't got a gun on me, Scratchy," he said. "Honest, I ain't." He was stiffening and steadying, but yet somewhere at the back of his mind a vision of the Pullman floated: the sea-green figured velvet, the shining brass, silver, and glass, the wood that gleamed as darkly brilliant as the surface of a pool of oil—all the glory of marriage, the environment of the new estate. "You know I fight when it comes to fighting, Scratchy Wilson; but I ain't got a gun on me. You'll have to do all the shootin' yourself."

His enemy's face went livid. He stepped forward, and lashed his weapon to and fro before Potter's chest. "Don't you tell me you ain't got no gun on you, you whelp. Don't tell me no lie like that. There ain't a man in Texas ever seen you without no gun. Don't take me for no kid." His eyes blazed with light, and his throat worked like a pump.

"I ain't takin' you for no kid," answered Potter. His heels had not moved an inch backward. "I'm takin' you for a damn fool. I tell you I ain't got a gun, and I ain't. If you're goin' to shoot me up, you better begin now; you'll never get a chance like this again."

So much enforced reasoning had told on Wilson's rage; he was calmer. "If you ain't got a gun, why ain't you got a gun?" he sneered. "Been to Sunday-school?"

"I ain't got a gun because I've just come from San Anton' with my wife. I'm married," said Potter. "And if I'd thought there was going to be any galoots like you prowling around when I brought my wife home, I'd had a gun, and don't you forget it."

"Married!" said Scratchy, not at all comprehending.

"Yes, married. I'm married," said Potter, distinctly.

"Married?" said Scratchy. Seemingly for the first time, he saw the drooping, drowning woman at the other man's side. "No!" he said. He was like a creature allowed a glimpse of another world. He moved a pace backward, and his arm, with the revolver, dropped to his side. "Is this the lady?" he asked.

"Yes; this is the lady," answered Potter.

There was another period of silence.

"Well," said Wilson at last, slowly, "I s'pose it's all off now."

"It's all off if you say so, Scratchy. You know I didn't make the trouble." Potter lifted his valise.

"Well, I 'low it's off, Jack," said Wilson. He was looking at the ground. "Married!" He was not a student of chivalry; it was merely that in the presence of this foreign condition he was a simple child of the earlier plains. He picked up his starboard revolver, and, placing both weapons in their holsters, he went away. His feet made funnel-shaped tracks in the heavy sand.

QUESTIONS

1. Scratchy is described in the final paragraph as "a simple child of the earlier plains." What does this mean? Was Potter ever a simple child of the earlier plains?   **2.** Early in the story we read that ". . . Jack Potter was beginning to find the shadow of a deed weigh upon him like a leaden slab. He, the town marshal of Yellow Sky, a man known, liked, and feared in his corner, a prominent person, had gone to San Antonio to meet a girl he believed he loved, and there, after the usual prayers, had actually induced her to marry him, without consulting Yellow Sky for any part of the transaction. He was now bringing his bride before an innocent and unsuspecting community." Jack Potter, like any man, has a right to marry. How do you account for his feelings as described in this passage?   **3.** A "drummer" is a traveling salesman. What effect does his presence have on the "myth of the West"?

WRITING TOPICS

1. How would you characterize Scratchy's behavior? How does it relate to the "myth of the West" preserved in films and Western novels? How does the description of Scratchy's shirt at the beginning of Part III affect that view of the West? Why is Scratchy disconsolate at the end?   **2.** Analyze Crane's metaphors and images. What function do they serve in the story?

Araby*

1914

JAMES JOYCE   [1882–1941]

North Richmond Street, being blind, was a quiet street except at the hour when the Christian Brothers' School set the boys free. An uninhabited house of two storeys stood at the blind end, detached from its neighbours in a square ground. The other houses of the street, conscious of decent lives within them, gazed at one another with brown imperturbable faces.

The former tenant of our house, a priest, had died in the back drawing-room. Air, musty from having been long enclosed, hung in all the rooms, and the waste room behind the kitchen was littered with old useless papers. Among these I found a few paper-covered books, the pages of which were curled and damp: *The Abbot*, by Walter Scott, *The Devout Communicant* and *The Memoirs of Vidocq*. I liked the last best because its leaves were yellow. The wild garden behind the house contained a central apple-tree and a few straggling bushes under one of which I found the late tenant's rusty bicycle pump. He had been a very charitable priest; in his will he had left all his money to institutions and the furniture of his house to his sister.

When the short days of winter came dusk fell before we had well eaten our dinners. When we met in the street the houses had grown sombre. The space of sky above us was the colour of ever-changing violet and towards it the lamps of the street lifted their feeble lanterns. The cold air stung us and we played till our bodies glowed. Our shouts echoed in the silent street. The career of our play brought us through the dark muddy lanes behind the houses where we ran the gauntlet of the rough tribes from the cottages, to the back doors of the dark dripping gardens where odours arose from the ashpits, to the dark odorous stables where a coachman smoothed and combed the horse or shook music from the buckled harness. When we returned to the street light from the kitchen windows had filled the areas. If my uncle was seen turning the corner we hid in the shadow until we had seen him safely housed. Or if Mangan's sister came out on the doorstep to call her brother in to his tea we watched her from our shadow peer up and down the street. We waited to see whether she would remain or go in and, if she remained, we left our shadow and walked up to Mangan's steps resignedly. She was waiting for us, her figure defined by the light from the half-opened door. Her brother always teased her before he obeyed and I stood by the railings looking at her. Her dress swung as she moved her body and the soft rope of her hair tossed from side to side.

---

* This story is considered in the essay "Reading Fiction" at the end of the book.

Every morning I lay on the floor in the front parlour watching her door. The blind was pulled down to within an inch of the sash so that I could not be seen. When she came out on the doorstep my heart leaped. I ran to the hall, seized my books and followed her. I kept her brown figure always in my eye and, when we came near the point at which our ways diverged, I quickened my pace and passed her. This happened morning after morning. I had never spoken to her, except for a few casual words, and yet her name was like a summons to all my foolish blood.

Her image accompanied me even in places the most hostile to romance. On Saturday evenings when my aunt went marketing I had to go to carry some of the parcels. We walked through the flaring streets, jostled by drunken men and bargaining women, amid the curses of labourers, the shrill litanies of shop-boys who stood on guard by the barrels of pigs' cheeks, the nasal chanting of street-singers, who sang a *come-all-you*[1] about O'Donovan Rossa, or a ballad about the troubles in our native land. These noises converged in a single sensation of life for me: I imagined that I bore my chalice safely through a throng of foes. Her name sprang to my lips at moments in strange prayers and praises which I myself did not understand. My eyes were often full of tears (I could not tell why) and at times a flood from my heart seemed to pour itself out into my bosom. I thought little of the future. I did not know whether I would ever speak to her or not or, if I spoke to her, how I could tell her of my confused adoration. But my body was like a harp and her words and gestures were like fingers running upon the wires.

One evening I went into the back drawing-room in which the priest had died. It was a dark rainy evening and there was no sound in the house. Through one of the broken panes I heard the rain impinge upon the earth, the fine incessant needles of water playing in the sodden beds. Some distant lamp or lighted window gleamed below me. I was thankful that I could see so little. All my senses seemed to desire to veil themselves and, feeling that I was about to slip from them, I pressed the palms of my hands together until they trembled, murmuring: "*O love! O love!*" many times.

At last she spoke to me. When she addressed the first words to me I was so confused that I did not know what to answer. She asked me was I going to *Araby*. I forgot whether I answered yes or no. It would be a splendid bazaar, she said she would love to go.

"And why can't you?" I asked.

While she spoke she turned a silver bracelet round and round her wrist. She could not go, she said, because there would be a retreat that week in her convent. Her brother and two other boys were fighting for their caps and I was alone at the railings. She held one of the spikes, bowing her head towards me. The light from the lamp opposite our door caught the white curve of her neck,

---

[1] A street ballad beginning with these words. This one is about Jeremiah Donovan, a nineteenth-century Irish nationalist popularly known as O'Donovan Rossa.

lit up her hair that rested there and, falling, lit up the hand upon the railing. It fell over one side of her dress and caught the white border of a petticoat, just visible as she stood at ease.

"It's well for you," she said.

"If I go," I said, "I will bring you something."

What innumerable follies laid waste my waking and sleeping thoughts after that evening! I wished to annihilate the tedious intervening days. I chafed against the work of school. At night in my bedroom and by day in the classroom her image came between me and the page I strove to read. The syllables of the word *Araby* were called to me through the silence in which my soul luxuriated and cast an Eastern enchantment over me. I asked for leave to go to the bazaar on Saturday night. My aunt was surprised and hoped it was not some Freemason affair. I answered few questions in class. I watched my master's face pass from amiability to sternness; he hoped I was not beginning to idle. I could not call my wandering thoughts together. I had hardly any patience with the serious work of life which, now that it stood between me and my desire, seemed to me child's play, ugly monotonous child's play.

On Saturday morning I reminded my uncle that I wished to go to the bazaar in the evening. He was fussing at the hallstand, looking for the hat-brush, and answered me curtly:

"Yes, boy, I know."

As he was in the hall I could not go into the front parlour and lie at the window. I left the house in bad humour and walked slowly towards the school. The air was pitilessly raw and already my heart misgave me.

When I came home to dinner my uncle had not yet been home. Still it was early. I sat staring at the clock for some time and, when its ticking began to irritate me, I left the room. I mounted the staircase and gained the upper part of the house. The high cold empty gloomy rooms liberated me and I went from room to room singing. From the front window I saw my companions playing below in the street. Their cries reached me weakened and indistinct and, leaning my forehead against the cool glass, I looked over at the dark house where she lived. I may have stood there for an hour, seeing nothing but the brown-clad figure cast by my imagination, touched discreetly by the lamplight at the curved neck, at the hand upon the railings and at the border below the dress.

When I came downstairs again I found Mrs. Mercer sitting at the fire. She was an old garrulous woman, a pawnbroker's widow, who collected used stamps for some pious purpose. I had to endure the gossip of the tea-table. The meal was prolonged beyond an hour and still my uncle did not come. Mrs. Mercer stood up to go: she was sorry she couldn't wait any longer, but it was after eight o'clock and she did not like to be out late, as the night air was bad for her. When she had gone I began to walk up and down the room, clenching my fists. My aunt said:

"I'm afraid you may put off your bazaar for this night of Our Lord."

At nine o'clock I heard my uncle's latchkey in the hall door. I heard him talking to himself and heard the hallstand rocking when it had received the

weight of his overcoat. I could interpret these signs. When he was midway
through his dinner I asked him to give me the money to go to the bazaar. He
had forgotten.

"The people are in bed and after their first sleep now," he said.

I did not smile. My aunt said to him energetically:

"Can't you give him the money and let him go? You've kept him late enough
as it is."

My uncle said he was very sorry he had forgotten. He said he believed in
the old saying: "All work and no play makes Jack a dull boy." He asked me
where I was going and, when I had told him a second time he asked me did I
know *The Arab's Farewell to His Steed*. When I left the kitchen he was about
to recite the opening lines of the piece to my aunt.

I held a florin tightly in my hand as I strode down Buckingham Street towards
the station. The sight of the streets thronged with buyers and glaring with gas
recalled to me the purpose of my journey. I took my seat in a third-class carriage
of a deserted train. After an intolerable delay the train moved out of the station
slowly. It crept onward among ruinous houses and over the twinkling river. At
Westland Row Station a crowd of people pressed to the carriage doors; but the
porters moved them back, saying that it was a special train for the bazaar. I
remained alone in the bare carriage. In a few minutes the train drew up beside
an improvised wooden platform. I passed out on to the road and saw by the
lighted dial of a clock that it was ten minutes to ten. In front of me was a large
building which displayed the magical name.

I could not find any sixpenny entrance and, fearing that the bazaar would
be closed, I passed in quickly through a turnstile, handing a shilling to a weary-
looking man. I found myself in a big hall girdled at half its height by a gallery.
Nearly all the stalls were closed and the greater part of the hall was in darkness.
I recognised a silence like that which pervades a church after a service. I walked
into the centre of the bazaar timidly. A few people were gathered about the
stalls which were still open. Before a curtain, over which the words *Café
Chantant* were written in coloured lamps, two men were counting money on
a salver. I listened to the fall of the coins.

Remembering with difficulty why I had come I went over to one of the stalls
and examined porcelain vases and flowered tea-sets. At the door of the stall a
young lady was talking and laughing with two young gentlemen. I remarked
their English accents and listened vaguely to their conversation.

"O, I never said such a thing!"

"O, but you did!"

"O, but I didn't!"

"Didn't she say that?"

"Yes. I heard her."

"O, there's a . . . fib!"

Observing me the young lady came over and asked me did I wish to buy
anything. The tone of her voice was not encouraging; she seemed to have

spoken to me out of a sense of duty. I looked humbly at the great jars that stood like Eastern guards at either side of the dark entrance to the stall and murmured:

"No, thank you."

The young lady changed the position of one of the vases and went back to the two young men. They began to talk of the same subject. Once or twice the young lady glanced at me over her shoulder.

I lingered before her stall, though I knew my stay was useless, to make my interest in her wares seem the more real. Then I turned away slowly and walked down the middle of the bazaar. I allowed the two pennies to fall against the sixpence in my pocket. I heard a voice call from one end of the gallery that the light was out. The upper part of the hall was now completely dark.

Gazing up into the darkness I saw myself as a creature driven and derided by vanity; and my eyes burned with anguish and anger.

A Clean, Well-Lighted Place 1933

ERNEST HEMINGWAY [1899–1961]

It was late and everyone had left the café except an old man who sat in the shadow the leaves of the tree made against the electric light. In the day time the street was dusty, but at night the dew settled the dust and the old man liked to sit late because he was deaf and now at night it was quiet and he felt the difference. The two waiters inside the café knew that the old man was a little drunk, and while he was a good client they knew that if he became too drunk he would leave without paying, so they kept watch on him.

"Last week he tried to commit suicide," one waiter said.

"Why?"

"He was in despair."

"What about?"

"Nothing."

"How do you know it was nothing?"

"He has plenty of money."

They sat together at a table that was close against the wall near the door of the café and looked at the terrace where the tables were all empty except where the old man sat in the shadow of the leaves of the tree that moved slightly in the wind. A girl and a soldier went by in the street. The street light shone on the brass number on his collar. The girl wore no head covering and hurried beside him.

"The guard will pick him up," one waiter said.

"What does it matter if he gets what he's after?"

"He had better get off the street now. The guard will get him. They went by five minutes ago."

The old man sitting in the shadow rapped on his saucer with his glass. The younger waiter went over to him.

"What do you want?"

The old man looked at him. "Another brandy," he said.

"You'll be drunk," the waiter said. The old man looked at him. The waiter went away.

"He'll stay all night," he said to his colleague. "I'm sleepy now. I never get into bed before three o'clock. He should have killed himself last week."

The waiter took the brandy bottle and another saucer from the counter inside the café and marched out to the old man's table. He put down the saucer and poured the glass full of brandy.

"You should have killed yourself last week," he said to the deaf man. The old man motioned with his finger. "A little more," he said. The waiter poured on into the glass so that the brandy slopped over and ran down the stem into the top saucer of the pile. "Thank you," the old man said. The waiter took the bottle back inside the café. He sat down at the table with his colleague again.

"He's drunk now," he said.

"He's drunk every night."

"What did he want to kill himself for?"

"How should I know."

"How did he do it?"

"He hung himself with a rope."

"Who cut him down?"

"His niece."

"Why did they do it?"

"Fear for his soul."

"How much money has he got?"

"He's got plenty."

"He must be eighty years old."

"Anyway I should say he was eighty."

"I wish he would go home. I never get to bed before three o'clock. What kind of hour is that to go to bed?"

"He stays up because he likes it."

"He's lonely. I'm not lonely. I have a wife waiting in bed for me."

"He had a wife once too."

"A wife would be no good to him now."

"You can't tell. He might be better with a wife."

"His niece looks after him."

"I know. You said she cut him down."

"I wouldn't want to be that old. An old man is a nasty thing."

"Not always. This old man is clean. He drinks without spilling. Even now, drunk. Look at him."

"I don't want to look at him. I wish he would go home. He has no regard for those who must work."

The old man looked from his glass across the square, then over at the waiters.

"Another brandy," he said, pointing to his glass. The waiter who was in a hurry came over.

"Finished," he said, speaking with that omission of syntax stupid people employ when talking to drunken people or foreigners. "No more tonight. Close now."

"Another," said the old man.

"No. Finished." The waiter wiped the edge of the table with a towel and shook his head.

The old man stood up, slowly counted the saucers, took a leather coin purse from his pocket and paid for the drinks, leaving half a peseta tip.

The waiter watched him go down the street, a very old man walking unsteadily but with dignity.

"Why didn't you let him stay and drink?" the unhurried waiter asked. They were putting up the shutters. "It is not half-past two."

"I want to go home to bed."

"What is an hour?"

"More to me than to him."

"An hour is the same."

"You talk like an old man yourself. He can buy a bottle and drink at home."

"It's not the same."

"No, it is not," agreed the waiter with a wife. He did not wish to be unjust. He was only in a hurry.

"And you? You have no fear of going home before your usual hour?"

"Are you trying to insult me?"

"No, hombre, only to make a joke."

"No," the waiter who was in a hurry said, rising from pulling down the metal shutters. "I have confidence. I am all confidence."

"You have youth, confidence, and a job," the older waiter said. "You have everything."

"And what do you lack?"

"Everything but work."

"You have everything I have."

"No. I have never had confidence and I am not young."

"Come on. Stop talking nonsense and lock up."

"I am of those who like to stay late at the café," the older waiter said. "With all those who do not want to go to bed. With all those who need a light for the night."

"I want to go home and into bed."

"We are of two different kinds," the older waiter said. He was now dressed to go home. "It is not only a question of youth and confidence although those things are very beautiful. Each night I am reluctant to close up because there may be some one who needs the café."

"Hombre, there are bodegas open all night long."

"You do not understand. This is a clean and pleasant café. It is well lighted. The light is very good and also, now, there are shadows of the leaves."

"Good night," said the younger waiter.

"Good night," the other said. Turning off the electric light he continued the conversation with himself. It is the light of course but it is necessary that the place be clean and pleasant. You do not want music. Certainly you do not want music. Nor can you stand before a bar with dignity although that is all that is provided for these hours. What did he fear? It was not fear or dread. It was a nothing that he knew too well. It was all a nothing and a man was nothing too. It was only that and light was all it needed and a certain cleanness and order. Some lived in it and never felt it but he knew it was nada y pues nada y pues nada.[1] Our nada who art in nada, nada be thy name thy kingdom

---

[1] Nothing, and then nothing, and then nothing.

nada thy will be nada in nada as it is in nada. Give us this nada our daily nada and nada us our nada as we nada our nadas and nada us not into nada but deliver us from nada; pues nada. Hail nothing full of nothing, nothing is with thee. He smiled and stood before a bar with a shining steam pressure coffee machine.

"What's yours?" asked the barman.

"Nada."

"Otro loco mas,"[2] said the barman and turned away.

"A little cup," said the waiter.

The barman poured it for him.

"The light is very bright and pleasant but the bar is unpolished," the waiter said.

The barman looked at him but did not answer. It was too late at night for conversation.

"You want another copita?" the barman asked.

"No, thank you," said the waiter and went out. He disliked bars and bodegas. A clean, well-lighted café was a very different thing. Now, without thinking further, he would go home to his room. He would lie in the bed and finally, with daylight, he would go to sleep. After all, he said to himself, it is probably only insomnia. Many must have it.

QUESTION

How do the two waiters differ in their attitudes toward the old man? What bearing does that difference have on the theme of the story?

---

[2] Another crazy one.

My Oedipus Complex

FRANK O'CONNOR   [1903–1966]

Father was in the army all through the war—the first war, I mean—so, up to the age of five, I never saw much of him, and what I saw did not worry me. Sometimes I woke and there was a big figure in khaki peering down at me in the candlelight. Sometimes in the early morning I heard the slamming of the front door and the clatter of nailed boots down the cobbles of the lane. These were Father's entrances and exits. Like Santa Claus he came and went mysteriously.

In fact, I rather liked his visits, though it was an uncomfortable squeeze between Mother and him when I got into the big bed in the early morning. He smoked, which gave him a pleasant musty smell, and shaved, an operation of astounding interest. Each time he left a trail of souvenirs—model tanks and Gurkha knives with handles made of bullet cases, and German helmets and cap badges and button-sticks, and all sorts of military equipment—carefully stowed away in a long box on top of the wardrobe, in case they ever came in handy. There was a bit of the magpie about Father; he expected everything to come in handy. When his back was turned, Mother let me get a chair and rummage through his treasures. She didn't seem to think so highly of them as he did.

The war was the most peaceful period of my life. The window of my attic faced southeast. My mother had curtained it, but that had small effect. I always woke with the first light and, with all the responsibilities of the previous day melted, feeling myself rather like the sun, ready to illumine and rejoice. Life never seemed so simple and clear and full of possibilities as then. I put my feet out from under the clothes—I called them Mrs. Left and Mrs. Right—and invented dramatic situations for them in which they discussed the problems of the day. At least Mrs. Right did; she was very demonstrative, but I hadn't the same control of Mrs. Left, so she mostly contented herself with nodding agreement.

They discussed what Mother and I should do during the day, what Santa Claus should give a fellow for Christmas, and what steps should be taken to brighten the home. There was that little matter of the baby, for instance. Mother and I could never agree about that. Ours was the only house in the terrace without a new baby, and Mother said we couldn't afford one till Father came back from the war because they cost seventeen and six. That showed how simple she was. The Geneys up the road had a baby, and everyone knew they couldn't afford seventeen and six. It was probably a cheap baby, and Mother wanted

36

something really good, but I felt she was too exclusive. The Geneys' baby would have done us fine.

Having settled my plans for the day, I got up, put a chair under the attic window, and lifted the frame high enough to stick out my head. The window overlooked the front gardens of the terrace behind ours, and beyond these it looked over a deep valley to the tall, red-brick houses terraced up the opposite hillside, which were all still in shadow, while those at our side of the valley were all lit up, though with long strange shadows that made them seem unfamiliar; rigid and painted.

After that I went into Mother's room and climbed into the big bed. She woke and I began to tell her of my schemes. By this time, though I never seem to have noticed it, I was petrified in my nightshirt, and I thawed as I talked until, the last frost melted, I fell asleep beside her and woke again only when I heard her below in the kitchen, making the breakfast.

After breakfast we went into town; heard Mass at St. Augustine's and said a prayer for Father, and did the shopping. If the afternoon was fine we either went for a walk in the country or a visit to Mother's great friend in the convent, Mother St. Dominic. Mother had them all praying for Father, and every night, going to bed, I asked God to send him back safe from the war to us. Little, indeed, did I know what I was praying for!

One morning, I got into the big bed, and there, sure enough, was Father in his usual Santa Claus manner, but later, instead of uniform, he put on his best blue suit, and Mother was as pleased as anything. I saw nothing to be pleased about, because, out of uniform, Father was altogether less interesting, but she only beamed, and explained that our prayers had been answered, and off we went to Mass to thank God for having brought Father safely home.

The irony of it! That very day when he came in to dinner he took off his boots and put on his slippers, donned the dirty old cap he wore about the house to save him from colds, crossed his legs, and began to talk gravely to Mother, who looked anxious. Naturally, I disliked her looking anxious, because it destroyed her good looks, so I interrupted him.

"Just a moment, Larry!" she said gently.

This was only what she said when we had boring visitors, so I attached no importance to it and went on talking.

"Do be quiet, Larry!" she said impatiently. "Don't you hear me talking to Daddy?"

This was the first time I had heard those ominous words, "talking to Daddy," and I couldn't help feeling that if this was how God answered prayers, he couldn't listen to them very attentively.

"Why are you talking to Daddy?" I asked with as great a show of indifference as I could muster.

"Because Daddy and I have business to discuss. Now, don't interrupt again!"

In the afternoon, at Mother's request, Father took me for a walk. This time we went into town instead of out to the country, and I thought at first, in my usual optimistic way, that it might be an improvement. It was nothing of the sort. Father and I had quite different notions of a walk in town. He had no proper interest in trams, ships, and horses, and the only thing that seemed to divert him was talking to fellows as old as himself. When I wanted to stop he simply went on, dragging me behind him by the hand; when he wanted to stop I had no alternative but to do the same. I noticed that it seemed to be a sign that he wanted to stop for a long time whenever he leaned against a wall. The second time I saw him do it I got wild. He seemed to be settling himself forever. I pulled him by the coat and trousers, but, unlike Mother who, if you were too persistent, got into a wax and said: "Larry, if you don't behave yourself, I'll give you a good slap," Father had an extraordinary capacity for amiable inattention. I sized him up and wondered would I cry, but he seemed to be too remote to be annoyed even by that. Really, it was like going for a walk with a mountain! He either ignored the wrenching and pummeling entirely, or else glanced down with a grin of amusement from his peak. I had never met anyone so absorbed in himself as he seemed.

At teatime, "talking to Daddy" began again, complicated this time by the fact that he had an evening paper, and every few minutes he put it down and told Mother something new out of it. I felt this was foul play. Man for man, I was prepared to compete with him any time for Mother's attention, but when he had it all made up for him by other people it left me no chance. Several times I tried to change the subject without success.

"You must be quiet while Daddy is reading, Larry," Mother said impatiently.

It was clear that she either genuinely liked talking to Father better than talking to me, or else that he had some terrible hold on her which made her afraid to admit the truth.

"Mummy," I said that night when she was tucking me up, "do you think if I prayed hard God would send Daddy back to the war?"

She seemed to think about that for a moment.

"No, dear," she said with a smile. "I don't think he would."

"Why wouldn't he, Mummy?"

"Because there isn't a war any longer, dear."

"But, Mummy, couldn't God make another war, if he liked?"

"He wouldn't like to, dear. It's not God who makes wars, but bad people."

"Oh!" I said.

I was disappointed about that. I began to think that God wasn't quite what he was cracked up to be.

Next morning I woke at my usual hour, feeling like a bottle of champagne. I put out my feet and invented a long conversation in which Mrs. Right talked of the trouble she had with her own father till she put him in the Home. I didn't quite know what the Home was but it sounded the right place for Father. Then I got my chair and stuck my head out of the attic window. Dawn was just breaking, with a guilty air that made me feel I had caught it in the act. My head bursting with stories and schemes, I stumbled in next door, and in the half-darkness scrambled into the big bed. There was no room at Mother's side so I had to get between her and Father. For the time being I had forgotten about him, and for several minutes I sat bolt upright, racking my brains to know what I could do with him. He was taking up more than his fair share of the bed, and I couldn't get comfortable, so I gave him several kicks that made him grunt and stretch. He made room all right, though. Mother waked and felt for me. I settled back comfortably in the warmth of the bed with my thumb in my mouth.

"Mummy!" I hummed, loudly and contentedly.

"Ssh! dear," she whispered. "Don't wake Daddy!"

This was a new development, which threatened to be even more serious than "talking to Daddy." Life without my early-morning conferences was unthinkable.

"Why?" I asked severely.

"Because poor Daddy is tired."

This seemed to me a quite inadequate reason, and I was sickened by the sentimentality of her "poor Daddy." I never liked that sort of gush; it always struck me as insincere.

"Oh!" I said lightly. Then in my most winning tone: "Do you know where I want to go with you today, Mummy?"

"No, dear," she sighed.

"I want to go down the Glen and fish for thornybacks with my new net, and then I want to go out to the Fox and Hounds, and—"

"Don't-wake-Daddy!" she hissed angrily, clapping her hand across my mouth.

But it was too late. He was awake, or nearly so. He grunted and reached for the matches. Then he stared incredulously at his watch.

"Like a cup of tea, dear?" asked Mother in a meek, hushed voice I had never heard her use before. It sounded almost as though she were afraid.

"Tea?" he exclaimed indignantly. "Do you know what the time is?"

"And after that I want to go up the Rathcooney Road," I said loudly, afraid I'd forget something in all those interruptions.

"Go to sleep at once, Larry!" she said sharply.

I began to snivel. I couldn't concentrate, the way that pair went on, and smothering my early-morning schemes was like burying a family from the cradle.

Father said nothing, but lit his pipe and sucked it, looking out into the shadows without minding Mother or me. I knew he was mad. Every time I made a remark Mother hushed me irritably. I was mortified. I felt it wasn't fair; there was even something sinister in it. Every time I had pointed out to her the waste of making two beds when we could both sleep in one, she had told me it was healthier like that, and now here was this man, this stranger, sleeping with her without the least regard for her health!

He got up early and made tea, but though he brought Mother a cup he brought none for me.

"Mummy," I shouted, "I want a cup of tea, too."

"Yes, dear," she said patiently. "You can drink from Mummy's saucer."

That settled it. Either Father or I would have to leave the house. I didn't want to drink from Mother's saucer; I wanted to be treated as an equal in my own home, so, just to spite her, I drank it all and left none for her. She took that quietly, too.

But that night when she was putting me to bed she said gently: "Larry, I want you to promise me something."

"What is it?" I asked.

"Not to come in and disturb poor Daddy in the morning. Promise?"

"Poor Daddy" again! I was becoming suspicious of everything involving that quite impossible man.

"Why?" I asked.

"Because poor Daddy is worried and tired and he doesn't sleep well."

"Why doesn't he, Mummy?"

"Well, you know, don't you, that while he was at the war Mummy got the pennies from the Post Office?"

"From Miss MacCarthy?"

"That's right. But now, you see, Miss MacCarthy hasn't any more pennies, so Daddy must go out and find us some. You know what would happen if he couldn't?"

"No," I said, "tell us."

"Well, I think we might have to go out and beg for them like the poor old woman on Fridays. We wouldn't like that, would we?"

"No," I agreed. "We wouldn't."

"So you'll promise not to come in and wake him?"

"Promise."

Mind you, I meant that. I knew pennies were a serious matter, and I was all against having to go out and beg like the old woman on Fridays. Mother laid out all my toys in a complete ring round the bed so that, whatever way I got out, I was bound to fall over one of them.

When I woke I remembered my promise all right. I got up and sat on the floor and played—for hours, it seemed to me. Then I got my chair and looked out the attic window for more hours. I wished it was time for Father to wake; I wished someone would make me a cup of tea. I didn't feel in the least like the sun; instead, I was bored and so very, very cold! I simply longed for the warmth and depth of the big featherbed.

At last I could stand it no longer. I went into the next room. As there was still no room at Mother's side I climbed over her and she woke with a start.

"Larry," she whispered, gripping my arm very tightly, "what did you promise?"

"But I did, Mummy," I wailed, caught in the very act. "I was quiet for ever so long."

"Oh, dear, and you're perished!" she said sadly, feeling me all over. "Now, if I let you stay will you promise not to talk?"

"But I want to talk, Mummy," I wailed.

"That has nothing to do with it," she said with a firmness that was new to me. "Daddy wants to sleep. Now, do you understand that?"

I understood it only too well. I wanted to talk, he wanted to sleep—whose house was it, anyway?

"Mummy," I said with equal firmness, "I think it would be healthier for Daddy to sleep in his own bed."

That seemed to stagger her, because she said nothing for a while.

"Now, once for all," she went on, "you're to be perfectly quiet or go back to your own bed. Which is it to be?"

The injustice of it got me down. I had convicted her out of her own mouth of inconsistency and unreasonableness, and she hadn't even attempted to reply. Full of spite, I gave Father a kick, which she didn't notice but which made him grunt and open his eyes in alarm.

"What time is it?" he asked in a panic-stricken voice, not looking at Mother but the door, as if he saw someone there.

"It's early yet," she replied soothingly. "It's only the child. Go to sleep again. . . . Now, Larry," she added, getting out of bed, "you've wakened Daddy and you must go back."

This time, for all her quiet air, I knew she meant it, and knew that my principal rights and privileges were as good as lost unless I asserted them at once. As she lifted me, I gave a screech, enough to wake the dead, not to mind Father. He groaned.

"That damn child! Doesn't he ever sleep?"

"It's only a habit, dear," she said quietly, though I could see she was vexed.

"Well, it's time he got out of it," shouted Father, beginning to heave in the bed. He suddenly gathered all the bedclothes about him, turned to the wall, and then looked back over his shoulder with nothing showing, only two small, spiteful, dark eyes. The man looked very wicked.

To open the bedroom door, Mother had to let me down, and I broke free and dashed for the farthest corner, screeching. Father sat bolt upright in bed.

"Shut up, you little puppy!" he said in a choking voice.

I was so astonished that I stopped screeching. Never, never had anyone spoken to me in that tone before. I looked at him incredulously and saw his face convulsed with rage. It was only then that I fully realized how God had codded me, listening to my prayers for the safe return of this monster.

"Shut up, you!" I bawled, beside myself.

"What's that you said?" shouted Father, making a wild leap out of bed.

"Mick, Mick!" cried Mother. "Don't you see the child isn't used to you?"

"I see he's better fed than taught," snarled Father, waving his arms wildly. "He wants his bottom smacked."

All his previous shouting was as nothing to these obscene words referring to my person. They really made my blood boil.

"Smack your own!" I screamed hysterically. "Smack your own! Shut up! Shut up!"

At this he lost his patience and let fly at me. He did it with the lack of conviction you'd expect of a man under Mother's horrified eyes, and it ended up as a mere tap, but the sheer indignity of being struck at all by a stranger, a total stranger who had cajoled his way back from the war into our big bed as a result of my innocent intercession, made me completely dotty. I shrieked and shrieked, and danced in my bare feet, and Father, looking awkward and hairy in nothing but a short grey army shirt, glared down at me like a mountain out for murder. I think it must have been then that I realized he was jealous too. And there stood Mother in her nightdress, looking as if her heart was broken between us. I hoped she felt as she looked. It seemed to me that she deserved it all.

From that morning out my life was a hell. Father and I were enemies, open and avowed. We conducted a series of skirmishes against one another, he trying to steal my time with Mother and I his. When she was sitting on my bed, telling me a story, he took to looking for some pair of old boots which he alleged he had left behind him at the beginning of the war. While he talked to Mother I played loudly with my toys to show my total lack of concern. He created a terrible scene one evening when he came in from work and found me at his box, playing with his regimental badges, Gurkha knives and button-sticks. Mother got up and took the box from me.

"You mustn't play with Daddy's toys unless he lets you, Larry," she said severely. "Daddy doesn't play with yours."

For some reason Father looked at her as if she had struck him and then turned away with a scowl.

"Those are not toys," he growled, taking down the box again to see had I lifted anything. "Some of those curios are very rare and valuable."

But as time went on I saw more and more how he managed to alienate Mother and me. What made it worse was that I couldn't grasp his method or see what attraction he had for Mother. In every possible way he was less winning than I. He had a common accent and made noises at his tea. I thought for a while that it might be the newspapers she was interested in, so I made up bits of news of my own to read to her. Then I thought it might be the smoking, which I personally thought attractive, and took his pipes and went round the house dribbling into them till he caught me. I even made noises at my tea, but Mother only told me I was disgusting. It all seemed to hinge round that unhealthy habit of sleeping together, so I made a point of dropping into their bedroom and nosing round, talking to myself, so that they wouldn't know I was watching them, but they were never up to anything that I could see. In the end it beat me. It seemed to depend on being grown-up and giving people rings, and I realized I'd have to wait.

But at the same time I wanted him to see that I was only waiting, not giving up the fight. One evening when he was being particularly obnoxious, chattering away well above my head, I let him have it.

"Mummy," I said, "do you know what I'm going to do when I grow up?"

"No, dear," she replied. "What?"

"I'm going to marry you," I said quietly.

Father gave a great guffaw out of him, but he didn't take me in. I knew it must only be pretense. And Mother, in spite of everything, was pleased. I felt she was probably relieved to know that one day Father's hold on her would be broken.

"Won't that be nice?" she said with a smile.

"It'll be very nice," I said confidentially. "Because we're going to have lots and lots of babies."

"That's right, dear," she said placidly. "I think we'll have one soon, and then you'll have plenty of company."

I was no end pleased about that because it showed that in spite of the way she gave in to Father she still considered my wishes. Besides, it would put the Geneys in their place.

It didn't turn out like that, though. To begin with, she was very preoccupied—I supposed about where she would get the seventeen and six—and though Father took to staying out late in the evenings it did me no particular good. She stopped taking me for walks, became as touchy as blazes, and smacked me for nothing at all. Sometimes I wished I'd never mentioned the confounded baby—I seemed to have a genius for bringing calamity on myself.

And calamity it was! Sonny arrived in the most appalling hullabaloo—even that much he couldn't do without a fuss—and from the first moment I disliked him. He was a difficult child—so far as I was concerned he was always difficult—and demanded far too much attention. Mother was simply silly about him, and couldn't see when he was only showing off. As company he was worse than useless. He slept all day, and I had to go round the house on tiptoe to avoid waking him. It wasn't any longer a question of not waking Father. The slogan now was "Don't-wake-Sonny!" I couldn't understand why the child wouldn't sleep at the proper time, so whenever Mother's back was turned I woke him. Sometimes to keep him awake I pinched him as well. Mother caught me at it one day and gave me a most unmerciful flaking.

One evening, when Father was coming from work, I was playing trains in the front garden. I let on not to notice him; instead, I pretended to be talking to myself, and said in a loud voice: "If another bloody baby comes into this house, I'm going out."

Father stopped dead and looked at me over his shoulder.

"What's that you said?" he asked sternly.

"I was only talking to myself," I replied, trying to conceal my panic. "It's private."

He turned and went in without a word. Mind you, I intended it as a solemn warning, but its effect was quite different. Father started being quite nice to me. I could understand that, of course. Mother was quite sickening about Sonny. Even at mealtimes she'd get up and gawk at him in the cradle with an idiotic smile, and tell Father to do the same. He was always polite about it, but he looked so puzzled you could see he didn't know what she was talking about. He complained of the way Sonny cried at night, but she only got cross and said that Sonny never cried except when there was something up with him—which was a flaming lie, because Sonny never had anything up with him, and only cried for attention. It was really painful to see how simple-minded she was. Father wasn't attractive, but he had a fine intelligence. He saw through Sonny, and now he knew that I saw through him as well.

One night I woke with a start. There was someone beside me in the bed. For one wild moment I felt sure it must be Mother, having come to her senses and left Father for good, but then I heard Sonny in convulsions in the next room, and Mother saying: "There! There! There!" and I knew it wasn't she. It was Father. He was lying beside me, wide awake, breathing hard and apparently as mad as hell.

After a while it came to me what he was mad about. It was his turn now. After turning me out of the big bed, he had been turned out himself. Mother had no consideration now for anyone but that poisonous pup, Sonny. I couldn't help feeling sorry for Father. I had been through it all myself, and even at that age I was magnanimous. I began to stroke him down and say: "There! There!" He wasn't exactly responsive.

"Aren't you asleep either?" he snarled.

"Ah, come on and put your arm around us, can't you?" I said, and he did, in a sort of way. Gingerly, I suppose, is how you'd describe it. He was very bony but better than nothing.

At Christmas he went out of his way to buy me a really nice model railway.

QUESTIONS

1. Is the story narrated from the point of view of a young child or a mature man? **2.** Note that the narrator's most ardent wishes—for the return of his father and for a new baby in the house—are granted. What are the consequences for him? **3.** What specific details in the story contribute to the appropriateness of its title? **4.** With whom does the reader sympathize? How does the author control those sympathies?

WRITING TOPIC

Focusing on the ironies embodied in this story, describe the shifting relationships among the main characters.

A Conversation with My Father   1972

GRACE PALEY   [b. 1922]

My father is eighty-six years old and in bed. His heart, that bloody motor, is equally old and will not do certain jobs any more. It still floods his head with brainy light. But it won't let his legs carry the weight of his body around the house. Despite my metaphors, this muscle failure is not due to his old heart, he says, but to a potassium shortage. Sitting on one pillow, leaning on three, he offers last-minute advice and makes a request.

"I would like you to write a simple story just once more," he says, "the kind de Maupassant wrote, or Chekhov,[1] the kind you used to write. Just recognizable people and then write down what happened to them next."

I say, "Yes, why not? That's possible." I want to please him, though I don't remember writing that way. I *would* like to try to tell such a story, if he means the kind that begins: "There was a woman . . ." followed by plot, the absolute line between two points which I've always despised. Not for literary reasons, but because it takes all hope away. Everyone, real or invented, deserves the open destiny of life.

Finally I thought of a story that had been happening for a couple of years right across the street. I wrote it down, then read it aloud. "Pa," I said, "how about this? Do you mean something like this?"

> Once in my time there was a woman and she had a son. They lived nicely, in a small apartment in Manhattan. This boy at about fifteen became a junkie, which is not unusual in our neighborhood. In order to maintain her close friendship with him, she became a junkie too. She said it was part of the youth culture, with which she felt very much at home. After a while, for a number of reasons, the boy gave it all up and left the city and his mother in disgust. Hopeless and alone, she grieved. We all visit her.

"O.K., Pa, that's it," I said, "an unadorned and miserable tale."

"But that's not what I mean," my father said. "You misunderstood me on purpose. You know there's a lot more to it. You know that. You left everything out. Turgenev[2] wouldn't do that. Chekhov wouldn't do that. There are in fact Russian writers you never heard of, you don't have an inkling of, as good as anyone, who can write a plain ordinary story, who would not leave out what you have left out. I object not to facts but to people sitting in trees talking senselessly, voices from who knows where. . . ."

---

[1] Guy de Maupassant (1850–1893) wrote stories that depended on ironic twists of plot for their effect. Anton Pavlovich Chekhov (1860–1904) wrote insistently realistic stories.

[2] Ivan Sergeyevich Turgenev (1818–1883), like Chekhov, wrote realistic fiction.

"Forget that one, Pa, what have I left out now? In this one?"

"Her looks, for instance."

"Oh. Quite handsome, I think. Yes."

"Her hair?"

"Dark, with heavy braids, as though she were a girl or a foreigner."

"What were her parents like, her stock? That she became such a person. It's interesting, you know."

"From out of town. Professional people. The first to be divorced in their county. How's that? Enough?" I asked.

"With you, it's all a joke," he said. "What about the boy's father? Why didn't you mention him? Who was he? Or was the boy born out of wedlock?"

"Yes," I said. "He was born out of wedlock."

"For Godsakes, doesn't anyone in your stories get married? Doesn't anyone have the time to run down to City Hall before they jump into bed?"

"No," I said. "In real life, yes. But in my stories, no."

"Why do you answer me like that?"

"Oh, Pa, this is a simple story about a smart woman who came to N.Y.C. full of interest love trust excitement very up to date, and about her son, what a hard time she had in this world. Married or not, it's of small consequence."

"It is of great consequence," he said.

"O.K.," I said.

"O.K. O.K. yourself," he said, "but listen. I believe you that she's good-looking, but I don't think she was so smart."

"That's true," I said. "Actually that's the trouble with stories. People start out fantastic. You think they're extraordinary, but it turns out as the work goes along, they're just average with a good education. Sometimes the other way around, the person's a kind of dumb innocent, but he outwits you and you can't even think of an ending good enough."

"What do you do then?" he asked. He had been a doctor for a couple of decades and then an artist for a couple of decades and he's still interested in details, craft, technique.

"Well, you just have to let the story lie around till some agreement can be reached between you and the stubborn hero."

"Aren't you talking silly now?" he asked. "Start again," he said. "It so happens I'm not going out this evening. Tell the story again. See what you can do this time."

"O.K.," I said. "But it's not a five-minute job." Second attempt:

> Once, across the street from us, there was a fine handsome woman, our neighbor. She had a son whom she loved because she'd known him since birth (in helpless chubby infancy, and in the wrestling, hugging ages, seven to ten, as well as earlier and later). This boy, when he fell into the fist of adolescence, became a junkie. He was not a hopeless one. He was in fact hopeful, an ideologue and successful converter. With his busy brilliance, he wrote persuasive articles for his high-school newspaper. Seeking a wider audience, using important connec-

tions, he drummed into Lower Manhattan newsstand distribution a periodical called *Oh! Golden Horse!*

In order to keep him from feeling guilty (because guilt is the stony heart of nine tenths of all clinically diagnosed cancers in America today, she said), and because she had always believed in giving bad habits room at home where one could keep an eye on them, she too became a junkie. Her kitchen was famous for a while—a center for intellectual addicts who knew what they were doing. A few felt artistic like Coleridge[3] and others were scientific and revolutionary like Leary.[4] Although she was often high herself, certain good mothering reflexes remained, and she saw to it that there was lots of orange juice around and honey and milk and vitamin pills. However, she never cooked anything but chili, and that no more than once a week. She explained, when we talked to her, seriously, with neighborly concern, that it was her part in the youth culture and she would rather be with the young, it was an honor, than with her own generation.

One week, while nodding through an Antonioni[5] film, this boy was severely jabbed by the elbow of a stern and proselytizing girl, sitting beside him. She offered immediate apricots and nuts for his sugar level, spoke to him sharply, and took him home.

She had heard of him and his work and she herself published, edited, and wrote a competitive journal called *Man Does Live by Bread Alone.* In the organic heat of her continuous presence he could not help but become interested once more in his muscles, his arteries, and nerve connections. In fact he began to love them, treasure them, praise them with funny little songs in *Man Does Live. . . .*

> the fingers of my flesh transcend
> my transcendental soul
> the tightness in my shoulders end
> my teeth have made me whole

To the mouth of his head (that glory of will and determination) he brought hard apples, nuts, wheat germ, and soybean oil. He said to his old friends, From now on, I guess I'll keep my wits about me. I'm going on the natch. He said he was about to begin a spiritual deep-breathing journey. How about you too, Mom? he asked kindly.

His conversion was so radiant, splendid, that neighborhood kids his age began to say that he had never been a real addict at all, only a journalist along for the smell of the story. The mother tried several times to give up what had become without her son and his friends a lonely habit. This effort only brought it to supportable levels. The boy and his girl took their electronic mimeograph and moved to the bushy edge of another borough. They were very strict. They said they would not see her again until she had been off drugs for sixty days.

At home alone in the evening, weeping, the mother read and reread the seven issues of *Oh! Golden Horse!* They seemed to her as truthful as ever. We often

---

[3] Samuel Taylor Coleridge (1772–1834), English poet who used opium.

[4] Timothy Leary (b. 1920), former professor of psychology at Harvard University, who promoted the use of psychedelic drugs.

[5] Michelangelo Antonioni (b. 1912), an Italian director of avant-garde films.

crossed the street to visit and console. But if we mentioned any of our children who were at college or in the hospital or dropouts at home, she would cry out, My baby! My baby! and burst into terrible, face-scarring, time-consuming tears. The End.

First my father was silent, then he said, "Number One: You have a nice sense of humor. Number Two: I see you can't tell a plain story. So don't waste time." Then he said sadly, "Number Three: I suppose that means she was alone, she was left like that, his mother. Alone. Probably sick?"

I said, "Yes."

"Poor woman. Poor girl, to be born in a time of fools, to live among fools. The end. The end. You were right to put that down. The end."

I didn't want to argue, but I had to say, "Well, it is not necessarily the end, Pa."

"Yes," he said, "what a tragedy. The end of a person."

"No, Pa," I begged him. "It doesn't have to be. She's only about forty. She could be a hundred different things in this world as time goes on. A teacher or a social worker. An ex-junkie! Sometimes it's better than having a master's in education."

"Jokes," he said. "As a writer that's your main trouble. You don't want to recognize it. Tragedy! Plain tragedy! Historical tragedy! No hope. The end."

"Oh, Pa," I said. "She could change."

"In your own life, too, you have to look it in the face." He took a couple of nitroglycerin. "Turn to five," he said, pointing to the dial on the oxygen tank. He inserted the tubes into his nostrils and breathed deep. He closed his eyes and said, "No."

I had promised the family to always let him have the last word when arguing, but in this case I had a different responsibility. That woman lives across the street. She's my knowledge and my invention. I'm sorry for her. I'm not going to leave her there in that house crying. (Actually neither would Life, which unlike me has no pity.)

Therefore: She did change. Of course her son never came home again. But right now, she's the receptionist in a storefront community clinic in the East Village. Most of the customers are young people, some old friends. The head doctor has said to her, "If we only had three people in this clinic with your experiences. . . ."

"The doctor said that?" My father took the oxygen tubes out of his nostrils and said, "Jokes. Jokes again."

"No, Pa, it could really happen that way, it's a funny world nowadays."

"No," he said. "Truth first. She will slide back. A person must have character. She does not."

"No, Pa," I said. "That's it. She's got a job. Forget it. She's in that storefront working."

"How long will it be?" he asked. "Tragedy! You too. When will you look it in the face?"

The Lesson   1972

TONI CADE BAMBARA   [b. 1939]

Back in the days when everyone was old and stupid or young and foolish and
me and Sugar were the only ones just right, this lady moved on our block with
nappy hair and proper speech and no makeup. And quite naturally we laughed
at her, laughed the way we did at the junk man who went about his business
like he was some big-time president and his sorry-ass horse his secretary. And
we kinda hated her too, hated the way we did the winos who cluttered up our
parks and pissed on our handball walls and stank up our hallways and stairs so
you couldn't halfway play hide-and-seek without a goddamn gas mask. Miss
Moore was her name. The only woman on the block with no first name. And
she was black as hell, cept for her feet, which were fish-white and spooky. And
she was always planning these boring-ass things for us to do, us being my
cousin, mostly, who lived on the block cause we all moved North the same
time and to the same apartment then spread out gradual to breathe. And our
parents would yank our heads into some kinda shape and crisp up our clothes
so we'd be presentable for travel with Miss Moore, who always looked like she
was going to church, though she never did. Which is just one of the things the
grownups talked about when they talked behind her back like a dog. But when
she came calling with some sachet she'd sewed up or some gingerbread she'd
made or some book, why then they'd all be too embarrassed to turn her down
and we'd get handed over all spruced up. She'd been to college and said it was
only right that she should take responsibility for the young ones' education, and
she not even related by marriage or blood. So they'd go for it. Specially Aunt
Gretchen. She was the main gofer in the family. You got some old dumb shit
foolishness you want somebody to go for, you send for Aunt Gretchen. She
been screwed into the go-along for so long, it's a blood-deep natural thing with
her. Which is how she got saddled with me and Sugar and Junior in the first
place while our mothers were in a la-de-da apartment up the block having a
good ole time.

So this one day Miss Moore rounds us all up at the mailbox and it's puredee
hot and she's knockin herself out about arithmetic. And school suppose to let
up in summer I heard, but she don't never let up. And the starch in my pinafore
scratching the shit outta me and I'm really hating this nappy-head bitch and
her goddamn college degree. I'd much rather go to the pool or to the show
where it's cool. So me and Sugar leaning on the mailbox being surly, which is
a Miss Moore word. And Flyboy checking out what everybody brought for
lunch. And Fat Butt already wasting his peanut-butter-and-jelly sandwich like
the pig he is. And Junebug punchin on Q.T.'s arm for potato chips. And Rosie

Giraffe shifting from one hip to the other waiting for somebody to step on her foot or ask her if she from Georgia so she can kick ass, preferably Mercedes'. And Miss Moore asking us do we know what money is, like we a bunch of retards. I mean real money, she say, like it's only poker chips or monopoly papers we lay on the grocer. So right away I'm tired of this and say so. And would much rather snatch Sugar and go to the Sunset and terrorize the West Indian kids and take their hair ribbons and their money too. And Miss Moore files that remark away for next week's lesson on brotherhood, I can tell. And finally I say we oughta get to the subway cause it's cooler and besides we might meet some cute boys. Sugar done swiped her mama's lipstick, so we ready.

So we heading down the street and she's boring us silly about what things cost and what our parents make and how much goes for rent and how money ain't divided up right in this country. And then she gets to the part about we all poor and live in the slums, which I don't feature. And I'm ready to speak on that, but she steps out in the street and hails two cabs just like that. Then she hustles half the crew in with her and hands me a five-dollar bill and tells me to calculate 10 percent tip for the driver. And we're off. Me and Sugar and Junebug and Flyboy hangin out the window and hollering to everybody, putting lipstick on each other cause Flyboy a faggot anyway, and making farts with our sweaty armpits. But I'm mostly trying to figure how to spend this money. But they all fascinated with the meter ticking and Junebug starts laying bets as to how much it'll read when Flyboy can't hold his breath no more. Then Sugar lays bets as to how much it'll be when we get there. So I'm stuck. Don't nobody want to go for my plan, which is to jump out at the next light and run off to the first bar-b-que we can find. Then the driver tells us to get the hell out cause we there already. And the meter reads eighty-five cents. And I'm stalling to figure out the tip and Sugar say give him a dime. And I decide he don't need it bad as I do, so later for him. But then he tries to take off with Junebug foot still in the door so we talk about his mama something ferocious. Then we check out that we on Fifth Avenue and everybody dressed up in stockings. One lady in a fur coat, hot as it is. White folks crazy.

"This is the place," Miss Moore say, presenting it to us in the voice she uses at the museum. "Let's look in the windows before we go in."

"Can we steal?" Sugar asks very serious like she's getting the ground rules squared away before she plays. "I beg your pardon," say Miss Moore, and we fall out. So she leads us around the windows of the toy store and me and Sugar screamin, "This is mine, that's mine, I gotta have that, that was made for me, I was born for that," till Big Butt drowns us out.

"Hey, I'm goin to buy that there."

"That there? You don't even know what it is, stupid."

"I do so," he say punchin on Rosie Giraffe. "It's a microscope."

"Whatcha gonna do with a microscope, fool?"

"Look at things."

"Like what, Ronald?" ask Miss Moore. And Big Butt ain't got the first notion.

So here go Miss Moore gabbing about the thousands of bacteria in a drop of water and the somethinorother in a speck of blood and the million and one living things in the air around us is invisible to the naked eye. And what she say that for? Junebug go to town on that "naked" and we rolling. Then Miss Moore ask what it cost. So we all jam into the window smudgin it up and the price tag say $300. So then she ask how long'd take for Big Butt and Junebug to save up their allowances. "Too long," I say. "Yeh," adds Sugar, "outgrown it by that time." And Miss Moore say no, you never outgrow learning instruments. "Why, even medical students and interns and," blah, blah, blah. And we ready to choke Big Butt for bringing it up in the first damn place.

"This here costs four hundred eighty dollars," say Rosie Giraffe. So we pile up all over her to see what she pointin out. My eyes tell me it's a chunk of glass cracked with something heavy, and different-color inks dripped into the splits, then the whole thing put into a oven or something. But for $480 it don't make sense.

"That's a paperweight made of semi-precious stones fused together under tremendous pressure," she explains slowly, with her hands doing the mining and all the factory work.

"So what's a paperweight?" asks Rosie Giraffe.

"To weigh paper with, dumbbell," say Flyboy, the wise man from the East.

"Not exactly," say Miss Moore, which is what she say when you warm or way off too. "It's to weigh paper down so it won't scatter and make your desk untidy." So right away me and Sugar curtsy to each other and then to Mercedes who is more the tidy type.

"We don't keep paper on top of the desk in my class," say Junebug, figuring Miss Moore crazy or lyin one.

"At home, then," she say. "Don't you have a calendar and pencil case and a blotter and a letter-opener on your desk at home where you do your homework?" And she know damn well what our homes look like cause she nosys around in them every chance she gets.

"I don't even have a desk," say Junebug. "Do we?"

"No. And I don't get no homework neither," says Big Butt.

"And I don't even have a home," say Flyboy like he do at school to keep the white folks off his back and sorry for him. Send this poor kid to camp posters, is his specialty.

"I do," says Mercedes. "I have a box of stationery on my desk and a picture of my cat. My godmother bought the stationery and the desk. There's a big rose on each sheet and the envelopes smell like roses."

"Who wants to know about your smelly-ass stationery," say Rosie Giraffe fore I can get my two cents in.

"It's important to have a work area all your own so that . . ."

"Will you look at this sailboat, please," say Flyboy, cuttin her off and pointin to the thing like it was his. So once again we tumble all over each other to gaze at this magnificent thing in the toy store which is just big enough to maybe sail two kittens across the pond if you strap them to the posts tight. We all start reciting the price tag like we in assembly. "Handcrafted sailboat of fiberglass at one thousand one hundred ninety-five dollars."

"Unbelievable," I hear myself say and am really stunned. I read it again for myself just in case the group recitation put me in a trance. Same thing. For some reason this pisses me off. We look at Miss Moore and she lookin at us, waiting for I dunno what.

"Who'd pay all that when you can buy a sailboat set for a quarter at Pop's, a tube of glue for a dime, and a ball of string for eight cents? It must have a motor and a whole lot else besides," I say. "My sailboat cost me about fifty cents."

"But will it take water?" say Mercedes with her smart ass.

"Took mine to Alley Pond Park once," say Flyboy. "String broke. Lost it. Pity."

"Sailed mine in Central Park and it keeled over and sank. Had to ask my father for another dollar."

"And you got the strap," laugh Big Butt. "The jerk didn't even have a string on it. My old man wailed on his behind."

Little Q.T. was staring hard at the sailboat and you could see he wanted it bad. But he too little and somebody'd just take it from him. So what the hell. "This boat for kids, Miss Moore?"

"Parents silly to buy something like that just to get all broke up," say Rosie Giraffe.

"That much money it should last forever," I figure.

"My father'd buy it for me if I wanted it."

"Your father, my ass," say Rosie Giraffe getting a chance to finally push Mercedes.

"Must be rich people shop here," say Q.T.

"You are a very bright boy," say Flyboy. "What was your first clue?" And he rap him on the head with the back of his knuckles, since Q.T. the only one he could get away with. Though Q.T. liable to come up behind you years later and get his licks in when you half expect it.

"What I want to know is," I says to Miss Moore though I never talk to her, I wouldn't give the bitch that satisfaction, "is how much a real boat costs? I figure a thousand'd get you a yacht any day."

"Why don't you check that out," she says, "and report back to the group?" Which really pains my ass. If you gonna mess up a perfectly good swim day least you could do is have some answers. "Let's go in," she say like she got something up her sleeve. Only she don't lead the way. So me and Sugar turn the corner to where the entrance is, but when we get there I kinda hang back. Not that I'm scared, what's there to be afraid of, just a toy store. But I feel funny, shame. But what I got to be shamed about? Got as much right to go in as anybody. But somehow I can't seem to get hold of the door, so I step away for Sugar to lead. But she hangs back too. And I look at her and she looks at me and this is ridiculous. I mean, damn, I have never ever been shy about doing nothing or going nowhere. But then Mercedes steps up and then Rosie Giraffe and Big Butt crowd in behind and shove, and next thing we all stuffed into the doorway with only Mercedes squeezing past us, smoothing out her jumper and walking right down the aisle. Then the rest of us tumble in like a glued-together jigsaw done all wrong. And people lookin at us. And it's like the time me and Sugar crashed into the Catholic church on a dare. But once we got in there and everything so hushed and holy and the candles and the bowin and the handkerchiefs on all the drooping heads, I just couldn't go through with the plan. Which was for me to run up to the altar and do a tap dance while Sugar played the nose flute and messed around in the holy water. And Sugar kept givin me the elbow. Then later teased me so bad I tied her up in the shower and turned it on and locked her in. And she'd be there till this day if Aunt Gretchen hadn't finally figured I was lyin about the boarder takin a shower.

Same thing in the store. We all walkin on tiptoe and hardly touchin the games and puzzles and things. And I watched Miss Moore who is steady watchin us like she waitin for a sign. Like Mama Drewery watches the sky and sniffs the air and takes note of just how much slant is in the bird formation. Then me and Sugar bump smack into each other, so busy gazing at the toys, 'specially the sailboat. But we don't laugh and go into our fat-lady bump-stomach routine. We just stare at that price tag. Then Sugar run a finger over the whole boat. And I'm jealous and want to hit her. Maybe not her, but I sure want to punch somebody in the mouth.

"Watcha bring us here for, Miss Moore?"

"You sound angry, Sylvia. Are you mad about something?" Givin me one of them grins like she tellin a grown-up joke that never turns out to be funny. And she's lookin very closely at me like maybe she planning to do my portrait from memory. I'm mad, but I won't give her that satisfaction. So I slouch around the store bein very bored and say, "Let's go."

Me and Sugar at the back of the train watchin the tracks whizzin by large then small then gettin gobbled up in the dark. I'm thinkin about this tricky toy I saw in the store. A clown that somersaults on a bar then does chin-ups just cause you yank lightly at his leg. Cost $35. I could see me askin my mother for a $35 birthday clown. "You wanna who that costs what?" she'd say, cocking her head to the side to get a better view of the hole in my head. Thirty-five dollars could buy new bunk beds for Junior and Gretchen's boy. Thirty-five dollars and the whole household could go visit Granddaddy Nelson in the country. Thirty-five dollars would pay for the rent and the piano bill too. Who are these people that spend that much for performing clowns and $1000 for toy sailboats? What kinda work they do and how they live and how come we ain't in on it? Where we are is who we are, Miss Moore always pointin out. But it don't necessarily have to be that way, she always adds then waits for somebody to say that poor people have to wake up and demand their share of the pie and don't none of us know what kind of pie she talking about in the first damn place. But she ain't so smart cause I still got her four dollars from the taxi and she sure ain't gettin it. Messin up my day with this shit. Sugar nudges me in my pocket and winks.

Miss Moore lines us up in front of the mailbox where we started from, seem like years ago, and I got a headache for thinkin so hard. And we lean all over each other so we can hold up under the draggy-ass lecture she always finishes us off with at the end before we thank her for borin us to tears. But she just looks at us like she readin tea leaves. Finally she say, "Well, what did you think of F. A. O. Schwarz?"

Rosie Giraffe mumbles, "White folks crazy."

"I'd like to go there again when I get my birthday money," says Mercedes, and we shove her out the pack so she has to lean on the mailbox by herself.

"I'd like a shower. Tiring day," say Flyboy.

Then Sugar surprises me by sayin, "You know, Miss Moore, I don't think all of us here put together eat in a year what that sailboat costs." And Miss Moore lights up like somebody goosed her. "And?" she say, urging Sugar on. Only I'm standin on her foot so she don't continue.

"Imagine for a minute what kind of society it is in which some people can spend on a toy what it would cost to feed a family of six or seven. What do you think?"

"I think," say Sugar pushing me off her feet like she never done before, cause I whip her ass in a minute, "that this is not much of a democracy if you ask me. Equal chance to pursue happiness means an equal crack at the dough, don't it?" Miss Moore is besides herself and I am disgusted with Sugar's treachery. So I stand on her foot one more time to see if she'll shove me. She shuts up, and Miss Moore looks at me, sorrowfully I'm thinkin. And somethin weird is goin on, I can feel it in my chest.

"Anybody else learn anything today?" lookin dead at me. I walk away and Sugar has to run to catch up and don't even seem to notice when I shrug her arm off my shoulder.

"Well, we got four dollars anyway," she says.

"Uh hunh."

"We could go to Hascombs and get half a chocolate layer and then go to the Sunset and still have plenty money for potato chips and ice cream sodas."

"Un hunh."

"Race you to Hascombs," she say.

We start down the block and she gets ahead which is O.K. by me cause I'm going to the West End and then over to the Drive to think this day through. She can run if she want to and even run faster. But ain't nobody gonna beat me at nuthin.

QUESTIONS

1. Characterize the narrator of this story.   **2.** How does the narrator describe her neighborhood? How does she feel when Miss Moore calls the neighborhood a slum?   **3.** F. A. O. Schwarz is a famous toy store on Fifth Avenue in New York

City, located about three miles south of Harlem where, doubtless, the children live. What lesson does Miss Moore convey by taking them there?

WRITING TOPIC
Is there any evidence at the end of the story that the narrator has been changed by the experience?

Orbiting

1988

BHARATI MUKHERJEE [b. 1940]

On Thanksgiving morning I'm still in my nightgown thinking of Vic when Dad raps on my apartment door. Who's he rolling joints for, who's he initiating now into the wonders of his inner space? What got me on Vic is remembering last Thanksgiving and his famous cranberry sauce with Grand Marnier, which Dad had interpreted as a sign of permanence in my life. A man who cooks like Vic is ready for other commitments. Dad cannot imagine cooking as self-expression. You cook *for* someone. Vic's sauce was a sign of his permanent isolation, if you really want to know.

Dad's come to drop off the turkey. It's a seventeen-pounder. Mr. Vitelli knows to reserve a biggish one for us every Thanksgiving and Christmas. But this November what with Danny in the Marines, Uncle Carmine having to be very careful after the bypass, and Vic taking off for outer space as well, we might as well have made do with one of those turkey rolls you pick out of the freezer. And in other years, Mr. Vitelli would not have given us a frozen bird. We were proud of that, our birds were fresh killed. I don't bring this up to Dad.

"Your mama took care of the thawing," Dad says. "She said you wouldn't have room in your Frigidaire."

"You mean Mom said Rindy shouldn't be living in a dump, right?" Mom has the simple, immigrant faith that children should do better than their parents, and her definition of better is comfortingly rigid. Fair enough—I believed it, too. But the fact is all I can afford is this third-floor studio with an art deco shower. The fridge fits under the kitchenette counter. The room has potential. I'm content with that. And I *like* my job even though it's selling, not designing, jewelry made out of seashells and semiprecious stones out of a boutique in Bellevue Plaza.

Dad shrugs. "You're an adult, Renata." He doesn't try to lower himself into one of my two deck chairs. He was a minor league catcher for a while and his knees went. The fake zebra-skin cushions piled as seats on the rug are out of the question for him. My futon bed folds up into a sofa, but the satin sheets are still lasciviously tangled. My father stands in a slat of sunlight, trying not to look embarrassed.

"Dad, I'd have come to the house and picked it up. You didn't have to make the extra trip out from Verona." A sixty-five-year-old man in wingtips and a Borsalino[1] hugging a wet, heavy bird is so poignant I have to laugh.

---

[1] A stylish brim hat.

"You wouldn't have gotten out of bed until noon, Renata." But Dad smiles. I know what he's saying. He's saying *he's* retired and *he* should be able to stay in bed till noon if he wants to, but he can't and he'd rather drive twenty miles with a soggy bird than read the *Ledger* one more time.

Grumbling and scolding are how we deMarcos express love. It's the North Italian way, Dad used to tell Cindi, Danny, and me when we were kids. Sicilians and Calabrians are emotional; we're contained. Actually, *he's* contained, the way Vic was contained for the most part. Mom's a Calabrian and she was born and raised there. Dad's very American, so Italy's a safe source of pride for him. I once figured it out: *his* father, Arturo deMarco, was a fifteen-week-old fetus when his mother planted her feet on Ellis Island. Dad, a proud son of North Italy, had one big adventure in his life, besides fighting in the Pacific, and that was marrying a Calabrian peasant. He made it sound as though Mom was a Korean or something, and their marriage was a kind of taming of the West, and that everything about her could be explained as a cultural deficiency. Actually, Vic could talk beautifully about his feelings. He'd brew espresso, pour it into tiny blue pottery cups and analyze our relationship. I should have listened. I mean really listened. I thought he was talking about us, but I know now he was only talking incessantly about himself. I put too much faith in mail-order nightgowns and bras.

"Your mama wanted me out of the house," Dad goes on. "She didn't used to be like this, Renata."

Renata and Carla are what we were christened. We changed to Rindy and Cindi in junior high. Danny didn't have to make such leaps, unless you count dropping out of Montclair State and joining the Marines. He was always Danny, or Junior.

I lug the turkey to the kitchen sink where it can drip away at a crazy angle until I have time to deal with it.

"Your mama must have told you girls I've been acting funny since I retired."

"No, Dad, she hasn't said anything about you acting funny." What she *has* said is do we think she ought to call Doc Brunetti and have a chat about Dad? Dad wouldn't have to know. He and Doc Brunetti are, or were, on the same church league bowling team. So is, or was, Vic's dad, Vinny Riccio.

"Your mama thinks a man should have an office to drive to every day. I sat at a desk for thirty-eight years and what did I get? Ask Doc, I'm too embarrassed to say." Dad told me once Doc—his real name was Frankie, though no one ever called him that—had been called Doc since he was six years old and growing up with Dad in Little Italy. There was never a time in his life when Doc wasn't Doc, which made his professional decision very easy. Dad used to say, no one ever called me Adjuster when I was a kid. Why didn't they call me something like Sarge or Teach? Then I would have known better.

I wish I had something breakfasty in my kitchen cupboard to offer him. He wants to stay and talk about Mom, which is the way old married people have. Let's talk about me means: What do you think of Mom? I'll take the turkey over means: When will Rindy settle down? I wish this morning I had bought the Goodwill sofa for ten dollars instead of letting Vic haul off the fancy deck chairs from Fortunoff's. Vic had flash. He'd left Jersey a long time before he actually took off.

"I can make you tea."

"None of that herbal stuff."

We don't talk about Mom, but I know what he's going through. She's just started to find herself. He's not burned out, he's merely stuck. I remember when Mom refused to learn to drive, wouldn't leave the house even to mail a letter. Her litany those days was: when you've spent the first fifteen years of your life in a mountain village, when you remember candles and gaslight and carrying water from a well, not to mention holding in your water at night because of wolves and the unlit outdoor privy, you *like* being housebound. She used those wolves for all they were worth, as though imaginary wolves still nipped her heels in the Clifton Mall.

Before Mom began to find herself and signed up for a class at Paterson, she used to nag Cindi and me about finding the right men. "Men," she said; she wasn't coy, never. Unembarrassed, she'd tell me about her wedding night, about her first sighting of Dad's "thing" ("Land Ho!" Cindi giggled. "Thar she blows!" I chipped in.) and she'd giggle at our word for it, the common word, and she'd use it around us, never around Dad. Mom's peasant, she's earthy but never coarse. If I could get that across to Dad, how I admire it in men or in women, I would feel somehow redeemed of all my little mistakes with them, with men, with myself. Cindi and Brent were married on a cruise ship by the ship's captain. Tony, Vic's older brother, made a play for me my senior year. Tony's solid now. He manages a funeral home but he's invested in crayfish ponds on the side.

"You don't even own a dining table." Dad sounds petulant. He uses "even" a lot around me. Not just a judgment, but a comparative judgment. Other people have dining tables. *Lots* of dining tables. He softens it a bit, not wanting to hurt me, wanting more for me to judge him a failure. "We've always had a sit-down dinner, hon."

Okay, so traditions change. This year dinner's potluck. So I don't have real furniture. I eat off stack-up plastic tables as I watch the evening news. I drink red wine and heat a pita bread on the gas burner and wrap it around alfalfa sprouts or green linguine. The Swedish knockdown dresser keeps popping its sides because Vic didn't glue it properly. Swedish engineering, he said, doesn't need glue. Think of Volvos, he said, and Ingmar Bergman. He isn't good with directions that come in four languages. At least he wasn't.

"Trust me, Dad." This isn't the time to spring new lovers on him. "A friend made me a table. It's in the basement."

"How about chairs?" Ah, my good father. He could have said, friend? What friend?

Marge, my landlady, has all kinds of junky stuff in the basement. "Jorge and I'll bring up what we need. You'd strain your back, Dad." Shot knees, bad back: daily pain but nothing fatal. Not like Carmine.

"Jorge? Is that the new boyfriend?"

Shocking him makes me feel good. It would serve him right if Jorge were my new boyfriend. But Jorge is Marge's other roomer. He gives Marge Spanish lessons, and does the heavy cleaning and the yard work. Jorge has family in El Salvador he's hoping to bring up. I haven't met Marge's husband yet. He works on an offshore oil rig in some emirate with a funny name.

"No, Dad." I explain about Jorge.

"El Salvador!" he repeats. "That means 'the Savior.'" He passes on the information with a kind of awe. It makes Jorge's homeland, which he's shown me pretty pictures of, seem messy and exotic, at the very rim of human comprehension.

After Dad leaves, I call Cindi, who lives fifteen minutes away on Upper Mountainside Road. She's eleven months younger and almost a natural blond, but we're close. Brent wasn't easy for me to take, not at first. He owns a discount camera and electronics store on Fifty-fourth in Manhattan. Cindi met him through Club Med. They sat on a gorgeous Caribbean beach and talked of hogs. His father is an Amish farmer in Kalona, Iowa. Brent, in spite of the obvious hairpiece and the gold chain, is a rebel. He was born Schwartzendruber, but changed his name to Schwartz. Now no one believes the Brent, either. They call him Bernie on the street and it makes everyone more comfortable. His father's never taken their buggy out of the county.

The first time Vic asked me out, he talked of feminism and holism and macrobiotics. Then he opened up on cinema and literature, and I was very impressed, as who wouldn't be? Ro, my current lover, is very different. He picked me up in an uptown singles bar that I and sometimes Cindi go to. He bought me a Cinzano and touched my breast in the dark. He was direct, and at the same time weirdly courtly. I took him home though usually I don't, at first. I learned in bed that night that the tall brown drink with the lemon twist he'd been drinking was Tab.

I went back on the singles circuit even though the break with Vic should have made me cautious. Cindi thinks Vic's a romantic. I've told her how it ended. One Sunday morning in March he kissed me awake as usual. He'd brought in the *Times* from the porch and was reading it. I made us some cinnamon rose tea. We had a ritual, starting with the real estate pages, passing remarks on the latest tacky towers. Not for us, we'd say, the view is terrible! No room for the servants, things like that. And our imaginary children's imaginary nanny. "Hi, gorgeous," I said. He is gorgeous, not strong, but showy. He said, "I'm leaving, babe. New Jersey doesn't do it for me anymore." I said, "Okay, so where're we going?" I had an awful job at the time, taking orders for MCI. Vic said, "I didn't say we, babe." So I asked, "You mean it's over? Just like that?" And he said, "Isn't that the best way? No fuss, no hang-ups." Then I got a little whiny. "*But* why?" I wanted to know. But he was macrobiotic in lots of things, including relationships. Yin and yang, hot and sour, green and yellow. "You know, Rindy, there are *places*. You don't fall off the earth when you leave Jersey, you know. Places you see pictures of and read about. Different weathers, different trees, different everything. Places that get the Cubs on cable instead of the Mets." He was into that. For all the sophisticated things he liked to talk about, he was a very local boy. "Vic," I pleaded, "you're crazy. You need help." "I need help because I want to get out of Jersey? You gotta be kidding!" He stood up and for a moment I thought he would do something crazy, like destroy something, or hurt me. "Don't ever call me crazy, got that? And give me the keys to the van."

He took the van. Danny had sold it to me when the Marines sent him overseas. I'd have given it to him anyway, even if he hadn't asked.

"Cindi, I need a turkey roaster," I tell my sister on the phone.

"I'll be right over," she says. "The brat's driving me crazy."

"Isn't Franny's visit working out?"

"I could kill her. I think up ways. How does that sound?"

"Why not send her home?" I'm joking. Franny is Brent's twelve-year-old and he's shelled out a lot of dough to lawyers in New Jersey and Florida to work out visitation rights.

"Poor Brent. He feels so *divided*," Cindi says. "He shouldn't have to take sides."

I want her to ask who my date is for this afternoon, but she doesn't. It's important to me that she like Ro, that Mom and Dad more than tolerate him.

All over the country, I tell myself, women are towing new lovers home to meet their families. Vic is simmering cranberries in somebody's kitchen and explaining yin and yang. I check out the stuffing recipe. The gravy calls for cream and freshly grated nutmeg. Ro brought me six whole nutmegs in a Ziplock bag from his friend, a Pakistani, who runs a spice store in SoHo.[2] The nuts look hard and ugly. I take one out of the bag and sniff it. The aroma's so exotic my head swims. On an impulse I call Ro.

The phone rings and rings. He doesn't have his own place yet. He has to crash with friends. He's been in the States three months, maybe less. I let it ring fifteen, sixteen, seventeen times.

Finally someone answers. "Yes?" The voice is guarded, the accent obviously foreign even though all I'm hearing is a one-syllable word. Ro has fled here from Kabul. He wants to take classes at NJIT and become an electrical engineer. He says he's lucky his father got him out. A friend of Ro's father, a man called Mumtaz, runs a fried chicken restaurant in Brooklyn in a neighborhood Ro calls "Little Kabul," though probably no one else has ever noticed. Mr. Mumtaz puts the legal immigrants to work as waiters out front. The illegals hide in a backroom as pluckers and gutters.

"Ro? I miss you. We're eating at three, remember?"

"Who is speaking, please?"

---

[2] A region, south of Houston Street on Manhattan Island, New York.

So I fell for the accent, but it isn't a malicious error. I *can* tell one Afghan tribe from another now, even by looking at them or by their names. I can make out some Pashto words. "Tell Ro it's Rindy. Please? I'm a friend. He wanted me to call this number."

"Not knowing any Ro."

"Hey, wait. Tell him it's Rindy deMarco."

The guy hangs up on me.

I'm crumbling cornbread into a bowl for the stuffing when Cindi honks half of "King Cotton" from the parking apron in the back. Brent bought her the BMW on the gray market and saved a bundle—once discount, always discount—then spent three hundred dollars to put in a horn that beeps a Sousa march. I wave a potato masher at her from the back window. She doesn't get out of the car. Instead she points to the pan in the back seat. I come down, wiping my hands on a dish towel.

"I should stay and help." Cindi sounds ready to cry. But I don't want her with me when Ro calls back.

"You're doing too much already, kiddo." My voice at least sounds comforting. "You promised one veg and the salad."

"I ought to come up and help. That or get drunk." She shifts the stick. When Brent bought her the car, the dealer threw in driving gloves to match the upholstery.

"Get Franny to shred the greens," I call as Cindi backs up the car. "Get her involved."

The phone is ringing in my apartment. I can hear it ring from the second-floor landing.

"Ro?"

"You're taking a chance, my treasure. It could have been any other admirer, then where would you be?"

"I don't have any other admirers." Ro is not a conventionally jealous man, not like the types I have known. He's totally unlike any man I have ever known. He wants men to come on to me. Lately when we go to a bar he makes me sit far enough from him so some poor lonely guy thinks I'm looking for action. Ro likes to swagger out of a dark booth as soon as someone buys me a drink. I go along. He comes from a macho culture.

"How else will I know you are as beautiful as I think you are? I would not want an unprized woman," he says. He is asking me for time, I know. In a few more months he'll know I'm something of a catch in my culture, or at least I've never had trouble finding boys. Even Brent Schwartzendruber has begged me to see him alone.

"I'm going to be a little late," Ro says. "I told you about my cousin, Abdul, no?"

Ro has three or four cousins that I know of in Manhattan. They're all named Abdul something. When I think of Abdul, I think of a giant black man with goggles on, running down a court. Abdul is the teenage cousin whom immigration officials nabbed as he was gutting chickens in Mumtaz's backroom. Abdul doesn't have the right papers to live and work in this country, and now he's been locked up in a detention center on Varick Street. Ro's afraid Abdul will be deported back to Afghanistan. If that happens, he'll be tortured.

"I have to visit him before I take the DeCamp bus. He's talking nonsense. He's talking of starting a hunger fast."

"A hunger strike! God!" When I'm with Ro I feel I am looking at America through the wrong end of a telescope. He makes it sound like a police state, with sudden raids, papers, detention centers, deportations, and torture and death waiting in the wings. I'm not a political person. Last fall I wore the Ferraro button because she's a woman and Italian.

"Rindy, all night I've been up and awake. All night I think of your splendid breasts. Like clusters of grapes, I think. I am stroking and fondling your grapes this very minute. My talk gets you excited?"

I tell him to test me, please get here before three. I remind him he can't buy his ticket on the bus.

"We got here too early, didn't we?" Dad stands just outside the door to my apartment, looking embarrassed. He's in his best dark suit, the one he wears every Thanksgiving and Christmas. This year he can't do up the top button of his jacket.

"Don't be so formal, Dad." I give him a showy hug and pull him indoors so Mom can come in.

"As if your papa ever listens to me!" Mom laughs. But she sits primly on the sofa bed in her velvet cloak, with her tote bag and evening purse on her lap. Before Dad started courting her, she worked as a seamstress. Dad rescued her from a sweatshop. He married down, she married well. That's the family story.

"She told me to rush."

Mom isn't in a mood to squabble. I think she's reached the point of knowing she won't have him forever. There was Carmine, at death's door just a month ago. Anything could happen to Dad. She says, "Renata, look what I made! Crostolis." She lifts a cake tin out of her tote bag. The pan still feels warm. And for dessert, I know, there'll be a jar of super-thick, super-rich Death by Chocolate.

The story about Grandma deMarco, Dad's mama, is that every Thanksgiving she served two full dinners, one American with the roast turkey, candied yams, pumpkin pie, the works, and another with Grandpa's favorite pastas.

Dad relaxes. He appoints himself bartender. "Don't you have more ice cubes, sweetheart?"

I tell him it's good Glenlivet. He shouldn't ruin it with ice, just a touch of water if he must. Dad pours sherry in Vic's pottery espresso cups for his women. Vic made them himself, and I used to think they were perfect blue jewels. Now I see they're lumpy, uneven in color.

"Go change into something pretty before Carla and Brent come." Mom believes in dressing up. Beaded dresses lift her spirits. She's wearing a beaded green dress today.

I take the sherry and vanish behind a four-panel screen, the kind long-legged showgirls change behind in black and white movies while their moustached lovers keep talking. My head barely shows above the screen's top, since I'm no long-legged showgirl. My best points, as Ro has said, are my clusters of grapes. Vic found the screen at a country auction in the Adirondacks. It had filled the van. Now I use the panels as a bulletin board and I'm worried Dad'll spot the notice for the next meeting of Amnesty International, which will bother him. He will think the two words stand for draft dodger and communist. I was going to drop my membership, a legacy of Vic, when Ro saw it and approved. Dad goes to the Sons of Italy Anti-Defamation dinners. He met Frank Sinatra at one. He voted for Reagan last time because the Democrats ran an Italian woman.

Instead of a thirties lover, it's my moustached papa talking to me from the other side of the screen. "So where's this dining table?"

"Ro's got the parts in the basement. He'll bring it up, Dad."

I hear them whispering. "Bo? Now she's messing with a Southerner?" and "Shh, it's her business."

I'm just smoothing on my pantyhose when Mom screams for the cops. Dad shouts too, at Mom for her to shut up. It's my fault, I should have warned Ro not to use his key this afternoon.

I peek over the screen's top and see my lover the way my parents see him. He's a slight, pretty man with hazel eyes and a tufty moustache, so whom can he intimidate? I've seen Jews and Greeks, not to mention Sons of Italy, darker-skinned than Ro. Poor Ro resorts to his Kabuli prep-school manners.

"How do you do, Madam! Sir! My name is Roashan."

Dad moves closer to Ro but doesn't hold out his hand. I can almost read his mind: *he speaks.* "Come again?" he says, baffled.

I cringe as he spells his name. My parents are so parochial. With each letter he does a graceful dip and bow. "Try it syllable by syllable, sir. Then it is not so hard."

Mom stares past him at me. The screen doesn't hide me because I've strayed too far in to watch the farce. "Renata, you're wearing only your camisole."

I pull my crew neck over my head, then kiss him. I make the kiss really sexy so they'll know I've slept with this man. Many times. And if he asks me, I will marry him. I had not known that till now. I think my mother guesses.

He's brought flowers: four long-stemmed, stylish purple blossoms in a florist's paper cone. "For you, madam." He glides over the dirty broadloom to Mom who fills up more than half the sofa bed. "This is my first Thanksgiving dinner, for which I have much to give thanks, no?"

"He was born in Afghanistan," I explain. But Dad gets continents wrong. He says, "We saw your famine camps on TV. Well, you won't starve this afternoon."

"They smell good," Mom says. "Thank you very much but you shouldn't spend a fortune."

"No, no, madam. What you smell good is my cologne. Flowers in New York have no fragrance."

"His father had a garden estate outside Kabul." I don't want Mom to think he's putting down American flowers, though in fact he is. Along with American fruits, meats, and vegetables. "The Russians bulldozed it," I add.

Dad doesn't want to talk politics. He senses, looking at Ro, this is not the face of Ethiopian starvation. "Well, what'll it be, Roy? Scotch and soda?" I wince. It's not going well.

"Thank you but no. I do not imbibe alcoholic spirits, though I have no objection for you, sir." My lover goes to the fridge and reaches down. He knows just where to find his Tab. My father is quietly livid, staring down at his drink.

In my father's world, grown men bowl in leagues and drink the best whiskey they can afford. Dad whistles "My Way." He must be under stress. That's his usual self-therapy: how would Francis Albert handle this?

"Muslims have taboos, Dad." Cindi didn't marry a Catholic, so he has no right to be upset about Ro, about us.

"Jews," Dad mutters. "So do Jews." He knows because catty-corner from Vitelli's is a kosher butcher. This isn't the time to parade new words before him, like *halal*, the Muslim kosher. An Italian-American man should be able to live sixty-five years never having heard the word, I can go along with that. Ro, fortunately, is cosmopolitan. Outside of pork and booze, he eats anything else I fix.

Brent and Cindi take forever to come. But finally we hear his MG squeal in the driveway. Ro glides to the front window; he seems to blend with the ficus tree and hanging ferns. Dad and I wait by the door.

"Party time!" Brent shouts as he maneuvers Cindi and Franny ahead of him up three flights of stairs. He looks very much the head of the family, a rich man steeply in debt to keep up appearances, to compete, to head off middle age. He's at that age—and Cindi's nowhere near that age—when people notice the difference and quietly judge it. I know these things from Cindi—I'd never guess it from looking at Brent. If he feels divided, as Cindi says he does, it doesn't show. Misery, anxiety, whatever, show on Cindi though; they bring her cheekbones out. When I'm depressed, my hair looks rough, my skin breaks out. Right now, I'm lustrous.

Brent does a lot of whooping and hugging at the door. He even hugs Dad who looks grave and funereal like an old-world Italian gentleman because of his outdated, pinched dark suit. Cindi makes straight for the fridge with her casserole of squash and browned marshmallow. Franny just stands in the middle of the room holding two biggish Baggies of salad greens and vinaigrette in an old Dijon mustard jar. Brent actually bought the mustard in Dijon, a story that Ro is bound to hear and not appreciate. Vic was mean enough last year to tell him that he could have gotten it for more or less the same price at the Italian specialty foods store down on Watchung Plaza. Franny doesn't seem to have her own winter clothes. She's wearing Cindi's car coat over a Dolphins sweat-shirt. Her mother moved down to Florida the very day the divorce became final. She's got a Walkman tucked into the pocket of her cords.

"You could have trusted me to make the salad dressing at least," I scold my sister.

Franny gives up the Baggies and the jar of dressing to me. She scrutinizes us—Mom, Dad, me and Ro, especially Ro, as though she can detect something strange about him—but doesn't take off her earphones. A smirk starts twitching her tanned, feral features. I see what she is seeing. Asian men carry their bodies differently, even these famed warriors from the Khyber Pass. Ro doesn't stand like Brent or Dad. His hands hang kind of stiffly from the shoulder joints, and when he moves, his palms are tucked tight against his thighs, his stomach sticks out like a slightly pregnant woman's. Each culture establishes its own manly posture, different ways of claiming space. Ro, hiding among my plants, holds himself in a way that seems both too effeminate and too macho. I hate Franny for what she's doing to me. I am twenty-seven years old, I should be more mature. But I see now how wrong Ro's clothes are. He shows too much white collar and cuff. His shirt and his wool-blend flare-leg pants were made to measure in Kabul. The jacket comes from a discount store on Canal Street, part of a discontinued line of two-trousered suits. I ought to know, I took him there. I want to shake Franny or smash the earphones.

Cindi catches my exasperated look. "Don't pay any attention to her. She's unsociable this weekend. We can't compete with the Depeche Mode."

I intend to compete.

Franny, her eyes very green and very hostile, turns on Brent. "How come she never gets it right, Dad?"

Brent hi-fives his daughter, which embarrasses her more than anyone else in the room. "It's a Howard Jones, hon," Brent tells Cindi.

Franny, close to tears, runs to the front window where Ro's been hanging back. She has an ungainly walk for a child whose support payments specify weekly ballet lessons. She bores in on Ro's hidey hole like Russian artillery. Ro moves back to the perimeter of family intimacy. I have no way of helping yet. I have to set out the dips and Tostitos. Brent and Dad are talking sports, Mom and Cindi are watching the turkey. Dad's going on about the Knicks. He's in despair, so early in the season. He's on his second Scotch. I see Brent try. "What do you think, Roy?" He's doing his best to get my lover involved. "Maybe we'll get lucky, huh? We can always hope for a top draft pick. End up with Patrick Ewing!" Dad brightens. "That guy'll change the game. Just wait and see. He'll fill the lane better than Russell." Brent gets angry, since for some strange Amish reason he's a Celtics fan. So was Vic. "Bird'll make a monkey out of him." He looks to Ro for support.

Ro nods. Even his headshake is foreign. "You are undoubtedly correct, Brent," he says. "I am deferring to your judgment because currently I have not familiarized myself with these practices."

Ro loves squash, but none of my relatives have ever picked up a racket. I want to tell Brent that Ro's skied in St. Moritz, lost a thousand dollars in a casino in Beirut, knows where to buy Havana cigars without getting hijacked. He's sophisticated, he could make monkeys out of us all, but they think he's a retard.

Brent drinks three Scotches to Dad's two; then all three men go down to the basement. Ro and Brent do the carrying, negotiating sharp turns in the stairwell. Dad supervises. There are two trestles and a wide, splintery plywood top. "Try not to take the wall down!" Dad yells.

When they make it back in, the men take off their jackets to assemble the table. Brent's wearing a red lamb's wool turtleneck under his camel hair blazer. Ro unfastens his cuff links—they are 24-karat gold and his father's told him to sell them if funds run low—and pushes up his very white shirt sleeves. There are scars on both arms, scars that bubble against his dark skin, scars like lightning flashes under his thick black hair. Scar tissue on Ro is the color of freshwater pearls. I want to kiss it.

Cindi checks the turkey one more time. "You guys better hurry. We'll be ready to eat in fifteen minutes."

Ro, the future engineer, adjusts the trestles. He's at his best now. He's become quite chatty. From under the plywood top, he's holding forth on the Soviet menace in Kabul. Brent may actually have an idea where Afghanistan is, in a general way, but Dad is lost. He's talking of being arrested for handing out pro-American pamphlets on his campus. Dad stiffens at "arrest" and blanks out the rest. He talks of this "so-called leader," this "criminal" named Babrak Karmal and I hear other buzz-words like Kandahār and Pamir, words that might have been Polish to me a month ago, and I can see even Brent is slightly embarrassed. It's his first exposure to Third World passion. He thought only Americans had informed political opinion—other people staged coups out of spite and misery. It's an unwelcome revelation to him that a reasonably educated and rational man like Ro would die for things that he, Brent, has never heard of and would rather laugh about. Ro was tortured in jail. Franny has taken off her earphones. Electrodes, canes, freezing tanks. He leaves nothing out. Something's gotten into Ro.

Dad looks sick. The meaning of Thanksgiving should not be so explicit. But Ro's in a daze. He goes on about how—*inshallah*[3]—his father, once a rich landlord, had stashed away enough to bribe a guard, sneak him out of this cell and hide him for four months in a tunnel dug under a servant's adobe hut until a forged American visa could be bought. Franny's eyes are wide, Dad joins Mom on the sofa bed, shaking his head. Jail, bribes, forged, what is this? I can read his mind. "For six days I must orbit one international airport to another," Ro is saying. "The main trick is having a valid ticket, that way the airline has to carry you, even if the country won't take you in. Colombo, Seoul, Bombay,

---

[3] "God willing." Here, it is apparently used to mean "Thank God."

Geneva, Frankfurt, I know too too well the transit lounges of many airports. We travel the world with our gym bags and prayer rugs, unrolling them in the transit lounges. The better airports have special rooms."

Brent tries to ease Dad's pain. "Say, buddy," he jokes, "you wouldn't be ripping us off, would you?"

Ro snakes his slender body from under the makeshift table. He hasn't been watching the effect of his monologue. "I am a working man," he says stiffly. I have seen his special permit. He's one of the lucky ones, though it might not last. He's saving for NJIT. Meantime he's gutting chickens to pay for room and board in Little Kabul. He describes the gutting process. His face is transformed as he sticks his fist into imaginary roasters and grabs for gizzards, pulls out the squishy stuff. He takes an Afghan dagger out of the pocket of his pants. You'd never guess, he looks like such a victim. "This," he says, eyes glinting. "This is all I need."

"Cool," Franny says.

"Time to eat," Mom shouts. "I made the gravy with the nutmeg as you said, Renata."

I lead Dad to the head of the table. "Everyone else sit where you want to."

Franny picks out the chair next to Ro before I can put Cindi there. I want Cindi to know him, I want her as an ally.

Dad tests the blade of the carving knife. Mom put the knife where Dad always sits when she set the table. He takes his thumb off the blade and pushes the switch. "That noise makes me feel good."

But I carry in the platter with the turkey and place it in front of Ro. "I want you to carve," I say.

He brings out his dagger all over again. Franny is practically licking his fingers. "You mean this is a professional job?"

We stare fascinated as my lover slashes and slices, swiftly, confidently, at the huge, browned, juicy beast. The dagger scoops out flesh.

Now I am the one in a daze. I am seeing Ro's naked body as though for the first time, his nicked, scarred, burned body. In his body, the blemishes seem embedded, more beautiful, like wood. I am seeing character made manifest. I am seeing Brent and Dad for the first time, too. They have their little scars, things they're proud of, football injuries and bowling elbows they brag about. Our scars are so innocent; they are invisible and come to us from rough-housing gone too far. Ro hates to talk about his scars. If I trace the puckered tissue on his left thigh and ask "How, Ro?" he becomes shy, dismissive: a pack of dogs attacked him when he was a boy. The skin on his back is speckled and lumpy from burns, but when I ask he laughs. A crazy villager whacked him with a burning stick for cheekiness, he explains. He's ashamed that he comes from a culture of pain.

The turkey is reduced to a drying, whitened skeleton. On our plates, the slices are symmetrical, elegant. I realize all in a rush how much I love this man with his blemished, tortured body. I will give him citizenship if he asks. Vic was beautiful, but Vic was self-sufficient. Ro's my chance to heal the world.

I shall teach him how to walk like an American, how to dress like Brent but better, how to fill up a room as Dad does instead of melting and blending but sticking out in the Afghan way. In spite of the funny way he holds himself and the funny way he moves his head from side to side when he wants to say yes, Ro is Clint Eastwood, scarred hero and survivor. Dad and Brent are children. I realize Ro's the only circumcised man I've slept with.

Mom asks, "Why are you grinning like that, Renata?"

QUESTIONS

1. During the conversation with her father, early in the story, Renata thinks: "This isn't the time to spring new lovers on him." Why not? Characterize Renata's previous lover, Vic. **2.** What do Brent and Renata's father talk about before dinner? What does Ro talk about? What do you make of the differences in their interests? **3.** How do the various members of Renata's family feel about Ro? Why? **4.** Explain the story's title.

WRITING TOPICS

1. Describe the cultural conflicts illustrated by this story. Is there any hope that those conflicts can be resolved? Explain. **2.** Describe from your personal life or knowledge an example of the kind of cultural conflict dealt with in this story.

Water Liars

1978

BARRY HANNAH   [b. 1942]

When I am run down and flocked around by the world, I go down to Farte Cove off the Yazoo River and take my beer to the end of the pier where the old liars are still snapping and wheezing at one another. The line-up is always different, because they're always dying out or succumbing to constipation, etc., whereupon they go back to the cabins and wait for a good day when they can come out and lie again, leaning on the rail with coats full of bran cookies. The son of the man the cove was named for is often out there. He pronounces his name far*tay*, with a great French stress on the last syllable. Otherwise you might laugh at his history or ignore it in favor of the name as it's spelled on the sign.

I'm glad it's not my name.

This poor dignified man has had to explain his nobility to the semiliterate of half of America before he could even begin a decent conversation with them. On the other hand, Farte, Jr., is a great liar himself. He tells about seeing ghost people around the lake and tells big loose ones about the size of the fish those ghosts took out of Farte Cove in years past.

Last year I turned thirty-three years old and, raised a Baptist, I had a sense of being Jesus and coming to something decided in my life—because we all know Jesus was crucified at thirty-three. It had all seemed especially important, what you do in this year, and holy with meaning.

On the morning after my birthday party, during which I and my wife almost drowned in vodka cocktails, we both woke up to the making of a truth session about the lovers we'd had before we met each other. I had a mildly exciting and usual history, and she had about the same, which surprised me. For ten years she'd sworn I was the first. I could not believe her history was exactly equal with mine. It hurt me to think that in the era when there were supposed to be virgins she had allowed anyone but *me*, and so on.

I was dazed and exhilarated by this information for several weeks. Finally, it drove me crazy, and I came out to Farte Cove to rest, under the pretense of a fishing week with my chum Wyatt.

I'm still figuring out why I couldn't handle it.

My sense of the past is vivid and slow. I hear every sign and see every shadow. The movement of every limb in every passionate event occupies my mind. I have a prurience on the grand scale. It makes no sense that I should be angry about happenings before she and I ever saw each other. Yet I feel an impotent homicidal urge in the matter of her lovers. She has excused my episodes as the course of things, though she has a vivid memory too. But there is a blurred nostalgia women have that men don't.

You could not believe how handsome and delicate my wife is naked.

I was driven wild by the bodies that had trespassed her twelve and thirteen years ago.

My vacation at Farte Cove wasn't like that easy little bit you get as a rich New Yorker. My finances weren't in great shape; to be true, they were about in ruin, and I left the house knowing my wife would have to answer the phone to hold off, for instance, the phone company itself. Everybody wanted money and I didn't have any.

I was going to take the next week in the house while she went away, watch our three kids and all the rest. When you both teach part-time in the high schools, the income can be slow in summer.

No poor-mouthing here. I don't want anybody's pity. I just want to explain. I've got good hopes of a job over at Alabama next year. Then I'll get myself among higher-paid liars, that's all.

Sidney Farte was out there prevaricating away at the end of the pier when Wyatt and I got there Friday evening. The old faces I recognized; a few new harkening idlers I didn't.

"Now, Doctor Mooney, he not only saw the ghost of Lily, he says he had intercourse with her. Said it was involuntary. Before he knew what he was doing, he was on her making cadence and all their clothes blown away off in the trees around the shore. She turned into a wax candle right under him."

"Intercourse," said an old-timer, breathing heavy. He sat up on the rail. It was a word of high danger to his old mind. He said it with a long disgust, glad, I guess, he was not involved.

"MacIntire, a Presbyterian preacher, I seen him come out here with his son-in-law, anchor near the bridge, and pull up fifty or more white perch big as small pumpkins. You know what they was using for bait?"

"What?" asked another geezer.

"*Nuthin.* Caught on the bare hook. It was Gawd made them fish bite," said Sidney Farte, going at it good.

"Naw. There be a season they bite a bare hook. Gawd didn't have to've done that," said another old guy, with a fringe of red hair and a racy Florida shirt.

"Nother night," said Sidney Farte, "I saw the ghost of Yazoo hisself with my pa, who's dead. A Indian king with four deer around him."

The old boys seemed to be used to this one. Nobody said anything. They ignored Sidney.

"Tell you what," said a well-built small old boy. "That was somethin when we come down here and had to chase that whole high-school party off the end of this pier, them drunken children. They was smokin dope and two-thirds a them nekid swimmin in the water. Good hunnerd of em. From your so-called *good* high school. What you think's happnin at the bad ones?"

I dropped my beer and grew suddenly sick. Wyatt asked me what was wrong. I could see my wife in 1960 in the group of high-schoolers she must have had. My jealousy went out into the stars of the night above me. I could not bear the roving carelessness of teen-agers, their judgeless tangling of wanting and bodies. But I was the worst back then. In the mad days back then, I dragged the panties off girls I hated and talked badly about them once the sun came up.

"Worst time in my life," said a new, younger man, maybe sixty but with the face of a man who had surrendered, "me and Woody was fishing. Had a lantern. It was about eleven. We was catching a few fish but rowed on into that little cove over there near town. We heard all these sounds, like they was ghosts. We was scared. We thought it might be the Yazoo hisself. We known of some fellows the Yazoo had killed to death just from fright. It was over the sounds of what was normal human sighin and amoanin. It was big unhuman sounds. We just stood still in the boat. Ain't nuthin else us to do. For thirty minutes."

"An what was it?" said the old geezer, letting himself off the rail.

"We had a big flashlight. There came up this rustlin in the brush and I beamed it over there. The two of em makin the sounds get up with half they clothes on. It was my own daughter Charlotte and an older guy I didn't even know with a mustache. My *own* daughter, and them sounds over the water scarin us like ghosts."

"My Gawd, that's awful," said the old geezer by the rail. "Is that the truth? I wouldn't've told that. That's terrible."

Sidney Farte was really upset.

"This ain't the place!" he said. "Tell your kind of story somewhere else."

The old man who'd told his story was calm and fixed to his place. He'd told the truth. The crowd on the pier was outraged and discomfited. He wasn't one of them. But he stood his place. He had a distressed pride. You could see he had never recovered from the thing he'd told about.

I told Wyatt to bring the old man back to the cabin. He was out here away from his wife the same as me and Wyatt. Just an older guy with a big hurting bosom. He wore a suit and the only way you'd know he was on vacation was he'd removed his tie. He didn't know where the bait house was. He didn't know what to do on vacation at all. But he got drunk with us and I can tell you he and I went out the next morning with our poles, Wyatt driving the motorboat, fishing for white perch in the cove near the town. And we were kindred.

We were both crucified by the truth.

The Red Convertible   1984

LYMAN LAMARTINE

LOUISE ERDRICH   [b. 1954]

I was the first one to drive a convertible on my reservation. And of course it was red, a red Olds. I owned that car along with my brother Henry Junior. We owned it together until his boots filled with water on a windy night and he bought out my share. Now Henry owns the whole car, and his youngest brother Lyman (that's myself), Lyman walks everywhere he goes.

How did I earn enough money to buy my share in the first place? My own talent was I could always make money. I had a touch for it, unusual in a Chippewa. From the first I was different that way, and everyone recognized it. I was the only kid they let in the American Legion Hall to shine shoes, for example, and one Christmas I sold spiritual bouquets for the mission door to door. The nuns let me keep a percentage. Once I started, it seemed the more money I made the easier the money came. Everyone encouraged it. When I was fifteen I got a job washing dishes at the Joliet Café, and that was where my first big break happened.

It wasn't long before I was promoted to bussing tables, and then the short-order cook quit and I was hired to take her place. No sooner than you know it I was managing the Joliet. The rest is history. I went on managing. I soon became part owner, and of course there was no stopping me then. It wasn't long before the whole thing was mine.

After I'd owned the Joliet for one year, it blew over in the worst tornado ever seen around here. The whole operation was smashed to bits. A total loss. The fryalator was up in a tree, the grill torn in half like it was paper. I was only sixteen. I had it all in my mother's name, and I lost it quick, but before I lost it I had every one of my relatives, and their relatives, to dinner, and I also bought that red Olds I mentioned, along with Henry.

The first time we saw it! I'll tell you when we first saw it. We had gotten a ride up to Winnipeg, and both of us had money. Don't ask me why, because we never mentioned a car or anything, we just had all our money. Mine was cash, a big bankroll from the Joliet's insurance. Henry had two checks—a week's extra pay for being laid off, and his regular check from the Jewel Bearing Plant.

We were walking down Portage anyway, seeing the sights, when we saw it. There it was, parked, large as life. Really as *if* it was alive. I thought of the word *repose*, because the car wasn't simply stopped, parked, or whatever. That car reposed, calm and gleaming, a FOR SALE sign in its left front window. Then, before we had thought it over at all, the car belonged to us and our pockets were empty. We had just enough money for gas back home.

We went places in that car, me and Henry. We took off driving all one whole summer. We started off toward the Little Knife River and Mandaree in Fort Berthold and then we found ourselves down in Wakpala somehow, and then suddenly we were over in Montana on the Rocky Boys, and yet the summer was not even half over. Some people hang on to details when they travel, but we didn't let them bother us and just lived our everyday lives here to there.

I do remember this one place with willows. I remember I laid under those trees and it was comfortable. So comfortable. The branches bent down all around me like a tent or a stable. And quiet, it was quiet, even though there was a powwow close enough so I could see it going on. The air was not too still, not too windy either. When the dust rises up and hangs in the air around the dancers like that, I feel good. Henry was asleep with his arms thrown wide. Later on, he woke up and we started driving again. We were somewhere in Montana, or maybe on the Blood Reserve—it could have been anywhere. Anyway it was where we met the girl.

All her hair was in buns around her ears, that's the first thing I noticed about her. She was posed alongside the road with her arm out, so we stopped. That girl was short, so short her lumber shirt looked comical on her, like a nightgown. She had jeans on and fancy moccasins and she carried a little suitcase.

"Hop on in," says Henry. So she climbs in between us.

"We'll take you home," I says. "Where do you live?"

"Chicken," she says.

"Where the hell's that?" I ask her.

"Alaska."

"Okay," says Henry, and we drive.

We got up there and never wanted to leave. The sun doesn't truly set there in summer, and the night is more a soft dusk. You might doze off, sometimes, but before you know it you're up again, like an animal in nature. You never feel like you have to sleep hard or put away the world. And things would grow up there. One day just dirt or moss, the next day flowers and long grass. The girl's name was Susy. Her family really took to us. They fed us and put us up. We had our own tent to live in by their house, and the kids would be in and out of there all day and night. They couldn't get over me and Henry being brothers, we looked so different. We told them we knew we had the same mother, anyway.

One night Susy came in to visit us. We sat around in the tent talking of this thing and that. The season was changing. It was getting darker by that time, and the cold was even getting just a little mean. I told her it was time for us to go. She stood up on a chair.

"You never seen my hair," Susy said.

That was true. She was standing on a chair, but still, when she unclipped her buns the hair reached all the way to the ground. Our eyes opened. You couldn't tell how much hair she had when it was rolled up so neatly. Then my brother Henry did something funny. He went up to the chair and said, "Jump on my shoulders." So she did that, and her hair reached down past his waist, and he started twirling, this way and that, so her hair was flung out from side to side.

"I always wondered what it was like to have long pretty hair," Henry says. Well we laughed. It was a funny sight, the way he did it. The next morning we got up and took leave of those people.

On to greener pastures, as they say. It was down through Spokane and across Idaho then Montana and very soon we were racing the weather right along under the Canadian border through Columbus, Des Lacs, and then we were in Bottineau County and soon home. We'd made most of the trip, that summer, without putting up the car hood at all. We got home just in time, it turned out, for the army to remember Henry had signed up to join it.

I don't wonder that the army was so glad to get my brother that they turned him into a Marine. He was built like a brick outhouse anyway. We liked to tease him that they really wanted him for his Indian nose. He had a nose big and sharp as a hatchet, like the nose on Red Tomahawk, the Indian who killed Sitting Bull, whose profile is on signs all along the North Dakota highways. Henry went off to training camp, came home once during Christmas, then the next thing you know we got an overseas letter from him. It was 1970, and he said he was stationed up in the northern hill country. Whereabouts I did not know. He wasn't such a hot letter writer, and only got off two before the enemy caught him. I could never keep it straight, which direction those good Vietnam soldiers were from.

I wrote him back several times, even though I didn't know if those letters would get through. I kept him informed all about the car. Most of the time I had it up on blocks in the yard or half taken apart, because that long trip did a hard job on it under the hood.

I always had good luck with numbers, and never worried about the draft myself. I never even had to think about what my number was. But Henry was never lucky in the same way as me. It was at least three years before Henry came home. By then I guess the whole war was solved in the government's mind, but for him it would keep on going. In those years I'd put his car into almost perfect shape. I always thought of it as his car while he was gone, even though when he left he said, "Now it's yours," and threw me his key.

"Thanks for the extra key," I'd say. "I'll put it up in your drawer just in case I need it." He laughed.

When he came home, though, Henry was very different, and I'll say this: the change was no good. You could hardly expect him to change for the better, I know. But he was quiet, so quiet, and never comfortable sitting still anywhere but always up and moving around. I thought back to times we'd sat still for whole afternoons, never moving a muscle, just shifting our weight along the ground, talking to whoever sat with us, watching things. He'd always had a joke, then, too, and now you couldn't get him to laugh, or when he did it was more the sound of a man choking, a sound that stopped up the throats of other people around him. They got to leaving him alone most of the time, and I didn't blame them. It was a fact: Henry was jumpy and mean.

I'd bought a color TV set for my mom and the rest of us while Henry was away. Money still came very easy. I was sorry I'd ever bought it though, because of Henry. I was also sorry I'd bought color, because with black-and-white the pictures seem older and farther away. But what are you going to do? He sat in front of it, watching it, and that was the only time he was completely still. But it was the kind of stillness that you see in a rabbit when it freezes and before it will bolt. He was not easy. He sat in his chair gripping the armrests with all his might, as if the chair itself was moving at a high speed and if he let go at all he would rocket forward and maybe crash right through the set.

Once I was in the room watching TV with Henry and I heard his teeth click at something. I looked over, and he'd bitten through his lip. Blood was going down his chin. I tell you right then I wanted to smash that tube to pieces. I went over to it but Henry must have known what I was up to. He rushed from his chair and shoved me out of the way, against the wall. I told myself he didn't know what he was doing.

My mom came in, turned the set off real quiet, and told us she had made something for supper. So we went and sat down. There was still blood going down Henry's chin, but he didn't notice it and no one said anything, even though every time he took a bit of his bread his blood fell onto it until he was eating his own blood mixed in with the food.

While Henry was not around we talked about what was going to happen to him. There were no Indian doctors on the reservation, and my mom was afraid of trusting Old Man Pillager because he courted her long ago and was jealous of her husbands. He might take revenge through her son. We were afraid that if we brought Henry to a regular hospital they would keep him.

"They don't fix them in those places," Mom said; "they just give them drugs."

"We wouldn't get him there in the first place," I agreed, "so let's just forget about it."

Then I thought about the car.

Henry had not even looked at the car since he'd gotten home, though like I said, it was in tip-top condition and ready to drive. I thought the car might bring the old Henry back somehow. So I bided my time and waited for my chance to interest him in the vehicle.

One night Henry was off somewhere. I took myself a hammer. I went out to that car and I did a number on its underside. Whacked it up. Bent the tail pipe double. Ripped the muffler loose. By the time I was done with the car it looked worse than any typical Indian car that has been driven all its life on reservation roads, which they always say are like government promises—full of holes. It just about hurt me, I'll tell you that! I threw dirt in the carburetor and

I ripped all the electric tape off the seats. I made it look just as beat up as I could. Then I sat back and waited for Henry to find it.

Still, it took him over a month. That was all right, because it was just getting warm enough, not melting, but warm enough to work outside.

"Lyman," he says, walking in one day, "that red car looks like shit."

"Well it's old," I says. "You got to expect that."

"No way!" says Henry. "That car's a classic! But you went and ran the piss right out of it, Lyman, and you know it don't deserve that. I kept that car in A-one shape. You don't remember. You're too young. But when I left, that car was running like a watch. Now I don't even know if I can get it to start again, let alone get it anywhere near its old condition."

"Well you try," I said, like I was getting mad, "but I say it's a piece of junk."

Then I walked out before he could realize I knew he'd strung together more than six words at once.

After that I thought he'd freeze himself to death working on that car. He was out there all day, and at night he rigged up a little lamp, ran a cord out the window, and had himself some light to see by while he worked. He was better than he had been before, but that's still not saying much. It was easier for him to do the things the rest of us did. He ate more slowly and didn't jump up and down during the meal to get this or that or look out the window. I put my hand in the back of the TV set, I admit, and fiddled around with it good, so that it was almost impossible now to get a clear picture. He didn't look at it very often anyway. He was always out with that car or going off to get parts for it. By the time it was really melting outside, he had it fixed.

I had been feeling down in the dumps about Henry around this time. We had always been together before. Henry and Lyman. But he was such a loner now that I didn't know how to take it. So I jumped at the chance one day when Henry seemed friendly. It's not that he smiled or anything. He just said, "Let's take that old shitbox for a spin." Just the way he said it made me think he could be coming around.

We went out to the car. It was spring. The sun was shining very bright. My only sister, Bonita, who was just eleven years old, came out and made us stand together for a picture. Henry leaned his elbow on the red car's windshield, and he took his other arm and put it over my shoulder, very carefully, as though it was heavy for him to lift and he didn't want to bring the weight down all at once.

"Smile," Bonita said, and he did.

That picture, I never look at it anymore. A few months ago, I don't know why, I got his picture out and tacked it on the wall. I felt good about Henry at the time, close to him. I felt good having his picture on the wall, until one night when I was looking at television. I was a little drunk and stoned. I looked up at the wall and Henry was staring at me. I don't know what it was, but his smile had changed, or maybe it was gone. All I know is I couldn't stay in the same room with that picture. I was shaking. I got up, closed the door, and went into the kitchen. A little later my friend Ray came over and we both went back into that room. We put the picture in a brown bag, folded the bag over and over tightly, then put it way back in a closet.

I still see that picture now, as if it tugs at me, whenever I pass that closet door. The picture is very clear in my mind. It was so sunny that day Henry had to squint against the glare. Or maybe the camera Bonita held flashed like a mirror, blinding him, before she snapped the picture. My face is right out in the sun, big and round. But he might have drawn back, because the shadows on his face are deep as holes. There are two shadows curved like little hooks around the ends of his smile, as if to frame it and try to keep it there—that one, first smile that looked like it might have hurt his face. He has his field jacket on and the worn-in clothes he'd come back in and kept wearing ever since. After Bonita took the picture, she went into the house and we got into the car. There was a full cooler in the trunk. We started off, east, toward Pembina and the Red River because Henry said he wanted to see the high water.

The trip over there was beautiful. When everything starts changing, drying up, clearing off, you feel like your whole life is starting. Henry felt it, too. The top was down and the car hummed like a top. He'd really put it back in shape, even the tape on the seats was very carefully put down and glued back in layers. It's not that he smiled again or even joked, but his face looked to me as if it was clear, more peaceful. It looked as though he wasn't thinking of anything in particular except the bare fields and windbreaks and houses we were passing.

The river was high and full of winter trash when we got there. The sun was still out, but it was colder by the river. There were still little clumps of dirty snow here and there on the banks. The water hadn't gone over the banks yet, but it would, you could tell. It was just at its limit, hard swollen glossy like an old gray scar. We made ourselves a fire, and we sat down and watched the current go. As I watched it I felt something squeezing inside me and tightening and trying to let go all at the same time. I knew I was not just feeling it myself; I knew I was feeling what Henry was going through at that moment. Except that I couldn't stand it, the closing and opening. I jumped to my feet. I took Henry by the shoulders and I started shaking him. "Wake up," I says, "wake up, wake up, wake up!" I didn't know what had come over me. I sat down beside him again.

His face was totally white and hard. Then it broke, like stones break all of a sudden when water boils up inside them.

"I know it," he says. "I know it. I can't help it. It's no use."

We start talking. He said he knew what I'd done with the car. It was obvious it had been whacked out of shape and not just neglected. He said he wanted to give the car to me for good now, it was no use. He said he'd fixed it just to give it back and I should take it.

"No way," I says, "I don't want it."

"That's okay," he says, "you take it."

"I don't want it, though," I says back to him, and then to emphasize, just to emphasize, you understand, I touch his shoulder. He slaps my hand off.

"Take that car," he says.

"No," I say, "make me," I say, and then he grabs my jacket and rips the arm loose. That jacket is a class act, suede with tags and zippers. I push Henry backwards, off the log. He jumps up and bowls me over. We go down in a clinch and come up swinging hard, for all we're worth, with our fists. He socks my jaw so hard I feel like it swings loose. Then I'm at his ribcage and land a good one under his chin so his head snaps back. He's dazzled. He looks at me and I look at him and then his eyes are full of tears and blood and at first I think he's crying. But no, he's laughing. "Ha! Ha!" he says. "Ha! Ha! Take good care of it."

"Okay," I says, "okay, no problem. Ha! Ha!"

I can't help it, and I start laughing, too. My face feels fat and strange, and after a while I get a beer from the cooler in the trunk, and when I hand it to Henry he takes his shirt and wipes my germs off. "Hoof-and-mouth disease," he says. For some reason this cracks me up, and so we're really laughing for a while, and then we drink all the rest of the beers one by one and throw them in the river and see how far, how fast, the current takes them before they fill up and sink.

"You want to go on back?" I ask after a while. "Maybe we could snag a couple nice Kashpaw girls."

He says nothing. But I can tell his mood is turning again.

"They're all crazy, the girls up here, every damn one of them."

"You're crazy too," I say, to jolly him up. "Crazy Lamartine boys!"

He looks as though he will take this wrong at first. His face twists, then clears, and he jumps up on his feet. "That's right!" he says. "Crazier 'n hell. Crazy Indians!"

I think it's the old Henry again. He throws off his jacket and starts swinging his legs out from the knees like a fancy dancer. He's down doing something between a grouse dance and a bunny hop, no kind of dance I ever saw before, but neither has anyone else on all this green growing earth. He's wild. He wants to pitch whoopee! He's up and at me and all over. All this time I'm laughing so hard, so hard my belly is getting tied up in a knot.

"Got to cool me off!" he shouts all of a sudden. Then he runs over to the river and jumps in.

There's boards and other things in the current. It's so high. No sound comes from the river after the splash he makes, so I run right over. I look around. It's getting dark. I see he's halfway across the water already, and I know he didn't swim there but the current took him. It's far. I hear his voice, though, very clearly across it.

"My boots are filling," he says.

He says this in a normal voice, like he just noticed and he doesn't know what to think of it. Then he's gone. A branch comes by. Another branch. And I go in.

By the time I get out of the river, off the snag I pulled myself onto, the sun is down. I walk back to the car, turn on the high beams, and drive it up the bank. I put it in first gear and then I take my foot off the clutch. I get out, close the door, and watch it plow softly into the water. The headlights reach in as they go down, searching, still lighted even after the water swirls over the back end. I wait. The wires short out. It is all finally dark. And then there is only the water, the sound of it going and running and going and running and running.

QUESTIONS
1. Characterize Lyman, the narrator. Why does he refer to himself in the third person in the opening paragraph?   **2.** In the sixth section of the story, why does Lyman move forward in time to describe the photograph taken by his sister and his feelings about it?   **3.** Why does Lyman feel that *repose* is the precise word to describe the red convertible?   **4.** How does the episode about Susy's hair relate to the theme of the story?   **5.** Does it make a difference that it is the Vietnam War (rather than, say, the Second World War) that Henry never recovers from? Explain.

WRITING TOPIC
1. Discuss the meaning of the red convertible to Lyman and Henry and its function in the story.   **2.** In what ways is it significant that Lyman and Henry are Native Americans?

INNOCENCE
AND
EXPERIENCE

Il castello di carte (The House of Cards) by Zinaida Serebriakova

POETRY

The Chimney Sweeper 1789

WILLIAM BLAKE [1757–1827]

When my mother died I was very young,
And my Father sold me while yet my tongue
Could scarcely cry "'weep! 'weep! 'weep! 'weep!"
So your chimneys I sweep, and in soot I sleep.

There's little Tom Dacre, who cried when his head,
That curled like a lamb's back, was shaved: so I said,
"Hush, Tom! never mind it, for when your head's bare
You know that the soot cannot spoil your white hair."

And so he was quiet and that very night
As Tom was a-sleeping, he had such a sight!   10
That thousands of sweepers, Dick, Joe, Ned, and Jack,
Were all of them locked up in coffins of black.

And by came an Angel who had a bright key,
And he opened the coffins and set them all free;
Then down a green plain leaping, laughing, they run,
And wash in a river, and shine in the Sun.

Then naked and white, all their bags left behind,
They rise upon clouds and sport in the wind;
And the Angel told Tom, if he'd be a good boy,
He'd have God for his father, and never want joy.   20

And so Tom awoke; and we rose in the dark,
And got with our bags and our brushes to work.
Though the morning was cold, Tom was happy and warm;
So if all do their duty they need not fear harm.

The Tyger   1794

WILLIAM BLAKE   [1757–1827]

Tyger! Tyger! burning bright
In the forests of the night,
What immortal hand or eye
Could frame thy fearful symmetry?

In what distant deeps or skies
Burnt the fire of thine eyes?
On what wings dare he aspire?
What the hand dare seize the fire?

And what shoulder, & what art,
Could twist the sinews of thy heart?   10
And when thy heart began to beat,
What dread hand? & what dread feet?

What the hammer? what the chain?
In what furnace was thy brain?
What the anvil? what dread grasp
Dare its deadly terrors clasp?

When the stars threw down their spears,
And water'd heaven with their tears,
Did he smile his work to see?
Did he who made the Lamb make thee?   20

Tyger! Tyger! burning bright
In the forests of the night,
What immortal hand or eye
Dare frame thy fearful symmetry?

The Garden of Love   1793

WILLIAM BLAKE   [1757–1827]

I went to the Garden of Love,
And saw what I never had seen:

A Chapel was built in the midst,
Where I used to play on the green.

And the gates of this Chapel were shut,
And "Thou shalt not" writ over the door;
So I turn'd to the Garden of Love,
That so many sweet flowers bore,

And I saw it was filled with graves,
And tomb-stones where flowers should be: 10
And Priests in black gowns were walking their rounds,
And binding with briars my joys & desires.

QUESTIONS
1. What meanings does the word "love" have in this poem?   **2.** What is Blake's
judgment on established religion?   **3.** Explain the meaning of "Chapel" (l. 3) and
of "briars" (l. 12).

WRITING TOPIC
Read the definition of irony in the glossary of literary terms. Write an essay in which
you distinguish between the types of irony used in "The Chimney Sweeper" and
"The Garden of Love."

London   1794

WILLIAM BLAKE   [1757–1827]

I wander through each chartered[1] street,
Near where the chartered Thames does flow
And mark in every face I meet
Marks of weakness, marks of woe.

In every cry of every man,
In every infant's cry of fear,
In every voice; in every ban,
The mind-forged manacles I hear:

London
    [1] Preempted by the state and leased out under royal patent.

How the chimney-sweeper's cry
Every blackening church appalls,   10
And the hapless soldier's sigh
Runs in blood down palace-walls.

But most, through midnight streets I hear
How the youthful harlot's curse
Blasts the new-born infant's tear,
And blights with plagues the marriage-hearse.

To a Mouse   1786
ON TURNING HER UP IN HER NEST WITH THE PLOUGH, NOVEMBER, 1785

ROBERT BURNS   [1759–1796]

Wee, sleekit,° cow'rin, tim'rous beastie,   sleek
O, what a panic's in thy breastie!
Thou need na start awa sae hasty,
    Wi' bickering° brattle!°   hurried/scamper
I wad be laith° to rin an' chase thee,   reluctant
    Wi' murd'ring pattle!°   plowstaff

I'm truly sorry man's dominion
Has broken Nature's social union,
An' justifies that ill opinion
    Which makes thee startle   10
At me, thy poor earth-born companion,
    An' fellow-mortal!

I doubt na, whiles,° but thou may thieve;   sometimes
What then? poor beastie, thou maun° live!   must
A daimen° icker° in a thrave°   occasional/corn-ear/shock
    'S a sma' request:
I'll get a blessin wi' the lave,°   rest
    And never miss't!

Thy wee bit housie, too, in ruin!
Its silly wa's the win's are strewin'
An' naething, now, to big° a new ane,   20
    O' foggage° green!   build
An' bleak December's winds ensuin,   mosses
    Baith snell° an' keen!   bitter

Thou saw the fields laid bare and waste,
An' weary winter comin fast,
An' cozie here, beneath the blast,
      Thou thought to dwell,
Till crash! the cruel coulter° past   *plowshare*
      Out thro' thy cell.   30

That wee bit heap o' leaves an' stibble
Has cost thee mony a weary nibble!
Now thou's turned out, for a' thy trouble,
      But° house or hald,   *without*
To thole° the winter's sleety dribble,   *endure*
      An' cranreuch° cauld!   *hoarfrost*

But, Mousie, thou art no thy lane°   *not alone*
In proving foresight may be vain:
The best laid schemes o' mice an' men
      Gang° aft a-gley.°   39
An' lea'e us nought but grief an' pain   *go/awry*
      For promised joy.

Still thou art blest, compared wi' me!
The present only toucheth thee:
But och! I backward cast my e'e
      On prospects drear!
An' forward, tho' I canna see,
      I guess an' fear!

Lines[1]   1798

COMPOSED A FEW MILES ABOVE TINTERN ABBEY
ON REVISITING THE BANKS OF THE WYE
DURING A TOUR. JULY 13, 1798

WILLIAM WORDSWORTH   [1770–1850]

Five years have passed;[2] five summers, with the length
Of five long winters! and again I hear

Lines
  [1] Wordsworth wrote this poem during a four- or five-day walking tour through the Wye valley with his sister Dorothy.
  [2] The poet had visited the region on a solitary walking tour in August of 1793 when he was twenty-three years old.

These waters, rolling from their mountain-springs
With a soft inland murmur. Once again
Do I behold these steep and lofty cliffs,
That on a wild secluded scene impress
Thoughts of more deep seclusion; and connect
The landscape with the quiet of the sky.
The day is come when I again repose
Here, under this dark sycamore, and view   10
These plots of cottage ground, these orchard tufts,
Which at this season, with their unripe fruits,
Are clad in one green hue, and lose themselves
'Mid groves and copses. Once again I see
These hedgerows, hardly hedgerows, little lines
Of sportive wood run wild; these pastoral farms,
Green to the very door; and wreaths of smoke
Sent up, in silence, from among the trees!
With some uncertain notice, as might seem
Of vagrant dwellers in the houseless woods,   20
Or of some Hermit's cave, where by his fire
The Hermit sits alone.

                              These beauteous forms,
Through a long absence, have not been to me
As is a landscape to a blind man's eye;
But oft, in lonely rooms, and 'mid the din
Of towns and cities, I have owed to them
In hours of weariness, sensations sweet,
Felt in the blood, and felt along the heart;
And passing even into my purer mind,
With tranquil restoration—feelings too   30
Of unremembered pleasure; such, perhaps,
As have no slight or trivial influence
On that best portion of a good man's life,
His little, nameless, unremembered, acts
Of kindness and of love. Nor less, I trust,
To them I may have owed another gift,
Of aspect more sublime; that blessed mood,
In which the burthen of the mystery,
In which the heavy and the weary weight
Of all this unintelligible world,   40
Is lightened—that serene and blessed mood,
In which the affections gently lead us on—
Until, the breath of this corporeal frame
And even the motion of our human blood
Almost suspended, we are laid asleep
In body, and become a living soul;

While with an eye made quiet by the power
Of harmony, and the deep power of joy,
We see into the life of things.

If this

Be but a vain belief, yet, oh! how oft—   50
In darkness and amid the many shapes
Of joyless daylight; when the fretful stir
Unprofitable, and the fever of the world,
Have hung upon the beatings of my heart—
How oft, in spirit, have I turned to thee,
O sylvan Wye! thou wanderer through the woods,
How often has my spirit turned to thee!

    And now, with gleams of half-extinguished thought
With many recognitions dim and faint,
And somewhat of a sad perplexity,   60
The picture of the mind revives again;
While here I stand, not only with the sense
Of present pleasure, but with pleasing thoughts
That in this moment there is life and food
For future years. And so I dare to hope,
Though changed, no doubt, from what I was when first
I came among these hills; when like a roe
I bounded o'er the mountains, by the sides
Of the deep rivers, and the lonely streams,
Wherever nature led—more like a man   70
Flying from something that he dreads than one
Who sought the thing he loved. For nature then
(The coarser pleasures of my boyish days,
And their glad animal movements all gone by)
To me was all in all.—I cannot paint
What then I was. The sounding cataract
Haunted me like a passion; the tall rock,
The mountain, and the deep and gloomy wood,
Their colors and their forms, were then to me
An appetite; a feeling and a love,   80
That had no need of a remoter charm,
By thought supplied, nor any interest
Unborrowed from the eye.—That time is past,
And all its aching joys are now no more,
And all its dizzy raptures. Not for this
Faint[3] I, nor mourn nor murmur; other gifts

---

[3] Lose heart.

Have followed; for such loss, I would believe,
Abundant recompense. For I have learned
To look on nature, not as in the hour
Of thoughtless youth; but hearing oftentimes   90
The still, sad music of humanity,
Nor harsh nor grating, though of ample power
To chasten and subdue. And I have felt
A presence that disturbs me with the joy
Of elevated thoughts; a sense sublime
Of something far more deeply interfused,
Whose dwelling is the light of setting suns,
And the round ocean and the living air,
And the blue sky, and in the mind of man:
A motion and a spirit, that impels   100
All thinking things, all objects of all thought,
And rolls through all things. Therefore am I still
A lover of the meadows and the woods,
And mountains; and of all that we behold
From this green earth; of all the mighty world
Of eye, and ear—both what they half create,
And what perceive; well pleased to recognize
In nature and the language of the sense
The anchor of my purest thoughts, the nurse,
The guide, the guardian of my heart, and soul   110
Of all my moral being.

                    Nor perchance,
If I were not thus taught, should I the more
Suffer my genial spirits to decay:
For thou art with me here upon the banks
Of this fair river; thou my dearest Friend,[4]
My dear, dear Friend; and in thy voice I catch
The language of my former heart, and read
My former pleasures in the shooting lights
Of thy wild eyes. Oh! yet a little while
May I behold in thee what I was once,   120
My dear, dear Sister! and this prayer I make,
Knowing that Nature never did betray
The heart that loved her; 'tis her privilege,
Through all the years of this our life, to lead
From joy to joy: for she can so inform
The mind that is within us, so impress

---

[4] The poet addresses his sister Dorothy.

With quietness and beauty, and so feed
With lofty thoughts, that neither evil tongues,
Rash judgments, nor the sneers of selfish men,
Nor greetings where no kindness is, nor all   130
The dreary intercourse of daily life,
Shall e'er prevail against us, or disturb
Our cheerful faith, that all which we behold
Is full of blessings. Therefore let the moon
Shine on thee in thy solitary walk;
And let the misty mountain winds be free
To blow against thee: and, in after years,
When these wild ecstasies shall be matured
Into a sober pleasure; when thy mind
Shall be a mansion for all lovely forms,   140
Thy memory be as a dwelling place
For all sweet sounds and harmonies; oh! then,
If solitude, or fear, or pain, or grief
Should be thy portion, with what healing thoughts
Of tender joy wilt thou remember me,
And these my exhortations! Nor, perchance—
If I should be where I no more can hear
Thy voice, nor catch from thy wild eyes these gleams
Of past existence⁵—wilt thou then forget
That on the banks of this delightful stream   150
We stood together; and that I, so long
A worshiper of Nature, hither came
Unwearied in that service; rather say
With warmer love—oh! with far deeper zeal
Of holier love. Nor wilt thou then forget,
That after many wanderings, many years
Of absence, these steep woods and lofty cliffs,
And this green pastoral landscape, were to me
More dear, both for themselves and for thy sake!

QUESTIONS

1. In this poem the poet distinguishes between two important periods in his life: the first is described in lines 65–83, and the second is described in lines 83–111. How does he characterize these two periods? **2.** The poem describes a visit to a familiar scene of the poet's youth and includes a meditation upon the changes that have occurred. Are the changes in the poet, the scene itself, or both?

---

⁵ I.e., the poet's past experience. Note lines 116–119.

WRITING TOPIC
Discuss the ways in which the poet contrasts the city and the countryside.

On First Looking into
Chapman's Homer[1]   1816

JOHN KEATS   [1795–1821]

Much have I travelled in the realms of gold,
And many goodly states and kingdoms seen:
Round many western islands have I been
Which bards in fealty to Apollo[2] hold.
Oft of one wide expanse had I been told
That deep-browed Homer ruled as his demesne;°   realm
Yet did I never breathe its pure serene°   clear air
Till I heard Chapman speak out loud and bold:
Then felt I like some watcher of the skies
When a new planet swims into his ken;   10
Or like stout Cortez[3] when with eagle eyes
He stared at the Pacific—and all his men
Looked at each other with a wild surmise—
    Silent, upon a peak in Darien.

My Last Duchess   1842

ROBERT BROWNING   [1812–1889]

FERRARA

That's my last Duchess painted on the wall,
Looking as if she were alive. I call
That piece a wonder, now: Frà Pandolf's[1] hands
Worked busily a day, and there she stands.
Will't please you sit and look at her? I said

On First Looking into Chapman's Homer
   [1] George Chapman published translations of *The Iliad* (1611) and *The Odyssey* (1616).
   [2] The god of poetry.
   [3] Keats mistakenly attributes the discovery of the Pacific Ocean by Europeans to Hernando Cortez (1485–1547), the Spanish conqueror of Mexico. Vasco Nuñez de Balboa (1475–1517) first saw the Pacific from a mountain located in eastern Panama.

My Last Duchess
   [1] Frà Pandolf and Claus of Innsbruck (mentioned in the last line) are fictitious artists.

"Frà Pandolf" by design, for never read
Strangers like you that pictured countenance,
The depth and passion of its earnest glance,
But to myself they turned (since none puts by
The curtain I have drawn for you, but I)   10
And seemed as they would ask me, if they durst,
How such a glance came there; so, not the first
Are you to turn and ask thus. Sir, 'twas not
Her husband's presence only, called that spot
Of joy into the Duchess' cheek: perhaps
Frà Pandolf chanced to say "Her mantle laps
"Over my lady's wrist too much," or "Paint
"Must never hope to reproduce the faint
"Half-flush that dies along her throat": such stuff
Was courtesy, she thought, and cause enough   20
For calling up that spot of joy. She had
A heart—how shall I say?—too soon made glad,
Too easily impressed; she liked whate'er
She looked on, and her looks went everywhere.
Sir, 'twas all one! My favor at her breast,
The dropping of the daylight in the West,
The bough of cherries some officious fool
Broke in the orchard for her, the white mule
She rode with round the terrace—all and each
Would draw from her alike the approving speech,   30
Or blush, at least. She thanked men—good! but thanked
Somehow—I know not how—as if she ranked
My gift of a nine-hundred-years-old name
With anybody's gift. Who'd stoop to blame
This sort of trifling? Even had you skill
In speech—which I have not—to make your will
Quite clear to such an one, and say, "Just this
"Or that in you disgusts me; here you miss,
"Or there exceed the mark"—and if she let
Herself be lessoned° so, nor plainly set   taught
Her wits to yours, forsooth, and made excuse,   41
—E'en then would be some stooping; and I choose
Never to stoop. Oh sir, she smiled, no doubt,
Whene'er I passed her; but who passed without
Much the same smile? This grew; I gave commands;
Then all smiles stopped together. There she stands
As if alive. Will't please you rise? We'll meet
The company below, then. I repeat,
The Count your master's known munificence°   generosity
Is ample warrant that no just pretense   50

Of mine for dowry will be disallowed;
Though his fair daughter's self, as I avowed
At starting, is my object. Nay, we'll go
Together down, sir. Notice Neptune, though,
Taming a sea-horse, thought a rarity,
Which Claus of Innsbruck cast in bronze for me!

QUESTIONS

1. To whom is the Duke speaking, and what is the occasion?   **2.** What does a
comparison between the Duke's feelings about his artworks and his feelings about
his last Duchess reveal about his character?   **3.** What became of the Duke's last
Duchess?   **4.** Does this poem rely upon irony? Explain.

WRITING TOPIC

Write an essay in which you argue that the reader is or is not meant to sympathize
with the Duke's characterization of his wife.

I Felt a Funeral, in My Brain   (1861)

EMILY DICKINSON   [1830–1886]

I felt a Funeral, in my Brain,
And Mourners to and fro
Kept treading—treading—till it seemed
That Sense was breaking through—

And when they all were seated,
A Service, like a Drum—
Kept beating—beating—till I thought
My Mind was going numb—

And then I heard them lift a Box
And creak across my Soul   10
With those same Boots of Lead, again,
Then Space—began to toll,

As all the Heavens were a Bell,
And Being, but an Ear,
And I, and Silence, some strange Race
Wrecked, solitary, here—

And then a Plank in Reason, broke,
And I dropped down, and down—
And hit a World, at every plunge,
And Finished knowing—then—   20

Hap   1898

THOMAS HARDY   [1840–1928]

If but some vengeful god would call to me
From up the sky, and laugh: "Thou suffering thing,
Know that thy sorrow is my ecstasy,
That thy love's loss is my hate's profiting!"

Then would I bear it, clench myself, and die,
Steeled by the sense of ire unmerited;
Half-eased in that a Powerfuller than I
Had willed and meted me the tears I shed.

But not so. How arrives it joy lies slain,
And why unblooms the best hope ever sown?   10
— Crass Casualty° obstructs the sun and rain,   chance
And dicing Time for gladness casts a moan. . . .
These purblind Doomsters[1] had as readily strown
Blisses about my pilgrimage as pain.

The Ruined Maid   1902

THOMAS HARDY   [1840–1928]

"O Melia, my dear, this does everything crown!
Who could have supposed I should meet you in Town?
And whence such fair garments, such prosperi-ty?"
"O didn't you know I'd been ruined?" said she.

"You left us in tatters, without shoes or socks,
Tired of digging potatoes, and spudding up docks;°   digging herbs
And now you've gay bracelets and bright feathers three!"
"Yes: that's how we dress when we're ruined," said she.

Hap
[1] Those who decide one's fate.

"At home in the barton° you said 'thee' and 'thou,'   farmyard
And 'thik onn,' and 'theäs oon,' and 't'other; but now   10
Your talking quite fits 'ee for high compa-ny!"
"Some polish is gained with one's ruin," said she.

"Your hands were like paws then, your face blue and bleak
But now I'm bewitched by your delicate cheek,
And your little gloves fit as on any la-dy!"
"We never do work when we're ruined," said she.

"You used to call home-life a hag-ridden dream,
And you'd sigh, and you'd sock; but at present you seem
To know not of megrims° or melancho-ly!"   sick headaches
"True. One's pretty lively when ruined," said she.   20

"I wish I had feathers, a fine sweeping gown,
And a delicate face, and could strut about Town!"
"My dear—a raw country girl, such as you be,
Cannot quite expect that. You ain't ruined," said she.

Spring and Fall   1880
TO A YOUNG CHILD

GERARD MANLEY HOPKINS [1844–1889]

Márgarét, áre you gríeving
Over Goldengrove unleaving?°   losing leaves
Leáves, líke the things of man, you
With your fresh thoughts care for, can you?
Áh! ás the heart grows older
It will come to such sights colder
By and by, nor spare a sigh
Though worlds of wanwood leafmeal[1] lie;
And yet you wíll weep and know why.
Now no matter, child, the name: 10
Sórrow's spríngs are the same.
Nor mouth had, no nor mind, expressed
What heart heard of, ghost° guessed: soul
It ís the blight man was born for,
It is Margaret you mourn for.

Spring and Fall
   [1] Pale woods littered with mouldering leaves.

QUESTIONS
1. In this poem Margaret grieves over the passing of spring and the coming of fall. What does the coming of fall symbolize? **2.** Why, when Margaret grows older, will she not sigh over the coming of fall? **3.** What are "Sorrow's springs" (l. 11)?

When I Was One-and-Twenty
1896

A. E. HOUSMAN   [1859–1936]

When I was one-and-twenty
    I heard a wise man say,
"Give crowns and pounds and guineas
    But not your heart away;
Give pearls away and rubies
    But keep your fancy free."
But I was one-and-twenty,
    No use to talk to me.

When I was one-and-twenty
    I heard him say again,   10
"The heart out of the bosom
    Was never given in vain;
'Tis paid with sighs a plenty
    And sold for endless rue."
And I am two-and-twenty,
    And oh, 'tis true, 'tis true.

Terence, This Is Stupid Stuff[1]
1896

A. E. HOUSMAN   [1859–1936]

   "Terence, this is stupid stuff:
You eat your victuals fast enough;
There can't be much amiss, 'tis clear,
To see the rate you drink your beer.

Terence, This Is Stupid Stuff
   [1] Housman originally titled the volume in which this poem appeared *The Poems of Terence Hearsay*. Terence was a Roman satiric playwright.

But oh, good Lord, the verse you make,
It gives a chap the bellyache.
The cow, the old cow, she is dead;
It sleeps well, the hornéd head:
We poor lads, 'tis our turn now
To hear such tunes as killed the cow.   10
Pretty friendship 'tis to rhyme
Your friends to death before their time
Moping melancholy mad:
Come, pipe a tune to dance to, lad."

    Why, if 'tis dancing you would be,
There's brisker pipes than poetry.
Say, for what were hopyards meant,
Or why was Burton built on Trent?[2]
Oh many a peer of England brews
Livelier liquor than the Muse,   20
And malt does more than Milton can
To justify God's ways to man.[3]
Ale, man, ale's the stuff to drink
For fellows whom it hurts to think:
Look into the pewter pot
To see the world as the world's not.
And faith, 'tis pleasant till 'tis past:
The mischief is that 'twill not last.

    Oh I have been to Ludlow fair
And left my necktie God knows where,   30
And carried halfway home, or near,
Pints and quarts of Ludlow beer:
Then the world seemed none so bad,
And I myself a sterling lad;
And down in lovely muck I've lain,
Happy till I woke again.
Then I saw the morning sky:
Heigho, the tale was all a lie;
The world, it was the old world yet,
I was I, my things were wet,   40
And nothing now remained to do
But begin the game anew.

---

[2] The river Trent provides water for the town's brewing industry.
[3] In the invocation to *Paradise Lost*, Milton declares that his epic will "justify the ways of God to men."

Therefore, since the world has still
Much good, but much less good than ill,
And while the sun and moon endure
Luck's a chance, but trouble's sure,
I'd face it as a wise man would,
And train for ill and not for good.
'Tis true the stuff I bring for sale
Is not so brisk a brew as ale: 50
Out of a stem that scored the hand
I wrung it in a weary land.
But take it: if the smack is sour,
The better for the embittered hour;
It should do good to heart and head
When your soul is in my soul's stead;
And I will friend you, if I may,
In the dark and cloudy day.

   There was a king reigned in the East:
There, when kings will sit to feast,   60
They get their fill before they think
With poisoned meat and poisoned drink.
He gathered all that springs to birth
From the many-venomed earth;
First a little, thence to more,
He sampled all her killing store;
And easy, smiling, seasoned sound,
Sate the king when healths went round.
They put arsenic in his meat
And stared aghast to watch him eat;   70
They poured strychnine in his cup
And shook to see him drink it up:
They shook, they stared as white's their shirt:
Them it was their poison hurt.
— I tell the tale that I heard told.
Mithridates, he died old.[4]

QUESTIONS

1. What does the speaker of the first fourteen lines object to in Terence's poetry?   **2.** What is Terence's response to the criticism of his verse? What function of true poetry is implied by his comparison of bad poetry with liquor?

---

  [4] Mithridates, the King of Pontus (in Asia Minor), reputedly immunized himself against poisons by administering to himself gradually increasing doses.

WRITING TOPIC
How does the story of Mithridates (ll. 59–76) illustrate the theme of the poem?

Adam's Curse   1902

WILLIAM BUTLER YEATS   [1865–1939]

We sat together at one summer's end,
That beautiful mild woman, your close friend,
And you and I, and talked of poetry.
I said, 'A line will take us hours maybe;
Yet if it does not seem a moment's thought,
Our stitching and unstitching has been naught.

Better go down upon your marrow-bones
And scrub a kitchen pavement, or break stones
Like an old pauper, in all kinds of weather;
For to articulate sweet sounds together   10
Is to work harder than all these, and yet
Be thought an idler by the noisy set
Of bankers, schoolmasters, and clergymen
The martyrs call the world.'

                              And thereupon
That beautiful mild woman for whose sake
There's many a one shall find out all heartache
On finding that her voice is sweet and low
Replied, 'To be born woman is to know —
Although they do not talk of it at school —   20
That we must labour to be beautiful.'

I said, 'It's certain there is no fine thing
Since Adam's fall but needs much labouring.
There have been lovers who thought love should be
So much compounded of high courtesy
That they would sigh and quote with learned looks
Precedents out of beautiful old books;
Yet now it seems an idle trade enough.'

We sat grown quiet at the name of love;
We saw the last embers of daylight die,   30
And in the trembling blue-green of the sky
A moon, worn as if it had been a shell

Washed by time's waters as they rose and fell
About the stars and broke in days and years.

I had a thought for no one's but your ears:
That you were beautiful, and that I strove
To love you in the old high way of love;
That it had all seemed happy, and yet we'd grown
As weary-hearted as that hollow moon.

Leda and the Swan[1]   1928

WILLIAM BUTLER YEATS   [1865–1939]

A sudden blow: the great wings beating still
Above the staggering girl, her thighs caressed
By the dark webs, her nape caught in his bill,
He holds her helpless breast upon his breast.

How can those terrified vague fingers push
The feathered glory from her loosening thighs?
And how can body, laid in that white rush,
But feel the strange heart beating where it lies?

A shudder in the loins engenders there
The broken wall, the burning roof and tower   10
And Agamemnon dead.
                        Being so caught up,
So mastered by the brute blood of the air,
Did she put on his knowledge with his power
Before the indifferent beak could let her drop?

Birches   1916

ROBERT FROST   [1874–1963]

When I see birches bend to left and right
Across the lines of straighter darker trees,

Leda and the Swan
   [1] In Greek myth, Zeus, in the form of a swan, rapes Leda. As a consequence, Helen and
Clytemnestra are born. Each sister marries the king of a city-state; Helen marries Menelaus and
Clytemnestra marries Agamemnon. Helen, the most beautiful woman on earth, elopes with Paris,
a prince of Troy, an act that precipitates the Trojan War in which Agamemnon commands the
combined Greek armies. The war ends with the destruction of Troy. Agamemnon, when he returns
to his home, is murdered by his unfaithful wife.

I like to think some boy's been swinging them.
But swinging doesn't bend them down to stay.
Ice-storms do that. Often you must have seen them
Loaded with ice a sunny winter morning
After a rain. They click upon themselves
As the breeze rises, and turn many-colored
As the stir cracks and crazes their enamel.
Soon the sun's warmth makes them shed crystal shells   10
Shattering and avalanching on the snow-crust —
Such heaps of broken glass to sweep away
You'd think the inner dome of heaven had fallen.
They are dragged to the withered bracken by the load,
And they seem not to break; though once they are bowed
So low for long, they never right themselves:
You may see their trunks arching in the woods
Years afterwards, trailing their leaves on the ground
Like girls on hands and knees that throw their hair
Before them over their heads to dry in the sun.   20
But I was going to say when Truth broke in
With all her matter-of-fact about the ice-storm
I should prefer to have some boy bend them
As he went out and in to fetch the cows —
Some boy too far from town to learn baseball,
Whose only play was what he found himself,
Summer or winter, and could play alone.
One by one he subdued his father's trees
By riding them down over and over again
Until he took the stiffness out of them,   30
And not one but hung limp, not one was left
For him to conquer. He learned all there was
To learn about not launching out too soon
And so not carrying the tree away
Clear to the ground. He always kept his poise
To the top branches, climbing carefully
With the same pains you use to fill a cup
Up to the brim, and even above the brim.
Then he flung outward, feet first, with a swish,
Kicking his way down through the air to the ground.   40
So was I once myself a swinger of birches.
And so I dream of going back to be.
It's when I'm weary of considerations,
And life is too much like a pathless wood
Where your face burns and tickles with the cobwebs
Broken across it, and one eye is weeping

From a twig's having lashed across it open.
I'd like to get away from earth awhile
And then come back to it and begin over.
May no fate willfully misunderstand me   50
And half grant what I wish and snatch me away
Not to return. Earth's the right place for love:
I don't know where it's likely to go better.
I'd like to go by climbing a birch tree,
And climb black branches up a snow-white trunk
Toward heaven, till the tree could bear no more,
But dipped its top and set me down again.
That would be good both going and coming back.
One could do worse than be a swinger of birches.

Provide, Provide   1936

ROBERT FROST   [1874–1963]

The witch that came (the withered hag)
To wash the steps with pail and rag,
Was once the beauty Abishag,[1]

The picture pride of Hollywood.
Too many fall from great and good
For you to doubt the likelihood.

Die early and avoid the fate.
Or if predestined to die late,
Make up your mind to die in state.

Make the whole stock exchange your own!   10
If need be occupy a throne,
Where nobody can call *you* crone.

Provide, Provide
    [1] "Now King David was old and advanced in years; and although they covered him with clothes,
he could not get warm. Therefore his servants said to him, 'Let a young maiden be sought for my
lord the king, and let her wait upon the king, and be his nurse; let her lie in your bosom, that my
lord the king may be warm.' So they sought for a beautiful maiden throughout all the territory of
Israel, and found Abishag, the Shunammite, and brought her to the king. The maiden was very
beautiful. . . ."—I Kings 1:1–4.

Some have relied on what they knew;
Others on being simply true.
What worked for them might work for you.

No memory of having starred
Atones for later disregard,
Or keeps the end from being hard.

Better to go down dignified
With boughten friendship at your side   20
Than none at all. Provide, provide!

Peter Quince at the Clavier[1]   1923

WALLACE STEVENS   [1879–1955]

1

Just as my fingers on these keys
Make music, so the selfsame sounds
On my spirit make a music, too.

Music is feeling, then, not sound;
And thus it is that what I feel,
Here in this room, desiring you,

Thinking of your blue-shadowed silk,
Is music. It is like the strain
Waked in the elders by Susanna.[2]

Of a green evening, clear and warm,   10
She bathed in her still garden, while
The red-eyed elders watching, felt

Peter Quince at the Clavier
   [1] A clavier is a keyboard instrument. The title is probably a whimsical reference to Peter Quince of Shakespeare's *A Midsummer Night's Dream*, who directs the mechanics' production of the "most cruel death of Pyramus and Thisby" to be performed at the king's wedding festival. One of the actors, Bottom, advises the director, "First, good Peter Quince, say what the play treats on, then read the names of the actors, and so grow on to a point." Peter Quince, here a musician, seems to follow that advice.
   [2] The Old Testament Apocrypha includes the story of Susanna, who is saved by the wisdom of Daniel from a death sentence for adultery based on the perjured testimony of the "elders."

The basses of their beings throb
In witching chords, and their thin blood
Pulse pizzicati of Hosanna.[3]

2

In the green water, clear and warm,
Susanna lay.

She searched
The touch of springs,
And found   20
Concealed imaginings.
She sighed,
For so much melody.

Upon the bank, she stood
In the cool
Of spent emotions.
She felt, among the leaves,
The dew
Of old devotions.

She walked upon the grass,   30
Still quavering.
The winds were like her maids,
On timid feet,
Fetching her woven scarves,
Yet wavering.

A breath upon her hand
Muted the night.

She turned—
A cymbal crashed,
And roaring horns.   40

3

Soon, with a noise like tambourines,
Came her attendant Byzantines.[4]

---

[3] Pizzicati notes are produced by plucking the strings rather than bowing. Hosanna is a cry of acclamation and adoration.

[4] From Byzantium (now Istanbul). The attendants are slaves.

They wondered why Susanna cried
Against the elders by her side;

And as they whispered, the refrain
Was like a willow swept by rain.

Anon, their lamps' uplifted flame
Revealed Susanna and her shame.

And then, the simpering Byzantines
Fled, with a noise like tambourines.   50

      4

Beauty is momentary in the mind—
The fitful tracing of a portal;
But in the flesh it is immortal.

The body dies; the body's beauty lives.
So evenings die, in their green going,
A wave, interminably flowing.
So gardens die, their meek breath scenting
The cowl of winter, done repenting.
So maidens die, to the auroral
Celebration of a maiden's choral.   60

Susanna's music touched the bawdy strings
Of those white elders; but, escaping,
Left only Death's ironic scraping.
Now, in its immortality, it plays
On the clear viol of her memory,
And makes a constant sacrament of praise.

QUESTIONS
1. What is the relationship of the narrative in lines 10–50 to lines 1–9 and to
section 4? **2.** Is the statement contained in lines 51–54 a paradox? Explain.

WRITING TOPIC
This poem is famous for its sound patterns. What are the dominating consonant and
vowel sounds in lines 1–11? What sounds dominate lines 12–15? Can you suggest
how these sounds reinforce the sense of the poem?

Thirteen Ways of Looking at a Blackbird

1923

WALLACE STEVENS   [1879–1955]

1

Among twenty snowy mountains,
The only moving thing
Was the eye of the blackbird.

2

I was of three minds,
Like a tree
In which there are three blackbirds.

3

The blackbird whirled in the autumn winds.
It was a small part of the pantomime.

4

A man and a woman
Are one.
A man and a woman and a blackbird
Are one.

10

5

I do not know which to prefer,
The beauty of inflections
Or the beauty of innuendoes,
The blackbird whistling
Or just after.

6

Icicles filled the long window
With barbaric glass.
The shadow of the blackbird

20

Crossed it, to and fro.
The mood
Traced in the shadow
An indecipherable cause.

7

O thin men of Haddam,°   a town in Connecticut
Why do you imagine golden birds?
Do you not see how the blackbird
Walks around the feet
Of the women about you?

8

I know noble accents   30
And lucid, inescapable rhythms;
But I know, too,
That the blackbird is involved
In what I know.

9

When the blackbird flew out of sight,
It marked the edge
Of one of many circles.

10

At the sight of blackbirds
Flying in a green light,
Even the bawds of euphony   40
Would cry out sharply.

11

He rode over Connecticut
In a glass coach.
Once, a fear pierced him,
In that he mistook
The shadow of his equipage
For blackbirds.

12

The river is moving.
The blackbird must be flying.

13

It was evening all afternoon.   50
It was snowing
And it was going to snow.
The blackbird sat
In the cedar-limbs.

QUESTION

1. Surely Stevens's blackbird is more than just a bird. What kinds of responses does the image of the blackbird evoke? A sense of pleasure or pain, life or death, light or darkness, good or evil?

To Carry the Child   1966

STEVIE SMITH   [1902–1971]

To carry the child into adult life
Is good? I say it is not,
To carry the child into adult life
Is to be handicapped.

The child in adult life is defenceless
And if he is grown-up, knows it,
And the grown-up looks at the childish part
And despises it.

The child, too, despises the clever grown-up,
The man-of-the-world, the frozen,   10
For the child has the tears alive on his cheek
And the man has none of them.

As the child has colours, and the man sees no
Colours or anything,
Being easy only in things of the mind,
The child is easy in feeling.

Easy in feeling, easily excessive
And in excess powerful,
For instance, if you do not speak to the child
He will make trouble.   20
You would say a man had the upper hand
Of the child, if a child survive,

But I say the child has fingers of strength
To strangle the man alive.

Oh! it is not happy, it is never happy,
To carry the child into adulthood,
Let the children lie down before full growth
And die in their infanthood
And be guilty of no man's blood.

But oh the poor child, the poor child, what can he do,   30
Trapped in a grown-up carapace,
But peer outside of his prison room
With the eye of an anarchist?

Not Waving but Drowning   1972

STEVIE SMITH [1902–1971]

Nobody heard him, the dead man,
But still he lay moaning:
I was much further out than you thought
And not waving but drowning.

Poor chap, he always loved larking
And now he's dead
It must have been too cold for him his heart gave way,
They said.

Oh, no no no, it was too cold always
(Still the dead one lay moaning)   10
I was much too far out all my life
And not waving but drowning.

QUESTIONS
1. Explain the paradox in the first and last stanzas, where the speaker describes
someone dead as moaning. **2.** Who do you suppose the *you* of line 3 is? And the
they of line 8? **3.** Explain the meaning of line 7. Can it be interpreted in more
than one way? Explain. **4.** Explain the meanings of *drowning*. **5.** The only thing
we learn about the dead man is that "he always loved larking." Why is this detail
significant? What kind of man do you think he was? **6.** Does the speaker know
more about the dead man than his friends did? Explain.

WRITING TOPICS
1. Write an essay describing how you or someone you know suffered the experience of "not waving but drowning." **2.** Write an essay describing how you came to the realization that someone close to you was not the person you thought he or she was.

Incident   1925

COUNTEE CULLEN   [1903–1946]

Once riding in old Baltimore,
    Heart-filled, head-filled with glee,
I saw a Baltimorean
    Keep looking straight at me.

Now I was eight and very small,
    And he was no whit bigger,
And so I smiled, but he poked out
    His tongue and called me, "Nigger."

I saw the whole of Baltimore
    From May until December: 10
Of all the things that happened there
    That's all that I remember.

Fern Hill   1946

DYLAN THOMAS   (1914–1953)

Now as I was young and easy under the apple boughs
About the lilting house and happy as the grass was green,
    The night above the dingle° starry,   _small wooded valley_
        Time let me hail and climb
        Golden in the heydays of his eyes,
And honored among wagons I was prince of the apple towns
And once below a time I lordly had the trees and leaves
        Trail with daisies and barley
        Down the rivers of the windfall light.

And I was green and carefree, famous among the barns   10
About the happy yard and singing as the farm was home,
        In the sun that is young once only,
           Time let me play and be

    Golden in the mercy of his means,
  1 green and golden I was huntsman and herdsman, the calves
  ıg to my horn, the foxes on the hills barked clear and cold,
       And the sabbath rang slowly
    In the pebbles of the holy streams.

All the sun long it was running, it was lovely, the hay
Fields high as the house, the tunes from the chimneys, it was air   20
      And playing, lovely and watery
      And fire green as grass.
      And nightly under the simple stars
As I rode to sleep the owls were bearing the farm away,
All the moon long I heard, blessed among stables, the nightjars[1]
    Flying with the ricks, and the horses
      Flashing into the dark.

And then to awake, and the farm, like a wanderer white
With the dew, come back, the cock on his shoulder: it was all
    Shining, it was Adam and maiden,   30
      The sky gathered again
    And the sun grew round that very day.
So it must have been after the birth of the simple light
In the first, spinning place, the spellbound horses walking warm
    Out of the whinnying green stable
      On to the fields of praise.

And honored among foxes and pheasants by the gay house
Under the new made clouds and happy as the heart was long,
    In the sun born over and over,
      I ran my heedless ways,   40
    My wishes raced through the house high hay
And nothing I cared, at my sky blue trades, that time allows
In all his tuneful turning so few and such morning songs
    Before the children green and golden
      Follow him out of grace.

Nothing I cared, in the lamb white days, that time would take me
Up to the swallow thronged loft by the shadow of my hand,
    In the moon that is always rising,
      Nor that riding to sleep
    I should hear him fly with the high fields   50

Fern Hill
[1] Nightjars are harsh-sounding nocturnal birds.

And wake to the farm forever fled from the childless land.
Oh as I was young and easy in the mercy of his means,
      Time held me green and dying
   Though I sang in my chains like the sea.

QUESTIONS

1. What emotional impact does the color imagery in the poem provide?   **2.** Trace the behavior of "time" in the poem.   **3.** Fairy tales often begin with the words "once upon a time." Why does Thomas alter that formula in line 7?   **4.** Explain the paradox in line 53.

WRITING TOPICS

1. Lines 17–18, 30, 45–46 incorporate religious language and biblical allusion. How do those allusions clarify the poet's vision of his childhood?   **2.** Compare this poem with Gerard Manley Hopkins's "Spring and Fall."

A Moment Please   1962

SAMUEL ALLEN   [b. 1917]

When I gaze at the sun
   I walked to the subway booth
   for change for a dime.
and know that this great earth
   Two adolescent girls stood there
   alive with eagerness to know
is but a fragment from it thrown
   all in their new found world
   there was for them to know
in heat and flame a billion years ago,   10
   they looked at me and brightly asked
   "Are you Arabian?"
that when this world was lifeless
   I smiled and cautiously
   —for one grows cautious—
   shook my head.
as, a billion hence,
   "Egyptian?"
It shall again be,
   Again I smiled and shook my head   20
   and walked away.
what moment is it that I am betrayed,

I've gone but seven paces now
oppressed, cast down,
    and from behind comes swift the sneer
or warm with love or triumph?
    "Or Nigger?"
    A moment, please
What is it that to fury I am roused?
    for still it takes a moment   30
What meaning for me
    and now
in this homeless clan
    I'll turn
the dupe of space
    and smile
the toy of time?
    and nod my head.

Disqualification   1973

ELIZABETH BREWSTER [b. 1922]

I am of puritan and loyalist ancestry
and of middle class tastes.
My father never swore in front of ladies,
as he always quaintly called women.
My mother thought that a man was no gentleman
if he smoked a cigar without asking her permission;
and she thought all men should be gentlemen,
even though a gentleman would not call himself one,
and all women should be ladies,
even though a lady would not call herself one.   10

I have never taken any drug
stronger than aspirin.
I have never been more than slightly drunk.
I think there are worse vices
than hypocrisy or gentility,
or even than voting Conservative.

If I wanted to be fucked
I should probably choose a different word.
(Anyhow, I am not quite sure
whether it is a transitive or an intransitive verb,   20
because it was never given to me to parse.)

Usually I can parse words, analyze sentences,
spell, punctuate,
and recognize the more common metrical forms.

It is almost impossible
that I shall ever be
a truly established poet.

This Be the Verse   1974

PHILIP LARKIN   [1922–1985]

They fuck you up, your mum and dad.
   They may not mean to, but they do.
They fill you with the faults they had
   And add some extra, just for you.

But they were fucked up in their turn
   By fools in old-style hats and coats,
Who half the time were soppy-stern
   And half at one another's throats.

Man hands on misery to man.
   It deepens like a coastal shelf.   10
Get out as early as you can,
   And don't have any kids yourself.

"More Light! More Light!"[1]   1961

FOR HEINRICH BLÜCHER AND HANNAH ARENDT[2]

ANTHONY HECHT   [b. 1923]

Composed in the Tower[3] before his execution
These moving verses, and being brought at that time
Painfully to the stake, submitted, declaring thus:
"I implore my God to witness that I have made no crime."

"More Light! More Light!"
  [1] These were the last words of the German poet Johann Wolfgang von Goethe (1749–1832).
  [2] Husband and wife who emigrated to the United States from Germany in 1941. Hannah Arendt has written extensively on political totalitarianism.
  [3] The Tower of London was used as a prison for eminent political prisoners. What follows is an account of a priest's execution for the crime of heresy. The punishment was death by fire, and often a sack of gunpowder was placed at the condemned's neck to shorten the agony.

Nor was he forsaken of courage, but the death was horrible,
The sack of gunpowder failing to ignite.
His legs were blistered sticks on which the black sap
Bubbled and burst as he howled for the Kindly Light.

And that was but one, and by no means one of the worst;
Permitted at least his pitiful dignity;   10
And such as were by made prayers in the name of Christ,
That shall judge all men, for his soul's tranquillity.

We move now to outside a German wood
Three men are there commanded to dig a hole
In which the two Jews are ordered to lie down
And be buried by the third, who is a Pole.

Not light from the shrine at Weimar⁴ beyond the hill
Nor light from heaven appeared. But he did refuse.
A Lüger⁵ settled back deeply in its glove.
He was ordered to change places with the Jews.   20

Much casual death had drained away their souls.
The thick dirt mounted toward the quivering chin.
When only the head was exposed the order came
To dig him out again and to get back in.

No light, no light in the blue Polish eye.
When he finished a riding boot packed down the earth.
The Lüger hovered lightly in its glove.
He was shot in the belly and in three hours bled to death.

No prayers or incense rose up in those hours
Which grew to be years, and every day came mute
Ghosts from the ovens, sifting through crisp air,
And settled upon his eyes in a black soot.

QUESTIONS
1. What relationship does the event (which occurred in sixteenth-century England) recounted in the first two stanzas of the poem bear to the event recounted in the last four stanzas?   **2.** What irony do you find in the title of the poem and the use of the word *light* in lines 8, 17, 18, and 25? How would you define *light* in each

---

⁴ Goethe spent most of his life in Weimar, and his humanistic achievements are honored there in the Goethe National Museum. The event recounted here occurred at Buchenwald, a German concentration camp north of Weimar.
⁵ A German automatic pistol.

case? Can you imagine yourself in the place of the three prisoners in line 14? What would you do?

Curiosity   1959

ALASTAIR REID   [b. 1926]

may have killed the cat; more likely
the cat was just unlucky, or else curious
to see what death was like, having no cause
to go on licking paws, or fathering
litter on litter of kittens, predictably.

    Nevertheless, to be curious
is dangerous enough. To distrust
what is always said, what seems,
to ask odd questions, interfere in dreams,
leave home, smell rats, have hunches   10
does not endear him to those doggy circles
where well-smelt baskets, suitable wives, good lunches
are the order of things and where prevails
much wagging of incurious heads and tails.

    Face it. Curiosity
will not cause him to die—
only lack of it will.
Never to want to see
the other side of the hill,
or that improbable country   20
where living is an idyll
(although a probable hell)
would kill us all.
Only the curious
have, if they live, a tale
worth telling at all.

    Dogs say he loves too much, is irresponsible,
is changeable, marries too many wives,
deserts his children, chills all dinner tables
with tales of his nine lives.   30
Well, he is lucky. Let him be
nine-lived and contradictory,
curious enough to change, prepared to pay
the cat price, which is to die

and die again and again,
each time with no less pain.
A cat minority of one
is all that can be counted on
to tell the truth. And what he has to tell
on each return from hell   40
is this: that dying is what the living do,
that dying is what the loving do,
and that dead dogs are those who do not know
that hell is where, to live, they have to go.

April Inventory   1959

W. D. SNODGRASS   [b. 1926]

The green catalpa tree has turned
All white; the cherry blooms once more.
In one whole year I haven't learned
A blessed thing they pay you for.
The blossoms snow down in my hair;
The trees and I will soon be bare.

The trees have more than I to spare.
The sleek, expensive girls I teach,
Younger and pinker every year,
Bloom gradually out of reach.   10
The pear tree lets its petals drop
Like dandruff on a tabletop.

The girls have grown so young by now
I have to nudge myself to stare.
This year they smile and mind me how
My teeth are falling with my hair.
In thirty years I may not get
Younger, shrewder, or out of debt.

The tenth time, just a year ago,
I made myself a little list   20
Of all the things I'd ought to know;
Then told my parents, analyst,
And everyone who's trusted me
I'd be substantial, presently.

I haven't read one book about
A book or memorized one plot.
Or found a mind I did not doubt.
I learned one date. And then forgot.
And one by one the solid scholars
Get the degrees, the jobs, the dollars.   30

And smile above their starchy collars.
I taught my classes Whitehead's notions;
One lovely girl, a song of Mahler's.
Lacking a source-book or promotions,
I showed one child the colors of
A luna moth and how to love.

I taught myself to name my name,
To bark back, loosen love and crying;
To ease my woman so she came,
To ease an old man who was dying.   40
I have not learned how often I
Can win, can love, but choose to die.

I have not learned there is a lie
Love shall be blonder, slimmer, younger;
That my equivocating eye
Loves only by my body's hunger;
That I have poems, true to feel,
Or that the lovely world is real.

While scholars speak authority
And wear their ulcers on their sleeves,   50
My eyes in spectacles shall see
These trees procure and spend their leaves.
There is a value underneath
The gold and silver in my teeth.

Though trees turn bare and girls turn wives,
We shall afford our costly seasons;
There is a gentleness survives
That will outspeak and has its reasons.
There is a loveliness exists,
Preserves us. Not for specialists.   60

QUESTIONS
1. What do the words "I have not learned" (ll. 41, 43) mean in the context of the poem? **2.** In what way does the tone of the first four stanzas differ from the tone of the last two? **3.** What is the meaning of "specialists" in the last line? **4.** What is the speaker's conception of teaching?

WRITING TOPIC
Explicate the final stanza of this poem. Is it an appropriate conclusion? Explain.

Cinderella   1971

ANNE SEXTON   [1928–1974]

You always read about it:
the plumber with twelve children
who wins the Irish Sweepstakes.
From toilets to riches.
That story.

Or the nursemaid,
some luscious sweet from Denmark
who captures the oldest son's heart.
From diapers to Dior.
That story.   10

Or a milkman who serves the wealthy,
eggs, cream, butter, yogurt, milk,
the white truck like an ambulance
who goes into real estate
and makes a pile.
From homogenized to martinis at lunch.

Or the charwoman
who is on the bus when it cracks up
and collects enough from the insurance.
From mops to Bonwit Teller.   20
That story.

Once
the wife of a rich man was on her deathbed
and she said to her daughter Cinderella:
Be devout. Be good. Then I will smile
down from heaven in the seam of a cloud.

The man took another wife who had
two daughters, pretty enough
but with hearts like blackjacks.
Cinderella was their maid.   30
She slept on the sooty hearth each night
and walked around looking like Al Jolson.
Her father brought presents home from town,
jewels and gowns for the other women
but the twig of a tree for Cinderella.
She planted that twig on her mother's grave
and it grew to a tree where a white dove sat.
Whenever she wished for anything the dove
would drop it like an egg upon the ground.
The bird is important, my dears, so heed him.   40

Next came the ball, as you all know.
It was a marriage market.
The prince was looking for a wife.
All but Cinderella were preparing
and gussying up for the big event.
Cinderella begged to go too.
Her stepmother threw a dish of lentils
into the cinders and said: Pick them
up in an hour and you shall go.
The white dove brought all his friends;   50
all the warm wings of the fatherland came,
and picked up the lentils in a jiffy.
No, Cinderella, said the stepmother,
you have no clothes and cannot dance.
That's the way with stepmothers.

Cinderella went to the tree at the grave
and cried forth like a gospel singer:
Mama! Mama! My turtledove,
send me to the prince's ball!
The bird dropped down a golden dress   60
and delicate little gold slippers.
Rather a large package for a simple bird.
So she went. Which is no surprise.
Her stepmother and sisters didn't
recognize her without her cinder face
and the prince took her hand on the spot
and danced with no other the whole day.

As nightfall came she thought she'd better
get home. The prince walked her home
and she disappeared into the pigeon house   70
and although the prince took an axe and broke
it open she was gone. Back to her cinders.
These events repeated themselves for three days.
However on the third day the prince
covered the palace steps with cobbler's wax
and Cinderella's gold shoe stuck upon it.

Now he would find whom the shoe fit
and find his strange dancing girl for keeps.
He went to their house and the two sisters
were delighted because they had lovely feet.   80
The eldest went into a room to try the slipper on
but her big toe got in the way so she simply
sliced it off and put on the slipper.
The prince rode away with her until the white dove
told him to look at the blood pouring forth.
That is the way with amputations.
They don't just heal up like a wish.
The other sister cut off her heel
but the blood told as blood will.
The prince was getting tired.   90
He began to feel like a shoe salesman
but he gave it one last try.
This time Cinderella fit into the shoe
like a love letter into its envelope.

At the wedding ceremony
the two sisters came to curry favor
and the white dove pecked their eyes out.
Two hollow spots were left
like soup spoons.

Cinderella and the prince   100
lived, they say, happily ever after,
like two dolls in a museum case
never bothered by diapers or dust,
never arguing over the timing of an egg,
never telling the same story twice,
never getting a middle-aged spread,

their darling smiles pasted on for eternity.
Regular Bobbsey Twins.[1]
That story.

QUESTIONS
1. Where does one usually find the first four "stories" mentioned in the poem? Why do such stories interest readers? **2.** The story of Cinderella, of course, is well known. Do you remember your feelings at the success of Cinderella? How are those feelings modified by the last stanza?

WRITING TOPIC
The language and formal structure of this poem are rather prosaic. Describe, by examining the image patterns and individual lines, the qualities that make the piece a poem.

First Confession   1961

X. J. KENNEDY [b. 1929]

Blood thudded in my ears. I scuffed,
    Steps stubborn, to the telltale booth
Beyond whose curtained portal coughed
    The robed repositor of truth.

The slat shot back. The universe
    Bowed down his cratered dome to hear
Enumerated my each curse,
    The sip snitched from my old man's beer.

My sloth pride envy lechery,
    The dime held back from Peter's Pence   10
With which I'd bribed my girl to pee
    That I might spy her instruments.

Hovering scale-pans when I'd done
    Settled their balance slow as silt
While in the restless dark I burned
    Bright as a brimstone in my guilt

Cinderella
  [1] The ever-cheerful central figures in a series of children's books.

Until as one feeds birds he doled
  Seven Our Fathers and a Hail
Which I to double-scrub my soul
  Intoned twice at the altar rail   20

Where Sunday in seraphic light
  I knelt, as full of grace as most,
And stuck my tongue out at the priest:
  A fresh roost for the Holy Ghost.

Advice to My Son   1965

PETER MEINKE   [b. 1932]

The trick is, to live your days
as if each one may be your last
(for they go fast, and young men lose their lives
in strange and unimaginable ways)
but at the same time, plan long range
(for they go slow: if you survive
the shattered windshield and the bursting shell
you will arrive
at our approximation here below
of heaven or hell).   10

To be specific, between the peony and the rose
plant squash and spinach, turnips and tomatoes;
beauty is nectar
and nectar, in a desert, saves—
but the stomach craves stronger sustenance
than the honied vine.

Therefore, marry a pretty girl
after seeing her mother;
show your soul to one man,
work with another;   20
and always serve bread with your wine.

But, son,
always serve wine.

QUESTIONS
1. Explain how the advice of lines 17–21 is logically related to the preceding lines.   **2.** What do the final two lines tell the reader about the speaker?

WRITING TOPIC
The advice of the first stanza seems contradictory. In what ways does the second stanza attempt to resolve the contradiction or explain "The trick" (l. 1)? What do the various plants and the bread and wine symbolize?

In a Spring Still Not Written Of 1965

ROBERT WALLACE [b. 1932]

This morning
with a class of girls outdoors, I saw
how frail poems are
in a world burning up with flowers,
in which, overhead,
the great elms
—green, and tall—
stood carrying leaves in their arms.

The girls listened equally
to my drone, reading, and to the bees'   10
ricocheting
among them for the blossom on the bone,
or gazed off at a distant mower's
astronomies of green
and clover, flashing,
threshing in the new, untarnished sunlight.

And all the while, dwindling,
tinier, the voices—Yeats, Marvell, Donne—
sank drowning
in a spring still not written of,   20
as only the sky
clear above the brick bell-tower
—blue, and white—
was shifting toward the hour.

Calm, indifferent, cross-legged
or on elbows half-lying in the grass—
how should the great dead
tell them of dying?
They will come to time for poems at last,
when they have found they are no more   30
the beautiful and young
all poems are for.

QUESTIONS
1. What is the speaker's attitude toward the "class of girls" he is teaching? Toward his job as a teacher?   **2.** Explain the meaning of the title.   **3.** Explain the various meanings of "drone" (l. 10).

WRITING TOPIC
Explain the paradox developed in this poem.

My Mother   1970

ROBERT MEZEY   [b. 1935]

My mother writes from Trenton,
a comedian to the bone
but underneath, serious
and all heart. "Honey," she says,
"be a mensch[1] and Mary too,
it's no good to worry, you
are doing the best you can
your Dad and everyone
thinks you turned out very well
as long as you pay your bills   10
nobody can say a word
you can tell them to drop dead
so save a dollar it can't
hurt—remember Frank you went
to highschool with? he still lives
with his wife's mother, his wife
works while he writes his books and
did he ever sell a one
the four kids run around naked
36 and he's never had,   20
you'll forgive my expression
even a pot to piss in
or a window to throw it,
such a smart boy he couldn't
read the footprints on the wall
honey you think you know all
the answers you don't, please try
to put some money away

My Mother
   [1] Man, in the sense of "human being."

believe me it wouldn't hurt
artist shmartist life's too short   30
for that kind of, forgive me,
horseshit, I know what you want
better than you, all that counts
is to make a good living
and the best of everything,
as Sholem Aleichem said
he was a great writer did
you ever read his books dear,
you should make what he makes a year
anyway he says some place   40
Poverty is no disgrace
but it's no honor either
that's what I say,
           love,
              Mother"

Memo: 1980

JUNE JORDAN   [b. 1936]

When I hear some woman say she
has finally decided you can spend time with
other women, I wonder what she means: Her
mother? My mother?
I've always despised my woman friends. Even
if they introduced me to a man I found
attractive I have never let them become
what you could call my intimates. Why
should I? Men are the ones with the money and
the big way with waiters and the passkey   10
to excitement in strange places of real
danger and the power to make things happen
like babies or war and all these great ideas
about mass magazines for members of the weaker sex
who need permission
to eat potatoes or a doctor's opinion on orgasm after death
or the latest word on what the female
executive should do, after hours, wearing
what. They must be morons: women!
Don't you think?   20
I guess you could say

I'm stuck in my ways
as
That Cosmopolitan Girl.

QUESTIONS
1. Explain the title. **2.** What do the first three lines mean? Why would a woman feel she *can't* spend time with other women? **3.** Does this poem accurately describe the power relations in our society? Explain. **4.** Describe the tone of this poem.

WRITING TOPIC
Examine a few issues of *Cosmopolitan* magazine to show how it inspired this poem.

First Light   1991

LINDA HOGAN [b. 1947]

In early morning
I forget I'm in this world
with crooked chiefs
who make federal deals.

In the first light
I remember who rewards me for living,
not bosses
but singing birds and blue sky.

I know I can bathe and stretch,
make jewelry and love   10
the witch and wise woman
living inside, needing to be silenced
and put at rest for work's long day.

In the first light
I offer cornmeal
and tobacco.
I say hello to those who came before me,
and to birds
under the eaves,
and budding plants.   20

I know the old ones are here.
And every morning I remember the song
about how buffalo left through a hole in the sky

and how the grandmothers look out from those holes
watching over us
from there and from there.

For Robin

QUESTIONS
1. Explain what "this world" of line 2 is.   **2.** Who are the "crooked chiefs"? What
is a "federal" deal?   **3.** Is the speaker part of the world of chiefs and federal deals?
Explain.   **4.** Why does the speaker offer cornmeal and tobacco?   **5.** Explain the
title.

WRITING TOPIC
Write an essay in which you speculate on who the poet is and what might have
led her to write this poem.

Our Room   1984

MOLLY PEACOCK   [b. 1947]

I tell the children in school sometimes
why I hate alcoholics: my father was one.
"Alcohol" and "disease" I use, and shun
the word "drunk" or even "drinking," since one time
the kids burst out laughing when I told them.
I felt as though they were laughing at me.
I waited for them, wounded, remembering how I imagined they'd howl at me
when I was in grade 5. Acting drunk
is a guaranteed screamer, especially   10
for boys. I'm quiet when I sort the junk
of my childhood for them, quiet so we
will all be quiet, and they can ask what
questions they have to and tell about what
happened to them, too. The classroom becomes
oddly lonely when we talk about our homes.

QUESTIONS
1. The implication of line 6 is that the children were laughing not at the speaker
but at something else. What might that have been?   **2.** Describe the speaker's
attitude toward her classmates.   **3.** Explain the title.

WRITING TOPIC

Have you ever experienced shame about your family? Describe what it was that caused the shame, your feelings at the time, and your present feelings about it.

Father Answers His Adversaries   1980

LAWRENCE KEARNEY

It's early March, Eisenhower still
president, & Mother's heating up supper
for the third time tonight.
We're at the table doing homework,
& she tells us Father's next in line
for foreman, that today he'll know for sure.
He's three hours late.

Half past eight the Chevy
screeches into the carport.
For a minute, nothing.   10
Then the sudden slam, & the thump downstairs
to the basement. Beneath our feet
Father lays into the workbench
with a sledgehammer—the jam jars
of nails, of screws, of nuts & bolts
he'd taken years to sort out
exploding against the wall.

Later, sheepish, he comes up,
slumps in his seat & asks for supper.
And when Mother brings his plate   20
& he looks up at her
& she takes his head on her breast,
he blushes, turns away, & spits out
that final, weary-mouthed answer
to all of it—General Motors & the bosses
& the union pimps & the punched-out Johnnies,
every yes-man goddam ass-lick
who'd ever been jumped to foreman
over him—*aah, crap's like cream,*
it rises.

QUESTIONS

1. How would you characterize the family? Happy? Unhappy? Close-knit? Explain.   **2.** Why do you suppose the father did not get the job as foreman?   **3.** Why is the father described as "sheepish" (l. 18)? Why does he blush (l. 23)?   **4.** Put into your own words the father's answer to his adversaries.

WRITING TOPIC
Write an essay describing someone you know who was unfairly passed over for a promotion (or fired from a job). Did he or she feel the same bitterness and helplessness as the father in this poem? What became of the person?

INNOCENCE
AND
EXPERIENCE

Belisarius and the Boy, 1802 by Benjamin West

DRAMA

Oedipus Rex*   (ca. 429 B.C.)

SOPHOCLES   [496?–406 B.C.]

PERSONS REPRESENTED

Oedipus
A Priest
Creon
Teiresias
Iocastê

Messenger
Shepherd of Laïos
Second Messenger
Chorus of Theban Elders

SCENE

Before the palace of Oedipus, King of Thebes. A central door and two lateral doors open onto a platform which runs the length of the facade. On the platform, right and left, are altars; and three steps lead down into the "orchestra," or chorus-ground. At the beginning of the action these steps are crowded by suppliants who have brought branches and chaplets of olive leaves and who lie in various attitudes of despair. Oedipus enters.

Prologue

Oedipus.   My children, generations of the living
In the line of Kadmos,[1] nursed at his ancient hearth:
Why have you strewn yourselves before these altars
In supplication, with your boughs and garlands?

---

* An English version by Dudley Fitts and Robert Fitzgerald.
[1] The legendary founder of Thebes.

The breath of incense rises from the city
With a sound of prayer and lamentation.

                                        Children,
I would not have you speak through messengers,
And therefore I have come myself to hear you—
I, Oedipus, who bear the famous name.
[*To a Priest.*] You, there, since you are eldest in the company,   10
Speak for them all, tell me what preys upon you,
Whether you come in dread, or crave some blessing:
Tell me, and never doubt that I will help you
In every way I can; I should be heartless
Were I not moved to find you suppliant here.
Priest.   Great Oedipus, O powerful King of Thebes!
You see how all the ages of our people
Cling to your altar steps: here are boys
Who can barely stand alone, and here are priests
By weight of age, as I am a priest of God,   20
And young men chosen from those yet unmarried;
As for the others, all that multitude,
They wait with olive chaplets in the squares,
At the two shrines of Pallas,[2] and where Apollo[3]
Speaks in the glowing embers.

                                  Your own eyes
Must tell you: Thebes is in her extremity
And can not lift her head from the surge of death.
A rust consumes the buds and fruits of the earth;
The herds are sick; children die unborn,
And labor is vain. The god of plague and pyre   30
Raids like detestable lightning through the city,
And all the house of Kadmos is laid waste,
All emptied, and all darkened: Death alone
Battens upon the misery of Thebes.

You are not one of the immortal gods, we know;
Yet we have come to you to make our prayer
As to the man of all men best in adversity
And wisest in the ways of God. You saved us
From the Sphinx,[4] that flinty singer, and the tribute

---

[2] Athena, goddess of wisdom.
[3] God of sunlight, medicine, and prophecy.
[4] A winged monster, with a woman's head and breasts and a lion's body, that destroyed those who failed to answer her riddle: "What walks on four feet in the morning, two at noon, and three in the evening?" When the young Oedipus correctly answered, "Man" ("three" alluding to a cane in old age), the Sphinx killed herself, and the plague ended.

We paid to her so long; yet you were never   40
Better informed than we, nor could we teach you:
It was some god breathed in you to set us free.
Therefore, O mighty King, we turn to you:
Find us our safety, find us a remedy,
Whether by counsel of the gods or men.
A king of wisdom tested in the past
Can act in a time of troubles, and act well.
Noblest of men, restore
Life to your city! Think how all men call you
Liberator for your triumph long ago;   50
Ah, when your years of kingship are remembered,
Let them not say *We rose, but later fell—*
Keep the State from going down in the storm!
Once, years ago, with happy augury,
You brought us fortune; be the same again!
No man questions your power to rule the land:
But rule over men, not over a dead city!
Ships are only hulls, citadels are nothing,
When no life moves in the empty passageways.

Oedipus.   Poor children! You may be sure I know   60
All that you longed for in your coming here.
I know that you are deathly sick; and yet,
Sick as you are, not one is as sick as I.
Each of you suffers in himself alone
His anguish, not another's; but my spirit
Groans for the city, for myself, for you.

I was not sleeping, you are not waking me.
No, I have been in tears for a long while
And in my restless thought walked many ways.
In all my search, I found one helpful course,   70
And that I have taken: I have sent Creon,
Son of Menoikeus, brother of the Queen,
To Delphi, Apollo's place of revelation,
To learn there, if he can,
What act or pledge of mine may save the city.
I have counted the days, and now, this very day,
I am troubled, for he has overstayed his time.
What is he doing? He has been gone too long.
Yet whenever he comes back, I should do ill
To scant whatever hint the god may give.   80

Priest.   It is a timely promise. At this instant
They tell me Creon is here.

Oedipus.   O Lord Apollo!
May his news be fair as his face is radiant!
Priest.   It could not be otherwise: he is crowned with bay,
The chaplet is thick with berries.
Oedipus.   We shall soon know;
He is near enough to hear us now.

[*Enter Creon.*]

                              O Prince:
Brother: son of Menoikeus:
What answer do you bring us from the god?
Creon.   It is favorable. I can tell you, great afflictions
Will turn out well, if they are taken well.   90
Oedipus.   What was the oracle? These vague words
Leave me still hanging between hope and fear.
Creon.   Is it your pleasure to hear me with all these
Gathered around us? I am prepared to speak,
But should we not go in?
Oedipus.   Let them all hear it.
It is for them I suffer, more than for myself.
Creon.   Then I will tell you what I heard at Delphi.

In plain words
The god commands us to expel from the land of Thebes
An old defilement that it seems we shelter.   100
It is a deathly thing, beyond expiation.
We must not let it feed upon us longer.
Oedipus.   What defilement? How shall we rid ourselves of it?
Creon.   By exile or death, blood for blood. It was
Murder that brought the plague-wind on the city.
Oedipus.   Murder of whom? Surely the god has named him?
Creon.   My lord: long ago Laïos was our king,
Before you came to govern us.
Oedipus.   I know;
I learned of him from others; I never saw him.
Creon.   He was murdered; and Apollo commands us now   110
To take revenge upon whoever killed him.
Oedipus.   Upon whom? Where are they? Where shall we find a clue
To solve that crime, after so many years?
Creon.   Here in this land, he said.
                              If we make enquiry,
We may touch things that otherwise escape us.
Oedipus.   Tell me: Was Laïos murdered in his house,
Or in the fields, or in some foreign country?

Creon.   He said he planned to make a pilgrimage.
He did not come home again.
Oedipus.   And was there no one,
No witness, no companion, to tell what happened?   120
Creon.   They were all killed but one, and he got away
So frightened that he could remember one thing only.
Oedipus.   What was that one thing? One may be the key
To everything, if we resolve to use it.
Creon.   He said that a band of highwaymen attacked them,
Outnumbered them, and overwhelmed the King.
Oedipus.   Strange, that a highwayman should be so daring—
Unless some faction here bribed him to do it.
Creon.   We thought of that. But after Laïos' death
New troubles arose and we had no avenger.   130
Oedipus.   What troubles could prevent your hunting down the killers?
Creon.   The riddling Sphinx's song
Made us deaf to all mysteries but her own.
Oedipus.   Then once more I must bring what is dark to light.
It is most fitting that Apollo shows,
As you do, this compunction for the dead.
You shall see how I stand by you, as I should,
To avenge the city and the city's god,
And not as though it were for some distant friend,
But for my own sake, to be rid of evil.   140
Whoever killed King Laïos might—who knows?—
Decide at any moment to kill me as well.
By avenging the murdered king I protect myself.
Come, then, my children: leave the altar steps,
Lift up your olive boughs!
                              One of you go
And summon the people of Kadmos to gather here.
I will do all that I can; you may tell them that.

[*Exit a page.*]

So, with the help of God,
We shall be saved—or else indeed we are lost.
Priest.   Let us rise, children. It was for this we came,   150
And now the King has promised it himself.
Phoibos[5] has sent us an oracle; may he descend
Himself to save us and drive out the plague.

---

[5] Phoebus Apollo, god of the sun.

[*Exeunt Oedipus and Creon into the palace by the central door. The Priest and the suppliants disperse R and L. After a short pause the Chorus enters the orchestra.*]

Párodos[6]

Chorus.   What is God singing in his profound   [*Strophe 1*]
    Delphi of gold and shadow?
    What oracle for Thebes, the sunwhipped city?
    Fear unjoints me, the roots of my heart tremble.
    Now I remember, O Healer, your power, and wonder;
    Will you send doom like a sudden cloud, or weave it
    Like nightfall of the past?
    Speak, speak to us, issue of holy sound:
    Dearest to our expectancy: be tender!

    Let me pray to Athenê, the immortal daughter of Zeus,   [*Antistrophe 1*]
    And to Artemis her sister   11
    Who keeps her famous throne in the market ring,
    And to Apollo, bowman at the far butts of heaven—

    O gods, descend! Like three streams leap against
    The fires of our grief, the fires of darkness;
    Be swift to bring us rest!

    As in the old time from the brilliant house
    Of air you stepped to save us, come again!

    Now our afflictions have no end,   [*Strophe 2*]
    Now all our stricken host lies down   20
    And no man fights off death with his mind;

    The noble plowland bears no grain,
    And groaning mothers can not bear—

    See, how our lives like birds take wing,
    Like sparks that fly when a fire soars,
    To the shore of the god of evening.

---

[6] The *Párodos* is the ode sung by the Chorus as it entered the theater and moved down the aisles to the playing area. The *strophe*, in Greek tragedy, is the unit of verse the Chorus chanted as it moved to the left in a dance rhythm. The Chorus sang the *antistrophe* as it moved to the right and the *epode* while standing still.

The plague burns on, it is pitiless,   [*Antistrophe 2*]
Though pallid children laden with death
Lie unwept in the stony ways,

And old gray women by every path   30
Flock to the strand about the altars
There to strike their breasts and cry
Worship of Phoibos in wailing prayers:
Be kind, God's golden child!

There are no swords in this attack by fire,   [*Strophe 3*]
No shields, but we are ringed with cries.
Send the besieger plunging from our homes
Into the vast sea-room of the Atlantic
Or into the waves that foam eastward of Thrace—
For the day ravages what the night spares—   40

Destroy our enemy, lord of the thunder!
Let him be riven by lightning from heaven!

Phoibus Apollo, stretch the sun's bowstring,   [*Antistrophe 3*]
That golden cord, until it sing for us,
Flashing arrows in heaven!
                        Artemis, Huntress
Race with flaring lights upon our mountains!

O scarlet god, O golden-banded brow,
O Theban Bacchos in a storm of Maenads,[7]

[*Enter Oedipus, C.*]

Whirl upon Death, that all the Undying hate!
Come with blinding cressets, come in joy!   50

Scene I

Oedipus.   Is this your prayer? It may be answered. Come,
    Listen to me, act as the crisis demands,
    And you shall have relief from all these evils.

---

[7] Bacchos is the god of wine and revelry, hence scarlet-faced. The Maenads were Bacchos'
female attendants.

Until now I was a stranger to this tale,
As I had been a stranger to the crime.
Could I track down the murderer without a clue?
But now, friends,
As one who became a citizen after the murder,
I make this proclamation to all Thebans:
If any man knows by whose hand Laïos, son of Labdakos,   10
Met his death, I direct that man to tell me everything,
No matter what he fears for having so long withheld it.
Let it stand as promised that no further trouble
Will come to him, but he may leave the land in safety.

Moreover: If anyone knows the murderer to be foreign,
Let him not keep silent: he shall have his reward from me.
However, if he does conceal it, if any man
Fearing for his friend or for himself disobeys this edict,
Hear what I propose to do:

I solemnly forbid the people of this country,   20
Where power and throne are mine, ever to receive that man
Or speak to him, no matter who he is, or let him
Join in sacrifice, lustration, or in prayer.
I decree that he be driven from every house,
Being, as he is, corruption itself to us: the Delphic
Voice of Zeus has pronounced this revelation.
Thus I associate myself with the oracle
And take the side of the murdered king.

As for the criminal, I pray to God—
Whether it be a lurking thief, or one of a number—   30
I pray that that man's life be consumed in evil and wretchedness.
And as for me, this curse applies no less
If it should turn out that the culprit is my guest here,
Sharing my hearth.
                    You have heard the penalty.
I lay it on you now to attend to this
For my sake, for Apollo's, for the sick
Sterile city that heaven has abandoned.
Suppose the oracle had given you no command:
Should this defilement go uncleansed for ever?
You should have found the murderer: your king,   40
A noble king, had been destroyed!
                    Now I,
Having the power that he held before me,
Having his bed, begetting children there

Upon his wife, as he would have, had he lived—
Their son would have been my children's brother,
If Laïos had had luck in fatherhood!
(But surely ill luck rushed upon his reign)—
I say I take the son's part, just as though
I were his son, to press the fight for him
And see it won! I'll find the hand that brought   50
Death to Labdakos' and Polydoros' child,
Heir of Kadmos's and Agenor's line.
And as for those who fail me,
May the gods deny them the fruit of the earth,
Fruit of the womb, and may they rot utterly!
Let them be wretched as we are wretched, and worse!

For you, for loyal Thebans, and for all
Who find my actions right, I pray the favor
Of justice, and of all the immortal gods.
Choragos.[8]   Since I am under oath, my lord, I swear   60
I did not do the murder. I can not name
The murderer. Might not the oracle
That has ordained the search tell where to find him?
Oedipus.   An honest question. But no man in the world
Can make the gods do more than the gods will.
Choragos.   There is one last expedient—
Oedipus.   Tell me what it is.
Though it seem slight, you must not hold it back.
Choragos.   A lord clairvoyant to the lord Apollo,
As we all know, is the skilled Teiresias.
One might learn much about this from him, Oedipus.   70
Oedipus.   I am not wasting time:
Creon spoke of this, and I have sent for him—
Twice, in fact; it is strange that he is not here.
Choragos.   The other matter—that old report—seems useless.
Oedipus.   Tell me. I am interested in all reports.
Choragos.   The King was said to have been killed by highwaymen.
Oedipus.   I know. But we have no witnesses to that.
Choragos.   If the killer can feel a particle of dread,
Your curse will bring him out of hiding!
Oedipus.   No.
The man who dared that act will fear no curse.   80

[*Enter the blind seer Teiresias, led by a page.*]

---

[8] Choragos is the leader of the Chorus.

Choragos.   But there is one man who may detect the criminal.
  This is Teiresias, this is the holy prophet
  In whom, alone of all men, truth was born.
Oedipus.   Teiresias: seer: student of mysteries,
  Of all that's taught and all that no man tells,
  Secrets of Heaven and secrets of the earth:
  Blind though you are, you know the city lies
  Sick with plague; and from this plague, my lord,
  We find that you alone can guard or save us.

  Possibly you did not hear the messengers?   90
  Apollo, when we sent to him,
  Sent us back word that this great pestilence
  Would lift, but only if we established clearly
  The identity of those who murdered Laïos.
  They must be killed or exiled.
                                   Can you use
  Birdflight or any art of divination
  To purify yourself, and Thebes, and me
  From this contagion? We are in your hands.
  There is no fairer duty
  Than that of helping others in distress.   100
Teiresias.   How dreadful knowledge of the truth can be
  When there's no help in truth! I knew this well,
  But did not act on it: else I should not have come.
Oedipus.   What is troubling you? Why are your eyes so cold?
Teiresias.   Let me go home. Bear your own fate, and I'll
  Bear mine. It is better so: trust what I say.
Oedipus.   What you say is ungracious and unhelpful
  To your native country. Do not refuse to speak.
Teiresias.   When it comes to speech, your own is neither temperate
  Nor opportune. I wish to be more prudent.   110
Oedipus.   In God's name, we all beg you—
Teiresias.   You are all ignorant.
  No; I will never tell you what I know.
  Now it is my misery; then, it would be yours.
Oedipus.   What! You do know something, and will not tell us?
  You would betray us all and wreck the State?
Teiresias.   I do not intend to torture myself, or you.
  Why persist in asking? You will not persuade me.
Oedipus.   What a wicked old man you are! You'd try a stone's
  Patience! Out with it! Have you no feeling at all?
Teiresias.   You call me unfeeling. If you could only see   120
  The nature of your own feelings . . .
Oedipus.   Why,

Who would not feel as I do? Who could endure
Your arrogance toward the city?
Teiresias.   What does it matter!
Whether I speak or not, it is bound to come.
Oedipus.   Then, if "it" is bound to come, you are bound to tell me.
Teiresias.   No, I will not go on. Rage as you please.
Oedipus.   Rage? Why not!
                                    And I'll tell you what I think:
You planned it, you had it done, you all but
Killed him with your own hands: if you had eyes,
I'd say the crime was yours, and yours alone.   130
Teiresias.   So? I charge you, then,
Abide by the proclamation you have made:
From this day forth
Never speak again to these men or to me;
You yourself are the pollution of this country.
Oedipus.   You dare say that! Can you possibly think you have
Some way of going free, after such insolence?
Teiresias.   I have gone free. It is the truth sustains me.
Oedipus.   Who taught you shamelessness? It was not your craft.
Teiresias.   You did. You made me speak. I did not want to.   140
Oedipus.   Speak what? Let me hear it again more clearly.
Teiresias.   Was it not clear before? Are you tempting me?
Oedipus.   I did not understand it. Say it again.
Teiresias.   I say that you are the murderer whom you seek.
Oedipus.   Now twice you have spat out infamy! You'll pay for it!
Teiresias.   Would you care for more? Do you wish to be really angry?
Oedipus.   Say what you will. Whatever you say is worthless.
Teiresias.   I say you live in hideous shame with those
Most dear to you. You can not see the evil.
Oedipus.   It seems you can go on mouthing like this for ever.   150
Teiresias.   I can, if there is power in truth.
Oedipus.   There is:
But not for you, not for you,
You sightless, witless, senseless, mad old man!
Teiresias.   You are the madman. There is no one here
Who will not curse you soon, as you curse me.
Oedipus.   You child of endless night! You can not hurt me
Or any other man who sees the sun.
Teiresias.   True: it is not from me your fate will come.
That lies within Apollo's competence,
As it is his concern.
Oedipus.   Tell me: 160
Are you speaking for Creon or for yourself?
Teiresias.   Creon is no threat. You weave your own doom.

Oedipus.   Wealth, power, craft of statesmanship!
Kingly position, everywhere admired!
What savage envy is stored up against these,
If Creon, whom I trusted, Creon my friend,
For this great office which the city once
Put in my hands unsought—if for this power
Creon desires in secret to destroy me!

He has brought this decrepit fortune-teller, this   170
Collector of dirty pennies, this prophet fraud—
Why, he is no more clairvoyant than I am!
                                              Tell us:
Has your mystic mummery ever approached the truth?
When that hellcat the Sphinx was performing here,
What help were you to these people?
Her magic was not for the first man who came along:
It demanded a real exorcist. Your birds—
What good were they? or the gods, for the matter of that?
But I came by,
Oedipus, the simple man, who knows nothing—   180
I thought it out for myself, no birds helped me!
And this is the man you think you can destroy,
That you may be close to Creon when he's king!
Well, you and your friend Creon, it seems to me,
Will suffer most. If you were not an old man,
You would have paid already for your plot.
Choragos.   We can not see that his words or yours
Have been spoken except in anger, Oedipus,
And of anger we have no need. How can God's will
Be accomplished best? That is what most concerns us.   190
Teiresias.   You are a king. But where argument's concerned
I am your man, as much a king as you.
I am not your servant, but Apollo's.
I have no need of Creon to speak for me.

Listen to me. You mock my blindness, do you?
But I say that you, with both your eyes, are blind:
You can not see the wretchedness of your life,
Nor in whose house you live, no, nor with whom.
Who are your father and mother? Can you tell me?
You do not even know the blind wrongs   200
That you have done them, on earth and in the world below.
But the double lash of your parents' curse will whip you
Out of this land some day, with only night
Upon your precious eyes.

Your cries then—where will they not be heard?
What fastness of Kithairon[9] will not echo them?
And that bridal-descant of yours—you'll know it then,
The song they sang when you came here to Thebes
And found your misguided berthing.
All this, and more, that you can not guess at now,   210
Will bring you to yourself among your children.

Be angry, then. Curse Creon. Curse my words.
I tell you, no man that walks upon the earth
Shall be rooted out more horribly than you.
Oedipus.   Am I to bear this from him?—Damnation
Take you! Out of this place! Out of my sight!
Teiresias.   I would not have come at all if you had not asked me.
Oedipus.   Could I have told that you'd talk nonsense, that
You'd come here to make a fool of yourself, and of me?
Teiresias.   A fool? Your parents thought me sane enough.   220
Oedipus.   My parents again!—Wait: who were my parents?
Teiresias.   This day will give you a father, and break your heart.
Oedipus.   Your infantile riddles! Your damned abracadabra!
Teiresias.   You were a great man once at solving riddles.
Oedipus.   Mock me with that if you like; you will find it true.
Teiresias.   It was true enough. It brought about your ruin.
Oedipus.   But if it saved this town?
Teiresias [*to the page*].   Boy, give me your hand.
Oedipus.   Yes, boy; lead him away.
                                                While you are here
We can do nothing. Go; leave us in peace.
Teiresias.   I will go when I have said what I have to say.   230
How can you hurt me? And I tell you again:
The man you have been looking for all this time,
The damned man, the murderer of Laïos,
That man is in Thebes. To your mind he is foreignborn,
But it will soon be shown that he is a Theban,
A revelation that will fail to please.
                                    A blind man,
Who has his eyes now; a penniless man, who is rich now;
And he will go tapping the strange earth with his staff;
To the children with whom he lives now he will be
Brother and father—the very same; to her   240
Who bore him, son and husband—the very same
Who came to his father's bed, wet with his father's blood.

---

[9] A mountain range near Thebes where the infant Oedipus was left to die.

Enough. Go think that over.
If later you find error in what I have said,
You may say that I have no skill in prophecy.

[*Exit Teiresias, led by his page. Oedipus goes into the palace.*]

Ode I

Chorus.   The Delphic stone of prophecies   [*Strophe 1*]
  Remembers ancient regicide
  And a still bloody hand.
  That killer's hour of flight has come.
  He must be stronger than riderless
  Coursers of untiring wind,
  For the son of Zeus[10] armed with his father's thunder
  Leaps in lightning after him;
  And the Furies follow him, the sad Furies.[11]

  Holy Parnassos' peak of snow   [*Antistrophe 1*]
  Flashes and blinds that secret man,   11
  That all shall hunt him down:
  Though he may roam the forest shade
  Like a bull gone wild from pasture
  To rage through glooms of stone.
  Doom comes down on him; flight will not avail him;
  For the world's heart calls him desolate,
  And the immortal Furies follow, for ever follow.

  But now a wilder thing is heard   [*Strophe 2*]
  From the old man skilled at hearing Fate in the wingbeat of a bird.   20
  Bewildered as a blown bird, my soul hovers and can not find
  Foothold in this debate, or any reason or rest of mind.
  But no man ever brought—none can bring
  Proof of strife between Thebes' royal house,
  Labdakos' line, and the son of Polybos;[12]
  And never until now has any man brought word
  Of Laïos' dark death staining Oedipus the King.

---

[10] I.e., Apollo (see note 3).
[11] The goddesses of divine vengeance.
[12] Labdakos was an early king of Thebes and an ancestor of Oedipus. Oedipus is mistakenly referred to as the son of Polybus.

Divine Zeus and Apollo hold   [*Antistrophe* 2]
Perfect intelligence alone of all tales ever told;
And well though this diviner works, he works in his own night;   30
No man can judge that rough unknown or trust in second sight,
For wisdom changes hands among the wise.
Shall I believe my great lord criminal
At a raging word that a blind old man let fall?
I saw him, when the carrion woman faced him of old,
Prove his heroic mind! These evil words are lies.

Scene II

Creon.   Men of Thebes:
  I am told that heavy accusations
  Have been brought against me by King Oedipus.

  I am not the kind of man to bear this tamely.

  If in these present difficulties
  He holds me accountable for any harm to him
  Through anything I have said or done—why, then,
  I do not value life in this dishonor.
  It is not as though this rumor touched upon
  Some private indiscretion. The matter is grave.   10
  The fact is that I am being called disloyal
  To the State, to my fellow citizens, to my friends.
Choragos.   He may have spoken in anger, not from his mind.
Creon.   But did you not hear him say I was the one
  Who seduced the old prophet into lying?
Choragos.   The thing was said; I do not know how seriously.
Creon.   But you were watching him! Were his eyes steady?
  Did he look like a man in his right mind?
Choragos.   I do not know.
  I can not judge the behavior of great men.
  But here is the King himself.

[*Enter Oedipus.*]

Oedipus.   So you dared come back.   20
  Why? How brazen of you to come to my house,
  You murderer!
                Do you think I do not know
  That you plotted to kill me, plotted to steal my throne?

Tell me, in God's name: am I coward, a fool,
That you should dream you could accomplish this?
A fool who could not see your slippery game?
A coward, not to fight back when I saw it?
You are the fool, Creon, are you not? hoping
Without support or friends to get a throne?
Thrones may be won or bought: you could do neither. 30

Creon.   Now listen to me. You have talked; let me talk, too.
You can not judge unless you know the facts.

Oedipus.   You speak well: there is one fact; but I find it hard
To learn from the deadliest enemy I have.

Creon.   That above all I must dispute with you.

Oedipus.   That above all I will not hear you deny.

Creon.   If you think there is anything good in being stubborn
Against all reason, then I say you are wrong.

Oedipus.   If you think a man can sin against his own kind
And not be punished for it, I say you are mad. 40

Creon.   I agree. But tell me: what have I done to you?

Oedipus.   You advised me to send for that wizard, did you not?

Creon.   I did. I should do it again.

Oedipus.   Very well. Now tell me:
How long has it been since Laïos—

Creon.   What of Laïos?

Oedipus.   Since he vanished in that onset by the road?

Creon.   It was long ago, a long time.

Oedipus.   And this prophet,
Was he practicing here then?

Creon.   He was; and with honor, as now.

Oedipus.   Did he speak of me at that time?

Creon.   He never did;
At least, not when I was present.

Oedipus.   But . . . the enquiry?
I suppose you held one?

Creon.   We did, but we learned nothing. 50

Oedipus.   Why did the prophet not speak against me then?

Creon.   I do not know; and I am the kind of man
Who holds his tongue when he has no facts to go on.

Oedipus.   There's one fact that you know, and you could tell it.

Creon.   What fact is that? If I know it, you shall have it.

Oedipus.   If he were not involved with you, he could not say
That it was I who murdered Laïos.

Creon.   If he says that, you are the one that knows it!—
But now it is my turn to question you.

Oedipus.   Put your questions. I am no murderer. 60

Creon.   First then: You married my sister?

Oedipus.   I married your sister.
Creon.   And you rule the kingdom equally with her?
Oedipus.   Everything that she wants she has from me.
Creon.   And I am the third, equal to both of you?
Oedipus.   That is why I call you a bad friend.
Creon.   No. Reason it out, as I have done.
Think of this first. Would any sane man prefer
Power, with all a king's anxieties,
To that same power and the grace of sleep?
Certainly not I.   70
I have never longed for the king's power—only his rights.
Would any wise man differ from me in this?
As matters stand, I have my way in everything
With your consent, and no responsibilities.
If I were king, I should be a slave to policy.

How could I desire a scepter more
Than what is now mine—untroubled influence?
No, I have not gone mad; I need no honors,
Except those with the perquisites I have now.
I am welcome everywhere; every man salutes me,   80
And those who want your favor seek my ear,
Since I know how to manage what they ask.
Should I exchange this ease for that anxiety?
Besides, no sober mind is treasonable.
I hate anarchy
And never would deal with any man who likes it.

Test what I have said. Go to the priestess
At Delphi, ask if I quoted her correctly.
And as for this other thing: if I am found
Guilty of treason with Teiresias,   90
Then sentence me to death! You have my word
It is a sentence I should cast my vote for—
But not without evidence!
                          You do wrong
When you take good men for bad, bad men for good.
A true friend thrown aside—why, life itself
Is not more precious!
                          In time you will know this well:
For time, and time alone, will show the just man,
Though scoundrels are discovered in a day.
Choragos.   This is well said, and a prudent man would ponder it.
Judgments too quickly formed are dangerous.   100

Oedipus.   But is he not quick in his duplicity?
    And shall I not be quick to parry him?
    Would you have me stand still, hold my peace, and let
    This man win everything, through my inaction?
Creon.   And you want—what is it, then? To banish me?
Oedipus.   No, not exile. It is your death I want,
    So that all the world may see what treason means.
Creon.   You will persist, then? You will not believe me?
Oedipus.   How can I believe you?
Creon.   Then you are a fool.
Oedipus.   To save myself?
Creon.   In justice, think of me.   110
Oedipus.   You are evil incarnate.
Creon.   But suppose that you are wrong?
Oedipus.   Still I must rule.
Creon.   But not if you rule badly.
Oedipus.   O city, city!
Creon.   It is my city, too!
Choragos.   Now, my lords, be still. I see the Queen,
    Iocastê, coming from her palace chambers;
    And it is time she came, for the sake of you both.
    This dreadful quarrel can be resolved through her.   120

[*Enter Iocastê.*]

Iocastê.   Poor foolish men, what wicked din is this?
    With Thebes sick to death, is it not shameful
    That you should rake some private quarrel up?
    [*To Oedipus.*] Come into the house.
                      —And you, Creon, go now:
    Let us have no more of this tumult over nothing.
Creon.   Nothing? No, sister: what your husband plans for me
    Is one of two great evils: exile or death.
Oedipus.   He is right.
              Why, woman I have caught him squarely
    Plotting against my life.
Creon.   No! Let me die
    Accurst if ever I have wished you harm!
Iocastê.   Ah, believe it, Oedipus!
    In the name of the gods, respect this oath of his
    For my sake, for the sake of these people here!   130

Choragos.   Open your mind to her my lord. Be ruled by her,   [*Strophe 1*]
    I beg you!
Oedipus.   What would you have me do?

Choragos.   Respect Creon's word. He has never spoken like a fool,
  And now he has sworn an oath.
Oedipus.   You know what you ask?
Choragos.   I do.
Oedipus.   Speak on, then.
Choragos.   A friend so sworn should not be baited so,
  In blind malice, and without final proof.
Oedipus.   You are aware, I hope, that what you say
  Means death for me, or exile at the least.

Choragos.   No, I swear by Helios,[13] first in Heaven!   [*Strophe 2*]
  May I die friendless and accurst,   140
  The worst of deaths, if ever I meant that!
    It is the withering fields
      That hurt my sick heart:
    Must we bear all these ills,
      And now your bad blood as well?
Oedipus.   Then let him go. And let me die, if I must,
  Or be driven by him in shame from the land of Thebes.
  It is your unhappiness, and not his talk,
  That touches me.
                As for him—
  Wherever he is, I will hate him as long as I live.   150
Creon.   Ugly in yielding, as you were ugly in rage!
  Natures like yours chiefly torment themselves.
Oedipus.   Can you not go? Can you not leave me?
Creon.   I can.
  You do not know me; but the city knows me,
  And in its eyes I am just, if not in yours.

[*Exit Creon.*]

Choragos.   Lady Iocastê, did you not ask the King to go   [*Antistrophe 1*]
  to his chambers?
Iocastê.   First tell me what has happened.
Choragos.   There was suspicion without evidence; yet it rankled
  As even false charges will.
Iocastê.   On both sides?
Choragos.   On both.
Iocastê.   But what was said?
Choragos.   Oh let it rest, let it be done with!   160
  Have we not suffered enough?

---

[13] The sun god.

Oedipus. You see to what your decency has brought you:
You have made difficulties where my heart saw none.

Choragos. Oedipus, it is not once only I have told you—   [*Antistrophe 2*]
You must know I should count myself unwise
To the point of madness, should I now forsake you—
    You, under whose hand,
        In the storm of another time,
    Our dear land sailed out free.
        But now stand fast at the helm!   170
Iocastê. In God's name, Oedipus, inform your wife as well:
Why are you so set in this hard anger?
Oedipus. I will tell you, for none of these men deserves
My confidence as you do. It is Creon's work,
His treachery, his plotting against me.
Iocastê. Go on, if you can make this clear to me.
Oedipus. He charges me with the murder of Laïos.
Iocastê. Has he some knowledge? Or does he speak from hearsay?
Oedipus. He would not commit himself to such a charge,
But he has brought in that damnable soothsayer   180
To tell his story.
Iocastê.   Set your mind at rest.
If it is a question of soothsayers, I tell you
That you will find no man whose craft gives knowledge
Of the unknowable.
                    Here is my proof:

An oracle was reported to Laïos once
(I will not say from Phoibos himself, but from
His appointed ministers, at any rate)
That his doom would be death at the hands of his own son—
His son, born of his flesh and of mine!

Now, you remember the story: Laïos was killed   190
By marauding strangers where three highways meet;
But his child had not been three days in this world
Before the King had pierced the baby's ankles
And left him to die on a lonely mountainside.

Thus, Apollo never caused that child
To kill his father, and it was not Laïos' fate
To die at the hands of his son, as he had feared.
This is what prophets and prophecies are worth!
Have no dread of them.

It is God himself
Who can show us what he wills, in his own way.   200
Oedipus.   How strange a shadowy memory crossed my mind,
Just now while you were speaking; it chilled my heart.
Iocastê.   What do you mean? What memory do you speak of?
Oedipus.   If I understand you, Laïos was killed
At a place where three roads meet.
Iocastê.   So it was said;
We have no later story.
Oedipus.   Where did it happen?
Iocastê.   Phokis, it is called: at a place where the Theban Way
Divides into the roads towards Delphi and Daulia.
Oedipus.   When?
Iocastê.   We had the news not long before you came
And proved the right to your succession here.   210
Oedipus.   Ah, what net has God been weaving for me?
Iocastê.   Oedipus! Why does this trouble you?
Oedipus.   Do not ask me yet.
First, tell me how Laïos looked, and tell me
How old he was.
Iocastê.   He was tall, his hair just touched
With white; his form was not unlike your own.
Oedipus.   I think that I myself may be accurst
By my own ignorant edict.
Iocastê.   You speak strangely.
It makes me tremble to look at you, my King.
Oedipus.   I am not sure that the blind man can not see.
But I should know better if you were to tell me—   220
Iocastê.   Anything—though I dread to hear you ask it.
Oedipus.   Was the King lightly escorted, or did he ride
With a large company, as a ruler should?
Iocastê.   There were five men with him in all: one was a herald;
And a single chariot, which he was driving.
Oedipus.   Alas, that makes it plain enough!
                                       But who—
Who told you how it happened?
Iocastê.   A household servant,
The only one to escape.
Oedipus.   And is he still
A servant of ours?
Iocastê.   No; for when he came back at last
And found you enthroned in the place of the dead king,   230
He came to me, touched my hand with his, and begged
That I would send him away to the frontier district
Where only the shepherds go—

As far away from the city as I could send him.
I granted his prayer; for although the man was a slave,
He had earned more than this favor at my hands.
Oedipus.   Can he be called back quickly?
Iocastê.   Easily.
But why?
Oedipus.   I have taken too much upon myself
Without enquiry; therefore I wish to consult him.
Iocastê.   Then he shall come.
                              But am I not one also   240
To whom you might confide these fears of yours?
Oedipus.   That is your right; it will not be denied you,
Now least of all; for I have reached a pitch
Of wild foreboding. Is there anyone
To whom I should sooner speak?
Polybos of Corinth is my father.
My mother is a Dorian: Meropê.
I grew up chief among the men of Corinth
Until a strange thing happened—
Not worth my passion, it may be, but strange.   250

At a feast, a drunken man maundering in his cups
Cries out that I am not my father's son!

I contained myself that night, though I felt anger
And a sinking heart. The next day I visited
My father and mother, and questioned them. They stormed,
Calling it all the slanderous rant of a fool;
And this relieved me. Yet the suspicion
Remained always aching in my mind;
I knew there was talk; I could not rest;
And finally, saying nothing to my parents,   260
I went to the shrine at Delphi.
The god dismissed my question without reply;
He spoke of other things.
                              Some were clear,
Full of wretchedness, dreadful, unbearable:
As, that I should lie with my own mother, breed
Children from whom all men would turn their eyes;
And that I should be my father's murderer.

I heard all this, and fled. And from that day
Corinth to me was only in the stars
Descending in that quarter of the sky,   270
As I wandered farther and farther on my way

To a land where I should never see the evil
Sung by the oracle. And I came to this country
Where, so you say, King Laïos was killed.

I will tell you all that happened there, my lady.

There were three highways
Coming together at a place I passed;
And there a herald came towards me, and a chariot
Drawn by horses, with a man such as you describe
Seated in it. The groom leading the horses   280
Forced me off the road at his lord's command;
But as this charioteer lurched over towards me
I struck him in my rage. The old man saw me
And brought his double goad down upon my head
As I came abreast.
            He was paid back, and more!
Swinging my club in this right hand I knocked him
Out of his car, and he rolled on the ground.
                    I killed him.

I killed them all.
Now if that stranger and Laïos were—kin,
Where is a man more miserable than I?   290
More hated by the gods? Citizen and alien alike
Must never shelter me or speak to me—
I must be shunned by all.
              And I myself
Pronounced this malediction upon myself!

Think of it: I have touched you with these hands,
These hands that killed your husband. What defilement!

Am I all evil, then? It must be so,
Since I must flee from Thebes, yet never again
See my own countrymen, my own country,
For fear of joining my mother in marriage   300
And killing Polybos, my father.
             Ah,
If I was created so, born to this fate,
Who could deny the savagery of God?

O holy majesty of heavenly powers!
May I never see that day! Never!

Rather let me vanish from the race of men
Than know the abomination destined me!
Choragos.   We too, my lord, have felt dismay at this.
But there is hope: you have yet to hear the shepherd.
Oedipus.   Indeed, I fear no other hope is left me.   310
Iocastê.   What do you hope from him when he comes?
Oedipus.   This much:
If his account of the murder tallies with yours,
Then I am cleared.
Iocastê.   What was it that I said
Of such importance?
Oedipus.   Why, "marauders," you said,
Killed the King, according to this man's story.
If he maintains that still, if there were several,
Clearly the guilt is not mine: I was alone.
But if he says one man, singlehanded, did it,
Then the evidence all points to me.
Iocastê.   You may be sure that he said there were several;   320
And can he call back that story now? He can not.
The whole city heard it as plainly as I.
But suppose he alters some detail of it:
He can not ever show that Laïos' death
Fulfilled the oracle: For Apollo said
My child was doomed to kill him; and my child—
Poor baby!—it was my child that died first.

No. From now on, where oracles are concerned,
I would not waste a second thought on any.
Oedipus.   You may be right.
                                        But come: let someone go   330
For the shepherd at once. This matter must be settled.
Iocastê.   I will send for him.
I would not wish to cross you in anything.
And surely not in this.—Let us go in.

[*Exeunt into the palace.*]

Ode II

Chorus.   Let me be reverent in the ways of right,   [*Strophe 1*]
Lowly the paths I journey on;
Let all my words and actions keep
The laws of the pure universe

From highest Heaven handed down.
For Heaven is their bright nurse,
Those generations of the realms of light;
Ah, never of mortal kind were they begot,
Nor are they slaves of memory, lost in sleep:
Their Father is greater than Time, and ages not.   10

The tyrant is a child of Pride   [*Antistrophe 1*]
Who drinks from his great sickening cup
Recklessness and vanity,
Until from his high crest headlong
He plummets to the dust of hope.
That strong man is not strong.
But let no fair ambition be denied;
May God protect the wrestler for the State
In government, in comely policy,
Who will fear God, and on His ordinance wait.   20

Haughtiness and the high hand of disdain   [*Strophe 2*]
Tempt and outrage God's holy law;
And any mortal who dares hold
No immortal Power in awe
Will be caught up in a net of pain:
The price for which his levity is sold.
Let each man take due earnings, then,
And keep his hands from holy things,
And from blasphemy stand apart—
Else the crackling blast of heaven   30
Blows on his head, and on his desperate heart;
Though fools will honor impious men,
In their cities no tragic poet sings.

Shall we lose faith in Delphi's obscurities,   [*Antistrophe 2*]
We who have heard the world's core
Discredited, and the sacred wood
Of Zeus at Elis praised no more?
The deeds and the strange prophecies
Must make a pattern yet to be understood.
Zeus, if indeed you are lord of all,   40
Throned in light over night and day,
Mirror this in your endless mind:
Our masters call the oracle
Words on the wind, and the Delphic vision blind!
Their hearts no longer know Apollo,
And reverence for the gods has died away.

Scene III

[*Enter Iocastê.*]

Iocastê.   Princes of Thebes, it has occurred to me
   To visit the altars of the gods, bearing
   These branches as a suppliant, and this incense.
   Our King is not himself: his noble soul
   Is overwrought with fantasies of dread,
   Else he would consider
   The new prophecies in the light of the old.
   He will listen to any voice that speaks disaster,
   And my advice goes for nothing.

[*She approaches the altar, R.*]

                              To you, then, Apollo,
   Lycean lord, since you are nearest, I turn in prayer.   10
   Receive these offerings, and grant us deliverance
   From defilement. Our hearts are heavy with fear
   When we see our leader distracted, as helpless sailors
   Are terrified by the confusion of their helmsman.

[*Enter Messenger.*]

Messenger.   Friends, no doubt you can direct me:
   Where shall I find the house of Oedipus,
   Or, better still, where is the King himself?
Choragos.   It is this very place, stranger; he is inside.
   This is his wife and mother of his children.
Messenger.   I wish her happiness in a happy house,   20
   Blest in all the fulfillment of her marriage.
Iocastê.   I wish as much for you: your courtesy
   Deserves a like good fortune. But now, tell me:
   Why have you come? What have you to say to us?
Messenger.   Good news, my lady, for your house and your husband.
Iocastê.   What news? Who sent you here?
Messenger.   I am from Corinth.
   The news I bring ought to mean joy for you,
   Though it may be you will find some grief in it.
Iocastê.   What is it? How can it touch us in both ways?
Messenger.   The people of Corinth, they say,   30
   Intend to call Oedipus to be their king.
Iocastê.   But old Polybos—is he not reigning still?
Messenger.   No. Death holds him in his sepulchre.

Iocastê.   What are you saying? Polybos is dead?
Messenger.   If I am not telling the truth, may I die myself.
Iocastê [to a maidservant].   Go in, go quickly; tell this to your master.
O riddlers of God's will, where are you now!
This was the man whom Oedipus, long ago,
Feared so, fled so, in dread of destroying him—
But it was another fate by which he died.   40

[Enter Oedipus, C.]

Oedipus.   Dearest Iocastê, why have you sent for me?
Iocastê.   Listen to what this man says, and then tell me
What has become of the solemn prophecies.
Oedipus.   Who is this man? What is his news for me?
Iocastê.   He has come from Corinth to announce your father's death!
Oedipus.   Is it true, stranger? Tell me in your own words.
Messenger.   I can not say it more clearly: the King is dead.
Oedipus.   Was it by treason? Or by an attack of illness?
Messenger.   A little thing brings old men to their rest.
Oedipus.   It was sickness, then?
Messenger.   Yes, and his many years.   50
Oedipus.   Ah!
Why should a man respect the Pythian hearth,[14] or
Give heed to the birds that jangle above his head?
They prophesied that I should kill Polybos,
Kill my own father; but he is dead and buried,
And I am here—I never touched him, never,
Unless he died of grief for my departure,
And thus, in a sense, through me. No. Polybos
Has packed the oracles off with him underground.
They are empty words.
Iocastê.   Had I not told you so?   60
Oedipus.   You had; it was my faint heart that betrayed me.
Iocastê.   From now on never think of those things again.
Oedipus.   And yet—must I not fear my mother's bed?
Iocastê.   Why should anyone in this world be afraid,
Since Fate rules us and nothing can be foreseen?
A man should live only for the present day.

Have no more fear of sleeping with your mother:
How many men, in dreams, have lain with their mothers!
No reasonable man is troubled by such things.

---

[14] Delphi, where Apollo spoke through an oracle.

Oedipus.   That is true; only—   70
  If only my mother were not still alive!
  But she is alive. I can not help my dread.
Iocastê.   Yet this news of your father's death is wonderful.
Oedipus.   Wonderful. But I fear the living woman.
Messenger.   Tell me, who is this woman that you fear?
Oedipus.   It is Meropê, man; the wife of King Polybos.
Messenger.   Meropê? Why should you be afraid of her?
Oedipus.   An oracle of the gods, a dreadful saying.
Messenger.   Can you tell me about it or are you sworn to silence?
Oedipus.   I can tell you, and I will.   80
  Apollo said through his prophet that I was the man
  Who should marry his own mother, shed his father's blood
  With his own hands. And so, for all these years
  I have kept clear of Corinth, and no harm has come—
  Though it would have been sweet to see my parents again.
Messenger.   And is this the fear that drove you out of Corinth?
Oedipus.   Would you have me kill my father?
Messenger.   As for that
  You must be reassured by the news I gave you.
Oedipus.   If you could reassure me, I would reward you.
Messenger.   I had that in mind, I will confess: I thought   90
  I could count on you when you returned to Corinth.
Oedipus.   No: I will never go near my parents again.
Messenger.   Ah, son, you still do not know what you are doing—
Oedipus.   What do you mean? In the name of God tell me!
Messenger.   —If these are your reasons for not going home.
Oedipus.   I tell you, I fear the oracle may come true.
Messenger.   And guilt may come upon you through your parents?
Oedipus.   That is the dread that is always in my heart.
Messenger.   Can you not see that all your fears are groundless?
Oedipus.   How can you say that? They are my parents, surely?   100
Messenger.   Polybos was not your father.
Oedipus.   Not my father?
Messenger.   No more your father than the man speaking to you.
Oedipus.   But you are nothing to me!
Messenger.   Neither was he.
Oedipus.   Then why did he call me son?
Messenger.   I will tell you:
  Long ago he had you from my hands, as a gift.
Oedipus.   Then how could he love me so, if I was not his?
Messenger.   He had no children, and his heart turned to you.
Oedipus.   What of you? Did you buy me? Did you find me by chance?
Messenger.   I came upon you in the crooked pass of Kithairon.
Oedipus.   And what were you doing there?

Messenger.	Tending my flocks.	110

Oedipus.   A wandering shepherd?

Messenger.   But your savior, son, that day.

Oedipus.   From what did you save me?

Messenger.   Your ankles should tell you that.

Oedipus.   Ah, stranger, why do you speak of that childhood pain?

Messenger.   I cut the bonds that tied your ankles together.

Oedipus.   I have had the mark as long as I can remember.

Messenger.   That was why you were given the name you bear.[15]

Oedipus.   God! Was it my father or my mother who did it?
     Tell me!

Messenger.   I do not know. The man who gave you to me
     Can tell you better than I.   120

Oedipus.   It was not you that found me, but another?

Messenger.   It was another shepherd gave you to me.

Oedipus.   Who was he? Can you tell me who he was?

Messenger.   I think he was said to be one of Laïos' people.

Oedipus.   You mean the Laïos who was king here years ago?

Messenger.   Yes; King Laïos; and the man was one of his herdsmen.

Oedipus.   Is he still alive? Can I see him?

Messenger.   These men here
     Know best about such things.

Oedipus.   Does anyone here
     Know this shepherd that he is talking about?
     Have you seen him in the fields, or in the town?   130
     If you have, tell me. It is time things were made plain.

Choragos.   I think the man he means is that same shepherd
     You have already asked to see. Iocastê perhaps
     Could tell you something.

Oedipus.   Do you know anything
     About him, Lady? Is he the man we have summoned?
     Is that the man this shepherd means?

Iocastê.   Why think of him?
     Forget this herdsman. Forget it all.
     This talk is a waste of time.

Oedipus.   How can you say that?
     When the clues to my true birth are in my hands?

Iocastê.   For God's love, let us have no more questioning!   140
     Is your life nothing to you?
     My own is pain enough for me to bear.

Oedipus.   You need not worry. Suppose my mother a slave,
     And born of slaves: no baseness can touch you.

Iocastê.   Listen to me, I beg you: do not do this thing!

---

[15] Oedipus literally means "swollen-foot."

Oedipus.   I will not listen; the truth must be made known.
Iocastê.   Everything that I say is for your own good!
Oedipus.   My own good
    Snaps my patience, then; I want none of it.
Iocastê.   You are fatally wrong! May you never learn who you are!
Oedipus.   Go, one of you, and bring the shepherd here.   150
    Let us leave this woman to brag of her royal name.
Iocastê.   Ah, miserable!
    That is the only word I have for you now.
    That is the only word I can ever have.

[*Exit into the palace.*]

Choragos.   Why has she left us, Oedipus? Why has she gone
    In such a passion of sorrow? I fear this silence:
    Something dreadful may come of it.
Oedipus.   Let it come!
    However base my birth, I must know about it.
    The Queen, like a woman, is perhaps ashamed
    To think of my low origin. But I   160
    Am a child of Luck; I can not be dishonored.
    Luck is my mother; the passing months, my brothers,
    Have seen me rich and poor.
                  If this is so,
    How could I wish that I were someone else?
    How could I not be glad to know my birth?

Ode III

Chorus.   If ever the coming time were known   [*Strophe*]
    To my heart's pondering,
    Kithairon, now by Heaven I see the torches
    At the festival of the next full moon,
    And see the dance, and hear the choir sing
    A grace to your gentle shade:
    Mountain where Oedipus was found,
    O mountain guard of a noble race!
    May the god who heals us lend his aid,
    And let that glory come to pass   10
    For our king's cradling-ground.

    Of the nymphs that flower beyond the years,   [*Antistrophe*]
    Who bore you, royal child,

To Pan of the hills or the timberline Apollo,
Cold in delight where the upland clears,
Or Hermês for whom Kyllenê's heights are piled?[16]
Or flushed as evening cloud,
Great Dionysos, roamer of mountains,
He—was it he who found you there,
And caught you up in his own proud   20
Arms from the sweet god-ravisher
Who laughed by the Muses' fountains?

Scene IV

Oedipus.   Sirs: though I do not know the man,
    I think I see him coming, this shepherd we want:
    He is old, like our friend here, and the men
    Bringing him seem to be servants of my house.
    But you can tell, if you have ever seen him.

[*Enter Shepherd escorted by servants.*]

Choragos.   I know him, he was Laïos' man. You can trust him.
Oedipus.   Tell me first, you from Corinth: is this the shepherd
    We were discussing?
Messenger.   This is the very man.
Oedipus [*to Shepherd*].   Come here. No, look at me. You must answer
    Everything I ask. You belonged to Laïos?   10
Shepherd.   Yes: born his slave, brought up in his house.
Oedipus.   Tell me what kind of work did you do for him?
Shepherd.   I was a shepherd of his, most of my life.
Oedipus.   Where mainly did you go for pasturage?
Shepherd.   Sometimes Kithairon, sometimes the hills near-by.
Oedipus.   Do you remember ever seeing this man out there?
Shepherd.   What would he be doing there? This man?
Oedipus.   This man standing here. Have you ever seen him before?
Shepherd.   No. At least, not to my recollection.
Messenger.   And that is not strange, my lord. But I'll refresh   20
    His memory: he must remember when we two
    Spent three whole seasons together, March to September,
    On Kithairon or thereabouts. He had two flocks;
    I had one. Each autumn I'd drive mine home

---

[16] Hermês, the herald of the Olympian gods, was born on the mountain of Kyllenê.

And he would go back with his to Laïos' sheepfold.—
Is this not true, just as I have described it?
Shepherd.   True, yes; but it was all so long ago.
Messenger.   Well, then: do you remember, back in those days
That you gave me a baby boy to bring up as my own?
Shepherd.   What if I did? What are you trying to say?   30
Messenger.   King Oedipus was once that little child.
Shepherd.   Damn you, hold your tongue!
Oedipus.   No more of that!
It is your tongue needs watching, not this man's.
Shepherd.   My King, my Master, what is it I have done wrong?
Oedipus.   You have not answered his question about the boy.
Shepherd.   He does not know . . . He is only making trouble . . .
Oedipus.   Come, speak plainly, or it will go hard with you.
Shepherd.   In God's name, do not torture an old man!
Oedipus.   Come here, one of you; bind his arms behind him.
Shepherd.   Unhappy king! What more do you wish to learn?   40
Oedipus.   Did you give this man the child he speaks of?
Shepherd.   I did.
And I would to God I had died that very day.
Oedipus.   You will die now unless you speak the truth.
Shepherd.   Yet if I speak the truth, I am worse than dead.
Oedipus.   Very well; since you insist on delaying—
Shepherd.   No! I have told you already that I gave him the boy.
Oedipus.   Where did you get him? From your house? From somewhere else?
Shepherd.   Not from mine, no. A man gave him to me.
Oedipus.   Is that man here? Do you know whose slave he was?
Shepherd.   For God's love, my King, do not ask me any more!   50
Oedipus.   You are a dead man if I have to ask you again.
Shepherd.   Then . . . Then the child was from the palace of Laïos.
Oedipus.   A slave child? or a child of his own line?
Shepherd.   Ah, I am on the brink of dreadful speech!
Oedipus.   And I of dreadful hearing. Yet I must hear.
Shepherd.   If you must be told, then . . .
                                                      They said it was Laïos' child,
But it is your wife who can tell you about that.
Oedipus.   My wife!—Did she give it to you?
Shepherd.   My lord, she did.
Oedipus.   Do you know why?
Shepherd.   I was told to get rid of it.
Oedipus.   An unspeakable mother!
Shepherd.   There had been prophecies . . .   60
Oedipus.   Tell me.
Shepherd.   It was said that the boy would kill his own father.
Oedipus.   Then why did you give him over to this old man?

Shepherd.   I pitied the baby, my King,
And I thought that this man would take him far away
To his own country.
                                He saved him—but for what a fate!
For if you are what this man says you are,
No man living is more wretched than Oedipus.
Oedipus.   Ah God!
It was true!
                    All the prophecies!
                                            —Now,
O Light, may I look on you for the last time!   70
I, Oedipus,
Oedipus, damned in his birth, in his marriage damned,
Damned in the blood he shed with his own hand!

[He rushes into the palace.]

Ode IV

Chorus.   Alas for the seed of men.   *[Strophe 1]*

What measure shall I give these generations
That breathe on the void and are void
And exist and do not exist?

Who bears more weight of joy
Than mass of sunlight shifting in images,
Or who shall make his thought stay on
That down time drifts away?

Your splendor is all fallen.

O naked brow of wrath and tears,   10
O change of Oedipus!
I who saw your days call no man blest—
Your great days like ghosts gone.

That mind was a strong bow.   *[Antistrophe 1]*

Deep, how deep you drew it then, hard archer,
At a dim fearful range,
And brought dear glory down!

You overcame the stranger—
The virgin with her hooking lion claws—
And though death sang, stood like a tower   20
To make pale Thebes take heart.

Fortress against our sorrow!

Divine king, giver of laws,
Majestic Oedipus!
No prince in Thebes had ever such renown,
No prince won such grace of power.

And now of all men ever known   [*Strophe* 2]
Most pitiful is this man's story:
His fortunes are most changed, his state
Fallen to a low slave's   30
Ground under bitter fate.

O Oedipus, most royal one!
The great door that expelled you to the light
Gave at night—ah, gave night to your glory:
As to the father, to the fathering son.

All understood too late.

How could that queen whom Laïos won,
The garden that he harrowed at his height,
Be silent when that act was done?

But all eyes fail before time's eye,   [*Antistrophe* 2]
All actions come to justice there   41
Though never willed, though far down the deep past,
Your bed, your dread sirings,
Are brought to book at last.

Child by Laïos doomed to die,
Then doomed to lose that fortunate little death,
Would God you never took breath in this air
That with my wailing lips I take to cry:

For I weep the world's outcast.

I was blind, and now I can tell why: 50
Asleep, for you had given ease of breath
To Thebes, while the false years went by.

Exodos

[Enter, from the palace, Second Messenger.]

Second Messenger.   Elders of Thebes, most honored in this land,
What horrors are yours to see and hear, what weight
Of sorrow to be endured, if, true to your birth,
You venerate the line of Labdakos!
I think neither Istros nor Phasis, those great rivers,
Could purify this place of the corruption
It shelters now, or soon must bring to light—
Evil not done unconsciously, but willed.

The greatest griefs are those we cause ourselves.
Choragos.   Surely, friend, we have grief enough already;   10
What new sorrow do you mean?
Second Messenger.   The Queen is dead.
Choragos.   Iocastê? Dead? But at whose hand?
Second Messenger.   Her own.
The full horror of what happened you can not know,
For you did not see it; but I, who did, will tell you
As clearly as I can how she met her death.

When she had left us,
In passionate silence, passing through the court,
She ran to her apartment in the house,
Her hair clutched by the fingers of both hands.

She closed the doors behind her; then, by that bed   20
Where long ago the fatal son was conceived—
The son who should bring about his father's death—
We heard her call upon Laïos, dead so many years,
And heard her wail for the double fruit of her marriage,
A husband by her husband, children by her child.

Exactly how she died I do not know:
For Oedipus burst in moaning and would not let us
Keep vigil to the end: it was by him
As he stormed about the room that our eyes were caught.
From one to another of us he went, begging a sword,   30
Cursing the wife who was not his wife, the mother
Whose womb had carried his own children and himself.
I do not know: it was none of us aided him,
But surely one of the gods was in control!
For with a dreadful cry

He hurled his weight, as though wrenched out of himself,
At the twin doors: the bolts gave, and he rushed in.
And there we saw her hanging, her body swaying
From the cruel cord she had noosed about her neck.
A great sob broke from him, heartbreaking to hear,   40
As he loosed the rope and lowered her to the ground.

I would blot out from my mind what happened next!
For the King ripped from her gown the golden brooches
That were her ornament, and raised them, and plunged them down
Straight into his own eyeballs, crying, "No more,
No more shall you look on the misery about me,
The horrors of my own doing! Too long have you known
The faces of those whom I should never have seen,
Too long been blind to those for whom I was searching!
From this hour, go in darkness!" And as he spoke,   50
He struck at his eyes—not once, but many times;
And the blood spattered his beard,
Bursting from his ruined sockets like red hail.

So from the unhappiness of two this evil has sprung,
A curse on the man and woman alike. The old
Happiness of the house of Labdakos
Was happiness enough: where is it today?
It is all wailing and ruin, disgrace, death—all
The misery of mankind that has a name—
And it is wholly and for ever theirs.   60
Choragos.   Is he in agony still? Is there no rest for him?
Second Messenger.   He is calling for someone to lead him to the gates
So that all the children of Kadmos may look upon
His father's murderer, his mother's—no,
I can not say it!
                    And then he will leave Thebes,
Self-exiled, in order that the curse
Which he himself pronounced may depart from the house.
He is weak, and there is none to lead him,
So terrible is his suffering.
                    But you will see:
Look, the doors are opening; in a moment   70
You will see a thing that would crush a heart of stone.

[*The central door is opened; Oedipus, blinded, is led in.*]

Choragos.   Dreadful indeed for men to see.
  Never have my own eyes
  Looked on a sight so full of fear.

  Oedipus!
  What madness came upon you, what daemon
  Leaped on your life with heavier
  Punishment than a mortal man can bear?
  No: I can not even
  Look at you, poor ruined one.   80
  And I would speak, question, ponder,
  If I were able. No.
  You make me shudder.
Oedipus.   God. God.
  Is there a sorrow greater?
  Where shall I find harbor in this world?
  My voice is hurled far on a dark wind.
  What has God done to me?
Choragos.   Too terrible to think of, or to see.

Oedipus.   O cloud of night,   [*Strophe 1*]
  Never to be turned away: night coming on,   91
  I can not tell how: night like a shroud!

  My fair winds brought me here.
                                    Oh God. Again
  The pain of the spikes where I had sight,
  The flooding pain
  Of memory, never to be gouged out.
Choragos.   This is not strange.
  You suffer it all twice over, remorse in pain,
  Pain in remorse.

Oedipus.   Ah dear friend   [*Antistrophe 1*]
  Are you faithful even yet, you alone?   101
  Are you still standing near me, will you stay here,
  Patient, to care for the blind?
                                    The blind man!
  Yet even blind I know who it is attends me,
  By the voice's tone—
  Though my new darkness hide the comforter.
Choragos.   Oh fearful act!
  What god was it drove you to rake black
  Night across your eyes?

Oedipus.   Apollo. Apollo. Dear   [*Strophe 2*]
Children, the god was Apollo.   111
He brought my sick, sick fate upon me.
But the blinding hand was my own!
How could I bear to see
When all my sight was horror everywhere?
Choragos.   Everywhere; that is true.
Oedipus.   And now what is left?
Images? Love? A greeting even,
Sweet to the senses? Is there anything?
Ah no, friends: lead me away.   120
Lead me away from Thebes.
Lead the great wreck
And hell of Oedipus, whom the gods hate.
Choragos.   Your fate is clear, you are not blind to that.
Would God you had never found it out!

Oedipus.   Death take the man who unbound   [*Antistrophe 2*]
My feet on that hillside
And delivered me from death to life! What life?
If only I had died,
This weight of monstrous doom
Could not have dragged me and my darlings down.   130
Choragos.   I would have wished the same.
Oedipus.   Oh never to have come here
With my father's blood upon me! Never
To have been the man they call his mother's husband!
Oh accurst! Oh child of evil,
To have entered that wretched bed—
the selfsame one!
More primal than sin itself, this fell to me.
Choragos.   I do not know how I can answer you.
You were better dead than alive and blind.
Oedipus.   Do not counsel me any more. This punishment   140
That I have laid upon myself is just.
If I had eyes,
I do not know how I could bear the sight
Of my father, when I came to the house of Death,
Or my mother: for I have sinned against them both
So vilely that I could not make my peace
By strangling my own life.
Or do you think my children,
Born as they were born, would be sweet to my eyes?

Ah never, never! Nor this town with its high walls,
Nor the holy images of the gods.
For I,   150
Thrice miserable!—Oedipus, noblest of all the line
Of Kadmos, have condemned myself to enjoy
These things no more, by my own malediction
Expelling that man whom the gods declared
To be a defilement in the house of Laïos.
After exposing the rankness of my own guilt,
How could I look men frankly in the eyes?
No, I swear it,
If I could have stifled my hearing at its source,
I would have done it and made all this body   160
A tight cell of misery, blank to light and sound:
So I should have been safe in a dark agony
Beyond all recollection.
Ah Kithairon!
Why did you shelter me? When I was cast upon you,
Why did I not die? Then I should never
Have shown the world my execrable birth.

Ah Polybos! Corinth, city that I believed
The ancient seat of my ancestors: how fair
I seemed, your child! And all the while this evil
Was cancerous within me!
For I am sick   170
In my daily life, sick in my origin.

O three roads, dark ravine, woodland and way
Where three roads met: you, drinking my father's blood,
My own blood, spilled by my own hand: can you remember
The unspeakable things I did there, and the things
I went on from there to do?
O marriage, marriage!
The act that engendered me, and again the act
Performed by the son in the same bed—
Ah, the net
Of incest, mingling fathers, brothers, sons,
With brides, wives, mothers; the last evil   180
That can be known by men: no tongue can say
How evil!
No. For the love of God, conceal me
Somewhere far from Thebes; or kill me; or hurl me
Into the sea, away from men's eyes for ever.

Come, lead me. You need not fear to touch me.
Of all men, I alone can bear this guilt.

[*Enter Creon.*]

Choragos.   We are not the ones to decide; but Creon here
  May fitly judge of what you ask. He only
  Is left to protect the city in your place.
Oedipus.   Alas, how can I speak to him? What right have I   190
  To beg his courtesy whom I have deeply wronged?
Creon.   I have not come to mock you, Oedipus,
  Or to reproach you, either.
  [*To attendants.*]   —You, standing there:
  If you have lost all respect for man's dignity,
  At least respect the flame of Lord Helios:
  Do not allow this pollution to show itself
  Openly here, an affront to the earth
  And Heaven's rain and the light of day. No, take him
  Into the house as quickly as you can.
  For it is proper   200
  That only the close kindred see his grief.
Oedipus.   I pray you in God's name, since your courtesy
  Ignores my dark expectation, visiting
  With mercy this man of all men most execrable:
  Give me what I ask—for your good, not for mine.
Creon.   And what is it that you would have me do?
Oedipus.   Drive me out of this country as quickly as may be
  To a place where no human voice can ever greet me.
Creon.   I should have done that before now—only,
  God's will had not been wholly revealed to me.   210
Oedipus.   But his command is plain: the parricide
  Must be destroyed. I am that evil man.
Creon.   That is the sense of it, yes; but as things are,
  We had best discover clearly what is to be done.
Oedipus.   You would learn more about a man like me?
Creon.   You are ready now to listen to the god.
Oedipus.   I will listen. But it is to you
  That I must turn for help. I beg you, hear me.

  The woman in there—
  Give her whatever funeral you think proper: 220
  She is your sister.
            —But let me go, Creon!
  Let me purge my father's Thebes of the pollution
  Of my living here, and go out to the wild hills,

To Kithairon, that has won such fame with me,
The tomb my mother and father appointed for me,
And let me die there, as they willed I should.
And yet I know
Death will not ever come to me through sickness
Or in any natural way: I have been preserved
For some unthinkable fate. But let that be.   230
As for my sons, you need not care for them.
They are men, they will find some way to live.
But my poor daughters, who have shared my table,
Who never before have been parted from their father—
Take care of them, Creon; do this for me.
And will you let me touch them with my hands
A last time, and let us weep together?
Be kind, my lord,
Great prince, be kind!
                    Could I but touch them,
They would be mine again, as when I had my eyes.   240

[*Enter Antigone and Ismene, attended.*]

Ah, God!
Is it my dearest children I hear weeping?
Has Creon pitied me and sent my daughters?
Creon.   Yes, Oedipus: I knew that they were dear to you
In the old days, and know you must love them still.
Oedipus.   May God bless you for this—and be a friendlier
Guardian to you than he has been to me!

Children, where are you?
Come quickly to my hands: they are your brother's—
Hands that have brought your father's once clear eyes   250
To this way of seeing—
                    Ah dearest ones,
I had neither sight nor knowledge then, your father
By the woman who was the source of his own life!
And I weep for you—having no strength to see you—,
I weep for you when I think of the bitterness
That men will visit upon you all your lives.
What homes, what festivals can you attend
Without being forced to depart again in tears?

And when you come to marriageable age,
Where is the man, my daughters, who would dare   260
Risk the bane that lies on all my children?

Is there any evil wanting? Your father killed
His father; sowed the womb of her who bore him;
Engendered you at the fount of his own existence!
That is what they will say of you.
                                        Then whom
Can you ever marry? There are no bridegrooms for you,
And your lives must wither away in sterile dreaming.
O Creon, son of Menoikeus!
You are the only father my daughters have,
Since we, their parents, are both of us gone for ever.   270
They are your own blood: you will not let them
Fall into beggary and loneliness;
You will keep them from the miseries that are mine!
Take pity on them; see, they are only children,
Friendless except for you. Promise me this,
Great Prince, and give me your hand in token of it.

[*Creon clasps his right hand.*]

Children:
I could say much, if you could understand me,
But as it is, I have only this prayer for you:
Live where you can, be as happy as you can—   280
Happier, please God, than God has made your father!
Creon.   Enough. You have wept enough. Now go within.
Oedipus.   I must; but it is hard.
Creon.   Time eases all things.
Oedipus.   But you must promise—
Creon.   Say what you desire.
Oedipus.   Send me from Thebes!
Creon.   God grant that I may!
Oedipus.   But since God hates me . . .
Creon.   No, he will grant your wish.
Oedipus.   You promise?
Creon.   I can not speak beyond my knowledge.
Oedipus.   Then lead me in.
Creon.   Come now, and leave your children.
Oedipus.   No! Do not take them from me!
Creon.   Think no longer
That you are in command here, but rather think   290
How, when you were, you served your own destruction.

[*Exeunt into the house all but the Chorus; the Choragos chants directly to the audience.*]

Choragos.   Men of Thebes: look upon Oedipus.

This is the king who solved the famous riddle
And towered up, most powerful of men.
No mortal eyes but looked on him with envy,
Yet in the end ruin swept over him.
Let every man in mankind's frailty
Consider his last day; and let none
Presume on his good fortune until he find
Life, at his death, a memory without pain.   300

QUESTIONS

1. How does the Prologue establish the mood and theme of the play? What aspects of Oedipus's character are revealed there?   **2.** Sophocles' audience knew the Oedipus story as you, for instance, know the story of the crucifixion. In the absence of suspense, what literary devices serve to hold the audience's attention?   **3.** To what extent and in what ways does the chorus contribute to the dramatic development and tension of the play?

WRITING TOPICS

1. In the Exodos, Oedipus declares that Apollo "brought my sick, sick fate upon me. / But the blinding hand was my own!" (ll. 112–113) and "This punishment / That I have laid upon myself is just" (ll. 140–141); later he declares, ". . . the parricide / Must be destroyed. I am that evil man" (ll. 211–212). How can Oedipus's acceptance of responsibility for his fate be reconciled with the fact that his fate was divinely ordained?   **2.** The play embodies a pattern of figurative and literal allusions to darkness and light, to vision and blindness. How does that figurative language function, and what relationship does it bear to Oedipus's self-inflicted punishment?

Major Barbara
1907

GEORGE BERNARD SHAW   [1856–1950]

CHARACTERS

Stephen Undershaft, son of Andrew Undershaft and Lady Britomart

Lady Britomart, daughter of the Earl of Stevenage and wife of Andrew Undershaft

Barbara Undershaft, daughter of Andrew Undershaft and Lady Britomart; a Major in the Salvation Army

Sarah Undershaft, daughter of Andrew Undershaft and Lady Britomart

Adolphus Cusins, fiancé of Barbara Undershaft

Charles Lomax, fiancé of Sarah Undershaft

Morrison, Lady Britomart's butler

Andrew Undershaft, husband of Lady Britomart; head of Undershaft and Lazarus, munitions makers

Rummy (Romola) Mitchens,

Snobby (Bronterre O'Brien) Price, regulars at the West Ham Salvation Army shelter

Peter Shirley, a discharged workman, poor but honest

Jenny Hill, a Salvation Army lass

Bill Walker, a young tough

Mrs. Baines, a Salvation Army Commissioner

Bilton, a foreman in Undershaft and Lazarus

Act One

It is after dinner in January 1906, in the library in Lady Britomart Undershaft's house in Wilton Crescent. A large and comfortable settee is in the middle of the room, upholstered in dark leather. A person sitting on it (it is vacant at present) would have, on his right, Lady Britomart's writing table, with the lady herself busy at it; a smaller writing table behind him on his left; the door behind him on Lady Britomart's side; and a window with a window seat directly on his left. Near the window is an armchair.

Lady Britomart is a woman of fifty or thereabouts, well dressed and yet careless of her dress, well bred and quite reckless of her breeding, well mannered and yet appallingly outspoken and indifferent to the opinion of her interlocutors, amiable and yet peremptory, arbitrary, and high-tempered to the last bearable degree, and withal a very typical managing matron of the upper class, treated as a naughty child until she grew into a scolding mother, and finally settling down with plenty of practical ability and worldly experience, limited in the oddest way with domestic and class limitations, conceiving the universe exactly as if it were a large house in Wilton Crescent, though handling her corner of it very effectively on that assumption, and being quite enlightened and liberal as to the books in the library, the pictures on the walls, the music in the portfolios, and the articles in the papers.

Her son, Stephen, comes in. He is a gravely correct young man under 25, taking himself very seriously, but still in some awe of his mother, from childish habit and bachelor shyness rather than from any weakness of character.

Stephen.   Whats the matter?

Lady Britomart.   Presently, Stephen.

Stephen submissively walks to the settee and sits down. He takes up a Liberal weekly called The Speaker.

Lady Britomart.   Dont begin to read, Stephen. I shall require all your attention.

Stephen.   It was only while I was waiting—

Lady Britomart.   Dont make excuses, Stephen. (He puts down The Speaker). Now! (She finishes her writing; rises; and comes to the settee). I have not kept you waiting very long, I think.

Stephen.   Not at all, mother.

Lady Britomart.   Bring me my cushion. (He takes the cushion from the chair at the desk and arranges it for her as she sits down on the settee). Sit down. (He sits down and fingers his tie nervously). Dont fiddle with your tie, Stephen: there is nothing the matter with it.

Stephen.   I beg your pardon. (He fiddles with his watch chain instead).

Lady Britomart.   Now are you attending to me, Stephen?

Stephen.   Of course, mother.

Lady Britomart.   No: it's not of course. I want something much more than your everyday matter-of-course attention. I am going to speak to you very seriously, Stephen. I wish you would let that chain alone.

Stephen (hastily relinquishing the chain).   Have I done anything to annoy you, mother? If so, it was quite unintentional.

Lady Britomart (astonished).   Nonsense! (With some remorse) My poor boy, did you think I was angry with you?

Stephen.   What is it, then, mother? You are making me very uneasy.

Lady Britomart (squaring herself at him rather aggressively).   Stephen: may I ask how soon you intend to realize that you are a grown-up man, and that I am only a woman?

Stephen (amazed).   Only a—

Lady Britomart.   Dont repeat my words, please: it is a most aggravating habit. You must learn to face life seriously, Stephen. I really cannot bear the whole burden of our family affairs any longer. You must advise me: you must assume the responsibility.

Stephen.   I!

Lady Britomart.   Yes, you, of course. You were 24 last June. Youve been at Harrow and Cambridge. Youve been to India and Japan. You must know a lot of things, now; unless you have wasted your time most scandalously. Well, advise me.

Stephen (*much perplexed*).   You know I have never interfered in the house-hold—

Lady Britomart.   No: I should think not. I dont want you to order the dinner.

Stephen.   I mean in our family affairs.

Lady Britomart.   Well, you must interfere now; for they are getting quite beyond me.

Stephen (*troubled*).   I have thought sometimes that perhaps I ought; but really, mother, I know so little about them; and what I do know is so painful! it is so impossible to mention some things to you— (*he stops, ashamed*).

Lady Britomart.   I suppose you mean your father.

Stephen (*almost inaudibly*).   Yes.

Lady Britomart.   My dear: we cant go on all our lives not mentioning him. Of course you were quite right not to open the subject until I asked you to; but you are old enough now to be taken into my confidence, and to help me to deal with him about the girls.

Stephen.   But the girls are all right. They are engaged.

Lady Britomart (*complacently*).   Yes: I have made a very good match for Sarah. Charles Lomax will be a millionaire at 35. But that is ten years ahead; and in the meantime his trustees cannot under the terms of his father's will allow him more than £800 a year.

Stephen.   But the will says also that if he increases his income by his own exertions, they may double the increase.

Lady Britomart.   Charles Lomax's exertions are much more likely to decrease his income than to increase it. Sarah will have to find at least another £800 a year for the next ten years; and even then they will be as poor as church mice. And what about Barbara? I thought Barbara was going to make the most brilliant career of all of you. And what does she do? Joins the Salvation Army; discharges her maid; lives on a pound a week; and walks in one evening with a professor of Greek whom she has picked up in the street, and who pretends to be a Salvationist, and actually plays the big drum for her in public because he has fallen head over ears in love with her.

Stephen.   I was certainly rather taken aback when I heard they were engaged. Cusins is a very nice fellow, certainly: nobody would ever guess that he was born in Australia; but—

Lady Britomart.   Oh, Adolphus Cusins will make a very good husband. After all, nobody can say a word against Greek: it stamps a man at once as an edu-cated gentleman. And my family, thank Heaven, is not a pig-headed Tory one. We are Whigs, and believe in liberty. Let snobbish people say what they please: Barbara shall marry, not the man they like, but the man *I* like.

Stephen.   Of course I was thinking only of his income. However, he is not likely to be extravagant.

Lady Britomart.   Dont be too sure of that, Stephen. I know your quiet, simple, refined, poetic people like Adolphus: quite content with the best of everything! They cost more than your extravagant people, who are always as mean as they are second rate. No: Barbara will need at least £2000 a year. You see it means two additional households. Besides, my dear, you must marry soon. I dont approve of the present fashion of philandering bachelors and late marriages; and I am trying to arrange something for you.

Stephen.   It's very good of you, mother; but perhaps I had better arrange that for myself.

Lady Britomart.   Nonsense! you are much too young to begin matchmaking: you would be taken in by some pretty little nobody. Of course I dont mean that you are not to be consulted: you know that as well as I do. *(Stephen closes his lips and is silent)*. Now dont sulk, Stephen.

Stephen.   I am not sulking, mother. What has all this got to do with—with—with my father?

Lady Britomart.   My dear Stephen: where is the money to come from? It is easy enough for you and the other children to live on my income as long as we are in the same house; but I cant keep four families in four separate houses. You know how poor my father is: he has barely seven thousand a year now; and really, if he were not the Earl of Stevenage, he would have to give up society. He can do nothing for us. He says, naturally enough, that it is absurd that he should be asked to provide for the children of a man who is rolling in money. You see, Stephen, your father must be fabulously wealthy, because there is always a war going on somewhere.

Stephen.   You need not remind me of that, mother. I have hardly ever opened a newspaper in my life without seeing our name in it. The Undershaft torpedo! The Undershaft quick firers! The Undershaft ten inch! The Undershaft disappearing rampart gun! The Undershaft submarine! and now the Undershaft aerial battleship! At Harrow they called me the Woolwich Infant. At Cambridge it was the same. A little brute at King's who was always trying to get up revivals, spoilt my Bible—your first birthday present to me—by writing under my name, 'Son and heir to Undershaft and Lazarus, Death and Destruction Dealers: address Christendom and Judea.' But that was not so bad as the way I was kowtowed to everywhere because my father was making millions by selling cannons.

Lady Britomart.   It is not only the cannons, but the war loans that Lazarus arranges under cover of giving credit for the cannons. You know, Stephen, it's perfectly scandalous. Those two men, Andrew Undershaft and Lazarus, positively have Europe under their thumbs. That is why your father is able to behave as he does. He is above the law. Do you think Bismarck or Gladstone or Disraeli could have openly defied every social and moral obligation all their lives as your father has? They simply wouldnt have dared. I asked Gladstone to take it up. I asked The Times to take it up. I asked the Lord Chamberlain to take it up. But it was just like asking them to declare war on the Sultan. They wouldnt. They said they couldnt touch him. I believe they were afraid.

Stephen.   What could they do? He does not actually break the law.

Lady Britomart. Not break the law! He is always breaking the law. He broke the law when he was born: his parents were not married.

Stephen. Mother! Is that true?

Lady Britomart. Of course it's true; that was why we separated.

Stephen. He married without letting you know this!

Lady Britomart (*rather taken aback by this inference*). Oh no. To do Andrew justice, that was not the sort of thing he did. Besides, you know the Undershaft motto: Unashamed. Everybody knew.

Stephen. But you said that was why you separated.

Lady Britomart. Yes, because he was not content with being a foundling himself: he wanted to disinherit you for another foundling. That was what I couldnt stand.

Stephen (*ashamed*). Do you mean for—for—for—

Lady Britomart. Dont stammer, Stephen. Speak distinctly.

Stephen. But this is so frightful to me, mother. To have to speak to you about such things!

Lady Britomart. It's not pleasant for me, either, especially if you are still so childish that you must make it worse by a display of embarrassment. It is only in the middle classes, Stephen, that people get into a state of dumb helpless horror when they find that there are wicked people in the world. In our class, we have to decide what is to be done with wicked people; and nothing should disturb our self-possession. Now ask your question properly.

Stephen. Mother: have you no consideration for me? Either treat me as a child, as you always do, and tell me nothing at all; or tell me everything and let me take it as best I can.

Lady Britomart. Treat you as a child! What do you mean? It is most unkind and ungrateful of you to say such a thing. You know I have never treated any of you as children. I have always made you my companions and friends, and allowed you perfect freedom to do and say whatever you liked, so long as you liked what I could approve of.

Stephen (*desperately*). I daresay we have been the very imperfect children of a very perfect mother; but I do beg you to let me alone for once, and tell me about this horrible business of my father wanting to set me aside for another son.

Lady Britomart (*amazed*). Another son! I never said anything of the kind. I never dreamt of such a thing. This is what comes of interrupting me.

Stephen. But you said—

Lady Britomart (*cutting him short*). Now be a good boy, Stephen, and listen to me patiently. The Undershafts are descended from a foundling in the parish of St Andrew Undershaft in the city. That was long ago, in the reign of James the First. Well, this foundling was adopted by an armorer and gunmaker. In the course of time the foundling succeeded to the business; and from some notion of gratitude, or some vow or something, he adopted another foundling, and left the business to him. And that foundling did the same. Ever since that, the cannon business has always been left to an adopted foundling named Andrew Undershaft.

Stephen. But did they never marry? Were there no legitimate sons?

Lady Britomart. Oh yes: they married just as your father did; and they were rich enough to buy land for their own children and leave them well provided for. But they always adopted and trained some foundling to succeed them in the business; and of course they always quarrelled with their wives furiously over it. Your father was adopted in that way; and he pretends to consider himself bound to keep up the tradition and adopt somebody to leave the business to. Of course I was not going to stand that. There may have been some reason for it when the Undershafts could only marry women in their own class, whose sons were not fit to govern great estates. But there could be no excuse for passing over my son.

Stephen (*dubiously*). I am afraid I should make a poor hand of managing a cannon foundry.

Lady Britomart. Nonsense! you could easily get a manager and pay him a salary.

Stephen. My father evidently had no great opinion of my capacity.

Lady Britomart. Stuff, child! you were only a baby: it had nothing to do with your capacity. Andrew did it on principle, just as he did every perverse and wicked thing on principle. When my father remonstrated, Andrew actually told him to his face that history tells us of only two successful institutions: one the Undershaft firm, and the other the Roman Empire under the Antonines. That was because the Antonine emperors all adopted their successors. Such rubbish! The Stevenages are as good as the Antonines, I hope; and you are a Stevenage. But that was Andrew all over. There you have the man! Always clever and unanswerable when he was defending nonsense and wickedness: always awkward and sullen when he had to behave sensibly and decently!

Stephen. Then it was on my account that your home life was broken up, mother. I am sorry.

Lady Britomart. Well, dear, there were other differences. I really cannot bear an immoral man. I am not a Pharisee, I hope; and I should not have minded his merely doing wrong things: we are none of us perfect. But your father didnt exactly do wrong things: he said them and thought them: that was what was so dreadful. He really had a sort of religion of wrongness. Just as one doesnt mind men practising immorality so long as they own that they are in the wrong by preaching morality; so I couldnt forgive Andrew for preaching immorality while he practised morality. You would all have grown up without principles, without any knowledge of right and wrong, if he had been in the house. You know, my dear, your father was a very attractive man in some ways. Children did not dislike him; and he took advantage of it to put the wickedest ideas into their heads, and make them quite unmanageable. I did not dislike him myself: very far from it; but nothing can bridge over moral disagreement.

Stephen. All this simply bewilders me, mother. People may differ about matters of opinion, or even about religion; but how can they differ about right and wrong? Right is right; and wrong is wrong; and if a man cannot distinguish them properly, he is either a fool or a rascal: thats all.

Lady Britomart *(touched).* Thats my own boy *(She pats his cheek)!* Your father never could answer that: he used to laugh and get out of it under cover of some affectionate nonsense. And now that you understand the situation, what do you advise me to do?

Stephen. Well, what can you do?

Lady Britomart. I must get the money somehow.

Stephen. We cannot take money from him. I had rather go and live in some cheap place like Bedford Square or even Hampstead than take a farthing of his money.

Lady Britomart. But after all, Stephen, our present income comes from Andrew.

Stephen *(shocked).* I never knew that.

Lady Britomart. Well, you surely didnt suppose your grandfather had anything to give me. The Stevenages could not do everything for you. We gave you social position. Andrew had to contribute something. He had a very good bargain, I think.

Stephen *(bitterly).* We are utterly dependent on him and his cannons, then?

Lady Britomart. Certainly not: the money is settled. But he provided it. So you see it is not a question of taking money from him or not: it is simply a question of how much. I dont want any more for myself.

Stephen. Nor do I.

Lady Britomart. But Sarah does; and Barbara does. That is, Charles Lomax and Adolphus Cusins will cost them more. So I must put my pride in my pocket and ask for it, I suppose. That is your advice, Stephen, is it not?

Stephen. No.

Lady Britomart *(sharply).* Stephen!

Stephen. Of course if you are determined—

Lady Britomart. I am not determined: I ask your advice; and I am waiting for it. I will not have all the responsibility thrown on my shoulders.

Stephen *(obstinately).* I would die sooner than ask him for another penny.

Lady Britomart *(resignedly).* You mean that *I* must ask him. Very well, Stephen: it shall be as you wish. You will be glad to know that your grandfather concurs. But he thinks I ought to ask Andrew to come here and see the girls. After all, he must have some natural affection for them.

Stephen. Ask him here!!!

Lady Britomart. Do not repeat my words, Stephen. Where else can I ask him?

Stephen. I never expected you to ask him at all.

Lady Britomart. Now dont tease, Stephen. Come! you see that it is necessary that he should pay us a visit, dont you?

Stephen *(reluctantly).* I suppose so, if the girls cannot do without his money.

Lady Britomart.   Thank you, Stephen: I knew you would give me the right advice when it was properly explained to you. I have asked your father to come this evening. *(Stephen bounds from his seat)*. Dont jump, Stephen: it fidgets me.

Stephen *(in utter consternation)*.   Do you mean to say that my father is coming here tonight—that he may be here at any moment?

Lady Britomart *(looking at her watch)*.   I said nine. *(He gasps. She rises)*. Ring the bell, please. *(Stephen goes to the smaller writing table; presses a button on it; and sits at it with his elbows on the table and his head in his hands, outwitted and overwhelmed)*. It is ten minutes to nine yet; and I have to prepare the girls. I asked Charles Lomax and Adolphus to dinner on purpose that they might be here. Andrew had better see them in case he should cherish any delusions as to their being capable of supporting their wives. *(The butler enters: Lady Britomart goes behind the settee to speak to him)*. Morrison: go up to the drawing room and tell everybody to come down here at once. *(Morrison withdraws. Lady Britomart turns to Stephen)*. Now remember, Stephen: I shall need all your countenance and authority. *(He rises and tries to recover some vestige of these attributes)*. Give me a chair, dear. *(He pushes a chair forward from the wall to where she stands, near the smaller writing table. She sits down; and he goes to the armchair, into which he throws himself)*. I dont know how Barbara will take it. Ever since they made her a major in the Salvation Army she has developed a propensity to have her own way and order people about which quite cows me sometimes. It's not ladylike: I'm sure I dont know where she picked it up. Anyhow, Barbara shant bully me; but still it's just as well that your father should be here before she has time to refuse to meet him or make a fuss. Dont look nervous, Stephen: it will only encourage Barbara to make difficulties. *I* am nervous enough, goodness knows; but I dont shew it.

Sarah and Barbara come in with their respective young men, Charles Lomax and Adolphus Cusins. Sarah is slender, bored, and mundane. Barbara is robuster, jollier, much more energetic. Sarah is fashionably dressed: Barbara is in Salvation Army uniform. Lomax, a young man about town, is like many other young men about town. He is afflicted with a frivolous sense of humor which plunges him at the most inopportune moments into paroxysms of imperfectly suppressed laughter. Cusins is a spectacled student, slight, thin haired, and sweet voiced, with a more complex form of Lomax's complaint. His sense of humor is intellectual and subtle, and is complicated by an appalling temper. The lifelong struggle of a benevolent temperament and a high conscience against impulses of inhuman ridicule and fierce impatience has set up a chronic strain which has visibly wrecked his constitution. He is a most implacable, determined, tenacious, intolerant person who by mere force of character presents himself as—and indeed actually is—considerate, gentle, explanatory, even mild and apologetic, capable possibly of murder, but not of cruelty or coarseness. By the operation of some instinct which is not merciful enough to blind him with the illusions of love, he is obstinately bent on marrying Barbara. Lomax likes Sarah and thinks it will be rather a lark to marry her. Consequently he has not attempted to resist Lady Britomart's arrangements to that end.

All four look as if they had been having a good deal of fun in the drawing room. The girls enter first, leaving the swains outside. Sarah comes to the settee. Barbara comes in after her and stops at the door.

Barbara.   Are Cholly and Dolly to come in?

Lady Britomart *(forcibly)*.   Barbara: I will not have Charles called Cholly: the vulgarity of it positively makes me ill.

Barbara.   It's all right, mother: Cholly is quite correct nowadays. Are they to come in?

Lady Britomart.   Yes, if they will behave themselves.

Barbara *(through the door)*.   Come in, Dolly; and behave yourself.

Barbara comes to her mother's writing table. Cusins enters smiling, and wanders towards Lady Britomart.

Sarah *(calling)*.   Come in, Cholly. *(Lomax enters, controlling his features very imperfectly, and places himself vaguely between Sarah and Barbara).*

Lady Britomart *(peremptorily)*.   Sit down, all of you. *(They sit. Cusins crosses to the window and seats himself there. Lomax takes a chair. Barbara sits at the writing table and Sarah on the settee).* I dont in the least know what you are laughing at, Adolphus. I am surprised at you, though I expected nothing better from Charles Lomax.

Cusins *(in a remarkably gentle voice)*.   Barbara has been trying to teach me the West Ham Salvation March.

Lady Britomart.   I see nothing to laugh at in that; nor should you if you are really converted.

Cusins *(sweetly)*.   You were not present. It was really funny, I believe.

Lomax.   Ripping.

Lady Britomart.   Be quiet, Charles. Now listen to me, children. Your father is coming here this evening.

General stupefaction. Lomax, Sarah, and Barbara rise: Sarah scared, and Barbara amused and expectant.

Lomax *(remonstrating)*.   Oh I say!

Lady Britomart.   You are not called on to say anything, Charles.

Sarah.   Are you serious, mother?

Lady Britomart.   Of course I am serious. It is on your account, Sarah, and also on Charles's. *(Silence. Sarah sits, with a shrug. Charles looks painfully unworthy).* I hope you are not going to object, Barbara.

Barbara. I! why should I? My father has a soul to be saved like anybody else. He's quite welcome as far as I am concerned. (*She sits on the table, and softly whistles 'Onward Christian Soldiers'*).

Lomax (*still remonstrant*). But really, dont you know! Oh I say!

Lady Britomart (*frigidly*). What do you wish to convey, Charles?

Lomax. Well, you must admit that this is a bit thick.

Lady Britomart (*turning with ominous suavity to Cusins*). Adolphus: you are a professor of Greek. Can you translate Charles Lomax's remarks into reputable English for us?

Cusins (*cautiously*). If I may say so, Lady Brit, I think Charles has rather happily expressed what we all feel. Homer, speaking of Autolycus, uses the same phrase. πυκινὸν δσμον ἐλθεῖν means a bit thick.

Lomax (*handsomely*). Not that I mind, you know, if Sarah dont. (*He sits*).

Lady Britomart (*crushingly*). Thank you. Have I your permission, Adolphus, to invite my own husband to my own house?

Cusins (*gallantly*). You have my unhesitating support in everything you do.

Lady Britomart. Tush! Sarah: have you nothing to say?

Sarah. Do you mean that he is coming regularly to live here?

Lady Britomart. Certainly not. The spare room is ready for him if he likes to stay for a day or two and see a little more of you; but there are limits.

Sarah. Well, he cant eat us, I suppose. *I* dont mind.

Lomax (*chuckling*). I wonder how the old man will take it.

Lady Britomart. Much as the old woman will, no doubt, Charles.

Lomax (*abashed*). I didnt mean—at least—

Lady Britomart. You didnt think, Charles. You never do; and the result is, you never mean anything. And now please attend to me, children. Your father will be quite a stranger to us.

Lomax. I suppose he hasnt seen Sarah since she was a little kid.

Lady Britomart. Not since she was a little kid, Charles, as you express it with that elegance of diction and refinement of thought that seem never to desert you. Accordingly—er— (*Impatiently*) Now I have forgotten what I was going to say. That comes of your provoking me to be sarcastic, Charles. Adolphus: will you kindly tell me where I was.

Cusins (*sweetly*). You were saying that as Mr Undershaft has not seen his children since they were babies, he will form his opinion of the way you have brought them up from their behavior tonight, and that therefore you wish us all to be particularly careful to conduct ourselves well, especially Charles.

Lady Britomart (*with emphatic approval*). Precisely.

Lomax. Look here, Dolly: Lady Brit didnt say that.

Lady Britomart (*vehemently*). I did, Charles. Adolphus's recollection is perfectly correct. It is most important that you should be good; and I do beg you for once not to pair off into opposite corners and giggle and whisper while I am speaking to your father.

Barbara. All right, mother. We'll do you credit. (*She comes off the table, and sits in her chair with ladylike elegance*).

Lady Britomart. Remember, Charles, that Sarah will want to feel proud of you instead of ashamed of you.

Lomax. Oh I say! theres nothing to be exactly proud of, dont you know.

Lady Britomart. Well, try and look as if there was.

Morrison, pale and dismayed, breaks into the room in unconcealed disorder.

Morrison. Might I speak a word to you, my lady?

Lady Britomart. Nonsense! Shew him up.

Morrison. Yes, my lady. (*He goes*).

Lomax. Does Morrison know who it is?

Lady Britomart. Of course. Morrison has always been with us.

Lomax. It must be a regular corker for him, dont you know.

Lady Britomart. Is this a moment to get on my nerves, Charles, with your outrageous expressions?

Lomax. But this is something out of the ordinary, really—

Morrison (*at the door*). The—er—Mr Undershaft. (*He retreats in confusion*).

Andrew Undershaft comes in. All rise. Lady Britomart meets him in the middle of the room behind the settee.

Andrew is, on the surface, a stoutish, easygoing elderly man, with kindly patient manners, and an engaging simplicity of character. But he has a watchful, deliberate, waiting, listening face, and formidable reserves of power, both bodily and mental, in his capacious chest and long head. His gentleness is partly that of a strong man who has learnt by experience that his natural grip hurts ordinary people unless he handles them very carefully, and partly the mellowness of age and success. He is also a little shy in his present very delicate situation.

Lady Britomart. Good evening, Andrew.

Undershaft. How d'ye do, my dear.

Lady Britomart. You look a good deal older.

Undershaft (*apologetically*). I am somewhat older. (*Taking her hand with a touch of courtship*) Time has stood still with you.

Lady Britomart (*throwing away his hand*). Rubbish! This is your family.

Undershaft (*surprised*). Is it so large? I am sorry to say my memory is failing very badly in some things. (*He offers his hand with paternal kindness to Lomax*).

Lomax (*jerkily shaking his hand*). Ahdedoo.

Undershaft. I can see you are my eldest. I am very glad to meet you again, my boy.

Lomax (*remonstrating*). No, but look here dont you know— (*Overcome*) Oh I say!

Lady Britomart (*recovering from momentary speechlessness*). Andrew: do you mean to say that you dont remember how many children you have?

Undershaft. Well, I am afraid I—. They have grown so much—er. Am I making any ridiculous mistake? I may as well confess: I recollect only one son. But so many things have happened since, of course—er—

Lady Britomart (*decisively*). Andrew: you are talking nonsense. Of course you have only one son.

Undershaft. Perhaps you will be good enough to introduce me, my dear.

Lady Britomart. That is Charles Lomax, who is engaged to Sarah.

Undershaft. My dear sir, I beg your pardon.

Lomax. Notatall. Delighted, I assure you.

Lady Britomart. This is Stephen.

Undershaft (*bowing*). Happy to make your acquaintance, Mr Stephen. (*Taking Cusins' hands in his*) How are you, my young friend? (*To Lady Britomart*) He is very like you, my love.

Cusins. You flatter me, Mr Undershaft. My name is Cusins: engaged to Barbara. (*Very explicitly*) That is Major Barbara Undershaft, of the Salvation Army. That is Sarah, your second daughter. This is Stephen Undershaft, your son.

Undershaft. My dear Stephen, I beg your pardon.

Stephen. Not at all.

Undershaft. Mr Cusins: I am much indebted to you for explaining so precisely. (*Turning to Sarah*) Barbara, my dear—

Sarah (*prompting him*). Sarah.

Undershaft. Sarah, of course. (*They shake hands. He goes over to Barbara*). Barbara—I am right this time, I hope?

Barbara. Quite right. (*They shake hands*).

Lady Britomart (*resuming command*). Sit down, all of you. Sit down, Andrew. (*She comes forward and sits on the settee. Cusins also brings his chair forward on her left. Barbara and Stephen resume their seats. Lomax gives his chair to Sarah and goes for another*).

Undershaft. Thank you, my love.

Lomax (*conversationally, as he brings a chair forward between the writing table and the settee, and offers it to Undershaft*). Takes you some time to find out exactly where you are, dont it?

Undershaft (*accepting the chair, but remaining standing*). That is not what embarrasses me, Mr Lomax. My difficulty is that if I play the part of a father, I shall produce the effect of an intrusive stranger; and if I play the part of a discreet stranger, I may appear a callous father.

Lady Britomart. There is no need for you to play any part at all, Andrew. You had much better be sincere and natural.

Undershaft (*submissively*). Yes, my dear: I daresay that will be best. (*He sits down comfortably*). Well, here I am. Now what can I do for you all?

Lady Britomart. You need not do anything, Andrew. You are one of the family. You can sit with us and enjoy yourself.

A painfully conscious pause. Barbara makes a face at Lomax, whose too long suppressed mirth immediately explodes in agonized neighings.

Lady Britomart (*outraged*).   Charles Lomax: if you can behave yourself, behave yourself. If not, leave the room.

Lomax.   I'm awfully sorry, Lady Brit; but really you know, upon my soul! (*He sits on the settee between Lady Britomart and Undershaft, quite overcome*).

Barbara.   Why dont you laugh if you want to, Cholly? It's good for your inside.

Lady Britomart.   Barbara: you have had the education of a lady. Please let your father see that; and dont talk like a street girl.

Undershaft.   Never mind me, my dear. As you know, I am not a gentleman; and I was never educated.

Lomax (*encouragingly*).   Nobody'd know it, I assure you. You look all right, you know.

Cusins.   Let me advise you to study Greek, Mr Undershaft. Greek scholars are privileged men. Few of them know Greek; and none of them know anything else; but their position is unchallengeable. Other languages are the qualifications of waiters and commercial travellers: Greek is to a man of position what the hallmark is to silver.

Barbara.   Dolly: dont be insincere. Cholly: fetch your concertina and play something for us.

Lomax (*jumps up eagerly, but checks himself to remark doubtfully to Undershaft*).   Perhaps that sort of thing isnt in your line, eh?

Undershaft.   I am particularly fond of music.

Lomax (*delighted*).   Are you? Then I'll get it. (*He goes upstairs for the instrument*).

Undershaft.   Do you play, Barbara?

Barbara.   Only the tambourine. But Cholly's teaching me the concertina.

Undershaft.   Is Cholly also a member of the Salvation Army?

Barbara.   No: he says it's bad form to be a dissenter.[1] But I dont despair of Cholly. I made him come yesterday to a meeting at the dock gates, and take the collection in his hat.

Undershaft (*looks whimsically at his wife*)!!

Lady Britomart.   It is not my doing, Andrew. Barbara is old enough to take her own way. She has no father to advise her.

Barbara.   Oh yes she has. There are no orphans in the Salvation Army.

Undershaft.   Your father there has a great many children and plenty of experience, eh?

Barbara (*looking at him with quick interest and nodding*).   Just so. How did you come to understand that? (*Lomax is heard at the door trying the concertina*).

Lady Britomart.   Come in, Charles. Play us something at once.

Lomax.   Righto! (*He sits down in his former place, and preludes*).

---

[1] One who refuses to accept the doctrines of the Church of England.

Undershaft.   One moment, Mr Lomax. I am rather interested in the Salvation Army. Its motto might be my own: Blood and Fire.

Lomax *(shocked).*   But not your sort of blood and fire, you know.

Undershaft.   My sort of blood cleanses: my sort of fire purifies.

Barbara.   So do ours. Come down tomorrow to my shelter—the West Ham shelter—and see what we're doing. We're going to march to a great meeting in the Assembly Hall at Mile End. Come and see the shelter and then march with us: it will do you a lot of good. Can you play anything?

Undershaft.   In my youth I earned pennies, and even shillings occasionally, in the streets and in public house parlors by my natural talent for stepdancing. Later on, I became a member of the Undershaft orchestral society, and performed passably on the tenor trombone.

Lomax *(scandalized—putting down the concertina).*   Oh I say!

Barbara.   Many a sinner has played himself into heaven on the trombone, thanks to the Army.

Lomax *(to Barbara, still rather shocked).*   Yes; but what about the cannon business, dont you know? *(To Undershaft)* Getting into heaven is not exactly in your line, is it?

Lady Britomart.   Charles!!!

Lomax.   Well; but it stands to reason, dont it? The cannon business may be necessary and all that: we cant get on without cannons; but it isnt right, you know. On the other hand, there may be a certain amount of tosh about the Salvation Army—I belong to the Established Church myself—but still you cant deny that it's religion; and you cant go against religion, can you? At least unless youre downright immoral, dont you know.

Undershaft.   You hardly appreciate my position, Mr Lomax—

Lomax *(hastily).*   I'm not saying anything against you personally—

Undershaft.   Quite so, quite so. But consider for a moment. Here I am, a profiteer in mutilation and murder. I find myself in a specially amiable humor just now because, this morning, down at the foundry, we blew twenty-seven dummy soldiers into fragments with a gun which formerly destroyed only thirteen.

Lomax *(leniently).*   Well, the more destructive war becomes, the sooner it will be abolished, eh?

Undershaft.   Not at all. The more destructive war becomes the more fascinating we find it. No, Mr Lomax: I am obliged to you for making the usual excuse for my trade; but I am not ashamed of it. I am not one of those men who keep their morals and their business in watertight compartments. All the spare money my trade rivals spend on hospitals, cathedrals, and other receptacles for conscience money, I devote to experiments and researches in improved methods of destroying life and property. I have always done so; and I always shall. Therefore your Christmas card moralities of peace on earth and goodwill among men are of no use to me. Your Christianity, which enjoins you to resist not evil, and to turn the other cheek, would make me a bankrupt. My morality—my religion—must have a place for cannons and torpedoes in it.

Stephen (*coldly—almost sullenly*).   You speak as if there were half a dozen moralities and religions to choose from, instead of one true morality and one true religion.

Undershaft.   For me there is only one true morality; but it might not fit you, as you do not manufacture aerial battleships. There is only one true morality for every man; but every man has not the same true morality.

Lomax (*overtaxed*).   Would you mind saying that again? I didn't quite follow it.

Cusins.   It's quite simple. As Euripides says, one man's meat is another man's poison morally as well as physically.

Undershaft.   Precisely.

Lomax.   Oh, that! Yes, yes, yes. True. True.

Stephen.   In other words, some men are honest and some are scoundrels.

Barbara.   Bosh! There are no scoundrels.

Undershaft.   Indeed? Are there any good men?

Barbara.   No. Not one. There are neither good men nor scoundrels: there are just children of one Father; and the sooner they stop calling one another names the better. You neednt talk to me: I know them. Ive had scores of them through my hands: scoundrels, criminals, infidels, philanthropists, missionaries, county councillors, all sorts. Theyre all just the same sort of sinner; and theres the same salvation ready for them all.

Undershaft.   May I ask have you ever saved a maker of cannons?

Barbara.   No. Will you let me try?

Undershaft.   Well, I will make a bargain with you. If I go to see you tomorrow in your Salvation Shelter, will you come the day after to see me in my cannon works?

Barbara.   Take care. It may end in your giving up the cannons for the sake of the Salvation Army.

Undershaft.   Are you sure it will not end in your giving up the Salvation Army for the sake of the cannons?

Barbara.   I will take my chance of that.

Undershaft.   And I will take my chance of the other. (*They shake hands on it*). Where is your shelter?

Barbara.   In West Ham. At the sign of the cross. Ask anybody in Canning Town. Where are your works?

Undershaft.   In Perivale St. Andrews. At the sign of the sword. Ask anybody in Europe.

Lomax.   Hadnt I better play something?

Barbara.   Yes. Give us Onward, Christian Soldiers.

Lomax.   Well, thats rather a strong order to begin with, dont you know. Suppose I sing Thourt passing hence, my brother. It's much the same tune.

Barbara.   It's too melancholy. You get saved, Cholly; and youll pass hence, my brother, without making such a fuss about it.

Lady Britomart. Really, Barbara, you go on as if religion were a pleasant subject. Do have some sense of propriety.

Undershaft. I do not find it an unpleasant subject, my dear. It is the only one that capable people really care for.

Lady Britomart (*looking at her watch*). Well, if you are determined to have it, I insist on having it in a proper and respectable way. Charles: ring for prayers.

General amazement. Stephen rises in dismay.

Lomax (*rising*). Oh I say!

Undershaft (*rising*). I am afraid I must be going.

Lady Britomart. You cannot go now, Andrew: it would be most improper. Sit down. What will the servants think?

Undershaft. My dear: I have conscientious scruples. May I suggest a compromise? If Barbara will conduct a little service in the drawing room, with Mr Lomax as organist, I will attend it willingly. I will even take part, if a trombone can be procured.

Lady Britomart. Dont mock, Andrew.

Undershaft (*shocked—to Barbara*). You dont think I am mocking, my love, I hope.

Barbara. No, of course not; and it wouldnt matter if you were: half the Army came to their first meeting for a lark. (*Rising*) Come along. (*She throws her arm round her father and sweeps him out, calling to the others from the threshold*). Come, Dolly. Come, Cholly.

Cusins rises.

Lady Britomart. I will not be disobeyed by everybody. Adolphus: sit down. (*He does not*). Charles: you may go. You are not fit for prayers: you cannot keep your countenance.

Lomax. Oh I say! (*He goes out*).

Lady Britomart (*continuing*). But you, Adolphus, can behave yourself if you choose to. I insist on your staying.

Cusins. My dear Lady Brit: there are things in the family prayer book that I couldnt bear to hear you say.

Lady Britomart. What things, pray?

Cusins. Well, you would have to say before all the servants that we have done things we ought not to have done, and left undone things we ought to have done, and that there is no health in us. I cannot bear to hear you doing yourself such an injustice, and Barbara such an injustice. As for myself, I flatly deny it: I have done my best. I shouldnt dare to marry Barbara—I couldnt look you in the face—if it were true. So I must go to the drawing room.

Lady Britomart *(offended)*.   Well, go. *(He starts for the door)*. And remember this, Adolphus *(he turns to listen)*: I have a very strong suspicion that you went to the Salvation Army to worship Barbara and nothing else. And I quite appreciate the very clever way in which you systematically humbug me. I have found you out. Take care Barbara doesnt. Thats all.

Cusins *(with unruffled sweetness)*.   Dont tell on me. *(He steals out)*.

Lady Britomart.   Sarah: if you want to go, go. Anything's better than to sit there as if you wished you were a thousand miles away.

Sarah *(languidly)*.   Very well, mamma. *(She goes)*.

Lady Britomart, with a sudden flounce, gives way to a little gust of tears.

Stephen *(going to her)*.   Mother: whats the matter?

Lady Britomart *(swishing away her tears with her handkerchief)*.   Nothing. Foolishness. You can go with him, too, if you like, and leave me with the servants.

Stephen.   Oh, you mustnt think that, mother. I—I dont like him.

Lady Britomart.   The others do. That is the injustice of a woman's lot. A woman has to bring up her children; and that means to restrain them, to deny them things they want, to set them tasks, to punish them when they do wrong, to do all the unpleasant things. And then the father, who has nothing to do but pet them and spoil them, comes in when all her work is done and steals their affection from her.

Stephen.   He has not stolen our affection from you. It is only curiosity.

Lady Britomart *(violently)*.   I wont be consoled, Stephen. There is nothing the matter with me. *(She rises and goes towards the door)*.

Stephen.   Where are you going, mother?

Lady Britomart.   To the drawing room, of course. *(She goes out. Onward, Christian Soldiers, on the concertina, with tambourine accompaniment, is heard when the door opens)*. Are you coming, Stephen?

Stephen.   No. Certainly not. *(She goes. He sits down on the settee, with compressed lips and an expression of strong dislike)*.

Act Two

The yard of the West Ham shelter of the Salvation Army is a cold place on a January morning. The building itself, an old warehouse, is newly whitewashed. Its gabled end projects into the yard in the middle, with a door on the ground floor, and another in the loft above it without any balcony or ladder, but with a pulley rigged over it for hoisting sacks. Those who come from this central gable end into the yard have the gateway leading to the street on their left, with a stone horsetrough just beyond it, and, on the right, a penthouse shielding a table from the weather. There are forms at the table; and on them are seated a man and a woman, both much down on their luck, finishing a meal of bread (one thick slice each, with margarine and golden syrup) and diluted milk.

The man, a workman out of employment, is young, agile, a talker, a poser, sharp enough to be capable of anything in reason except honesty or altruistic considerations of any kind. The woman is a commonplace old bundle of poverty and hard-worn humanity. She looks sixty and probably is forty-five. If they were rich people, gloved and muffed and well wrapped up in furs and overcoats, they would be numbed and miserable; for it is a grindingly cold raw January day; and a glance at the background of grimy warehouses and leaden sky visible over the whitewashed walls of the yard would drive any idle rich person straight to the Mediterranean. But these two, being no more troubled with visions of the Mediterranean than of the moon, and being compelled to keep more of their clothes in the pawnshop, and less on their persons, in winter than in summer, are not depressed by the cold: rather are they stung into vivacity, to which their meal has just now given an almost jolly turn. The man takes a pull at his mug, then gets up and moves about the yard with his hands deep in his pockets, occasionally breaking into a stepdance.

The Woman.   Feel better arter your meal, sir?

The Man.   No. Call that a meal! Good enough for you, praps; but wot is it to me, an intelligent workin man.

The Woman.   Workin man! Wot are you?

The Man.   Painter.

The Woman *(sceptically)*.   Yus, I dessay.

The Man.   Yus, you dessay! I know. Every loafer that cant do nothink calls isself a painter. Well, I'm a real painter: grainer, finisher, thirty-eight bob a week when I can get it.

The Woman.   Then why dont you go and get it?

The Man.   I'll tell you why. Fust: I'm intelligent—fffff! it's rotten cold here. *(he dances a step or two)*—yes: intelligent beyond the station o life into which it has pleased the capitalists to call me; and they dont like a man that sees through em. Second, an intelligent bein needs a doo share of appiness; so I drink somethink cruel when I get the chawnce. Third, I stand by my class and do as little as I can so's to leave arf the job for me fellow workers. Fourth, I'm fly enough to know wots inside the law and wots outside it; and inside I do as the capitalists do: pinch wot I can lay me ands on. In a proper state of society I am sober, industrious and honest: in Rome, so to speak, I do as the Romans do. Wots the consequence? When trade is bad—and it's rotten bad just now—and the employers az to sack arf their men, they generally start on me.

The Woman.   Whats your name?

The Man.   Price. Bronterre O'Brien Price. Usually called Snobby Price, for short.

The Woman.   Snobby's a carpenter, aint it? You said you was a painter.

Price.   Not that kind of snob, but the genteel sort. I'm too uppish, owing to my intelligence, and my father being a Chartist[2] and a reading, thinking man: a stationer, too. I'm none of your common hewers of wood and drawers of water; and dont you forget it. *(He returns to his seat at the table, and takes up his mug).* Wots your name?

The Woman.   Rummy Mitchens, sir.

Price *(quaffing the remains of his milk to her).*   Your elth, Miss Mitchens.

Rummy *(correcting him).*   Missis Mitchens.

Price.   Wot! Oh Rummy, Rummy! Respectable married woman, Rummy, gittin rescued by the Salvation Army by pretendin to be a bad un. Same old game!

Rummy.   What am I to do? I cant starve. Them Salvation lasses is dear good girls; but the better you are, the worse they likes to think you were before they rescued you. Why shouldnt they av a bit o credit, poor loves? Theyre worn to rags by their work. And where would they get the money to rescue us if we was to let on we're no worse than other people? You know what ladies and gentlemen are.

Price.   Thievin swine! Wish I ad their job, Rummy, all the same. Wot does Rummy stand for? Pet name praps?

Rummy.   Short for Romola.

Price.   For wot!?

Rummy.   Romola. It was out of a new book. Somebody me mother wanted me to grow up like.

Price.   We're companions in misfortune, Rummy. Both of us got names that nobody cawnt pronounce. Consequently I'm Snobby and youre Rummy because Bill and Sally wasnt good enough for our parents. Such is life!

Rummy.   Who saved you, Mr Price? Was it Major Barbara?

Price.   No: I come here on my own. I'm going to be Bronterre O'Brien Price, the converted painter. I know wot they like. I'll tell em how I blasphemed and gambled and wopped my poor old mother—

Rummy *(shocked).*   Used you to beat your mother?

Price.   Not likely. She used to beat me. No matter: you come and listen to the converted painter, and youll hear how she was a pious woman that taught me prayers at er knee, an how I used to come home drunk and drag her out o bed be er snow white airs, an lam into er with the poker.

Rummy.   Thats whats so unfair to us women. Your confessions is just as big lies as ours: you dont tell what you really done no more than us; but you men can tell your lies right out at the meetins and be made much of for it; while the sort o confessions we az to make az to be whispered to one lady at a time. It aint right, spite of all their piety.

Price.   Right! Do you spose the Army'd be allowed if it went and did right?

---

[2] Chartism was a movement for democratic and social reform set forth in the People's Charter (1838).

Not much. It combs our air and makes us good little blokes to be robbed and put upon. But I'll play the game as good as any of em. I'll see somebody struck by lightnin, or hear a voice saying 'Snobby Price: where will you spend eternity?' I'll av a time of it, I tell you.

Rummy.   You wont be let drink, though.

Price.   I'll take it out in gorspellin, then. I dont want to drink if I can get fun enough any other way.

Jenny Hill, a pale, overwrought, pretty Salvation lass of 18, comes in through the yard gate, leading Peter Shirley, a half hardened, half worn-out elderly man, weak with hunger.

Jenny (*supporting him*).   Come! pluck up. I'll get you something to eat. Youll be all right then.

Price (*rising and hurrying officiously to take the old man off Jenny's hands*).   Poor old man! Cheer up, brother: youll find rest and peace and appiness ere. Hurry up with the food, miss: e's fair done. (*Jenny hurries into the shelter*). Ere, buck up, daddy! she's fetchin y'a thick slice of breadn treacle, an a mug o skyblue. (*He seats him at the corner of the table*).

Rummy (*gaily*).   Keep up your old art! Never say die!

Shirley.   I'm not an old man. I'm only 46. I'm as good as ever I was. The grey patch come in my hair before I was thirty. All it wants is three pennorth o hair dye: am I to be turned on the streets to starve for it? Holy God! Ive worked ten to twelve hours a day since I was thirteen, and paid my way all through; and now am I to be thrown into the gutter and my job given to a young man that can do it no better than me because Ive black hair that goes white at the first change?

Price (*cheerfully*).   No good jawrin about it. Your only a jumped-up, jerked-off, orspittle-turned-out incurable of an ole working man: who cares about you? Eh? Make the thievin swine give you a meal: theyve stole many a one from you. Get a bit o your own back. (*Jenny returns with the usual meal*). There you are, brother. Awsk a blessin an tuck that into you.

Shirley (*looking at it ravenously but not touching it, and crying like a child*). I never took anything before.

Jenny (*petting him*).   Come, come! the Lord sends it to you: he wasnt above taking bread from his friends; and why should you be? Besides, when we find you a job you can pay us for it if you like.

Shirley (*eagerly*).   Yes, yes: thats true. I can pay you back: it's only a loan. (*Shivering*) Oh Lord! oh Lord! (*He turns to the table and attacks the meal ravenously*).

Jenny.   Well, Rummy, are you more comfortable now?

Rummy.   God bless you, lovey! youve fed my body and saved my soul, havnt you?(*Jenny, touched, kisses her*). Sit down and rest a bit: you must be ready to drop.

Jenny.   Ive been going hard since morning. But theres more work than we can do. I mustnt stop.

Rummy.   Try a prayer for just two minutes. Youll work all the better after.

Jenny *(her eyes lighting up).*   Oh isnt it wonderful how a few minutes prayer revives you! I was quite lightheaded at twelve o'clock, I was so tired; but Major Barbara just sent me to pray for five minutes; and I was able to go on as if I had only just begun. *(To Price)* Did you have a piece of bread?

Price *(with unction).*   Yes, miss; but Ive got the piece that I value more; and thats the peace that passeth hall hannerstennin.

Rummy *(fervently).*   Glory Hallelujah!

Bill Walker, a rough customer of about 25, appears at the yard gate and looks malevolently at Jenny.

Jenny.   That makes me so happy. When you say that, I feel wicked for loitering here. I must get to work again.

She is hurrying to the shelter, when the newcomer moves quickly up to the door and intercepts her. His manner is so threatening that she retreats as he comes at her truculently, driving her down the yard.

Bill.   Aw knaow. Youre the one that took away maw girl. Youre the one that set er agen me. Well, I'm gowin to ev er aht. Not that Aw care a carse for er or you: see? Bat Aw'll let er knaow; and Aw'll let you knaow. Aw'm gowing to give her a doin thatll teach er to cat away from me. Nah in wiv you and tell er to cam aht afore Aw cam in and kick er aht. Tell er Bill Walker wants er. She'll knaow wot thet means; and if she keeps me witin itll be worse. You stop to jawr beck at me; and Aw'll stawt on you: d'ye eah? Theres your wy. In you gow. *(He takes her by the arm and slings her towards the door of the shelter. She falls on her hand and knee. Rummy helps her up again).*

Price *(rising, and venturing irresolutely towards Bill).*   Easy there, mate. She aint doin you no arm.

Bill.   Oo are you callin mite? *(Standing over him threateningly)* Youre goin to stend ap for er, aw yer? Put ap your ends.

Rummy *(running indignantly to him to scold him).*   Oh, you great brute— *(He instantly swings his left hand back against her face. She screams and reels back to the trough, where she sits down, covering her bruised face with her hands and rocking herself and moaning with pain).*

Jenny *(going to her).*   Oh, God forgive you! How could you strike an old woman like that?

Bill *(seizing her by the hair so violently that she also screams, and tearing her away from the old woman).*   You Gawd forgimme again an Aw'll Gawd forgive you one on the jawr thetll stop you pryin for a week. *(Holding her and turning fiercely on Price)* Ev you ennything to sy agen it?

Price *(intimidated).*   No, matey: she aint anything to do with me.

Bill. Good job for you! Aw'd pat two meals into you and fawt you with one finger arter, you stawved cur. *(To Jenny)* Nah are you gowin to fetch aht Mog Ebbijem; or em Aw to knock your fice off you and fetch her meself?

Jenny *(writhing in his grasp).* Oh please someone go in and tell Major Barbara— *(She screams again as he wrenches her head down; and Price and Rummy flee into the shelter).*

Bill. You want to gow in and tell your Mijor of me, do you?

Jenny. Oh please dont drag my hair. Let me go.

Bill. Do you or downt you? *(She stifles a scream).* Yus or nao?

Jenny. God give me strength—

Bill *(striking her with his fist in the face).* Gow an shaow her thet, and tell her if she wants one lawk it to cam and interfere with me. *(Jenny, crying with pain, goes into the shed. He goes to the form and addresses the old man).* Eah: finish your mess; an git aht o maw wy.

Shirley *(springing up and facing him fiercely, with the mug in his hand).* You take a liberty with me, and I'll smash you over the face with the mug and cut your eye out. Aint you satisfied—young whelps like you—with takin the bread out o the mouths of your elders that have brought you up and slaved for you, but you must come shovin and cheekin and bullyin in here, where the bread o charity is sickenin in our stummicks?

Bill *(contemptuously, but backing a little).* Wot good are you, you aold palsy mag? Wot good are you?

Shirley. As good as you and better. I'll do a day's work agen you or any fat young soaker of your age. Go and take my job at Horrockses, where I worked for ten year. They want young men there: they cant afford to keep men over forty-five. Theyre very sorry—give you a character and happy to help you to get anything suited to your years—sure a steady man wont be long out of a job. Well, let em try you. Theyll find the differ. What do you know? Not as much as how to beeyave yourself—layin your dirty fist across the mouth of a respectable woman!

Bill. Downt provowk me to ly it acrost yours: d'ye eah?

Shirley *(with blighting contempt).* Yes: you like an old man to hit, dont you, when youve finished with the women. I aint seen you hit a young one yet.

Bill *(stung).* You loy, you aold soupkitchener, you. There was a yang menn eah. Did Aw offer to itt him or did Aw not?

Shirley. Was he starvin or was he not? Was he a man or only a crosseyed thief an a loafer? Would you hit my son-in-law's brother?

Bill. Oo's ee?

Shirley. Todger Fairmile o Balls Pond. Him that won £20 off the Japanese wrastler at the music hall by standin out 17 minutes 4 seconds agen him.

Bill *(sullenly).* Aw'm nao music awl wrastler. Ken he box?

Shirley. Yes: an you cant.

Bill. Wot! Aw cawnt, cawnt Aw? Wots thet you sy *(threatening him)*?

Shirley *(not budging an inch).* Will you box Todger Fairmile if I put him on to you? Say the word.

Bill *(subsiding with a slouch).*   Aw'll stend ap to enny menn alawv, if he was ten Todger Fairmawls. But Aw dont set ap to be a perfeshnal.

Shirley *(looking down on him with unfathomable disdain).*   You box! Slap an old woman with the back o your hand! You hadnt even the sense to hit her where a magistrate couldnt see the mark of it, you silly young lump of conceit and ignorance. Hit a girl in the jaw and ony make her cry! If Todger Fairmile'd done it, she wouldnt a got up inside o ten minutes, no more than you would if he got on to you. Yah! I'd set about you myself if I had a week's feedin in me instead o two months' starvation. *(He turns his back on him and sits down moodily at the table).*

Bill *(following him and stooping over him to drive the taunt in).*   You loy! youve the bread and treacle in you that you cam eah to beg.

Shirley *(bursting into tears).*   Oh God! it's true: I'm only an old pauper on the scrap heap. *(Furiously)* But youll come to it yourself; and then youll know. Youll come to it sooner than a teetotaller like me, fillin yourself with gin at this hour o the mornin!

Bill.   Aw'm nao gin drinker, you aold lawr; bat wen Aw want to give my girl a bloomin good awdin Aw lawk to ev a bit o devil in me: see? An eah emm, talkin to a rotten aold blawter like you sted o givin her wot for. *(Working himself into a rage)* Aw'm gowin in there to fetch her aht. *(He makes vengefully for the shelter door).*

Shirley.   Youre going to the station on a stretcher, more likely; and theyll take the gin and the devil out of you there when they get you inside. You mind what youre about: the major here is the Earl o Stevenage's granddaughter.

Bill *(checked).*   Garn!

Shirley.   Youll see.

Bill *(his resolution oozing).*   Well, Aw aint dan nathin to er.

Shirley.   Spose she said you did! who'd believe you?

Bill *(very uneasy, skulking back to the corner of the penthouse).*   Gawd! theres no jastice in this cantry. To think wot them people can do! Aw'm as good as er.

Shirley.   Tell her so. It's just what a fool like you would do.

Barbara, brisk and businesslike, comes from the shelter with a note book, and addresses herself to Shirley. Bill, cowed, sits down in the corner on a form, and turns his back on them.

Barbara.   Good morning.

Shirley *(standing up and taking off his hat).*   Good morning, miss.

Barbara.   Sit down: make yourself at home. *(He hesitates; but she puts a friendly hand on his shoulder and makes him obey).* Now then! since youve made friends with us, we want to know all about you. Names and addresses and trades.

Shirley.   Peter Shirley. Fitter. Chucked out two months ago because I was too old.

Barbara *(not at all surprised)*.   Youd pass still. Why didnt you dye your hair?

Shirley.   I did. Me age come out at a coroner's inquest on me daughter.

Barbara.   Steady?

Shirley.   Teetotaller. Never out of a job before. Good worker. And sent to the knackers like an old horse!

Barbara.   No matter: if you did your part God will do his.

Shirley *(suddenly stubborn)*.   My religion's no concern of anybody but myself.

Barbara *(guessing)*.   I know. Secularist?

Shirley *(hotly)*.   Did I offer to deny it?

Barbara.   Why should you? My own father's a Secularist, I think. Our Father—yours and mine—fulfills himself in many ways; and I daresay he knew what he was about when he made a Secularist of you. So buck up, Peter! we can always find a job for a steady man like you. *(Shirley, disarmed and a little bewildered, touches his hat. She turns from him to Bill)*. Whats your name?

Bill *(insolently)*.   Wots thet to you?

Barbara *(calmly making a note)*.   Afraid to give his name. Any trade?

Bill.   Oo's afride to give is nime? *(Doggedly, with a sense of heroically defying the House of Lords in the person of Lord Stevenage)* If you want to bring a chawge agen me, bring it. *(She waits, unruffled)*. Moy nime's Bill Walker.

Barbara *(as if the name were familiar: trying to remember how)*.   Bill Walker? *(Recollecting)* Oh, I know: youre the man that Jenny Hill was praying for inside just now. *(She enters his name in her note book)*.

Bill.   Oo's Jenny Ill? And wot call as she to pry for me?

Barbara.   I dont know. Perhaps it was you that cut her lip.

Bill *(defiantly)*.   Yus, it was me that cat her lip. Aw aint afride o you.

Barbara.   How could you be, since youre not afraid of God? Youre a brave man, Mr Walker. It takes some pluck to do our work here; but none of us dare lift our hand against a girl like that, for fear of her father in heaven.

Bill *(sullenly)*.   I want nan of your kentin jawr. I spowse you think Aw cam eah to beg from you, like this demmiged lot eah. Not me. Aw downt want your bread and scripe and ketlep. Aw dont blieve in your Gawd, no more than you do yourself.

Barbara *(sunnily apologetic and ladylike, as on a new footing with him)*.   Oh, I beg your pardon for putting your name down, Mr Walker. I didnt understand. I'll strike it out.

Bill *(taking this as a slight, and deeply wounded by it)*.   Eah! you let maw nime alown. Aint it good enaff to be in your book?

Barbara *(considering)*.   Well, you see, theres no use putting down your name unless I can do something for you, is there? Whats your trade?

Bill *(still smarting)*.   Thets nao concern o yours.

Barbara.   Just so. *(Very businesslike)* I'll put you down as *(writing)* the man who—struck—poor little Jenny Hill—in the mouth.

Bill *(rising threateningly)*.   See eah. Awve ed enaff o this.

Barbara *(quite sunny and fearless)*.   What did you come to us for?

Bill.   Aw cam for maw gel, see? Aw cam to tike her aht o this and to brike er jawr for er.

Barbara *(complacently)*.   You see I was right about your trade. *(Bill, on the point of retorting furiously, finds himself, to his great shame and terror, in danger of crying instead. He sits down again suddenly)*. Whats her name?

Bill *(dogged)*.   Er nime's Mog Ebbijem: thets wot her nime is.

Barbara.   Mog Habbijam! Oh, she's gone to Canning Town, to our barracks there.

Bill *(fortified by his resentment of Mog's perfidy)*.   Is she? *(Vindictively)* Then Aw'm gowin to Kennintahn arter her. *(He crosses to the gate; hesitates; finally comes back at Barbara)*. Are you loyin to me to git shat o me?

Barbara.   I dont want to get shut of you. I want to keep you here and save your soul. Youd better stay: youre going to have a bad time today, Bill.

Bill.   Oo's gowin to give it to me? You, preps?

Barbara.   Someone you dont believe in. But youll be glad afterwards.

Bill *(slinking off)*.   Aw'll gow to Kennintahn to be aht o reach o your tangue. *(Suddenly turning on her with intense malice)* And if Aw downt fawnd Mog there, Aw'll cam beck and do two years for you, selp me Gawd if Aw downt!

Barbara *(a shade kindlier, if possible)*.   It's no use, Bill. She's got another bloke.

Bill.   Wot!

Barbara.   One of her converts. He fell in love with her when he saw her with her soul saved, and her face clean, and her hair washed.

Bill *(surprised)*.   Wottud she wash it for, the carroty slat? It's red.

Barbara.   It's quite lovely now, because she wears a new look in her eyes with it. It's a pity youre too late. The new bloke has put your nose out of joint, Bill.

Bill.   Aw'll put his nowse aht o joint for him. Not that Aw care a carse for er, mawnd thet. But Aw'll teach her to drop me as if Aw was dirt. And Aw'll teach him to meddle with maw judy. Wots iz bleedin nime?

Barbara.   Sergeant Todger Fairmile.

Shirley *(rising with grim joy)*.   I'll go with him, miss. I want to see them two meet. I'll take him to the infirmary when it's over.

Bill *(to Shirley, with undissembled misgiving)*.   Is thet im you was speakin on?

Shirley.   Thats him.

Bill.   Im that wrastled in the music awl?

Shirley.   The competitions at the National Sportin Club was worth nigh a hundred a year to him. He's gev em up now for religion; so he's a bit fresh for want of the exercise he was accustomed to. He'll be glad to see you. Come along.

Bill.   Wots is wight?

Shirley.   Thirteen four. *(Bill's last hope expires)*.

Barbara.   Go and talk to him, Bill. He'll convert you.

Shirley.   He'll convert your head into a mashed potato.

Bill *(sullenly)*.   Aw aint afride of im. Aw aint afride of ennybody. Bat e can lick me. She's dan me. *(He sits down moodily on the edge of the horse trough)*.

Shirley.   You aint going. I thought not. *(He resumes his seat)*.

Barbara *(calling)*.   Jenny!

Jenny *(appearing at the shelter door with a plaster on the corner of her mouth)*.   Yes, Major.

Barbara.   Send Rummy Mitchens out to clear away here.

Jenny.   I think she's afraid.

Barbara *(her resemblance to her mother flashing out for a moment)*.   Nonsense! she must do as she's told.

Jenny *(calling into the shelter)*.   Rummy: the Major says you must come.

Jenny comes to Barbara, purposely keeping on the side next Bill, lest he should suppose that she shrank from him or bore malice.

Barbara.   Poor little Jenny! Are you tired? *(Looking at the wounded cheek)* Does it hurt?

Jenny.   No: it's all right now. It was nothing.

Barbara *(critically)*.   It was as hard as he could hit, I expect. Poor Bill! You dont feel angry with him, do you?

Jenny.   Oh no, no, no: indeed I dont, Major, bless his poor heart! *(Barbara kisses her; and she runs away merrily into the shelter. Bill writhes with an agonizing return of his new and alarming symptoms, but says nothing. Rummy Mitchens comes from the shelter)*.

Barbara *(going to meet Rummy)*.   Now Rummy, bustle. Take in those mugs and plates to be washed; and throw the crumbs about for the birds.

Rummy takes the three plates and mugs; but Shirley takes back his mug from her, as there is still some milk left in it.

Rummy.   There aint any crumbs. This aint a time to waste good bread on birds.

Price *(appearing at the shelter door)*.   Gentleman come to see the shelter, Major. Says he's your father.

Barbara.   All right. Coming. *(Snobby goes back into the shelter, followed by Barbara)*.

Rummy *(stealing across to Bill and addressing him in a subdued voice, but with intense conviction)*.   I'd av the lor of you, you flat eared pignosed potwalloper, if she'd let me. Youre no gentleman, to hit a lady in the face. *(Bill, with greater things moving in him, takes no notice)*.

Shirley *(following her)*.   Here! in with you and dont get yourself into more trouble by talking.

Rummy *(with hauteur)*. I aint ad the pleasure o being hintroduced to you, as I can remember. *(She goes into the shelter with the plates)*.

Shirley. Thats the—

Bill *(savagely)*. Downt you talk to me, d'ye eah? You lea me alown, or Aw'll do you a mischief. Aw'm not dirt under your feet, ennywy.

Shirley *(calmly)*. Dont you be afeered. You aint such prime company that you need expect to be sought after. *(He is about to go into the shelter when Barbara comes out, with Undershaft on her right)*.

Barbara. Oh, there you are, Mr Shirley! *(Between them)* This is my father: I told you he was a Secularist, didnt I? Perhaps youll be able to comfort one another.

Undershaft *(startled)*. A Secularist! Not the least in the world: on the contrary, a confirmed mystic.

Barbara. Sorry, I'm sure. By the way, papa, what is your religion? in case I have to introduce you again.

Undershaft. My religion? Well, my dear, I am a Millionaire. That is my religion.

Barbara. Then I'm afraid you and Mr Shirley wont be able to comfort one another after all. Youre not a Millionaire, are you, Peter?

Shirley. No; and proud of it.

Undershaft *(gravely)*. Poverty, my friend, is not a thing to be proud of.

Shirley *(angrily)*. Who made your millions for you? Me and my like. Whats kep us poor? Keepin you rich. I wouldnt have your conscience, not for all your income.

Undershaft. I wouldnt have your income, not for all your conscience, Mr Shirley. *(He goes to the penthouse and sits down on a form)*.

Barbara *(stopping Shirley adroitly as he is about to retort)*. You wouldnt think he was my father, would you, Peter? Will you go into the shelter and lend the lasses a hand for a while: we're worked off our feet.

Shirley *(bitterly)*. Yes: I'm in their debt for a meal, aint I?

Barbara. Oh, not because youre in their debt, but for love of them, Peter, for love of them. *(He cannot understand, and is rather scandalized)*. There! dont stare at me. In with you; and give that conscience of yours a holiday. *(Bustling him into the shelter)*.

Shirley *(as he goes in)*. Ah! it's a pity you never was trained to use your reason, miss. Youd have been a very taking lecturer on Secularism.

Barbara turns to her father.

Undershaft. Never mind me, my dear. Go about your work; and let me watch it for a while.

Barbara. All right.

Undershaft. For instance, whats the matter with that outpatient over there?

Barbara *(looking at Bill, whose attitude has never changed, and whose expression of brooding wrath has deepened)*. Oh, we shall cure him in no time. Just watch. *(She goes over to Bill and waits. He glances up at her and casts his eyes down again, uneasy, but grimmer than ever)*. It would be nice to just stamp on Mog Habbijam's face, wouldnt it, Bill?

Bill *(starting up from the trough in consternation)*.   It's a loy: Aw never said so. *(She shakes her head)*. Oo taold you wot was in moy mawnd?

Barbara.   Only your new friend.

Bill.   Wot new friend?

Barbara.   The devil, Bill. When he gets round people they get miserable, just like you.

Bill *(with a heartbreaking attempt at devil-may-care cheerfulness)*.   Aw aint miserable. *(He sits down again, and stretches his legs in an attempt to seem indifferent)*.

Barbara.   Well, if youre happy, why dont you look happy, as we do?

Bill *(his legs curling back in spite of him)*.   Aw'm eppy enaff, Aw tell you. Woy cawnt you lea me alown? Wot ev I dan to you? Aw aint smashed your fice, ev Aw?

Barbara *(softly: wooing his soul)*.   It's not me thats getting at you, Bill.

Bill.   Oo else is it?

Barbara.   Somebody that doesnt intend you to smash women's faces, I suppose. Somebody or something that wants to make a man of you.

Bill *(blustering)*.   Mike a menn o me! Aint Aw a menn? eh? Oo sez Aw'm not a menn?

Barbara.   Theres a man in you somewhere, I suppose. But why did he let you hit poor little Jenny Hill? That wasnt very manly of him, was it?

Bill *(tormented)*.   Ev dan wiv it, Aw tell you. Chack it. Aw'm sick o your Jenny Ill and er silly little fice.

Barbara.   Then why do you keep thinking about it? Why does it keep coming up against you in your mind? Youre not getting converted, are you?

Bill *(with conviction)*.   Not ME. Not lawkly.

Barbara.   Thats right, Bill. Hold out against it. Put out your strength. Dont lets get you cheap. Todger Fairmile said he wrestled for three nights against his salvation harder than he ever wrestled with the Jap at the music hall. He gave in to the Jap when his arm was going to break. But he didnt give in to his salvation until his heart was going to break. Perhaps youll escape that. You havnt any heart, have you?

Bill.   Wot d'ye mean? Woy aint Aw got a awt the sime as ennybody else?

Barbara.   A man with a heart wouldnt have bashed poor little Jenny's face, would he?

Bill *(almost crying)*.   Ow, will you lea me alown? Ev Aw ever offered to meddle with you, that you cam neggin and provowkin me lawk this? *(He writhes convulsively from his eyes to his toes)*.

Barbara *(with a steady soothing hand on his arm and a gentle voice that never lets him go)*.   It's your soul thats hurting you, Bill, and not me. Weve been through it all ourselves. Come with us, Bill. *(He looks wildly round)*. To brave manhood on earth and eternal glory in heaven. *(He is on the point of* *breaking down).* Come. *(A drum is heard in the shelter; and Bill, with a gasp, escapes from the spell as Barbara turns quickly. Adolphus enters from the shelter with a big drum).* Oh! there you are, Dolly. Let me introduce a new friend of mine, Mr Bill Walker. This is my bloke, Bill: Mr Cusins. *(Cusins salutes with his drumstick).*

Bill.   Gowin to merry him?

Barbara.   Yes.

Bill *(fervently).*   Gawd elp im! Gaw-aw-aw-awd elp im!

Barbara.   Why? Do you think he wont be happy with me?

Bill.   Awve aony ed to stend it for a mawnin: e'll ev to stend it for a lawftawm.

Cusins.   That is a frightful reflection, Mr Walker. But I cant tear myself away from her.

Bill.   Well, Aw ken. *(To Barbara)* Eah! do you knaow where Aw'm gowin to, and wot Aw'm gowin to do?

Barbara.   Yes: youre going to heaven; and youre coming back here before the week's out to tell me so.

Bill.   You loy. Aw'm gowin to Kennintahn, to spit in Todger Fairmawl's eye. Aw beshed Jenny Ill's fice; an nar Aw'll git me aown fice beshed and cam beck and shaow it to er. Ee'll itt me ardern Aw itt her. Thatll mike us square. *(To Adolphus)* Is thet fair or is it not? Youre a genlmn: you oughter knaow.

Barbara.   Two black eyes wont make one white one, Bill.

Bill.   Aw didnt awst you. Cawnt you never keep your mahth shat? Oy awst the genlmn.

Cusins *(reflectively).*   Yes: I think youre right, Mr Walker. Yes: I should do it. It's curious: it's exactly what an ancient Greek would have done.

Barbara.   But what good will it do?

Cusins.   Well, it will give Mr Fairmile some exercise; and it will satisfy Mr Walker's soul.

Bill.   Rot! there aint nao sach a thing as a saoul. Ah kin you tell wevver Awve a saoul or not? You never seen it.

Barbara.   Ive seen it hurting you when you went against it.

Bill *(with compressed aggravation).*   If you was maw gel and took the word aht o me mahth lawk thet, Aw'd give you sathink youd feel urtin, Aw would. *(To Adolphus)* You tike maw tip, mite. Stop er jawr; or youll doy afoah your tawm. *(With intense expression)* Wore aht: thets wot youll be: wore aht. *(He goes away through the gate).*

Cusins *(looking after him).*   I wonder!

Barbara.   Dolly! *(Indignant, in her mother's manner).*

Cusins.   Yes, my dear, it's very wearing to be in love with you. If it lasts, I quite think I shall die young.

Barbara.   Should you mind?

Cusins.   Not at all. *(He is suddenly softened, and kisses her over the drum, evidently not for the first time, as people cannot kiss over a big drum without practice. Undershaft coughs).*

Barbara.   It's all right papa, weve not forgotten you. Dolly: explain the place to papa: I havnt time. (*She goes busily into the shelter*).

Undershaft and Adolphus now have the yard to themselves. Undershaft, seated on a form, and still keenly attentive, looks hard at Adolphus. Adolphus looks hard at him.

Undershaft.   I fancy you guess something of what is in my mind, Mr Cusins. (*Cusins flourishes his drumsticks as if in the act of beating a lively rataplan, but makes no sound*). Exactly so. But suppose Barbara finds you out!

Cusins.   You know, I do not admit that I am imposing on Barbara. I am quite genuinely interested in the views of the Salvation Army. The fact is, I am a sort of collector of religions; and the curious thing is that I find I can believe them all. By the way, have you any religion?

Undershaft.   Yes.

Cusins.   Anything out of the common?

Undershaft.   Only that there are two things necessary to Salvation.

Cusins (*disappointed, but polite*).   Ah, the Church Catechism. Charles Lomax also belongs to the Established Church.

Undershaft.   The two things are—

Cusins.   Baptism and—

Undershaft.   No. Money and gunpowder.

Cusins (*surprised, but interested*).   That is the general opinion of our governing classes. The novelty is in hearing any man confess it.

Undershaft.   Just so.

Cusins.   Excuse me: is there any place in your religion for honor, justice, truth, love, mercy and so forth?

Undershaft.   Yes: they are the graces and luxuries of a rich, strong, and safe life.

Cusins.   Suppose one is forced to choose between them and money or gunpowder?

Undershaft.   Choose money and gunpowder; for without enough of both you cannot afford the others.

Cusins.   That is your religion?

Undershaft.   Yes.

The cadence of this reply makes a full close in the conversation, Cusins twists his face dubiously and contemplates Undershaft. Undershaft contemplates him.

Cusins.   Barbara wont stand that. You will have to choose between your religion and Barbara.

Undershaft.   So will you, my friend. She will find out that that drum of yours is hollow.

Cusins.   Father Undershaft: you are mistaken: I am a sincere Salvationist. You do not understand the Salvation Army. It is the army of joy, of love, of courage: it has banished the fear and remorse and despair of the old hell-ridden evangelical sects: it marches to fight the devil with trumpet and drum, with music and dancing, with banner and palm, as becomes a sally from heaven by its happy garrison. It picks the waster out of the public house and makes a man of him: it finds a worm wriggling in a back kitchen, and lo! a woman! Men and women of rank too, sons and daughters of the Highest. It takes the poor professor of Greek, the most artificial and self-suppressed of human creatures, from his meal of roots, and lets loose the rhapsodist in him; reveals the true worship of Dionysos to him; sends him down the public street drumming dithyrambs (*he plays a thundering flourish on the drum*).
Undershaft.   You will alarm the shelter.
Cusins.   Oh, they are accustomed to these sudden ecstasies. However, if the drum worries you— (*He pockets the drumsticks; unhooks the drum; and stands it on the ground opposite the gateway*).
Undershaft.   Thank you.
Cusins.   You remember what Euripides says about your money and gunpowder?
Undershaft.   No.
Cusins (*declaiming*).

> One and another
> In money and guns may outpass his brother;
> And men in their millions float and flow
> And seethe with a million hopes as leaven;
> And they win their will; or they miss their will;
> And their hopes are dead or are pined for still;
> But who'er can know
> As the long days go
> That to live is happy, has found his heaven.

My translation: what do you think of it?
Undershaft.   I think, my friend, that if you wish to know, as the long days go, that to live is happy, you must first acquire money enough for a decent life, and power enough to be your own master.
Cusins.   You are damnably discouraging. (*He resumes his declamation*).

> Is it so hard a thing to see
> That the spirit of God—whate'er it be—
> The law that abides and changes not, ages long,
> The Eternal and Nature-born: these things be strong?
> What else is Wisdom? What of Man's endeavor,
> Or God's high grace so lovely and so great?
> To stand from fear set free? to breathe and wait?

To hold a hand uplifted over Fate?
And shall not Barbara be loved for ever?

Undershaft. Euripides mentions Barbara, does he?

Cusins. It is a fair translation. The word means Loveliness.

Undershaft. May I ask—as Barbara's father—how much a year she is to be loved for ever on?

Cusins. As for Barbara's father, that is more your affair than mine. I can feed her by teaching Greek: that is about all.

Undershaft. Do you consider it a good match for her?

Cusins *(with polite obstinacy)*. Mr Undershaft: I am in many ways a weak, timid, ineffectual person; and my health is far from satisfactory. But whenever I feel that I must have anything, I get it, sooner or later. I feel that way about Barbara. I dont like marriage: I feel intensely afraid of it; and I dont know what I shall do with Barbara or what she will do with me. But I feel that I and nobody else must marry her. Please regard that as settled.—Not that I wish to be arbitrary; but why should I waste your time in discussing what is inevitable?

Undershaft. You mean that you will stick at nothing: not even the conversion of the Salvation Army to the worship of Dionysos.

Cusins. The business of the Salvation Army is to save, not to wrangle about the name of the pathfinder. Dionysos or another: what does it matter?

Undershaft *(rising and approaching him)*. Professor Cusins: you are a young man after my own heart.

Cusins. Mr Undershaft: you are, as far as I am able to gather, a most infernal old rascal; but you appeal very strongly to my sense of ironic humor.

Undershaft mutely offers his hand. They shake.

Undershaft *(suddenly concentrating himself)*. And now to business.

Cusins. Pardon me. We are discussing religion. Why go back to such an uninteresting and unimportant subject as business?

Undershaft. Religion is our business at present, because it is through religion alone that we can win Barbara.

Cusins. Have you, too, fallen in love with Barbara?

Undershaft. Yes, with a father's love.

Cusins. A father's love for a grown-up daughter is the most dangerous of all infatuations. I apologize for mentioning my own pale, coy, mistrustful fancy in the same breath with it.

Undershaft. Keep to the point. We have to win her; and we are neither of us Methodists.

Cusins. That doesnt matter. The power Barbara wields here—the power that wields Barbara herself—is not Calvinism, not Presbyterianism, not Methodism—

Undershaft. Not Greek Paganism either, eh?

Cusins. I admit that. Barbara is quite original in her religion.

Undershaft *(triumphantly).* Aha! Barbara Undershaft would be. Her inspiration comes from within herself.

Cusins. How do you suppose it got there?

Undershaft *(in towering excitement).* It is the Undershaft inheritance. I shall hand on my torch to my daughter. She shall make my converts and preach my gospel—

Cusins. What! Money and gunpowder!

Undershaft. Yes, money and gunpowder. Freedom and power. Command of life and command of death.

Cusins *(urbanely: trying to bring him down to earth).* This is extremely interesting, Mr Undershaft. Of course you know that you are mad.

Undershaft *(with redoubled force).* And you?

Cusins. Oh, mad as a hatter. You are welcome to my secret since I have discovered yours. But I am astonished. Can a madman make cannons?

Undershaft. Would anyone else than a madman make them? And now *(with surging energy)* question for question. Can a sane man translate Euripides?

Cusins. No.

Undershaft *(seizing him by the shoulder).* Can a sane woman make a man of a waster or a woman of a worm?

Cusins *(reeling before the storm).* Father Colossus—Mammoth Millionaire—

Undershaft *(pressing him).* Are there two mad people or three in this Salvation shelter today?

Cusins. You mean Barbara is as mad as we are?

Undershaft *(pushing him lightly off and resuming his equanimity suddenly and completely).* Pooh, Professor! let us call things by their proper names. I am a millionaire; you are a poet; Barbara is a savior of souls. What have we three to do with the common mob of slaves and idolators? *(He sits down again with a shrug of contempt for the mob).*

Cusins. Take care! Barbara is in love with the common people. So am I. Have you never felt the romance of that love?

Undershaft *(cold and sardonic).* Have you ever been in love with Poverty, like St Francis? Have you ever been in love with Dirt, like St Simeon! Have you ever been in love with disease and suffering, like our nurses and philanthropists? Such passions are not virtues, but the most unnatural of all the vices. This love of the common people may please an earl's granddaughter and a university professor; but I have been a common man and a poor man; and it has no romance for me. Leave it to the poor to pretend that poverty is a blessing: leave it to the coward to make a religion of his cowardice by preaching humility: we know better than that. We three must stand together above the common people: how else can we help their children to climb up beside us? Barbara must belong to us, not to the Salvation Army.

Cusins. Well, I can only say that if you think you will get her away from the Salvation Army by talking to her as you have been talking to me, you dont know Barbara.

Undershaft.   My friend: I never ask for what I can buy.

Cusins *(in a white fury).*   Do I understand you to imply that you can buy Barbara?

Undershaft.   No; but I can buy the Salvation Army.

Cusins.   Quite impossible.

Undershaft.   You shall see. All religious organizations exist by selling themselves to the rich.

Cusins.   Not the Army. That is the Church of the poor.

Undershaft.   All the more reason for buying it.

Cusins.   I dont think you quite know what the Army does for the poor.

Undershaft.   Oh yes I do. It draws their teeth: that is enough for me as a man of business.

Cusins.   Nonsense! It makes them sober—

Undershaft.   I prefer sober workmen. The profits are larger.

Cusins.   —honest—

Undershaft.   Honest workmen are the most economical.

Cusins.   —attached to their homes—

Undershaft.   So much the better: they will put up with anything sooner than change their shop.

Cusins.   —happy—

Undershaft.   An invaluable safeguard against revolution.

Cusins.   —unselfish—

Undershaft.   Indifferent to their own interests, which suits me exactly.

Cusins.   —with their thoughts on heavenly things—

Undershaft *(rising).*   And not on Trade Unionism nor Socialism. Excellent.

Cusins *(revolted).*   You really are an infernal old rascal.

Undershaft *(indicating Peter Shirley, who has just come from the shelter and strolled dejectedly down the yard between them).*   And this is an honest man!

Shirley.   Yes; and what av I got by it? *(He passes on bitterly and sits on the form, in the corner of the penthouse).*

Snobby Price, beaming sanctimoniously, and Jenny Hill, with a tambourine full of coppers, come from the shelter and go to the drum, on which Jenny begins to count the money.

Undershaft *(replying to Shirley).*   Oh, your employers must have got a good deal by it from first to last. *(He sits on the table, with one foot on the side form. Cusins, overwhelmed, sits down on the same form nearer the shelter. Barbara comes from the shelter to the middle of the yard. She is excited and a little overwrought).*

Barbara.   Weve just had a splendid experience meeting at the other gate in Cripp's lane. Ive hardly ever seen them so much moved as they were by your confession, Mr Price.

Price.   I could almost be glad of my past wickedness if I could believe that it would elp to keep hathers stright.

Barbara.   So it will, Snobby. How much, Jenny?

Jenny.   Four and tenpence, Major.

Barbara.   Oh Snobby, if you had given your poor mother just one more kick, we should have got the whole five shillings!

Price.   If she heard you say that, miss, she'd be sorry I didnt. But I'm glad. Oh what a joy it will be to her when she hears I'm saved!

Undershaft.   Shall I contribute the odd twopence, Barbara? The millionaire's mite, eh? *(He takes a couple of pennies from his pocket).*

Barbara.   How did you make that twopence?

Undershaft.   As usual. By selling cannons, torpedoes, submarines, and my new patent Grand Duke hand grenade.

Barbara.   Put it back in your pocket. You cant buy your salvation here for twopence: you must work it out.

Undershaft.   Is twopence not enough? I can afford a little more, if you press me.

Barbara.   Two million millions would not be enough. There is bad blood on your hands; and nothing but good blood can cleanse them. Money is no use. Take it away. *(She turns to Cusins).* Dolly: you must write another letter for me to the papers. *(He makes a wry face).* Yes: I know you dont like it; but it must be done. The starvation this winter is beating us: everybody is unemployed. The General says we must close this shelter if we cant get more money. I force the collections at the meetings until I am ashamed: dont I, Snobby?

Price.   It's a fair treat to see you work it, miss. The way you got them up from three-and-six to four-and-ten with that hymn, penny by penny and verse by verse, was a caution. Not a Cheap Jack on Mile End Waste could touch you at it.

Barbara.   Yes; but I wish we could do without it. I am getting at last to think more of the collection than of the people's souls. And what are those hatfuls of pence and halfpence? We want thousands! I want to convert people, not to be always begging for the Army in a way I'd die sooner than beg for myself.

Undershaft *(in profound irony).*   Genuine unselfishness is capable of anything, my dear.

Barbara *(unsuspectingly, as she turns away to take the money from the drum and put it in a cash bag she carries).*   Yes, isnt it? *(Undershaft looks sardonically at Cusins).*

Cusins *(aside to Undershaft).*   Mephistopheles! Machiavelli!

Barbara *(tears coming into her eyes as she ties the bag and pockets it).*   How are we to feed them? I cant talk religion to a man with bodily hunger in his eyes. *(Almost breaking down)* It's frightful.

Jenny *(running to her).*   Major, dear—

Barbara *(rebounding).*   No: dont comfort me. It will be all right. We shall get the money.

Undershaft.   How?

Jenny.   By praying for it, of course. Mrs Baines says she prayed for it last night; and she has never prayed for it in vain: never once. *(She goes to the gate and looks out into the street).*

Barbara *(who has dried her eyes and regained her composure).*   By the way, dad, Mrs Baines has come to march with us to our big meeting this afternoon; and she is very anxious to meet you, for some reason or other. Perhaps she'll convert you.

Undershaft.   I shall be delighted, my dear.

Jenny *(at the gate: excitedly).*   Major! Major! heres that man back again.

Barbara.   What man?

Jenny.   The man that hit me. Oh, I hope he's coming back to join us.

Bill Walker, with frost on his jacket, comes through the gate, his hands deep in his pockets and his chin sunk between his shoulders, like a cleaned-out gambler. He halts between Barbara and the drum.

Barbara.   Hullo, Bill! Back already!

Bill *(nagging at her).*   Bin talkin ever sence, ev you?

Barbara.   Pretty nearly. Well, has Todger paid you out for poor Jenny's jaw?

Bill.   Nao e aint.

Barbara.   I thought your jacket looked a bit snowy.

Bill.   Sao it is snaowy. You want to knaow where the snaow cam from, downt you?

Barbara.   Yes.

Bill.   Well, it cam from orf the grahnd in Pawkinses Corner in Kenningtahn. It got rabbed orf be maw shaoulders: see?

Barbara.   Pity you didnt rub some off with your knees, Bill! That would have done you a lot of good.

Bill *(with sour mirthless humor).*   Aw was sivin anather menn's knees at the tawm. E was kneelin on moy ed, e was.

Jenny.   Who was kneeling on your head?

Bill.   Todger was. E was pryin for me: pryin camfortable wiv me as a cawpet. Sow was Mog. Sao was the aol bloomin meetin. Mog she sez 'Ow Lawd brike is stabborn sperrit; bat downt urt is dear art.' Thet was wot she said. 'Downt urt is dear art'! An er blowk—thirteen stun four!—kneelin wiv all is wight on me. Fanny, aint it?

Jenny.   Oh no. We're so sorry, Mr Walker.

Barbara *(enjoying it frankly).*   Nonsense! of course it's funny. Served you right, Bill! You must have done something to him first.

Bill *(doggedly).*   Aw did wot Aw said Aw'd do. Aw spit in is eye. E looks ap at the skoy and sez, 'Ow that Aw should be fahnd worthy to be spit upon for the gospel's sike!' e sez; an Mog sez 'Glaory Allelloolier!'; and then e called me Braddher, an dahned me as if Aw was a kid and e was me mather worshin me a Setterda nawt. Aw ednt jast nao shaow wiv im at all. Arf the street pryed; and the tather arf larfed fit to split theirselves. *(To Barbara)* There! are you settisfawd nah?

Barbara *(her eyes dancing)*.   Wish I'd been there, Bill.

Bill.   Yus: youd a got in a hextra bit o talk on me, wouldnt you?

Jenny.   I'm so sorry, Mr Walker.

Bill *(fiercely)*.   Downt you gow bein sorry for me: youve no call. Listen eah. Aw browk your jawr.

Jenny.   No, it didnt hurt me: indeed it didnt, except for a moment. It was only that I was frightened.

Bill.   Aw downt want to be forgiven be you, or be ennybody. Wot Aw did Aw'll py for. Aw trawd to gat me aown jawr browk to settisfaw you—

Jenny *(distressed)*.   Oh no—

Bill *(impatiently)*.   Tell y' Aw did: cawnt you listen to wots bein taold you? All Aw got be it was bein mide a sawt of in the pablic street for me pines. Well, if Aw cawnt settisfaw you one wy, Aw ken anather. Listen eah! Aw ed two quid sived agen the frost; and Awve a pahnd of it left. A mite o mawn last week ed words with the judy e's gowing to merry. E give er wot-for; an e's bin fawnd fifteen bob. E ed a rawt to itt er cause they was gowin to be merrid; but Aw ednt nao rawt to itt you; sao put anather fawv bob on an call it a pahnd's worth. *(He produces a sovereign)*. Eahs the manney. Tike it; and lets ev no more o your forgivin an pryin and your Mijor jawrin me. Let wot Aw dan be dan an pide for; and let there be a end of it.

Jenny.   Oh, I couldnt take it, Mr Walker. But if you would give a shilling or two to poor Rummy Mitchens! you really did hurt her; and she's old.

Bill *(contemptuously)*.   Not lawkly. Aw'd give her anather as soon as look at er. Let her ev the lawr o me as she threatened! She aint forgiven me: not mach. Wot Aw dan to er is not on me mawnd—wot she *(indicating Barbara)* mawt call on me conscience—no more than stickin a pig. It's this Christian gime o yours that Aw wownt ev plyed agen me: this bloomin forgivin an neggin an jawrin that mikes a menn thet sore that iz lawf's a burdn to im. Aw wownt ev it, Aw tell you; sao tike your manney and stop thraowin your silly beshed fice hap agen me.

Jenny.   Major: may I take a little of it for the Army?

Barbara.   No: the Army is not to be bought. We want your soul, Bill; and we'll take nothing less.

Bill *(bitterly)*.   Aw knaow. Me an maw few shillins is not good enaff for you. Youre a earl's grendorter, you are. Nathink less than a andered pahnd for you.

Undershaft.   Come, Barbara! you could do a great deal of good with a hundred pounds. If you will set this gentleman's mind at ease by taking his pound, I will give the other ninety-nine.

Bill, dazed by such opulence, instinctively touches his cap.

Barbara.   Oh, youre too extravagant, papa. Bill offers twenty pieces of silver. All you need offer is the other ten. That will make the standard price to buy anybody who's for sale. I'm not; and the Army's not. *(To Bill)* Youll never have another quiet moment, Bill, until you come round to us. You cant stand out against your salvation.

Bill *(sullenly)*.   Aw cawnt stend aht agen music awl wrastlers and awtful tangued women. Awve offered to py. Aw can do no more. Tike it or leave it. There it is. *(He throws the sovereign on the drum, and sits down on the horsetrough. The coin fascinates Snobby Price, who takes an early opportunity of dropping his cap on it).*

Mrs Baines comes from the shelter. She is dressed as a Salvation Army Commissioner. She is an earnest looking woman of about 40, with a caressing, urgent voice, and an appealing manner.

Barbara.   This is my father, Mrs Baines. *(Undershaft comes from the table, taking his hat off with marked civility).* Try what you can do with him. He wont listen to me, because he remembers what a fool I was when I was a baby. *(She leaves them together and chats with Jenny).*

Mrs Baines.   Have you been shewn over the shelter, Mr Undershaft? You know the work we're doing, of course.

Undershaft *(very civilly)*.   The whole nation knows it, Mrs Baines.

Mrs Baines.   No, sir: the whole nation does not know it, or we should not be crippled as we are for want of money to carry our work through the length and breadth of the land. Let me tell you that there would have been rioting this winter in London but for us.

Undershaft.   You really think so?

Mrs Baines.   I know it. I remember 1886, when you rich gentlemen hardened your hearts against the cry of the poor. They broke the windows of your clubs in Pall Mall.

Undershaft *(gleaming with approval of their method)*.   And the Mansion House Fund went up next day from thirty thousand pounds to seventy-nine thousand! I remember quite well.

Mrs Baines.   Well, wont you help me to get at the people? They wont break windows then. Come here, Price. Let me shew you to this gentleman *(Price comes to be inspected)*. Do you remember the window breaking?

Price.   My ole father thought it was the revolution, maam.

Mrs Baines.   Would you break windows now?

Price.   Oh no, maam. The windows of eaven ave bin opened to me. I know now that the rich man is a sinner like myself.

Rummy *(appearing above at the loft door)*.   Snobby Price!

Snobby.   Wot is it?

Rummy.   Your mother's askin for you at the other gate in Cripp's Lane. She's heard about your confession *(Price turns pale)*.

Mrs Baines.   Go, Mr Price; and pray with her.

Jenny.   You can go through the shelter, Snobby.

Price *(to Mrs Baines).*   I couldnt face her now, maam, with all the weight of my sins fresh on me. Tell her she'll find her son at ome, waitin for her in prayer. *(He skulks off through the gate, incidentally stealing the sovereign on his way out by picking up his cap from the drum).*

Mrs Baines *(with swimming eyes).*   You see how we take the anger and the bitterness against you out of their hearts, Mr Undershaft.

Undershaft.   It is certainly most convenient and gratifying to all large employers of labor, Mrs Baines.

Mrs Baines.   Barbara: Jenny: I have good news: most wonderful news. *(Jenny runs to her).* My prayers have been answered. I told you they would, Jenny, didnt I?

Jenny.   Yes, yes.

Barbara *(moving nearer to the drum).*   Have we got money enough to keep the shelter open?

Mrs Baines.   I hope we shall have enough to keep all the shelters open. Lord Saxmundham has promised us five thousand pounds—

Barbara.   Hooray!

Jenny.   Glory!

Mrs Baines.   —if—

Barbara.   'If!' If what?

Mrs Baines.   —if five other gentlemen will give a thousand each to make it up to ten thousand.

Barbara.   Who is Lord Saxmundham? I never heard of him.

Undershaft *(who has pricked up his ears at the peer's name, and is now watching Barbara curiously).*   A new creation, my dear. You have heard of Sir Horace Bodger?

Barbara.   Bodger! Do you mean the distiller? Bodger's whisky!

Undershaft.   That is the man. He is one of the greatest of our public benefactors. He restored the cathedral at Hakington. They made him a baronet for that. He gave half a million to the funds of his party: they made him a baron for that.

Shirley.   What will they give him for the five thousand?

Undershaft.   There is nothing left to give him. So the five thousand, I should think, is to save his soul.

Mrs Baines.   Heaven grant it may! Oh Mr Undershaft, you have some very rich friends. Cant you help us towards the other five thousand? We are going to hold a great meeting this afternoon at the Assembly Hall in the Mile End Road. If I could only announce that one gentleman had come forward to support Lord Saxmundham, others would follow. Dont you know somebody? couldnt you? wouldnt you? *(her eyes fill with tears)* oh, think of those poor people, Mr Undershaft: think of how much it means to them, and how little to a great man like you.

Undershaft *(sardonically gallant)*.   Mrs Baines: you are irresistible. I cant disappoint you; and I cant deny myself the satisfaction of making Bodger pay up. You shall have your five thousand pounds.

Mrs Baines.   Thank God!

Undershaft.   You dont thank me?

Mrs Baines.   Oh sir, dont try to be cynical: dont be ashamed of being a good man. The Lord will bless you abundantly; and our prayers will be like a strong fortification round you all the days of your life. *(With a touch of caution)* You will let me have the cheque to shew at the meeting, wont you? Jenny: go in and fetch a pen and ink. *(Jenny runs to the shelter door)*.

Undershaft.   Do not disturb Miss Hill: I have a fountain pen. *(Jenny halts. He sits at the table, writes the cheque. Cusins rises to make room for him. They all watch him silently)*.

Bill *(cynically, aside to Barbara, his voice and accent horribly debased)*.   Wot prawce selvytion nah?

Barbara.   Stop. *(Undershaft stops writing: they all turn to her in surprise)*. Mrs Baines: are you really going to take this money?

Mrs Baines *(astonished)*.   Why not, dear?

Barbara.   Why not! Do you know what my father is? Have you forgotten that Lord Saxmundham is Bodger the whisky man? Do you remember how we implored the County Council to stop him from writing Bodger's Whisky in letters of fire against the sky; so that the poor drink-ruined creatures on the Embankment could not wake up from their snatches of sleep without being reminded of their deadly thirst by that wicked sky sign? Do you know that the worst thing I have had to fight here is not the devil, but Bodger, Bodger, Bodger, with his whisky, his distilleries, and his tied houses? Are you going to make our shelter another tied house for him, and ask me to keep it?

Bill.   Rotten dranken whisky it is too.

Mrs Baines.   Dear Barbara: Lord Saxmundham has a soul to be saved like any of us. If heaven has found the way to make a good use of his money, are we to set ourselves up against the answer to our prayers?

Barbara.   I know he has a soul to be saved. Let him come down here; and I'll do my best to help him to his salvation. But he wants to send his cheque down to buy us, and go on being as wicked as ever.

Undershaft *(with a reasonableness which Cusins alone perceives to be ironical)*.   My dear Barbara: alcohol is a very necessary article. It heals the sick—

Barbara.   It does nothing of the sort.

Undershaft.   Well, it assists the doctor: that is perhaps a less questionable way of putting it. It makes life bearable to millions of people who could not endure their existence if they were quite sober. It enables Parliament to do things at eleven at night that no sane person would do at eleven in the morning. Is it Bodger's fault that this inestimable gift is deplorably abused by less than one per cent of the poor? *(He turns again to the table; signs the cheque; and crosses it)*.

Mrs Baines.   Barbara: will there be less drinking or more if all those poor souls we are saving come tomorrow and find the doors of our shelters shut in their faces? Lord Saxmundham gives us the money to stop drinking—to take his own business from him.

Cusins *(impishly)*.   Pure self-sacrifice on Bodger's part, clearly! Bless dear Bodger! *(Barbara almost breaks down as Adolphus, too, fails her)*.

Undershaft *(tearing out the cheque and pocketing the book as he rises and goes past Cusins to Mrs Baines)*.   I also, Mrs Baines, may claim a little disinterestedness. Think of my business! think of the widows and orphans! the men and lads torn to pieces with shrapnel and poisoned with lyddite! *(Mrs Baines shrinks; but he goes on remorselessly)* the oceans of blood, not one drop of which is shed in a really just cause! the ravaged crops! the peaceful peasants forced, women and men, to till their fields under the fire of opposing armies on pain of starvation! the bad blood of the fierce little cowards at home who egg on others to fight for the gratification of their national vanity! All this makes money for me: I am never richer, never busier than when the papers are full of it. Well, it is your work to preach peace on earth and good will to men. *(Mrs Baines's face lights up again)*. Every convert you make is a vote against war. *(Her lips move in prayer)*. Yet I give you this money to help you to hasten my own commercial ruin. *(He gives her the cheque)*.

Cusins *(mounting the form in an ecstasy of mischief)*.   The millennium will be inaugurated by the unselfishness of Undershaft and Bodger. Oh be joyful! *(He takes the drumsticks from his pocket and flourishes them)*.

Mrs Baines *(taking the cheque)*.   The longer I live the more proof I see that there is an Infinite Goodness that turns everything to the work of salvation sooner or later. Who would have thought that any good could have come out of war and drink? And yet their profits are brought today to the feet of salvation to do its blessed work. *(She is affected to tears)*.

Jenny *(running to Mrs Baines and throwing her arms round her)*.   Oh dear! how blessed, how glorious it all is!

Cusins *(in a convulsion of irony)*.   Let us seize this unspeakable moment. Let us march to the great meeting at once. Excuse me just an instant. *(He rushes into the shelter. Jenny takes her tambourine from the drum head)*.

Mrs Baines.   Mr Undershaft: have you ever seen a thousand people fall on their knees with one impulse and pray? Come with us to the meeting. Barbara shall tell them that the Army is saved, and saved through you.

Cusins *(returning impetuously from the shelter with a flag and a trombone, and coming between Mrs Baines and Undershaft)*.   You shall carry the flag down the first street, Mrs Baines. *(He gives her the flag)*. Mr Undershaft is a gifted trombonist: he shall intone an Olympian diapason to the West Ham Salvation March. *(Aside to Undershaft, as he forces the trombone on him)* Blow, Machiavelli, blow.

Undershaft *(aside to him, as he takes the trombone)*.   The trumpet in Zion! *(Cusins rushes to the drum, which he takes up and puts on. Undershaft continues, aloud)* I will do my best. I could vamp a bass if I knew the tune.

Cusins. It is a wedding chorus from one of Donizetti's operas; but we have converted it. We convert everything to good here, including Bodger. You remember the chorus. 'For thee immense rejoicing—immenso giubilo— immenso giubilo.' *(With drum obbligato)* Rum tum ti tum tum, tum tum ti ta—

Barbara. Dolly: you are breaking my heart.

Cusins. What is a broken heart more or less here? Dionysos Undershaft has descended. I am possessed.

Mrs Baines. Come, Barbara: I must have my dear Major to carry the flag with me.

Jenny. Yes, yes, Major darling.

Cusins snatches the tambourine out of Jenny's hand and mutely offers it to Barbara.

Barbara *(coming forward a little as she puts the offer behind her with a shudder, whilst Cusins recklessly tosses the tambourine back to Jenny and goes to the gate).* I cant come.

Jenny. Not come!

Mrs Baines *(with tears in her eyes).* Barbara: do you think I am wrong to take the money?

Barbara *(impulsively going to her and kissing her).* No, no: God help you, dear, you must: you are saving the Army. Go; and may you have a great meeting!

Jenny. But arnt you coming?

Barbara. No. *(She begins taking off the silver S brooch from her collar).*

Mrs Baines. Barbara: what are you doing?

Jenny. Why are you taking your badge off? You cant be going to leave us, Major.

Barbara *(quietly).* Father: come here.

Undershaft *(coming to her).* My dear! *(Seeing that she is going to pin the badge on his collar, he retreats to the penthouse in some alarm).*

Barbara *(following him).* Dont be frightened. *(She pins the badge on and steps back towards the table, shewing him to the others).* There! It's not much for £5000, is it?

Mrs Baines. Barbara: if you wont come and pray with us, promise me you will pray for us.

Barbara. I cant pray now. Perhaps I shall never pray again.

Mrs Baines. Barbara!

Jenny. Major!

Barbara *(almost delirious).* I cant bear any more. Quick march!

Cusins *(calling to the procession in the street outside).* Off we go. Play up, there! Immenso giubilo. *(He gives the time with his drum; and the band strikes up the march, which rapidly becomes more distant as the procession moves briskly away).*

Mrs Baines.   I must go, dear. Youre overworked: you will be all right tomorrow. We'll never lose you. Now Jenny: step out with the old flag. Blood and Fire! *(She marches out through the gate with her flag).*

Jenny.   Glory Hallelujah! *(Flourishing her tambourine and marching).*

Undershaft *(to Cusins, as he marches out past him easing the slide of his trombone).*   'My ducats and my daughter'!

Cusins *(following him out).*   Money and gunpowder!

Barbara.   Drunkenness and Murder! My God: why hast thou forsaken me?

She sinks on the form with her face buried in her hands. The march passes away into silence. Bill Walker steals across to her.

Bill *(taunting).*   Wot prawce selvytion nah?

Shirley.   Dont you hit her when she's down.

Bill.   She itt me wen aw wiz dahn. Waw shouldnt Aw git a bit o me aown beck?

Barbara *(raising her head).*   I didnt take your money, Bill. *(She crosses the yard to the gate and turns her back on the two men to hide her face from them).*

Bill *(sneering after her).*   Naow, it warnt enaff for you. *(Turning to the drum, he misses the money)* Ellow! If you aint took it sammun else ez. Weres it gorn? Bly me if Jenny Ill didnt tike it arter all!

Rummy *(screaming at him from the loft).*   You lie, you dirty blackguard! Snobby Price pinched it off the drum when he took up his cap. I was up here all the time an see im do it.

Bill.   Wot! Stowl maw manney! Waw didnt you call thief on him, you silly aold macker you?

Rummy.   To serve you aht for ittin me acrost the fice. It's cost y'pahnd, that az. *(Raising a paean of squalid triumph)* I done you. I'm even with you. Uve ad it aht o y—(Bill snatches up Shirley's mug and hurls it at her. She slams the loft door and vanishes. The mug smashes against the door and falls in fragments).

Bill *(beginning to chuckle).*   Tell us, aol menn, wot o'clock this mawnin was it wen im as they call Snobby Prawce was sived?

Barbara *(turning to him more composedly, and with unspoiled sweetness).*   About half past twelve, Bill. And he pinched your pound at a quarter to two. *I* know. Well, you cant afford to lose it. I'll send it to you.

Bill *(his voice and accent suddenly improving).*   Not if Aw wiz to stawve for it. Aw aint to be bought.

Shirley.   Aint you? Youd sell yourself to the devil for a pint o beer; only there aint no devil to make the offer.

Bill *(unashamed).*   Sao Aw would, mite, and often ev, cheerful. But she cawnt baw me. *(Approaching Barbara)* You wanted maw saoul, did you? Well, you aint got it.

Barbara.   I nearly got it, Bill. But weve sold it back to you for ten thousand pounds.

Shirley.   And dear at the money!

Barbara.   No, Peter: it was worth more than money.

Bill *(salvationproof)*.   It's nao good: you cawnt get rahnd me nah. Aw downt blieve in it; and Awve seen tody that Aw was rawt. *(Going)* Sao long, aol soupkitchener! Ta, ta, Mijor Earl's Grendorter! *(Turning at the gate)* Wot Prawce selvytion nah? Snobby Prawce! Ha! ha!

Barbara *(offering her hand)*.   Goodbye, Bill.

Bill *(taken aback, half plucks his cap off; then shoves it on again defiantly)*.   Git aht. *(Barbara drops her hand, discouraged. He has a twinge of remorse)*. But thets aw rawt, you knaow. Nathink pasnl. Naow mellice. Sao long, Judy. *(He goes)*.

Barbara.   No malice. So long, Bill.

Shirley *(shaking his head)*.   You make too much of him, miss, in your innocence.

Barbara *(going to him)*.   Peter: I'm like you now. Cleaned out, and lost my job.

Shirley.   Youve youth an hope. Thats two better than me.

Barbara.   I'll get you a job, Peter. Thats hope for you: the youth will have to be enough for me. *(She counts her money)*. I have just enough left for two teas at Lockharts, a Rowton doss for you, and my tram and bus home. *(He frowns and rises with offended pride. She takes his arm)*. Dont be proud, Peter: it's sharing between friends. And promise me youll talk to me and not let me cry. *(She draws him towards the gate)*.

Shirley.   Well, I'm not accustomed to talk to the like of you—

Barbara *(urgently)*.   Yes, yes: you must talk to me. Tell me about Tom Paine's books and Bradlaugh's lectures. Come along.

Shirley.   Ah, if you would only read Tom Paine in the proper spirit, miss! *(They go out through the gate together)*.

Act Three

Next day after lunch Lady Britomart is writing in the library in Wilton Crescent. Sarah is reading in the armchair near the window. Barbara, in ordinary fashionable dress, pale and brooding, is on the settee. Charles Lomax enters. He starts on seeing Barbara fashionably attired and in low spirits.

Lomax.   Youve left off your uniform!

Barbara says nothing; but an expression of pain passes over her face.

Lady Britomart *(warning him in low tones to be careful)*.   Charles!

Lomax *(much concerned, coming behind the settee and bending sympathetically over Barbara)*.   I'm awfully sorry, Barbara. You know I helped you all I could with the concertina and so forth. *(Momentously)* Still, I have never shut my eyes to the fact that there is a certain amount of tosh about the Salvation Army. Now the claims of the Church of England—

Lady Britomart.   That's enough, Charles. Speak of something suited to your mental capacity.

Lomax.   But surely the Church of England is suited to all our capacities.

Barbara *(pressing his hand)*.   Thank you for your sympathy, Cholly. Now go and spoon with Sarah.

Lomax *(dragging a chair from the writing table and seating himself affectionately by Sarah's side)*.   How is my ownest today?

Sarah.   I wish you wouldnt tell Cholly to do things, Barbara. He always comes straight and does them. Cholly: we're going to the works this afternoon.

Lomax.   What works?

Sarah.   The cannon works.

Lomax.   What? your governor's shop!

Sarah.   Yes.

Lomax.   Oh I say!

Cusins enters in poor condition. He also starts visibly when he sees Barbara without her uniform.

Barbara.   I expected you this morning, Dolly. Didnt you guess that?

Cusins *(sitting down beside her)*.   I'm sorry. I have only just breakfasted.

Sarah.   But weve just finished lunch.

Barbara.   Have you had one of your bad nights?

Cusins.   No: I had rather a good night: in fact, one of the most remarkable nights I have ever passed.

Barbara.   The meeting?

Cusins.   No: after the meeting.

Lady Britomart.   You should have gone to bed after the meeting. What were you doing?

Cusins.   Drinking.

Lady Britomart.		Adolphus!
Sarah.		Dolly!
Barbara.		Dolly!
Lomax.		Oh I say!

Lady Britomart.   What were you drinking, may I ask?

Cusins.   A most devilish kind of Spanish burgundy, warranted free from added alcohol: a Temperance burgundy in fact. Its richness in natural alcohol made any addition superfluous.

Barbara.   Are you joking, Dolly?

Cusins *(patiently)*.   No. I have been making a night of it with the nominal head of this household: that is all.

Lady Britomart.   Andrew made you drunk!

Cusins. No: he only provided the wine. I think it was Dionysos who made me drunk. *(To Barbara)* I told you I was possessed.

Lady Britomart. Youre not sober yet. Go home to bed at once.

Cusins. I have never before ventured to reproach you, Lady Brit; but how could you marry the Prince of Darkness?

Lady Britomart. It was much more excusable to marry him than to get drunk with him. That is a new accomplishment of Andrew's, by the way. He usent to drink.

Cusins. He doesnt now. He only sat there and completed the wreck of my moral basis, the rout of my convictions, the purchase of my soul. He cares for you, Barbara. That is what makes him so dangerous to me.

Barbara. That has nothing to do with it, Dolly. There are larger loves and diviner dreams than the fireside ones. You know that, dont you?

Cusins. Yes: that is our understanding. I know it. I hold to it. Unless he can win me on that holier ground he may amuse me for a while; but he can get no deeper hold, strong as he is.

Barbara. Keep to that; and the end will be right. Now tell me what happened at the meeting?

Cusins. It was an amazing meeting. Mrs Baines almost died of emotion. Jenny Hill simply gibbered with hysteria. The Prince of Darkness played his trombone like a madman: its brazen roarings were like the laughter of the damned. 117 conversions took place then and there. They prayed with the most touching sincerity and gratitude for Bodger, and for the anonymous donor of the £5000. Your father would not let his name be given.

Lomax. That was rather fine of the old man, you know. Most chaps would have wanted the advertisement.

Cusins. He said all the charitable institutions would be down on him like kites on a battlefield if he gave his name.

Lady Britomart. Thats Andrew all over. He never does a proper thing without giving an improper reason for it.

Cusins. He convinced me that I have all my life been doing improper things for proper reasons.

Lady Britomart. Adolphus: now that Barbara has left the Salvation Army, you had better leave it too. I will not have you playing that drum in the streets.

Cusins. Your orders are already obeyed, Lady Brit.

Barbara. Dolly: were you ever really in earnest about it? Would you have joined if you had never seen me?

Cusins *(disingenuously)*. Well—er—well, possibly, as a collector of religions—

Lomax *(cunningly)*. Not as a drummer, though, you know. You are a very clearheaded brainy chap, Dolly; and it must have been apparent to you that there is a certain amount of tosh about—

Lady Britomart. Charles: if you must drivel, drivel like a grown-up man and not like a schoolboy.

Lomax *(out of countenance)*.   Well, drivel is drivel, dont you know, whatever a man's age.

Lady Britomart.   In good society in England, Charles, men drivel at all ages by repeating silly formulas with an air of wisdom. Schoolboys make their own formulas out of slang, like you. When they reach your age, and get political private secretaryships and things of that sort, they drop slang and get their formulas out of The Spectator or The Times. You had better confine yourself to The Times. You will find that there is a certain amount of tosh about The Times; but at least its language is reputable.

Lomax *(overwhelmed)*.   You are so awfully strong-minded, Lady Brit—

Lady Britomart.   Rubbish! *(Morrison comes in)*. What is it?

Morrison.   If you please, my lady, Mr Undershaft has just drove up to the door.

Lady Britomart.   Well, let him in. *(Morrison hesitates)*. Whats the matter with you?

Morrison.   Shall I announce him, my lady; or is he at home here, so to speak, my lady?

Lady Britomart.   Announce him.

Morrison.   Thank you, my lady. You wont mind my asking, I hope. The occasion is in a manner of speaking new to me.

Lady Britomart.   Quite right. Go and let him in.

Morrison.   Thank you, my lady. *(He withdraws)*.

Lady Britomart.   Children: go and get ready. *(Sarah and Barbara go upstairs for their out-of-door wraps)*. Charles: go and tell Stephen to come down here in five minutes: you will find him in the drawing room. *(Charles goes)*. Adolphus: tell them to send round the carriage in about fifteen minutes. *(Adolphus goes)*.

Morrison *(at the door)*.   Mr Undershaft.

Undershaft comes in. Morrison goes out.

Undershaft.   Alone! How fortunate!

Lady Britomart *(rising)*.   Dont be sentimental, Andrew. Sit down. *(She sits on the settee: he sits beside her, on her left. She comes to the point before he has time to breathe)*. Sarah must have £800 a year until Charles Lomax comes into his property. Barbara will need more, and need it permanently, because Adolphus hasnt any property.

Undershaft *(resignedly)*.   Yes, my dear: I will see to it. Anything else? for yourself, for instance?

Lady Britomart.   I want to talk to you about Stephen.

Undershaft *(rather wearily)*.   Dont, my dear. Stephen doesnt interest me.

Lady Britomart.   He does interest me. He is our son.

Undershaft.   Do you really think so? He has induced us to bring him into the world; but he chose his parents very incongruously, I think. I see nothing of myself in him, and less of you.

Lady Britomart.   Andrew: Stephen is an excellent son, and a most steady, capable, high-minded young man. You are simply trying to find an excuse for disinheriting him.

Undershaft.   My dear Biddy: the Undershaft tradition disinherits him. It would be dishonest of me to leave the cannon foundry to my son.

Lady Britomart.   It would be most unnatural and improper of you to leave it to anyone else, Andrew. Do you suppose this wicked and immoral tradition can be kept up for ever? Do you pretend that Stephen could not carry on the foundry just as well as the other sons of the big business houses?

Undershaft.   Yes: he could learn the office routine without understanding the business, like all the other sons; and the firm would go on by its own momentum until the real Undershaft—probably an Italian or a German— would invent a new method and cut him out.

Lady Britomart.   There is nothing that any Italian or German could do that Stephen could not do. And Stephen at least has breeding.

Undershaft.   The son of a foundling! Nonsense!

Lady Britomart.   My son, Andrew! And even you may have good blood in your veins for all you know.

Undershaft.   True. Probably I have. That is another argument in favour of a foundling.

Lady Britomart.   Andrew: dont be aggravating. And dont be wicked. At present you are both.

Undershaft.   This conversation is part of the Undershaft tradition, Biddy. Every Undershaft's wife has treated him to it ever since the house was founded. It is a mere waste of breath. If the tradition be ever broken it will be for an abler man than Stephen.

Lady Britomart *(pouting)*.   Then go away.

Undershaft *(deprecatory)*.   Go away!

Lady Britomart.   Yes: go away. If you will do nothing for Stephen, you are not wanted here. Go to your foundling, whoever he is; and look after him.

Undershaft.   The fact is, Biddy—

Lady Britomart.   Dont call me Biddy. I dont call you Andy.

Undershaft.   I will not call my wife Britomart: it is not good sense. Seriously, my love, the Undershaft tradition has landed me in a difficulty. I am getting on in years; and my partner Lazarus has at last made a stand and insisted that the succession must be settled one way or the other; and of course he is quite right. You see, I havent found a fit successor yet.

Lady Britomart *(obstinately)*.   There is Stephen.

Undershaft.   Thats just it: all the foundlings I can find are exactly like Stephen.

Lady Britomart.   Andrew!!

Undershaft.   I want a man with no relations and no schooling: that is, a man who would be out of the running altogether if he were not a strong man. And I cant find him. Every blessed foundling nowadays is snapped up in his infancy by Barnardo homes, or School Board officers, or Boards of Guardians; and if he shews the least ability he is fastened on by schoolmasters; trained to win scholarships like a racehorse; crammed with secondhand ideas; drilled and disciplined in docility and what they call good taste; and lamed for life so that he is fit for nothing but teaching. If you want to keep the foundry in the family, you had better find an eligible foundling and marry him to Barbara.

Lady Britomart.   Ah! Barbara! Your pet! You would sacrifice Stephen to Barbara.

Undershaft.   Cheerfully. And you, my dear, would boil Barbara to make soup for Stephen.

Lady Britomart.   Andrew: this is not a question of our likings and dislikings: it is a question of duty. It is your duty to make Stephen your successor.

Undershaft.   Just as much as it is your duty to submit to your husband. Come, Biddy! these tricks of the governing class are of no use with me. I am one of the governing class myself; and it is a waste of time giving tracts to a missionary. I have the power in this matter; and I am not to be humbugged into using it for your purposes.

Lady Britomart.   Andrew: you can talk my head off; but you cant change wrong into right. And your tie is all on one side. Put it straight.

Undershaft *(disconcerted)*.   It wont stay unless it's pinned—*(He fumbles at it with childish grimaces)*.

Stephen comes in.

Stephen *(at the door)*.   I beg your pardon *(about to retire)*.

Lady Britomart.   No: come in, Stephen. *(Stephen comes forward to his mother's writing table)*.

Undershaft *(not very cordially)*.   Good afternoon.

Stephen *(coldly)*.   Good afternoon.

Undershaft *(to Lady Britomart)*.   He knows all about the tradition, I suppose?

Lady Britomart.   Yes. *(To Stephen)* It is what I told you last night, Stephen.

Undershaft *(sulkily)*.   I understand you want to come into the cannon business.

Stephen.   *I* go into trade! Certainly not.

Undershaft *(opening his eyes, greatly eased in mind and manner)*.   Oh! in that case—

Lady Britomart.   Cannons are not trade, Stephen. They are enterprise.

Stephen.   I have no intention of becoming a man of business in any sense. I have no capacity for business and no taste for it. I intend to devote myself to politics.

Undershaft *(rising)*.   My dear boy: this is an immense relief to me. And I trust it may prove an equally good thing for the country. I was afraid you would consider yourself disparaged and slighted. *(He moves towards Stephen as if to shake hands with him)*.

Lady Britomart *(rising and interposing)*.   Stephen: I cannot allow you to throw away an enormous property like this.

Stephen (*stiffly*).   Mother: there must be an end of treating me as a child, if you please. (*Lady Britomart recoils, deeply wounded by his tone*). Until last night I did not take your attitude seriously, because I did not think you meant it seriously. But I find now that you left me in the dark as to matters which you should have explained to me years ago. I am extremely hurt and offended. Any further discussion of my intentions had better take place with my father, as between one man and another.

Lady Britomart.   Stephen! (*She sits down again, her eyes filling with tears*).

Undershaft (*with grave compassion*).   You see, my dear, it is only the big men who can be treated as children.

Stephen.   I am sorry, mother, that you have forced me—

Undershaft (*stopping him*).   Yes, yes, yes, yes: thats all right, Stephen. She wont interfere with you any more: your independence is achieved: you have won your latchkey. Dont rub it in; and above all, dont apologize. (*He resumes his seat*). Now what about your future, as between one man and another—I beg your pardon, Biddy: as between two men and a woman.

Lady Britomart (*who has pulled herself together strongly*).   I quite understand, Stephen. By all means go your own way if you feel strong enough. (*Stephen sits down magisterially in the chair at the writing table with an air of affirming his majority*).

Undershaft.   It is settled that you do not ask for the succession to the cannon business.

Stephen.   I hope it is settled that I repudiate the cannon business.

Undershaft.   Come, come! dont be so devilishly sulky: it's boyish. Freedom should be generous. Besides, I owe you a fair start in life in exchange for disinheriting you. You cant become prime minister all at once. Havnt you a turn for something? What about literature, art, and so forth?

Stephen.   I have nothing of the artist about me, either in faculty or character, thank Heaven!

Undershaft.   A philosopher, perhaps? Eh?

Stephen.   I make no such ridiculous pretension.

Undershaft.   Just so. Well, there is the army, the navy, the Church, the Bar. The Bar requires some ability. What about the Bar?

Stephen.   I have not studied law. And I am afraid I have not the necessary push—I believe that is the name barristers give to their vulgarity—for success in pleading.

Undershaft.   Rather a difficult case, Stephen. Hardly anything left but the stage, is there? (*Stephen makes an impatient movement*). Well, come! is there anything you know or care for?

Stephen (*rising and looking at him steadily*).   I know the difference between right and wrong.

Undershaft (*hugely tickled*).   You dont say so! What! no capacity for business, no knowledge of law, no sympathy with art, no pretension to philosophy; only a simple knowledge of the secret that has puzzled all the philosophers, baffled all the lawyers, muddled all the men of business, and ruined most of the artists: the secret of right and wrong. Why, man, youre a genius, a master of masters, a god! At twenty-four, too!

Stephen *(keeping his temper with difficulty)*. You are pleased to be facetious. I pretend to be nothing more than any honorable English gentleman claims as his birthright. *(He sits down angrily)*.

Undershaft. Oh, thats everybody's birthright. Look at poor little Jenny Hill, the Salvation lassie! she would think you were laughing at her if you asked her to stand up in the street and teach grammar or geography or mathematics or even drawing room dancing; but it never occurs to her to doubt that she can teach morals and religion. You are all alike, you respectable people. You cant tell me the bursting strain of a ten-inch gun, which is a very simple matter; but you all think you can tell me the bursting strain of a man under temptation. You darent handle high explosives; but youre all ready to handle honesty and truth and justice and the whole duty of man, and kill one another at that game. What a country! What a world!

Lady Britomart *(uneasily)*. What do you think he had better do, Andrew?

Undershaft. Oh, just what he wants to do. He knows nothing and he thinks he knows everything. That points clearly to a political career. Get him a private secretaryship to someone who can get him an Under Secretaryship; and then leave him alone. He will find his natural and proper place in the end on the Treasury Bench.

Stephen *(springing up again)*. I am sorry, sir, that you force me to forget the respect due to you as my father. I am an Englishman and I will not hear the Government of my country insulted. *(He thrusts his hands in his pockets, and walks angrily across to the window)*.

Undershaft *(with a touch of brutality)*. The government of your country! I am the government of your country: I, and Lazarus. Do you suppose that you and half a dozen amateurs like you, sitting in a row in that foolish gabble shop, can govern Undershaft and Lazarus? No, my friend: you will do what pays us. You will make war when it suits us, and keep peace when it doesnt. You will find out that trade requires certain measures when we have decided on those measures. When I want anything to keep my dividends up, you will discover that my want is a national need. When other people want something to keep my dividends down, you will call out the police and military. And in return you shall have the support and applause of my newspapers, and the delight of imagining that you are a great statesman. Government of your country! Be off with you, my boy, and play with your caucuses and leading articles and historic parties and great leaders and burning questions and the rest of your toys. *I* am going back to my counting-house to pay the piper and call the tune.

Stephen *(actually smiling, and putting his hand on his father's shoulder with indulgent patronage)*. Really, my dear father, it is impossible to be angry with you. You dont know how absurd all this sounds to me. You are very properly proud of having been industrious enough to make money; and it is greatly to your credit that you have made so much of it. But it has kept you in circles where you are valued for your money and deferred to for it, instead of in the doubtless very old-fashioned and behind-the-times public school and university where I formed my habits of mind. It is natural for you to think that money governs England; but you must allow me to think I know better.

Undershaft.   And what does govern England, pray?

Stephen.   Character, father, character.

Undershaft.   Whose character? Yours or mine?

Stephen.   Neither yours nor mine, father, but the best elements in the English national character.

Undershaft.   Stephen: Ive found your profession for you. Youre a born journalist. I'll start you with a high-toned weekly review. There!

Before Stephen can reply Sarah, Barbara, Lomax, and Cusins come in ready for walking. Barbara crosses the room to the window and looks out. Cusins drifts amiably to the armchair. Lomax remains near the door, whilst Sarah comes to her mother.

Stephen goes to the smaller writing table and busies himself with his letters.

Sarah.   Go and get ready, mamma: the carriage is waiting. *(Lady Britomart leaves the room).*

Undershaft *(to Sarah).*   Good day, my dear. Good afternoon, Mr Lomax.

Lomax *(vaguely).*   Ahdedoo.

Undershaft *(to Cusins).*   Quite well after last night, Euripides, eh?

Cusins.   As well as can be expected.

Undershaft.   Thats right. *(To Barbara)* So you are coming to see my death and devastation factory, Barbara?

Barbara *(at the window).*   You came yesterday to see my salvation factory. I promised you a return visit.

Lomax *(coming forward between Sarah and Undershaft).*   Youll find it awfully interesting. Ive been through the Woolwich Arsenal; and it gives you a ripping feeling of security, you know, to think of the lot of beggars we could kill if it came to fighting. *(To Undershaft, with sudden solemnity)* Still, it must be rather an awful reflection for you, from the religious point of view as it were. Youre getting on, you know, and all that.

Sarah.   You dont mind Cholly's imbecility, papa, do you?

Lomax *(much taken aback).*   Oh I say!

Undershaft.   Mr Lomax looks at the matter in a very proper spirit, my dear.

Lomax.   Just so. Thats all I meant, I assure you.

Sarah.   Are you coming, Stephen?

Stephen.   Well, I am rather busy—er—*(Magnanimously)* Oh well, yes: I'll come. That is, if there is room for me.

Undershaft.   I can take two with me in a little motor I am experimenting with for field use. You wont mind its being rather unfashionable. It's not painted yet; but it's bullet proof.

Lomax (*appalled at the prospect of confronting Wilton Crescent in an unpainted motor*). Oh I say!

Sarah. The carriage for me, thank you. Barbara doesnt mind what she's seen in.

Lomax. I say, Dolly, old chap: do you really mind the car being a guy? Because of course if you do I'll go in it. Still—

Cusins. I prefer it.

Lomax. Thanks awfully, old man. Come, my ownest. (*He hurries out to secure his seat in the carriage. Sarah follows him*).

Cusins (*moodily walking across to Lady Britomart's writing table*). Why are we two coming to this Works Department of Hell? that is what I ask myself.

Barbara. I have always thought of it as a sort of pit where lost creatures with blackened faces stirred up smoky fires and were driven and tormented by my father. Is it like that, dad?

Undershaft (*scandalized*). My dear! It is a spotlessly clean and beautiful hill-side town.

Cusins. With a Methodist chapel? Oh do say theres a Methodist chapel.

Undershaft. There are two: a Primitive one and a sophisticated one. There is even an Ethical Society; but it is not much patronized, as my men are all strongly religious. In the High Explosives Sheds they object to the presence of Agnostics as unsafe.

Cusins. And yet they dont object to you!

Barbara. Do they obey all your orders?

Undershaft. I never give them any orders. When I speak to one of them it is 'Well, Jones, is the baby doing well? and has Mrs Jones made a good recovery?' 'Nicely, thank you, sir.' And thats all.

Cusins. But Jones has to be kept in order. How do you maintain discipline among your men?

Undershaft. I dont. They do. You see, the one thing Jones wont stand is any rebellion from the man under him, or any assertion of social equality between the wife of the man with 4 shillings a week less than himself, and Mrs Jones! Of course they all rebel against me, theoretically. Practically, every man of them keeps the man just below him in his place. I never meddle with them. I never bully them. I dont even bully Lazarus. I say that certain things are to be done; but I dont order anybody to do them. I dont say, mind you, that there is no ordering about and snubbing and even bullying. The men snub the boys and order them about; the carmen snub the sweepers; the artisans snub the unskilled laborers; the foremen drive and bully both the laborers and artisans; the assistant engineers find fault with the foremen; the chief engineers drop on the assistants; the departmental managers worry the chiefs; and the clerks have tall hats and hymnbooks and keep up the social tone by refusing to associate on equal terms with anybody. The result is a colossal profit, which comes to me.

Cusins (*revolted*). You really are a—well, what I was saying yesterday.

Barbara. What was he saying yesterday?

Undershaft.   Never mind, my dear. He thinks I have made you unhappy. Have I?

Barbara.   Do you think I can be happy in this vulgar silly dress? I! who have worn the uniform. Do you understand what you have done to me? Yesterday I had a man's soul in my hand. I set him in the way of life with his face to salvation. But when we took your money he turned back to drunkenness and derision. (*With intense conviction*) I will never forgive you that. If I had a child, and you destroyed its body with your explosives—if you murdered Dolly with your horrible guns—I could forgive you if my forgiveness would open the gates of heaven to you. But to take a human soul from me, and turn it into the soul of a wolf! that is worse than any murder.

Undershaft.   Does my daughter despair so easily? Can you strike a man to the heart and leave no mark on him?

Barbara (*her face lighting up*).   Oh, you are right: he can never be lost now: where was my faith?

Cusins.   Oh, clever clever devil!

Barbara.   You may be a devil; but God speaks through you sometimes. (*She takes her father's hands and kisses them*). You have given me back my happiness: I feel it deep down now, though my spirit is troubled.

Undershaft.   You have learnt something. That always feels at first as if you had lost something.

Barbara.   Well, take me to the factory of death; and let me learn something more. There must be some truth or other behind all this frightful irony. Come, Dolly. (*She goes out*).

Cusins.   My guardian angel! (*To Undershaft*) Avaunt! (*He follows Barbara*).

Stephen (*quietly, at the writing table*).   You must not mind Cusins, father. He is a very amiable good fellow; but he is a Greek scholar and naturally a little eccentric.

Undershaft.   Ah, quite so. Thank you, Stephen. Thank you. (*He goes out*).

Stephen smiles patronizingly; buttons his coat responsibly; and crosses the room to the door. Lady Britomart, dressed for out-of-doors, opens it before he reaches it. She looks round for others; looks at Stephen; and turns to go without a word.

Stephen (*embarrassed*).   Mother—

Lady Britomart.   Dont be apologetic, Stephen. And dont forget that you have outgrown your mother. (*She goes out*).

Perivale St Andrews lies between two Middlesex hills, half climbing the northern one. It is an almost smokeless town of white walls, roofs of narrow green slates or red tiles, tall trees, domes, campaniles, and slender chimney shafts, beautifully situated and beautiful in itself. The best view of it is obtained from the crest of a slope about half a mile to the east, where the high explosives are dealt with. The foundry lies hidden in the depths between, the tops of its chimneys sprouting like huge skittles into the middle distance. Across the crest runs an emplacement of concrete, with a firestep, and a parapet which suggests a fortification, because there is a huge cannon of the obsolete Woolwich Infant pattern peering across it at the town. The cannon is mounted on an experimental gun carriage: possibly the original model of the Undershaft disappearing rampart gun alluded to by Stephen. The firestep, being a convenient place to sit, is furnished here and there with straw disc cushions; and at one place there is the additional luxury of a fur rug.

Barbara is standing on the firestep, looking over the parapet towards the town. On her right is the cannon; on her left the end of a shed raised on piles, with a ladder of three or four steps up to the door, which opens outwards and has a little wooden landing at the threshold, with a fire bucket in the corner of the landing. Several dummy soldiers more or less mutilated, with straw protruding from their gashes, have been shoved out of the way under the landing. A few others are nearly upright against the shed; and one has fallen forward and lies, like a grotesque corpse, on the emplacement. The parapet stops short of the shed, leaving a gap which is the beginning of the path down the hill through the foundry to the town. The rug is on the firestep near this gap. Down on the emplacement behind the cannon is a trolley carrying a huge conical bombshell with a red band painted on it. Further to the right is the door of an office, which, like the sheds, is of the lightest possible construction.

Cusins arrives by the path from the town.

Barbara.   Well?

Cusins.   Not a ray of hope. Everything perfect! wonderful! real! It only needs a cathedral to be a heavenly city instead of a hellish one.

Barbara.   Have you found out whether they have done anything for old Peter Shirley?

Cusins.   They have found him a job as gatekeeper and timekeeper. He's frightfully miserable. He calls the timekeeping brainwork, and says he isnt used to it; and his gate lodge is so splendid that he's ashamed to use the rooms, and skulks in the scullery.

Barbara.   Poor Peter!

Stephen arrives from town. He carries a fieldglass.

Stephen (*enthusiastically*).   Have you two seen the place? Why did you leave us?

Cusins.   I wanted to see everything I was not intended to see; and Barbara wanted to make the men talk.

Stephen.   Have you found anything discreditable?

Cusins.   No. They call him Dandy Andy and are proud of his being a cunning old rascal; but it's all horribly, frightfully, immorally, unanswerably perfect.

Sarah arrives.

Sarah.   Heavens! what a place! *(She crosses to the trolley).* Did you see the nursing home!? *(She sits down on the shell).*

Stephen.   Did you see the libraries and schools!?

Sarah.   Did you see the ball room and the banqueting chamber in the Town Hall!?

Stephen.   Have you gone into the insurance fund, the pension fund, the building society, the various applications of cooperation!?

Undershaft comes from the office, with a sheaf of telegrams in his hand.

Undershaft.   Well, have you seen everything? I'm sorry I was called away. *(Indicating the telegrams)* Good news from Manchuria.

Stephen.   Another Japanese victory?

Undershaft.   Oh, I dont know. Which side wins does not concern us here. No: the good news is that the aerial battleship is a tremendous success. At the first trial it has wiped out a fort with three hundred soldiers in it.

Cusins *(from the platform).*   Dummy soldiers?

Undershaft *(striding across to Stephen and kicking the prostrate dummy brutally out of his way).*   No: the real thing.

Cusins and Barbara exchange glances. Then Cusins sits on the step and buries his face in his hands. Barbara gravely lays her hand on his shoulder. He looks up at her in whimsical desperation.

Undershaft.   Well, Stephen, what do you think of the place?

Stephen.   Oh, magnificent. A perfect triumph of modern industry. Frankly, my dear father, I have been a fool: I had no idea of what it all meant: of the wonderful forethought, the power of organization, the administrative capacity, the financial genius, the colossal capital it represents. I have been repeating to myself as I came through your streets 'Peace hath her victories no less renowned than War.' I have only one misgiving about it all.

Undershaft.   Out with it.

Stephen.   Well, I cannot help thinking that all this provision for every want of your workmen may sap their independence and weaken their sense of responsibility. And greatly as we enjoyed our tea at that splendid restaurant— how they gave us all that luxury and cake and jam and cream for threepence I really cannot imagine!—still you must remember that restaurants break up home life. Look at the continent, for instance! Are you sure so much pampering is really good for the men's characters?

Undershaft.   Well you see, my dear boy, when you are organizing civilization you have to make up your mind whether trouble and anxiety are good things or not. If you decide that they are, then, I take it, you simply dont organize civilization; and there you are, with trouble and anxiety enough to make us all angels! But if you decide the other way, you may as well go through with it. However, Stephen, our characters are safe here. A sufficient dose of anxiety is always provided by the fact that we may be blown to smithereens at any moment.

Sarah.   By the way, papa, where do you make the explosives?

Undershaft.   In separate little sheds, like that one. When one of them blows up, it costs very little; and only the people quite close to it are killed.

Stephen, who is quite close to it, looks at it rather scaredly, and moves away quickly to the cannon. At the same moment the door of the shed is thrown abruptly open; and a foreman in overalls and list slippers comes out on the little landing and holds the door for Lomax, who appears in the doorway.

Lomax *(with studied coolness)*.   My good fellow: you neednt get into a state of nerves. Nothing's going to happen to you; and I suppose it wouldnt be the end of the world if anything did. A little bit of British pluck is what you want, old chap. *(He descends and strolls across to Sarah)*.

Undershaft *(to the foreman)*.   Anything wrong, Bilton?

Bilton *(with ironic calm)*.   Gentleman walked into the high explosives shed and lit a cigaret, sir: thats all.

Undershaft.   Ah, quite so. *(Going over to Lomax)* Do you happen to remember what you did with the match?

Lomax.   Oh come! I'm not a fool. I took jolly good care to blow it out before I chucked it away.

Bilton.   The top of it was red hot inside, sir.

Lomax.   Well, suppose it was! I didn't chuck it into any of your messes.

Undershaft.   Think no more of it, Mr Lomax. By the way, would you mind lending me your matches.

Lomax *(offering his box)*.   Certainly.

Undershaft.   Thanks. *(He pockets the matches)*.

Lomax *(lecturing to the company generally)*.   You know, these high explosives dont go off like gunpowder, except when theyre in a gun. When theyre spread loose, you can put a match to them without the least risk: they just burn quietly like a bit of paper. *(Warming to the scientific interest of the subject)* Did you know that, Undershaft? Have you ever tried?

Undershaft.   Not on a large scale, Mr Lomax. Bilton will give you a sample of gun cotton when you are leaving if you ask him. You can experiment with it at home. *(Bilton looks puzzled)*.

Sarah.   Bilton will do nothing of the sort, papa. I suppose it's your business to blow up the Russians and Japs; but you might really stop short of blowing up poor Cholly. *(Bilton gives it up and retires into the shed)*.

Lomax.   My ownest, there is no danger. *(He sits beside her on the shell)*.

Lady Britomart arrives from the town with a bouquet.

Lady Britomart *(impetuously)*.   Andrew: you shouldnt have let me see this place.

Undershaft.   Why, my dear?

Lady Britomart.   Never mind why: you shouldnt have: thats all. To think of all that *(indicating the town)* being yours! and that you have kept it to yourself all these years!

Undershaft.   It does not belong to me. I belong to it. It is the Undershaft inheritance.

Lady Britomart.   It is not. Your ridiculous cannons and that noisy banging foundry may be the Undershaft inheritance; but all that plate and linen, all that furniture and those houses and orchards and gardens belong to us. They belong to me: they are not a man's business. I wont give them up. You must be out of your senses to throw them all away; and if you persist in such folly, I will call in a doctor.

Undershaft *(stooping to smell the bouquet)*.   Where did you get the flowers, my dear?

Lady Britomart.   Your men presented them to me in your William Morris[3] Labor Church.

Cusins.   Oh! It needed only that. A Labor Church! *(He mounts the firestep distractedly, and leans with his elbows on the parapet, turning his back to them)*.

Lady Britomart.   Yes, with Morris's words in mosaic letters ten feet high round the dome. NO MAN IS GOOD ENOUGH TO BE ANOTHER MAN'S MASTER. The cynicism of it!

Undershaft.   It shocked the men at first, I am afraid. But now they take no more notice of it than of the ten commandments in church.

Lady Britomart.   Andrew: you are trying to put me off the subject of the inheritance by profane jokes. Well, you shant. I dont ask it any longer for Stephen: he has inherited far too much of your perversity to be fit for it. But Barbara has rights as well as Stephen. Why should not Adolphus succeed to the inheritance? I could manage the town for him; and he can look after the cannons, if they are really necessary.

Undershaft.   I should ask nothing better if Adolphus were a foundling. He is exactly the sort of new blood that is wanted in English business. But he's not a foundling; and theres an end of it. *(He makes for the office door)*.

Cusins *(turning to them)*.   Not quite. *(They all turn and stare at him)*. I think—Mind! I am not committing myself in any way as to my future course—but I think the foundling difficulty can be got over. *(He jumps down to the emplacement)*.

Undershaft *(coming back to him)*.   What do you mean?

Cusins.   Well, I have something to say which is in the nature of a confession.

Sarah.
Lady Britomart. } Confession!
Barbara.
Stephen.

Lomax.   Oh I say!

Cusins.   Yes, a confession. Listen, all. Until I met Barbara I thought myself

---

[3] William Morris (1834–1896) was an English poet, artist, craftsman, and socialist.

in the main an honorable, truthful man, because I wanted the approval of my conscience more than I wanted anything else. But the moment I saw Barbara, I wanted her far more than the approval of my conscience.

Lady Britomart.   Adolphus!

Cusins.   It is true. You accused me yourself, Lady Brit, of joining the Army to worship Barbara; and so I did. She bought my soul like a flower at a street corner; but she bought it for herself.

Undershaft.   What! Not for Dionysos or another?

Cusins.   Dionysos and all the others are in herself. I adored what was divine in her, and was therefore a true worshipper. But I was romantic about her too. I thought she was a woman of the people, and that a marriage with a professor of Greek would be far beyond the wildest social ambitions of her rank.

Lady Britomart.   Adolphus!!

Lomax.   Oh I say!!!

Cusins.   When I learnt the horrible truth—

Lady Britomart.   What do you mean by the horrible truth, pray?

Cusins.   That she was enormously rich; that her grandfather was an earl; that her father was the Prince of Darkness—

Undershaft.   Chut!

Cusins.   —and that I was only an adventurer trying to catch a rich wife, then I stooped to deceive her about my birth.

Barbara (*rising*).   Dolly!

Lady Britomart.   Your birth! Now Adolphus, dont dare to make up a wicked story for the sake of these wretched cannons. Remember: I have seen photographs of your parents; and the Agent General for South Western Australia knows them personally and has assured me that they are most respectable married people.

Cusins.   So they are in Australia; but here they are outcasts. Their marriage is legal in Australia, but not in England. My mother is my father's deceased wife's sister; and in this island I am consequently a foundling. (*Sensation*).

Barbara.   Silly! (*She climbs to the cannon, and leans, listening, in the angle it makes with the parapet*).

Cusins.   Is the subterfuge good enough, Machiavelli?

Undershaft (*thoughtfully*).   Biddy: this may be a way out of the difficulty.

Lady Britomart.   Stuff! A man cant make cannons any the better for being his own cousin instead of his proper self. (*She sits down on the rug with a bounce that expresses her downright contempt for their casuistry*).

Undershaft (*to Cusins*).   You are an educated man. That is against the tradition.

Cusins.   Once in ten thousand times it happens that the schoolboy is a born master of what they try to teach him. Greek has not destroyed my mind: it has nourished it. Besides, I did not learn it at an English public school.

Undershaft.   Hm! Well, I cannot afford to be too particular: you have cornered the foundling market. Let it pass. You are eligible, Euripides: you are eligible.

Barbara.   Dolly: yesterday morning, when Stephen told us all about the tradition, you became very silent; and you have been strange and excited ever since. Were you thinking of your birth then?

Cusins.   When the finger of Destiny suddenly points at a man in the middle of his breakfast, it makes him thoughtful.

Undershaft.   Aha! You have had your eye on the business, my young friend, have you?

Cusins.   Take care! There is an abyss of moral horror between me and your accursed aerial battleships.

Undershaft.   Never mind the abyss for the present. Let us settle the practical details and leave your final decision open. You know that you will have to change your name. Do you object to that?

Cusins.   Would any man named Adolphus—any man called Dolly!—object to be called something else?

Undershaft.   Good. Now, as to money! I propose to treat you handsomely from the beginning. You shall start at a thousand a year.

Cusins (*with sudden heat, his spectacles twinkling with mischief*).   A thousand! You dare offer a miserable thousand to the son-in-law of a millionaire! No, by Heavens, Machiavelli! you shall not cheat me. You cannot do without me; and I can do without you. I must have two thousand five hundred a year for two years. At the end of that time, if I am a failure, I go. But if I am a success, and stay on, you must give me the other five thousand.

Undershaft.   What other five thousand?

Cusins.   To make the two years up to five thousand a year. The two thousand five hundred is only half pay in case I should turn out a failure. The third year I must have ten per cent on the profits.

Undershaft (*taken aback*).   Ten per cent! Why, man, do you know what my profits are?

Cusins.   Enormous, I hope: otherwise I shall require twenty-five per cent.

Undershaft.   But, Mr Cusins, this is a serious matter of business. You are not bringing any capital into the concern.

Cusins.   What! no capital! Is my mastery of Greek no capital? Is my access to the subtlest thought, the loftiest poetry yet attained by humanity, no capital? My character! my intellect! my life! my career! what Barbara calls my soul! are these no capital? Say another word; and I double my salary.

Undershaft.   Be reasonable—

Cusins (*peremptorily*).   Mr Undershaft: you have my terms. Take them or leave them.

Undershaft (*recovering himself*).   Very well. I note your terms; and I offer you half.

Cusins (*disgusted*).   Half!

Undershaft (*firmly*).   Half.

Cusins.   You call yourself a gentleman; and you offer me half!!

Undershaft.   I do not call myself a gentleman; but I offer you half.

Cusins.   This to your future partner! your successor! your son-in-law!

Barbara.   You are selling your own soul, Dolly, not mine. Leave me out of the bargain, please.

Undershaft.   Come! I will go a step further for Barbara's sake. I will give you three fifths; but that is my last word.

Cusins.   Done!

Lomax.   Done in the eye! Why, *I* get only eight hundred, you know.

Cusins.   By the way, Mac, I am a classical scholar, not an arithmetical one. Is three fifths more than half or less?

Undershaft.   More, of course.

Cusins.   I would have taken two hundred and fifty. How you can succeed in business when you are willing to pay all that money to a University don who is obviously not worth a junior clerk's wages!—well! What will Lazarus say?

Undershaft.   Lazarus is a gentle romantic Jew who cares for nothing but string quartets and stalls at fashionable theatres. He will be blamed for your rapacity in money matters, poor fellow! as he has hitherto been blamed for mine. You are a shark of the first order, Euripides. So much the better for the firm!

Barbara.   Is the bargain closed, Dolly? Does your soul belong to him now?

Cusins.   No: the price is settled: that is all. The real tug of war is still to come. What about the moral question?

Lady Britomart.   There is no moral question in the matter at all, Adolphus. You must simply sell cannons and weapons to people whose cause is right and just, and refuse them to foreigners and criminals.

Undershaft *(determinedly)*.   No: none of that. You must keep the true faith of an Armorer, or you dont come in here.

Cusins.   What on earth is the true faith of an Armorer?

Undershaft.   To give arms to all men who offer an honest price for them, without respect of persons or principles: to aristocrat and republican, to Nihilist and Tsar, to Capitalist and Socialist, to Protestant and Catholic, to burglar and policeman, to black man, white man and yellow man, to all sorts and conditions, all nationalities, all faiths, all follies, all causes and all crimes. The first Undershaft wrote up in his shop IF GOD GAVE THE HAND, LET NOT MAN WITHHOLD THE SWORD. The second wrote up ALL HAVE THE RIGHT TO FIGHT: NONE HAVE THE RIGHT TO JUDGE. The third wrote up TO MAN THE WEAPON: TO HEAVEN THE VICTORY. The fourth had no literary turn; so he did not write up anything; but he sold cannons to Napoleon under the nose of George the Third. The fifth wrote up PEACE SHALL NOT PREVAIL SAVE WITH A SWORD IN HER HAND. The sixth, my master, was the best of all. He wrote up NOTHING IS EVER DONE IN THIS WORLD UNTIL MEN ARE PREPARED TO KILL ONE ANOTHER IF IT IS NOT DONE. After that, there was nothing left for the seventh to say. So he wrote up, simply, UNASHAMED.

Cusins.   My good Machiavelli, I shall certainly write something up on the wall; only, as I shall write it in Greek, you wont be able to read it. But as to your Armorer's faith, if I take my neck out of the noose of my own morality I am not going to put it into the noose of yours. I shall sell cannons to whom I please and refuse them to whom I please. So there!

Undershaft.   From the moment when you become Andrew Undershaft, you will never do as you please again. Dont come here lusting for power, young man.

Cusins.   If power were my aim I should not come here for it. You have no power.

Undershaft.   None of my own, certainly.

Cusins.   I have more power than you, more will. You do not drive this place: it drives you. And what drives the place?

Undershaft (*enigmatically*).   A will of which I am a part.

Barbara (*startled*).   Father! Do you know what you are saying; or are you laying a snare for my soul?

Cusins.   Dont listen to his metaphysics, Barbara. The place is driven by the most rascally part of society, the money hunters, the pleasure hunters, the military promotion hunters; and he is their slave.

Undershaft.   Not necessarily. Remember the Armorer's Faith. I will take an order from a good man as cheerfully as from a bad one. If you good people prefer preaching and shirking to buying my weapons and fighting the rascals, dont blame me. I can make cannons: I cannot make courage and conviction. Bah! you tire me, Euripides, with your morality mongering. Ask Barbara: she understands. (*He suddenly reaches up and takes Barbara's hands, looking powerfully into her eyes*). Tell him, my love, what power really means.

Barbara (*hypnotized*).   Before I joined the Salvation Army, I was in my own power; and the consequence was that I never knew what to do with myself. When I joined it, I had not time enough for all the things I had to do.

Undershaft (*approvingly*).   Just so. And why was that, do you suppose?

Barbara.   Yesterday I should have said, because I was in the power of God. (*She resumes her self-possession, withdrawing her hands from his with a power equal to his own*). But you came and shewed me that I was in the power of Bodger and Undershaft. Today I feel—oh! how can I put it into words? Sarah: do you remember the earthquake at Cannes, when we were little children?—how little the surprise of the first shock mattered compared to the dread and horror of waiting for the second? That is how I feel in this place today. I stood on the rock I thought eternal; and without a word of warning it reeled and crumbled under me. I was safe with an infinite wisdom watching me, an army marching to Salvation with me; and in a moment, at a stroke of your pen in a cheque book, I stood alone; and the heavens were empty. That was the first shock of the earthquake: I am waiting for the second.

Undershaft.   Come, come, my daughter! dont make too much of your little tinpot tragedy. What do we do here when we spend years of work and thought and thousands of pounds of solid cash on a new gun or an aerial battleship that turns out just a hairsbreadth wrong after all? Scrap it. Scrap it without wasting another hour or another pound on it. Well, you have made for yourself something that you call a morality or a religion or what not. It doesnt fit the facts. Well, scrap it. Scrap it and get one that does fit. That is what is wrong with the world at present. It scraps its obsolete steam engines and dynamos; but it wont scrap its old prejudices and its old moralities and its old religions and its old political constitutions. Whats the result? In machinery it does very well; but in morals and religion and politics it is working at a loss that brings it nearer bankruptcy every year. Dont persist in that folly. If your old religion broke down yesterday, get a newer and a better one for tomorrow.

Barbara.   Oh how gladly I would take a better one to my soul! But you offer me a worse one. *(Turning on him with sudden vehemence)* Justify yourself: shew me some light through the darkness of this dreadful place, with its beautifully clean workshops, and respectable workmen, and model homes.

Undershaft.   Cleanliness and respectability do not need justification, Barbara: they justify themselves. I see no darkness here, no dreadfulness. In your Salvation shelter I saw poverty, misery, cold and hunger. You gave them bread and treacle and dreams of heaven. I give from thirty shillings a week to twelve thousand a year. They find their own dreams; but I look after the drainage.

Barbara.   And their souls?

Undershaft.   I save their souls just as I saved yours.

Barbara *(revolted)*.   You saved my soul! What do you mean?

Undershaft.   I fed you and clothed you and housed you. I took care that you should have money enough to live handsomely—more than enough; so that you could be wasteful, careless, generous. That saved your soul from the seven deadly sins.

Barbara *(bewildered)*.   The seven deadly sins!

Undershaft.   Yes, the deadly seven. *(Counting on his fingers)* Food, clothing, firing, rent, taxes, respectability and children. Nothing can lift those seven millstones from Man's neck but money; and the spirit cannot soar until the millstones are lifted. I lifted them from your spirit. I enabled Barbara to become Major Barbara; and I saved her from the crime of poverty.

Cusins.   Do you call poverty a crime?

Undershaft.   The worst of crimes. All the other crimes are virtues beside it: all the other dishonors are chivalry itself by comparison. Poverty blights whole cities; spreads horrible pestilences; strikes dead the very souls of all who come within sight, sound, or smell of it. What you call crime is nothing: a murder here and a theft there, a blow now and a curse then: what do they matter? they are only the accidents and illnesses of life: there are not fifty genuine professional criminals in London. But there are millions of poor people, abject people, dirty people, ill fed, ill clothed people. They poison us morally and physically: they kill the happiness of society: they force us to do away with our own liberties and to organize unnatural cruelties for fear they should rise against us and drag us down into their abyss. Only fools fear crime: we all fear poverty. Pah! *(turning on Barbara)* you talk of your half-saved ruffian in West Ham: you accuse me of dragging his soul back to perdition. Well, bring him to me here; and I will drag his soul back again to salvation for you. Not by words and dreams; but by thirty-eight shillings a week, a sound house in a handsome street, and a permanent job. In three weeks he will have a fancy waistcoat; in three months a tall hat and a chapel sitting; before the end of the year he will shake hands with a duchess at a Primrose League meeting, and join the Conservative Party.

Barbara.   And will he be the better for that?

Undershaft.   You know he will. Dont be a hypocrite, Barbara. He will be better fed, better housed, better clothed, better behaved; and his children will be pounds heavier and bigger. That will be better than an American cloth mattress in a shelter, chopping firewood, eating bread and treacle, and being forced to kneel down from time to time to thank heaven for it: knee drill, I think you call it. It is cheap work converting starving men with a Bible in one hand and a slice of bread in the other. I will undertake to convert West Ham to Mahometanism on the same terms. Try your hand on my men: their souls are hungry because their bodies are full.

Barbara.   And leave the east end to starve?

Undershaft (*his energetic tone dropping into one of bitter and brooding remembrance*).   I was an east ender. I moralized and starved until one day I swore that I would be a full-fed free man at all costs; that nothing should stop me except a bullet, neither reason nor morals nor the lives of other men. I said 'Thou shalt starve ere I starve'; and with that word I became free and great. I was a dangerous man until I had my will: now I am a useful, beneficent, kindly person. That is the history of most self-made millionaires, I fancy. When it is the history of every Englishman we shall have an England worth living in.

Lady Britomart.   Stop making speeches, Andrew. This is not the place for them.

Undershaft (*punctured*).   My dear: I have no other means of conveying my ideas.

Lady Britomart.   Your ideas are nonsense. You got on because you were selfish and unscrupulous.

Undershaft.   Not at all. I had the strongest scruples about poverty and starvation. Your moralists are quite unscrupulous about both: they make virtues of them. I had rather be a thief than a pauper. I had rather be a murderer than a slave. I dont want to be either; but if you force the alternative on me, then, by Heaven, I'll choose the braver and more moral one. I hate poverty and slavery worse than any other crimes whatsoever. And let me tell you this. Poverty and slavery have stood up for centuries to your sermons and leading articles: they will not stand up to my machine guns. Dont preach at them: dont reason with them. Kill them.

Barbara.   Killing. Is that your remedy for everything?

Undershaft.   It is the final test of conviction, the only lever strong enough to overturn a social system, the only way of saying Must. Let six hundred and seventy fools loose in the streets; and three policemen can scatter them. But huddle them together in a certain house in Westminster; and let them go through certain ceremonies and call themselves certain names until at last they get the courage to kill; and your six hundred and seventy fools become a government. Your pious mob fills up ballot papers and imagines it is governing its masters; but the ballot paper that really governs is the paper that has a bullet wrapped up in it.

Cusins.   That is perhaps why, like most intelligent people, I never vote.

Undershaft.   Vote! Bah! When you vote, you only change the names of the cabinet. When you shoot, you pull down governments, inaugurate new epochs, abolish old orders and set up new. Is that historically true, Mr Learned Man, or is it not?

Cusins.   It is historically true. I loathe having to admit it. I repudiate your sentiments. I abhor your nature. I defy you in every possible way. Still, it is true. But it ought not to be true.

Undershaft.   Ought! ought! ought! ought! ought! Are you going to spend your life saying ought, like the rest of our moralists? Turn your oughts into shalls, man. Come and make explosives with me. Whatever can blow men up can blow society up. The history of the world is the history of those who had courage enough to embrace this truth. Have you the courage to embrace it, Barbara?

Lady Britomart.   Barbara: I positively forbid you to listen to your father's abominable wickedness. And you, Adolphus, ought to know better than to go about saying that wrong things are true. What does it matter whether they are true if they are wrong?

Undershaft.   What does it matter whether they are wrong if they are true?

Lady Britomart *(rising)*.   Children: come home instantly. Andrew: I am exceedingly sorry I allowed you to call on us. You are wickeder than ever. Come at once.

Barbara *(shaking her head)*.   It's no use running away from wicked people, mamma.

Lady Britomart.   It is every use. It shews your disapprobation of them.

Barbara.   It does not save them.

Lady Britomart.   I can see that you are going to disobey me. Sarah: are you coming home or are you not?

Sarah.   I daresay it's very wicked of papa to make cannons; but I dont think I shall cut him on that account.

Lomax *(pouring oil on the troubled waters)*.   The fact is, you know, there is a certain amount of tosh about this notion of wickedness. It doesnt work. You must look at facts. Not that I would say a word in favor of anything wrong; but then, you see, all sorts of chaps are always doing all sorts of things; and we have to fit them in somehow, dont you know. What I mean is that you cant go cutting everybody; and thats about what it comes to. *(Their rapt attention to his eloquence makes him nervous)*. Perhaps I dont make myself clear.

Lady Britomart.   You are lucidity itself, Charles. Because Andrew is successful
and has plenty of money to give to Sarah, you will flatter him and encourage
him in his wickedness.

Lomax *(unruffled)*.   Well, where the carcase is, there will the eagles be gathered, dont you know. *(To Undershaft)* Eh? What?

Undershaft.   Precisely. By the way, may I call you Charles?

Lomax.   Delighted. Cholly is the usual ticket.

Undershaft *(to Lady Britomart)*.   Biddy—

Lady Britomart *(violently)*.   Dont dare call me Biddy. Charles Lomax: you are
a fool. Adolphus Cusins: you are a Jesuit. Stephen: you are a prig. Barbara:
you are a lunatic. Andrew: you are a vulgar tradesman. Now you all know
my opinion; and my conscience is clear, at all events. *(She sits down with a
vehemence that the rug fortunately softens)*.

Undershaft.   My dear: you are the incarnation of morality. *(She snorts)*. Your
conscience is clear and your duty done when you have called everybody
names. Come, Euripides! it is getting late; and we all want to go home.
Make up your mind.

Cusins.   Understand this, you old demon—

Lady Britomart.   Adolphus!

Undershaft.   Let him alone, Biddy. Proceed, Euripides.

Cusins.   You have me in a horrible dilemma. I want Barbara.

Undershaft.   Like all young men, you greatly exaggerate the difference between
one young woman and another.

Barbara.   Quite true, Dolly.

Cusins.   I also want to avoid being a rascal.

Undershaft *(with biting contempt)*.   You lust for personal righteousness, for
self-approval, for what you call a good conscience, for what Barbara calls
salvation, for what I call patronizing people who are not so lucky as yourself.

Cusins.   I do not: all the poet in me recoils from being a good man. But there
are things in me that I must reckon with. Pity—

Undershaft.   Pity! The scavenger of misery.

Cusins.   Well, love.

Undershaft.   I know. You love the needy and the outcast: you love the oppressed races, the negro, the Indian ryot, the underdog everywhere. Do you
love the Japanese? Do you love the French? Do you love the English?

Cusins.   No. Every true Englishman detests the English. We are the wickedest
nation on earth; and our success is a moral horror.

Undershaft.   That is what comes of your gospel of love, is it?

Cusins.   May I not love even my father-in-law?

Undershaft.   Who wants your love, man? By what right do you take the liberty
of offering it to me? I will have your due heed and respect, or I will kill you.
But your love! Damn your impertinence!

Cusins *(grinning)*.   I may not be able to control my affections, Mac.

Undershaft. You are fencing, Euripides. You are weakening: your grip is slipping. Come! try your last weapon. Pity and love have broken in your hand: forgiveness is still left.

Cusins. No: forgiveness is a beggar's refuge. I am with you there: we must pay our debts.

Undershaft. Well said. Come! you will suit me. Remember the words of Plato.

Cusins (*starting*). Plato! You dare quote Plato to me!

Undershaft. Plato says, my friend, that society cannot be saved until either the Professors of Greek take to making gunpowder, or else the makers of gunpowder become Professors of Greek.

Cusins. Oh, tempter, cunning tempter!

Undershaft. Come! choose, man, choose.

Cusins. But perhaps Barbara will not marry me if I make the wrong choice.

Barbara. Perhaps not.

Cusins (*desperately perplexed*). You hear!

Barbara. Father: do you love nobody?

Undershaft. I love my best friend.

Lady Britomart. And who is that, pray?

Undershaft. My bravest enemy. That is the man who keeps me up to the mark.

Cusins. You know, the creature is really a sort of poet in his way. Suppose he is a great man, after all!

Undershaft. Suppose you stop talking and make up your mind, my young friend.

Cusins. But you are driving me against my nature. I hate war.

Undershaft. Hatred is the coward's revenge for being intimidated. Dare you make war on war? Here are the means: my friend Mr Lomax is sitting on them.

Lomax (*springing up*). Oh I say! You dont mean that this thing is loaded, do you? My ownest: come off it.

Sarah (*sitting placidly on the shell*). If I am to be blown up, the more thoroughly it is done the better. Dont fuss, Cholly.

Lomax (*to Undershaft, strongly remonstrant*). Your own daughter, you know!

Undershaft. So I see. (*To Cusins*) Well, my friend, may we expect you here at six tomorrow morning?

Cusins (*firmly*). Not on any account. I will see the whole establishment blown up with its own dynamite before I will get up at five. My hours are healthy, rational hours: eleven to five.

Undershaft. Come when you please: before a week you will come at six and stay until I turn you out for the sake of your health. (*Calling*) Bilton! (*He turns to Lady Britomart, who rises*). My dear: let us leave these two young people to themselves for a moment. (*Bilton comes from the shed*). I am going to take you through the gun cotton shed.

Bilton (*barring the way*). You cant take anything explosive in here, sir.

Lady Britomart.   What do you mean? Are you alluding to me?

Bilton *(unmoved).*   No, maam. Mr Undershaft has the other gentleman's matches in his pocket.

Lady Britomart *(abruptly).*   Oh! I beg your pardon. *(She goes into the shed).*

Undershaft.   Quite right, Bilton, quite right: here you are. *(He gives Bilton the box of matches).* Come, Stephen. Come, Charles. Bring Sarah. *(He passes into the shed).*

Bilton opens the box and deliberately drops the matches into the fire-bucket.

Lomax.   Oh I say! *(Bilton stolidly hands him the empty box).* Infernal nonsense! Pure scientific ignorance! *(He goes in).*

Sarah.   Am I all right, Bilton?

Bilton.   Youll have to put on list slippers, miss: that's all. Weve got em inside. *(She goes in).*

Stephen *(very seriously to Cusins).*   Dolly, old fellow, think. Think before you decide. Do you feel that you are a sufficiently practical man? It is a huge undertaking, an enormous responsibility. All this mass of business will be Greek to you.

Cusins.   Oh, I think it will be much less difficult than Greek.

Stephen.   Well, I just want to say this before I leave you to yourselves. Dont let anything I have said about right and wrong prejudice you against this great chance in life. I have satisfied myself that the business is one of the highest character and a credit to our country. *(Emotionally)* I am very proud of my father. I—*(Unable to proceed, he presses Cusins' hand and goes hastily into the shed, followed by Bilton).*

Barbara and Cusins, left alone together, look at one another silently.

Cusins.   Barbara: I am going to accept this offer.

Barbara.   I thought you would.

Cusins.   You understand, dont you, that I had to decide without consulting you. If I had thrown the burden of the choice on you, you would sooner or later have despised me for it.

Barbara.   Yes: I did not want you to sell your soul for me any more than for this inheritance.

Cusins.   It is not the sale of my soul that troubles me: I have sold it too often to care about that. I have sold it for a professorship. I have sold it for an income. I have sold it to escape being imprisoned for refusing to pay taxes for hangmen's ropes and unjust wars and things that I abhor. What is all human conduct but the daily and hourly sale of our souls for trifles? What I am now selling it for is neither money nor position nor comfort, but for reality and for power.

Barbara.   You know that you will have no power, and that he has none.

Cusins.   I know. It is not for myself alone. I want to make power for the world.

Barbara. I want to make power for the world too; but it must be spiritual power.

Cusins. I think all power is spiritual: these cannons will not go off by themselves. I have tried to make spiritual power by teaching Greek. But the world can never be really touched by a dead language and a dead civilization. The people must have power; and the people cannot have Greek. Now the power that is made here can be wielded by all men.

Barbara. Power to burn women's houses down and kill their sons and tear their husbands to pieces.

Cusins. You cannot have power for good without having power for evil too. Even mother's milk nourishes murderers as well as heroes. This power which only tears men's bodies to pieces has never been so horribly abused as the intellectual power, the imaginative power, the poetic, religious power that can enslave men's souls. As a teacher of Greek I gave the intellectual man weapons against the common man. I now want to give the common man weapons against the intellectual man. I love the common people. I want to arm them against the lawyers, the doctors, the priests, the literary men, the professors, the artists, and the politicians, who, once in authority, are more disastrous and tyrannical than all the fools, rascals, and impostors. I want a power simple enough for common men to use, yet strong enough to force the intellectual oligarchy to use its genius for the general good.

Barbara. Is there no higher power than that (*pointing to the shell*)?

Cusins. Yes; but that power can destroy the higher powers just as a tiger can destroy a man: therefore Man must master that power first. I admitted this when the Turks and Greeks were last at war. My best pupil went out to fight for Hellas. My parting gift to him was not a copy of Plato's Republic, but a revolver and a hundred Undershaft cartridges. The blood of every Turk he shot—if he shot any—is on my head as well as on Undershaft's. That act committed me to this place for ever. Your father's challenge has beaten me. Dare I make war on war? I must. I will. And now, is it all over between us?

Barbara (*touched by his evident dread of her answer*). Silly baby Dolly! How could it be!

Cusins (*overjoyed*). Then you—you—you—Oh for my drum! (*He flourishes imaginery drumsticks*).

Barbara (*angered by his levity*). Take care, Dolly, take care. Oh, if only I could get away from you and from father and from it all! if I could have the wings of a dove and fly away to heaven!

Cusins. And leave me!

Barbara. Yes, you, and all the other naughty mischievous children of men. But I cant. I was happy in the Salvation Army for a moment. I escaped from the world into a paradise of enthusiasm and prayer and soul saving; but the moment our money ran short, it all came back to Bodger: it was he who saved our people: he, and the Prince of Darkness, my papa. Undershaft and Bodger: their hands stretch everywhere: when we feed a starving fellow creature, it is with their bread, because there is no other bread; when we tend the sick, it is in the hospitals they endow; if we turn from the churches they build, we must kneel on the stones of the streets they pave. As long as that lasts, there is no getting away from them. Turning our backs on Bodger and Undershaft is turning our backs on life.

Cusins. I thought you were determined to turn your back on the wicked side of life.

Barbara. There is no wicked side: life is all one. And I never wanted to shirk my share in whatever evil must be endured, whether it be sin or suffering. I wish I could cure you of middle-class ideas, Dolly.

Cusins *(gasping).* Middle cl—! A snub! A social snub to me! from the daughter of a foundling!

Barbara. That is why I have no class, Dolly: I come straight out of the heart of the whole people. If I were middle-class I should turn my back on my father's business; and we should both live in an artistic drawing room, with you reading the reviews in one corner, and I in the other at the piano, playing Schumann: both very superior persons, and neither of us a bit of use. Sooner than that, I would sweep out the guncotton shed, or be one of Bodger's barmaids. Do you know what would have happened if you had refused papa's offer?

Cusins. I wonder!

Barbara. I should have given you up and married the man who accepted it. After all, my dear old mother has more sense than any of you. I felt like her when I saw this place—felt that I must have it—that never, never, never could I let it go; only she thought it was the houses and the kitchen ranges and the linen and china, when it was really all the human souls to be saved: not weak souls in starved bodies, sobbing with gratitude for a scrap of bread and treacle, but fullfed, quarrelsome, snobbish, uppish creatures, all standing on their little rights and dignities, and thinking that my father ought to be greatly obliged to them for making so much money for him—and so he ought. That is where salvation is really wanted. My father shall never throw it in my teeth again that my converts were bribed with bread. *(She is transfigured).* I have got rid of the bribe of bread. I have got rid of the bribe of heaven. Let God's work be done for its own sake: the work he had to create us to do because it cannot be done except by living men and women. When I die, let him be in my debt, not I in his; and let me forgive him as becomes a woman of my rank.

Cusins. Then the way of life lies through the factory of death?

Barbara. Yes, through the raising of hell to heaven and of man to God, through the unveiling of an eternal light in the Valley of The Shadow. *(Seizing him with both hands)* Oh, did you think my courage would never come back? did you believe that I was a deserter? that I, who have stood in the streets, and taken my people to my heart, and talked of the holiest and greatest things with them, could ever turn back and chatter foolishly to fashionable people about nothing in a drawing room? Never, never, never, never: Major Barbara will die with the colors. Oh! and I have my dear little Dolly boy still; and he has found me my place and my work. Glory Hallelujah! *(She kisses him)*.

Cusins.   My dearest: consider my delicate health. I cannot stand as much happiness as you can.

Barbara.   Yes: it is not easy work being in love with me, is it? But its good for you. *(She runs to the shed, and calls, childlike)* Mamma! Mamma! *(Bilton comes out of the shed, followed by Undershaft)*. I want Mamma.

Undershaft.   She is taking off her list slippers, dear. *(He passes on to Cusins)*. Well? What does she say?

Cusins.   She has gone right up into the skies.

Lady Britomart *(coming from the shed and stopping on the steps, obstructing Sarah, who follows with Lomax. Barbara clutches like a baby at her mother's skirt)*.   Barbara: when will you learn to be independent and to act and think for yourself? I know as well as possible what that cry of 'Mamma, Mamma,' means. Always running to me!

Sarah *(touching Lady Britomart's ribs with her finger tips and imitating a bicycle horn)*.   Pip! pip!

Lady Britomart *(highly indignant)*.   How dare you say Pip! pip! to me, Sarah? You are both very naughty children. What do you want, Barbara?

Barbara.   I want a house in the village to live in with Dolly. *(Dragging at the skirt)* Come and tell me which one to take.

Undershaft *(to Cusins)*.   Six o'clock tomorrow morning, Euripides.

THE END

QUESTIONS

1. What commonly held social, political, moral, and religious attitudes does Undershaft attack in this play? Justify or refute his position.   **2.** What differing viewpoints are represented by Lady Britomart, Stephen, and Charles Lomax? How, in the creation of these characters, does Shaw manipulate the audience's response to these points of view?   **3.** What function does the episode involving Bill Walker serve in the play? In what way does he differ from Snobby Price?   **4.** In Act III Stephen asserts that he knows "the difference between right and wrong." Why does Undershaft ridicule that assertion? Does Undershaft know the difference between right and wrong? Explain.   **5.** Briefly state Undershaft's argument against charity. Do you agree with him? Can you offer any examples from your own experience or knowledge that would support or challenge Undershaft's views?   **6.** Although Undershaft's factory manufactures the instruments of warfare and death, and although Undershaft makes no moral distinctions among his customers, he has created (given the harsh economic conditions of early twentieth-century England) an almost utopian economic and social community for his own employees. Is Undershaft's behavior "evil" or "good"? Defend your answer.

WRITING TOPICS

1. Undershaft quotes the Undershaft maxims in Act III. Do you accept or reject the underlying ethical principles they illustrate? Explain.   **2.** If Undershaft represents power and Barbara represents religion, what does Cusins represent in the play? Do you find Cusins's decision to become Undershaft's successor satisfying? Explain.

Dutchman   1964

IMAMU AMIRI BARAKA (LEROI JONES)   [b. 1934]

CHARACTERS

Clay, twenty-year-old Negro   **Young Negro**
Lula, thirty-year-old white woman   **Conductor**
Riders of coach, white and black

In the flying underbelly of the city. Steaming hot, and summer on top, outside. Underground. The subway heaped in modern myth.

Opening scene is a man sitting in a subway seat, holding a magazine but looking vacantly just above its wilting pages. Occasionally he looks blankly toward the window on his right. Dim lights and darkness whistling against the glass. (Or paste the lights, as admitted props, right on the subway windows. Have them move, even dim and flicker. But give the sense of speed. Also stations, whether the train is stopped or the glitter and activity of these stations merely flashes by the windows.)

The man is sitting alone. That is, only his seat is visible, though the rest of the car is outfitted as a complete subway car. But only his seat is shown. There might be, for a time, as the play begins, a loud scream of the actual train. And it can recur throughout the play, or continue on a lower key once the dialogue starts.

The train slows after a time, pulling to a brief stop at one of the stations. The man looks idly up, until he sees a woman's face staring at him through the window; when it realizes that the man has noticed the face, it begins very premeditatedly to smile. The man smiles too, for a moment, without a trace of self-consciousness. Almost an instinctive though undesirable response. Then a kind of awkwardness or embarrassment sets in, and the man makes to look away, is further embarrassed, so he brings back his eyes to where the face was, but by now the train is moving again, and the face would seem to be left behind by the way the man turns his head to look back through the other windows at the slowly fading platform. He smiles then; more comfortably confident, hoping perhaps that his memory of this brief encounter will be pleasant. And then he is idle again.

Scene 1

Train roars. Lights flash outside the windows.

Lula enters from the rear of the car in bright, skimpy summer clothes and sandals. She carries a net bag full of paper books, fruit, and other anonymous articles. She is wearing sunglasses, which she pushes up on her forehead from time to time. Lula is a tall, slender, beautiful woman with long red hair hanging straight down her back, wearing only loud lipstick in somebody's good taste. She is eating an apple, very daintily. Coming down the car toward Clay.

She stops beside Clay's seat and hangs languidly from the strap, still managing to eat the apple. It is apparent that she is going to sit in the seat next to Clay, and that she is only waiting for him to notice her before she sits.

Clay sits as before, looking just beyond his magazine, now and again pulling the magazine slowly back and forth in front of his face in a hopeless effort to fan himself. Then he sees the woman hanging there beside him and he looks up into her face, smiling quizzically.

Lula.   Hello.
Clay.   Uh, hi're you?
Lula.   I'm going to sit down. . . . O.K.?
Clay.   Sure.
Lula (*swings down onto the seat, pushing her legs straight out as if she is very weary*).   Oooof! Too much weight.
Clay.   Ha, doesn't look like much to me. (*Leaning back against the window, a little surprised and maybe stiff.*)
Lula.   It's so anyway.

(*And she moves her toes in the sandals, then pulls her right leg up on the left knee, better to inspect the bottom of the sandals and the back of her heel. She appears for a second not to notice that Clay is sitting next to her or that she has spoken to him just a second before. Clay looks at the magazine, then out the black window. As he does this, she turns very quickly toward him.*)

Lula.   Weren't you staring at me through the window?
Clay (*wheeling around and very much stiffened*).   What?
Lula.   Weren't you staring at me through the window? At the last stop?
Clay.   Staring at you? What do you mean?
Lula.   Don't you know what staring means?
Clay.   I saw you through the window . . . if that's what it means. I don't know if I was staring. Seems to me you were staring through the window at me.
Lula.   I was. But only after I'd turned around and saw you staring through that window down in the vicinity of my ass and legs.
Clay.   Really?
Lula.   Really. I guess you were just taking those idle potshots. Nothing else to do. Run your mind over people's flesh.
Clay.   Oh boy. Wow, now I admit I was looking in your direction. But the rest of that weight is yours.
Lula.   I suppose.

Clay. Staring through train windows is weird business. Much weirder than staring very sedately at abstract asses.

Lula. That's why I came looking through the window . . . so you'd have more than that to go on. I even smiled at you.

Clay. That's right.

Lula. I even got into this train, going some other way than mine. Walked down the aisle . . . searching you out.

Clay. Really? That's pretty funny.

Lula. That's pretty funny. . . . God, you're dull.

Clay. Well, I'm sorry, lady, but I really wasn't prepared for party talk.

Lula. No, you're not. What are you prepared for? (*Wrapping the apple core in a Kleenex and dropping it on the floor.*)

Clay (*takes her conversation as pure sex talk. He turns to confront her squarely with this idea*). I'm prepared for anything. How about you?

Lula (*laughing loudly and cutting it off abruptly*). What do you think you're doing?

Clay. What?

Lula. You think I want to pick you up, get you to take me somewhere and screw me, huh?

Clay. Is that the way I look?

Lula. You look like you been trying to grow a beard. That's exactly what you look like. You look like you live in New Jersey with your parents and are trying to grow a beard. That's what. You look like you've been reading Chinese poetry and drinking lukewarm sugarless tea. (*Laughs, uncrossing and recrossing her legs.*) You look like death eating a soda cracker.

Clay (*cocking his head from one side to the other, embarrassed and trying to make some comeback, but also intrigued by what the woman is saying . . . even the sharp city coarseness of her voice, which is still a kind of gentle sidewalk throb*). Really? I look like all that?

Lula. Not all of it. (*She feints a seriousness to cover an actual somber tone.*) I lie a lot. (*Smiling.*) It helps me control the world.

Clay (*relieved and laughing louder than the humor*). Yeah, I bet.

Lula. But it's true, most of it, right? Jersey? Your bumpy neck?

Clay. How'd you know all that? Huh? Really, I mean about Jersey . . . and even the beard. I met you before? You know Warren Enright?

Lula. You tried to make it with your sister when you were ten.

(*Clay leans back hard against the back of the seat, his eyes opening now, still trying to look amused.*)

Lula. But I succeeded a few weeks ago. (*She starts to laugh again.*)

Clay. What're you talking about? Warren tell you that? You're a friend of Georgia's?

Lula. I told you I lie. I don't know your sister. I don't know Warren Enright.

Clay. You mean you're just picking these things out of the air?

Lula. Is Warren Enright a tall skinny black boy with a phony English accent?

Clay. I figured you knew him.

Lula. But I don't. I just figured you would know somebody like that. *(Laughs.)*

Clay. Yeah, yeah.

Lula. You're probably on your way to his house now.

Clay. That's right.

Lula *(putting her hand on Clay's closest knee, drawing it from the knee up to the thigh's hinge, then removing it, watching his face very closely, and continuing to laugh, perhaps more gently than before).*   Dull, dull, dull. I bet you think I'm exciting.

Clay. You're O.K.

Lula. Am I exciting you now?

Clay. Right. That's not what's supposed to happen?

Lula. How do I know? *(She returns her hand, without moving it, then takes it away and plunges it in her bag to draw out an apple.)* You want this?

Clay. Sure.

Lula *(she gets one out of her bag for herself).*   Eating apples together is always the first step. Or walking up uninhabited Seventh Avenue in the twenties on weekends. *(Bites and giggles, glancing at Clay and speaking in loose singsong.)* Can you get involved . . . boy! Get us involved. Um-huh. *(Mock seriousness.)* Would you like to get involved with me, Mister Man?

Clay *(trying to be as flippant as Lula, whacking happily at the apple).*   Sure. Why not? A beautiful woman like you. Huh, I'd be a fool not to.

Lula. And I bet you're sure you know what you're talking about. *(Taking him a little roughly by the wrist, so he cannot eat the apple, then shaking the wrist.)* I bet you're sure of almost everything anybody ever asked you about . . . right? *(Shakes his wrist harder.)* Right?

Clay. Yeah, right. . . . Wow, you're pretty strong, you know? Whatta you, a lady wrestler or something?

Lula. What's wrong with lady wrestlers? And don't answer because you never knew any. Huh. *(Cynically.)* That's for sure. They don't have any lady wrestlers in that part of Jersey. That's for sure.

Clay. Hey, you still haven't told me how you know so much about me.

Lula. I told you I didn't know anything about *you* . . . you're a well-known type.

Clay. Really?

Lula. Or at least I know the type very well. And your skinny English friend too.

Clay. Anonymously?

Lula *(settles back in seat, single-mindedly finishing her apple and humming snatches of rhythm and blues song).* What?

Clay. Without knowing us specifically?

Lula. Oh boy. *(Looking quickly at Clay.)* What a face. You know, you could be a handsome man.

Clay. I can't argue with you.

Lula *(vague, off-center response).* What?

Clay *(raising his voice, thinking the train noise has drowned part of his sentence).* I can't argue with you.

Lula. My hair is turning gray. A gray hair for each year and type I've come through.

Clay. Why do you want to sound so old?

Lula. But it's always gentle when it starts. *(Attention drifting.)* Hugged against tenements, day or night.

Clay. What?

Lula *(refocusing).* Hey, why don't you take me to that party you're going to?

Clay. You must be a friend of Warren's to know about the party.

Lula. Wouldn't you like to take me to the party? *(Imitates clinging vine.)* Oh, come on, ask me to your party.

Clay. Of course I'll ask you to come with me to the party. And I'll bet you're a friend of Warren's.

Lula. Why not be a friend of Warren's? Why not? *(Taking his arm.)* Have you asked me yet?

Clay. How can I ask you when I don't know your name?

Lula. Are you talking to my name?

Clay. What is it, a secret?

Lula. I'm Lena the Hyena.

Clay. The famous woman poet?

Lula. Poetess! The same!

Clay. Well, you know so much about me . . . what's my name?

Lula. Morris the Hyena.

Clay. The famous woman poet?

Lula. The same. *(Laughing and going into her bag.)* You want another apple?

Clay. Can't make it, lady. I only have to keep one doctor away a day.

Lula. I bet your name is . . . something like . . . uh, Gerald or Walter. Huh?

Clay. God, no.

Lula. Lloyd, Norman? One of those hopeless colored names creeping out of New Jersey. Leonard? Gag. . . .

Clay. Like Warren?

Lula. Definitely. Just exactly like Warren. Or Everett.

Clay. Gag. . . .

Lula. Well, for sure, it's not Willie.

Clay. It's Clay.

Lula. Clay? Really? Clay what?

Clay. Take your pick. Jackson, Johnson, or Williams.

Lula. Oh, really? Good for you. But it's got to be Williams. You're too pretentious to be a Jackson or Johnson.

Clay. Thass right.

Lula. But Clay's O.K.

Clay. So's Lena.

Lula. It's Lula.

Clay. Oh?

Lula. Lula the Hyena.

Clay. Very good.

Lula (*starts laughing again*).   Now you say to me, "Lula, Lula, why don't you go to this party with me tonight?" It's your turn, and let those be your lines.

Clay. Lula, why don't you go to this party with me tonight, huh?

Lula. Say my name twice before you ask, and no huh's.

Clay. Lula, Lula, why don't you go to this party with me tonight?

Lula. I'd like to go, Clay, but how can you ask me to go when you barely know me?

Clay. That is strange, isn't it?

Lula. What kind of reaction is that? You're supposed to say, "Aw, come on, we'll get to know each other better at the party."

Clay. That's pretty corny.

Lula. What are you into anyway? (*Looking at him half sullenly but still amused.*) What thing are you playing at, Mister? Mister Clay Williams? (*Grabs his thigh, up near the crotch.*) What are *you* thinking about?

Clay. Watch it now, you're gonna excite me for real.

Lula (*taking her hand away and throwing her apple core through the window*).   I bet. (*She slumps in the seat and is heavily silent.*)

Clay. I thought you knew everything about me? What happened?

(*Lula looks at him, then looks slowly away, then over where the other aisle would be. Noise of the train. She reaches in her bag and pulls out one of the paper books. She puts it on her leg and thumbs the pages listlessly. Clay cocks his head to see the title of the book. Noise of the train. Lula flips pages and her eyes drift. Both remain silent.*)

Clay. Are you going to the party with me, Lula?

Lula (*bored and not even looking*).   I don't even know you.

Clay. You said you know my type.

Lula (*strangely irritated*).   Don't get smart with me, Buster. I know you like the palm of my hand.

Clay. The one you eat the apples with?

Lula. Yeh. And the one I open doors late Saturday evening with. That's my door. Up at the top of the stairs. Five flights. Above a lot of Italians and lying Americans. And scrape carrots with. Also . . . (*looks at him*) the same hand I unbutton my dress with, or let my skirt fall down. Same hand. Lover.

Clay. Are you angry about anything? Did I say something wrong?

Lula. Everything you say is wrong. (*Mock smile.*) That's what makes you so attractive. Ha. In that funnybook jacket with all the buttons. (*More animate, taking hold of his jacket.*) What've you got that jacket and tie on in all this heat for? And why're you wearing a jacket and tie like that? Did your people ever burn witches or start revolutions over the price of tea? Boy, those narrow-shoulder clothes come from a tradition you ought to feel oppressed by. A three-button suit. What right do you have to be wearing a three-button suit and striped tie? Your grandfather was a slave, he didn't go to Harvard.

Clay.   My grandfather was a night watchman.

Lula.   And you went to a colored college where everybody thought they were Averell Harriman.[1]

Clay.   All except me.

Lula.   And who did you think you were? Who do you think you are now?

Clay (*laughs as if to make light of the whole trend of the conversation*).   Well, in college I thought I was Baudelaire.[2] But I've slowed down since.

Lula.   I bet you never once thought you were a black nigger.

(*Mock serious, then she howls with laughter. Clay is stunned but after initial reaction, he quickly tries to appreciate the humor. Lula almost shrieks.*)

Lula.   A black Baudelaire.

Clay.   That's right.

Lula.   Boy, are you corny. I take back what I said before. Everything you say is not wrong. It's perfect. You should be on television.

Clay.   You act like you're on television already.

Lula.   That's because I'm an actress.

Clay.   I thought so.

Lula.   Well, you're wrong. I'm no actress. I told you I always lie. I'm nothing, honey, and don't you ever forget it. (*Lighter.*) Although my mother was a Communist. The only person in my family ever to amount to anything.

Clay.   My mother was a Republican.

Lula.   And your father voted for the man rather than the party.

Clay.   Right!

Lula.   Yea for him. Yea, yea for him.

Clay.   Yea!

Lula.   And yea for America where he is free to vote for the mediocrity of his choice! Yea!

Clay.   Yea!

Lula.   And yea for both your parents who even though they differ about so crucial a matter as the body politic still forged a union of love and sacrifice that was destined to flower at the birth of the noble Clay . . . what's your middle name?

Clay.   Clay.

Lula.   A union of love and sacrifice that was destined to flower at the birth of the noble Clay Clay Williams. Yea! And most of all yea yea for you, Clay, Clay. The Black Baudelaire! Yes! (*And with knifelike cynicism.*) My Christ. My Christ.

---

[1] Averell Harriman (1891–1986), governor of New York (1955–1959) and eminent, politically liberal white statesman.

[2] Charles Pierre Baudelaire (1821–1867), French symbolist poet.

Clay. Thank you, ma'am.

Lula. May the people accept you as a ghost of the future. And love you, that you might not kill them when you can.

Clay. What?

Lula. You're a murderer, Clay, and you know it. (*Her voice darkening with significance.*) You know goddamn well what I mean.

Clay. I do?

Lula. So we'll pretend the air is light and full of perfume.

Clay (*sniffing at her blouse*). It is.

Lula. And we'll pretend the people cannot see you. That is, the citizens. And that you are free of your own history. And I am free of my history. We'll pretend that we are both anonymous beauties smashing along through the city's entrails. (*She yells as loud as she can.*) GROOVE!

Black

Scene 2

Scene is the same as before, though now there are other seats visible in the car. And throughout the scene other people get on the subway. There are maybe one or two seated in the car as the scene opens, though neither Clay nor Lula notices them. Clay's tie is open. Lula is hugging his arm.

Clay. The party!

Lula. I know it'll be something good. You can come in with me, looking casual and significant. I'll be strange, haughty, and silent, and walk with long slow strides.

Clay. Right.

Lula. When you get drunk, pat me once, very lovingly on the flanks, and I'll look at you cryptically, licking my lips.

Clay. It sounds like something we can do.

Lula. You'll go around talking to young men about your mind, and to old men about your plans. If you meet a very close friend who is also with someone like me, we can stand together, sipping our drinks and exchanging codes of lust. The atmosphere will be slithering in love and half-love and very open moral decision.

Clay. Great. Great.

Lula. And everyone will pretend they don't know your name, and then . . . (*she pauses heavily*) later, when they have to, they'll claim a friendship that denies your sterling character.

Clay (*kissing her neck and fingers*). And then what?

Lula. Then? Well, then we'll go down the street, late night, eating apples and winding very deliberately toward my house.

Clay.   Deliberately?

Lula.   I mean, we'll look in all the shopwindows, and make fun of the queers. Maybe we'll meet a Jewish Buddhist and flatten his conceits over some very pretentious coffee.

Clay.   In honor of whose God?

Lula.   Mine.

Clay.   Who is . . .?

Lula.   Me . . . and you?

Clay.   A corporate Godhead.

Lula.   Exactly. Exactly. *(Notices one of the other people entering.)*

Clay.   Go on with the chronicle. Then what happens to us?

Lula *(a mild depression, but she still makes her description triumphant and increasingly direct).*   To my house, of course.

Clay.   Of course.

Lula.   And up the narrow steps of the tenement.

Clay.   You live in a tenement?

Lula.   Wouldn't live anywhere else. Reminds me specifically of my novel form of insanity.

Clay.   Up the tenement stairs.

Lula.   And with my apple-eating hand I push open the door and lead you, my tender big-eyed prey, into my . . . God, what can I call it . . . into my hovel.

Clay.   Then what happens?

Lula.   After the dancing and games, after the long drinks and long walks, the real fun begins.

Clay.   Ah, the real fun. *(Embarrassed, in spite of himself.)* Which is . . .?

Lula *(laughs at him).*   Real fun in the dark house. Hah! Real fun in the dark house, high up above the street and the ignorant cowboys. I lead you in, holding your wet hand gently in my hand . . .

Clay.   Which is not wet?

Lula.   Which is dry as ashes.

Clay.   And cold?

Lula.   Don't think you'll get out of your responsibility that way. It's not cold at all. You Fascist! Into my dark living room. Where we'll sit and talk endlessly, endlessly.

Clay.   About what?

Lula.   About what? About your manhood, what do you think? What do you think we've been talking about all this time?

Clay.   Well, I didn't know it was that. That's for sure. Every other thing in the world but that. *(Notices another person entering, looks quickly, almost involuntarily up and down the car, seeing the other people in the car.)* Hey, I didn't even notice when those people got on.

Lula.   Yeah, I know.

Clay.   Man, this subway is slow.

Lula.   Yeah, I know.

Clay.   Well, go on. We were talking about my manhood.

Lula.   We still are. All the time.

Clay.   We were in your living room.

Lula.   My dark living room. Talking endlessly.

Clay.   About my manhood.

Lula.   I'll make you a map of it. Just as soon as we get to my house.

Clay.   Well, that's great.

Lula.   One of the things we do while we talk. And screw.

Clay (*trying to make his smile broader and less shaky*).   We finally got there.

Lula.   And you'll call my rooms black as a grave. You'll say, "This place is like Juliet's tomb."

Clay (*laughs*).   I might.

Lula.   I know. You've probably said it before.

Clay.   And is that all? The whole grand tour?

Lula.   Not all. You'll say to me very close to my face, many, many times, you'll say, even whisper, that you love me.

Clay.   Maybe I will.

Lula.   And you'll be lying.

Clay.   I wouldn't lie about something like that.

Lula.   Hah. It's the only kind of thing you will lie about. Especially if you think it'll keep me alive.

Clay.   Keep you alive? I don't understand.

Lula (*bursting out laughing, but too shrilly*).   Don't understand? Well, don't look at me. It's the path I take, that's all. Where both feet take me when I set them down. One in front of the other.

Clay.   Morbid. Morbid. You sure you're not an actress? All that self-aggrandizement.

Lula.   Well, I told you I wasn't an actress . . . but I also told you I lie all the time. Draw your own conclusions.

Clay.   Morbid. Morbid. You sure you're not an actress? All scribed? There's no more?

Lula.   I've told you all I know. Or almost all.

Clay.   There's no funny parts?

Lula.   I thought it was all funny.

Clay.   But you mean peculiar, not ha-ha.

Lula.   You don't know what I mean.

Clay.   Well, tell me the almost part then. You said almost all. What else? I want the whole story.

Lula (*searching aimlessly through her bag. She begins to talk breathlessly, with a light and silly tone*).   All stories are whole stories. All of 'em. Our whole story . . . nothing but change. How could things go on like that forever? Huh? (*Slaps him on the shoulder, begins finding things in her bag, taking them out and throwing them over her shoulder into the aisle.*) Except I do go on as I do. Apples and long walks with deathless intelligent lovers. But you mix it up. Look out the window, all the time. Turning pages. Change change

change. Till, shit, I don't know you. Wouldn't, for that matter. You're too serious. I bet you're even too serious to be psychoanalyzed. Like all those Jewish poets from Yonkers, who leave their mothers looking for other mothers, or others' mothers, on whose baggy tits they lay their fumbling heads. Their poems are always funny, and all about sex.

Clay.   They sound great. Like movies.

Lula.   But you change. *(Blankly.)* And things work on you till you hate them.

(More people come into the train. They come closer to the couple, some of them not sitting, but swinging drearily on the straps, staring at the two with uncertain interest.)

Clay.   Wow. All these people, so suddenly. They must all come from the same place.

Lula.   Right. That they do.

Clay.   Oh? You know about them too?

Lula.   Oh yeah. About them more than I know about you. Do they frighten you?

Clay.   Frighten me? Why should they frighten me?

Lula.   'Cause you're an escaped nigger.

Clay.   Yeah?

Lula.   'Cause you crawled through the wire and made tracks to my side.

Clay.   Wire?

Lula.   Don't they have wire around plantations?

Clay.   You must be Jewish. All you can think about is wire. Plantations didn't have any wire. Plantations were big open white-washed places like heaven, and everybody on 'em was grooved to be there. Just strummin' and hummin' all day.

Lula.   Yes, yes.

Clay.   And that's how the blues was born.

Lula.   Yes, yes. And that's how the blues was born. *(Begins to make up a song that becomes quickly hysterical. As she sings she rises from her seat, still throwing things out of her bag into the aisle, beginning a rhythmical shudder and twistlike wiggle, which she continues up and down the aisle, bumping into many of the standing people and tripping over the feet of those sitting. Each time she runs into a person she lets out a very vicious piece of profanity, wiggling and stepping all the time.)* And that's how the blues was born. Yes. Yes. Son of a bitch, get out of the way. Yes. Quack. Yes. Yes. And that's how the blues was born. Ten little niggers sitting on a limb, but none of them ever looked like him. *(Points to Clay, returns toward the seat, with her hands extended for him to rise and dance with her.)* And that's how blues was born. Yes. Come on, Clay. Let's do the nasty. Rub bellies. Rub bellies.

Clay *(waves his hands to refuse. He is embarrassed, but determined to get a kick out of the proceedings).*   Hey, what was in those apples? Mirror, mirror on the wall, who's the fairest one of all? Snow White, baby, and don't you forget it.

Lula (*grabbing for his hands, which he draws away*).   Come on, Clay. Let's rub bellies on the train. The nasty. The nasty. Do the gritty grind, like your ol' rag-head mammy. Grind till you lose your mind. Shake it, shake it, shake it, shake it! OOOOweeee! Come on, Clay. Let's do the choochoo train shuffle, the navel scratcher.

Clay.   Hey, you coming on like the lady who smoked up her grass skirt.

Lula (*becoming annoyed that he will not dance, and becoming more animated as if to embarrass him still further*).   Come on, Clay . . . let's do the thing. Uhh! Uhh! Clay! Clay! You middle-class black bastard. Forget your social-working mother for a few seconds and let's knock stomachs. Clay, you liver-lipped white man. You would-be Christian. You ain't no nigger, you're just a dirty white man. Get up, Clay. Dance with me, Clay.

Clay.   Lula! Sit down, now. Be cool.

Lula (*mocking him, in wild dance*).   Be cool. Be cool. That's all you know . . . shaking that wildroot cream-oil on your knotty head, jackets buttoning up to your chin, so full of white man's words. Christ. God. Get up and scream at these people. Like scream meaningless shit in these hopeless faces. (*She screams at people in train, still dancing.*) Red trains cough Jewish underwear for keeps! Expanding smells of silence. Gravy snot whistling like sea birds. Clay. Clay, you got to break out. Don't sit there dying the way they want you to die. Get up.

Clay.   Oh, sit the fuck down. (*He moves to restrain her.*) Sit down, goddamn it.

Lula (*twisting out of his reach*).   Screw yourself, Uncle Tom. Thomas Woolly-Head. (*Begins to dance a kind of jig, mocking Clay with loud forced humor.*) There is Uncle Tom . . . I mean, Uncle Thomas Woolly-Head. With old white matted mane. He hobbles on his wooden cane. Old Tom. Old Tom. Let the white man hump his ol' mama, and he jes' shuffle off in the woods and hide his gentle gray head. Ol' Thomas Woolly-Head.

(*Some of the other riders are laughing now. A drunk gets up and joins Lula in her dance, singing, as best he can, her "song." Clay gets up out of his seat and visibly scans the faces of the other riders.*)

Clay.   Lula! Lula!

(*She is dancing and turning, still shouting as loud as she can. The drunk too is shouting, and waving his hands wildly.*)

Clay.   Lula . . . you dumb bitch. Why don't you stop it? (*He rushes half stumbling from his seat, and grabs one of her flailing arms.*)

Lula.   Let me go! You black son of a bitch. (*She struggles against him.*) Let me go! Help!

(Clay is dragging her toward her seat, and the drunk seeks to interfere. He grabs Clay around the shoulders and begins wrestling with him. Clay clubs the drunk to the floor without releasing Lula, who is still screaming. Clay finally gets her to the seat and throws her into it.)

Clay.   Now you shut the hell up. *(Grabbing her shoulders.)* Just shut up. You don't know what you're talking about. You don't know anything. So just keep your stupid mouth closed.

Lula.   You're afraid of white people. And your father was. Uncle Tom Big Lip!

Clay *(slaps her as hard as he can, across the mouth. Lula's head bangs against the back of the seat. When she raises it again, Clay slaps her again).*   Now shut up and let me talk.

(He turns toward the other riders, some of whom are sitting on the edge of their seats. The drunk is on one knee, rubbing his head, and singing softly the same song. He shuts up too when he sees Clay watching him. The others go back to newspapers or stare out the windows.)

Clay.   Shit, you don't have any sense, Lula, nor feelings either. I could murder you now. Such a tiny ugly throat. I could squeeze it flat, and watch you turn blue, on a humble. For dull kicks. And all these weak-faced ofays[3] squatting around here, staring over their papers at me. Murder them too. Even if they expected it. That man there . . . *(Points to a well-dressed man.)* I could rip that *Times* right out of his hand, as skinny and middle-classed as I am, I could rip that paper out of his hand and just as easily rip out his throat. It takes no great effort. For what? To kill you soft idiots? You don't understand anything but luxury.

Lula.   You fool!

Clay *(pushing her against the seat).*   I'm not telling you again, Tallulah Bankhead![4] Luxury. In your face and your fingers. You telling me what I ought to do. *(Sudden scream frightening the whole coach.)* Well, don't! Don't you tell me anything! If I'm a middle-class fake white man . . . let me be. And let me be in the way I want. *(Through his teeth.)* I'll rip your lousy breasts off! Let me be who I feel like being. Uncle Tom. Thomas. Whoever. It's none of your business. You don't know anything except what's there for you to see. An act. Lies. Device. Not the pure heart, the pumping black heart. You don't ever know that. And I sit here, in this buttoned-up suit, to keep myself from cutting all your throats. I mean wantonly. You great liberated whore! You fuck some black man, and right away you're an expert on black

---

[3] Derogatory black street slang for a Caucasian, probably pig latin for *foe*.
[4] Tallulah Bankhead (1903–1968), stage and screen actress.

people. What a lotta shit that is. The only thing you know is that you come if he bangs you hard enough. And that's all. The belly rub? You wanted to do the belly rub? Shit, you don't even know how. You don't know how. That ol' dipty-dip shit you do, rolling your ass like an elephant. That's not my kind of belly rub. Belly rub is not Queens. Belly rub is dark places, with big hats and overcoats held up with one arm. Belly rub hates you. Old bald-headed four-eyed ofays popping their fingers . . . and don't know yet what they're doing. They say, "I love Bessie Smith."[5] And don't even understand that Bessie Smith is saying, "Kiss my ass, kiss my black unruly ass." Before love, suffering, desire, anything you can explain, she's saying, and very plainly, "Kiss my black ass." And if you don't know that, it's you that's doing the kissing.

Charlie Parker?[6] Charlie Parker. All the hip white boys scream for Bird. And Bird saying, "Up your ass, feeble-minded ofay! Up your ass." And they sit there talking about the tortured genius of Charlie Parker. Bird would've played not a note of music if he just walked up to East Sixty-seventh Street and killed the first ten white people he saw. Not a note! And I'm the great would-be poet. Yes. That's right! Poet. Some kind of bastard literature . . . all it needs is a simple knife thrust. Just let me bleed you, you loud whore, and one poem vanished. A whole people of neurotics, struggling to keep from being sane. And the only thing that would cure the neurosis would be your murder. Simple as that. I mean if I murdered you, then other white people would begin to understand me. You understand? No. I guess not. If Bessie Smith had killed some white people she wouldn't have needed that music. She could have talked very straight and plain about the world. No metaphors. No grunts. No wiggles in the dark of her soul. Just straight two and two are four. Money. Power. Luxury. Like that. All of them. Crazy niggers turning their backs on sanity. When all it needs is that simple act. Murder. Just murder! Would make us all sane.

(Suddenly weary.) Ahhh. Shit. But who needs it? I'd rather be a fool. Insane. Safe with my words, and no deaths, and clean, hard thoughts, urging me to new conquests. My people's madness. Hah! That's a laugh. My people. They don't need me to claim them. They got legs and arms of their own. Personal insanities. Mirrors. They don't need all those words. They don't need any defense. But listen, though, one more thing. And you tell this to your father, who's probably the kind of man who needs to know at once. So he can plan ahead. Tell him not to preach so much rationalism and cold logic to these niggers. Let them alone. Let them sing curses at you in code and see your filth as simple lack of style. Don't make the mistake, through some irresponsible surge of Christian charity, of talking too much about the advantages of Western rationalism, or the great intellectual legacy of the

---

[5] Bessie Smith (1898?–1937) was a black Jazz singer. Severely injured in an automobile accident while on tour in Mississippi, she died at the segregated hospital in Clarksdale, Mississippi.

[6] Charlie (Bird) Parker (1920–1955) was an innovative black Jazz musician.

white man, or maybe they'll begin to listen. And then, maybe one day, you'll find they actually do understand exactly what you are talking about, all these fantasy people. All these blues people. And on that day, as sure as shit, when you really believe you can "accept" them into your fold, as half-white trusties late of the subject peoples. With no more blues, except the very old ones, and not a watermelon in sight, the great missionary heart will have triumphed, and all of those ex-coons will be stand-up Western men, with eyes for clean hard useful lives, sober, pious and sane, and they'll murder you. They'll murder you, and have very rational explanations. Very much like your own. They'll cut your throats, and drag you out to the edge of your cities so the flesh can fall away from your bones, in sanitary isolation.

Lula *(her voice takes on a different, more businesslike quality)*. I've heard enough.

Clay *(reaching for his books)*. I bet you have. I guess I better collect my stuff and get off this train. Looks like we won't be acting out that little pageant you outlined before.

Lula. No. We won't. You're right about that, at least. *(She turns to look quickly around the rest of the car.)* All right!

(The others respond.)

Clay *(bending across the girl to retrieve his belongings)*. Sorry, baby, I don't think we could make it.

(As he is bending over her, the girl brings up a small knife and plunges it into Clay's chest. Twice. He slumps across her knees, his mouth working stupidly.)

Lula. Sorry is right. *(Turning to the others in the car who have already gotten up from their seats.)* Sorry is the rightest thing you've said. Get this man off me! Hurry, now! *(The others come and drag Clay's body down the aisle.)* Open the door and throw his body out. *(They throw him off.)* And all of you get off at the next stop.

(Lula busies herself straightening her things. Getting everything in order. She takes out a notebook and makes a quick scribbling note. Drops it in her bag. The train apparently stops and all the others get off, leaving her alone in the coach.

Very soon a young Negro of about twenty comes into the coach, with a couple of books under his arm. He sits a few seats in back of Lula. When he is seated she turns and gives him a long slow look. He looks up from his book and drops the book on his lap. Then an old Negro conductor comes into the car, doing a sort of restrained soft shoe, and half mumbling the words of some song. He looks at the young man, briefly, with a quick greeting.)

Conductor. Hey, brother!

Young man.   Hey.

(The conductor continues down the aisle with his little dance and the mumbled song. Lula turns to stare at him, and follows his movements down the aisle. The conductor tips his hat when he reaches her seat, and continues out the car.)

Curtain

QUESTIONS

1. The opening stage direction sets the play in "the flying underbelly of the city." How might a set designer respond to that direction?   **2.** When Lula enters the subway car, she is eating an apple. Later, she offers an apple to Clay. What do these events suggest?   **3.** Lula accuses Clay of being a "well-known type." What type is he? What type is Lula?   **4.** In the first scene, Lula says, "I lie a lot. It helps me control the world." In what sense does Lula control the world?   **5.** Late in the play, Clay's long speech beginning "I'm not telling you again, Tallulah Bankhead," comments on the sources of the music of Bessie Smith and Charlie Parker. What are those sources? What would have silenced them?   **6.** Clay changes toward the end of the play. Describe that change. Does your response to him change at the same time? If so, explain why and how. Do you like him more or less as he changes, for instance? How do you think the author feels about the two Clays he has created? Do you think he likes one of them more than the other? Why or why not?   **7.** In what way is Lula's final act a logical extension of Clay's long speech just before his death?

WRITING TOPIC

Baraka once argued that "the Black Artist's role in America is to aid in the destruction of America as he knows it. His role is to report and reflect so precisely the nature of the society, that other men will be moved by the exactness of his rendering and, if they are black men, grow strong through this moving, having seen their own strength, and weakness; and if they are white men, tremble, curse, and go mad, because they will be drenched with the filth of their evil." Is *Dutchman* such a report? Base your essay, pro or con, on a close analysis of the play.

M. Butterfly

1988

DAVID HENRY HWANG [b. 1957]

CHARACTERS

Rene Gallimard	**Comrade Chin / Suzuki / Shu-Fang**
Song Liling	**Helga**
Marc / Man No. 2 / Consul Sharpless	**Toulon / Man No. 1 / Judge**
Renee / Woman at Party / Pinup Girl	**Dancers**

Playwright's Notes

This play was suggested by international newspaper accounts of a recent espionage trial. For purposes of dramatization, names have been changed, characters created, and incidents devised or altered, and this play does not purport to be a factual record of real events or real people.

> A former French diplomat and a Chinese opera singer have been sentenced to six years in jail for spying for China after a two-day trial that traced a story of clandestine love and mistaken sexual identity. . . .
> Mr. Bouriscot was accused of passing information to China after he fell in love with Mr. Shi, whom he believed for twenty years to be a woman.
> —*The New York Times,* May 11, 1986

> I could escape this feeling
> With my China girl . . .
> —David Bowie & Iggy Pop

Time and Place

The action of the play takes place in a Paris prison in the present, and, in recall, during the decade 1960–1970 in Beijing, and from 1966 to the present in Paris.

Act I

SCENE I. M. Gallimard's prison cell. Paris. 1988.

Lights fade up to reveal Rene Gallimard, sixty-five, in a prison cell. He wears a comfortable bathrobe, and looks old and tired. The sparsely furnished cell contains a wooden crate, upon which sits a hot plate with a kettle, and a portable tape recorder. Gallimard sits on the crate staring at the recorder, a sad smile on his face.

Upstage Song, who appears as a beautiful woman in traditional Chinese garb, dances a traditional piece from the Peking Opera, surrounded by the percussive clatter of Chinese music.

Then, slowly, lights and sound cross-fade; the Chinese opera music dissolves into a Western opera, the "Love Duet" from Puccini's Madame Butterfly. *Song continues dancing, now to the Western accompaniment. Though her movements are the same, the difference in music now gives them a balletic quality.*

Gallimard rises, and turns upstage towards the figure of Song, who dances without acknowledging him.

Gallimard.   Butterfly, Butterfly . . .

He forces himself to turn away, as the image of Song fades out, and talks to us.

Gallimard.   The limits of my cell are as such: four-and-a-half meters by five. There's one window against the far wall; a door, very strong, to protect me from autograph hounds. I'm responsible for the tape recorder, the hot plate, and this charming coffee table.

When I want to eat, I'm marched off to the dining room—hot, steaming slop appears on my plate. When I want to sleep, the light bulb turns itself off—the work of fairies. It's an enchanted space I occupy. The French—we know how to run a prison.

But, to be honest, I'm not treated like an ordinary prisoner. Why? Because I'm a celebrity. You see, I make people laugh.

I never dreamed this day would arrive. I've never been considered witty or clever. In fact, as a young boy, in an informal poll among my grammar school classmates, I was voted "least likely to be invited to a party." It's a title I managed to hold on to for many years. Despite some stiff competition.

But now, how the tables turn! Look at me: the life of every social function in Paris. Paris? Why be modest: My fame has spread to Amsterdam, London, New York. Listen to them! In the world's smartest parlors, I'm the one who lifts their spirits!

With a flourish, Gallimard directs our attention to another part of the stage.

SCENE II.   A party. 1988.

Lights go up on a chic-looking parlor, where a well-dressed trio, two men and one woman, make conversation. Gallimard also remains lit; he observes them from his cell.

Woman.   And what of Gallimard?

Man 1.   Gallimard?

Man 2.   Gallimard!

Gallimard *(to us).*   You see? They're all determined to say my name, as if it were some new dance.

Woman.   He still claims not to believe the truth.

Man 1.   What? Still? Even since the trial?

Woman.   Yes. Isn't it mad?

Man 2 *(laughing).*   He says . . . it was dark . . . and she was very modest!

The trio break into laughter.

Man 1.   So—what? He never touched her with his hands?

Man 2.   Perhaps he did, and simply misidentified the equipment. A compelling case for sex education in the schools.

Woman.   To protect the National Security—the Church can't argue with that.

Man 1.   That's impossible! How could he not know?

Man 2.   Simple ignorance.

Man 1.   For twenty years?

Man 2.   Time flies when you're being stupid.

Woman.   Well, I thought the French were ladies' men.

Man 2.   It seems Monsieur Gallimard was overly anxious to live up to his national reputation.

Woman.   Well, he's not very good-looking.

Man 1.   No, he's not.

Man 2.   Certainly not.

Woman.   Actually, I feel sorry for him.

Man 2.   A toast! To Monsieur Gallimard!

Woman.   Yes! To Gallimard!

Man 1.   To Gallimard!

Man 2.   *Vive la différence!*

They toast, laughing. Lights down on them.

SCENE III.   M. Gallimard's cell.

Gallimard *(smiling).*   You see? They toast me. I've become a patron saint of the socially inept. Can they really be so foolish? Men like that—they should be scratching at my door, begging to learn my secrets! For I, Rene Gallimard, you see, I have known, and been loved by . . . the Perfect Woman.

Alone in this cell, I sit night after night, watching our story play through my head, always searching for a new ending, one which redeems my honor, where she returns at last to my arms. And I imagine you—my ideal audience—who come to understand and even, perhaps just a little, to envy me.

He turns on his tape recorder. Over the house speakers, we hear the opening phrases of Madame Butterfly.

Gallimard.   In order for you to understand what I did and why, I must introduce you to my favorite opera: *Madame Butterfly.* By Giacomo Puccini. First produced at La Scala, Milan, in 1904, it is now beloved throughout the Western world.

As Gallimard describes the opera, the tape segues in and out to sections he may be describing.

Gallimard.   And why not? Its heroine, Cio-Cio-San, also known as Butterfly, is a feminine ideal, beautiful and brave. And its hero, the man for whom she gives up everything, is—*(He pulls out a naval officer's cap from under his crate, pops it on his head, and struts about)*—not very good-looking, not too bright, and pretty much a wimp: Benjamin Franklin Pinkerton of the U.S. Navy. As the curtain rises, he's just closed on two great bargains: one on a house, the other on a woman—call it a package deal.
  Pinkerton purchased the rights to Butterfly for one hundred yen—in modern currency, equivalent to about . . . sixty-six cents. So, he's feeling pretty pleased with himself as Sharpless, the American consul, arrives to witness the marriage.

Marc, wearing an official cap to designate Sharpless, enters and plays the character.

Sharpless/Marc.   Pinkerton!
Pinkerton/Gallimard.   Sharpless! How's it hangin'? It's a great day, just great. Between my house, my wife, and the rickshaw ride in from town, I've saved nineteen cents just this morning.
Sharpless.   Wonderful. I can see the inscription on your tombstone already: "I saved a dollar, here I lie." *(He looks around.)* Nice house.
Pinkerton.   It's artistic. Artistic, don't you think? Like the way the shoji screens slide open to reveal the wet bar and disco mirror ball? Classy, huh? Great for impressing the chicks.
Sharpless.   "Chicks"? Pinkerton, you're going to be a married man!
Pinkerton.   Well, sort of.
Sharpless.   What do you mean?
Pinkerton.   This country—Sharpless, it is okay. You got all these geisha girls running around—
Sharpless.   I know! I live here!
Pinkerton.   Then, you know the marriage laws, right? I split for one month, it's annulled!
Sharpless.   Leave it to you to read the fine print. Who's the lucky girl?

Pinkerton.   Cio-Cio-San. Her friends call her Butterfly. Sharpless, she eats out of my hand!

Sharpless.   She's probably very hungry.

Pinkerton.   Not like American girls. It's true what they say about Oriental girls. They want to be treated bad!

Sharpless.   Oh, please!

Pinkerton.   It's true!

Sharpless.   Are you serious about this girl?

Pinkerton.   I'm marrying her, aren't I?

Sharpless.   Yes—with generous trade-in terms.

Pinkerton.   When I leave, she'll know what it's like to have loved a real man. And I'll even buy her a few nylons.

Sharpless.   You aren't planning to take her with you?

Pinkerton.   Huh? Where?

Sharpless.   Home!

Pinkerton.   You mean, America? Are you crazy? Can you see her trying to buy rice in St. Louis?

Sharpless.   So, you're not serious.

Pause

Pinkerton/Gallimard *(as Pinkerton).*   Consul, I am a sailor in port. *(As Gallimard.)* They then proceed to sing the famous duet, "The Whole World Over."

The duet plays on the speakers. Gallimard, as Pinkerton, lip-syncs his lines from the opera.

Gallimard.   To give a rough translation: "The whole world over, the Yankee travels, casting his anchor wherever he wants. Life's not worth living unless he can win the hearts of the fairest maidens, then hotfoot it off the premises ASAP." *(He turns towards Marc.)* In the preceding scene, I played Pinkerton, the womanizing cad, and my friend Marc from school . . . *(Marc bows grandly for our benefit.)* played Sharpless, the sensitive soul of reason. In life, however, our positions were usually—no, always—reversed.

SCENE IV.   École Nationale.[1] Aix-en-Provence. 1947.

Gallimard.   No, Marc, I think I'd rather stay home.

Marc.   Are you crazy?! We are going to Dad's condo in Marseilles! You know what happened last time?

---

[1] National School.

Gallimard. Of course I do.

Marc. Of course you don't! You never know. . . . They stripped, Rene!

Gallimard. Who stripped?

Marc. The girls!

Gallimard. Girls? Who said anything about girls?

Marc. Rene, we're a buncha university guys goin' up to the woods. What are we gonna do — talk philosophy?

Gallimard. What girls? Where do you get them?

Marc. Who cares? The point is, they come. On trucks. Packed in like sardines. The back flips open, babes hop out, we're ready to roll.

Gallimard. You mean, they just—?

Marc. Before you know it, every last one of them—they're stripped and splashing around my pool. There's no moon out, they can't see what's going on, their boobs are flapping, right? You close your eyes, reach out—it's grab bag, get it? Doesn't matter whose ass is between whose legs, whose teeth are sinking into who. You're just in there, going at it, eyes closed, on and on for as long as you can stand. *(Pause.)* Some fun, huh?

Gallimard. What happens in the morning?

Marc. In the morning, you're ready to talk some philosophy. *(Beat.)* So how 'bout it?

Gallimard. Marc, I can't . . . I'm afraid they'll say no—the girls. So I never ask.

Marc. You don't have to ask! That's the beauty—don't you see? They don't have to say yes. It's perfect for a guy like you, really.

Gallimard. You go ahead . . . I may come later.

Marc. Hey, Rene—it doesn't matter that you're clumsy and got zits—they're not looking!

Gallimard. Thank you very much.

Marc. Wimp.

Marc walks over to the other side of the stage, and starts waving and smiling at women in the audience.

Gallimard *(to us)*. We now return to my version of *Madame Butterfly* and the events leading to my recent conviction for treason.

Gallimard notices Marc making lewd gestures.

Gallimard. Marc, what are you doing?

Marc. Huh? *(Sotto voce.)* Rene, there're a lotta great babes out there. They're probably lookin' at me and thinking, "What a dangerous guy."

Gallimard. Yes—how could they help but be impressed by your cool sophistication?

Gallimard pops the Sharpless cap on Marc's head, and points him offstage. Marc exits, leering.

    SCENE V.   M. Gallimard's cell.

Gallimard.   Next, Butterfly makes her entrance. We learn her age—fifteen . . . but very mature for her years.

Lights come up on the area where we saw Song dancing at the top of the play. She appears there again, now dressed as Madame Butterfly, moving to the "Love Duet." Gallimard turns upstage slightly to watch, transfixed.

Gallimard.   But as she glides past him, beautiful, laughing softly behind her fan, don't we who are men sigh with hope? We, who are not handsome, nor brave, nor powerful, yet somehow believe, like Pinkerton, that we deserve a Butterfly. She arrives with all her possessions in the folds of her sleeves, lays them all out, for her man to do with as he pleases. Even her life itself— she bows her head as she whispers that she's not even worth the hundred yen he paid for her. He's already given too much, when we know he's really had to give nothing at all.

Music and lights on Song out. Gallimard sits at his crate.

Gallimard.   In real life, women who put their total worth at less than sixty-six cents are quite hard to find. The closest we come is in the pages of these magazines. (*He reaches into his crate, pulls out a stack of girlie magazines, and begins flipping through them.*) Quite a necessity in prison. For three or four dollars, you get seven or eight women.
    I first discovered these magazines at my uncle's house. One day, as a boy of twelve. The first time I saw them in his closet . . . all lined up—my body shook. Not with lust—no, with power. Here were women—a shelf-full—who would do exactly as I wanted.

The "Love Duet" creeps in over the speakers. Special comes up, revealing, not Song this time, but a pinup girl in a sexy negligee, her back to us. Gallimard turns upstage and looks at her.

Girl.   I know you're watching me.
Gallimard.   My throat . . . it's dry.
Girl.   I leave my blinds open every night before I go to bed.
Gallimard.   I can't move.
Girl.   I leave my blinds open and the lights on.
Gallimard.   I'm shaking. My skin is hot, but my penis is soft. Why?
Girl.   I stand in front of the window.

Gallimard. What is she going to do?

Girl. I toss my hair, and I let my lips part . . . barely.

Gallimard. I shouldn't be seeing this. It's so dirty. I'm so bad.

Girl. Then, slowly, I lift off my nightdress.

Gallimard. Oh, god. I can't believe it. I can't—

Girl. I toss it to the ground.

Gallimard. Now, she's going to walk away. She's going to—

Girl. I stand there, in the light, displaying myself.

Gallimard. No. She's—why is she naked?

Girl. To you.

Gallimard. In front of a window? This is wrong. No—

Girl. Without shame.

Gallimard. No, she must . . . like it.

Girl. I like it.

Gallimard. She . . . she wants me to see.

Girl. I want you to see.

Gallimard. I can't believe it! She's getting excited!

Girl. I can't see you. You can do whatever you want.

Gallimard. I can't do a thing. Why?

Girl. What would you like me to do . . . next?

Lights go down on her. Music off. Silence, as Gallimard puts away his magazines. Then he resumes talking to us.

Gallimard. Act Two begins with Butterfly staring at the ocean. Pinkerton's been called back to the U.S., and he's given his wife a detailed schedule of his plans. In the column marked "return date," he's written "when the robins nest." This failed to ignite her suspicions. Now, three years have passed without a peep from him. Which brings a response from her faithful servant, Suzuki.

Comrade Chin enters, playing Suzuki.

Suzuki. Girl, he's a loser. What'd he ever give you? Nineteen cents and those ugly Day-Glo stockings? Look, it's finished! Kaput! Done! And you should be glad! I mean, the guy was a woofer! He tried before, you know—before he met you, he went down to geisha central and plunked down his spare change in front of the usual candidates—everyone else gagged! These are hungry prostitutes, and they were not interested, get the picture? Now, stop slathering when an American ship sails in, and let's make some bucks—I mean, yen! We are broke!

 Now, what about Yamadori? Hey, hey—don't look away—the man is a prince—figuratively, and, what's even better, literally. He's rich, he's handsome, he says he'll die if you don't marry him—and he's even willing to overlook the little fact that you've been deflowered all over the place by a foreign devil. What do you mean, "But he's Japanese?" What do you think you are? You think you've been touched by the whitey god? He was a sailor with dirty hands!

Suzuki stalks offstage.

Gallimard.   She's also visited by Consul Sharpless, sent by Pinkerton on a minor errand.

Marc enters, as Sharpless.

Sharpless.   I hate this job.
Gallimard.   This Pinkerton—he doesn't show up personally to tell his wife he's abandoning her. No, he sends a government diplomat . . . at taxpayers' expense.
Sharpless.   Butterfly? Butterfly? I have some bad—I'm going to be ill. Butterfly, I came to tell you—
Gallimard.   Butterfly says she knows he'll return and if he doesn't she'll kill herself rather than go back to her own people. *(Beat.)* This causes a lull in the conversation.
Sharpless.   Let's put it this way . . .
Gallimard.   Butterfly runs into the next room, and returns holding—

Sound cue: a baby crying. Sharpless, "seeing" this, backs away.

Sharpless.   Well, good. Happy to see things going so well. I suppose I'll be going now. Ta ta. Ciao. *(He turns away. Sound cue out.)* I hate this job. *(He exits.)*
Gallimard.   At that moment, Butterfly spots in the harbor an American ship— the *Abramo Lincoln!*

Music cue: "The Flower Duet." Song, still dressed as Butterfly, changes into a wedding kimono, moving to the music.

Gallimard.   This is the moment that redeems her years of waiting. With Suzuki's help, they cover the room with flowers—

Chin, as Suzuki, trudges onstage and drops a lone flower without much enthusiasm.

Gallimard.   —and she changes into her wedding dress to prepare for Pinkerton's arrival.

Suzuki helps Butterfly change. Helga enters, and helps Gallimard change into a tuxedo.

Gallimard.   I married a woman older than myself—Helga.

Helga.   My father was ambassador to Australia. I grew up among criminals and kangaroos.

Gallimard.   Hearing that brought me to the altar—

Helga exits.

Gallimard.   —where I took a vow renouncing love. No fantasy woman would ever want me, so, yes, I would settle for a quick leap up the career ladder. Passion, I banish, and in its place—practicality!

But my vows had long since lost their charm by the time we arrived in China. The sad truth is that all men want a beautiful woman, and the uglier the man, the greater the want.

Suzuki makes final adjustments of Butterfly's costume, as does Gallimard of his tuxedo.

Gallimard.   I married late, at age thirty-one. I was faithful to my marriage for eight years. Until the day when, as a junior-level diplomat in puritanical Peking, in a parlor at the German ambassador's house, during the "Reign of a Hundred Flowers,"[2] I first saw her . . . singing the death scene from *Madame Butterfly.*

Suzuki runs offstage.

SCENE VI.   German ambassador's house. Beijing. 1960.

The upstage special area now becomes a stage. Several chairs face upstage, representing seating for some twenty guests in the parlor. A few "diplomats"— Renee, Marc, Toulon—in formal dress enter and take seats.

Gallimard also sits down, but turns towards us and continues to talk. Orchestral accompaniment on the tape is now replaced by a simple piano. Song picks up the death scene from the point where Butterfly uncovers the hara-kiri knife.

Gallimard.   The ending is pitiful. Pinkerton, in an act of great courage, stays home and sends his American wife to pick up Butterfly's child. The truth, long deferred, has come up to her door.

Song, playing Butterfly, sings the lines from the opera in her own voice—which, though not classical, should be decent.

---

[2] The name given to a short-lived encouragement of free expression in China in 1957.

Song.   *"Con onor muore / chi non puo serbar / vita con onore."*
Gallimard *(simultaneously).*   "Death with honor / Is better than life / Life with dishonor."

The stage is illuminated; we are now completely within an elegant diplomat's residence. Song proceeds to play out an abbreviated death scene. Everyone in the room applauds. Song, shyly, takes her bows. Others in the room rush to congratulate her. Gallimard remains with us.

Gallimard.   They say in opera the voice is everything. That's probably why I'd never before enjoyed opera. Here . . . here was a Butterfly with little or no voice—but she had the grace, the delicacy . . . I believed this girl. I believed her suffering. I wanted to take her in my arms—so delicate, even I could protect her, take her home, pamper her until she smiled.

Over the course of the preceding speech, Song has broken from the upstage crowd and moved directly upstage of Gallimard.

Song.   Excuse me. Monsieur . . . ?

Gallimard turns upstage, shocked.

Gallimard.   Oh! Gallimard. Mademoiselle . . . ? A beautiful . . .
Song.   Song Liling.
Gallimard.   A beautiful performance.
Song.   Oh, please.
Gallimard.   I usually—
Song.   You make me blush. I'm no opera singer at all.
Gallimard.   I usually don't like *Butterfly.*
Song.   I can't blame you in the least.
Gallimard.   I mean, the story—
Song.   Ridiculous.
Gallimard.   I like the story, but . . . what?
Song.   Oh, you like it?
Gallimard.   I . . . what I mean is, I've always seen it played by huge women in so much bad makeup.
Song.   Bad makeup is not unique to the West.
Gallimard.   But, who can believe them?
Song.   And you believe me?
Gallimard.   Absolutely. You were utterly convincing. It's the first time—
Song.   Convincing? As a Japanese woman? The Japanese used hundreds of our people for medical experiments during the war, you know. But I gather such an irony is lost on you.
Gallimard.   No! I was about to say, it's the first time I've seen the beauty of the story.

Song. Really?

Gallimard. Of her death. It's a . . . a pure sacrifice. He's unworthy, but what can she do? She loves him . . . so much. It's a very beautiful story.

Song. Well, yes, to a Westerner.

Gallimard. Excuse me?

Song. It's one of your favorite fantasies, isn't it? The submissive Oriental woman and the cruel white man.

Gallimard. Well, I didn't quite mean . . .

Song. Consider it this way: what would you say if a blonde homecoming queen fell in love with a short Japanese businessman? He treats her cruelly, then goes home for three years, during which time she prays to his picture and turns down marriage from a young Kennedy. Then, when she learns he has remarried, she kills herself. Now, I believe you would consider this girl to be a deranged idiot, correct? But because it's an Oriental who kills herself for a Westerner—ah!—you find it beautiful.

Silence.

Gallimard. Yes . . . well . . . I see your point . . .

Song. I will never do Butterfly again, Monsieur Gallimard. If you wish to see some real theater, come to the Peking Opera sometime. Expand your mind.

Song walks offstage. Other guests exit with her.

Gallimard *(to us).* So much for protecting her in my big Western arms.

SCENE VII. M. Gallimard's apartment. Beijing. 1960.

Gallimard changes from his tux into a casual suit. Helga enters.

Gallimard. The Chinese are an incredibly arrogant people.

Helga. They warned us about that in Paris, remember?

Gallimard. Even Parisians consider them arrogant. That's a switch.

Helga. What is it that Madame Su says? "We are a very old civilization." I never know if she's talking about her country or herself.

Gallimard. I walk around here, all I hear every day, everywhere is how *old* this culture is. The fact that "old" may be synonymous with "senile" doesn't occur to them.

Helga. You're not going to change them. "East is east, west is west, and . . ." whatever that guy said.

Gallimard. It's just that—silly. I met . . . at Ambassador Koening's tonight—you should've been there.

Helga. Koening? Oh god, no. Did he enchant you all again with the history of Bavaria?

Gallimard.   No. I met, I suppose, the Chinese equivalent of a diva. She's a singer in the Chinese opera.

Helga.   They have an opera, too? Do they sing in Chinese? Or maybe—in Italian?

Gallimard.   Tonight, she did sing in Italian.

Helga.   How'd she manage that?

Gallimard.   She must've been educated in the West before the Revolution. Her French is very good also. Anyway, she sang the death scene from *Madame Butterfly.*

Helga.   *Madame Butterfly!* Then I should have come. *(She begins humming, floating around the room as if dragging long kimono sleeves.)* Did she have a nice costume? I think it's a classic piece of music.

Gallimard.   That's what *I* thought, too. Don't let her hear you say that.

Helga.   What's wrong?

Gallimard.   Evidently the Chinese hate it.

Helga.   She hated it, but she performed it anyway? Is she perverse?

Gallimard.   They hate it because the white man gets the girl. Sour grapes if you ask me.

Helga.   Politics again? Why can't they just hear it as a piece of beautiful music? So, what's in their opera?

Gallimard.   I don't know. But, whatever it is, I'm sure it must be *old.*

Helga exits.

SCENE VIII.   Chinese opera house and the streets of Beijing. 1960.

The sound of gongs clanging fills the stage.

Gallimard.   My wife's innocent question kept ringing in my ears. I asked around, but no one knew anything about the Chinese opera. It took four weeks, but my curiosity overcame my cowardice. This Chinese diva—this unwilling Butterfly—what did she do to make her so proud?

The room was hot, and full of smoke. Wrinkled faces, old women, teeth missing—a man with a growth on his neck, like a human toad. All smiling, pipes falling from their mouths, cracking nuts between their teeth, a live chicken pecking at my foot—all looking, screaming, gawking . . . at her.

The upstage area is suddenly hit with a harsh white light. It has become the stage for the Chinese opera performance. Two dancers enter, along with Song. Gallimard stands apart, watching. Song glides gracefully amidst the two dancers. Drums suddenly slam to a halt. Song strikes a pose, looking straight at Gallimard. Dancers exit. Light change. Pause, then Song walks right off the stage and straight up to Gallimard.

Song.   Yes. You. White man. I'm looking straight at you.

Gallimard. Me?

Song. You see any other white men? It was too easy to spot you. How often does a man in my audience come in a tie?

Song starts to remove her costume. Underneath, she wears simple baggy clothes. They are now backstage. The show is over.

Song. So, you are an adventurous imperialist?

Gallimard. I . . . thought it would further my education.

Song. It took you four weeks. Why?

Gallimard. I've been busy.

Song. Well, education has always been undervalued in the West, hasn't it?

Gallimard *(laughing)*. I don't think that's true.

Song. No, you wouldn't. You're a Westerner. How can you objectively judge your own values?

Gallimard. I think it's possible to achieve some distance.

Song. Do you? *(Pause.)* It stinks in here. Let's go.

Gallimard. These are the smells of your loyal fans.

Song. I love them for being my fans, I hate the smell they leave behind. I too can distance myself from my people. *(She looks around, then whispers in his ear.)* "Art for the masses" is a shitty excuse to keep artists poor. *(She pops a cigarette in her mouth.)* Be a gentleman, will you? And light my cigarette.

Gallimard fumbles for a match.

Gallimard. I don't . . . smoke.

Song *(lighting her own)*. Your loss. Had you lit my cigarette, I might have blown a puff of smoke right between your eyes. Come.

They start to walk about the stage. It is a summer night on the Beijing streets. Sounds of the city play on the house speakers.

Song. How I wish there were even a tiny café to sit in. With cappuccinos, and men in tuxedos and bad expatriate jazz.

Gallimard. If my history serves me correctly, you weren't even allowed into the clubs in Shanghai before the Revolution.

Song. Your history serves you poorly, Monsieur Gallimard. True, there were signs reading "No dogs and Chinamen." But a woman, especially a delicate Oriental woman—we always go where we please. Could you imagine it otherwise? Clubs in China filled with pasty, big-thighed white women, while thousands of slender lotus blossoms wait just outside the door? Never. The clubs would be empty. *(Beat.)* We have always held a certain fascination for you Caucasian men, have we not?

Gallimard. But . . . that fascination is imperialist, or so you tell me.

Song. Do you believe everything I tell you? Yes. It is always imperialist. But sometimes . . . sometimes, it is also mutual. Oh—this is my flat.

Gallimard. I didn't even—

Song. Thank you. Come another time and we will further expand your mind.

Song exits. Gallimard continues roaming the streets as he speaks to us.

Gallimard. What was that? What did she mean, "Sometimes . . . it is mutual"? Women do not flirt with me. And I normally can't talk to them. But tonight, I held up my end of the conversation.

SCENE IX. Gallimard's bedroom. Beijing. 1960.

Helga enters.

Helga. You didn't tell me you'd be home late.

Gallimard. I didn't intend to. Something came up.

Helga. Oh? Like what?

Gallimard. I went to the . . . to the Dutch ambassador's home.

Helga. Again?

Gallimard. There was a reception for a visiting scholar. He's writing a six-volume treatise on the Chinese revolution. We all gathered that meant he'd have to live here long enough to actually write six volumes, and we all expressed our deepest sympathies.

Helga. Well, I had a good night too. I went with the ladies to a martial arts demonstration. Some of those men—when they break those thick boards— *(she mimes fanning herself.)* whoo-whoo!

Helga exits. Lights dim.

Gallimard. I lied to my wife. Why? I've never had any reason to lie before. But what reason did I have tonight? I didn't do anything wrong. That night, I had a dream. Other people, I've been told, have dreams when angels appear. Or dragons, or Sophia Loren in a towel. In my dream, Marc from school appeared.

Marc enters, in a nightshirt and cap.

Marc. Rene! You met a girl!

Gallimard and Marc stumble down the Beijing streets. Night sounds over the speakers.

Gallimard. It's not that amazing, thank you.

Marc.   No! It's so monumental, I heard about it halfway around the world in my sleep!

Gallimard.   I've met girls before, you know.

Marc.   Name one. I've come across time and space to congratulate you. *(He hands Gallimard a bottle of wine.)*

Gallimard.   Marc, this is expensive.

Marc.   On those rare occasions when you become a formless spirit, why not steal the best?

Marc pops open the bottle, begins to share it with Gallimard.

Gallimard.   You embarrass me. She . . . there's no reason to think she likes me.

Marc.   "Sometimes, it is mutual"?

Gallimard.   Oh.

Marc.   "Mutual"? "Mutual"? What does that mean?

Gallimard.   You heard?

Marc.   It means the money is in the bank, you only have to write the check!

Gallimard.   I am a married man!

Marc.   And an excellent one too. I cheated after . . . six months. Then again and again, until now—three hundred girls in twelve years.

Gallimard.   I don't think we should hold that up as a model.

Marc.   Of course not! My life—it is disgusting! Phooey! Phooey! But, you— you are the model husband.

Gallimard.   Anyway, it's impossible. I'm a foreigner.

Marc.   Ah, yes. She cannot love you, it is taboo, but something deep inside her heart . . . she cannot help herself . . . she must surrender to you. It is her destiny.

Gallimard.   How do you imagine all this?

Marc.   The same way you do. It's an old story. It's in our blood. They fear us, Rene. Their women fear us. And their men—their men hate us. And, you know something? They are all correct.

They spot a light in a window.

Marc.   There! There, Rene!

Gallimard.   It's her window.

Marc.   Late at night—it burns. The light—it burns for you.

Gallimard.   I won't look. It's not respectful.

Marc.   We don't have to be respectful. We're foreign devils.

Enter Song, in a sheer robe, her face completely swathed in black cloth. The "One Fine Day" aria creeps in over the speakers. With her back to us, Song mimes attending to her toilette. Her robe comes loose, revealing her white shoulders.

Marc.   All your life you've waited for a beautiful girl who would lay down for you. All your life you've smiled like a saint when it's happened to every other man you know. And you see them in magazines and you see them in movies. And you wonder, what's wrong with me? Will anyone beautiful ever want me? As the years pass, your hair thins and you struggle to hold on to even your hopes. Stop struggling, Rene. The wait is over. *(He exits.)*

Gallimard.   Marc? Marc?

At that moment, Song, her back still towards us, drops her robe. A second of her naked back, then a sound cue: a phone ringing, very loud. Blackout, followed in the next beat by a special up on the bedroom area, where a phone now sits. Gallimard stumbles across the stage and picks up the phone. Sound cue out. Over the course of his conversation, area lights fill in the vicinity of his bed. It is the following morning.

Gallimard.   Yes? Hello?

Song *(offstage)*.   Is it very early?

Gallimard.   Why, yes.

Song *(offstage)*.   How early?

Gallimard.   It's . . . it's 5:30. Why are you—?

Song *(offstage)*.   But it's light outside. Already.

Gallimard.   It is. The sun must be in confusion today.

Over the course of Song's next speech, her upstage special comes up again. She sits in a chair, legs crossed, in a robe, telephone to her ear.

Song.   I waited until I saw the sun. That was as much discipline as I could manage for one night. Do you forgive me?

Gallimard.   Of course . . . for what?

Song.   Then I'll ask you quickly. Are you really interested in the opera?

Gallimard.   Why, yes. Yes I am.

Song.   Then come again next Thursday. I am playing *The Drunken Beauty*. May I count on you?

Gallimard.   Yes. You may.

Song.   Perfect. Well, I must be getting to bed. I'm exhausted. It's been a very long night for me.

Song hangs up; special on her goes off. Gallimard begins to dress for work.

SCENE X.   Song Liling's apartment. Beijing. 1960.

Gallimard.   I returned to the opera that next week, and the week after that . . . she keeps our meetings so short—perhaps fifteen, twenty minutes at most. So I am left each week with a thirst which is intensified. In this way, fifteen weeks have gone by. I am starting to doubt the words of my friend Marc. But no, not really. In my heart, I know she has . . . an interest in me. I suspect this is her way. She is outwardly bold and outspoken, yet her heart is shy and afraid. It is the Oriental in her at war with her Western education.

Song (*offstage*).   I will be out in an instant. Ask the servant for anything you want.

Gallimard.   Tonight, I have finally been invited to enter her apartment. Though the idea is almost beyond belief, I believe she is afraid of me.

Gallimard looks around the room. He picks up a picture in a frame, studies it. Without his noticing, Song enters, dressed elegantly in a black gown from the twenties. She stands in the doorway looking like Anna May Wong. [3]

Song.   That is my father.

Gallimard (*surprised*).   Mademoiselle Song . . .

She glides up to him, snatches away the picture.

Song.   It is very good that he did not live to see the Revolution. They would, no doubt, have made him kneel on broken glass. Not that he didn't deserve such a punishment. But he is my father. I would've hated to see it happen.

Gallimard.   I'm very honored that you've allowed me to visit your home.

Song curtseys.

Song.   Thank you. Oh! Haven't you been poured any tea?

Gallimard.   I'm really not—

Song (*to her offstage servant*).   Shu-Fang! Cha! Kwai-lah! (*To Gallimard.*) I'm sorry. You want everything to be perfect—

Gallimard.   Please.

Song.   —and before the evening even begins—

Gallimard.   I'm really not thirsty.

Song.   —it's ruined.

Gallimard (*sharply*).   Mademoiselle Song!

Song sits down.

Song.   I'm sorry.

Gallimard.   What are you apologizing for now?

Pause; Song starts to giggle.

---

[3] (1905–1961), a beautiful Chinese-American actress.

Song.   I don't know!

Gallimard laughs.

Gallimard.   Exactly my point.
Song.   Oh, I am silly. Light-headed. I promise not to apologize for anything else tonight, do you hear me?
Gallimard.   That's a good girl.

Shu-Fang, a servant girl, comes out with a tea tray and starts to pour.

Song *(to Shu-Fang).*   No! I'll pour myself for the gentleman!

Shu-Fang, staring at Gallimard, exits.

Gallimard.   You have a beautiful home.
Song.   No, I . . . I don't even know why I invited you up.
Gallimard.   Well, I'm glad you did.

Song looks around the room.

Song.   There is an element of danger to your presence.
Gallimard.   Oh?
Song.   You must know.
Gallimard.   It doesn't concern me. We both know why I'm here.
Song.   It doesn't concern me either. No . . . well perhaps . . .
Gallimard.   What?
Song.   Perhaps I am slightly afraid of scandal.
Gallimard.   What are we doing?
Song.   I'm entertaining you. In my parlor.
Gallimard.   In France, that would hardly—
Song.   France. France is a country living in the modern era. Perhaps even ahead of it. China is a nation whose soul is firmly rooted two thousand years in the past. What I do, even pouring the tea for you now . . . it has . . . implications. The walls and windows say so. Even my own heart, strapped inside this Western dress . . . even it says things—things I don't care to hear.

Song hands Gallimard a cup of tea. Gallimard puts his hand over both the teacup and Song's hand.

Gallimard.   This is a beautiful dress.
Song.   Don't.
Gallimard.   What?
Song.   I don't even know if it looks right on me.

Gallimard.   Believe me—
Song.   You are from France. You see so many beautiful women.
Gallimard.   France? Since when are the European women—?
Song.   Oh! What am I trying to do, anyway?!

Song runs to the door, composes herself, then turns towards Gallimard.

Song.   Monsieur Gallimard, perhaps you should go.
Gallimard.   But . . . why?
Song.   There's something wrong about this.
Gallimard.   I don't see what.
Song.   I feel . . . I am not myself.
Gallimard.   No. You're nervous.
Song.   Please. Hard as I try to be modern, to speak like a man, to hold a
    Western woman's strong face up to my own . . . in the end, I fail. A small,
    frightened heart beats too quickly and gives me away. Monsieur Gallimard,
    I'm a Chinese girl. I've never . . . never invited a man up to my flat before.
    The forwardness of my actions makes my skin burn.
Gallimard.   What are you afraid of? Certainly not me, I hope.
Song.   I'm a modest girl.
Gallimard.   I know. And very beautiful. *(He touches her hair.)*
Song.   Please—go now. The next time you see me, I shall again be myself.
Gallimard.   I like you the way you are right now.
Song.   You are a cad.
Gallimard.   What do you expect? I'm a foreign devil.

Gallimard walks downstage. Song exits.

Gallimard *(to us).*   Did you hear the way she talked about Western women?
    Much differently than the first night. She does—she feels inferior to them—
    and to me.

SCENE XI.   The French embassy. Beijing. 1960.

Gallimard moves towards a desk.

Gallimard.   I determined to try an experiment. In *Madame Butterfly*, Cio-
    Cio-San fears that the Western man who catches a butterfly will pierce its
    heart with a needle, then leave it to perish. I began to wonder: had I, too,
    caught a butterfly who would writhe on a needle?

*Marc enters, dressed as a bureaucrat, holding a stack of papers. As Gallimard
speaks, Marc hands papers to him. He peruses, then signs, stamps, or rejects
them.*

Gallimard. Over the next five weeks, I worked like a dynamo. I stopped going to the opera, I didn't phone or write her. I knew this little flower was waiting for me to call, and, as I wickedly refused to do so, I felt for the first time that rush of power—the absolute power of a man.

Marc continues acting as the bureaucrat, but he now speaks as himself.

Marc. Rene! It's me.

Gallimard. Marc—I hear your voice everywhere now. Even in the midst of work.

Marc. That's because I'm watching you—all the time.

Gallimard. You were always the most popular guy in school.

Marc. Well, there's no guarantee of failure in life like happiness in high school. Somehow I knew I'd end up in the suburbs working for Renault and you'd be in the Orient picking exotic women off the trees. And they say there's no justice.

Gallimard. That's why you were my friend?

Marc. I gave you a little of my life, so that now you can give me some of yours. *(Pause.)* Remember Isabelle?

Gallimard. Of course I remember! She was my first experience.

Marc. We all wanted to ball her. But she only wanted me.

Gallimard. I had her.

Marc. Right. You balled her.

Gallimard. You were the only one who ever believed me.

Marc. Well, there's a good reason for that. *(Beat.)* C'mon. You must've guessed.

Gallimard. You told me to wait in the bushes by the cafeteria that night. The next thing I knew, she was on me. Dress up in the air.

Marc. She never wore underwear.

Gallimard. My arms were pinned to the dirt.

Marc. She loved the superior position. A girl ahead of her time.

Gallimard. I looked up, and there was this woman . . . bouncing up and down on my loins.

Marc. Screaming, right?

Gallimard. Screaming, and breaking off the branches all around me, and pounding my butt up and down into the dirt.

Marc. Huffing and puffing like a locomotive.

Gallimard. And in the middle of all this, the leaves were getting into my mouth, my legs were losing circulation, I thought, "God. So this is *it?*"

Marc. You thought that?

Gallimard. Well, I was worried about my legs falling off.

Marc. You didn't have a good time?

Gallimard. No, that's not what I—I had a great time!

Marc. You're sure?

Gallimard. Yeah. Really.

Marc.   'Cuz I wanted you to have a good time.
Gallimard.   I did.

Pause.

Marc.   Shit. *(Pause.)* When all is said and done, she was kind of a lousy lay, wasn't she? I mean, there was a lot of energy there, but you never knew what she was doing with it. Like when she yelled "I'm coming!"—hell, it was so loud, you wanted to go, "Look, it's not that big a deal."
Gallimard.   I got scared. I thought she meant someone was actually coming. *(Pause.)* But, Marc?
Marc.   What?
Gallimard.   Thanks.
Marc.   Oh, don't mention it.
Gallimard.   It was my first experience.
Marc.   Yeah. You got her.
Gallimard.   I got her.
Marc.   Wait! Look at that letter again!

Gallimard picks up one of the papers he's been stamping, and rereads it.

Gallimard *(to us)*.   After six weeks, they began to arrive. The letters.

Upstage special on Song, as Madame Butterfly. The scene is underscored by the "Love Duet."

Song.   Did we fight? I do not know. Is the opera no longer of interest to you? Please come—my audiences miss the white devil in their midst.

Gallimard looks up from the letter, towards us.

Gallimard *(to us)*.   A concession, but much too dignified. *(Beat; he discards the letter.)* I skipped the opera again that week to complete a position paper on trade.

The bureaucrat hands him another letter.

Song.   Six weeks have passed since last we met. Is this your practice—to leave friends in the lurch? Sometimes I hate you, sometimes I hate myself, but always I miss you.
Gallimard *(to us)*.   Better, but I don't like the way she calls me "friend." When a woman calls a man her "friend," she's calling him a eunuch or a homo-

sexual. *(Beat; he discards the letter.)* I was absent from the opera for the seventh week, feeling a sudden urge to clean out my files.

Bureaucrat hands him another letter.

Song.   Your rudeness is beyond belief. I don't deserve this cruelty. Don't bother to call. I'll have you turned away at the door.

Gallimard *(to us)*.   I didn't. *(He discards the letter; bureaucrat hands him another.)* And then finally, the letter that concluded my experiment.

Song.   I am out of words. I can hide behind dignity no longer. What do you want? I have already given you my shame.

Gallimard gives the letter back to Marc, slowly. Special on Song fades out.

Gallimard *(to us)*.   Reading it, I became suddenly ashamed. Yes, my experiment had been a success. She was turning on my needle. But the victory seemed hollow.

Marc.   Hollow?! Are you crazy?

Gallimard.   Nothing, Marc. Please go away.

Marc *(exiting, with papers)*.   Haven't I taught you anything?

Gallimard.   "I have already given you my shame." I had to attend a reception that evening. On the way, I felt sick. If there is a God, surely he would punish me now. I had finally gained power over a beautiful woman, only to abuse it cruelly. There must be justice in the world. I had the strange feeling that the ax would fall this very evening.

   SCENE XII.   Ambassador Toulon's residence. Beijing. 1960.

Sound cue: party noises. Light change. We are now in a spacious residence. Toulon, the French ambassador, enters and taps Gallimard on the shoulder.

Toulon.   Gallimard? Can I have a word? Over here.

Gallimard *(to us)*.   Manuel Toulon. French ambassador to China. He likes to think of us all as his children. Rather like God.

Toulon.   Look, Gallimard, there's not much to say. I've liked you. From the day you walked in. You were no leader, but you were tidy and efficient.

Gallimard.   Thank you, sir.

Toulon.   Don't jump the gun. Okay, our needs in China are changing. It's embarrassing that we lost Indochina. Someone just wasn't on the ball there. I don't mean you personally, of course.

Gallimard.   Thank you, sir.

Toulon.   We're going to be doing a lot more information-gathering in the future. The nature of our work here is changing. Some people are just going to have to go. It's nothing personal.

Gallimard.   Oh.

Toulon. Want to know a secret? Vice-Consul LeBon is being transferred.
Gallimard *(to us)*. My immediate superior!
Toulon. And most of his department.
Gallimard *(to us)*. Just as I feared! God has seen my evil heart—
Toulon. But not you.
Gallimard *(to us)*. —and he's taking her away just as . . . *(To Toulon.)* Excuse me, sir?
Toulon. Scare you? I think I did. Cheer up, Gallimard. I want you to replace LeBon as vice-consul.
Gallimard. You—? Yes, well, thank you, sir.
Toulon. Anytime.
Gallimard. I . . . accept with great humility.
Toulon. Humility won't be part of the job. You're going to coordinate the revamped intelligence division. Want to know a secret? A year ago, you would've been out. But the past few months, I don't know how it happened, you've become this new aggressive confident . . . thing. And they also tell me you get along with the Chinese. So I think you're a lucky man, Gallimard. Congratulations.

They shake hands. Toulon exits. Party noises out. Gallimard stumbles across a darkened stage.

Gallimard. Vice-consul? Impossible! As I stumbled out of the party, I saw it written across the sky: There is no God. Or, no—say that there is a God. But that God . . . understands. Of course! God who creates Eve to serve Adam, who blesses Solomon with his harem but ties Jezebel to a burning bed[4]—that God is a man. And he understands! At age thirty-nine, I was suddenly initiated into the way of the world.

SCENE XIII. Song Liling's apartment. Beijing. 1960.

Song enters, in a sheer dressing gown.

Song. Are you crazy?
Gallimard. Mademoiselle Song—
Song. To come here—at this hour? After . . . after eight weeks?
Gallimard. It's the most amazing—
Song. You bang on my door? Scare my servants, scandalize the neighbors?
Gallimard. I've been promoted. To vice-consul.

Pause.

---

[4] Biblical allusions. See Genesis 2:18–25, I Kings 11:1–8, and II Kings 9:30–37.

Song.   And what is that supposed to mean to me?

Gallimard.   Are you my Butterfly?

Song.   What are you saying?

Gallimard.   I've come tonight for an answer: are you my Butterfly?

Song.   Don't you know already?

Gallimard.   I want you to say it.

Song.   I don't want to say it.

Gallimard.   So, that is your answer?

Song.   You know how I feel about—

Gallimard.   I do remember one thing.

Song.   What?

Gallimard.   In the letter I received today.

Song.   Don't.

Gallimard.   "I have already given you my shame."

Song.   It's enough that I even wrote it.

Gallimard.   Well, then—

Song.   I shouldn't have it splashed across my face.

Gallimard.   —if that's all true—

Song.   Stop!

Gallimard.   Then what is one more short answer?

Song.   I don't want to!

Gallimard.   Are you my Butterfly? *(Silence; he crosses the room and begins to touch her hair.)* I want from you honesty. There should be nothing false between us. No false pride.

Pause.

Song.   Yes, I am. I am your Butterfly.

Gallimard.   Then let me be honest with you. It is because of you that I was promoted tonight. You have changed my life forever. My little Butterfly, there should be no more secrets: I love you.

He starts to kiss her roughly. She resists slightly.

Song.   No . . . no . . . gently . . . please, I've never . . .

Gallimard.   No?

Song.   I've tried to appear experienced, but . . . the truth is . . . no.

Gallimard.   Are you cold?

Song.   Yes. Cold.

Gallimard.   Then we will go very, very slowly.

He starts to caress her; her gown begins to open.

Song.   No . . . let me . . . keep my clothes . . .

Gallimard. But . . .

Song. Please . . . it all frightens me. I'm a modest Chinese girl.

Gallimard. My poor little treasure.

Song. I am your treasure. Though inexperienced, I am not . . . ignorant. They teach us things, our mothers, about pleasing a man.

Gallimard. Yes?

Song. I'll do my best to make you happy. Turn off the lights.

Gallimard gets up and heads for a lamp. Song, propped up on one elbow, tosses her hair back and smiles.

Song.   Monsieur Gallimard?

Gallimard.   Yes, Butterfly?

Song: *"Vieni, vieni!"*

Gallimard.   "Come, darling."

Song: *"Ah! Dolce notte!"*

Gallimard.   "Beautiful night."

Song: *"Tutto estatico d'amor ride il ciel!"*

Gallimard.   "All ecstatic with love, the heavens are filled with laughter."

He turns off the lamp. Blackout.

Act II

SCENE I. M. Gallimard's cell. Paris. 1988.

Lights up on Gallimard. He sits in his cell, reading from a leaflet.

Gallimard.   This, from a contemporary critic's commentary on *Madame Butterfly*: "Pinkerton suffers from . . . being an obnoxious bounder whom every man in the audience itches to kick." Bully for us men in the audience! Then, in the same note: "Butterfly is the most irresistibly appealing of Puccini's 'Little Women.' Watching the succession of her humiliations is like watching a child under torture." *(He tosses the pamphlet over his shoulder.)* I suggest that, while we men may all want to kick Pinkerton, very few of us would pass up the opportunity to *be* Pinkerton.

Gallimard moves out of his cell.

SCENE II.   Gallimard and Butterfly's flat. Beijing. 1960.

We are in a simple but well-decorated parlor. Gallimard moves to sit on a sofa, while Song, dressed in a chong sam,[5] enters and curls up at his feet.

Gallimard *(to us).*   We secured a flat on the outskirts of Peking. Butterfly, as I was calling her now, decorated our "home" with Western furniture and Chinese antiques. And there, on a few stolen afternoons or evenings each week, Butterfly commenced her education.
Song.   The Chinese men—they keep us down.
Gallimard.   Even in the "New Society"?
Song.   In the "New Society," we are all kept ignorant equally. That's one of the exciting things about loving a Western man. I know you are not threatened by a woman's education.
Gallimard.   I'm no saint, Butterfly.
Song.   But you come from a progressive society.
Gallimard.   We're not always reminding each other how "old" we are, if that's what you mean.
Song.   Exactly. We Chinese—once, I suppose, it is true, we ruled the world. But so what? How much more exciting to be part of the society ruling the world today. Tell me—what's happening in Vietnam?
Gallimard.   Oh, Butterfly—you want me to bring my work home?
Song.   I want to know what you know. To be impressed by my man. It's not the particulars so much as the fact that you're making decisions which change the shape of the world.
Gallimard.   Not the world. At best, a small corner.

Toulon enters, and sits at a desk upstage.

SCENE III.   French embassy. Beijing. 1961.

Gallimard moves downstage, to Toulon's desk. Song remains upstage, watching.

Toulon.   And a more troublesome corner is hard to imagine.
Gallimard.   So, the Americans plan to begin bombing?
Toulon.   This is very secret, Gallimard: yes. The Americans don't have an embassy here. They're asking us to be their eyes and ears. Say Jack Kennedy signed an order to bomb North Vietnam, Laos. How would the Chinese react?
Gallimard.   I think the Chinese will squawk—
Toulon.   Uh-huh.

---

[5] A tight-fitting dress with side slits in the skirt.

Gallimard.   —but, in their hearts, they don't even like Ho Chi Minh.[6]

Pause.

Toulon.   What a bunch of jerks. Vietnam was *our* colony. Not only didn't the Americans help us fight to keep them, but now, seven years later, they've come back to grab the territory for themselves. It's very irritating.

Gallimard.   With all due respect, sir, why should the Americans have won our war for us back in 'fifty-four if we didn't have the will to win it ourselves?

Toulon.   You're kidding, aren't you?

Pause.

Gallimard.   The Orientals simply want to be associated with whoever shows the most strength and power. You live with the Chinese, sir. Do you think they like Communism?

Toulon.   I live in China. Not with the Chinese.

Gallimard.   Well, I—

Toulon.   *You* live with the Chinese.

Gallimard.   Excuse me?

Toulon.   I can't keep a secret.

Gallimard.   What are you saying?

Toulon.   Only that I'm not immune to gossip. So, you're keeping a native mistress? Don't answer. It's none of my business. *(Pause.)* I'm sure she must be gorgeous.

Gallimard.   Well . . .

Toulon.   I'm impressed. You had the stamina to go out into the streets and hunt one down. Some of us have to be content with the wives of the expatriate community.

Gallimard.   I do feel . . . fortunate.

Toulon.   So, Gallimard, you've got the inside knowledge—what *do* the Chinese think?

Gallimard.   Deep down, they miss the old days. You know, cappuccinos, men in tuxedos—

Toulon.   So what do we tell the Americans about Vietnam?

Gallimard.   Tell them there's a natural affinity between the West and the Orient.

Toulon.   And that you speak from experience?

Gallimard.   The Orientals are people too. They want the good things we can give them. If the Americans demonstrate the will to win, the Vietnamese will welcome them into a mutually beneficial union.

Toulon.   I don't see how the Vietnamese can stand up to American firepower.

---

[6] Revolutionary leader and president of North Vietnam, 1945–1969.

Gallimard.   Orientals will always submit to a greater force.

Toulon.   I'll note your opinions in my report. The Americans always love to hear how "welcome" they'll be. *(He starts to exit.)*

Gallimard.   Sir?

Toulon.   Mmmm?

Gallimard.   This . . . rumor you've heard.

Toulon.   Uh-huh?

Gallimard.   How . . . widespread do you think it is?

Toulon.   It's only widespread within this embassy. Where nobody talks because everybody is guilty. We were worried about you, Gallimard. We thought you were the only one here without a secret. Now you go and find a lotus blossom . . . and top us all. *(He exits.)*

Gallimard *(to us).*   Toulon knows! And he approves! I was learning the benefits of being a man. We form our own clubs, sit behind thick doors, smoke— and celebrate the fact that we're still boys. *(He starts to move downstage, towards Song.)* So, over the—

Suddenly Comrade Chin enters. Gallimard backs away.

Gallimard *(to Song).*   No! Why does she have to come in?

Song.   Rene, be sensible. How can they understand the story without her? Now, don't embarrass yourself.

Gallimard moves down center.

Gallimard *(to us).*   Now, you will see why my story is so amusing to so many people. Why they snicker at parties in disbelief. Please—try to understand it from my point of view. We are all prisoners of our time and place. *(He exits.)*

SCENE IV.   Gallimard and Butterfly's flat. Beijing. 1961.

Song *(to us).*   1961. The flat Monsieur Gallimard rented for us. An evening after he has gone.

Chin.   Okay, see if you can find out when the Americans plan to start bombing Vietnam. If you can find out what cities, even better.

Song.   I'll do my best, but I don't want to arouse his suspicions.

Chin.   Yeah, sure, of course. So, what else?

Song.   The Americans will increase troops in Vietnam to 170,000 soldiers with 120,000 militia and 11,000 American advisors.

Chin *(writing).*   Wait, wait, 120,000 militia and—

Song.   —11,000 American—

Chin.   —American advisors. *(Beat.)* How do you remember so much?

Song.   I'm an actor.

Chin.   Yeah. *(Beat.)* Is that how come you dress like that?

Song.   Like what, Miss Chin?

Chin.   Like that dress! You're wearing a dress. And every time I come here, you're wearing a dress. Is that because you're an actor? Or what?

Song.   It's a . . . disguise, Miss Chin.

Chin.   Actors, I think they're all weirdos. My mother tells me actors are like gamblers or prostitutes or—

Song.   It helps me in my assignment.

Pause.

Chin.   You're not gathering information in any way that violates Communist Party principles, are you?

Song.   Why would I do that?

Chin.   Just checking. Remember: when working for the Great Proletarian State, you represent our Chairman Mao in every position you take.

Song.   I'll try to imagine the Chairman taking my positions.

Chin.   We all think of him this way. Good-bye, comrade. *(She starts to exit.)* Comrade?

Song.   Yes?

Chin.   Don't forget: there is no homosexuality in China!

Song.   Yes, I've heard.

Chin.   Just checking. *(She exits.)*

Song *(to us)*.   What passes for a woman in modern China.

Gallimard sticks his head out from the wings.

Gallimard.   Is she gone?

Song.   Yes, Rene. Please continue in your own fashion.

SCENE V.   Beijing. 1961–1963.

Gallimard moves to the couch where Song still sits. He lies down in her lap, and she strokes his forehead.

Gallimard *(to us)*.   And so, over the years 1961, '62, '63, we settled into our routine, Butterfly and I. She would always have prepared a light snack and then, ever so delicately, and only if I agreed, she would start to pleasure me. With her hands, her mouth . . . too many ways to explain, and too sad, given my present situation. But mostly we would talk. About my life. Perhaps there is nothing more rare than to find a woman who passionately listens.

Song remains upstage, listening, as Helga enters and plays a scene downstage with Gallimard.

Helga.   Rene, I visited Dr. Bolleart this morning.

Gallimard.   Why? Are you ill?

Helga.   No, no. You see, I wanted to ask him . . . that question we've been discussing.

Gallimard.   And I told you, it's only a matter of time. Why did you bring a doctor into this? We just have to keep trying—like a crapshoot, actually.

Helga.   I went, I'm sorry. But listen: he says there's nothing wrong with me.

Gallimard.   You see? Now, will you stop—?

Helga.   Rene, he says he'd like you to go in and take some tests.

Gallimard.   Why? So he can find there's nothing wrong with both of us?

Helga.   Rene, I don't ask for much. One trip! One visit! And then, whatever you want to do about it—you decide.

Gallimard.   You're assuming he'll find something defective!

Helga.   No! Of course not! Whatever he finds—if he finds nothing, we decide what to do about nothing! But go!

Gallimard.   If he finds nothing, we keep trying. Just like we do now.

Helga.   But at least we'll know! *(Pause.)* I'm sorry. *(She starts to exit.)*

Gallimard.   Do you really want me to see Dr. Bolleart?

Helga.   Only if you want a child, Rene. We have to face the fact that time is running out. Only if you want a child. *(She exits.)*

Gallimard *(to Song).*   I'm a modern man, Butterfly. And yet, I don't want to go. It's the same old voodoo. I feel like God himself is laughing at me if I can't produce a child.

Song.   You men of the West—you're obsessed by your odd desire for equality. Your wife can't give you a child, and *you're* going to the doctor?

Gallimard.   Well, you see, she's already gone.

Song.   And because this incompetent can't find the defect, you now have to subject yourself to him? It's unnatural.

Gallimard.   Well, what is the "natural" solution?

Song.   In Imperial China, when a man found that one wife was inadequate, he turned to another—to give him his son.

Gallimard.   What do you—? I can't . . . marry you, yet.

Song.   Please. I'm not asking you to be my husband. But I am already your wife.

Gallimard.   Do you want to . . . have my child?

Song.   I thought you'd never ask.

Gallimard.   But, your career . . . your—

Song.   Phooey on my career! That's your Western mind, twisting itself into strange shapes again. Of course I love my career. But what would I love most of all? To feel something inside me—day and night—something I know is yours. *(Pause.)* Promise me . . . you won't go to this doctor. Who is this Western quack to set himself as judge over the man I love? I know who is a man, and who is not. *(She exits.)*

Gallimard *(to us).*   Dr. Bolleart? Of course I didn't go. What man would?

SCENE VI. Beijing. 1963.

Party noises over the house speakers. Renee enters, wearing a revealing gown.

Gallimard.   1963. A party at the Austrian embassy. None of us could remember the Austrian ambassador's name, which seemed somehow appropriate. *(To Renee.)* So, I tell the Americans, Diem[7] must go. The U.S. wants to be respected by the Vietnamese, and yet they're propping up this nobody seminarian as her president. A man whose claim to fame is his sister-in-law imposing fanatic "moral order" campaigns? Oriental women—when they're good, they're very good, but when they're bad, they're Christians.
Renee.   Yeah.
Gallimard.   And what do you do?
Renee.   I'm a student. My father exports a lot of useless stuff to the Third World.
Gallimard.   How useless?
Renee.   You know. Squirt guns, confectioner's sugar, Hula Hoops . . .
Gallimard.   I'm sure they appreciate the sugar.
Renee.   I'm here for two years to study Chinese.
Gallimard.   Two years!
Renee.   That's what everybody says.
Gallimard.   When did you arrive?
Renee.   Three weeks ago.
Gallimard.   And?
Renee.   I like it. It's primitive, but . . . well, this is the place to learn Chinese, so here I am.
Gallimard.   Why Chinese?
Renee.   I think it'll be important someday.
Gallimard.   You do?
Renee.   Don't ask me when, but . . . that's what I think.
Gallimard.   Well, I agree with you. One hundred percent. That's very farsighted.
Renee.   Yeah. Well of course, my father thinks I'm a complete weirdo.
Gallimard.   He'll thank you someday.
Renee.   Like when the Chinese start buying Hula Hoops?
Gallimard.   There're a billion bellies out there.
Renee.   And if they end up taking over the world—well, then I'll be lucky to know Chinese too, right?

Pause.

---

[7] Ngo Dinh Diem (1901–1963), president of South Vietnam, 1955–1963. He was assassinated in a U.S.-supported coup d'etat.

Gallimard.   At this point, I don't see how the Chinese can possibly take—

Renee.   You know what I *don't* like about China?

Gallimard.   Excuse me? No—what?

Renee.   Nothing to do at night.

Gallimard.   You come to parties at embassies like everyone else.

Renee.   Yeah, but they get out at ten. And then what?

Gallimard.   I'm afraid the Chinese idea of a dance hall is a dirt floor and a man with a flute.

Renee.   Are you married?

Gallimard.   Yes. Why?

Renee.   You wanna . . . fool around?

Pause.

Gallimard.   Sure.

Renee.   I'll wait for you outside. What's your name?

Gallimard.   Gallimard. Rene.

Renee.   Weird. I'm Renee too. *(She exits.)*

Gallimard *(to us).*   And so, I embarked on my first extra-extramarital affair. Renee was picture perfect. With a body like those girls in the magazines. If I put a tissue paper over my eyes, I wouldn't have been able to tell the difference. And it was exciting to be with someone who wasn't afraid to be seen completely naked. But is it possible for a woman to be *too* uninhibited, *too* willing, so as to seem almost too . . . masculine?

Chuck Berry blares from the house speakers, then comes down in volume as Renee enters, toweling her hair.

Renee.   You have a nice weenie.

Gallimard.   What?

Renee.   Penis. You have a nice penis.

Gallimard.   Oh. Well, thank you. That's very . . .

Renee.   What—can't take a compliment?

Gallimard.   No, it's very . . . reassuring.

Renee.   But most girls don't come out and say it, huh?

Gallimard.   And also . . . what did you call it?

Renee.   Oh. Most girls don't call it a "weenie," huh?

Gallimard.   It sounds very—

Renee.   Small, I know.

Gallimard.   I was going to say, "young."

Renee.   Yeah. Young, small, same thing. Most guys are pretty, uh, sensitive about that. Like, you know, I had a boyfriend back home in Denmark. I got mad at him once and called him a little weeniehead. He got so mad! He said at least I should call him a great big weeniehead.

Gallimard.   I suppose I just say "penis."

Renee.   Yeah. That's pretty clinical. There's "cock," but that sounds like a chicken. And "prick" is painful, and "dick" is like you're talking about someone who's not in the room.

Gallimard.   Yes. It's a . . . bigger problem than I imagined.

Renee.   I—I think maybe it's because I really don't know what to do with them—that's why I call them "weenies."

Gallimard.   Well, you did quite well with . . . mine.

Renee.   Thanks, but I mean, really *do* with them. Like, okay, have you ever looked at one? I mean, really?

Gallimard.   No, I suppose when it's part of you, you sort of take it for granted.

Renee.   I guess. But, like, it just hangs there. This little . . . flap of flesh. And there's so much fuss that we make about it. Like, I think the reason we fight wars is because we wear clothes. Because no one knows—between the men, I mean—who has the biggest . . . weenie. So, if I'm a guy with a small one, I'm going to build a really big building or take over a really big piece of land or write a really long book so the other men don't know, right? But, see, it never really works, that's the problem. I mean, you conquer the country, or whatever, but you're still wearing clothes, so there's no way to prove absolutely whose is bigger or smaller. And that's what we call a civilized society. The whole world run by a bunch of men with pricks the size of pins. *(She exits.)*

Gallimard *(to us).*   This was simply not acceptable.

A high-pitched chime rings through the air. Song, dressed as Butterfly, appears in the upstage special. She is obviously distressed. Her body swoons as she attempts to clip the stems of flowers she's arranging in a vase.

Gallimard.   But I kept up our affair, wildly, for several months. Why? I believe because of Butterfly. She knew the secret I was trying to hide. But, unlike a Western woman, she didn't confront me, threaten, even pout. I remembered the words of Puccini's *Butterfly*:

Song.   *"Noi siamo gente avvezza / alle piccole cose / umili e silenziose."*

Gallimard.   "I come from a people / Who are accustomed to little / Humble and silent." I saw Pinkerton and Butterfly, and what she would say if he were unfaithful . . . nothing. She would cry, alone, into those wildly soft sleeves, once full of possessions, now empty to collect her tears. It was her tears and her silence that excited me, every time I visited Renee.

Toulon *(offstage).*   Gallimard!

Toulon enters. Gallimard turns towards him. During the next section, Song, up center, begins to dance with the flowers. It is a drunken, reckless dance, where she breaks small pieces off the stems.

Toulon.   They're killing him.

Gallimard.   Who? I'm sorry? What?

Toulon.   Bother you to come over at this late hour?

Gallimard.   No . . . of course not.

Toulon.   Not after you hear my secret. Champagne?

Gallimard.   Um . . . thank you.

Toulon.   You're surprised. There's something that you've wanted, Gallimard. No, not a promotion. Next time. Something in the world. You're not aware of this, but there's an informal gossip circle among intelligence agents. And some of ours heard from some of the Americans—

Gallimard.   Yes?

Toulon.   That the U.S. will allow the Vietnamese generals to stage a coup . . . and assassinate President Diem.

The chime rings again. Toulon freezes. Gallimard turns upstage and looks at Butterfly, who slowly and deliberately clips a flower off its stem. Gallimard turns back towards Toulon.

Gallimard.   I think . . . that's a very wise move!

Toulon unfreezes.

Toulon.   It's what you've been advocating. A toast?

Gallimard.   Sure. I consider this a vindication.

Toulon.   Not exactly. "To the test. Let's hope you pass."

They drink. The chime rings again. Toulon freezes. Gallimard turns upstage, and Song clips another flower.

Gallimard *(to Toulon)*.   The test?

Toulon *(unfreezing)*.   It's a test of everything you've been saying. I personally think the generals probably will stop the Communists. And you'll be a hero. But if anything goes wrong, then your opinions won't be worth a pig's ear. I'm sure that won't happen. But sometimes it's easier when they don't listen to you.

Gallimard.   They're your opinions too, aren't they?

Toulon.   Personally, yes.

Gallimard.   So we agree.

Toulon.   But my opinions aren't on that report. Yours are. Cheers.

Toulon turns away from Gallimard and raises his glass. At that instant Song picks up the vase and hurls it to the ground. It shatters. Song sinks down amidst the shards of the vase, in a calm, childlike trance. She sings softly, as if reciting a child's nursery rhyme.

Song (*repeat as necessary*).   "The whole world over, the white man travels, setting anchor, wherever he likes. Life's not worth living, unless he finds, the finest maidens, of every land . . ."

Gallimard turns downstage towards us. Song continues singing.

Gallimard.   I shook as I left his house. That coward! That worm! To put the burden for his decisions on my shoulders!
    I started for Renee's. But no, that was all I needed. A schoolgirl who would question the role of the penis in modern society. What I wanted was revenge. A vessel to contain my humiliation. Though I hadn't seen her in several weeks, I headed for Butterfly's.

Gallimard enters Song's apartment.

Song.   Oh! Rene . . . I was dreaming!
Gallimard.   You've been drinking?
Song.   If I can't sleep, then yes, I drink. But then, it gives me these dreams which—Rene, it's been almost three weeks since you visited me last.
Gallimard.   I know. There's been a lot going on in the world.
Song.   Fortunately I am drunk. So I can speak freely. It's not the world, it's you and me. And an old problem. Even the softest skin becomes like leather to a man who's touched it too often. I confess I don't know how to stop it. I don't know how to become another woman.
Gallimard.   I have a request.
Song.   Is this a solution? Or are you ready to give up the flat?
Gallimard.   It may be a solution. But I'm sure you won't like it.
Song.   Oh well, that's very important. "Like it?" Do you think I "like" lying here alone, waiting, always waiting for your return? Please—don't worry about what I may not "like."
Gallimard.   I want to see you . . . naked.

Silence.

Song.   I thought you understood my modesty. So you want me to—what—strip? Like a big cowboy girl? Shiny pasties on my breasts? Shall I fling my kimono over my head and yell "ya-hoo" in the process? I thought you respected my shame!
Gallimard.   I believe you gave me your shame many years ago.
Song.   Yes—and it is just like a white devil to use it against me. I can't believe it. I thought myself so repulsed by the passive Oriental and the cruel white man. Now I see—we are always most revolted by the things hidden within us.
Gallimard.   I just mean—
Song.   Yes?

Gallimard.   —that it will remove the only barrier left between us.

Song.   No, Rene. Don't couch your request in sweet words. Be yourself—a cad—and know that my love is enough, that I submit—submit to the worst you can give me. *(Pause.)* Well, come. Strip me. Whatever happens, know that you have willed it. Our love, in your hands. I'm helpless before my man.

Gallimard starts to cross the room.

Gallimard.   Did I not undress her because I knew, somewhere deep down, what I would find? Perhaps. Happiness is so rare that our mind can turn somersaults to protect it.

At the time, I only knew that I was seeing Pinkerton stalking towards his Butterfly, ready to reward her love with his lecherous hands. The image sickened me, pulled me to my knees, so I was crawling towards her like a worm. By the time I reached her, Pinkerton . . . had vanished from my heart. To be replaced by something new, something unnatural, that flew in the face of all I'd learned in the world—something very close to love.

He grabs her around the waist; she strokes his hair.

Gallimard.   Butterfly, forgive me.

Song.   Rene . . .

Gallimard.   For everything. From the start.

Song.   I'm . . .

Gallimard.   I want to—

Song.   I'm pregnant. *(Beat.)* I'm pregnant. *(Beat.)* I'm pregnant.

Beat.

Gallimard.   I want to marry you!

SCENE VII.   Gallimard and Butterfly's flat. Beijing. 1963.

Downstage, Song paces as Comrade Chin reads from her notepad. Upstage, Gallimard is still kneeling. He remains on his knees throughout the scene, watching it.

Song.   I need a baby.

Chin *(from pad).*   He's been spotted going to a dorm.

Song.   I need a baby.

Chin.   At the Foreign Language Institute.

Song.   I need a baby.

Chin.   The room of a Danish girl. . . . What do you mean, you need a baby?!

Song. Tell Comrade Kang—last night, the entire mission, it could've ended.
Chin. What do you mean?
Song. Tell Kang—he told me to strip.
Chin. Strip?!
Song. Write!
Chin. I tell you, I don't understand nothing about this case anymore. Nothing.
Song. He told me to strip, and I took a chance. Oh, we Chinese, we know how to gamble.
Chin (*writing*). ". . . told him to strip."
Song. My palms were wet, I had to make a split-second decision.
Chin. Hey! Can you slow down?!

Pause.

Song. You write faster, I'm the artist here. Suddenly, it hit me—"All he wants is for her to submit. Once a woman submits, a man is always ready to become 'generous.' "
Chin. You're just gonna end up with rough notes.
Song. And it worked! He gave in! Now, if I can just present him with a baby. A Chinese baby with blond hair—he'll be mine for life!
Chin. Kang will never agree! The trading of babies has to be a counterrevolutionary act!
Song. Sometimes, a counterrevolutionary act is necessary to counter a counterrevolutionary act.

Pause.

Chin. Wait.
Song. I need one . . . in seven months. Make sure it's a boy.
Chin. This doesn't sound like something the Chairman would do. Maybe you'd better talk to Comrade Kang yourself.
Song. Good. I will.

Chin gets up to leave.

Song. Miss Chin? Why, in the Peking Opera, are women's roles played by men?
Chin. I don't know. Maybe, a reactionary remnant of male—
Song. No. (*Beat.*) Because only a man knows how a woman is supposed to act.

Chin exits. Song turns upstage, towards Gallimard.

Gallimard *(calling after Chin).*   Good riddance! *(To Song.)* I could forget all that betrayal in an instant, you know. If you'd just come back and become Butterfly again.

Song.   Fat chance. You're here in prison, rotting in a cell. And I'm on a plane, winging my way back to China. Your President pardoned me of our treason, you know.

Gallimard.   Yes, I read about that.

Song.   Must make you feel . . . lower than shit.

Gallimard.   But don't you, even a little bit, wish you were here with me?

Song.   I'm an artist, Rene. You were my greatest . . . acting challenge. *(She laughs.)* It doesn't matter how rotten I answer, does it? You still adore me. That's why I love you, Rene. *(She points to us.)* So—you were telling your audience about the night I announced I was pregnant.

Gallimard puts his arms around Song's waist. He and Song are in the positions they were in at the end of Scene VI.

SCENE VIII.   Same.

Gallimard.   I'll divorce my wife. We'll live together here, and then later in France.

Song.   I feel so . . . ashamed.

Gallimard.   Why?

Song.   I had begun to lose faith. And now, you shame me with your generosity.

Gallimard.   Generosity? No, I'm proposing for very selfish reasons.

Song.   Your apologies only make me feel more ashamed. My outburst a moment ago!

Gallimard.   Your outburst? What about my request?!

Song.   You've been very patient dealing with my . . . eccentricities. A Western man, used to women freer with their bodies—

Gallimard.   It was sick! Don't make excuses for me.

Song.   I have to. You don't seem willing to make them for yourself.

Pause.

Gallimard.   You're crazy.

Song.   I'm happy. Which often looks like crazy.

Gallimard.   Then make me crazy. Marry me.

Pause.

Song.   No.

Gallimard.   What?

Song.   Do I sound silly, a slave, if I say I'm not worthy?

Gallimard.   Yes. In fact you do. No one has loved me like you.

Song.   Thank you. And no one ever will. I'll see to that.

Gallimard.   So what is the problem?

Song.   Rene, we Chinese are realists. We understand rice, gold, and guns. You are a diplomat. Your career is skyrocketing. Now, what would happen if you divorced your wife to marry a Communist Chinese actress?

Gallimard.   That's not being realistic. That's defeating yourself before you begin.

Song.   We conserve our strength for the battles we can win.

Gallimard.   That sounds like a fortune cookie!

Song.   Where do you think fortune cookies come from!

Gallimard.   I don't care.

Song.   You do. So do I. And we should. That is why I say I'm not worthy. I'm worthy to love and even to be loved by you. But I am not worthy to end the career of one of the West's most promising diplomats.

Gallimard.   It's not that great a career! I made it sound like more than it is!

Song.   Modesty will get you nowhere. Flatter yourself, and you flatter me. I'm flattered to decline your offer. *(She exits.)*

Gallimard *(to us)*.   Butterfly and I argued all night. And, in the end, I left, knowing I would never be her husband. She went away for several months— to the countryside, like a small animal. Until the night I received her call.

A baby's cry from offstage. Song enters, carrying a child.

Song.   He looks like you.

Gallimard.   Oh! *(Beat; he approaches the baby.)* Well, babies are never very attractive at birth.

Song.   Stop!

Gallimard.   I'm sure he'll grow more beautiful with age. More like his mother.

Song.   *"Chi vide mai / a bimbo del Giappon . . ."*

Gallimard.   "What baby, I wonder, was ever born in Japan"—or China, for that matter—

Song.   *". . . occhi azzurrini?"*

Gallimard.   "With azure eyes"—they're actually sort of brown, wouldn't you say?

Song.   *"E il labbro."*

Gallimard.   "And such lips!" *(He kisses Song.)* And such lips.

Song.   *"E i ricciolini d'oro schietto?"*

Gallimard.   "And such a head of golden"—if slightly patchy—"curls?"

Song.   I'm going to call him "Peepee."

Gallimard.   Darling, could you repeat that because I'm sure a rickshaw just flew by overhead.

Song.   You heard me.

Gallimard.   "Song Peepee"? May I suggest Michael, or Stephan, or Adolph?

Song.   You may, but I won't listen.

Gallimard.   You can't be serious. Can you imagine the time this child will have in school?
Song.   In the West, yes.
Gallimard.   It's worse than naming him Ping Pong or Long Dong or—
Song.   But he's never going to live in the West, is he?

Pause.

Gallimard.   That wasn't my choice.
Song.   It is mine. And this is my promise to you: I will raise him, he will be our child, but he will never burden you outside of China.
Gallimard.   Why do you make these promises? I want to be burdened! I want a scandal to cover the papers!
Song *(to us).*   Prophetic.
Gallimard.   I'm serious.
Song.   So am I. His name is as I registered it. And he will never live in the West.

Song exits with the child.

Gallimard *(to us).*   It is possible that her stubbornness only made me want her more. That drawing back at the moment of my capitulation was the most brilliant strategy she could have chosen. It is possible. But it is also possible that by this point she could have said, could have done . . . anything, and I would have adored her still.

SCENE IX.   Beijing. 1966.

A driving rhythm of Chinese percussion fills the stage.

Gallimard.   And then, China began to change. Mao became very old, and his cult became very strong. And, like many old men, he entered his second childhood. So he handed over the reins of state to those with minds like his own. And children ruled the Middle Kingdom[8] with complete caprice. The doctrine of the Cultural Revolution[9] implied continuous anarchy. Contact between Chinese and foreigners became impossible. Our flat was confiscated. Her fame and my money now counted against us.

Two dancers in Mao suits and red-starred caps enter, and begin crudely mimicking revolutionary violence, in an agitprop fashion.

---

[8] From early in its history, the Chinese have called their country the Middle (or Central) Kingdom.
[9] The name given to the period from 1965 to 1967 during which any opposition to the ideological ideas of Chinese leader Mao Tse-tung were fiercely suppressed.

Gallimard.   And somehow the American war went wrong too. Four hundred thousand dollars were being spent for every Viet Cong[10] killed; so General Westmoreland's[11] remark that the Oriental does not value life the way Americans do was oddly accurate. Why weren't the Vietnamese people giving in? Why were they content instead to die and die and die again?

Toulon enters. Percussion and dancers continue upstage.

Toulon.   Congratulations, Gallimard.
Gallimard.   Excuse me, sir?
Toulon.   Not a promotion. That was last time. You're going home.
Gallimard.   What?
Toulon.   Don't say I didn't warn you.
Gallimard.   I'm being transferred . . . because I was wrong about the American war?
Toulon.   Of course not. We don't care about the Americans. We care about your mind. The quality of your analysis. In general, everything you've predicted here in the Orient . . . just hasn't happened.
Gallimard.   I think that's premature.
Toulon.   Don't force me to be blunt. Okay, you said China was ready to open to Western trade. The only thing they're trading out there are Western heads. And, yes, you said the Americans would succeed in Indochina. You were kidding, right?
Gallimard.   I think the end is in sight.
Toulon.   Don't be pathetic. And don't take this personally. You were wrong. It's not your fault.
Gallimard.   But I'm going home.
Toulon.   Right. Could I have the number of your mistress? *(Beat.)* Joke! Joke! Eat a croissant for me.

Toulon exits. Song, wearing a Mao suit, is dragged in from the wings as part of the upstage dance. They "beat" her, then lampoon the acrobatics of the Chinese opera, as she is made to kneel onstage.

Gallimard *(simultaneously).*   I don't care to recall how Butterfly and I said our hurried farewell. Perhaps it was better to end our affair before it killed her.

Gallimard exits. Percussion rises in volume. The lampooning becomes faster, more frenetic. At its height, Comrade Chin walks across the stage with a banner reading: "The Actor Renounces His Decadent Profession!" She reaches the kneel-

---

[10] Those in the Vietnamese Communist movement rebelling against the South Vietnam government. U.S. military forces were sent to suppress the Viet Cong.

[11] William Westmoreland commanded American military forces in Vietnam from 1964 to 1968.

ing Song. At the moment Chin touches Song's chin, percussion stops with a thud. Dancers strike poses.

Chin.   Actor-oppressor, for years you have lived above the common people and looked down on their labor. While the farmer ate millet—
Song.   I ate pastries from France and sweetmeats from silver trays.
Chin.   And how did you come to live in such an exalted position?
Song.   I was a plaything for the imperialists!
Chin.   What did you do?
Song.   I shamed China by allowing myself to be corrupted by a foreigner . . .
Chin.   What does this mean? The People demand a full confession!
Song.   I engaged in the lowest perversions with China's enemies!
Chin.   What perversions? Be more clear!
Song.   I let him put it up my ass!

Dancers look over, disgusted.

Chin.   Aaaa-ya! How can you use such sickening language?!
Song.   My language . . . is only as foul as the crimes I committed . . .
Chin.   Yeah. That's better. So—what do you want to do . . . now?
Song.   I want to serve the people

Percussion starts up, with Chinese strings.

Chin.   What?
Song.   I want to serve the people!

Dancers regain their revolutionary smiles, and begin a dance of victory.

Chin.   What?!
Song.   I want to serve the people!!

Dancers unveil a banner: "The Actor Is Re-Habilitated!" Song remains kneeling before Chin, as the dancers bounce around them, then exit. Music out.

SCENE X.   A commune. Hunan Province. 1970.

Chin.   How you planning to do that?
Song.   I've already worked four years in the fields of Hunan, Comrade Chin.
Chin.   So? Farmers work all their lives. Let me see your hands.

Song holds them out for her inspection.

Chin.   Goddamn! Still so smooth! How long does it take to turn you actors into good anythings? Hunh. You've just spent too many years in luxury to be any good to the Revolution.

Song.   I served the Revolution.

Chin.   Served the Revolution? Bullshit! You wore dresses! Don't tell me—I was there. I saw you! You and your white vice-consul! Stuck up there in your flat, living off the People's Treasury! Yeah, I knew what was going on! You two . . . homos! Homos! Homos! (*Pause; she composes herself.*) Ah! Well . . . you will serve the people, all right. But not with the Revolution's money. This time, you use your own money.

Song.   I have no money.

Chin.   Shut up! And you won't stink up China anymore with your pervert stuff. You'll pollute the place where pollution begins—the West.

Song.   What do you mean?

Chin.   Shut up! You're going to France. Without a cent in your pocket. You find your consul's house, you make him pay your expenses—

Song.   No.

Chin.   And you give us weekly reports! Useful information!

Song.   That's crazy. It's been four years.

Chin.   Either that, or back to the rehabilitation center!

Song.   Comrade Chin, he's not going to support me! Not in France! He's a white man! I was just his plaything—

Chin.   Oh yuck! Again with the sickening language? Where's my stick?

Song.   You don't understand the mind of a man.

Pause.

Chin.   Oh no? No I don't? Then how come I'm married, huh? How come I got a man? Five, six years ago, you always tell me those kind of things, I felt very bad. But not now! Because what does the Chairman say? He tells us *I'm* now the smart one, you're now the nincompoop! *You're* the blockhead, the harebrain, the nitwit! You think you're so smart? You understand "The Mind of a Man"? Good! Then *you* go to France and be a pervert for Chairman Mao!

Chin and Song exit in opposite directions.

SCENE XI.   Paris. 1968–1970.

Gallimard enters.

Gallimard.   And what was waiting for me back in Paris? Well, better Chinese food than I'd eaten in China. Friends and relatives. A little accounting, regular schedule, keeping track of traffic violations in the suburbs. . . . And the indignity of students shouting the slogans of Chairman Mao at me—in French.

Helga. Rene? Rene? *(She enters, soaking wet.)* I've had a . . . problem. *(She sneezes.)*

Gallimard. You're wet.

Helga. Yes, I . . . coming back from the grocer's. A group of students, waving red flags, they—

Gallimard fetches a towel.

Helga. — they ran by, I was caught up along with them. Before I knew what was happening—

Gallimard gives her the towel.

Helga. Thank you. The police started firing water cannons at us. I tried to shout, to tell them I was the wife of a diplomat, but—you know how it is . . . *(Pause.)* Needless to say, I lost the groceries. Rene, what's happening to France?

Gallimard. What's—? Well, nothing, really.

Helga. Nothing?! The storefronts are in flames, there's glass in the streets, buildings are toppling—and I'm wet!

Gallimard. Nothing! . . . that I care to think about.

Helga. And is that why you stay in this room?

Gallimard. Yes, in fact.

Helga. With the incense burning? You know something? I hate incense. It smells so sickly sweet.

Gallimard. Well, I hate the French. Who just smell—period!

Helga. And the Chinese were better?

Gallimard. Please—don't start.

Helga. When we left, this exact same thing, the riots—

Gallimard. No, no . . .

Helga. Students screaming slogans, smashing down doors—

Gallimard. Helga—

Helga. It was all going on in China, too. Don't you remember?!

Gallimard. Helga! Please! *(Pause.)* You have never understood China, have you? You walk in here with these ridiculous ideas, that the West is falling apart, that China was spitting in our faces. You come in, dripping of the streets, and you leave water all over my floor. *(He grabs Helga's towel, begins mopping up the floor.)*

Helga. But it's the truth!

Gallimard. Helga, I want a divorce.

Pause; Gallimard continues mopping the floor.

Helga.   I take it back. China is . . . beautiful. Incense, I like incense.

Gallimard.   I've had a mistress.

Helga.   So?

Gallimard.   For eight years.

Helga.   I knew you would. I knew you would the day I married you. And now what? You want to marry her?

Gallimard.   I can't. She's in China.

Helga.   I see. You know that no one else is ever going to marry me, right?

Gallimard.   I'm sorry.

Helga.   And you want to leave. For someone who's not here, is that right?

Gallimard.   That's right.

Helga.   You can't live with her, but still you don't want to live with me.

Gallimard.   That's right.

Pause.

Helga.   Shit. How terrible that I can figure that out. *(Pause.)* I never thought I'd say it. But, in China, I was happy. I knew, in my own way, I knew that you were not everything you pretended to be. But the pretense—going on your arm to the embassy ball, visiting your office and the guards saying, "Good morning, good morning, Madame Gallimard"—the pretense . . . was very good indeed. *(Pause.)* I hope everyone is mean to you for the rest of your life. *(She exits.)*

Gallimard *(to us).*   Prophetic.

Marc enters with two drinks.

Gallimard *(to Marc).*   In China, I was different from all other men.

Marc.   Sure. You were white. Here's your drink.

Gallimard.   I felt . . . touched.

Marc.   In the head? Rene, I don't want to hear about the Oriental love goddess. Okay? One night—can we just drink and throw up without a lot of conversation?

Gallimard.   You still don't believe me, do you?

Marc.   Sure I do. She was the most beautiful, et cetera, et cetera, blasé, blasé.

Pause.

Gallimard.   My life in the West has been such a disappointment.

Marc.   Life in the West is like that. You'll get used to it. Look, you're driving me away. I'm leaving. Happy, now? *(He exits, then returns.)* Look, I have a date tomorrow night. You wanna come? I can fix you up with—

Gallimard.   Of course. I would love to come.

Pause.

Marc.   Uh—on second thought, no. You'd better get ahold of yourself first.

He exits; Gallimard nurses his drink.

Gallimard *(to us).*   This is the ultimate cruelty, isn't it? That I can talk and talk and to anyone listening, it's only air—too rich a diet to be swallowed by a mundane world. Why can't anyone understand? That in China, I once loved, and was loved by, very simply, the Perfect Woman.

Song enters, dressed as Butterfly in wedding dress.

Gallimard *(to Song).*   Not again. My imagination is hell. Am I asleep this time? Or did I drink too much?
Song.   Rene!
Gallimard.   God, it's too painful! That you speak?
Song.   What are you talking about? Rene—touch me.
Gallimard.   Why?
Song.   I'm real. Take my hand.
Gallimard.   Why? So you can disappear again and leave me clutching at the air? For the entertainment of my neighbors who—?

Song touches Gallimard.

Song.   Rene?

Gallimard takes Song's hand. Silence.

Gallimard.   Butterfly? I never doubted you'd return.
Song.   You hadn't . . . forgotten—?
Gallimard.   Yes, actually, I've forgotten everything. My mind, you see—there wasn't enough room in this hard head—not for the world *and* for you. No, there was only room for one. *(Beat.)* Come, look. See? Your bed has been waiting, with the Klimt[12] poster you like, and—see? The *xiang lu*[13] you gave me?
Song.   I . . . I don't know what to say.
Gallimard.   There's nothing to say. Not at the end of a long trip. Can I make you some tea?
Song.   But where's your wife?
Gallimard.   She's by my side. She's by my side at last.

Gallimard reaches to embrace Song. Song sidesteps, dodging him.

---

[12] Gustav Klimt (1862–1918), an Austrian painter.
[13] Incense burner.

Gallimard.   Why?!

Song (*to us*).   So I did return to Rene in Paris. Where I found—

Gallimard.   Why do you run away? Can't we show them how we embraced that evening?

Song.   Please. I'm talking.

Gallimard.   You have to do what I say! I'm conjuring you up in *my* mind!

Song.   Rene, I've never done what you've said. Why should it be any different in your mind? Now split—the story moves on, and I must change.

Gallimard.   I welcomed you into my home! I didn't have to, you know! I could've left you penniless on the streets of Paris! But I took you in!

Song.   Thank you.

Gallimard.   So . . . please . . . don't change.

Song.   You know I have to. You know I will. And anyway, what difference does it make? No matter what your eyes tell you, you can't ignore the truth. You already know too much.

Gallimard exits. Song turns to us.

Song.   The change I'm going to make requires about five minutes. So I thought you might want to take this opportunity to stretch your legs, enjoy a drink, or listen to the musicians. I'll be here, when you return, right where you left me.

Song goes to a mirror in front of which is a washbasin of water. She starts to remove her makeup as stagelights go to half and houselights come up.

Act III

SCENE I.   A courthouse in Paris. 1986.

As he promised, Song has completed the bulk of his transformation onstage by the time the houselights go down and the stagelights come up full. As he speaks to us, he removes his wig and kimono, leaving them on the floor. Underneath, he wears a well-cut suit.

Song.   So I'd done my job better than I had a right to expect. Well, give him some credit, too. He's right—I was in a fix when I arrived in Paris. I walked from the airport into town, then I located, by blind groping, the Chinatown district. Let me make one thing clear: whatever else may be said about the Chinese, they are stingy! I slept in doorways three days until I could find a tailor who would make me this kimono on credit. As it turns out, maybe I didn't even need it. Maybe he would've been happy to see me in a simple shift and mascara. But . . . better safe than sorry.

That was 1970, when I arrived in Paris. For the next fifteen years, yes, I lived a very comfy life. Some relief, believe me, after four years on a fucking commune in Nowheresville, China. Rene supported the boy and me, and I did some demonstrations around the country as part of my "cultural exchange" cover. And then there was the spying.

Song moves upstage, to a chair. Toulon enters as a judge, wearing the appropriate wig and robes. He sits near Song. It's 1986, and Song is testifying in a courtroom.

Song.   Not much at first. Rene had lost all his high-level contacts. Comrade Chin wasn't very interested in parking-ticket statistics. But finally, at my urging, Rene got a job as a courier, handling sensitive documents. He'd photograph them for me, and I'd pass them on to the Chinese embassy.

Judge.   Did he understand the extent of his activity?

Song.   He didn't ask. He knew that I needed those documents, and that was enough.

Judge.   But he must've known he was passing classified information.

Song.   I can't say.

Judge.   He never asked what you were going to do with them?

Song.   Nope.

Pause.

Judge.   There is one thing that the court—indeed, that all of France—would like to know.

Song.   Fire away.

Judge.   Did Monsieur Gallimard know you were a man?

Song.   Well, he never saw me completely naked. Ever.

Judge.   But surely, he must've . . . how can I put this?

Song.   Put it however you like. I'm not shy. He must've felt around?

Judge.   Mmmmm.

Song.   Not really. I did all the work. He just laid back. Of course we did enjoy more . . . complete union, and I suppose he *might* have wondered why I was always on my stomach, but. . . . But what you're thinking is, "Of course a wrist must've brushed . . . a hand hit . . . over twenty years!" Yeah. Well, Your Honor, it was my job to make him think I was a woman. And chew on this: it wasn't all that hard. See, my mother was a prostitute along the Bundt before the Revolution. And, uh, I think it's fair to say she learned a few things about Western men. So I borrowed her knowledge. In service to my country.

Judge.   Would you care to enlighten the court with this secret knowledge? I'm sure we're all very curious.

Song.   I'm sure you are. *(Pause.)* Okay, Rule One is: Men always believe what they want to hear. So a girl can tell the most obnoxious lies and the guys will believe them every time—"This is my first time"—"That's the biggest I've ever seen"—or *both*, which, if you really think about it, is not possible in a single lifetime. You've maybe heard those phrases a few times in your own life, yes, Your Honor?

Judge. It's not my life, Monsieur Song, which is on trial today.

Song. Okay, okay, just trying to lighten up the proceedings. Tough room.

Judge. Go on.

Song. Rule Two: As soon as a Western man comes into contact with the East—he's already confused. The West has sort of an international rape mentality towards the East. Do you know rape mentality?

Judge. Give us your definition, please.

Song. Basically, "Her mouth says no, but her eyes say yes."

The West thinks of itself as masculine—big guns, big industry, big money—so the East is feminine—weak, delicate, poor . . . but good at art, and full of inscrutable wisdom—the feminine mystique.

Her mouth says no, but her eyes say yes. The West believes the East, deep down, *wants* to be dominated—because a woman can't think for herself.

Judge. What does this have to do with my question?

Song. You expect Oriental countries to submit to your guns, and you expect Oriental women to be submissive to your men. That's why you say they make the best wives.

Judge. But why would that make it possible for you to fool Monsieur Galli-mard? Please—get to the point.

Song. One, because when he finally met his fantasy woman, he wanted more than anything to believe that she was, in fact, a woman. And second, I am an Oriental. And being an Oriental, I could never be completely a man.

Pause.

Judge. Your armchair political theory is tenuous, Monsieur Song.

Song. You think so? That's why you'll lose in all your dealings with the East.

Judge. Just answer my question: did he know you were a man?

Pause.

Song. You know, Your Honor, I never asked.

SCENE II. Same.

Music from the "Death Scene" from Butterfly blares over the house speakers. It is the loudest thing we've heard in this play.

Gallimard enters, crawling towards Song's wig and kimono.

Gallimard. Butterfly? Butterfly?

Song remains a man, in the witness box, delivering a testimony we do not hear.

Gallimard (*to us*).   In my moment of greatest shame, here, in this courtroom—with that . . . person up there, telling the world. . . . What strikes me especially is how shallow he is, how glib and obsequious . . . completely . . . without substance! The type that prowls around discos with a gold medallion stinking of garlic. So little like my Butterfly.

Yet even in this moment my mind remains agile, flip-flopping like a man on a trampoline. Even now, my picture dissolves, and I see that . . . witness . . . talking to me.

Song suddenly stands straight up in his witness box, and looks at Gallimard.

Song.   Yes. You. White man.

Song steps out of the witness box, and moves downstage towards Gallimard. Light change.

Gallimard (*to Song*).   Who? Me?
Song.   Do you see any other white men?
Gallimard.   Yes. There're white men all around. This is a French courtroom.
Song.   So you are an adventurous imperialist. Tell me, why did it take you so long? To come back to this place?
Gallimard.   What place?
Song.   This theater in China. Where we met many years ago.
Gallimard (*to us*).   And once again, against my will, I am transported.

Chinese opera music comes up on the speakers. Song begins to do opera moves, as he did the night they met.

Song.   Do you remember? The night you gave your heart?
Gallimard.   It was a long time ago.
Song.   Not long enough. A night that turned your world upside down.
Gallimard.   Perhaps.
Song.   Oh, be honest with me. What's another bit of flattery when you've already given me twenty years' worth? It's a wonder my head hasn't swollen to the size of China.
Gallimard.   Who's to say it hasn't?
Song.   Who's to say? And what's the shame? In pride? You think I could've pulled this off if I wasn't already full of pride when we met? No, not just pride. Arrogance. It takes arrogance, really—to believe you can will, with your eyes and your lips, the destiny of another. (*He dances.*) C'mon. Admit it. You still want me. Even in slacks and a button-down collar.
Gallimard.   I don't see what the point of—
Song.   You don't? Well maybe, Rene, just maybe—I want you.
Gallimard.   You do?

Song.   Then again, maybe I'm just playing with you. How can you tell? (*Reprising his feminine character, he sidles up to Gallimard.*) "How I wish there were even a small café to sit in. With men in tuxedos, and cappuccinos, and bad expatriate jazz." Now you want to kiss me, don't you?

Gallimard (*pulling away*).   What makes you—?

Song.   —so sure? See? I take the words from your mouth. Then I wait for you to come and retrieve them. (*He reclines on the floor.*)

Gallimard.   Why?! Why do you treat me so cruelly?

Song.   Perhaps I *was* treating you cruelly. But now—I'm being nice. Come here, my little one.

Gallimard.   I'm not your little one!

Song.   My mistake. It's I who am *your* little one, right?

Gallimard.   Yes, I—

Song.   So come get your little one. If you like, I may even let you strip me.

Gallimard.   I mean, you were! Before . . . but not like this!

Song.   I was? Then perhaps I still am. If you look hard enough. (*He starts to remove his clothes.*)

Gallimard.   What—what are you doing?

Song.   Helping you to see through my act.

Gallimard.   Stop that! I don't want to! I don't—

Song.   Oh, but you asked me to strip, remember?

Gallimard.   What? That was years ago! And I took it back!

Song.   No. You postponed it. Postponed the inevitable. Today, the inevitable has come calling.

From the speakers, cacophony: Butterfly mixed in with Chinese gongs.

Gallimard.   No! Stop! I don't want to see!

Song.   Then look away.

Gallimard.   You're only in my mind! All this is in my mind! I order you! To stop!

Song.   To what? To strip? That's just what I'm—

Gallimard.   No! Stop! I want you—!

Song.   You want me?

Gallimard.   To stop!

Song.   You know something, Rene? Your mouth says no, but your eyes say yes. Turn them away. I dare you.

Gallimard.   I don't have to! Every night, you say you're going to strip, but then I beg you and you stop!

Song.   I guess tonight is different.

Gallimard.   Why? Why should that be?

Song.   Maybe I've become frustrated. Maybe I'm saying "Look at me, you fool!" Or maybe I'm just feeling . . . sexy. (*He is down to his briefs.*)

Gallimard.   Please. This is unnecessary. I know what you are.

Song.   You do? What am I?

Gallimard. A—a man.

Song. You don't really believe that.

Gallimard. Yes I do! I knew all the time somewhere that my happiness was temporary, my love a deception. But my mind kept the knowledge at bay. To make the wait bearable.

Song. Monsieur Gallimard—the wait is over.

Song drops his briefs. He is naked. Sound cue out. Slowly, we and Song come to the realization that what we had thought to be Gallimard's sobbing is actually his laughter.

Gallimard. Oh god! What an idiot! Of course!

Song. Rene—what?

Gallimard. Look at you! You're a man! *(He bursts into laughter again.)*

Song. I fail to see what's so funny!

Gallimard. "You fail to see—!" I mean, you never did have much of a sense of humor, did you? I just think it's ridiculously funny that I've wasted so much time on just a man!

Song. Wait. I'm not "just a man."

Gallimard. No? Isn't that what you've been trying to convince me of?

Song. Yes, but what I mean—

Gallimard. And now, I finally believe you, and you tell me it's not true? I think you must have some kind of identity problem.

Song. Will you listen to me?

Gallimard. Why?! I've been listening to you for twenty years. Don't I deserve a vacation?

Song. I'm not just any man!

Gallimard. Then, what exactly are you?

Song. Rene, how can you ask—? Okay, what about this?

He picks up Butterfly's robes, starts to dance around. No music.

Gallimard. Yes, that's very nice. I have to admit.

Song holds out his arm to Gallimard.

Song. It's the same skin you've worshipped for years. Touch it.

Gallimard. Yes, it does feel the same.

Song. Now—close your eyes.

Song covers Gallimard's eyes with one hand. With the other, Song draws Gallimard's hand up to his face. Gallimard, like a blind man, lets his hands run over Song's face.

Gallimard.   This skin, I remember. The curve of her face, the softness of her cheek, her hair against the back of my hand . . .

Song.   I'm your Butterfly. Under the robes, beneath everything, it was always me. Now, open your eyes and admit it—you adore me. *(He removes his hand from Gallimard's eyes.)*

Gallimard.   You, who knew every inch of my desires—how could you, of all people, have made such a mistake?

Song.   What?

Gallimard.   You showed me your true self. When all I loved was the lie. A perfect lie, which you let fall to the ground—and now, it's old and soiled.

Song.   So—you never really loved me? Only when I was playing a part?

Gallimard.   I'm a man who loved a woman created by a man. Everything else—simply falls short.

Pause.

Song.   What am I supposed to do now?

Gallimard.   You were a fine spy, Monsieur Song, with an even finer accomplice. But now I believe you should go. Get out of my life!

Song.   Go where? Rene, you can't live without me. Not after twenty years.

Gallimard.   I certainly can't live with you—not after twenty years of betrayal.

Song.   Don't be stubborn! Where will you go?

Gallimard.   I have a date . . . with my Butterfly.

Song.   So, throw away your pride. And come . . .

Gallimard.   Get away from me! Tonight, I've finally learned to tell fantasy from reality. And, knowing the difference, I choose fantasy.

Song.   *I'm* your fantasy!

Gallimard.   You? You're as real as hamburger. Now get out! I have a date with my Butterfly and I don't want your body polluting the room! *(He tosses Song's suit at him.)* Look at these—you dress like a pimp.

Song.   Hey! These are Armani slacks and—! *(He puts on his briefs and slacks.)* Let's just say . . . I'm disappointed in you, Rene. In the crush of your adoration, I thought you'd become something more. More like . . . a woman.

But no. Men. You're like the rest of them. It's all in the way we dress, and make up our faces, and bat our eyelashes. You really have so little imagination!

Gallimard.   You, Monsieur Song? Accuse me of too little imagination? You, if anyone, should know—I am pure imagination. And in imagination I will remain. Now get out!

Gallimard bodily removes Song from the stage, taking his kimono.

Song.   Rene! I'll never put on those robes again! You'll be sorry!

Gallimard *(to Song).*   I'm already sorry! *(Looking at the kimono in his hands.)* Exactly as sorry . . . as a Butterfly.

SCENE III.   M. Gallimard's prison cell. Paris. 1988.

Gallimard.   I've played out the events of my life night after night, always searching for a new ending to my story, one where I leave this cell and return forever to my Butterfly's arms.

Tonight I realize my search is over. That I've looked all along in the wrong place. And now, to you, I will prove that my love was not in vain— by returning to the world of fantasy where I first met her.

He picks up the kimono; dancers enter.

Gallimard.   There is a vision of the Orient that I have. Of slender women in chong sams and kimonos who die for the love of unworthy foreign devils. Who are born and raised to be the perfect women. Who take whatever punishment we give them, and bounce back, strengthened by love, unconditionally. It is a vision that has become my life.

Dancers bring the washbasin to him and help him make up his face.

Gallimard.   In public, I have continued to deny that Song Liling is a man. This brings me headlines, and is a source of great embarrassment to my French colleagues, who can now be sent into a coughing fit by the mere mention of Chinese food. But alone, in my cell, I have long since faced the truth.

And the truth demands a sacrifice. For mistakes made over the course of a lifetime. My mistakes were simple and absolute—the man I loved was a cad, a bounder. He deserved nothing but a kick in the behind, and instead I gave him . . . all my love.

Yes—love. Why not admit it all? That was my undoing, wasn't it? Love warped my judgment, blinded my eyes, rearranged the very lines on my face . . . until I could look in the mirror and see nothing but . . . a woman.

Dancers help him put on the Butterfly wig.

Gallimard.   I have a vision. Of the Orient. That, deep within its almond eyes, there are still women. Women willing to sacrifice themselves for the love of a man. Even a man whose love is completely without worth.

Dancers assist Gallimard in donning the kimono. They hand him a knife.

Gallimard.   Death with honor is better than life . . . life with dishonor. *(He sets himself center stage, in a seppuku position.)* The love of a Butterfly can withstand many things—unfaithfulness, loss, even abandonment. But how can it face the one sin that implies all others? The devastating knowledge that, underneath it all, the object of her love was nothing more, nothing less than . . . a man. *(He sets the tip of the knife against his body.)* It is 1988. And I have found her at last. In a prison on the outskirts of Paris. My name is Rene Gallimard—also known as Madame Butterfly.

Gallimard turns upstage and plunges the knife into his body, as music from the "Love Duet" blares over the speakers. He collapses into the arms of the dancers, who lay him reverently on the floor. The image holds for several beats. Then a tight special up on Song, who stands as a man, staring at the dead Gallimard. He smokes a cigarette; the smoke filters up through the lights. Two words leave his lips.

Song.   Butterfly? Butterfly?

Smoke rises as lights fade slowly to black.

QUESTIONS

1. Explain the title of the play. Who was Madame Butterfly? What happened to her? Why does Hwang use the abbreviation *M.*?   **2.** Examine the Western stereotypes of Chinese and Japanese women that occur in the play. What are those stereotypes? How do they contribute to the play's impact? Are such stereotypes widely accepted in your community?   **3.** What function is served by minor characters such as Marc and Helga?   **4.** Is this play about international spying? Odd and obsessive sexuality? Political systems? Or something else? Explain.

WRITING TOPICS

1. How does *M. Butterfly*'s complex structure (its movements back and forth in time, in and out of the story of *Madame Butterfly* and the Chinese Opera) contribute to the play's central themes?   **2.** In an essay, describe the implications of the play's ending. Who does Gallimard emulate? How has he changed?

Innocence and Experience

QUESTIONS AND WRITING TOPICS

1. What support do the works in this section provide for Thomas Gray's well-known observation that "where ignorance is bliss, / 'Tis folly to be wise"? **Writing Topic:** Use Gray's observation as the basis for an analysis of Frank O'Connor's "My Oedipus Complex" or Toni Cade Bambara's "The Lesson."

2. In such poems as William Blake's "The Garden of Love," William Wordsworth's "Lines Composed a Few Miles above Tintern Abbey," Robert Frost's "Birches," and Stevie Smith's "To Carry the Child," growing up is seen as a growing away from a kind of truth and reality; in other poems, such as Gerard Manley Hopkins's "Spring and Fall," Dylan Thomas's "Fern Hill," and Robert Wallace's "In a Spring Still Not Written Of," growing up is seen as growing into truth and reality. Do these two groups of poems embody contradictory and mutually exclusive conceptions of childhood? Explain. **Writing Topic:** Select one poem from each of these two groups and contrast the conception of childhood embodied in each.

3. An eighteenth-century novelist wrote: "Oh Innocence, how glorious and happy a portion art thou to the breast that possesses thee! Thou fearest neither the eyes nor the tongues of men. Truth, the most powerful of all things, is thy strongest friend; and the brighter the light is in which thou art displayed, the more it discovers thy transcendent beauties." Which works in this section support this assessment of innocence? Which works contradict it? How would you characterize the relationship between "truth" and "innocence" in the fiction and the drama presented here? **Writing Topic:** Use this observation as the basis for an analysis of *Oedipus Rex*.

4. A certain arrogance is associated with the innocence of Oedipus in Sophocles' *Oedipus Rex,* and Brown in Hawthorne's "Young Goodman Brown." On what is their arrogance based, and how is it modified? **Writing Topic:** Contrast the nature and the consequences of the central characters' arrogance in these works.

5. James Joyce's "Araby," and Frank O'Connor's "My Oedipus Complex" deal with some aspect of sexuality as a force that moves the protagonist from innocence toward experience. How does the recognition of sexuality function in each of the stories? **Writing Topic:** Discuss the relationship between sexuality and innocence in these stories.

6. Which poems in this section depend largely on irony for their force? Can you suggest why irony is a useful device in literature that portrays innocence and experience? **Writing Topics:** a.) Show how Sophocles uses irony in *Oedipus Rex* to advance the plot and create suspense. b.) Write an analysis of the function of irony in Blake's "The Garden of Love" and Hardy's "The Ruined Maid."

7. Hwang's *M. Butterfly* turns on Gallimard's conventional ideas about Asian women. What are those ideas and how do they empower his antagonist? Shaw's *Major Barbara* examines conventional attitudes toward charitable works and weapons manufacture. Which turns out to be more socially useful? **Writing Topic:** Discuss the conventional attitudes that *M. Butterfly* and *Major Barbara* attack. Do you find those attacks successful? Which do you find to be more socially and politically relevant? Explain.

8. Some authors treat the passage from innocence to experience as comedy, while others treat it more seriously, even as tragedy. Do you find one or the other treatment more satisfying? Explain. **Writing Topic:** Select one short story and show how the author achieves either a comic or serious tone.

Conformity and Rebellion

LE VENTRE LÉGISLATIF.

Aspect des bancs ministériels de la chambre improstituée de 1834.

Le Ventre Législatif, 1834 by Honore Daumier

Although the works in this section, like those in "Innocence and Experience," may also feature a violation of innocence, the events are usually based on the clash between the two well-articulated positions; the rebel, on principle, confronts and struggles with established authority. Central in these works is the sense of tremendous external forces—the state, the church, tradition—which can be obeyed only at the expense of conscience and humanity. At the most general level, these works confront a dilemma older than Antigonê's Thebes: the very organizations men and women establish to protect and nurture the individual demand—on pain of economic ruin, social ostracism, even spiritual or physical death—that they violate their most deeply cherished beliefs. When individuals refuse such a demand, they translate their awareness of a hostile social order into action against it and precipitate a crisis. In *Antigonê*, the issue is drawn with utter clarity: Antigonê must obey either the state (Creon) or the gods. In *An Enemy of the People*, Dr. Stockmann realizes that dehumanization is too high a price to pay for domestic prosperity. On a different note, in "Bartleby the Scrivener," Bartleby's "preference" not to conform to the established structures of Wall Street results in a crisis of passive resistance.

Many of the works in this section, particularly the poems, do not treat the theme of conformity and rebellion quite so explicitly and dramatically. Some, like "Eleanor Rigby," describe a world devoid of human communion and community without directly accounting for it; others, like W. H. Auden's "The Unknown Citizen," tell us that the price exacted for total conformity to the industrial superstate is spiritual death. In "Easter 1916," William Butler Yeats meditates upon the awesome meaning of the lives and deaths of political revolutionaries, and in "Harlem," Langston Hughes warns that an inflexible and constricting social order will generate explosion.

Two basic modes, then, inform the literary treatment of conformity and rebellion. While in many of the works, the individual is caught up in a crisis that forces him or her into rebellion, in other works, especially the poems, the focus may be on the individual's failure to move from awareness into action, as in Amy Lowell's "Patterns." Indeed, the portraits of Auden's unknown citizen and of E. E. Cummings's "Cambridge ladies" affirm the necessity for rebellion by rendering so effectively the hollow life of mindless conformity.

However diverse in treatment and technique, all the works in this section are about individuals trapped by complex sets of external forces that regulate and define their lives. Social beings—men and women—sometimes submit to these forces, but it is always an uneasy submission, for the purpose of these forces is to curb and control people. Individuals may recognize that they must be controlled for some larger good; yet they are aware that established social power is often abusive. The tendency of power, at its best, is to act as a conserving force that brakes the disruptive impulse to abandon and destroy, without cause, old ways and ideas. At its worst, power is self-serving. The individual must constantly judge which tendency power is enhancing. And because the power of the individual is most often negligible beside that of frequently abusive social forces, it is not surprising that many artists since the advent of the great nation-states have found a fundamental human dignity in the resistance of the individual to organized society. One of humanity's ancient and profound recognitions, after all, is that the impulse of a Creon is always to make unknown citizens of us all.

FOR THINKING AND WRITING

As you read the selections in this section, consider the following questions. You may want to write out your thoughts informally in a journal or notebook as a way of preparing to respond to the selections, or you may wish to make one of these questions the basis for a formal essay.

1. How would you define *conformity?* What forms of rebellion are possible for a person in your situation? Do you perceive yourself as a conformist? A rebel? Some combination of the two? Explain.

2. How would you define *sanity?* Based on your own definition, do you know an insane person? What form does that insanity take? Do you agree or disagree with Emily Dickinson's assertion that "Much Madness is divinest Sense"? Explain.

3. Discuss this proposition: Governments routinely engage in behavior that would cause an individual to be imprisoned or institutionalized.

4. Give an extended response to each of the following questions. Is war sane? Should one obey an "unjust" law? Should one be guided absolutely by religious principles?

CONFORMITY
AND
REBELLION

The Trial, 1950 by Keith Vaughan

FICTION

Bartleby the Scrivener
A STORY OF WALL STREET

1853

HERMAN MELVILLE [1819–1891]

I am a rather elderly man. The nature of my avocations, for the last thirty years, has brought me into more than ordinary contact with what would seem an interesting and somewhat singular set of men, of whom, as yet, nothing, that I know of, has ever been written—I mean, the law-copyists, or scriveners. I have known very many of them, professionally and privately, and, if I pleased, could relate divers histories, at which good-natured gentlemen might smile, and sentimental souls might weep. But I waive the biographies of all other scriveners, for a few passages in the life of Bartleby, who was a scrivener, the strangest I ever saw, or heard of. While, of other law-copyists, I might write the complete life, of Bartleby nothing of that sort can be done. I believe that no materials exist for a full and satisfactory biography of this man. It is an irreparable loss to literature. Bartleby was one of those beings of whom nothing is ascertainable, except from the original sources, and, in his case, those are very small. What my own astonished eyes saw of Bartleby, *that* is all I know of him, except, indeed, one vague report, which will appear in the sequel.

Ere introducing the scrivener, as he first appeared to me, it is fit I make some mention of myself, my employees, my business, my chambers, and general surroundings; because some such description is indispensable to an adequate understanding of the chief character about to be presented. Imprimis: I am a man who, from his youth upwards, has been filled with a profound conviction that the easiest way of life is the best. Hence, though I belong to a profession proverbially energetic and nervous, even to turbulence, at times, yet nothing of that sort have I ever suffered to invade my peace. I am one of those unambitious lawyers who never addresses a jury, or in any way draws down public applause; but, in the cool tranquillity of a snug retreat, do a snug business among rich men's bonds, and mortgages, and title-deeds. All who know me, consider me an eminently *safe* man. The late John Jacob

Astor,[1] a personage little given to poetic enthusiasm, had no hesitation in pronouncing my first grand point to be prudence; my next, method. I do not speak it in vanity, but simply record the fact, that I was not unemployed in my profession by the late John Jacob Astor; a name which, I admit, I love to repeat; for it hath a rounded and orbicular sound to it, and rings like unto bullion. I will freely add, that I was not insensible to the late John Jacob Astor's good opinion.

Some time prior to the period at which this little history begins, my avocations had been largely increased. The good old office, now extinct in the State of New York, of a Master in Chancery,[2] had been conferred upon me. It was not a very arduous office, but very pleasantly remunerative. I seldom lose my temper; much more seldom indulge in dangerous indignation at wrongs and outrages; but, I must be permitted to be rash here, and declare that I consider the sudden and violent abrogation of the office of Master in Chancery, by the new Constitution, as a—premature act; inasmuch as I had counted upon a life-lease of the profits, whereas I only received those of a few short years. But this is by the way.

My chambers were up stairs, at No. ——— Wall Street. At one end, they looked upon the white wall of the interior of a spacious sky-light shaft, penetrating the building from top to bottom.

This view might have been considered rather tame than otherwise, deficient in what landscape painters call "life." But, if so, the view from the other end of my chambers offered, at least, a contrast, if nothing more. In that direction, my windows commanded an unobstructed view of a lofty brick wall, black by age and everlasting shade; which wall required no spyglass to bring out its lurking beauties, but, for the benefit of all near-sighted spectators, was pushed up to within ten feet of my window panes. Owing to the great height of the surrounding buildings, and my chambers being on the second floor, the interval between this wall and mine not a little resembled a huge square cistern.

At the period just preceding the advent of Bartleby, I had two persons as copyists in my employment, and a promising lad as an office-boy. First, Turkey; second, Nippers; third, Ginger Nut. These may seem names, the like of which are not usually found in the Directory. In truth, they were nicknames, mutually conferred upon each other by my three clerks, and were deemed expressive of their respective persons or characters. Turkey was a short, pursy Englishman, of about my own age—that is, somewhere not far from sixty. In the morning, one might say, his face was of a fine florid hue, but after twelve o'clock, meridian— his dinner hour—it blazed like a grate full of Christmas coals; and continued blazing—but, as it were, with a gradual wane—till six o'clock P.M., or thereabouts; after which, I saw no more of the proprietor of the face, which, gaining

---

[1] A poor immigrant who rose to become one of the great business tycoons of the nineteenth century.

[2] Courts of Chancery often adjudicated business disputes.

its meridian with the sun, seemed to set with it, to rise, culminate, and decline the following day, with the like regularity and undiminished glory. There are many singular coincidences I have known in the course of my life, not the least among which was the fact, that, exactly when Turkey displayed his fullest beams from his red and radiant countenance, just then, too, at that critical moment, began the daily period when I considered his business capacities as seriously disturbed for the remainder of the twenty-four hours. Not that he was absolutely idle, or averse to business, then; far from it. The difficulty was, he was apt to be altogether too energetic. There was a strange, inflamed, flurried, flighty recklessness of activity about him. He would be incautious in dipping his pen into his inkstand. All his blots upon my documents were dropped there after twelve o'clock meridian. Indeed, not only would he be reckless, and sadly given to making blots in the afternoon, but, some days, he went further, and was rather noisy. At such times, too, his face flamed with augmented blazonry, as if cannel coal had been heaped on anthracite. He made an unpleasant racket with his chair; spilled his sand-box; in mending his pens, impatiently split them all to pieces, and threw them on the floor in a sudden passion; stood up, and leaned over his table, boxing his papers about in a most indecorous manner, very sad to behold in an elderly man like him. Nevertheless, as he was in many ways a most valuable person to me, and all the time before twelve o'clock meridian, was the quickest, steadiest creature, too, accomplishing a great deal of work in a style not easily to be matched—for these reasons, I was willing to overlook his eccentricities, though, indeed, occasionally, I remonstrated with him. I did this very gently, however, because, though the civilest, nay, the blandest and most reverential of men in the morning, yet, in the afternoon, he was disposed, upon provocation, to be slightly rash with his tongue—in fact, insolent. Now, valuing his morning services as I did, and resolved not to lose them—yet, at the same time, made uncomfortable by his inflamed ways after twelve o'clock—and being a man of peace, unwilling by my admonitions to call forth unseemly retorts from him, I took upon me, one Saturday noon (he was always worse on Saturdays) to hint to him, very kindly, that, perhaps, now that he was growing old, it might be well to abridge his labors; in short, he need not come to my chambers after twelve o'clock, but, dinner over, had best go home to his lodgings, and rest himself till tea-time. But no; he insisted upon his afternoon devotions. His countenance became intolerably fervid, as he oratorically assured me—gesticulating with a long ruler at the other end of the room—that if his services in the morning were useful, how indispensable, then, in the afternoon?

"With submission, sir," said Turkey, on this occasion, "I consider myself your right-hand man. In the morning I but marshal and deploy my columns; but in the afternoon I put myself at their head, and gallantly charge the foe, thus"—and he made a violent thrust with the ruler.

"But the blots, Turkey," intimated I.

"True; but, with submission, sir, behold these hairs! I am getting old. Surely, sir, a blot or two of a warm afternoon is not to be severely urged against gray hairs. Old age—even if it blot the page—is honorable. With submission, sir, we *both* are getting old."

This appeal to my fellow-feeling was hardly to be resisted. At all events, I saw that go he would not. So, I made up my mind to let him stay, resolving, nevertheless, to see to it that, during the afternoon, he had to do with my less important papers.

Nippers, the second on my list, was a whiskered, sallow, and, upon the whole, rather piratical-looking young man, of about five and twenty. I always deemed him the victim of two evil powers—ambition and indigestion. The ambition was evinced by a certain impatience of the duties of a mere copyist, an unwarrantable usurpation of strictly professional affairs, such as the original drawing up of legal documents. The indigestion seemed betokened in an oc-casional nervous testiness and grinning irritability, causing the teeth to audibly grind together over mistakes committed in copying; unnecessary maledictions, hissed, rather than spoken, in the heat of business; and especially by a continual discontent with the height of the table where he worked. Though of a very ingenious, mechanical turn, Nippers could never get this table to suit him. He put chips under it, blocks of various sorts, bits of pasteboard, and at last went so far as to attempt an exquisite adjustment, by final pieces of folded blotting-paper. But no invention would answer. If, for the sake of easing his back, he brought the table-lid at a sharp angle well up towards his chin, and wrote there like a man using the steep roof of a Dutch house for his desk, then he declared that it stopped the circulation in his arms. If now he lowered the table to his waistbands, and stooped over it in writing, then there was a sore aching in his back. In short, the truth of the matter was, Nippers knew not what he wanted. Or, if he wanted anything, it was to be rid of a scrivener's table altogether. Among the manifestations of his diseased ambition was a fondness he had for receiving visits from certain ambiguous-looking fellows in seedy coats, whom he called his clients. Indeed, I was aware that not only was he, at times, considerable of a ward-politician, but he occasionally did a little business at the Justices' courts, and was not unknown on the steps of the Tombs.[3] I have good reason to believe, however, that one individual who called upon him at my chambers, and who, with a grand air, he insisted was his client, was no other than a dun, and the alleged title-deed, a bill. But, with all his failings, and the annoyances he caused me, Nippers, like his compatriot Turkey, was a very useful man to me; wrote a neat, swift hand; and, when he chose, was not deficient in a gentlemanly sort of deportment. Added to this, he always dressed in a gentlemanly sort of way; and so, incidentally, reflected credit upon my chambers. Whereas, with respect to Turkey, I had much ado to keep him from being a reproach to me. His clothes were apt to look oily, and smell of eating houses. He wore his pantaloons very loose and baggy in summer. His coats

---

[3] A prison in New York City.

were execrable, his hat not to be handled. But while the hat was a thing of indifference to me, inasmuch as his natural civility and deference, as a dependent Englishman, always led him to doff it the moment he entered the room, yet his coat was another matter. Concerning his coats, I reasoned with him; but with no effect. The truth was, I suppose, that a man with so small an income could not afford to sport such a lustrous face and a lustrous coat at one and the same time. As Nippers once observed, Turkey's money went chiefly for red ink. One winter day, I presented Turkey with a highly respectable-looking coat of my own—a padded gray coat, of a most comfortable warmth, and which buttoned straight up from the knee to the neck. I thought Turkey would appreciate the favor, and abate his rashness and obstreperousness of afternoons. But no; I verily believe that buttoning himself up in so downy and blanket-like a coat had a pernicious effect upon him—upon the same principle that too much oats are bad for horses. In fact, precisely as a rash, restive horse is said to feel his oats, so Turkey felt his coat. It made him insolent. He was a man whom prosperity harmed.

Though, concerning the self-indulgent habits of Turkey, I had my own private surmises, yet, touching Nippers, I was well persuaded that, whatever might be his faults in other respects, he was, at least, a temperate young man. But, indeed, nature herself seemed to have been his vintner, and, at his birth, charged him so thoroughly with an irritable, brandy-like disposition, that all subsequent potations were needless. When I consider how, amid the stillness of my chambers, Nippers would sometimes impatiently rise from his seat, and stooping over his table, spread his arms wide apart, seize the whole desk, and move it, and jerk it, with a grim, grinding motion on the floor, as if the table were a perverse voluntary agent and vexing him, I plainly perceive that, for Nippers, brandy-and-water were altogether superfluous.

It was fortunate for me that, owing to its peculiar cause—indigestion—the irritability and consequent nervousness of Nippers were mainly observable in the morning, while in the afternoon he was comparatively mild. So that, Turkey's paroxysms only coming on about twelve o'clock, I never had to do with their eccentricities at one time. Their fits relieved each other, like guards. When Nippers's was on, Turkey's was off; and *vice versa*. This was a good natural arrangement, under the circumstances.

Ginger Nut, the third on my list, was a lad, some twelve years old. His father was a car-man, ambitious of seeing his son on the bench instead of a cart, before he died. So he sent him to my office, as student at law, errand-boy, cleaner and sweeper, at the rate of one dollar a week. He had a little desk to himself; but he did not use it much. Upon inspection, the drawer exhibited a great array of shells of various sorts of nuts. Indeed, to this quick-witted youth, the whole noble science of the law was contained in a nutshell. Not the least among the employments of Ginger Nut, as well as one which he discharged with the most alacrity, was his duty as cake and apple purveyor for Turkey and Nippers. Copying law-papers being proverbially a dry, husky sort of business,

my two scriveners were fain to moisten their mouths very often with Spitzen-
bergs,[4] to be had at the numerous stalls nigh the Custom House and Post Office.
Also, they sent Ginger Nut very frequently for that peculiar cake—small, flat,
round, and very spicy—after which he had been named by them. Of a cold
morning, when business was but dull, Turkey would gobble up scores of these
cakes, as if they were mere wafers—indeed, they sell them at the rate of six or
eight for a penny—the scrape of his pen blending with the crunching of the
crisp particles in his mouth. Rashest of all the fiery afternoon blunders and
flurried rashnesses of Turkey, was his once moistening a ginger-cake between
his lips, and clapping it on to a mortgage, for a seal. I came within an ace of
dismissing him then. But he mollified me by making an oriental bow, and
saying—

"With submission, sir, it was generous of me to find you in stationery on
my own account."

Now my original business—that of a conveyancer and title hunter, and
drawer-up of recondite documents of all sorts—was considerably increased by
receiving the master's office. There was now great work for scriveners. Not only
must I push the clerks already with me, but I must have additional help.

In answer to my advertisement, a motionless young man one morning stood
upon my office threshold, the door being open, for it was summer. I can see
that figure now—pallidly neat, pitiably respectable, incurably forlorn! It was
Bartleby.

After a few words touching his qualifications, I engaged him, glad to have
among my corps of copyists a man of so singularly sedate an aspect, which I
thought might operate beneficially upon the flighty temper of Turkey, and the
fiery one of Nippers.

I should have stated before that ground-glass folding-doors divided my premises into two parts, one of which was occupied by my scriveners, the other by
myself. According to my humor, I threw open these doors, or closed them. I
resolved to assign Bartleby a corner by the folding-doors, but on my side of
them, so as to have this quiet man within easy call, in case any trifling thing
was to be done. I placed his desk close up to a small side-window in that part
of the room, a window which originally had afforded a lateral view of certain
grimy backyards and bricks, but which, owing to subsequent erections, commanded at present no view at all, though it gave some light. Within three feet
of the panes was a wall, and the light came down from far above, between two
lofty buildings, as from a very small opening in a dome. Still further to a
satisfactory arrangement, I procured a high green folding screen, which might
entirely isolate Bartleby from my sight, though not remove him from my voice.
And thus, in a manner, privacy and society were conjoined.

At first, Bartleby did an extraordinary quantity of writing. As if long famishing
for something to copy, he seemed to gorge himself on my documents. There

---

[4] A variety of apple.

was no pause for digestion. He ran a day and night line, copying by sun-light and by candle-light. I should have been quite delighted with his application, had he been cheerfully industrious. But he wrote on silently, palely, mechanically.

It is, of course, an indispensable part of a scrivener's business to verify the accuracy of his copy, word by word. Where there are two or more scriveners in an office, they assist each other in this examination, one reading from the copy, the other holding the original. It is a very dull, wearisome, and lethargic affair. I can readily imagine that, to some sanguine temperaments, it would be altogether intolerable. For example, I cannot credit that the mettlesome poet, Byron, would have contentedly sat down with Bartleby to examine a law document of, say five hundred pages, closely written in a crimpy hand.

Now and then, in the haste of business, it had been my habit to assist in comparing some brief document myself, calling Turkey or Nippers for this purpose. One object I had, in placing Bartleby so handy to me behind the screen, was to avail myself of his services on such trivial occasions. It was on the third day, I think, of his being with me, and before any necessity had arisen for having his own writing examined, that, being much hurried to complete a small affair I had in hand, I abruptly called to Bartleby. In my haste and natural expectancy of instant compliance, I sat with my head bent over the original on my desk, and my right hand sideways, and somewhat nervously extended with the copy, so that, immediately upon emerging from his retreat, Bartleby might snatch it and proceed to business without the least delay.

In this very attitude did I sit when I called to him, rapidly stating what it was I wanted him to do—namely, to examine a small paper with me. Imagine my surprise, nay, my consternation, when, without moving from his privacy, Bartleby, in a singularly mild, firm voice, replied, "I would prefer not to."

I sat awhile in perfect silence, rallying my stunned faculties. Immediately it occurred to me that my ears had deceived me, or Bartleby had entirely misunderstood my meaning. I repeated my request in the clearest tone I could assume; but in quite as clear a one came the previous reply, "I would prefer not to."

"Prefer not to," echoed I, rising in high excitement, and crossing the room with a stride. "What do you mean? Are you moon-struck? I want you to help me compare this sheet here—take it," and I thrust it towards him.

"I would prefer not to," said he.

I looked at him steadfastly. His face was leanly composed; his gray eye dimly calm. Not a wrinkle of agitation rippled him. Had there been the least uneasiness, anger, impatience, or impertinence in his manner; in other words, had there been any thing ordinarily human about him, doubtless I should have violently dismissed him from the premises. But as it was, I should have as soon thought of turning my pale plaster-of-paris bust of Cicero out of doors. I stood gazing at him awhile, as he went on with his own writing, and then reseated myself at my desk. This is very strange, thought I. What had one best do? But my business hurried me. I concluded to forget the matter for the present, reserving it for my future leisure. So calling Nippers from the other room, the paper was speedily examined.

A few days after this, Bartleby concluded four lengthy documents, being quadruplicates of a week's testimony taken before me in my High Court of Chancery. It became necessary to examine them. It was an important suit, and great accuracy was imperative. Having all things arranged, I called Turkey, Nippers, and Ginger Nut from the next room, meaning to place the four copies in the hands of my four clerks, while I should read from the original. Accordingly, Turkey, Nippers, and Ginger Nut had taken their seats in a row, each with his document in his hand, when I called to Bartleby to join this interesting group.

"Bartleby! quick, I am waiting."

I heard a slow scrape of his chair legs on the uncarpeted floor, and soon he appeared standing at the entrance of his hermitage.

"What is wanted?" said he, mildly.

"The copies, the copies," said I, hurriedly. "We are going to examine them. There—" and I held towards him the fourth quadruplicate.

"I would prefer not to," he said, and gently disappeared behind the screen.

For a few moments I was turned into a pillar of salt, standing at the head of my seated column of clerks. Recovering myself, I advanced towards the screen, and demanded the reason for such extraordinary conduct.

"*Why* do you refuse?"

"I would prefer not to."

With any other man I should have flown outright into a dreadful passion, scorned all further words, and thrust him ignominiously from my presence. But there was something about Bartleby that not only strangely disarmed me, but in a wonderful manner, touched and disconcerted me. I began to reason with him.

"These are your own copies we are about to examine. It is labor saving to you, because one examination will answer for your four papers. It is common usage. Every copyist is bound to help examine his copy. Is it not so? Will you not speak? Answer!"

"I prefer not to," he replied in a flutelike tone. It seemed to me that, while I had been addressing him, he carefully revolved every statement that I made; fully comprehended the meaning; could not gainsay the irresistible conclusion; but, at the same time, some paramount consideration prevailed with him to reply as he did.

"You are decided, then, not to comply with my request—a request made according to common usage and common sense?"

He briefly gave me to understand, that on that point my judgment was sound. Yes: his decision was irreversible.

It is not seldom the case that, when a man is browbeaten in some unprecedented and violently unreasonable way, he begins to stagger in his own plainest faith. He begins, as it were, vaguely to surmise that, wonderful as it may be, all the justice and all the reason is on the other side. Accordingly, if any disinterested persons are present, he turns to them for some reinforcement of his own faltering mind.

"Turkey," said I, "what do you think of this? Am I not right?"

"With submission, sir," said Turkey, in his blandest tone, "I think that you are."

"Nippers," said I, "what do *you* think of it?"

"I think I should kick him out of the office."

(The reader, of nice perceptions, will here perceive that, it being morning, Turkey's answer is couched in polite and tranquil terms, but Nippers replies in ill-tempered ones. Or, to repeat a previous sentence, Nippers's ugly mood was on duty, and Turkey's off.)

"Ginger Nut," said I, willing to enlist the smallest suffrage in my behalf, "what do *you* think of it?"

"I think, sir, he's a little *luny*," replied Ginger Nut, with a grin.

"You hear what they say," said I, turning towards the screen, "come forth and do your duty."

But he vouchsafed no reply. I pondered a moment in sore perplexity. But once more business hurried me. I determined again to postpone the consideration of this dilemma to my future leisure. With a little trouble we made out to examine the papers without Bartleby, though at every page or two Turkey deferentially dropped his opinion, that this proceeding was quite out of the common; while Nippers, twitching in his chair with a dyspeptic nervousness, ground out, between his set teeth, occasional hissing maledictions against the stubborn oaf behind the screen. And for his (Nippers's) part, this was the first and the last time he would do another man's business without pay.

Meanwhile Bartleby sat in his hermitage, oblivious to everything but his own peculiar business there.

Some days passed, the scrivener being employed upon another lengthy work. His late remarkable conduct led me to regard his ways narrowly. I observed that he never went to dinner; indeed, that he never went anywhere. As yet I had never, of my personal knowledge, known him to be outside of my office. He was a perpetual sentry in the corner. At about eleven o'clock though, in the morning, I noticed that Ginger Nut would advance toward the opening in Bartleby's screen, as if silently beckoned thither by a gesture invisible to me where I sat. The boy would then leave the office, jingling a few pence, and reappear with a handful of ginger-nuts, which he delivered in the hermitage, receiving two of the cakes for his trouble.

He lives, then, on ginger-nuts, thought I; never eats a dinner, properly speaking; he must be a vegetarian, then; but no; he never eats even vegetables; he eats nothing but ginger-nuts. My mind then ran on in reveries concerning the probable effects upon the human constitution of living entirely on ginger-nuts. Ginger-nuts are so called, because they contain ginger as one of their peculiar constituents, and the final flavoring one. Now, what was ginger? A hot, spicy thing. Was Bartleby hot and spicy? Not at all. Ginger, then, had no effect upon Bartleby. Probably he preferred it should have none.

Nothing so aggravates an earnest person as a passive resistance. If the individual so resisted be of a not inhumane temper, and the resisting one perfectly harmless in his passivity, then, in the better moods of the former, he will endeavor charitably to construe to his imagination what proves impossible to be solved by his judgement. Even so, for the most part, I regarded Bartleby and his ways. Poor fellow! thought I, he means no mischief; it is plain he intends no insolence; his aspect sufficiently evinces that his eccentricities are involuntary. He is useful to me. I can get along with him. If I turn him away, the chances are he will fall in with some less-indulgent employer, and then he will be rudely treated, and perhaps driven forth miserably to starve. Yes. Here I can cheaply purchase a delicious self-approval. To befriend Bartleby; to humor him in his strange willfulness, will cost me little or nothing, while I lay up in my soul what will eventually prove a sweet morsel for my conscience. But this mood was not invariable with me. The passiveness of Bartleby sometimes irritated me. I felt strangely goaded on to encounter him in new opposition— to elicit some angry spark from him answerable to my own. But, indeed, I might as well have essayed to strike fire with my knuckles against a bit of Windsor soap. But one afternoon the evil impulse in me mastered me, and the following little scene ensued:

"Bartleby," said I, "when those papers are all copied, I will compare them with you."

"I would prefer not to."

"How? Surely you do not mean to persist in that mulish vagary?"

No answer.

I threw open the folding-doors near by, and, turning upon Turkey and Nippers, exclaimed:

"Bartleby a second time says, he won't examine his papers. What do you think of it, Turkey?"

It was afternoon, be it remembered. Turkey sat glowing like a brass boiler; his bald head steaming; his hands reeling among his blotted papers.

"Think of it?" roared Turkey; "I think I'll just step behind his screen, and black his eyes for him!"

So saying, Turkey rose to his feet and threw his arms into a pugilistic position. He was hurrying away to make good his promise, when I detained him, alarmed at the effect of incautiously rousing Turkey's combativeness after dinner.

"Sit down, Turkey," said I, "and hear what Nippers has to say. What do you think of it, Nippers? Would I not be justified in immediately dismissing Bartleby?"

"Excuse me, that is for you to decide, sir. I think his conduct quite unusual, and, indeed, unjust, as regards Turkey and myself. But it may only be a passing whim."

"Ah," exclaimed I, "you have strangely changed your mind, then—you speak very gently of him now."

"All beer," cried Turkey; "gentleness is effects of beer—Nippers and I dined together to-day. You see how gentle *I* am, sir. Shall I go and black his eyes?"

"You refer to Bartleby, I suppose. No, not to-day, Turkey," I replied; "pray, put up your fists."

I closed the doors, and again advanced towards Bartleby. I felt additional incentives tempting me to my fate. I burned to be rebelled against again. I remembered that Bartleby never left the office.

"Bartleby," said I, "Ginger Nut is away; just step around to the post office, won't you? (it was but a three minutes' walk), and see if there is anything for me."

"I would prefer not to."

"You *will* not?"

"I *prefer* not."

I staggered to my desk, and sat there in a deep study. My blind inveteracy returned. Was there any other thing in which I could procure myself to be ignominiously repulsed by this lean, penniless wight?—my hired clerk? What added thing is there, perfectly reasonable, that he will be sure to refuse to do? "Bartleby!"

No answer.

"Bartleby," in a louder tone.

No answer.

"Bartleby," I roared.

Like a very ghost, agreeably to the laws of magical invocation, at the third summons, he appeared at the entrance of his hermitage.

"Go to the next room, and tell Nippers to come to me."

"I prefer not to," he respectfully and slowly said and mildly disappeared.

"Very good, Bartleby," said I, in a quiet sort of serenely-severe, self-possessed tone, intimating the unalterable purpose of some terrible retribution very close at hand. At the moment I half intended something of the kind. But upon the whole, as it was drawing towards my dinner-hour, I thought it best to put on my hat and walk home for the day, suffering much from perplexity and distress of mind.

Shall I acknowledge it? The conclusion of this whole business was, that it soon became a fixed fact of my chambers, that a pale young scrivener, by the name of Bartleby, had a desk there; that he copied for me at the usual rate of four cents a folio (one hundred words); but he was permanently exempt from examining the work done by him, that duty being transferred to Turkey and Nippers, out of compliment, doubtless, to their superior acuteness; moreover, said Bartleby was never, on any account, to be dispatched on the most trivial errand of any sort; and that even if entreated to take upon him such a matter, it was generally understood that he would "prefer not to"—in other words, he would refuse point blank.

As days passed on, I became considerably reconciled to Bartleby. His steadiness, his freedom from all dissipation, his incessant industry (except when he chose to throw himself into a standing revery behind his screen), his great stillness, his unalterableness of demeanor under all circumstances, made him a valuable acquisition. One prime thing was this—*he was always there*—first in the morning, continually through the day, and the last at night. I had a singular confidence in his honesty. I felt my most precious papers perfectly safe in his hands. Sometimes, to be sure, I could not, for the very soul of me, avoid falling into sudden spasmodic passions with him. For it was exceeding difficult to bear in mind all the time those strange peculiarities, privileges, and unheard of exemptions, forming the tacit stipulations on Bartleby's part under which he remained in my office. Now and then, in the eagerness of dispatching pressing business, I would inadvertently summon Bartleby, in a short, rapid tone, to put his finger, say, on the incipient tie of a bit of red tape with which I was about compressing some papers. Of course, from behind the screen the usual answer, "I prefer not to," was sure to come; and then, how could a human creature, with the common infirmities of our nature, refrain from bitterly exclaiming upon such perverseness—such unreasonableness? However, every added repulse of this sort which I received only tended to lessen the probability of my repeating the inadvertence.

Here it must be said, that according to the custom of most legal gentlemen occupying chambers in densely-populated law buildings, there were several keys to my door. One was kept by a woman residing in the attic, which person weekly scrubbed and daily swept and dusted my apartments. Another was kept by Turkey for convenience sake. The third I sometimes carried in my own pocket. The fourth I knew not who had.

Now, one Sunday morning I happened to go to Trinity Church, to hear a celebrated preacher, and finding myself rather early on the ground I thought I would walk round to my chambers for a while. Luckily I had my key with me; but upon applying it to the lock, I found it resisted by something inserted from the inside. Quite surprised, I called out; when to my consternation a key was turned from within; and thrusting his lean visage at me, and holding the door ajar, the apparition of Bartleby appeared, in his shirt sleeves, and otherwise in a strangely tattered *déshabillé*, saying quietly that he was sorry, but he was deeply engaged just then, and—preferred not admitting me at present. In a brief word or two, he moreover added, that perhaps I had better walk around the block two or three times, and by that time he would probably have concluded his affairs.

Now, the utterly unsurmised appearance of Bartleby, tenanting my law-chambers of a Sunday morning, with his cadaverously gentlemanly *nonchalance*, yet withal firm and self-possessed, had such a strange effect upon me, that incontinently I slunk away from my own door, and did as desired. But not without sundry twinges of impotent rebellion against the mild effrontery of this unaccountable scrivener. Indeed, it was his wonderful mildness chiefly, which not only disarmed me, but unmanned me as it were. For I consider that one, for the time, is somehow unmanned when he tranquilly permits his hired clerk to dictate to him, and order him away from his own premises. Furthermore, I was full of uneasiness as to what Bartleby could possibly be doing in my office in his shirt sleeves, and in an otherwise dismantled condition of a Sunday morning. Was anything amiss going on? Nay, that was out of the question. It was not to be thought of for a moment that Bartleby was an immoral person. But what could he be doing there?—copying? Nay again, whatever might be his eccentricities, Bartleby was an eminently decorous person. He would be the last man to sit down to his desk in any state approaching to nudity. Besides, it was Sunday; and there was something about Bartleby that forbade the supposition that he would by any secular occupation violate the proprieties of the day.

Nevertheless, my mind was not pacified; and full of a restless curiosity, at last I returned to the door. Without hindrance I inserted my key, opened it, and entered. Bartleby was not to be seen. I looked round anxiously, peeped behind his screen; but it was very plain that he was gone. Upon more closely examining the place, I surmised that for an indefinite period Bartleby must have eaten, dressed, and slept in my office, and that, too, without plate, mirror, or bed. The cushioned seat of a rickety old sofa in one corner bore the faint impress of a lean, reclining form. Rolled away under his desk, I found a blanket; under the empty grate, a blacking box and brush; on a chair, a tin basin, with soap and a ragged towel; in a newspaper a few crumbs of ginger-nuts and a morsel of cheese. Yes, thought I, it is evident enough that Bartleby has been making his home here, keeping bachelor's hall all by himself. Immediately then the thought came sweeping across me, what miserable friendlessness and loneliness are here revealed! His poverty is great; but his solitude, how horrible! Think of it. Of a Sunday, Wall Street is deserted as Petra;[5] and every night of every day it is an emptiness. This building, too, which of week-days hums with industry and life, at nightfall echoes with sheer vacancy, and all through Sunday is forlorn. And here Bartleby makes his home; sole spectator of a solitude which he has seen all populous—a sort of innocent and transformed Marius brooding among the ruins of Carthage![6]

For the first time in my life a feeling of over-powering stinging melancholy seized me. Before, I had never experienced aught but a not unpleasing sadness. The bond of a common humanity now drew me irresistibly to gloom. A fraternal melancholy! For both I and Bartleby were sons of Adam. I remembered the bright silks and sparkling faces I had seen that day, in gala trim, swan-like sailing down the Mississippi of Broadway; and I contrasted them with the pallid copyist, and thought to myself, Ah, happiness courts the light, so we deem the world is gay; but misery hides aloof, so we deem that misery there is none. These sad fancyings—chimeras, doubtless, of a sick and silly brain—led on to other and more special thoughts, concerning the eccentricities of Bartleby. Presentiments of strange discoveries hovered round me. The scrivener's pale form appeared to me laid out, among uncaring strangers, in its shivering winding sheet.

---

[5] A city in Palestine found by explorers in 1812. It had been deserted and lost for centuries.
[6] Gaius Marius (155–86 B.C.), a plebeian general who was forced to flee from Rome. Nineteenth-century democratic literature sometimes pictured him old and alone among the ruins of Carthage.

Suddenly I was attracted by Bartleby's closed desk, the key in open sight left in the lock.

I mean no mischief, seek the gratification of no heartless curiosity, thought I; besides, the desk is mine, and its contents, too, so I will make bold to look within. Everything was methodically arranged, the papers smoothly placed. The pigeon holes were deep, and removing the files of documents, I groped into their recesses. Presently I felt something there, and dragged it out. It was an old bandanna handkerchief, heavy and knotted. I opened it, and saw it was a saving's bank.

I now recalled all the quiet mysteries which I had noted in the man. I remembered that he never spoke but to answer; that, though at intervals he had considerable time to himself, yet I had never seen him reading—no, not even a newspaper; that for long periods he would stand looking out, at his pale window behind the screen, upon the dead brick wall; I was quite sure he never visited any refectory or eating house; while his pale face clearly indicated that he never drank beer like Turkey; or tea and coffee even, like other men; that he never went anywhere in particular that I could learn; never went out for a walk, unless, indeed, that was the case at present; that he had declined telling who he was, or whence he came, or whether he had any relatives in the world; that though so thin and pale, he never complained of ill health. And more than all, I remembered a certain unconscious air of pallid—how shall I call it?—of pallid haughtiness, say, or rather an austere reserve about him, which had positively awed me into my tame compliance with his eccentricities, when I had feared to ask him to do the slightest incidental thing for me, even though I might know, from his long-continued motionlessness, that behind his screen he must be standing in one of those dead-wall reveries of his.

Revolving all these things, and coupling them with the recently discovered fact, that he made my office his constant abiding place and home, and not forgetful of his morbid moodiness; revolving all these things, a prudential feeling began to steal over me. My first emotions had been those of pure melancholy and sincerest pity; but just in proportion as the forlornness of Bartleby grew and grew to my imagination, did that same melancholy merge into fear, that pity into repulsion. So true it is, and so terrible, too, that up to a certain point the thought or sight of misery enlists our best affections; but, in certain special cases, beyond that point it does not. They err who would assert that invariably this is owing to the inherent selfishness of the human heart. It rather proceeds from a certain hopelessness of remedying excessive and organic ill. To a sensitive being, pity is not seldom pain. And when at last it is perceived that such pity cannot lead to effectual succor, common sense bids the soul be rid of it. What I saw that morning persuaded me that the scrivener was the victim of innate and incurable disorder. I might give alms to his body; but his body did not pain him; it was his soul that suffered, and his soul I could not reach.

I did not accomplish the purpose of going to Trinity Church that morning. Somehow, the things I had seen disqualified me for the time from church-going. I walked homeward, thinking what I would do with Bartleby. Finally, I resolved upon this—I would put certain calm questions to him the next morning, touching his history, etc., and if he declined to answer them openly and unreservedly (and I supposed he would prefer not), then to give him a twenty dollar bill over and above whatever I might owe him, and tell him his services were no longer required; but that if in any other way I could assist him, I would be happy to do so, especially if he desired to return to his native place, wherever that might be, I would willingly help to defray the expenses. Moreover, if, after reaching home, he found himself at any time in want of aid, a letter from him would be sure of a reply.

The next morning came.

"Bartleby," said I, gently calling to him behind his screen.

No reply.

"Bartleby," said I, in a still gentler tone, "come here; I am not going to ask you to do anything you would prefer not to do—I simply wish to speak to you."

Upon this he noiselessly slid into view.

"Will you tell me, Bartleby, where you were born?"

"I would prefer not to."

"Will you tell me *anything* about yourself?"

"I would prefer not to."

"But what reasonable objection can you have to speak to me? I feel friendly towards you."

He did not look at me while I spoke, but kept his glance fixed upon my bust of Cicero, which, as I then sat, was directly behind me, some six inches above my head.

"What is your answer, Bartleby," said I, after waiting a considerable time for a reply, during which his countenance remained immovable, only there was the faintest conceivable tremor of the white attenuated mouth.

"At present I prefer to give no answer," he said, and retired into his hermitage.

It was rather weak in me I confess, but his manner, on this occasion, nettled me. Not only did there seem to lurk in it a certain calm disdain, but his perverseness seemed ungrateful, considering the undeniable good usage and indulgence he had received from me.

Again I sat ruminating what I should do. Mortified as I was at his behavior, and resolved as I had been to dismiss him when I entered my office, nevertheless I strangely felt something superstitious knocking at my heart, and forbidding me to carry out my purpose, and denouncing me for a villain if I dared to breathe one bitter word against this forlornest of mankind. At last, familiarly drawing my chair behind his screen, I sat down and said: "Bartleby, never mind, then, about revealing your history; but let me entreat you, as a friend, to comply as far as may be with the usages of this office. Say now, you will help to examine papers to-morrow or next day: in short, say now, that in a day or two you will begin to be a little reasonable:—say so, Bartleby."

"At present I would prefer not to be a little reasonable," was his mildly cadaverous reply.

Just then the folding-doors opened, and Nippers approached. He seemed suffering from an unusually bad night's rest, induced by severer indigestion than common. He overheard those final words of Bartleby.

"*Prefer not*, eh?" gritted Nippers—"I'd *prefer* him, if I were you, sir," addressing me—"I'd *prefer* him; I'd give him preferences, the stubborn mule! What is it, sir, pray, that he *prefers* not to do now?"

Bartleby moved not a limb.

"Mr. Nippers," said I, "I'd prefer that you would withdraw for the present."

Somehow, of late, I had got into the way of involuntarily using this word "prefer" upon all sorts of not exactly suitable occasions. And I trembled to think that my contact with the scrivener had already and seriously affected me in a mental way. And what further and deeper aberration might it not yet produce? This apprehension had not been without efficacy in determining me to summary measures.

As Nippers, looking very sour and sulky, was departing, Turkey blandly and deferentially approached.

"With submission, sir," said he, "yesterday I was thinking about Bartleby here, and I think that if he would but prefer to take a quart of good ale every day, it would do much towards mending him, and enabling him to assist in examining his papers."

"So you have got the word, too," said I, slightly excited.

"With submission, what word, sir," asked Turkey, respectfully crowding himself into the contracted space behind the screen, and by so doing, making me jostle the scrivener. "What word, sir?"

"I would prefer to be left alone here," said Bartleby, as if offended at being mobbed in his privacy.

"*That's* the word, Turkey," said I—"*that's* it."

"Oh, *prefer?* oh yes—queer word. I never use it myself. But, sir, as I was saying, if he would but prefer—"

"Turkey," interrupted I, "you will please withdraw."

"Oh certainly, sir, if you prefer that I should."

As he opened the folding-door to retire, Nippers at his desk caught a glimpse of me, and asked whether I would prefer to have a certain paper copied on blue paper or white. He did not in the least roguishly accent the word prefer. It was plain that it involuntarily rolled from his tongue. I thought to myself, surely I must get rid of a demented man, who already has in some degree turned the tongues, if not the heads of myself and clerks. But I thought it prudent not to break the dismission at once.

The next day I noticed that Bartleby did nothing but stand at his window in his dead-wall revery. Upon asking him why he did not write, he said that he had decided upon doing no more writing.

"Why, how now? What next?" exclaimed I, "do no more writing?"

"No more."

"And what is the reason?"

"Do you not see the reason for yourself?" he indifferently replied.

I looked steadfastly at him, and perceived that his eyes looked dull and glazed. Instantly it occurred to me, that his unexampled diligence in copying by his dim window for the first few weeks of his stay with me might have temporarily impaired his vision.

I was touched. I said something in condolence with him. I hinted that of course he did wisely in abstaining from writing for a while; and urged him to embrace that opportunity of taking wholesome exercise in the open air. This, however, he did not do. A few days after this, my other clerks being absent, and being in a great hurry to dispatch certain letters by the mail, I thought that, having nothing else earthly to do, Bartleby would surely be less inflexible than usual, and carry these letters to the post office. But he blankly declined. So, much to my inconvenience, I went myself.

Still added days went by. Whether Bartleby's eyes improved or not, I could not say. To all appearance, I thought they did. But when I asked him if they did, he vouchsafed no answer. At all events, he would do no copying. At last, in reply to my urgings, he informed me that he had permanently given up copying.

"What!" exclaimed I; "suppose your eyes should get entirely well—better than ever before—would you not copy then?"

"I have given up copying," he answered, and slid aside.

He remained as ever, a fixture in my chamber. Nay—if that were possible—he became still more of a fixture than before. What was to be done? He would do nothing in the office; why should he stay there? In plain fact, he had now become a millstone to me, not only useless as a necklace, but afflictive to bear. Yet I was sorry for him. I speak less than truth when I say that, on his own account, he occasioned me uneasiness. If he would but have named a single relative or friend, I would instantly have written, and urged their taking the poor fellow away to some convenient retreat. But he seemed alone, absolutely alone in the universe. A bit of wreck in the mid-Atlantic. At length, necessities connected with my business tyrannized over all other considerations. Decently as I could, I told Bartleby that in six days time he must unconditionally leave the office. I warned him to take measures, in the interval, for procuring some other abode. I offered to assist him in this endeavor, if he himself would but take the first step towards a removal. "And when you finally quit me, Bartleby," added I, "I shall see that you go not away entirely unprovided. Six days from this hour, remember."

At the expiration of that period, I peeped behind the screen, and lo! Bartleby was there.

I buttoned up my coat, balanced myself; advanced slowly towards him, touched his shoulder, and said, "The time has come; you must quit this place; I am sorry for you; here is money; but you must go."

"I would prefer not," he replied, with his back still towards me.

"You *must*."

He remained silent.

Now I had an unbounded confidence in this man's common honesty. He had frequently restored to me sixpences and shillings carelessly dropped upon the floor, for I am apt to be very reckless in such shirt-button affairs. The proceeding, then, which followed will not be deemed extraordinary.

"Bartleby," said I, "I owe you twelve dollars on account; here are thirty-two, the odd twenty are yours—Will you take it?" and I handed the bills towards him.

But he made no motion.

"I will leave them here, then," putting them under a weight on the table. Then taking my hat and cane and going to the door, I tranquilly turned and added—"After you have removed your things from these offices, Bartleby, you will of course lock the door—since every one is now gone for the day but you—and if you please, slip your key underneath the mat, so that I may have it in the morning. I shall not see you again; so good-by to you. If, hereafter, in your new place of abode, I can be of any service to you, do not fail to advise me by letter. Good-by, Bartleby, and fare you well."

But he answered not a word; like the last column of some ruined temple, he remained standing mute and solitary in the middle of the otherwise deserted room.

As I walked home in a pensive mood, my vanity got the better of my pity. I could not but highly plume myself on my masterly management in getting rid of Bartleby. Masterly I call it, and such it must appear to any dispassionate thinker. The beauty of my procedure seemed to consist in its perfect quietness. There was no vulgar bullying, no bravado of any sort, no choleric hectoring, and striding to and fro across the apartment, jerking out vehement commands for Bartleby to bundle himself off with his beggarly traps. Nothing of the kind. Without loudly bidding Bartleby depart—as an inferior genius might have done—I *assumed* the ground that depart he must; and upon that assumption built all I had to say. The more I thought over my procedure, the more I was charmed with it. Nevertheless, next morning, upon awakening, I had my doubts—I had somehow slept off the fumes of vanity. One of the coolest and wisest hours a man has, is just after he awakes in the morning. My procedure seemed as sagacious as ever—but only in theory. How it would prove in practice—there was the rub. It was truly a beautiful thought to have assumed Bartleby's departure; but, after all, that assumption was simply my own, and none of Bartleby's. The great point was, not whether I had assumed that he would quit me, but whether he would prefer to do so. He was more a man of preferences than assumptions.

After breakfast, I walked down town, arguing the probabilities *pro* and *con*. One moment I thought it would prove a miserable failure, and Bartleby would be found all alive at my office as usual; the next moment it seemed certain that I should find his chair empty. And so I kept veering about. At the corner of Broadway and Canal Street, I saw quite an excited group of people standing in earnest conversation.

"I'll take odds he doesn't," said a voice as I passed.

"Doesn't go?—done!" said I; "put up your money."

I was instinctively putting my hand in my pocket to produce my own, when

I remembered that this was an election day. The words I had overheard bore no reference to Bartleby, but to the success or non-success of some candidate for the mayoralty. In my intent frame of mind, I had, as it were, imagined that all Broadway shared in my excitement, and were debating the same question with me. I passed on, very thankful that the uproar of the street screened my momentary absent-mindedness.

As I had intended, I was earlier than usual at my office door. I stood listening for a moment. All was still. He must be gone. I tried the knob. The door was locked. Yes, my procedure had worked to a charm; he indeed must be vanished. Yet a certain melancholy mixed with this: I was almost sorry for my brilliant success. I was fumbling under the door mat for the key, which Bartleby was to have left there for me, when accidentally my knee knocked against a panel, producing a summoning sound, and in response a voice came to me from within—"Not yet; I am occupied."

It was Bartleby.

I was thunderstruck. For an instant I stood like the man who, pipe in mouth, was killed one cloudless afternoon long ago in Virginia, by summer lightning; at his own warm open window he was killed, and remained leaning out there upon the dreamy afternoon, till some one touched him, when he fell.

"Not gone!" I murmured at last. But again obeying that wondrous ascendancy which the inscrutable scrivener had over me, and from which ascendancy, for all my chafing, I could not completely escape, I slowly went down stairs and out into the street, and while walking round the block, considered what I should next do in this unheard-of perplexity. Turn the man out by an actual thrusting I could not; to drive him away by calling him hard names would not do; calling in the police was an unpleasant idea; and yet, permit him to enjoy his cadaverous triumph over me—this, too, I could not think of. What was to be done? or, if nothing could be done, was there anything further that I could *assume* in the matter? Yes, as before I had prospectively assumed that Bartleby would depart, so now I might retrospectively assume that departed he was. In the legitimate carrying out of this assumption, I might enter my office in a great hurry, and pretending not to see Bartleby at all, walk straight against him as if he were air. Such a proceeding would in a singular degree have the appearance of a home-thrust. It was hardly possible that Bartleby could withstand such an application of the doctrine of assumption. But upon second thoughts the success of the plan seemed rather dubious. I resolved to argue the matter over with him again.

"Bartleby," said I, entering the office, with a quietly severe expression, "I am seriously displeased. I am pained, Bartleby. I had thought better of you. I had imagined you of such a gentlemanly organization, that in any delicate dilemma a slight hint would suffice—in short, an assumption. But it appears I am deceived. Why," I added, unaffectedly starting, "you have not even touched that money yet," pointing to it, just where I had left it the evening previous.

He answered nothing.

"Will you, or will you not, quit me?" I now demanded in a sudden passion, advancing close to him.

"I would prefer *not* to quit you," he replied, gently emphasizing the *not*.

"What earthly right have you to stay here? Do you pay any rent? Do you pay my taxes? Or is this property yours?"

He answered nothing.

"Are you ready to go on and write now? Are your eyes recovered? Could you copy a small paper for me this morning? or help examine a few lines? or step round to the post office? In a word, will you do anything at all, to give a coloring to your refusal to depart the premises?"

He silently retired into his hermitage.

I was now in such a state of nervous resentment that I thought it but prudent to check myself at present from further demonstrations. Bartleby and I were alone. I remembered the tragedy of the unfortunate Adams and the still more unfortunate Colt in the solitary office of the latter; and how poor Colt, being dreadfully incensed by Adams, and imprudently permitting himself to get wildly excited, was at unawares hurried into his fatal act—an act which certainly no man could possibly deplore more than the actor himself.[7] Often it had occurred to me in my ponderings upon the subject that had that altercation taken place in the public street, or at a private residence, it would not have terminated as it did. It was the circumstance of being alone in a solitary office, up stairs, of a building entirely unhallowed by humanizing domestic associations—an uncarpeted office, doubtless, of a dusty, haggard sort of appearance—this it must have been, which greatly helped to enhance the irritable desperation of the hapless Colt.

But when this old Adam of resentment rose in me and tempted me concerning Bartleby, I grappled him and threw him. How? Why, simply by recalling the divine injunction: "A new commandment give I unto you, that ye love one another." Yes, this it was that saved me. Aside from higher considerations, charity often operates as a vastly wise and prudent principle—a great safeguard to its possessor. Men have committed murder for jealousy's sake, and anger's sake, and hatred's sake, and selfishness' sake, and spiritual pride's sake; but no man, that ever I heard of, ever committed a diabolical murder for sweet charity's sake. Mere self-interest, then, if no better motive can be enlisted, should, especially with high-tempered men, prompt all beings to charity and philanthropy. At any rate, upon the occasion in question, I strove to drown my exasperated feelings towards the scrivener by benevolently construing his conduct. Poor fellow, poor fellow! thought I, he don't mean anything; and besides, he has seen hard times, and ought to be indulged.

I endeavored, also, immediately to occupy myself, and at the same time to comfort my despondency. I tried to fancy, that in the course of the morning, at such time as might prove agreeable to him, Bartleby, of his own free accord, would emerge from his hermitage and take up some decided line of march in the direction of the door. But no. Half-past twelve o'clock came; Turkey began

---

[7] A sensational homicide case in which Colt murdered Adams in a fit of passion.

to glow in the face, overturn his inkstand, and become generally obstreperous; Nippers abated down into quietude and courtesy; Ginger Nut munched his noon apple; and Bartleby remained standing at his window in one of his profoundest dead-wall reveries. Will it be credited? Ought I to acknowledge it? That afternoon I left the office without saying one further word to him.

Some days now passed, during which, at leisure intervals I looked a little into "Edwards on the Will," and "Priestley on Necessity."[8] Under the circumstances, those books induced a salutary feeling. Gradually I slid into the persuasion that these troubles of mine, touching the scrivener, had been all predestinated from eternity, and Bartleby was billeted upon me for some mysterious purpose of an all-wise Providence, which it was not for a mere mortal like me to fathom. Yes, Bartleby, stay there behind your screen, thought I; I shall persecute you no more; you are harmless and noiseless as any of these old chairs; in short, I never feel so private as when I know you are here. At last I see it, I feel it; I penetrate to the predestinated purpose of my life. I am content. Others may have loftier parts to enact; but my mission in this world, Bartleby, is to furnish you with office-room for such period as you may see fit to remain.

I believe that this wise and blessed frame of mind would have continued with me, had it not been for the unsolicited and uncharitable remarks obtruded upon me by my professional friends who visited the rooms. But thus it often is, that the constant friction of illiberal minds wears out at last the best resolves of the more generous. Though to be sure, when I reflected upon it, it was not strange that people entering my office should be struck by the peculiar aspect of the unaccountable Bartleby, and so be tempted to throw out some sinister observations concerning him. Sometimes an attorney, having business with me, and calling at my office, and finding no one but the scrivener there, would undertake to obtain some sort of precise information from him touching my whereabouts; but without heeding his idle talk, Bartleby would remain standing immovable in the middle of the room. So after contemplating him in that position for a time, the attorney would depart, no wiser than he came.

Also, when a reference was going on, and the room full of lawyers and witnesses, and business driving fast, some deeply-occupied legal gentleman present, seeing Bartleby wholly unemployed, would request him to run round to his (the legal gentleman's) office and fetch some papers for him. Thereupon, Bartleby would tranquilly decline, and yet remain idle as before. Then the lawyer would give a great stare, and turn to me. And what could I say? At last I was made aware that all through the circle of my professional acquaintance, a whisper of wonder was running round, having reference to the strange creature I kept at my office. This worried me very much. And as the idea came upon me of his possibly turning out a long-lived man, and keep occupying my chambers, and denying my authority; and perplexing my visitors; and scandal-

---

[8] Jonathan Edwards (1703–1758), American theologian, and Joseph Priestley (1733–1804), English clergyman and chemist, both held that man's life was predetermined.

izing my professional reputation; and casting a general gloom over the premises; keeping soul and body together to the last upon his savings (for doubtless he spent but half a dime a day), and in the end perhaps outlive me, and claim possession of my office by right of his perpetual occupancy: as all these dark anticipations crowded upon me more and more, and my friends continually intruded their relentless remarks upon the apparition in my room; a great change was wrought in me. I resolved to gather all my faculties together, and forever rid me of this intolerable incubus.

Ere revolving any complicated project, however, adapted to this end, I first simply suggested to Bartleby the propriety of his permanent departure. In a calm and serious tone, I commended the idea to his careful and mature consideration. But, having taken three days to meditate upon it, he apprised me, that his original determination remained the same; in short, that he still preferred to abide with me.

What shall I do? I now said to myself, buttoning up my coat to the last button. What shall I do? what ought I to do? what does conscience say I *should* do with this man, or, rather, ghost. Rid myself of him, I must; go, he shall. But how? You will not thrust him, the poor, pale, passive mortal—you will not thrust such a helpless creature out of your door? you will not dishonor yourself by such cruelty? No, I will not, I cannot do that. Rather would I let him live and die here, and then mason up his remains in the wall. What, then, will you do? For all your coaxing, he will not budge. Bribes he leaves under your own paper-weight on your table; in short, it is quite plain that he prefers to cling to you.

Then something severe, something unusual must be done. What! surely you will not have him collared by a constable, and commit his innocent pallor to the common jail? And upon what ground could you procure such a thing to be done?—a vagrant, is he? What! he a vagrant, a wanderer, who refuses to budge? It is because he will *not* be a vagrant, then, that you seek to count him *as* a vagrant. That is too absurd. No visible means of support: there I have him. Wrong again: for indubitably he *does* support himself, and that is the only unanswerable proof that any man can show of his possessing the means so to do. No more, then. Since he will not quit me, I must quit him. I will change my offices; I will move elsewhere, and give him fair notice, that if I find him on my new premises I will then proceed against him as a common trespasser.

Acting accordingly, next day I thus addressed him: "I find these chambers too far from the City Hall; the air is unwholesome. In a word, I propose to remove my offices next week, and shall no longer require your services. I tell you this now, in order that you may seek another place."

He made no reply, and nothing more was said.

On the appointed day I engaged carts and men, proceeded to my chambers, and, having but little furniture, everything was removed in a few hours. Throughout, the scrivener remained standing behind the screen, which I directed to be removed the last thing. It was withdrawn; and, being folded up like a huge folio, left him the motionless occupant of a naked room. I stood in the entry watching him a moment, while something from within me upbraided me.

I re-entered, with my hand in my pocket—and—and my heart in my mouth.

"Good-by, Bartleby; I am going—good-by, and God some way bless you; and take that," slipping something in his hand. But it dropped upon the floor, and then—strange to say—I tore myself from him whom I had so longed to be rid of.

Established in my new quarters, for a day or two I kept the door locked, and started at every footfall in the passages. When I returned to my rooms, after any little absence, I would pause at the threshold for an instant, and attentively listen, ere applying my key. But these fears were needless. Bartleby never came nigh me.

I thought all was going well, when a perturbed-looking stranger visited me, inquiring whether I was the person who had recently occupied rooms at No. —— Wall Street.

Full of forebodings, I replied that I was.

"Then, sir," said the stranger, who proved a lawyer, "you are responsible for the man you left there. He refuses to do any copying; he refuses to do anything; he says he prefers not to; and he refuses to quit the premises."

"I am very sorry, sir," said I, with assumed tranquillity, but an inward tremor, "but, really, the man you allude to is nothing to me—he is no relation or apprentice of mine, that you should hold me responsible for him."

"In mercy's name, who is he?"

"I certainly cannot inform you. I know nothing about him. Formerly I employed him as a copyist; but he has done nothing for me now for some time past."

"I shall settle him, then—good morning, sir."

Several days passed, and I heard nothing more; and, though I often felt a charitable prompting to call at the place and see poor Bartleby, yet a certain squeamishness, of I know not what, withheld me.

All is over with him, by this time, thought I, at last, when, through another week, no further intelligence reached me. But, coming to my room the day after, I found several persons waiting at my door in a high state of nervous excitement.

"That's the man—here he comes," cried the foremost one, whom I recognized as the lawyer who had previously called upon me alone.

"You must take him away, sir, at once," cried a portly person among them, advancing upon me, and whom I knew to be the landlord of No. —— Wall Street. "These gentlemen, my tenants, cannot stand it any longer; Mr. B——," pointing to the lawyer, "has turned him out of his room, and he now persists in haunting the building generally, sitting upon the banisters of the stairs by day, and sleeping in the entry by night. Everybody is concerned; clients are leaving the offices; some fears are entertained of a mob; something you must do, and that without delay."

Aghast at this torrent, I fell back before it, and would fain have locked myself in my new quarters. In vain I persisted that Bartleby was nothing to me—no more than to any one else. In vain—I was the last person known to have anything to do with him, and they held me to the terrible account. Fearful, then, of being exposed in the papers (as one person present obscurely threatened), I considered the matter, and, at length, said, that if the lawyer would give me a confidential interview with the scrivener, in his (the lawyer's) own room, I would, that afternoon, strive my best to rid them of the nuisance they complained of.

Going up stairs to my old haunt, there was Bartleby silently sitting upon the banister at the landing.

"What are you doing here, Bartleby?" said I.

"Sitting upon the banister," he mildly replied.

I motioned him into the lawyer's room, who then left us.

"Bartleby," said I, "are you aware that you are the cause of great tribulation to me, by persisting in occupying the entry after being dismissed from the office?"

No answer.

"Now one of two things must take place. Either you must do something, or something must be done to you. Now what sort of business would you like to engage in? Would you like to re-engage in copying for some one?"

"No; I would prefer not to make any change."

"Would you like a clerkship in a dry-goods store?"

"There is too much confinement about that. No, I would not like a clerkship; but I am not particular."

"Too much confinement," I cried, "why, you keep yourself confined all the time!"

"I would prefer not to take a clerkship," he rejoined, as if to settle that little item at once.

"How would a bar-tender's business suit you? There is no trying of the eyesight in that."

"I would not like it at all; though, as I said before, I am not particular."

His unwonted wordiness inspirited me. I returned to the charge.

"Well, then, would you like to travel through the country collecting bills for the merchants? That would improve your health."

"No, I would prefer to be doing something else."

"How, then, would going as a companion to Europe, to entertain some young gentleman with your conversation—how would that suit you?"

"Not at all. It does not strike me that there is anything definite about that. I like to be stationary. But I am not particular."

"Stationary you shall be, then," I cried, now losing all patience, and, for the first time in all my exasperating connection with him, fairly flying into a passion. "If you do not go away from these premises before night, I shall feel bound—indeed, I *am* bound—to—to—to quit the premises myself!" I rather absurdly concluded, knowing not with what possible threat to try to frighten his immobility into compliance. Despairing of all further efforts, I was precipitately leaving him, when a final thought occurred to me—one which had not been wholly unindulged before.

"Bartleby," said I, in the kindest tone I could assume under such exciting circumstances, "will you go home with me now—not to my office, but my dwelling—and remain there till we can conclude upon some convenient arrangement for you at our leisure? Come, let us start now, right away."

"No: at present I would prefer not to make any change at all."

I answered nothing; but, effectually dodging every one by the suddenness and rapidity of my flight, rushed from the building, ran up Wall Street towards Broadway, and, jumping into the first omnibus, was soon removed from pursuit. As soon as tranquillity returned, I distinctly perceived that I had now done all that I possibly could, both in respect to the demands of the landlord and his tenants, and with regard to my own desire and sense of duty, to benefit Bartleby, and shield him from rude persecution. I now strove to be entirely care-free and quiescent; and my conscience justified me in the attempt; though, indeed, it was not so successful as I could have wished. So fearful was I of being again hunted out by the incensed landlord and his exasperated tenants, that, surrendering my business to Nippers, for a few days, I drove about the upper part of the town and through the suburbs, in my rockaway; crossed over to Jersey City and Hoboken, and paid fugitive visits to Manhattanville and Astoria. In fact, I almost lived in my rockaway for the time.

When again I entered my office, lo, a note from the landlord lay upon the desk. I opened it with trembling hands. It informed me that the writer had sent to the police, and had Bartleby removed to the Tombs as a vagrant. Moreover, since I knew more about him than any one else, he wished me to appear at that place, and make a suitable statement of the facts. These tidings had a conflicting effect upon me. At first I was indignant; but, at last, almost approved. The landlord's energetic, summary disposition, had led him to adopt a procedure which I do not think I would have decided upon myself; and yet, as a last resort, under such peculiar circumstances, it seemed the only plan.

As I afterwards learned, the poor scrivener, when told that he must be conducted to the Tombs, offered not the slightest obstacle, but, in his pale, unmoving way, silently acquiesced.

Some of the compassionate and curious by-standers joined the party; and headed by one of the constables arm in arm with Bartleby, the silent procession filed its way through all the noise, and heat, and joy of the roaring thoroughfares at noon.

The same day I received the note, I went to the Tombs, or, to speak more properly, the Halls of Justice. Seeking the right officer, I stated the purpose of my call, and was informed that the individual I described was, indeed, within. I then assured the functionary that Bartleby was a perfectly honest man, and greatly to be compassionated, however unaccountably eccentric. I narrated all I knew, and closed by suggesting the idea of letting him remain in as indulgent confinement as possible, till something less harsh might be done—though, indeed, I hardly knew what. At all events, if nothing else could be decided upon, the alms-house must receive him. I then begged to have an interview.

Being under no disgraceful charge, and quite serene and harmless in all his ways, they had permitted him freely to wander about the prison, and, especially, in the inclosed grass-platted yards thereof. And so I found him there, standing all alone in the quietest of the yards, his face towards a high wall, while all around, from the narrow slits of the jail windows, I thought I saw peering out upon him the eyes of murderers and thieves.

"Bartleby!"

"I know you," he said, without looking round—"and I want nothing to say to you."

"It was not I that brought you here, Bartleby," said I, keenly pained at his implied suspicion. "And to you, this should not be so vile a place. Nothing reproachful attaches to you by being here. And see, it is not so sad a place as one might think. Look, there is the sky, and here is the grass."

"I know where I am," he replied, but would say nothing more, and so I left him.

As I entered the corridor again, a broad meat-like man, in an apron, accosted me, and, jerking his thumb over his shoulder, said—"Is that your friend?"

"Yes."

"Does he want to starve? If he does, let him live on the prison fare, that's all."

"Who are you?" asked I, not knowing what to make of such an unofficially speaking person in such a place.

"I am the grub-man. Such gentlemen as have friends here, hire me to provide them with something good to eat."

"Is this so?" said I, turning the turnkey.

He said it was.

"Well, then," said I, slipping some silver into the grub-man's hands (for so they called him), "I want you to give particular attention to my friend there; let him have the best dinner you can get. And you must be as polite to him as possible."

"Introduce me, will you?" said the grub-man, looking at me with an expression which seemed to say he was all impatience for an opportunity to give a specimen of his breeding.

Thinking it would prove of benefit to the scrivener, I acquiesced; and, asking the grub-man his name, went up with him to Bartleby.

"Bartleby, this is a friend; you will find him very useful to you."

"Your sarvant, sir, your sarvant," said the grub-man, making a low salutation behind his apron. "Hope you find it pleasant here, sir; nice grounds—cool apartments—hope you'll stay with us some time—try to make it agreeable. What will you have for dinner to-day?"

"I prefer not to dine to-day," said Bartleby, turning away. "It would disagree with me; I am unused to dinners." So saying, he slowly moved to the other side of the inclosure, and took up a position fronting the deadwall.

"How's this?" said the grub-man, addressing me with a stare of astonishment. "He's odd, ain't he?"

"I think he is a little deranged," said I, sadly.

"Deranged? deranged is it? Well, now, upon my word, I thought that friend of yourn was a gentleman forger; they are always pale and genteel-like, them forgers. I can't help pity 'em—can't help it, sir. Did you know Monroe Edwards?" he added, touchingly, and paused. Then, laying his hand piteously on my shoulder, sighed, "he died of consumption at Sing-Sing.⁹ So you weren't acquainted with Monroe?"

"No, I was never socially acquainted with any forgers. But I cannot stop longer. Look to my friend yonder. You will not lose by it. I will see you again."

Some few days after this, I again obtained admission to the Tombs, and went through the corridors in quest of Bartleby; but without finding him.

"I saw him coming from his cell not long ago," said a turnkey, "may be he's gone to loiter in the yards."

So I went in that direction.

"Are you looking for the silent man?" said another turnkey, passing me. "Yonder he lies—sleeping in the yard there. 'Tis not twenty minutes since I saw him lie down."

The yard was entirely quiet. It was not accessible to the common prisoners. The surrounding walls of amazing thickness, kept off all sounds behind them. The Egyptian character of the masonry weighed upon me with its gloom. But a soft imprisoned turf grew under foot. The heart of the eternal pyramids, it seemed, wherein, by some strange magic, through the clefts, grass-seed, dropped by birds, had sprung.

Strangely huddled at the base of the wall, his knees drawn up, and lying on his side, his head touching the cold stones, I saw the wasted Bartleby. But nothing stirred. I paused; then went close up to him; stooped over, and saw that his dim eyes were open; otherwise he seemed profoundly sleeping. Something prompted me to touch him. I felt his hand, when a tingling shiver ran up my arm and down my spine to my feet.

The round face of the grub-man peered upon me now. "His dinner is ready. Won't he dine to-day, either? Or does he live without dining?"

"Lives without dining," said I, and closed the eyes.

"Eh!—He's asleep, ain't he?"

"With kings and counselors," murmured I.

There would seem little need for proceeding further in this history. Imagination will readily supply the meagre recital of poor Bartleby's interment. But, ere parting with the reader, let me say, that if this little narrative has sufficiently interested him, to awaken curiosity as to who Bartleby was, and what manner of life he led prior to the present narrator's making his acquaintance, I can only

---

⁹ The state prison near Ossining, New York.

reply, that in such curiosity I fully share, but am wholly unable to gratify it. Yet here I hardly know whether I should divulge one little item of rumor, which came to my ear a few months after the scrivener's decease. Upon what basis it rested, I could never ascertain; and hence, how true it is I cannot now tell. But, inasmuch as this vague report has not been without a certain suggestive interest to me, however said, it may prove the same with some others; and so I will briefly mention it. The report was this: that Bartleby had been a subordinate clerk in the Dead Letter[10] Office at Washington, from which he had been suddenly removed by a change in the administration. When I think over this rumor, hardly can I express the emotions which seize me. Dead letters! does it not sound like dead men? Conceive a man by nature and misfortune prone to a pallid hopelessness, can any business seem more fitted to heighten it than that of continually handling these dead letters, and assorting them for the flames? For by the cart-load they are annually burned. Some times from out the folded paper the pale clerk takes a ring—the finger it was meant for, perhaps, moulders in the grave; a bank-note sent in swiftest charity—he whom it would relieve, nor eats nor hungers any more; pardon for those who died despairing; hope for those who died unhoping; good tidings for those who died stifled by unrelieved calamities. On errands of life, these letters speed to death.

Ah, Bartleby! Ah, humanity!

QUESTIONS

1. What is it about Bartleby that so intrigues and fascinates the narrator? Why does the narrator continue to feel a moral obligation to an employee who refuses to work and curtly rejects kindly offers of help?   **2.** With his final utterance, "Ah, Bartleby! Ah, humanity!" the narrator apparently penetrates the mystery of Bartleby. The comments seem to suggest that for the narrator Bartleby is a representative of humanity. In what sense might the narrator come to see Bartleby in this light?   **3.** What functions do Turkey and Nippers serve?   **4.** Would it be fair to describe Bartleby as a rebel without a cause, as a young man who refuses to participate in a comfortable and well-ordered business world but fails to offer any alternative way of life? Justify your answer.

WRITING TOPICS

1. Readers differ as to whether this is the story of Bartleby or the story of the lawyer-narrator. What is your view?   **2.** Why does Melville allow the narrator (and the reader) to discover so little about Bartleby and the causes of his behavior? All we learn of Bartleby's past is contained in the next-to-last paragraph. What, if anything, in this paragraph establishes a link between Bartleby and the narrator?

---

[10] A letter that is undeliverable because it lacks a correct address and unreturned to the sender.

War*   1918

LUIGI PIRANDELLO   [1867–1936]

The passengers who had left Rome by the night express had had to stop until dawn at the small station of Fabriano in order to continue their journey by the small old-fashioned "local" joining the main line with Sulmona.

At dawn, in a stuffy and smoky second-class carriage in which five people had already spent the night, a bulky woman in deep mourning was hoisted in— almost like a shapeless bundle. Behind her—puffing and moaning, followed her husband—a tiny man, thin and weakly, his face death-white, his eyes small and bright and looking shy and uneasy.

Having at last taken a seat he politely thanked the passengers who had helped his wife and who had made room for her; then he turned round to the woman trying to pull down the collar of her coat and politely enquired:

"Are you all right, dear?"

The wife, instead of answering, pulled up her collar again to her eyes, so as to hide her face.

"Nasty world," muttered the husband with a sad smile.

And he felt it his duty to explain to his travelling companions that the poor woman was to be pitied for the war was taking away from her her only son, a boy of twenty to whom both had devoted their entire life, even breaking up their home at Sulmona to follow him to Rome where he had to go as a student, then allowing him to volunteer for war with an assurance, however, that at least for six months he would not be sent to the front and now, all of a sudden, receiving a wire saying that he was due to leave in three days' time and asking them to go and see him off.

The woman under the big coat was twisting and wriggling, at times growling like a wild animal, feeling certain that all those explanations would not have aroused even a shadow of sympathy from those people who—most likely—were in the same plight as herself. One of them, who had been listening with particular attention, said:

"You should thank God that your son is only leaving now for the front. Mine has been sent there the first day of the war. He has already come back twice wounded and been sent back again to the front."

"What about me? I have two sons and three nephews at the front," said another passenger.

"Maybe, but in our case it is our *only* son," ventured the husband.

---

* Translated by Michele Pettinati.

"What difference can it make? You may spoil your only son with excessive attentions, but you cannot love him more than you would all your other children if you had any. Paternal love is not like bread that can be broken into pieces and split amongst the children in equal shares. A father gives *all* his love to each one of his children without discrimination, whether it be one or ten, and if I am suffering now for my two sons, I am not suffering half for each of them but double. . . ."

"True . . . true . . ." sighed the embarrassed husband, "but suppose (of course we all hope it will never be your case) a father has two sons at the front and he loses one of them, there is still one left to console him . . . while . . ."

"Yes," answered the other, getting cross, "a son left to console him but also a son left for whom he must survive, while in the case of the father of an only son if the son dies the father can die too and put an end to his distress. Which of the two positions is the worse? Don't you see how my case would be worse than yours?"

"Nonsense," interrupted another traveller, a fat, red-faced man with blood-shot eyes of the palest grey.

He was panting. From his bulging eyes seemed to spurt inner violence of an uncontrolled vitality which his weakened body could hardly contain.

"Nonsense," he repeated, trying to cover his mouth with his hand so as to hide the two missing front teeth. "Nonsense. Do we give life to our children for our own benefit?"

The other travellers stared at him in distress. The one who had had his son at the front since the first day of the war sighed: "You are right. Our children do not belong to us, they belong to the Country. . . ."

"Bosh," retorted the fat traveller. "Do we think of the Country when we give life to our children? Our sons are born because . . . well, because they must be born and when they come to life they take our own life with them. This is the truth. We belong to them but they never belong to us. And when they reach twenty they are exactly what we were at their age. We too had a father and mother, but there were so many other things as well . . . girls, cigarettes, illusions, new ties . . . and the Country, of course, whose call we would have answered—when we were twenty—even if father and mother had said no. Now, at our age, the love of our Country is still great, of course, but stronger than it is the love for our children. Is there any one of us here who wouldn't gladly take his son's place at the front if he could?"

There was a silence all round, everybody nodding as to approve.

"Why then," continued the fat man, "shouldn't we consider the feelings of our children when they are twenty? Isn't it *natural* that at their age they should consider the love for their Country (I am speaking of decent boys, of course) even greater than the love for us? Isn't it *natural* that it should be so, as after all they must look upon us as upon old boys who cannot move any more and must stay at home? If Country exists, if Country is a natural necessity like bread, of which each of us must eat in order not to die of hunger, somebody must go to defend it. And our sons go, when they are twenty, and they don't want tears, because if they die, they die inflamed and happy (I am speaking, of course, of decent boys). Now, if one dies young and happy, without having the ugly sides of life, the boredom of it, the pettiness, the bitterness of disillusion . . . what more can we ask for him? Everyone should stop crying: everyone should laugh, as I do . . . or at least thank God—as I do—because my son, before dying, sent me a message saying that he was dying satisfied at having ended his life in the best way he could have wished. That is why, as you see, I do not even wear mourning. . . ."

He shook his light fawn coat as to show it; his livid lip over his missing teeth was trembling, his eyes were watery and motionless and soon after he ended with a shrill laugh which might well have been a sob.

"Quite so . . . quite so . . ." agreed the others.

The woman who, bundled in a corner under her coat, had been sitting and listening had—for the last three months—tried to find in the words of her husband and her friends something to console her in her deep sorrow, something that might show her how a mother should resign herself to send her son not even to death but to a probable danger of life. Yet not a word had she found amongst the many which had been said . . . and her grief had been greater in seeing that nobody—as she thought—could share her feelings.

But now the words of the traveller amazed and almost stunned her. She suddenly realized that it wasn't the others who were wrong and could not understand her but herself who could not rise up to the same height of those fathers and mothers willing to resign themselves, without crying, not only to the departure of their sons but even to their death.

She lifted her head, she bent over from her corner trying to listen with great attention to the details which the fat man was giving to his companions about the way his son had fallen as a hero, for his King and his Country, happy and without regrets. It seemed to her that she had stumbled into a world she had never dreamt of, a world so far unknown to her and she was so pleased to hear everyone joining in congratulating that brave father who could so stoically speak of his child's death.

Then suddenly, just as if she had heard nothing of what had been said and almost as if waking up from a dream, she turned to the old man, asking him:

"Then . . . is your son really dead?"

Everybody stared at her. The old man, too, turned to look at her, fixing his great, bulging, horribly watery light grey eyes, deep in her face. For some little time he tried to answer, but words failed him. He looked and looked at her, almost as if only then—at that silly, incongruous question—he had suddenly realized at last that his son was really dead . . . gone for ever . . . for ever. His face contracted, became horribly distorted, then he snatched in haste a handkerchief from his pocket and, to the amazement of everyone, broke into harrowing, heart-rending, uncontrollable sobs.

Gladius Dei*

1902

THOMAS MANN [1875–1955]

Munich was radiant. Above the gay squares and white columned temples, the classicistic monuments and the baroque churches, the leaping fountains, the palaces and parks of the Residence there stretched a sky of luminous blue silk. Well-arranged leafy vistas laced with sun and shade lay basking in the sunshine of a beautiful day in early June.

There was a twittering of birds and a blithe holiday spirit in all the little streets. And in the squares and past the rows of villas there swelled, rolled, and hummed the leisurely, entertaining traffic of that easy-going, charming town. Travellers of all nationalities drove about in the slow little droshkies, looking right and left in aimless curiosity at the house-fronts; they mounted and descended museum stairs. Many windows stood open and music was heard from within: practising on piano, cello, or violin—earnest and well-meant amateur efforts; while from the Odeon came the sound of serious work on several grand pianos.

Young people, the kind that can whistle the Nothung motif,[1] who fill the pit of the Schauspielhaus every evening, wandered in and out of the University and Library with literary magazines in their coat pockets. A court carriage stood before the Academy, the home of the plastic arts, which spreads its white wings between the Türkenstrasse and the Siegestor. And colourful groups of models, picturesque old men, women and children in Albanian costume, stood or lounged at the top of the balustrade.

Indolent, unhurried sauntering was the mode in all the long streets of the northern quarter. There life is lived for pleasanter ends than the driving greed of gain. Young artists with little round hats on the backs of their heads, flowing cravats and no canes—carefree bachelors who paid for their lodgings with colour-sketches—were strolling up and down to let the clear blue morning play upon their mood, also to look at the little girls, the pretty, rather plump type, with the brunette bandeaux, the too large feet, and the unobjectionable morals. Every fifth house had studio windows blinking in the sun. Sometimes a fine piece of architecture stood out from a middle-class row, the work of some imaginative young architect; a wide front with shallow bays and decorations in a bizarre style very expressive and full of invention. Or the door to some

---

* Translated by H. T. Lowe-Porter. *Gladius Dei* means "sword of God."
[1] *Nothung* means "sword." The Nothung motif is a musical passage from Richard Wagner's opera *Siegfried. Schauspielhaus* means "theater."

monotonous façade would be framed in a bold improvisation of flowing lines and sunny colours, with bacchantes, naiads,[2] and rosy-skinned nudes.

It was always a joy to linger before the windows of the cabinet-makers and the shops for modern articles *de luxe*. What a sense for luxurious nothings and amusing, significant line was displayed in the shape of everything! Little shops that sold picture frames, sculptures, and antiques there were in endless number; in their windows you might see those busts of Florentine women of the Renaissance, so full of noble poise and poignant charm. And the owners of the smallest and meanest of these shops spoke of Mino da Fiesole and Donatello[3] as though he had received the rights of reproduction from them personally.

But on the Odeonsplatz, in view of the mighty loggia with the spacious mosaic pavement before it, diagonally opposite to the Regent's palace, people were crowding round the large windows and glass show-cases of the big art-shop owned by M. Blüthenzweig. What a glorious display! There were reproductions of the masterpieces of all the galleries in the world, in costly decorated and tinted frames, the good taste of which was precious in its very simplicity. There were copies of modern paintings, works of a joyously sensuous fantasy, in which the antiques seemed born again in humorous and realistic guise; bronze nudes and fragile ornamental glassware; tall, thin earthenware vases with an iridescent glaze produced by a bath in metal steam; *éditions de luxe* which were triumphs of modern binding and presswork, containing the works of the most modish poets, set out with every possible advantage of sumptuous elegance. Cheek by jowl with these, the portraits of artists, musicians, philosophers, actors, writers, displayed to gratify the public taste for personalities.—In the first window, next the book-shop, a large picture stood on an easel, with a crowd of people in front of it, a fine sepia photograph in a wide old-gold frame, a very striking reproduction of the sensation at this year's great international exhibition, to which public attention is always invited by means of effective and artistic posters stuck up everywhere on hoardings among concert programmes and clever advertisements of toilet preparations.

If you looked into the windows of the book-shop your eye met such titles as *Interior Decoration Since the Renaissance, The Renaissance in Modern Decorative Art, The Book as Work of Art, The Decorative Arts, Hunger for Art,* and many more. And you would remember that these thought-provoking pamphlets were sold and read by the thousand and that discussions on these subjects were the preoccupation of all the salons.

You might be lucky enough to meet in person one of the famous fair ones whom less fortunate folk know only through the medium of art; one of those rich and beautiful women whose Titian-blond colouring Nature's most sweet and cunning hand did *not* lay on, but whose diamond parures and beguiling charms had received immortality from the hand of some portrait-painter of

---

[2] Bacchantes are female followers of Bacchus, the god of wine; naiads are water nymphs.

[3] Mino da Fiesole and Donatello were fourteenth-century Italian artists.

genius and whose love-affairs were the talk of the town. These were the queens of the artist balls at carnival-time. They were a little painted, a little made up, full of haughty caprices, worthy of adoration, avid of praise. You might see a carriage rolling up the Ludwigstrasse, with such a great painter and his mistress inside. People would be pointing out the sight, standing still to gaze after the pair. Some of them would curtsy. A little more and the very policemen would stand at attention.

Art flourished, art swayed the destinies of the town, art stretched above it her rose-bound sceptre and smiled. On every hand obsequious interest was displayed in her prosperity, on every hand she was served with industry and devotion. There was a downright cult of line, decoration, form, significance, beauty. Munich was radiant.

A youth was coming down the Schellingstrasse. With the bells of cyclists ringing about him he strode across the wooden pavement towards the broad façade of the Ludwigskirche. Looking at him it was as though a shadow passed across the sky, or cast over the spirit some memory of melancholy hours. Did he not love the sun which bathed the lovely city in its festal light? Why did he walk wrapped in his own thoughts, his eyes directed on the ground?

No one in that tolerant and variety-loving town would have taken offence at his wearing no hat; but why need the hood of his ample black cloak have been drawn over his head, shadowing his low, prominent, and peaked forehead, covering his ears and framing his haggard cheeks? What pangs of conscience, what scruples and self-tortures had so availed to hollow out these cheeks? It is frightful, on such a sunny day, to see care sitting in the hollows of the human face. His dark brows thickened at the narrow base of his hooked and prominent nose. His lips were unpleasantly full, his eyes brown and close-lying. When he lifted them, diagonal folds appeared on the peaked brow. His gaze expressed knowledge, limitation, and suffering. Seen in profile his face was strikingly like an old painting preserved at Florence in a narrow cloister cell whence once a frightful and shattering protest issued against life and her triumphs.[4]

Hieronymus walked along the Schellingstrasse with a slow, firm stride, holding his wide cloak together with both hands from inside. Two little girls, two of those pretty, plump little creatures with the bandeaux, the big feet, and the unobjectionable morals, strolled towards him arm in arm, on pleasure bent. They poked each other and laughed, they bent double with laughter, they even

---

[4] We are grateful to Professor George W. Walton of Abilene Christian University for pointing out that the painting described is Fra Bartolommeo's portrait of Girolamo Savonarola (1452–1498), an Italian friar disturbed by the moral decay of the city of Florence. On April 5, 1492, Savonarola experienced his famous vision of a suspended sword of divine justice together with the words: *Ecce gladius Domini super terram cito et velociter* ("Behold the sword of the Lord over the earth swiftly and quickly"). Note that Hieronymus quotes these words at the end of the story. Savonarola's influence in Florence led to the flight of the governor, Piero de' Medici, and in 1497 the friar led a "burning of the vanities" in which the citizens of Florence hurled worldly clothing, paintings, and books into bonfires.

broke into a run and ran away still laughing, at his hood and his face. But he paid them no heed. With bent head, looking neither to the right nor to the left, he crossed the Ludwigstrasse and mounted the church steps.

The great wings of the middle portal stood wide open. From somewhere within the consecrated twilight, cool, dank, incense-laden, there came a pale red glow. An old woman with inflamed eyes rose from a prayer-stool and slipped on crutches through the columns. Otherwise the church was empty.

Hieronymus sprinkled brow and breast at the stoup, bent the knee before the high altar, and then paused in the centre nave. Here in the church his stature seemed to have grown. He stood upright and immovable; his head was flung up and his great hooked nose jutted domineeringly above the thick lips. His eyes no longer sought the ground, but looked straight and boldly into the distance, at the crucifix on the high altar. Thus he stood awhile, then retreating he bent the knee again and left the church.

He strode up the Ludwigstrasse, slowly, firmly, with bent head, in the centre of the wide unpaved road, towards the mighty loggia with its statues. But arrived at the Odeonsplatz, he looked up, so that the folds came out on his peaked forehead, and checked his step, his attention being called to the crowd at the windows of the big art-shop of M. Blüthenzweig.

People moved from window to window, pointing out to each other the treasures displayed and exchanging views as they looked over one another's shoulders. Hieronymus mingled among them and did as they did, taking in all these things with his eyes, one by one.

He saw the reproductions of masterpieces from all the galleries in the world, the priceless frames so precious in their simplicity, the Renaissance sculpture, the bronze nudes, the exquisitely bound volumes, the iridescent vases, the portraits of artists, musicians, philosophers, actors, writers; he looked at everything and turned a moment of his scrutiny upon each object. Holding his mantle closely together with both hands from inside, he moved his hood-covered head in short turns from one thing to the next, gazing at each awhile with a dull, inimical, and remotely surprised air, lifting the dark brows which grew so thick at the base of the nose. At length he stood in front of the last window, which contained the startling picture. For a while he looked over the shoulders of people before him and then in his turn reached a position directly in front of the window.

The large red-brown photograph in the choice old-gold frame stood on an easel in the centre. It was a Madonna, but an utterly unconventional one, a work of entirely modern feeling. The figure of the Holy Mother was revealed as enchantingly feminine and beautiful. Her great smouldering eyes were rimmed with darkness, and her delicate and strangely smiling lips were half-parted. Her slender fingers held in a somewhat nervous grasp the hips of a Child, a nude boy of pronounced, almost primitive leanness. He was playing with her breast and glancing aside at the beholder with a wise look in his eyes.

Two other youths stood near Hieronymus, talking about the picture. They were two young men with books under their arms, which they had fetched from the Library or were taking thither. Humanistically educated people, that is, equipped with science and with art.

"The little chap is in luck, devil take me!" said one.

"He seems to be trying to make one envious," replied the other. "A bewildering female!"

"A female to drive a man crazy! Gives you funny ideas about the Immaculate Conception."

"No, she doesn't look exactly immaculate. Have you seen the original?"

"Of course; I was quite bowled over. She makes an even more aphrodisiac impression in colour. Especially the eyes."

"The likeness is pretty plain."

"How so?"

"Don't you know the model? Of course he used his little dressmaker. It is almost a portrait, only with a lot more emphasis on the corruptible. The girl is more innocent."

"I hope so. Life would be altogether too much of a strain if there were many like this *mater amata.*"[5]

"The Pinakothek has bought it."

"Really? Well, well! They knew what they were about, anyhow. The treatment of the flesh and the flow of the linen garment are really first-class."

"Yes, an incredibly gifted chap."

"Do you know him?"

"A little. He will have a career, that is certain. He has been invited twice by the Prince Regent."

This last was said as they were taking leave of each other.

"Shall I see you this evening at the theatre?" asked the first. "The Dramatic Club is giving Machiavelli's *Mandragola.*"[6]

"Oh, bravo! That will be great, of course. I had meant to go the Variété, but I shall probably choose our stout Niccolò after all. Good-bye."

They parted, going off to right and left. New people took their places and looked at the famous picture. But Hieronymus stood where he was, motionless, with his head thrust out; his hands clutched convulsively at the mantle as they held it together from inside. His brows were no longer lifted with that cool and unpleasantly surprised expression; they were drawn and darkened; his cheeks, half-shrouded in the black hood, seemed more sunken than ever and his thick lips had gone pale. Slowly his head dropped lower and lower, so that finally his eyes stared upwards at the work of art, while the nostrils of his great nose dilated.

Thus he remained for perhaps a quarter of an hour. The crowd about him melted away, but he did not stir from the spot. At last he turned slowly on the balls of his feet and went hence.

---

[5] Beloved mother. The Pinakothek is a municipal art gallery.

[6] Niccolò Machiavelli (1469–1527) was a playwright as well as a political philosopher. His play, *Mandragola,* is a sex comedy.

But the picture of the Madonna went with him. Always and ever, whether in his hard and narrow little room or kneeling in the cool church, it stood before his outraged soul, with its smouldering, dark-rimmed eyes, its riddlingly smiling lips—stark and beautiful. And no prayer availed to exorcise it.

But the third night it happened that a command and summons from on high came to Hieronymus, to intercede and lift his voice against the frivolity, blasphemy, and arrogance of beauty. In vain like Moses he protested that he had not the gift of tongues. God's will remained unshaken; in a loud voice He demanded that the faint-hearted Hieronymus go forth to sacrifice amid the jeers of the foe.

And since God would have it so, he set forth one morning and wended his way to the great art-shop of M. Blüthenzweig. He wore his hood over his head and held his mantle together in front from inside with both hands as he went.

The air had grown heavy, the sky was livid and thunder threatened. Once more crowds were besieging the show-cases at the art-shop and especially the window where the photograph of the Madonna stood. Hieronymus cast one brief glance thither; then he pushed up the latch of the glass door hung with placards and art magazines. "As God wills," said he, and entered the shop.

A young girl was somewhere at a desk writing in a big book. She was a pretty brunette thing with bandeaux of hair and big feet. She came up to him and asked pleasantly what he would like.

"Thank you," said Hieronymus in a low voice and looked her earnestly in the face, with diagonal wrinkles in his peaked brow. "I would speak not to you but to the owner of this shop, Herr Blüthenzweig."

She hesitated a little, turned away, and took up her work once more. He stood there in the middle of the shop.

Instead of the single specimens in the show-windows there was here a riot and a heaping-up of luxury, a fullness of colour, line, form, style, invention, good taste, and beauty. Hieronymus looked slowly round him, drawing his mantle close with both hands.

There were several people in the shop besides him. At one of the broad tables running across the room sat a man in a yellow suit, with a black goat's-beard, looking at a portfolio of French drawings, over which he now and then emitted a bleating laugh. He was being waited on by an undernourished and vegetarian young man, who kept on dragging up fresh portfolios. Diagonally opposite the bleating man sat an elegant old dame, examining art embroideries with a pattern of fabulous flowers in pale tones standing together on tall perpendicular stalks. An attendant hovered about her too. A leisurely Englishman in a travelling-cap, with his pipe in his mouth, sat at another table. Cold and smooth-shaven, of indefinite age, in his good English clothes, he sat examining bronzes brought to him by M. Blüthenzweig in person. He was holding up by the head the dainty figure of a nude young girl, immature and delicately articulated, her hands crossed in coquettish innocence upon her breast. He studied her thoroughly, turning her slowly about. M. Blüthenzweig, a man with a short, heavy brown beard and bright brown eyes of exactly the same colour, moved in a semicircle round him, rubbing his hands, praising the statuette with all the terms his vocabulary possessed.

"A hundred and fifty marks, sir," he said in English. "Munich art—very charming, in fact. Simply full of charm, you know. Grace itself. Really extremely pretty, good, admirable, in fact." Then he thought of some more and went on: "Highly attractive, fascinating." Then he began again from the beginning.

His nose lay a little flat on his upper lip, so that he breathed constantly with a slight sniff into his moustache. Sometimes he did this as he approached a customer, stooping over as though he were smelling at him. When Hieronymus entered, M. Blüthenzweig had examined him cursorily in this way, then devoted himself again to his Englishman.

The elegant old dame made her selection and left the shop. A man entered. M. Blüthenzweig sniffed briefly at him as though to scent out his capacity to buy and left him to the young bookkeeper. The man purchased a faience bust of young Piero de' Medici, son of Lorenzo, and went out again. The Englishman began to depart. He had acquired the statuette of the young girl and left amid bowings from M. Blüthenzweig. Then the art-dealer turned to Hieronymus and came forward.

"You wanted something?" he said, without any particular courtesy.

Hieronymus held his cloak together with both hands and looked the other in the face almost without winking an eyelash. He parted his big lips slowly and said:

"I have come to you on account of the picture in the window there, the big photograph, the Madonna." His voice was thick and without modulation.

"Yes, quite right," said M. Blüthenzweig briskly and began rubbing his hands. "Seventy marks in the frame. It is unfadable—a first-class reproduction. Highly attractive and full of charm."

Hieronymus was silent. He nodded his head in the hood and shrank a little into himself as the dealer spoke. Then he drew himself up again and said:

"I would remark to you first of all that I am not in the position to purchase anything, nor have I the desire. I am sorry to have to disappoint your expectations. I regret if it upsets you. But in the first place I am poor and in the second I do not love the things you sell. No, I cannot buy anything."

"No? Well, then?" asked M. Blüthenzweig, sniffing a good deal. "Then may I ask—"

"I suppose," Hieronymus went on, "that being what you are you look down on me because I am not in a position to buy."

"Oh—er—not at all," said M. Blüthenzweig. "Not at all. Only—"

"And yet I beg you to hear me and give some consideration to my words."

"Consideration to your words. H'm—may I ask—"

"You may ask," said Hieronymus, "and I will answer you. I have come to beg you to remove that picture, the big photograph, the Madonna, out of your window and never display it again."

M. Blüthenzweig looked awhile dumbly into Hieronymus's face—as though he expected him to be abashed at the words he had just uttered. But as this did not happen he gave a violent sniff and spoke himself:

"Will you be so good as to tell me whether you are here in any official capacity which authorizes you to dictate to me, or what does bring you here?"

"Oh, no," replied Hieronymus, "I have neither office nor dignity from the state. I have no power on my side, sir. What brings me hither is my conscience alone."

M. Blüthenzweig, searching for words, snorted violently into his moustache. At length he said:

"Your conscience . . . well, you will kindly understand that I take not the faintest interest in your conscience." With which he turned round and moved quickly to his desk at the back of the shop, where he began to write. Both attendants laughed heartily. The pretty Fräulein giggled over her account-book. As for the yellow gentleman with the goat's beard, he was evidently a foreigner, for he gave no sign of comprehension but went on studying the French drawings and emitting from time to time his bleating laugh.

"Just get rid of the man for me," said M. Blüthenzweig shortly over his shoulder to his assistant. He went on writing. The poorly paid young vegetarian approached Hieronymus, smothering his laughter, and the other salesman came up too.

"May we be of service to you in any other way?" the first asked mildly. Hieronymus fixed him with his glazed and suffering eyes.

"No," he said, "you cannot. I beg you to take the Madonna picture out of the window, at once and forever."

"But—why?"

"It is the Holy Mother of God," said Hieronymus in a subdued voice.

"Quite. But you have heard that Herr Blüthenzweig is not inclined to accede to your request."

"We must bear in mind that it is the Holy Mother of God," said Hieronymus again and his head trembled on his neck.

"So we must. But should we not be allowed to exhibit any Madonnas—or paint any?"

"It is not that," said Hieronymus, almost whispering. He drew himself up and shook his head energetically several times. His peaked brow under the hood was entirely furrowed with long, deep cross-folds. "You know very well that it is vice itself that is painted there—naked sensuality. I was standing near two simple young people and overheard with my own ears that it led them astray upon the doctrine of the Immaculate Conception."

"Oh, permit me—that is not the point," said the young salesman, smiling. In his leisure hours he was writing a brochure on the modern movement in art and was well qualified to conduct a cultured conversation. "The picture is a work of art," he went on, "and one must measure it by the appropriate standards as such. It has been very highly praised on all hands. The state has purchased it."

"I know that the state has purchased it," said Hieronymus. "I also know that the artist has twice dined with the Prince Regent. It is common talk—and God knows how people interpret the fact that a man can become famous by such work as this. What does such a fact bear witness to? To the blindness of the world, a blindness inconceivable, if not indeed shamelessly hypocritical. This picture has its origin in sensual lust and is enjoyed in the same—is that true or not? Answer me! And you too answer me, Herr Blüthenzweig!"

A pause ensued. Hieronymus seemed in all seriousness to demand an answer to his question, looking by turns at the staring attendants and the round back M. Blüthenzweig turned upon him, with his own piercing and anguishing brown eyes. Silence reigned. Only the yellow man with the goat's beard, bending over the French drawings, broke it with his bleating laugh.

"It is true," Hieronymus went on in a hoarse voice that shook with his profound indignation. "You do not dare deny it. How then can honour be done to its creator, as though he had endowed mankind with a new ideal possession? How can one stand before it and surrender unthinkingly to the base enjoyment which it purveys, persuading oneself in all seriousness that one is yielding to a noble and elevated sentiment, highly creditable to the human race? Is this reckless ignorance or abandoned hypocrisy? My understanding falters, it is completely at a loss when confronted by the absurd fact that a man can achieve renown on this earth by the stupid and shameless exploitation of the animal instincts. Beauty? What is beauty? What forces are they which use beauty as their tool today—and upon what does it work? No one can fail to know this, Herr Blüthenzweig. But who, understanding it clearly, can fail to feel disgust and pain? It is criminal to play upon the ignorance of the immature, the lewd, the brazen, and the unscrupulous by elevating beauty into an idol to be worshipped, to give it even more power over those who know not affliction and have no knowledge of redemption. You are unknown to me, and you look at me with black looks—yet answer me! Knowledge, I tell you, is the profoundest torture in the world; but it is the purgatory without whose purifying pangs no soul can reach salvation. It is not infantile, blasphemous shallowness that can save us, Herr Blüthenzweig; only knowledge can avail, knowledge in which the passions of our loathsome flesh die away and are quenched."

Silence.—The yellow man with the goat's beard gave a sudden little bleat.

"I think you really must go now," said the underpaid assistant mildly.

But Hieronymus made no move to do so. Drawn up in his hooded cape, he stood with blazing eyes in the centre of the shop and his thick lips poured out condemnation in a voice that was harsh and rusty and clanking.

"Art, you cry; enjoyment, beauty! Enfold the world in beauty and endow all things with the noble grace of style!—Profligate, away! Do you think to wash over with lurid colours the misery of the world? Do you think with the sounds of feasting and music to drown out the voice of the tortured earth? Shameless one, you err! God lets not Himself be mocked, and your impudent deification of the glistering surface of things is an abomination in His eyes. You tell me that I blaspheme art. I say to you that you lie. I do not blaspheme art. Art is no conscienceless delusion, lending itself to reinforce the allurements of the fleshly. Art is the holy torch which turns its light upon all the frightful depths, all the shameful and woeful abysses of life; art is the godly fire laid to the world that, being redeemed by pity, it may flame up and dissolve altogether with its shames and torments.—Take it out, Herr Blüthenzweig, take away the work of that famous painter out of your window—you would do well to burn it with a hot fire and strew its ashes to the four winds—yes, to all the four winds—"

His harsh voice broke off. He had taken a violent backwards step, snatched one arm from his black wrappings, and stretched it passionately forth, gesturing towards the window with a hand that shook as though palsied. And in this commanding attitude he paused. His great hooked nose seemed to jut more than ever, his dark brows were gathered so thick and high that folds crowded upon the peaked forehead shaded by the hood; a hectic flush mantled his hollow cheeks.

But at this point M. Blüthenzweig turned round. Perhaps he was outraged by the idea of burning his seventy-mark reproduction; perhaps Hieronymus's speech had completely exhausted his patience. In any case he was a picture of stern and righteous anger. He pointed with his pen to the door of the shop, gave several short, excited snorts into his moustache, struggled for words, and uttered with the maximum of energy those which he found:

"My fine fellow, if you don't get out at once I will have my packer help you—do you understand?"

"Oh, you cannot intimidate me, you cannot drive me away, you cannot silence my voice!" cried Hieronymus as he clutched his cloak over his chest with his fists and shook his head doughtily. "I know that I am single-handed and powerless, but yet I will not cease until you hear me, Herr Blüthenzweig! Take the picture out of your window and burn it even today! Ah, burn not it alone! Burn all these statues and busts, the sight of which plunges the beholder into sin! Burn these vases and ornaments, these shameless revivals of paganism, these elegantly bound volumes of erotic verse! Burn everything in your shop, Herr Blüthenzweig, for it is a filthiness in God's sight. Burn it, burn it!" he shrieked, beside himself, describing a wild, all-embracing circle with his arm. "The harvest is ripe for the reaper, the measure of the age's shamelessness is full—but I say unto you—"

"Krauthuber!" Herr Blüthenzweig raised his voice and shouted towards a door at the back of the shop. "Come in here at once!"

And in answer to the summons there appeared upon the scene a massive overpowering presence, a vast and awe-inspiring, swollen human bulk, whose limbs merged into each other like links of sausage—a gigantic son of the people, malt-nourished and immoderate, who weighed in, with puffings, bursting with energy, from the packing-room. His appearance in the upper reaches of his form was notable for a fringe of walrus beard; a hide apron fouled with paste covered his body from the waist down, and his yellow shirt-sleeves were rolled back from his heroic arms.

"Will you open the door for this gentleman, Krauthuber?" said M. Blüthenzweig; "and if he should not find the way to it, just help him into the street."

"Huh," said the man, looking from his enraged employer to Hieronymus and back with his little elephant eyes. It was a heavy monosyllable, suggesting reserve force restrained with difficulty. The floor shook with his tread as he went to the door and opened it.

Hieronymus had grown very pale. "Burn—" he shouted once more. He was about to go on when he felt himself turned round by an irresistible power, by a physical preponderance to which no resistance was even thinkable. Slowly and inexorably he was propelled towards the door.

"I am weak," he managed to ejaculate. "My flesh cannot bear the force . . . it cannot hold its ground, no . . . but what does that prove? Burn—"

He stopped. He found himself outside the art-shop. M. Blüthenzweig's giant packer had let him go with one final shove, which set him down on the stone threshold of the shop, supporting himself with one hand. Behind him the door closed with a rattle of glass.

He picked himself up. He stood erect, breathing heavily, and pulled his cloak together with one fist over his breast, letting the other hang down inside. His hollow cheeks had a grey pallor; the nostrils of his great hooked nose opened and closed; his ugly lips were writhen in an expression of hatred and despair and his red-rimmed eyes wandered over the beautiful square like those of a man in a frenzy.

He did not see that people were looking at him with amusement and curiosity. For what he beheld upon the mosaic pavement before the great loggia were all the vanities of this world: the masked costumes of the artist balls, the decorations, vases and art objects, the nude statues, the female busts, the picturesque rebirths of the pagan age, the portraits of famous beauties by the hands of masters, the elegantly bound erotic verse, the art brochures—all these he saw heaped in a pyramid and going up in crackling flames amid loud exultations from the people enthralled by his own frightful words. A yellow background of cloud had drawn up over the Theatinerstrasse, and from it issued wild rumblings; but what he saw was a burning fiery sword, towering in sulphurous light above the joyous city.

"*Gladius Dei super terram* . . ." his thick lips whispered; and drawing himself still higher in his hooded cloak while the hand hanging down inside it twitched convulsively, he murmured, quaking: "*cito et velociter!*"[7]

QUESTIONS

1. How would you characterize Munich as it is described in the first six paragraphs? Does it sound attractive? **2.** What effect does the conversation between the two youths (p. 360) have on the reader? On Hieronymus?

WRITING TOPIC

What finally does the story say about the relationship between art, religion, and morality?

---

[7] *Gladius Dei super terram* means "sword of God over the earth"; *cito et velociter* means "swiftly and quickly."

The Greatest Man in the World   1935

JAMES THURBER   [1894–1961]

Looking back on it now, from the vantage point of 1950, one can only marvel that it hadn't happened long before it did. The United States of America had been, ever since Kitty Hawk, blindly constructing the elaborate petard by which, sooner or later, it must be hoist. It was inevitable that some day there would come roaring out of the skies a national hero of insufficient intelligence, background, and character successfully to endure the mounting orgies of glory prepared for aviators who stayed up a long time or flew a great distance. Both Lindbergh and Byrd, fortunately for national decorum and international amity, had been gentlemen; so had our other famous aviators. They wore their laurels gracefully, withstood the awful weather of publicity, married excellent women, usually of fine family, and quietly retired to private life and the enjoyment of their varying fortunes. No untoward incidents, on a worldwide scale, marred the perfection of their conduct on the perilous heights of fame. The exception to the rule was, however, bound to occur and it did, in July, 1937, when Jack ("Pal") Smurch, erstwhile mechanics' helper in a small garage in Westfield, Iowa, flew a second-hand, single-motored Bresthaven Dragon-Fly III monoplane all the way around the world, without stopping.

Never before in the history of aviation had such a flight as Smurch's ever been dreamed of. No one had even taken seriously the weird floating auxiliary gas tanks, invention of the mad New Hampshire professor of astronomy, Dr. Charles Lewis Gresham, upon which Smurch placed full reliance. When the garage worker, a slightly built, surly, unprepossessing young man of twenty-two, appeared at Roosevelt Field in early July, 1937, slowly chewing a great quid of scrap tobacco, and announced "Nobody ain't seen no flyin' yet," the newspapers touched briefly and satirically upon his projected twenty-five-thousand-mile flight. Aeronautical and automotive experts dismissed the idea curtly, implying that it was a hoax, a publicity stunt. The rusty, battered, second-hand plane wouldn't go. The Gresham auxiliary tanks wouldn't work. It was simply a cheap joke.

Smurch, however, after calling on a girl in Brooklyn who worked in the flap-folding department of a large paper-box factory, a girl whom he later described as his "sweet patootie," climbed nonchalantly into his ridiculous plane at dawn of the memorable seventh of July, 1937, spat a curve of tobacco juice into the still air, and took off, carrying with him only a gallon of bootleg gin and six pounds of salami.

When the garage boy thundered out over the ocean the papers were forced to record, in all seriousness, that a mad, unknown young man—his name was variously misspelled—had actually set out upon a preposterous attempt to span the world in a rickety, one-engined contraption, trusting to the long-distance refueling device of a crazy schoolmaster. When, nine days later, without having stopped once, the tiny plane appeared above San Francisco Bay, headed for New York, spluttering and choking, to be sure, but still magnificently and miraculously aloft, the headlines, which long since had crowded everything else off the front page—even the shooting of the Governor of Illinois by the Vileti gang—swelled to unprecedented size, and the news stories began to run to twenty-five and thirty columns. It was noticeable, however, that the accounts of the epoch-making flight touched rather lightly upon the aviator himself. This was not because facts about the hero as a man were too meagre, but because they were too complete.

Reporters, who had been rushed out to Iowa when Smurch's plane was first sighted over the little French coast town of Serly-le-Mar, to dig up the story of the great man's life, had promptly discovered that the story of his life could not be printed. His mother, a sullen short-order cook in a shack restaurant on the edge of a tourists' camping ground near Westfield, met all enquiries as to her son with an angry, "Ah, the hell with him; I hope he drowns." His father appeared to be in jail somewhere for stealing spotlights and laprobes from tourists' automobiles; his younger brother, a weak-minded lad, had but recently escaped from the Preston, Iowa, Reformatory and was already wanted in several Western towns for the theft of money-order blanks from post offices. These alarming discoveries were still piling up at the very time that Pal Smurch, the greatest hero of the twentieth century, blear-eyed, dead for sleep, half-starved, was piloting his crazy junk-heap high above the region in which the lamentable story of his private life was being unearthed, headed for New York under greater glory than any man of his time had ever known.

The necessity for printing some account in the papers of the young man's career and personality had led to a remarkable predicament. It was of course impossible to reveal the facts, for a tremendous popular feeling in favor of the young hero had sprung up, like a grass fire, when he was halfway across Europe on his flight around the globe. He was, therefore, described as a modest chap, taciturn, blond, popular with his friends, popular with girls. The only available snapshot of Smurch, taken at the wheel of a phony automobile in a cheap photo studio at an amusement park, was touched up so that the little vulgarian looked quite handsome. His twisted leer was smoothed into a pleasant smile. The truth was, in this way, kept from the youth's ecstatic compatriots; they did not dream that the Smurch family was despised and feared by its neighbors in the obscure Iowa town, nor that the hero himself, because of numerous unsavory exploits, had come to be regarded in Westfield as a nuisance and a menace. He had, the reporters discovered, once knifed the principal of his high school— not mortally, to be sure, but he had knifed him; and on another occasion, surprised in the act of stealing an altar-cloth from a church, he had bashed the sacristan over the head with a pot of Easter lilies; for each of these offences he had served a sentence in the reformatory.

Inwardly, the authorities, both in New York and in Washington, prayed that an understanding Providence might, however awful such a thing seemed, bring disaster to the rusty, battered plane and its illustrious pilot, whose unheard-of flight had aroused the civilized world to hosannas of hysterical praise. The authorities were convinced that the character of the renowned aviator was such that the limelight of adulation was bound to reveal him to all the world, as a congenital hooligan mentally and morally unequipped to cope with his own prodigious fame. "I trust," said the Secretary of State, at one of many secret Cabinet meetings called to consider the national dilemma, "I trust that his mother's prayer will be answered," by which he referred to Mrs. Emma Smurch's wish that her son might be drowned. It was, however, too late for that—Smurch had leaped the Atlantic and then the Pacific as if they were millponds. At three minutes after two o'clock in the afternoon of 17 July, 1937, the garage boy brought his idiotic plane into Roosevelt Field for a perfect three-point landing.

It had, of course, been out of the question to arrange a modest little reception for the greatest flier in the history of the world. He was received at Roosevelt Field with such elaborate and pretentious ceremonies as rocked the world. Fortunately, however, the worn and spent hero promptly swooned, had to be removed bodily from his plane, and was spirited from the field without having opened his mouth once. Thus he did not jeopardize the dignity of this first reception, a reception illumined by the presence of the Secretaries of War and the Navy, Mayor Michael J. Moriarity of New York, the Premier of Canada, Governors Fanniman, Groves, McFeely, and Critchfield, and a brilliant array of European diplomats. Smurch did not, in fact, come to in time to take part in the gigantic hullabaloo arranged at City Hall for the next day. He was rushed to a secluded nursing home and confined to bed. It was nine days before he was able to get up, or to be more exact, before he was permitted to get up. Meanwhile the greatest minds in the country, in solemn assembly, had arranged a secret conference of city, state and government officials, which Smurch was to attend for the purpose of being instructed in the ethics and behavior of heroism.

On the day that the little mechanic was finally allowed to get up and dress and, for the first time in two weeks, took a great chew of tobacco, he was permitted to receive the newspapermen—this by way of testing him out. Smurch did not wait for questions. "Youse guys," he said—and the *Times* man winced— "youse guys can tell the cock-eyed world dat I put it over on Lindbergh, see? Yes—an' made an ass o' them two frogs." The "two frogs" was a reference to a pair of gallant French fliers who, in attempting a flight only halfway round the world, had, two weeks before, unhappily been lost at sea. The *Times* man was bold enough, at this point, to sketch out for Smurch the accepted formula for interviews in cases of this kind; he explained that there should be no arrogant statements belittling the achievements of other heroes, particularly heroes of foreign nations. "Ah, the hell with that," said Smurch. "I did it, see? I did it, an' I'm talkin' about it." And he did talk about it.

None of this extraordinary interview was, of course, printed. On the contrary, the newspapers, already under the disciplined direction of a secret directorate created for the occasion and composed of statesmen and editors, gave out to a panting and restless world that "Jacky," as he had been arbitrarily nicknamed, would consent to say only that he was very happy and that anyone could have done what he did. "My achievement has been, I fear, slightly exaggerated," the *Times* man's article had him protest, with a modest smile. These newspaper stories were kept from the hero, a restriction which did not serve to abate the rising malevolence of his temper. The situation was, indeed, extremely grave, for Pal Smurch was, as he kept insisting, "rarin' to go." He could not much longer be kept from a nation clamorous to lionize him. It was the most desperate crisis the United States of America had faced since the sinking of the *Lusitania*.

On the afternoon of the twenty-seventh of July, Smurch was spirited away to a conference-room in which were gathered mayors, governors, government officials, behaviorist psychologists, and editors. He gave them each a limp, moist paw and a brief unlovely grin. "Hah ya?" he said. When Smurch was seated, the Mayor of New York arose and, with obvious pessimism, attempted to explain what he must say and how he must act when presented to the world, ending his talk with a high tribute to the hero's courage and integrity. The Mayor was followed by Governor Fanniman of New York, who, after a touching declaration of faith, introduced Cameron Spottiswood, Second Secretary of the American Embassy in Paris, the gentlemen selected to coach Smurch in the amenities of public ceremonies. Sitting in a chair, with a soiled yellow tie in his hand and his shirt open at the throat, unshaved, smoking a rolled cigarette, Jack Smurch listened with a leer on his lips. "I get ya, I get ya," he cut in nastily. "Ya want me to ack like a softy, huh? Ya want me to ack like that— baby-faced Lindbergh, huh? Well, nuts to that, see?" Everyone took in his breath sharply; it was a sigh and a hiss. "Mr. Lindbergh," began a United States Senator, purple with rage, "and Mr. Byrd—" Smurch, who was paring his nails with a jackknife, cut in again. "Byrd!" he exclaimed. "Aw fa God's sake, dat big—" Somebody shut off his blasphemies with a sharp word. A newcomer had entered the room. Everyone stood up, except Smurch, who, still busy with his nails, did not even glance up. "Mr. Smurch," said someone sternly, "the President of the United States!" It had been thought that the presence of the Chief Executive might have a chastening effect upon the young hero, and the former had been, thanks to the remarkable co-operation of the press, secretly brought to the obscure conference-room.

A great, painful silence fell. Smurch looked up, waved a hand at the President. "How ya comin'?" he asked, and began rolling a fresh cigarette. The silence deepened. Someone coughed in a strained way. "Geez, it's hot, ain't it?" said Smurch. He loosened two more shirt buttons, revealing a hairy chest and the tattooed word "Sadie" enclosed in a stenciled heart. The great and important men in the room, faced by the most serious crisis in recent American history, exchanged worried frowns. Nobody seemed to know how to proceed. "Come awn, come awn," said Smurch. "Let's get the hell out of here! When do I start cuttin' in on de parties, huh? And what's they goin' to be *in* it?" He rubbed a thumb and a forefinger together meaningly. "Money!" exclaimed a state senator, shocked, pale. "Yeh, money," said Pal, flipping his cigarette out of a window, "an' big money." He began rolling a fresh cigarette. "Big money," he repeated, frowning over the rice paper. He tilted back in his chair, and leered at each gentleman, separately, the leer of an animal that knows its power, the leer of a leopard loose in a bird-and-dog shop. "Aw, fa God's sake, let's get some place where it's cooler," he said. "I been cooped up plenty for three weeks!"

Smurch stood up and walked over to an open window, where he stood staring down into the street, nine floors below. The faint shouting of newsboys floated up to him. He made out his name. "Hot dog!" he cried, grinning, ecstatic. He leaned out over the sill. "You tell 'em, babies!" he shouted down. "Hot diggity dog!" In the tense little knot of men standing behind him, a quick, mad impulse flared up. An unspoken word of appeal, of command, seemed to ring through the room. Yet it was deadly silent. Charles K. L. Brand, secretary to the Mayor of New York City, happened to be standing nearest Smurch; he looked inquiringly at the President of the United States. The President, pale, grim, nodded shortly. Brand, a tall, powerfully built man, once a tackle at Rutgers, stepped forward, seized the greatest man in the world by his left shoulder and the seat of his pants, and pushed him out of the window.

"My God, he's fallen out the window!" cried a quick-witted editor.

"Get me out of here!" cried the President. Several men sprang to his side and he was hurriedly escorted out of a door toward a side-entrance to the building. The editor of the Associated Press took charge, being used to such things. Crisply he ordered certain men to leave, others to stay; quickly he outlined a story which all the papers were to agree on, sent two men to the street to handle that end of the tragedy, commanded a Senator to sob and two Congressmen to go to pieces nervously. In a word, he skillfully set the stage for the gigantic task that was to follow, the task of breaking to a grief-stricken world the sad story of the untimely, accidental death of its most illustrious and spectacular figure.

The funeral was, as you know, the most elaborate, the finest, the solemnest, and the saddest ever held in the United States of America. The monument in Arlington Cemetery, with its clean white shaft of marble and the simple device of a tiny plane carved on its base, is a place for pilgrims, in deep reverence, to visit. The nations of the world paid lofty tributes to little Jacky Smurch, America's greatest hero. At a given hour there were two minutes of silence throughout the nation. Even the inhabitants of the small, bewildered town of Westfield, Iowa, observed this touching ceremony; agents of the Department of Justice saw to that. One of them was especially assigned to stand grimly in the doorway of a little shack restaurant on the edge of the tourists' camping ground just outside the town. There, under his stern scrutiny, Mrs. Emma Smurch bowed her head above two hamburger steaks sizzling on her grill—bowed her head and turned away, so that the Secret Service man could not see the twisted, strangely familiar, leer on her lips.

The Second Tree
from the Corner

1947

E. B. WHITE   [1899–1985]

"Ever have any bizarre thoughts?" asked the doctor.

Mr. Trexler failed to catch the word. "What kind?" he said.

"Bizarre," repeated the doctor, his voice steady. He watched his patient for any slight change of expression, any wince. It seemed to Trexler that the doctor was not only watching him closely, but was creeping slowly toward him, like a lizard toward a bug. Trexler shoved his chair back an inch and gathered himself for a reply. He was about to say "Yes" when he realized that if he said yes the next question would be unanswerable. Bizarre thoughts, bizarre thoughts? Ever have any bizarre thoughts? What kind of thoughts *except* bizarre had he had since the age of two?

Trexler felt the time passing, the necessity for an answer. These psychiatrists were busy men, overloaded, not to be kept waiting. The next patient was probably already perched out there in the waiting room, lonely, worried, shifting around on the sofa, his mind stuffed with bizarre thoughts and amorphous fears. Poor bastard, thought Trexler. Out there all alone in that misshapen antechamber, staring at the filing cabinet and wondering whether to tell the doctor about that day on the Madison Avenue bus.

Let's see, bizarre thoughts. Trexler dodged back along the dreadful corridor of the years to see what he could find. He felt the doctor's eyes upon him and knew that time was running out. Don't be so conscientious, he said to himself. If a bizarre thought is indicated here, just reach into the bag and pick anything at all. A man as well supplied with bizarre thoughts as you are should have no difficulty producing one for the record. Trexler darted into the bag, hung for a moment before one of his thoughts, as a hummingbird pauses in the delphinium. No, he said, not that one. He darted to another (the one about the rhesus monkey), paused, considered. No, he said, not that.

Trexler knew he must hurry. He had already used up pretty nearly four seconds since the question had been put. But it was an impossible situation—just one more lousy, impossible situation such as he was always getting himself into. When, he asked himself, are you going to quit maneuvering yourself into a pocket? He made one more effort. This time he stopped at the asylum, only the bars were lucite—fluted, retractable. Not here, he said. Not this one.

He looked straight at the doctor. "No," he said quietly. "I never have any bizarre thoughts."

The doctor sucked in on his pipe, blew a plume of smoke toward the rows of medical books. Trexler's gaze followed the smoke. He managed to make out one of the titles. "The Genito-Urinary System." A bright wave of fear swept cleanly over him, and he winced under the first pain of kidney stones. He remembered when he was a child, the first time he ever entered a doctor's office, sneaking a look at the titles of the books—and the flush of fear, the shirt wet under the arms, the book on T.B., the sudden knowledge that he was in the advanced stages of consumption, the quick vision of the hemorrhage. Trexler sighed wearily. Forty years, he thought, and I still get thrown by the title of a medical book. Forty years and I still can't stay on life's little bucky horse. No wonder I'm sitting here in this dreary joint at the end of this woebegone afternoon, lying about my bizarre thoughts to a doctor who looks, come to think of it, rather tired.

The session dragged on. After about twenty minutes, the doctor rose and knocked his pipe out. Trexler got up, knocked the ashes out of his brain, and waited. The doctor smiled warmly and stuck out his hand. "There's nothing the matter with you—you're just scared. Want to know how I know you're scared?"

"How?" asked Trexler.

"Look at the chair you've been sitting in! See how it has moved back away from my desk? You kept inching away from me while I asked you questions. That means you're scared."

"Does it?" said Trexler, faking a grin. "Yeah, I suppose it does."

They finished shaking hands. Trexler turned and walked out uncertainly along the passage, then into the waiting room and out past the next patient, a ruddy pin-striped man who was seated on the sofa twirling his hat nervously and staring straight ahead at the files. Poor, frightened guy, thought Trexler, he's probably read in the *Times* that one American male out of every two is going to die of heart disease by twelve o'clock next Thursday. It says that in the paper almost every morning. And he's also probably thinking about that day on the Madison Avenue bus.

A week later, Trexler was back in the patient's chair. And for several weeks thereafter he continued to visit the doctor, always toward the end of the afternoon, when the vapors hung thick above the pool of the mind and darkened the whole region of the East Seventies.[1] He felt no better as time went on, and he found it impossible to work. He discovered that the visits were becoming routine and that although the routine was one to which he certainly did not look forward, at least he could accept it with cool resignation, as once, years ago, he had accepted a long spell with a dentist who had settled down to a steady fooling with a couple of dead teeth. The visits, moreover, were now assuming a pattern recognizable to the patient.

Each session would begin with a résumé of symptoms—the dizziness in the streets, the constricting pain in the back of the neck, the apprehensions, the

---

[1] The East Seventies is a neighborhood, much of it elegant and expensive, in Manhattan.

tightness of the scalp, the inability to concentrate, the despondency and the melancholy times, the feeling of pressure and tension, the anger at not being able to work, the anxiety over work not done, the gas on the stomach. Dullest set of neurotic symptoms in the world, Trexler would think, as he obediently trudged back over them for the doctor's benefit. And then, having listened attentively to the recital, the doctor would spring his question: "Have you ever found anything that gives you relief?" And Trexler would answer, "Yes. A drink." And the doctor would nod his head knowingly.

As he became familiar with the pattern Trexler found that he increasingly tended to identify himself with the doctor, transferring himself into the doctor's seat—probably (he thought) some rather slick form of escapism. At any rate, it was nothing new for Trexler to identify himself with other people. Whenever he got into a cab, he instantly became the driver, saw everything from the hackman's angle (and the reaching over with the right hand, the nudging of the flag, the pushing it down, all the way down along the side of the meter), saw everything—traffic, fare, everything—through the eyes of Anthony Rocco, or Isidore Freedman, or Matthew Scott. In a barbershop, Trexler was the barber, his fingers curled around the comb, his hand on the tonic. Perfectly natural, then, that Trexler should soon be occupying the doctor's chair, asking the questions, waiting for the answers. He got quite interested in the doctor, in this way. He liked him, and he found him a not too difficult patient.

It was on the fifth visit, about halfway through, that the doctor turned to Trexler and said, suddenly, "What do you want?" He gave the word "want" special emphasis.

"I d'know," replied Trexler uneasily. "I guess nobody knows the answer to that one."

"Sure they do," replied the doctor.

"Do *you* know what *you* want?" asked Trexler narrowly.

"Certainly," said the doctor. Trexler noticed that at this point the doctor's chair slid slightly backward, away from him. Trexler stifled a small, internal smile. Scared as a rabbit, he said to himself. Look at him scoot!

"What *do* you want?" continued Trexler, pressing his advantage, pressing it hard.

The doctor glided back another inch away from his inquisitor. "I want a wing on the small house I own in Westport. I want more money, and more leisure to do the things I want to do."

Trexler was just about to say, "And what are those things you want to do, Doctor?" when he caught himself. Better not go too far, he mused. Better not lose possession of the ball. And besides, he thought, what the hell goes on here, anyway—me paying fifteen bucks a throw for these séances and then doing the work myself, asking the questions, weighing the answers. So he wants a new wing! There's a fine piece of theatrical gauze for you! A new wing.

Trexler settled down again and resumed the role of patient for the rest of the visit. It ended on a kindly, friendly note. The doctor reassured him that his fears were the cause of his sickness, and that his fears were unsubstantial. They shook hands, smiling.

Trexler walked dizzily through the empty waiting room and the doctor followed along to let him out. It was late; the secretary had shut up shop and gone home. Another day over the dam. "Goodbye," said Trexler. He stepped into the street, turned west toward Madison, and thought of the doctor all alone there, after hours, in that desolate hole—a man who worked longer hours than his secretary. Poor, scared, overworked bastard, thought Trexler. And that new wing!

It was an evening of clearing weather, the Park showing green and desirable in the distance, the last daylight applying a high lacquer to the brick and brownstone walls and giving the street scene a luminous and intoxicating splendor. Trexler meditated, as he walked, on what he wanted. "What do you want?" he heard again. Trexler knew what he wanted, and what, in general, all men wanted; and he was glad, in a way, that it was both inexpressible and unattainable, and that it wasn't a wing. He was satisfied to remember that it was deep, formless, enduring, and impossible of fulfillment, and that it made men sick, and that when you sauntered along Third Avenue and looked through the doorways into the dim saloons, you could sometimes pick out from the unregenerate ranks the ones who had not forgotten, gazing steadily into the bottoms of the glasses on the long chance that they could get another little peek at it. Trexler found himself renewed by the remembrance that what he wanted was at once great and microscopic, and that although it borrowed from the nature of large deeds and of youthful love and of old songs and early intimations, it was not any one of these things, and that it had not been isolated or pinned down, and that a man who attempted to define it in the privacy of a doctor's office would fall flat on his face.

Trexler felt invigorated. Suddenly his sickness seemed health, his dizziness stability. A small tree, rising between him and the light, stood there saturated with the evening, each gilt-edged leaf perfectly drunk with excellence and delicacy. Trexler's spine registered an ever so slight tremor as it picked up this natural disturbance in the lovely scene. "I want the second tree from the corner, just as it stands," he said, answering an imaginary question from an imaginary physician. And he felt a slow pride in realizing that what he wanted none could bestow, and that what he had none could take away. He felt content to be sick, unembarrassed at being afraid; and in the jungle of his fear he glimpsed (as he had so often glimpsed them before) the flashy tail feathers of the bird courage.

Then he thought once again of the doctor, and of his being left there all alone, tired, frightened. (The poor, scared guy, thought Trexler.) Trexler began humming "Moonshine Lullaby," his spirit reacting instantly to the hypodermic of Merman's[2] healthy voice. He crossed Madison, boarded a downtown bus,

---

[2] Ethel Merman (1909–1984), a musical comedy star with a strong voice.

and rode all the way to Fifty-second Street before he had a thought that could rightly have been called bizarre.

QUESTIONS

1. At the beginning of the story, the doctor asks Trexler if he ever had any bizarre thoughts. What is Trexler's reply? Why does he give that reply? Can you imagine from Trexler's ruminations, what sort of bizarre thoughts he might have had? Would it be more effective if White indicated precisely what Trexler's thoughts had been? Explain.   **2.** The seminal question in this story is put by the doctor to Trexler: "What do you want?" What is Trexler's answer? What is the doctor's response? What do *you* want?   **3.** Trexler, we are told, knew what he wanted and was glad "that it was both inexpressible and unattainable." In what sense is Trexler's desire inexpressible and unattainable?   **4.** In what sense might this be a story about the difference between being afraid and unafraid?

WRITING TOPIC

How does Trexler's recognition that he wants "the second tree from the corner, just as it stands" result in his feeling "content to be sick"?

The Man Who Lived Underground

1944

RICHARD WRIGHT [1908–1960]

I've got to hide, he told himself. His chest heaved as he waited, crouching in a dark corner of the vestibule. He was tired of running and dodging. Either he had to find a place to hide, or he had to surrender. A police car swished by through the rain, its siren rising sharply. They're looking for me all over . . . He crept to the door and squinted through the fogged plate glass. He stiffened as the siren rose and died in the distance. Yes, he had to hide, but where? He gritted his teeth. Then a sudden movement in the street caught his attention. A throng of tiny columns of water snaked into the air from the perforations of a manhole cover. The columns stopped abruptly, as though the perforations had become clogged; a gray spout of sewer water jutted up from underground and lifted the circular metal cover, juggled it for a moment, then let it fall with a clang.

He hatched a tentative plan: he would wait until the siren sounded far off, then he would go out. He smoked and waited, tense. At last the siren gave him his signal; it wailed, dying, going away from him. He stepped to the sidewalk, then paused and looked curiously at the open manhole, half expecting the cover to leap up again. He went to the center of the street and stooped and peered into the hole, but could see nothing. Water rustled in the black depths.

He started with terror; the siren sounded so near that he had the idea that he had been dreaming and had awakened to find the car upon him. He dropped instinctively to his knees and his hands grasped the rim of the manhole. The siren seemed to hoot directly above him and with a wild gasp of exertion he snatched the cover far enough off to admit his body. He swung his legs over the opening and lowered himself into watery darkness. He hung for an eternal moment to the rim by his finger tips, then he felt rough metal prongs and at once, he knew that sewer workmen used these ridges to lower themselves into manholes. Fist over fist, he let his body sink until he could feel no more prongs. He swayed in dank space; the siren seemed to howl at the very rim of the manhole. He dropped and was washed violently into an ocean of warm, leaping water. His head was battered against a wall and he wondered if this were death. Frenziedly his fingers clawed and sank into a crevice. He steadied himself and measured the strength of the current with his own muscular tension. He stood slowly in water that dashed past his knees with fearful velocity.

He heard a prolonged scream of brakes and the siren broke off. Oh, God! They had found him! Looming above his head in the rain a white face hovered over the hole. "How did this damn thing get off?" he heard a policeman ask. He saw the steel cover move slowly until the hole looked like a quarter moon turned black. "Give me a hand here," someone called. The cover clanged into place, muffling the sights and sounds of the upper world. Knee-deep in the pulsing current, he breathed with aching chest, filling his lungs with the hot stench of yeasty rot.

From the perforations of the manhole cover, delicate lances of hazy violet sifted down and wove a mottled pattern upon the surface of the streaking current. His lips parted as a car swept past along the wet pavement overhead, its heavy rumble soon dying out, like the hum of a plane speeding through a dense cloud. He had never thought that cars could sound like that; everything seemed strange and unreal under here. He stood in darkness for a long time, knee-deep in rustling water, musing.

The odor of rot had become so general that he no longer smelled it. He got his cigarettes, but discovered that his matches were wet. He searched and found a dry folder in the pocket of his shirt and managed to strike one; it flared weirdly in the wet gloom, glowing greenishly, turning red, orange, then yellow. He lit a crumpled cigarette; then, by the flickering light of the match, he looked for support so that he would not have to keep his muscles flexed against the pouring water. His pupils narrowed and he saw to either side of him two steaming walls that rose and curved inward some six feet above his head to form a dripping, mouse-colored dome. The bottom of the sewer was a sloping V-trough. To the left, the sewer vanished in ashen fog. To the right was a deep down-curve into which water plunged.

He saw now that had he not regained his feet in time, he would have been swept to death, or had he entered any other manhole he would have probably drowned. Above the rush of the current he heard sharper juttings of water; tiny streams were spewing into the sewer from smaller conduits. The match died; he struck another and saw a mass of debris sweep past him and clog the throat of the down-curve. At once the water began rising rapidly. Could he climb out before he drowned? A long hiss sounded and the debris was sucked from sight; the current lowered. He understood now what had made the water toss the manhole cover; the down-curve had become temporarily obstructed and the perforations had become clogged.

He was in danger; he might slide into a down-curve; he might wander with a lighted match into a pocket of gas and blow himself up; or he might contract some horrible disease . . . Though he wanted to leave, an irrational impulse held him rooted. To the left, the convex ceiling swooped to a height of less than five feet. With cigarette slanting from pursed lips, he waded with taut muscles, his feet sloshing over the slimy bottom, his shoes sinking into spongy slop, the slate-colored water cracking in creamy foam against his knees. Pressing flat his left palm against the lowered ceiling, he struck another match and saw a metal pole nestling in a niche of the wall. Yes, some sewer workman had left it. He reached for it, then jerked his head away as a whisper of scurrying life whisked past and was still. He held the match close and saw a huge rat, wet with slime, blinking beady eyes and baring tiny fangs. The light blinded the rat and the frizzled head moved aimlessly. He grabbed the pole and let it fly against the rat's soft body; there was shrill piping and the grizzly body splashed into the dun-colored water and was snatched out of sight, spinning in the scuttling stream.

He swallowed and pushed on, following the curve of the misty cavern, sounding the water with the pole. By the faint light of another manhole cover he saw, amid loose wet brick, a hole with walls of damp earth leading into blackness. Gingerly he poked the pole into it; it was hollow and went beyond the length of the pole. He shoved the pole before him, hoisted himself upward, got to his hands and knees, and crawled. After a few yards he paused, struck to wonderment by the silence; it seemed that he had traveled a million miles away from the world. As he inched forward again he could sense the bottom of the dirt tunnel becoming dry and lowering slightly. Slowly he rose and to his astonishment he stood erect. He could not hear the rustling of the water now and he felt confoundingly alone, yet lured by the darkness and silence.

He crept a long way, then stopped, curious, afraid. He put his right foot forward and it dangled in space; he drew back in fear. He thrust the pole outward and it swung in emptiness. He trembled, imagining the earth crumbling and burying him alive. He scratched a match and saw that the dirt floor sheered away steeply and widened into a sort of cave some five feet below him. An old sewer, he muttered. He cocked his head, hearing a feathery cadence which he could not identify. The match ceased to burn.

Using the pole as a kind of ladder, he slid down and stood in darkness. The air was a little fresher and he could still hear vague noises. Where was he? He felt suddenly that someone was standing near him and he turned sharply, but there was only darkness. He poked cautiously and felt a brick wall; he followed it and the strange sounds grew louder. He ought to get out of here. This was crazy. He could not remain here for any length of time; there was no food and no place to sleep. But the faint sounds tantalized him; they were strange but familiar. Was it a motor? A baby crying? Music? A siren? He groped on, and the sounds came so clearly that he could feel the pitch and timbre of human voices. Yes, singing! That was it! He listened with open mouth. It was a church service. Enchanted, he groped toward the waves of melody.

> *Jesus, take me to your home above*
> *And fold me in the bosom of Thy love . . .*

The singing was on the other side of the brick wall. Excited, he wanted to watch the service without being seen. Whose church was it? He knew most of the churches in this area aboveground, but the singing sounded too strange and detached for him to guess. He looked to the left, to the right, down to the black dirt, then upward and was startled to see a bright sliver of light slicing the darkness like the blade of a razor. He struck one of his two remaining matches and saw rusty pipes running along an old concrete ceiling. Photographically he located the exact position of the pipes in his mind. The match flame sank and he sprang upward; his hands clutched a pipe. He swung his legs and tossed his body onto the bed of pipes and they creaked, swaying up and down; he thought that the tier was about to crash, but nothing happened. He edged to the crevice and saw a segment of black men and women, dressed in white robes, singing, holding tattered songbooks in their black palms. His first impulse was to laugh, but he checked himself.

What was he doing? He was crushed with a sense of guilt. Would God strike him dead for that? The singing swept on and he shook his head, disagreeing in spite of himself. They oughtn't to do that, he thought. But he could think of no reason *why* they should not do it. Just singing with the air of the sewer blowing in on them . . . He felt that he was gazing upon something abysmally obscene, yet he could not bring himself to leave.

After a long time he grew numb and dropped to the dirt. Pain throbbed in his legs and a deeper pain, induced by the sight of those black people groveling and begging for something they could never get, churned in him. A vague conviction made him feel that those people should stand unrepentant and yield no quarter in singing and praying, yet *he* had run away from the police, had pleaded with them to believe in *his* innocence. He shook his head, bewildered.

How long had he been down here? He did not know. This was a new kind of living for him; the intensity of feelings he had experienced when looking at the church people sing made him certain that he had been down here a long time, but his mind told him that the time must have been short. In this darkness the only notion he had of time was when a match flared and measured time by its fleeting light. He groped back through the hole toward the sewer and the waves of song subsided and finally he could not hear them at all. He came to where the earth hole ended and he heard the noise of the current and time lived again for him, measuring the moments by the wash of the water.

The rain must have slackened, for the flow of water had lessened and came only to his ankles. Ought he to go up into the streets and take his chances on hiding somewhere else? But they would surely catch him. The mere thought of dodging and running again from the police made him tense. No, he would stay and plot how to elude them. But what could he do down here? He walked forward into the sewer and came to another manhole cover; he stood beneath it, debating. Fine pencils of gold spilled suddenly from the little circles in the manhole cover and trembled on the surface of the current. Yes, street lamps . . . It must be night . . .

He went forward for about a quarter of an hour, wading aimlessly, poking the pole carefully before him. Then he stopped, his eyes fixed and intent. What's that? A strangely familiar image attracted and repelled him. Lit by the yellow stems from another manhole cover was a tiny nude body of a baby snagged by debris and half-submerged in water. Thinking that the baby was alive, he moved impulsively to save it, but his roused feelings told him that it was dead, cold, nothing, the same nothingness he had felt while watching the men and women singing in the church. Water blossomed about the tiny legs, the tiny arms, the tiny head, and rushed onward. The eyes were closed, as though in sleep; the fists were clenched, as though in protest; and the mouth gaped black in a soundless cry.

He straightened and drew in his breath, feeling that he had been staring for all eternity at the ripples of veined water skimming impersonally over the shriveled limbs. He felt as condemned as when the policemen had accused him. Involuntarily he lifted his hand to brush the vision away, but his arm fell listlessly to his side. Then he acted; he closed his eyes and reached forward slowly with the soggy shoe of his right foot and shoved the dead baby from where it had been lodged. He kept his eyes closed, seeing the little body twisting in the current as it floated from sight. He opened his eyes, shivered, placed his knuckles in the sockets, hearing the water speed in the somber shadows.

He tramped on, sensing at times a sudden quickening in the current as he passed some conduit whose waters were swelling the stream that slid by his feet. A few minutes later he was standing under another manhole cover, listening to the faint rumble of noises aboveground. Streetcars and trucks, he mused. He looked down and saw a stagnant pool of gray-green sludge; at intervals a balloon pocket rose from the scum, glistening a bluish-purple, and burst. Then another. He turned, shook his head, and tramped back to the dirt cave by the church, his lips quivering.

Back in the cave, he sat and leaned his back against a dirt wall. His body was trembling slightly. Finally his senses quieted and he slept. When he awakened he felt stiff and cold. He had to leave this foul place, but leaving meant facing those policemen who had wrongly accused him. No he could not go back aboveground. He remembered the beating they had given him and how he had signed his name to a confession, a confession which he had not even read. He had been too tired when they had shouted at him, demanding that he sign his name; he had signed it to end his pain.

He stood and groped about in the darkness. The church singing had stopped. How long had he slept? He did not know. But he felt refreshed and hungry. He doubled his fist nervously, realizing that he could not make a decision. As he walked about he stumbled over an old rusty iron pipe. He picked it up and felt a jagged edge. Yes, there was a brick wall and he could dig into it. What would he find? Smiling, he groped to the brick wall, sat, and began digging idly into damp cement. I can't make any noise, he cautioned himself. As time passed he grew thirsty, but there was no water. He had to kill time or go aboveground. The cement came out of the wall easily; he extracted four bricks and felt a soft draft blowing into his face. He stopped, afraid. What was beyond? He waited a long time and nothing happened; then he began digging again, soundlessly, slowly; he enlarged the hole and crawled through into a dark room and collided with another wall. He felt his way to the right; the wall ended and his fingers toyed in space, like the antennae of an insect.

He fumbled on and his feet struck something hollow, like wood. What's this? He felt with his fingers. Steps . . . He stooped and pulled off his shoes and mounted the stairs and saw a yellow chink of light shining and heard a low voice speaking. He placed his eye to a keyhole and saw the nude waxen figure of a man stretched out upon a white table. The voice, low-pitched and vibrant, mumbled indistinguishable words, neither rising nor falling. He craned his neck and squinted to see the man who was talking, but he could not locate him. Above the naked figure was suspended a huge glass container filled with a bloodred liquid from which a white rubber tube dangled. He crouched closer to the door and saw the tip end of a black object lined with pink satin. A coffin, he breathed. This is an undertaker's establishment . . . A fine-spun lace of ice covered his body and he shuddered. A throaty chuckle sounded in the depths of the yellow room.

He turned to leave. Three steps down it occurred to him that a light switch should be nearby; he felt along the wall, found an electric button, pressed it, and a blinding glare smote his pupils so hard that he was sightless, defenseless. His pupils contracted and he wrinkled his nostrils at a peculiar odor. At once he knew that he had been dimly aware of this odor in the darkness, but the light had brought it sharply to his attention. Some kind of stuff they use to embalm, he thought. He went down the steps and saw piles of lumber, coffins, and a long workbench. In one corner was a tool chest. Yes, he could use tools, could tunnel through walls with them. He lifted the lid of the chest and saw nails, a hammer, a crowbar, a screwdriver, a light bulb, and a long length of electric wire. Good! He would lug these back to his cave.

He was about to hoist the chest to his shoulders when he discovered a door behind the furnace. Where did it lead? He tried to open it and found it securely bolted. Using the crowbar so as to make no sound, he pried the door open; it swung on creaking hinges, outward. Fresh air came to his face and he caught the faint roar of faraway sound. Easy now, he told himself. He widened the door and a lump of coal rattled toward him. A coalbin . . . Evidently the door led into another basement. The roaring noise was louder, but he could not identify it. Where was he? He groped slowly over the coal pile, then ranged in darkness over a gritty floor. The roaring noise seemed to come from above him, then below. His fingers followed a wall until he touched a wooden ridge. A door, he breathed.

The noise died to a low pitch; he felt his skin prickle. It seemed that he was playing a game with an unseen person whose intelligence outstripped his. He put his ear to the flat surface of the door. Yes, voices . . . Was this a prize fight stadium? The sound of the voices came near and sharp, but he could not tell if they were joyous or despairing. He twisted the knob until he heard a soft click and felt the springy weight of the door swinging toward him. He was afraid to open it, yet captured by curiosity and wonder. He jerked the door wide and saw on the far side of the basement a furnace glowing red. Ten feet away was still another door, half ajar. He crossed and peered through the door into an empty, high-ceilinged corridor that terminated in a dark complex of shadow. The belling voices rolled about him and his eagerness mounted. He stepped into the corridor and the voices swelled louder. He crept on and came to a narrow stairway leading circularly upward; there was no question but that he was going to ascend those stairs.

Mounting the spiraled staircase, he heard the voices roll in a steady wave, then leap to crescendo, only to die away, but always remaining audible. Ahead of him glowed red letters: E—X—I—T. At the top of the steps he paused in front of a black curtain that fluttered uncertainly. He parted the folds and looked into a convex depth that gleamed with clusters of shimmering lights. Sprawled below him was a stretch of human faces, tilted upward, chanting, whistling, screaming, laughing. Dangling before the faces, high upon a screen of silver, were jerking shadows. A movie, he said with slow laughter breaking from his lips.

He stood in a box in the reserved section of a movie house and the impulse he had had to tell the people in the church to stop their singing seized him. These people were laughing at their lives, he thought with amazement. They were shouting and yelling at the animated shadows of themselves. His compassion fired his imagination and he stepped out of the box, walked out upon thin air, walked on down to the audience; and, hovering in the air just above them, he stretched out his hand to touch them . . . His tension snapped and he found himself back in the box, looking down into the sea of faces. No; it could not be done; he could not awaken them. He sighed. Yes, these people were children, sleeping in their living, awake in their dying.

He turned away, parted the black curtain, and looked out. He saw no one. He started down the white stone steps and when he reached the bottom he saw a man in trim blue uniform coming toward him. So used had he become to being underground that he thought that he could walk past the man, as though he were a ghost. But the man stopped. And he stopped.

"Looking for the men's room, sir?" the man asked, and without waiting for an answer, he turned and pointed. "This way, sir. The first door to your right."

He watched the man turn and walk up the steps and go out of sight. Then he laughed. What a funny fellow! He went back to the basement and stood in the red darkness, watching the glowing embers in the furnace. He went to the sink and turned the faucet and the water flowed in a smooth silent stream that looked like a spout of blood. He brushed the mad image from his mind and began to wash his hands leisurely, looking about for the usual bar of soap. He found one and rubbed it in his palms until a rich lather bloomed in his cupped fingers, like a scarlet sponge. He scrubbed and rinsed his hands meticulously, then hunted for a towel; there was none. He shut off the water, pulled off his shirt, dried his hands on it; when he put it on again he was grateful for the cool dampness that came to his skin.

Yes, he was thirsty; he turned on the faucet again, bowled his fingers and when the water bubbled over the brim of his cupped palms, he drank in long, slow swallows. His bladder grew tight; he shut off the water, faced the wall, bent his head, and watched a red stream strike the floor. His nostrils wrinkled against acrid wisps of vapor; though he had tramped in the waters of the sewer, he stepped back from the wall so that his shoes, wet with sewer slime, would not touch his urine.

He heard footsteps and crawled quickly into the coalbin. Lumps rattled noisily. The footsteps came into the basement and stopped. Who was it? Had someone heard him and come down to investigate? He waited, crouching, sweating. For a long time there was silence, then he heard the clang of metal and a brighter glow lit the room. Somebody's tending the furnace, he thought. Footsteps came closer and he stiffened. Looming before him was a white face lined with coal dust, the face of an old man with watery blue eyes. Highlights spotted his gaunt cheekbones, and he held a huge shovel. There was a screechy scrape of metal against stone, and the old man lifted a shovelful of coal and went from sight.

The room dimmed momentarily, then a yellow glare came as coal flared at the furnace door. Six times the old man came to the bin and went to the furnace with shovels of coal, but not once did he lift his eyes. Finally he dropped the shovel, mopped his face with a dirty handkerchief, and sighed: "Wheeew!" He turned slowly and trudged out of the basement, his footsteps dying away.

He stood, and lumps of coal clattered down the pile. He stepped from the bin and was startled to see the shadowy outline of an electric bulb hanging above his head. Why had not the old man turned it on? Oh, yes . . . He understood. The old man had worked here for so long that he had no need for light; he had learned a way of seeing in his dark world, like those sightless worms that inch along underground by a sense of touch.

His eyes fell upon a lunch pail and he was afraid to hope that it was full. He picked it up; it was heavy. He opened it. *Sandwiches!* He looked guiltily around; he was alone. He searched farther and found a folder of matches and a half-empty tin of tobacco; he put them eagerly into his pocket and clicked off the light. With the lunch pail under his arm, he went through the door, groped over the pile of coal, and stood again in the lighted basement of the undertaking establishment. I've got to get those tools, he told himself. And turn off that light. He tiptoed back up the steps and switched off the light; the invisible voice still droned on behind the door. He crept down and, seeing with his fingers, opened the lunch pail and tore off a piece of paper bag and brought out the tin and spilled grains of tobacco into the makeshift concave. He rolled it and wet it with spittle, then inserted one end into his mouth and lit it: he sucked smoke that bit his lungs. The nicotine reached his brain, went out along his arms to his finger tips, down to his stomach, and over all the tired nerves of his body.

He carted the tools to the hole he had made in the wall. Would the noise of the falling chest betray him? But he would have to take a chance; he had to have those tools. He lifted the chest and shoved it; it hit the dirt on the other side of the wall with a loud clatter. He waited, listening; nothing happened. Head first, he slithered through and stood in the cave. He grinned, filled with a cunning idea. Yes, he would now go back into the basement of the undertaking establishment and crouch behind the coal pile and dig another hole. Sure! Fumbling, he opened the tool chest and extracted a crowbar, a screwdriver, and a hammer; he fastened them securely about his person.

With another lumpish cigarette in his flexed lips, he crawled back through the hole and over the coal pile and sat, facing the brick wall. He jabbed with the crowbar and the cement sheered away; quicker than he thought, a brick came loose. He worked an hour; the other bricks did not come easily. He sighed, weak from effort. I ought to rest a little, he thought. I'm hungry. He felt his way back to the cave and stumbled along the wall till he came to the tool chest. He sat upon it, opened the lunch pail, and took out two thick sandwiches. He smelled them. Pork chops . . . His mouth watered. He closed his eyes and devoured a sandwich, savoring the smooth rye bread and juicy meat. He ate rapidly, gulping down lumpy mouthfuls that made him long for water. He ate the other sandwich and found an apple and gobbled that up too, sucking the core till the last trace of flavor was drained from it. Then, like a dog, he ground the meat bones with his teeth, enjoying the salty, tangy marrow. He finished and stretched out full length on the ground and went to sleep. . . .

. . . His body was washed by cold water that gradually turned warm and he was buoyed upon a stream and swept out to sea where waves rolled gently and suddenly he found himself walking upon the water how strange and delightful to walk upon the water and he came upon a nude woman holding a nude baby in her arms and the woman was sinking into the water holding the baby above her head and screaming *help* and he ran over the water to the woman and he reached her just before she went down and he took the baby from her hands and stood watching the breaking bubbles where the woman sank and he called *lady* and still no answer yes dive down there and rescue that woman but he could not take this baby with him and he stooped and laid the baby tenderly upon the surface of the water expecting it to sink but it floated and he leaped into the water and held his breath and strained his eyes to see through the gloomy volume of water but there was no woman and he opened his mouth and called *lady* and the water bubbled and his chest ached and his arms were tired but he could not see the woman and he called again *lady lady* and his feet touched sand at the bottom of the sea and his chest felt as though it would burst and he bent his knees and propelled himself upward and water rushed past him and his head bobbed out and he breathed deeply and looked around where was the baby the baby was gone and he rushed over the water looking for the baby calling *where is it* and the empty sky and sea threw back his voice *where is it* and he began to doubt that he could stand upon the water and then he was sinking and as he struggled the water rushed him downward spinning dizzily and he opened his mouth to call for help and water surged into his lungs and he choked . . .

He groaned and leaped erect in the dark, his eyes wide. The images of terror that thronged his brain would not let him sleep. He rose, made sure that the tools were hitched to his belt, and groped his way to the coal pile and found the rectangular gap from which he had taken the bricks. He took out the crowbar and hacked. Then dread paralyzed him. How long had he slept? Was it day or night now? He had to be careful. Someone might hear him if it were day. He hewed softly for hours at the cement, working silently. Faintly quivering in the air above him was the dim sound of yelling voices. Crazy people, he muttered. They're still there in that movie . . .

Having rested, he found the digging much easier. He soon had a dozen bricks out. His spirits rose. He took out another brick and his fingers fluttered in space. Good! What lay ahead of him? Another basement? He made the hole larger, climbed through, walked over an uneven floor and felt a metal surface. He lighted a match and saw that he was standing behind a furnace in a basement; before him, on the far side of the room, was a door. He crossed and opened it; it was full of odds and ends. Daylight spilled from a window above his head.

Then he was aware of a soft, continuous tapping. What was it? A clock? No, it was louder than a clock and more irregular. He placed an old empty box beneath the window, stood upon it, and looked into an areaway. He eased the window up and crawled through; the sound of the tapping came clearly now. He glanced about; he was alone. Then he looked upward at a series of window ledges. The tapping identified itself. That's a typewriter, he said to himself. It seemed to be coming from just above. He grasped the ridges of a rain pipe and lifted himself upward; through a half-inch opening of window he saw a doorknob about three feet away. No, it was not a doorknob; it was a small circular disk made of stainless steel with many fine markings upon it. He held his breath; an eerie white hand, seemingly detached from its arm, touched the metal knob and whirled it, first to the left, then to the right. It's a safe! . . . Suddenly he could see the dial no more; a huge metal door swung slowly toward him and he was looking into a safe filled with green wads of paper money, rows of coins wrapped in brown paper, and glass jars and boxes of various sizes. His heart quickened. Good Lord! The white hand went in and out of the safe, taking wads of bills and cylinders of coins. The hand vanished and he heard the muffled click of the big door as it closed. Only the steel dial was visible now. The typewriter still tapped in his ears, but he could not see it. He blinked, wondering if what he had seen was real. There was more money in that safe than he had seen in all his life.

As he clung to the rain pipe, a daring idea came to him and he pulled the screwdriver from his belt. If the white hand twirled that dial again, he would be able to see how far to left and right it spun and he would have the combination! His blood tingled. I can scratch the numbers right here, he thought. Holding the pipe with one hand, he made the sharp edge of the screwdriver bite into the brick wall. Yes, he could do it. Now, he was set. Now, he had a reason for staying here in the underground. He waited for a long time, but the white hand did not return. Goddamn! Had he been more alert, he could have counted the twirls and he would have had the combination. He got down and stood in the areaway, sunk in reflection.

How could he get into that room? He climbed back into the basement and saw wooden steps leading upward. Was that the room where the safe stood? Fearing that the dial was now being twirled, he clambered through the window, hoisted himself up the rain pipe, and peered; he saw only the naked gleam of the steel dial. He got down and doubled his fists. Well, he would explore the basement. He returned to the basement room and mounted the steps to the door and squinted through the keyhole; all was dark, but the tapping was still somewhere near, still faint and directionless. He pushed the door in; along one wall of a room was a table piled with radios and electrical equipment. A radio shop, he muttered.

Well, he could rig up a radio in his cave. He found a sack, slid the radio into it, and slung it across his back. Closing the door, he went down the steps and stood again in the basement, disappointed. He had not solved the problem of the steel dial and he was irked. He set the radio on the floor and again hoisted himself through the window and up the rain pipe and squinted; the metal door was swinging shut. Goddamn! He's worked the combination again. If I had been patient, I'd have had it! How could he get into that room? He *had* to get into it. He could jimmy the window, but it would be much better if he could get in without any traces. To the right of him, he calculated, should be the basement of the building that held the safe; therefore, if he dug a hole right *here*, he ought to reach his goal.

He began a quiet scraping; it was hard work, for the bricks were not damp. He eventually got one out and lowered it softly to the floor. He had to be careful; perhaps people were beyond this wall. He extracted a second layer of brick and found still another. He gritted his teeth, ready to quit. I'll dig one more, he resolved. When the next brick came out he felt air blowing into his face. He waited to be challenged, but nothing happened.

He enlarged the hole and pulled himself through and stood in quiet darkness. He scratched a match to flame and saw steps; he mounted and peered through a keyhole; Darkness . . . He strained to hear the typewriter, but there was only silence. Maybe the office had closed? He twisted the knob and swung the door in; a frigid blast made him shiver. In the shadows before him were halves and quarters of hogs and lambs and steers hanging from metal hooks on the low ceiling, red meat encased in folds of cold white fat. Fronting him was frost-coated glass from behind which came indistinguishable sounds. The odor of fresh raw meat sickened him and he backed away. A meat market, he whispered.

He ducked his head, suddenly blinded by light. He narrowed his eyes; the red-white rows of meat were drenched in yellow glare. A man wearing a crimson spotted jacket came in and took down a bloody meat cleaver. He eased the door to, holding it ajar just enough to watch the man, hoping that the darkness in which he stood would keep him from being seen. The man took down a hunk of steer and placed it upon a bloody wooden block and bent forward and whacked with the cleaver. The man's face was hard, square, grim; a jet of mustache smudged his upper lip and a glistening cowlick of hair fell over his left eye. Each time he lifted the cleaver and brought it down upon the meat, he let out a short, deep-chested grunt. After he had cut the meat, he wiped blood off the wooden block with a sticky wad of gunny sack and hung the cleaver upon a hook. His face was proud as he placed the chunk of meat in the crook of his elbow and left.

The door slammed and the light went off; once more he stood in shadow. His tension ebbed. From behind the frosted glass he heard the man's voice: "Forty-eight cents a pound, ma'am." He shuddered, feeling that there was something he had to do. But what? He stared fixedly at the cleaver, then he sneezed and was terrified for fear that the man had heard him. But the door did not open. He took down the cleaver and examined the sharp edge smeared with cold blood. Behind the ice-coated glass a cash register rang with a vibrating, musical tinkle.

Absent-mindedly holding the meat cleaver, he rubbed the glass with his thumb and cleared a spot that enabled him to see into the front of the store. The shop was empty, save for the man who was now putting on his hat and coat. Beyond the front window a wan sun shone in the streets; people passed and now and then a fragment of laughter or the whir of a speeding auto came to him. He peered closer and saw on the right counter of the shop a mosquito netting covering pears, grapes, lemons, oranges, bananas, peaches, and plums. His stomach contracted.

The man clicked out the light and he gritted his teeth, muttering, Don't lock the icebox door . . . The man went through the door of the shop and locked it from the outside. Thank God! Now, he would eat some more! He waited, trembling. The sun died and its rays lingered on in the sky, turning the streets to dusk. He opened the door and stepped inside the shop. In reverse letters across the front window was: NICK'S FRUITS AND MEATS. He laughed, picked up a soft ripe yellow pear and bit into it; juice squirted; his mouth ached as his saliva glands reacted to the acid of the fruit. He ate three pears, gobbled six bananas, and made away with several oranges, taking a bite out of their tops and holding them to his lips and squeezing them as he hungrily sucked the juice.

He found a faucet, turned it on, laid the cleaver aside, pursed his lips under the stream until his stomach felt about to burst. He straightened and belched, feeling satisfied for the first time since he had been underground. He sat upon the floor, rolled and lit a cigarette, his bloodshot eyes squinting against the film of drifting smoke. He watched a patch of sky turn red, then purple; night fell and he lit another cigarette, brooding. Some part of him was trying to remember the world he had left, and another part of him did not want to remember it. Sprawling before him in his mind was his wife, Mrs. Wooten for whom he worked, the three policemen who had picked him up . . . He possessed them now more completely than he had ever possessed them when he had lived aboveground. How this had come about he could not say, but he had no desire to go back to them. He laughed, crushed the cigarette, and stood up.

He went to the front door and gazed out. Emotionally he hovered between the world aboveground and the world underground. He longed to go out, but sober judgment urged him to remain here. Then impulsively he pried the lock loose with one swift twist of the crowbar; the door swung outward. Through the twilight he saw a white man and a white woman coming toward him. He held himself tense, waiting for them to pass; but they came directly to the door and confronted him.

"I want to buy a pound of grapes," the woman said.

Terrified, he stepped back into the store. The white man stood to one side and the woman entered.

"Give me a pound of dark ones," the woman said.

The white man came slowly forward, blinking his eyes.

"Where's Nick?" the man asked.

"Were you just closing?" the woman asked.

"Yes, ma'am," he mumbled. For a second he did not breathe, then he mumbled again: "Yes, ma'am."

"I'm sorry," the woman said.

The street lamps came on, lighting the store somewhat. Ought he run? But that would raise an alarm. He moved slowly, dreamily, to a counter and lifted up a bunch of grapes and showed them to the woman.

"Fine," the woman said. "But isn't that more than a pound?"

He did not answer. The man was staring at him intently.

"Put them in a bag for me," the woman said, fumbling with her purse.

"Yes, ma'am."

He saw a pile of paper bags under a narrow ledge; he opened one and put the grapes in.

"Thanks," the woman said, taking the bag and placing a dime in his dark palm.

"Where's Nick?" the man asked again. "At supper?"

"Sir? Yes, sir," he breathed.

They left the store and he stood trembling in the doorway. When they were out of sight, he burst out laughing and crying. A trolley car rolled noisily past and he controlled himself quickly. He flung the dime to the pavement with a gesture of contempt and stepped into the warm night air. A few shy stars trembled above him. The look of things was beautiful, yet he felt a lurking threat. He went to an unattended newsstand and looked at a stack of papers. He saw a headline: HUNT NEGRO FOR MURDER.

He felt that someone had slipped up on him from behind and was stripping off his clothes; he looked about wildly, went quickly back into the store, picked up the meat cleaver where he had left it near the sink, then made his way through the icebox to the basement. He stood for a long time, breathing heavily. They know I didn't do anything, he muttered. But how could he prove it? He had signed a confession. Though innocent, he felt guilty, condemned. He struck a match and held it near the steel blade, fascinated and repelled by the dried blotches of blood. Then his fingers gripped the handle of the cleaver with all the strength of his body, he wanted to fling the cleaver from him, but he could not. The match flame wavered and fled; he struggled through the hole and put the cleaver in the sack with the radio. He was determined to keep it for what purpose he did not know.

He was about to leave when he remembered the safe. Where was it? He wanted to give up, but felt that he ought to make one more try. Opposite the last hole he had dug, he tunneled again, plying the crowbar. Once he was so exhausted that he lay on the concrete floor and panted. Finally he made another hole. He wriggled through and his nostrils filled with the fresh smell of coal. He struck a match; yes, the usual steps led upward. He tiptoed to a door and eased it open. A fair-haired white girl stood in front of a steel cabinet, her blue eyes wide upon him. She turned chalky and gave a high-pitched scream. He bounded down the steps and raced to his hole and clambered through, replacing the bricks with nervous haste. He paused, hearing loud voices.

"What's the matter, Alice?"

"A man . . ."

"What man? Where?"

"A man was at that door . . ."

"Oh, nonsense!"

"He was looking at me through the door!"

"Aw, you're dreaming."

"I *did* see a man!"

The girl was crying now.

"There's nobody here."

Another man's voice sounded.

"What is it, Bob?"

"Alice says she saw a man in here, in that door!"

"Let's take a look."

He waited, poised for flight. Footsteps descended the stairs.

"There's nobody down here."

"The window's locked."

"And there's no door."

"You ought to fire that dame."

"Oh, I don't know. Women are that way."

"She's too hysterical."

The men laughed. Footsteps sounded again on the stairs. A door slammed. He sighed, relieved that he had escaped. But he had not done what he had set out to do; his glimpse of the room had been too brief to determine if the safe was there. He had to know. Boldly he groped through the hole once more; he reached the steps and pulled off his shoes and tiptoed up and peered through the keyhole. His head accidentally touched the door and it swung silently in a fraction of an inch; he saw the girl bent over the cabinet, her back to him. Beyond her was the safe. He crept back down the steps, thinking exultingly: I found it!

Now he had to get the combination. Even if the window in the areaway was locked and bolted, he could gain entrance when the office closed. He scoured through the holes he had dug and stood again in the basement where he had left the radio and the cleaver. Again he crawled out of the window and lifted himself up the rain pipe and peered. The steel dial showed lonely and bright, reflecting the yellow glow of an unseen light. Resigned to a long wait, he sat and leaned against the wall. From far off came the faint sounds of life above-ground; once he looked with a baffled expression at the dark sky. Frequently he rose and climbed the pipe to see the white hand spin the dial, but nothing happened. He bit his lip with impatience. It was not the money that was luring him, but the mere fact that he could get it with impunity. Was the hand now twirling the dial? He rose and looked, but the white hand was not in sight.

Perhaps it would be better to watch continuously? Yes; he clung to the pipe and watched the dial until his eyes thickened with tears. Exhausted, he stood again in the areaway. He heard a door being shut and he clawed up the pipe and looked. He jerked tense as a vague figure passed in front of him. He stared unblinkingly, hugging the pipe with one hand and holding the screwdriver with the other, ready to etch the combination upon the wall. His ears caught: *Dong . . . Dong . . . Dong . . . Dong . . . Dong . . . Dong . . . Dong. . . .* Seven o'clock, he whispered. Maybe they were closing now? What kind of a store would be open as late as this? he wondered. Did anyone live in the rear? Was there a night watchman? Perhaps the safe was *already* locked for the night! Goddamn! While he had been eating in that shop, they had locked up every-thing . . . Then, just as he was about to give up, the white hand touched the dial and turned it once to the right and stopped at six. With quivering fingers, he etched 1—R—6 upon the brick wall with the tip of the screwdriver. The hand twisted the dial twice to the left and stopped at two, and he engraved 2—L—2 upon the wall. The dial was spun four times to the right and stopped at six again: he wrote 4—R—6. The dial rotated three times to the left and was centered straight up and down; he wrote 3—L—0. The door swung open and again he saw the piles of green money and the rows of wrapped coins. I got it, he said grimly.

Then he was stone still, astonished. There were two hands now. A right hand lifted a wad of green bills and deftly slipped it up the sleeve of the left arm. The hands trembled; again the right hand slipped a packet of bills up the left sleeve. He's stealing he said to himself. He grew indignant, as if the money belonged to him. Though *he* had planned to steal the money, he despised and pitied the man. He felt that his stealing the money and the man's stealing were two entirely different things. He wanted to steal the money merely for the sensation involved in getting it, and he had no intention whatever of spending a penny of it; but he knew that the man who was now stealing it was going to spend it, perhaps for pleasure. The huge steel door closed with a soft click.

Though angry, he was somewhat satisfied. The office would close soon. I'll clean the place out, he mused. He imagined the entire office staff cringing with fear; the police would question everyone for a crime they had not committed, just as they had questioned him. And they would have no idea of how the money had been stolen until they discovered the holes he had tunneled in the walls of the basements. He lowered himself and laughed mischievously, with the abandoned glee of an adolescent.

He flattened himself against the wall as the window above him closed with a rasping sound. He looked; somebody was bolting the window securely with a metal screen. That won't help you, he snickered to himself. He clung to the rain pipe until the yellow light in the office went out. He went back into the basement, picked up the sack containing the radio and cleaver, and crawled through the two holes he had dug and groped his way into the basement of the building that held the safe. He moved in slow motion, breathing softly. Be careful now, he told himself. There might be a night watchman . . . In his memory was the combination written in bold white characters as upon a blackboard. Eel-like he squeezed through the last hole and crept up the steps and put his hand on the knob and pushed the door in about three inches. Then his courage ebbed; his imagination wove dangers for him.

Perhaps the night watchman was waiting in there, ready to shoot. He dangled his cap on a forefinger and poked it past the jamb of the door. If anyone fired, they would hit his cap; but nothing happened. He widened the door, holding the crowbar high above his head, ready to beat off an assailant. He stood like that for five minutes; the rumble of a streetcar brought him to himself. He entered the room. Moonlight floated in from a side window. He confronted the safe, then checked himself. Better take a look around first . . . He stepped about and found a closed door. Was the night watchman in there? He opened it and saw a washbowl, a faucet, and a commode. To the left was still another door that opened into a huge dark room that seemed empty; on the far side of that room he made out the shadow of still another door. Nobody's here, he told himself.

He turned back to the safe and fingered the dial; it spun with ease. He laughed and twirled it just for fun. Get to work, he told himself. He turned the dial to the figures he saw on the blackboard of his memory; it was so easy that he felt that the safe had not been locked at all. The heavy door eased loose and he caught hold of the handle and pulled hard, but the door swung open with a slow momentum of its own. Breathless, he gaped at wads of green bills, rows of wrapped coins, curious glass jars full of white pellets, and many oblong green metal boxes. He glanced guiltily over his shoulder; it seemed impossible that someone should not call to him to stop.

They'll be surprised in the morning, he thought. He opened the top of the sack and lifted a wad of compactly tied bills; the money was crisp and new. He admired the smooth, cleancut edges. The fellows in Washington sure know how to make this stuff, he mused. He rubbed the money with his fingers, as though expecting it to reveal hidden qualities. He lifted the wad to his nose and smelled the fresh odor of ink. Just like any other paper, he mumbled. He dropped the wad into the sack and picked up another. Holding the bag, he thought and laughed.

There was in him no sense of possessiveness; he was intrigued with the form and color of the money, with the manifold reactions which he knew that men aboveground held toward it. The sack was one-third full when it occurred to him to examine the denominations of the bills; without realizing it, he had put many wads of one-dollar bills into the sack. Aw, nuts, he said in disgust. Take the big ones . . . He dumped the one-dollar bills onto the floor and swept all the hundred-dollar bills he could find into the sack, then he raked in rolls of coins with crooked fingers.

He walked to a desk upon which sat a typewriter, the same machine which the blond girl had used. He was fascinated by it; never in his life had he used one of them. It was a queer instrument of business, something beyond the rim of his life. Whenever he had been in an office where a girl was typing, he had almost always spoken in whispers. Remembering vaguely what he had seen others do, he inserted a sheet of paper into the machine; it went in lopsided and he did not know how to straighten it. Spelling in a soft diffident voice, he pecked out his name on the keys: *freddaniels*. He looked at it and laughed. He would learn to type correctly one of these days.

Yes, he would take the typewriter too. He lifted the machine and placed it atop the bulk of money in the sack. He did not feel that he was stealing, for the cleaver, the radio, the money, and the typewriter were all on the same level of value, all meant the same thing to him. They were the serious toys of the men who lived in the dead world of sunshine and rain he had left, the world that had condemned him, branded him guilty.

But what kind of a place is this? he wondered. What was in that dark room to his rear? He felt for his matches and found that he had only one left. He leaned the sack against the safe and groped forward into the room, encountering smooth, metallic objects that felt like machines. Baffled, he touched a wall and tried vainly to locate an electric switch. Well, he *had* to strike his last match. He knelt and struck it, cupping the flame near the floor with his palms. The place seemed to be a factory, with benches and tables. There were bulbs with green shades spaced about the tables; he turned on a light and twisted it low so that the glare was limited. He saw a half-filled packet of cigarettes and appropriated it. There were stools at the benches and he concluded that men worked here at some trade. He wandered and found a few half-used folders of matches. If only he could find more cigarettes! But there were none.

But what kind of a place was this? On a bench he saw a pad of paper captioned: PEER'S—MANUFACTURING JEWELERS. His lips formed an "O," then he snapped off the light and ran back to the safe and lifted one of the glass jars and stared at the tiny white pellets. Gingerly he picked up one and found that it was wrapped in tissue paper. He peeled the paper and saw a glittering stone that looked like glass, glinting white and blue sparks. Diamonds, he breathed.

Roughly he tore the paper from the pellets and soon his palm quivered with precious fire. Trembling, he took all four glass jars from the safe and put them into the sack. He grabbed one of the metal boxes, shook it, and heard a tinny rattle. He pried off the lid with the screwdriver. Rings! Hundreds of them . . . Were they worth anything? He scooped up a handful and jets of fire shot fitfully from the stones. These are diamonds too, he said. He pried open another box. Watches! A chorus of soft, metallic ticking filled his ears. For a moment he could not move, then he dumped all the boxes into the sack.

He shut the safe door, then stood looking around, anxious not to overlook anything. Oh! He had seen a door in the room where the machines were. What was in there? More valuables? He re-entered the room, crossed the floor, and stood undecided before the door. He finally caught hold of the knob and pushed the door in; the room beyond was dark. He advanced cautiously inside and ran his fingers along the wall for the usual switch, then he was stark still. *Something had moved in the room!* What was it? Ought he to creep out, taking the rings and diamonds and money? Why risk what he already had? He waited and the ensuing silence gave him confidence to explore further. Dare he strike a match? Would not a match flame make him a good target? He tensed again as he heard a faint sigh; he was now convinced that there was something alive near him, something that lived and breathed. On tiptoe he felt slowly along the wall, hoping that he would not collide with anything. Luck was with him; he found the light switch.

No; don't turn the light on . . . Then suddenly he realized that he did not know in what direction the door was. Goddamn! He had to turn the light on or strike a match. He fingered the switch for a long time, then thought of an idea. He knelt upon the floor, reached his arm up to the switch and flicked the button, hoping that if anyone shot, the bullet would go above his head. The moment the light came on he narrowed his eyes to see quickly. He sucked in his breath and his body gave a violent twitch and was still. In front of him, so close that it made him want to bound up and scream, was a human face.

He was afraid to move lest he touch the man. If the man had opened his eyes at that moment, there was no telling what he might have done. The man— long and rawboned—was stretched out on his back upon a little cot, sleeping in his clothes, his head cushioned by a dirty pillow; his face, clouded by a dark stubble of beard, looked straight up to the ceiling. The man sighed, and he grew tense to defend himself; the man mumbled and turned his face away from the light. I've got to turn off that light, he thought. Just as he was about to rise, he saw a gun and cartridge belt on the floor at the man's side. Yes, he would take the gun and cartridge belt, not to use them, but just to keep them, as one takes a memento from a country fair. He picked them up and was about to click off the light when his eyes fell upon a photograph perched upon a chair near the man's head; it was the picture of a woman, smiling, shown against a background of open fields; at the woman's side were two young children, a boy and a girl. He smiled indulgently; he could send a bullet into that man's brain and time would be over for him. . . .

He clicked off the light and crept silently back into the room where the safe stood; he fastened the cartridge belt about him and adjusted the holster at his right hip. He strutted about the room on tiptoe, lolling his head nonchalantly, then paused, abruptly pulled the gun, and pointed it with grim face toward an imaginary foe. "Boom!" he whispered fiercely. Then he bent forward with silent laughter. That's just like they do it in the movies, he said.

He contemplated his loot for a long time, then got a towel from the washroom and tied the sack securely. When he looked up he was momentarily frightened by his shadow looming on the wall before him. He lifted the sack, dragged it down the basement steps, lugged it across the basement, gasping for breath. After he had struggled through the hole, he clumsily replaced the bricks, then tussled with the sack until he got it to the cave. He stood in the dark, wet with sweat, brooding about the diamonds, the rings, the watches, the money; he remembered the singing in the church, the people yelling in the movie, the dead baby, the nude man stretched out upon the white table . . . He saw these items hovering before his eyes and felt that some dim meaning linked them together, that some magical relationship made them kin. He stared with vacant eyes, convinced that all of these images, with their tongueless reality, were striving to tell him something . . .

Later, seeing with his fingers, he untied the sack and set each item neatly upon the dirt floor. Exploring, he took the bulb, the socket, and the wire out of the tool chest; he was elated to find a double socket at one end of the wire. He crammed the stuff into his pockets and hoisted himself upon the rusty pipes and squinted into the church; it was dim and empty. Somewhere in this wall were live electric wires; but where? He lowered himself, groped and tapped the wall with the butt of the screwdriver, listening vainly for hollow sounds. I'll just take a chance and dig, he said.

For an hour he tried to dislodge a brick, and when he struck a match, he found that he had dug a depth of only an inch! No use in digging here, he sighed. By the flickering light of a match, he looked upward, then lowered his eyes, only to glance up again, startled. Directly above his head, beyond the pipes, was a wealth of electric wiring. I'll be damned, he snickered.

He got an old dull knife from the chest and, seeing again with his fingers, separated the two strands of wire and cut away the insulation. Twice he received a slight shock. He scraped the wiring clean and managed to join the two twin ends, then screwed in the bulb. The sudden illumination blinded him and he shut his lids to kill the pain in his eyeballs. I've got that much done, he thought jubilantly.

He placed the bulb on the dirt floor and the light cast a blatant glare on the bleak clay walls. Next he plugged one end of the wire that dangled from the radio into the light socket and bent down and switched on the button; almost at once there was the harsh sound of static, but no words or music. Why won't it work? he wondered. Had he damaged the mechanism in any way? Maybe it needed grounding? Yes . . . He rummaged in the tool chest and found another length of wire, fastened it to the ground of the radio, and then tied the opposite end to a pipe. Rising and growing distinct, a slow strain of music entranced him with its measured sound. He sat upon the chest, deliriously happy.

Later he searched again in the chest and found a half-gallon can of glue; he opened it and smelled a sharp odor. Then he recalled that he had not even looked at the money. He took a wad of green bills and weighed it in his palm, then broke the seal and held one of the bills up to the light and studied it closely. *The United States of America will pay to the bearer on demand one hundred dollars,* he read in slow speech; then: *This note is legal tender for all debts, public and private* . . . He broke into a musing laugh, feeling that he was reading of the doings of people who lived on some far-off planet. He turned the bill over and saw on the other side of it a delicately beautiful building gleaming with paint and set amidst green grass. He had no desire whatever to count the money; it was what it stood for—the various currents of life swirling aboveground—that captivated him. Next he opened the rolls of coins and let them slide from their paper wrappings to the ground; the bright, new gleaming pennies and nickels and dimes piled high at his feet, a glowing mound of shimmering copper and silver. He sifted them through his fingers, listening to their tinkle as they struck the conical heap.

Oh, yes! He had forgotten. He would now write his name on the typewriter. He inserted a piece of paper and poised his fingers to write. But what was his name? He stared, trying to remember. He stood and glared about the dirt cave, his name on the tip of his lips. But it would not come to him. Why was he here? Yes, he had been running away from the police. But why? His mind was blank. He bit his lips and sat again, feeling a vague terror. But why worry? He laughed, then pecked slowly: *itwasalonghotday.* He was determined to type the sentence without making any mistakes. How did one make capital letters? He experimented and luckily discovered how to lock the machine for capital letters and then shift it back to lower case. Next he discovered how to make spaces, then he wrote neatly and correctly: *It was a long hot day.* Just why he selected that sentence he did not know; it was merely the ritual of performing the thing that appealed to him. He took the sheet out of the machine and looked around with stiff neck and hard eyes and spoke to an imaginary person:

"Yes, I'll have the contracts ready tomorrow."

He laughed. That's just the way they talk, he said. He grew weary of the game and pushed the machine aside. His eyes fell upon the can of glue, and a mischievous idea bloomed in him, filling him with nervous eagerness. He leaped up and opened the can of glue, then broke the seals on all the wads of money. I'm going to have some wallpaper, he said with a luxurious, physical laugh that made him bend at the knees. He took the towel with which he had tied the sack and balled it into a swab and dipped it into the can of glue and dabbed glue onto the wall; then he pasted one green bill by the side of another. He stepped back and cocked his head. Jesus! That's funny . . . He slapped his thighs and guffawed. He had triumphed over the world aboveground! He was free! If only people could see this! He wanted to run from this cave and yell his discovery to the world.

He swabbed all the dirt walls of the cave and pasted them with green bills; when he had finished the walls blazed with a yellow-green fire. Yes, this room would be his hide-out; between him and the world that had branded him guilty would stand this mocking symbol. He had not stolen the money; he had simply picked it up, just as a man would pick up firewood in a forest. And that was how the world aboveground now seemed to him, a wild forest filled with death.

The walls of money finally palled on him and he looked about for new interests to feed his emotions. The cleaver! He drove a nail into the wall and hung the bloody cleaver upon it. Still another idea welled up. He pried open the metal boxes and lined them side by side on the dirt floor. He grinned at the gold and fire. From one box he lifted up a fistful of ticking gold watches and dangled them by their gleaming chains. He stared with an idle smile, then began to wind them up; he did not attempt to set them at any given hour, for there was no time for him now. He took a fistful of nails and drove them into the papered walls and hung the watches upon them, letting them swing down by their glittering chains, trembling and ticking busily against the backdrop of green with the lemon sheen of the electric light shining upon the metal watch casings, converting the golden disks into blobs of liquid yellow. Hardly had he hung up the last watch than the idea extended itself; he took more nails from the chest and drove them into the green paper and took the boxes of rings and went from nail to nail and hung up the golden bands. The blue and white sparks from the stones filled the cave with brittle laughter, as though enjoying his hilarious secret. People certainly can do some funny things, he said to himself.

He sat upon the tool chest, alternately laughing and shaking his head soberly. Hours later he became conscious of the gun sagging at his hip and he pulled it from the holster. He had seen men fire guns in movies, but somehow his life had never led him into contact with firearms. A desire to feel the sensation others felt in firing came over him. But someone might hear . . . Well, what if they did? They would not know where the shot had come from. Not in their wildest notions would they think that it had come from under the streets! He tightened his fingers on the trigger; there was a deafening report and it seemed that the entire underground had caved in upon his eardrums; and in the same instant there flashed an orange-blue spurt of flame that died quickly but lingered on as a vivid after-image. He smelled the acrid stench of burnt powder filling his lungs and he dropped the gun abruptly.

The intensity of his feelings died and he hung the gun and cartridge belt upon the wall. Next he lifted the jars of diamonds and turned them bottom upward, dumping the white pellets upon the ground. One by one he picked them up and peeled the tissue paper from them and piled them in a neat heap. He wiped his sweaty hands on his trousers, lit a cigarette, and commenced playing another game. He imagined that he was a rich man who lived above-ground in the obscene sunshine and he was strolling through a park of a summer morning, smiling, nodding to his neighbors, sucking an after-breakfast cigar. Many times he crossed the floor of the cave, avoiding the diamonds with his feet, yet subtly gauging his footsteps so that his shoes, wet with sewer slime, would strike the diamonds at some undetermined moment. After twenty minutes of sauntering, his right foot smashed into the heap and diamonds lay scattered in all directions, glinting with a million tiny chuckles of icy laughter. Oh, shucks, he mumbled in mock regret, intrigued by the damage he had wrought. He continued walking, ignoring the brittle fire. He felt that he had a glorious victory locked in his heart.

He stooped and flung the diamonds more evenly over the floor and they showered rich sparks, collaborating with him. He went over the floor and trampled the stones just deeply enough for them to be faintly visible, as though they were set deliberately in the prongs of a thousand rings. A ghostly light bathed the cave. He sat on the chest and frowned. Maybe *any*thing's right, he mumbled. Yes, if the world as men had made it was right, then anything else was right, any act a man took to satisfy himself, murder, theft, torture.

He straightened with a start. What was happening to him? He was drawn to these crazy thoughts, yet they made him feel vaguely guilty. He would stretch out upon the ground, then get up; he would want to crawl again through the holes he had dug, but would restrain himself; he would think of going up into the streets, but fear would hold him still. He stood in the middle of the cave, surrounded by green walls and a laughing floor, trembling. He was going to do something, but what? Yes, he was afraid of himself, afraid of doing some nameless thing.

To control himself, he turned on the radio. A melancholy piece of music rose. Brooding over the diamonds on the floor was like looking up into a sky full of restless stars; then the illusion turned into its opposite: he was high up in the air looking down at the twinkling lights of a sprawling city. The music ended and a man recited news events. In the same attitude in which he had contemplated the city, so now, as he heard the cultivated tone, he looked down upon land and sea as men fought, as cities were razed, as planes scattered death upon open towns, as long lines of trenches wavered and broke. He heard the names of generals and the names of mountains and the names of countries and the names and numbers of divisions that were in action on different battle fronts. He saw black smoke billowing from the stacks of warships as they neared each other over wastes of water and he heard their huge thunder as red-hot shells screamed across the surface of night seas. He saw hundreds of planes wheeling and droning in the sky and heard the clatter of machine guns as they fought each other and he saw planes falling in plumes of smoke and a blaze of fire. He saw steel tanks rumbling across fields of ripe wheat to meet other tanks and there was a loud clang of steel as numberless tanks collided. He saw troops with fixed bayonets charging in waves against other troops who held fixed bayonets and men groaned as steel ripped into their bodies and they went down to die . . . The voice of the radio faded and he was staring at the diamonds on the floor at his feet.

He shut off the radio, fighting an irrational compulsion to act. He walked aimlessly about the cave, touching the walls with his finger tips. Suddenly he stood still. *What was the matter with him?* Yes, he knew . . . It was these walls; these crazy walls were filling him with a wild urge to climb out into the dark sunshine aboveground. Quickly he doused the light to banish the shouting walls, then sat again upon the tool chest. Yes, he was trapped. His muscles were flexed taut and sweat ran down his face. He knew now that he could not stay here and he could not go out. He lit a cigarette with shaking fingers; the match flame revealed the green-papered walls with militant distinctness; the purple on the gun barrel glinted like a threat; the meat cleaver brooded with its eloquent splotches of blood; the mound of silver and copper smoldered angrily; the diamonds winked at him from the floor, and the gold watches ticked and trembled, crowning time the king of consciousness, defining the limits of living . . . The match blaze died and he bolted from where he stood and collided brutally with the nails upon the walls. The spell was broken. He shuddered, feeling that, in spite of his fear, sooner or later he would go up into that dead sunshine and somehow say something to somebody about all this.

He sat again upon the tool chest. Fatigue weighed upon his forehead and eyes. Minutes passed and he relaxed. He dozed, but his imagination was alert. He saw himself rising, wading again in the sweeping water of the sewer; he came to a manhole and climbed out and was amazed to discover that he hoisted himself into a room filled with armed policemen who were watching him intently. He jumped awake in the dark; he had not moved. He sighed, closed his eyes, and slept again; this time his imagination designed a scheme of protection for him. His dreaming made him feel that he was standing in a room watching over his own nude body lying stiff and cold upon a white table. At the far end of the room he saw a crowd of people huddled in a corner, afraid of his body. Though lying dead upon the table, he was standing in some mysterious way at his side, warding off the people, guarding his body, and laughing to himself as he observed the situation. They're scared of me, he thought.

He awakened with a start, leaped to his feet, and stood in the center of the black cave. It was a full minute before he moved again. He hovered between sleeping and waking, unprotected, a prey of wild fears. He could neither see nor hear. One part of him was asleep; his blood coursed slowly and his flesh was numb. On the other hand he was roused to a strange, high pitch of tension. He lifted his fingers to his face, as though about to weep. Gradually his hands lowered and he struck a match, looking about, expecting to see a door through which he could walk to safety; but there was no door, only the green walls and the moving floor. The match flame died and it was dark again.

Five minutes later he was still standing when the thought came to him that he had been asleep. Yes . . . But he was not yet fully awake; he was still queerly blind and deaf. How long had he slept? Where was he? Then suddenly he recalled the green-papered walls of the cave and in the same instant he heard loud singing coming from the church beyond the wall. Yes, they woke me up, he muttered. He hoisted himself and lay atop the bed of pipes and brought his face to the narrow slit. Men and women stood here and there between pews. A song ended and a young black girl tossed back her head and closed her eyes and broke plaintively into another hymn:

> Glad, glad, glad, oh, so glad
> I got Jesus in my soul . . .

Those few words were all she sang, but what her words did not say, her emotions said as she repeated the lines, varying the mood and tempo, making her tone express meanings which her conscious mind did not know. Another woman melted her voice with the girl's, and then an old man's voice merged with that of the two women. Soon the entire congregation was singing:

> Glad, glad, glad, oh, so glad
> I got Jesus in my soul . . .

They're wrong, he whispered in the lyric darkness. He felt that their search for a happiness they could never find made them feel that they had committed some dreadful offense which they could not remember or understand. He was now in possession of the feeling that had gripped him when he had first come into the underground. It came to him in a series of questions: Why was this sense of guilt so seemingly innate, so easy to come by, to think, to feel, so verily physical? It seemed that when one felt this guilt one was retracing in one's feelings a faint pattern designed long before; it seemed that one was always trying to remember a gigantic shock that had left a haunting impression upon one's body which one could not forget or shake off, but which had been forgotten by the conscious mind, creating in one's life a state of eternal anxiety.

He had to tear himself away from this; he got down from the pipes. His nerves were so taut that he seemed to feel his brain pushing through his skull. He felt that he had to do something, but he could not figure out what it was. Yet he knew that if he stood here until he made up his mind, he would never move. He crawled through the hole he had made in the brick wall and the exertion afforded him respite from tension. When he entered the basement of the radio store, he stopped in fear, hearing loud voices.

"Come on, boy! Tell us what you did with the radio!"

"Mister, I didn't steal the radio! I swear!"

He heard a dull thumping sound and he imagined a boy being struck violently.

"Please, mister!"

"Did you take it to a pawn shop?"

"No, sir! I didn't steal the radio! I got a radio at home," the boy's voice pleaded hysterically. "Go to my home and look!"

There came to his ears the sound of another blow. It was so funny that he had to clap his hand over his mouth to keep from laughing out loud. They're beating some poor boy, he whispered to himself, shaking his head. He felt a sort of distant pity for the boy and wondered if he ought to bring back the radio and leave it in the basement. No. Perhaps it was a good thing that they were beating the boy; perhaps the beating would bring to the boy's attention, for the first time in his life, the secret of his existence, the guilt that he could never get rid of.

Smiling, he scampered over a coal pile and stood again in the basement of the building where he had stolen the money and jewelry. He lifted himself into the areaway, climbed the rain pipe, and squinted through a two-inch opening of window. The guilty familiarity of what he saw made his muscles tighten. Framed before him in a bright tableau of daylight was the night watchman sitting upon the edge of a chair, stripped to the waist, his head sagging forward, his eyes red and puffy. The watchman's face and shoulders were stippled with red and black welts. Back of the watchman stood the safe, the steel door wide open showing the empty vault. Yes, they think he did it, he mused.

Footsteps sounded in the room and a man in a blue suit passed in front of him, then another, then still another. Policemen, he breathed. Yes, they were trying to make the watchman confess, just as they had once made him confess to a crime he had not done. He stared into the room, trying to recall something. Oh . . . Those were the same policemen who had beaten him, had made him sign that paper when he had been too tired and sick to care. Now, they were doing the same thing to the watchman. His heart pounded as he saw one of the policemen shake a finger into the watchman's face.

"Why don't you admit it's an inside job, Thompson?" the policeman said.

"I've told you all I know," the watchman mumbled through swollen lips.

"But nobody was here but you!" the policeman shouted.

"I was sleeping," the watchman said. "It was wrong, but I was sleeping all that night!"

"Stop telling us that lie!"

"It's the truth!"

"When did you get the combination?"

"I don't know how to open the safe," the watchman said.

He clung to the rain pipe, tense; he wanted to laugh, but he controlled himself. He felt a great sense of power; yes, he could go back to the cave, rip the money off the walls, pick up the diamonds and rings, and bring them here and write a note, telling them where to look for their foolish toys. No . . . What good would that do? It was not worth the effort. The watchman was guilty; although he was not guilty of the crime of which he had been accused, he was guilty, had always been guilty. The only thing that worried him was that the man who had been really stealing was not being accused. But he consoled himself: they'll catch him sometime during his life.

He saw one of the policemen slap the watchman across the mouth.

"Come clean, you bastard!"

"I've told you all I know," the watchman mumbled like a child.

One of the police went to the rear of the watchman's chair and jerked it from under him; the watchman pitched forward upon his face.

"Get up!" a policeman said.

Trembling, the watchman pulled himself up and sat limply again in the chair.

"Now, are you going to talk?"

"I've told you all I know," the watchman gasped.

"Where did you hide the stuff?"

"I didn't take it!"

"Thompson, your brains are in your feet," one of the policemen said. "We're going to string you up and get them back into your skull."

He watched the policemen clamp handcuffs on the watchman's wrists and ankles; then they lifted the watchman and swung him upside-down and hoisted his feet to the edge of a door. The watchman hung, head down, his eyes bulging. They're crazy, he whispered to himself as he clung to the ridges of the pipe.

"You going to talk?" a policeman shouted into the watchman's ear.

He heard the watchman groan.

"We'll let you hang there till you talk, see?"

He saw the watchman close his eyes.

"Let's take 'im down. He passed out," a policeman said.

He grinned as he watched them take the body down and dump it carelessly upon the floor. The policemen took off the handcuffs.

"Let 'im come to. Let's get a smoke," a policeman said.

The three policemen left the scope of his vision. A door slammed. He had an impulse to yell to the watchman that he could escape through the hole in the basement and live with him in the cave. But he wouldn't understand, he told himself. After a moment he saw the watchman rise and stand, swaying from weakness. He stumbled across the room to a desk, opened a drawer, and took out a gun. He's going to kill himself, he thought, intent, eager, detached, yearning to see the end of the man's actions. As the watchman stared vaguely about he lifted the gun to his temple; he stood like that for some minutes, biting his lips until a line of blood etched its way down a corner of his chin. No, he oughtn't do that, he said to himself in a mood of pity.

"Don't!" he half whispered and half yelled.

The watchman looked wildly about; he had heard him. But it did not help; there was a loud report and the watchman's head jerked violently and he fell like a log and lay prone, the gun clattering over the floor.

The three policemen came running into the room with drawn guns. One of the policemen knelt and rolled the watchman's body over and stared at a ragged, scarlet hole in the temple.

"Our hunch was right," the kneeling policeman said. "He was guilty, all right."

"Well, this ends the case," another policeman said.

"He knew he was licked," the third one said with grim satisfaction.

He eased down the rain pipe, crawled back through the holes he had made, and went back into his cave. A fever burned in his bones. He had to act, yet he was afraid. His eyes stared in the darkness as though propped open by invisible hands, as though they had become lidless. His muscles were rigid and he stood for what seemed to him a thousand years.

When he moved again his actions were informed with precision, his muscular system reinforced from a reservoir of energy. He crawled through the hole of earth, dropped into the gray sewer current, and sloshed ahead. When his right foot went forward at a street intersection, he fell backward and shot down into water. In a spasm of terror his right hand grabbed the concrete ledge of a down-curve and he felt the streaking water tugging violently at his body. The current reached his neck and for a moment he was still. He knew if he moved clumsily he would be sucked under. He held onto the ledge with both hands and slowly pulled himself up. He sighed, standing once more in the sweeping water, thankful that he had missed death.

He waded on through sludge, moving with care, until he came to a web of light sifting down from a manhole cover. He saw steel hooks running up the side of the sewer wall; he caught hold and lifted himself and put his shoulder to the cover and moved it an inch. A crash of sound came to him as he looked into a hot glare of sunshine through which blurred shapes moved. Fear scalded him and he dropped back into the pallid current and stood paralyzed in the shadows. A heavy car rumbled past overhead, jarring the pavement, warning him to stay in his world of dark light, knocking the cover back into place with an imperious clang.

He did not know how much fear he felt, for fear claimed him completely; yet it was not a fear of the police or of people, but a cold dread at the thought of the actions he knew he would perform if he went out into that cruel sunshine. His mind said no; his body said yes; and his mind could not understand his feelings. A low whine broke from him and he was in the act of uncoiling. He climbed upward and heard the faint honking of auto horns. Like a frantic cat clutching a rag, he clung to the steel prongs and heaved his shoulder against the cover and pushed it off halfway. For a split second his eyes were drowned in the terror of yellow light and he was in a deeper darkness than he had ever known in the underground.

Partly out of the hole, he blinked, regaining enough sight to make out meaningful forms. An odd thing was happening: No one was rushing forward to challenge him. He had imagined the moment of his emergence as a desperate tussle with men who wanted to cart him off to be killed; instead, life froze about him as the traffic stopped. He pushed the cover aside, stood, swaying in a world so fragile that he expected it to collapse and drop him into some deep void. But nobody seemed to pay him heed. The cars were now swerving to shun him and the gaping hole.

"Why in hell don't you put up a red light, dummy?" a raucous voice yelled.

He understood; they thought that he was a sewer workman. He walked toward the sidewalk, weaving unsteadily through the moving traffic.

"Look where you're going, nigger!"

"That's right! Stay there and get killed!"

"You blind, you bastard?"

"Go home and sleep your drunk off!"

A policeman stood at the curb, looking in the opposite direction. When he passed the policeman, he feared that he would be grabbed, but nothing happened. Where was he? Was this real? He wanted to look about to get his bearings, but felt that something awful would happen to him if he did. He wandered into a spacious doorway of a store that sold men's clothing and saw his reflection in a long mirror: his cheekbones protruded from a hairy black face; his greasy cap was perched askew upon his head and his eyes were red and glassy. His shirt and trousers were caked with mud and hung loosely. His hands were gummed with a black stickiness. He threw back his head and laughed so loudly that passers-by stopped and stared.

He ambled on down the sidewalk, not having the merest notion of where he was going. Yet, sleeping within him, was the drive to go somewhere and say something to somebody. Half an hour later his ears caught the sound of spirited singing.

> The Lamb, the Lamb, the Lamb
> > I hear thy voice a-calling
> The Lamb, the Lamb, the Lamb
> > I feel thy grace a-falling

A church! he exclaimed. He broke into a run and came to brick steps leading downward to a subbasement. This is it! The church into which he had peered. Yes, he was going in and tell them. What? He did not know; but, once face to face with them, he would think of what to say. Must be Sunday, he mused. He ran down the steps and jerked the door open; the church was crowded and a deluge of song swept over him.

> The Lamb, the Lamb, the Lamb
> > Tell me again your story
> The Lamb, the Lamb, the Lamb
> > Flood my soul with your glory

He stared at the singing faces with a trembling smile.

"Say!" he shouted.

Many turned to look at him, but the song rolled on. His arm was jerked violently.

"I'm sorry, Brother, but you can't do that in here," a man said.

"But, mister!"

"You can't act rowdy in God's house," the man said.

"He's filthy," another man said.

"But I want to tell 'em," he said loudly.

"He stinks," someone muttered.

The song had stopped, but at once another one began.

> Oh, wondrous sight upon the cross
> > Vision sweet and divine
> Oh, wondrous sight upon the cross
> > Full of such love sublime

He attempted to twist away, but other hands grabbed him and rushed him into the doorway.

"Let me alone!" he screamed, struggling.

"Get out!"

"He's drunk," somebody said. "He ought to be ashamed!"

"He acts crazy!"

He felt that he was failing and he grew frantic.

"But, mister, let me tell—"

"Get away from this door, or I'll call the police!"

He stared, his trembling smile fading in a sense of wonderment.

"The police," he repeated vacantly.

"Now, get!"

He was pushed toward the brick steps and the door banged shut. The waves of song came.

> *Oh, wondrous sight, wondrous sight*
> *Lift my heavy heart above*
> *Oh, wondrous sight, wondrous sight*
> *Fill my weary soul with love*

He was smiling again now. Yes, the police . . . That was it! Why had he not thought of it before? The idea had been deep down in him, and only now did it assume supreme importance. He looked up and saw a street sign: COURT STREET—HARTSDALE AVENUE. He turned and walked northward, his mind filled with the image of the police station. Yes, that was where they had beaten him, accused him, and had made him sign a confession of his guilt. He would go there and clear up everything, make a statement. What statement? He did not know. He was the statement, and since it was all so clear to him, surely he would be able to make it clear to others.

He came to the corner of Hartsdale Avenue and turned westward. Yeah, there's the station . . . A policeman came down the steps and walked past him without a glance. He mounted the stone steps and went through the door, paused; he was in a hallway where several policemen were standing, talking, smoking. One turned to him.

"What do you want, boy?"

He looked at the policeman and laughed.

"What in hell are you laughing about?" the policeman asked.

He stopped laughing and stared. His whole being was full of what he wanted to say to them, but he could not say it.

"Are you looking for the Desk Sergeant?"

"Yes, sir," he said quickly; then: "Oh, no, sir."

"Well, make up your mind, now."

Four policemen grouped themselves around him.

"I'm looking for the men," he said.

"What men?"

Peculiarly, at that moment he could not remember the names of the policemen; he recalled their beating him, the confession he had signed, and how he had run away from them. He saw the cave next to the church, the money on the walls, the gun, the rings, the cleaver, the watches, and the diamonds on the floor.

"They brought me here," he began.

"When?"

His mind flew back over the blur of the time lived in the underground blackness. He had no idea of how much time had elapsed, but the intensity of what had happened to him told him that it could not have transpired in a short space of time, yet his mind told him that time must have been brief.

"It was a long time ago." He spoke like a child relating a dimly remembered dream. "It was a long time," he repeated, following the promptings of his emotions. "They beat me . . . I was scared . . . I ran away."

A policeman raised a finger to his temple and made a derisive circle.

"Nuts," the policeman said.

"Do you know what place this is, boy?"

"Yes, sir. The police station," he answered sturdily, almost proudly.

"Well, who do you want to see?"

"The men," he said again, feeling that surely they knew the men. "You know the men," he said in a hurt tone.

"What's your name?"

He opened his lips to answer and no words came. He had forgotten. But what did it matter if he had? It was not important.

"Where do you live?"

Where did he live? It had been so long ago since he had lived up here in this strange world that he felt it was foolish even to try to remember. Then for a moment the old mood that had dominated him in the underground surged back. He leaned forward and spoke eagerly.

"They said I killed the woman."

"What woman?" a policeman asked.

"And I signed a paper that said I was guilty," he went on, ignoring their questions. "Then I ran off . . ."

"Did you run off from an institution?"

"No, sir," he said, blinking and shaking his head. "I came from under the ground. I pushed off the manhole cover and climbed out . . ."

"All right, now," a policeman said, placing an arm about his shoulder. "We'll send you to the psycho and you'll be taken care of."

"Maybe he's a Fifth Columnist!" a policeman shouted.

There was laughter and, despite his anxiety, he joined in. But the laughter lasted so long that it irked him.

"I got to find those men," he protested mildly.

"Say, boy, what have you been drinking?"

"Water," he said. "I got some water in a basement."

"Were the men you ran away from dressed in white, boy?"

"No, sir," he said brightly. "They were men like you."

An elderly policeman caught hold of his arm.

"Try and think hard. Where did they pick you up?"

He knotted his brows in an effort to remember, but he was blank inside. The policeman stood before him demanding logical answers and he could no longer think with his mind; he thought with his feelings and no words came.

"I was guilty," he said. "Oh, no, sir. I wasn't then, I mean, mister!"

"Aw, talk sense. Now, where did they pick you up?"

He felt challenged and his mind began reconstructing events in reverse; his feelings ranged back over the long hours and he saw the cave, the sewer, the bloody room where it was said that a woman had been killed.

"Oh, yes, sir," he said, smiling. "I was coming from Mrs. Wooten's."

"Who is she?"

"I work for her."

"Where does she live?"

"Next door to Mrs. Peabody, the woman who was killed."

The policemen were very quiet now, looking at him intently.

"What do you know about Mrs. Peabody's death, boy?"

"Nothing, sir. But they said I killed her. But it doesn't make any difference, I'm guilty!"

"What are you talking about, boy?"

His smile faded and he was possessed with memories of the underground; he saw the cave next to the church and his lips moved to speak. But how could he say it? The distance between what he felt and what these men meant was vast. Something told him, as he stood there looking into their faces, that he would never be able to tell them, that they would never believe him if he told them.

"All the people I saw was guilty," he began slowly.

"Aw, nuts," a policeman muttered.

"Say," another policeman said, "that Peabody woman was killed over on Winewood. That's Number Ten's beat."

"Where's Number Ten?" a policeman asked.

"Upstairs in the swing room," someone answered.

"Take this boy up, Sam," a policeman ordered.

"O.K. Come along, boy."

An elderly policeman caught hold of his arm and led him up a flight of wooden stairs, down a long hall, and to a door.

"Squad Ten!" the policeman called through the door.

"What?" a gruff voice answered.

"Someone to see you!"

"About what?"

The old policeman pushed the door in and then shoved him into the room.

He stared, his lips open, his heart barely beating. Before him were the three policemen who had picked him up and had beaten him to extract the confession. They were seated about a small table, playing cards. The air was blue with smoke and sunshine poured through a high window, lighting up fantastic smoke shapes. He saw one of the policemen look up; the policeman's face was tired and a cigarette drooped limply from one corner of his mouth and both of his fat, puffy eyes were squinting and his hands gripped his cards.

"Lawson!" the man exclaimed.

The moment the man's name sounded he remembered the names of all of them: Lawson, Murphy, and Johnson. How simple it was. He waited, smiling, wondering how they would react when they knew that he had come back.

"Looking for me?" the man who had been called Lawson mumbled, sorting his cards. "For what?"

So far only Murphy, the red-headed one, had recognized him.

"Don't you-all remember me?" he blurted, running to the table.

All three of the policemen were looking at him now. Lawson, who seemed the leader, jumped to his feet.

"Where in hell have you been?"

"Do you know 'im, Lawson?" the old policeman asked.

"Huh?" Lawson frowned. "Oh, yes. I'll handle 'im." The old policeman left the room and Lawson crossed to the door and turned the key in the lock. "Come here, boy," he ordered in a cold tone.

He did not move; he looked from face to face. Yes, he would tell them about his cave.

"He looks batty to me," Johnson said, the one who had not spoken before.

"Why in hell did you come back here?" Lawson said.

"I—I just didn't want to run away no more," he said. "I'm all right, now." He paused; the men's attitude puzzled him.

"You've been hiding, huh?" Lawson asked in a tone that denoted that he had not heard his previous words. "You told us you were sick, and when we left you in the room, you jumped out of the window and ran away."

Panic filled him. Yes, they were indifferent to what he would say! They were waiting for him to speak and they would laugh at him. He had to rescue himself from this bog; he had to force the reality of himself upon them.

"Mister, I took a sackful of money and pasted it on the walls . . ." he began.

"I'll be damned," Lawson said.

"Listen," said Murphy, "let me tell you something for your own good. We don't want you, see? You're free, free as air. Now go home and forget it. It was all a mistake. We caught the guy who did the Peabody job. He wasn't colored at all. He was an Eyetalian."

"Shut up!" Lawson yelled. "Have you no sense!"

"But I want to tell 'im," Murphy said.

"We can't let this crazy fool go," Lawson exploded. "He acts nuts, but this may be a stunt . . ."

"I was down in the basement," he began in a childlike tone, as though repeating a lesson learned by heart; "and I went into a movie . . ." His voice failed. He was getting ahead of his story. First, he ought to tell them about the singing in the church, but what words could he use? He looked at them appealingly. "I went into a shop and took a sackful of money and diamonds and watches and rings . . . I didn't steal 'em, I'll give 'em all back. I just took 'em to play with . . ." He paused, stunned by their disbelieving eyes.

Lawson lit a cigarette and looked at him coldly.

"What did you do with the money?" he asked in a quiet, waiting voice.

"I pasted the hundred-dollar bills on the walls."

"What walls?" Lawson asked.

"The walls of the dirt room," he said, smiling, "the room next to the church. I hung up the rings and the watches and I stamped the diamonds into the dirt . . ." He saw that they were not understanding what he was saying. He grew frantic to make them believe, his voice tumbled on eagerly. "I saw a dead baby and a dead man . . ."

"Aw, you're nuts," Lawson snarled, shoving him into a chair.

"But mister . . ."

"Johnson, where's the paper he signed?" Lawson asked.

"What paper?"

"The confession, fool!"

Johnson pulled out his billfold and extracted a crumpled piece of paper.

"Yes, sir, mister," he said, stretching forth his hand. "That's the paper I signed . . ."

Lawson slapped him and he would have toppled had his chair not struck a wall behind him. Lawson scratched a match and held the paper over the flame; the confession burned down to Lawson's finger tips.

He stared, thunderstruck; the sun of the underground was fleeting and the terrible darkness of the day stood before him. They did not believe him, but he *had* to make them believe him!

"But mister . . ."

"It's going to be all right, boy," Lawson said with a quiet, soothing laugh. "I've burned your confession, see? You didn't sign anything." Lawson came close to him with the black ashes in his palm. "You don't remember a thing about this, do you?"

"Don't you-all be scared of me," he pleaded, sensing their uneasiness. "I'll sign another paper, if you want me to. I'll show you the cave."

"What's your game, boy?" Lawson asked suddenly.

"What are you trying to find out?" Johnson asked.

"Who sent you here?" Murphy demanded.

"Nobody sent me, mister," he said. "I just want to show you the room . . ."

"Aw, he's plumb bats," Murphy said. "Let's ship 'im to the psycho."

"No," Lawson said. "He's playing a game and I wish to God I knew what it was."

There flashed through his mind a definite way to make them believe him; he rose from the chair with nervous excitement.

"Mister, I saw the night watchman blow his brains out because you accused him of stealing," he told them. "But he didn't steal the money and diamonds. I took 'em."

Tigerishly Lawson grabbed his collar and lifted him bodily.

"*Who told you about that?*"

"Don't get excited, Lawson," Johnson said. "He read about it in the papers."

Lawson flung him away.

"He couldn't have," Lawson said, pulling papers from his pocket. "I haven't turned in the reports yet."

"Then how *did* he find out?" Murphy asked.

"Let's get out of here," Lawson said with quick resolution. "Listen, boy, we're going to take you to a nice, quiet place, see?"

"Yes, sir," he said. "And I'll show you the underground."

"Goddamn," Lawson muttered, fastening the gun at his hip. He narrowed his eyes at Johnson and Murphy. "Listen," he spoke just above a whisper, "say nothing about this, you hear?"

"O.K.," Johnson said.

"Sure," Murphy said.

Lawson unlocked the door and Johnson and Murphy led him down the stairs. The hallway was crowded with policemen.

"What have you got there, Lawson?"

"What did he do, Lawson?"

"He's psycho, ain't he, Lawson?"

Lawson did not answer; Johnson and Murphy led him to the car parked at the curb, pushed him into the back seat. Lawson got behind the steering wheel and the car rolled forward.

"What's up, Lawson?" Murphy asked.

"Listen," Lawson began slowly, "we tell the papers that he spilled about the Peabody job, then he escapes. The Wop is caught and we tell the papers that we steered them wrong to trap the real guy, see? Now this dope shows up and acts nuts. If we let him go, he'll squeal that we framed him, see?"

"I'm all right, mister," he said, feeling Murphy's and Johnson's arms locked rigidly into his. "I'm guilty . . . I'll show you everything in the underground. I laughed and laughed . . ."

"Shut that fool up!" Lawson ordered.

Johnson tapped him across the head with a blackjack and he fell back against the seat cushion, dazed.

"Yes, sir," he mumbled. "I'm all right."

The car sped along Hartsdale Avenue, then swung onto Pine Street and rolled to State Street, then turned south. It slowed to a stop, turned in the middle of a block, and headed north again.

"You're going around in circles, Lawson," Murphy said.

Lawson did not answer; he was hunched over the steering wheel. Finally he pulled the car to a stop at a curb.

"Say, boy, tell us the truth," Lawson asked quietly. "Where did you hide?"

"I didn't hide, mister."

The three policemen were staring at him now; he felt that for the first time they were willing to understand him.

"Then what happened?"

"Mister, when I looked through all of those holes and saw how people were living, I loved 'em . . ."

"Cut out that crazy talk!" Lawson snapped. "Who sent you back here?"

"Nobody, mister."

"Maybe he's talking straight," Johnson ventured.

"All right," Lawson said. "Nobody hid you. Now, tell us *where* you hid."

"I went underground . . ."

"What goddamn underground do you keep talking about?"

"I just went . . ." He paused and looked into the street, then pointed to a manhole cover. "I went down in there and stayed."

"In the *sewer*?"

"Yes, sir."

The policemen burst into a sudden laugh and ended quickly. Lawson swung the car around and drove to Woodside Avenue; he brought the car to a stop in front of a tall apartment building.

"What're we going to do, Lawson?" Murphy asked.

"I'm taking him up to my place," Lawson said. "We've got to wait until night. There's nothing we can do now."

They took him out of the car and led him into a vestibule.

"Take the steps," Lawson muttered.

They led him up four flights of stairs and into the living room of a small apartment. Johnson and Murphy let go of his arms and he stood uncertainly in the middle of the room.

"Now, listen, boy," Lawson began, "forget those wild lies you've been telling us. Where did you hide?"

"I just went underground, like I told you."

The room rocked with laughter. Lawson went to a cabinet and got a bottle of whiskey; he placed glasses for Johnson and Murphy. The three of them drank.

He felt that he could not explain himself to them. He tried to muster all the sprawling images that floated in him; the images stood out sharply in his mind, but he could not make them have the meaning for others that they had for him. He felt so helpless that he began to cry.

"He's nuts, all right," Johnson said. "All nuts cry like that."

Murphy crossed the room and slapped him.

"Stop that raving!"

A sense of excitement flooded him; he ran to Murphy and grabbed his arm.

"Let me show you the cave," he said. "Come on, and you'll see!"

Before he knew it a sharp blow had clipped him on the chin; darkness covered his eyes. He dimly felt himself being lifted and laid out on the sofa. He heard low voices and struggled to rise, but hard hands held him down. His brain was clearing now. He pulled to a sitting posture and stared with glazed eyes. It had grown dark. How long had he been out?

"Say, boy," Lawson said soothingly, "will you show us the underground?"

His eyes shone and his heart swelled with gratitude. Lawson believed him! He rose, glad; he grabbed Lawson's arm, making the policeman spill whiskey from the glass to his shirt.

"Take it easy, goddammit," Lawson said.

"Yes, sir."

"O.K. We'll take you down. But you'd better be telling us the truth, you hear?"

He clapped his hands in wild joy.

"I'll show you everything!"

He had triumphed at last! He would now do what he had felt was compelling him all along. At last he would be free of his burden.

"Take 'im down," Lawson ordered.

They led him down to the vestibule; when he reached the sidewalk he saw that it was night and a fine rain was falling.

"It's just like when I went down," he told them.

"What?" Lawson asked.

"The rain," he said, sweeping his arm in a wide arc. "It was raining when I went down. The rain made the water rise and lift the cover off."

"Cut it out," Lawson snapped.

They did not believe him now, but they would. A mood of high selflessness throbbed in him. He could barely contain his rising spirits. They would see what he had seen; they would feel what he had felt. He would lead them through all the holes he had dug and . . . He wanted to make a hymn, prance about in physical ecstasy, throw his arm about the policemen in fellowship.

"Get into the car," Lawson ordered.

He climbed in and Johnson and Murphy sat at either side of him; Lawson slid behind the steering wheel and started the motor.

"Now, tell us where to go," Lawson said.

"It's right around the corner from where the lady was killed," he said.

The car rolled slowly and he closed his eyes, remembering the song he had heard in the church, the song that had wrought him to such a high pitch of terror and pity. He sang softly, lolling his head:

> Glad, glad, glad, oh, so glad
> I got Jesus in my soul . . .

"Mister," he said, stopping his song, "you ought to see how funny the rings look on the wall." He giggled. "I fired a pistol, too. Just once, to see how it felt."

"What do you suppose he's suffering from?" Johnson asked.

"Delusions of grandeur, maybe," Murphy said.

"Maybe it's because he lives in a white man's world," Lawson said.

"Say, boy, what did you eat down there?" Murphy asked, prodding Johnson anticipatorily with his elbow.

"Pears, oranges, bananas, and pork chops," he said.

The car filled with laughter.

"You didn't eat any watermelon?" Lawson asked, smiling.

"No, sir," he answered calmly. "I didn't see any."

The three policemen roared harder and louder.

"Boy, you're sure some case," Murphy said, shaking his head in wonder.

The car pulled to a curb.

"All right, boy," Lawson said. "Tell us where to go."

He peered through the rain and saw where he had gone down. The streets, save for a few dim lamps glowing softly through the rain, were dark and empty.

"Right there, mister," he said, pointing.

"Come on; let's take a look," Lawson said.

"Well, suppose he did hide down there," Johnson said, "what is that supposed to prove?"

"I don't believe he hid down there," Murphy said.

"It won't hurt to look," Lawson said. "Leave things to me."

Lawson got out of the car and looked up and down the street.

He was eager to show them the cave now. If he could show them what he had seen, then they would feel what he had felt and they in turn would show it to others and those others would feel as they had felt, and soon everybody would be governed by the same impulse of pity.

"Take 'im out," Lawson ordered.

Johnson and Murphy opened the door and pushed him out; he stood trembling in the rain, smiling. Again Lawson looked up and down the street; no one was in sight. The rain came down hard, slanting like black wires across the wind-swept air.

"All right," Lawson said. "Show us."

He walked to the center of the street, stopped and inserted a finger in one of the tiny holes of the cover and tugged, but he was too weak to budge it.

"Did you really go down in there, boy?" Lawson asked; there was a doubt in his voice.

"Yes, sir. Just a minute. I'll show you."

"Help 'im get that damn thing off," Lawson said.

Johnson stepped forward and lifted the cover; it clanged against the wet pavement. The hole gaped round and black.

"I went down in there," he announced with pride.

Lawson gazed at him for a long time without speaking, then he reached his right hand to his holster and drew his gun.

"Mister, I got a gun just like that down there," he said, laughing, and looking into Lawson's face. "I fired it once then hung it on the wall. I'll show you."

"Show us how you went down," Lawson said quietly.

"I'll go down first, mister, and then you-all can come after me, hear?" he spoke like a little boy playing a game.

"Sure, sure," Lawson said soothingly. "Go ahead. We'll come."

He looked brightly at the policemen; he was bursting with happiness. He bent down and placed his hands on the rim of the hole and sat on the edge, his feet dangling into watery darkness. He heard the familiar drone of the gray current. He lowered his body and hung for a moment by his fingers, then he went downward on the steel prongs, hand over hand, until he reached the last rung. He dropped and his feet hit the water and he felt the stiff current trying to suck him away. He balanced himself quickly and looked back upward at the policemen.

"Come on, you-all!" he yelled, casting his voice above the rustling at his feet.

The vague forms that towered above him in the rain did not move. He laughed, feeling that they doubted him. But, once they saw the things he had done, they would never doubt again.

"Come on! The cave isn't far!" he yelled. "But be careful when your feet hit the water, because the current's pretty rough down here!"

Lawson still held the gun. Murphy and Johnson looked at Lawson quizzically.

"What are we going to do, Lawson?" Murphy asked.

"We are not going to follow that crazy nigger down into that sewer, are we?" Johnson asked.

"Come on, you-all!" he begged in a shout.

He saw Lawson raise the gun and point it directly at him. Lawson's face twitched, as though he were hesitating.

Then there was a thunderous report and a streak of fire ripped through his chest. He was hurled into the water, flat on his back. He looked in amazement at the blurred white faces above him. They shot me, he said to himself. The water flowed past him, blossoming in foam about his arms, his legs, and his head. His jaw sagged and his mouth gaped soundless. A vast pain gripped his head and gradually squeezed out consciousness. As from a great distance he heard hollow voices.

"What did you shoot him for, Lawson?"

"I had to."

"Why?"

"You've got to shoot his kind. They'd wreck things."

As though in a deep dream, he heard a metallic clank; they had replaced the manhole cover, shutting out forever the sound of wind and rain. From overhead came the muffled roar of a powerful motor and the swish of a speeding car. He felt the strong tide pushing him slowly into the middle of the sewer, turning him about. For a split second there hovered before his eyes the glittering cave, the shouting walls, and the laughing floor . . . Then his mouth was full of thick, bitter water. The current spun him around. He sighed and closed his eyes, a whirling object rushing alone in the darkness, veering, tossing, lost in the heart of the earth.

QUESTIONS

1. The police officer who kills Daniels sees him as a dangerous rebel, as the kind who'd "wreck things." In what sense could Daniels be seen as a rebel?   **2.** What is the significance of Fred Daniels's pecking out his own name on the typewriter?   **3.** What significance do you see in the fact that Daniels tries to communicate his joyous feelings at a church and a police station? What is it that he wants to communicate?

WRITING TOPICS
1. Fred Daniels goes underground to escape punishment for a crime he did not commit. He is a black man, and the underground is an appropriate metaphor for the position white America has accorded blacks. The underground is more than a place of escape for him, however; it is a place where he comes to understand what the society he lives in, black and white, is about. How do various episodes—the discovery of the dead baby, the funeral parlor, the movie house, the meat market, the black church—contribute to this understanding?   **2.** What significance do Fred Daniels's two dreams have in this story?

Something for the Time Being   1965

NADINE GORDIMER   [b. 1923]

He thought of it as discussing things with her, but the truth was that she did
not help him out at all. She said nothing, while she ran her hand up the ridge
of bone behind the rim of her child-sized yellow-brown ear, and raked her
fingers tenderly into her hairline along the back of her neck as if feeling out
some symptom in herself. Yet her listening was very demanding; when he
stopped at the end of a supposition or a suggestion, her silence made the stop
inconclusive. He had to take up again what he had said, carry it—where?

"Ve vant to give you a tsance, but you von't let us," he mimicked; and made
a loud glottal click, half angry, resentfully amused. He knew it wasn't because
Kalzin Brothers were Jews that he had lost his job at last, but just because he
had lost it, Mr. Solly's accent suddenly presented to him the irresistibly vulnerable. He had come out of prison nine days before after spending three
months as an awaiting-trial prisoner in a political case that had just been
quashed—he was one of those who would not accept bail. He had been in
prison three or four times since 1952; his wife Ella and the Kalzin Brothers
were used to it. Until now, his employers had always given him his job back
when he came out. They were importers of china and glass and he was head
packer in a team of black men who ran the dispatch department. "Well, what
the hell, I'll get something else," he said. "Hey?"

She stopped the self-absorbed examination of the surface of her skin for a
slow moment and shrugged, looking at him.

He smiled.

Her gaze loosened hold like hands falling away from a grasp. The ends of
her nails pressed at small imperfections in the skin of her neck. He drank his
tea and tore off pieces of bread to dip in it; then he noticed the tin of sardines
she had opened, and sopped up the pale matrix of oil in which ragged flecks of
silver were suspended. She offered him more tea, without speaking.

They lived in one room of a three-roomed house belonging to someone else;
it was better for her that way, since he was often likely to have to be away for
long stretches. She worked in a textile factory that made knitted socks; there
was no one at home to look after their one child, a girl, and the child lived
with a grandmother in a dusty peaceful village a day's train journey from the
city.

He said, dismissing it as of no importance, "I wonder what chance they meant?
You can imagine. I don't suppose they were going to give me an office with
my name on it." He spoke as if she would appreciate the joke. She had known
when she married him that he was a political man; she had been proud of him

because he didn't merely want something for himself, like the other young men she knew, but everything, and for *the people*. It had excited her, under his influence, to change her awareness of herself as a young black girl to awareness of herself as belonging to the people. She knew that everything wasn't like something—a hand-out, a wangled privilege, a trinket you could hold. She would never get something from him.

Her hand went on searching over her skin as if it must come soon, come anxiously, to the flaw, the sickness, the evidence of what was wrong with her; for on this Saturday afternoon, all these things that she knew had deserted her. She had lost her wits. All that she could understand was the one room, the child growing up far away in the mud house, and the fact that you couldn't keep a job if you kept being away from work for weeks at a time.

"I think I'd better look up Flora Donaldson," he said. Flora Donaldson was a white woman who had set up an office to help political prisoners. "Sooner the better. Perhaps she'll dig up something for me by Monday. It's the beginning of the month."

He got on all right with those people. Ella had met Flora Donaldson once; she was a pretty white woman who looked just like any white woman who would automatically send a black face round to the back door, but she didn't seem to know that she was white and you were black.

He pulled the curtain that hung across one corner of the room and took out his suit. It was a thin suit, of the kind associated with holiday-makers in American clothing advertisements, and when he was dressed in it, with a sharp-brimmed grey hat tilted back on his small head, he looked a wiry, boyish figure, rather like one of those boy-men who sing and shake before a microphone, and whose clothes admirers try to touch as a talisman.

He kissed her good-bye, obliging her to put down, the lowering of a defence, the piece of sewing she held. She had cleared away the dishes from the table and set up the sewing machine, and he saw that the shapes of cut material that lay on the table were the parts of a small girl's dress.

She spoke suddenly. "And when the next lot gets tired of you?"

"When that lot gets tired of me, I'll get another job again, that's all."

She nodded, very slowly, and her hand crept back to her neck.

"Who was that?" Madge Chadders asked.

Her husband had been out into the hall to answer the telephone.

"Flora Donaldson. I wish you'd explain to these people exactly what sort of factory I've got. It's so embarrassing. She's trying to find a job for some chap, he's a skilled packer. There's no skilled packing done in my workshop, no skilled jobs at all done by black men. What on earth can I offer the fellow? She says he's desperate and anything will do."

Madge had the broken pieces of a bowl on a newspaper spread on the Persian carpet. "Mind the glue, darling! There, just next to your foot. Well, anything is better than nothing. I suppose it's someone who was in the Soganiland sedition case. Three months awaiting trial taken out of their lives, and now they're chucked back to fend for themselves."

William Chadders had not had any black friends or mixed with coloured people in any but master-servant terms until he married Madge, but his views on the immorality and absurdity of the colour bar were sound; sounder, she often felt, than her own, for they were backed by the impersonal authority of a familiarity with the views of great thinkers, saints, and philosophers, with history, political economy, sociology, and anthropology. She knew only what she felt. And she always did something, at once, to express what she felt. She never measured the smallness of her personal protest against the establishment she opposed; she marched with Flora and five hundred black women in a demonstration against African women's being forced to carry passes; outside the university where she had once been a student, she stood between sandwich-boards bearing messages of mourning because a bill had been passed closing the university, for the future, to all but white students; she had living in her house for three months a young African who wanted to write and hadn't the peace or space to get on with it in a Location.[1] She did not stop to consider the varying degrees of usefulness of the things she did, and if others pointed this out to her and suggested that she might make up her mind to throw her weight on the side of either politics or philanthropy, she was not resentful but answered candidly that there was so little it was possible to do that she simply took any and every chance to get off her chest her disgust at the colour bar. When she had married William Chadders, her friends had thought that her protestant activities would stop; they underestimated not only Madge, but also William, who, although he was a wealthy businessman, subscribed to the necessity of personal freedom as strictly as any bohemian. Besides he was not fool enough to want to change in any way the person who had enchanted him just as she was.

She reacted upon him, rather than he upon her; she, of course, would not hesitate to go ahead and change anybody. (But why not? she would have said, astonished. If it's to the good?) The attitude she sought to change would occur to her as something of independent existence, she would not see it as a cell in the organism of personality, whose whole structure would have to regroup itself round the change. She had the boldness of being unaware of these consequences.

William did not carry a banner in the streets, of course; he worked up there, among his first principles and historical precedents and economic necessities, but now they were translated from theory to practice of an anonymous, large-scale, and behind-the-scenes sort—he was the brains and some of the money in a scheme to get Africans some economic power besides their labour, through the setting up of an all-African trust company and investment corporation. A

---

[1] A township where Africans, who make up a majority of South Africa's population, were forced to live under *apartheid*, the white South African system of racial separation.

number of Madge's political friends, both white and black, thought this was putting the middle-class cart before the proletarian horse, but most of the African leaders welcomed the attempt as an essential backing to popular movements on other levels—something to count on outside the unpredictability of mobs. Sometimes it amused Madge to think that William, making a point at a meeting in a boardroom, fifteen floors above life in the streets, might achieve in five minutes something of more value than she did in all her days of turning her hand to anything—from sorting old clothes to duplicating a manifesto or driving people during a bus boycott. Yet this did not knock the meaning out of her own life, for her; she knew that she had to see, touch, and talk to people in order to care about them, that was all there was to it.

Before she and her husband dressed to go out that evening, she finished sticking together the broken Chinese bowl, and showed it to him with satisfaction. To her, it was whole again. But it was one of a set, that had belonged together, and whose unity had illustrated certain philosophical concepts. William had bought them long ago, in London; for him, the whole set was damaged forever.

He said nothing to her, but he was thinking of the bowls when she said to him as they drove off, "Will you see that chap, on Monday, yourself?"

He changed gear deliberately, attempting to follow her out of his preoccupation. But she said, "The man Flora's sending. What was his name?"

He opened his hand on the steering wheel, indicating that the name escaped him.

"See him yourself?"

"I'll have to leave it to the works manager to find something for him to do," he said.

"Yes, I know. But see him yourself, too?"

Her anxious voice made him feel very fond of her. He turned and smiled at her suspiciously. "Why?"

She was embarrassed at his indulgent manner. She said, frank and wheedling, "Just to show him. You know. That you know about him and it's not much of a job."

"All right," he said, "I'll see him myself."

He met her in town straight from the office on Monday and they went to the opening of an exhibition of paintings and on to dinner and to see a play, with friends. He had not been home at all, until they returned after midnight. It was a summer night and they sat for a few minutes on their terrace, where it was still mild with the warmth of the day's sun coming from the walls in the darkness, and drank lime juice and water to quench the thirst that wine and the stuffy theatre had given them. Madge made gasps and groans of pleasure at the release from the pressures of company and noise. Then she lay quiet for a while, her voice lifting now and then in fragments of unrelated comment on the evening—the occasional chirp of a bird that has already put its head under its wing for the night.

By the time they went in, they were free of the evening. Her black dress, her earrings, and her bracelets felt like fancy dress; she shed the character and sat on the bedroom carpet, and, passing her, he said, "Oh—that chap of Flora's came today, but I don't think he'll last. I explained to him that I didn't have the sort of job he was looking for."

"Well, that's all right, then," she said, inquiringly. "What more could you do?"

"Yes," he said, deprecating. "But I could see he didn't like the idea much. It's a cleaner's job; nothing for him. He's an intelligent chap. I didn't like having to offer it to him."

She was moving about her dressing table, piling out upon it the contents of her handbag. "Then I'm sure he'll understand. It'll give him something for the time being, anyway, darling. You can't help it if you don't need the sort of work he does."

"Huh, he won't last. I could see that. He accepted it, but only with his head. He'll get fed up. Probably won't turn up tomorrow. I had to speak to him about his Congress[2] button, too. The works manager came to me."

"What about his Congress button?" she said.

He was unfastening his shirt and his eyes were on the evening paper that lay folded on the bed. "He was wearing one," he said inattentively.

"I know, but what did you have to speak to him about it for?"

"He was wearing it in the workshop all day."

"Well, what about it?" She was sitting at her dressing table, legs spread, as if she had sat heavily and suddenly. She was not looking at him, but at her own face.

He gave the paper a push and drew his pyjamas from under the pillow. Vulnerable and naked, he said authoritatively, "You can't wear a button like that among the men in the workshop."

"Good heavens," she said, almost in relief, laughing, backing away from the edge of tension, chivvying him out of a piece of stuffiness. "And why can't you?"

"You can't have someone clearly representing a political organization like Congress."

"But he's not there *representing* anything, he's there as a workman!" Her mouth was still twitching with something between amusement and nerves.

"Exactly."

"Then why can't he wear a button that signifies his allegiance to an organization in his private life outside the workshop? There's no rule about not wearing tie-pins or club buttons or anything, in the workshop, is there?"

"No, there isn't, but that's not quite the same thing."

"My dear William," she said, "it is exactly the same. It's nothing to do with the works manager whether the man wears a Rotary button, or an Elvis Presley button, or an African National Congress button. It's damn all his business."

---

[2] The African National Congress, a predominantly black political party, continues to struggle, sometimes violently, to replace *apartheid* with majority rule.

"No, Madge, I'm sorry," William said, patient, "but it's not the same. I can give the man a job because I feel sympathetic toward the struggle he's in, but I can't put him in the workshop as a Congress man. I mean that wouldn't be fair to Fowler. That I can't do to Fowler." He was smiling as he went towards the bathroom but his profile, as he turned into the doorway, was incisive.

She sat on at her dressing table, pulling a comb through her hair, dragging it down through knots. Then she rested her face on her palms, caught sight of herself, and became aware, against her fingers, of the curving shelf of bone, like the lip of a strong shell, under each eye. Everyone has his own intimations of mortality. For her, the feel of the bone beneath the face, in any living creature, brought her the message of the skull. Once hollowed out of this, outside the world, too. For what it's worth. It's worth a lot, the world, she affirmed, as she always did, life rising at once in her as a fish opens its jaws to a fly. It's worth a lot; and she sighed and got up with the sigh.

She went into the bathroom and sat down on the edge of the bath. He was lying there in the water, his chin relaxed on his chest, and he smiled at her. She said, "You mean you don't want Fowler to know."

"Oh," he said, seeing where they were, again. "What is it I don't want Fowler to know?"

"You don't want your partner to know that you slip black men with political ideas into your workshop. Cheeky kaffir agitators. Specially a man who's just been in jail for getting people to defy the government!—What was his name; you never said?"

"Daniel something. I don't know. Mongoma or Ngoma. Something like that."

A line like a cut appeared between her eyebrows. "Why can't you remember his name?" Then she went on at once, "You don't want Fowler to know what you think, do you? That's it? You want to pretend you're like him, you don't mind the native in his place. You want to pretend that to please Fowler. You don't want Fowler to think you're cracked, or Communist, or whatever it is that good-natured, kind, jolly rich people like old Fowler think about people like us."

"I couldn't have less interest in what Fowler thinks outside our boardroom. And inside it, he never thinks about anything but how to sell more earth-moving gear."

"I don't mind the native in his place. You want him to think you go along with all that." She spoke aloud, but she seemed to be telling herself rather than him.

"Fowler and I run a factory. Our only common interest is the efficient running of that factory. Our *only* one. The factory depends on a stable, satisfied black labour force, and that we've got. Right, you and I know that the whole black wage standard is too low, right, we know that they haven't a legal union to speak for them, *right*, we know that the conditions they live under make it impossible for them really to be stable. All that. But the fact is, so far as accepted standards go in this crazy country, they're a stable, satisfied labour force with better working conditions than most. So long as I'm a partner in a business that lives by them, I can't officially admit an element that represents dissatisfaction with their lot."

"A green badge with a map of Africa on it," she said.

"If you make up your mind not to understand, you don't, and there it is," he said indulgently.

"You give him a job but you make him hide his Congress button."

He began to soap himself. She wanted everything to stop while she inquired into things, she could not go on while a remark was unexplained or a problem unsettled, but he represented a principle she subscribed to but found so hard to follow, that life must go on, trivially, commonplace, the trailing hem of the only power worth clinging to. She smoothed the film of her thin nightgown over the shape of her knees, again and again, and presently she said, in exactly the flat tone of statement that she had used before, the flat tone that was the height of belligerence in her, "He can say and do what he likes, he can call for strikes and boycotts and anything he likes, outside the factory, but he mustn't wear his Congress button at work."

He was standing up, washing his body that was full of scars; she knew them all, from the place on his left breast where a piece of shrapnel had gone in, all the way back to the place under his arm where he had torn himself on barbed wire as a child. "Yes, of course, anything he likes."

Anything except his self-respect. Pretend, pretend. Pretend he doesn't belong to a political organization. Pretend he doesn't want to be a man. Pretend he hasn't been to prison for what he believes. Suddenly she spoke to her husband. "You'll let him have anything except the one thing worth giving."

They stood in uncomfortable proximity to each other, in the smallness of the bathroom. They were at once aware of each other as people who live in intimacy are only when hostility returns each to the confines of himself. He felt himself naked before her, where he had stepped out onto the towelling mat, and he took a towel and slowly covered himself, pushing the free end in round his waist. She felt herself an intrusion and, in silence, went out.

Her hands were tingling. She walked up and down the bedroom floor like someone waiting to be summoned, called to account. I'll forget about it, she kept thinking, very fast, I'll forget about it again. Take a sip of water. Read another chapter. Let things flow, cover up, go on.

But when he came into the room with his wet hair combed and his stranger's face, and he said, "You're angry," it came from her lips, a black bird in the room, before she could understand what she had released—"I'm not angry. I'm beginning to get to know you."

Ella Mgoma knew he was going to a meeting that evening and didn't expect him home early. She put the paraffin lamp on the table so that she could see to finish the child's dress. It was done, buttons and all, by the time he came in at half past ten.

"Well, now we'll see what happens. I've got them to accept, *in principle,* that in future we won't take bail. You should have seen Ben Tsolo's face when I said that we lent the government our money interest-free when we paid bail. That really hit him. That was language he understood." He laughed, and did not seem to want to sit down, the heat of the meeting still upon him. "*In principle*. Yes, it's easy to accept in principle. We'll see."

She pumped the primus and set a pot of stew to warm up for him. "Ah, that's nice"—he saw the dress. "Finished already?" And she nodded vociferously in pleasure; but at once she noticed his forefinger run lightly along the line of braid round the neck, and the traces of failure that were always at the bottom of her cup tasted on her tongue again. Probably he was not even aware of it, or perhaps his instinct for what was true—the plumb line, the coin with the right ring—led him absently to it, but the fact was that she had botched the neck.

She had an almost Oriental delicacy about not badgering him, and she waited until he had washed and sat down to eat before she asked, "How did the job go?"

"Oh that," he said. "It went." He was eating quickly, moving his tongue strongly round his mouth to marshal the bits of meat that escaped his teeth. She was sitting with him, feeling, in spite of herself, the rest of satisfaction in her evening's work. "Didn't you get it?"

"It got *me*. But I got loose again, all right."

She watched his face to see what he meant. "They don't want you to come back tomorrow?"

He shook his head, no, no, no, to stem the irritation of her suppositions. He finished his mouthful and said, "Everything very nice. Boss takes me into his office, apologizes for the pay, he knows it's not the sort of job I should have and so forth. So I go off and clean up in the assembly shop. Then at lunch time he calls me into the office again: they don't want me to wear my ANC badge at work. Flora Donaldson's sympathetic white man, who's going to do me the great favour of paying me three pounds a week." He laughed. "Well, there you are."

She kept on looking at him. Her eyes widened and her mouth tightened; she was trying to prime herself to speak, or was trying not to cry. The idea of tears exasperated him and he held her with a firm, almost belligerently inquiring gaze. Her hand went up round the back of her neck under her collar, anxiously exploratory. "Don't do that!" he said. "You're like a monkey catching lice."

She took her hand down swiftly and broke into trembling, like a sweat. She began to breathe hysterically. "You couldn't put it in your pocket, for the day," she said wildly, grimacing at the bitterness of malice towards him.

He jumped up from the table. "Christ! I knew you'd say it! I've been waiting for you to say it. You've been wanting to say it for five years. Well, now it's out. Out with it. Spit it out!" She began to scream softly as if he were hitting her. The impulse to cruelty left him and he sat down before his dirty plate, where the battered spoon lay among bits of gristle and potato eyes. Presently he spoke. "You come out and you think there's everybody waiting for you. The truth is, there isn't anybody. You think straight in prison because you've got nothing to lose. Nobody thinks straight, outside. They don't want to hear you. What are you all going to do with me, Ella? Send me back to prison as quickly as possible? Perhaps I'll get a banishment order next time. That'd do. That's what you've got for me. I must keep myself busy with that kind of thing."

He went over to her and said, in a kindly voice, kneading her shoulder with spread fingers, "Don't cry. Don't cry. You're just like any other woman."

QUESTIONS

1. What do the contrasting reactions of Ella Mgoma and Madge Chadders to Daniel's wearing of the badge tell us about the theme of the story? **2.** What do Daniel's final words mean? **3.** What does the author mean when she says that Madge "would not hesitate to go ahead and change anybody. . . . The attitude she sought to change would occur to her as something of independent existence, she would not see it as a cell in the organism of personality, whose whole structure would have to regroup itself round the change. She had the boldness of being unaware of these consequences."? **4.** How do the contrasting reactions of Madge and William reflect their attitudes toward Daniel? **5.** Does the portrayal of the two wives and the two husbands reflect gender differences?

WRITING TOPIC

Daniel's political activities are the focus of the story. How would you characterize his politics? Compare and contrast the reaction to his political activities of his wife, Ella; William Chadders; and Madge Chadders. Which of the four characters do you find most sympathetic? Which the least? Explain.

The Ones Who Walk Away from Omelas

1974

URSULA K. LE GUIN [b. 1929]

With a clamor of bells that set the swallows soaring, the Festival of Summer came to the city Omelas, bright-towered by the sea. The rigging of the boats in harbor sparkled with flags. In the streets between houses with red roofs and painted walls, between old moss-grown gardens and under avenues of trees, past great parks and public buildings, processions moved. Some were decorous: old people in long stiff robes of mauve and grey, grave master workmen, quiet, merry women carrying their babies and chatting as they walked. In other streets the music beat faster, a shimmering of gong and tambourine, and the people went dancing, the procession was a dance. Children dodged in and out, their high calls rising like the swallows' crossing flights over the music and the singing. All the processions wound towards the north side of the city, where on the great water-meadow called the Green Fields boys and girls, naked in the bright air, with mud-stained feet and ankles and long, lithe arms, exercised their restive horses before the race. The horses wore no gear at all but a halter without bit. Their manes were braided with streamers of silver, gold, and green. They flared their nostrils and pranced and boasted to one another; they were vastly excited, the horse being the only animal who has adopted our ceremonies as his own. Far off to the north and west the mountains stood up half encircling Omelas on her bay. The air of morning was so clear that the snow still crowning the Eighteen Peaks burned with white-gold fire across the miles of sunlit air, under the dark blue of the sky. There was just enough wind to make the banners that marked the racecourse snap and flutter now and then. In the silence of the broad green meadows one could hear the music winding through the city streets, farther and nearer and ever approaching, a cheerful faint sweetness of the air that from time to time trembled and gathered together and broke out into the great joyous clanging of the bells.

Joyous! How is one to tell about joy? How describe the citizens of Omelas?

They were not simple folk, you see, though they were happy. But we do not say the words of cheer much any more. All smiles have become archaic. Given a description such as this one tends to make certain assumptions. Given a description such as this one tends to look next for the King, mounted on a splendid stallion and surrounded by his noble knights, or perhaps in a golden litter borne by great-muscled slaves. But there was no king. They did not use swords, or keep slaves. They were not barbarians. I do not know the rules and laws of their society, but I suspect that they were singularly few. As they did without monarchy and slavery, so they also got on without the stock exchange, the advertisement, the secret police, and the bomb. Yet I repeat that these were not simple folk, not dulcet shepherds, noble savages, bland utopians. They were not less complex than us. The trouble is that we have a bad habit, encouraged by pedants and sophisticates, of considering happiness as something rather stupid. Only pain is intellectual, only evil interesting. This is the treason of the artist: a refusal to admit the banality of evil and the terrible boredom of pain. If you can't lick 'em, join 'em. If it hurts, repeat it. But to praise despair is to condemn delight, to embrace violence is to lose hold of everything else. We have almost lost hold; we can no longer describe a happy man, nor make any celebration of joy. How can I tell you about the people of Omelas? They were not naïve and happy children—though their children were, in fact, happy. They were mature, intelligent, passionate adults whose lives were not wretched. O miracle! but I wish I could describe it better. I wish I could convince you. Omelas sounds in my words like a city in a fairy tale, long ago and far away, once upon a time. Perhaps it would be best if you imagined it as your own fancy bids, assuming it will rise to the occasion, for certainly I cannot suit you all. For instance, how about technology? I think that there would be no cars or helicopters in and above the streets; this follows from the fact that the people of Omelas are happy people. Happiness is based on a just discrimination of what is necessary, what is neither necessary nor destructive, and what is destructive. In the middle category, however—that of the unnecessary but undestructive, that of comfort, luxury, exuberance, etc.—they could perfectly well have central heating, subway trains, washing machines, and all kinds of marvelous devices not yet invented here, floating light-sources, fuelless power, a cure for the common cold. Or they could have none of that: it doesn't matter. As you like it. I incline to think that people from towns up and down the coast have been coming in to Omelas during the last days before the Festival on very fast little trains and double-decker trams, and that the train station of Omelas is actually the handsomest building in town, though plainer than the magnificent Farmers' Market. But even granted trains, I fear that Omelas so far strikes some of you as goody-goody. Smiles, bells, parades, horses, bleh. If so, please add an orgy. If an orgy would help, don't hesitate. Let us not, however, have temples from which issue beautiful nude priests and priestesses already half in ecstasy and ready to copulate with any man or woman, lover or stranger, who desires union with the deep godhead of the blood, although that was my first idea. But really it would be better not to have any temples in Omelas—at least, not manned temples. Religion yes, clergy no. Surely the beautiful nudes can just wander about, offering themselves like divine soufflés to the hunger of the needy and the rapture of the flesh. Let them join the processions. Let tambourines be struck above the copulations, and the glory of desire be proclaimed upon the gongs, and (a not unimportant point) let the offspring of these delightful rituals be beloved and looked after by all. One thing I know there is none of in Omelas is guilt. But what else should there be? I thought at first there were no drugs, but that is puritanical. For those who like it, the faint insistent sweetness of *drooz* may perfume the ways of the city, *drooz* which first brings a great lightness and brilliance to the mind and limbs, and then after some hours a dreamy languor, and wonderful visions at last of the very arcana and inmost secrets of the Universe, as well as exciting the pleasure of sex beyond all belief; and it is not habit-forming. For more modest tastes I think there ought to be beer. What else, what else belongs in the joyous city? The sense of victory, surely, the celebration of courage. But as we did without clergy, let us do without soldiers. The joy built upon successful slaughter is not the right kind of joy; it will not do; it is fearful and it is trivial. A boundless and generous contentment, a magnanimous triumph felt not against some outer enemy but in communion with the finest and fairest in the souls of all men everywhere and the splendor of the world's summer: this is what swells the hearts of the people of Omelas, and the victory they celebrate is that of life. I really don't think many of them need to take *drooz*.

Most of the processions have reached the Green Fields by now. A marvelous smell of cooking goes forth from the red and blue tents of the provisioners. The faces of small children are amiably sticky; in the benign grey beard of a man a couple of crumbs of rich pastry are entangled. The youths and girls have mounted their horses and are beginning to group around the starting line of the course. An old woman, small, fat, and laughing, is passing out flowers from a basket, and tall young men wear her flowers in their shining hair. A child of nine or ten sits at the edge of the crowd, alone, playing on a wooden flute. People pause to listen, and they smile, but they do not speak to him, for he never ceases playing and never sees them, his dark eyes wholly rapt in the sweet, thin magic of the tune.

He finishes, and slowly lowers his hands holding the wooden flute.

As if that little private silence were the signal, all at once a trumpet sounds from the pavilion near the starting line: imperious, melancholy, piercing. The horses rear on their slender legs, and some of them neigh in answer. Sober-faced, the young riders stroke the horses' necks and soothe them, whispering, "Quiet, quiet, there my beauty, my hope. . . ." They begin to form in rank along the starting line. The crowds along the racecourse are like a field of grass and flowers in the wind. The Festival of Summer has begun.

Do you believe? Do you accept the festival, the city, the joy? No? Then let me describe one more thing.

In a basement under one of the beautiful public buildings of Omelas, or perhaps in the cellar of one of its spacious private homes, there is a room. It has one locked door, and no window. A little light seeps in dustily between cracks in the boards, secondhand from a cobwebbed window somewhere across the cellar. In one corner of the little room a couple of mops, with stiff, clotted, foul-smelling heads, stand near a rusty bucket. The floor is dirt, a little damp to the touch, as cellar dirt usually is. The room is about three paces long and two wide: a mere broom closet or disused tool room. In the room a child is sitting. It could be a boy or a girl. It looks about six, but actually is nearly ten. It is feeble-minded. Perhaps it was born defective, or perhaps it has become imbecile through fear, malnutrition, and neglect. It picks its nose and occasionally fumbles vaguely with its toes or genitals, as it sits hunched in the corner farthest from the bucket and the two mops. It is afraid of the mops. It finds them horrible. It shuts its eyes, but it knows the mops are still standing there; and the door is locked; and nobody will come. The door is always locked; and nobody ever comes, except that sometimes—the child has no understanding of time or interval—sometimes the door rattles terribly and opens, and a person, or several people, are there. One of them may come in and kick the child to make it stand up. The others never come close, but peer in at it with frightened, disgusted eyes. The food bowl and the water jug are hastily filled, the door is locked, the eyes disappear. The people at the door never say anything, but the child, who has not always lived in the tool room, and can remember sunlight and its mother's voice, sometimes speaks. "I will be good," it says. "Please let me out. I will be good!" They never answer. The child used to scream for help at night, and cry a good deal, but now it only makes a kind of whining, "eh-haa, eh-haa," and it speaks less and less often. It is so thin there are no calves to its legs; its belly protrudes; it lives on a half-bowl of corn meal and grease a day. It is naked. Its buttocks and thighs are a mass of festered sores, as it sits in its own excrement continually.

They all know it is there, all the people of Omelas. Some of them have come to see it, others are content merely to know it is there. They all know that it has to be there. Some of them understand why, and some do not, but all understand that their happiness, the beauty of their city, the tenderness of their friendships, the health of their children, the wisdom of their scholars, the skill of their makers, even the abundance of their harvest and the kindly weathers of their skies, depend wholly on this child's abominable misery.

This is usually explained to children when they are between eight and twelve, whenever they seem capable of understanding; and most of those who come to see the child are young people, though often enough an adult comes, or comes back, to see the child. No matter how well the matter has been explained to them, these young spectators are always shocked and sickened at the sight. They feel disgust, which they had thought themselves superior to. They feel anger, outrage, impotence, despite all the explanations. They would like to do something for the child. But there is nothing they can do. If the child were brought up into the sunlight out of that vile place, if it were cleaned and fed and comforted, that would be a good thing, indeed; but if it were done, in that day and hour all the prosperity and beauty and delight of Omelas would wither and be destroyed. Those are the terms. To exchange all the goodness and grace of every life in Omelas for that single, small improvement: to throw away the happiness of thousands for the chance of the happiness of one: that would be to let guilt within the walls indeed.

The terms are strict and absolute; there may not even be a kind word spoken to the child.

Often the young people go home in tears, or in a tearless rage, when they have seen the child and faced this terrible paradox. They may brood over it for weeks or years. But as time goes on they begin to realize that even if the child could be released, it would not get much good of its freedom: a little vague pleasure of warmth and food, no doubt, but little more. It is too degraded and imbecile to know any real joy. It has been afraid too long ever to be free of fear. Its habits are too uncouth for it to respond to humane treatment. Indeed, after so long it would probably be wretched without walls about it to protect it, and darkness for its eyes, and its own excrement to sit in. Their tears at the bitter injustice dry when they begin to perceive the terrible justice of reality, and to accept it. Yet it is their tears and anger, the trying of their generosity and the acceptance of their helplessness, which are perhaps the true source of the splendor of their lives. Theirs is no vapid, irresponsible happiness. They know that they, like the child, are not free. They know compassion. It is the existence of the child, and their knowledge of its existence, that makes possible the nobility of their architecture, the poignancy of their music, the profundity of their science. It is because of the child that they are so gentle with children. They know that if the wretched one were not there snivelling in the dark, the other one, the flute-player, could make no joyful music as the young riders line up in their beauty for the race in the sunlight of the first morning of summer.

Now do you believe in them? Are they not more credible? But there is one more thing to tell, and this is quite incredible.

At times one of the adolescent girls or boys who go to see the child does not go home to weep or rage, does not, in fact, go home at all. Sometimes also a man or woman much older falls silent for a day or two, and then leaves home. These people go out into the street, and walk down the street alone. They keep walking, and walk straight out of the city of Omelas, through the beautiful gates. They keep walking across the farmlands of Omelas. Each one goes alone, youth or girl, man or woman. Night falls; the traveler must pass down village streets, between the houses with yellow-lit windows, and on out into the darkness of the fields. Each alone, they go west or north, towards the mountains. They go on. They leave Omelas, they walk ahead into the darkness, and they do not come back. The place they go towards is a place even less imaginable to most of us than the city of happiness. I cannot describe it at all. It is possible that it does not exist. But they seem to know where they are going, the ones who walk away from Omelas.

The Sandman

1972

DONALD BARTHELME   [1931–1989]

Dear Dr. Hodder, I realize that it is probably wrong to write a letter to one's girl friend's shrink but there are several things going on here that I think ought to be pointed out to you. I thought of making a personal visit but the situation then, as I'm sure you understand, would be completely untenable—I would be *visiting a psychiatrist.* I also understand that in writing to you I am in some sense interfering with the process but you don't have to discuss with Susan what I have said. Please consider this an "eyes only" letter. Please think of it as personal and confidential.

You must be aware, first, that because Susan is my girl friend pretty much everything she discusses with you she also discusses with me. She tells me what she said and what you said. We have been seeing each other for about six months now and I am pretty familiar with her story, or stories. Similarly, with your responses, or at least the general pattern. I know, for example, that my habit of referring to you as "the sandman" annoys you but let me assure you that I mean nothing unpleasant by it. It is simply a nickname. The reference is to the old rhyme: "Sea-sand does the Sandman bring/Sleep to end the day/He dusts the children's eyes with sand/And steals their dreams away." (This is a variant; there are other versions, but this is the one I prefer.) I also understand that you are a little bit shaky because the prestige of analysis is now, as I'm sure you know far better than I, at a nadir. This must tend to make you nervous and who can blame you? One always tends to get a little bit shook when one's methodology is in question. Of course! (By the bye, let me say that I am very pleased that you are one of the ones that talk, instead of just sitting there. I think that's a good thing, an excellent thing, I congratulate you.)

To the point. I fully understand that Susan's wish to terminate with you and buy a piano instead has disturbed you. You have every right to be disturbed and to say that she is not electing the proper course, that what she says conceals something else, that she is evading reality, etc., etc. Go ahead. But there is one possibility here that you might be, just might be, missing. Which is that she means it.

Susan says: "I want to buy a piano."

You think: She wishes to terminate the analysis and escape into the piano.

Or: Yes, it is true that her father wanted her to be a concert pianist and that she studied for twelve years with Goetzmann. But she does not really want to reopen that can of maggots. She wants me to disapprove.

Or: Having failed to achieve a career as a concert pianist, she wishes to fail

430

again. She is now too old to achieve the original objective. The spontaneous organization of defeat!

Or: She is flirting again.

Or:

Or:

Or:

Or:

The one thing you cannot consider, by the nature of your training and of the discipline itself, is that she really might want to terminate the analysis and buy a piano. That the piano might be more necessary and valuable to her than the analysis.[1]

What we really have to consider here is the locus of hope. Does hope reside in the analysis or rather in the piano? As a shrink rather than a piano salesman you would naturally tend to opt for the analysis. But there are differences. The piano salesman can stand behind his product; you, unfortunately, cannot. A Steinway is a known quantity, whereas an analysis can succeed or fail. I don't reproach you for this, I simply note it. (An interesting question: Why do laymen feel such a desire to, in plain language, fuck over shrinks? As I am doing here, in a sense? I don't mean hostility in the psychoanalytic encounter, I mean in general. That is an interesting phenomenon and should be investigated by somebody.)

It might be useful if I gave you a little taste of my own experience of analysis. I only went five or six times. Dr. Behring was a tall thin man who never said anything much. If you could get a "What comes to mind?" out of him you were doing splendidly. There was a little incident that is, perhaps, illustrative. I went for my hour one day and told him about something I was worried about. (I was then working for a newspaper down in Texas.) There was a story that four black teenagers had come across a little white boy, about ten, in a vacant lot, sodomized him repeatedly and then put him inside a refrigerator and closed the door (this was before they had that requirement that abandoned refrigerators had to have their doors removed) and he suffocated. I don't know to this day what actually happened, but the cops had picked up *some* black kids and were reportedly beating the shit out of them in an effort to make them confess. I was not on the police run at that time but one of the police reporters told me about it and I told Dr. Behring. A good liberal, he grew white with anger and said what was I doing about it? It was the first time he had talked. So I was shaken— it hadn't occurred to me that I was required to do something about it, he was right—and after I left I called my then sister-in-law, who was at that time secretary to a City Councilman. As you can imagine, such a position is a very

---

[1] For an admirable discussion of this sort of communication failure and many other matters of interest see Percy, "Toward a Triadic Theory of Meaning," *Psychiatry*, Vol. 35 (February 1972), pp. 6–14 *et seq.* [Editor's note: This and all subsequent footnotes to this story are part of the text.]

powerful one—the councilmen are mostly off making business deals and the executive secretaries run the office—and she got on to the chief of police with an inquiry as to what was going on and if there was any police brutality involved and if so, how much. The case was a very sensational one, you see; *Ebony* had a writer down there trying to cover it but he couldn't get in to see the boys and the cops had roughed him up some, they couldn't understand at that time that there could be such a thing as a black reporter. They understood that they had to be a little careful with the white reporters, but a black reporter was beyond them. But my sister-in-law threw her weight (her Councilman's weight) around a bit and suggested to the chief that if there was a serious amount of brutality going on the cops had better stop it, because there was too much outside interest in the case and it would be extremely bad PR if the brutality stuff got out. I also called a guy I knew pretty high up in the sheriff's department and suggested that *he* suggest to his colleagues that they cool it. I hinted at unspeakable political urgencies and he picked it up. The sheriff's department was separate from the police department but they both operated out of the Courthouse Building and they interacted quite a bit, in the normal course. So the long and short of it was that the cops decided to show the four black kids at a press conference to demonstrate that they weren't really beat all to rags, and that took place at four in the afternoon. I went and the kids looked O.K., except for one whose teeth were out and who the cops said had fallen down the stairs. Well, we all know the falling-down-the-stairs story but the point was the *degree* of mishandling and it was clear that the kids had not been half-killed by the cops, as the rumor stated. They were walking and talking naturally, although scared to death, as who would not be? There weren't any TV pictures because the newspaper people always pulled out the plugs of the TV people, at important moments, in those days—it was a standard thing. Now while I admit it sounds callous to be talking about the degree of brutality being minimal, let me tell you that it was no small matter, in that time and place, to force the cops to show the kids to the press at all. It was an achievement, of sorts. So about eight o'clock I called Dr. Behring at home, I hope interrupting his supper, and told him that the kids were O.K., relatively, and he said that was fine, he was glad to hear it. They were later no-billed and I stopped seeing him. That was my experience of analysis and that it may have left me a little sour, I freely grant. Allow for this bias.

To continue. I take exception to your remark that Susan's "openness" is a form of voyeurism. This remark interested me for a while, until I thought about it. Voyeurism I take to be an eroticized expression of curiosity whose chief phenomenological characteristic is the distance maintained between the voyeur and the object. The tension between the desire to draw near the object and the necessity to maintain the distance becomes a libidinous energy nondischarge, which is what the voyeur seeks.[2] The tension. But your remark indicates, in

---

[2] See, for example, Straus, "Shame As a Historiological Problem," in *Phenomenological Psychology.* (New York: Basic Books, 1966), p. 219.

my opinion, a radical misreading of the problem. Susan's "openness"—a willingness of the heart, if you will allow such a term—is not at all comparable to the activities of the voyeur. Susan draws near. Distance is not her thing—not by a long chalk. Frequently, as you know, she gets burned, but she always tries again. What is operating here, I suggest, is an attempt on your part to "stabilize" Susan's behavior in reference to a state-of-affairs that you feel should obtain. Susan gets married and lives happily ever after. Or: There is within Susan a certain amount of creativity which should be liberated and actualized. Susan becomes an artist and lives happily ever after.

But your norms are, I suggest, skewing your view of the problem, and very badly.

Let us take the first case. You reason: If Susan is happy or at least functioning in the present state of affairs (that is, moving from man to man as a silver dollar moves from hand to hand), then why is she seeing a shrink? Something is wrong. New behavior is indicated. Susan is to get married and live happily ever after. May I offer another view? That is, that "seeing a shrink" might be precisely a maneuver in a situation in which Susan *does not want* to get married and live happily ever after? That getting married and living happily ever after might be, for Susan, the worst of fates, and that in order to validate her nonacceptance of this norm she defines herself to herself as shrink-needing? That you are actually certifying the behavior which you seek to change? (When she says to you that she's not shrinkable, you should listen.)

Perhaps, Dr. Hodder, my logic is feeble, perhaps my intuitions are frail. It is, God knows, a complex and difficult question. Your perception that Susan is an artist of some kind *in potentia* is, I think, an acute one. But the proposition "Susan becomes an artist and lives happily ever after" is ridiculous. (I realize that I am couching the proposition in such terms—"happily ever after"—that it is ridiculous on the face of it, but there is ridiculousness piled upon ridiculousness.) Let me point out, if it has escaped your notice, that what an artist does, is fail. Any reading of the literature[3] (I mean the theory of artistic creation), however summary, will persuade you instantly that the paradigmatic artistic experience is that of failure. The actualization fails to meet, equal, the intuition. There is something "out there" which cannot be brought "here." This is standard. I don't mean bad artists, I mean good artists. There is no such thing as a "successful artist" (except, of course, in worldly terms). The proposition should read, "Susan becomes an artist and lives unhappily ever after." This is the case. Don't be deceived.

What I am saying is, that the therapy of choice is not clear. I deeply sympathize. You have a dilemma.

I ask you to note, by the way, that Susan's is not a seeking after instant gratification as dealt out by so-called encounter or sensitivity groups, nude

---

[3] Especially, perhaps, Ehrenzweig, *The Hidden Order of Art* (University of California Press, 1966), pp. 234–9.

marathons, or dope. None of this is what is going down. "Joy" is not Susan's bag. I praise her for seeking out you rather than getting involved with any of this other idiocy. Her forte, I would suggest, is mind, and if there are games being played they are being conducted with taste, decorum, and some amount of intellectual rigor. Not-bad games. When I take Susan out to dinner she does not order chocolate-covered ants, even if they are on the menu. (Have you, by the way, tried Alfredo's, at the corner of Bank and Hudson streets? It's wonderful.) (Parenthetically, the problem of analysts sleeping with their patients is well known and I understand that Susan has been routinely seducing you—a reflex, she can't help it—throughout the analysis. I understand that there is a new splinter group of therapists, behaviorists of some kind, who take this to be some kind of ethic? Is this true? Does this mean that they do it only when they want to, or whether they want to or not? At a dinner party the other evening a lady analyst was saying that three cases of this kind had recently come to her attention and she seemed to think that this was rather a lot. The problem of maintaining mentorship is, as we know, not easy. I think you have done very well in this regard, and God knows it must have been difficult, given those skirts Susan wears that unbutton up to the crotch and which she routinely leaves unbuttoned to the third button.)

Am I wandering too much for you? Bear with me. The world is waiting for the sunrise.

We are left, I submit, with the problem of her depressions. They are, I agree, terrible. Your idea that I am not "supportive" enough is, I think, wrong. I have found, as a practical matter, that the best thing to do is to just do ordinary things, read the newspaper for example, or watch basketball, or wash the dishes. That seems to allow her to come out of it better than any amount of so-called "support." (About the *chasmus hystericus* or hysterical yawning I don't worry any more. It is masking behavior, of course, but after all, you must allow us our tics. The world is waiting for the sunrise.) What do you do with a patient who finds the world unsatisfactory? The world *is* unsatisfactory; only a fool would deny it. I know that your own ongoing psychic structuralization is still going on—you are thirty-seven and I am forty-one—but you must be old enough by now to realize that shit is shit. Susan's perception that America has somehow got hold of the greed ethic and that the greed ethic has turned America into a tidy little hell is not, I think, wrong. What do you do with such a perception? Apply Band-Aids, I suppose. About her depressions, I wouldn't do anything. I'd leave them alone. Put on a record.[4]

Let me tell you a story.

One night we were at her place, about three a.m., and this man called, another lover, quite a well-known musician who is very good, very fast—a good man. He asked Susan "Is he there?," meaning me, and she said "Yes," and he said, "What are you doing?," and she said, "What do you think?," and he said,

---

[4] For example, Harrison, "Wah Wah," Apple Records, STCH 639, Side One, Track 3.

"When will you be finished?," and she said, "Never." Are you, Doctor dear, in a position to appreciate the beauty of this reply, in this context?

What I am saying is that Susan is wonderful. *As is*. There are not so many things around to which that word can be accurately applied. Therefore I must view your efforts to improve her with, let us say, a certain amount of ambivalence. If this makes me a negative factor in the analysis, so be it. I will be a negative factor until the cows come home, and cheerfully. I can't help it, Doctor, I am voting for the piano.

With best wishes,

"Repent, Harlequin!" Said the Ticktockman

1965

HARLAN ELLISON [b. 1934]

There are always those who ask, what is it all about? For those who need to ask, for those who need points sharply made, who need to know "where it's at," this:

> *The mass of men serve the state thus, not as men mainly, but as machines, with their bodies. They are the standing army, and the militia, jailors, constables, posse comitatus, etc. In most cases there is no free exercise whatever of the judgment or of the moral sense; but they put themselves on a level with wood and earth and stones; and wooden men can perhaps be manufactured that will serve the purpose as well. Such command no more respect than men of straw or a lump of dirt. They have the same sort of worth only as horses and dogs. Yet such as these even are commonly esteemed good citizens. Others—as most legislators, politicians, lawyers, ministers, and officeholders—serve the state chiefly with their heads; and, as they rarely make any moral distinctions, they are as likely to serve the Devil, without intending it, as God. A very few, as heroes, patriots, martyrs, reformers in the great sense, and* men, *serve the state with their consciences also, and so necessarily resist it for the most part; and they are commonly treated as enemies by it.*
>
> Henry David Thoreau
CIVIL DISOBEDIENCE

That is the heart of it. Now begin in the middle, and later learn the beginning; the end will take care of itself.

But because it was the very world it was, the very world they had allowed it to *become*, for months his activities did not come to the alarmed attention of The Ones Who Kept The Machine Functioning Smoothly, the ones who poured the very best butter over the cams and mainsprings of the culture. Not until it had become obvious that somehow, someway, he had become a notoriety, a celebrity, perhaps even a hero for (what Officialdom inescapably tagged) "an emotionally disturbed segment of the populace," did they turn it over to the Ticktockman and his legal machinery. But by then, because it was the very world it was, and they had no way to predict he would happen—possibly a strain of disease long-defunct, now, suddenly, reborn in a system where immunity had been forgotten, had lapsed—he had been allowed to become too real. Now he had form and substance.

He had become a *personality*, something they had filtered out of the system many decades before. But there it was, and there *he* was, a very definitely imposing personality. In certain circles—middle-class circles—it was thought disgusting. Vulgar ostentation. Anarchistic. Shameful. In others, there was only sniggering: those strata where thought is subjugated to form and ritual, niceties, proprieties. But down below, ah, down below, where the people always needed their saints and sinners, their bread and circuses, their heroes and villains, he was considered a Bolivar; a Napoleon; a Robin Hood; a Dick Bong (Ace of Aces); a Jesus; a Jomo Kenyatta.

And at the top—where, like socially-attuned Shipwreck Kellys, every tremor and vibration threatening to dislodge the wealthy, powerful and titled from their flagpoles—he was considered a menace; a heretic; a rebel; a disgrace; a peril. He was known down the line, to the very heart-meat core, but the important reactions were high above and far below. At the very top, at the very bottom.

So his file was turned over, along with his time-card and his cardioplate, to the office of the Ticktockman.

The Ticktockman: very much over six feet tall, often silent, a soft purring man when things went timewise. The Ticktockman.

Even in the cubicles of the hierarchy, where fear was generated, seldom suffered, he was called the Ticktockman. But no one called him that to his mask.

You don't call a man a hated name, not when that man, behind his mask, is capable of revoking the minutes, the hours, the days and nights, the years of your life. He was called the Master Timekeeper to his mask. It was safer that way.

"That is *what* he is," said the Ticktockman with genuine softness, "but not *who* he is. This time-card I'm holding in my left hand has a name on it, but it is the name of *what* he is, not *who* he is. The cardioplate here in my right hand is also named, but not *whom* named, merely *what* named. Before I can exercise proper revocation, I have to know *who* this *what* is."

To his staff, all the ferrets, all the loggers, all the finks, all the commex, even the mineez, he said, "Who is this Harlequin?"

He was not purring smoothly. Timewise, it was jangle.

However, it *was* the longest speech they had ever heard him utter at one time, the staff, the ferrets, the loggers, the finks, the commex, but not the mineez, who usually weren't around to know, in any case. But even they scurried to find out.

Who is the Harlequin?

High above the third level of the city, he crouched on the humming aluminum-frame platform of the air-boat (foof! air-boat, indeed! swizzleskid is what it was, with a tow-rack jerry-rigged) and he stared down at the neat Mondrian arrangement of the buildings.

Somewhere nearby, he could hear the metronomic left-right-left of the 2:47 PM shift, entering the Timkin roller-bearing plant in their sneakers. A minute later, precisely, he heard the softer right-left-right of the 5:00 AM formation, going home.

An elfin grin spread across his tanned features, and his dimples appeared for a moment. Then, scratching at his thatch of auburn hair, he shrugged within his motley, as though girding himself for what came next, and threw the joystick forward, and bent into the wind as the air-boat dropped. He skimmed over a slidewalk, purposely dropping a few feet to crease the tassels of the ladies of fashion, and—inserting thumbs in large ears—he stuck out his tongue, rolled his eyes and went wugga-wugga-wugga. It was a minor diversion. One pedestrian skittered and tumbled, sending parcels everywhichway, another wet herself, a third keeled slantwise and the walk was stopped automatically by the servitors till she could be resuscitated. It was a minor diversion.

Then he swirled away on a vagrant breeze, and was gone. Hi-ho.

As he rounded the cornice of the Time-Motion Study Building, he saw the shift, just boarding the slidewalk. With practiced motion and an absolute conservation of movement, they sidestepped up onto the slow-strip and (in a chorus line reminiscent of a Busby Berkeley film of the antediluvian 1930s) advanced across the strips ostrich-walking till they were lined up on the express-strip.

Once more, in anticipation, the elfin grin spread, and there was a tooth missing back there on the left side. He dipped, skimmed, and swooped over them; and then, scrunching about on the air-boat, he released the holding pins that fastened shut the ends of the home-made pouring troughs that kept his cargo from dumping prematurely. And as he pulled the trough-pins, the air-boat slid over the factory workers and one hundred and fifty thousand dollars' worth of jelly beans cascaded down on the expresstrip.

Jelly beans! Millions and billions of purples and yellows and greens and licorice and grape and raspberry and mint and round and smooth and crunchy outside and soft-mealy inside and sugary and bouncing jouncing tumbling clittering clattering skittering fell on the heads and shoulders and hardhats and carapaces of the Timkin workers, tinkling on the slidewalk and bouncing away and rolling about underfoot and filling the sky on their way down with all the colors of joy and childhood and holidays, coming down in a steady rain, a solid wash, a torrent of color and sweetness out of the sky from above, and entering a universe of sanity and metronomic order with quite-mad coocoo newness. Jelly beans!

The shift workers howled and laughed and were pelted, and broke ranks, and the jelly beans managed to work their way into the mechanism of the slidewalks after which there was a hideous scraping as the sound of a million fingernails rasped down a quarter of a million blackboards, followed by a coughing and a sputtering, and then the slidewalks all stopped and everyone was dumped thisawayandthataway in a jackstraw tumble, still laughing and popping little jelly bean eggs of childish color into their mouths. It was a holiday, and a jollity, an absolute insanity, a giggle. But . . .

The shift was delayed seven minutes.

They did not get home for seven minutes.

The master schedule was thrown off by seven minutes.

Quotas were delayed by inoperative slidewalks for seven minutes.

He had tapped the first domino in the line, and one after another, like chik chik chik, the others had fallen.

He had tapped the first domino in the line, and one after another, like chik chik chik, the others had fallen.

The System had been seven minutes' worth of disrupted. It was a tiny matter, one hardly worthy of note, but in a society where the single driving force was order and unity and equality and promptness and clocklike precision and attention to the clock, reverence of the gods of the passage of time, it was a disaster of major importance.

So he was ordered to appear before the Ticktockman. It was broadcast across every channel of the communications web. He was ordered to be *there* at 7:00 dammit on time. And they waited, and they waited, but he didn't show up till almost ten-thirty, at which time he merely sang a little song about moonlight in a place no one had ever heard of, called Vermont, and vanished again. But they had all been waiting since seven, and it wrecked *hell* with their schedules. So the question remained: Who is the Harlequin?

But the *unasked* question (more important of the two) was: how did we get *into* this position, where a laughing, irresponsible japer of jabberwocky and jive could disrupt our entire economic and cultural life with a hundred and fifty thousand dollars' worth of jelly beans . . .

Jelly for God's sake *beans!* This is madness! Where did he get the money to buy a hundred and fifty thousand dollars' worth of jelly beans? (They knew it would have cost that much, because they had a team of Situation Analysts pulled off another assignment, and rushed to the slidewalk scene to sweep up and count the candies, and produce findings, which disrupted *their* schedules and threw their entire branch at least a day behind.) Jelly beans! Jelly . . . *beans?* Now wait a second—a second accounted for—no one has manufactured jelly beans for over a hundred years. Where did he get jelly beans?

That's another good question. More than likely it will never be answered to your complete satisfaction. But then, how many questions ever are?

The middle you know. Here is the beginning. How it starts:

A desk pad. Day for day, and turn each day. 9:00—open the mail. 9:45—appointment with planning commission board. 10:30—discuss installation progress charts with J.L. 11:45—pray for rain. 12:00—lunch. *And so it goes.*

"I'm sorry, Miss Grant, but the time for interviews was set at 2:30, and it's almost five now. I'm sorry you're late, but those are the rules. You'll have to wait till next year to submit application for this college again." *And so it goes.*

The 10:10 local stops at Cresthaven, Galesville, Tonawanda Junction, Selby and Farnhurst, but not at Indiana City, Lucasville and Colton, except on Sunday. The 10:35 express stops at Galesville, Selby and Indiana City, except on Sundays & Holidays, at which time it stops at . . . *and so it goes.*

"I couldn't wait, Fred. I had to be at Pierre Cartain's by 3:00, and you said you'd meet me under the clock in the terminal at 2:45, and you weren't there, so I had to go on. You're always late, Fred. If you'd been there, we could have sewed it up together, but as it was, well, I took the order alone . . ." *And so it goes.*

Dear Mr. and Mrs. Atterley: In reference to your son Gerold's constant tardiness, I am afraid we will have to suspend him from school unless some more reliable method can be instituted guaranteeing he will arrive at his classes on time. Granted he is an exemplary student, and his marks are high, his constant flouting of the schedules of this school makes it impractical to maintain him in a system where the other children seem capable of getting where they are supposed to be on time *and so it goes.*

YOU CANNOT VOTE UNLESS YOU APPEAR AT 8:45 AM.

"I don't care if the script is *good*, I need it Thursday!"

CHECK-OUT TIME IS 2:00 PM.

"You got here late. The job's taken. Sorry."

YOUR SALARY HAS BEEN DOCKED FOR TWENTY MINUTES TIME LOST.

"God, what time is it, I've gotta run!"

And so it goes. And so it goes. And so it goes. And so it goes goes goes goes goes tick tock tick tock tick tock and one day we no longer let time serve us, we serve time and we are slaves of the schedule, worshippers of the sun's passing, bound into a life predicated on restrictions because the system will not function if we don't keep the schedule tight.

Until it becomes more than a minor inconvenience to be late. It becomes a sin. Then a crime. Then a crime punishable by this:

EFFECTIVE 15 JULY 2389 12:00:00 midnight, the office of the Master Timekeeper will require all citizens to submit their time-cards and cardioplates for processing. In accordance with Statute 555-7-SGH-999 governing the revocation of time per capita, all cardioplates will be keyed to the individual holder and—

What they had done, was devise a method of curtailing the amount of life a person could have. If he was ten minutes late, he lost ten minutes of his life. An hour was proportionately worth more revocation. If someone was consistently tardy, he might find himself, on a Sunday night, receiving a communiqué from the Master Timekeeper that his time had run out, and he would be "turned off" at high noon on Monday, please straighten your affairs, sir, madame or bisex.

And so, by this simple scientific expedient (utilizing a scientific process held dearly secret by the Ticktockman's office) the System was maintained. It was the only expedient thing to do. It was, after all, patriotic. The schedules had to be met. After all, there *was* a war on!

But, wasn't there always?

"Now that is really disgusting," the Harlequin said, when Pretty Alice showed him the wanted poster. "Disgusting and *highly* improbable. After all, this isn't the Day of the Desperado. A *wanted* poster!"

"You know," Pretty Alice noted, "you speak with a great deal of inflection."

"I'm sorry," said the Harlequin, humbly.

"No need to be sorry. You're always saying 'I'm sorry.' You have such massive guilt, Everett, it's really very sad."

"I'm sorry," he said again, then pursed his lips so the dimples appeared momentarily. He hadn't wanted to say that at all. "I have to go out again. I have to *do* something."

Pretty Alice slammed her coffee-bulb down on the counter. "Oh for God's *sake*, Everett, can't you stay home just *one* night! Must you always be out in that ghastly clown suit, running around an*noy*ing people?"

"I'm—" He stopped, and clapped the jester's hat onto his auburn thatch with a tiny tingling of bells. He rose, rinsed out his coffee-bulb at the spray, and put it into the dryer for a moment. "I have to go."

She didn't answer. The faxbox was purring, and she pulled a sheet out, read it, threw it toward him on the counter. "It's about you. Of course. You're ridiculous."

He read it quickly. It said the Ticktockman was trying to locate him. He didn't care, he was going out to be late again. At the door, dredging for an exit line, he hurled back petulantly, "Well, *you* speak with inflection, *too!*"

Pretty Alice rolled her pretty eyes heavenward. "You're ridiculous." The Harlequin stalked out, slamming the door, which sighed shut softly, and locked itself.

There was a gentle knock, and Pretty Alice got up with an exhalation of exasperated breath, and opened the door. He stood there. "I'll be back about ten-thirty, okay?"

She pulled a rueful face. "Why do you tell me that? Why? You *know* you'll be late! You *know* it! You're *always* late, so why do you tell me these dumb things?" She closed the door.

On the other side, the Harlequin nodded to himself. *She's right. She's always right. I'll be late. I'm always late. Why do I tell her these dumb things?*

He shrugged again, and went off to be late once more.

He had fired off the firecracker rockets that said: I will attend the 115th annual International Medical Association Invocation at 8:00 PM precisely. I do hope you will all be able to join me.

The words had burned in the sky, and of course the authorities were there, lying in wait for him. They assumed, naturally, that he would be late. He arrived twenty minutes early, while they were setting up the spiderwebs to trap and hold him. Blowing a large bullhorn, he frightened and unnerved them so, their own moisturized encirclement webs sucked closed, and they were hauled up, kicking and shrieking, high above the amphitheater's floor. The Harlequin laughed and laughed, and apologized profusely. The physicians, gathered in solemn conclave, roared with laughter, and accepted the Harlequin's apologies with exaggerated bowing and posturing, and a merry time was had by all, who thought the Harlequin was a regular foofaraw in fancy pants; all, that is, but the authorities, who had been sent out by the office of the Ticktockman; they hung there like so much dockside cargo, hauled up above the floor of the amphitheater in a most unseemly fashion.

(In another part of the same city where the Harlequin carried on his "activities," totally unrelated in every way to what concerns us here, save that it illustrates the Ticktockman's power and import, a man named Marshall Delahanty received his turn-off notice from the Ticktockman's office. His wife received the notification from the gray-suited minee who delivered it, with the traditional "look of sorrow" plastered hideously across his face. She knew what it was, even without unsealing it. It was a billet-doux of immediate recognition to everyone these days. She gasped, and held it as though it were a glass slide tinged with botulism, and prayed it was not for her. Let it be for Marsh, she thought, brutally, realistically, or one of the kids, but not for me, please dear God, not for me. And then she opened it, and it *was* for Marsh, and she was at one and the same time horrified and relieved. The next trooper in the line had caught the bullet. "Marshall," she screamed, "Marshall! Termination, Marshall! OhmiGod, Marshall, whattl we do, whattl we do, Marshall omigodmarshall . . ." and in their home that night was the sound of tearing paper and fear, and the stink of madness went up the flue and there was nothing, absolutely nothing they could do about it.

(But Marshall Delahanty tried to run. And early the next day, when turn-off time came, he was deep in the Canadian forest two hundred miles away, and the office of the Ticktockman blanked his cardioplate, and Marshall Delahanty keeled over, running, and his heart stopped, and the blood dried up on its way to his brain, and he was dead that's all. One light went out on the sector map in the office of the Master Timekeeper, while notification was entered for fax reproduction, and Georgette Delahanty's name was entered on the dole roles till she could remarry. Which is the end of the footnote, and all the point that need be made, except don't laugh, because that is what would happen to the Harlequin if ever the Ticktockman found out his real name. It isn't funny.)

The shopping level of the city was thronged with the Thursday-colors of the buyers. Women in canary yellow chitons and men in pseudo-Tyrolean outfits that were jade and leather and fit very tightly, save for the balloon pants.

When the Harlequin appeared on the still-being-constructed shell of the new Efficiency Shopping Center, his bullhorn to his elfishly-laughing lips, everyone pointed and stared, and he berated them:

"Why let them order you about? Why let them tell you to hurry and scurry like ants or maggots? Take your time! Saunter a while! Enjoy the sunshine, enjoy the breeze, let life carry you at your own pace! Don't be slaves of time, it's a helluva way to die, slowly, by degrees . . . down with the Ticktockman!"

Who's the nut? most of the shoppers wanted to know. Who's the nut oh wow I'm gonna be late I gotta run . . .

And the construction gang on the Shopping Center received an urgent order from the office of the Master Timekeeper that the dangerous criminal known as the Harlequin was atop their spire, and their aid was urgently needed in apprehending him. The work crew said no, they would lose time on their construction schedule, but the Ticktockman managed to pull the proper threads of governmental webbing, and they were told to cease work and catch that nitwit up there on the spire; up there with the bullhorn. So a dozen and more burly workers began climbing into their construction platforms, releasing the a-grav plates, and rising toward the Harlequin.

After the debacle (in which, through the Harlequin's attention to personal safety, no one was seriously injured), the workers tried to reassemble, and assault him again, but it was too late. He had vanished. It had attracted quite a crowd, however, and the shopping cycle was thrown off by hours, simply hours. The purchasing needs of the system were therefore falling behind, and so measures were taken to accelerate the cycle for the rest of the day, but it got bogged down and speeded up and they sold too many float-valves and not nearly enough wegglers, which meant that the popli ratio was off, which made it necessary to rush cases and cases of spoiling Smash-O to stores that usually needed a case only every three or four hours. The shipments were bollixed, the transshipments were misrouted, and in the end, even the swizzleskid industries felt it.

"Don't come back till you have him!" the Ticktockman said, very quietly, very sincerely, extremely dangerously.

They used dogs. They used probes. They used cardioplate crossoffs. They used teepers. They used bribery. They used stiktytes. They used intimidation. They used torment. They used torture. They used finks. They used cops. They used search&seizure. They used fallaron. They used betterment incentive. They used fingerprints. They used the Bertillon system. They used cunning. They used guile. They used treachery. They used Raoul Mitgong, but he didn't help much. They used applied physics. They used techniques of criminology.

And what the hell: they caught him.

After all, his name was Everett C. Marm, and he wasn't much to begin with, except a man who had no sense of time.

"Repent, Harlequin!" said the Ticktockman.

"Get stuffed!" the Harlequin replied, sneering.

"You've been late a total of sixty-three years, five months, three weeks, two days, twelve hours, forty-one minutes, fifty-nine seconds, point oh three six one one one microseconds. You've used up everything you can, and more. I'm going to turn you off."

"Scare someone else. I'd rather be dead than live in a dumb world with a bogeyman like you."

"It's my job."

"You're full of it. You're a tyrant. You have no right to order people around and kill them if they show up late."

"You can't adjust. You can't fit in."

"Unstrap me, and I'll fit my fist into your mouth."

"You're a nonconformist."

"That didn't used to be a felony."

"It is now. Live in the world around you."

"I hate it. It's a terrible world."

"Not everyone thinks so. Most people enjoy order."

"I don't, and most of the people I know don't."

"That's not true. How do you think we caught you?"

"I'm not interested."

"A girl named Pretty Alice told us who you were."

"That's a lie."

"It's true. You unnerve her. She wants to belong; she wants to conform; I'm going to turn you off."

"Then do it already, and stop arguing with me."

"I'm not going to turn you off."

"You're an idiot!"

"Repent, Harlequin!" said the Ticktockman.

"Get stuffed."

So they sent him to Coventry. And in Coventry they worked him over. It was just like what they did to Winston Smith in NINETEEN EIGHTY-FOUR, which was a book none of them knew about, but the techniques are really quite ancient, and so they did it to Everett C. Marm; and one day, quite a long time later, the Harlequin appeared on the communications web, appearing elfin and dimpled and bright-eyed, and not at all brainwashed, and he said he had been wrong, that it was a good, a very good thing indeed, to belong, to be right on time hip-ho and away we go, and everyone stared up at him on the public screens that covered an entire city block, and they said to themselves, well, you see, he was just a nut after all, and if that's the way the system is run, then let's do it that way, because it doesn't pay to fight city hall, or in this case, the Ticktockman. So Everett C. Marm was destroyed, which was a loss, because of what Thoreau said earlier, but you can't make an omelet without breaking a few eggs, and in every revolution a few die who shouldn't, but they have to, because that's the way it happens, and if you make only a little change, then it seems to be worthwhile. Or, to make the point lucidly:

"Uh, excuse me, sir, I, uh, don't know how to uh, to uh, tell you this, but you were three minutes late. The schedule is a little, uh, bit off."

He grinned sheepishly.

"That's ridiculous!" murmured the Ticktockman behind his mask. "Check your watch." And then he went into his office, going *mrmee, mrmee, mrmee, mrmee.*

Everyday Use 1973
FOR YOUR GRANDMAMA
ALICE WALKER [b. 1944]

I will wait for her in the yard that Maggie and I made so clean and wavy yesterday afternoon. A yard like this is more comfortable than most people know. It is not just a yard. It is like an extended living room. When the hard clay is swept clean as a floor and the fine sand around the edges lined with tiny, irregular grooves anyone can come and sit and look up into the elm tree and wait for the breezes that never come inside the house.

Maggie will be nervous until after her sister goes: she will stand hopelessly in corners homely and ashamed of the burn scars down her arms and legs, eyeing her sister with a mixture of envy and awe. She thinks her sister has held life always in the palm of one hand, that "no" is a word the world never learned to say to her.

You've no doubt seen those TV shows where the child who has "made it" is confronted, as a surprise, by her own mother and father, tottering in weakly from backstage. (A pleasant surprise, of course: What would they do if parent and child came on the show only to curse out and insult each other?) On TV mother and child embrace and smile into each other's faces. Sometimes the mother and father weep, the child wraps them in her arms and leans across the table to tell how she would not have made it without their help. I have seen these programs.

Sometimes I dream a dream in which Dee and I are suddenly brought together on a TV program of this sort. Out of a dark and soft-seated limousine I am ushered into a bright room filled with many people. There I meet a smiling, gray, sporty man like Johnny Carson who shakes my hand and tells me what a fine girl I have. Then we are on the stage and Dee is embracing me with tears in her eyes. She pins on my dress a large orchid, even though she has told me once that she thinks orchids are tacky flowers.

In real life I am a large, big-boned woman with rough, man-working hands. In the winter I wear flannel nightgowns to bed and overalls during the day. I can kill and clean a hog as mercilessly as a man. My fat keeps me hot in zero weather. I can work outside all day, breaking ice to get water for washing. I can eat pork liver cooked over the open fire minutes after it comes steaming from the hog. One winter I knocked a bull calf straight in the brain between the eyes with a sledge hammer and had the meat hung up to chill before nightfall. But of course all this does not show on television. I am the way my daughter would want me to be: a hundred pounds lighter, my skin like an uncooked barley pancake. My hair glistens in the hot bright lights. Johnny Carson has much to do to keep up with my quick and witty tongue.

But that is a mistake. I know even before I wake up. Who ever knew a Johnson with a quick tongue? Who can even imagine me looking a strange white man in the eye? It seems to me I have talked to them always with one foot raised in flight, with my head turned in whichever way is farthest from them. Dee, though. She would always look anyone in the eye. Hesitation was no part of her nature.

"How do I look, Mama?" Maggie says, showing just enough of her thin body enveloped in pink skirt and red blouse for me to know she's there, almost hidden by the door.

"Come out into the yard," I say.

Have you ever seen a lame animal, perhaps a dog run over by some careless person rich enough to own a car, sidle up to someone who is ignorant enough to be kind to him? That is the way my Maggie walks. She has been like this, chin on chest, eyes on ground, feet in shuffle, ever since the fire that burned the other house to the ground.

Dee is lighter than Maggie, with nicer hair and a fuller figure. She's a woman now, though sometimes I forget. How long ago was it that the other house burned? Ten, twelve years? Sometimes I can still hear the flames and feel Maggie's arms sticking to me, her hair smoking and her dress falling off her in little black papery flakes. Her eyes seemed stretched open, blazed open by the flames reflected in them. And Dee. I see her standing off under the sweet gum tree she used to dig gum out of; a look of concentration on her face as she watched the last dingy gray board of the house fall in toward the red-hot brick chimney. Why don't you do a dance around the ashes? I'd wanted to ask her. She had hated the house that much.

I used to think she hated Maggie, too. But that was before we raised the money, the church and me, to send her to Augusta to school. She used to read to us without pity; forcing words, lies, other folks' habits, whole lives upon us two, sitting trapped and ignorant underneath her voice. She washed us in a river of make-believe, burned us with a lot of knowledge we didn't necessarily need to know. Pressed us to her with the serious way she read, to shove us away at just the moment, like dimwits, we seemed about to understand.

Dee wanted nice things. A yellow organdy dress to wear to her graduation from high school; black pumps to match a green suit she'd made from an old suit somebody gave me. She was determined to stare down any disaster in her efforts. Her eyelids would not flicker for minutes at a time. Often I fought off the temptation to shake her. At sixteen she had a style of her own: and knew what style was.

I never had an education myself. After second grade the school was closed down. Don't ask me why: in 1927 colored asked fewer questions than they do now. Sometimes Maggie reads to me. She stumbles along good-naturedly but can't see well. She knows she is not bright. Like good looks and money, quickness passed her by. She will marry John Thomas (who has mossy teeth in an earnest face) and then I'll be free to sit here and I guess just sing church songs to myself. Although I never was a good singer. Never could carry a tune. I was always better at a man's job. I used to love to milk till I was hoofed in the side in '49. Cows are soothing and slow and don't bother you, unless you try to milk them the wrong way.

I have deliberately turned my back on the house. It is three rooms, just like the one that burned, except the roof is tin; they don't make shingle roofs any more. There are no real windows, just some holes cut in the sides, like the portholes in a ship, but not round and not square, with rawhide holding the shutters up on the outside. This house is in a pasture, too, like the other one. No doubt when Dee sees it she will want to tear it down. She wrote me once that no matter where we "choose" to live, she will manage to come see us. But she will never bring her friends. Maggie and I thought about this and Maggie asked me, "Mama, when did Dee ever *have* any friends?"

She had a few. Furtive boys in pink shirts hanging about on washday after school. Nervous girls who never laughed. Impressed with her they worshiped the well-turned phrase, the cute shape, the scalding humor that erupted like bubbles in lye. She read to them.

When she was courting Jimmy T she didn't have much time to pay to us, but turned all her faultfinding power on him. He *flew* to marry a cheap gal from a family of ignorant flashy people. She hardly had time to recompose herself.

When she comes I will meet — but there they are!

Maggie attempts to make a dash for the house, in her shuffling way, but I stay her with my hand. "Come back here," I say. And she stops and tries to dig a well in the sand with her toe.

It is hard to see them clearly through the strong sun. But even the first glimpse of leg out of the car tells me it is Dee. Her feet were always neat-looking, as if God himself had shaped them with a certain style. From the other side of the car comes a short, stocky man. Hair is all over his head a foot long and hanging from his chin like a kinky mule tail. I hear Maggie suck in her breath. "Uhnnnh," is what it sounds like. Like when you see the wriggling end of a snake just in front of your foot on the road. "Uhnnnh."

Dee next. A dress down to the ground, in this hot weather. A dress so loud it hurts my eyes. There are yellows and oranges enough to throw back the light of the sun. I feel my whole face warming from the heat waves it throws out. Earrings, too, gold and hanging down to her shoulders. Bracelets dangling and making noises when she moves her arm up to shake the folds of the dress out of her armpits. The dress is loose and flows, and as she walks closer, I like it. I hear Maggie go "Uhnnnh" again. It is her sister's hair. It stands straight up like the wool on a sheep. It is black as night and around the edges are two long pigtails that rope about like small lizards disappearing behind her ears.

"Wa-su-zo-Tean-o!" she says, coming on in that gliding way the dress makes her move. The short stocky fellow with the hair to his navel is all grinning and he follows up with "Asalamalakim, my mother and sister!" He moves to hug Maggie but she falls back, right up against the back of my chair. I feel her trembling there and when I look up I see the perspiration falling off her chin.

"Don't get up," says Dee. Since I am stout it takes something of a push. You can see me trying to move a second or two before I make it. She turns, showing white heels through her sandals, and goes back to the car. Out she peeks next with a Polaroid. She stoops down quickly and lines up picture after picture of me sitting there in front of the house with Maggie cowering behind me. She never takes a shot without making sure the house is included. When a cow comes nibbling around the edge of the yard she snaps it and me and Maggie *and* the house. Then she puts the Polaroid in the back seat of the car, and comes up and kisses me on the forehead.

Meanwhile Asalamalakim is going through motions with Maggie's hand. Maggie's hand is as limp as a fish, and probably as cold, despite the sweat, and she keeps trying to pull it back. It looks like Asalamalakim wants to shake hands but wants to do it fancy. Or maybe he don't know how people shake hands. Anyhow, he soon gives up on Maggie.

"Well," I say. "Dee."

"No, Mama," she says. "Not 'Dee,' Wangero Leewanika Kemanjo!"

"What happened to 'Dee'?" I wanted to know.

"She's dead," Wangero said. "I couldn't bear it any longer being named after the people who oppress me."

"You know as well as me you was named after your aunt Dicie," I said. Dicie is my sister. She named Dee. We called her "Big Dee" after Dee was born.

"But who was *she* named after?" asked Wangero.

"I guess after Grandma Dee," I said.

"And who was she named after?" asked Wangero.

"Her mother," I said, and saw Wangero was getting tired. "That's about as far back as I can trace it," I said. Though, in fact, I probably could have carried it back beyond the Civil War through the branches.

"Well," said Asalamalakim, "there you are."

"Uhnnnh," I heard Maggie say.

"There I was not," I said, "before 'Dicie' cropped up in our family, so why should I try to trace it that far back?"

He just stood there grinning, looking down on me like somebody inspecting a Model A car. Every once in a while he and Wangero sent eye signals over my head.

"How do you pronounce this name?" I asked.

"You don't have to call me by it if you don't want to," said Wangero.

"Why shouldn't I?" I asked. "If that's what you want us to call you, we'll call you."

"I know it might sound awkward at first," said Wangero.

"I'll get used to it," I said. "Ream it out again."

Well, soon we got the name out of the way. Asalamalakim had a name twice as long and three times as hard. After I tripped over it two or three times he told me to just call him Hakim-a-barber. I wanted to ask him was he a barber, but I didn't really think he was, so I didn't ask.

"You must belong to those beef-cattle peoples down the road," I said. They said "Asalamalakim" when they met you, too, but they didn't shake hands. Always too busy: feeding the cattle, fixing the fences, putting up salt-lick shelters, throwing down hay. When the white folks poisoned some of the herd the men stayed up all night with rifles in their hands. I walked a mile and a half just to see the sight.

Hakim-a-barber said, "I accept some of their doctrines, but farming and raising cattle is not my style." (They didn't tell me, and I didn't ask, whether Wangero [Dee] had really gone and married him.)

We sat down to eat and right away he said he didn't eat collards and pork was unclean. Wangero, though, went on through the chitlins and corn bread, the greens and everything else. She talked a blue streak over the sweet potatoes. Everything delighted her. Even the fact that we still used the benches her daddy made for the table when we couldn't afford to buy chairs.

"Oh, Mama!" she cried. Then turned to Hakim-a-barber. "I never knew how lovely these benches are. You can feel the rump prints," she said, running her hands underneath her and along the bench. Then she gave a sigh and her hand closed over Grandma Dee's butter dish. "That's it!" she said. "I knew there was something I wanted to ask you if I could have." She jumped up from the table and went over in the corner where the churn stood, the milk in its clabber by now. She looked at the churn and looked at it.

"This churn top is what I need," she said. "Didn't Uncle Buddy whittle it out of a tree you all used to have?"

"Yes," I said.

"Uh huh," she said happily. "And I want the dasher, too."

"Uncle Buddy whittle that, too?" asked the barber.

Dee (Wangero) looked up at me.

"Aunt Dee's first husband whittled the dash," said Maggie so low you almost couldn't hear her. "His name was Henry, but they called him Stash."

"Maggie's brain is like an elephant's," Wangero said, laughing. "I can use the churn top as a centerpiece for the alcove table," she said, sliding a plate over the churn, "and I'll think of something artistic to do with the dasher."

When she finished wrapping the dasher the handle stuck out. I took it for a moment in my hands. You didn't even have to look close to see where hands pushing the dasher up and down to make butter had left a kind of sink in the wood. In fact, there were a lot of small sinks; you could see where thumbs and fingers had sunk into the wood. It was beautiful light yellow wood, from a tree that grew in the yard where Big Dee and Stash had lived.

After dinner Dee (Wangero) went to the trunk at the foot of my bed and started rifling through it. Maggie hung back in the kitchen over the dishpan. Out came Wangero with two quilts. They had been pieced by Grandma Dee and then Big Dee and me had hung them on the quilt frames on the front porch and quilted them. One was in the Lone Star pattern. The other was Walk Around the Mountain. In both of them were scraps of dresses Grandma Dee had worn fifty and more years ago. Bits and pieces of Grandpa Jarrell's Paisley shirts. And one teeny faded blue piece, about the size of a penny matchbox, that was from Great Grandpa Ezra's uniform that he wore in the Civil War.

"Mama," Wangero said sweet as a bird. "Can I have these old quilts?"

I heard something fall in the kitchen, and a minute later the kitchen door slammed.

"Why don't you take one or two of the others?" I asked. "These old things was just done by me and Big Dee from some tops your grandma pieced before she died."

"No," said Wangero. "I don't want those. They are stitched around the borders by machine."

"That'll make them last better," I said.

"That's not the point," said Wangero. "These are all pieces of dresses Grandma used to wear. She did all this stitching by hand. Imagine!" She held the quilts securely in her arms, stroking them.

"Some of the pieces, like those lavender ones, come from old clothes her mother handed down to her," I said, moving up to touch the quilts. Dee (Wangero) moved back just enough so that I couldn't reach the quilts. They already belonged to her.

"Imagine!" she breathed again, clutching them closely to her bosom.

"The truth is," I said, "I promised to give them quilts to Maggie, for when she marries John Thomas."

She gasped like a bee had stung her.

"Maggie can't appreciate these quilts!" she said. "She'd probably be backward enough to put them to everyday use."

"I reckon she would," I said. "God knows I been saving 'em for long enough with nobody using 'em. I hope she will!" I didn't want to bring up how I had offered Dee (Wangero) a quilt when she went away to college. Then she had told me they were old-fashioned, out of style.

"But they're *priceless!*" she was saying now, furiously; for she has a temper. "Maggie would put them on the bed and in five years they'd be in rags. Less than that!"

"She can always make some more," I said. "Maggie knows how to quilt."

Dee (Wangero) looked at me with hatred. "You just will not understand. The point is these quilts, *these* quilts!"

"Well," I said, stumped. "What would *you* do with them?"

"Hang them," she said. As if that was the only thing you *could* do with quilts.

Maggie by now was standing in the door. I could almost hear the sound her feet made as they scraped over each other.

"She can have them, Mama," she said, like somebody used to never winning anything, or having anything reserved for her. "I can 'member Grandma Dee without the quilts."

I looked at her hard. She had filled her bottom lip with checkerberry snuff and it gave her face a kind of dopey, hangdog look. It was Grandma Dee and Big Dee who taught her how to quilt herself. She stood there with her scarred hands hidden in the folds of her skirt. She looked at her sister with something like fear but she wasn't mad at her. This was Maggie's portion. This was the way she knew God to work.

When I looked at her like that something hit me in the top of my head and ran down to the soles of my feet. Just like when I'm in church and the spirit of God touches me and I get happy and shout. I did something I never had done before: hugged Maggie to me, then dragged her on into the room, snatched the quilts out of Miss Wangero's hands and dumped them into Maggie's lap. Maggie just sat there on my bed with her mouth open.

"Take one or two of the others," I said to Dee.

But she turned without a word and went out to Hakim-a-barber.

"You just don't understand," she said, as Maggie and I came out to the car.

"What don't I understand?" I wanted to know.

"Your heritage," she said. And then she turned to Maggie, kissed her, and said, "You ought to try to make something of yourself, too, Maggie. It's really a new day for us. But from the way you and Mama still live you'd never know it."

She put on some sunglasses that hid everything above the tip of her nose and her chin.

Maggie smiled; maybe at the sunglasses. But a real smile, not scared. After we watched the car dust settle I asked Maggie to bring me a dip of snuff. And then the two of us sat there just enjoying, until it was time to go in the house and go to bed.

Winter Count 1973: Geese, They Flew Over in a Storm 1981

BARRY HOLSTUN LOPEZ [b. 1945]

He followed the bellboy off the elevator, through a foyer with forlorn leather couches, noting how low the ceiling was, with its white plaster flowers in bas-relief—and that there were no windows. He followed him down a long corridor dank with an air of fugitives, past dark, impenetrable doors. At the distant end of the next corridor he saw gray thunderheads and the black ironwork of a fire escape. The boy slowed down and reached out to slide a thick key into the lock and he heard the sudden alignment of steel tumblers and their ratchet click. The door swung open and the boy entered, with the suitcase bouncing against the crook at the back of his knee.

He tipped the boy, having no idea what amount was now thought proper. The boy departed, leaving the room sealed off as if in a vacuum. The key with the ornate brass fob lay on a glass table. The man stood by the bed with his hands folded at his lips as though in prayer. Slowly he cleared away the drapes, the curtains and the blinds and stared out at the bare sky. Wind whipped rain in streaks across the glass. He had never been to New Orleans. It was a vague streamer blowing in his memory, like a boyhood acquaintance with Lafcadio Hearn. Natchez Trace. Did Choctaw live here? he wondered. Or Chitamacha? Before them, worshippers of the sun.

He knew the plains better. Best. The high plains north of the Platte River.

He took off his shoes and lay on the bed. He was glad for the feel of the candlewick bedspread. Or was it chenille? He had had this kind of spread on his bed when he was a child. He removed his glasses and pinched the bridge of his nose. In all these years he had delivered so few papers, had come to enjoy much more listening to them, to the stories unfolding in them. It did not matter to him that the arguments were so abstruse they were all but impregnable, that the thought in them would turn to vapor, an arrested breath. He came to hear a story unfold, to regard its shape and effect. He thought one unpacked history, that it came like pemmican in a parfleche and was to be consumed in a hard winter.

The wind sucked at the windows and released them suddenly to rattle in their metal frames. It made him think of home, of the Sand Hills. He lay motionless on the bed and thought of the wind. Crow men racing naked in an April rain, with their hair, five-foot-long black banners, spiraling behind, splashing on the muscled rumps of white horses with brown ears.

1847 One man alone defended the Hat in a fight with the Crow

1847 White buffalo, Dusk killed it

1847 Daughter of Turtle Head, her clothes caught fire and she was burned up

1847 Three men who were women came

He got up and went to his bag. He took out three stout willow sticks and bound them as a tripod. From its apex he hung a beaded bag of white elk hide with long fringe. The fringe was wrinkled from having been folded against itself in his suit pocket.

1891 Medicine bundles, police tore them open

What did they want from him? A teacher. He taught, he did not write papers. He told the story of people coming up from the Tigris-Euphrates, starting there. Other years he would start in a different place—Olduvai, Afar Valley. Or in Tierra del Fuego with the Onas. He could as easily start in the First World of the Navajo. The point, he told his students, was not this. There was no point. It was a slab of meat. It was a rhythm to dance to. It was a cloak that cut the wind when it blew hard enough to crack your soul.

1859 Ravens froze, fell over

1804 Heavy spring snow. Even the dogs went snow-blind

He slept. In his rumpled suit. In the flat, reflected storm light his face appeared ironed smooth. The wind fell away from the building and he dreamed.

For a moment he was lost. Starlight Room. Tarpon Room. Oak Room. He was due—he thought suddenly of aging, of illness: *when our children, they had strangulations of the throat,* of the cure for *any* illness as he scanned the long program—in the Creole Room. He was due in the Creole Room. Roger Callahan, Nebraska State College: "Winter Counts from the Dakota, the Crow and the Blackfeet: Personal Histories." Jesus, he thought, why had he come? He had been asked. They had asked.
"Aha, Roger."
"I'm on time? I got—"
"You come right this way. I want you in front here. Everyone is very excited, very excited, you know. We're very glad you came. And how is Margaret?"
"Yes—. Margaret died. She died two years ago."

1837 Straight Calf took six horses from the Crow and gave them to Blue Cloud
    Woman's father and took her

1875 White Hair, he was killed in a river by an Omaha man

1943 John Badger Heart killed in an automobile crash

He did not hear the man. He sat. The histories began to cover him over like willows, thick as creek willows, and he reached out to steady himself in the pool of time.

He listened patiently to the other papers. Edward Rice Phillips, Purdue: "The Okipa Ceremony and Mandan Sexual Habits." The Mandan, he thought, they were all dead. Who would defend them? Renata Morrison, University of Texas: "The Role of Women in Northern Plains Religious Ceremonials."

> 1818 Sparrow Woman promised the Sun Dance in winter if the Cree didn't find us

> 1872 Comes Out of the Water, she ran off the Assiniboine horses

> 1904 Moving Gently, his sister hung herself

He tried to listen, but the words fell away like tumbled leaves. Cottonwoods. Winters so bad they would have to cut down cottonwood trees for the horses to eat. *So cold we got water from beaver holes only.* And years when they had to eat the horses. *We killed our ponies and ate them. No buffalo.*

Inside the windowless room (he could not remember which floor the elevator had opened on) everyone was seated in long rows. From the first row he could not see anyone. He shifted in his seat and his leather bag fell with a slap against the linoleum floor. How long had he been carrying papers from one place to another like this? He remembered a friend's poem about a snowy owl dead behind glass in a museum, no more to soar, to hunch and spread his wings and tail and fall silent as moonlight.

> 1809 Blue feathers found on the ground from unknown birds

> 1811 Weasel Sits Down came into camp with blue feathers tied in his hair

There was distant applause, like dry brush rattling in the wind.

Years before, defense of theory had concerned him. Not now. "I've thrown away everything that is no good," he told a colleague one summer afternoon on his porch, as though shouting over the roar of a storm. "I can no longer think of anything worse than proving you are right." He took what was left and he went on from there.

> 1851 No meat in camp. A man went to look for buffalo and was killed by two Arapaho

> 1854 The year they dragged the Arapaho's head through camp

". . . and my purpose in aligning these four examples is to clearly demonstrate an irrefutable, or what I consider an irrefutable, relationship: the Arikara never . . ."

When he was a boy his father had taken him one April morning to watch whooping cranes on estuaries of the Platte, headed for Alberta. The morning was crucial in the unfolding of his own life.

> 1916 My father drives east for hours in silence. We walk out into a field covered
> all over with river fog. The cranes, just their legs are visible

His own count would be personal, more personal, as though he were the only one.

> 1918 Father, shot dead. Argonne forest

The other years came around him now like soft velvet noses of horses touching his arms in the dark.

". . . while the Cheyenne, contrary to what Greenwold has had to say on this point but reinforcing what has been stated previously by Gregg and Houston, were more inclined . . ."

He wished for something to hold, something to touch, to strip leaves bare-handed from a chokecherry branch or to hear rain falling on the surface of a lake. In this windowless room he ached.

> 1833 Stars blowing around like snow. Some fall to the earth

> 1856 Reaches into the Enemy's Tipi has a dream and can't speak

> 1869 Fire Wagon, it comes

Applause.

He stood up and walked in quiet shoes to the stage. (Once in the middle of class he had stopped to explain his feeling about walking everywhere in silence.) He set his notes on the podium and covered them with his hands. In a clear voice, without apology for his informality or a look at his papers, he unfolded the winter counts of the Sioux warrior Blue Thunder, of the Blackfeet Bad Head, and of the Crow Extends His Paw. He stated that these were personal views of history, sometimes metaphorical, bearing on a larger, tribal history. He spoke of the confusion caused by translators who had tried to force agreement among several winter counts or who mistook mythic time for some other kind of real time. He concluded by urging less contention. "As professional historians, we have too often subordinated one system to another and forgotten all together the individual view, the poetic view, which is as close to the truth as the consensus. Or it can be as distant."

He felt the necklace of hawk talons pressing against his clavicles under the weight of his shirt.

The applause was respectful, thin, distracted. As he stepped away from the podium he realized it was perhaps foolish to have accepted the invitation. He could no longer make a final point. He had long ago lost touch with the definitive, the awful distance of reason. He wanted to go back to the podium. You can only tell the story as it was given to you, he wanted to say. Do not lie. Do not make it up.

He hesitated for a moment at the edge of the stage. He wished he were back in Nebraska with his students, to warn them: it is too dangerous for everyone to have the same story. The same things do not happen to everyone.

He passed through the murmuring crowd, through a steel fire door, down a hallway, up a flight of stairs, another, and emerged into palms in the lobby.

> 1823 A man, he was called Fifteen Horses, who was heyoka, a contrary, sacred clown, ran at the Crow backwards, shooting arrows at his own people. The Crow shot him in midair like a quail. He couldn't fool them

He felt the edge of self-pity, standing before a plate-glass window as wide as the spread of his arms and as tall as his house. He watched the storm that still raged, which he could not hear, which he had not been able to hear, bend trees to breaking, slash the surface of Lake Pontchartrain and raise air boiling over the gulf beyond. "Everything is held together with stories," he thought. "That is all that is holding us together, stories and compassion."

He turned quickly from the cold glass and went up in the silent elevator and ordered dinner. When it came, he threw back the drapes and curtains and opened the windows. The storm howled through his room and roared through his head. He breathed the wet air deep into his lungs. In the deepest distance, once, he heard the barking-dog sounds of geese, running like horses before a prairie thunderstorm.

QUESTIONS

1. Why do you suppose Roger Callahan carries a "medicine bag" and wears a hawk talon necklace?   **2.** What did tribal historians record in their "winter counts"? How do such records differ from the events recorded by academic historians?   **3.** Locate Callahan's own winter count observation. How does it differ from typical historical treatments of World War I?   **4.** Is there any relationship between the last winter count anecdote about the "contrary" who ran backwards and Callahan? Explain.

WRITING TOPICS

1. In an essay, expand on Callahan's statement to his colleague: "I can no longer think of anything worse than proving you are right."   **2.** Mindful of the contrast between Indian historical observations and the learned papers being read at the academic meeting, discuss Callahan's concluding remark: "As professional historians we have too often subordinated one system to another and forgotten all together the individual view, the poetic view, which is as close to the truth as the consensus. Or it can be as distant."

CONFORMITY
AND
REBELLION

Adam and Eve, Sistine Chapel (restored figures) by Michelangelo.

POETRY

Sonnet XVII   (1655)

JOHN MILTON   [1608–1674]

When I consider how my light is spent,[1]
    Ere half my days, in this dark world and wide,
    And that one talent[2] which is death to hide
    Lodged with me useless, though my soul more bent
To serve therewith my maker, and present
    My true account, lest he, returning, chide.
    'Doth God exact day-labour, light denied?'
    I fondly° ask; but Patience, to prevent   *foolishly*
That murmur, soon replies: 'God doth not need
    Either man's work or his own gifts; who best   10
    Bear his mild yoke, they serve him best; his state
Is kingly—thousands at his bidding speed
    And post o'er land and ocean without rest:
    They also serve who only stand and wait.'

from
Paradise Lost[1]   1667

JOHN MILTON   [1608–1674]

  "Is this the region, this the soil, the clime,"
Said then the lost archangel, "this the seat

Sonnet XVII
  [1] Milton was blind when he wrote this sonnet.
  [2] The parable of the Master who gave his servants "talents" (literally, coins of precious metal) occurs in Matthew 25:14–30.
Paradise Lost
  [1] The first part of *Paradise Lost*, a poem on the expulsion of Adam and Eve from the Garden of Eden, tells the story of Satan's rebellion against God, his defeat and expulsion from heaven. In this passage, Satan surveys the infernal region to which God has banished him.

That we must change for Heaven? this mournful gloom
For that celestial light? Be it so, since he
Who now is sovereign can dispose and bid
What shall be right: farthest from him is best,
Whom reason hath equaled, force hath made supreme
Above his equals. Farewell, happy fields,
Where joy forever dwells! Hail, horrors! hail,
Infernal world! and thou, profoundest Hell,   10
Receive thy new possessor, one who brings
A mind not to be changed by place or time.
The mind is its own place, and in itself
Can make a Heaven of Hell, a Hell of Heaven.
What matter where, if I be still the same,
And what I should be, all but° less than he   only
Whom thunder hath made greater? Here at least
We shall be free; th' Almighty hath not built
Here for his envy, will not drive us hence:
Here we may reign secure; and, in my choice,   20
To reign is worth ambition, though in Hell:
Better to reign in Hell than serve in Heaven.
But wherefore let we then our faithful friends,
Th' associates and copartners of our loss,
Lie thus astonished on th' oblivious pool,
And call them not to share with us their part
In this unhappy mansion, or once more
With rallied arms to try what may be yet
Regained in Heaven, or what more lost in Hell?"

QUESTIONS
1. Is the statement in line 22 a logical extension of the statement in lines 13–14?
Explain.   **2.** Is the rebellious Satan heroic or ignoble? Defend your answer.
3. What are the political implications of Satan's analysis of power (ll. 4–8)?

from

An Essay on Man   1733

ALEXANDER POPE   [1688–1744]

Cease then, nor ORDER imperfection name:
Our proper bliss depends on what we blame.
Know thy own point: this kind, this due degree
Of blindness, weakness, Heaven bestows on thee.
Submit—In this, or any other sphere,

Secure to be as blest as thou canst bear:
Safe in the hand of one disposing Power,
Or in the natal, or the mortal hour.
All Nature is but art, unknown to thee;
All chance, direction, which thou canst not see;   10
All discord, harmony not understood;
All partial evil, universal good:
And, spite of pride, in erring reason's spite,
One truth is clear: Whatever IS, is RIGHT.

The World Is
Too Much with Us   1807

WILLIAM WORDSWORTH   [1770–1850]

The world is too much with us; late and soon,
Getting and spending, we lay waste our powers;
Little we see in Nature that is ours;
We have given our hearts away, a sordid boon!
This Sea that bares her bosom to the moon,
The winds that will be howling at all hours,
And are up-gathered now like sleeping flowers,
For this, for everything, we are out of tune;
It moves us not.—Great God! I'd rather be
A Pagan suckled in a creed outworn;   10
So might I, standing on this pleasant lea,
Have glimpses that would make me less forlorn;
Have sight of Proteus rising from the sea;
Or hear old Triton blow his wreathèd horn.[1]

QUESTIONS
1. What does "world" mean in line 1?   **2.** What does Wordsworth complain of
in the first four lines?   **3.** In lines 4–8 Wordsworth tells us what we have lost; in
the concluding lines he suggests a remedy. What is that remedy? What do Proteus
and Triton symbolize?

The World . . .
   [1] Proteus and Triton are both figures from Greek mythology. Proteus had the power to assume
different forms; Triton was often represented as blowing on a conch shell.

WRITING TOPIC
In what ways does Wordsworth's use of images both define what we have lost and suggest a remedy for this loss?

Ulysses[1]   (1833)

ALFRED, LORD TENNYSON   [1809–1892]

It little profits that an idle king,
By this still hearth, among these barren crags,
Matched with an aged wife, I mete and dole
Unequal laws unto a savage race,
That hoard, and sleep, and feed, and know not me.

   I cannot rest from travel; I will drink
Life to the lees. All times I have enjoyed
Greatly, have suffered greatly, both with those
That loved me, and alone; on shore, and when
Through scudding drifts the rainy Hyades[2]   10
Vexed the dim sea. I am become a name;
For always roaming with a hungry heart
Much have I seen and known—cities of men
And manners, climates, councils, governments,
Myself not least, but honored of them all—
And drunk delight of battle with my peers,
Far on the ringing plains of windy Troy.
I am a part of all that I have met;
Yet all experience is an arch wherethrough
Gleams that untraveled world whose margin fades   20
Forever and forever when I move.
How dull it is to pause, to make an end,
To rust unburnished, not to shine in use!
As though to breathe were life. Life piled on life
Were all too little, and of one to me
Little remains; but every hour is saved
From that eternal silence, something more,
A bringer of new things; and vile it were
For some three suns to store and hoard myself,

Ulysses
  [1] Ulysses, according to Greek legend, was the king of Ithaca and a hero of the Trojan War. Tennyson represents him as eager to resume the life of travel and adventure.
  [2] A group of stars in the constellation Taurus. According to Greek mythology, the rising of these stars with the sun foretold rain.

And this gray spirit yearning in desire   30
To follow knowledge like a sinking star,
Beyond the utmost bound of human thought.

   This is my son, mine own Telemachus,
To whom I leave the scepter and the isle—
Well-loved of me, discerning to fulfill
This labor, by slow prudence to make mild
A rugged people, and through soft degrees
Subdue them to the useful and the good.
Most blameless is he, centered in the sphere
Of common duties, decent not to fail   40
In offices of tenderness, and pay
Meet° adoration to my household gods,   proper
When I am gone. He works his work, I mine.

   There lies the port; the vessel puffs her sail;
There gloom the dark, broad seas. My mariners,
Souls that have toiled, and wrought, and thought with me—
That ever with a frolic welcome took
The thunder and the sunshine, and opposed
Free hearts, free foreheads—you and I are old;
Old age hath yet his honor and his toil.   50
Death closes all; but something ere the end,
Some work of noble note, may yet be done,
Not unbecoming men that strove with Gods.
The lights begin to twinkle from the rocks;
The long day wanes; the slow moon climbs; the deep
Moans round with many voices. Come, my friends,
'Tis not too late to seek a newer world.
Push off, and sitting well in order smite
The sounding furrows; for my purpose holds
To sail beyond the sunset, and the baths   60
Of all the western stars, until I die.
It may be that the gulfs will wash us down;
It may be we shall touch the Happy Isles,[3]
And see the great Achilles, whom we knew.
Though much is taken, much abides; and though
We are not now that strength which in old days
Moved earth and heaven, that which we are, we are—
One equal temper of heroic hearts,

---

   [3] The Islands of the Blessed (also Elysium), thought to be in the far western oceans, where those favored by the gods, such as Achilles, enjoyed life after death.

Made weak by time and fate, but strong in will
To strive, to seek, to find, and not to yield.   70

QUESTIONS
1. Is Ulysses' desire to abdicate his duties as king irresponsible? Defend your
answer.   **2.** Contrast Ulysses with his son Telemachus as the latter is described in
lines 33–43. Is Telemachus admirable? Explain.

WRITING TOPIC
At the conclusion of the poem Ulysses is determined not to yield. Yield to what?

Much Madness
Is Divinest Sense   (1862)

EMILY DICKINSON   [1830–1886]

Much Madness is divinest Sense—
To a discerning Eye—
Much Sense—the starkest Madness—
'Tis the Majority
In this, as All, prevail—
Assent—and you are sane—
Demur—you're straightway dangerous—
And handled with a Chain—

What Soft—
Cherubic Creatures   (ca. 1862)

EMILY DICKINSON   [1830–1886]

What Soft—Cherubic Creatures—
These Gentlewomen are—
One would as soon assault a Plush—
Or violate a Star—

Such Dimity Convictions—
A Horror so refined
Of freckled Human Nature—
Of Deity—ashamed—

It's such a common-Glory—
A Fisherman's—Degree—   10
Redemption—Brittle Lady—
Be so—ashamed of Thee—

She Rose to His Requirement (ca. 1863)

EMILY DICKINSON   [1830–1886]

She rose to His Requirement—dropt
The Playthings of Her Life
To take the honorable Work
Of Woman, and of Wife—

If ought° She missed in Her new Day,   anything
Of Amplitude, or Awe—
Or first Prospective—Or the Gold
In using, wear away,

It lay unmentioned—as the Sea
Develope Pearl, and Weed,   10
But only to Himself—be known
The Fathoms they abide—

QUESTIONS
1. What are the "Playthings" referred to in line 2? Could the word be construed as ironic? Explain.   **2.** Why does the poet refer to both "Woman" and "Wife" in line 4, since a wife is also a woman?   **3.** The second stanza alludes to some losses the woman might have suffered in "Her new Day" (i.e., her marriage). Look up in your dictionary *amplitude, awe,* and *prospective,* and consider how these words help you to understand what those losses are.   **4.** What does "It" in the third stanza refer to?   **5.** Why is the sea image at the end of the poem appropriate? What does the contrast between "Pearl" and "Weed" suggest?   **6.** The last word of the poem, *abide,* has several meanings. Which of them are relevant to the meaning of the poem?

WRITING TOPIC
1. Write an essay describing a woman you know who gave up an important part of herself to be a wife.   **2.** Write an essay comparing and contrasting the attitudes toward marriage in this poem and in Helen Sorrells' "From a Correct Address in a Suburb of a Major City" (p. 483).

Thou Art Indeed Just, Lord   (1889)

GERARD MANLEY HOPKINS   [1844–1889]

> *Justus quidem tu es, Domine, si disputem tecum: verumtamen
> justa loquar ad te: Quare via impiorum prosperatur? & c.*[1]

Thou art indeed just, Lord, if I contend
With thee; but, sir, so what I plead is just.
Why do sinners' ways prosper? and why must
Disappointment all I endeavour end?
   Wert thou my enemy, O thou my friend,
How wouldst thou worse, I wonder, than thou dost
Defeat, thwart me? Oh, the sots and thralls of lust
Do in spare hours more thrive than I that spend,
Sir, life upon thy cause. See, banks and brakes
Now, leavèd how thick! lacèd they are again   10
With fretty chervil,° look, and fresh wind shakes   parsley
Them; birds build—but not I build; no, but strain,
Time's eunuch, and not breed one work that wakes.
Mine, O thou lord of life, send my roots rain.

QUESTIONS

1. How is the nature imagery used to indicate the speaker's plight?   **2.** How would
you characterize the poet's attitude toward God?

WRITING TOPIC

Summarize the debate in this poem. What implications about divine justice emerge
from the poet's questions in lines 3 and 4?

Easter 1916[1]   (1916)

WILLIAM BUTLER YEATS   [1865–1939]

I have met them at close of day
Coming with vivid faces

Thou Art Indeed . . .
   [1] The first three lines of the poem translate the Latin epigraph.
Easter 1916
   [1] On Easter Sunday of 1916, a group of Irish nationalists seized key points in Ireland, including
the Dublin Post Office, from which they proclaimed an independent Irish Republic. At first, most

From counter or desk among grey
Eighteenth-century houses.
I have passed with a nod of the head
Or polite meaningless words,
Or have lingered awhile and said
Polite meaningless words,
And thought before I had done
Of a mocking tale or a gibe   10
To please a companion
Around the fire at the club,
Being certain that they and I
But lived where motley is worn:
All changed, changed utterly:
A terrible beauty is born.

That woman's days were spent
In ignorant good-will,
Her nights in argument
Until her voice grew shrill.   20
What voice more sweet than hers
When, young and beautiful,
She rode to harriers?
This man had kept a school
And rode our wingéd horse;[2]
This other his helper and friend
Was coming into his force;
He might have won fame in the end,
So sensitive his nature seemed,
So daring and sweet his thought.   30
This other man I had dreamed
A drunken, vainglorious lout.
He had done most bitter wrong
To some who are near my heart,
Yet I number him in the song;
He, too, has resigned his part
In the casual comedy;
He, too, has been changed in his turn,
Transformed utterly:
A terrible beauty is born.   40

Irishmen were indifferent to the nationalists' futile and heroic gesture, but as the rebellion was crushed and the leaders executed, they became heroes in their countrymen's eyes. Some of those leaders are alluded to in the second stanza and are named in lines 75 and 76.

   [2] In Greek mythology, a winged horse is associated with poetic inspiration.

Hearts with one purpose alone
Through summer and winter seem
Enchanted to a stone
To trouble the living stream.
The horse that comes from the road,
The rider, the birds that range
From cloud to tumbling cloud,
Minute by minute they change;
A shadow of cloud on the stream
Changes minute by minute;   50
A horse-hoof slides on the brim,
And a horse plashes within it;
The long-legged moor-hens dive,
And hens to moor-cocks call;
Minute by minute they live:
The stone's in the midst of all.

Too long a sacrifice
Can make a stone of the heart.
O when may it suffice?
That is Heaven's part, our part   60
To murmur name upon name,
As a mother names her child
When sleep at last has come
On limbs that had run wild.
What is it but nightfall?
No, no, not night but death;
Was it needless death after all?
For England may keep faith
For all that is done and said.
We know their dream; enough   70
To know they dreamed and are dead;
And what if excess of love
Bewildered them till they died?
I write it out in a verse—
MacDonagh and MacBride
And Connolly and Pearse
Now and in time to be,
Wherever green is worn,
Are changed, changed utterly:
A terrible beauty is born.   80

QUESTIONS

1. What is "changed utterly," and in what sense can beauty be "terrible"?   **2.** What does "they" in line 55 refer to? What does the "stone" in lines 43 and 56 symbolize? What is Yeats contrasting?   **3.** How does the poet answer the question he asks in line 67?

WRITING TOPIC

In the first stanza the attitude of the poet toward the people he is describing is indifferent, even contemptuous. How is that attitude modified in the rest of the poem?

Miniver Cheevy   1910

EDWIN ARLINGTON ROBINSON   [1869–1935]

Miniver Cheevy, child of scorn,
    Grew lean while he assailed the seasons;
He wept that he was ever born,
    And he had reasons.

Miniver loved the days of old
    When swords were bright and steeds were prancing;
The vision of a warrior bold
    Would set him dancing.

Miniver sighed for what was not,
    And dreamed, and rested from his labors;   10
He dreamed of Thebes and Camelot,
    And Priam's neighbors.[1]

Miniver mourned the ripe renown
    That made so many a name so fragrant,
He mourned Romance, now on the town,
    And Art, a vagrant.

Miniver loved the Medici,[2]
    Albeit he had never seen one;

Miniver Cheevy
    [1] Thebes was an ancient Greek city, famous in history and legend; Camelot was the site of the legendary King Arthur's court; Priam was king of Troy during the Trojan War.
    [2] A family of bankers and statesmen, notorious for their cruelty, who ruled Florence for nearly two centuries during the Italian Renaissance.

He would have sinned incessantly
    Could he have been one.   20

Miniver cursed the commonplace
    And eyed a khaki suit with loathing;
He missed the medieval grace
    Of iron clothing.

Miniver scorned the gold he sought,
    But sore annoyed was he without it;
Miniver thought, and thought, and thought,
    And thought about it.

Miniver Cheevy, born too late,
    Scratched his head and kept on thinking;   30
Miniver coughed, and called it fate,
    And kept on drinking.

We Wear the Mask   1896

PAUL LAURENCE DUNBAR   [1872–1906]

We wear the mask that grins and lies,
It hides our cheeks and shades our eyes—
This debt we pay to human guile;
With torn and bleeding hearts we smile,
And mouth with myriad subtleties.

Why should the world be over-wise,
In counting all our tears and sighs?
Nay, let them only see us, while
    We wear the mask.

We smile, but, O great Christ, our cries   10
To thee from tortured souls arise.
We sing, but oh the clay is vile
Beneath our feet, and long the mile;
But let the world dream otherwise,
    We wear the mask!

Departmental

1936

ROBERT FROST   [1874–1963]

An ant on the table cloth
Ran into a dormant moth
Of many times his size.
He showed not the least surprise.
His business wasn't with such.
He gave it scarcely a touch,
And was off on his duty run.
Yet if he encountered one
Of the hive's enquiry squad
Whose work is to find out God   10
And the nature of time and space,
He would put him onto the case.
Ants are a curious race;
One crossing with hurried tread
The body of one of their dead
Isn't given a moment's arrest—
Seems not even impressed.
But he no doubt reports to any
With whom he crosses antennae,
And they no doubt report   20
To the higher up at court.
Then word goes forth in Formic:
"Death's come to Jerry McCormic,
Our selfless forager Jerry.
Will the special Janizary
Whose office it is to bury
The dead of the commissary
Go bring him home to his people.
Lay him in state on a sepal.
Wrap him for shroud in a petal.   30
Embalm him with ichor of nettle.
This is the word of your Queen."
And presently on the scene
Appears a solemn mortician;
And taking formal position
With feelers calmly atwiddle,
Seizes the dead by the middle,
And heaving him high in air,
Carries him out of there.

No one stands round to stare.   40
It is nobody else's affair.
It couldn't be called ungentle.
But how thoroughly departmental.

QUESTIONS
1. What comment does this poem make on human society? Is ant society a good
metaphor for human society? Explain.   **2.** How do the diction and rhyme help
establish the tone?

WRITING TOPIC
How does the diction in this poem convey the speaker's attitude toward the social
order he describes?

Patterns   1916

AMY LOWELL   [1874–1925]

I walk down the garden-paths,
And all the daffodils
Are blowing, and the bright blue squills.
I walk down the patterned garden-paths
In my stiff, brocaded gown.
With my powdered hair and jeweled fan,
I too am a rare
Pattern. As I wander down
The garden-paths.
My dress is richly figured,   10
And the train
Makes a pink and silver stain
On the gravel, and the thrift
Of the borders.
Just a plate of current fashion,
Tripping by in high-heeled, ribboned shoes.
Not a softness anywhere about me,
Only whalebone and brocade.
And I sink on a seat in the shade
Of a lime tree. For my passion   20
Wars against the stiff brocade.
The daffodils and squills
Flutter in the breeze
As they please.

And I weep;
For the lime-tree is in blossom
And one small flower has dropped upon my bosom.

And the plashing of waterdrops
In the marble fountain
Comes down the garden-paths.   30
The dripping never stops.
Underneath my stiffened gown
Is the softness of a woman bathing in a marble basin,
A basin in the midst of hedges grown
So thick, she cannot see her lover hiding,
But she guesses he is near,
And the sliding of the water
Seems the stroking of a dear
Hand upon her.
What is Summer in a fine brocaded gown!   40
I should like to see it lying in a heap upon the ground.
All the pink and silver crumpled up on the ground.

I would be the pink and silver as I ran along the paths,
And he would stumble after,
Bewildered by my laughter.
I should see the sun flashing from his sword-hilt and the buckles on his
    shoes.
I would choose
To lead him in a maze along the patterned paths,
A bright and laughing maze for my heavy-booted lover.
Till he caught me in the shade,   50
And the buttons of his waistcoat bruised my body as he clasped me,
Aching, melting, unafraid.
With the shadows of the leaves and the sundrops,
And the plopping of the waterdrops,
All about us in the open afternoon—
I am very like to swoon
With the weight of this brocade,
For the sun sifts through the shade.

Underneath the fallen blossom
In my bosom   60
Is a letter I have hid.
It was brought to me this morning by a rider from the Duke.
"Madam, we regret to inform you that Lord Hartwell

Died in action Thursday se'nnight."[1]
As I read it in the white, morning sunlight,
The letters squirmed like snakes.
"Any answer, Madam," said my footman.
"No," I told him.
"See that the messenger takes some refreshment.
No, no answer."   70
And I walked into the garden,
Up and down the patterned paths,
In my stiff, correct brocade.
The blue and yellow flowers stood up proudly in the sun,
Each one.
I stood upright too,
Held rigid to the pattern
By the stiffness of my gown;
Up and down I walked,
Up and down.   80

In a month he would have been my husband.
In a month, here, underneath this lime,
We would have broke the pattern;
He for me, and I for him,
He as Colonel, I as Lady,
On this shady seat.
He had a whim
That sunlight carried blessing.
And I answered, "It shall be as you have said."
Now he is dead.   90

In Summer and in Winter I shall walk
Up and down
The patterned garden-paths
In my stiff, brocaded gown.
The squills and daffodils
Will give place to pillared roses, and to asters, and to snow.
I shall go
Up and down
In my gown.
Gorgeously arrayed,   100
Boned and stayed.
And the softness of my body will be guarded from embrace

---

[1] Seven nights (i.e., a week) ago.

By each button, hook, and lace.
For the man who should loose me is dead,
Fighting with the Duke in Flanders,[2]
In a pattern called a war.
Christ! What are patterns for?

QUESTIONS

1. What period of time does the poem seem to be set in? Explain.   **2.** Identify the various kinds of patterns in the poem.   **3.** In line 83, the speaker refers to the pattern "We would have broke." What is that pattern? How might it have been broken?   **4.** Does the poem provide an answer to the question the speaker asks in the final line? Explain.

WRITING TOPICS

1. Describe a pattern in your family that has limited your life.   **2.** Describe a societal pattern that has limited your life.   **3.** Write an essay in which you argue that patterns, while perhaps limiting, are necessary.

Sunday Morning   1923

WALLACE STEVENS   [1879–1955]

I

Complacencies of the peignoir, and late
Coffee and oranges in a sunny chair,
And the green freedom of a cockatoo
Upon a rug mingle to dissipate
The holy hush of ancient sacrifice.
She dreams a little, and she feels the dark
Encroachment of that old catastrophe,
As a calm darkens among water-lights.
The pungent oranges and bright, green wings
Seem things in some procession of the dead,   10
Winding across wide water, without sound.
The day is like wide water, without sound,
Stilled for the passing of her dreaming feet
Over the seas, to silent Palestine,
Dominion of the blood and sepulchre.

Patterns
    [2] A region of Belgium where battles were fought during wars in the eighteenth, nineteenth, and twentieth centuries.

II

Why should she give her bounty to the dead?
What is divinity if it can come
Only in silent shadows and in dreams?
Shall she not find in comforts of the sun,
In pungent fruit and bright, green wings, or else   20
In any balm or beauty of the earth,
Things to be cherished like the thought of heaven?
Divinity must live within herself:
Passions of rain, or moods in falling snow;
Grievings in loneliness, or unsubdued
Elations when the forest blooms; gusty
Emotions on wet roads on autumn nights;
All pleasures and all pains, remembering
The bough of summer and the winter branch.
These are the measures destined for her soul.   30

III

Jove in the clouds had his inhuman birth.[1]
No mother suckled him, no sweet land gave
Large-mannered motions to his mythy mind
He moved among us, as a muttering king,
Magnificent, would move among his hinds,°   farm servants
Until our blood, commingling, virginal,
With heaven, brought such requital to desire
The very hinds discerned it, in a star.
Shall our blood fail? Or shall it come to be
The blood of paradise? And shall the earth   40
Seem all of paradise that we shall know?
The sky will be much friendlier then than now,
A part of labor and a part of pain,
And next in glory to enduring love,
Not this dividing and indifferent blue.

IV

She says, "I am content when wakened birds,
Before they fly, test the reality
Of misty fields, by their sweet questionings;

---

[1] Jove is Jupiter, the principal god of the Romans, who, unlike Jesus, had an "inhuman birth."

But when the birds are gone, and their warm fields
Return no more, where, then, is paradise?"   50
There is not any haunt of prophecy,
Nor any old chimera² of the grave,
Neither the golden underground, nor isle
Melodious, where spirits gat them home,
Nor visionary south, nor cloudy palm
Remote on heaven's hill, that has endured
As April's green endures; or will endure
Like her remembrance of awakened birds,
Or her desire for June and evening, tipped
By the consummation of the swallow's wings.   60

V

She says, "But in contentment I still feel
The need of some imperishable bliss."
Death is the mother of beauty; hence from her,
Alone, shall come fulfilment to our dreams
And our desires. Although she strews the leaves
Of sure obliteration on our paths,
The path sick sorrow took, the many paths
Where triumph rang its brassy phrase, or love
Whispered a little out of tenderness,
She makes the willow shiver in the sun   70
For maidens who were wont to sit and gaze
Upon the grass, relinquished to their feet.
She causes boys to pile new plums and pears
On disregarded plate. The maidens taste
And stray impassioned in the littering leaves.

VI

Is there no change of death in paradise?
Does ripe fruit never fall? Or do the boughs
Hang always heavy in that perfect sky,
Unchanging, yet so like our perishing earth,
With rivers like our own that seek for seas   80
They never find, the same receding shores
That never touch with inarticulate pang?

---

² A monster with a lion's head, a goat's body, and a serpent's tail. Here an emblem for the belief in other worlds described in the following lines.

Why set the pear upon those river-banks
Or spice the shores with odors of the plum?
Alas, that they should wear our colors there,
The silken weavings of our afternoons,
And pick the strings of our insipid lutes!
Death is the mother of beauty, mystical,
Within whose burning bosom we devise
Our earthly mothers waiting, sleeplessly.   90

VII

Supple and turbulent, a ring of men
Shall chant in orgy on a summer morn
Their boisterous devotion to the sun,
Not as a god, but as a god might be,
Naked among them, like a savage source.
Their chant shall be a chant of paradise,
Out of their blood, returning to the sky;
And in their chant shall enter, voice by voice,
The windy lake wherein their lord delights,
The trees, like serafin, and echoing hills,   100
That choir among themselves long afterward.
They shall know well the heavenly fellowship
Of men that perish and of summer morn.
And whence they came and whither they shall go
The dew upon their feet shall manifest.

VIII

She hears, upon that water without sound,
A voice that cries, "The tomb in Palestine
Is not the porch of spirits lingering.
It is the grave of Jesus, where he lay."
We live in an old chaos of the sun,   110
Or old dependency of day and night,
Or island solitude, unsponsored, free,
Of that wide water, inescapable.
Deer walk upon our mountains, and the quail
Whistle about us their spontaneous cries;
Sweet berries ripen in the wilderness;
And, in the isolation of the sky,
At evening, casual flocks of pigeons make
Ambiguous undulations as they sink,
Downward to darkness, on extended wings.   120

QUESTIONS

1. In the opening stanza, the woman's enjoyment of a late Sunday morning breakfast in a relaxed and sensuous atmosphere is troubled by thoughts of what Sunday morning should mean to her. What are the thoughts that disturb her complacency?   **2.** What does the speaker mean when he says, "Death is the mother of beauty" (ll. 63 and 88)?   **3.** In stanza VI, what is the speaker's attitude toward the conventional Christian conception of paradise?   **4.** Stanza VII presents the speaker's vision of an alternative religion. How does it differ from the paradise of stanza VI?   **5.** In what ways does the cry of the voice in the final stanza (ll. 107–109) state the woman's dilemma? How do the lines about the pigeons at the end of the poem sum up the speaker's belief?

WRITING TOPIC

This poem is, in a sense, a commentary by the speaker on the woman's desire for truth and certainty more enduring than the physical world can provide. Is the speaker sympathetic to her quest? Explain.

If We Must Die   1922

CLAUDE MCKAY   [1890–1948]

If we must die, let it not be like hogs
Hunted and penned in an inglorious spot,
While round us bark the mad and hungry dogs,
Making their mock at our accursèd lot.
If we must die, O let us nobly die,
So that our precious blood may not be shed
In vain; then even the monsters we defy
Shall be constrained to honor us though dead!
O kinsmen! we must meet the common foe!
Though far outnumbered let us show us brave,   10
And for their thousand blows deal one deathblow!
What though before us lies the open grave?
Like men we'll face the murderous, cowardly pack,
Pressed to the wall, dying, but fighting back!

the Cambridge ladies
who live in furnished souls   1923

E. E. CUMMINGS   [1894–1962]

the Cambridge ladies who live in furnished souls
are unbeautiful and have comfortable minds

(also, with the church's protestant blessings
daughters, unscented shapeless spirited)
they believe in Christ and Longfellow, both dead,
are invariably interested in so many things—
at the present writing one still finds
delighted fingers knitting for the is it Poles?
perhaps. While permanent faces coyly bandy
scandal of Mrs. N. and Professor D   10
. . . . the Cambridge ladies do not care, above
Cambridge if sometimes in its box of
sky lavender and cornerless, the
moon rattles like a fragment of angry candy

QUESTIONS

1. What images does the poet use to describe "the Cambridge ladies"? What do the images suggest?   **2.** What is the effect of the interruption "is it" in line 8?   **3.** In the final lines, the moon seems to protest against the superficiality of these women. What is the effect of comparing the moon to a fragment of candy?

WRITING TOPIC

Compare this poem with Emily Dickinson's "What Soft—Cherubic Creatures."

Tilth   1975

ROBERT GRAVES [1895–1985]

"Robert Graves, the British Veteran, is no longer in the poetic swim. He still resorts to traditional metres and rhyme, and to such outdated words as *tilth*; withholding his 100% approbation also from contemporary poems that favour sexual freedom."[1]

Gone are the sad monosyllabic days
When 'agricultural labour' still was *tilth*;
And '100% approbation', *praise*;
And 'pornographic modernism', *filth*—
And still I stand by *tilth* and *filth* and *praise*.

Tilth
    [1] Graves is quoting (or pretending to quote) a reviewer.

Harlem   1951

LANGSTON HUGHES   [1902–1967]

What happens to a dream deferred?

> Does it dry up
> like a raisin in the sun?
> Or fester like a sore—
> And then run?
> Does it stink like rotten meat?
> Or crust and sugar over—
> like a syrupy sweet?

> Maybe it just sags
> like a heavy load.   10

> *Or does it explode?*

Same in Blues   1951

LANGSTON HUGHES   [1902–1967]

I said to my baby,
Baby take it slow.
I can't, she said, I can't!
I got to go!

> *There's a certain*
> *amount of traveling*
> *in a dream deferred.*

Lulu said to Leonard,
I want a diamond ring.
Leonard said to Lulu,   10
You won't get a goddam thing!

> *A certain*
> *amount of nothing*
> *in a dream deferred.*

ldy, daddy, daddy,
    I want is you.
    u can have me, baby—
but my lovin' days is through.

    A *certain*
    amount of impotence
    in a dream deferred.   20

Three parties
On my party line—
But that third party,
Lord, ain't mine!

    There's liable
    to be confusion
    in a dream deferred.

From river to river
Uptown and down,   30
There's liable to be confusion
when a dream gets kicked around.

The Unknown Citizen   1940

(TO JS/07/M/378
THIS MARBLE MONUMENT
IS ERECTED BY THE STATE)

W. H. AUDEN   [1907–1973]

He was found by the Bureau of Statistics to be
One against whom there was no official complaint,
And all the reports on his conduct agree
That, in the modern sense of an old-fashioned word, he was a saint,
For in everything he did he served the Greater Community.
Except for the War till the day he retired
He worked in a factory and never got fired,
But satisfied his employers, Fudge Motors Inc.
Yet he wasn't a scab or odd in his views,
For his Union reports that he paid his dues,   10
(Our report on his Union shows it was sound)
And our Social Psychology workers found
That he was popular with his mates and liked a drink.

The Press are convinced that he bought a paper every day
And that his reactions to advertisements were normal in every way.
Policies taken out in his name prove that he was fully insured,
And his Health-card shows he was once in hospital but left it cured.
Both Producers Research and High-Grade Living declare
He was fully sensible to the advantages of the Installment Plan
And had everything necessary to the Modern Man,   20
A phonograph, radio, a car and a frigidaire.
Our researchers into Public Opinion are content
That he held the proper opinions for the time of year;
When there was peace, he was for peace; when there was war, he went.
He was married and added five children to the population,
Which our Eugenist says was the right number for a parent of his generation,
And our teachers report that he never interfered with their education.
Was he free? Was he happy? The question is absurd:
Had anything been wrong, we should certainly have heard.

From a Correct Address in a Suburb of a Major City   1971

HELEN SORRELLS [b. 1908]

She wears her middle age like a cowled
gown, sleeved in it, folded high
at the breast,

charming, proper at cocktails
but the inner one raging
and how to hide her,

how to keep her leashed, contain
the heat of her, the soaring cry
never yet loosed,

demanding a chance before the years devour her,   10
before the marrow of her fine long legs
congeals and she

settles forever for this street, this house,
her face set to the world
sweet, sweet

above the shocked, astonished
hunger.

Myth   1973

MURIEL RUKEYSER   [1913–1980]

Long afterward, Oedipus, old and blinded, walked the
roads.[1]   He smelled a familiar smell.   It was
the Sphinx.   Oedipus said, "I want to ask one question.
Why didn't I recognize my mother?"   "You gave the
wrong answer," said the Sphinx.   "But that was what
made everything possible," said Oedipus.   "No," she said.
"When I asked, What walks on four legs in the morning,
two at noon, and three in the evening, you answered,
Man.   You didn't say anything about woman."
"When you say Man," said Oedipus, "you include women   10
too. Everyone knows that."   She said, "That's what
you think."

Ballad of Birmingham   1969

(On the Bombing of a Church in Birmingham, Alabama, 1963)

DUDLEY RANDALL   [b. 1914]

"Mother dear, may I go downtown
Instead of out to play,
And march the streets of Birmingham
In a Freedom March today?"

"No, baby, no, you may not go,
For the dogs are fierce and wild,
And clubs and hoses, guns and jails
Aren't good for a little child."

"But, mother, I won't be alone.
Other children will go with me,   10
And march the streets of Birmingham
To make our country free."

Myth
      [1] Oedipus became King of Thebes when he solved the riddle of the Sphinx quoted in the poem.
He blinded himself when he discovered that he had married his own mother.

"No, baby, no, you may not go,
For I fear those guns will fire.
But you may go to church instead
And sing in the children's choir."

She has combed and brushed her night-dark hair,
And bathed rose petal sweet.
And drawn white gloves on her small brown hands,
And white shoes on her feet.   20

The mother smiled to know her child
Was in the sacred place,
But that smile was the last smile
To come upon her face.

For when she heard the explosion,
Her eyes grew wet and wild.
She raced through the streets of Birmingham
Calling for her child.

She clawed through bits of glass and brick,
Then lifted out a shoe.   30
"Oh, here's the shoe my baby wore,
But, baby, where are you?"

Naming of Parts   1946

HENRY REED   [b. 1914]

Today we have naming of parts. Yesterday,
We had daily cleaning. And tomorrow morning
We shall have what to do after firing. But today,
Today we have naming of parts. Japonica
Glistens like coral in all of the neighboring gardens,
        And today we have naming of parts.

This is the lower sling swivel. And this
Is the upper sling swivel, whose use you will see,
When you are given your slings. And this is the piling swivel,
Which in your case you have not got. The branches   10
Hold in the gardens their silent, eloquent gestures,
        Which in our case we have not got.

This is the safety-catch, which is always released
With an easy flick of the thumb. And please do not let me
See anyone using his finger. You can do it quite easy
If you have any strength in your thumb. The blossoms
Are fragile and motionless, never letting anyone see
    Any of them using their finger.

And this you can see is the bolt. The purpose of this
Is to open the breech, as you see. We can slide it   20
Rapidly backwards and forwards: we call this
Easing the spring. And rapidly backwards and forwards
The early bees are assaulting and fumbling the flowers:
    They call it easing the Spring.

They call it easing the Spring: it is perfectly easy
If you have any strength in your thumb: like the bolt,
And the breech, and the cocking-piece, and the point of balance,
Which in our case we have not got; and the almond-blossom
Silent in all of the gardens and the bees going backwards and forwards,
    For today we have naming of parts.   30

QUESTIONS
1. The poem has two speakers. Identify their voices, and characterize the speakers.   **2.** The last line of each stanza repeats a phrase from within the stanza. What is the effect of the repetition?

WRITING TOPIC
This poem incorporates a subtle underlying sexuality. Trace the language that generates it. What function does that sexuality serve in the poem?

from
The Children of the Poor   (1949)

GWENDOLYN BROOKS [b. 1917]

4

First fight. Then fiddle. Ply the slipping string
With feathery sorcery; muzzle the note
With hurting love, the music that they wrote
Bewitch, bewilder. Qualify to sing
Threadwise. Devise no salt, no hempen thing
For the dear instrument to bear. Devote

The bow to silks and honey. Be remote
A while from malice and from murdering.
But first to arms, to armor. Carry hate
In front of you and harmony behind.   10
Be deaf to music and to beauty blind.
Win war. Rise bloody, maybe not too late
For having first to civilize a space
Wherein to play your violin with grace.

11

Life for my child is simple, and is good.
He knows his wish. Yes, but that is not all.
Because I know mine too.
And we both want joy of undeep and unabiding things,
Like kicking over a chair or throwing blocks out of a window
Or tipping over an icebox pan
Or snatching down curtains or fingering an electric outlet
Or a journey or a friend or an illegal kiss.
No. There is more to it than that.
It is that he has never been afraid.   10
Rather, he reaches out and lo the chair falls with a beautiful crash,
And the blocks fall, down on the people's heads,
And the water comes slooshing sloppily out across the floor.
And so forth.
Not that success, for him, is sure, infallible.
But never has he been afraid to reach.
His lesions are legion.
But reaching is his rule.

QUESTIONS

1. In sonnet 4, the poet advises the children: "First fight, Then fiddle." The meaning of "fight" is clear. What does "fiddle" symbolize? **2.** Why does the poet advocate violence? **3.** Is the child described in poem 11 different from the children addressed in sonnet 4? **4.** Explain the meaning of line 4 in poem 11. **5.** What does "reaching" in the last line mean?

In Goya's Greatest Scenes   1958

LAWRENCE FERLINGHETTI   [b. 1919]

In Goya's greatest scenes[1] we seem to see
        the people of the world
  exactly at the moment when
    they first attained the title of
       'suffering humanity'
  They writhe upon the page
     in a veritable rage
       of adversity
 Heaped up
    groaning with babies and bayonets   10
      under cement skies
  in an abstract landscape of blasted trees
   bent statues bats wings and beaks
     slippery gibbets
    cadavers and carnivorous cocks
 and all the final hollering monsters
   of the
     'imagination of disaster'
 they are so bloody real
     it is as if they really still existed   20

  And they do
    Only the landscape is changed

They still are ranged along the roads
   plagued by legionaires
     false windmills and demented roosters

They are the same people
     only further from home
  on freeways fifty lanes wide
    on a concrete continent
      spaced with bland billboards   30
    illustrating imbecile illusions of happiness

---

[1] Francisco José de Goya (1746–1828), famous Spanish artist, celebrated for his representations of "suffering humanity."

The scene shows fewer tumbrils²
      but more maimed citizens
           in painted cars
  and they have strange license plates
and engines
    that devour America

QUESTIONS
1. To whom does the word "they" refer in line 26? **2.** What is responsible for
the "suffering" of modern American "humanity"?

Formal Application   (1963)

DONALD W. BAKER [b. 1923]

"The poets apparently want to rejoin the human race."   TIME

I shall begin by learning to throw
the knife, first at trees, until it sticks
in the trunk and quivers every time;

next from a chair, using only wrist
and fingers, at a thing on the ground,
a fresh ant hill or a fallen leaf;

then at a moving object, perhaps
a pine cone swinging on twine, until
I pot it at least twice in three tries.

Meanwhile, I shall be teaching the birds   10
that the skinny fellow in sneakers
is a source of suet and bread crumbs,

first putting them on a shingle nailed
to a pine tree, next scattering them
on the needles, closer and closer

to my seat, until the proper bird,
a towhee, I think, in black and rust
and gray, takes tossed crumbs six feet away.

In Goya's Greatest Scenes
   ² Carts in which prisoners were conducted to the place of execution.

Finally, I shall coordinate
conditioned reflex and functional   20
form and qualify as Modern Man.

You see the splash of blood and feathers
and the blade pinning it to the tree?
It's called an "Audubon Crucifix."

The phrase has pleasing (even pious)
connotations, like *Arbeit Macht Frei*,
"Molotov Cocktail," and *Enola Gay*.[1]

QUESTIONS

1. What did *Time* mean by the line Baker uses as an epigraph to this poem? How, for example, are poets not members of the human race? What does the title of the poem mean?   **2.** In what sense does "Audubon Crucifix" have "pleasing (even pious) connotations"? What are the pleasing connotations of the expressions in the last two lines? According to this poem, what are the attributes necessary to join the human race?

Hard Rock Returns to Prison from the Hospital for the Criminal Insane   1968

ETHERIDGE KNIGHT   [1933–1991]

Hard Rock was "known not to take no shit
From nobody," and he had the scars to prove it:
Split purple lips, lumped ears, welts above
His yellow eyes, and one long scar that cut
Across his temple and plowed through a thick
Canopy of kinky hair.

The WORD was that Hard Rock wasn't a mean nigger
Anymore, that the doctors had bored a hole in his head,
Cut out part of his brain, and shot electricity

Formal Application

[1] *Arbeit Macht Frei*, the motto of the German Nazi party, means "labor liberates." A Molotov cocktail is a homemade hand grenade named after Vyacheslav M. Molotov, the foreign minister of the Soviet Union during the reign of Joseph Stalin. *Enola Gay* was the name of the United States plane that dropped the atomic bomb on Hiroshima in 1945.

Through the rest. When they brought Hard Rock back,   10
Handcuffed and chained, he was turned loose,
Like a freshly gelded stallion, to try his new status.
And we all waited and watched, like Indians at a corral,
To see if the WORD was true.

As we waited we wrapped ourselves in the cloak
Of his exploits: "Man, the last time, it took eight
Screws to put him in the Hole." "Yeah, remember when he
Smacked the captain with his dinner tray?" "He set
The record for time in the Hole—67 straight days!"
"Ol Hard Rock! man, that's one crazy nigger."   20
And then the jewel of a myth that Hard Rock had once bit
A screw on the thumb and poisoned him with syphilitic spit.

The testing came, to see if Hard Rock was really tame.
A hillbilly called him a black son of a bitch
And didn't lose his teeth, a screw who knew Hard Rock
From before shook him down and barked in his face.
And Hard Rock did *nothing*. Just grinned and looked silly,
His eyes empty like knot holes in a fence.

And even after we discovered that it took Hard Rock
Exactly 3 minutes to tell you his first name,   30
We told ourselves that he had just wised up,
Was being cool; but we could not fool ourselves for long,
And we turned away, our eyes on the ground. Crushed.

He had been our Destroyer, the doer of things
We dreamed of doing but could not bring ourselves to do,
The fears of years, like a biting whip,
Had cut grooves too deeply across our backs.

The Stranglehold of English Lit.   1961
(For Molara Ogundipe-Leslie)

FELIX MNTHALI   [b. 1933]

Those questions, sister,
those questions
                    stand
                    stab
                    jab

                      and gore
too close to the centre!

For if we had asked
why Jane Austen's people[1]
carouse all day   10
and do no work

would Europe in Africa
have stood
the test of time?
and would she still maul
the flower of our youth
in the south?
Would she?

Your elegance of deceit,
Jane Austen,   20
lulled the sons and daughters
of the dispossessed
into a calf-love
with irony and satire
around imaginary people.

While history went on mocking
the victims of branding irons
and sugar-plantations
that made Jane Austen's people
wealthy beyond compare!   30

Eng. Lit., my sister,
was more than a cruel joke—
it was the heart
of alien conquest.

How could questions be asked
at Makerere and Ibadan,
Dakar and Ford Hare[2]—
with Jane Austen

---

[1] Characters in the novels of Jane Austen (1775–1817), a standard author in English literature courses. Her ironic domestic comedies are peopled with English country gentlefolk who, apparently, do not have to work for a living.

[2] The sites of major African Universities whose students, among others, participated in Africa's struggle to free itself from European domination.

at the centre?
How could they be answered?   40

QUESTIONS
1. Malawi, the poet's birthplace, was a part of British South Africa, a colonial possession, before it achieved independence. How would the school curriculum reflect this fact?   **2.** Some would argue that studying Jane Austen is appropriate because her work embodies "universal" values. Does the poet agree? Explain.   **3.** In the fifth stanza, the poet moves from derision to an attack; discuss the issues he raises.   **4.** Do you agree with the assertion of the sixth stanza? Explain.

WRITING TOPIC
Discuss the political and cultural implications of the poem's title.

I Would Like   (trans. 1962)

YEVGENY YEVTUSHENKO   [b. 1933]

I would like
            to be born
                        in every country,
have a passport
            for them all,
to throw
            all foreign offices
                        into panic,
be every fish
            in every ocean   10
and every dog
            along the path.
I don't want to bow down
                        before any idols
or play at being
                        an Orthodox church hippy,
but I would like to plunge
                        deep into Lake Baikal[1]
and surface snorting
                        somewhere,   20
                        why not in the Mississippi?

I Would Like
   [1] A large lake in Siberia, just north of Mongolia.

In my beloved universe
                    I would like
to be a lonely weed,
                    but not a delicate Narcissus[2]
kissing his own mug
                    in the mirror.
I would like to be
                    any of God's creatures
right down to the last mangy hyena—   30
but never a tyrant
                    or even the cat of a tyrant.
I would like to be
                    reincarnated as a man
                              in any circumstance:
a victim of Paraguayan prison tortures,
a homeless child in the slums of Hong Kong,
a living skeleton in Bangladesh,
a holy beggar in Tibet,
a black in Cape Town,   40
but never
          in the image of Rambo
The only people whom I hate
                    are the hypocrites—
pickled hyenas
          in heavy syrup.
I would like to lie
                    under the knives of all the surgeons in the world,
be hunchbacked, blind,
                    suffer all kinds of diseases,   50
                              wounds and scars,
be a victim of war,
                    or a sweeper of cigarette butts,
just so a filthy microbe of superiority
                    doesn't creep inside.
I would not like to be in the elite,
nor of course,
          in the cowardly herd,
nor be a guard-dog of that herd,
nor a shepherd,   60
          sheltered by that herd.
And I would like happiness,

---

    [2] In Greek myth, a beautiful youth who pined away for love of his own reflection and was
changed into a flower.

but not at the expense of the unhappy,
and I would like freedom,
but not at the expense of the unfree.
I would like to love
all the women in the world,
and I would like to be a woman, too—
just once. . . .
Men have been diminished   70
by Mother Nature.
Suppose she'd given motherhood
to men?
If an innocent child
stirred
below his heart,
man would probably
not be so cruel.
I would like to be man's daily bread—
say,   80
a cup of rice
for a Vietnamese woman in mourning,
cheap wine
in a Neapolitan workers' trattoria,³
or a tiny tube of cheese
in orbit round the moon:
let them eat me,
let them drink me,
only let my death
be of some use.   90
I would like to belong to all times,
shock all history so much
that it would be amazed
what a smart aleck I was.
I would like to bring Nefertiti
to Pushkin in a troika.⁴
I would like to increase
the space of a moment
a hundredfold,
so that in the same moment   100
I could drink vodka with fishermen in Siberia
and sit together with Homer,

---

³ A small inexpensive restaurant in Italy.
⁴ Nefertiti was a famously beautiful fourteenth-century B.C. queen of Egypt. Aleksandr Sergeyevich Pushkin (1799–1837) was, perhaps, the greatest Russian writer and poet of his time. A troika is a Russian vehicle drawn by a team of three horses.

Dante,
Shakespeare,
and Tolstoy,
drinking anything,
except of course,
Coca-Cola,
—dance to the tom-toms in the Congo,
—strike at Renault,   110
—chase a ball with Brazilian boys
at Copacabana Beach.
I would like
to know every language,
the secret waters under the earth,
and do all kinds of work at once.
I would make sure
that one Yevtushenko was merely a poet,
the second—an underground fighter,
somewhere,   120
I couldn't say where
for security reasons,
the third—a student at Berkeley,
the fourth—a jolly Georgian[5] drinker,
and the fifth—
maybe a teacher of Eskimo children in Alaska,
the sixth—
a young president,
somewhere, say even in Sierra Leone,
the seventh—   130
would still be shaking a rattle in his stroller,
and the tenth . . .
the hundredth . . .
the millionth . . .
For me it's not enough to be myself,
let me be everyone!
Every creature
usually has a double,
but God was stingy
with the carbon paper,   140
and in his Paradise Publishing Company
made a unique copy of me.
But I shall muddle up

---

[5] Georgia is one of the republics that made up the former Soviet Union. It lies along the east coast of the Black Sea.

all God's cards—
                    I shall confound God!
I shall be in a thousand copies
                    to the end of my days,
so that the earth buzzes with me,
                    and computers go berserk
in the world census of me.   150
I would like to fight on all your barricades,
                              humanity,
dying each night
              an exhausted moon,
and being resurrected each morning
                              like a newborn sun,
with an immortal soft spot
                    on my skull.
And when I die,
              a smart-aleck Siberian François Villon,[6]   160
do not lay me in the earth
                    of France
                         or Italy,
but in our Russian, Siberian earth,
                    on a still green hill,
where I first felt
              that I was
                    everyone.

QUESTIONS

1. The poet declares that he would like to be a certain kind of person. What kind of person? What concrete images lead you to your judgment? **2.** What kind of person does he *not* wish to be? What images support your conclusion? **3.** Discuss the images that address chronological time. Discuss those that address geographical distance. Discuss those that address a sort of chain of being among creatures, moving from "low" to "high." How does Yevtushenko use these images to define his social and political views?

WRITING TOPIC

In an essay, characterize the poet's notion of an ideal person, and speculate on how that person would get along in the real world. Do you accept, or would you modify, Yevtushenko's ideal? Explain.

---

[6] A French balladeer, born in 1431, who was often in trouble with the law.

Eleanor Rigby

1966

JOHN LENNON   [1940–1980] **and** **PAUL McCARTNEY**   [b. 1942]

Ah, look at all the lonely people!
Ah, look at all the lonely people!
Eleanor Rigby picks up the rice
   in the church
Where a wedding has been.
Lives in a dream.
Waits at the window, wearing the face
   that she keeps in a jar by the door.
Who is it for?

All the lonely people,   10
   where do they all come from?
All the lonely people,
   where do they all belong?

Father McKenzie writing the words
   of a sermon that no one will hear—
No one comes near. Look at him
   working, darning his socks in the night
   when there's nobody there.
What does he care?

All the lonely people,   20
   where do they all come from?
All the lonely people,
   where do they all belong?

Ah, look at all the lonely people!
Ah, look at all the lonely people!
Eleanor Rigby died in the church and
   was buried along with her name.
Nobody came.
Father McKenzie wiping the dirt from
   his hands as he walks from the grave.   30
No one was saved.

All the lonely people,
   where do they all come from?

All the lonely people,
  where do they all belong?

QUESTIONS
1. How does the first stanza establish Eleanor Rigby's character? What is the meaning of lines 7–8?   **2.** What does the portrait of Father McKenzie contribute to our understanding of the theme of the lyric?   **3.** What significance has the juxtaposition of Father McKenzie's writing "a sermon that no one will hear" and "darning his socks in the night" (stanza 3)?   **4.** What is the significance of Eleanor Rigby's dying in the church? Why was "No one saved" (l. 31)?   **5.** What answers, if any, does the poem suggest to the questions in the last stanza?

Conversation with a Fireman from Brooklyn

1984

TESS GALLAGHER   [b. 1943]

He offers, between planes,
to buy me a drink. I've never talked
to a fireman before, not one from Brooklyn
anyway. Okay. Fine, I say. Somehow
the subject is bound to come up, women
firefighters, and since I'm
a woman and he's a fireman, between
the two of us, we know something
about this subject. Already
he's telling me he doesn't mind   10
women firefighters, but what
they look like
after fighting a fire, well
they lose all respect. He's sorry, but
he looks at them
covered with the cinders of someone's
lost hope, and he feels disgust, he just
wants to turn the hose on them, they
are that sweaty and stinking, just like
him, of course, but not the woman he   20
wants, you get me? and to come to that—
isn't it too bad, to be despised
for what you do to prove yourself
among men
who want to love you, to love you,
love you.

QUESTIONS
1. Do you think the speaker agrees to have a drink with the fireman because she is sexually attracted to him? Explain. **2.** Why does the speaker describe a woman firefighter as "covered with the cinders of someone's / lost hope" (ll. 16–17)? **3.** How does the phrase "You get me?" (l. 21) help establish the tone of the poem? **4.** Why does the speaker repeat "to love you" at the end of the poem? **5.** In a few sentences, summarize the speaker's response to the fireman.

WRITING TOPIC
Write an essay in which you argue that women should or should not be excluded from such traditional male occupations as firefighting.

Dreams   1968

NIKKI GIOVANNI [b. 1943]

i used to dream militant
dreams of taking
over america to show
these white folks how it should be
done
i used to dream radical dreams
of blowing everyone away with my perceptive powers
of correct analysis
i even used to think i'd be the one
to stop the riot and negotiate the peace   10
then i awoke and dug
that if i dreamed natural
dreams of being a natural
woman doing what a woman
does when she's natural
i would have a revolution

The Colonel   1981

CAROLYN FORCHÉ [b. 1950]

What you have heard is true. I was in his house. His wife carried a tray of coffee and sugar. His daughter filed her nails, his son went out for the night. There were daily papers, pet dogs, a pistol on the cushion beside him. The moon swung bare on its black cord over the house. On the television was a cop show. It was in English. Broken bottles were embedded in the walls round the house to scoop the kneecaps from a man's legs or cut his hands to lace. On the windows there were gratings like those in liquor stores. We had dinner, rack of lamb, good wine, a gold bell was on the table for calling the maid. The maid brought green mangoes, salt, a type of bread. I was asked how I enjoyed the country. There was a brief commercial in Spanish. His wife took everything away. There was some talk then of how difficult it had become to govern. The parrot said hello on the terrace. The colonel told it to shut up, and pushed himself from the table. My friend said to me with his eyes: say nothing. The colonel returned with a sack used to bring groceries home. He spilled many human ears on the table. They were like dried peach halves. There is no other way to say this. He took one of them in his hands, shook it in our faces, dropped it into a water glass. It came alive there. I am tired of fooling around he said. As for the rights of anyone, tell your people they can go fuck themselves. He swept the ears to the floor with his arm and held the last of his wine in the air. Something for your poetry, no? he said. Some of the ears on the floor caught this scrap of his voice. Some of the ears on the floor were pressed to the ground.

QUESTIONS

1. What is the occasion of this poem? Where is it set? How would you characterize the colonel's family?   **2.** "There was some talk then of how difficult it had become to govern." Can you suggest why it had become difficult to govern? How does the colonel respond to these difficulties?   **3.** What does the last sentence suggest?

WRITING TOPIC

This piece is printed as if it were prose. Does it have any of the formal characteristics of a poem?

CONFORMITY
AND
REBELLION

Self-Portrait, c. 1900, by Gwen John.

DRAMA

Antigonê*

(ca. 441 B.C.)

SOPHOCLES   [496?–406 B.C.]

CHARACTERS

Antigonê	Teiresias
Ismenê	A Sentry
Eurydicê	A Messenger
Creon	Chorus
Haimon	

SCENE

Before the Palace of Creon, King of Thebes. A central double door, and two lateral doors. A platform extends the length of the façade, and from this platform three steps lead down into the "orchestra," or chorus-ground.

TIME

Dawn of the day after the repulse of the Argive army from the assault on Thebes.

Prologue

[*Antigonê and Ismenê enter from the central door of the Palace.*]

Antigonê.   Ismenê, dear sister,
   You would think that we had already suffered enough

---

* An English version by Dudley Fitts and Robert Fitzgerald.

For the curse on Oedipus:[1]
I cannot imagine any grief
That you and I have not gone through. And now—
Have they told you of the new decree of our King Creon?
Ismenê.   I have heard nothing: I know
That two sisters lost two brothers, a double death
In a single hour; and I know that the Argive army
Fled in the night; but beyond this, nothing.   10
Antigonê.   I thought so. And that is why I wanted you
To come out here with me. There is something we must do.
Ismenê.   Why do you speak so strangely?
Antigonê.   Listen, Ismenê:
Creon buried our brother Eteoclês
With military honors, gave him a soldier's funeral,
And it was right that he should; but Polyneicês,
Who fought as bravely and died as miserably,—
They say that Creon has sworn
No one shall bury him, no one mourn for him,   20
But his body must lie in the fields, a sweet treasure
For carrion birds to find as they search for food.
That is what they say, and our good Creon is coming here
To announce it publicly; and the penalty—
Stoning to death in the public square!
                                                    There it is,
And now you can prove what you are:
A true sister, or a traitor to your family.
Ismenê.   Antigonê, you are mad! What could I possibly do?
Antigonê.   You must decide whether you will help me or not.
Ismenê.   I do not understand you. Help you in what?   30
Antigonê.   Ismenê, I am going to bury him. Will you come?
Ismenê.   Bury him! You have just said the new law forbids it.
Antigonê.   He is my brother. And he is your brother, too.
Ismenê.   But think of the danger! Think what Creon will do!
Antigonê.   Creon is not strong enough to stand in my way.
Ismenê.   Ah sister!
Oedipus died, everyone hating him
For what his own search brought to light, his eyes

---

[1] Oedipus, a former king of Thebes, unwittingly killed his father and married his own mother, Iocastê. By her he had four children, the sisters Antigonê and Ismenê and the brothers Polyneicês and Eteoclês. When Oedipus realized what he had done, he blinded himself and left Thebes. Eteoclês drove Polyneicês out of Thebes after a quarrel, but Polyneicês returned with an army and laid siege to Thebes. In the ensuing struggle, the brothers killed each other. Creon became king and, as a punishment, decreed that Polyneicês be denied the rites of burial.

Ripped out by his own hand; and Iocastê died,
His mother and wife at once: she twisted the cords   40
That strangled her life; and our two brothers died,
Each killed by the other's sword. And we are left:
But oh, Antigonê,
Think how much more terrible than these
Our own death would be if we should go against Creon
And do what he has forbidden! We are only women,
We cannot fight with men, Antigonê!
The law is strong, we must give in to the law
In this thing, and in worse. I beg the Dead
To forgive me, but I am helpless: I must yield   50
To those in authority. And I think it is dangerous business
To be always meddling.
Antigonê.   If that is what you think,
I should not want you, even if you asked to come.
You have made your choice, you can be what you want to be.
But I will bury him; and if I must die,
I say that this crime is holy: I shall lie down
With him in death, and I shall be as dear
To him as he to me.
                    It is the dead,
Not the living, who make the longest demands:
We die for ever . . .
                    You may do as you like,   60
Since apparently the laws of the gods mean nothing to you.
Ismenê.   They mean a great deal to me; but I have no strength
To break laws that were made for the public good.
Antigonê.   That must be your excuse, I suppose. But as for me,
I will bury the brother I love.
Ismenê.   Antigonê,
I am so afraid for you!
Antigonê.   You need not be:
You have yourself to consider, after all.
Ismenê.   But no one must hear of this, you must tell no one!
I will keep it a secret, I promise!
Antigonê.   Oh tell it! Tell everyone!
Think how they'll hate you when it all comes out   70
If they learn that you knew about it all the time!
Ismenê.   So fiery! You should be cold with fear.
Antigonê.   Perhaps. But I am doing only what I must.
Ismenê.   But can you do it? I say that you cannot.
Antigonê.   Very well: when my strength gives out, I shall do no more.
Ismenê.   Impossible things should not be tried at all.

Antigonê. Go away, Ismenê:
  I shall be hating you soon, and the dead will too,
  For your words are hateful. Leave me my foolish plan:
  I am not afraid of the danger; if it means death,   80
  It will not be the worst of deaths—death without honor.
Ismenê. Go then, if you feel you must.
  You are unwise,
  But a loyal friend indeed to those who love you.

[*Exit into the Palace. Antigonê goes off, L. Enter the Chorus.*]

Párodos[2]

Chorus. Now the long blade of the sun, lying   [*Strophe 1*]
  Level east to west, touches with glory
  Thebes of the Seven Gates. Open, unlidded
  Eye of golden day! O marching light
  Across the eddy and rush of Dircê's stream,[3]
  Striking the white shields of the enemy
  Thrown headlong backward from the blaze of morning!
Choragos.[4] Polyneicês their commander
  Roused them with windy phrases,
  He the wild eagle screaming   10
  Insults above our land,
  His wings their shields of snow,
  His crest their marshalled helms.

Chorus. Against our seven gates in a yawning ring   [*Antistrophe 1*]
  The famished spears came onward in the night;
  But before his jaws were sated with our blood,
  Or pinefire took the garland of our towers,
  He was thrown back; and as he turned, great Thebes—
  No tender victim for his noisy power—
  Rose like a dragon behind him, shouting war.   20
Choragos. For God hates utterly
  The bray of bragging tongues;
  And when he beheld their smiling,

---

  [2] The *Párodos* is the ode sung by the Chorus as it entered the theater and moved down the
aisles to the playing area. The *strophe*, in Greek tragedy, is the unit of verse the Chorus chanted
as it moved to the left in a dance rhythm. The Chorus sang the *antistrophe* as it moved to the
right, and the *epode* while standing still.
  [3] A stream near Thebes.
  [4] Choragos is the leader of the Chorus.

Their swagger of golden helms,
The frown of his thunder blasted
Their first man from our walls.

Chorus.   We heard his shout of triumph high in the air   [*Strophe* 2]
    Turn to a scream; far out in a flaming arc
    He fell with his windy torch, and the earth struck him.
    And others storming in fury no less than his   30
    Found shock of death in the dusty joy of battle.
Choragos.   Seven captains at seven gates
    Yielded their clanging arms to the god
    That bends the battle-line and breaks it.
    These two only, brothers in blood,
    Face to face in matchless rage,
    Mirroring each the other's death,
    Clashed in long combat.

Chorus.   But now in the beautiful morning of victory   [*Antistrophe* 2]
    Let Thebes of the many chariots sing for joy!   40
    With hearts for dancing we'll take leave of war:
    Our temples shall be sweet with hymns of praise,
    And the long night shall echo with our chorus.

Scene I

Choragos.   But now at last our new King is coming:
    Creon of Thebes, Menoikeus' son.
    In this auspicious dawn of his reign
    What are the new complexities
    That shifting Fate has woven for him?
    What is his counsel? Why has he summoned
    The old men to hear him?

[*Enter Creon from the Palace, C. He addresses the Chorus from the top step.*]

Creon.   Gentlemen: I have the honor to inform you that our Ship of State,
    which recent storms have threatened to destroy, has come safely to harbor
    at last, guided by the merciful wisdom of Heaven. I have summoned you
    here this morning because I know that I can depend upon you: your devotion
    to King Laïos was absolute; you never hesitated in your duty to our late ruler
    Oedipus; and when Oedipus died, your loyalty was transferred to his children.
    Unfortunately, as you know, his two sons, the princes Eteoclês and Poly-

neicês, have killed each other in battle; and I, as the next in blood, have succeeded to the full power of the throne.

I am aware, of course, that no Ruler can expect complete loyalty from his subjects until he has been tested in office. Nevertheless, I say to you at the very outset that I have nothing but contempt for the kind of Governor who is afraid, for whatever reason, to follow the course that he knows is best for the State; and as for the man who sets private friendship above the public welfare,—I have no use for him, either. I call God to witness that if I saw my country headed for ruin, I should not be afraid to speak out plainly; and I need hardly remind you that I would never have any dealings with an enemy of the people. No one values friendship more highly than I; but we must remember that friends made at the risk of wrecking our Ship are not real friends at all.

These are my principles, at any rate, and that is why I have made the following decision concerning the sons of Oedipus: Eteoclês, who died as a man should die, fighting for his country, is to be buried with full military honors, with all the ceremony that is usual when the greatest heroes die; but his brother Polyneicês, who broke his exile to come back with fire and sword against his native city and the shrines of his fathers' gods, whose one idea was to spill the blood of his blood and sell his own people into slavery— Polyneicês, I say, is to have no burial: no man is to touch him or say the least prayer for him; he shall lie on the plain, unburied; and the birds and the scavenging dogs can do with him whatever they like.

This is my command, and you can see the wisdom behind it. As long as I am King, no traitor is going to be honored with the loyal man. But whoever shows by word and deed that he is on the side of the State,—he shall have my respect while he is living and my reverence when he is dead.

Choragos. If that is your will, Creon, son of Menoikeus,

You have the right to enforce it: we are yours.

Creon. That is my will. Take care that you do your part.

Choragos. We are old men: let the younger ones carry it out.

Creon. I do not mean that: the sentries have been appointed.

Choragos. Then what is it that you would have us do?

Creon. You will give no support to whoever breaks this law.

Choragos. Only a crazy man is in love with death!

Creon. And death it is; yet money talks, and the wisest

Have sometimes been known to count a few coins too many.

[*Enter Sentry from L.*]

Sentry. I'll not say that I'm out of breath from running, King, because every time I stopped to think about what I have to tell you, I felt like going back. And all the time a voice kept saying, "You fool, don't you know you're walking straight into trouble?"; and then another voice: "Yes, but if you let somebody else get the news to Creon first, it will be even worse than that

for you!" But good sense won out, at least I hope it was good sense, and
here I am with a story that makes no sense at all; but I'll tell it anyhow,
because, as they say, what's going to happen's going to happen, and—
Creon.   Come to the point. What have you to say?
Sentry.   I did not do it. I did not see who did it. You must not punish me for
what someone else has done.
Creon.   A comprehensive defense! More effective, perhaps,
    If I knew its purpose. Come: what is it?
Sentry.   A dreadful thing . . . I don't know how to put it—
Creon.   Out with it!
Sentry.   Well, then;
    The dead man—
                            Polyneicês—

[*Pause. The Sentry is overcome, fumbles for words. Creon waits impassively.*]

                            out there—
                                        someone,—
    New dust on the slimy flesh!

[*Pause. No sign from Creon.*]

    Someone has given it burial that way, and
    Gone . . .

[*Long pause. Creon finally speaks with deadly control.*]

Creon.   And the man who dared do this?
Sentry.   I swear I
    Do not know! You must believe me!
                                        Listen:
    The ground was dry, not a sign of digging, no,
    Not a wheeltrack in the dust, no trace of anyone.
    It was when they relieved us this morning: and one of them,
    The corporal, pointed to it.
                            There it was,
    The strangest—
                    Look:
    The body, just mounded over with light dust: you see?
    Not buried really, but as if they'd covered it
    Just enough for the ghost's peace. And no sign
    Of dogs or any wild animal that had been there.

    And then what a scene there was! Every man of us
    Accusing the other: we all proved the other man did it,

We all had proof that we could not have done it.
We were ready to take hot iron in our hands,
Walk through fire, swear by all the gods,
It was not I!
I do not know who it was, but it was not I!

[*Creon's rage has been mounting steadily, but the Sentry is too intent upon his story to notice it.*]

And then, when this came to nothing, someone said
A thing that silenced us and made us stare
Down at the ground: you had to be told the news,
And one of us had to do it! We threw the dice,
And the bad luck fell to me. So here I am,
No happier to be here than you are to have me:
Nobody likes the man who brings bad news.

Choragos.   I have been wondering, King: can it be that the gods have done this?

Creon [*furiously*].   Stop!
Must you doddering wrecks
Go out of your heads entirely? "The gods!"
Intolerable!
The gods favor this corpse? Why? How had he served them?
Tried to loot their temples, burn their images,
Yes, and the whole State, and its laws with it!
Is it your senile opinion that the gods love to honor bad men?
A pious thought!—
No, from the very beginning
There have been those who have whispered together,
Stiff-necked anarchists, putting their heads together,
Scheming against me in alleys. These are the men,
And they have bribed my own guard to do this thing.
[*Sententiously.*] Money!
There's nothing in the world so demoralizing as money.
Down go your cities,
Homes gone, men gone, honest hearts corrupted,
Crookedness of all kinds, and all for money!
[*To Sentry.*]   But you—!
I swear by God and by the throne of God,
The man who has done this thing shall pay for it!
Find that man, bring him here to me, or your death
Will be the least of your problems: I'll string you up
Alive, and there will be certain ways to make you
Discover your employer before you die;
And the process may teach you a lesson you seem to have missed:

The dearest profit is sometimes all too dear:
That depends on the source. Do you understand me?
A fortune won is often misfortune.

Sentry.   King, may I speak?

Creon.   Your very voice distresses me.

Sentry.   Are you sure that it is my voice, and not your conscience?

Creon.   By God, he wants to analyze me now!

Sentry.   It is not what I say, but what has been done, that hurts you.

Creon.   You talk too much.

Sentry.   Maybe; but I've done nothing.

Creon.   Sold your soul for some silver: that's all you've done.

Sentry.   How dreadful it is when the right judge judges wrong!

Creon.   Your figures of speech
May entertain you now; but unless you bring me the man,
You will get little profit from them in the end.

[Exit Creon into the Palace.]

Sentry.   "Bring me the man"—!
I'd like nothing better than bringing him the man!
But bring him or not, you have seen the last of me here.
At any rate, I am safe!

[Exit Sentry.]

Ode I

Chorus.   Numberless are the world's wonders, but none   *[Strophe 1]*
More wonderful than man; the stormgray sea
Yields to his prows, the huge crests bear him high;
Earth, holy and inexhaustible, is graven
With shining furrows where his plows have gone
Year after year, the timeless labor of stallions.

The lightboned birds and beasts that cling to cover,   *[Antistrophe 1]*
The lithe fish lighting their reaches of dim water,
All are taken, tamed in the net of his mind;
The lion on the hill, the wild horse windy-maned,   10
Resign to him; and his blunt yoke has broken
The sultry shoulders of the mountain bull.

Words also, and thought as rapid as air,   *[Strophe 2]*
He fashions to his good use; statecraft is his,

And his the skill that deflects the arrows of snow,
The spears of winter rain: from every wind
He has made himself secure—from all but one:
In the late wind of death he cannot stand.

O clear intelligence, force beyond all measure!   [*Antistrophe* 2]
O fate of man, working both good and evil!   20
When the laws are kept, how proudly his city stands!
When the laws are broken, what of his city then?
Never may the anarchic man find rest at my hearth,
Never be it said that my thoughts are his thoughts.

Scene II

[*Re-enter Sentry leading Antigonê.*]

Choragos.   What does this mean? Surely this captive woman
   Is the Princess, Antigonê. Why should she be taken?
Sentry.   Here is the one who did it! We caught her
   In the very act of burying him.—Where is Creon?
Choragos.   Just coming from the house.

[*Enter Creon, C.*]

Creon.   What has happened?
   Why have you come back so soon?
Sentry [*expansively*].   O King,
   A man should never be too sure of anything:
   I would have sworn
   That you'd not see me here again: your anger
   Frightened me so, and the things you threatened me with;   10
   But how could I tell then
   That I'd be able to solve the case so soon?
   No dice-throwing this time: I was only too glad to come!

   Here is this woman. She is the guilty one:
   We found her trying to bury him.
   Take her, then; question her; judge her as you will.
   I am through with the whole thing now, and glad of it.
Creon.   But this is Antigonê! Why have you brought her here?
Sentry.   She was burying him, I tell you!
Creon [*severely*].   Is this the truth?
Sentry.   I saw her with my own eyes. Can I say more?   20

Creon.   The details: come, tell me quickly!
Sentry.   It was like this:
  After those terrible threats of yours, King,
  We went back and brushed the dust away from the body.
  The flesh was soft by now, and stinking,
  So we sat on a hill to windward and kept guard.
  No napping this time! We kept each other awake.
  But nothing happened until the white round sun
  Whirled in the center of the round sky over us:
  Then, suddenly,
  A storm of dust roared up from the earth, and the sky   30
  Went out, the plain vanished with all its trees
  In the stinging dark. We closed our eyes and endured it.
  The whirlwind lasted a long time, but it passed;
  And then we looked, and there was Antigonê!
  I have seen
  A mother bird come back to a stripped nest, heard
  Her crying bitterly a broken note or two
  For the young ones stolen. Just so, when this girl
  Found the bare corpse, and all her love's work wasted,
  She wept, and cried on heaven to damn the hands   40
  That had done this thing.
                    And then she brought more dust
  And sprinkled wine three times for her brother's ghost.
  We ran and took her at once. She was not afraid,
  Not even when we charged her with what she had done.
  She denied nothing.
              And this was a comfort to me,
  And some uneasiness: for it is a good thing
  To escape from death, but it is no great pleasure
  To bring death to a friend.
                  Yet I always say
  There is nothing so comfortable as your own safe skin!
Creon [*slowly, dangerously*].   And you, Antigonê,   50
  You with your head hanging,—do you confess this thing?
Antigonê.   I do. I deny nothing.
Creon [*to Sentry*].   You may go.

[*Exit Sentry.*]

[*To Antigonê.*] Tell me, tell me briefly:
  Had you heard my proclamation touching this matter?
Antigonê.   It was public. Could I help hearing it?
Creon.   And yet you dared defy the law.

Antigonê.   I dared.
   It was not God's proclamation. That final Justice
   That rules the world below makes no such laws.

   Your edict, King, was strong,
   But all your strength is weakness itself against   60
   The immortal unrecorded laws of God.
   They are not merely now: they were, and shall be,
   Operative for ever, beyond man utterly.

   I knew I must die, even without your decree:
   I am only mortal. And if I must die
   Now, before it is my time to die,
   Surely this is no hardship: can anyone
   Living, as I live, with evil all about me,
   Think Death less than a friend? This death of mine
   Is of no importance; but if I had left my brother   70
   Lying in death unburied, I should have suffered.
   Now I do not.
                  You smile at me. Ah Creon,
   Think me a fool, if you like; but it may well be
   That a fool convicts me of folly.
Choragos.   Like father, like daughter: both headstrong, deaf to reason!
   She has never learned to yield.
Creon.   She has much to learn.
   The inflexible heart breaks first, the toughest iron
   Cracks first, and the wildest horses bend their necks
   At the pull of the smallest curb.
                                 Pride? In a slave?
   This girl is guilty of a double insolence,   80
   Breaking the given laws and boasting of it.
   Who is the man here,
   She or I, if this crime goes unpunished?
   Sister's child, or more than sister's child,
   Or closer yet in blood—she and her sister
   Win bitter death for this!
   [*To servants.*]   Go, some of you,
   Arrest Ismenê. I accuse her equally.
   Bring her: you will find her sniffling in the house there.

   Her mind's a traitor: crimes kept in the dark
   Cry for light, and the guardian brain shudders;   90
   But how much worse than this
   Is brazen boasting of barefaced anarchy!

Antigonê.   Creon, what more do you want than my death?
Creon.   Nothing.
  That gives me everything.
Antigonê.   Then I beg you: kill me.
  This talking is a great weariness: your words
  Are distasteful to me, and I am sure that mine
  Seem so to you. And yet they should not seem so:
  I should have praise and honor for what I have done.
  All these men here would praise me
  Were their lips not frozen shut with fear of you.   100
  [*Bitterly.*] Ah the good fortune of kings,
  Licensed to say and do whatever they please!
Creon.   You are alone here in that opinion.
Antigonê.   No, they are with me. But they keep their tongues in leash.
Creon.   Maybe. But you are guilty, and they are not.
Antigonê.   There is no guilt in reverence for the dead.
Creon.   But Eteoclês—was he not your brother too?
Antigonê.   My brother too.
Creon.   And you insult his memory?
Antigonê [*softly*].   The dead man would not say that I insult it.
Creon.   He would: for you honor a traitor as much as him.   110
Antigonê.   His own brother, traitor or not, and equal in blood.
Creon.   He made war on his country. Eteoclês defended it.
Antigonê.   Nevertheless, there are honors due all the dead.
Creon.   But not the same for the wicked as for the just.
Antigonê.   Ah Creon, Creon,
  Which of us can say what the gods hold wicked?
Creon.   An enemy is an enemy, even dead.
Antigonê.   It is my nature to join in love, not hate.
Creon [*finally losing patience*].   Go join them, then; if you must have your
    love,
      Find it in hell!   120
Choragos.   But see, Ismenê comes:

[*Enter Ismenê, guarded.*]

  Those tears are sisterly, the cloud
  That shadows her eyes rains down gentle sorrow.
Creon.   You too, Ismenê,
  Snake in my ordered house, sucking my blood
  Stealthily—and all the time I never knew
  That these two sisters were aiming at my throne!
                                                                                  Ismenê,
  Do you confess your share in this crime, or deny it?
  Answer me.

Ismenê.   Yes, if she will let me say so. I am guilty.   130
Antigonê [*coldly*].   No, Ismenê. You have no right to say so.
  You would not help me, and I will not have you help me.
Ismenê.   But now I know what you meant; and I am here
  To join you, to take my share of punishment.
Antigonê.   The dead man and the gods who rule the dead
  Know whose act this was. Words are not friends.
Ismenê.   Do you refuse me, Antigonê? I want to die with you:
  I too have a duty that I must discharge to the dead.
Antigonê.   You shall not lessen my death by sharing it.
Ismenê.   What do I care for life when you are dead?   140
Antigonê.   Ask Creon. You're always hanging on his opinions.
Ismenê.   You are laughing at me. Why, Antigonê?
Antigonê.   It's a joyless laughter, Ismenê.
Ismenê.   But can I do nothing?
Antigonê.   Yes. Save yourself. I shall not envy you.
  There are those who will praise you; I shall have honor, too.
Ismenê.   But we are equally guilty!
Antigonê.   No more, Ismenê.
  You are alive, but I belong to Death.
Creon [*to the Chorus*].   Gentlemen, I beg you to observe these girls:
  One has just now lost her mind; the other,
  It seems, has never had a mind at all.   150
Ismenê.   Grief teaches the steadiest minds to waver, King.
Creon.   Yours certainly did, when you assumed guilt with the guilty!
Ismenê.   But how could I go on living without her?
Creon.   You are.
  She is already dead.
Ismenê.   But your own son's bride!
Creon.   There are places enough for him to push his plow.
  I want no wicked women for my sons!
Ismenê.   O dearest Haimon, how your father wrongs you!
Creon.   I've had enough of your childish talk of marriage!
Choragos.   Do you really intend to steal this girl from your son?
Creon.   No; Death will do that for me.
Choragos.   Then she must die?   160
Creon [*ironically*].   You dazzle me.
                                    —But enough of this talk!
  [*To Guards.*] You there, take them away and guard them well:
  For they are but women, and even brave men run
  When they see Death coming.

[*Exeunt Ismenê, Antigonê, and Guards.*]

Ode II

Chorus.   Fortunate is the man who has never tasted   [*Strophe 1*]
      God's vengeance!
Where once the anger of heaven has struck, that house is shaken
For ever: damnation rises behind each child
Like a wave cresting out of the black northeast,
When the long darkness under sea roars up
And bursts drumming death upon the windwhipped sand.

I have seen this gathering sorrow from time long past   [*Antistrophe 1*]
Loom upon Oedipus' children: generation from generation
Takes the compulsive rage of the enemy god.
So lately this last flower of Oedipus' line   10
Drank the sunlight! but now a passionate word
And a handful of dust have closed up all its beauty.

    What mortal arrogance   [*Strophe 2*]
    Transcends the wrath of Zeus?
Sleep cannot lull him, nor the effortless long months
Of the timeless gods: but he is young for ever,
And his house is the shining day of high Olympos.
      And that is and shall be,
      And all the past, is his.
No pride on earth is free of the curse of heaven.   20

    The straying dreams of men   [*Antistrophe 2*]
    May bring them ghosts of joy:
But as they drowse, the waking embers burn them;
Or they walk with fixed eyes, as blind men walk.
But the ancient wisdom speaks for our own time:
    Fate works most for woe
    With Folly's fairest show.
Man's little pleasure is the spring of sorrow.

Scene III

Choragos.   But here is Haimon, King, the last of all your sons.
    Is it grief for Antigonê that brings him here,
    And bitterness at being robbed of his bride?

[*Enter Haimon.*]

Creon.   We shall soon see, and no need of diviners.

                                                    —Son,

    You have heard my final judgment on that girl:
    Have you come here hating me, or have you come
    With deference and with love, whatever I do?
Haimon.   I am your son, father. You are my guide.
    You make things clear for me, and I obey you.
    No marriage means more to me than your continuing wisdom.   10
Creon.   Good. That is the way to behave: subordinate
    Everything else, my son, to your father's will.
    This is what a man prays for, that he may get
    Sons attentive and dutiful in his house,
    Each one hating his father's enemies,
    Honoring his father's friends. But if his sons
    Fail him, if they turn out unprofitably,
    What has he fathered but trouble for himself
    And amusement for the malicious?

                                 So you are right

    Not to lose your head over this woman.   20
    Your pleasure with her would soon grow cold, Haimon,
    And then you'd have a hellcat in bed and elsewhere.
    Let her find her husband in Hell!
    Of all the people in this city, only she
    Has had contempt for my law and broken it.

    Do you want me to show myself weak before the people?
    Or to break my sworn word? No, and I will not.
    The woman dies.
    I suppose she'll plead "family ties." Well, let her.
    If I permit my own family to rebel,   30
    How shall I earn the world's obedience?
    Show me the man who keeps his house in hand,
    He's fit for public authority.

                                   I'll have no dealings

    With law-breakers, critics of the government:
    Whoever is chosen to govern should be obeyed—
    Must be obeyed, in all things, great and small,
    Just and unjust! O Haimon,
    The man who knows how to obey, and that man only,
    Knows how to give commands when the time comes.
    You can depend on him, no matter how fast   40
    The spears come: he's a good soldier, he'll stick it out.

Anarchy, anarchy! Show me a greater evil!
This is why cities tumble and the great houses rain down,
This is what scatters armies!

No, no: good lives are made so by discipline.
We keep the laws then, and the lawmakers,
And no woman shall seduce us. If we must lose,
Let's lose to a man, at least! Is a woman stronger than we?
Choragos.   Unless time has rusted my wits,
What you say, King, is said with point and dignity.   50
Haimon [*boyishly earnest*].   Father:
Reason is God's crowning gift to man, and you are right
To warn me against losing mine. I cannot say—
I hope that I shall never want to say!—that you
Have reasoned badly. Yet there are other men
Who can reason, too; and their opinions might be helpful.
You are not in a position to know everything
That people say or do, or what they feel:
Your temper terrifies them—everyone
Will tell you only what you like to hear.   60
But I, at any rate, can listen; and I have heard them
Muttering and whispering in the dark about this girl.
They say no woman has ever, so unreasonably,
Died so shameful a death for a generous act:
"She covered her brother's body. Is this indecent?
She kept him from dogs and vultures. Is this a crime?
Death?—She should have all the honor that we can give her!"

This is the way they talk out there in the city.

You must believe me:
Nothing is closer to me than your happiness.   70
What could be closer? Must not any son
Value his father's fortune as his father does his?
I beg you, do not be unchangeable:
Do not believe that you alone can be right.
The man who thinks that,
The man who maintains that only he has the power
To reason correctly, the gift to speak, the soul—
A man like that, when you know him, turns out empty.
It is not reason never to yield to reason!

In flood time you can see how some trees bend   80
And because they bend, even their twigs are safe,
While stubborn trees are torn up, roots and all.

And the same thing happens in sailing:
Make your sheet fast, never slacken—and over you go,
Head over heels and under: and there's your voyage.
Forget you are angry! Let yourself be moved!
I know I am young; but please let me say this:
The ideal condition
Would be, I admit, that men should be right by instinct;
But since we are all too likely to go astray,   90
The reasonable thing is to learn from those who can teach.

Choragos.   You will do well to listen to him, King,
If what he says is sensible. And you, Haimon,
Must listen to your father.—Both speak well.

Creon.   You consider it right for a man of my years and experience
To go to school to a boy?

Haimon.   It is not right
If I am wrong. But if I am young, and right,
What does my age matter?

Creon.   You think it right to stand up for an anarchist?

Haimon.   Not at all. I pay no respect to criminals.   100

Creon.   Then she is not a criminal?

Haimon.   The City would deny it, to a man.

Creon.   And the City proposes to teach me how to rule?

Haimon.   Ah. Who is it that's talking like a boy now?

Creon.   My voice is the one voice giving orders in this City!

Haimon.   It is no City if it takes orders from one voice.

Creon.   The State is the King!

Haimon.   Yes, if the State is a desert.

[*Pause.*]

Creon.   This boy, it seems, has sold out to a woman.

Haimon.   If you are a woman: my concern is only for you.

Creon.   So? Your "concern"! In a public brawl with your father!   110

Haimon.   How about you, in a public brawl with justice?

Creon.   With justice, when all that I do is within my rights?

Haimon.   You have no right to trample on God's right.

Creon [*completely out of control*].   Fool, adolescent fool! Taken in by a woman!

Haimon.   You'll never see me taken in by anything vile.

Creon.   Every word you say is for her!

Haimon [*quietly, darkly*].   And for you.
And for me. And for the gods under the earth.

Creon.   You'll never marry her while she lives.

Haimon.   Then she must die.—But her death will cause another.

Creon.   Another?   120
   Have you lost your senses? Is this an open threat?
Haimon.   There is no threat in speaking to emptiness.
Creon.   I swear you'll regret this superior tone of yours!
   You are the empty one!
Haimon.   If you were not my father,
   I'd say you were perverse.
Creon.   You girlstruck fool, don't play at words with me!
Haimon.   I am sorry. You prefer silence.
Creon.   Now, by God—!
   I swear, by all the gods in heaven above us,
   You'll watch it, I swear you shall!
   [*To the servants.*]   Bring her out!
   Bring the woman out! Let her die before his eyes!   130
   Here, this instant, with her bridegroom beside her!
Haimon.   Not here, no; she will not die here, King.
   And you will never see my face again.
   Go on raving as long as you've a friend to endure you.

[*Exit Haimon.*]

Choragos.   Gone, gone.
   Creon, a young man in a rage is dangerous!
Creon.   Let him do, or dream to do, more than a man can.
   He shall not save these girls from death.
Choragos.   These girls?
   You have sentenced them both?
Creon.   No, you are right.
   I will not kill the one whose hands are clean.   140
Choragos.   But Antigonê?
Creon [*somberly*].   I will carry her far away
   Out there in the wilderness, and lock her
   Living in a vault of stone. She shall have food,
   As the custom is, to absolve the State of her death.
   And there let her pray to the gods of hell:
   They are her only gods:
   Perhaps they will show her an escape from death,
   Or she may learn,
                       though late,
   That piety shown the dead is pity in vain.

[*Exit Creon.*]

Ode III

Chorus.   Love, unconquerable   [*Strophe*]
 Waster of rich men, keeper
 Of warm lights and all-night vigil
 In the soft face of a girl:
 Sea-wanderer, forest-visitor!
 Even the pure Immortals cannot escape you,
 And mortal man, in his one day's dusk,
 Trembles before your glory.

 Surely you swerve upon ruin   [*Antistrophe*]
 The just man's consenting heart,   10
 As here you have made bright anger
 Strike between father and son—
 And none had conquered but Love!
 A girl's glance working the will of heaven:
 Pleasure to her alone who mocks us,
 Merciless Aphroditê.[5]

Scene IV

Choragos [*as Antigonê enters guarded*].   But I can no longer stand in awe of
  this,
 Nor, seeing what I see, keep back my tears.
 Here is Antigonê, passing to that chamber
 Where all find sleep at last.

Antigonê.   Look upon me, friends, and pity me   [*Strophe 1*]
 Turning back at the night's edge to say
 Good-by to the sun that shines for me no longer;
 Now sleepy Death
 Summons me down to Acheron,[6] that cold shore:
 There is no bridesong there, nor any music.   10
Chorus.   Yet not unpraised, not without a kind of honor,
 You walk at last into the underworld;
 Untouched by sickness, broken by no sword.
 What woman has ever found your way to death?

---

[5] Aphroditê is the goddess of love.
[6] A river of Hades.

Antigonê.   How often I have heard the story of Niobê,[7]   [*Antistrophe 1*]
Tantalos' wretched daughter, how the stone
Clung fast about her, ivy-close: and they say
The rain falls endlessly
And sifting soft snow; her tears are never done.
I feel the loneliness of her death in mine.   20
Chorus.   But she was born of heaven, and you
Are woman, woman-born. If her death is yours,
A mortal woman's, is this not for you
Glory in our world and in the world beyond?

Antigonê.   You laugh at me. Ah, friends, friends,   [*Strophe 2*]
Can you not wait until I am dead? O Thebes,
O men many-charioted, in love with Fortune,
Dear springs of Dircê, sacred Theban grove,
Be witnesses for me, denied all pity,
Unjustly judged! and think a word of love   30
For her whose path turns
Under dark earth, where there are no more tears.
Chorus.   You have passed beyond human daring and come at last
Into a place of stone where Justice sits.
I cannot tell
What shape of your father's guilt appears in this.

Antigonê.   You have touched it at last: that bridal bed   [*Antistrophe 2*]
Unspeakable, horror of son and mother mingling:
Their crime, infection of all our family!
O Oedipus, father and brother!   40
Your marriage strikes from the grave to murder mine.
I have been a stranger here in my own land:
All my life
The blasphemy of my birth has followed me.
Chorus.   Reverence is a virtue, but strength
Lives in established law: that must prevail.
You have made your choice,
Your death is the doing of your conscious hand.

Antigonê.   Then let me go, since all your words are bitter,   [*Epode*]
And the very light of the sun is cold to me.   50

---

[7] Niobê married an ancestor of Oedipus named Amphion. Her fourteen children were killed
by Apollo and Artemis after Niobê boasted to their mother, Leto, that her children were superior
to them. She wept incessantly and was finally transformed into a rock on Mt. Sipylos, whose
streams are her tears.

Lead me to my vigil, where I must have
Neither love nor lamentation; no song, but silence.

[*Creon interrupts impatiently.*]

Creon.   If dirges and planned lamentations could put off death,
Men would be singing for ever.
[*To the servants.*]   Take her, go!
You know your orders: take her to the vault
And leave her alone there. And if she lives or dies,
That's her affair, not ours: our hands are clean.

Antigonê.   O tomb, vaulted bride-bed in eternal rock,
Soon I shall be with my own again
Where Persephonê[8] welcomes the thin ghosts underground: 60
And I shall see my father again, and you, mother,
And dearest Polyneicês—
                         dearest indeed
To me, since it was my hand
That washed him clean and poured the ritual wine:
And my reward is death before my time!

And yet, as men's hearts know, I have done no wrong,
I have not sinned before God. Or if I have,
I shall know the truth in death. But if the guilt
Lies upon Creon who judged me, then, I pray,
May his punishment equal my own.
Choragos.   O passionate heart,   70
Unyielding, tormented still by the same winds!
Creon.   Her guards shall have good cause to regret their delaying.
Antigonê.   Ah! That voice is like the voice of death!
Creon.   I can give you no reason to think you are mistaken.
Antigonê.   Thebes, and you my fathers' gods,
And rulers of Thebes, you see me now, the last
Unhappy daughter of a line of kings,
Your kings, led away to death. You will remember
What things I suffer, and at what men's hands,
Because I would not transgress the laws of heaven.   80
[*To the guards, simply.*] Come: let us wait no longer.

[*Exit Antigonê, L., guarded.*]

---

[8] Queen of Hades.

Ode IV

Chorus.   All Danaê's[9] beauty was locked away   [*Strophe 1*]
    In a brazen cell where the sunlight could not come:
    A small room, still as any grave, enclosed her.
    Yet she was a princess too,
    And Zeus in a rain of gold poured love upon her.
    O child, child,
    No power in wealth or war
    Or tough sea-blackened ships
    Can prevail against untiring Destiny!

    And Dryas' son[10] also, that furious king,   [*Antistrophe 1*]
    Bore the god's prisoning anger for his pride: 11
    Sealed up by Dionysos in deaf stone,
    His madness died among echoes.
    So at the last he learned what dreadful power
    His tongue had mocked:
    For he had profaned the revels,
    And fired the wrath of the nine
    Implacable Sisters[11] that love the sound of the flute.

    And old men tell a half-remembered tale   [*Strophe 2*]
    Of horror where a dark ledge splits the sea   20
    And a double surf beats on the gray shores:
    How a king's new woman,[12] sick
    With hatred for the queen he had imprisoned,
    Ripped out his two sons' eyes with her bloody hands
    While grinning Arês[13] watched the shuttle plunge
    Four times: four blind wounds crying for revenge,

    Crying, tears and blood mingled.—Piteously born,   [*Antistrophe 2*]
    Those sons whose mother was of heavenly birth!
    Her father was the god of the North Wind
    And she was cradled by gales,   30
    She raced with young colts on the glittering hills

---

[9] Though Danaê, a beautiful princess of Àrgos, was confined by her father, Zeus visited her in the form of a shower of gold, and she gave birth to Perseus as a result.

[10] Lycurgus, King of Thrace, who was driven mad by Dionysos, the god of wine.

[11] The Muses.

[12] The ode alludes to a story indicating the uselessness of high birth against implacable fate. The king's new woman is Eidothea, the second wife of King Phineus. Though Cleopatra, his first wife, was the daughter of Boreas, the north wind, and Phineus was descended from kings, yet Eidothea, out of hatred for Cleopatra, blinded her two sons.

[13] The god of war.

And walked untrammeled in the open light:
But in her marriage deathless Fate found means
To build a tomb like yours for all her joy.

Scene V

[*Enter blind Teiresias, led by a boy. The opening speeches of Teiresias should be in singsong contrast to the realistic lines of Creon.*]

Teiresias.   This is the way the blind man comes, Princes, Princes,
    Lock-step, two heads lit by the eyes of one.
Creon.   What new thing have you to tell us, old Teiresias?
Teiresias.   I have much to tell you: listen to the prophet, Creon.
Creon.   I am not aware that I have ever failed to listen.
Teiresias.   Then you have done wisely, King, and ruled well.
Creon.   I admit my debt to you. But what have you to say?
Teiresias.   This, Creon: you stand once more on the edge of fate.
Creon.   What do you mean? Your words are a kind of dread.
Teiresias.   Listen, Creon: 10
    I was sitting in my chair of augury, at the place
    Where the birds gather about me. They were all a-chatter,
    As is their habit, when suddenly I heard
    A strange note in their jangling, a scream, a
    Whirring fury; I knew that they were fighting,
    Tearing each other, dying
    In a whirlwind of wings clashing. And I was afraid.
    I began the rites of burnt-offering at the altar,
    But Hephaistos[14] failed me: instead of bright flame,
    There was only the sputtering slime of the fat thigh-flesh   20
    Melting: the entrails dissolved in gray smoke;
    The bare bone burst from the welter. And no blaze!

    This was a sign from heaven. My boy described it,
    Seeing for me as I see for others.

    I tell you, Creon, you yourself have brought
    This new calamity upon us. Our hearths and altars
    Are stained with the corruption of dogs and carrion birds
    That glut themselves on the corpse of Oedipus' son.
    The gods are deaf when we pray to them, their fire
    Recoils from our offering, their birds of omen   30

---

[14] The god of fire.

Have no cry of comfort, for they are gorged
With the thick blood of the dead.
O my son,
These are no trifles! Think: all men make mistakes,
But a good man yields when he knows his course is wrong,
And repairs the evil. The only crime is pride.

Give in to the dead man, then: do not fight with a corpse—
What glory is it to kill a man who is dead?
Think, I beg you:
It is for your own good that I speak as I do.
You should be able to yield for your own good.   40
Creon.   It seems that prophets have made me their especial province.
All my life long
I have been a kind of butt for the dull arrows
Of doddering fortune-tellers!
No, Teiresias:
If your birds—if the great eagles of God himself
Should carry him stinking bit by bit to heaven,
I would not yield. I am not afraid of pollution:
No man can defile the gods.
Do what you will,
Go into business, make money, speculate
In India gold or that synthetic gold from Sardis,   50
Get rich otherwise than by my consent to bury him.
Teiresias, it is a sorry thing when a wise man
Sells his wisdom, lets out his words for hire!
Teiresias.   Ah Creon! Is there no man left in the world—
Creon.   To do what?—Come, let's have the aphorism!
Teiresias.   No man who knows that wisdom outweighs any wealth?
Creon.   As surely as bribes are baser than any baseness.
Teiresias.   You are sick, Creon! You are deathly sick!
Creon.   As you say: it is not my place to challenge a prophet.
Teiresias.   Yet you have said my prophecy is for sale.   60
Creon.   The generation of prophets has always loved gold.
Teiresias.   The generation of kings has always loved brass.
Creon.   You forget yourself! You are speaking to your King.
Teiresias.   I know it. You are a king because of me.
Creon.   You have a certain skill; but you have sold out.
Teiresias.   King, you will drive me to words that—
Creon.   Say them, say them!
Only remember: I will not pay you for them.
Teiresias.   No, you will find them too costly.
Creon.   No doubt. Speak:
Whatever you say, you will not change my will.

Teiresias.   Then take this, and take it to heart!   70
     The time is not far off when you shall pay back
     Corpse for corpse, flesh of your own flesh.
     You have thrust the child of this world into living night,
     You have kept from the gods below the child that is theirs:
     The one in a grave before her death, the other,
     Dead, denied the grave. This is your crime:
     And the Furies and the dark gods of Hell
     Are swift with terrible punishment for you.

     Do you want to buy me now, Creon?
                                                        Not many days,
     And your house will be full of men and women weeping,   80
     And curses will be hurled at you from far
     Cities grieving for sons unburied, left to rot
     Before the walls of Thebes.
     These are my arrows, Creon: they are all for you.

     [*To boy.*] But come, child: lead me home.
     Let him waste his fine anger upon younger men.
     Maybe he will learn at last
     To control a wiser tongue in a better head.

[*Exit Teiresias.*]

Choragos.   The old man has gone, King, but his words
     Remain to plague us. I am old, too,   90
     But I cannot remember that he was ever false.
Creon.   That is true. . . . It troubles me.
     Oh it is hard to give in! but it is worse
     To risk everything for stubborn pride.
Choragos.   Creon: take my advice.
Creon.   What shall I do?
Choragos.   Go quickly: free Antigonê from her vault
     And build a tomb for the body of Polyneicês.
Creon.   You would have me do this?
Choragos.   Creon, yes!
     And it must be done at once: God moves
     Swiftly to cancel the folly of stubborn men.   100
Creon.   It is hard to deny the heart! But I
     Will do it: I will not fight with destiny.
Choragos.   You must go yourself, you cannot leave it to others.
Creon.   I will go.
                  —Bring axes, servants:
     Come with me to the tomb. I buried her, I

Will set her free.
          Oh quickly!
My mind misgives—
The laws of the gods are mighty, and a man must serve them
To the last days of his life!

[*Exit Creon.*]

Paean[15]

Choragos. God of many names		[*Strophe 1*]
Chorus. O Iacchos[16]		

                     son
of Kadmeian Sémelê
              O born of the Thunder!
Guardian of the West
              Regent
of Eleusis's plain
            O Prince of maenad Thebes
and the Dragon Field by rippling Ismenos:[17]

Choragos. God of many names   [*Antistrophe 1*]
Chorus.   the flame of torches
flares on our hills
           the nymphs of Iacchos
dance at the spring of Castalia:[18]
from the vine-close mountain
                come ah come in ivy:
Evohé evohé! sings through the streets of Thebes   10

Choragos. God of many names   [*Strophe 2*]
Chorus.   Iacchos of Thebes
heavenly Child
           of Sémelê bride of the Thunderer!
The shadow of plague is upon us:
                come

---

[15] A hymn.
[16] Iacchos is a name for Dionysos. His mother was Sémelê, daughter of Kadmos, the founder
of Thebes. His father was Zeus. The Maenads were priestesses of Dionysos who cry "evohé evohé."
[17] A river of Thebes, sacred to Apollo. Dragon Field refers to the legend that the ancestors of
Thebes sprang from the dragon's teeth sown by Kadmos.
[18] A spring on Mt. Parnasos.

with clement feet
                    oh come from Parnasos
down the long slopes
                    across the lamenting water

Choragos.   Iô Fire! Chorister of the throbbing stars!   [*Antistrophe 2*]
    O purest among the voices of the night!
    Thou son of God, blaze for us!
Chorus.   Come with choric rapture of circling Maenads
    Who cry *Iô Iacche!*
                    God of many names!   20

Exodos

[*Enter Messenger, L.*]

Messenger.   Men of the line of Kadmos, you who live
    Near Amphion's[19] citadel:
                    I cannot say
    Of any condition of human life "This is fixed,
    This is clearly good, or bad." Fate raises up,
    And Fate casts down the happy and unhappy alike:
    No man can foretell his Fate.
                    Take the case of Creon:
    Creon was happy once, as I count happiness:
    Victorious in battle, sole governor of the land,
    Fortunate father of children nobly born.
    And now it has all gone from him! Who can say   10
    That a man is still alive when his life's joy fails?
    He is a walking dead man. Grant him rich,
    Let him live like a king in his great house:
    If his pleasure is gone, I would not give
    So much as the shadow of smoke for all he owns.
Choragos.   Your words hint at sorrow: what is your news for us?
Messenger.   They are dead. The living are guilty of their death.
Choragos.   Who is guilty? Who is dead? Speak!
Messenger.   Haimon.
    Haimon is dead; and the hand that killed him
    Is his own hand.
Choragos.   His father's? or his own?   20

---

[19] A child of Zeus and Antiope. He is noted for building the walls of Thebes by charming the stones into place with a lyre.

Messenger.   His own, driven mad by the murder his father had done.
Choragos.   Teiresias, Teiresias, how clearly you saw it all!
Messenger.   This is my news: you must draw what conclusions you can from it.
Choragos.   But look: Eurydicê, our Queen:
Has she overheard us?

[*Enter Eurydicê from the Palace, C.*]

Eurydicê.   I have heard something, friends:
As I was unlocking the gate of Pallas'[20] shrine,
For I needed her help today, I heard a voice
Telling of some new sorrow. And I fainted
There at the temple with all my maidens about me.   30
But speak again: whatever it is, I can bear it:
Grief and I are no strangers.
Messenger.   Dearest lady,
I will tell you plainly all that I have seen.
I shall not try to comfort you: what is the use,
Since comfort could lie only in what is not true?
The truth is always best.

                  I went with Creon
To the outer plain where Polyneicês was lying,
No friend to pity him, his body shredded by dogs.
We made our prayers in that place to Hecatê[21]
And Pluto,[22] that they would be merciful. And we bathed   40
The corpse with holy water, and we brought
Fresh-broken branches to burn what was left of it,
And upon the urn we heaped up a towering barrow
Of the earth of his own land.

                  When we were done, we ran
To the vault where Antigonê lay on her couch of stone.
One of the servants had gone ahead,
And while he was yet far off he heard a voice
Grieving within the chamber, and he came back
And told Creon. And as the King went closer,
The air was full of wailing, the words lost,   50
And he begged us to make all haste. "Am I a prophet?"
He said, weeping, "And must I walk this road,
The saddest of all that I have gone before?

---

[20] Pallas Athene, goddess of wisdom.
[21] Hecatê is often identified with Persephone, a goddess of Hades; generally Hecatê is a goddess of sorcery and witchcraft.
[22] King of Hades and brother of Zeus and Poseidon.

My son's voice calls me on. Oh quickly, quickly!
Look through the crevice there, and tell me
If it is Haimon, or some deception of the gods!"

We obeyed; and in the cavern's farthest corner
We saw her lying:
She had made a noose of her fine linen veil
And hanged herself. Haimon lay beside her,   60
His arms about her waist, lamenting her,
His love lost under ground, crying out
That his father had stolen her away from him.

When Creon saw him the tears rushed to his eyes
And he called to him: "What have you done, child? Speak to me.
What are you thinking that makes your eyes so strange?
O my son, my son, I come to you on my knees!"
But Haimon spat in his face. He said not a word,
Staring—
          And suddenly drew his sword
And lunged. Creon shrank back, the blade missed; and the boy,   70
Desperate against himself, drove it half its length
Into his own side, and fell. And as he died
He gathered Antigonê close in his arms again,
Choking, his blood bright red on her white cheek.
And now he lies dead with the dead, and she is his
At last, his bride in the houses of the dead.

[*Exit Eurydicê into the Palace.*]

Choragos.   She has left us without a word. What can this mean?
Messenger.   It troubles me, too; yet she knows what is best,
    Her grief is too great for public lamentation,
    And doubtless she has gone to her chamber to weep   80
    For her dead son, leading her maidens in his dirge.
Choragos.   It may be so: but I fear this deep silence.

[*Pause.*]

Messenger.   I will see what she is doing. I will go in.

[*Exit Messenger into the Palace.*]
[*Enter Creon with attendants, bearing Haimon's body.*]

Choragos.   But here is the King himself: oh look at him,
    Bearing his own damnation in his arms.

Creon.   Nothing you say can touch me any more.
    My own blind heart has brought me
    From darkness to final darkness. Here you see
    The father murdering, the murdered son—
    And all my civic wisdom!   90
    Haimon my son, so young to die,
    I was the fool, not you; and you died for me.
Choragos.   That is the truth; but you were late in learning it.
Creon.   This truth is hard to bear. Surely a god
    Has crushed me beneath the hugest weight of heaven,
    And driven me headlong a barbaric way
    To trample out the thing I held most dear.

    The pains that men will take to come to pain!

[*Enter Messenger from the Palace.*]

Messenger.   The burden you carry in your hands is heavy,
    But it is not all: you will find more in your house.   100
Creon.   What burden worse than this shall I find there?
Messenger.   The Queen is dead.
Creon.   O port of death, deaf world,
    Is there no pity for me? And you, Angel of evil,
    I was dead, and your words are death again.
    Is it true, boy? Can it be true?
    Is my wife dead? Has death bred death?
Messenger.   You can see for yourself.

[*The doors are opened, and the body of Eurydicê is disclosed within.*]

Creon.   Oh pity!
    All true, all true, and more than I can bear!   110
    O my wife, my son!
Messenger.   She stood before the altar, and her heart
    Welcomed the knife her own hand guided,
    And a great cry burst from her lips for Megareus[23] dead,
    And for Haimon dead, her sons; and her last breath
    Was a curse for their father, the murderer of her sons,
    And she fell, and the dark flowed in through her closing eyes.
Creon.   O God, I am sick with fear.
    Are there no swords here? Has no one a blow for me?
Messenger.   Her curse is upon you for the deaths of both.   120

---

[23] Son of Creon who was killed in the attack on Thebes.

Creon. It is right that it should be. I alone am guilty.
    I know it, and I say it. Lead me in,
    Quickly, friends.
    I have neither life nor substance. Lead me in.
Choragos. You are right, if there can be right in so much wrong.
    The briefest way is best in a world of sorrow.
Creon. Let it come,
    Let death come quickly, and be kind to me.
    I would not ever see the sun again.
Choragos. All that will come when it will; but we, meanwhile,   130
    Have much to do. Leave the future to itself.
Creon. All my heart was in that prayer!
Choragos. Then do not pray any more: the sky is deaf.
Creon. Lead me away. I have been rash and foolish.
    I have killed my son and my wife.
    I look for comfort; my comfort lies here dead.
    Whatever my hands have touched has come to nothing.
    Fate has brought all my pride to a thought of dust.

[*As Creon is being led into the house, the Choragos advances and speaks directly to the audience.*]

Choragos. There is no happiness where there is no wisdom;
    No wisdom but in submission to the gods.   140
    Big words are always punished,
    And proud men in old age learn to be wise.

QUESTIONS

1. Critics have traditionally divided over the question of whether Antigonê or Creon is the protagonist in the play. How does the answer to this question affect one's interpretation of the play? **2.** How does the Prologue establish the mood and theme of the play? **3.** Does the character of Antigonê change during the course of the play? **4.** Does the action of the play prepare us for the change in Creon— that is, for his realization that he has been wrong? **5.** Is there any justification for Antigonê's cold refusal to allow Ismenê to share her martyrdom? Explain.

WRITING TOPICS

1. Can *Antigonê* be read as a justification for civil disobedience? Explain. **2.** To what extent and in what ways does the Chorus contribute to the dramatic development and tension of the play?

An Enemy of the People*   1882

HENRIK IBSEN   [1828–1906]

DRAMATIS PERSONAE

Dr. Thomas Stockmann, Medical Officer of the Municipal Baths.
Mrs. Stockmann, his wife.
Petra, their daughter, a teacher.
Ejlif ⎱ their sons (aged 13 and 10
Morten ⎰ respectively).
Peter Stockmann, the Doctor's elder brother; Mayor of the Town and Chief Constable, Chairman of the Baths' Committee, etc., etc.

Morten Kiil, a tanner (Mrs. Stockmann's adoptive father).
Hovstad, editor of the "People's Messenger."
Billing, sub-editor.
Captain Horster.
Aslaksen, a printer.
Men of various conditions and occupations, some few women, and a troop of schoolboys—the audience at a public meeting.

(The action takes place in a coast town in southern Norway.)

Act I

SCENE.   *Dr. Stockmann's sitting-room. It is evening. The room is plainly but neatly appointed and furnished. In the right-hand wall are two doors; the farther leads out to the hall, the nearer to the doctor's study. In the left-hand wall, opposite the door leading to the hall, is a door leading to the other rooms occupied by the family. In the middle of the same wall stands the stove, and, further forward, a couch with a looking-glass hanging over it and an oval table in front of it. On the table, a lighted lamp, with a lampshade. At the back of the room, an open door leads to the dining-room. Billing is seen sitting at the dining table, on which a lamp is burning. He has a napkin tucked under his chin, and Mrs. Stockmann is standing by the table handing him a large platefull of roast beef. The other places at the table are empty, and the table somewhat in disorder, a meal having evidently recently been finished.*

Mrs. Stockmann.   You see, if you come an hour late, Mr. Billing, you have to put up with cold meat.
Billing *(as he eats).*   It is uncommonly good, thank you—remarkably good.
Mrs. Stockmann.   My husband makes such a point of having his meals punctually, you know—

---

* Translated by R. Farquharson Sharp.

Billing.   That doesn't affect me a bit. Indeed, I almost think I enjoy a meal all the better when I can sit down and eat all by myself and undisturbed.

Mrs. Stockmann.   Oh well, as long as you are enjoying it—. *(Turns to the hall door, listening.)* I expect that is Mr. Hovstad coming too.

Billing.   Very likely.

(Peter Stockmann comes in. He wears an overcoat and his official hat, and carries a stick.)

Peter Stockmann.   Good evening, Katherine.

Mrs. Stockmann *(coming forward into the sitting-room)*.   Ah, good evening— is it you? How good of you to come up and see us!

Peter Stockmann.   I happened to be passing, and so—*(looks into the dining-room)*. But you have company with you, I see.

Mrs. Stockmann *(a little embarrassed)*.   Oh, no—it was quite by chance he came in. *(Hurriedly.)* Won't you come in and have something, too?

Peter Stockmann.   I! No, thank you. Good gracious—hot meat at night! Not with my digestion.

Mrs. Stockmann.   Oh, but just once in a way—

Peter Stockmann.   No, no, my dear lady; I stick to my tea and bread and butter. It is much more wholesome in the long run—and a little more economical, too.

Mrs. Stockmann *(smiling)*.   Now you mustn't think that Thomas and I are spendthrifts.

Peter Stockmann.   Not you, my dear; I would never think that of you. *(Points to the Doctor's study.)* Is he not at home?

Mrs. Stockmann.   No, he went for a little turn after supper—he and the boys.

Peter Stockmann.   I doubt if that is a wise thing to do. *(Listens.)* I fancy I hear him coming now.

Mrs. Stockmann.   No, I don't think it is he. *(A knock is heard at the door.)* Come in! *(Hovstad comes in from the hall.)* Oh, it is you, Mr. Hovstad!

Hovstad.   Yes, I hope you will forgive me, but I was delayed at the printers. Good evening, Mr. Mayor.

Peter Stockmann *(bowing a little distantly)*.   Good evening. You have come on business, no doubt.

Hovstad.   Partly. It's about an article for the paper.

Peter Stockmann.   So I imagined. I hear my brother has become a prolific contributor to the "People's Messenger."

Hovstad.   Yes, he is good enough to write in the "People's Messenger" when he has any home truths to tell.

Mrs. Stockmann *(to Hovstad)*.   But won't you—? *(Points to the dining-room.)*

Peter Stockmann.   Quite so, quite so. I don't blame him in the least, as a writer, for addressing himself to the quarters where he will find the readiest sympathy. And, besides that, I personally have no reason to bear any ill will to your paper, Mr. Hovstad.

Hovstad.   I quite agree with you.

Peter Stockmann.   Taking one thing with another, there is an excellent spirit of toleration in the town—an admirable municipal spirit. And it all springs from the fact of our having a great common interest to unite us—an interest that is in an equally high degree the concern of every right-minded citizen—

Hovstad.   The Baths, yes.

Peter Stockmann.   Exactly—our fine, new handsome Baths. Mark my words, Mr. Hovstad—the Baths will become the focus of our municipal life! Not a doubt of it!

Mrs. Stockmann.   That is just what Thomas says.

Peter Stockmann.   Think how extraordinarily the place has developed within the last year or two! Money has been flowing in, and there is some life and some business doing in the town. Houses and landed property are rising in value every day.

Hovstad.   And unemployment is diminishing.

Peter Stockmann.   Yes, that is another thing. The burden of the poor rates has been lightened, to the great relief of the propertied classes; and that relief will be even greater if only we get a really good summer this year, and lots of visitors—plenty of invalids, who will make the Baths talked about.

Hovstad.   And there is a good prospect of that, I hear.

Peter Stockmann.   It looks very promising. Enquiries about apartments and that sort of thing are reaching us every day.

Hovstad.   Well, the doctor's article will come in very suitably.

Peter Stockmann.   Has he been writing something just lately?

Hovstad.   This is something he wrote in the winter; a recommendation of the Baths—an account of the excellent sanitary conditions here. But I held the article over, temporarily.

Peter Stockmann.   Ah,—some little difficulty about it, I suppose?

Hovstad.   No, not at all; I thought it would be better to wait till the spring, because it is just at this time that people begin to think seriously about their summer quarters.

Peter Stockmann.   Quite right; you were perfectly right, Mr. Hovstad.

Hovstad.   Yes, Thomas is really indefatigable when it is a question of the Baths.

Peter Stockmann.   Well—remember, he is the Medical Officer to the Baths.

Hovstad.   Yes, and what is more, they owe their existence to him.

Peter Stockmann.   To him? Indeed! It is true I have heard from time to time that some people are of that opinion. At the same time I must say I imagined that I took a modest part in the enterprise.

Mrs. Stockmann.   Yes, that is what Thomas is always saying.

Hovstad.   But who denies it, Mr. Stockmann? You set the thing going and made a practical concern of it; we all know that. I only meant that the idea of it came first from the doctor.

Peter Stockmann.   Oh, ideas—yes! My brother has had plenty of them in his time—unfortunately. But when it is a question of putting an idea into practical shape, you have to apply to a man of different mettle, Mr. Hovstad. And I certainly should have thought that in this house at least—

Mrs. Stockmann. My dear Peter—

Hovstad. How can you think that—?

Mrs. Stockmann. Won't you go in and have something, Mr. Hovstad? My husband is sure to be back directly.

Hovstad. Thank you, perhaps just a morsel. (*Goes into the dining-room.*)

Peter Stockmann (*lowering his voice a little*). It is a curious thing that these farmers' sons never seem to lose their want of tact.

Mrs. Stockmann. Surely it is not worth bothering about! Cannot you and Thomas share the credit as brothers?

Peter Stockmann. I should have thought so; but apparently some people are not satisfied with a share.

Mrs. Stockmann. What nonsense! You and Thomas get on so capitally together. (*Listens.*) There he is at last, I think. (*Goes out and opens the door leading to the hall.*)

Dr. Stockmann (*laughing and talking outside*). Look here—here is another guest for you, Katherine. Isn't that jolly! Come in, Captain Horster; hang your coat upon this peg. Ah, you don't wear an overcoat. Just think, Katherine; I met him in the street and could hardly persuade him to come up! (*Captain Horster comes into the room and greets Mrs. Stockmann. He is followed by Dr. Stockmann.*) Come along in, boys. They are ravenously hungry again, you know. Come along, Captain Horster; you must have a slice of beef. (*Pushes Horster into the dining-room. Ejlif and Morten go in after them.*)

Mrs. Stockmann. But, Thomas, don't you see—?

Dr. Stockmann (*turning in the doorway*). Oh, is it you, Peter? (*Shakes hands with him.*) Now that is very delightful.

Peter Stockmann. Unfortunately I must go in a moment—

Dr. Stockmann. Rubbish! There is some toddy just coming in. You haven't forgotten the toddy, Katherine?

Mrs. Stockmann. Of course not; the water is boiling now. (*Goes into the dining-room.*)

Peter Stockmann. Toddy too!

Dr. Stockmann. Yes, sit down and we will have it comfortably.

Peter Stockmann. Thanks, I never care about an evening's drinking.

Dr. Stockmann. But this isn't an evening's drinking.

Peter Stockmann. It seems to me—. (*Looks towards the dining-room.*) It is extraordinary how they can put away all that food.

Dr. Stockmann (*rubbing his hands*). Yes, isn't it splendid to see young people eat? They have always got an appetite, you know! That's as it should be. Lots of food—to build up their strength! They are the people who are going to stir up the fermenting forces of the future, Peter.

Peter Stockmann. May I ask what they will find here to "stir up," as you put it?

Dr. Stockmann. Ah, you must ask the young people that—when the time comes. We shan't be able to see it, of course. That stands to reason—two old fogies, like us—

Peter Stockmann. Really, really! I must say that is an extremely odd expression to—

Dr. Stockmann. Oh, you mustn't take me too literally, Peter. I am so heartily happy and contented, you know. I think it is such an extraordinary piece of good fortune to be in the middle of all this growing, germinating life. It is a splendid time to live in! It is as if a whole new world were being created around one.

Peter Stockmann. Do you really think so?

Dr. Stockmann. Ah, naturally you can't appreciate it as keenly as I. You have lived all your life in these surroundings, and your impressions have got blunted. But I, who have been buried all these years in my little corner up north, almost without ever seeing a stranger who might bring new ideas with him—well, in my case it has just the same effect as if I had been transported into the middle of a crowded city.

Peter Stockmann. Oh, a city—!

Dr. Stockmann. I know, I know; it is all cramped enough here, compared with many other places. But there is life here—there is promise—there are innumerable things to work for and fight for; and that is the main thing. (*Calls.*) Katherine, hasn't the postman been here?

Mrs. Stockmann (*from the dining-room*). No.

Dr. Stockmann. And then to be comfortably off, Peter! That is something one learns to value, when one has been on the brink of starvation, as we have.

Peter Stockmann. Oh, surely—

Dr. Stockmann. Indeed I can assure you we have often been very hard put to it, up there. And now to be able to live like a lord! To-day, for instance, we had roast beef for dinner—and, what is more, for supper too. Won't you come and have a little bit? Or let me show it you, at any rate? Come here—

Peter Stockmann. No, no—not for worlds!

Dr. Stockmann. Well, but just come here then. Do you see, we have got a table-cover?

Peter Stockmann. Yes, I noticed it.

Dr. Stockmann. And we have got a lamp-shade too. Do you see? All out of Katherine's savings! It makes the room so cosy. Don't you think so? Just stand here for a moment—no, no, not there—just here, that's it! Look now, when you get the light on it altogether—I really think it looks very nice, doesn't it?

Peter Stockmann. Oh, if you can afford luxuries of this kind—

Dr. Stockmann. Yes, I can afford it now. Katherine tells me I earn almost as much as we spend.

Peter Stockmann. Almost—yes!

Dr. Stockmann. But a scientific man must live in a little bit of style. I am quite sure an ordinary civil servant spends more in a year than I do.

Peter Stockmann. I daresay. A civil servant—a man in a well-paid position—

Dr. Stockmann.   Well, any ordinary merchant, then! A man in that position spends two or three times as much as—

Peter Stockmann.   It just depends on circumstances.

Dr. Stockmann.   At all events I assure you I don't waste money unprofitably. But I can't find it in my heart to deny myself the pleasure of entertaining my friends. I need that sort of thing, you know. I have lived for so long shut out of it all, that it is a necessity of life to me to mix with young, eager, ambitious men, men of liberal and active minds; and that describes every one of those fellows who are enjoying their supper in there. I wish you knew more of Hovstad—

Peter Stockmann.   By the way, Hovstad was telling me he was going to print another article of yours.

Dr. Stockmann.   An article of mine?

Peter Stockmann.   Yes, about the Baths. An article you wrote in the winter.

Dr. Stockmann.   Oh, that one! No, I don't intend that to appear just for the present.

Peter Stockmann.   Why not? It seems to me that this would be the most opportune moment.

Dr. Stockmann.   Yes, very likely—under normal conditions. (*Crosses the room.*)

Peter Stockmann (*following him with his eyes*).   Is there anything abnormal about the present conditions?

Dr. Stockmann (*standing still*).   To tell you the truth, Peter, I can't say just at this moment—at all events not tonight. There may be much that is very abnormal about the present conditions—and it is possible there may be nothing abnormal about them at all. It is quite possible it may be merely my imagination.

Peter Stockmann.   I must say it all sounds most mysterious. Is there something going on that I am to be kept in ignorance of? I should have imagined that I, as Chairman of the governing body of the Baths—

Dr. Stockmann.   And I should have imagined that I—. Oh, come, don't let us fly out at one another, Peter.

Peter Stockmann.   Heaven forbid! I am not in the habit of flying out at people, as you call it. But I am entitled to request most emphatically that all arrangements shall be made in a business-like manner, through the proper channels, and shall be dealt with by the legally constituted authorities. I can allow no going behind our backs by any roundabout means.

Dr. Stockmann.   Have I ever at any time tried to go behind your backs!

Peter Stockmann.   You have an ingrained tendency to take your own way, at all events; and that is almost equally inadmissible in a well ordered community. The individual ought undoubtedly to acquiesce in subordinating himself to the community—or, to speak more accurately, to the authorities who have the care of the community's welfare.

Dr. Stockmann.   Very likely. But what the deuce has all this got to do with me?

Peter Stockmann.   That is exactly what you never appear to be willing to learn, my dear Thomas. But, mark my words, some day you will have to suffer for it—sooner or later. Now I have told you. Good-bye.

Dr. Stockmann.   Have you taken leave of your senses? You are on the wrong scent altogether.

Peter Stockmann.   I am not usually that. You must excuse me now if I— *(calls into the dining-room)*. Good night, Katherine. Good night, gentlemen. *(Goes out.)*

Mrs. Stockmann *(coming from the dining-room)*.   Has he gone?

Dr. Stockmann.   Yes, and in such a bad temper.

Mrs. Stockmann.   But, dear Thomas, what have you been doing to him again?

Dr. Stockmann.   Nothing at all. And, anyhow, he can't oblige me to make my report before the proper time.

Mrs. Stockmann.   What have you got to make a report to him about?

Dr. Stockmann.   Hm! Leave that to me, Katherine.—It is an extraordinary thing that the postman doesn't come.

(Hovstad, Billing, and Horster have got up from the table and come into the sitting-room. Ejlif and Morten come in after them.)

Billing *(stretching himself)*.   Ah!—one feels a new man after a meal like that.

Hovstad.   The mayor wasn't in a very sweet temper tonight, then.

Dr. Stockmann.   It is his stomach; he has a wretched digestion.

Hovstad.   I rather think it was us two of the "People's Messenger" that he couldn't digest.

Mrs. Stockmann.   I thought you came out of it pretty well with him.

Hovstad.   Oh yes; but it isn't anything more than a sort of truce.

Billing.   That is just what it is! That word sums up the situation.

Dr. Stockmann.   We must remember that Peter is a lonely man, poor chap. He has no home comforts of any kind; nothing but everlasting business. And all that infernal weak tea wash that he pours into himself! Now then, my boys, bring chairs up to the table. Aren't we going to have that toddy, Katherine?

Mrs. Stockmann *(going into the dining-room)*.   I am just getting it.

Dr. Stockmann.   Sit down here on the couch beside me, Captain Horster. We so seldom see you—. Please sit down, my friends. *(They sit down at the table. Mrs. Stockmann brings a tray, with a spirit-lamp, glasses, bottles, etc., upon it.)*

Mrs. Stockmann.   There you are! This is arrack, and this is rum, and this one is the brandy. Now everyone must help themselves.

Dr. Stockmann *(taking a glass)*.   We will. *(They all mix themselves some toddy.)* And let us have the cigars. Ejlif, you know where the box is. And you, Morten, can fetch my pipe. *(The two boys go into the room on the right.)* I have a suspicion that Ejlif pockets a cigar now and then!—but I take no notice of it. *(Calls out.)* And my smoking-cap too, Morten. Katherine, you can tell him where I left it. Ah, he has got it. *(The boys bring the various things.)* Now, my friends. I stick to my pipe, you know. This one has seen plenty of bad weather with me up north. *(Touches glasses with them.)* Your good health! Ah, it is good to be sitting snug and warm here.

Mrs. Stockmann *(who sits knitting).*   Do you sail soon, Captain Horster?

Horster.   I expect to be ready to sail next week.

Mrs. Stockmann.   I suppose you are going to America?

Horster.   Yes, that is the plan.

Mrs. Stockmann.   Then you won't be able to take part in the coming election.

Horster.   Is there going to be an election?

Billing.   Didn't you know?

Horster.   No, I don't mix myself up with those things.

Billing.   But do you not take an interest in public affairs?

Horster.   No, I don't know anything about politics.

Billing.   All the same, one ought to vote, at any rate.

Horster.   Even if one doesn't know anything about what is going on?

Billing.   Doesn't know! What do you mean by that? A community is like a ship; every one ought to be prepared to take the helm.

Horster.   Maybe that is all very well on shore; but on board ship it wouldn't work.

Hovstad.   It is astonishing how little most sailors care about what goes on on shore.

Billing.   Very extraordinary.

Dr. Stockmann.   Sailors are like birds of passage; they feel equally at home in any latitude. And that is only an additional reason for our being all the more keen, Hovstad. Is there to be anything of public interest in tomorrow's "Messenger"?

Hovstad.   Nothing about municipal affairs. But the day after to-morrow I was thinking of printing your article—

Dr. Stockmann.   Ah, devil take it—my article! Look here, that must wait a bit.

Hovstad.   Really? We had just got convenient space for it, and I thought it was just the opportune moment—

Dr. Stockmann.   Yes, yes, very likely you are right; but it must wait all the same. I will explain to you later. *(Petra comes in from the hall, in hat and cloak and with a bundle of exercise books under her arm.)*

Petra.   Good evening.

Dr. Stockmann.   Good evening, Petra; come along. *(Mutual greetings; Petra takes off her things and puts them down on a chair by the door.)*

Petra.   And you have all been sitting here enjoying yourselves, while I have been out slaving!

Dr. Stockmann.   Well, come and enjoy yourself too!

Billing.   May I mix a glass for you?

Petra (*coming to the table*).   Thanks, I would rather do it; you always mix it too strong. But I forgot, father—I have a letter for you. (*Goes to the chair where she has laid her things.*)

Dr. Stockmann.   A letter? From whom?

Petra (*looking in her coat pocket*).   The postman gave it to me just as I was going out—

Dr. Stockmann (*getting up and going to her*).   And you only give it to me now!

Petra.   I really had not time to run up again. There it is!

Dr. Stockmann (*seizing the letter*).   Let's see, let's see, child! (*Looks at the address.*) Yes, that's all right!

Mrs. Stockmann.   Is it the one you have been expecting so anxiously, Thomas?

Dr. Stockmann.   Yes, it is. I must go to my room now and—. Where shall I get a light, Katherine? Is there no lamp in my room again?

Mrs. Stockmann.   Yes, your lamp is all ready lit on your desk.

Dr. Stockmann.   Good, good. Excuse me for a moment—. (*Goes into his study.*)

Petra.   What do you suppose it is, mother?

Mrs. Stockmann.   I don't know; for the last day or two he has always been asking if the postman has not been.

Billing.   Probably some country patient.

Petra.   Poor old dad!—he will overwork himself soon. (*Mixes a glass for herself.*) There, that will taste good!

Hovstad.   Have you been teaching in the evening school again to-day?

Petra (*sipping from her glass*).   Two hours.

Billing.   And four hours of school in the morning—

Petra.   Five hours.

Mrs. Stockmann.   And you have still got exercises to correct, I see.

Petra.   A whole heap, yes.

Horster.   You are pretty full up with work too, it seems to me.

Petra.   Yes—but that is good. One is so delightfully tired after it.

Billing.   Do you like that?

Petra.   Yes, because one sleeps so well then.

Morten.   You must be dreadfully wicked, Petra.

Petra.   Wicked?

Morten.   Yes, because you work so much. Mr. Rörlund says work is a punishment for our sins.

Ejlif.   Pooh, what a duffer you are, to believe a thing like that!

Mrs. Stockmann.   Come, come, Ejlif!

Billing (*laughing*).   That's capital!

Hovstad.   Don't you want to work as hard as that, Morten?

Morten.   No, indeed I don't.

Hovstad.   What do you want to be, then?

Morten.   I should like best to be a Viking.

Ejlif. You would have to be a pagan then.

Morten. Well, I could become a pagan, couldn't I?

Billing. I agree with you, Morten! My sentiments, exactly.

Mrs. Stockmann *(signalling to him).* I am sure that is not true, Mr. Billing.

Billing. Yes, I swear it is! I am a pagan, and I am proud of it. Believe me, before long we shall all be pagans.

Morten. And then shall we be allowed to do anything we like?

Billing. Well, you see, Morten—.

Mrs. Stockmann. You must go to your room now, boys; I am sure you have some lessons to learn for to-morrow.

Ejlif. I should like so much to stay a little longer—

Mrs. Stockmann. No, no; away you go, both of you. *(The boys say good night and go into the room on the left.)*

Hovstad. Do you really think it can do the boys any harm to hear such things?

Mrs. Stockmann. I don't know; but I don't like it.

Petra. But you know, mother, I think you really are wrong about it.

Mrs. Stockmann. Maybe, but I don't like it—not in our own home.

Petra. There is so much falsehood both at home and at school. At home one must not speak, and at school we have to stand and tell lies to the children.

Horster. Tell lies?

Petra. Yes, don't you suppose we have to teach them all sorts of things that we don't believe?

Billing. That is perfectly true.

Petra. If only I had the means I would start a school of my own, and it would be conducted on very different lines.

Billing. Oh, bother the means—!

Horster. Well if you are thinking of that, Miss Stockmann, I shall be delighted to provide you with a schoolroom. The great big old house my father left me is standing almost empty; there is an immense dining-room downstairs—

Petra *(laughing).* Thank you very much; but I am afraid nothing will come of it.

Hovstad. No, Miss Petra is much more likely to take to journalism, I expect. By the way, have you had time to do anything with that English story you promised to translate for us?

Petra. No, not yet; but you shall have it in good time.

(Dr. Stockmann comes in from his room with an open letter in his hand.)

Dr. Stockmann *(waving the letter).* Well, now the town will have something new to talk about, I can tell you!

Billing. Something new?

Mrs. Stockmann. What is this?

Dr. Stockmann. A great discovery, Katherine.

Hovstad. Really?

Mrs. Stockmann. A discovery of yours?

Dr. Stockmann.   A discovery of mine. *(Walks up and down.)* Just let them come saying, as usual, that it is all fancy and a crazy man's imagination! But they will be careful what they say this time, I can tell you!

Petra.   But, father, tell us what it is.

Dr. Stockmann.   Yes, yes—only give me time, and you shall know all about it. If only I had Peter here now! It just shows how we men can go about forming our judgments, when in reality we are as blind as any moles—

Hovstad.   What are you driving at, Doctor?

Dr. Stockmann *(standing still by the table).*   Isn't it the universal opinion that our town is a healthy spot?

Hovstad.   Certainly.

Dr. Stockmann.   Quite an unusually healthy spot, in fact—a place that deserves to be recommended in the warmest possible manner either for invalids or for people who are well—

Mrs. Stockmann.   Yes, but my dear Thomas—

Dr. Stockmann.   And we have been recommending it and praising it—I have written and written, both in the "Messenger" and in pamphlets—

Hovstad.   Well, what then?

Dr. Stockmann.   And the Baths—we have called them the "main artery of the town's life-blood," the "nerve-centre of our town," and the devil knows what else—

Billing.   "The town's pulsating heart" was the expression I once used on an important occasion—

Dr. Stockmann.   Quite so. Well, do you know what they really are, these great, splendid, much praised Baths, that have cost so much money—do you know what they are?

Hovstad.   No, what are they?

Mrs. Stockmann.   Yes, what are they?

Dr. Stockmann.   The whole place is a pesthouse!

Petra.   The Baths, father?

Mrs. Stockmann *(at the same time).*   Our Baths!

Hovstad.   But, Doctor—

Billing.   Absolutely incredible!

Dr. Stockmann.   The whole Bath establishment is a whited, poisoned sepulchre, I tell you—the gravest possible danger to the public health! All the nastiness up at Mölledal, all that stinking filth, is infecting the water in the conduit-pipes leading to the reservoir; and the same cursed, filthy poison oozes out on the shore too—

Horster.   Where the bathing-place is?

Dr. Stockmann.   Just there.

Hovstad.   How do you come to be so certain of all this, Doctor?

Dr. Stockmann.   I have investigated the matter most conscientiously. For a long time past I have suspected something of the kind. Last year we had some very strange cases of illness among the visitors—typhoid cases, and cases of gastric fever—

Mrs. Stockmann. Yes, that is quite true.

Dr. Stockmann. At the time, we supposed the visitors had been infected before they came; but later on, in the winter, I began to have a different opinion; and so I set myself to examine the water, as well as I could.

Mrs. Stockmann. Then that is what you have been so busy with?

Dr. Stockmann. Indeed I have been busy, Katherine. But here I had none of the necessary scientific apparatus; so I sent samples, both of the drinking-water and of the sea-water, up to the University, to have an accurate analysis made by a chemist.

Hovstad. And have you got that?

Dr. Stockmann (*showing him the letter*). Here it is! It proves the presence of decomposing organic matter in the water—it is full of infusoria. The water is absolutely dangerous to use, either internally or externally.

Mrs. Stockmann. What a mercy you discovered it in time.

Dr. Stockmann. You may well say so.

Hovstad. And what do you propose to do now, Doctor?

Dr. Stockmann. To see the matter put right—naturally.

Hovstad. Can that be done?

Dr. Stockmann. It must be done. Otherwise the Baths will be absolutely useless and wasted. But we need not anticipate that; I have a very clear idea what we shall have to do.

Mrs. Stockmann. But why have you kept this all so secret, dear?

Dr. Stockmann. Do you suppose I was going to run about the town gossiping about it, before I had absolute proof? No, thank you. I am not such a fool.

Petra. Still, you might have told us—

Dr. Stockmann. Not a living soul. But to-morrow you may run around to the old Badger—

Mrs. Stockmann. Oh, Thomas! Thomas!

Dr. Stockmann. Well, to your grandfather, then. The old boy will have something to be astonished at! I know he thinks I am cracked—and there are lots of other people think so too, I have noticed. But now these good folks shall see—they shall just see—! (*Walks about, rubbing his hands.*) There will be a nice upset in the town, Katherine; you can't imagine what it will be. All the conduit-pipes will have to be relaid.

Hovstad (*getting up*). All the conduit-pipes—?

Dr. Stockmann. Yes, of course. The intake is too low down; it will have to be lifted to a position much higher up.

Petra. Then you were right after all.

Dr. Stockmann. Ah, you remember, Petra—I wrote opposing the plans before the work was begun. But at that time no one would listen to me. Well, I am going to let them have it, now! Of course I have prepared a report for the Baths Committee; I have had it ready for a week, and was only waiting for this to come. (*Shows the letter.*) Now it shall go off at once. (*Goes into his room and comes back with some papers.*) Look at that! Four closely written sheets!—and the letter shall go with them. Give me a bit of paper, Kather-

ine—something to wrap them up in. That will do! Now give it to—to—
(*stamps his foot*)—what the deuce is her name?—give it to the maid, and
tell her to take it at once to the Mayor.

(*Mrs. Stockmann takes the packet and goes out through the dining-room.*)

Petra.   What do you think uncle Peter will say, father?

Dr. Stockmann.   What is there for him to say? I should think he would be
very glad that such an important truth has been brought to light.

Hovstad.   Will you let me print a short note about your discovery in the
"Messenger"?

Dr. Stockmann.   I shall be very much obliged if you will.

Hovstad.   It is very desirable that the public should be informed of it without
delay.

Dr. Stockmann.   Certainly.

Mrs. Stockmann (*coming back*).   She has just gone with it.

Billing.   Upon my soul, Doctor, you are going to be the foremost man in the
town!

Dr. Stockmann (*walking about happily*).   Nonsense! As a matter of fact I have
done nothing more than my duty. I have only made a lucky find—that's all.
Still, all the same—

Billing.   Hovstad, don't you think the town ought to give Dr. Stockmann some
sort of testimonial?

Hovstad.   I will suggest it, anyway.

Billing.   And I will speak to Aslaksen about it.

Dr. Stockmann.   No, my good friends, don't let us have any of that nonsense.
I won't hear of anything of the kind. And if the Baths Committee should
think of voting me an increase of salary, I will not accept it. Do you hear,
Katherine?—I won't accept it.

Mrs. Stockmann.   You are quite right, Thomas.

Petra (*lifting her glass*).   Your health, father!

Hovstad and Billing.   Your health, Doctor! Good health!

Horster (*touches glasses with Dr. Stockmann*).   I hope it will bring you nothing
but good luck.

Dr. Stockmann.   Thank you, thank you, my dear fellows! I feel tremendously
happy! It is a splendid thing for a man to be able to feel that he has done a
service to his native town and to his fellow-citizens. Hurrah, Katherine! (*He
puts his arms round her and whirls her round and round, while she protests
with laughing cries. They all laugh, clap their hands, and cheer the Doctor.
The boys put their heads in at the door to see what is going on.*)

Act II

SCENE. *The same. The door into the dining-room is shut. It is morning. Mrs. Stockmann, with a sealed letter in her hand, comes in from the dining-room, goes to the door of the Doctor's study, and peeps in.*

Mrs. Stockmann.   Are you in, Thomas?

Dr. Stockmann *(from within his room)*.   Yes, I have just come in. *(Comes into the room.)* What is it?

Mrs. Stockmann.   A letter from your brother.

Dr. Stockmann.   Aha, let us see! *(Opens the letter and reads:)* "I return herewith the manuscript you sent me"—*(reads on in a low murmur)* Hm!—

Mrs. Stockmann.   What does he say?

Dr. Stockmann *(putting the papers in his pocket)*.   Oh, he only writes that he will come up here himself about midday.

Mrs. Stockmann.   Well, try and remember to be at home this time.

Dr. Stockmann.   That will be all right; I have got through all my morning visits.

Mrs. Stockmann.   I am extremely curious to know how he takes it.

Dr. Stockmann.   You will see he won't like its having been I, and not he, that made the discovery.

Mrs. Stockmann.   Aren't you a little nervous about that?

Dr. Stockmann.   Oh, he really will be pleased enough, you know. But, at the same time, Peter is so confoundedly afraid of anyone's doing any service to the town except himself.

Mrs. Stockmann.   I will tell you what, Thomas—you should be good natured, and share the credit of this with him. Couldn't you make out that it was he who set you on the scent of this discovery?

Dr. Stockmann.   I am quite willing. If only I can get the thing set right. I—

(Morten Kiil puts his head in through the door leading from the hall, looks round in an enquiring manner, and chuckles.)

Morten Kiil *(slyly)*.   Is it—is it true?

Mrs. Stockmann *(going to the door)*.   Father!—is it you?

Dr. Stockmann.   Ah, Mr. Kiil—good morning, good morning!

Mrs. Stockmann.   But come along in.

Morten Kiil.   If it is true, I will; if not, I am off.

Dr. Stockmann.   If what is true?

Morten Kiil.   This tale about the water supply. Is it true?

Dr. Stockmann.   Certainly it is true. But how did you come to hear it?

Morten Kiil *(coming in)*.   Petra ran in on her way to the school—

Dr. Stockmann.   Did she?

Morten Kiil.   Yes; and she declares that—. I thought she was only making a fool of me, but it isn't like Petra to do that.

Dr. Stockmann.   Of course not. How could you imagine such a thing!

Morten Kiil.   Oh well, it is better never to trust anybody; you may find you have been made a fool of before you know where you are. But it is really true, all the same?

Dr. Stockmann.   You can depend upon it that it is true. Won't you sit down? *(Settles him on the couch.)* Isn't it a real bit of luck for the town—

Morten Kiil *(suppressing his laughter).*   A bit of luck for the town?

Dr. Stockmann.   Yes, that I made the discovery in good time.

Morten Kiil *(as before).*   Yes, yes, yes!—But I should never have thought you the sort of man to pull your own brother's leg like this!

Dr. Stockmann.   Pull his leg!

Mrs. Stockmann.   Really, father dear—

Morten Kiil *(resting his hands and his chin on the handle of his stick and winking slyly at the Doctor).*   Let me see, what was the story? Some kind of beast that had got into the water-pipes, wasn't it?

Dr. Stockmann.   Infusoria—yes.

Morten Kiil.   And a lot of these beasts had got in, according to Petra—a tremendous lot.

Dr. Stockmann.   Certainly; hundreds of thousands of them, probably.

Morten Kiil.   But no one can see them—isn't that so?

Dr. Stockmann.   Yes; you can't see them.

Morten Kiil *(with a quiet chuckle).*   Damme—it's the finest story I have ever heard!

Dr. Stockmann.   What do you mean?

Morten Kiil.   But you will never get the Mayor to believe a thing like that.

Dr. Stockmann.   We shall see.

Morten Kiil.   Do you think he will be fool enough to—?

Dr. Stockmann.   I hope the whole town will be fools enough.

Morten Kiil.   The whole town! Well, it wouldn't be a bad thing. It would just serve them right, and teach them a lesson. They think themselves so much cleverer than we old fellows. They hounded me out of the council; they did, I tell you—they hounded me out. Now they shall pay for it. You pull their legs too, Thomas!

Dr. Stockmann.   Really, I—

Morten Kiil.   You pull their legs! *(Gets up.)* If you can work it so that the Mayor and his friends all swallow the same bait, I will give ten pounds to a charity—like a shot!

Dr. Stockmann.   That is very kind of you.

Morten Kiil.   Yes, I haven't got much money to throw away, I can tell you; but if you can work this, I will give five pounds to a charity at Christmas.

(Hovstad comes in by the hall door.)

Hovstad.   Good morning! *(Stops.)* Oh, I beg your pardon—

Dr. Stockmann.   Not at all; come in.

Morten Kiil *(with another chuckle).* Oho!—is he in this too?

Hovstad. What do you mean?

Dr. Stockmann. Certainly he is.

Morten Kiil. I might have known it! It must get into the papers. You know how to do it, Thomas! Set your wits to work. Now I must go.

Dr. Stockmann. Won't you stay a little while?

Morten Kiil. No, I must be off now. You keep up this game for all it is worth; you won't repent it, I'm damned if you will!

(He goes out; Mrs. Stockmann follows him into the hall.)

Dr. Stockmann *(laughing).* Just imagine—the old chap doesn't believe a word of all this about the water supply.

Hovstad. Oh that was it, then?

Dr. Stockmann. Yes, that was what we were talking about. Perhaps it is the same thing that brings you here?

Hovstad. Yes, it is. Can you spare me a few minutes, Doctor?

Dr. Stockmann. As long as you like, my dear fellow.

Hovstad. Have you heard from the Mayor yet?

Dr. Stockmann. Not yet. He is coming here later.

Hovstad. I have given the matter a great deal of thought since last night.

Dr. Stockmann. Well?

Hovstad. From your point of view, as a doctor and a man of science, this affair of the water-supply is an isolated matter. I mean, you do not realise that it involves a great many other things.

Dr. Stockmann. How do you mean?—Let us sit down, my dear fellow. No, sit here on the couch. *(Hovstad sits down on the couch, Dr. Stockmann on a chair on the other side of the table.)* Now then. You mean that—?

Hovstad. You said yesterday that the pollution of the water was due to impurities in the soil.

Dr. Stockmann. Yes, unquestionably it is due to that poisonous morass up at Mölledal.

Hovstad. Begging your pardon, doctor, I fancy it is due to quite another morass altogether.

Dr. Stockmann. What morass?

Hovstad. The morass that the whole life of our town is built on and is rotting in.

Dr. Stockmann. What the deuce are you driving at, Hovstad?

Hovstad. The whole of the town's interests have, little by little, got into the hands of a pack of officials.

Dr. Stockmann. Oh, come!—they are not all officials.

Hovstad. No, but those that are not officials are at any rate the officials' friends and adherents; it is the wealthy folk, the old families in the town, that have got us entirely in their hands.

Dr. Stockmann. Yes, but after all they are men of ability and knowledge.

Hovstad. Did they show any ability or knowledge when they laid the conduit-pipes where they are now?

Dr. Stockmann. No, of course that was a great piece of stupidity on their part. But that is going to be set right now.

Hovstad. Do you think that will be such plain sailing?

Dr. Stockmann. Plain sailing or no, it has got to be done, anyway.

Hovstad. Yes, provided the press takes up the question.

Dr. Stockmann. I don't think that will be necessary, my dear fellow, I am certain my brother—

Hovstad. Excuse me, doctor; I feel bound to tell you I am inclined to take the matter up.

Dr. Stockmann. In the paper?

Hovstad. Yes. When I took over the "People's Messenger" my idea was to break up this ring of self-opinionated old fossils who had got hold of all the influence.

Dr. Stockmann. But you know you told me yourself what the result had been; you nearly ruined your paper.

Hovstad. Yes, at the time we were obliged to climb down a peg or two, it is quite true; because there was a danger of the whole project of the Baths coming to nothing if they failed us. But now the scheme has been carried through, and we can dispense with these grand gentlemen.

Dr. Stockmann. Dispense with them, yes; but we owe them a great debt of gratitude.

Hovstad. That shall be recognised ungrudgingly. But a journalist of my democratic tendencies cannot let such an opportunity as this slip. The bubble of official infallibility must be pricked. This superstition must be destroyed, like any other.

Dr. Stockmann. I am whole-heartedly with you in that, Mr. Hovstad; if it is a superstition, away with it!

Hovstad. I should be very reluctant to bring the Mayor into it, because he is your brother. But I am sure you will agree with me that truth should be the first consideration.

Dr. Stockmann. That goes without saying. *(With sudden emphasis.)* Yes, but—but—

Hovstad. You must not misjudge me. I am neither more self-interested nor more ambitious than most men.

Dr. Stockmann. My dear fellow—who suggests anything of that kind?

Hovstad. I am of humble origin, as you know; and that has given me opportunities of knowing what is the most crying need in the humbler ranks of life. It is that they should be allowed some part in the direction of public affairs, Doctor. That is what will develop their faculties and intelligence and self-respect—

Dr. Stockmann. I quite appreciate that.

Hovstad. Yes—and in my opinion a journalist incurs a heavy responsibility if he neglects a favourable opportunity of emancipating the masses—the humble and oppressed. I know well enough that in exalted circles I shall be called an agitator, and all that sort of thing; but they may call what they like. If only my conscience doesn't reproach me, then—

Dr. Stockmann. Quite right! Quite right, Mr. Hovstad. But all the same—devil take it! *(A knock is heard at the door.)* Come in!

(Aslaksen appears at the door. He is poorly but decently dressed, in black, with a slightly crumpled white neckcloth; he wears gloves and has a felt hat in his hand.)

Aslaksen *(bowing).* Excuse my taking the liberty, Doctor—

Dr. Stockmann *(getting up).* Ah, it is you, Aslaksen!

Aslaksen. Yes, Doctor.

Hovstad *(standing up).* Is it me you want, Aslaksen?

Aslaksen. No; I didn't know I should find you here. No, it was the Doctor I—

Dr. Stockmann. I am quite at your service. What is it?

Aslaksen. Is what I heard from Mr. Billing true, sir—that you mean to improve our water-supply?

Dr. Stockmann. Yes, for the Baths.

Aslaksen. Quite so, I understand. Well, I have come to say that I will back that up by every means in my power.

Hovstad *(to the Doctor).* You see!

Dr. Stockmann. I shall be very grateful to you, but—

Aslaksen. Because it may be no bad thing to have us small tradesmen at your back. We form, as it were, a compact majority in the town—if we choose. And it is always a good thing to have the majority with you, Doctor.

Dr. Stockmann. This is undeniably true; but I confess I don't see why such unusual precautions should be necessary in this case. It seems to me that such a plain, straightforward thing—

Aslaksen. Oh, it may be very desirable, all the same. I know our local authorities so well; officials are not generally very ready to act on proposals that come from other people. That is why I think it would not be at all amiss if we made a little demonstration.

Hovstad. That's right.

Dr. Stockmann. Demonstration, did you say? What on earth are you going to make a demonstration about?

Aslaksen. We shall proceed with the greatest moderation, Doctor. Moderation is always my aim; it is the greatest virtue in a citizen—at least, I think so.

Dr. Stockmann. It is well known to be a characteristic of yours, Mr. Aslaksen.

Aslaksen. Yes, I think I may pride myself on that. And this matter of the water-supply is of the greatest importance to us small tradesmen. The Baths promise to be a regular gold-mine for the town. We shall all make our living out of them, especially those of us who are householders. That is why we will back up the project as strongly as possible. And as I am at present Chairman of the Householders' Association—

Dr. Stockmann.   Yes—?

Aslaksen.   And, what is more, local secretary of the Temperance Society— you know, sir, I suppose, that I am a worker in the temperance cause?

Dr. Stockmann.   Of course, of course.

Aslaksen.   Well, you can understand that I come into contact with a great many people. And as I have the reputation of a temperate and law-abiding citizen—like yourself, Doctor—I have a certain influence in the town, a little bit of power, if I may be allowed to say so.

Dr. Stockmann.   I know that quite well, Mr. Aslaksen.

Aslaksen.   So you see it would be an easy matter for me to set on foot some testimonial, if necessary.

Dr. Stockmann.   A testimonial?

Aslaksen.   Yes, some kind of an address of thanks from the townsmen for your share in a matter of such importance to the community. I need scarcely say that it would have to be drawn up with the greatest regard to moderation, so as not to offend the authorities—who, after all, have the reins in their hands. If we pay strict attention to that, no one can take it amiss, I should think!

Hovstad.   Well, and even supposing they didn't like it—

Aslaksen.   No, no, no; there must be no discourtesy to the authorities, Mr. Hovstad. It is no use falling foul of those upon whom our welfare so closely depends. I have done that in my time, and no good ever comes of it. But no one can take exception to a reasonable and frank expression of a citizen's views.

Dr. Stockmann (*shaking him by the hand*).   I can't tell you, dear Mr. Aslaksen, how extremely pleased I am to find such hearty support among my fellow-citizens. I am delighted—delighted! Now, you will take a small glass of sherry, eh?

Aslaksen.   No, thank you; I never drink alcohol of that kind.

Dr. Stockmann.   Well, what do you say to a glass of beer, then?

Aslaksen.   Nor that either, thank you, Doctor. I never drink anything as early as this. I am going into town now to talk this over with one or two house-holders, and prepare the ground.

Dr. Stockmann.   It is tremendously kind of you, Mr. Aslaksen; but I really cannot understand the necessity for all these precautions. It seems to me that the thing should go of itself.

Aslaksen.   The authorities are somewhat slow to move, Doctor. Far be it from me to seem to blame them—

Hovstad.   We are going to stir them up in the paper tomorrow, Aslaksen.

Aslaksen.   But not violently, I trust, Mr. Hovstad. Proceed with moderation, or you will do nothing with them. You may take my advice; I have gathered my experience in the school of life. Well, I must say good-bye, Doctor. You know now that we small tradesmen are at your back at all events, like a solid wall. You have the compact majority on your side, Doctor.

Dr. Stockmann. I am very much obliged, dear Mr. Aslaksen. *(Shakes hands with him.)* Good-bye, good-bye.

Aslaksen. Are you going my way, towards the printing-office, Mr. Hovstad?

Hovstad. I will come later; I have something to settle up first.

Aslaksen. Very well. *(Bows and goes out; Stockmann follows him into the hall.)*

Hovstad *(as Stockmann comes in again).* Well, what do you think of that, Doctor? Don't you think it is high time we stirred a little life into all this slackness and vacillation and cowardice?

Dr. Stockmann. Are you referring to Aslaksen?

Hovstad. Yes, I am. He is one of those who are floundering in a bog—decent enough fellow though he may be, otherwise. And most of the people here are in just the same case—see-sawing and edging first to one side and then to the other, so overcome with caution and scruple that they never dare to take any decided step.

Dr. Stockmann. Yes, but Aslaksen seemed to me so thoroughly well-intentioned.

Hovstad. There is one thing I esteem higher than that; and that is for a man to be self-reliant and sure of himself.

Dr. Stockmann. I think you are perfectly right there.

Hovstad. That is why I want to seize this opportunity, and try if I cannot manage to put a little virility into these well-intentioned people for once. The idol of Authority must be shattered in this town. This gross and inexcusable blunder about the water-supply must be brought home to the mind of every municipal voter.

Dr. Stockmann. Very well; if you are of opinion that it is for the good of the community, so be it. But not until I have had a talk with my brother.

Hovstad. Anyway, I will get a leading article ready; and if the Mayor refuses to take the matter up—

Dr. Stockmann. How can you suppose such a thing possible?

Hovstad. It is conceivable. And in that case—

Dr. Stockmann. In that case I promise you—. Look here, in that case you may print my report—every word of it.

Hovstad. May I? Have I your word for it?

Dr. Stockmann *(giving him the MS).* Here it is; take it with you. It can do no harm for you to read it through, and you can give it back to me later on.

Hovstad. Good, good! That is what I will do. And now good-bye, Doctor.

Dr. Stockmann. Good-bye, good-bye. You will see everything will run quite smoothly, Mr. Hovstad—quite smoothly.

Hovstad. Hm!—we shall see. *(Bows and goes out.)*

Dr. Stockmann *(opens the dining-room door and looks in).* Katherine! Oh, you are back, Petra?

Petra *(coming in).* Yes, I have just come from the school.

Mrs. Stockmann *(coming in).* Has he not been here yet?

Dr. Stockmann. Peter? No. But I have had a long talk with Hovstad. He is quite excited about my discovery. I find it has a much wider bearing than I at first imagined. And he has put his paper at my disposal if necessity should arise.

Mrs. Stockmann.   Do you think it will?

Dr. Stockmann.   Not for a moment. But at all events it makes me feel proud to know that I have the liberal-minded independent press on my side. Yes, and—just imagine—I have had a visit from the Chairman of the House-holders' Association!

Mrs. Stockmann.   Oh! What did he want?

Dr. Stockmann.   To offer me his support too. They will support me in a body if it should be necessary. Katherine—do you know what I have got behind me?

Mrs. Stockmann.   Behind you? No, what have you got behind you?

Dr. Stockmann.   The compact majority.

Mrs. Stockmann.   Really? Is that a good thing for you, Thomas?

Dr. Stockmann.   I should think it was a good thing. (*Walks up and down rubbing his hands.*) By Jove, it's a fine thing to feel this bond of brotherhood between oneself and one's fellow citizens!

Petra.   And to be able to do so much that is good and useful, father!

Dr. Stockmann.   And for one's own native town into the bargain, my child!

Mrs. Stockmann.   That was a ring at the bell.

Dr. Stockmann.   It must be he, then. (*A knock is heard at the door.*) Come in!

Peter Stockmann (*comes in from the hall*).   Good morning.

Dr. Stockmann.   Glad to see you, Peter!

Mrs. Stockmann.   Good morning, Peter. How are you?

Peter Stockmann.   So so, thank you. (*To Dr. Stockmann.*) I received from you yesterday, after office hours, a report dealing with the condition of the water at the Baths.

Dr. Stockmann.   Yes. Have you read it?

Peter Stockmann.   Yes, I have.

Dr. Stockmann.   And what have you to say to it?

Peter Stockmann (*with a sidelong glance*).   Hm!—

Mrs. Stockmann.   Come along, Petra. (*She and Petra go into the room on the left.*)

Peter Stockmann (*after a pause*).   Was it necessary to make all these investigations behind my back?

Dr. Stockmann.   Yes, because until I was absolutely certain about it—

Peter Stockmann.   Then you mean that you are absolutely certain now?

Dr. Stockmann.   Surely you are convinced of that.

Peter Stockmann.   Is it your intention to bring this document before the Baths Committee as a sort of official communication?

Dr. Stockmann.   Certainly. Something must be done in the matter—and that quickly.

Peter Stockmann.   As usual, you employ violent expressions in your report. You say, amongst other things, that what we offer visitors in our Baths is a permanent supply of poison.

Dr. Stockmann. Well, can you describe it any other way, Peter? Just think—water that is poisonous, whether you drink it or bathe in it! And this we offer to the poor sick folk who come to us trustfully and pay us at an exorbitant rate to be made well again!

Peter Stockmann. And your reasoning leads you to this conclusion, that we must build a sewer to draw off the alleged impurities from Mölledal and must relay the water-conduits.

Dr. Stockmann. Yes. Do you see any other way out of it? I don't.

Peter Stockmann. I made a pretext this morning to go and see the town engineer, and, as if only half seriously, broached the subject of these proposals as a thing we might perhaps have to take under consideration some time later on.

Dr. Stockmann. Some time later on!

Peter Stockmann. He smiled at what he considered to be my extravagance, naturally. Have you taken the trouble to consider what your proposed alterations would cost? According to the information I obtained, the expenses would probably mount up to fifteen or twenty thousand pounds.

Dr. Stockmann. Would it cost so much?

Peter Stockmann. Yes; and the worst part of it would be that the work would take at least two years.

Dr. Stockmann. Two years? Two whole years?

Peter Stockmann. At least. And what are we to do with the Baths in the meantime? Close them? Indeed we should be obliged to. And do you suppose any one would come near the place after it had got about that the water was dangerous?

Dr. Stockmann. Yes, but, Peter, that is what it is.

Peter Stockmann. And all this at this juncture—just as the Baths are beginning to be known. There are other towns in the neighbourhood with qualifications to attract visitors for bathing purposes. Don't you suppose they would immediately strain every nerve to divert the entire stream of strangers to themselves? Unquestionably they would; and then where should we be? We should probably have to abandon the whole thing, which has cost us so much money—and then you would have ruined your native town.

Dr. Stockmann. I—should have ruined—!

Peter Stockmann. It is simply and solely through the Baths that the town has before it any future worth mentioning. You know that just as well as I.

Dr. Stockmann. But what do you think ought to be done, then?

Peter Stockmann. Your report has not convinced me that the condition of the water at the Baths is as bad as you represent it to be.

Dr. Stockmann. I tell you it is even worse!—or at all events it will be in summer, when the warm weather comes.

Peter Stockmann. As I said, I believe you exaggerate the matter considerably. A capable physician ought to know what measures to take—he ought to be capable of preventing injurious influences or of remedying them if they become obviously persistent.

Dr. Stockmann.   Well? What more?

Peter Stockmann.   The water supply for the Baths is now an established fact, and in consequence must be treated as such. But probably the Committee, at its discretion, will not be disinclined to consider the question of how far it might be possible to introduce certain improvements consistently with a reasonable expenditure.

Dr. Stockmann.   And do you suppose that I will have anything to do with such a piece of trickery as that?

Peter Stockmann.   Trickery!!

Dr. Stockmann.   Yes, it would be a trick—a fraud, a lie, a downright crime towards the public, towards the whole community!

Peter Stockmann.   I have not, as I remarked before, been able to convince myself that there is actually any imminent danger.

Dr. Stockmann.   You have! It is impossible that you should not be convinced. I know I have represented the facts absolutely truthfully and fairly. And you know it very well, Peter, only you won't acknowledge it. It was owing to your action that both the Baths and the water-conduits were built where they are; and that is what you won't acknowledge—that damnable blunder of yours. Pooh!—do you suppose I don't see through you?

Peter Stockmann.   And even if that were true? If I perhaps guard my reputation somewhat anxiously, it is in the best interests of the town. Without moral authority I am powerless to direct public affairs as seems, to my judgment, to be best for the common good. And on that account—and for various other reasons too—it appears to me to be a matter of importance that your report should not be delivered to the Committee. In the interests of the public, you must withhold it. Then, later on, I will raise the question and we will do our best, privately; but nothing of this unfortunate affair—not a single word of it—must come to the ears of the public.

Dr. Stockmann.   I am afraid you will not be able to prevent that now, my dear Peter.

Peter Stockmann.   It must and shall be prevented.

Dr. Stockmann.   It is no use, I tell you. There are too many people that know about it.

Peter Stockmann.   That know about it? Who? Surely you don't mean those fellows on the "People's Messenger"?

Dr. Stockmann.   Yes, they know. The liberal-minded independent press is going to see that you do your duty.

Peter Stockmann (*after a short pause*).   You are an extraordinarily independent man, Thomas. Have you given no thought to the consequences this may have for yourself?

Dr. Stockmann.   Consequences?—for me?

Peter Stockmann.   For you and yours, yes.

Dr. Stockmann.   What the deuce do you mean?

Peter Stockmann.   I believe I have always behaved in a brotherly way to you— have always been ready to oblige or to help you?

Dr. Stockmann.   Yes, you have, and I am grateful to you for it.

Peter Stockmann.   There is no need. Indeed, to some extent I was forced to do so—for my own sake. I always hoped that, if I helped to improve your financial position, I should be able to keep some check on you.

Dr. Stockmann.   What!! Then it was only for your own sake—!

Peter Stockmann.   Up to a certain point, yes. It is painful for a man in an official position to have his nearest relative compromising himself time after time.

Dr. Stockmann.   And do you consider that I do that?

Peter Stockmann.   Yes, unfortunately, you do, without even being aware of it. You have a restless, pugnacious, rebellious disposition. And then there is that disastrous propensity of yours to want to write about every sort of possible and impossible thing. The moment an idea comes into your head, you must needs go and write a newspaper article or a whole pamphlet about it.

Dr. Stockmann.   Well, but is it not the duty of a citizen to let the public share in any new ideas he may have?

Peter Stockmann.   Oh, the public doesn't require any new ideas. The public is best served by the good, old-established ideas it already has.

Dr. Stockmann.   And that is your honest opinion?

Peter Stockmann.   Yes, and for once I must talk frankly to you. Hitherto I have tried to avoid doing so, because I know how irritable you are; but now I must tell you the truth, Thomas. You have no conception what an amount of harm you do yourself by your impetuosity. You complain of the author-ities, you even complain of the government—you are always pulling them to pieces; you insist that you have been neglected and persecuted. But what else can such a cantankerous man as you expect?

Dr. Stockmann.   What next! Cantankerous, am I?

Peter Stockmann.   Yes, Thomas, you are an extremely cantankerous man to work with—I know that to my cost. You disregard everything that you ought to have consideration for. You seem completely to forget that it is me you have to thank for your appointment here as medical officer to the Baths—

Dr. Stockmann.   I was entitled to it as a matter of course!—I and nobody else! I was the first person to see that the town could be made into a flourishing watering-place, and I was the only one who saw it at that time. I had to fight single-handed in support of the idea for many years; and I wrote and wrote—

Peter Stockmann.   Undoubtedly. But things were not ripe for the scheme then—though, of course, you could not judge of that in your out-of-the-way corner up north. But as soon as the opportune moment came I—and the others—took the matter into our hands—

Dr. Stockmann.   Yes, and made this mess of all my beautiful plan. It is pretty obvious now what clever fellows you were!

Peter Stockmann.   To my mind the whole thing only seems to mean that you are seeking another outlet for your combativeness. You want to pick a quarrel with your superiors—an old habit of yours. You cannot put up with any authority over you. You look askance at anyone who occupies a superior official position; you regard him as a personal enemy, and then any stick is good enough to beat him with. But now I have called your attention to the fact that the town's interests are at stake—and, incidentally, my own too. And therefore I must tell you, Thomas, that you will find me inexorable with regard to what I am about to require you to do.

Dr. Stockmann.   And what is that?

Peter Stockmann.   As you have been so indiscreet as to speak of this delicate matter to outsiders, despite the fact that you ought to have treated it as entirely official and confidential, it is obviously impossible to hush it up now. All sorts of rumours will get about directly, and everybody who has a grudge against us will take care to embellish these rumours. So it will be necessary for you to refute them publicly.

Dr. Stockmann.   I! How? I don't understand.

Peter Stockmann.   What we shall expect is that, after making further investigations, you will come to the conclusion that the matter is not by any means as dangerous or as critical as you imagined in the first instance.

Dr. Stockmann.   Oho!—so that is what you expect!

Peter Stockmann.   And, what is more, we shall expect you to make public profession of your confidence in the Committee and in their readiness to consider fully and conscientiously what steps may be necessary to remedy any possible defects.

Dr. Stockmann.   But you will never be able to do that by patching and tinkering at it—never! Take my word for it, Peter; I mean what I say, as deliberately and emphatically as possible.

Peter Stockmann.   As an officer under the Committee, you have no right to any individual opinion.

Dr. Stockmann (*amazed*).   No right?

Peter Stockmann.   In your official capacity, no. As a private person, it is quite another matter. But as a subordinate member of the staff of the Baths, you have no right to express any opinion which runs contrary to that of your superiors.

Dr. Stockmann.   This is too much! I, a doctor, a man of science, have no right to—!

Peter Stockmann.   The matter in hand is not simply a scientific one. It is a complicated matter, and has its economic as well as its technical side.

Dr. Stockmann.   I don't care what it is! I intend to be free to express my opinion on any subject under the sun.

Peter Stockmann.   As you please—but not on any subject concerning the Baths. That we forbid.

Dr. Stockmann (*shouting*).   You forbid—! You! A pack of—

Peter Stockmann.   *I* forbid it—I, your chief; and if I forbid it, you have to obey.

Dr. Stockmann (*controlling himself*).   Peter—if you were not my brother—
Petra (*throwing open the door*).   Father, you shan't stand this!
Mrs. Stockmann (*coming in after her*).   Petra, Petra!
Peter Stockmann.   Oh, so you have been eavesdropping.
Mrs. Stockmann.   You were talking so loud, we couldn't help—
Petra.   Yes, I was listening.
Peter Stockmann.   Well, after all, I am very glad—
Dr. Stockmann (*going up to him*).   You were saying something about forbidding and obeying?
Peter Stockmann.   You obliged me to take that tone with you.
Dr. Stockmann.   And so I am to give myself the lie, publicly?
Peter Stockmann.   We consider it absolutely necessary that you should make some such public statement as I have asked for.
Dr. Stockmann.   And if I do not—obey?
Peter Stockmann.   Then we shall publish a statement ourselves to reassure the public.
Dr. Stockmann.   Very well; but in that case I shall use my pen against you. I stick to what I have said; I will show that I am right and that you are wrong. And what will you do then?
Peter Stockmann.   Then I shall not be able to prevent your being dismissed.
Dr. Stockmann.   What—!
Petra.   Father—dismissed!
Mrs. Stockmann.   Dismissed!
Peter Stockmann.   Dismissed from the staff of the Baths. I shall be obliged to propose that you shall immediately be given notice, and shall not be allowed any further participation in the Baths' affairs.
Dr. Stockmann.   You would dare to do that!
Peter Stockmann.   It is you that are playing the daring game.
Petra.   Uncle, that is a shameful way to treat a man like father!
Mrs. Stockmann.   Do hold your tongue, Petra!
Peter Stockmann (*looking at Petra*).   Oh, so we volunteer our opinions already, do we? Of course. (*To Mrs. Stockmann.*) Katherine, I imagine you are the most sensible person in this house. Use any influence you may have over your husband, and make him see what this will entail for his family as well as—
Dr. Stockmann.   My family is my own concern and nobody else's!
Peter Stockmann.   —for his own family, as I was saying, as well as for the town he lives in.
Dr. Stockmann.   It is I who have the real good of the town at heart! I want to lay bare the defects that sooner or later must come to the light of day. I will show whether I love my native town.
Peter Stockmann.   You, who in your blind obstinacy want to cut off the most important source of the town's welfare?
Dr. Stockmann.   The source is poisoned, man! Are you mad? We are making

our living by retailing filth and corruption! The whole of our flourishing municipal life derives its sustenance from a lie!

Peter Stockmann. All imagination—or something even worse. The man who can throw out such offensive insinuations about his native town must be an enemy to our community.

Dr. Stockmann (*going up to him*). Do you dare to—!

Mrs. Stockmann (*throwing herself between them*). Thomas!

Petra (*catching her father by the arm*). Don't lose your temper, father!

Peter Stockmann. I will not expose myself to violence. Now you have had a warning; so reflect on what you owe to yourself and your family. Good-bye. (*Goes out.*)

Dr. Stockmann (*walking up and down*). Am I to put up with such treatment as this? In my own house, Katherine! What do you think of that!

Mrs. Stockmann. Indeed it is both shameful and absurd, Thomas—

Petra. If only I could give uncle a piece of my mind—

Dr. Stockmann. It is my own fault. I ought to have flown out at him long ago!—shown my teeth!—bitten! To hear him call me an enemy to our community! Me! I shall not take that lying down, upon my soul!

Mrs. Stockmann. But, dear Thomas, your brother has power on his side—

Dr. Stockmann. Yes, but I have right on mine, I tell you.

Mrs. Stockmann. Oh yes, right—right. What is the use of having right on your side if you have not got might?

Petra. Oh, mother!—how can you say such a thing!

Dr. Stockmann. Do you imagine that in a free country it is no use having right on your side? You are absurd, Katherine. Besides, haven't I got the liberal-minded independent press to lead the way, and the compact majority behind me? That is might enough, I should think!

Mrs. Stockmann. But, good heavens, Thomas, you don't mean to—?

Dr. Stockmann. Don't mean to what?

Mrs. Stockmann. To set yourself up in opposition to your brother.

Dr. Stockmann. In God's name, what else do you suppose I should do but take my stand on right and truth?

Petra. Yes, I was just going to say that.

Mrs. Stockmann. But it won't do you any earthly good. If they won't do it, they won't.

Dr. Stockmann. Oho, Katherine! Just give me time, and you will see how I will carry the war into their camp.

Mrs. Stockmann. Yes, you carry the war into their camp, and you get your dismissal—that is what you will do.

Dr. Stockmann. In any case I shall have done my duty towards the public— towards the community. I, who am called its enemy!

Mrs. Stockmann. But towards your family, Thomas? Towards your own home! Do you think that is doing your duty towards those you have to provide for?

Petra.   Ah, don't think always first of us, mother.

Mrs. Stockmann.   Oh, it is easy for you to talk; you are able to shift for yourself, if need be. But remember the boys, Thomas; and think a little too of yourself, and of me—

Dr. Stockmann.   I think you are out of your senses, Katherine! If I were to be such a miserable coward as to go on my knees to Peter and his damned crew, do you suppose I should ever know an hour's peace of mind all my life afterwards?

Mrs. Stockmann.   I don't know anything about that; but God preserve us from the peace of mind we shall have, all the same, if you go on defying him! You will find yourself again without the means of subsistence, with no income to count upon. I should think we had had enough of that in the old days. Remember that, Thomas; think what that means.

Dr. Stockmann *(collecting himself with a struggle and clenching his fists).*   And this is what this slavery can bring upon a free, honourable man! Isn't it horrible, Katherine?

Mrs. Stockmann.   Yes, it is sinful to treat you so, it is perfectly true. But, good heavens, one has to put up with so much injustice in this world.— There are the boys, Thomas! Look at them! What is to become of them? Oh, no, you can never have the heart—. *(Ejlif and Morten have come in while she was speaking, with their school books in their hands.)*

Dr. Stockmann.   The boys—! *(Recovers himself suddenly.)* No, even if the whole world goes to pieces, I will never bow my neck to this yoke! *(Goes towards his room.)*

Mrs. Stockmann *(following him).*   Thomas—what are you going to do!

Dr. Stockmann *(at his door).*   I mean to have the right to look my sons in the face when they are grown men. *(Goes into his room.)*

Mrs. Stockmann *(bursting into tears).*   God help us all!

Petra.   Father is splendid! He will not give in.

(The boys look on in amazement; Petra signs to them not to speak.)

Act III

SCENE.   *The editorial office of the "People's Messenger." The entrance door is on the left-hand side of the back wall; on the right-hand side is another door with glass panels through which the printing-room can be seen. Another door in the right-hand wall. In the middle of the room is a large table covered with papers, newspapers and books. In the foreground on the left a window, before which stands a desk and a high stool. There are a couple of easy chairs by the table, and other chairs standing along the wall. The room is dingy and uncomfortable; the furniture is old, the chairs stained and torn. In the printing-room the compositors are seen at work, and a printer is working a hand-press. Hovstad* *is sitting at the desk, writing. Billing comes in from the right with Dr. Stockmann's manuscript in his hand.*

Billing.   Well, I must say!

Hovstad *(still writing).*   Have you read it through?

Billing *(laying the MS on the desk).*   Yes, indeed I have.

Hovstad.   Don't you think the Doctor hits them pretty hard?

Billing.   Hard? Bless my soul, he's crushing! Every word falls like—how shall I put it?—like the blow of a sledge-hammer.

Hovstad.   Yes, but they are not the people to throw up the sponge at the first blow.

Billing.   That is true; and for that reason we must strike blow upon blow until the whole of this aristocracy tumbles to pieces. As I sat there reading this, I almost seemed to see a revolution in being.

Hovstad *(turning round).*   Hush!—Speak so that Aslaksen cannot hear you.

Billing *(lowering his voice).*   Aslaksen is a chicken-hearted chap, a coward; there is nothing of the man in him. But this time you will insist on your own way, won't you? You will put the Doctor's article in?

Hovstad.   Yes, and if the Mayor doesn't like it—

Billing.   That will be the devil of a nuisance.

Hovstad.   Well, fortunately we can turn the situation to good account, whatever happens. If the Mayor will not fall in with the Doctor's project, he will have all the small tradesmen down on him—the whole of the Householders' Association and the rest of them. And if he does fall in with it, he will fall out with the whole crowd of large shareholders in the Baths, who up to now have been his most valuable supporters—

Billing.   Yes, because they will certainly have to fork out a pretty penny—

Hovstad.   Yes, you may be sure they will. And in this way the ring will be broken up, you see, and then in every issue of the paper we will enlighten the public on the Mayor's incapability on one point and another, and make it clear that all the positions of trust in the town, the whole control of municipal affairs, ought to be put in the hands of the Liberals.

Billing.   That is perfectly true! I see it coming—I see it coming; we are on the threshold of a revolution!

(A knock is heard at the door.)

Hovstad.   Hush! *(Calls out.)* Come in! *(Dr. Stockmann comes in by the street door. Hovstad goes to meet him.)* Ah, it is you, Doctor! Well?

Dr. Stockmann.   You may set to work and print it, Mr. Hovstad!

Hovstad.   Has it come to that, then?

Billing.   Hurrah!

Dr. Stockmann.   Yes, print away. Undoubtedly it has come to that. Now they must take what they get. There is going to be a fight in the town, Mr. Billing!

Billing.   War to the knife, I hope! We will get our knives to their throats, Doctor!

Dr. Stockmann.   This article is only a beginning. I have already got four or five more sketched out in my head. Where is Aslaksen?

Billing *(calls into the printing-room).*   Aslaksen, just come here for a minute!

Hovstad.   Four or five more articles, did you say? On the same subject?

Dr. Stockmann.   No—far from it, my dear fellow. No, they are about quite another matter. But they all spring from the question of the water-supply and the drainage. One thing leads to another, you know. It is like beginning to pull down an old house, exactly.

Billing.   Upon my soul, it's true; you find you are not done till you have pulled all the old rubbish down.

Aslaksen *(coming in).*   Pulled down? You are not thinking of pulling down the Baths surely, Doctor?

Hovstad.   Far from it, don't be afraid.

Dr. Stockmann.   No, we meant something quite different. Well, what do you think of my article, Mr. Hovstad?

Hovstad.   I think it is simply a masterpiece—

Dr. Stockmann.   Do you really think so? Well, I am very pleased, very pleased.

Hovstad.   It is so clear and intelligible. One need have no special knowledge to understand the bearing of it. You will have every enlightened man on your side.

Aslaksen.   And every prudent man too, I hope?

Billing.   The prudent and the imprudent—almost the whole town.

Aslaksen.   In that case we may venture to print it.

Dr. Stockmann.   I should think so!

Hovstad.   We will put it in to-morrow morning.

Dr. Stockmann.   Of course—you must not lose a single day. What I wanted to ask you, Mr. Aslaksen, was if you would supervise the printing of it yourself.

Aslaksen.   With pleasure.

Dr. Stockmann.   Take care of it as if it were a treasure! No misprints—every word is important. I will look in again a little later; perhaps you will be able to let me see a proof. I can't tell you how eager I am to see it in print, and see it burst upon the public—

Billing.   Burst upon them—yes, like a flash of lightning!

Dr. Stockmann.   —and to have it submitted to the judgment of my intelligent fellow-townsmen. You cannot imagine what I have gone through to-day. I have been threatened first with one thing and then with another; they have tried to rob me of my most elementary rights as a man—

Billing.   What! Your rights as a man!

Dr. Stockmann.   —they have tried to degrade me, to make a coward of me, to force me to put personal interests before my most sacred convictions—

Billing.   That is too much—I'm damned if it isn't.

Hovstad. Oh, you mustn't be surprised at anything from that quarter.

Dr. Stockmann. Well, they will get the worst of it with me; they may assure themselves of that. I shall consider the "People's Messenger" my sheet-anchor now, and every single day I will bombard them with one article after another, like bomb-shells—

Aslaksen. Yes, but—

Billing. Hurrah!—it is war, it is war!

Dr. Stockmann. I shall smite them to the ground—I shall crush them—I shall break down all their defences, before the eyes of the honest public! That is what I shall do!

Aslaksen. Yes, but in moderation, Doctor—proceed with moderation—

Billing. Not a bit of it, not a bit of it! Don't spare the dynamite!

Dr. Stockmann. Because it is not merely a question of water-supply and drains now, you know. No—it is the whole of our social life that we have got to purify and disinfect—

Billing. Spoken like a deliverer!

Dr. Stockmann. All the incapables must be turned out, you understand— and that in every walk of life! Endless vistas have opened themselves to my mind's eye to-day. I cannot see it all quite clearly yet, but I shall in time. Young and vigorous standard-bearers—those are what we need and must seek, my friends; we must have new men in command at all our outposts.

Billing. Hear, hear!

Dr. Stockmann. We only need to stand by one another, and it will all be perfectly easy. The revolution will be launched like a ship that runs smoothly off the stocks. Don't you think so?

Hovstad. For my part I think we have now a prospect of getting the municipal authority into the hands where it should lie.

Aslaksen. And if only we proceed with moderation, I cannot imagine that there will be any risk.

Dr. Stockmann. Who the devil cares whether there is any risk or not! What I am doing, I am doing in the name of truth and for the sake of my conscience.

Hovstad. You are a man who deserves to be supported, Doctor.

Aslaksen. Yes, there is no denying that the Doctor is a true friend to the town—a real friend to the community, that he is.

Billing. Take my word for it, Aslaksen, Dr. Stockmann is a friend of the people.

Aslaksen. I fancy the Householders' Association will make use of that expression before long.

Dr. Stockmann (*affected, grasps their hands*). Thank you, thank you, my dear staunch friends. It is very refreshing to me to hear you say that; my brother called me something quite different. By Jove, he shall have it back, with interest! But now I must be off to see a poor devil—. I will come back, as I said. Keep a very careful eye on the manuscript, Aslaksen, and don't for worlds leave out any of my notes of exclamation! Rather put one or two more in! Capital, capital! Well, good-bye for the present—good-bye, good-bye!

(They show him to the door, and bow him out.)

Hovstad. He may prove an invaluably useful man to us.

Aslaksen. Yes, so long as he confines himself to this matter of the Baths. But if he goes farther afield, I don't think it would be advisable to follow him.

Hovstad. Hm!—that all depends—

Billing. You are so infernally timid, Aslaksen!

Aslaksen. Timid? Yes, when it is a question of the local authorities, I am timid, Mr. Billing; it is a lesson I have learnt in the school of experience, let me tell you. But try me in higher politics, in matters that concern the government itself, and then see if I am timid.

Billing. No, you aren't, I admit. But this is simply contradicting yourself.

Aslaksen. I am a man with a conscience, and that is the whole matter. If you attack the government, you don't do the community any harm, anyway; those fellows pay no attention to attacks, you see—they go on just as they are, in spite of them. But *local* authorities are different; they *can* be turned out, and then perhaps you may get an ignorant lot into office who may do irreparable harm to the householders and everybody else.

Hovstad. But what of the education of citizens by self-government—don't you attach any importance to that?

Aslaksen. When a man has interests of his own to protect, he cannot think of everything, Mr. Hovstad.

Hovstad. Then I hope I shall never have interests of my own to protect!

Billing. Hear, hear!

Aslaksen *(with a smile)*. Hm! *(Points to the desk.)* Mr. Sheriff Stensgaard was your predecessor at that editorial desk.

Billing *(spitting)*. Bah! That turncoat.

Hovstad. I am not a weathercock—and never will be.

Aslaksen. A politician should never be too certain of anything, Mr. Hovstad. And as for you, Mr. Billing, I should think it is time for you to be taking in a reef or two in your sails, seeing that you are applying for the post of secretary to the Bench.

Billing. I—!

Hovstad. Are you, Billing?

Billing. Well, yes—but you must clearly understand I am only doing it to annoy the bigwigs.

Aslaksen. Anyhow, it is no business of mine. But if I am to be accused of timidity and of inconsistency in my principles, this is what I want to point out: my political past is an open book. I have never changed, except to become a little more moderate, you see. My heart is still with the people;

but I don't deny that my reason has a certain bias towards the authorities—the local ones, I mean. (*Goes into the printing-room.*)

Billing. Oughtn't we to try and get rid of him, Hovstad?

Hovstad. Do you know anyone else who will advance the money for our paper and printing bill?

Billing. It is an infernal nuisance that we don't possess some capital to trade on.

Hovstad (*sitting down at his desk*). Yes, if we only had that, then—

Billing. Suppose you were to apply to Dr. Stockmann?

Hovstad (*turning over some papers*). What is the use? He has got nothing.

Billing. No, but he has got a warm man in the background, old Morten Kiil—"the Badger," as they call him.

Hovstad (*writing*). Are you so sure *he* has got anything?

Billing. Good Lord, of course he has! And some of it must come to the Stockmanns. Most probably he will do something for the children, at all events.

Hovstad (*turning half round*). Are you counting on that?

Billing. Counting on it? Of course I am not counting on anything.

Hovstad. That is right. And I should not count on the secretaryship to the Bench either, if I were you; for I can assure you—you won't get it.

Billing. Do you think I am not quite aware of that? My object is precisely *not* to get it. A slight of that kind stimulates a man's fighting power—it is like getting a supply of fresh bile—and I am sure one needs that badly enough in a hole-and-corner place like this, where it is so seldom anything happens to stir one up.

Hovstad (*writing*). Quite so, quite so.

Billing. Ah, I shall be heard of yet!—Now I shall go and write the appeal to the Householders' Association. (*Goes into the room on the right.*)

Hovstad (*sitting at his desk, biting his penholder, says slowly*). Hm!—that's it, is it. (*A knock is heard.*) Come in! (*Petra comes in by the outer door. Hovstad gets up.*) What, you!—here?

Petra. Yes, you must forgive me—

Hovstad (*pulling a chair forward*). Won't you sit down?

Petra. No, thank you; I must go again in a moment.

Hovstad. Have you come with a message from your father, by any chance?

Petra. No, I have come on my own account. (*Takes a book out of her coat pocket.*) Here is the English story.

Hovstad. Why have you brought it back?

Petra. Because I am not going to translate it.

Hovstad. But you promised me faithfully—

Petra. Yes, but then I had not read it. I don't suppose you have read it either?

Hovstad. No, you know quite well I don't understand English; but—

Petra. Quite so. That is why I wanted to tell you that you must find something else. (*Lays the book on the table.*) You can't use this for the "People's Messenger."

Hovstad. Why not?

Petra. Because it conflicts with all your opinions.

Hovstad. Oh, for that matter—

Petra. You don't understand me. The burden of this story is that there is a supernatural power that looks after the so-called good people in this world and makes everything happen for the best in their case—while all the so-called bad people are punished.

Hovstad. Well, but that is all right. That is just what our readers want.

Petra. And are you going to be the one to give it to them? For myself, I do not believe a word of it. You know quite well that things do not happen so in reality.

Hovstad. You are perfectly right; but an editor cannot always act as he would prefer. He is often obliged to bow to the wishes of the public in unimportant matters. Politics are the most important thing in life—for a newspaper, anyway; and if I want to carry my public with me on the path that leads to liberty and progress, I must not frighten them away. If they find a moral tale of this sort in the serial at the bottom of the page, they will be all the more ready to read what is printed above it; they feel more secure, as it were.

Petra. For shame! You would never go and set a snare like that for your readers; you are not a spider!

Hovstad (*smiling*). Thank you for having such a good opinion of me. No; as a matter of fact that is Billing's idea and not mine.

Petra. Billing's!

Hovstad. Yes; anyway he propounded that theory here one day. And it is Billing who is so anxious to have that story in the paper; I don't know anything about the book.

Petra. But how can Billing, with his emancipated views—

Hovstad. Oh, Billing is a many-sided man. He is applying for the post of secretary to the Bench, too, I hear.

Petra. I don't believe it, Mr. Hovstad. How could he possibly bring himself to do such a thing?

Hovstad. Ah, you must ask him that.

Petra. I should never have thought it of him.

Hovstad (*looking more closely at her*). No? Does it really surprise you so much?

Petra. Yes. Or perhaps not altogether. Really, I don't quite know—

Hovstad. We journalists are not much worth, Miss Stockmann.

Petra. Do you really mean that?

Hovstad. I think so sometimes.

Petra. Yes, in the ordinary affairs of everyday life, perhaps; I can understand that. But now, when you have taken a weighty matter in hand—

Hovstad. This matter of your father's, you mean?

Petra. Exactly. It seems to me that now you must feel you are a man worth more than most.

Hovstad. Yes, to-day I do feel something of that sort.

Petra. Of course you do, don't you? It is a splendid vocation you have chosen—to smooth the way for the march of unappreciated truths, and new and courageous lines of thought. If it were nothing more than because you stand fearlessly in the open and take up the cause of an injured man—

Hovstad. Especially when that injured man is—ahem!—I don't rightly know how to—

Petra. When that man is so upright and so honest, you mean?

Hovstad (*more gently*). Especially when he is your father, I meant.

Petra (*suddenly checked*). That?

Hovstad. Yes, Petra—Miss Petra.

Petra. Is it *that*, that is first and foremost with you? Not the matter itself? Not the truth?—not my father's big generous heart?

Hovstad. Certainly—of course—that too.

Petra. No, thank you; you have betrayed yourself, Mr. Hovstad, and now I shall never trust you again in anything.

Hovstad. Can you really take it so amiss in me that it is mostly for your sake—?

Petra. What I am angry with you for, is for not having been honest with my father. You talked to him as if the truth and the good of the community were what lay nearest to your heart. You have made fools of both my father and me. You are not the man you made yourself out to be. And that I shall never forgive you—never!

Hovstad. You ought not to speak so bitterly, Miss Petra—least of all now.

Petra. Why not now, especially?

Hovstad. Because your father cannot do without my help.

Petra (*looking him up and down*). Are you that sort of man too? For shame!

Hovstad. No, no, I am not. This came upon me so unexpectedly—you must believe that.

Petra. I know what to believe. Good-bye.

Aslaksen (*coming from the printing-room, hurriedly and with an air of mystery*). Damnation, Hovstad!—(*Sees Petra.*) Oh, this is awkward—

Petra. There is the book; you must give it to some one else. (*Goes towards the door.*)

Hovstad (*following her*). But, Miss Stockmann—

Petra. Good-bye. (*Goes out.*)

Aslaksen. I say—Mr. Hovstad—

Hovstad. Well, well!—what is it?

Aslaksen. The Mayor is outside in the printing-room.

Hovstad. The Mayor, did you say?

Aslaksen. Yes, he wants to speak to you. He came in by the back door—didn't want to be seen, you understand.

Hovstad. What can he want? Wait a bit—I will go myself. (*Goes to the door of the printing-room, opens it, bows and invites Peter Stockmann in.*) Just see, Aslaksen, that no one—

Aslaksen. Quite so. (*Goes into the printing-room.*)

Peter Stockmann. You did not expect to see me here, Mr. Hovstad?

Hovstad. No, I confess I did not.

Peter Stockmann (*looking round*). You are very snug in here—very nice indeed.

Hovstad. Oh—

Peter Stockmann. And here I come, without any notice, to take up your time!

Hovstad. By all means, Mr. Mayor. I am at your service. But let me relieve you of your— (*takes Stockmann's hat and stick and puts them on a chair*). Won't you sit down?

Peter Stockmann (*sitting down by the table*). Thank you. (*Hovstad sits down.*) I have had an extremely annoying experience to-day, Mr. Hovstad.

Hovstad. Really? Ah well, I expect with all the various business you have to attend to—

Peter Stockmann. The Medical Officer of the Baths is responsible for what happened to-day.

Hovstad. Indeed? The Doctor?

Peter Stockmann. He has addressed a kind of report to the Baths Committee on the subject of certain supposed defects in the Baths.

Hovstad. Has he indeed?

Peter Stockmann. Yes—has he not told you? I thought he said—

Hovstad. Ah, yes—it is true he did mention something about—

Aslaksen (*coming from the printing-room*). I ought to have that copy—

Hovstad (*angrily*). Ahem!—there it is on the desk.

Aslaksen (*taking it*). Right.

Peter Stockmann. But look there—that is the thing I was speaking of!

Aslaksen. Yes, that is the Doctor's article, Mr. Mayor.

Hovstad. Oh, is *that* what you were speaking about?

Peter Stockmann. Yes, that is it. What do you think of it?

Hovstad. Oh, I am only a layman—and I have only taken a very cursory glance at it.

Peter Stockmann. But you are going to print it?

Hovstad. I cannot very well refuse a distinguished man—

Aslaksen. I have nothing to do with editing the paper, Mr. Mayor—

Peter Stockmann. I understand.

Aslaksen. I merely print what is put into my hands.

Peter Stockmann. Quite so.

Aslaksen. And so I must—(*moves off towards the printing-room*).

Peter Stockmann. No, wait a moment, Mr. Aslaksen. You will allow me, Mr. Hovstad?

Hovstad. If you please, Mr. Mayor.

Peter Stockmann. You are a discreet and thoughtful man, Mr. Aslaksen.

Aslaksen. I am delighted to hear you think so, sir.

Peter Stockmann. And a man of very considerable influence.

Aslaksen. Chiefly among the small tradesmen, sir.

Peter Stockmann.   The small tax-payers are the majority—here as everywhere else.

Aslaksen.   That is true.

Peter Stockmann.   And I have no doubt you know the general trend of opinion among them, don't you?

Aslaksen.   Yes, I think I may say I do, Mr. Mayor.

Peter Stockmann.   Yes. Well, since there is such a praiseworthy spirit of self-sacrifice among the less wealthy citizens of our town—

Aslaksen.   What?

Hovstad.   Self-sacrifice?

Peter Stockmann.   It is pleasing evidence of a public-spirited feeling, extremely pleasing evidence. I might almost say I hardly expected it. But you have a closer knowledge of public opinion than I.

Aslaksen.   But, Mr. Mayor—

Peter Stockmann.   And indeed it is no small sacrifice that the town is going to make.

Hovstad.   The town?

Aslaksen.   But I don't understand. Is it the Baths—?

Peter Stockmann.   At a provisional estimate, the alterations that the Medical Officer asserts to be desirable will cost somewhere about twenty thousand pounds.

Aslaksen.   That is a lot of money, but—

Peter Stockmann.   Of course it will be necessary to raise a municipal loan.

Hovstad (*getting up*).   Surely you don't mean that the town must pay—?

Aslaksen.   Do you mean that it must come out of the municipal funds?—out of the ill-filled pockets of the small tradesmen?

Peter Stockmann.   Well, my dear Mr. Aslaksen, where else is the money to come from?

Aslaksen.   The gentlemen who own the Baths ought to provide that.

Peter Stockmann.   The proprietors of the Baths are not in a position to incur any further expense.

Aslaksen.   Is that absolutely certain, Mr. Mayor?

Peter Stockmann.   I have satisfied myself that it is so. If the town wants these very extensive alterations, it will have to pay for them.

Aslaksen.   But, damn it all—I beg your pardon—this is quite another matter, Mr. Hovstad!

Hovstad.   It is, indeed.

Peter Stockmann.   The most fatal part of it is that we shall be obliged to shut the Baths for a couple of years.

Hovstad.   Shut them? Shut them altogether?

Aslaksen.   For two years?

Peter Stockmann.   Yes, the work will take as long as that—at least.

Aslaksen.   I'm damned if we will stand that, Mr. Mayor! What are we house-holders to live upon in the meantime?

Peter Stockmann.   Unfortunately that is an extremely difficult question to answer, Mr. Aslaksen. But what would you have us do? Do you suppose we shall have a single visitor in the town, if we go about proclaiming that our water is polluted, that we are living over a plague spot, that the entire town—

Aslaksen.   And the whole thing is merely imagination?

Peter Stockmann.   With the best will in the world, I have not been able to come to any other conclusion.

Aslaksen.   Well then I must say it is absolutely unjustifiable of Dr. Stockmann—I beg your pardon, Mr. Mayor—

Peter Stockmann.   What you say is lamentably true, Mr. Aslaksen. My brother has unfortunately always been a headstrong man.

Aslaksen.   After this, do you mean to give him your support, Mr. Hovstad?

Hovstad.   Can you suppose for a moment that I—?

Peter Stockmann.   I have drawn up a short *résumé* of the situation as it appears from a reasonable man's point of view. In it I have indicated how certain possible defects might suitably be remedied without out-running the resources of the Baths Committee.

Hovstad.   Have you got it with you, Mr. Mayor?

Peter Stockmann *(fumbling in his pocket)*.   Yes, I brought it with me in case you should—

Aslaksen.   Good Lord, there he is!

Peter Stockmann.   Who? My brother?

Hovstad.   Where? Where?

Aslaksen.   He has just gone through the printing-room.

Peter Stockmann.   How unlucky! I don't want to meet him here, and I had still several things to speak to you about.

Hovstad *(pointing to the door on the right)*.   Go in there for the present.

Peter Stockmann.   But—?

Hovstad.   You will only find Billing in there.

Aslaksen.   Quick, quick, Mr. Mayor—he is just coming.

Peter Stockmann.   Yes, very well; but see that you get rid of him quickly. *(Goes out through the door on the right, which Aslaksen opens for him and shuts after him.)*

Hovstad.   Pretend to be doing something, Aslaksen. *(Sits down and writes. Aslaksen begins foraging among a heap of newspapers that are lying on a chair.)*

Dr. Stockmann *(coming in from the printing-room)*.   Here I am again. *(Puts down his hat and stick.)*

Hovstad *(writing)*.   Already, Doctor? Hurry up with what we were speaking about, Aslaksen. We are very pressed for time to-day.

Dr. Stockmann *(to Aslaksen)*.   No proof for me to see yet, I hear.

Aslaksen *(without turning round)*.   You couldn't expect it yet, Doctor.

Dr. Stockmann.   No, no; but I am impatient, as you can understand. I shall not know a moment's peace of mind till I see it in print.

Hovstad.   Hm!—It will take a good while yet, won't it, Aslaksen?

Aslaksen.   Yes, I am almost afraid it will.

Dr. Stockmann.   All right, my dear friends; I will come back. I do not mind coming back twice if necessary. A matter of such great importance—the welfare of the town at stake—it is no time to shirk trouble. (*Is just going, but stops and comes back.*) Look here—there is one thing more I want to speak to you about.

Hovstad.   Excuse me, but could it not wait till some other time?

Dr. Stockmann.   I can tell you in half a dozen words. It is only this. When my article is read to-morrow and it is realised that I have been quietly working the whole winter for the welfare of the town—

Hovstad.   Yes but, Doctor—

Dr. Stockmann.   I know what you are going to say. You don't see how on earth it was any more than my duty—my obvious duty as a citizen. Of course it wasn't; I know that as well as you. But my fellow citizens, you know—! Good Lord, think of all the good souls who think so highly of me—!

Aslaksen.   Yes, our townsfolk have had a very high opinion of you so far, Doctor.

Dr. Stockmann.   Yes, and that is just why I am afraid they—. Well, this is the point; when this reaches them, especially the poorer classes, and sounds in their ears like a summons to take the town's affairs into their own hands for the future—

Hovstad (*getting up*).   Ahem! Doctor, I won't conceal from you the fact—

Dr. Stockmann.   Ah!—I knew there was something in the wind! But I won't hear a word of it. If anything of that sort is being set on foot—

Hovstad.   Of what sort?

Dr. Stockmann.   Well, whatever it is—whether it is a demonstration in my honour, or a banquet, or a subscription list for some presentation to me—whatever it is, you must promise me solemnly and faithfully to put a stop to it. You too, Mr. Aslaksen; do you understand?

Hovstad.   You must forgive me, Doctor, but sooner or later we must tell you the plain truth—

(*He is interrupted by the entrance of Mrs. Stockmann, who comes in from the street door.*)

Mrs. Stockmann (*seeing her husband*).   Just as I thought!

Hovstad (*going towards her*).   You too, Mrs. Stockmann?

Dr. Stockmann.   What on earth do *you* want here, Katherine?

Mrs. Stockmann.   I should think you know very well what I want.

Hovstad.   Won't you sit down? Or perhaps—

Mrs. Stockmann.   No, thank you; don't trouble. And you must not be offended at my coming to fetch my husband; I am the mother of three children, you know.

Dr. Stockmann.   Nonsense!—we know all about that.

Mrs. Stockmann.   Well, one would not give you credit for much thought for your wife and the children to-day; if you had had that, you would not have gone and dragged us all into misfortune.

Dr. Stockmann.   Are you out of your senses, Katherine! Because a man has a wife and children, is he not to be allowed to do a service to his native town!

Mrs. Stockmann.   Yes, Thomas—in reason.

Aslaksen.   Just what I say. Moderation in everything.

Mrs. Stockmann.   And that is why you wrong us, Mr. Hovstad, in enticing my husband away from his home and making a dupe of him in all this.

Hovstad.   I certainly am making a dupe of no one—

Dr. Stockmann.   Making a dupe of me! Do you suppose I should allow myself to be duped!

Mrs. Stockmann.   It is just what you do. I know quite well you have more brains than anyone in the town, but you are extremely easily duped, Thomas. *(To Hovstad.)* Please realise that he loses his post at the Baths if you print what he has written—

Aslaksen.   What?

Hovstad.   Look here, Doctor—

Dr. Stockmann *(laughing).*   Ha—ha!—just let them try! No, no—they will take good care not to. I have got the compact majority behind me, let me tell you!

Mrs. Stockmann.   Yes, that is just the worst of it—your having any such horrid thing behind you.

Dr. Stockmann.   Rubbish, Katherine!—Go home and look after your house and leave me to look after the community. How can you be so afraid, when I am so confident and happy? *(Walks up and down, rubbing his hands.)* Truth and the People will win the fight, you may be certain! I see the whole of the broad-minded middle class marching like a victorious army—! *(Stops beside a chair.)* What the deuce is that lying there?

Aslaksen.   Good Lord!

Hovstad.   Ahem!

Dr. Stockmann.   Here we have the topmost pinnacle of authority. *(Takes the Mayor's official hat carefully between his finger-tips and holds it up in the air.)*

Mrs. Stockmann.   The Mayor's hat!

Dr. Stockmann.   And here is the staff of office too. How in the name of all that's wonderful—?

Hovstad.   Well, you see—

Dr. Stockmann.   Oh, I understand. He has been here trying to talk you over. Ha—ha!—he made rather a mistake there! And as soon as he caught sight of me in the printing-room—. *(Bursts out laughing.)* Did he run away, Mr. Aslaksen?

Aslaksen *(hurriedly).*   Yes, he ran away, Doctor.

Dr. Stockmann.   Ran away without his stick or his—. Fiddlesticks! Peter doesn't run away and leave his belongings behind him. But what the deuce have you done with him? Ah!—in there, of course. Now you shall see, Katherine!

Mrs. Stockmann.   Thomas—please don't—!

Aslaksen.   Don't be rash, Doctor.

(Dr. Stockmann has put on the Mayor's hat and taken his stick in his hand. He goes up to the door, opens it, and stands with his hand to his hat at the salute. Peter Stockmann comes in, red with anger. Billing follows him.)

Peter Stockmann.   What does this tomfoolery mean?

Dr. Stockmann.   Be respectful, my good Peter. I am the chief authority in the town now. *(Walks up and down.)*

Mrs. Stockmann *(almost in tears).*   Really, Thomas!

Peter Stockmann *(following him about).*   Give me my hat and stick.

Dr. Stockmann *(in the same tone as before).*   If you are chief constable, let me tell you that I am the Mayor—I am the master of the whole town, please understand!

Peter Stockmann.   Take off my hat, I tell you. Remember it is part of an official uniform.

Dr. Stockmann.   Pooh! Do you think the newly awakened lion-hearted people are going to be frightened by an official hat? There is going to be a revolution in the town to-morrow, let me tell you. You thought you could turn me out; but now I shall turn you out—turn you out of all your various offices. Do you think I cannot? Listen to me. I have triumphant social forces behind me. Hovstad and Billing will thunder in the "People's Messenger," and Aslaksen will take the field at the head of the whole Householders' Association—

Aslaksen.   That I won't, Doctor.

Dr. Stockmann.   Of course you will—

Peter Stockmann.   Ah!—may I ask then if Mr. Hovstad intends to join this agitation.

Hovstad.   No, Mr. Mayor.

Aslaksen.   No, Mr. Hovstad is not such a fool as to go and ruin his paper and himself for the sake of an imaginary grievance.

Dr. Stockmann *(looking round him).*   What does this mean?

Hovstad.   You have represented your case in a false light, Doctor, and therefore I am unable to give you my support.

Billing.   And after what the Mayor was so kind as to tell me just now, I—

Dr. Stockmann.   A false light! Leave that part of it to me. Only print my article; I am quite capable of defending it.

Hovstad.   I am not going to print it. I cannot and will not and dare not print it.

Dr. Stockmann.   You dare not? What nonsense!—you are the editor; and an editor controls his paper, I suppose!

Aslaksen.   No, it is the subscribers, Doctor.

Peter Stockmann.   Fortunately, yes.

Aslaksen.   It is public opinion—the enlightened public—householders and people of that kind; they control the newspapers.

Dr. Stockmann (*composedly*).   And I have all these influences against me?

Aslaksen.   Yes, you have. It would mean the absolute ruin of the community if your article were to appear.

Dr. Stockmann.   Indeed.

Peter Stockmann.   My hat and stick, if you please. (*Dr. Stockmann takes off the hat and lays it on the table with the stick. Peter Stockmann takes them up.*) Your authority as mayor has come to an untimely end.

Dr. Stockmann.   We have not got to the end yet. (*To Hovstad.*) Then it is quite impossible for you to print my article in the "People's Messenger"?

Hovstad.   Quite impossible—out of regard for your family as well.

Mrs. Stockmann.   You need not concern yourself about his family, thank you, Mr. Hovstad.

Peter Stockmann (*taking a paper from his pocket*).   It will be sufficient, for the guidance of the public, if this appears. It is an official statement. May I trouble you?

Hovstad (*taking the paper*).   Certainly; I will see that it is printed.

Dr. Stockmann.   But not mine. Do you imagine that you can silence me and stifle the truth! You will not find it so easy as you suppose. Mr. Aslaksen, kindly take my manuscript at once and print it as a pamphlet—at my expense. I will have four hundred copies—no, five—six hundred.

Aslaksen.   If you offered me its weight in gold, I could not lend my press for any such purpose, Doctor. It would be flying in the face of public opinion. You will not get it printed anywhere in the town.

Dr. Stockmann.   Then give it back to me.

Hovstad (*giving him the MS*).   Here it is.

Dr. Stockmann (*taking his hat and stick*).   It shall be made public all the same. I will read it out at a mass meeting of the townspeople. All my fellow-citizens shall hear the voice of truth!

Peter Stockmann.   You will not find any public body in the town that will give you the use of their hall for such a purpose.

Aslaksen.   Not a single one, I am certain.

Billing.   No, I'm damned if you will find one.

Mrs. Stockmann.   But this is too shameful! Why should every one turn against you like that?

Dr. Stockmann (*angrily*).   I will tell you why. It is because all the men in this town are old women—like you; they all think of nothing but their families, and never of the community.

Mrs. Stockmann (*putting her arm into his*).   Then I will show them that an— an old woman can be a man for once. I am going to stand by you, Thomas!

Dr. Stockmann.   Bravely said, Katherine! It shall be made public—as I am a living soul! If I can't hire a hall, I shall hire a drum, and parade the town with it and read it at every street-corner.

Peter Stockmann.   You are surely not such an arrant fool as that!

Dr. Stockmann.   Yes, I am.

Aslaksen.   You won't find a single man in the whole town to go with you.

Billing.   No, I'm damned if you will.

Mrs. Stockmann.   Don't give in, Thomas. I will tell the boys to go with you.

Dr. Stockmann.   That is a splendid idea!

Mrs. Stockmann.   Morten will be delighted; and Ejlif will do whatever he does.

Dr. Stockmann.   Yes, and Petra!—and you too, Katherine!

Mrs. Stockmann.   No, I won't do that; but I will stand at the window and watch you, that's what I will do.

Dr. Stockmann (*puts his arms round her and kisses her*).   Thank you, my dear! Now you and I are going to try a fall, my fine gentlemen! I am going to see whether a pack of cowards can succeed in gagging a patriot who wants to purify society! (*He and his wife go out by the street door.*)

Peter Stockmann (*shaking his head seriously*).   Now he has sent *her* out of her senses, too.

ACT IV

SCENE.   *A big old-fashioned room in Captain Horster's house. At the back folding-doors, which are standing open, lead to an ante-room. Three windows in the left-hand wall. In the middle of the opposite wall a platform has been erected. On this is a small table with two candles, a water-bottle and glass, and a bell. The room is lit by lamps placed between the windows. In the foreground on the left there is a table with candles and a chair. To the right is a door and some chairs standing near it. The room is nearly filled with a crowd of towns- people of all sorts, a few women and schoolboys being amongst them. People are still streaming in from the back, and the room is soon filled.*

1st Citizen (*meeting another*).   Hullo, Lamstad! You here too?

2nd Citizen.   I go to every public meeting, I do.

3rd Citizen.   Brought your whistle too, I expect!

2nd Citizen.   I should think so. Haven't you?

3rd Citizen.   Rather! And old Evensen said he was going to bring a cow-horn, he did.

2nd Citizen.   Good old Evensen! (*Laughter among the crowd.*)

4th Citizen (*coming up to them*).   I say, tell me what is going on here to- night.

2nd Citizen.   Dr. Stockmann is going to deliver an address attacking the Mayor.

4th Citizen.   But the Mayor is his brother.

1st Citizen.   That doesn't matter; Dr. Stockmann's not the chap to be afraid.

3rd Citizen.   But he is in the wrong; it said so in the "People's Messenger."

2nd Citizen.   Yes, I expect he must be in the wrong this time, because neither the Householders' Association nor the Citizens' Club would lend him their hall for this meeting.

1st Citizen.   He couldn't even get the loan of the hall at the Baths.

2nd Citizen.   No, I should think not.

A Man in another part of the crowd.   I say—who are we to back up in this?

Another Man, beside him.   Watch Aslaksen, and do as he does.

Billing (*pushing his way through the crowd, with a writing-case under his arm*).   Excuse me, gentlemen—do you mind letting me through? I am reporting for the "People's Messenger." Thank you very much! (*He sits down at the table on the left.*)

A Workman.   Who was that?

Second Workman.   Don't you know him? It's Billing, who writes for Aslaksen's paper.

(*Captain Horster brings in Mrs. Stockmann and Petra through the door on the right. Ejlif and Morten follow them in.*)

Horster.   I thought you might all sit here; you can slip out easily from here, if things get too lively.

Mrs. Stockmann.   Do you think there will be a disturbance?

Horster.   One can never tell—with such a crowd. But sit down, and don't be uneasy.

Mrs. Stockmann (*sitting down*).   It was extremely kind of you to offer my husband the room.

Horster.   Well, if nobody else would—

Petra (*who has sat down beside her mother*).   And it was a plucky thing to do, Captain Horster.

Horster.   Oh, it is not such a great matter as all that.

(*Hovstad and Aslaksen make their way through the crowd.*)

Aslaksen (*going up to Horster*).   Has the Doctor not come yet?

Horster.   He is waiting in the next room. (*Movement in the crowd by the door at the back.*)

Hovstad.   Look—here comes the Mayor!

Billing.   Yes, I'm damned if he hasn't come after all!

(*Peter Stockmann makes his way gradually through the crowd, bows courteously, and takes up a position by the wall on the left. Shortly afterwards Dr. Stockmann comes in by the right-hand door. He is dressed in a black frock-coat, with a white tie. There is a little feeble applause, which is hushed down. Silence is obtained.*)

Dr. Stockmann (*in an undertone*).   How do you feel, Katherine?

Mrs. Stockmann.   All right, thank you. *(Lowering her voice.)* Be sure not to lose your temper, Thomas.

Dr. Stockmann.   Oh, I know how to control myself. *(Looks at his watch, steps on to the platform, and bows.)* It is a quarter past—so I will begin. *(Takes his MS out of his pocket.)*

Aslaksen.   I think we ought to elect a chairman first.

Dr. Stockmann.   No, it is quite unnecessary.

Some of the Crowd.   Yes—yes!

Peter Stockmann.   I certainly think too that we ought to have a chairman.

Dr. Stockmann.   But I have called this meeting to deliver a lecture, Peter.

Peter Stockmann.   Dr. Stockmann's lecture may possibly lead to a considerable conflict of opinion.

Voices in the Crowd.   A chairman! A chairman!

Hovstad.   The general wish of the meeting seems to be that a chairman should be elected.

Dr. Stockmann *(restraining himself)*.   Very well—let the meeting have its way.

Aslaksen.   Will the Mayor be good enough to undertake the task?

Three Men *(clapping their hands)*.   Bravo! Bravo!

Peter Stockmann.   For various reasons, which you will easily understand, I must beg to be excused. But fortunately we have amongst us a man who I think will be acceptable to you all. I refer to the President of the House-holders' Association, Mr. Aslaksen!

Several Voices.   Yes—Aslaksen! Bravo Aslaksen!

(Dr. Stockmann takes up his MS and walks up and down the platform.)

Aslaksen.   Since my fellow-citizens choose to entrust me with this duty, I cannot refuse.

(Loud applause. Aslaksen mounts the platform.)

Billing *(writing)*.   "Mr. Aslaksen was elected with enthusiasm."

Aslaksen.   And now, as I am in this position, I should like to say a few brief words. I am a quiet and peaceable man, who believes in discreet moderation, and—and—in moderate discretion. All my friends can bear witness to that.

Several Voices.   That's right! That's right, Aslaksen!

Aslaksen.   I have learnt in the school of life and experience that moderation is the most valuable virtue a citizen can possess—

Peter Stockmann.   Hear, hear!

Aslaksen.   —And moreover that discretion and moderation are what enable a man to be of most service to the community. I would therefore suggest to our esteemed fellow-citizen, who has called this meeting, that he should strive to keep strictly within the bounds of moderation.

A Man by the Door.   Three cheers for the Moderation Society!

A Voice.   Shame!

Several Voices. Sh!—Sh!

Aslaksen. No interruptions, gentlemen, please! Does anyone wish to make any remarks?

Peter Stockmann. Mr. Chairman.

Aslaksen. The Mayor will address the meeting.

Peter Stockmann. In consideration of the close relationship in which, as you all know, I stand to the present Medical Officer of the Baths, I should have preferred not to speak this evening. But my official position with regard to the Baths and my solicitude for the vital interests of the town compel me to bring forward a motion. I venture to presume that there is not a single one of our citizens present who considers it desirable that unreliable and exaggerated accounts of the sanitary condition of the Baths and the town should be spread abroad.

Several Voices. No, no! Certainly not! We protest against it!

Peter Stockmann. Therefore I should like to propose that the meeting should not permit the Medical Officer either to read or to comment on his proposed lecture.

Dr. Stockmann *(impatiently)*. Not permit—! What the devil—!

Mrs. Stockmann *(coughing)*. Ahem!—ahem!

Dr. Stockmann *(collecting himself)*. Very well. Go ahead!

Peter Stockmann. In my communication to the "People's Messenger," I have put the essential facts before the public in such a way that every fair-minded citizen can easily form his own opinion. From it you will see that the main result of the Medical Officer's proposals—apart from their constituting a vote of censure on the leading men of the town—would be to saddle the ratepayers with an unnecessary expenditure of at least some thousands of pounds.

(Sounds of disapproval among the audience, and some cat-calls.)

Aslaksen *(ringing his bell)*. Silence, please, gentlemen! I beg to support the Mayor's motion. I quite agree with him that there is something behind this agitation started by the Doctor. He talks about the Baths; but it is a revolution he is aiming at—he wants to get the administration of the town put into new hands. No one doubts the honesty of the Doctor's intentions—no one will suggest that there can be any two opinions as to that. I myself am a believer in self-government for the people, provided it does not fall too heavily on the ratepayers. But that would be the case here; and that is why I will see Dr. Stockmann damned—I beg your pardon—before I go with him in the matter. You can pay too dearly for a thing sometimes; that is my opinion.

(Loud applause on all sides.)

Hovstad.   I, too, feel called upon to explain my position. Dr. Stockmann's agitation appeared to be gaining a certain amount of sympathy at first, so I supported it as impartially as I could. But presently we had reason to suspect that we had allowed ourselves to be misled by misrepresentation of the state of affairs—

Dr. Stockmann.   Misrepresentation—!

Hovstad.   Well, let us say a not entirely trustworthy representation. The Mayor's statement has proved that. I hope no one here has any doubt as to my liberal principles; the attitude of the "People's Messenger" towards important political questions is well known to every one. But the advice of experienced and thoughtful men has convinced me that in purely local matters a newspaper ought to proceed with a certain caution.

Aslaksen.   I entirely agree with the speaker.

Hovstad.   And, in the matter before us, it is now an undoubted fact that Dr. Stockmann has public opinion against him. Now, what is an editor's first and most obvious duty, gentlemen? Is it not to work in harmony with his readers? Has he not received a sort of tacit mandate to work persistently and assiduously for the welfare of those whose opinions he represents? Or is it possible I am mistaken in that?

Voices from the crowd.   No, No! You are quite right!

Hovstad.   It has cost me a severe struggle to break with a man in whose house I have been lately a frequent guest—a man who till to-day has been able to pride himself on the undivided goodwill of his fellow-citizens—a man whose only, or at all events whose essential failing, is that he is swayed by his heart rather than his head.

A few scattered voices.   That is true! Bravo, Stockmann!

Hovstad.   But my duty to the community obliged me to break with him. And there is another consideration that impels me to oppose him, and, as far as possible, to arrest him on the perilous course he has adopted; that is, consideration for his family—

Dr. Stockmann.   Please stick to the water-supply and drainage!

Hovstad.   —consideration, I repeat, for his wife and his children for whom he has made no provision.

Morten.   Is that us, mother?

Mrs. Stockmann.   Hush!

Aslaksen.   I will now put the Mayor's proposition to the vote.

Dr. Stockmann.   There is no necessity! To-night I have no intention of dealing with all that filth down at the Baths. No; I have something quite different to say to you.

Peter Stockmann *(aside)*.   What is coming now?

A Drunken Man *(by the entrance door)*.   I am a ratepayer! And therefore I have a right to speak too! And my entire—firm—inconceivable opinion is—

A number of voices.   Be quiet, at the back there!

Others.   He is drunk! Turn him out! *(They turn him out.)*

Dr. Stockmann.   Am I allowed to speak?

Aslaksen *(ringing his bell)*.   Dr. Stockmann will address the meeting.

Dr. Stockmann.   I should like to have seen anyone, a few days ago, dare to attempt to silence me as has been done to-night! I would have defended my sacred rights as a man, like a lion! But now it is all one to me; I have something of even weightier importance to say to you. *(The crowd presses nearer to him, Morten Kiil conspicuous among them.)*

Dr. Stockmann *(continuing)*.   I have thought and pondered a great deal, these last few days—pondered over such a variety of things that in the end my head seemed too full to hold them—

Peter Stockmann *(with a cough)*.   Ahem!

Dr. Stockmann.   —but I got them clear in my mind at last, and then I saw the whole situation lucidly. And that is why I am standing here to-night. I have a great revelation to make to you, my fellow-citizens! I will impart to you a discovery of a far wider scope than the trifling matter that our water-supply is poisoned and our medicinal Baths are standing on pestiferous soil.

A number of voices *(shouting)*.   Don't talk about the Baths! We won't hear you! None of that!

Dr. Stockmann.   I have already told you that what I want to speak about is the great discovery I have made lately—the discovery that all the sources of our *moral* life are poisoned and that the whole fabric of our civic community is founded on the pestiferous soil of falsehood.

Voices of disconcerted Citizens.   What is that he says?

Peter Stockmann.   Such an insinuation—!

Aslaksen *(with his hand on his bell)*.   I call upon the speaker to moderate his language.

Dr. Stockmann.   I have always loved my native town as a man only can love the home of his youthful days. I was not old when I went away from here; and exile, longing and memories cast as it were an additional halo over both the town and its inhabitants. *(Some clapping and applause.)* And there I stayed, for many years, in a horrible hole far away up north. When I came into contact with some of the people that lived scattered about among the rocks, I often thought it would have been more service to the poor half-starved creatures if a veterinary doctor had been sent up there, instead of a man like me. *(Murmurs among the crowd.)*

Billing *(laying down his pen)*.   I'm damned if I have ever heard—!

Hovstad.   It is an insult to a respectable population!

Dr. Stockmann.   Wait a bit! I do not think anyone will charge me with having forgotten my native town up there. I was like one of the eider-ducks brooding on its nest, and what I hatched was—the plans for these Baths. *(Applause and protests.)* And then when fate at last decreed for me the great happiness of coming home again—I assure you, gentlemen, I thought I had nothing more in the world to wish for. Or rather, there was one thing I wished for—eagerly, untiringly, ardently—and that was to be able to be of service to my native town and the good of the community.

Peter Stockmann *(looking at the ceiling)*.   You chose a strange way of doing it—ahem!

Dr. Stockmann.   And so, with my eyes blinded to the real facts, I revelled in happiness. But yesterday morning—no, to be precise, it was yesterday after-noon—the eyes of my mind were opened wide, and the first thing I realised was the colossal stupidity of the authorities—. *(Uproar, shouts and laughter. Mrs. Stockmann coughs persistently.)*

Peter Stockmann.   Mr. Chairman!

Aslaksen *(ringing his bell)*.   By virtue of my authority—!

Dr. Stockmann.   It is a petty thing to catch me up on a word, Mr. Aslaksen. What I mean is only that I got scent of the unbelievable piggishness our leading men had been responsible for down at the Baths. I can't stand leading men at any price!—I have had enough of such people in my time. They are like billy-goats in a young plantation; they do mischief everywhere. They stand in a free man's way, whichever way he turns, and what I should like best would be to see them exterminated like any other vermin—. *(Uproar.)*

Peter Stockmann.   Mr. Chairman, can we allow such expressions to pass?

Aslaksen *(with his hand on his bell)*.   Doctor—!

Dr. Stockmann.   I cannot understand how it is that I have only now acquired a clear conception of what these gentry are, when I had almost daily before my eyes in this town such an excellent specimen of them—my brother Peter—slow-witted and hide-bound in prejudice—. *(Laughter, uproar and hisses. Mrs. Stockmann sits coughing assiduously. Aslaksen rings his bell violently.)*

The Drunken Man *(who has got in again)*.   Is it me he is talking about? My name's Petersen, all right—but devil take me if I—

Angry Voices.   Turn out that drunken man! Turn him out. *(He is turned out again.)*

Peter Stockmann.   Who was that person?

1st Citizen.   I don't know who he is, Mr. Mayor.

2nd Citizen.   He doesn't belong here.

3rd Citizen.   I expect he is a navvy from over at—*(the rest is inaudible)*.

Aslaksen.   He had obviously had too much beer.—Proceed, Doctor; but please strive to be moderate in your language.

Dr. Stockmann.   Very well, gentlemen, I will say no more about our leading men. And if anyone imagines, from what I have just said, that my object is to attack these people this evening, he is wrong—absolutely wide of the mark. For I cherish the comforting conviction that these parasites—all these venerable relics of a dying school of thought—are most admirably paving the way for their own extinction; they need no doctor's help to hasten their end. Nor is it folk of that kind who constitute the most pressing danger to the community. It is not they who are most instrumental in poisoning the sources of our moral life and infecting the ground on which we stand. It is not they who are the most dangerous enemies of truth and freedom amongst us.

Shouts from all sides.   Who then? Who is it? Name! Name!

Dr. Stockmann.   You may depend upon it I shall name them! That is precisely the great discovery I made yesterday. *(Raises his voice.)* The most dangerous enemy of truth and freedom amongst us is the compact majority—yes, the damned compact Liberal majority—that is it! Now you know!

(Tremendous uproar. Most of the crowd are shouting, stamping and hissing. Some of the older men among them exchange stolen glances and seem to be enjoying themselves. Mrs. Stockmann gets up, looking anxious. Ejlif and Morten advance threateningly upon some schoolboys who are playing pranks. Aslaksen rings his bell and begs for silence. Hovstad and Billing both talk at once, but are inaudible. At last quiet is restored.)

Aslaksen.   As chairman, I call upon the speaker to withdraw the ill-considered expressions he has just used.

Dr. Stockmann.   Never, Mr. Aslaksen! It is the majority in our community that denies me my freedom and seeks to prevent my speaking the truth.

Hovstad.   The majority always has right on its side.

Billing.   And truth too, by God!

Dr. Stockmann.   The majority *never* has right on its side. Never, I say! That is one of these social lies against which an independent, intelligent man must wage war. Who is it that constitute the majority of the population in a country? Is it the clever folk or the stupid? I don't imagine you will dispute the fact that at present the stupid people are in an absolutely overwhelming majority all the world over. But, good Lord!—you can never pretend that it is right that the stupid folk should govern the clever ones! *(Uproar and cries.)* Oh, yes—you can shout me down, I know! but you cannot answer me. The majority has *might* on its side—unfortunately; but *right* it has *not*. I am in the right—I and a few other scattered individuals. The minority is always in the right. *(Renewed uproar.)*

Hovstad.   Aha!—so Dr. Stockmann has become an aristocrat since the day before yesterday!

Dr. Stockmann.   I have already said that I don't intend to waste a word on the puny, narrow-chested, short-winded crew whom we are leaving astern. Pulsating life no longer concerns itself with them. I am thinking of the few, the scattered few amongst us, who have absorbed new and vigorous truths. Such men stand, as it were, at the outposts, so far ahead that the compact majority has not yet been able to come up with them; and there they are fighting for truths that are too newly-born into the world of consciousness to have any considerable number of people on their side as yet.

Hovstad.   So the Doctor is a revolutionary now!

Dr. Stockmann.   Good heavens—of course I am, Mr. Hovstad! I propose to raise a revolution against the lie that the majority has the monopoly on the truth. What sort of truths are they that the majority usually supports? They are truths that are of such advanced age that they are beginning to break up.

And if a truth is as old as that, it is also in a fair way to become a lie, gentlemen. *(Laughter and mocking cries.)* Yes, believe me or not, as you like; but truths are by no means as long-lived as Methuselah—as some folks imagine. A normally constituted truth lives, let us say, as a rule seventeen or eighteen, or at most twenty years; seldom longer. But truths as aged as that are always worn frightfully thin, and nevertheless it is only then that the majority recognises them and recommends them to the community as whole-some moral nourishment. There is no great nutritive value in that sort of fare, I can assure you; and, as a doctor, I ought to know. These "majority truths" are like last year's cured meat—like rancid, tainted ham; and they are the origin of the moral scurvy that is rampant in our communities.

Aslaksen.   It appears to me that the speaker is wandering a long way from his subject.

Peter Stockmann.   I quite agree with the Chairman.

Dr. Stockmann.   Have you gone clean out of your senses, Peter? I am sticking as closely to my subject as I can; for my subject is precisely this, that it is the masses, the majority—this infernal compact majority—that poisons the sources of our moral life and infects the ground we stand on.

Hovstad.   And all this because the great, broad-minded majority of the people is prudent enough to show deference only to well-ascertained and well-approved truths?

Dr. Stockmann.   Ah, my good Mr. Hovstad, don't talk nonsense about well-ascertained truths! The truths of which the masses now approve are the very truths that the fighters at the outposts held to in the days of our grandfathers. We fighters at the outposts nowadays no longer approve of them; and I do not believe there is any other well-ascertained truth except this, that no community can live a healthy life if it is nourished only on such old marrowless truths.

Hovstad.   But instead of standing there using vague generalities, it would be interesting if you would tell us what these old marrowless truths are, that we are nourished on.

(Applause from many quarters.)

Dr. Stockmann.   Oh, I could give you a whole string of such abominations; but to begin with I will confine myself to one well-approved truth, which at bottom is a foul lie, but upon which nevertheless Mr. Hovstad and the "People's Messenger" and all the "Messenger's" supporters are nourished.

Hovstad.   And that is—?

Dr. Stockmann.   That is, the doctrine you have inherited from your forefathers and proclaim thoughtlessly far and wide—the doctrine that the public, the crowd, the masses, are the essential part of the population—that they con-stitute the People—that the common folk, the ignorant and incomplete element in the community, have the same right to pronounce judgment and to approve, to direct and to govern, as the isolated, intellectually superior personalities in it.

Billing. Well, damn me if ever I—

Hovstad (*at the same time, shouting out*). Fellow-citizens, take good note of that!

A number of voices (*angrily*). Oho!—we are not the People! Only the superior folk are to govern, are they!

A Workman. Turn the fellow out, for talking such rubbish!

Another. Out with him!

Another (*calling out*). Blow your horn, Evensen!

(*A horn is blown loudly, amidst hisses and an angry uproar.*)

Dr. Stockmann (*when the noise has somewhat abated*). Be reasonable! Can't you stand hearing the voice of truth for once? I don't in the least expect you to agree with me all at once; but I must say I did expect Mr. Hovstad to admit I was right, when he had recovered his composure a little. He claims to be a freethinker—

Voices (*in murmurs of astonishment*). Freethinker, did he say? Is Hovstad a freethinker?

Hovstad (*shouting*). Prove it, Dr. Stockmann! When have I said so in print?

Dr. Stockmann (*reflecting*). No, confound it, you are right!—you have never had the courage to. Well, I won't put you in a hole, Mr. Hovstad. Let us say it is I that am the freethinker, then. I am going to prove to you, scientifically, that the "People's Messenger" leads you by the nose in a shameful manner when it tells you that you—that the common people, the crowd, the masses, are the real essence of the People. That is only a newspaper lie, I tell you! The common people are nothing more than the raw material of which a People is made. (*Groans, laughter and uproar.*) Well, isn't that the case? Isn't there an enormous difference between a well-bred and an ill-bred strain of animals? Take, for instance, a common barn-door hen. What sort of eating do you get from a shrivelled up old scrag of a fowl like that? Not much, do you! And what sort of eggs does it lay? A fairly good crow or a raven can lay pretty nearly as good an egg. But take a well-bred Spanish or Japanese hen, or a good pheasant or a turkey—then you will see the difference. Or take the case of dogs, with whom we humans are on such intimate terms. Think first of an ordinary common cur—I mean one of the horrible, coarse-haired, low-bred curs that do nothing but run about the streets and befoul the walls of the houses. Compare one of these curs with a poodle whose sires for many generations have been bred in a gentleman's house, where they have had the best of food and had the opportunity of hearing soft voices and music. Do you not think that the poodle's brain is developed to quite a different degree from that of the cur? Of course it is. It is puppies of well-bred poodles like that, that showmen train to do incredibly clever tricks—things that a common cur could never learn to do even if it stood on its head. *(Uproar and mocking cries.)*

A Citizen *(calls out).*   Are you going to make out we are dogs, now?

Another Citizen.   We are not animals, Doctor!

Dr. Stockmann.   Yes, but, bless my soul, we *are*, my friend! It is true we are the finest animals anyone could wish for; but, even amongst us, exceptionally fine animals are rare. There is a tremendous difference between poodle-men and cur-men. And the amusing part of it is, that Mr. Hovstad quite agrees with me as long as it is a question of four-footed animals—

Hovstad.   Yes, it is true enough as far as they are concerned.

Dr. Stockmann.   Very well. But as soon as I extend the principle and apply it to two-legged animals, Mr. Hovstad stops short. He no longer dares to think independently, or to pursue his ideas to their logical conclusion; so he turns the whole theory upside down and proclaims in the "People's Messenger" that it is the barn-door hens and street curs that are the finest specimens in the menagerie. But that is always the way, as long as a man retains the traces of common origin and has not worked his way up to intellectual distinction.

Hovstad.   I lay no claim to any sort of distinction. I am the son of humble countryfolk, and I am proud that the stock I come from is rooted deep among the common people he insults.

Voices.   Bravo, Hovstad! Bravo! Bravo!

Dr. Stockmann.   The kind of common people I mean are not only to be found low down in the social scale; they crawl and swarm all around us—even in the highest social positions. You have only to look at your own fine, distinguished Mayor! My brother Peter is every bit as plebeian as anyone that walks in two shoes—*(laughter and hisses.)*

Peter Stockmann.   I protest against personal allusions of this kind.

Dr. Stockmann *(imperturbably).*   —and that, not because he is, like myself, descended from some old rascal of a pirate from Pomerania or thereabouts—because that is who we are descended from—

Peter Stockmann.   An absurd legend. I deny it!

Dr. Stockmann.   —but because he thinks what his superiors think and holds the same opinions as they. People who do that are, intellectually speaking, common people; and that is why my magnificent brother Peter is in reality so very far from any distinction—and consequently also so far from being liberal-minded.

Peter Stockmann.   Mr. Chairman—!

Hovstad.   So it is only the distinguished men that are liberal-minded in this country? We are learning something quite new! *(Laughter.)*

Dr. Stockmann.   Yes, that is part of my new discovery too. And another part of it is that broad-mindedness is almost precisely the same thing as morality. That is why I maintain that it is absolutely inexcusable in the "People's Messenger" to proclaim, day in and day out, the false doctrine that it is the masses, the crowd, the compact majority, that have the monopoly of broad-mindedness and morality—and that vice and corruption and every kind of intellectual depravity are the result of culture, just as all the filth that is draining into our Baths is the result of the tanneries up at Mölledal! *(Uproar and interruptions. Dr. Stockmann is undisturbed, and goes on, carried away by his ardour, with a smile.)* And yet this same "People's Messenger" can go on preaching that the masses ought to be elevated to higher conditions of life! But, bless my soul, if the "Messenger's" teaching is to be depended upon, this very raising up the masses would mean nothing more or less than setting them straightway upon the paths of depravity! Happily the theory that culture demoralises is only an old falsehood that our forefathers believed in and we have inherited. No, it is ignorance, poverty, ugly conditions of life, that do the devil's work! In a house which does not get aired and swept every day—my wife Katherine maintains that the floor ought to be scrubbed as well, but that is a debatable question—in such a house, let me tell you, people will lose within two or three years the power of thinking or acting in a moral manner. Lack of oxygen weakens the conscience. And there must be a plentiful lack of oxygen in very many houses in this town, I should think, judging from the fact that the whole compact majority can be unconscientious enough to wish to build the town's prosperity on a quagmire of falsehood and deceit.

Aslaksen. We cannot allow such a grave accusation to be flung at a citizen community.

A Citizen. I move that the Chairman direct the speaker to sit down.

Voices *(angrily)*. Hear, hear! Quite right! Make him sit down!

Dr. Stockmann *(losing his self-control)*. Then I will go and shout the truth at every street corner! I will write it in other towns' newspapers! The whole country shall know what is going on here!

Hovstad. It almost seems as if Dr. Stockmann's intention were to ruin the town.

Dr. Stockmann. Yes, my native town is so dear to me that I would rather ruin it than see it flourishing upon a lie.

Aslaksen. This is really serious. *(Uproar and cat-calls. Mrs. Stockmann coughs, but to no purpose; her husband does not listen to her any longer.)*

Hovstad *(shouting above the din)*. A man must be a public enemy to wish to ruin a whole community!

Dr. Stockmann *(with growing fervour)*. What does the destruction of a community matter, if it lives on lies! It ought to be razed to the ground, I tell you! All who live by lies ought to be exterminated like vermin! You will end by infecting the whole country; you will bring about such a state of things that the whole country will deserve to be ruined. And if things come to that pass, I shall say from the bottom of my heart: Let the whole country perish, let all these people be exterminated!

Voices from the crowd. That is talking like an out-and-out enemy of the people!

Billing. There sounded the voice of the people, by all that's holy!

The whole crowd *(shouting).* Yes, yes! He is an enemy of the people! He hates his country! He hates his own people!

Aslaksen. Both as a citizen and as an individual, I am profoundly disturbed by what we have had to listen to. Dr. Stockmann has shown himself in a light I should never have dreamed of. I am unhappily obliged to subscribe to the opinion which I have just heard my estimable fellow-citizens utter; and I propose that we should give expression to that opinion in a resolution. I propose a resolution as follows: "This meeting declares that it considers Dr. Thomas Stockmann, Medical Officer of the Baths, to be an enemy of the people." *(A storm of cheers and applause. A number of men surround the Doctor and hiss him. Mrs. Stockmann and Petra have got up from their seats. Morten and Ejlif are fighting the other schoolboys for hissing; some of their elders separate them.)*

Dr. Stockmann *(to the men who are hissing him).* Oh, you fools! I tell you that—

Aslaksen *(ringing his bell).* We cannot hear you now, Doctor. A formal vote is about to be taken; but, out of regard for personal feelings, it shall be by ballot and not verbal. Have you any clean paper, Mr. Billing?

Billing. I have both blue and white here.

Aslaksen *(going to him).* That will do nicely; we shall get on more quickly that way. Cut it up into small strips—yes, that's it. *(To the meeting.)* Blue means no; white means yes. I will come round myself and collect votes. *(Peter Stockmann leaves the hall. Aslaksen and one or two others go round the room with the slips of paper in their hats.)*

1st Citizen *(to Hovstad).* I say, what has come to the Doctor? What are we to think of it?

Hovstad. Oh, you know how headstrong he is.

2nd Citizen *(to Billing).* Billing, you go to their house—have you ever noticed if the fellow drinks?

Billing. Well I'm hanged if I know what to say. There are always spirits on the table when you go.

3rd Citizen. I rather think he goes quite off his head sometimes.

1st Citizen. I wonder if there is any madness in his family?

Billing. I shouldn't wonder if there were.

4th Citizen. No, it is nothing more than sheer malice; he wants to get even with somebody for something or other.

Billing. Well certainly he suggested a rise in his salary on one occasion lately, and did not get it.

The Citizens *(together).* Ah!—then it is easy to understand how it is!

The Drunken Man *(who has got amongst the audience again).* I want a blue one, I do! And I want a white one too!

Voices. It's that drunken chap again! Turn him out!

Morten Kiil *(going up to Dr. Stockmann).* Well, Stockmann, do you see what these monkey tricks of yours lead to?

Dr. Stockmann. I have done my duty.

Morten Kiil. What was that you said about the tanneries at Mölledal?

Dr. Stockmann. You heard well enough. I said they were the source of all the filth.

Morten Kiil. My tannery too?

Dr. Stockmann. Unfortunately your tannery is by far the worst.

Morten Kiil. Are you going to put that in the papers?

Dr. Stockmann. I shall conceal nothing.

Morten Kiil. That may cost you dear, Stockmann. *(Goes out.)*

A Stout Man *(going up to Captain Horster, without taking any notice of the ladies).* Well, Captain, so you lend your house to enemies of the people?

Horster. I imagine I can do what I like with my own possessions, Mr. Vik.

The Stout Man. Then you can have no objection to my doing the same with mine.

Horster. What do you mean, sir?

The Stout Man. You shall hear from me in the morning. *(Turns his back on him and moves off.)*

Petra. Was that not your owner, Captain Horster?

Aslaksen *(with the voting-papers in his hands, gets up on to the platform, and rings his bell).* Gentlemen, allow me to announce the result. By the votes of every one here except one person—

A Young Man. That is the drunk chap!

Aslaksen. By the votes of everyone here except a tipsy man, this meeting of citizens declares Dr. Thomas Stockmann to be an enemy of the people. *(Shouts and applause.)* Three cheers for our ancient and honourable citizen community! *(Renewed applause.)* Three cheers for our able and energetic Mayor, who has so loyally suppressed the promptings of family feeling! *(Cheers.)* The meeting is dissolved. *(Gets down.)*

Billing. Three cheers for the Chairman!

The whole crowd. Three cheers for Aslaksen! Hurrah!

Dr. Stockmann. My hat and coat, Petra! Captain, have you room on your ship for passengers to the New World?

Horster. For you and yours we will make room, Doctor.

Dr. Stockmann *(as Petra helps him into his coat).* Good. Come, Katherine! Come, boys!

Mrs. Stockmann *(in an undertone).* Thomas, dear, let us go out by the back way.

Dr. Stockmann. No back ways for me, Katherine. *(Raising his voice.)* You will hear more of this enemy of the people, before he shakes the dust off his shoes upon you! I am not so forgiving as a certain Person; I do not say: "I forgive you, for ye know not what ye do."

Aslaksen *(shouting).* That is a blasphemous comparison, Dr. Stockmann!

Billing. It is, by God! It's dreadful for an earnest man to listen to.

A Coarse Voice. Threatens us now, does he!

Other Voices *(excitedly)*.   Let's go and break his windows! Duck him in the fjord!

Another Voice.   Blow your horn, Evensen! Pip, pip!

(Horn-blowing, hisses, and wild cries. Dr. Stockmann goes out through the hall with his family, Horster elbowing a way for them.)

The Whole Crowd *(howling after them as they go)*.   Enemy of the People! Enemy of the People!

Billing *(as he puts his papers together)*.   Well, I'm damned if I go and drink toddy with the Stockmanns to-night!

(The crowd press towards the exit. The uproar continues outside; shouts of "Enemy of the People!" are heard from without.)

Act V

SCENE.   *Dr. Stockmann's study. Bookcases, and cabinets containing specimens, line the walls. At the back is a door leading to the hall; in the foreground on the left, a door leading to the sitting-room. In the right-hand wall are two windows, of which all the panes are broken. The Doctor's desk, littered with books and papers, stands in the middle of the room, which is in disorder. It is morning. Dr. Stockmann in dressing-gown, slippers and a smoking-cap, is bending down and raking with an umbrella under one of the cabinets. After a little while he rakes out a stone.*

Dr. Stockmann *(calling through the open sitting-room door)*.   Katherine, I have found another one.

Mrs. Stockmann *(from the sitting-room)*.   Oh, you will find a lot more yet, I expect.

Dr. Stockmann *(adding the stone to a heap of others on the table)*.   I shall treasure these stones as relics. Ejlif and Morten shall look at them every day, and when they are grown up they shall inherit them as heirlooms. *(Rakes about under a bookcase.)* Hasn't—what the deuce is her name?—the girl, you know—hasn't she been to fetch the glazier yet?

Mrs. Stockmann *(coming in)*.   Yes, but he said he didn't know if he would be able to come to-day.

Dr. Stockmann.   You will see he won't dare to come.

Mrs. Stockmann.   Well, that is just what Randine thought—that he didn't dare to, on account of the neighbours. *(Calls into the sitting-room)*. What is it you want, Randine? Give it to me. *(Goes in, and comes out again directly.)* Here is a letter for you, Thomas.

Dr. Stockmann.   Let me see it. *(Opens and reads it.)* Ah!—of course.

Mrs. Stockmann.   Who is it from?

Dr. Stockmann.   From the landlord. Notice to quit.

Mrs. Stockmann.   Is it possible? Such a nice man—

Dr. Stockmann *(looking at the letter)*.   Does not dare do otherwise, he says. Doesn't like doing it, but dare not do otherwise—on account of his fellow-citizens—out of regard for public opinion. Is in a dependent position—dare not offend certain influential men—

Mrs. Stockmann.   There, you see, Thomas!

Dr. Stockmann.   Yes, yes, I see well enough; the whole lot of them in the town are cowards; not a man among them dares do anything for fear of the others. *(Throws the letter on to the table.)* But it doesn't matter to us, Katherine. We are going to sail away to the New World, and—

Mrs. Stockmann.   But, Thomas, are you sure we are well advised to take this step?

Dr. Stockmann.   Are you suggesting that I should stay here, where they have pilloried me as an enemy of the people—branded me—broken my windows! And just look here, Katherine—they have torn a great rent in my black trousers too!

Mrs. Stockmann.   Oh, dear!—and they are the best pair you have got!

Dr. Stockmann.   You should never wear your best trousers when you go out to fight for freedom and truth. It is not that I care so much about the trousers, you know; you can always sew them up again for me. But that the common herd should dare to make this attack on me, as if they were my equals—that is what I cannot, for the life of me, swallow!

Mrs. Stockmann.   There is no doubt they have behaved very ill to you, Thomas; but is that sufficient reason for our leaving our native country for good and all?

Dr. Stockmann.   If we went to another town, do you suppose we should not find the common people just as insolent as they are here? Depend upon it, there is not much to choose between them. Oh, well, let the curs snap—that is not the worst part of it. The worst is that, from one end of this country to the other, every man is the slave of his Party. Although, as far as that goes, I daresay it is not much better in the free West either; the compact majority, and liberal public opinion, and all that infernal old bag of tricks are probably rampant there too. But there things are done on a larger scale, you see. They may kill you, but they won't put you to death by slow torture. They don't squeeze a free man's soul in a vice, as they do here. And, if need be, one can live in solitude. *(Walks up and down.)* If only I knew where there was a virgin forest or a small South Sea island for sale, cheap—

Mrs. Stockmann.   But think of the boys, Thomas!

Dr. Stockmann *(standing still)*.   What a strange woman you are, Katherine! Would you prefer to have the boys grow up in a society like this? You saw for yourself last night that half the population are out of their minds; and if the other half have not lost their senses, it is because they are mere brutes, with no sense to lose.

Mrs. Stockmann.   But, Thomas dear, the imprudent things you said had something to do with it, you know.

Dr. Stockmann.   Well, isn't what I said perfectly true? Don't they turn every idea topsy-turvy? Don't they make a regular hotch-potch of right and wrong? Don't they say that the things I know are true, are lies? The craziest part of it all is the fact of these "liberals," men of full age, going about in crowds imagining that they are the broad-minded party! Did you ever hear anything like it, Katherine!

Mrs. Stockmann.   Yes, yes, it's mad enough of them, certainly; but—*(Petra comes in from the sitting-room).* Back from school already?

Petra.   Yes. I have been given notice of dismissal.

Mrs. Stockmann.   Dismissal?

Dr. Stockmann.   You too?

Petra.   Mrs. Busk gave me my notice; so I thought it was best to go at once.

Dr. Stockmann.   You were perfectly right, too!

Mrs. Stockmann.   Who would have thought Mrs. Busk was a woman like that!

Petra.   Mrs. Busk isn't a bit like that, mother; I saw quite plainly how it hurt her to do it. But she didn't dare do otherwise, she said; and so I got my notice.

Dr. Stockmann *(laughing and rubbing his hands).*   She didn't dare do otherwise, either! It's delicious!

Mrs. Stockmann.   Well, after the dreadful scenes last night—

Petra.   It was not only that. Just listen to this, father!

Dr. Stockmann.   Well?

Petra.   Mrs. Busk showed me no less than three letters she received this morning—

Dr. Stockmann.   Anonymous, I suppose?

Petra.   Yes.

Dr. Stockmann.   Yes, because they didn't dare to risk signing their names, Katherine!

Petra.   And two of them were to the effect that a man, who has been our guest here, was declaring last night at the Club that my views on various subjects are extremely emancipated—

Dr. Stockmann.   You did not deny that, I hope?

Petra.   No, you know I wouldn't. Mrs. Busk's own views are tolerably emancipated, when we are alone together; but now that this report about me is being spread, she dare not keep me on any longer.

Mrs. Stockmann.   And someone who had been a guest of ours! That shows you the return you get for your hospitality, Thomas!

Dr. Stockmann.   We won't live in such a disgusting hole any longer. Pack up as quickly as you can, Katherine; the sooner we can get away, the better.

Mrs. Stockmann.   Be quiet—I think I hear someone in the hall. See who it is, Petra.

Petra *(opening the door)*.   Oh, it's you, Captain Horster! Do come in.

Horster *(coming in)*.   Good morning. I thought I would just come in and see how you were.

Dr. Stockmann *(shaking his hand)*.   Thanks—that is really kind of you.

Mrs. Stockmann.   And thank you, too, for helping us through the crowd, Captain Horster.

Petra.   How did you manage to get home again?

Horster.   Oh, somehow or other. I am fairly strong, and there is more sound than fury about these folk.

Dr. Stockmann.   Yes, isn't their swinish cowardice astonishing? Look here, I will show you something! There are all the stones they have thrown through my windows. Just look at them! I'm hanged if there are more than two decently large bits of hardstone in the whole heap; the rest are nothing but gravel—wretched little things. And yet they stood out there bawling and swearing that they would do me some violence; but as for *doing* anything— you don't see much of that in this town.

Horster.   Just as well for you this time, Doctor!

Dr. Stockmann.   True enough. But it makes one angry all the same; because if some day it should be a question of a national fight in real earnest, you will see that public opinion will be in favor of taking to one's heels, and the compact majority will turn tail like a flock of sheep, Captain Horster. That is what is so mournful to think of; it gives me so much concern, that—. No, devil take it, it is ridiculous to care about it! They have called me an enemy of the people, so an enemy of the people let me be!

Mrs. Stockmann.   You will never be that, Thomas.

Dr. Stockmann.   Don't swear to that, Katherine. To be called an ugly name may have the same effect as a pin-scratch in the lung. And that hateful name—I can't get quit of it. It is sticking here in the pit of my stomach, eating into me like a corrosive acid. And no magnesia will remove it.

Petra.   Bah!—you should only laugh at them, father.

Horster.   They will change their minds some day, Doctor.

Mrs. Stockmann.   Yes, Thomas, as sure as you are standing here.

Dr. Stockmann.   Perhaps, when it is too late. Much good may it do them! They may wallow in their filth then and rue the day when they drove a patriot into exile. When do you sail, Captain Horster?

Horster.   Hm!—that was just what I had come to speak about—

Dr. Stockmann.   Why, has anything gone wrong with the ship?

Horster.   No; but what has happened is that I am not to sail in it.

Petra.   Do you mean that you have been dismissed from your command?

Horster *(smiling)*.   Yes, that's just it.

Petra.   You too.

Mrs. Stockmann.   There, you see, Thomas!

Dr. Stockmann.   And that for the truth's sake! Oh, if I had thought such a thing possible—

Horster.   You mustn't take it to heart; I shall be sure to find a job with some ship-owner or other, elsewhere.

Dr. Stockmann.   And that is this man Vik—a wealthy man, independent of everyone and everything—! Shame on him!

Horster.   He is quite an excellent fellow otherwise; he told me himself he would willingly have kept me on, if only he had dared—

Dr. Stockmann.   But he didn't dare? No, of course not.

Horster.   It is not such an easy matter, he said, for a party man—

Dr. Stockmann.   The worthy man spoke the truth. A party is like a sausage machine; it mashes up all sorts of heads together into the same mincemeat— fatheads and blockheads, all in one mash!

Mrs. Stockmann.   Come, come, Thomas dear!

Petra *(to Horster)*.   If only you had not come home with us, things might not have come to this pass.

Horster.   I do not regret it.

Petra *(holding out her hand to him)*.   Thank you for that!

Horster *(to Dr. Stockmann)*.   And so what I came to say was that if you are determined to go away, I have thought of another plan—

Dr. Stockmann.   That's splendid!—if only we can get away at once.

Mrs. Stockmann.   Hush!—wasn't that someone knocking?

Petra.   That is uncle, surely.

Dr. Stockmann.   Aha! *(Calls out.)* Come in!

Mrs. Stockmann.   Dear Thomas, promise me definitely—.

(Peter Stockmann comes in from the hall.)

Peter Stockmann.   Oh, you are engaged. In that case, I will—

Dr. Stockmann.   No, no, come in.

Peter Stockmann.   But I wanted to speak to you alone.

Mrs. Stockmann.   We will go into the sitting-room in the meanwhile.

Horster.   And I will look in again later.

Dr. Stockmann.   No, go in there with them, Captain Horster; I want to hear more about—.

Horster.   Very well, I will wait, then. *(He follows Mrs. Stockmann and Petra into the sitting-room.)*

Dr. Stockmann.   I daresay you find it rather draughty here to-day. Put your hat on.

Peter Stockmann.   Thank you, if I may. *(Does so.)* I think I caught cold last night; I stood and shivered—

Dr. Stockmann.   Really! I found it warm enough.

Peter Stockmann.   I regret that it was not in my power to prevent those excesses last night.

Dr. Stockmann.   Have you anything particular to say to me besides that?

Peter Stockmann *(taking a big letter from his pocket).*   I have this document for you, from the Baths Committee.

Dr. Stockmann.   My dismissal?

Peter Stockmann.   Yes, dating from to-day. *(Lays the letter on the table.)* It gives us pain to do it; but, to speak frankly, we dared not do otherwise on account of public opinion.

Dr. Stockmann *(smiling).*   Dared not? I seem to have heard that word before, to-day.

Peter Stockmann.   I must beg you to understand your position clearly. For the future you must not count on any practice whatever in the town.

Dr. Stockmann.   Devil take the practice! But why are you so sure of that?

Peter Stockmann.   The Householders' Association is circulating a list from house to house. All right-minded citizens are being called upon to give up employing you; and I can assure you that not a single head of a family will risk refusing his signature. They simply dare not.

Dr. Stockmann.   No, no; I don't doubt it. But what then?

Peter Stockmann.   If I might advise you, it would be best to leave the place for a little while—

Dr. Stockmann.   Yes, the propriety of leaving the place *has* occurred to me.

Peter Stockmann.   Good. And then, when you have had six months to think things over, if, after mature consideration, you can persuade yourself to write a few words of regret, acknowledging your error—

Dr. Stockmann.   I might have my appointment restored to me, do you mean?

Peter Stockmann.   Perhaps. It is not at all impossible.

Dr. Stockmann.   But what about public opinion, then? Surely you would not dare to do it on account of public feeling.

Peter Stockmann.   Public opinion is an extremely mutable thing. And, to be quite candid with you, it is a matter of great importance to us to have some admission of that sort from you in writing.

Dr. Stockmann.   Oh, that's what you are after, is it! I will just trouble you to remember what I said to you lately about foxy tricks of that sort!

Peter Stockmann.   Your position was quite different then. At that time you had reason to suppose you had the whole town at your back—

Dr. Stockmann.   Yes, and now I feel I have the whole town *on* my back— *(flaring up).* I would not do it if I had the devil and his dam on my back—! Never—never, I tell you!

Peter Stockmann.   A man with a family has no right to behave as you do. You have no right to do it, Thomas.

Dr. Stockmann.   I have no right! There is only one single thing in the world a free man has no right to do. Do you know what that is?

Peter Stockmann.   No.

Dr. Stockmann.   Of course you don't, but I will tell you. A free man has no right to soil himself with filth; he has no right to behave in a way that would justify his spitting in his own face.

Peter Stockmann. This sort of thing sounds extremely plausible, of course; and if there were no other explanation for your obstinacy—. But as it happens that there is.

Dr. Stockmann. What do you mean?

Peter Stockmann. You understand very well what I mean. But, as your brother and as a man of discretion, I advise you not to build too much upon expectations and prospects that may so very easily fail you.

Dr. Stockmann. What in the world is all this about?

Peter Stockmann. Do you really ask me to believe that you are ignorant of the terms of Mr. Kiil's will?

Dr. Stockmann. I know that the small amount he possesses is to go to an institution for indigent old workpeople. How does that concern me?

Peter Stockmann. In the first place, it is by no means a small amount that is in question. Mr. Kiil is a fairly wealthy man.

Dr. Stockmann. I had no notion of that!

Peter Stockmann. Hm!—hadn't you really? Then I suppose you had no notion, either, that a considerable portion of his wealth will come to your children, you and your wife having a life-rent of the capital. Has he never told you so?

Dr. Stockmann. Never, on my honour! Quite the reverse; he has consistently done nothing but fume at being so unconscionably heavily taxed. But are you perfectly certain of this, Peter?

Peter Stockmann. I have it from an absolutely reliable source.

Dr. Stockmann. Then, thank God, Katherine is provided for—and the children too! I must tell her this at once— *(calls out)* Katherine, Katherine!

Peter Stockmann *(restraining him).* Hush, don't say a word yet!

Mrs. Stockmann *(opening the door).* What is the matter?

Dr. Stockmann. Oh, nothing, nothing; you can go back. *(She shuts the door. Dr. Stockmann walks up and down in his excitement.)* Provided for!—Just think of it, we are all provided for! And for life! What a blessed feeling it is to know one is provided for!

Peter Stockmann. Yes, but that is just exactly what you are not. Mr. Kiil can alter his will any day he likes.

Dr. Stockmann. But he won't do that, my dear Peter. The "Badger" is much too delighted at my attack on you and your wise friends.

Peter Stockmann *(starts and looks intently at him).* Ah, that throws a light on various things.

Dr. Stockmann. What things?

Peter Stockmann. I see that the whole thing was a combined manœuvre on your part and his. These violent, reckless attacks that you have made against the leading men of the town, under the pretence that it was in the name of truth—

Dr. Stockmann. What about them?

Peter Stockmann. I see that they were nothing else than the stipulated price for that vindictive old man's will.

Dr. Stockmann *(almost speechless).* Peter—you are the most disgusting plebeian I have ever met in all my life.

Peter Stockmann. All is over between us. Your dismissal is irrevocable—we have a weapon against you now. *(Goes out.)*

Dr. Stockmann. For shame! For shame! *(Calls out.)* Katherine, you must have the floor scrubbed after him! Let—what's her name—devil take it, the girl who has always got soot on her nose—

Mrs. Stockmann *(in the sitting-room).* Hush, Thomas, be quiet!

Petra *(coming to the door).* Father, grandfather is here, asking if he may speak to you alone.

Dr. Stockmann. Certainly he may. *(Going to the door.)* Come in, Mr. Kiil. *(Morten Kiil comes in. Dr. Stockmann shuts the door after him.)* What can I do for you? Won't you sit down?

Morten Kiil. I won't sit. *(Looks around.)* You look very comfortable here to-day, Thomas.

Dr. Stockmann. Yes, don't we!

Morten Kiil. Very comfortable—plenty of fresh air. I should think you have got enough to-day of that oxygen you were talking about yesterday. Your conscience must be in splendid order to-day, I should think.

Dr. Stockmann. It is.

Morten Kiil. So I should think. *(Taps his chest.)* Do you know what I have got here?

Dr. Stockmann. A good conscience, too, I hope.

Morten Kiil. Bah!—No, it is something better than that. *(He takes a thick pocket-book from his breast-pocket, opens it, and displays a packet of papers.)*

Dr. Stockmann *(looking at him in astonishment).* Shares in the Baths?

Morten Kiil. They were not difficult to get to-day.

Dr. Stockmann. And you have been buying—?

Morten Kiil. As many as I could pay for.

Dr. Stockmann. But, my dear Mr. Kiil—consider the state of the Baths' affairs!

Morten Kiil. If you behave like a reasonable man, you can soon set the Baths on their feet again.

Dr. Stockmann. Well, you can see for yourself that I have done all I can, but—. They are all mad in this town!

Morten Kiil. You said yesterday that the worst of this pollution came from my tannery. If that is true, then my grandfather and my father before me, and I myself, for many years past, have been poisoning the town like three destroying angels. Do you think I am going to sit quiet under that reproach?

Dr. Stockmann. Unfortunately I am afraid you will have to.

Morten Kiil. No, thank you. I am jealous of my name and reputation. They call me "the Badger," I am told. A badger is a kind of pig, I believe; but I am not going to give them the right to call me that. I mean to live and die a clean man.

Dr. Stockmann. And how are you going to set about it?

Morten Kiil. You shall cleanse me, Thomas.

Dr. Stockmann.   I!

Morten Kiil.   Do you know what money I have bought these shares with? No, of course you can't know—but I will tell you. It is the money that Katherine and Petra and the boys will have when I am gone. Because I have been able to save a little bit after all, you know.

Dr. Stockmann *(flaring up)*.   And you have gone and taken Katherine's money for *this!*

Morten Kiil.   Yes, the whole of the money is invested in the Baths now. And now I just want to see whether you are quite stark, staring mad, Thomas! If you still make out that these animals and other nasty things of that sort come from my tannery, it will be exactly as if you were to flay broad strips of skin from Katherine's body, and Petra's, and the boys'; and no decent man would do that—unless he were mad.

Dr. Stockmann *(walking up and down)*.   Yes, but I *am* mad; I *am* mad!

Morten Kiil.   You cannot be so absurdly mad as all that, when it is a question of your wife and children.

Dr. Stockmann *(standing still in front of him)*.   Why couldn't you consult me about it, before you went and bought all that trash?

Morten Kiil.   What is done cannot be undone.

Dr. Stockmann *(walks about uneasily)*.   If only I were not so certain about it—! But I am absolutely convinced that I am right.

Morten Kiil *(weighing the pocket-book in his hand)*.   If you stick to your mad idea, this won't be worth much, you know. *(Puts the pocket-book in his pocket.)*

Dr. Stockmann.   But, hang it all! it might be possible for science to discover some prophylactic, I should think—or some antidote of some kind—

Morten Kiil.   To kill these animals, do you mean?

Dr. Stockmann.   Yes, or to make them innocuous.

Morten Kiil.   Couldn't you try some rat's-bane?

Dr. Stockmann.   Don't talk nonsense! They all say it is only imagination, you know. Well, let it go at that! Let them have their own way about it! Haven't the ignorant, narrow-minded curs reviled me as an enemy of the people?—and haven't they been ready to tear the clothes off my back too?

Morten Kiil.   And broken all your windows to pieces!

Dr. Stockmann.   And then there is my duty to my family. I must talk it over with Katherine; she is great on those things.

Morten Kiil.   That is right; be guided by a reasonable woman's advice.

Dr. Stockmann *(advancing towards him)*.   To think you could do such a preposterous thing! Risking Katherine's money in this way, and putting me in such a horribly painful dilemma! When I look at you, I think I see the devil himself—.

Morten Kiil.   Then I had better go. But I must have an answer from you before two o'clock—yes or no. If it is no, the shares go to a charity, and that this very day.

Dr. Stockmann.   And what does Katherine get?

Morten Kiil. Not a halfpenny. *(The door leading to the hall opens, and Hovstad and Aslaksen make their appearance.)* Look at those two!

Dr. Stockmann *(staring at them).* What the devil!—have *you* actually the face to come into my house?

Hovstad. Certainly.

Aslaksen. We have something to say to you, you see.

Morten Kiil *(in a whisper).* Yes or no—before two o'clock.

Aslaksen *(glancing at Hovstad).* Aha! *(Morten Kiil goes out.)*

Dr. Stockmann. Well, what do you want with me? Be brief.

Hovstad. I can quite understand that you are annoyed with us for our attitude at the meeting yesterday—

Dr. Stockmann. Attitude, do you call it? Yes, it was a charming attitude! I call it weak, womanish—damnably shameful!

Hovstad. Call it what you like, we could not do otherwise.

Dr. Stockmann. You *dared* not do otherwise—isn't that it?

Hovstad. Well, if you like to put it that way.

Aslaksen. But why did you not let us have word of it beforehand?—just a hint to Mr. Hovstad or to me?

Dr. Stockmann. A hint? Of what?

Aslaksen. Of what was behind it all.

Dr. Stockmann. I don't understand you in the least.

Aslaksen *(with a confidential nod).* Oh yes, you do, Dr. Stockmann.

Hovstad. It is no good making a mystery of it any longer.

Dr. Stockmann *(looking first at one of them and then at the other).* What the devil do you both mean?

Aslaksen. May I ask if your father-in-law is not going round the town buying up all the shares in the Baths?

Dr. Stockmann. Yes, he has been buying Baths shares to-day; but—

Aslaksen. It would have been more prudent to get someone else to do it—someone less nearly related to you.

Hovstad. And you should not have let your name appear in the affair. There was no need for anyone to know that the attack on the Baths came from you. You ought to have consulted me, Dr. Stockmann.

Dr. Stockmann *(looks in front of him; then a light seems to dawn on him and he says in amazement:)* Are such things conceivable? Are such things possible?

Aslaksen *(with a smile).* Evidently they are. But it is better to use a little *finesse*, you know.

Hovstad. And it is much better to have several persons in a thing of that sort; because the responsibility of each individual is lessened, when there are others with him.

Dr. Stockmann *(composedly).* Come to the point, gentlemen. What do you want?

Aslaksen. Perhaps Mr. Hovstad had better—

Hovstad. No, you tell him, Aslaksen.

Aslaksen. Well, the fact is that, now we know the bearings of the whole affair, we think we might venture to put the "People's Messenger" at your disposal.

Dr. Stockmann. Do you dare do that now? What about public opinion? Are you not afraid of a storm breaking upon our heads?

Hovstad. We will try to weather it.

Aslaksen. And you must be ready to go off quickly on a new tack, Doctor. As soon as your invective has done its work—

Dr. Stockmann. Do you mean, as soon as my father-in-law and I have got hold of the shares at a low figure?

Hovstad. Your reasons for wishing to get the control of the Baths are mainly scientific, I take it.

Dr. Stockmann. Of course; it was for scientific reasons that I persuaded the old "Badger" to stand in with me in the matter. So we will tinker at the conduit-pipes a little, and dig up a little bit of the shore, and it shan't cost the town a sixpence. That will be all right—eh?

Hovstad. I think so—if you have the "People's Messenger" behind you.

Aslaksen. The Press is a power in a free community, Doctor.

Dr. Stockmann. Quite so. And so is public opinion. And you, Mr. Aslaksen— I suppose you will be answerable for the Householders' Association?

Aslaksen. Yes, and for the Temperance Society. You may rely on that.

Dr. Stockmann. But gentlemen—I really am ashamed to ask the question— but, what return do you—?

Hovstad. We should prefer to help you without any return whatever, believe me. But the "People's Messenger" is in rather a shaky condition; it doesn't go really well; and I should be very unwilling to suspend the paper now, when there is so much work to do here in the political way.

Dr. Stockmann. Quite so; that would be a great trial to such a friend of the people as you are. (*Flares up.*) But I am an enemy of the people, remember! (*Walks about the room.*) Where have I put my stick? Where the devil is my stick?

Hovstad. What's that?

Aslaksen. Surely you never mean—?

Dr. Stockmann (*standing still*). And suppose I don't give you a single penny of all I get out of it? Money is not very easy to get out of us rich folk, please to remember!

Hovstad. And you please to remember that this affair of the shares can be represented in two ways!

Dr. Stockmann. Yes, and you are just the man to do it. If I don't come to the rescue of the "People's Messenger," you will certainly take an evil view of the affair; you will hunt me down, I can well imagine—pursue me—try to throttle me as a dog does a hare.

Hovstad. It is a natural law; every animal must fight for its own livelihood.

Aslaksen. And get its food where it can, you know.

Dr. Stockmann (*walking about the room*). Then you go and look for yours in the gutter; because I am going to show you which is the strongest animal of us three! *(Finds an umbrella and brandishes it above his head.)* Ah, now—!

Hovstad. You are surely not going to use violence!

Aslaksen. Take care what you are doing with that umbrella.

Dr. Stockmann. Out of the window with you, Mr. Hovstad!

Hovstad *(edging to the door).* Are you quite mad!

Dr. Stockmann. Out of the window, Mr. Aslaksen! Jump, I tell you! You will have to do it, sooner or later.

Aslaksen *(running round the writing-table).* Moderation, Doctor—I am a delicate man—I can stand so little—*(calls out)* help, help!

(Mrs. Stockmann, Petra and Horster come in from the sitting-room.)

Mrs. Stockmann. Good gracious, Thomas! What is happening?

Dr. Stockmann *(brandishing the umbrella).* Jump out, I tell you! Out into the gutter!

Hovstad. An assault on an unoffending man! I call you to witness, Captain Horster. *(Hurries out through the hall.)*

Aslaksen *(irresolutely).* If only I knew the way about here—. *(Steals out through the sitting-room.)*

Mrs. Stockmann *(holding her husband back).* Control yourself, Thomas!

Dr. Stockmann *(throwing down the umbrella).* Upon my soul, they have escaped after all.

Mrs. Stockmann. What did they want you to do?

Dr. Stockmann. I will tell you later on; I have something else to think about now. *(Goes to the table and writes something on a calling-card.)* Look there, Katherine; what is written there?

Mrs. Stockmann. Three big *Noes;* what does that mean?

Dr. Stockmann. I will tell you that too, later on. *(Holds out the card to Petra.)* There, Petra; tell sooty-face to run over to the "Badger's" with that, as quick as she can. Hurry up! *(Petra takes the card and goes out to the hall.)*

Dr. Stockmann. Well, I think I have had a visit from every one of the devil's messengers to-day! But now I am going to sharpen my pen till they can feel its point; I shall dip it in venom and gall; I shall hurl my ink-pot at their heads!

Mrs. Stockmann. Yes, but we are going away, you know, Thomas.

(Petra comes back.)

Dr. Stockmann. Well?

Petra. She has gone with it.

Dr. Stockmann. Good.—Going away, did you say? No, I'll be hanged if we are going away! We are going to stay where we are, Katherine!

Petra. Stay here?

Mrs. Stockmann. Here, in the town?

Dr. Stockmann.   Yes, here. This is the field of battle—this is where the fight will be. This is where I shall triumph! As soon as I have had my trousers sewn up I shall go out and look for another house. We must have a roof over our heads for the winter.

Horster.   That you shall have in my house.

Dr. Stockmann.   Can I?

Horster.   Yes, quite well. I have plenty of room, and I am almost never at home.

Mrs. Stockmann.   How good of you, Captain Horster!

Petra.   Thank you!

Dr. Stockmann (*grasping his hand*).   Thank you, thank you! That is one trouble over! Now I can set to work in earnest at once. There is an endless amount of things to look through here, Katherine! Luckily I shall have all my time at my disposal; because I have been dismissed from the Baths, you know.

Mrs. Stockmann (*with a sigh*).   Oh yes, I expected that.

Dr. Stockmann.   And they want to take my practice away from me too. Let them! I have got the poor people to fall back upon, anyway—those that don't pay anything! and, after all, they need me most, too. But, by Jove, they will have to listen to me; I shall preach to them in season and out of season, as it says somewhere.

Mrs. Stockmann.   But, dear Thomas, I should have thought events had showed you what use it is to preach.

Dr. Stockmann.   You are really ridiculous, Katherine. Do you want me to let myself be beaten off the field by public opinion and the compact majority and all that deviltry? No, thank you! And what I want to do is so simple and clear and straightforward. I only want to drum into the heads of these curs the fact that the liberals are the most insidious enemies of freedom—that party programmes strangle every young and vigorous truth—that considerations of expediency turn morality and justice upside down—and that they will end by making life here unbearable. Don't you think, Captain Horster, that I ought to be able to make people understand that?

Horster.   Very likely; I don't know much about such things myself.

Dr. Stockmann.   Well, look here—I will explain! It is the party leaders that must be exterminated. A party leader is like a wolf, you see—like a voracious wolf. He requires a certain number of smaller victims to prey upon every year, if he is to live. Just look at Hovstad and Aslaksen! How many smaller victims have they not put an end to—or at any rate maimed and mangled until they are fit for nothing except to be householders or subscribers to the "People's Messenger"! (*Sits down on the edge of the table.*) Come here, Katherine—look how beautifully the sun shines to-day! And this lovely spring air I am drinking in!

Mrs. Stockmann.   Yes, if only we could live on sunshine and spring air, Thomas.

Dr. Stockmann.   Oh, you will have to pinch and save a bit—then we shall get along. That gives me very little concern. What is much worse is, that I know of no one who is liberal-minded and high-minded enough to venture to take up my work after me.

Petra.   Don't think about that, father; you have plenty of time before you.— Hullo, here are the boys already!

(Ejlif and Morten come in from the sitting-room.)

Mrs. Stockmann.   Have you got a holiday?

Morten.   No; but we were fighting with the other boys between lessons—

Ejlif.   That isn't true; it was the other boys were fighting with us.

Morten.   Well, and then Mr. Rörlund said we had better stay at home for a day or two.

Dr. Stockmann *(snapping his fingers and getting up from the table).*   I have it! I have it, by Jove! You shall never set foot in the school again!

The Boys.   No more school!

Mrs. Stockmann.   But, Thomas—

Dr. Stockmann.   Never, I say. I will educate you myself; that is to say, you shan't learn a blessed thing—

Morten.   Hooray!

Dr. Stockmann.   —but I will make liberal-minded and high-minded men of you. You must help me with that, Petra.

Petra.   Yes, father, you may be sure I will.

Dr. Stockmann.   And my school shall be in the room where they insulted me and called me an enemy of the people. But we are too few as we are; I must have at least twelve boys to begin with.

Mrs. Stockmann.   You will certainly never get them in this town.

Dr. Stockmann.   We shall. *(To the boys.)* Don't you know any street urchins— regular ragamuffins—?

Morten.   Yes, father, I know lots!

Dr. Stockmann.   That's capital! Bring me some specimens of them. I am going to experiment with curs, just for once; there may be some exceptional heads amongst them.

Morten.   And what are we going to do, when you have made liberal-minded and high-minded men of us?

Dr. Stockmann.   Then you shall drive all the wolves out of the country, my boys!

(Ejlif looks rather doubtful about it; Morten jumps about crying "Hurrah!")

Mrs. Stockmann.   Let us hope it won't be the wolves that will drive you out of the country, Thomas.

Dr. Stockmann.   Are you out of your mind, Katherine? Drive me out! Now— when I am the strongest man in the town!

Mrs. Stockmann.   The strongest—now?

Dr. Stockmann.   Yes, and I will go so far as to say that now I am the strongest man in the whole world.

Morten.   I say!

Dr. Stockmann (*lowering his voice*).   Hush! You mustn't say anything about it yet; but I have made a great discovery.

Mrs. Stockmann.   Another one?

Dr. Stockmann.   Yes. (*Gathers them round him, and says confidentially:*) It is this, let me tell you—that the strongest man in the world is he who stands most alone.

Mrs. Stockmann (*smiling and shaking her head*).   Oh, Thomas, Thomas!

Petra (*encouragingly, as she grasps her father's hands*).   Father!

QUESTIONS

1. In Act I Peter Stockmann says to his brother, "You have an ingrained tendency to take your own way, at all events; and that is almost equally inadmissable in a well ordered community. The individual ought undoubtedly to acquiesce in subordinating himself to the community—or, to speak more accurately, to the authorities who have the care of the community's welfare." How does this speech serve to characterize the mayor? What does Peter Stockmann mean by "community"?   **2.** What political position do Hovstad and Billing represent? Why do they support Dr. Stockmann in Act I? What political position does Aslaksen represent? Why does he switch sides in the course of the action?   **3.** How do Petra's reasons for refusing to translate an English story for the newspaper (Act III) relate to the main action of the play?   **4.** At the public meeting in Act IV, Dr. Stockmann says, "The majority *never* has right on its side. Never, I say! That is one of these social lies against which an independent, intelligent man must wage war. Who is it that constitute the majority of the population in a country? Is it the clever folk or the stupid? I don't imagine you will dispute the fact that at present the stupid people are in an absolutely overwhelming majority all the world over. But, good Lord!— you can never pretend that it is right that the stupid folk should govern the clever ones! . . . The minority is always in the right." In what way does this speech embody the theme of the play? Contrast it with Peter Stockmann's speech quoted in question 1. Are the brothers' positions antagonistic or parallel? Explain.   **5.** In Act V Morten Kiil buys stock in the Baths and tells Dr. Stockmann he has purchased the shares with Mrs. Stockmann's inheritance. What function does this event serve in the play?

WRITING TOPICS

1. At the end of the play, Dr. Stockmann looks to the future with great hope. Is his optimism justified?   **2.** Dr. Stockmann's final words are, "the strongest man in the world is he who stands most alone." Does the play vindicate his position? In any case, do you agree with Stockmann's statement?   **3.** Support or defend Dr. Stockmann's attack on political parties.   **4.** Describe a public event which pitted environmentalists against private interests. Describe the issue, the arguments on both sides, and your own position on the issue.

Trifles

1916

SUSAN GLASPELL   [1882–1948]

CHARACTERS

George Henderson, county attorney
Henry Peters, sheriff
Lewis Hale, a neighboring farmer
Mrs. Peters
Mrs. Hale

SCENE

The kitchen in the now abandoned farmhouse of John Wright, a gloomy kitchen, and left without having been put in order—the walls covered with a faded wall paper. Down right is a door leading to the parlor. On the right wall above this door is a built-in kitchen cupboard with shelves in the upper portion and drawers below. In the rear wall at right, up two steps is a door opening onto stairs leading to the second floor. In the rear wall at left is a door to the shed and from there to the outside. Between these two doors is an old-fashioned black iron stove. Running along the left wall from the shed door is an old iron sink and sink shelf, in which is set a hand pump. Downstage of the sink is an uncurtained window. Near the window is an old wooden rocker. Center stage is an unpainted wooden kitchen table with straight chairs on either side. There is a small chair down right. Unwashed pans under the sink, a loaf of bread outside the breadbox, a dish towel on the table—other signs of incompleted work. At the rear the shed door opens and the Sheriff comes in followed by the County Attorney and Hale. The Sheriff and Hale are men in middle life, the County Attorney is a young man; all are much bundled up and go at once to the stove. They are followed by the two women—the Sheriff's wife, Mrs. Peters, first; she is a slightly wiry woman, with a thin nervous face. Mrs. Hale is larger and would ordinarily be called more comfortable looking, but she is disturbed now and looks fearfully about as she enters. The women have come in slowly, and stand close together near the door.

County Attorney *(at stove rubbing his hands).*   This feels good. Come up to
the fire, ladies.

Mrs. Peters *(after taking a step forward).*   I'm not—cold.

Sheriff *(unbuttoning his overcoat and stepping away from the stove to right of
table as if to mark the beginning of official business).*   Now, Mr. Hale,
before we move things about, you explain to Mr. Henderson just what you
saw when you came here yesterday morning.

County Attorney (*crossing down to left of the table*).   By the way, has anything been moved? Are things just as you left them yesterday?

Sheriff (*looking about*).   It's just about the same. When it dropped below zero last night I thought I'd better send Frank out this morning to make a fire for us—(*sits right of center table*) no use getting pneumonia with a big case on, but I told him not to touch anything except the stove—and you know Frank.

County Attorney.   Somebody should have been left here yesterday.

Sheriff.   Oh—yesterday. When I had to send Frank to Morris Center for that man who went crazy—I want you to know I had my hands full yesterday. I knew you could get back from Omaha by today and as long as I went over everything here myself—

County Attorney.   Well, Mr. Hale, tell just what happened when you came here yesterday morning.

Hale (*crossing down to above table*).   Harry and I started to town with a load of potatoes. We came along the road from my place and as I got here I said, "I'm going to see if I can't get John Wright to go in with me on a party telephone." I spoke to Wright about it once before and he put me off, saying folks talked too much anyway, and all he asked was peace and quiet—I guess you know about how much he talked himself; but I thought maybe if I went to the house and talked about it before his wife, though I said to Harry that I didn't know as what his wife wanted made much difference to John———

County Attorney.   Let's talk about that later, Mr. Hale. I do want to talk about that, but tell now just what happened when you got to the house.

Hale.   I didn't hear or see anything; I knocked at the door, and still it was all quiet inside. I knew they must be up, it was past eight o'clock. So I knocked again, and I thought I heard somebody say, "Come in." I wasn't sure. I'm not sure yet, but I opened the door—this door (*indicating the door by which the two women are still standing*) and there in that rocker—(*pointing at it*) sat Mrs. Wright. (*They all look at the rocker down left.*)

County Attorney.   What—was she doing?

Hale.   She was rockin' back and forth. She had her apron in her hand and was kind of—pleating it.

County Attorney.   And how did she—look?

Hale.   Well, she looked queer.

County Attorney.   How do you mean—queer?

Hale.   Well, as if she didn't know what she was going to do next. And kind of done up.

County Attorney (*takes out notebook and pencil and sits left of center table*).   How did she seem to feel about your coming?

Hale.   Why, I don't think she minded—one way or another. She didn't pay much attention. I said, "How do, Mrs. Wright, it's cold, ain't it?" And she said, "Is it?"—and went on kind of pleating at her apron. Well, I was surprised; she didn't ask me to come up to the stove, or to set down, but just sat there, not even looking at me, so I said, "I want to see John." And then she—laughed. I guess you would call it a laugh. I thought of Harry and the team outside, so I said a little sharp: "Can't I see John?" "No," she says, kind o' dull like. "Ain't he home?" says I. "Yes," says she, "he's home." "Then why can't I see him?" I asked her, out of patience. "'Cause he's dead," says she. "*Dead?*" says I. She just nodded her head, not getting a bit excited, but rockin' back and forth. "Why—where is he?" says I, not knowing what to say. She just pointed upstairs—like that. (*Himself pointing to the room above.*) I started for the stairs, with the idea of going up there. I walked from there to here—then I says, "Why, what did he die of?" "He died of a rope round his neck," says she, and just went on, pleatin' at her apron. Well, I went out and called Harry. I thought I might—need help. We went upstairs and there he was lyin'———

County Attorney.   I think I'd rather have you go into that upstairs, where you can point it all out. Just go on now with the rest of the story.

Hale.   Well, my first thought was to get that rope off. It looked . . . (*stops; his face twitches*) . . . but Harry, he went up to him, and he said, "No, he's dead all right, and we'd better not touch anything." So we went back downstairs. She was still sitting that same way. "Has anybody been notified?" I asked. "No," says she, unconcerned. "Who did this, Mrs. Wright?" said Harry. He said it businesslike—and she stopped pleatin' of her apron. "I don't know," she says. "You don't *know*?" says Harry. "No," says she. "Weren't you sleepin' in the bed with him?" says Harry. "Yes," says she, "but I was on the inside." "Somebody slipped a rope round his neck and strangled him and you didn't wake up?" says Harry. "I didn't wake up," she said after him. We must 'a' looked as if we didn't see how that could be, for after a minute she said, "I sleep sound." Harry was going to ask her more questions but I said maybe we ought to let her tell her story first to the coroner, or the sheriff, so Harry went fast as he could to Rivers' place, where there's a telephone.

County Attorney.   And what did Mrs. Wright do when she knew that you had gone for the coroner?

Hale.   She moved from the rocker to that chair over there (*pointing to a small chair in the down right corner*) and just sat there with her hands held together and looking down. I got a feeling that I ought to make some conversation, so I said I had come in to see if John wanted to put in a telephone, and at that she started to laugh, and then she stopped and looked at me—scared. (*The County Attorney, who has had his notebook out, makes a note.*) I dunno, maybe it wasn't scared. I wouldn't like to say it was. Soon Harry got back, and then Dr. Lloyd came and you, Mr. Peters, and so I guess that's all I know that you don't.

County Attorney (*rising and looking around*).   I guess we'll go upstairs first— and then out to the barn and around there. (*To the Sheriff.*) You're convinced that there was nothing important here—nothing that would point to any motive?

Sheriff.   Nothing here but kitchen things.

(The County Attorney, after again looking around the kitchen, opens the door of a cupboard closet in right wall. He brings a small chair from right—gets on it and looks on a shelf. Pulls his hand away, sticky.)

County Attorney.   Here's a nice mess. *(The women draw nearer up center.)*

Mrs. Peters *(to the other woman).*   Oh, her fruit; it did freeze. *(To the Lawyer.)* She worried about that when it turned so cold. She said the fire'd go out and her jars would break.

Sheriff *(rises).*   Well, can you beat the women! Held for murder and worryin' about her preserves.

County Attorney *(getting down from chair).*   I guess before we're through she may have something more serious than preserves to worry about. *(Crosses down right center.)*

Hale.   Well, women are used to worrying over trifles. *(The two women move a little closer together.)*

County Attorney *(with the gallantry of a young politician).*   And yet, for all their worries, what would we do without the ladies? *(The women do not unbend. He goes below the center table to the sink, takes a dipperful of water from the pail, and pouring it into a basin, washes his hands. While he is doing this the Sheriff and Hale cross to cupboard, which they inspect. The County Attorney starts to wipe his hands on the roller towel, turns it for a cleaner place.)* Dirty towels! *(Kicks his foot against the pans under the sink.)* Not much of a housekeeper, would you say, ladies?

Mrs. Hale *(stiffly).*   There's a great deal of work to be done on a farm.

County Attorney.   To be sure. And yet *(with a little bow to her)* I know there are some Dickson County farmhouses which do not have such roller towels.

(He gives it a pull to expose its full length again.)

Mrs. Hale.   Those towels get dirty awful quick. Men's hands aren't always as clean as they might be.

County Attorney.   Ah, loyal to your sex, I see. But you and Mrs. Wright were neighbors. I suppose you were friends, too.

Mrs. Hale *(shaking her head).*   I've not seen much of her of late years. I've not been in this house—it's more than a year.

County Attorney *(crossing to women up center).*   And why was that? You didn't like her?

Mrs. Hale.   I liked her all well enough. Farmers' wives have their hands full, Mr. Henderson. And then————

County Attorney.   Yes————?

Mrs. Hale *(looking about).*   It never seemed a very cheerful place.

County Attorney. No—it's not cheerful. I shouldn't say she had the home-making instinct.

Mrs. Hale. Well, I don't know as Wright had, either.

County Attorney. You mean that they didn't get on very well?

Mrs. Hale. No, I don't mean anything. But I don't think a place'd be any cheerfuller for John Wright's being in it.

County Attorney. I'd like to talk more of that a little later. I want to get the lay of things upstairs now.

(He goes past the women to up right where steps lead to a stair door.)

Sheriff. I suppose anything Mrs. Peters does'll be all right. She was to take in some clothes for her, you know, and a few little things. We left in such a hurry, yesterday.

County Attorney. Yes, but I would like to see what you take, Mrs. Peters, and keep an eye out for anything that might be of use to us.

Mrs. Peters. Yes, Mr. Henderson.

(The men leave by up right door to stairs. The women listen to the men's steps on the stairs, then look about the kitchen.)

Mrs. Hale *(crossing left to sink).* I'd hate to have men coming into my kitchen, snooping around and criticizing.

(She arranges the pans under sink which the Lawyer had shoved out of place.)

Mrs. Peters. Of course it's no more than their duty.

(Crosses to cupboard up right.)

Mrs. Hale. Duty's all right, but I guess that deputy sheriff that came out to make the fire might have got a little of this on. *(Gives the roller towel a pull.)* Wish I'd thought of that sooner. Seems mean to talk about her for not having things slicked up when she had to come away in such a hurry.

(Crosses right to Mrs. Peters at cupboard.)

Mrs. Peters *(who has been looking through cupboard, lifts one end of towel that covers a pan).* She had bread set.

(Stands still.)

Mrs. Hale *(eyes fixed on a loaf of bread beside the breadbox, which is on a low shelf of the cupboard).* She was going to put this in there. *(Picks up a loaf, abruptly drops it. In a manner of returning to familiar things.)* It's a shame about her fruit. I wonder if it's all gone. *(Gets up on the chair and looks.)* I think there's some here that's all right, Mrs. Peters. Yes—here; *(holding it toward the window)* this is cherries, too. *(Looking again.)* I declare I believe that's the only one. *(Gets down, jar in her hand. Goes to the sink and wipes it off on the outside.)* She'll feel awful bad after all her hard work in the hot weather. I remember the afternoon I put up my cherries last summer.

(She puts the jar on the big kitchen table, center of the room. With a sigh, is about to sit down in the rocking chair. Before she is seated realizes what chair it is; with a slow look at it, steps back. The chair which she has touched rocks back and forth. Mrs. Peters moves to center table and they both watch the chair rock for a moment or two.)

Mrs. Peters *(shaking off the mood which the empty rocking chair has evoked. Now in a businesslike manner she speaks).*   Well I must get those things from the front room closet. *(She goes to the door at the right but, after looking into the other room, steps back.)* You coming with me, Mrs. Hale? You could help me carry them. *(They go in the other room; reappear, Mrs. Peters carrying a dress, petticoat, and skirt, Mrs. Hale following with a pair of shoes.)* My, it's cold in there.

(She puts the clothes on the big table and hurries to the stove.)

Mrs. Hale *(right of center table examining the skirt).*   Wright was close. I think maybe that's why she kept so much to herself. She didn't even belong to the Ladies' Aid. I suppose she felt she couldn't do her part, and then you don't enjoy things when you feel shabby. I heard she used to wear pretty clothes and be lively, when she was Minnie Foster, one of the town girls singing in the choir. But that—oh, that was thirty years ago. This all you want to take in?

Mrs. Peters.   She said she wanted an apron. Funny thing to want, for there isn't much to get you dirty in jail, goodness knows. But I suppose just to make her feel more natural. *(Crosses to cupboard.)* She said they was in the top drawer in this cupboard. Yes, here. And then her little shawl that always hung behind the door. *(Opens stair door and looks.)* Yes, here it is.

(Quickly shuts door leading upstairs.)

Mrs. Hale *(abruptly moving toward her).*   Mrs. Peters?
Mrs. Peters.   Yes, Mrs. Hale?

(At up right door.)

Mrs. Hale.   Do you think she did it?
Mrs. Peters *(in a frightened voice).*   Oh, I don't know.

Mrs. Hale.   Well, I don't think she did. Asking for an apron and her little shawl. Worrying about her fruit.

Mrs. Peters *(starts to speak, glances up, where footsteps are heard in the room above. In a low voice).*   Mr. Peters says it looks bad for her. Mr. Henderson is awful sarcastic in a speech and he'll make fun of her sayin' she didn't wake up.

Mrs. Hale.   Well, I guess John Wright didn't wake when they was slipping that rope under his neck.

Mrs. Peters *(crossing slowly to table and placing shawl and apron on table with other clothing).*   No, it's strange. It must have been done awful crafty and still. They say it was such a—funny way to kill a man, rigging it all up like that.

Mrs. Hale *(crossing to left of Mrs. Peters at table).*   That's just what Mr. Hale said. There was a gun in the house. He says that's what he can't understand.

Mrs. Peters.   Mr. Henderson said coming out that what was needed for the case was a motive; something to show anger, or—sudden feeling.

Mrs. Hale *(who is standing by the table).*   Well, I don't see any signs of anger around here. *(She puts her hand on the dish towel, which lies on the table, stands looking down at table, one-half of which is clean, the other half messy.)* It's wiped to here. *(Makes a move as if to finish work, then turns and looks at loaf of bread outside the breadbox. Drops towel. In that voice of coming back to familiar things.)* Wonder how they are finding things upstairs. *(Crossing below table to down right.)* I hope she had it a little more red-up[1] up there. You know, it seems kind of *sneaking.* Locking her up in town and then coming out here and trying to get her own house to turn against her!

Mrs. Peters.   But, Mrs. Hale, the law is the law.

Mrs. Hale.   I s'pose 'tis. *(Unbuttoning her coat.)* Better loosen up your things, Mrs. Peters. You won't feel them when you go out.

(Mrs. Peters takes off her fur tippet, goes to hang it on chair back left of table, stands looking at the work basket on floor near down left window.)

Mrs. Peters.   She was piecing a quilt.

(She brings the large sewing basket to the center table and they look at the bright pieces, Mrs. Hale above the table and Mrs. Peters left of it.)

Mrs. Hale.   It's a log cabin pattern. Pretty, isn't it? I wonder if she was goin' to quilt it or just knot it?

(Footsteps have been heard coming down the stairs. The Sheriff enters followed by Hale and the County Attorney.)

---

[1] A slang expression for "made attractive."

Sheriff. They wonder if she was going to quilt it or just knot it!

(The men laugh, the women look abashed.)

County Attorney *(rubbing his hands over the stove).* Frank's fire didn't do much up there, did it? Well, let's go out to the barn and get that cleared up.

(The men go outside by up left door.)

Mrs. Hale *(resentfully).* I don't know as there's anything so strange, our takin' up our time with little things while we're waiting for them to get the evidence. *(She sits in chair right of table smoothing out a block with decision.)* I don't see as it's anything to laugh about.

Mrs. Peters *(apologetically).* Of course they've got awful important things on their minds.

(Pulls up a chair and joins Mrs. Hale at the left of the table.)

Mrs. Hale *(examining another block).* Mrs. Peters, look at this one. Here, this is the one she was working on, and look at the sewing! All the rest of it has been so nice and even. And look at this! It's all over the place! Why, it looks as if she didn't know what she was about!

(After she has said this they look at each other, then start to glance back at the door. After an instant Mrs. Hale has pulled at a knot and ripped the sewing.)

Mrs. Peters. Oh, what are you doing, Mrs. Hale?

Mrs. Hale *(mildly).* Just pulling out a stitch or two that's not sewed very good. *(Threading a needle.)* Bad sewing always made me fidgety.

Mrs. Peters *(with a glance at door, nervously).* I don't think we ought to touch things.

Mrs. Hale. I'll just finish up this end. *(Suddenly stopping and leaning forward.)* Mrs. Peters?

Mrs. Peters. Yes, Mrs. Hale?

Mrs. Hale. What do you suppose she was so nervous about?

Mrs. Peters. Oh—I don't know. I don't know as she was nervous. I sometimes sew awful queer when I'm just tired. *(Mrs. Hale starts to say something, looks at Mrs. Peters, then goes on sewing.)* Well, I must get these things wrapped up. They may be through sooner than we think. *(Putting apron and other things together.)* I wonder where I can find a piece of paper, and string.

(Rises.)

Mrs. Hale. In that cupboard, maybe.

Mrs. Peters *(crosses right looking in cupboard).* Why, here's a bird-cage. *(Holds it up.)* Did she have a bird, Mrs. Hale?

Mrs. Hale. Why, I don't know whether she did or not—I've not been here for so long. There was a man around last year selling canaries cheap, but I don't know as she took one; maybe she did. She used to sing real pretty herself.

Mrs. Peters *(glancing around).* Seems funny to think of a bird here. But she must have had one, or why would she have a cage? I wonder what happened to it?

Mrs. Hale. I s'pose maybe the cat got it.

Mrs. Peters. No, she didn't have a cat. She's got that feeling some people have about cats—being afraid of them. My cat got in her room and she was real upset and asked me to take it out.

Mrs. Hale. My sister Bessie was like that. Queer, ain't it?

Mrs. Peters *(examining the cage).* Why, look at this door. It's broke. One hinge is pulled apart.

(Takes a step down to Mrs. Hale's right.)

Mrs. Hale *(looking too).* Looks as if someone must have been rough with it.

Mrs. Peters. Why, yes.

(She brings the cage forward and puts it on the table.)

Mrs. Hale *(glancing toward up left door).* I wish if they're going to find any evidence they'd be about it. I don't like this place.

Mrs. Peters. But I'm awful glad you came with me, Mrs. Hale. It would be lonesome for me sitting here alone.

Mrs. Hale. It would, wouldn't it? *(Dropping her sewing.)* But I tell you what I do wish, Mrs. Peters. I wish I had come over sometimes when *she* was here. I—*(looking around the room)*—wish I had.

Mrs. Peters. But of course you were awful busy, Mrs. Hale—your house and your children.

Mrs. Hale *(rises and crosses left).* I could've come. I stayed away because it weren't cheerful—and that's why I ought to have come. I—*(looking out left window)*—I've never liked this place. Maybe because it's down in a hollow and you don't see the road. I dunno what it is, but it's a lonesome place and always was. I wish I had come over to see Minnie Foster sometimes. I can see now—

(Shakes her head.)

Mrs. Peters *(left of table and above it).* Well, you mustn't reproach yourself, Mrs. Hale. Somehow we just don't see how it is with other folks until—something turns up.

Mrs. Hale.   Not having children makes less work—but it makes a quiet house, and Wright out to work all day, and no company when he did come in. *(Turning from window.)* Did you know John Wright, Mrs. Peters?

Mrs. Peters.   Not to know him; I've seen him in town. They say he was a good man.

Mrs. Hale.   Yes—good; he didn't drink, and kept his word as well as most, I guess, and paid his debts. But he was a hard man, Mrs. Peters. Just to pass the time of day with him—*(Shivers.)* Like a raw wind that gets to the bone. *(Pauses, her eye falling on the cage.)* I should think she would 'a' wanted a bird. But what do you suppose went with it?

Mrs. Peters.   I don't know, unless it got sick and died.

(She reaches over and swings the broken door, swings it again, both women watch it.)

Mrs. Hale.   You weren't raised round here, were you? *(Mrs. Peters shakes her head.)* You didn't know—her?

Mrs. Peters.   Not till they brought her yesterday.

Mrs. Hale.   She—come to think of it, she was kind of like a bird herself— real sweet and pretty, but kind of timid and—fluttery. How—she—did— change. *(Silence: then as if struck by a happy thought and relieved to get back to everyday things. Crosses right above Mrs. Peters to cupboard, replaces small chair used to stand on to its original place down right.)* Tell you what, Mrs. Peters, why don't you take the quilt in with you? It might take up her mind.

Mrs. Peters.   Why, I think that's a real nice idea, Mrs. Hale. There couldn't possibly be any objection to it could there? Now, just what would I take? I wonder if her patches are in here—and her things.

(They look in the sewing basket.)

Mrs. Hale *(crosses to right of table).*   Here's some red. I expect this has got sewing things in it. *(Brings out a fancy box.)* What a pretty box. Looks like something somebody would give you. Maybe her scissors are in here. *(Opens box. Suddenly puts her hand to her nose.)* Why———*(Mrs. Peters bends nearer, then turns her face away.)* There's something wrapped up in this piece of silk.

Mrs. Peters.   Why, this isn't her scissors.

Mrs. Hale *(lifting the silk).*   Oh, Mrs. Peters—it's———

(Mrs. Peters bends closer.)

Mrs. Peters.   It's the bird.

Mrs. Hale.   But, Mrs. Peters—look at it! Its neck! Look at its neck! It's all— other side *to.*

Mrs. Peters.   Somebody—wrung—its—neck.

(Their eyes meet. A look of growing comprehension, of horror. Steps are heard outside. Mrs. Hale slips box under quilt pieces, and sinks into her chair. Enter Sheriff and County Attorney. Mrs. Peters steps down left and stands looking out of window.)

County Attorney *(as one turning from serious things to little pleasantries).* Well, ladies, have you decided whether she was going to quilt it or knot it?

(Crosses to center above table.)

Mrs. Peters. We think she was going to—knot it.

(Sheriff crosses to right of stove, lifts stove lid, and glances at fire, then stands warming hands at stove.)

County Attorney. Well, that's interesting, I'm sure. *(Seeing the bird-cage.)* Has the bird flown?
Mrs. Hale *(putting more quilt pieces over the box).* We think the—cat got it.
County Attorney *(preoccupied).* Is there a cat?

(Mrs. Hale glances in a quick covert way at Mrs. Peters.)

Mrs. Peters *(turning from window takes a step in).* Well, not *now.* They're superstitious, you know. They leave.
County Attorney *(to Sheriff Peters, continuing an interrupted conversation).* No sign at all of anyone having come from the outside. Their own rope. Now let's go up again and go over it piece by piece. *(They start upstairs.)* It would have to have been someone who knew just the——

(Mrs. Peters sits down left of table. The two women sit there not looking at one another, but as if peering into something and at the same time holding back. When they talk now it is in the manner of feeling their way over strange ground, as if afraid of what they are saying, but as if they cannot help saying it.)

Mrs. Hale *(hesitatively and in hushed voice).* She liked the bird. She was going to bury it in that pretty box.
Mrs. Peters *(in a whisper).* When I was a girl—my kitten—there was a boy took a hatchet, and before my eyes—and before I could get there—— *(Covers her face an instant.)* If they hadn't held me back I would have— *(catches herself, looks upstairs where steps are heard, falters weakly)*—hurt him.
Mrs. Hale *(with a slow look around her).* I wonder how it would seem never to have had any children around. *(Pause.)* No, Wright wouldn't like the bird—a thing that sang. She used to sing. He killed that, too.

Mrs. Peters *(moving uneasily)*.   We don't know who killed the bird.

Mrs. Hale.   I knew John Wright.

Mrs. Peters.   It was an awful thing was done in this house that night, Mrs. Hale. Killing a man while he slept, slipping a rope around his neck that choked the life out of him.

Mrs. Hale.   His neck. Choked the life out of him.

(Her hand goes out and rests on the bird-cage.)

Mrs. Peters *(with rising voice)*.   We don't know who killed him. We don't *know.*

Mrs. Hale *(her own feeling not interrupted)*.   If there'd been years and years of nothing, then a bird to sing to you, it would be awful—still, after the bird was still.

Mrs. Peters *(something within her speaking)*.   I know what stillness is. When we homesteaded in Dakota, and my first baby died—after he was two years old, and me with no other then———

Mrs. Hale *(moving)*.   How soon do you suppose they'll be through looking for the evidence?

Mrs. Peters.   I know what stillness is. *(Pulling herself back.)* The law has got to punish crime, Mrs. Hale.

Mrs. Hale *(not as if answering that)*.   I wish you'd seen Minnie Foster when she wore a white dress with blue ribbons and stood up there in the choir and sang. *(A look around the room.)* Oh, I *wish* I'd come over here once in a while! That was a crime! That was a crime! Who's going to punish that?

Mrs. Peters *(looking upstairs)*.   We mustn't—take on.

Mrs. Hale.   I might have known she needed help! I know how things can be—for women. I tell you, it's queer, Mrs. Peters. We live close together and we live far apart. We all go through the same things—it's all just a different kind of the same thing. *(Brushes her eyes, noticing the jar of fruit, reaches out for it.)* If I was you I wouldn't tell her her fruit was gone. Tell her it *ain't.* Tell her it's all right. Take this in to prove it to her. She—she may never know whether it was broke or not.

Mrs. Peters *(takes the jar, looks about for something to wrap it in; takes petticoat from the clothes brought from the other room, very nervously begins winding this around the jar. In a false voice)*.   My, it's a good thing the men couldn't hear us. Wouldn't they just laugh! Getting all stirred up over a little thing like a—dead canary. As if that could have anything to do with—with— wouldn't they *laugh!*

(The men are heard coming downstairs.)

Mrs. Hale *(under her breath)*.   Maybe they would—maybe they wouldn't.

County Attorney.   No, Peters, it's all perfectly clear except a reason for doing it. But you know juries when it comes to women. If there was some definite thing. *(Crosses slowly to above table. Sheriff crosses down right. Mrs. Hale and Mrs. Peters remain seated at either side of table.)* Something to show—something to make a story about—a thing that would connect up with this strange way of doing it———

(The women's eyes meet for an instant. Enter Hale from outer door.)

Hale *(remaining by door).* Well, I've got the team around. Pretty cold out there.

County Attorney. I'm going to stay awhile by myself. *(To the Sheriff.)* You can send Frank out for me, can't you? I want to go over everything. I'm not satisfied that we can't do better.

Sheriff. Do you want to see what Mrs. Peters is going to take in?

(The Lawyer picks up the apron, laughs.)

County Attorney. Oh, I guess they're not very dangerous things the ladies have picked out. *(Moves a few things about, disturbing the quilt pieces which cover the box. Steps back.)* No, Mrs. Peters doesn't need supervising. For that matter a sheriff's wife is married to the law. Ever think of it that way, Mrs. Peters?

Mrs. Peters. Not—just that way.

Sheriff *(chuckling).* Married to the law. *(Moves to down right door to the other room.)* I just want you to come in here a minute, George. We ought to take a look at these windows.

County Attorney *(scoffingly).* Oh, windows!

Sheriff. We'll be right out, Mr. Hale.

(Hale goes outside. The Sheriff follows the County Attorney into the room. Then Mrs. Hale rises, hands tight together, looking intensely at Mrs. Peters, whose eyes make a slow turn, finally meeting Mrs. Hale's. A moment Mrs. Hale holds her, then her own eyes point the way to where the box is concealed. Suddenly Mrs. Peters throws back quilt pieces and tries to put the box in the bag she is carrying. It is too big. She opens box, starts to take bird out, cannot touch it, goes to pieces, stands there helpless. Sound of a knob turning in the other room. Mrs. Hale snatches the box and puts it in the pocket of her big coat. Enter County Attorney and Sheriff, who remain down right.)

County Attorney *(crosses to up left door facetiously).* Well, Henry, at least we found out that she was not going to quilt it. She was going to—what is it you call it, ladies?

Mrs. Hale *(standing center below table facing front, her hand against her pocket).* We call it—knot it, Mr. Henderson.

Curtain.

QUESTIONS
1. What is the meaning of the title? Glaspell titled a short-story version of the play "A Jury of Her Peers." Is this a better title than *Trifles*?   **2.** What are the major differences between Mrs. Hale and Mrs. Peters?   **3.** At one point, Mrs. Peters tells Mrs. Hale that when she was a child, a boy killed her cat. What is the significance of this event?   **4.** Why are the men unable to see the clues the women discover?   **5.** Why are the women determined to conceal the evidence of Mrs. Wright's guilt?

WRITING TOPIC
Show how the discussions of Minnie Wright's quilt embody the major themes of the play.

Conformity and Rebellion

QUESTIONS AND WRITING TOPICS

1. What support do the works in this section offer for Emily Dickinson's assertion that "Much Madness Is Divinest Sense"? **Writing Topic:** The central characters in Melville's "Bartleby the Scrivener," Mann's "Gladius Dei," and Ellison's "'Repent, Harlequin!' Said the Ticktockman" are viewed by society as mad. How might it be argued that they exhibit "divinest sense"?

2. Which works in this section can be criticized on the grounds that while they attack the established order, they fail to provide any alternatives? **Writing Topic:** Discuss the validity of this objection for two of the following poems: Wordsworth's "The World Is Too Much with Us," Lowell's "Patterns," Frost's "Departmental," Reed's "Naming of Parts."

3. In a number of these works, a single individual rebels against society and suffers defeat or death. Are these works therefore pessimistic and despairing? If not, then what is the purpose of the rebellions, and why do the authors choose to bring their characters to such ends? **Writing Topic:** Compare two works from this section that offer support for the idea that a single individual can have a decisive effect on society.

4. Examine some of the representatives of established order—the lawyer in "Bartleby the Scrivener," Peter Stockmann in *An Enemy of the People,* Herr Blüthenzweig in "Gladius Dei," the Ticktockman—and discuss what attitudes they share and how effectively they function as spokespeople for law and order. **Writing Topic:** Compare and evaluate the kinds of order that each represents.

5. Amy Lowell's "Patterns," Lawrence Ferlinghetti's "In Goya's Greatest Scenes," and Henry Reed's "Naming of Parts" are, in different ways, antiwar poems. Which of these poems do you find the most articulate and convincing antiwar statement? **Writing Topic:** Discuss the argument that, while condemning war, none of these poems examines the specific reasons that a nation may be obliged to fight—self-defense and national self-interest, for example—and that consequently they are irresponsible.

6. Most of us live out our lives in the ordinary and humdrum world that is rejected in such poems as Wordsworth's "The World Is Too Much with Us," Auden's "The Unknown Citizen," and Lennon and McCartney's "Eleanor Rigby." Can it be said that these poems are counsels to social irresponsibility? **Writing Topic:** Consider whether "we" in Wordsworth's poem, the unknown citizen, Father McKenzie, and Eleanor Rigby are simply objects of scorn or whether they deserve sympathy and perhaps even respect.

7. Characters in two of the plays included here, Antigonê and Dr. Stockmann, are rebels. Are they comparable? **Writing Topic:** Explain how the attitudes and actions of these characters constitute an attack on the status quo.

Love
and
Hate

Mr. and Mrs. Clark and Percy, 1970–1971 by David Hockney.

Love and death, it is often noted, are the two great themes of literature. Many of the literary works we have placed in the sections "Innocence and Experience" and "Conformity and Rebellion" speak of love and death as well. But in those works, other thematic interests dominate. In this section, we gather a number of works in which love and hate are thematically central.

The rosy conception of love presented in many popular and sentimental stories ill prepares us for the complicated reality we face. We know that the course of true love never runs smooth, but in those popular stories the obstacles that hinder the lovers are simple and external. If the young lover can land the high-paying job or convince the beloved's parents that he or she is worthy despite social differences, all will be well. But love in life is rarely that simple. The external obstacles may be insuperable, or the obstacles may lie deep within the personality. The major obstacle may well be an individual's difficult and painful effort to understand that he or she has been deceived by an immature and sentimental conception of love.

In this age of psychoanalytic awareness, the claims of the flesh are well recognized. But psychoanalytic theory teaches us, as well, to recognize the aggressive aspect of the human condition. The omnipresent selfishness that civilization attempts to check may be aggressively violent as well as lustful. Thus, on one hand, we have the simple eroticism of Kate Chopin's "The Storm," and on the other, the macabre behavior of Faulkner's Emily Grierson in "A Rose for Emily." And Matthew Arnold in "Dover Beach" finds love the only refuge from a chaotic world in which "ignorant armies clash by night."

The cliché has it that love and hate are closely related, and much evidence supports this proposition. But why should love and hate, seeming opposites, lie so close together in the emotional lives of men and women? We are all egos, separate from each other. And as separate individuals, we develop elaborate behavior mechanisms that defend us from each other. But the erotic love relationship differs from other relationships in that it may be defined as a rejection of separateness. The common metaphor speaks of two lovers as joining, as merging into one. That surrender of the "me" to join in an "us" leaves lovers uniquely vulnerable to psychic injury. In short, the defenses are down, and the self-esteem of each of the lovers depends importantly on the behavior of the other. If the lover is betrayed by the beloved, the emotional consequences are uniquely disastrous—hence the peculiarly close relationship of passionate hatred with erotic love.

Words like *love* and *hate* are so general that poets rarely use them except as one term in a metaphor designed to project sharply some aspect of emotional life. The simple sexuality in such poems as Marvell's "To His Coy Mistress,"

Marlowe's "The Passionate Shepherd to His Love," and Campion's "I Care Not for These Ladies" may be juxtaposed with the hatred and violence generated in Othello by sexual jealousy or with the quick reprisal of the slighted Barbara Allan. And Shakespeare's description of lust in "Th' expense of spirit in a waste of shame" notes an aspect of love quite overlooked by Edmund Waller in his song, "Go, Lovely Rose!"

Perhaps more than anything, the works in this section celebrate the elemental impulses of men and women that run counter to those rational formulations by which we govern our lives. We pursue Othello's love for Desdemona and Iago's hate for Othello and arrive at an irreducible mystery, for neither Othello's love nor Iago's hate yields satisfactorily to rational explanation. Reason does not tell us why Othello and Desdemona love one another or why Iago hates rather than honors Othello.

Love is an act of faith springing from our deep-seated need to join with another human being not only in physical nakedness but in emotional and spiritual nakedness as well. While hate is a denial of that faith and, therefore, a retreat into spiritual isolation, love is an attempt to break out of the isolation.

FOR THINKING AND WRITING

As you read the selections in this section, consider the following questions. You may want to write out your thoughts informally in a journal or notebook as a way of preparing to respond to the selections, or you may wish to make one of these questions the basis for a formal essay.

1. What is love? What is the source of your definition (literature, personal observation, discussions with those you trust)? Have you ever been in love? How did you know? Do you know someone who is in love? How do you know?

2. Have you ever truly hated someone or something? Describe the circumstances, and characterize your hatred.

3. Do you believe that love and hate are closely related? Have you experienced a change from love to hatred, or do you know someone who has? Explain.

4. There are different kinds of love—love of family, of humankind, of God. There are, of course, sexual love and the love of a cause. Characterize several different kinds of love, and examine your own motives and behavior in different love relationships. In what ways do certain kinds of love necessarily generate certain hatreds?

LOVE
AND
HATE

A Husband Parting from His Wife and Child, 1799 by William Blake

FICTION

The Storm (1898)

KATE CHOPIN [1851–1904]

I

The leaves were so still that even Bibi thought it was going to rain. Bobinôt, who was accustomed to converse on terms of perfect equality with his little son, called the child's attention to certain sombre clouds that were rolling with sinister intention from the west, accompanied by a sullen, threatening roar. They were at Friedheimer's store and decided to remain there till the storm had passed. They sat within the door on two empty kegs. Bibi was four years old and looked very wise.

"Mama'll be 'fraid, yes," he suggested with blinking eyes.

"She'll shut the house. Maybe she got Sylvie helpin' her this evenin'," Bobinôt responded reassuringly.

"No; she ent got Sylvie. Sylvie was helpin' her yistiday," piped Bibi.

Bobinôt arose and going across to the counter purchased a can of shrimps, of which Calixta was very fond. Then he returned to his perch on the keg and sat stolidly holding the can of shrimps while the storm burst. It shook the wooden store and seemed to be ripping great furrows in the distant field. Bibi laid his little hand on his father's knee and was not afraid.

II

Calixta, at home, felt no uneasiness for their safety. She sat at a side window sewing furiously on a sewing machine. She was greatly occupied and did not notice the approaching storm. But she felt very warm and often stopped to mop her face on which the perspiration gathered in beads. She unfastened her white sacque at the throat. It began to grow dark, and suddenly realizing the situation she got up hurriedly and went about closing windows and doors.

Out on the small front gallery she had hung Bobinôt's Sunday clothes to air and she hastened out to gather them before the rain fell. As she stepped outside,

Alcée Laballière rode in at the gate. She had not seen him very often since her marriage, and never alone. She stood there with Bobinôt's coat in her hands, and the big rain drops began to fall. Alcée rode his horse under the shelter of a side projection where the chickens had huddled and there were plows and a harrow piled up in the corner.

"May I come and wait on your gallery till the storm is over, Calixta?" he asked.

"Come 'long in, M'sieur Alcée."

His voice and her own startled her as if from a trance, and she seized Bobinôt's vest. Alcée, mounting to the porch, grabbed the trousers and snatched Bibi's braided jacket that was about to be carried away by a sudden gust of wind. He expressed an intention to remain outside, but it was soon apparent that he might as well have been out in the open: the water beat in upon the boards in driving sheets, and he went inside, closing the door after him. It was even necessary to put something beneath the door to keep the water out.

"My! what a rain! It's good two years sence it rain' like that," exclaimed Calixta as she rolled up a piece of bagging and Alcée helped her to thrust it beneath the crack.

She was a little fuller of figure than five years before when she married; but she had lost nothing of her vivacity. Her blue eyes still retained their melting quality; and her yellow hair, dishevelled by the wind and rain, kinked more stubbornly than ever about her ears and temples.

The rain beat upon the low, shingled roof with a force and clatter that threatened to break an entrance and deluge them there. They were in the dining room—the sitting room—the general utility room. Adjoining was her bed room, with Bibi's couch along side her own. The door stood open, and the room with its white, monumental bed, its closed shutters, looked dim and mysterious.

Alcée flung himself into a rocker and Calixta nervously began to gather up from the floor the lengths of a cotton sheet which she had been sewing.

"If this keeps up, *Dieu sait*[1] if the levees goin' to stan' it!" she exclaimed.

"What have you got to do with the levees?"

"I got enough to do! An' there's Bobinôt with Bibi out in that storm—if he only didn' left Friedheimer's!"

"Let us hope, Calixta, that Bobinôt's got sense enough to come in out of a cyclone."

She went and stood at the window with a greatly disturbed look on her face. She wiped the frame that was clouded with moisture. It was stiflingly hot. Alcée got up and joined her at the window, looking over her shoulder. The rain was coming down in sheets obscuring the view of far-off cabins and enveloping the distant wood in a gray mist. The playing of the lightning was incessant. A bolt struck a tall chinaberry tree at the edge of the field. It filled all visible space

---

[1] God knows.

with a blinding glare and the crash seemed to invade the very boards they stood upon.

Calixta put her hands to her eyes, and with a cry, staggered backward. Alcée's arm encircled her, and for an instant he drew her close and spasmodically to him.

"*Bonté!*"[2] she cried, releasing herself from his encircling arm and retreating from the window, "the house'll go next! If I only knew w'ere Bibi was!" She would not compose herself; she would not be seated. Alcée clasped her shoulders and looked into her face. The contact of her warm, palpitating body when he had unthinkingly drawn her into his arms, had aroused all the old-time infatuation and desire for her flesh.

"Calixta," he said, "don't be frightened. Nothing can happen. The house is too low to be struck, with so many tall trees standing about. There! aren't you going to be quiet? say, aren't you?" He pushed her hair back from her face that was warm and steaming. Her lips were as red and moist as pomegranate seed. Her white neck and a glimpse of her full, firm bosom disturbed him powerfully. As she glanced up at him the fear in her liquid blue eyes had given place to a drowsy gleam that unconsciously betrayed a sensuous desire. He looked down into her eyes and there was nothing for him to do but to gather her lips in a kiss. It reminded him of Assumption.[3]

"Do you remember—in Assumption, Calixta?" he asked in a low voice broken by passion. Oh! she remembered; for in Assumption he had kissed her and kissed and kissed her; until his senses would well nigh fail, and to save her he would resort to a desperate flight. If she was not an immaculate dove in those days, she was still inviolate; a passionate creature whose very defenselessness had made her defense, against which his honor forbade him to prevail. Now—well, now—her lips seemed in a manner free to be tasted, as well as her round, white throat and her whiter breasts.

They did not heed the crashing torrents, and the roar of the elements made her laugh as she lay in his arms. She was a revelation in that dim, mysterious chamber; as white as the couch she lay upon. Her firm, elastic flesh that was knowing for the first time its birthright, was like a creamy lily that the sun invites to contribute its breath and perfume to the undying life of the world.

The generous abundance of her passion, without guile or trickery, was like a white flame which penetrated and found response in depths of his own sensuous nature that had never yet been reached.

When he touched her breasts they gave themselves up in quivering ecstasy, inviting his lips. Her mouth was a fountain of delight. And when he possessed her, they seemed to swoon together at the very borderland of life's mystery.

He stayed cushioned upon her, breathless, dazed, enervated, with his heart

---

[2] An exclamation: Goodness!

[3] A holiday commemorating the ascent of the Virgin Mary to heaven. Assumption is also the name of a Louisiana parish (county) where Calixta and Alcée had had a rendezvous in an earlier story.

beating like a hammer upon her. With one hand she clasped his head, her lips lightly touching his forehead. The other hand stroked with a soothing rhythm his muscular shoulders.

The growl of the thunder was distant and passing away. The rain beat softly upon the shingles, inviting them to drowsiness and sleep. But they dared not yield.

The rain was over; and the sun was turning the glistening green world into a palace of gems. Calixta, on the gallery, watched Alcée ride away. He turned and smiled at her with a beaming face; and she lifted her pretty chin in the air and laughed aloud.

III

Bobinôt and Bibi, trudging home, stopped without at the cistern to make themselves presentable.

"My! Bibi, w'at will yo' mama say! You ought to be ashame'. You oughtn' put on those good pants. Look at 'em! An' that mud on yo' collar! How you got that mud on yo' collar, Bibi? I never saw such a boy!" Bibi was the picture of pathetic resignation. Bobinôt was the embodiment of serious solicitude as he strove to remove from his own person and his son's the signs of their tramp over heavy roads and through wet fields. He scraped the mud off Bibi's bare legs and feet with a stick and carefully removed all traces from his heavy brogans. Then, prepared for the worst—the meeting with an over-scrupulous housewife, they entered cautiously at the back door.

Calixta was preparing supper. She had set the table and was dripping coffee at the hearth. She sprang up as they came in.

"Oh, Bobinôt! You back! My! but I was uneasy. W'ere you been during the rain? An' Bibi? he ain't wet? he ain't hurt?" She had clasped Bibi and was kissing him effusively. Bobinôt's explanations and apologies which he had been composing all along the way, died on his lips as Calixta felt him to see if he were dry, and seemed to express nothing but satisfaction at their safe return.

"I brought you some shrimps, Calixta," offered Bobinôt, hauling the can from his ample side pocket and laying it on the table.

"Shrimps! Oh, Bobinôt! you too good fo' anything!" and she gave him a smacking kiss on the cheek that resounded. "*J'vous réponds,*[4] we'll have a feas' to night! umph-umph!"

Bobinôt and Bibi began to relax and enjoy themselves, and when the three seated themselves at table they laughed much and so loud that anyone might have heard them as far away as Laballière's.

---

[4] I'm telling you.

IV

Alcée Laballière wrote to his wife, Clarisse, that night. It was a loving letter, full of tender solicitude. He told her not to hurry back, but if she and the babies liked it at Biloxi, to stay a month longer. He was getting on nicely; and though he missed them, he was willing to bear the separation a while longer—realizing that their health and pleasure were the first things to be considered.

V

As for Clarisse, she was charmed upon receiving her husband's letter. She and the babies were doing well. The society was agreeable; many of her old friends and acquaintances were at the bay. And the first free breath since her marriage seemed to restore the pleasant liberty of her maiden days. Devoted as she was to her husband, their intimate conjugal life was something which she was more than willing to forego for a while.

So the storm passed and everyone was happy.

Theater

1923

JEAN TOOMER [1894–1967]

Life of nigger alleys, of pool rooms and restaurants and near-beer saloons soaks into the walls of Howard Theater and sets them throbbing jazz songs. Black-skinned, they dance and shout above the tick and trill of white-walled buildings. At night, they open doors to people who come in to stamp their feet and shout. At night, road-shows volley songs into the mass-heart of black people. Songs soak the walls and seep out to the nigger life of alleys and near-beer saloons, of the Poodle Dog and Black Bear cabarets. Afternoons, the house is dark, and the walls are sleeping singers until rehearsal begins. Or until John comes within them. Then they start throbbing to a subtle syncopation. And the space-dark air grows softly luminous.

John is the manager's brother. He is seated at the center of the theater, just before rehearsal. Light streaks down upon him from a window high above. One half his face is orange in it. One half his face is in shadow. The soft glow of the house rushes to, and compacts about, the shaft of light. John's mind coincides with the shaft of light. Thoughts rush to, and compact about it. Life of the house and of the slowly awakening stage swirls to the body of John, and thrills it. John's body is separate from the thoughts that pack his mind.

Stage-lights, soft, as if they shine through clear pink fingers. Beneath them, hid by the shadow of a set, Dorris. Other chorus girls drift in. John feels them in the mass. And as if his own body were the mass-heart of a black audience listening to them singing, he wants to stamp his feet and shout. His mind, contained above desires of his body, singles the girls out, and tries to trace origins and plot destinies.

A pianist slips into the pit and improvises jazz. The walls awake. Arms of the girls, and their limbs, which . . . jazz, jazz . . . by lifting up their tight street skirts they set free, jab the air and clog the floor in rhythm to the music. (Lift your skirts, Baby, and talk to papa!) Crude, individualized, and yet . . . monotonous. . . .

John: Soon the director will herd you, my full-lipped, distant beauties, and tame you, and blunt your sharp thrusts in loosely suggestive movements, appropriate to Broadway. (O dance!) Soon the audience will paint your dusk faces white, and call you beautiful. (O dance!) Soon I . . . (O dance!) I'd like . . .

Girls laugh and shout. Sing discordant snatches of other jazz songs. Whirl with loose passion into the arms of passing show-men.

John: Too thick. Too easy. Too monotonous. Her whom I'd love I'd leave before she knew that I was with her. Her? Which? (O dance!) I'd like to . . .

Girls dance and sing. Men clap. The walls sing and press inward. They press the men and girls, they press John towards a center of physical ecstasy. Go to it, Baby! Fan yourself, and feed your papa! Put . . . nobody lied . . . and take . . . when they said I cried over you. No lie! The glitter and color of stacked scenes, the gilt and brass and crimson of the house, converge towards a center of physical ecstasy. John's feet and torso and his blood press in. He wills thought to rid his mind of passion.

"All right, girls. Alaska. Miss Reynolds, please."

The director wants to get the rehearsal through with.

The girls line up. John sees the front row: dancing ponies. The rest are in shadow. The leading lady fits loosely in the front. Lack-life, monotonous. "One, two, three—" Music starts. The song is somewhere where it will not strain the leading lady's throat. The dance is somewhere where it will not strain the girls. Above the staleness, one dancer throws herself into it. Dorris. John sees her. Her hair, crisp-curled, is bobbed. Bushy, black hair bobbing about her lemon-colored face. Her lips are curiously full, and very red. Her limbs in silk purple stockings are lovely. John feels them. Desires her. Holds off.

John: Stage-door johnny; chorus-girl. No, that would be all right. Dictie,[1] educated, stuck-up; show-girl. Yep. Her suspicion would be stronger than her passion. It wouldn't work. Keep her loveliness. Let her go.

Dorris sees John and knows that he is looking at her. Her own glowing is too rich a thing to let her feel the slimness of his diluted passion.

"Who's that?" she asks her dancing partner.

"Th manager's brother. Dictie. Nothin doin, hon."

Dorris tosses her head and dances for him until she feels she has him. Then, withdrawing disdainfully, she flirts with the director.

Dorris: Nothin doin? How come? Aint I as good as him? Couldnt I have got an education if I'd wanted one? Dont I know respectable folks, lots of em, in Philadelphia and New York and Chicago? Aint I had men as good as him? Better. Doctors an lawyers. Whats a manager's brother, anyhow?

Two steps back, and two steps front.

"Say, Mame, where do you get that stuff?"

"Whatshmean, Dorris?"

"If you two girls cant listen to what I'm telling you, I know where I can get some who can. Now listen."

Mame: Go to hell, you black bastard.

Dorris: Whats eatin at him, anyway?

"Now follow me in this, you girls. Its three counts to the right, three counts to the left, and then you shimmy—"

John:—and then you shimmy. I'll bet she can. Some good cabaret, with rooms upstairs. And what in hell do you think you'd get from it? Youre going wrong. Here's right: get her to herself—(Christ, but how she'd bore you after the first five minutes)—not if you get her right she wouldnt. Touch her, I

---

[1] A snob.

mean. To herself—in some room perhaps. Some cheap, dingy bedroom. Hell no. Cant be done. But the point is, brother John, it can be done. Get her to herself somewhere, anywhere. Go down in yourself—and she'd be calling you all sorts of asses while you were in the process of going down. Hold em, bud. Cant be done. Let her go. (Dance and I'll love you!) And keep her loveliness.

"All right now, Chicken Chaser. Dorris and girls. Where's Dorris? I told you to stay on the stage, didnt I? Well? Now thats enough. All right. All right there, Professor?[2] All right. One, two, three—"

Dorris swings to the front. The line of girls, four deep, blurs within the shadow of suspended scenes. Dorris wants to dance. The director feels that and steps to one side. He smiles, and picks her for a leading lady, one of these days. Odd ends of stage-men emerge from the wings, and stare and clap. A crap game in the alley suddenly ends. Black faces crowd the rear stage doors. The girls, catching joy from Dorris, whip up within the footlights' glow. They forget set steps; they find their own. The director forgets to bawl them out. Dorris dances.

John: Her head bobs to Broadway. Dance from yourself. Dance! O just a little more.

Dorris' eyes burn across the space of seats to him.

Dorris: I bet he can love. Hell, he cant love. He's too skinny. His lips are too skinny. He wouldn't love me anyway, only for that. But I'd get a pair of silk stockings out of it. Red silk. I got purple. Cut it, kid. You cant win him to respect you that away. He wouldnt anyway. Maybe he would. Maybe he'd love. I've heard em say that men who look like him (what does he look like?) will marry if they love. O will you love me? And give me kids, and a home, and everything? (I'd like to make your nest, and honest, hon, I wouldnt run out on you.) You will if I make you. Just watch me.

Dorris dances. She forgets her tricks. She dances.

Glorious songs are the muscles of her limbs.

And her singing is of canebrake loves and mangrove feastings.

The walls press in, singing. Flesh of a throbbing body, they press close to John and Dorris. They close them in. John's heart beats tensely against her dancing body. Walls press his mind within his heart. And then, the shaft of light goes out the window high above him. John's mind sweeps up to follow it. Mind pulls him upward into dream. Dorris dances . . . John dreams:

> Dorris is dressed in a loose black gown, splashed with lemon ribbons. Her feet taper long and slim from trim ankles. She waits for him just inside the stage door. John, collar and tie colorful and flaring, walks towards the stage door. There are no trees in the alley. But his feet feel as though they step on autumn leaves whose rustle has been pressed out of them by the passing of a million satin slippers. The air is sweet with roasting chestnuts, sweet with bonfires of old leaves. John's

---

[2] A piano player.

melancholy is a deep thing that seals all senses but his eyes, and makes him whole.

Dorris knows that he is coming. Just at the right moment she steps from the door, as if there were no door. Her face is tinted like the autumn alley. Of old flowers, or of a southern canefield, her perfume. "Glorious Dorris." So his eyes speak. And their sadness is too deep for sweet untruth. She barely touches his arm. They glide off with footfalls softened on the leaves, the old leaves powdered by a million satin slippers.

They are in a room. John knows nothing of it. Only, that the flesh and blood of Dorris are its walls. Singing walls. Lights, soft, as if they shine through clear pink fingers. Soft lights, and warm.

John reaches for a manuscript of his, and reads. Dorris, who has no eyes, has eyes to understand him. He comes to a dancing scene. The scene is Dorris. She dances. Dorris dances. Glorious Dorris. Dorris whirls, whirls, dances. . . .

Dorris dances. The pianist crashes a bumper chord. The whole stage claps. Dorris, flushed, looks quick at John. His whole face is in shadow. She seeks for her dance in it. She finds it a dead thing in the shadow which is his dream. She rushes from the stage. Falls down the steps into her dressing-room. Pulls her hair. Her eyes, over a flood of tears, stare at the whitewashed ceiling. (Smell of dry paste, and paint, and soiled clothing.) Her pal comes in. Dorris flings herself into the old safe arms, and cries bitterly.

"I told you nothin doing," is what Mame says to comfort her.

QUESTIONS

1. State the nature of the conflict in John.   **2.** How does Toomer achieve dramatic conflict between John and Dorris even though they do not speak to each other?   **3.** How does the opening paragraph establish the mood and the values of the story?

A Rose for Emily   1931

WILLIAM FAULKNER   [1897–1962]

I

When Miss Emily Grierson died, our whole town went to her funeral: the men through a sort of respectful affection for a fallen monument, the women mostly out of curiosity to see the inside of her house, which no one save an old manservant—a combined gardener and cook—had seen in at least ten years.

It was a big, squarish frame house that had once been white, decorated with cupolas and spires and scrolled balconies in the heavily lightsome style of the seventies, set on what had once been our most select street. But garages and cotton gins had encroached and obliterated even the august names of that neighborhood; only Miss Emily's house was left, lifting its stubborn and co-quettish decay above the cotton wagons and the gasoline pumps—an eyesore among eyesores. And now Miss Emily had gone to join the representatives of those august names where they lay in the cedar-bemused cemetery among the ranked and anonymous graves of Union and Confederate soldiers who fell at the battle of Jefferson.

Alive, Miss Emily had been a tradition, a duty, and a care; a sort of hereditary obligation upon the town, dating from that day in 1894 when Colonel Sartoris, the mayor—he who fathered the edict that no Negro woman should appear on the streets without an apron—remitted her taxes, the dispensation dating from the death of her father on into perpetuity. Not that Miss Emily would have accepted charity. Colonel Sartoris invented an involved tale to the effect that Miss Emily's father had loaned money to the town, which the town, as a matter of business, preferred this way of repaying. Only a man of Colonel Sartoris' generation and thought could have invented it, and only a woman could have believed it.

When the next generation, with its more modern ideas, became mayors and aldermen, this arrangement created some little dissatisfaction. On the first of the year they mailed her a tax notice. February came, and there was no reply. They wrote her a formal letter, asking her to call at the sheriff's office at her convenience. A week later the mayor wrote her himself, offering to call or to send his car for her, and received in reply a note on paper of an archaic shape, in a thin, flowing calligraphy in faded ink, to the effect that she no longer went out at all. The tax notice was also enclosed, without comment.

They called a special meeting of the Board of Aldermen. A deputation waited upon her, knocked at the door through which no visitor had passed since she ceased giving china-painting lessons eight or ten years earlier. They were admitted by the old Negro into a dim hall from which a stairway mounted into still more shadow. It smelled of dust and disuse—a close, dank smell. The Negro led them into the parlor. It was furnished in heavy, leather-covered furniture. When the Negro opened the blinds of one window, they could see that the leather was cracked; and when they sat down, a faint dust rose sluggishly about their thighs, spinning with slow motions in the single sun-ray. On a tarnished gilt easel before the fireplace stood a crayon portrait of Miss Emily's father.

They rose when she entered—a small, fat woman in black, with a thin gold chain descending to her waist and vanishing into her belt, leaning on an ebony cane with a tarnished gold head. Her skeleton was small and spare; perhaps that was why what would have been merely plumpness in another was obesity in her. She looked bloated, like a body long submerged in motionless water, and of that pallid hue. Her eyes, lost in the fatty ridges of her face, looked like two small pieces of coal pressed into a lump of dough as they moved from one face to another while the visitors stated their errand.

She did not ask them to sit. She just stood in the door and listened quietly until the spokesman came to a stumbling halt. Then they could hear the invisible watch ticking at the end of the gold chain.

Her voice was dry and cold. "I have no taxes in Jefferson. Colonel Sartoris explained it to me. Perhaps one of you can gain access to the city records and satisfy yourselves."

"But we have. We are the city authorities, Miss Emily. Didn't you get a notice from the sheriff, signed by him?"

"I received a paper, yes," Miss Emily said. "Perhaps he considers himself the sheriff . . . I have no taxes in Jefferson."

"But there is nothing on the books to show that, you see. We must go by the—"

"See Colonel Sartoris." (Colonel Sartoris had been dead almost ten years.) "I have no taxes in Jefferson. Tobe!" The Negro appeared. "Show these gentlemen out."

II

So she vanquished them, horse and foot, just as she had vanquished their fathers thirty years before about the smell. That was two years after her father's death and a short time after her sweetheart—the one we believed would marry her—had deserted her. After her father's death she went out very little; after her sweetheart went away, people hardly saw her at all. A few of the ladies had the temerity to call, but were not received, and the only sign of life about the place was the Negro man—a young man then—going in and out with a market basket.

"Just as if a man—any man—could keep a kitchen properly," the ladies said;

so they were not surprised when the smell developed. It was another link between the gross, teeming world and the high and mighty Griersons.

A neighbor, a woman, complained to the mayor, Judge Stevens, eighty years old.

"But what will you have me do about it, madam?" he said.

"Why, send her word to stop it," the woman said. "Isn't there a law?"

"I'm sure that won't be necessary," Judge Stevens said. "It's probably just a snake or a rat that nigger of hers killed in the yard. I'll speak to him about it."

The next day he received two more complaints, one from a man who came in diffident deprecation. "We really must do something about it, Judge. I'd be the last one in the world to bother Miss Emily, but we've got to do something." That night the Board of Aldermen met—three graybeards and one younger man, a member of the rising generation.

"It's simple enough," he said. "Send her word to have her place cleaned up. Give her a certain time to do it in, and if she don't . . ."

"Dammit, sir," Judge Stevens said, "will you accuse a lady to her face of smelling bad?"

So the next night, after midnight, four men crossed Miss Emily's lawn and slunk about the house like burglars, sniffing along the base of the brickwork and at the cellar openings while one of them performed a regular sowing motion with his hand out of a sack slung from his shoulder. They broke open the cellar door and sprinkled lime there, and in all the outbuildings. As they recrossed the lawn, a window that had been dark was lighted and Miss Emily sat in it, the light behind her, and her upright torso motionless as that of an idol. They crept quietly across the lawn and into the shadow of the locusts that lined the street. After a week or two the smell went away.

That was when people had begun to feel really sorry for her. People in our town, remembering how old lady Wyatt, her great-aunt, had gone completely crazy at last, believed that the Griersons held themselves a little too high for what they really were. None of the young men were quite good enough for Miss Emily and such. We had long thought of them as a tableau, Miss Emily a slender figure in white in the background, her father a spraddled silhouette in the foreground, his back to her and clutching a horsewhip, the two of them framed by the back-flung front door. So when she got to be thirty and was still single, we were not pleased exactly, but vindicated; even with insanity in the family she wouldn't have turned down all of her chances if they had really materialized.

When her father died, it got about that the house was all that was left to her; and in a way, people were glad. At last they could pity Miss Emily. Being left alone, and a pauper, she had become humanized. Now she too would know the old thrill and the old despair of a penny more or less.

The day after his death all the ladies prepared to call at the house and offer condolence and aid, as is our custom. Miss Emily met them at the door, dressed as usual and with no trace of grief on her face. She told them that her father was not dead. She did that for three days, with the ministers calling on her, and the doctors, trying to persuade her to let them dispose of the body. Just as they were about to resort to law and force, she broke down, and they buried her father quickly.

We did not say she was crazy then. We believed she had to do that. We remembered all the young men her father had driven away, and we knew that with nothing left, she would have to cling to that which had robbed her, as people will.

III

She was sick for a long time. When we saw her again, her hair was cut short, making her look like a girl, with a vague resemblance to those angels in colored church windows—sort of tragic and serene.

The town had just let the contracts for paving the sidewalks, and in the summer after her father's death they began the work. The construction company came with niggers and mules and machinery, and a foreman named Homer Barron, a Yankee—a big, dark, ready man, with a big voice and eyes lighter than his face. The little boys would follow in groups to hear him cuss the niggers, and the niggers singing in time to the rise and fall of picks. Pretty soon he knew everybody in town. Whenever you heard a lot of laughing anywhere about the square, Homer Barron would be in the center of the group. Presently we began to see him and Miss Emily on Sunday afternoons driving in the yellow-wheeled buggy and the matched team of bays from the livery stable.

At first we were glad that Miss Emily would have an interest, because the ladies all said, "Of course a Grierson would not think seriously of a Northerner, a day laborer." But there were still others, older people, who said that even grief could not cause a real lady to forget *noblesse oblige*—without calling it *noblesse oblige*. They just said, "Poor Emily. Her kinsfolk should come to her." She had some kin in Alabama; but years ago her father had fallen out with them over the estate of old lady Wyatt, the crazy woman, and there was no communication between the two families. They had not even been represented at the funeral.

And as soon as the old people said, "Poor Emily," the whispering began. "Do you suppose it's really so?" they said to one another. "Of course it is. What else could . . ." This behind their hands; rustling of craned silk and satin behind jalousies closed upon the sun of Sunday afternoon as the thin, swift clop-clop-clop of the matched team passed: "Poor Emily."

She carried her head high enough—even when we believed that she was fallen. It was as if she demanded more than ever the recognition of her dignity as the last Grierson; as if it had wanted that touch of earthiness to reaffirm her imperviousness. Like when she bought the rat poison, the arsenic. That was over a year after they had begun to say "Poor Emily," and while the two female cousins were visiting her.

"I want some poison," she said to the druggist. She was over thirty then, still a slight woman, though thinner than usual, with cold, haughty black eyes in a face the flesh of which was strained across the temples and about the eye-sockets as you imagine a lighthouse-keeper's face ought to look. "I want some poison," she said.

"Yes, Miss Emily. What kind? For rats and such? I'd recom—"

"I want the best you have. I don't care what kind."

The druggist named several. "They'll kill anything up to an elephant. But what you want is—"

"Arsenic," Miss Emily said. "Is that a good one?"

"Is . . . arsenic? Yes, ma'am. But what you want—"

"I want arsenic."

The druggist looked down at her. She looked back at him, erect, her face like a strained flag. "Why, of course," the druggist said. "If that's what you want. But the law requires you to tell what you are going to use it for."

Miss Emily just stared at him, her head tilted back in order to look him eye for eye, until he looked away and went and got the arsenic and wrapped it up. The Negro delivery boy brought her package; the druggist didn't come back. When she opened the package at home there was written on the box, under the skull and bones: "For rats."

IV

So the next day we all said, "She will kill herself"; and we said it would be the best thing. When she had first begun to be seen with Homer Barron, we had said, "She will marry him." Then we said, "She will persuade him yet," because Homer himself had remarked—he liked men, and it was known that he drank with the younger men in the Elks' Club—that he was not a marrying man. Later we said, "Poor Emily" behind the jalousies as they passed on Sunday afternoon in the glittering buggy, Miss Emily with her head high and Homer Barron with his hat cocked and a cigar in his teeth, reins and whip in a yellow glove.

Then some of the ladies began to say that it was a disgrace to the town and a bad example to the young people. The men did not want to interfere, but at last the ladies forced the Baptist minister—Miss Emily's people were Episcopal—to call upon her. He would never divulge what happened during that interview, but he refused to go back again. The next Sunday they again drove about the streets, and the following day the minister's wife wrote to Miss Emily's relations in Alabama.

So she had blood-kin under her roof again and we sat back to watch developments. At first nothing happened. Then we were sure that they were to be married. We learned that Miss Emily had been to the jeweler's and ordered a man's toilet set in silver, with the letters H.B. on each piece. Two days later we learned that she had bought a complete outfit of men's clothing, including a nightshirt, and we said, "They are married." We were really glad. We were glad because the two female cousins were even more Grierson than Miss Emily had ever been.

So we were not surprised when Homer Barron—the streets had been finished some time since—was gone. We were a little disappointed that there was not a public blowing-off, but we believed that he had gone on to prepare for Miss Emily's coming, or to give her a chance to get rid of the cousins. (By that time it was a cabal, and we were all Miss Emily's allies to help circumvent the cousins.) Sure enough, after another week they departed. And, as we had expected all along, within three days Homer Barron was back in town. A neighbor saw the Negro man admit him at the kitchen door at dusk one evening.

And that was the last we saw of Homer Barron. And of Miss Emily for some time. The Negro man went in and out with the market basket, but the front door remained closed. Now and then we would see her at the window for a moment, as the men did that night when they sprinkled the lime, but for almost six months she did not appear on the streets. Then we knew that this was to be expected too; as if that quality of her father which had thwarted her woman's life so many times had been too virulent and too furious to die.

When we next saw Miss Emily, she had grown fat and her hair was turning gray. During the next few years it grew grayer and grayer until it attained an even pepper-and-salt iron-gray, when it ceased turning. Up to the day of her death at seventy-four it was still that vigorous iron-gray, like the hair of an active man.

From that time on her front door remained closed, save during a period of six or seven years, when she was about forty, during which she gave lessons in china-painting. She fitted up a studio in one of the downstairs rooms, where the daughters and granddaughters of Colonel Sartoris' contemporaries were sent to her with the same regularity and in the same spirit that they were sent to church on Sundays with a twenty-five-cent piece for the collection plate. Meanwhile her taxes had been remitted.

Then the newer generation became the backbone and the spirit of the town, and the painting pupils grew up and fell away and did not send their children to her with boxes of color and tedious brushes and pictures cut from the ladies' magazines. The front door closed upon the last one and remained closed for good. When the town got free postal delivery, Miss Emily alone refused to let them fasten the metal numbers above her door and attach a mailbox to it. She would not listen to them.

Daily, monthly, yearly we watched the Negro grow grayer and more stooped, going in and out with the market basket. Each December we sent her a tax notice, which would be returned by the post office a week later, unclaimed. Now and then we would see her in one of the downstairs windows—she had evidently shut up the top floor of the house—like the carven torso of an idol in a niche, looking or not looking at us, we could never tell which. Thus she passed from generation to generation—dear, inescapable, impervious, tranquil, and perverse.

And so she died. Fell ill in the house filled with dust and shadows, with only a doddering Negro man to wait on her. We did not even know she was sick; we had long since given up trying to get any information from the Negro. He talked to no one, probably not even to her, for his voice had grown harsh and rusty, as if from disuse.

She died in one of the downstairs rooms, in a heavy walnut bed with a curtain, her gray head propped on a pillow yellow and moldy with age and lack of sunlight.

V

The Negro met the first of the ladies at the front door and let them in, with their hushed, sibilant voices and their quick, curious glances, and then he disappeared. He walked right through the house and out the back and was not seen again.

The two female cousins came at once. They held the funeral on the second day, with the town coming to look at Miss Emily beneath a mass of bought flowers, with the crayon face of her father musing profoundly above the bier and the ladies sibilant and macabre; and the very old men—some in their brushed Confederate uniforms—on the porch and the lawn, talking of Miss Emily as if she had been a contemporary of theirs, believing they had danced with her and courted her perhaps, confusing time with its mathematical progression, as the old do, to whom all the past is not a diminishing road but, instead, a huge meadow which no winter ever quite touches, divided from them now by the narrow bottle-neck of the most recent decade of years.

Already we knew that there was one room in that region above stairs which no one had seen in forty years, and which would have to be forced. They waited until Miss Emily was decently in the ground before they opened it.

The violence of breaking down the door seemed to fill this room with pervading dust. A thin, acrid pall as of the tomb seemed to lie everywhere upon this room decked and furnished as for a bridal: upon the valance curtains of faded rose color, upon the rose-shaded lights, upon the dressing table, upon the delicate array of crystal and the man's toilet things backed with tarnished silver, silver so tarnished that the monogram was obscured. Among them lay a collar and tie, as if they had just been removed, which, lifted, left upon the surface a pale crescent in the dust. Upon a chair hung the suit, carefully folded; beneath it the two mute shoes and the discarded socks.

The man himself lay in the bed.

For a long while we just stood there, looking down at the profound and fleshless grin. The body had apparently once lain in the attitude of an embrace, but now the long sleep that outlasts love, that conquers even the grimace of love, had cuckolded him. What was left of him, rotted beneath what was left of the nightshirt, had become inextricable from the bed in which he lay; and upon him and upon the pillow beside him lay that even coating of the patient and biding dust.

Then we noticed that in the second pillow was the indentation of a head.

One of us lifted something from it, and leaning forward, that faint and invisible dust dry and acrid in the nostrils, we saw a long strand of iron-gray hair.

QUESTIONS
1. Describe the narrator. Is he sympathetic to Emily? Explain. Why does Faulkner title the narrative "A Rose for Emily"?   **2.** Why does Faulkner devote the second paragraph to a description of Emily's house?   **3.** Why doesn't Faulkner present the story in chronological order?   **4.** What is the effect of the final paragraph?

WRITING TOPIC
In the second paragraph of part V, the narrator refers to some old men "talking of Miss Emily as if she had been a contemporary of theirs, believing that they had danced with her and courted her perhaps, confusing time with its mathematical progression, as the old do, to whom all the past is not a diminishing road but, instead, a huge meadow which no winter ever quite touches, divided from them now by the narrow bottle-neck of the most recent decade of years." Use this passage as the basis for a comparison of the narrator's and Emily's view of time.

The Intruder*

1966

JORGE LUIS BORGES [1899–1986]

2 Samuel 1:26[1]

They claim (improbably) that the story was told by Eduardo, the younger of the Nilsen brothers, at the wake for Cristian, the elder, who died of natural causes at some point in the 1890s, in the district of Morón. Someone must certainly have heard it from someone else, in the course of that long, idle night, between servings of maté, and passed it on to Santiago Dabove, from whom I learned it. Years later, they told it to me again in Turdera, where it had all happened. The second version, considerably more detailed, substantiated Santiago's, with the usual small variations and departures. I write it down now because, if I am not wrong, it reflects briefly and tragically the whole temper of life in those days along the banks of the River Plate. I shall put it down scrupulously; but already I see myself yielding to the writer's temptation to heighten or amplify some detail or other.

In Turdera, they were referred to as the Nilsens. The parish priest told me that his predecessor remembered with some astonishment seeing in that house a worn Bible, bound in black, with Gothic characters; in the end pages, he glimpsed handwritten names and dates. It was the only book in the house. The recorded misfortunes of the Nilsens, lost as all will be lost. The old house, now no longer in existence, was built of unstuccoed brick; beyond the hallway, one could make out a patio of colored tile, and another with an earth floor. In any case, very few ever went there; the Nilsens were jealous of their privacy. In the dilapidated rooms, they slept on camp beds; their indulgences were horses, riding gear, short-bladed daggers, a substantial fling on Saturdays, and belligerent drinking. I know that they were tall, with red hair which they wore long. Denmark, Ireland, places they would never hear tell of, stirred in the blood of those two *criollos*.[2] The neighborhood feared them, as they did all red-haired people; nor is it impossible that they might have been responsible for someone's death. Once, shoulder to shoulder, they tangled with the police. The younger one was said to have had an altercation with Juan Iberra in which he did not

---

* Translated by Alastair Reid.
[1] A verse from David's lament upon the death of his brother-in-law and friend Jonathan: "I am distressed for you, my brother Jonathan; / very pleasant have you been to me, / your love to me was wonderful, passing the love of woman."
[2] Creole, a person of European parentage born in South America, Central America, or the West Indies.

come off worst; which, according to what we hear, is indeed something. They were cowboys, team drivers, rustlers, and, at times, cheats. They had a reputation for meanness, except when drinking and gambling made them expansive. Of their ancestry or where they came from, nothing was known. They owned a wagon and a yoke of oxen.

Physically, they were quite distinct from the roughneck crowd of settlers who lent the Costa Brava their own bad name. This, and other things we do not know, helps to explain how close they were; to cross one of them meant having two enemies.

The Nilsens were roisterers, but their amorous escapades had until then been confined to hallways and houses of ill fame. Hence, there was no lack of local comment when Cristian brought Juliana Burgos to live with him. True enough, in that way he got himself a servant; but it is also true that he showered her with gaudy trinkets, and showed her off at fiestas—the poor tenement fiestas, where the more intimate figures of the tango were forbidden and where the dancers still kept a respectable space between them. Juliana was dark-complexioned, with large wide eyes; one had only to look at her to make her smile. In a poor neighborhood, where work and neglect wear out the women, she was not at all bad looking.

At first, Eduardo went about with them. Later, he took a journey to Arrecifes on some business or other; he brought back home with him a girl he had picked up along the way. After a few days, he threw her out. He grew more sullen; he would get drunk alone at the local bar, and would have nothing to do with anyone. He was in love with Cristian's woman. The neighborhood, aware of it possibly before he was, looked forward with malicious glee to the subterranean rivalry between the brothers.

One night, when he came back late from the bar at the corner, Eduardo saw Cristian's black horse tethered to the fence. In the patio, the elder brother was waiting for him, all dressed up. The woman came and went, carrying maté. Cristian said to Eduardo:

"I'm off to a brawl at the Farías'. There's Juliana for you. If you want her, make use of her."

His tone was half-commanding, half-cordial. Eduardo kept still, gazing at him; he did not know what to do. Cristian rose, said goodbye to Eduardo but not to Juliana, who was an object to him, mounted, and trotted off, casually.

From that night on, they shared her. No one knew the details of that sordid conjunction, which outraged the proprieties of the poor locality. The arrangement worked well for some weeks, but it could not last. Between them, the brothers never uttered the name of Juliana, not even to summon her, but they sought out and found reasons for disagreeing. They argued over the sale of some skins, but they were really arguing about something else. Cristian would habitually raise his voice, while Eduardo kept quiet. Without realizing it, they were growing jealous. In that rough settlement, no man ever let on to others, or to himself, that a woman would matter, except as something desired or possessed, but the two of them were in love. For them, that in its way was a humiliation.

One afternoon, in the Plaza de Lomos, Eduardo ran into Juan Iberra, who congratulated him on the beautiful "dish" he had fixed up for himself. It was then, I think, that Eduardo roughed him up. No one, in his presence, was going to make fun of Cristian.

The woman waited on the two of them with animal submissiveness; but she could not conceal her preference, unquestionably for the younger one, who, although he had not rejected the arrangement, had not sought it out.

One day, they told Juliana to get two chairs from the first patio, and to keep out of the way, for they had to talk. Expecting a long discussion, she lay down for her siesta, but soon they summoned her. They had her pack a bag with all she possessed, not forgetting the glass rosary and the little crucifix her mother had left her. Without any explanation, they put her on the wagon, and set out on a wordless and wearisome journey. It had rained; the roads were heavy going and it was eleven in the evening when they arrived at Morón. There they passed her over to the *patrona* of the house of prostitution. The deal had already been made; Cristian picked up the money, and later on he divided it with Eduardo.

In Turdera, the Nilsens, floundering in the meshes of that outrageous love (which was also something of a routine), sought to recover their old ways, of men among men. They went back to their poker games, to fighting, to occasional binges. At times, perhaps, they felt themselves liberated, but one or other of them would quite often be away, perhaps genuinely, perhaps not. A little before the end of the year, the younger one announced that he had business in Buenos Aires. Cristian went to Morón; in the yard of the house we already know, he recognized Eduardo's piebald. He entered; the other was inside, waiting his turn. It seems that Cristian said to him, "If we go on like this, we'll wear out the horses. It's better that we do something about her."

He spoke with the *patrona*, took some coins from his money belt, and they went off with her. Juliana went with Cristian; Eduardo spurred his horse so as not to see them.

They returned to what has already been told. The cruel solution had failed; both had given in to the temptation to dissimulate. Cain's mark was there, but the bond between the Nilsens was strong—who knows what trials and dangers they had shared—and they preferred to vent their furies on others. On a stranger, on the dogs, on Juliana, who had brought discord into their lives.

March was almost over and the heat did not break. One Sunday (on Sundays it is the custom to retire early), Eduardo, coming back from the corner bar, saw Cristian yoking up the oxen. Cristian said to him, "Come on. We have to leave some hides off at the Pardos'. I've already loaded them. Let us take advantage of the cool."

The Pardo place lay, I think, to the south of them; they took the Camino de las Tropas, and then a detour. The landscape was spreading out slowly under the night.

They skirted a clump of dry reeds. Cristian threw away the cigarette he had lit and said casually, "Now, brother, to work. Later on, the buzzards will give us a hand. Today I killed her. Let her stay here with all her finery, and not do us any more harm."

They embraced, almost in tears. Now they shared an extra bond; the woman sorrowfully sacrificed and the obligation to forget her.

The Chase*

1967

ALBERTO MORAVIA [1907–1990]

I have never been a sportsman—or, rather, I have been a sportsman only once, and that was the first and last time. I was a child, and one day, for some reason or other, I found myself together with my father, who was holding a gun in his hand, behind a bush, watching a bird that had perched on a branch not very far away. It was a large, gray bird—or perhaps it was brown—with a long—or perhaps a short—beak; I don't remember. I only remember what I felt at that moment as I looked at it. It was like watching an animal whose vitality was rendered more intense by the very fact of my watching it and of the animal's not knowing that I was watching it.

At that moment, I say, the notion of wildness entered my mind, never again to leave it; everything is wild which is autonomous and unpredictable and does not depend upon us. Then all of a sudden there was an explosion; I could no longer see the bird and I thought it had flown away. But my father was leading the way, walking in front of me through the undergrowth. Finally he stooped down, picked up something and put it in my hand. I was aware of something warm and soft and I lowered my eyes: there was a bird in the palm of my hand, its dangling, shattered head crowned with a plume of already-thickening blood. I burst into tears and dropped the corpse on the ground, and that was the end of my shooting experience.

I thought again of this remote episode in my life this very day after watching my wife, for the first and also the last time, as she was walking through the streets of the city. But let us take things in order.

What had my wife been like; what was she like now? She once had been, to put it briefly, "wild"—that is, entirely autonomous and unpredictable; latterly she had become "tame"—that is, predictable and dependent. For a long time she had been like the bird that, on that far-off morning in my childhood, I had seen perching on the bough; latterly, I am sorry to say, she had become like a hen about which one knows everything in advance—how it moves, how it eats, how it lays eggs, how it sleeps, and so on.

Nevertheless I would not wish anyone to think that my wife's wildness consisted of an uncouth, rough, rebellious character. Apart from being extremely beautiful, she is the gentlest, politest, most discreet person in the world. Rather her wildness consisted of the air of charming unpredictability, of independence in her way of living, with which during the first years of our marriage

---

* Translated by Angus Davidson.

she acted in my presence, both at home and abroad. Wildness signified intimacy, privacy, secrecy. Yes, my wife as she sat in front of her dressing table, her eyes fixed on the looking glass, passing the hairbrush with a repeated motion over her long, loose hair, was just as wild as the solitary quail hopping forward along a sun-filled furrow or the furtive fox coming out into a clearing and stopping to look around before running on. She was wild because I, as I looked at her, could never manage to foresee when she would give a last stroke with the hairbrush and rise and come toward me; wild to such a degree that sometimes when I went into our bedroom the smell of her, floating in the air, would have something of the acrid quality of a wild beast's lair.

Gradually she became less wild, tamer. I had had a fox, a quail, in the house, as I have said; then one day I realized that I had a hen. What effect does a hen have on someone who watches it? It has the effect of being, so to speak, an automaton in the form of a bird; automatic are the brief, rapid steps with which it moves about; automatic its hard, terse pecking; automatic the glance of the round eyes in its head that nods and turns; automatic its ready crouching down under the cock; automatic the dropping of the egg wherever it may be and the cry with which it announces that the egg has been laid. Good-by to the fox; good-by to the quail. And her smell—this no longer brought to my mind, in any way, the innocent odor of a wild animal; rather I detected in it the chemical suavity of some ordinary French perfume.

Our flat is on the first floor of a big building in a modern quarter of the town; our windows look out on a square in which there is a small public garden, the haunt of nurses and children and dogs. One day I was standing at the window, looking in a melancholy way at the garden. My wife, shortly before, had dressed to go out; and once again, watching her, I had noticed the irrevocable and, so to speak, invisible character of her gestures and personality: something which gave one the feeling of a thing already seen and already done and which therefore evaded even the most determined observation. And now, as I stood looking at the garden and at the same time wondering why the adorable wildness of former times had so completely disappeared, suddenly my wife came into my range of vision as she walked quickly across the garden in the direction of the bus stop. I watched her and then I almost jumped for joy; in a movement she was making to pull down a fold of her narrow skirt and smooth it over her thigh with the tips of her long, sharp nails, in this movement I recognized the wildness that in the past had made me love her. It was only an instant, but in that instant I said to myself: She's become wild again because she's convinced that I am not there and am not watching her. Then I left the window and rushed out.

But I did not join her at the bus stop; I felt that I must not allow myself to be seen. Instead I hurried to my car, which was standing nearby, got in and waited. A bus came and she got in together with some other people; the bus started off again and I began following it. Then there came back to me the memory of that one shooting expedition in which I had taken part as a child, and I saw that the bus was the undergrowth with its bushes and trees, my wife the bird perching on the bough while I, unseen, watched it living before my eyes. And the whole town, during this pursuit, became, as though by magic, a fact of nature like the countryside: the houses were hills, the streets valleys, the vehicles hedges and woods, and even the passers-by on the pavements had something unpredictable and autonomous—that is, wild—about them. And in my mouth, behind my clenched teeth, there was the acrid, metallic taste of gunfire; and my eyes, usually listless and wandering, had become sharp, watchful, attentive.

These eyes were fixed intently upon the exit door when the bus came to the end of its run. A number of people got out, and then I saw my wife getting out. Once again I recognized, in the manner in which she broke free of the crowd and started off toward a neighboring street, the wildness that pleased me so much. I jumped out of the car and started following her.

She was walking in front of me, ignorant of my presence, a tall woman with an elegant figure, long-legged, narrow-hipped, broad-backed, her brown hair falling on her shoulders.

Men turned around as she went past; perhaps they were aware of what I myself was now sensing with an intensity that quickened the beating of my heart and took my breath away: the unrestricted, steadily increasing, irresistible character of her mysterious wildness.

She walked hurriedly, having evidently some purpose in view, and even the fact that she had a purpose of which I was ignorant added to her wildness; I did not know where she was going, just as on that far-off morning I had not known what the bird perching on the bough was about to do. Moreover I thought the gradual, steady increase in this quality of wildness came partly from the fact that as she drew nearer to the object of this mysterious walk there was an increase in her—how shall I express it?—of biological tension, of existential excitement, of vital effervescence. Then, unexpectedly, with the suddenness of a film, her purpose was revealed.

A fair-haired young man in a leather jacket and a pair of corduroy trousers was leaning against the wall of a house in that ancient, narrow street. He was idly smoking as he looked in front of him. But as my wife passed close to him, he threw away his cigarette with a decisive gesture, took a step forward and seized her arm. I was expecting her to rebuff him, to move away from him, but nothing happened: evidently obeying the rules of some kind of erotic ritual, she went on walking beside the young man. Then after a few steps, with a movement that confirmed her own complicity, she put her arm around her companion's waist and he put his around her.

I understood then that this unknown man who took such liberties with my wife was also attracted by wildness. And so, instead of making a conventional appointment with her, instead of meeting in a café with a handshake, a falsely friendly and respectful welcome, he had preferred, by agreement with her, to take her by surprise—or, rather, to pretend to do so—while she was apparently taking a walk on her own account. All this I perceived by intuition, noticing that at the very moment when he stepped forward and took her arm her wildness had, so to speak, given an upward bound. It was years since I had seen my wife so alive, but alas, the source of this life could not be traced to me.

They walked on thus entwined and then, without any preliminaries, just like two wild animals, they did an unexpected thing: they went into one of the dark doorways in order to kiss. I stopped and watched them from a distance, peering into the darkness of the entrance. My wife was turned away from me and was bending back with the pressure of his body, her hair hanging free. I looked at that long, thick mane of brown hair, which as she leaned back fell free of her shoulders, and I felt at that moment her vitality reached its diapason, just as happens with wild animals when they couple and their customary wildness is redoubled by the violence of love. I watched for a long time and then, since this kiss went on and on and in fact seemed to be prolonged beyond the limits of my power of endurance, I saw that I would have to intervene.

I would have to go forward, seize my wife by the arm—or actually by that hair, which hung down and conveyed so well the feeling of feminine passivity— then hurl myself with clenched fists upon the blond young man. After this encounter I would carry off my wife, weeping, mortified, ashamed, while I was raging and broken-hearted, upbraiding her and pouring scorn upon her.

But what else would this intervention amount to but the shot my father fired at that free, unknowing bird as it perched on the bough? The disorder and confusion, the mortification, the shame, that would follow would irreparably destroy the rare and precious moment of wildness that I was witnessing inside the dark doorway. It was true that this wildness was directed against me; but I had to remember that wildness, always and everywhere, is directed against everything and everybody. After the scene of my intervention it might be possible for me to regain control of my wife, but I should find her shattered and lifeless in my arms like the bird that my father placed in my hand so that I might throw it into the shooting bag.

The kiss went on and on: well, it was a kiss of passion—that could not be denied. I waited until they finished, until they came out of the doorway, until they walked on again still linked together. Then I turned back.

The Girls in Their Summer Dresses

1939

IRWIN SHAW [1913–1984]

Fifth Avenue was shining in the sun when they left the Brevoort.[1] The sun was warm, even though it was February, and everything looked like Sunday morning—the buses and the well-dressed people walking slowly in couples and the quiet buildings with the windows closed.

Michael held Frances' arm tightly as they walked toward Washington Square[2] in the sunlight. They walked lightly, almost smiling, because they had slept late and had a good breakfast and it was Sunday. Michael unbuttoned his coat and let it flap around him in the mild wind.

"Look out," Frances said as they crossed Eighth Street. "You'll break your neck." Michael laughed and Frances laughed with him.

"She's not so pretty," Frances said. "Anyway, not pretty enough to take a chance of breaking your neck."

Michael laughed again. "How did you know I was looking at her?"

Frances cocked her head to one side and smiled at her husband under the brim of her hat. "Mike, darling," she said.

"O.K.," he said. "Excuse me."

Frances patted his arm lightly and pulled him along a little faster toward Washington Square. "Let's not see anybody all day," she said. "Let's just hang around with each other. You and me. We're always up to our neck in people, drinking their Scotch or drinking our Scotch; we only see each other in bed. I want to go out with my husband all day long. I want him to talk only to me and listen only to me."

"What's to stop us?" Michael asked.

"The Stevensons. They want us to drop by around one o'clock and they'll drive us into the country."

"The cunning Stevensons," Mike said. "Transparent. They can whistle. They can go driving in the country by themselves."

"Is it a date?"

"It's a date."

Frances leaned over and kissed him on the tip of the ear.

---

[1] The Brevoort was a New York hotel on lower Fifth Avenue. At the time that this story was written, the Brevoort's bar was famous as a gathering place for literary people.
[2] A park at the south end of Fifth Avenue.

"Darling," Michael said, "this is Fifth Avenue."

"Let me arrange a program," Frances said. "A planned Sunday in New York for a young couple with money to throw away."

"Go easy."

"First let's go to the Metropolitan Museum of Art," Frances suggested, because Michael had said during the week he wanted to go. "I haven't been there in three years and there're at least ten pictures I want to see again. Then we can take the bus down to Radio City and watch them skate. And later we'll go down to Cavanagh's and get a steak as big as a blacksmith's apron, with a bottle of wine, and after that there's a French picture at the Filmarte that everybody says—say, are you listening to me?"

"Sure," he said. He took his eyes off the hatless girl with the dark hair, cut dancer-style like a helmet, who was walking past him.

"That's the program for the day," Frances said flatly. "Or maybe you'd just rather walk up and down Fifth Avenue."

"No," Michael said. "Not at all."

"You always look at other women," Frances said. "Everywhere. Every damned place we go."

"No, darling," Michael said, "I look at everything. God gave me eyes and I look at women and men in subway excavations and moving pictures and the little flowers of the field. I casually inspect the universe."

"You ought to see the look in your eye," Frances said, "as you casually inspect the universe on Fifth Avenue."

"I'm a happily married man." Michael pressed her elbow tenderly. "Example for the whole twentieth century—Mr. and Mrs. Mike Loomis. Hey, let's have a drink," he said, stopping.

"We just had breakfast."

"Now listen, darling," Mike said, choosing his words with care, "it's a nice day and we both felt good and there's no reason why we have to break it up. Let's have a nice Sunday."

"All right. I don't know why I started this. Let's drop it. Let's have a good time."

They joined hands consciously and walked without talking among the baby carriages and the old Italian men in their Sunday clothes and the young women with Scotties in Washington Square Park.

"At least once a year everyone should go to the Metropolitan Museum of Art," Frances said after a while, her tone a good imitation of the tone she had used at breakfast and at the beginning of their walk. "And it's nice on Sunday. There're a lot of people looking at the pictures and you get the feeling maybe Art isn't on the decline in New York City, after all—"

"I want to tell you something," Michael said very seriously. "I have not touched another woman. Not once. In all the five years."

"All right," Frances said.

"You believe that, don't you?"

"All right."

They walked between the crowded benches, under the scrubby city-park trees.

"I try not to notice it," Frances said, "but I feel rotten inside, in my stomach, when we pass a woman and you look at her and I see that look in your eye and that's the way you looked at me the first time. In Alice Maxwell's house. Standing there in the living room, next to the radio, with a green hat on and all those people."

"I remember the hat," Michael said.

"The same look," Frances said. "And it makes me feel bad. It makes me feel terrible."

"Sh-h-h, please, darling, sh-h-h."

"I think I would like a drink now," Frances said.

They walked over to a bar on Eighth Street, not saying anything, Michael automatically helping her over curbstones and guiding her past automobiles. They sat near a window in the bar and the sun streamed in and there was a small, cheerful fire in the fireplace. A little Japanese waiter came over and put down some pretzels and smiled happily at them.

"What do you order after breakfast?" Michael asked.

"Brandy, I suppose," Frances said.

"Courvoisier," Michael told the waiter. "Two Courvoisiers."

The waiter came with the glasses and they sat drinking the brandy in the sunlight. Michael finished half his and drank a little water.

"I look at women," he said. "Correct. I don't say it's wrong or right. I look at them. If I pass them on the street and I don't look at them, I'm fooling you, I'm fooling myself."

"You look at them as though you want them," Frances said, playing with her brandy glass. "Every one of them."

"In a way," Michael said, speaking softly and not to his wife, "in a way that's true. I don't do anything about it, but it's true."

"I know it. That's why I feel bad."

"Another brandy," Michael called. "Waiter, two more brandies."

He sighed and closed his eyes and rubbed them gently with his fingers. "I love the way women look. One of the things I like best about New York is the battalions of women. When I first came to New York from Ohio that was the first thing I noticed, the million wonderful women, all over the city. I walked around with my heart in my throat."

"A kid," Frances said. "That's a kid's feeling."

"Guess again," Michael said. "Guess again. I'm older now. I'm a man getting near middle age, putting on a little fat, and I still love to walk along Fifth Avenue at three o'clock on the east side of the street between Fiftieth and Fifty-seventh Streets. They're all out then, shopping, in their furs and their crazy hats, everything all concentrated from all over the world into seven blocks—the best furs, the best clothes, the handsomest women, out to spend money and feeling good about it."

The Japanese waiter put the two drinks down, smiling with great happiness.

"Everything is all right?" he asked.

"Everything is wonderful," Michael said.

"If it's just a couple of fur coats," Frances said, "and forty-five dollar hats—"

"It's not the fur coats. Or the hats. That's just the scenery for that particular kind of woman. Understand," he said, "you don't have to listen to this."

"I want to listen."

"I like the girls in the offices. Neat with their eyeglasses, smart, chipper, knowing what everything is about. I like the girls on Forty-fourth Street at lunchtime, the actresses, all dressed up on nothing a week. I like the salesgirls in the stores, paying attention to you first because you're a man, leaving the lady customers waiting. I got all this stuff accumulated in me because I've been thinking about it for ten years and now you've asked for it and here it is."

"Go ahead," Frances said.

"When I think of New York City, I think of all the girls on parade in the city. I don't know whether it's something special with me or whether every man in the city walks around with the same feeling inside him, but I feel as though I'm at a picnic in this city. I like to sit near the women in the theatres, the famous beauties who've taken six hours to get ready and look it. And the young girls at the football games, with the red cheeks, and when the warm weather comes, the girls in their summer dresses." He finished his drink. "That's the story."

Frances finished her drink and swallowed two or three times extra. "You say you love me?"

"I love you."

"I'm pretty, too," Frances said. "As pretty as any of them."

"You're beautiful," Michael said.

"I'm good for you," Frances said, pleading. "I've made a good wife, a good housekeeper, a good friend. I'd do any damn thing for you."

"I know," Michael said. He put his hand out and grasped hers.

"You'd like to be free to—" Frances said.

"Sh-h-h."

"Tell the truth." She took her hand away from under his.

Michael flicked the edge of his glass with his finger. "O.K.," he said gently. "Sometimes I feel I would like to be free."

"Well," Frances said, "any time you say."

"Don't be foolish." Michael swung his chair around to her side of the table and patted her thigh.

She began to cry silently into her handkerchief, bent over just enough so that nobody else in the bar would notice. "Someday," she said, crying, "you're going to make a move."

Michael didn't say anything. He sat watching the bartender slowly peel a lemon.

"Aren't you?" Frances asked harshly. "Come on, tell me. Talk. Aren't you?"

"Maybe," Michael said. He moved his chair back again. "How the hell do I know?"

"You know," Frances persisted. "Don't you know?"

"Yes," Michael said after a while, "I know."

Frances stopped crying then. Two or three snuffles into the handkerchief and she put it away and her face didn't tell anything to anybody. "At least do me one favor," she said.

"Sure."

"Stop talking about how pretty this woman is or that one. Nice eyes, nice breasts, a pretty figure, good voice." She mimicked his voice. "Keep it to yourself. I'm not interested."

Michael waved to the waiter. "I'll keep it to myself," he said.

Frances flicked the corners of her eyes. "Another brandy," she told the waiter.

"Two," Michael said.

"Yes, ma'am, yes, sir," said the waiter, backing away.

Frances regarded Michael coolly across the table. "Do you want me to call the Stevensons?" she asked. "It'll be nice in the country."

"Sure," Michael said. "Call them."

She got up from the table and walked across the room toward the telephone. Michael watched her walk, thinking what a pretty girl, what nice legs.

QUESTIONS

1. Is Frances's anger justified? Explain. **2.** What is the effect of the final sentence of the story?

To Room Nineteen 1963

DORIS LESSING [b. 1919]

This is a story, I suppose, about a failure in intelligence: the Rawlings' marriage was grounded in intelligence.

They were older when they married than most of their married friends: in their well-seasoned late twenties. Both had had a number of affairs, sweet rather than bitter; and when they fell in love—for they did fall in love—had known each other for some time. They joked that they had saved each other "for the real thing." That they had waited so long (but not too long) for this real thing was to them a proof of their sensible discrimination. A good many of their friends had married young, and now (they felt) probably regretted lost opportunities; while others, still unmarried, seemed to them arid, self-doubting, and likely to make desperate or romantic marriages.

Not only they, but others, felt they were well-matched: their friends' delight was an additional proof of their happiness. They had played the same roles, male and female, in this group or set, if such a wide, loosely connected, constantly changing constellation of people could be called a set. They had both become, by virtue of their moderation, their humour, and their abstinence from painful experience, people to whom others came for advice. They could be, and were, relied on. It was one of those cases of a man and a woman linking themselves whom no one else had ever thought of linking, probably because of their similarities. But then everyone exclaimed: Of course! How right! How was it we never thought of it before!

And so they married amid general rejoicing, and because of their foresight and their sense for what was probable, nothing was a surprise to them.

Both had well-paid jobs. Matthew was a subeditor on a large London newspaper, and Susan worked in an advertising firm. He was not the stuff of which editors or publicised journalists are made, but he was much more than "a subeditor," being one of the essential background people who in fact steady, inspire, and make possible the people in the limelight. He was content with this position. Susan had a talent for commercial drawing. She was humorous about the advertisements she was responsible for, but she did not feel strongly about them one way or the other.

Both, before they married, had had pleasant flats, but they felt it unwise to base a marriage on either flat, because it might seem like a submission of personality on the part of the one whose flat it was not. They moved into a new flat in South Kensington on the clear understanding that when their marriage had settled down (a process they knew would not take long, and was

657

in fact more a humorous concession to popular wisdom than what was due to themselves) they would buy a house and start a family.

And this is what happened. They lived in their charming flat for two years, giving parties and going to them, being a popular young married couple, and then Susan became pregnant, she gave up her job, and they bought a house in Richmond. It was typical of this couple that they had a son first, then a daughter, then twins, son and daughter. Everything right, appropriate, and what everyone would wish for, if they could choose. But people did feel these two had chosen; this balanced and sensible family was no more than what was due to them because of their infallible sense for *choosing* right.

And so they lived with their four children in their gardened house in Richmond and were happy. They had everything they had wanted and had planned for.

And yet . . .

Well, even this was expected, that there must be a certain flatness. . . .

Yes, yes, of course, it was natural they sometimes felt like this. Like what?

Their life seemed to be like a snake biting its tail. Matthew's job for the sake of Susan, children, house, and garden—which caravanserai needed a well-paid job to maintain it. And Susan's practical intelligence for the sake of Matthew, the children, the house, and the garden—which unit would have collapsed in a week without her.

But there was no point about which either could say: "For the sake of *this* is all the rest." Children? But children can't be a centre of life and a reason for being. They can be a thousand things that are delightful, interesting, satisfying, but they can't be a wellspring to live from. Or they shouldn't be. Susan and Matthew knew that well enough.

Matthew's job? Ridiculous. It was an interesting job, but scarcely a reason for living. Matthew took pride in doing it well, but he could hardly be expected to be proud of the newspaper; the newspaper he read, *his* newspaper, was not the one he worked for.

Their love for each other? Well, that was nearest it. If this wasn't a centre, what was? Yes, it was around this point, their love, that the whole extraordinary structure revolved. For extraordinary it certainly was. Both Susan and Matthew had moments of thinking so, of looking in secret disbelief at this thing they had created: marriage, four children, big house, garden, charwomen, friends, cars . . . and this *thing*, this entity, all of it had come into existence, been blown into being out of nowhere, because Susan loved Matthew and Matthew loved Susan. Extraordinary. So that was the central point, the wellspring.

And if one felt that it simply was not strong enough, important enough, to support it all, well whose fault was that? Certainly neither Susan's nor Matthew's. It was in the nature of things. And they sensibly blamed neither themselves nor each other.

On the contrary, they used their intelligence to preserve what they had created from a painful and explosive world: they looked around them, and took lessons. All around them, marriages collapsing, or breaking, or rubbing along (even worse, they felt). They must not make the same mistakes, they must not.

They had avoided the pitfall so many of their friends had fallen into—of buying a house in the country *for the sake of the children;* so that the husband became a weekend husband, a weekend father, and the wife always careful not to ask what went on in the town flat which they called (in joke) a bachelor flat. No, Matthew was a full-time husband, a full-time father, and at night, in the big married bed in the big married bedroom (which had an attractive view of the river), they lay beside each other talking and he told her about his day, and what he had done, and whom he had met; and she told him about her day (not as interesting, but that was not her fault), for both knew of the hidden resentments and deprivations of the woman who has lived her own life—and above all, has earned her own living—and is now dependent on a husband for outside interests and money.

Nor did Susan make the mistake of taking a job for the sake of her independence, which she might very well have done, since her old firm, missing her qualities of humour, balance, and sense, invited her often to go back. Children needed their mother to a certain age, that both parents knew and agreed on; and when these four healthy wisely brought-up children were of the right age, Susan would work again, because she knew, and so did he, what happened to women of fifty at the height of their energy and ability, with grown-up children who no longer needed their full devotion.

So here was this couple, testing their marriage, looking after it, treating it like a small boat full of helpless people in a very stormy sea. Well, of course, so it was. . . . The storms of the world were bad, but not too close—which is not to say they were selfishly felt: Susan and Matthew were both well-informed and responsible people. And the inner storms and quicksands were understood and charted. So everything was all right. Everything was in order. Yes, things were under control.

So what did it matter if they felt dry, flat? People like themselves, fed on a hundred books (psychological, anthropological, sociological), could scarcely be unprepared for the dry, controlled wistfulness which is the distinguishing mark of the intelligent marriage. Two people, endowed with education, with discrimination, with judgement, linked together voluntarily from their will to be happy together and to be of use to others—one sees them everywhere, one knows them, one even is that thing oneself: sadness because so much is after all so little. These two, unsurprised, turned towards each other with even more courtesy and gentle love: this was life, that two people, no matter how carefully chosen, could not be everything to each other. In fact, even to say so, to think in such a way, was banal; they were ashamed to do it.

It was banal, too, when one night Matthew came home late and confessed he had been to a party, taken a girl home, and slept with her. Susan forgave him, of course. Except that forgiveness is hardly the word. Understanding, yes. But if you understand something, you don't forgive it, you are the thing itself:

forgiveness is for what you *don't* understand. Nor had he *confessed*—what sort of word is that?

The whole thing was not important. After all, years ago they had joked: Of course I'm not going to be faithful to you, no one can be faithful to one other person for a whole lifetime. (And there was the word *faithful*—stupid, all these words, stupid, belonging to a savage old world.) But the incident left both of them irritable. Strange, but they were both bad-tempered, annoyed. There was something unassimilable about it.

Making love splendidly after he had come home that night, both had felt that the idea that Myra Jenkins, a pretty girl met at a party, could be even relevant was ridiculous. They had loved each other for over a decade, would love each other for years more. Who, then, was Myra Jenkins?

Except, thought Susan, unaccountably bad-tempered, she was (is?) the first. In ten years. So either the ten years' fidelity was not important, or she isn't. (No, no, there is something wrong with this way of thinking, there must be.) But if she isn't important, presumably it wasn't important either when Matthew and I first went to bed with each other that afternoon whose delight even now (like a very long shadow at sundown) lays a long, wandlike finger over us. (Why did I say sundown?) Well, if what we felt that afternoon was not important, nothing is important, because if it hadn't been for what we felt, we wouldn't be Mr. and Mrs. Rawlings with four children, etc., etc. The whole thing is *absurd*—for him to have come home and told me was absurd. For him not to have told me was absurd. For me to care or, for that matter, not to care, is absurd . . . and who is Myra Jenkins? Why, no one at all.

There was only one thing to do, and of course these sensible people did it: they put the thing behind them, and consciously, knowing what they were doing, moved forward into a different phase of their marriage, giving thanks for the past good fortune as they did so.

For it was inevitable that the handsome, blond, attractive, manly man, Matthew Rawlings, should be at times tempted (oh, what a word!) by the attractive girls at parties she could not attend because of the four children; and that sometimes he would succumb (a word even more repulsive, if possible) and that she, a good-looking woman in the big well-tended garden at Richmond, would sometimes be pierced as by an arrow from the sky with bitterness. Except that bitterness was not in order, it was out of court. Did the casual girls touch the marriage? They did not. Rather it was they who knew defeat because of the handsome Matthew Rawlings' marriage body and soul to Susan Rawlings.

In that case why did Susan feel (though luckily not for longer than a few seconds at a time) as if life had become a desert, and that nothing mattered, and that her children were not her own?

Meanwhile her intelligence continued to assert that all was well. What if her Matthew did have an occasional sweet afternoon, the odd affair? For she knew quite well, except in her moments of aridity, that they were very happy, that the affairs were not important.

Perhaps that was the trouble? It was in the nature of things that the adventures and delights could no longer be hers, because of the four children and the big house that needed so much attention. But perhaps she was secretly wishing, and even knowing that she did, that the wildness and the beauty could be his. But he was married to her. She was married to him. They were married inextricably. And therefore the gods could not strike him with the real magic, not really. Well, was it Susan's fault that after he came home from an adventure he looked harassed rather than fulfilled? (In fact, that was how she knew he had been *unfaithful*, because of his sullen air, and his glances at her, similar to hers at him: What is it that I share with this person that shields all delight from me?) But none of it by anybody's fault. (But what did they feel ought to be somebody's fault?) Nobody's fault, nothing to be at fault, no one to blame, no one to offer or to take it . . . and nothing wrong, either, except that Matthew never was really struck, as he wanted to be, by joy; and that Susan was more and more often threatened by emptiness. (It was usually in the garden that she was invaded by this feeling: she was coming to avoid the garden, unless the children or Matthew were with her.) There was no need to use the dramatic words, unfaithful, forgive, and the rest: intelligence forbade them. Intelligence barred, too, quarrelling, sulking, anger, silences of withdrawal, accusations, and tears. Above all, intelligence forbids tears.

A high price has to be paid for the happy marriage with the four healthy children in the large white gardened house.

And they were paying it, willingly, knowing what they were doing. When they lay side by side or breast to breast in the big civilised bedroom overlooking the wild sullied river, they laughed, often, for no particular reason; but they knew it was really because of these two small people, Susan and Matthew, supporting such an edifice on their intelligent love. The laugh comforted them; it saved them both, though from what, they did not know.

They were now both fortyish. The older children, boy and girl, were ten and eight, at school. The twins, six, were still at home. Susan did not have nurses or girls to help her: childhood is short; and she did not regret the hard work. Often enough she was bored, since small children can be boring; she was often very tired; but she regretted nothing. In another decade, she would turn herself back into being a woman with a life of her own.

Soon the twins would go to school, and they would be away from home from nine until four. These hours, so Susan saw it, would be the preparation for her own slow emancipation away from the role of hub-of-the-family into woman-with-her-own-life. She was already planning for the hours of freedom when all the children would be "off her hands." That was the phrase used by Matthew and by Susan and by their friends, for the moment when the youngest child went off to school. "They'll be off your hands, darling Susan, and you'll have time to yourself." So said Matthew, the intelligent husband, who had often enough commended and consoled Susan, standing by her in spirit during the years when her soul was not her own, as she said, but her children's.

What it amounted to was that Susan saw herself as she had been at twenty-eight, unmarried; and then again somewhere about fifty, blossoming from the root of what she had been twenty years before. As if the essential Susan were in abeyance, as if she were in cold storage. Matthew said something like this to Susan one night: and she agreed that it was true—she did feel something like that. What, then, was this essential Susan? She did not know. Put like that it sounded ridiculous, and she did not really feel it. Anyway, they had a long discussion about the whole thing before going off to sleep in each other's arms.

So the twins were off to their school, two bright affectionate children who had no problems about it, since their older brother and sister had trodden this path so successfully before them. And now Susan was going to be alone in the big house, every day of the school term, except for the daily woman who came in to clean.

It was now, for the first time in this marriage, that something happened which neither of them had foreseen.

This is what happened. She returned, at nine-thirty, from taking the twins to the school by car, looking forward to seven blissful hours of freedom. On the first morning she was simply restless, worrying about the twins "naturally enough" since this was their first day away at school. She was hardly able to contain herself until they came back. Which they did happily, excited by the world of school, looking forward to the next day. And the next day Susan took them, dropped them, came back, and found herself reluctant to enter her big and beautiful home because it was as if something was waiting for her there that she did not wish to confront. Sensibly, however, she parked the car in the garage, entered the house, spoke to Mrs. Parkes, the daily woman, about her duties, and went up to her bedroom. She was possessed by a fever which drove her out again, downstairs, into the kitchen, where Mrs. Parkes was making cake and did not need her, and into the garden. There she sat on a bench and tried to calm herself, looking at trees, at a brown glimpse of the river. But she was filled with tension, like a panic: as if an enemy was in the garden with her. She spoke to herself severely, thus: All this is quite natural. First, I spent twelve years of my adult life working, *living my own life*. Then I married, and from the moment I became pregnant for the first time I signed myself over, so to speak, to other people. To the children. Not for one moment in twelve years have I been alone, had time to myself. So now I have to learn to be myself again. That's all.

And she went indoors to help Mrs. Parkes cook and clean, and found some sewing to do for the children. She kept herself occupied every day. At the end of the first term she understood she felt two contrary emotions. First: secret astonishment and dismay that during those weeks when the house was empty of children she had in fact been more occupied (had been careful to keep herself occupied) than ever she had been when the children were around her needing her continual attention. Second: that now she knew the house would be full of them, and for five weeks, she resented the fact she would never be alone. She was already looking back at those hours of sewing, cooking (but by herself), as at a lost freedom which would not be hers for five long weeks. And the two months of term which would succeed the five weeks stretched alluringly open to her—freedom. But what freedom—when in fact she had been so careful *not* to be free of small duties during the last weeks? She looked at herself, Susan Rawlings, sitting in a big chair by the window in the bedroom, sewing shirts or dresses, which she might just as well have bought. She saw herself making cakes for hours at a time in the big family kitchen: yet usually she bought cakes. What she saw was a woman alone, that was true, but she had not felt alone. For instance, Mrs. Parkes was always somewhere in the house. And she did not like being in the garden at all, because of the closeness there of the enemy—irritation, restlessness, emptiness, whatever it was, which keeping her hands occupied made less dangerous for some reason.

Susan did not tell Matthew of these thoughts. They were not sensible. She did not recognize herself in them. What should she say to her dear friend and husband Matthew? "When I go into the garden, that is, if the children are not there, I feel as if there is an enemy there waiting to invade me." "What enemy, Susan darling?" "Well I don't know, really. . . ." "Perhaps you should see a doctor?"

No, clearly this conversation should not take place. The holidays began and Susan welcomed them. Four children, lively, energetic, intelligent, demanding: she was never, not for a moment of her day, alone. If she was in a room, they would be in the next room, or waiting for her to do something for them; or it would soon be time for lunch or tea, or to take one of them to the dentist. Something to do: five weeks of it, thank goodness.

On the fourth day of these so welcome holidays, she found she was storming with anger at the twins, two shrinking beautiful children who (and this is what checked her) stood hand in hand looking at her with sheer dismayed disbelief. This was their calm mother, shouting at them. And for what? They had come to her with some game, some bit of nonsense. They looked at each other, moved closer for support, and went off hand in hand, leaving Susan holding on to the windowsill of the living room, breathing deep, feeling sick. She went to lie down, telling the older children she had a headache. She heard the boy Harry telling the little ones: "It's all right, Mother's got a headache." She heard that *It's all right* with pain.

That night she said to her husband: "Today I shouted at the twins, quite unfairly." She sounded miserable, and he said gently: "Well, what of it?"

"It's more of an adjustment than I thought, their going to school."

"But Susie, Susie darling. . . ." For she was crouched weeping on the bed. He comforted her: "Susan, what is all this about? You shouted at them? What of it? If you shouted at them fifty times a day it wouldn't be more than the little devils deserve." But she wouldn't laugh. She wept. Soon he comforted her with his body. She became calm. Calm, she wondered what was wrong with her, and why she should mind so much that she might, just once, have behaved unjustly with the children. What did it matter? They had forgotten it all long ago: Mother had a headache and everything was all right.

It was a long time later that Susan understood that that night, when she had wept and Matthew had driven the misery out of her with his big solid body, was the last time, ever in their married life, that they had been—to use their mutual language—with each other. And even that was a lie, because she had not told him of her real fears at all.

The five weeks passed, and Susan was in control of herself, and good and kind, and she looked forward to the holidays with a mixture of fear and longing. She did not know what to expect. She took the twins off to school (the elder children took themselves to school) and she returned to the house determined to face the enemy wherever he was, in the house, or the garden or—where?

She was again restless, she was possessed by restlessness. She cooked and sewed and worked as before, day after day, while Mrs. Parkes remonstrated: "Mrs. Rawlings, what's the need for it? I can do that, it's what you pay me for."

And it was so irrational that she checked herself. She would put the car into the garage, go up to her bedroom, and sit, hands in her lap, forcing herself to be quiet. She listened to Mrs. Parkes moving around the house. She looked out into the garden and saw the branches shake the trees. She sat defeating the enemy, restlessness. Emptiness. She ought to be thinking about her life, about herself. But she did not. Or perhaps she could not. As soon as she forced her mind to think about Susan (for what else did she want to be alone for?) it skipped off to thoughts of butter or school clothes. Or it thought of Mrs. Parkes. She realised that she sat listening for the movements of the cleaning woman, following her every turn, bend, thought. She followed her in her mind from kitchen to bathroom, from table to oven, and it was as if the duster, the cleaning cloth, the saucepan, were in her own hand. She would hear herself saying: No, not like that, don't put that there. . . . Yet she did not give a damn what Mrs. Parkes did, or if she did it at all. Yet she could not prevent herself from being conscious of her, every minute. Yes, this was what was wrong with her: she needed, when she was alone, to be really alone, with no one near. She could not endure the knowledge that in ten minutes or in half an hour Mrs. Parkes would call up the stairs: "Mrs. Rawlings, there's no silver polish. Madam, we're out of flour."

So she left the house and went to sit in the garden where she was screened from the house by trees. She waited for the demon to appear and claim her, but he did not.

She was keeping him off, because she had not, after all, come to an end of arranging herself.

She was planning how to be somewhere where Mrs. Parkes would not come after her with a cup of tea, or a demand to be allowed to telephone (always irritating, since Susan did not care who she telephoned or how often), or just a nice talk about something. Yes, she needed a place, or a state of affairs, where it would not be necessary to keep reminding herself: In ten minutes I must telephone Matthew about . . . and at half past three I must leave early for the children because the car needs cleaning. And at ten o'clock tomorrow I must remember. . . . She was possessed with resentment that the seven hours of freedom in every day (during the weekdays in the school term) were not free, that never, not for one second, ever, was she free from the pressure of time, from having to remember this or that. She could never forget herself; never really let herself go into forgetfulness.

Resentment. It was poisoning her. (She looked at this emotion and thought it was absurd. Yet she felt it.) She was a prisoner. (She looked at this thought too, and it was no good telling herself it was a ridiculous one.) She must tell Matthew—but what? She was filled with emotions that were utterly ridiculous, that she despised, yet that nevertheless she was feeling so strongly she could not shake them off.

The school holidays came round, and this time they were for nearly two months, and she behaved with a conscious controlled decency that nearly drove her crazy. She would lock herself in the bathroom, and sit on the edge of the bath, breathing deep, trying to let go into some kind of calm. Or she went up into the spare room, usually empty, where no one would expect her to be. She heard the children calling "Mother, Mother," and kept silent, feeling guilty. Or she went to the very end of the garden, by herself, and looked at the slow-moving brown river; she looked at the river and closed her eyes and breathed slow and deep, taking it into her being, into her veins.

Then she returned to the family, wife and mother, smiling and responsible, feeling as if the pressure of these people—four lively children and her husband—were a painful pressure on the surface of her skin, a hand pressing on her brain. She did not once break down into irritation during these holidays, but it was like living out a prison sentence, and when the children went back to school, she sat on a white stone seat near the flowing river, and she thought: It is not even a year since the twins went to school, since *they were off my hands* (What on earth did I think I meant when I used that stupid phrase?) and yet I'm a different person. I'm simply not myself. I don't understand it.

Yet she had to understand it. For she knew that this structure—big white house, on which the mortgage still cost four hundred a year, a husband, so good and kind and insightful, four children, all doing so nicely, and the garden where she sat, and Mrs. Parkes the cleaning woman—all this depended on her, and yet she could not understand why, or even what it was she contributed to it.

She said to Matthew in their bedroom: "I think there must be something wrong with me."

And he said: "Surely not, Susan? You look marvellous—you're as lovely as ever."

She looked at the handsome blond man, with his clear, intelligent, blue-eyed face, and thought: Why is it I can't tell him? Why not? And she said: "I need to be alone more than I am."

At which he swung his slow blue gaze at her, and she saw what she had been dreading: Incredulity. Disbelief. And fear. An incredulous blue stare from a stranger who was her husband, as close to her as her own breath.

He said: "But the children are at school and off your hands."

She said to herself: I've got to force myself to say: Yes, but do you realize that I never feel free? There's never a moment I can say to myself: There's nothing I have to remind myself about, nothing I have to do in half an hour, or an hour, or two hours. . . .

But she said: "I don't feel well."

He said: "Perhaps you need a holiday."

She said, appalled: "But not without you, surely?" For she could not imagine herself going off without him. Yet that was what he meant. Seeing her face, he laughed, and opened his arms, and she went into them, thinking: Yes, yes, but why can't I say it? And what is it I have to say?

She tried to tell him, about never being free. And he listened and said: "But Susan, what sort of freedom can you possibly want—short of being dead! Am I ever free? I go to the office, and I have to be there at ten—all right, half past ten, sometimes. And I have to do this or that, don't I? Then I've got to come home at a certain time—I don't mind it, you know I don't—but if I'm not going to be back home at six I telephone you. When can I ever say to myself: I have nothing to be responsible for in the next six hours?"

Susan, hearing this, was remorseful. Because it was true. The good marriage, the house, the children, depended just as much on his voluntary bondage as it did on hers. But why did he not feel bound? Why didn't he chafe and become restless? No, there was something really wrong with her and this proved it.

And that word *bondage*—why had she used it? She had never felt marriage, or the children, as bondage. Neither had he, or surely they wouldn't be together lying in each other's arms content after twelve years of marriage.

No, her state (whatever it was) was irrelevant, nothing to do with her real good life with her family. She had to accept the fact that after all, she was an irrational person and to live with it. Some people had to live with crippled arms, or stammers, or being deaf. She would have to live knowing she was subject to a state of mind she could not own.

Nevertheless, as a result of this conversation with her husband, there was a new regime next holidays.

The spare room at the top of the house now had a cardboard sign saying: PRIVATE! DO NOT DISTURB! on it. (This sign had been drawn in coloured chalks by the children, after a discussion between the parents in which it was decided this was psychologically the right thing.) The family and Mrs. Parkes knew this was "Mother's Room" and that she was entitled to her privacy. Many serious conversations took place between Matthew and the children about not taking Mother for granted. Susan overheard the first, between father and Harry, the older boy, and was surprised at her irritation over it. Surely she could have a room somewhere in that big house and retire into it without such a fuss being made? Without it being so solemnly discussed? Why couldn't she simply have announced: "I'm going to fit out the little top room for myself, and when I'm in it I'm not to be disturbed for anything short of fire"? Just that, and finished; instead of long earnest discussions. When she heard Harry and Matthew explaining it to the twins with Mrs. Parkes coming in—"Yes, well, a family sometimes gets on top of a woman"—she had to go right away to the bottom of her garden until the devils of exasperation had finished their dance in her blood.

But now there was a room, and she could go there when she liked, she used it seldom: she felt even more caged there than in her bedroom. One day she had gone up there after a lunch for ten children she had cooked and served because Mrs. Parkes was not there, and had sat alone for a while looking into the garden. She saw the children stream out from the kitchen and stand looking up at the window where she sat behind the curtains. They were all—her children and their friends—discussing Mother's Room. A few minutes later, the chase of children in some game came pounding up the stairs, but ended as abruptly as if they had fallen over a ravine, so sudden was the silence. They had remembered she was there, and had gone silent in a great gale of "Hush! Shhhhh! Quiet, you'll disturb her. . . ." And they went tiptoeing downstairs like criminal conspirators. When she came down to make tea for them, they all apologised. The twins put their arms around her, from front and back, making a human cage of loving limbs, and promised it would never occur again. "We forgot, Mummy, we forgot all about it!"

What it amounted to was that Mother's Room, and her need for privacy, had become a valuable lesson in respect for other people's rights. Quite soon Susan was going up to the room only because it was a lesson it was a pity to drop. Then she took sewing up there, and the children and Mrs. Parkes came in and out: it had become another family room.

She sighed, and smiled, and resigned herself—she made jokes at her own expense with Matthew over the room. That is, she did from the self she liked, she respected. But at the same time, something inside her howled with impatience, with rage. . . . And she was frightened. One day she found herself kneeling by her bed and praying: "Dear God, keep it away from me, keep him away from me." She meant the devil, for she now thought of it, not caring if she were irrational, as some sort of demon. She imagined him, or it, as a youngish man, or perhaps a middle-aged man pretending to be young. Or a man young-looking from immaturity? At any rate, she saw the young-looking face which, when she drew closer, had dry lines about mouth and eyes. He was thinnish, meagre in build. And he had a reddish complexion, and ginger hair. That was he—a gingery, energetic man, and he wore a reddish hairy jacket, unpleasant to the touch.

Well, one day she saw him. She was standing at the bottom of the garden, watching the river ebb past, when she raised her eyes and saw this person, or being, sitting on the white stone bench. He was looking at her, and grinning. In his hand was a long crooked stick, which he had picked off the ground, or broken off the tree above him. He was absent-mindedly, out of an absent-minded or freakish impulse of spite, using the stick to stir around in the coils of a blindworm or a grass snake (or some kind of snakelike creature: it was whitish and unhealthy to look at, unpleasant). The snake was twisting about, flinging its coils from side to side in a kind of dance of protest against the teasing prodding stick.

Susan looked at him, thinking: Who is the stranger? What is he doing in our garden? Then she recognised the man around whom her terrors had crystallised. As she did so, he vanished. She made herself walk over to the bench.

A shadow from a branch lay across thin emerald grass, moving jerkily over its roughness, and she could see why she had taken it for a snake, lashing and twisting. She went back to the house thinking: Right, then, so I've seen him with my own eyes, so I'm not crazy after all—there *is* a danger because I've seen him. He is lurking in the garden and sometimes even in the house, and he wants *to get into me and to take me over.*

She dreamed of having a room or a place, anywhere, where she could go and sit, by herself, no one knowing where she was.

Once, near Victoria, she found herself outside a news agent that had Rooms to Let advertised. She decided to rent a room, telling no one. Sometimes she could take the train into Richmond and sit alone in it for an hour or two. Yet how could she? A room would cost three or four pounds a week, and she earned no money, and how could she explain to Matthew that she needed such a sum? What for? It did not occur to her that she was taking it for granted she wasn't going to tell him about the room.

Well, it was out of the question, having a room; yet she knew she must.

One day, when a school term was well established, and none of the children had measles or other ailments, and everything seemed in order, she did the shopping early, explained to Mrs. Parkes she was meeting an old school friend, took the train to Victoria, searched until she found a small quiet hotel, and asked for a room for the day. They did not let rooms by the day, the manageress said, looking doubtful, since Susan so obviously was not the kind of woman who needed a room for unrespectable reasons. Susan made a long explanation about not being well, being unable to shop without frequent rests for lying down. At last she was allowed to rent the room provided she paid a full night's price for it. She was taken up by the manageress and a maid, both concerned over the state of her health . . . which must be pretty bad if, living at Richmond (she had signed her name and address in the register), she needed a shelter at Victoria.

The room was ordinary and anonymous, and was just what Susan needed. She put a shilling in the gas fire, and sat, eyes shut, in a dingy armchair with her back to a dingy window. She was alone. She was alone. She was alone. She could feel pressures lifting off her. First the sounds of traffic came very loud; then they seemed to vanish; she might even have slept a little. A knock on the door: it was Miss Townsend, the manageress, bringing her a cup of tea with her own hands, so concerned was she over Susan's long silence and possible illness.

Miss Townsend was a lonely woman of fifty, running this hotel with all the rectitude expected of her, and she sensed in Susan the possibility of understanding companionship. She stayed to talk. Susan found herself in the middle of a fantastic story about her illness, which got more and more impossible as she tried to make it tally with the large house at Richmond, well-off husband, and four children. Suppose she said instead: Miss Townsend, I'm here in your hotel because I need to be alone for a few hours, above all *alone and with no one knowing where I am.* She said it mentally, and saw, mentally, the look that would inevitably come on Miss Townsend's elderly maiden's face. "Miss Town-

send, my four children and my husband are driving me insane, do you understand that? Yes, I can see from the gleam of hysteria in your eyes that comes
from loneliness controlled but only just contained that I've got everything in
the world you've ever longed for. Well, Miss Townsend, I don't want any of it.
You can have it, Miss Townsend. I wish I was absolutely alone in the world,
like you. Miss Townsend, I'm besieged by seven devils, Miss Townsend, Miss
Townsend, let me stay here in your hotel where the devils can't get me. . . ."
Instead of saying all this, she described her anaemia, agreed to try Miss Townsend's remedy for it, which was raw liver, minced, between whole-meal bread,
and said yes, perhaps it would be better if she stayed at home and let a friend
do shopping for her. She paid her bill and left the hotel, defeated.

At home Mrs. Parkes said she didn't really like it, no, not really, when Mrs.
Rawlings was away from nine in the morning until five. The teacher had
telephoned from school to say Joan's teeth were paining her, and she hadn't
known what to say; and what was she to make for the children's tea, Mrs.
Rawlings hadn't said.

All this was nonsense, of course. Mrs. Parkes's complaint was that Susan
had withdrawn herself spiritually, leaving the burden of the big house on her.

Susan looked back at her day of "freedom" which had resulted in her
becoming a friend of the lonely Miss Townsend, and in Mrs. Parkes's remon-
strances. Yet she remembered the short blissful hour of being alone, really
alone. She was determined to arrange her life, no matter what it cost, so that
she could have that solitude more often. An absolute solitude, where no one
knew her or cared about her.

But how? She thought of saying to her old employer: I want to back you up
in a story with Matthew that I am doing part-time work for you. The truth is
that . . . but she would have to tell him a lie too, and which lie? She could
not say: I want to sit by myself three or four times a week in a rented room.
And besides, he knew Matthew, and she could not really ask him to tell lies on
her behalf, apart from his being bound to think it meant a lover.

Suppose she really took a part-time job, which she could get through fast
and efficiently, leaving time for herself. What job? Addressing envelopes? Can-
vassing?

And there was Mrs. Parkes, working widow, who knew exactly what she was
prepared to give to the house, who knew by instinct when her mistress withdrew
in spirit from her responsibilities. Mrs. Parkes was one of the servers of this
world, but she needed someone to serve. She had to have Mrs. Rawlings, her
madam, at the top of the house or in the garden, so that she could come and
get support from her: "Yes, the bread's not what it was when I was a girl. . . .
Yes, Harry's got a wonderful appetite, I wonder where he puts it all. . . . Yes,
it's lucky the twins are so much of a size, they can wear each other's shoes,
that's a saving in these hard times. . . . Yes, the cherry jam from Switzerland
is not a patch on the jam from Poland, and three times the price. . . ." And
so on. That sort of talk Mrs. Parkes must have, every day, or she would leave,
not knowing herself why she left.

Susan Rawlings, thinking these thoughts, found that she was prowling through the great thicketed garden like a wild cat: she was walking up the stairs, down the stairs, through the rooms into the garden, along the brown running river, back, up through the house, down again. . . . It was a wonder Mrs. Parkes did not think it strange. But, on the contrary, Mrs. Rawlings could do what she liked, she could stand on her head if she wanted, provided she was *there*. Susan Rawlings prowled and muttered through her house, hating Mrs. Parkes, hating poor Miss Townsend, dreaming of her hour of solitude in the dingy respectability of Miss Townsend's hotel bedroom, and she knew quite well she was mad. Yes, she was mad.

She said to Matthew that she must have a holiday. Matthew agreed with her. This was not as things had been once—how they had talked in each other's arms in the marriage bed. He had, she knew, diagnosed her finally as *unreasonable*. She had become someone outside himself that he had to manage. They were living side by side in this house like two tolerably friendly strangers.

Having told Mrs. Parkes—or rather, asked for her permission—she went off on a walking holiday in Wales. She chose the remotest place she knew of. Every morning the children telephoned her before they went off to school, to encourage and support her, just as they had over Mother's Room. Every evening she telephoned them, spoke to each child in turn, and then to Matthew. Mrs. Parkes, given permission to telephone for instructions or advice, did so every day at lunchtime. When, as happened three times, Mrs. Rawlings was out on the mountainside, Mrs. Parkes asked that she should ring back at such and such a time, for she would not be happy in what she was doing without Mrs. Rawlings' blessing.

Susan prowled over wild country with the telephone wire holding her to her duty like a leash. The next time she must telephone, or wait to be telephoned, nailed her to her cross. The mountains themselves seemed trammelled by her unfreedom. Everywhere on the mountains, where she met no one at all, from breakfast time to dusk, excepting sheep, or a shepherd, she came face to face with her own craziness, which might attack her in the broadest valleys, so that they seemed too small; or on a mountaintop from which she could see a hundred other mountains and valleys, so that they seemed too low, too small, with the sky pressing down too close. She would stand gazing at a hillside brilliant with ferns and bracken, jewelled with running water, and see nothing but her devil, who lifted inhuman eyes at her from where he leaned negligently on a rock, switching at his ugly yellow boots with a leafy twig.

She returned to her home and family, with the Welsh emptiness at the back of her mind like a promise of freedom.

She told her husband she wanted to have an *au pair* girl.

They were in their bedroom, it was late at night, the children slept. He sat, shirted and slippered, in a chair by the window, looking out. She sat brushing her hair and watching him in the mirror. A time-hallowed scene in the connubial bedroom. He said nothing, while she heard the arguments coming into his mind, only to be rejected because every one was *reasonable*.

"It seems strange to get one now, after all, the children are in school most of the day. Surely the time for you to have help was when you were stuck with them day and night. Why don't you ask Mrs. Parkes to cook for you? She's even offered to—I can understand if you are tired of cooking for six people. But you know that an *au pair* girl means all kinds of problems; it's not like having an ordinary char in during the day. . . ."

Finally he said carefully: "Are you thinking of going back to work?"

"No," she said, "no, not really." She made herself sound vague, rather stupid. She went on brushing her black hair and peering at herself so as to be oblivious of the short uneasy glances her Matthew kept giving her. "Do you think we can't afford it?" she went on vaguely, not at all the old efficient Susan who knew exactly what they could afford.

"It's not that," he said, looking out of the window at dark trees, so as not to look at her. Meanwhile she examined a round, candid, pleasant face with clear dark brows and clear grey eyes. A sensible face. She brushed thick healthy black hair and thought: Yet that's the reflection of a madwoman. How very strange! Much more to the point if what looked back at me was the gingery green-eyed demon with his dry meagre smile. . . . Why wasn't Matthew agreeing? After all, what else could he do? She was breaking her part of the bargain and there was no way of forcing her to keep it: that her spirit, her soul, should live in this house, so that the people in it could grow like plants in water, and Mrs. Parkes remain content in their service. In return for this, he would be a good loving husband, and responsible towards the children. Well, nothing like this had been true of either of them for a long time. He did his duty, perfunctorily; she did not even pretend to do hers. And he had become like other husbands, with his real life in his work and the people he met there, and very likely a serious affair. All this was her fault.

At last he drew heavy curtains, blotting out the trees, and turned to force her attention: "Susan, are you really sure we need a girl?" But she would not meet his appeal at all. She was running the brush over her hair again and again, lifting fine black clouds in a small hiss of electricity. She was peering in and smiling as if she were amused at the clinging hissing hair that followed the brush.

"Yes, I think it would be a good idea, on the whole," she said, with the cunning of a madwoman evading the real point.

In the mirror she could see her Matthew lying on his back, his hands behind his head, staring upwards, his face sad and hard. She felt her heart (the old heart of Susan Rawlings) soften and call out to him. But she set it to be indifferent.

He said: "Susan, the children?" It was an appeal that *almost* reached her. He opened his arms, lifting them from where they had lain by his sides, palms up, empty. She had only to run across and fling herself into them, onto his hard, warm chest, and melt into herself, into Susan. But she could not. She would not see his lifted arms. She said vaguely: "Well, surely it'll be even better for them? We'll get a French or a German girl and they'll learn the language."

In the dark she lay beside him, feeling frozen, a stranger. She felt as if Susan had been spirited away. She disliked very much this woman who lay here, cold and indifferent beside a suffering man, but she could not change her.

Next morning she set about getting a girl, and very soon came Sophie Traub from Hamburg, a girl of twenty, laughing, healthy, blue-eyed, pretending to learn English. Indeed, she already spoke a good deal. In return for a room— "Mother's Room"—and her food, she undertook to do some light cooking, and to be with the children when Mrs. Rawlings asked. She was an intelligent girl and understood perfectly what was needed. Susan said: "I go off sometimes, for the morning or for the day—well, sometimes the children run home from school, or they ring up, or a teacher rings up. I should be here, really. And there's the daily woman. . . ." And Sophie laughed her deep fruity *Fräulein's* laugh, showed her fine white teeth and her dimples, and said: "You want some person to play mistress of the house sometimes, not so?"

"Yes, that is just so," said Susan, a bit dry, despite herself, thinking in secret fear how easy it was, how much nearer to the end she was than she thought. Healthy Fräulein Traub's instant understanding of their position proved this to be true.

The *au pair* girl, because of her own common sense, or (as Susan said to herself with her new inward shudder) because she had been *chosen* so well by Susan, was a success with everyone, the children liking her, Mrs. Parkes forgetting almost at once that she was German, and Matthew finding her "nice to have around the house." For he was now taking things as they came, from the surface of life, withdrawn both as a husband and a father from the household.

One day Susan saw how Sophie and Mrs. Parkes were talking and laughing in the kitchen, and she announced that she would be away until teatime. She knew exactly where to go and what she must look for. She took the District Line to South Kensington, changed to the Circle, got off at Paddington, and walked around looking at the smaller hotels until she was satisfied with one which had FRED'S HOTEL painted on windowpanes that needed cleaning. The façade was a faded shiny yellow, like unhealthy skin. A door at the end of a passage said she must knock; she did, and Fred appeared. He was not at all attractive, not in any way, being fattish, and run-down, and wearing a tasteless striped suit. He had small sharp eyes in a white creased face, and was quite prepared to let Mrs. Jones (she chose the farcical name deliberately, staring him out) have a room three days a week from ten until six. Provided of course that she paid in advance each time she came? Susan produced fifteen shillings (no price had been set by him) and held it out, still fixing him with a bold unblinking challenge she had not known until then she could use at will. Looking at her still, he took up a ten-shilling note from her palm between thumb and forefinger, fingered it; then shuffled up two half-crowns, held out his own palm with these bits of money displayed thereon, and let his gaze lower broodingly at them. They were standing in the passage, a red-shaded light above, bare boards beneath, and a strong smell of floor polish rising about them. He shot his gaze up at her over the still-extended palm, and smiled as if to say: What do you take me for? "I shan't," said Susan, "be using this room for the purposes of making money." He still waited. She added another five shillings, at which he nodded and said: "You pay, and I ask no questions." "Good," said Susan. He now went past her to the stairs, and there waited a moment: the light from the street door being in her eyes, she lost sight of him momentarily. Then she saw a sober-suited, white-faced, white-balding little man trotting up the stairs like a waiter, and she went after him. They proceeded in utter silence up the stairs of this house where no questions were asked—Fred's Hotel, which could afford the freedom for its visitors that poor Miss Townsend's hotel could not. The room was hideous. It had a single window, with thin green brocade curtains, a three-quarter bed that had a cheap green satin bedspread on it, a fireplace with a gas fire and a shilling meter by it, a chest of drawers, and a green wicker armchair.

"Thank you," said Susan, knowing that Fred (if this was Fred, and not George, or Herbert or Charlie) was looking at her, not so much with curiosity, an emotion he would not own to, for professional reasons, but with a philo-sophical sense of what was appropriate. Having taken her money and shown her up and agreed to everything, he was clearly disapproving of her for coming here. She did not belong here at all, so his look said. (But she knew, already, how very much she did belong: the room had been waiting for her to join it.) "Would you have me called at five o'clock, please?" and he nodded and went downstairs.

It was twelve in the morning. She was free. She sat in the armchair, she simply sat, she closed her eyes and sat and let herself be alone. She was alone and no one knew where she was. When a knock came on the door she was annoyed, and prepared to show it: but it was Fred himself; it was five o'clock and he was calling her as ordered. He flicked his sharp little eyes over the room—bed, first. It was undisturbed. She might never have been in the room at all. She thanked him, said she would be returning the day after tomorrow, and left. She was back home in time to cook supper, to put the children to bed, to cook a second supper for her husband and herself later. And to welcome Sophie back from the pictures where she had gone with a friend. All these things she did cheerfully, willingly. But she was thinking all the time of the hotel room; she was longing for it with her whole being.

Three times a week. She arrived promptly at ten, looked Fred in the eyes, gave him twenty shillings, followed him up the stairs, went into the room, and shut the door on him with gentle firmness. For Fred, disapproving of her being here at all, was quite ready to let friendship, or at least acquaintanceship, follow his disapproval, if only she would let him. But he was content to go off on her dismissing nod, with the twenty shillings in his hand.

She sat in the armchair and shut her eyes.

What did she *do* in the room? Why, nothing at all. From the chair, when it had rested her, she went to the window, stretching her arms, smiling, trea-suring her anonymity, to look out. She was no longer Susan Rawlings, mother of four, wife of Matthew, employer of Mrs. Parkes and of Sophie Traub, with these and those relations with friends, schoolteachers, tradesmen. She no longer was mistress of the big white house and garden, owning clothes suitable for this and that activity or occasion. She was Mrs. Jones, and she was alone, and she had no past and no future. Here I am, she thought, after all these years of being married and having children and playing those roles of responsibility— and I'm just the same. Yet there have been times I thought that nothing existed of me except the roles that went with being Mrs. Matthew Rawlings. Yes, here I am, and if I never saw any of my family again, here I would still be . . . how very strange that is! And she leaned on the sill, and looked into the street, loving the men and women who passed, because she did not know them. She looked at the downtrodden buildings over the street, and at the sky, wet and dingy, or sometimes blue, and she felt she had never seen buildings or sky before. And then she went back to the chair, empty, her mind a blank. Sometimes she talked aloud, saying nothing—an exclamation, meaningless, followed by a comment about the floral pattern on the thin rug, or a stain on the green satin coverlet. For the most part, she wool-gathered—what word is there for it?—brooded, wandered, simply went dark, feeling emptiness run deliciously through her veins like the movement of her blood.

This room had become more her own than the house she lived in. One morning she found Fred taking her a flight higher than usual. She stopped, refusing to go up, and demanded her usual room, Number 19. "Well, you'll have to wait half an hour then," he said. Willingly she descended to the dark disinfectant-smelling hall, and sat waiting until the two, man and woman, came down the stairs, giving her swift indifferent glances before they hurried out into the street, separating at the door. She went up to the room, *her* room, which they had just vacated. It was no less hers, though the windows were set wide open, and a maid was straightening the bed as she came in.

After these days of solitude, it was both easy to play her part as mother and wife, and difficult—because it was so easy: she felt an impostor. She felt as if her shell moved here, with her family, answering to Mummy, Mother, Susan, Mrs. Rawlings. She was surprised no one saw through her, that she wasn't turned out of doors, as a fake. On the contrary, it seemed the children loved her more; Matthew and she "got on" pleasantly, and Mrs. Parkes was happy in her work under (for the most part, it must be confessed) Sophie Traub. At night she lay beside her husband, and they made love again, apparently just as they used to, when they were really married. But she, Susan, or the being who answered so readily and improbably to the name of Susan, was not there: she was in Fred's Hotel, in Paddington, waiting for the easing hours of solitude to begin.

Soon she made a new arrangement with Fred and with Sophie. It was for five days a week. As for the money, five pounds, she simply asked Matthew for it. She saw that she was not even frightened he might ask what for: he would give it to her, she knew that, and yet it was terrifying it could be so, for this close couple, these partners, had once known the destination of every shilling they must spend. He agreed to give her five pounds a week. She asked for just so much, not a penny more. He sounded indifferent about it. It was as if he were paying her, she thought: *paying her off*—yes, that was it. Terror came back for a moment when she understood this, but she stilled it: things had gone too far for that. Now, every week, on Sunday nights, he gave her five pounds, turning away from her before their eyes could meet on the transaction. As for Sophie Traub, she was to be somewhere in or near the house until six at night, after which she was free. She was not to cook, or to clean, she was simply to be there. So she gardened or sewed, and asked friends in, being a person who was bound to have a lot of friends. If the children were sick, she nursed them. If teachers telephoned, she answered them sensibly. For the five daytimes in the school week, she was altogether the mistress of the house.

One night in the bedroom, Matthew asked: "Susan, I don't want to interfere—don't think that, please—but are you sure you are well?"

She was brushing her hair at the mirror. She made two more strokes on either side of her head, before she replied: "Yes, dear, I am sure I am well."

He was again lying on his back, his blond head on his hands, his elbows angled up and part-concealing his face. He said: "Then Susan, I have to ask you this question, though you must understand, I'm not putting any sort of pressure on you." (Susan heard the word *pressure* with dismay, because this was inevitable; of course she could not go on like this.) "Are things going to go on like this?"

"Well," she said, going vague and bright and idiotic again, so as to escape: "Well, I don't see why not."

He was jerking his elbows up and down, in annoyance or in pain, and, looking at him, she saw he had got thin, even gaunt; and restless angry movements were not what she remembered of him. He said: "Do you want a divorce, is that it?"

At this, Susan only with the greatest difficulty stopped herself from laughing: she could hear the bright bubbling laughter she *would* have emitted, had she let herself. He could only mean one thing: she had a lover, and that was why she spent her days in London, as lost to him as if she had vanished to another continent.

Then the small panic set in again: she understood that he hoped she did have a lover, he was begging her to say so, because otherwise it would be too terrifying.

She thought this out, as she brushed her hair, watching the fine black stuff fly up to make its little clouds of electricity, hiss, hiss, hiss. Behind her head, across the room, was a blue wall. She realised she was absorbed in watching the black hair making shapes against the blue. She should be answering him. "Do *you* want a divorce, Matthew?"

He said: "That surely isn't the point, is it?"

"You brought it up, I didn't," she said, brightly, suppressing meaningless tinkling laughter.

Next day she asked Fred: "Have enquiries been made for me?"

He hesitated, and she said: "I've been coming here a year now. I've made no trouble, and you've been paid every day. I have a right to be told."

"As a matter of fact, Mrs. Jones, a man did come asking."

"A man from a detective agency?"

"Well, he could have been, couldn't he?"

"I was asking you . . . Well, what did you tell him?"

"I told him a Mrs. Jones came every weekday from ten until five or six and stayed in Number 19 by herself."

"Describing me?"

"Well, Mrs. Jones, I had no alternative. Put yourself in my place."

"By rights I should deduct what that man gave you for the information."

He raised shocked eyes: she was not the sort of person to make jokes like this! Then he chose to laugh: a pinkish wet slit appeared across his white crinkled face: his eyes positively begged her to laugh, otherwise he might lose some money. She remained grave, looking at him.

He stopped laughing and said: "You want to go up now?"—returning to the familiarity, the comradeship, of the country where no questions are asked, on which (and he knew it) she depended completely.

She went up to sit in her wicker chair. But it was not the same. Her husband had searched her out. (The world had searched her out.) The pressures were on her. She was here with his connivance. He might walk in at any moment, here, into Room 19. She imagined the report from the detective agency: "A woman calling herself Mrs. Jones, fitting the description of your wife (etc., etc., etc.), stays alone all day in Room No. 19. She insists on this room, waits for it if it is engaged. As far as the proprietor knows, she receives no visitors there, male or female." A report something on these lines, Matthew must have received.

Well, of course he was right: things couldn't go on like this. He had put an end to it all simply by sending a detective after her.

She tried to shrink herself back into the shelter of the room, a snail pecked out of its shell and trying to squirm back. But the peace of the room had gone. She was trying consciously to revive it, trying to let go into the dark creative trance (or whatever it was) that she had found there. It was no use, yet she craved for it, she was as ill as a suddenly deprived addict.

Several times she returned to the room, to look for herself there, but instead she found the unnamed spirit of restlessness, a prickling fevered hunger for movement, an irritable self-consciousness that made her brain feel as if it had coloured lights going on and off inside it. Instead of the soft dark that had been the room's air, were now waiting for her demons that made her dash blindly about, muttering words of hate; she was impelling herself from point to point like a moth dashing itself against a windowpane, sliding to the bottom, fluttering off on broken wings, then crashing into the invisible barrier again. And again and again. Soon she was exhausted, and she told Fred that for a while she would not be needing the room, she was going on a holiday. Home she went, to the big white house by the river. The middle of a weekday, and she felt guilty at returning to her own home when not expected. She stood unseen, looking in at the kitchen window. Mrs. Parkes, wearing a discarded floral overall of Susan's, was stooping to slide something into the oven. Sophie, arms folded, was leaning her back against a cupboard and laughing at some joke made by a girl not seen before by Susan—a dark foreign girl, Sophie's visitor. In an armchair Molly, one of the twins, lay curled, sucking her thumb and watching the grownups. She must have some sickness, to be kept from school. The child's listless face, the dark circles under her eyes, hurt Susan: Molly was looking at the three grownups working and talking in exactly the same way Susan looked at the four through the kitchen window: she was remote, shut off from them.

But then, just as Susan imagined herself going in, picking up the little girl, and sitting in an armchair with her, stroking her probably heated forehead, Sophie did just that: she had been standing on one leg, the other knee flexed, its foot set against the wall. Now she let her foot in its ribbon-tied red shoe slide down the wall, stood solid on two feet, clapping her hands before and behind her, and sang a couple of lines in German, so that the child lifted her heavy eyes at her and began to smile. Then she walked, or rather skipped, over to the child, swung her up, and let her fall into her lap at the same moment she sat herself. She said "Hopla! Hopla! Molly . . ." and began stroking the dark untidy young head that Molly laid on her shoulder for comfort.

Well. . . . Susan blinked the tears of farewell out of her eyes, and went quietly up the house to her bedroom. There she sat looking at the river through the trees. She felt at peace, but in a way that was new to her. She had no desire to move, to talk, to do anything at all. The devils that had haunted the house, the garden, were not there; but she knew it was because her soul was in Room 19 in Fred's Hotel; she was not really here at all. It was a sensation that should have been frightening: to sit at her own bedroom window, listening to Sophie's rich young voice sing German nursery songs to her child, listening to Mrs. Parkes clatter and move below, and to know that all this had nothing to do with her: she was already out of it.

Later, she made herself go down and say she was home: it was unfair to be here unannounced. She took lunch with Mrs. Parkes, Sophie, Sophie's Italian friend Maria, and her daughter Molly, and felt like a visitor.

A few days later, at bedtime, Matthew said: "Here's your five pounds," and pushed them over at her. Yet he must have known she had not been leaving the house at all.

She shook her head, gave it back to him, and said, in explanation, not in accusation: "As soon as you knew where I was, there was no point."

He nodded, not looking at her. He was turned away from her: thinking, she knew, how best to handle this wife who terrified him.

He said: "I wasn't trying to . . . It's just that I was worried."

"Yes, I know."

"I must confess that I was beginning to wonder . . ."

"You thought I had a lover?"

"Yes, I am afraid I did."

She knew that he wished she had. She sat wondering how to say: "For a year now I've been spending all my days in a very sordid hotel room. It's the place where I'm happy. In fact, without it I don't exist." She heard herself saying this, and understood how terrified he was that she might. So instead she said: "Well, perhaps you're not far wrong."

Probably Matthew would think the hotel proprietor lied: he would want to think so.

"Well," he said, and she could hear his voice spring up, so to speak, with relief, "in that case I must confess I've got a bit of an affair on myself."

She said, detached and interested: "Really? Who is she?" and saw Matthew's startled look because of this reaction.

"It's Phil. Phil Hunt."

She had known Phil Hunt well in the old unmarried days. She was thinking: No, she won't do, she's too neurotic and difficult. She's never been happy yet. Sophie's much better. Well Matthew will see that himself, as sensible as he is.

This line of thought went on in silence, while she said aloud: "It's no point telling you about mine, because you don't know him."

Quick, quick, invent, she thought. Remember how you invented all that nonsense for Miss Townsend.

She began slowly, careful not to contradict herself: "His name is Michael"—(*Michael What?*)—"Michael Plant." (What a silly name!) "He's rather like you—in looks, I mean." And indeed, she could imagine herself being touched by no one but Matthew himself. "He's a publisher." (Really? Why?) "He's got a wife already and two children."

She brought out this fantasy, proud of herself.

Matthew said: "Are you two thinking of marrying?"

She said, before she could stop herself: "Good God, *no!*"

She realised, if Matthew wanted to marry Phil Hunt, that this was too emphatic, but apparently it was all right, for his voice sounded relieved as he said: "It is a bit impossible to imagine oneself married to anyone else, isn't it?" With which he pulled her to him, so that her head lay on his shoulder. She turned her face into the dark of his flesh, and listened to the blood pounding through her ears saying: I am alone, I am alone, I am alone.

In the morning Susan lay in bed while he dressed.

He had been thinking things out in the night, because now he said: "Susan, why don't we make a foursome?"

Of course, she said to herself, of course he would be bound to say that. If one is sensible, if one is reasonable, if one never allows oneself a base thought or an envious emotion, naturally one says: Let's make a foursome!

"Why not?" she said.

"We could all meet for lunch. I mean, it's ridiculous, you sneaking off to filthy hotels, and me staying late at the office, and all the lies everyone has to tell."

What on earth did I say his name was?—she panicked, then said: "I think it's a good idea, but Michael is away at the moment. When he comes back, though—and I'm sure you two would like each other."

"He's away, is he? So that's why you've been . . ." Her husband put his hand to the knot of his tie in a gesture of male coquetry she would not before have associated with him; and he bent to kiss her cheek with the expression that goes with the words: Oh you naughty little puss! And she felt its answering look, naughty and coy, come onto her face.

Inside she was dissolving in horror at them both, at how far they had both sunk from honesty of emotion.

So now she was saddled with a lover, and he had a mistress! How ordinary, how reassuring, how jolly! And now they would make a foursome of it, and go about to theatres and restaurants. After all, the Rawlings could well afford that sort of thing, and presumably the publisher Michael Plant could afford to do himself and his mistress quite well. No, there was nothing to stop the four of them developing the most intricate relationship of civilised tolerance, all enveloped in a charming afterglow of autumnal passion. Perhaps they would all go off on holidays together? She had known people who did. Or perhaps Matthew would draw the line there? Why should he, though, if he was capable of talking about "foursomes" at all?

She lay in the empty bedroom, listening to the car drive off with Matthew in it, off to work. Then she heard the children clattering off to school to the accompaniment of Sophie's cheerfully ringing voice. She slid down into the hollow of the bed, for shelter against her own irrelevance. And she stretched out her hand to the hollow where her husband's body had lain, but found no comfort there: he was not her husband. She curled herself up in a small tight ball under the clothes: she could stay here all day, all week, indeed, all her life.

But in a few days she must produce Michael Plant, and—but how? She must presumably find some agreeable man prepared to impersonate a publisher called Michael Plant. And in return for which she would—what? Well, for one thing they would make love. The idea made her want to cry with sheer exhaustion. Oh no, she had finished with all that—the proof of it was that the words "make love," or even imagining it, trying hard to revive no more than the pleasures of sensuality, let alone affection, or love, made her want to run away and hide from the sheer effort of the thing. . . . Good Lord, why make love at all? Why make love with anyone? Or if you are going to make love, what does it matter who with? Why shouldn't she simply walk into the street, pick up a man, and have a roaring sexual affair with him? Why not? Or even with Fred? What difference did it make?

But she had let herself in for it—an interminable stretch of time with a lover, called Michael, as part of a gallant civilised foursome. Well, she could not, and she would not.

She got up, dressed, went down to find Mrs. Parkes, and asked her for the loan of a pound, since Matthew, she said, had forgotten to leave her money. She exchanged with Mrs. Parkes variations on the theme that husbands are all the same, they don't think, and without saying a word to Sophie, whose voice could be heard upstairs from the telephone, walked to the underground, travelled to South Kensington, changed to the Inner Circle, got out at Paddington, and walked to Fred's Hotel. There she told Fred that she wasn't going on holiday after all, she needed the room. She would have to wait an hour, Fred said. She went to a busy tearoom-cum-restaurant around the corner, and sat watching the people flow in and out the door that kept swinging open and shut, watched them mingle and merge and separate, felt her being flow into them, into their movement. When the hour was up she left a half crown for her pot of tea, and left the place without looking back at it, just as she had left her house, the big, beautiful white house, without another look, but silently dedicating it to Sophie. She returned to Fred, received the key of No. 19, now free, and ascended the grimy stairs slowly, letting floor after floor fall away below her, keeping her eyes lifted, so that floor after floor descended jerkily to her level of vision, and fell away out of sight.

No. 19 was the same. She saw everything with an acute, narrow, checking glance: the cheap shine of the satin spread, which had been replaced carelessly after the two bodies had finished their convulsions under it; a trace of powder on the glass that topped the chest of drawers; an intense green shade in a fold of the curtain. She stood at the window, looking down, watching people pass and pass and pass until her mind went dark from the constant movement. Then she sat in the wicker chair, letting herself go slack. But she had to be careful, because she did not want, today, to be surprised by Fred's knock at five o'clock.

The demons were not here. They had gone forever, because she was buying her freedom from them. She was slipping already into the dark fructifying dream that seemed to caress her inwardly, like the movement of her blood . . . but she had to think about Matthew first. Should she write a letter for the coroner? But what should she say? She would like to leave him with the look on his face she had seen this morning—banal, admittedly, but at least confidently healthy. Well, that was impossible, one did not look like that with a wife dead from suicide. But how to leave him believing she was dying because of a man— because of the fascinating publisher Michael Plant? Oh, how ridiculous! How absurd! How humiliating! But she decided not to trouble about it, simply not to think about the living. If he wanted to believe she had a lover, he would believe it. And he *did* want to believe it. Even when he had found out that there was no publisher in London called Michael Plant, he would think: Oh poor Susan, she was afraid to give me his real name.

And what did it matter whether he married Phil Hunt or Sophie? Though it ought to be Sophie, who was already the mother of those children . . . and what hypocrisy to sit here worrying about the children, when she was going to leave them because she had not got the energy to stay.

She had about four hours. She spent them delightfully, darkly, sweetly, letting herself slide gently, gently, to the edge of the river. Then, with hardly a break in her consciousness, she got up, pushed the thin rug against the door, made sure the windows were tight shut, put two shillings in the meter, and turned on the gas. For the first time since she had been in the room she lay on the hard bed that smelled stale, that smelled of sweat and sex.

She lay on her back on the green satin cover, but her legs were chilly. She got up, found a blanket folded in the bottom of the chest of drawers, and carefully covered her legs with it. She was quite content lying there, listening to the faint soft hiss of the gas that poured into the room, into her lungs, into her brain, as she drifted off into the dark river.

QUESTIONS

1. In what sense is the Rawlings's marriage "grounded in intelligence"?   **2.** Are the sources of Susan's growing discontent clear? Explain.   **3.** Why does Matthew assume that Susan is having an affair? Why does Susan encourage him in this mistaken belief?   **4.** In what sense is Susan's suicide a "failure in intelligence"?

WRITING TOPIC

Do you believe that Susan was justified in taking her own life? Explain.

What We Talk about
When We Talk about Love   1981

RAYMOND CARVER   [1938–1989]

My friend Mel McGinnis was talking. Mel McGinnis is a cardiologist, and
sometimes that gives him the right.

The four of us were sitting around his kitchen table drinking gin. Sunlight
filled the kitchen from the big window behind the sink. There were Mel and
me and his second wife, Teresa—Terri, we called her—and my wife, Laura.
We lived in Albuquerque then. But we were all from somewhere else.

There was an ice bucket on the table. The gin and the tonic water kept
going around, and we somehow got on the subject of love. Mel thought real
love was nothing less than spiritual love. He said he'd spent five years in a
seminary before quitting to go to medical school. He said he still looked back
on those years in the seminary as the most important years in his life.

Terri said the man she lived with before she lived with Mel loved her so
much he tried to kill her. Then Terri said, "He beat me up one night. He
dragged me around the living room by my ankles. He kept saying, 'I love you,
I love you, you bitch.' He went on dragging me around the living room. My
head kept knocking on things." Terri looked around the table. "What do you
do with love like that?"

She was a bone-thin woman with a pretty face, dark eyes, and brown hair
that hung down her back. She liked necklaces made of turquoise, and long
pendant earrings.

"My God, don't be silly. That's not love, and you know it," Mel said. "I
don't know what you'd call it, but I sure know you wouldn't call it love."

"Say what you want to, but I know it was," Terri said. "It may sound crazy
to you, but it's true just the same. People are different, Mel. Sure, sometimes
he may have acted crazy. Okay. But he loved me. In his own way maybe, but
he loved me. There was love there, Mel. Don't say there wasn't."

Mel let out his breath. He held his glass and turned to Laura and me. "The
man threatened to kill me," Mel said. He finished his drink and reached for
the gin bottle. "Terri's a romantic. Terri's of the kick-me-so-I'll-know-you-love-
me school. Terri, hon, don't look that way." Mel reached across the table and
touched Terri's cheek with his fingers. He grinned at her.

"Now he wants to make up," Terri said.

"Make up what?" Mel said. "What is there to make up? I know what I know.
That's all."

"How'd we get started on this subject, anyway?" Terri said. She raised her glass and drank from it. "Mel always has love on his mind," she said. "Don't you, honey?" She smiled, and I thought that was the last of it.

"I just wouldn't call Ed's behavior love. That's all I'm saying, honey," Mel said. "What about you guys?" Mel said to Laura and me. "Does that sound like love to you?"

"I'm the wrong person to ask," I said. "I didn't even know the man. I've only heard his name mentioned in passing. I wouldn't know. You'd have to know the particulars. But I think what you're saying is that love is an absolute."

Mel said, "The kind of love I'm talking about is. The kind of love I'm talking about, you don't try to kill people."

Laura said, "I don't know anything about Ed, or anything about the situation. But who can judge anyone else's situation?"

I touched the back of Laura's hand. She gave me a quick smile. I picked up Laura's hand. It was warm, the nails polished, perfectly manicured. I encircled the broad wrist with my fingers, and I held her.

"When I left, he drank rat poison," Terri said. She clasped her arms with her hands. "They took him to the hospital in Sante Fe. That's where we lived then, about ten miles out. They saved his life. But his gums went crazy from it. I mean they pulled away from his teeth. After that, his teeth stood out like fangs. My God," Terri said. She waited a minute, then let go of her arms and picked up her glass.

"What people won't do!" Laura said.

"He's out of the action now," Mel said. "He's dead."

Mel handed me the saucer of limes. I took a section, squeezed it over my drink, and stirred the ice cubes with my finger.

"It gets worse," Terri said. "He shot himself in the mouth. But he bungled that too. Poor Ed," she said. Terri shook her head.

"Poor Ed nothing," Mel said. "He was dangerous."

Mel was forty-five years old. He was tall and rangy with curly soft hair. His face and arms were brown from the tennis he played. When he was sober, his gestures, all his movements, were precise, very careful.

"He did love me though, Mel. Grant me that," Terri said. "That's all I'm asking. He didn't love me the way you love me. I'm not saying that. But he loved me. You can grant me that, can't you?"

"What do you mean, he bungled it?" I said.

Laura leaned forward with her glass. She put her elbows on the table and held her glass in both hands. She glanced from Mel to Terri and waited with a look of bewilderment on her open face, as if amazed that such things happened to people you were friendly with.

"How'd he bungle it when he killed himself?" I said.

"I'll tell you what happened," Mel said. "He took this twenty-two pistol he'd bought to threaten Terri and me with. Oh, I'm serious, the man was always threatening. You should have seen the way we lived in those days. Like fugitives. I even bought a gun myself. Can you believe it? A guy like me? But I did. I bought one for self-defense and carried it in the glove compartment. Sometimes

I'd have to leave the apartment in the middle of the night. To go to the hospital, you know? Terri and I weren't married then, and my first wife had the house and kids, the dog, everything, and Terri and I were living in this apartment here. Sometimes, as I say, I'd get a call in the middle of the night and have to go in to the hospital at two or three in the morning. It'd be dark out there in the parking lot, and I'd break into a sweat before I could even get to my car. I never knew if he was going to come up out of the shrubbery or from behind a car and start shooting. I mean, the man was crazy. He was capable of wiring a bomb, anything. He used to call my service at all hours and say he needed to talk to the doctor, and when I'd return the call, he'd say, 'Son of a bitch, your days are numbered.' Little things like that. It was scary, I'm telling you."

"I still feel sorry for him," Terri said.

"It sounds like a nightmare," Laura said. "But what exactly happened after he shot himself?"

Laura is a legal secretary. We'd met in a professional capacity. Before we knew it, it was a courtship. She's thirty-five, three years younger than I am. In addition to being in love, we like each other and enjoy one another's company. She's easy to be with.

"What happened?" Laura said.

Mel said, "He shot himself in the mouth in his room. Someone heard the shot and told the manager. They came in with a passkey, saw what had happened, and called an ambulance. I happened to be there when they brought him in, alive but past recall. The man lived for three days. His head swelled up to twice the size of a normal head. I'd never seen anything like it, and I hope I never do again. Terri wanted to go in and sit with him when she found out about it. We had a fight over it. I didn't think she should see him like that. I didn't think she should see him, and I still don't."

"Who won the fight?" Laura said.

"I was in the room with him when he died," Terri said. "He never came up out of it. But I sat with him. He didn't have anyone else."

"He was dangerous," Mel said. "If you call that love, you can have it."

"It was love," Terri said. "Sure, it's abnormal in most people's eyes. But he was willing to die for it. He did die for it."

"I sure as hell wouldn't call it love," Mel said. "I mean, no one knows what he did it for. I've seen a lot of suicides, and I couldn't say anyone ever knew what they did it for."

Mel put his hands behind his neck and tilted his chair back. "I'm not interested in that kind of love," he said. "If that's love, you can have it."

Terri said, "We were afraid. Mel even made a will out and wrote to his brother in California who used to be a Green Beret. Mel told him who to look for if something happened to him."

Terri drank from her glass. She said, "But Mel's right—we lived like fugitives. We were afraid. Mel was, weren't you, honey? I even called the police at one point, but they were no help. They said they couldn't do anything until Ed actually did something. Isn't that a laugh?" Terry said.

She poured the last of the gin into her glass and waggled the bottle. Mel got up from the table and went to the cupboard. He took down another bottle.

"Well, Nick and I know what love is," Laura said. "For us, I mean," Laura said. She bumped my knee with her knee. "You're supposed to say something now," Laura said, and turned her smile on me.

For an answer, I took Laura's hand and raised it to my lips. I made a big production out of kissing her hand. Everyone was amused.

"We're lucky," I said.

"You guys," Terri said. "Stop that now. You're making me sick. You're still on the honeymoon, for God's sake. You're still gaga, for crying out loud. Just wait. How long have you been together now? How long has it been? A year? Longer than a year?"

"Going on a year and a half," Laura said, flushed and smiling.

"Oh, now," Terri said. "Wait a while."

She held her drink and gazed at Laura.

"I'm only kidding," Terri said.

Mel opened the gin and went around the table with the bottle.

"Here, you guys," he said. "Let's have a toast. I want to propose a toast. A toast to love. To true love," Mel said.

We touched glasses.

"To love," we said.

Outside in the backyard, one of the dogs began to bark. The leaves of the aspen that leaned past the window ticked against the glass. The afternoon sun was like a presence in this room, the spacious light of ease and generosity. We could have been anywhere, somewhere enchanted. We raised our glasses again and grinned at each other like children who had agreed on something forbidden.

"I'll tell you what real love is," Mel said. "I mean, I'll give you a good example. And then you can draw your own conclusions." He poured more gin into his glass. He added an ice cube and a sliver of lime. We waited and sipped our drinks. Laura and I touched knees again. I put a hand on her warm thigh and left it there.

"What do any of us really know about love?" Mel said. "It seems to me we're just beginners at love. We say we love each other and we do, I don't doubt it. I love Terri and Terri loves me, and you guys love each other too. You know the kind of love I'm talking about now. Physical love, that impulse that drives you to someone special, as well as love of the other person's being, his or her essence, as it were. Carnal love and, well, call it sentimental love, the day-to-day caring about the other person. But sometimes I have a hard time accounting for the fact that I must have loved my first wife too. But I did, I know I did. So I suppose I am like Terri in that regard. Terri and Ed." He thought about it and then he went on. "There was a time when I thought I loved my first wife more than life itself. But now I hate her guts. I do. How do you explain that? What happened to that love? What happened to it, is what I'd like to know. I wish someone could tell me. Then there's Ed. Okay, we're back to Ed. He loves Terri so much he tries to kill her and he winds up killing himself." Mel stopped talking and swallowed from his glass. "You guys have been together eighteen months and you love each other. It shows all over you. You glow with it. But you both loved other people before you met each other. You've both been married before, just like us. And you probably loved other people before that too, even. Terri and I have been together five years, been married for four. And the terrible thing, the terrible thing is, but the good thing too, the saving grace, you might say, is that if something happened to one of us—excuse me for saying this—but if something happened to one of us tomorrow I think the other one, the other person, would grieve for a while, you know, but then the surviving party would go out and love again, have someone else soon enough. All this, all of this love we're talking about, it would just be a memory. Maybe not even a memory. Am I wrong? Am I way off base? Because I want you to set me straight if you think I'm wrong. I want to know. I mean, I don't know anything, and I'm the first one to admit it."

"Mel, for God's sake," Terri said. She reached out and took hold of his wrist. "Are you getting drunk? Honey? Are you drunk?"

"Honey, I'm just talking," Mel said. "All right? I don't have to be drunk to say what I think. I mean, we're all just talking, right?" Mel said. He fixed his eyes on her.

"Sweetie, I'm not criticizing," Terri said.

She picked up her glass.

"I'm not on call today," Mel said. "Let me remind you of that. I am not on call," he said.

"Mel, we love you," Laura said.

Mel looked at Laura. He looked at her as if he could not place her, as if she was not the woman she was.

"Love you too, Laura," Mel said. "And you, Nick, love you too. You know something?" Mel said. "You guys are our pals," Mel said.

He picked up his glass.

Mel said, "I was going to tell you about something. I mean, I was going to prove a point. You see, this happened a few months ago, but it's still going on right now, and it ought to make us feel ashamed when we talk like we know what we're talking about when we talk above love."

"Come on now," Terri said. "Don't talk like you're drunk if you're not drunk."

"Just shut up for once in your life," Mel said very quietly. "Will you do me a favor and do that for a minute? So as I was saying, there's this old couple who had this car wreck out on the interstate. A kid hit them and they were all torn to shit and nobody was giving them much chance to pull through."

Terri looked at us and then back at Mel. She seemed anxious, or maybe that's too strong a word.

Mel was handing the bottle around the table.

"I was on call that night," Mel said. "It was May or maybe it was June. Terri and I had just sat down to dinner when the hospital called. There'd been this thing out on the interstate. Drunk kid, teenager, plowed his dad's pickup into this camper with this old couple in it. They were up in their mid-seventies, that couple. The kid—eighteen, nineteen, something—he was DOA. Taken the steering wheel through his sternum. The old couple, they were alive, you understand. I mean, just barely. But they had everything. Multiple fractures, internal injuries, hemorrhaging, contusions, lacerations, the works, and they each of them had themselves concussions. They were in a bad way, believe me. And, of course, their age was two strikes against them. I'd say she was worse off than he was. Ruptured spleen along with everything else. Both kneecaps broken. But they'd been wearing their seatbelts and, God knows, that's what saved them for the time being."

"Folks, this is an advertisement for the National Safety Council," Terri said. "This is your spokesman, Dr. Melvin R. McGinnis, talking." Terri laughed. "Mel," she said, "sometimes you're just too much. But I love you, hon," she said.

"Honey, I love you," Mel said.

He leaned across the table. Terri met him halfway. They kissed.

"Terri's right," Mel said as he settled himself again. "Get those seatbelts on. But seriously, they were in some shape, those oldsters. By the time I got down there, the kid was dead, as I said. He was off in a corner, laid out on a gurney. I took one look at the old couple and told the ER nurse to get me a neurologist and an orthopedic man and a couple of surgeons down there right away."

He drank from his glass. "I'll try to keep this short," he said. "So we took the two of them up to the OR and worked like fuck on them most of the night. They had these incredible reserves, those two. You see that once in a while. So we did everything that could be done, and toward morning we're giving them a fifty-fifty chance, maybe less than that for her. So here they are, still alive the next morning. So, okay, we move them into the ICU, which is where they both kept plugging away at it for two weeks, hitting it better and better on all the scopes. So we transfer them out to their own room."

Mel stopped talking. "Here," he said, "let's drink this cheapo gin the hell up. Then we're going to dinner, right? Terri and I know a new place. That's where we'll go, to this new place we know about. But we're not going until we finish up this cut-rate, lousy gin."

Terri said, "We haven't actually eaten there yet. But it looks good. From the outside, you know."

"I like food," Mel said. "If I had it to do all over again, I'd be a chef, you know? Right, Terri?" Mel said.

He laughed. He fingered the ice in his glass.

"Terri knows," he said. "Terri can tell you. But let me say this. If I could come back again in a different life, a different time and all, you know what? I'd like to come back as a knight. You were pretty safe wearing all that armor. It was all right being a knight until gunpowder and muskets and pistols came along."

"Mel would like to ride a horse and carry a lance," Terri said.

"Carry a woman's scarf with you everywhere," Laura said.

"Or just a woman," Mel said.

"Shame on you," Laura said.

Terri said, "Suppose you came back as a serf. The serfs didn't have it so good in those days," Terri said.

"The serfs never had it good," Mel said. "But I guess even the knights were vessels to someone. Isn't that the way it worked? But then everyone is always a vessel to someone. Isn't that right? Terri? But what I liked about knights, besides their ladies, was that they had that suit of armor, you know, and they couldn't get hurt very easy. No cars in those days, you know? No drunk teenagers to tear into your ass."

"Vassals," Terri said.

"What?" Mel said.

"Vassals," Terri said. "They were called vassals, not vessels."

"Vassals, vessels," Mel said, "what the fuck's the difference? You knew what I meant anyway. All right," Mel said. "So I'm not educated. I learned my stuff. I'm a heart surgeon, sure, but I'm just a mechanic. I go in and I fuck around and I fix things. Shit," Mel said.

"Modesty doesn't become you," Terri said.

"He's just a humble sawbones," I said. "But sometimes they suffocated in all that armor, Mel. They'd even have heart attacks if it got too hot and they were too tired and worn out. I read somewhere that they'd fall off their horses and not be able to get up because they were too tired to stand with all that armor on them. They got trampled by their own horses sometimes."

"That's terrible," Mel said. "That's a terrible thing, Nicky. I guess they'd just lay there and wait until somebody came along and made a shish kebab out of them."

"Some other vessel," Terri said.

"That's right," Mel said. "Some vassal would come along and spear the bastard in the name of love. Or whatever the fuck it was they fought over in those days."

"Same things we fight over these days," Terri said.

Laura said, "Nothing's changed."

The color was still high in Laura's cheeks. Her eyes were bright. She brought her glass to her lips.

Mel poured himself another drink. He looked at the label closely as if studying a long row of numbers. Then he slowly put the bottle down on the table and slowly reached for the tonic water.

"What about the old couple?" Laura said. "You didn't finish that story you started."

Laura was having a hard time lighting her cigarette. Her matches kept going out.

The sunshine inside the room was different now, changing, getting thinner. But the leaves outside the window were still shimmering, and I stared at the pattern they made on the panes and on the Formica counter. They weren't the same patterns, of course.

"What about the old couple?" I said.

"Older but wiser," Terri said.

Mel stared at her.

Terri said, "Go on with your story, hon. I was only kidding. Then what happened?"

"Terri, sometimes," Mel said.

"Please, Mel," Terri said. "Don't always be so serious, sweetie. Can't you take a joke?"

"Where's the joke?" Mel said.

He held his glass and gazed steadily at his wife.

"What happened?" Laura said.

Mel fastened his eyes on Laura. He said, "Laura, if I didn't have Terri and if I didn't love her so much, and if Nick wasn't my best friend, I'd fall in love with you, I'd carry you off, honey," he said.

"Tell your story," Terri said. "Then we'll go to that new place, okay?"

"Okay," Mel said. "Where was I?" he said. He stared at the table and then he began again.

"I dropped in to see each of them every day, sometimes twice a day if I was up doing other calls anyway. Casts and bandages, head to foot, the both of them. You know, you've seen it in the movies. That's just the way they looked, just like in the movies. Little eye-holes and nose-holes and mouth-holes. And she had to have her legs slung up on top of it. Well, the husband was very depressed for the longest while. Even after he found out that his wife was going to pull through, he was still very depressed. Not about the accident, though. I mean, the accident was one thing, but it wasn't everything. I'd get up to his mouth-hole, you know, and he'd say no, it wasn't the accident exactly but it was because he couldn't see her through his eye-holes. He said that was what was making him feel so bad. Can you imagine? I'm telling you, the man's heart was breaking because he couldn't turn his goddamn head and *see* his goddamn wife."

Mel looked around the table and shook his head at what he was going to say.

"I mean, it was killing the old fart just because he couldn't *look* at the fucking woman."

We all looked at Mel.

"Do you see what I'm saying?" he said.

Maybe we were a little drunk by then. I know it was hard keeping things in focus. The light was draining out of the room, going back through the window where it had come from. Yet nobody made a move to get up from the table to turn on the overhead light.

"Listen," Mel said. "Let's finish this fucking gin. There's about enough left here for one shooter all around. Then let's go eat. Let's go to the new place."

"He's depressed," Terri said. "Mel, why don't you take a pill?"

Mel shook his head. "I've taken everything there is."

"We all need a pill now and then," I said.

"Some people are born needing them," Terri said.

She was using her finger to rub at something on the table. Then she stopped rubbing.

"I think I want to call my kids," Mel said. "Is that all right with everybody? I'll call my kids," he said.

Terri said, "What if Marjorie answers the phone? You guys, you've heard us on the subject of Marjorie? Honey, you know you don't want to talk to Marjorie. It'll make you feel even worse."

"I don't want to talk to Marjorie," Mel said. "But I want to talk to my kids."

"There isn't a day goes by that Mel doesn't say he wishes she'd get married again. Or else die," Terri said. "For one thing," Terri said, "she's bankrupting us. Mel says it's just to spite him that she won't get married again. She has a boyfriend who lives with her and the kids, so Mel is supporting the boyfriend too."

"She's allergic to bees," Mel said. "If I'm not praying she'll get married again, I'm praying she'll get herself stung to death by a swarm of fucking bees."

"Shame on you," Laura said.

"Bzzzzzzz," Mel said, turning his fingers into bees and buzzing them at Terri's throat. Then he let his hands drop all the way to his sides.

"She's vicious," Mel said. "Sometimes I think I'll go up there dressed like a beekeeper. You know, that hat that's like a helmet with the plate that comes down over your face, the big gloves, and the padded coat? I'll knock on the door and let loose a hive of bees in the house. But first I'd make sure the kids were out, of course."

He crossed one leg over the other. It seemed to take him a lot of time to do it. Then he put both feet on the floor and leaned forward, elbows on the table, his chin cupped in his hands.

"Maybe I won't call the kids, after all. Maybe it isn't such a hot idea. Maybe we'll just go eat. How does that sound?"

"Sounds fine to me," I said. "Eat or not eat. Or keep drinking. I could head right on out into the sunset."

"What does that mean, honey?" Laura said.

"It just means what I said," I said. "It means I could just keep going. That's all it means."

"I could eat something myself," Laura said. "I don't think I've ever been so hungry in my life. Is there something to nibble on?"

"I'll put out some cheese and crackers," Terri said.

But Terri just sat there. She did not get up to get anything.

Mel turned his glass over. He spilled it out on the table.

"Gin's gone," Mel said.

Terri said, "Now what?"

I could hear my heart beating. I could hear everyone's heart. I could hear the human noise we sat there making, not one of us moving, not even when the room went dark.

QUESTIONS

1. How would you characterize the relationship between Mel and Terri? Between Nick and Laura?   **2.** What is your reaction to Mel? Is he likable? Why does Carver make him a scientist and a cardiologist?   **3.** The story begins in the sunlight of midday and ends in darkness. Does this transition help us understand what the author is saying about love and marriage? Explain.   **4.** Do you agree with Mel or with Terri about Ed? Explain.

WRITING TOPIC

Examine the various marriages (including the relationship between Terri and Ed) and discuss how they provide an explanation for the title of the story.

Today Will Be a Quiet Day

1985

AMY HEMPEL [b. 1951]

"I think it's the other way around," the boy said. "I think if the quake hit now the *bridge* would collapse and the *ramps* would be left."

He looked at his sister with satisfaction.

"You are just trying to scare your sister," the father said. "You know that is not true."

"No, really," the boy insisted, "and I heard birds in the middle of the night. Isn't that a warning?"

The girl gave her brother a toxic look and ate a handful of Raisinets. The three of them were stalled in traffic on the Golden Gate Bridge.

That morning, before waking his children, the father had canceled their music lessons and decided to make a day of it. He wanted to know how they were, is all. Just—how were they. He thought his kids were as self-contained as one of those dogs you sometimes see carrying home its own leash. But you could read things wrong.

Could you ever.

The boy had a friend who jumped from a floor of Langley Porter.[1] The friend had been there for two weeks, mostly playing Ping-Pong. All the friend said the day the boy visited and lost every game was never play Ping-Pong with a mental patient because it's all we do and we'll kill you. That night the friend had cut the red belt he wore in two and left the other half on his bed. That was this time last year when the boy was twelve years old.

You think you're safe, the father thought, but it's thinking you're invisible because you closed your eyes.

This day they were headed for Petaluma—the chicken, egg, and arm-wrestling capital of the nation—for lunch. The father had offered to take them to the men's arm-wrestling semifinals. But it was said that arm-wrestling wasn't so interesting since the new safety precautions, that hardly anyone broke an arm or a wrist anymore. The best anyone could hope to see would be dislocation, so they said they would rather go to Pete's. Pete's was a gas station turned into a place to eat. The hamburgers there were named after cars, and the gas pumps in front still pumped gas.

"Can I have one?" the boy asked, meaning the Raisinets.

---

[1] A psychiatric hospital in San Francisco.

"No," his sister said.

"Can I have two?"

"Neither of you should be eating candy before lunch," the father said. He said it with the good sport of a father who enjoys his kids and gets a kick out of saying Dad things.

"You mean dinner," said the girl. "It will be dinner before we get to Pete's."

Only the northbound lanes were stopped. Southbound traffic flashed past at the normal speed.

"Check it out," the boy said from the back seat. "Did you see the bumper sticker on that Porsche? 'If you don't like the way I drive, stay off the sidewalk.'"

He spoke directly to his sister. "I've just solved my Christmas shopping."

"I got the highest score in my class in Driver's Ed," she said.

"I thought I would let your sister drive home today," the father said.

From the back seat came sirens, screams for help, and then a dirge.

The girl spoke to her father in a voice rich with complicity. "Don't people make you want to give up?"

"Don't the two of you know any jokes? I haven't laughed all day," the father said.

"Did I tell you the guillotine joke?" the girl said.

"He hasn't laughed all day, so you must've," her brother said.

The girl gave her brother a look you could iron clothes with. Then her gaze dropped down. "Oh-oh," she said, "Johnny's out of jail."

Her brother zipped his pants back up. He said, "Tell the joke."

"Two Frenchmen and a Belgian were about to be beheaded," the girl began. "The first Frenchman was led to the block and blindfolded. The executioner let the blade go. But it stopped a quarter inch above the Frenchman's neck. So he was allowed to go free, and ran off shouting, '*C'est un miracle! C'est un miracle!*'"

"What does that mean?" her brother asked.

"It's a miracle," the father said.

"Then the second Frenchman was led to the block, and same thing—the blade stopped just before cutting off his head. So *he* got to go free, and ran off shouting '*C'est un miracle!*'

"Finally the Belgian was led to the block. But before they could blindfold him, he looked up, pointed to the guillotine, and cried, '*Voilà la difficulté!*'"

She doubled over.

"Maybe *I* would be wetting *my* pants if I knew what that meant," the boy said.

"You can't explain after the punchline," the girl said, "and have it still be funny."

"There's the problem," said the father.

The waitress handed out menus to the party of three seated in the corner booth of what used to be the lube bay. She told them the specialty of the day was Moroccan chicken.

"That's what I want," the boy said, "Morerotten chicken."

But he changed his order to a Studeburger and fries after his father and sister had ordered.

"So," the father said, "who misses music lessons?"

"I'm serious about what I asked you last week," the girl said. "About switching to piano? My teacher says a real flutist only breathes with the stomach, and I can't."

"The real reason she wants to change," said the boy, "is her waist will get two inches bigger when she learns to stomach-breathe. That's what *else* her teacher said."

The boy buttered a piece of sourdough bread and flipped a chunk of cold butter onto his sister's sleeve.

"Jeezo-beezo," the girl said, "why don't they skip the knife and fork and just set his place with a slingshot!"

"Who will ever adopt you if you don't mind your manners?" the father said. "Maybe we could try a little quiet today."

"You sound like your tombstone," the girl said. "Remember what you wanted it to say?"

Her brother joined in with his mouth full: "Today will be a quiet day."

"Because it never is with us around," the boy said.

"You guys," said the father.

The waitress brought plates. The father passed sugar to the boy and salt to the girl without being asked. He watched the girl shake out salt onto the fries.

"If I had a sore throat, I would gargle with those," he said.

"Looks like she's trying to melt a driveway," the boy offered.

The father watched his children eat. They ate fast. They called it Hoovering. He finished while they sucked at straws in empty drinks.

"Funny," he said thoughtfully, "I'm not hungry anymore."

Every meal ended this way. It was his benediction, one of the Dad things they expected him to say.

"That reminds me," the girl said. "Did you feed Rocky before we left?"

"Uh-uh," her brother said. "I fed him yesterday."

"*I* fed him yesterday!" the girl said.

"Okay, we'll compromise," the boy said. "We won't feed the cat today."

"I'd say you are out of bounds on that one," the father said.

He meant you could not tease her about animals. Once, during dinner, that cat ran into the dining room shot from guns. He ran around the table at top speed, then spun out on the parquet floor into a leg of the table. He fell onto his side and made short coughing sounds. "Isn't he smart?" the girl had crooned, kneeling beside him. "He knows he's hurt."

For years, her father had to say that the animals seen on shoulders of roads were napping.

"He never would have not fed Homer," she said to her father.

"Homer was a dog," the boy said. "If I forgot to feed him, he could just go into the hills and bite a deer."

"Or a Campfire Girl selling candy at the front door," their father reminded them.

"Homer," the girl sighed. "I hope he likes chasing sheep on that ranch in the mountains."

The boy looked at her, incredulous.

"You *believed* that? You actually *believed* that?"

In her head, a clumsy magician yanked the cloth and the dishes all crashed to the floor. She took air into her lungs until they filled, and then she filled her stomach, too.

"I thought she knew," the boy said.

The dog was five years ago.

"The girl's parents insisted," the father said. "It's the law in California."

"Then I hate California," she said. "I hate its guts."

The boy said he would wait for them in the car, and left the table.

"What would help?" the father asked.

"For Homer to be alive," she said.

"What would help?"

"Nothing."

"Help."

She pinched a trail of salt on her plate.

"A ride," she said. "I'll drive."

The girl started the car and screamed. "Goddammit!"

With the power off, the boy had tuned in the Spanish station. Mariachis exploded on ignition.

"Dammit isn't God's last name," the boy said, quoting another bumper sticker.

"Don't people make you want to give up?" the father said.

"No talking," the girl said to the rearview mirror, and put the car in gear.

She drove for hours. Through groves of eucalyptus with their damp peeling bark, past acacia bushes with yellow flowers pulsing off their stems. She cut over to the coast route and the stony-green tones of Inverness.[2]

"What you'd call scenic," the boy tried.

Otherwise, they were quiet.

No one said anything else until the sky started to close, and then it was the boy again, asking shouldn't they be going home.

---

[2] A small town northwest of San Francisco.

"No, no," the father said, and made a show of looking out the window, up at the sky and back at his watch. "No," he said, "keep driving—it's getting earlier."

But the sky spilled rain, and the girl headed south towards the bridge. She turned on the headlights and the dashboard lit up green. She read off the odometer on the way home: "Twenty-six thousand, three hundred eighty-three and eight-tenths miles."

"Today?" the boy said.

The boy got to Rocky first. "Let's play the cat," he said, and carried the Siamese to the upright piano. He sat on the bench holding the cat in his lap and pressed its paws to the keys. Rocky played "Born Free." He tried to twist away.

"Come on, Rocky, ten more minutes and we'll break."

"Give him to me," the girl said.

She puckered up and gave the cat a five-lipper.

"Bring the Rock upstairs," the father called. "Bring sleeping bags, too."

Pretty soon three sleeping bags formed a triangle in the master bedroom. The father was the hypotenuse. The girl asked him to brush out her hair, which he did while the boy ate a tangerine, peeling it up close to his face, inhaling the mist. Then he held each segment to the light to find seeds. In his lap, cat paws fluttered like dreaming eyes.

"What are you thinking?" the father asked.

"Me?" the girl said. "Fifty-seven T-bird, white with red interior, convertible. I drive it to Texas and wear skirts with rick-rack. I'm changing my name to Ruby," she said, "or else Easy."

The father considered her dream of a checkered future.

"Early ripe, early rot," he warned.

A wet wind slammed the window in its warped sash, and the boy jumped.

"I hate rain," he said. "I hate its guts."

The father got up and closed the window tighter against the storm. "It's a real frog-choker," he said.

In darkness, lying still, it was no less camplike than if they had been under the stars singing to a stone-ringed fire burned down to embers.

They had already said good-night some minutes earlier when the boy and girl heard their father's voice in the dark.

"Kids, I just remembered—I have some good news and some bad news. Which do you want first?"

It was his daughter who spoke. "Let's get it over with," she said. "Let's get the bad news over with."

The father smiled. They are all right, he decided. My kids are as right as this rain. He smiled at the exact spots he knew their heads were turned to his, and doubted he would ever feel—not better, but *more* than he did now.

"I lied," he said. "There is no bad news."

QUESTIONS

1. At the outset, we learn that the father has decided to "make a day of it" in order to learn how his children are doing. At the end, he concludes that they are all right, "as right as this rain." Do you agree with the father's conclusion? Explain.   **2.** Explain the meaning of the title.   **3.** What is the thematic relevance of the account of the boy's friend who committed suicide, the story of Homer, the family dog, and the joke about the guillotine?   **4.** How would you characterize the relationship between the brother and sister? Between the children and the father?

WRITING TOPIC

Write an essay in which you speculate on the history of the family. You might consider such questions as: Does there seem to be any particular reason why the father and his two children are spending the day together? Why is there no mention of a mother? Does the father seem to have a good relationship with his children? Do the children seem to love their father? In your opinion, are they a "normal" or "healthy" family?

A Place I've Never Been   1990

DAVID LEAVITT   [b. 1961]

I had known Nathan for years—too many years, since we were in college—so when he went to Europe I wasn't sure how I'd survive it; he was my best friend, after all, my constant companion at Sunday afternoon double bills at the Thalia, my ever-present source of consolation and conversation. Still, such a turn can prove to be a blessing in disguise. It threw me off at first, his not being there— I had no one to watch *Jeopardy!* with, or talk to on the phone late at night— but then, gradually, I got over it, and I realized that maybe it was a good thing after all, that maybe now, with Nathan gone, I would be forced to go out into the world more, make new friends, maybe even find a boyfriend. And I had started: I lost weight, I went shopping. I was at Bloomingdale's one day on my lunch hour when a very skinny black woman with a French accent asked me if I'd like to have a makeover. I had always run away from such things, but this time, before I had a chance, this woman put her long hands on my cheeks and looked into my face—not my eyes, my face—and said, "You're really beautiful. You know that?" And I absolutely couldn't answer. After she was through with me I didn't even know what I looked like, but everyone at my office was amazed. "Celia," they said, "you look great. What happened?" I smiled, won-dering if I'd be allowed to go back every day for a makeover, if I offered to pay.

There was even some interest from a man—a guy named Roy who works downstairs, in contracts—and I was feeling pretty good about myself again, when the phone rang, and it was Nathan. At first I thought he must have been calling me from some European capital, but he said no, he was back in New York. "Celia," he said, "I have to see you. Something awful has happened."

Hearing those words, I pitched over—I assumed the worst. (And why not? He had been assuming the worst for over a year.) But he said, "No, no, I'm fine. I'm perfectly healthy. It's my apartment. Oh, Celia, it's awful. Could you come over?"

"Were you broken into?" I asked.

"I might as well have been!"

"Okay," I said. "I'll come over after work."

"I just got back last night. This is too much."

"I'll be there by six, Nathan."

"Thank you," he said, a little breathlessly, and hung up.

I drummed my nails—newly painted by another skinny woman at Bloom-ingdale's—against the black Formica of my desk, mostly to try out the sound. In truth I was a little happy he was back—I had missed him—and not at all surprised that he'd cut his trip short. Rich people are like that, I've observed; because they don't have to buy bargain-basement tickets on weird charter airlines, they feel free to change their minds. Probably he just got bored tooting around Europe, missed his old life, missed *Jeopardy!*, his friends. Oh, Nathan! How could I tell him the Thalia had closed?

I had to take several buses to get from my office to his neighborhood—a route I had once traversed almost daily, but which, since Nathan's departure, I hadn't had much occasion to take. Sitting on the Madison Avenue bus, I looked out the window at the rows of unaffordable shops, some still exactly what they'd been before, others boarded up, or reopened under new auspices— such a familiar panorama, unfolding, block by block, like a Chinese scroll I'd once been shown on a museum trip in junior high school. It was raining a little, and in the warm bus the long, unvarying progress of my love for Nathan seemed to unscroll as well—all the dinners and lunches and arguments, and all the trips back alone to my apartment, feeling ugly and fat, because Nathan had once again confirmed he could never love me the way he assured me he would someday love a man. How many hundreds of times I received that confirmation! And yet, somehow, it never occurred to me to give up that love I had nurtured for him since our earliest time together, that love which belonged to those days just past the brink of childhood, before I understood about Nathan, or rather, before Nathan understood about himself. So I persisted, and Nathan, in spite of his embarrassment at my occasional outbursts, continued to depend on me. I think he hoped that my feeling for him would one day transform itself into a more maternal kind of affection, that I would one day become the sort of woman who could tend to him without expecting anything in return. And that was, perhaps, a reasonable hope on his part, given my behavior. But: "If only," he said to me once, "you didn't have to act so crazy, Celia—" And that was how I realized I had to get out.

I got off the bus and walked the block and a half to his building—its façade, I noted, like almost every façade in the neighborhood, blemished by a bit of scaffolding—and, standing in that vestibule where I'd stood so often, waiting for him to buzz me up. I read for diversion the now familiar list of tenants' names. The only difference today was that there were ragged ends of Scotch tape stuck around Nathan's name; probably his subletter had put his own name over Nathan's, and Nathan, returning, had torn the piece of paper off and left the ends of the tape. This didn't seem like him, and it made me suspicious. He was a scrupulous person about such things.

In due time—though slowly, for him—he let me in, and I walked the three flights of stairs to find him standing in the doorway, unshaven, looking as if he'd just gotten out of bed. He wasn't wearing any shoes, and he'd gained some weight. Almost immediately he fell into me—that is the only way to describe it, his big body limp in my arms. "Oh, God," he murmured into my hair, "am I glad to see you."

"Nathan," I said. "Nathan." And held him there. Usually he wriggled out of physical affection; kisses from him were little nips; hugs were tight, jerky chokeholds. Now he lay absolutely still, his arms slung under mine, and I tried to keep from gasping from the weight of him. But finally—reluctantly—he let go, and putting his hand on his forehead, gestured toward the open door. "Prepare yourself," he said. "It's worse than you can imagine."

He led me into the apartment. I have to admit, I was shocked by what I saw. Nathan, unlike me, is a chronically neat person, everything in its place, all his perfect furniture glowing, polished, every state-of-the-art fountain pen and pencil tip-up in the blue glass jar on his desk. Today, however, the place was in havoc—newspapers and old Entenmann's cookie boxes spread over the floor, records piled on top of each other, inner sleeves crumpled behind the radiator, the blue glass jar overturned. The carpet was covered with dark mottlings, and a stench of old cigarette smoke and sweat and urine inhabited the place. "It gets worse," he said. "Look at the kitchen." A thick, yellowing layer of grease encrusted the stove-top. The bathroom was beyond the pale of my descriptive capacity for filth.

"Those bastards," Nathan was saying, shaking his head.

"Hold on to the security deposit," I suggested. "Make them pay for it."

He sat down on the sofa, the arms of which appeared to have been ground with cigarette butts, and shook his head. "There *is* no security deposit," he moaned. "I didn't take one because supposedly Denny was my friend, and this other guy—Hoop, or whatever his name was—he was Denny's friend. And look at this!" From the coffee table he handed me a thick stack of utility and phone bills, all unopened. "The phone's disconnected," he said. "Two of the rent checks have bounced. The landlord's about to evict me. I'm sure my credit rating has gone to hell. Jesus, why'd I do it?" He stood, marched into the corner, then turned again to face me. "You know what? I'm going to call my father. I'm going to have him sick every one of his bastard lawyers on those assholes until they pay."

"Nathan," I reminded, "they're unemployed actors. They're poor."

"Then let them rot in jail!" Nathan screamed. His voice was loud and sharp in my ears. It had been a long time since I'd had to witness another person's misery, a long time since anyone had asked of me what Nathan was now asking of me: to take care, to resolve, to smooth. Nonetheless I rallied my energies. I stood. "Look," I said. "I'm going to go out and buy sponges, Comet, Spic and Span, Fantastik, Windex. Everything. We're going to clean this place up. We're going to wash the sheets and shampoo the rug, we're going to scrub the toilet until it shines. I promise you, by the time you go to sleep tonight, it'll be what it was."

He stood silent in the corner.

"Okay?" I said.

"Okay."

"So you wait here," I said. "I'll be right back."

"Thank you."

I picked up my purse and closed the door, thus, once again, saving him from disaster.

But there were certain things I could not save Nathan from. A year ago, his ex-lover Martin had called him up and told him he had tested positive. This was the secret fact he had to live with every day of his life, the secret fact that had brought him to Xanax and Halcion, Darvon and Valium—all crude efforts to cut the fear firing through his blood, exploding like the tiny viral time bombs he believed were lying in wait, expertly planted. It was the day after he found out that he started talking about clearing out. He had no obligations—he had quit his job a few months before and was just doing free-lance work anyway— and so, he reasoned, what was keeping him in New York? "I need to get away from all this," he said, gesturing frantically at the air. I believe he really thought back then that by running away to somewhere where it was less well known, he might be able to escape the disease. This is something I've noticed: The men act as if they think the power of infection exists in direct proportion to its publicity, that in places far from New York City it can, in effect, be outrun. And who's to say they are wrong, with all this talk about stress and the immune system? In Italy, in the countryside, Nathan seemed to feel he'd feel safer. And probably he was right; he would feel safer. Over there, away from the American cityscape with its streets full of gaunt sufferers, you're able to forget the last ten years, you can remember how old the world is and how there was a time when sex wasn't something likely to kill you.

It should be pointed out that Nathan had no symptoms; he hadn't even had the test for the virus itself. He refused to have it, saying he could think of no reason to give up at least the hope of freedom. Not that this made any difference, of course. The fear itself is a brutal enough enemy.

But he gave up sex. No sex, he said, was safe enough for him. He bought a VCR and began to hoard pornographic videotapes. And I think he was having phone sex too, because once I picked up the phone in his apartment and before I could say hello, a husky-voiced man said, "You stud," and then, when I said "Excuse me?" got flustered-sounding and hung up. Some people would probably count that as sex, but I'm not sure I would.

All the time, meanwhile, he was frenzied. I could never guess what time he'd call—six in the morning, sometimes, he'd drag me from sleep. "I figured you'd still be up," he'd say, which gave me a clue to how he was living. It got so bad that by the time he actually left I felt as if a great burden had been lifted from my shoulders. Not that I didn't miss him, but from that day on my time was, miraculously, my own. Nathan is a terrible correspondent—I don't think he's sent me one postcard or letter in all the time we've known each other— and so for months my only news of him came through the phone. Strangers would call me, Germans, Italians, nervous-sounding young men who spoke bad English, who were staying at the YMCA, who were in New York for the first time and to whom he had given my number. I don't think any of them actually wanted to see me; I think they just wanted me to tell them which bars were good and which subway lines were safe—information I happily dispensed. Of course, there was a time when I would have taken them on the subways, shown them around the bars, but I have thankfully passed out of that phase.

And of course, as sex became more and more a possibility, then a likelihood once again in my life, I began to worry myself about the very things that were torturing Nathan. What should I say, say, to Roy in contracts, when he asked me to sleep with him, which I was fairly sure he was going to do within a lunch or two? Certainly I wanted to sleep with him. But did I dare ask him to use a condom? Did I dare even broach the subject? I was frightened that he might get furious, that he might overreact, and I considered saying nothing, taking my chances. Then again, for me in particular, it was a very big chance to take; I have a pattern of falling in love with men who at some point or other have fallen in love with other men. All trivial, selfish, this line of worry, I recognize now, but at that point Nathan was gone, and I had no one around to remind me of how high the stakes were for other people. I slipped back into a kind of women's-magazine attitude toward the whole thing: for the moment, at least, *I* was safe, and I cherished that safety without even knowing it, I gloried in it. All my speculations were merely matters of prevention; that place where Nathan had been exiled was a place I'd never been. I am ashamed to admit it, but there was even a moment when I took a kind of vengeful pleasure in the whole matter—the years I had hardly slept with anyone, for which I had been taught to feel ashamed and freakish, I now wanted to rub in someone's face: I was right and you were wrong! I wanted to say. I'm not proud of having had such thoughts, and I can only say, in my defense, that they passed quickly—but a strict accounting of all feelings, at this point, seems to me necessary. We have to be rigorous with ourselves these days.

In any case, Nathan was back, and I didn't dare think about myself. I went to the grocery store, I bought every cleaner I could find. And when I got back to the apartment he was still standing where he'd been standing, in the corner. "Nate," I said, "here's everything. Let's get to work."

"Okay," he said glumly, even though he is an ace cleaner, and we began.

As we cleaned, the truth came out. This Denny to whom he'd sublet the apartment, Nathan had had a crush on. "To the extent that a crush is a relevant thing in my life anymore," he said, "since God knows, there's nothing to be done about it. But there you are. The libido doesn't stop, the heart doesn't stop, no matter how hard you try to make them."

None of this—especially that last part—was news to me, though Nathan had managed to overlook that aspect of our relationship for years. I had understood from the beginning about the skipping-over of the security payment, the laxness of the setup, because these were the sorts of things I would have willingly done for Nathan at a different time. I think he was privately so excited at the prospect of this virile young man, Denny, sleeping, and perhaps having sex, between his sheets, that he would have taken any number of risks to assure it. Crush: what an oddly appropriate word, considering what it makes you do to yourself.

His apartment was, in a sense, the most Nathan could offer, and probably the most Denny would accept. I understood: You want to get as close as you can, even if it's only at arm's length. And when you come back, maybe, you want to breathe in the smell of the person you love loving someone else.

Europe, he said, had been a failure. He had wandered, having dinner with old friends of his parents, visiting college acquaintances who were busy with exotic lives. He'd gone to bars, which was merely frustrating; there was nothing to be done. "What about safe sex?" I asked, and he said, "Celia, please. There is no such thing, as far as I'm concerned." Once again this started a panicked thumping in my chest as I thought about Roy, and Nathan said, "It's really true. Suppose something lands on you—you know what I'm saying—and there's a microscopic cut in your skin. Bingo."

"Nathan, come on," I said. "That sounds crazy to me."

"Yeah?" he said. "Just wait till some ex-lover of yours calls you up with a little piece of news. Then see how you feel."

He returned to his furious scrubbing of the bathroom sink. I returned to my furious scrubbing of the tub. Somehow, even now, I'm always stuck with the worst of it.

Finally we were done. The place looked okay—it didn't smell anymore—though it was hardly what it had been. Some long-preserved pristineness was gone from the apartment, and both of us knew without saying a word that it would never be restored. We breathed in exhausted—no, not exhausted triumph. It was more like relief. We had beaten something back, yet again.

My hands were red from detergents, my stomach and forehead sweaty. I went into the now-bearable bathroom and washed up, and then Nathan said he would take me out to dinner—my choice. And so we ended up, as we had a thousand other nights, sitting by the window at the Empire Szechuan down the block from his apartment, eating cold noodles with sesame sauce, which, when we had finished them, Nathan ordered more of. "God, how I've missed these," he said, as he scooped the brown slimy noodles into his mouth. "You don't know."

In between slurps he looked at me and said, "You look good, Celia. Have you lost weight?"

"Yes, as a matter of fact," I said.

"I thought so."

I looked back at him, trying to recreate the expression on the French woman's face, and didn't say anything, but as it turned out I didn't need to. "I know what you're thinking," he said, "and you're right. Twelve pounds since you last saw me. But I don't care. I mean, you lose weight when you're sick. At least this way, gaining weight, I know I don't have it."

He continued eating. I looked outside. Past the plate-glass window that separated us from the sidewalk, crowds of people walked, young and old, good-looking and bad-looking, healthy and sick, some of them staring in at our food and our eating. Suddenly—urgently—I wanted to be out among them, I wanted to be walking in that crowd, pushed along in it, and not sitting here, locked into this tiny two-person table with Nathan. And yet I knew that escape was probably impossible. I looked once again at Nathan, eating happily, resigned, perhaps, to the fate of his apartment, and the knowledge that everything would work out, that this had, in fact, been merely a run-of-the-mill crisis. For the moment he was appeased, his hungry anxiety sated; for the moment. But who could guess what would set him off next? I steadied my chin on my palm, drank some water, watched Nathan eat like a happy child.

The next few weeks were thorny with events. Nathan bought a new sofa, had his place recarpeted, threw several small dinners. Then it was time for Lizzie Fischman's birthday party—one of the few annual events in our lives. We had known Lizzie since college—she was a tragic, trying sort of person, the sort who carries with her a constant aura of fatedness, of doom. So many bad things happen to Lizzie you can't help but wonder, after a while, if she doesn't hold out a beacon for disaster. This year alone, she was in a taxi that got hit by a bus; then she was mugged in the subway by a man who called her an "ugly dyke bitch"; then she started feeling sick all the time, and no one could figure out what was wrong, until it was revealed that her building's heating system was leaking small quantities of carbon monoxide into her awful little apartment. The tenants sued, and in the course of the suit, Lizzie, exposed as an illegal subletter, was evicted. She now lived with her father in one half of a two-family house in Plainfield, New Jersey, because she couldn't find another apartment she could afford. (Her job, incidentally, in addition to being wretchedly low-paying, is one of the dreariest I know of: proofreading accounting textbooks in an office on Forty-second Street.)

Anyway, each year Lizzie threw a big birthday party for herself in her father's house in Plainfield, and we all went, her friends, because of course we couldn't bear to disappoint her and add ourselves to her roster of worldwide enemies. It was invariably a miserable party—everyone drunk on bourbon, and Lizzie, eager to recreate the slumber parties of her childhood, dancing around in pink pajamas with feet. We were making s'mores over the gas stove—shoving the chocolate bars and the graham crackers onto fondue forks rather than old sticks—and *Beach Blanket Bingo* was playing on the VCR and no one was having a good time, particularly Nathan, who was overdressed in a beige Giorgio Armani linen suit he'd bought in Italy, and was standing in the corner idly pressing his neck, feeling for swollen lymph nodes. Lizzie's circle dwindled each year, as her friends moved on, or found ways to get out of it. This year eight of us had made it to the party, plus a newcomer from Lizzie's office, a very fat girl with very red nails named Dorrie Friedman, who, in spite of her heaviness, was what my mother would have called dainty. She ate a lot, but unless you were observant, you'd never have noticed it. The image of the fat person stuffing food into her face is mythic: I know from experience, when fat you eat slowly, chew methodically, in order not to draw attention to your mouth. Over the course of an hour I watched Dorrie Friedman put away six of those s'mores with a tidiness worthy of Emily Post, I watched her dab her cheek with her napkin after each bite, and I understood: This was shame, but also, in some peculiar way, this was innocence. A state to envy.

There is a point in Lizzie's parties when she invariably suggests we play Deprivation, a game that had been terribly popular among our crowd in college. The way you play it is you sit in a big circle, and everyone is given ten pennies. (In this case the pennies were unceremoniously taken from a huge bowl that sat on top of Lizzie's mother's refrigerator, and that she had upended on the linoleum floor—no doubt a long-contemplated act of desecration.) You go around the circle, and each person announces something he or she has never done, or a place they've never been—"I've never been to Borneo" is a good example—and then everyone who has been to Borneo is obliged to throw you a penny. Needless to say, especially in college, the game degenerates rather quickly to matters of sex and drugs.

I remembered the first time I ever played Deprivation, my sophomore year, I had been reading Blake's *Songs of Innocence* and *Songs of Experience*. Everything in our lives seemed a question of innocence and experience back then, so this seemed appropriate. There was a tacit assumption among my friends that "experience"—by that term we meant, I think, almost exclusively sex and drugs—was something you strove to get as much of as you could, that innocence, for all the praise it received in literature, was a state so essentially tedious that those of us still stuck in it deserved the childish recompense of shiny new pennies. (None of us, of course, imagining that five years from now the "experiences" we urged on one another might spread a murderous germ, that five years from now some of our friends, still in their youth, would be lost. Youth! You were supposed to sow your wild oats, weren't you? Those of us who didn't—we were the ones who failed, weren't we?)

One problem with Deprivation is that the older you get, the less interesting it becomes; every year, it seemed, my friends had fewer gaps in their lives to confess, and as our embarrassments began to stack up on the positive side, it was what we *had* done that was titillating. Indeed, Nick Walsh, who was to Lizzie what Nathan was to me, complained as the game began, "I can't play this. There's nothing I haven't done." But Lizzie, who has a naive faith in ritual, merely smiled and said, "Oh come on, Nick. No one's done *everything*. For instance, you could say, 'I've never been to Togo,' or 'I've never been made love to simultaneously by twelve Arab boys in a back alley on Mott Street.'"

"Well, Lizzie," Nick said, "it *is* true that I've never been to Togo." His leering smile surveyed the circle, and of course, there *was* someone there— Gracie Wong, I think—who had, in fact, been to Togo.

The next person in the circle was Nathan. He's never liked this game, but he also plays it more cleverly than anyone. "Hmm," he said, stroking his chin as if there were a beard there, "let's see . . . Ah, I've got it. I've never had sex with anyone in this group." He smiled boldly, and everyone laughed—everyone, that is, except for me and Bill Darlington, and Lizzie herself—all three of us now, for the wretched experiments of our early youth, obliged to throw Nathan a penny.

Next was Dorrie Friedman's turn, which I had been dreading. She sat on the floor, her legs crossed under her, her very fat fingers intertwined, and said, "Hmm . . . Something I've never done. Well—I've never ridden a bicycle."

An awful silence greeted this confession, and then a tinkling sound, like wind chimes, as the pennies flew. "Gee," Dorrie Friedman said, "I won big that time." I couldn't tell if she was genuinely pleased.

And as the game went on, we settled, all of us, into more or less parallel states of innocence and experience, except for Lizzie and Nick, whose piles had rapidly dwindled, and Dorrie Friedman, who, it seemed, by virtue of lifelong fatness, had done nearly nothing. She had never been to Europe; she had never swum; she had never played tennis; she had never skied; she had never been on a boat. Even someone else's turn could be an awful moment for Dorrie, as when Nick said, "I've never had a vaginal orgasm." But fortunately, there, she did throw in her penny. I was relieved; I don't think I could have stood it if she hadn't.

After a while, in an effort not to look at Dorrie and her immense pile of pennies, we all started trying to trip up Lizzie and Nick, whose respective caches of sexual experience seemed limitless. "I've never had sex in my parents' bed," I offered. The pennies flew. "I've never had sex under a dry-docked boat." "I've never had sex with more than one other person." "Two other people." "Three other people." By then Lizzie was out of pennies, and declared the game over.

"I guess I won," Dorrie said rather softly. She had her pennies neatly piled in identically sized stacks.

I wondered if Lizzie was worried. I wondered if she was thinking about the disease, if she was frightened, the way Nathan was, or if she just assumed death was coming anyway, the final blow in her life of unendurable misfortunes. She started to gather the pennies back into their bowl, and I glanced across the room at Nathan, to see if he was ready to go. All through the game, of course, he had been looking pretty miserable—he always looks miserable at parties. Worse, he has a way of turning his misery around, making me responsible for it. Across the circle of our nearest and dearest friends he glared at me angrily, and I knew that by the time we were back in his car and on our way home to Manhattan he would have contrived a way for the evening to be my fault. And yet tonight, his occasional knowing sneers, inviting my complicity in looking down on the party, only enraged me. I was angry at him, in advance, for what I was sure he was going to do in the car, and I was also angry at him for being such a snob, for having no sympathy toward this evening, which, in spite of all its displeasures, was nevertheless an event of some interest, perhaps the very last hurrah of our youth, our own little big chill. And that was something: Up until now I had always assumed Nathan's version of things to be the correct one, and cast my own into the background. Now his perception seemed meager, insufficient: Here was an historic night, after all, and all he seemed to want to think about was his own boredom, his own unhappiness.

Finally, reluctantly, Lizzie let us go, and relinquished from her grip, we got into Nathan's car and headed onto the Garden State Parkway. "Never again,"

Nathan was saying, "will I allow you to convince me to attend one of Lizzie Fischman's awful parties. This is the last." I didn't even bother answering, it all seemed so predictable. Instead I just settled back into the comfortable velour of the car seat and switched on the radio. Dionne Warwick and Elton John were singing "That's What Friends Are For," and Nathan said, "You know, of course, that that's the song they wrote to raise money for AIDS."

"I'd heard," I said.

"Have you seen the video? It makes me furious. All these famous singers up there, grinning these huge grins, rocking back and forth. Why the hell are they smiling, I'd like to ask?"

For a second, I considered answering that question, then decided I'd better not. We were slipping into the Holland Tunnel, and by the time we got through to Manhattan I was ready to call it a night. I wanted to get back to my apartment and see if Roy had left a message on my answering machine. But Nathan said, "It's Saturday night, Celia, it's still early. Won't you have a drink with me or something?"

"I don't want to go to any more gay bars, Nathan, I told you that."

"So we'll go to a straight bar. I don't care. I just can't bear to go back to my apartment at eleven o'clock." We stopped for a red light, and he leaned closer to me. "The truth is, I don't think I can bear to be alone. Please."

"All right," I said. What else could I say?

"Goody," Nathan said.

We parked the car in a garage and walked to a darkish café on Greenwich Avenue, just a few doors down from the huge gay bar Nathan used to frequent, and which he jokingly referred to as "the airport." No mention was made of that bar in the café, however, where he ordered latte machiato for both of us. "Aren't you going to have some dessert?" he said. "I know I am. Baba au rhum, perhaps. Or tiramisu. You know '*tirami su*' means 'pick me up,' but if you want to offend an Italian waiter, you say 'I'll have the *tiramilo su*,' which means 'pick up my dick.'"

"I'm trying to lose weight, Nathan," I said. "Please don't encourage me to eat desserts."

"Sorry." He coughed. Our latte machiatos came, and Nathan raised his cup and said, "Here's to us. Here's to Lizzie Fischman. Here's to never playing that dumb game again as long as we live." These days, I noticed, Nathan used the phrase "as long as we live" a bit too frequently for comfort.

Reluctantly I touched my glass to his. "You know," he said, "I think I've always hated that game. Even in college, when I won, it made me jealous. Everyone else had done so much more than me. Back then I figured I'd have time to explore the sexual world. Guess the joke's on me, huh?"

I shrugged. I wasn't sure.

"What's with you tonight, anyway?" he said. "You're so distant."

"I just have things on my mind, Nathan, that's all."

"You've been acting weird ever since I got back from Europe, Celia. Sometimes I think you don't even want to see me."

Clearly he was expecting reassurances to the contrary. I didn't say anything.

"Well," he said, "is that it? You don't want to see me?"

I twisted my shoulders in confusion. "Nathan—"

"Great," he said, and laughed so that I couldn't tell if he was kidding. "Your best friend for nearly ten years. Jesus."

"Look, Nathan, don't melodramatize," I said. "It's not that simple. It's just that I have to think a little about myself. My own life, my own needs. I mean, I'm going to be thirty soon. You know how long it's been since I've had a boyfriend?"

"I'm not against your having a boyfriend," Nathan said. "Have I ever tried to stop you from having a boyfriend?"

"But, Nathan," I said, "I never get to meet anyone when I'm with you all the time. I love you and I want to be your friend, but you can't expect me to just keep giving and giving and giving my time to you without anything in return. It's not fair."

I was looking away from him as I said this. From the corner of my vision I could see him glancing to the side, his mouth a small, tight line.

"You're all I have," he said quietly.

"That's not true, Nathan," I said.

"Yes it is true, Celia."

"Nathan, you have lots of other friends."

"But none of them count. No one but you counts."

The waitress arrived with his goblet of tiramisu, put it down in front of him. "Go on with your life, you say," he was muttering. "Find a boyfriend. Don't you think I'd do the same thing if I could? But all those options are closed to me, Celia. There's nowhere for me to go, no route that isn't dangerous. I mean, getting on with my life—I just can't talk about that simply anymore, the way you can." He leaned closer, over the table. "Do you want to know something?" he said. "Every time I see someone I'm attracted to I go into a cold sweat. And I imagine that they're dead, that if I touch them, the part of them I touch will die. Don't you see? It's bad enough to be afraid you might get it. But to be afraid you might give it—and to someone you loved—" He shook his head, put his hand to his forehead.

What could I say to that? What possibly was there to say? I took his hand, suddenly, I squeezed his hand until the edges of his fingers were white. I was remembering how Nathan looked the first time I saw him, in line at a college dining hall, his hands on his hips, his head erect, staring worriedly at the old lady dishing out food, as if he feared she might run out, or not give him enough. I have always loved the boyish hungers—for food, for sex—because they are so perpetual, so faithful in their daily revival, and even though I hadn't met Nathan yet, I think, in my mind, I already understood: I wanted to feed him, to fill him up; I wanted to give him everything.

Across from us, now, two girls were smoking cigarettes and talking about what art was. A man and a woman, in love, intertwined their fingers. Nathan's hand was getting warm and damp in mine, so I let it go, and eventually he blew his nose and lit a cigarette.

"You know," he said after a while, "it's not the sex, really. That's not what I regret missing. It's just that— Do you realize, Celia, I've never been in love? Never once in my life have I actually been in love?" And he looked at me very earnestly, not knowing, not having the slightest idea, that once again he was counting me for nothing.

"Nathan," I said. "Oh, my Nathan." Still, he didn't seem satisfied, and I knew he had been hoping for something better than my limp consolation. He looked away from me, across the café, listening, I suppose, for that wind-chime peal as all the world's pennies flew his way.

QUESTIONS

1. Characterize the relationship between Celia and Nathan. Do you find that relationship believable?   **2.** Why did Nathan leave New York? How does Celia respond to his absence?   **3.** How does the danger of AIDS affect Celia's feelings about her own sexual experiences? Explain Celia's notion that the "place where Nathan had been exiled was a place I'd never been."   **4.** Although the fat girl, Dorrie, wins the game of Deprivation, how might Nathan have won?

WRITING TOPIC

How would you conduct your life if you shared Nathan's dilemma?

How to Talk to a Hunter

1990

PAM HOUSTON   [b. 1962]

When he says "Skins or blankets?" it will take you a moment to realize that he's asking which you want to sleep under. And in your hesitation he'll decide that he wants to see your skin wrapped in the big black moosehide. He carried it, he'll say, soaking wet and heavier than a dead man, across the tundra for two—was it hours or days or weeks? But the payoff, now, will be to see it fall across one of your white breasts. It's December, and your skin is never really warm, so you will pull the bulk of it around you and pose for him, pose for his camera, without having to narrate this moose's death.

You will spend every night in this man's bed without asking yourself why he listens to top-forty country. Why he donated money to the Republican party. Why he won't play back his messages while you are in the room. You are there so often the messages pile up. Once, you noticed the bright green counter reading as high as fifteen.

He will have lured you here out of a careful independence that you spent months cultivating; though it will finally be winter, the dwindling daylight and the threat of Christmas, that makes you give in. Spending nights with this man means suffering the long face of your sheep dog, who likes to sleep on your bed, who worries when you don't come home. But the hunter's house is so much warmer than yours, and he'll give you a key, and just like a woman, you'll think that means something. It will snow hard for thirteen straight days. Then it will really get cold. When it is sixty below there will be no wind and no clouds, just still air and cold sunshine. The sun on the windows will lure you out of bed, but he'll pull you back under. The next two hours he'll devote to your body. With his hands, with his tongue, he'll express what will seem to you like the most eternal of loves. Like the house key, this is just another kind of lie. Even in bed; especially in bed, you and he cannot speak the same language. The machine will answer the incoming calls. From under an ocean of passion and hide and hair you'll hear a woman's muffled voice between the beeps.

Your best female friend will say, "So what did you think? That a man who sleeps under a dead moose is capable of commitment?"

This is what you learned in college: A man desires the satisfaction of his desire; a woman desires the condition of desiring.

The hunter will talk about spring in Hawaii, summer in Alaska. The man who says he was always better at math will form the sentences so carefully it will be impossible to tell if you are included in these plans. When he asks you if you would like to open a small guest ranch way out in the country, understand that this is a rhetorical question. Label these conversations future perfect, but don't expect the present to catch up with them. Spring is an inconceivable distance from the December days that just keep getting shorter and gray.

He'll ask you if you've ever shot anything, if you'd like to, if you ever thought about teaching your dog to retrieve. Your dog will like him too much, will drop the stick at his feet every time, will roll over and let the hunter scratch his belly.

One day he'll leave you sleeping to go split wood or get the mail and his phone will ring again. You'll sit very still while a woman who calls herself something like Patty Coyote leaves a message on his machine: she's leaving work, she'll say, and the last thing she wanted to hear was the sound of his beautiful voice. Maybe she'll talk only in rhyme. Maybe the counter will change to sixteen. You'll look a question at the mule deer on the wall, and the dark spots on either side of his mouth will tell you he shares more with this hunter than you ever will. One night, drunk, the hunter told you he was sorry for taking that deer, that every now and then there's an animal that isn't meant to be taken, and he should have known that deer was one.

Your best male friend will say, "No one who needs to call herself Patty Coyote can hold a candle to you, but why not let him sleep alone a few nights, just to make sure?"

The hunter will fill your freezer with elk burger, venison sausage, organic potatoes, fresh pecans. He'll tell you to wear your seat belt, to dress warmly, to drive safely. He'll say you are always on his mind, that you're the best thing that's ever happened to him, that you make him glad that he's a man.

Tell him it don't come easy, tell him freedom's just another word for nothing left to lose.

These are the things you'll know without asking: The coyote woman wears her hair in braids. She uses words like "howdy." She's man enough to shoot a deer.

A week before Christmas you'll rent *It's a Wonderful Life* and watch it together, curled on your couch, faces touching. Then you'll bring up the word "monogamy." He'll tell you how badly he was hurt by your predecessor. He'll tell you he couldn't be happier spending every night with you. He'll say there's just a few questions he doesn't have the answers for. He'll say he's just scared and confused. Of course this isn't exactly what he means. Tell him you understand. Tell him you are scared too. Tell him to take all the time he needs. Know that you could never shoot an animal, and be glad of it.

Your best female friend will say, "You didn't tell him you loved him, did you?" Don't even tell her the truth. If you do, you'll have to tell her that he said this: "I feel exactly the same way."

Your best male friend will say, "Didn't you know what would happen when you said the word 'commitment'?"
But that isn't the word that you said.
He'll say, "Commitment, monogamy, it all means just one thing."

The coyote woman will come from Montana with the heavier snows. The hunter will call you on the day of the solstice to say he has a friend in town and can't see you. He'll leave you hanging your Christmas lights; he'll give new meaning to the phrase "longest night of the year." The man who has said he's not so good with words will manage to say eight things about his friend without using a gender-determining pronoun. Get out of the house quickly. Call the most understanding person you know that will let you sleep in his bed.

Your best female friend will say, "So what did you think? That he was capable of living outside his gender?"

When you get home in the morning there's a candy tin on your pillow. Santa, obese and grotesque, fondles two small children on the lid. The card will say something like, From your not-so-secret admirer. Open it. Examine each carefully made truffle. Feed them, one at a time, to the dog. Call the hunter's machine. Tell him you don't speak chocolate.

Your best female friend will say, "At this point, what is it about him that you could possibly find appealing?"

Your best male friend will say, "Can't you understand that this is a good sign? Can't you understand that this proves how deep he's in with you?" Hug your best male friend. Give him the truffles the dog wouldn't eat.

Of course the weather will cooperate with the coyote woman. The highways will close, she will stay another night. He'll tell her he's going to work so he can come and see you. He'll even leave her your number and write "Me at Work" on the yellow pad of paper by his phone. Although you shouldn't, you'll have to be there. It will be you and your nauseous dog and your half-trimmed tree all waiting for him like a series of questions.

This is what you learned in graduate school: in every assumption is contained the possibility of its opposite.

In your kitchen he'll hug you like you might both die there. Sniff him for coyote. Don't hug him back.

He will say whatever he needs to win. He'll say it's just an old friend. He'll say the visit was all the friend's idea. He'll say the night away from you has given him time to think about how much you mean to him. Realize that nothing short of sleeping alone will ever make him realize how much you mean to him. He'll say that if you can just be a little patient, some good will come out of this for the two of you after all. He still won't use a gender-specific pronoun.

Put your head in your hands. Think about what it means to be patient. Think about the beautiful, smart, strong, clever woman you thought he saw when he looked at you. Pull on your hair. Rock your body back and forth. Don't cry.

He'll say that after holding you it doesn't feel right holding anyone else. For "holding," substitute "fucking." Then take it as a compliment.

He will get frustrated and rise to leave. He may or may not be bluffing. Stall for time. Ask a question he can't immediately answer. Tell him you want to make love on the floor. When he tells you your body is beautiful, say, "I feel exactly the same way." Don't, under any circumstances, stand in front of the door.

Your best female friend will say, "They lie to us, they cheat on us, and we love them more for it." She'll say, "It's our fault. We raise them to be like that."

Tell her it can't be your fault. You've never raised anything but dogs.

The hunter will say it's late and he has to go home to sleep. He'll emphasize the last word in the sentence. Give him one kiss that he'll remember while he's fucking the coyote woman. Give him one kiss that ought to make him cry if he's capable of it, but don't notice when he does. Tell him to have a good night.

Your best male friend will say, "We all do it. We can't help it. We're self-destructive. It's the old bad-boy routine. You have a male dog, don't you?"

The next day the sun will be out and the coyote woman will leave. Think about how easy it must be for the coyote woman and a man who listens to top-forty country. The coyote woman would never use a word like "monogamy"; the coyote woman will stay gentle on his mind.

If you can, let him sleep alone for at least one night. If you can't, invite him over to finish trimming your Christmas tree. When he asks how you are, tell him you think it's a good idea to keep your sense of humor during the holidays.

Plan to be breezy and aloof and full of interesting anecdotes about all the other men you've ever known. Plan to be hotter than ever before in bed, and a little cold out of it. Remember that necessity is the mother of invention. Be flexible.

First, he will find the faulty bulb that's been keeping all the others from lighting. He will explain in great detail the most elementary electrical principles. You will take turns placing the ornaments you and other men, he and other women, have spent years carefully choosing. Under the circumstances, try to let this be a comforting thought.

He will thin the clusters of tinsel you put on the tree. He'll say something ambiguous like, Next year you should string popcorn and cranberries. Finally, his arm will stretch just high enough to place the angel on the top of the tree.

Your best female friend will say, "Why can't you ever fall in love with a man who will be your friend?"

Your best male friend will say, "You ought to know this by now: Men always cheat on the best women."

This is what you learned in the pop psychology book: Love means letting go of fear.

Play Willie Nelson's "Pretty Paper." He'll ask you to dance, and before you can answer he'll be spinning you around your wood stove, he'll be humming in your ear. Before the song ends he'll be taking off your clothes, setting you lightly under the tree, hovering above you with tinsel in his hair. Through the spread of the branches the all-white lights you insisted on will shudder and blur, outlining the ornaments he brought: a pheasant, a snow goose, a deer.

The record will end. Above the crackle of the wood stove and the rasp of the hunter's breathing you'll hear one long low howl break the quiet of the frozen night: your dog, chained and lonely and cold. You'll wonder if he knows enough to stay in his dog house. You'll wonder if he knows that the nights are getting shorter now.

QUESTIONS
1. What is the difference between the advice offered by the male and the female friend? Which is more accurate and useful? Explain.   **2.** Describe the difference between the narrator and the "coyote woman." What does the narrator think of the "coyote woman"?   **3.** What specific advice does the narrator give about talking to a hunter?   **4.** Why does the story end with the narrator's thoughts about the dog?

WRITING TOPIC
What common relationship between men and women does this story reflect? Does the relationship in this story parallel your own courtship experiences?

LOVE
AND
HATE

La Fontana della Giovinezza, 15th century by Giacomo Jaquerio.

POETRY

With His Venom*

SAPPHO   [ca. 610–ca. 580 B.C.]

With his venom

Irresistible
and bittersweet

that loosener
of limbs, Love

reptile-like
strikes me down

Bonny Barbara Allan

ANONYMOUS

It was in and about the Martinmas[1] time,
  When the green leaves were a falling,
That Sir John Graeme, in the West Country,
  Fell in love with Barbara Allan.

He sent his man down through the town,
  To the place where she was dwelling:
"O haste and come to my master dear,
  Gin° ye be Barbara Allan."   if

With His Venom
  * Translated by Mary Barnard.
Bonny Barbara Allan
  [1] November 11.

O hooly,° hooly rose she up,   slowly
   To the place where he was lying,   10
And when she drew the curtain by:
   "Young man, I think you're dying."

"O it's I'm sick, and very, very sick,
   And 'tis a' for Barbara Allan."
"O the better for me ye s'° never be,   ye shall
   Tho your heart's blood were a-spilling.

"O dinna° ye mind,° young man," said she,   don't/remember
   "When ye was in the tavern a drinking,
That ye made the healths gae° round and round,   go
   And slighted Barbara Allan?"   20

He turned his face unto the wall,
   And death was with him dealing:
"Adieu, adieu, my dear friends all,
   And be kind to Barbara Allan."

And slowly, slowly raise she up,
   And slowly, slowly left him,
And sighing said she could not stay,
   Since death of life had reft him.

She had not gane a mile but twa,
   When she heard the dead-bell ringing,   30
And every jow° that the dead-bell geid,°   stroke/gave
   It cried, "Woe to Barbara Allan!"

"O mother, mother, make my bed!
   O make it saft and narrow!
Since my love died for me to-day,
   I'll die for him to-morrow."

They Flee from Me   1557

SIR THOMAS WYATT [1503?–1542]

They flee from me, that sometime did me seek,[1]
With naked foot stalking in my chamber.

They Flee from Me
  [1] I.e., formerly pursued me.

I have seen them, gentle, tame, and meek,
That now are wild, and do not remember
That sometime they put themselves in danger
To take bread at my hand; and now they range,
Busily seeking with a continual change.

Thanked be Fortune, it hath been otherwise
Twenty times better; but once in special,
In thin array, after a pleasant guise,   10
When her loose gown from her shoulders did fall,
And she me caught in her arms long and small,°   slender
And therewith all sweetly did me kiss
And softly said, "Dear heart, how like you this?"

It was no dream, I lay broad waking.
But all is turned, thorough° my gentleness,   through
Into a strange fashion of forsaking;
And I have leave to go, of her goodness,
And she also to use newfangleness.°   fickleness
But since that I so kindely² am served,   20
I fain would know what she hath deserved.

QUESTIONS
1. Who are "they" in line 1 and for what are they a metaphor?   **2.** What sort of
relationship is described in the last stanza? How does the poet feel about
it?   **3.** How does the first stanza serve to introduce the theme of the poem?

WRITING TOPIC
How does the poet use the extended hunting metaphor to develop his theme?

Since There's No Help, Come
Let Us Kiss and Part   1619

MICHAEL DRAYTON   [1563–1631]

Since there's no help, come let us kiss and part;
Nay, I have done, you get no more of me,
And I am glad, yea glad with all my heart
That thus so cleanly I myself can free;

They Flee from Me
² I.e., served in kind. The pun on the modern meaning of *kindly* is intended.

Shake hands forever, cancel all our vows,
And when we meet at any time again,
Be it not seen in either of our brows
That we one jot of former love retain.
Now at the last gasp of Love's latest breath,
When, his pulse failing, Passion speechless lies,   10
When faith is kneeling by his bed of death,
And innocence is closing up his eyes,
    Now if thou wouldst, when all have given him over,
    From death to life thou mightst him yet recover.

QUESTIONS
1. Describe the scene in lines 9–12. Why is "innocence" described as closing "Love's" eyes? **2.** How might the lady save Love from death?

The Passionate Shepherd to His Love[1]

1600

CHRISTOPHER MARLOWE   [1564–1593]

Come live with me and be my love,
And we will all the pleasures prove
That valleys, groves, hills, and fields,
Woods, or steepy mountain yields.

And we will sit upon the rocks,
Seeing the shepherds feed their flocks,
By shallow rivers to whose falls
Melodious birds sing madrigals.

And I will make thee beds of roses
And a thousand fragrant posies,   10
A cap of flowers, and a kirtle°   skirt
Embroidered all with leaves of myrtle;

A gown made of the finest wool
Which from our pretty lambs we pull;

The Passionate Shepherd . . .
  [1] This poem has elicited many responses over the centuries. Sir Walter Ralegh's early answer follows. C. Day Lewis's twentieth-century response appears on p. 747.

Fair lined slippers for the cold,
With buckles of the purest gold;

A belt of straw and ivy buds,
With coral clasps and amber studs:
And if these pleasures may thee move,
Come live with me, and be my love.   20

The shepherds' swains shall dance and sing
For thy delight each May morning:
If these delights thy mind may move,
Then live with me and be my love.

The Nymph's Reply
to the Shepherd   1600

SIR WALTER RALEGH   [1552?–1618][1]

If all the world and love were young,
And truth in every shepherd's tongue,
These pretty pleasures might me move
To live with thee and be thy love.

Time drives the flocks from field to fold,
When rivers rage and rocks grow cold,
And Philomel° becometh dumb;   the nightingale
The rest complains of cares to come.

The flowers do fade, and wanton fields
To wayward winter reckoning yields;   10
A honey tongue, a heart of gall,
Is fancy's spring, but sorrow's fall.

Thy gowns, thy shoes, thy beds of roses,
Thy cap, thy kirtle, and thy posies
Soon break, soon wither, soon forgotten—
In folly ripe, in reason rotten.

The Nymph's Reply
   [1] Chronology has been dispensed with here to facilitate comparison with Marlowe's "Passionate Shepherd."

Thy belt of straw and ivy buds,
Thy coral clasps and amber studs,
All these in me no means can move
To come to thee and be thy love.   20

But could youth last and love still breed,
Had joys no date° nor age no need,   end
Then these delights my mind might move
To live with thee and be thy love.

Sonnets   1609

WILLIAM SHAKESPEARE   [1564–1616]

18

Shall I compare thee to a summer's day?
Thou art more lovely and more temperate:
Rough winds do shake the darling buds of May,
And summer's lease hath all too short a date:
Sometime too hot the eye of heaven shines,
And often is his gold complexion dimmed;
And every fair from fair sometimes declines,
By chance or nature's changing course untrimmed;
But thy eternal summer shall not fade,
Nor lose possession of that fair thou ow'st,°   owns
Nor shall death brag thou wander'st in his shade,   11
When in eternal lines to time thou grow'st:
     So long as men can breathe, or eyes can see,
     So long lives this, and this gives life to thee.

QUESTIONS
1. Why does the poet argue that "a summer's day" is an inappropriate metaphor for his beloved?   **2.** What is "this" in line 14?

29

When, in disgrace with fortune and men's eyes,
I all alone beweep my outcast state
And trouble deaf heaven with my bootless cries
And look upon myself and curse my fate,
Wishing me like to one more rich in hope,

Featured like him, like him with friends possessed,
Desiring this man's art and that man's scope,
With what I most enjoy contented least;
Yet in these thoughts myself almost despising,
Haply I think on thee, and then my state,   10
Like to the lark at break of day arising
From sullen earth, sings hymns at heaven's gate;
　　For thy sweet love remembered such wealth brings
　　That then I scorn to change my state with kings.

116

Let me not to the marriage of true minds
Admit impediments;[1] love is not love
Which alters when it alteration finds,
Or bends with the remover to remove.[2]
Oh no! it is an ever-fixed mark
That looks on tempests and is never shaken;
It is the star to every wandering bark,
Whose worth's unknown although his height be taken,[3]
Love's not Time's fool, though rosy lips and cheeks
Within his bending sickle's compass come;   10
Love alters not with his brief hours and weeks,
But bears it out!° even to the edge of the doom.   endures
　　If this be error and upon me proved,
　　I never writ, nor no man ever loved.

129

Th' expense of spirit in a waste of shame
Is lust in action; and till action, lust
Is perjured, murderous, bloody, full of blame,
Savage, extreme, rude, cruel, not to trust;
Enjoyed no sooner but despiséd straight;
Past reason hunted; and no sooner had,
Past reason hated, as a swallowed bait,
On purpose laid to make the taker mad:
Mad in pursuit, and in possession so;

Sonnet 116
　　[1] An echo of the marriage service: "If any of you know cause or just impediments why these persons should not be joined together . . ."
　　[2] I.e., love does not change when a rival attempts to remove its object.
　　[3] The star serves the navigator who measures its height above the horizon but does not understand its value.

Had, having, and in quest to have, extreme;   10
A bliss in proof,° and proved, a very woe;   experience
Before, a joy proposed; behind, a dream.
     All this the world well knows; yet none knows well
     To shun the heaven that leads men to this hell.

QUESTIONS
1. Paraphrase "Th' expense of spirit in a waste of shame / Is lust in action."
2. Describe the sound patterns and metrical variations in lines 3 and 4. What do
they contribute to the "sense" of the lines?

WRITING TOPIC
How do the sound patterns, the metrical variations, and the paradox in the final
couplet contribute to the sense of this sonnet?

130

My mistress' eyes are nothing like the sun;
Coral is far more red than her lips' red;
If snow be white, why then her breasts are dun;
If hairs be wires, black wires grow on her head.
I have seen roses damasked,° red and white,   variegated
But no such roses see I in her cheeks;
And in some perfumes is there more delight
Than in the breath that from my mistress reeks.
I love to hear her speak, yet well I know
That music hath a far more pleasing sound;   10
I grant I never saw a goddess go;
My mistress, when she walks, treads on the ground.
     And yet, by heaven, I think my love as rare
     As any she belied with false compare.¹

I Care Not for These Ladies   1601

THOMAS CAMPION   [1567–1620]

I care not for these ladies,
That must be wooed and prayed:

Sonnet 130
     ¹ I.e., as any woman misrepresented with false comparisons.

Give me kind Amaryllis,[1]
The wanton country maid.
Nature art disdaineth,
Her beauty is her own.
　　Who, when we court and kiss,
　　She cries, "Forsooth, let go!"
　　But when we come where comfort is,
　　She never will say no.　　　　　　　　　　10

If I love Amaryllis,
She gives me fruit and flowers:
But if we love these ladies,
We must give golden showers.
Give them gold, that sell love,
Give me the nut-brown lass,
　　Who, when we court and kiss,
　　She cries, "Forsooth, let go!"
　　But when we come where comfort is,
　　She never will say no.　　　　　　　　　　20

These ladies must have pillows,
And beds by strangers wrought;
Give me a bower of willows,
Of moss and leaves unbought,
And fresh Amaryllis,
With milk and honey fed;
　　Who, when we court and kiss,
　　She cries, "Forsooth, let go!"
　　But when we come where comfort is,
　　She never will say no.　　　　　　　　　　30

The Flea   1633

JOHN DONNE　[1572–1631]

Mark but this flea, and mark in this,
How little that which thou deniest me is;
It sucked me first, and now sucks thee,
And in this flea our two bloods mingled be;
Thou know'st that this cannot be said

I Care Not for These Ladies
　[1] A conventional name for a country girl in pastoral poetry.

A sin, nor shame, nor loss of maidenhead,
   Yet this enjoys before it woo,
   And pampered swells with one blood made of two,
   And this, alas, is more than we would do.

Oh stay, three lives in one flea spare,   10
Where we almost, yea more than married, are.
This flea is you and I, and this
Our marriage bed and marriage temple is;
Though parents grudge, and you, we are met,
And cloistered in these living walls of jet.
   Though use° make you apt to kill me   *custom*
   Let not to that, self-murder added be,
   And sacrilege, three sins in killing three.

Cruel and sudden, hast thou since
Purpled thy nail, in blood of innocence?   20
Wherein could this flea guilty be,
Except in that drop which it sucked from thee?
Yet thou triumph'st, and say'st that thou
Find'st not thy self nor me the weaker now;
   'Tis true, then learn how false fears be;
   Just so much honor, when thou yield'st to me,
   Will waste, as this flea's death took life from thee.

A Valediction: Forbidding Mourning   1633

JOHN DONNE [1572–1631]

As virtuous men pass mildly away,
   And whisper to their souls to go,
Whilst some of their sad friends do say
   The breath goes now, and some say, No;

So let us melt, and make no noise,
   No tear-floods, nor sigh-tempests move,
'Twere profanation of our joys
   To tell the laity our love.

Moving of th' earth° brings harms and fears,   *earthquake*
   Men reckon what it did and meant;   10

But trepidation of the spheres,
   Though greater far, is innocent.[1]

Dull sublunary° lovers' love   under the moon
   (Whose soul is sense) cannot admit
Absence, because it doth remove
   Those things which elemented it.

But we by a love so much refined
   That our selves know not what it is,
Inter-assuréd of the mind,
   Care less, eyes, lips, and hands to miss.   20

Our two souls therefore, which are one,
   Though I must go, endure not yet
A breach, but an expansion,
   Like gold to airy thinness beat.

If they be two, they are two so
   As stiff twin compasses are two;
Thy soul, the fixed foot, makes no show
   To move, but doth, if th' other do.

And though it in the center sit,
   Yet when the other far doth roam,   30
It leans and harkens after it,
   And grows erect, as that comes home.

Such wilt thou be to me, who must
   Like th' other foot, obliquely run;
Thy firmness makes my circle just,
   And makes me end where I begun.

QUESTIONS

1. Two kinds of love are described in this poem—spiritual and physical. How does the simile drawn in the first two stanzas help define the differences between them? **2.** How does the contrast between earthquakes and the movement of the spheres in stanza three further develop the contrast between the two types of lovers? **3.** Explain the comparison between a drawing compass and the lovers in the last three stanzas.

A Valediction: Forbidding Mourning
  [1] The movement of the heavenly spheres is harmless.

Delight in Disorder   1648

ROBERT HERRICK [1591–1674]

A sweet disorder in the dress
Kindles in clothes a wantonness:
A lawn[1] about the shoulders thrown
Into a fine distraction,
An erring lace, which here and there
Enthralls the crimson stomacher,[2]
A cuff neglectful, and thereby
Ribbands to flow confusedly,
A winning wave (deserving note)
In the tempestuous petticoat,   10
A careless shoe-string, in whose tie
I see a wild civility;
Do more bewitch me, than when art
Is too precise in every part.

QUESTIONS
1. State in your own words the speaker's views on art and "disorder." **2.** Does
the speaker explain—directly or indirectly—why he values "disorder"? How so?

Upon Julia's Clothes   1648

ROBERT HERRICK [1591–1674]

Whenas° in silks my Julia goes   *when*
Then, then (methinks) how sweetly flows
That liquefaction of her clothes.

Next, when I cast mine eyes and see
That brave vibration each way free;
O how that glittering taketh me!

Delight in Disorder
  [1] A linen scarf.
  [2] An ornamental covering for the chest.

QUESTIONS
1. What is the effect of the repetition in line 2?   **2.** Show how this poem exemplifies Alexander Pope's dictum that in poetry "the sound should seem an echo to the sense."

Go, Lovely Rose!   1645

EDMUND WALLER [1606–1687]

   Go, lovely rose!
Tell her that wastes her time and me
   That now she knows,
When I resemble° her to thee,   compare
How sweet and fair she seems to be.

   Tell her that's young,
And shuns to have her graces spied,
   That hadst thou sprung
In deserts, where no men abide,
Thou must have uncommended died.   10

   Small is the worth
Of beauty from the light retired;
   Bid her come forth,
Suffer herself to be desired,
And not blush so to be admired.

   Then die! that she
The common fate of all things rare
   May read in thee;
How small a part of time they share
That are so wondrous sweet and fair!   20

To His Coy Mistress   1681

ANDREW MARVELL [1621–1678]

   Had we but world enough, and time,
This coyness, lady, were no crime.
We would sit down, and think which way
To walk, and pass our long love's day.
Thou by the Indian Ganges' side
Shouldst rubies find; I by the tide

Of Humber would complain. I would
Love you ten years before the flood,
And you should, if you please, refuse
Til the conversion of the Jews.   10
My vegetable love should grow
Vaster than empires and more slow;
An hundred years should go to praise
Thine eyes, and on thy forehead gaze;
Two hundred to adore each breast,
But thirty thousand to the rest;
An age at least to every part,
And the last age should show your heart.
For, lady, you deserve this state,
Nor would I love at lower rate.   20
    But at my back I always hear
Time's wingéd chariot hurrying near;
And yonder all before us lie
Deserts of vast eternity.
Thy beauty shall no more be found,
Nor, in thy marble vault, shall sound
My echoing song; then worms shall try
That long-preserved virginity,
And your quaint honor turn to dust,
And into ashes all my lust: 30
The grave's a fine and private place,
But none, I think, do there embrace.
    Now therefore, while the youthful hue
Sits on thy skin like morning dew,
And while thy willing soul transpires
At every pore with instant fires,
Now let us sport us while we may,
And now, like amorous birds of prey,
Rather at once our time devour   39
Than languish in his slow-chapped° power.   slow-jawed
Let us roll our strength and all
Our sweetness up into one ball,
And tear our pleasures with rough strife
Thorough° the iron gates of life: through
Thus, though we cannot make our sun
Stand still, yet we will make him run.

QUESTIONS

1. State the argument of the poem (see ll. 1–2, 21–22, 33–34). **2.** Compare the figures of speech in the first verse paragraph with those in the last. How do they differ? **3.** Characterize the attitude toward life recommended by the poet.

WRITING TOPIC
In what ways does the conception of love in this poem differ from that in Donne's
"A Valediction: Forbidding Mourning"? In your discussion consider the imagery in
both poems.

A Poison Tree   1794

WILLIAM BLAKE   [1757–1827]

I was angry with my friend:
I told my wrath, my wrath did end.
I was angry with my foe:
I told it not, my wrath did grow.

And I watered it in fears,
Night & morning with my tears;
And I sunnéd it with smiles,
And with soft deceitful wiles.

And it grew both day and night,
Till it bore an apple bright.   10
And my foe beheld it shine,
And he knew that it was mine,

And into my garden stole,
When the night had veil'd the pole;
In the morning glad I see
My foe outstretched beneath the tree.

QUESTIONS
1. Is anything gained from the parallel readers might draw between this tree and
the tree in the Garden of Eden? Explain.   **2.** Can you articulate what the "poison"
is?   **3.** Does your own experience verify the first stanza of the poem?

A Red, Red Rose   1796

ROBERT BURNS   [1759–1796]

O My Luve's like a red, red rose,
    That's newly sprung in June;
O My Luve's like a melodie
    That's sweetly played in tune.

As fair art thou, my bonnie lass,
  So deep in luve am I;
And I will luve thee still, my dear,
  Til a' the seas gang dry.

Till a' the seas gang dry, my dear,
  And the rocks melt wi' the sun: 10
O I will love thee still, my dear,
  While the sands o' life shall run.

And fare thee weel, my only luve,
  And fare thee weel awhile!
And I will come again, my luve,
  Though it were ten thousand mile.

Porphyria's Lover[1]   1842

ROBERT BROWNING   [1812–1889]

The rain set early in tonight,
  The sullen wind was soon awake,
It tore the elm-tops down for spite,
  And did its worst to vex the lake:
  I listened with heart fit to break.
When glided in Porphyria; straight
  She shut the cold out and the storm,
And kneeled and made the cheerless grate
  Blaze up, and all the cottage warm;
  Which done, she rose, and from her form   10
Withdrew the dripping cloak and shawl,
  And laid her soiled gloves by, untied
Her hat and let the damp hair fall,
  And, last, she sat down by my side
  And called me. When no voice replied,
She put my arm about her waist,
  And made her smooth white shoulder bare,
And all her yellow hair displaced,
  And, stooping, made my cheek lie there,
  And spread, o'er all, her yellow hair,   20
Murmuring how she loved me—she

Porphyria's Lover
  [1] First published with a complementary poem, whose speaker is also a psychopath, under the cover title *Madhouse Cells*.

Too weak, for all her heart's endeavor,
To set its struggling passion free
    From pride, and vainer ties dissever,
    And give herself to me forever.
But passion sometimes would prevail,
    Nor could tonight's gay feast restrain
A sudden thought of one so pale
    For love of her, and all in vain:
    So, she was come through wind and rain.   30
Be sure I looked up at her eyes
    Happy and proud; at last I knew
Porphyria worshiped me: surprise
    Made my heart swell, and still it grew
    While I debated what to do.
That moment she was mine, mine, fair,
    Perfectly pure and good: I found
A thing to do, and all her hair
    In one long yellow string I wound
    Three times her little throat around,   40
And strangled her. No pain felt she;
    I am quite sure she felt no pain.
As a shut bud that holds a bee,
    I warily oped her lids: again
    Laughed the blue eyes without a stain.
And I untightened next the tress
    About her neck; her cheek once more
Blushed bright beneath my burning kiss:
    I propped her head up as before,
    Only, this time my shoulder bore   50
Her head, which droops upon it still:
    The smiling rosy little head,
So glad it has its utmost will,
    That all it scorned at once is fled,
    And I, its love, am gained instead!
Porphyria's love: she guessed not how
    Her darling one wish would be heard.
And thus we sit together now,
    And all night long we have not stirred,
    And yet God has not said a word!   60

QUESTIONS

1. How do the first five lines set the scene and suggest that there may be something strange about the speaker?   **2.** What kind of person is Porphyria?   **3.** Some critics find the poem weak because it relies on horror rather than character. Do you agree? Explain.   **4.** Why does the speaker's realization that "at last I knew / Porphyria worshiped me" lead him to murder her?   **5.** The speaker declares his intent to kill Porphyria with the words, "I found / A thing to do. . . ." How does this phrasing help establish the tone of the poem? What would be the difference if he had said instead, "I had / To kill her now"?   **6.** How do the meter and rhythm help create the tone?

WRITING TOPIC
Write a character sketch of Porphyria's lover. Use your imagination in speculating on his past.

from

Song of Myself   1855

WALT WHITMAN   [1819–1892]

11

Twenty-eight young men bathe by the shore,
Twenty-eight young men and all so friendly;
Twenty-eight years of womanly life and all so lonesome.

She owns the fine house by the rise of the bank,
She hides handsome and richly drest aft the blinds of the window.

Which of the young men does she like the best?
Ah the homeliest of them is beautiful to her.

Where are you off to, lady? for I see you,
You splash in the water there, yet stay stock still in your room.

Dancing and laughing along the beach came the twenty-ninth bather,   10
The rest did not see her, but she saw them and loved them.

The beards of the young men glisten'd with wet, it ran from their long
    hair,
Little streams pass'd all over their bodies.

An unseen hand also pass'd over their bodies,
It descended tremblingly from their temples and ribs.

The young men float on their backs, their white bellies bulge to the sun,
   they do not ask who seizes fast to them,
They do not know who puffs and declines with pendant and bending
   arch,
They do not think whom they souse with spray.

Dover Beach   1867

MATTHEW ARNOLD   [1822–1888]

The sea is calm tonight.
The tide is full, the moon lies fair
Upon the straits; on the French coast the light
Gleams and is gone; the cliffs of England stand,
Glimmering and vast, out in the tranquil bay.
Come to the window, sweet is the night-air!
Only, from the long line of spray
Where the sea meets the moon-blanched land,
Listen! you hear the grating roar
Of pebbles which the waves draw back, and fling,   10
At their return, up the high strand,
Begin, and cease, and then again begin,
With tremulous cadence slow, and bring
The eternal note of sadness in.

Sophocles long ago
Heard it on the Aegean, and it brought
Into his mind the turbid ebb and flow
Of human misery; we
Find also in the sound a thought,
Hearing it by this distant northern sea.   20

The Sea of Faith
Was once, too, at the full, and round earth's shore
Lay like the folds of a bright girdle furled.
But now I only hear
Its melancholy, long, withdrawing roar,
Retreating, to the breath
Of the night-wind, down the vast edges drear
And naked shingles° of the world.   pebble beaches

Ah, love, let us be true
To one another! for the world, which seems   30

To lie before us like a land of dreams,
So various, so beautiful, so new,
Hath really neither joy, nor love, nor light,
Nor certitude, nor peace, nor help for pain;
And we are here as on a darkling plain
Swept with confused alarms of struggle and flight,
Where ignorant armies clash by night.

from
Modern Love   1862

GEORGE MEREDITH   [1828–1909]

17

At dinner, she is hostess, I am host.
Went the feast ever cheerfuller? She keeps
The Topic over intellectual deeps
In buoyancy afloat. They see no ghost.
With sparkling surface-eyes we ply the ball:
It is in truth a most contagious game:
HIDING THE SKELETON, shall be its name.
Such play as this the devils might appall!
But here's the greater wonder: in that we,
Enamored of an acting naught can tire,   10
Each other, like true hypocrites, admire;
Warm-lighted looks, Love's ephemeridae,°   short-lived insects
Shoot gayly o'er the dishes and the wine.
We waken envy of our happy lot.
Fast, sweet, and golden, shows the marriage knot.
Dear guests, you now have seen Love's corpse-light[1] shine.

QUESTIONS
1. What, precisely, is "Love's corpse-light" (l. 16) a metaphor for in this
poem?   **2.** Is the "marriage knot" really "fast, sweet, and golden" (l. 15)? Explain.

Modern Love
   [1] I.e., corpse-candle, a soft light which, when seen in churchyards, portends a funeral.

Mine Enemy Is
Growing Old

(ca. 1881)

EMILY DICKINSON   [1830–1886]

Mine Enemy is growing old—
I have at last Revenge—
The Palate of the Hate departs—
If any would avenge

Let him be quick—the Viand flits—
It is a faded Meat—
Anger as soon as fed is dead—
'Tis starving makes it fat—

QUESTION
1. Explain the paradox contained in the last two lines.

WRITING TOPIC
Compare this poem with Blake's "A Poison Tree."

The Windhover[1]
TO CHRIST OUR LORD

1877

GERARD MANLEY HOPKINS   [1844–1889]

I caught this morning morning's minion,° king-   favorite
    dom of daylight's dauphin,[2] dapple-dawn-drawn Falcon, in his riding
    Of the rolling level underneath him steady air, and striding
High there, how he rung upon the rein of a wimpling° wing   rippling
In his ecstasy! then off, off forth on swing,

The Windhover
   [1] A small hawk, so called because it is able to hover in the wind.
   [2] Heir to kingly splendor.

As a skate's heel sweeps smooth on a bow-bend: the hurl and gliding
    Rebuffed the big wind. My heart in hiding
Stirred for a bird,—the achieve of, the mastery of the thing!

Brute beauty and valour and act, oh, air, pride, plume, here
    Buckle! AND the fire that breaks from thee then, a billion   10
Times told lovelier, more dangerous, O my chevalier!

    No wonder of it: shéer plód makes plough down sillion³
Shine, and blue-bleak embers, ah my dear,
    Fall, gall themselves, and gash gold-vermilion.

QUESTIONS

1. The poem expresses a love of God. On what is that love, or awe, of God based? **2.** Do the sound patterns of the poem convey emotional intensity? Explain. **3.** "Buckle" in line 10 may mean "collapse" or "join." How do you read it? Explain.

WRITING TOPIC

Although the metrical quality of this poem is unique to Hopkins, it is structured as a sonnet. How do each of its parts—that is, the octave and each of the three-line divisions of the sestet—function?

Pied Beauty   1877

GERARD MANLEY HOPKINS   [1844–1889]

Glory be to God for dappled things—
    For skies of couple-colour as a brinded° cow;   brindled
        For rose-moles all in stipple upon trout that swim;
Fresh-firecoal chestnut-falls;¹ finches' wings;
    Landscape plotted and pieced²—fold, fallow, and plough;
        And all trades, their gear and tackle, and trim.°   equipment
All things counter,° original, spare, strange;   contrasted
    Whatever is fickle, freckled (who knows how?)
        With swift, slow; sweet, sour; adazzle, dim;

The Windhover
  ³ The ridge between ploughed furrows.
Pied Beauty
  ¹ Fallen chestnuts, with the outer husks removed, colored like fresh fire coal.
  ² Reference to the variegated pattern of land put to different uses.

He fathers-forth whose beauty is past change: 10
          Praise him.

Fire and Ice   1923

ROBERT FROST   [1874–1963]

Some say the world will end in fire,
Some say in ice,
From what I've tasted of desire
I hold with those who favor fire.
But if it had to perish twice,
I think I know enough of hate
To say that for destruction ice
Is also great
And would suffice.

The Silken Tent   1942

ROBERT FROST   [1874–1963]

She is as in a field a silken tent
At midday when a sunny summer breeze
Has dried the dew and all its ropes relent,
So that in guys it gently sways at ease,
And its supporting central cedar pole,
That is its pinnacle to heavenward
And signifies the sureness of the soul,
Seems to owe naught to any single cord,
But strictly held by none, is loosely bound
By countless silken ties of love and thought   10
To everything on earth the compass round,
And only by one's going slightly taut
In the capriciousness of summer air
Is of the slightest bondage made aware.

The Love Song
of J. Alfred Prufrock

1917

T. S. ELIOT   [1888–1965]

S'io credessi che mia risposta fosse
a persona che mai tornasse al mondo,
questa fiamma staria senza più scosse.
Ma per ciò che giammai di questo fondo
non tornò vivo alcun, s'i'odo il vero,
senza tema d'infamia ti rispondo.[1]

Let us go then, you and I,
When the evening is spread out against the sky
Like a patient etherized upon a table;
Let us go, through certain half-deserted streets,
The muttering retreats
Of restless nights in one-night cheap hotels
And sawdust restaurants with oyster shells:
Streets that follow like a tedious argument
Of insidious intent
To lead you to an overwhelming question . . .   10
Oh, do not ask, "What is it?"
Let us go and make our visit.

In the room the women come and go
Talking of Michelangelo.

The yellow fog that rubs its back upon the windowpanes,
The yellow smoke that rubs its muzzle on the windowpanes
Licked its tongue into the corners of the evening,
Lingered upon the pools that stand in drains,
Let fall upon its back the soot that falls from chimneys,
Slipped by the terrace, made a sudden leap,   20

. . . *Prufrock*
   [1] From Dante, *Inferno*, XXVII, 61–66. The speaker is Guido da Montefeltro, who is imprisoned in a flame in the level of Hell reserved for false counselors. He tells Dante and Virgil, "If I thought my answer were given to one who might return to the world, this flame would stay without further movement. But since from this depth none has ever returned alive, if what I hear is true, I answer you without fear of infamy."

And seeing that it was a soft October night,
Curled once about the house, and fell asleep.

And indeed there will be time
For the yellow smoke that slides along the street,
Rubbing its back upon the windowpanes;
There will be time, there will be time
To prepare a face to meet the faces that you meet;
There will be time to murder and create,
And time for all the works and days of hands
That lift and drop a question on your plate;   30
Time for you and time for me,
And time yet for a hundred indecisions,
And for a hundred visions and revisions,
Before the taking of a toast and tea.

In the room the women come and go
Talking of Michelangelo.

And indeed there will be time
To wonder, "Do I dare?" and, "Do I dare?"
Time to turn back and descend the stair,
With a bald spot in the middle of my hair—   40
(They will say: "How his hair is growing thin!")
My morning coat, my collar mounting firmly to the chin,
My necktie rich and modest, but asserted by a simple pin—
(They will say: "But how his arms and legs are thin!")
Do I dare
Disturb the universe?
In a minute there is time
For decisions and revisions which a minute will reverse.

For I have known them all already, known them all—
Have known the evenings, mornings, afternoons,   50
I have measured out my life with coffee spoons;
I know the voices dying with a dying fall
Beneath the music from a farther room.
    So how should I presume?

And I have known the eyes already, known them all—
The eyes that fix you in a formulated phrase,
And when I am formulated, sprawling on a pin,
When I am pinned and wriggling on the wall,
Then how should I begin

To spit out all the butt-ends of my days and ways?   60
   And how should I presume?

And I have known the arms already, known them all—
Arms that are braceleted and white and bare
(But in the lamplight, downed with light brown hair!)
Is it perfume from a dress
That makes me so digress?
Arms that lie along a table, or wrap about a shawl.
   And should I then presume?
   And how should I begin?

         .   .   .   .

Shall I say, I have gone at dusk through narrow streets   70
And watched the smoke that rises from the pipes
Of lonely men in shirt-sleeves, leaning out of windows? . . .

I should have been a pair of ragged claws
Scuttling across the floors of silent seas.

         .   .   .   .

And the afternoon, the evening, sleeps so peacefully!
Smoothed by long fingers,
Asleep . . . tired . . . or it malingers,
Stretched on the floor, here beside you and me.
Should I, after tea and cakes and ices,
Have the strength to force the moment to its crisis?   80
But though I have wept and fasted, wept and prayed,
Though I have seen my head (grown slightly bald) brought in upon a platter,[2]
I am no prophet—and here's no great matter;
I have seen the moment of my greatness flicker,
And I have seen the eternal Footman hold my coat, and snicker,
And in short, I was afraid.

And would it have been worth it, after all,
After the cups, the marmalade, the tea,
Among the porcelain, among some talk of you and me,
Would it have been worth while,   90
To have bitten off the matter with a smile,
To have squeezed the universe into a ball
To roll it toward some overwhelming question,
To say: "I am Lazarus,[3] come from the dead,

---

[2] Like the head of John the Baptist. See Matthew 14:3–12.
[3] See John 11:1–14 and Luke 16:19–26.

Come back to tell you all, I shall tell you all"—
If one, settling a pillow by her head,
   Should say: "That is not what I meant at all.
   That is not it, at all."

And would it have been worth it, after all,
Would it have been worth while,   100
After the sunsets and the dooryards and the sprinkled streets,
After the novels, after the teacups, after the skirts that trail along the floor—
And this, and so much more?—
It is impossible to say just what I mean!
But as if a magic lantern threw the nerves in patterns on a screen:
Would it have been worth while
If one, settling a pillow or throwing off a shawl,
And turning toward the window, should say:
   "That is not it at all,
   That is not what I meant, at all."   110
       .   .   .   .

No! I am not Prince Hamlet, nor was meant to be;
Am an attendant lord, one that will do
To swell a progress,° start a scene or two,   *state journey*
Advise the prince; no doubt, an easy tool,
Deferential, glad to be of use,
Politic, cautious, and meticulous;
Full of high sentence,° but a bit obtuse;   *sententiousness*
At times, indeed, almost ridiculous—
Almost, at times, the Fool.

I grow old . . . I grow old . . .   120
I shall wear the bottoms of my trousers rolled.°   *cuffed*

Shall I part my hair behind? Do I dare to eat a peach?
I shall wear white flannel trousers, and walk upon the beach.
I have heard the mermaids singing, each to each.

I do not think that they will sing to me.

I have seen them riding seaward on the waves
Combing the white hair of the waves blown back
When the wind blows the water white and black.

We have lingered in the chambers of the sea
By sea-girls wreathed with seaweed red and brown   130
Till human voices wake us, and we drown.

QUESTIONS
1. This poem may be understood as a stream of consciousness passing through the
mind of Prufrock. The "you and I" of line 1 may be different aspects of his personality. Or perhaps the "you and I" is parallel to Guido who speaks the epigraph and
Dante to whom he tells the story that resulted in his damnation—hence, "you" is
the reader and "I" is Prufrock. Apparently, Prufrock is on his way to a tea and is
pondering his relationship with a certain woman. The poem is disjointed because
it proceeds by psychological rather than logical stages. To what social class does
Prufrock belong? How does Prufrock respond to the attitudes and values of his
class? Does he change in the course of the poem?   **2.** Line 92 provides a good
example of literary allusion (see the last stanza of Marvell, "To His Coy Mistress,"
especially ll. 41–42). How does an awareness of the allusion contribute to the
reader's response to the stanza here?   **3.** What might the song of the mermaids
(l. 124) signify, and why does Prufrock think they will not sing to him (l. 125)?
4. T. S. Eliot once said that some poetry "can communicate without being understood." Is this such a poem?

WRITING TOPIC
What sort of man is J. Alfred Prufrock? How does the poet establish his characteristics?

Love Is Not All   1931

EDNA ST. VINCENT MILLAY   [1892–1950]

Love is not all: it is not meat nor drink
Nor slumber nor a roof against the rain;
Nor yet a floating spar to men that sink
And rise and sink and rise and sink again;
Love can not fill the thickened lung with breath,
Nor clean the blood, nor set the fractured bone;
Yet many a man is making friends with death
Even as I speak, for lack of love alone.
It well may be that in a difficult hour,
Pinned down by pain and moaning for release,   10
Or nagged by want past resolution's power,
I might be driven to sell your love for peace,
Or trade the memory of this night for food.
It well may be. I do not think I would.

if everything happens
that can't be done   1944

E. E. CUMMINGS   [1894–1962]

if everything happens that can't be done
(and anything's righter
than books
could plan)
the stupidest teacher will almost guess
(with a run
skip
around we go yes)
there's nothing as something as one

one hasn't a why or because or although   10
(and buds know better
than books
don't grow)
one's anything old being everything new
(with a what
which
around we come who)
one's everyanything so

so world is a leaf so tree is a bough
(and birds sing sweeter   20
than books
tell how)
so here is away and so your is a my
(with a down
up
around again fly)
forever was never till now

now i love you and you love me
(and books are shuter
than books   30
can be)
and deep in the high that does nothing but fall
(with a shout

each
around we go all)
there's somebody calling who's we

we're anything brighter than even the sun
(we're everything greater
than books
might mean)   40
we're everyanything more than believe
(with a spin
leap
alive we're alive)
we're wonderful one times one

QUESTIONS
1. What fundamental contrast is stated by the poem?   **2.** Lines 2–4 and 6–8 of
each stanza could be printed as single lines. Why do you think Cummings decided
to print them as he does?   **3.** What common attitude toward lovers is expressed
by the last lines of the stanzas?   **4.** Is the poem free verse or formal verse?

WRITING TOPIC
What relation do the parenthetical lines in each stanza bear to the poem as a whole?

The Dream   1941

LOUISE BOGAN   [1897–1970]

O God, in the dream the terrible horse began
To paw at the air, and make for me with his blows.
Fear kept for thirty-five years poured through his mane,
And retribution equally old, or nearly, breathed through his nose.

Coward complete, I lay and wept on the ground
When some strong creature appeared, and leapt for the rein.
Another woman, as I lay half in a swound,
Leapt in the air, and clutched at the leather and chain.

Give him, she said, something of yours as a charm.
Throw him, she said, some poor thing you alone claim.   10
No, no, I cried, he hates me; he's out for harm,
And whether I yield or not, it is all the same.

But, like a lion in a legend, when I flung the glove
Pulled from my sweating, my cold right hand,
The terrible beast, that no one may understand,
Came to my side, and put down his head in love.

QUESTIONS

1. The "terrible horse" of the speaker's dream advances through "fear kept for thirty-five years" while breathing "retribution" through his nose. What might the speaker have done (or felt) to account for the horse's attack? In other words, what might the aggressive horse symbolize?   **2.** What is the significance of the strong woman's advice?   **3.** Explain the allusion to the "lion in a legend." What function does the allusion serve in the poem?   **4.** What might the flung glove symbolize? Suggest some reasons to account for the assertion "that no one may understand" the "terrible beast." What accounts for the transformation in the horse's behavior?

Song[1]   1935

C. DAY LEWIS   [1904–1972]

Come, live with me and be my love,
And we will all the pleasures prove
Of peace and plenty, bed and board,
That chance employment may afford.

I'll handle dainties on the docks
And thou shalt read of summer frocks:
At evening by the sour canals
We'll hope to hear some madrigals.

Care on thy maiden brow shall put
A wreath of wrinkles, and thy foot   10
Be shod with pain: not silken dress
But toil shall tire thy loveliness.

Hunger shall make thy modest zone
And cheat fond death of all but bone—
If these delights thy mind may move,
Then live with me and be my love.

Song
   [1] See Christopher Marlowe's "The Passionate Shepherd to His Love," pp. 720–721.

from
Five Songs   (1937)

W. H. AUDEN   [1907–1973]

That night when joy began
Our narrowest veins to flush,
We waited for the flash
Of morning's levelled gun.

But morning let us pass,
And day by day relief
Outgrew his nervous laugh,
Grows credulous of peace.

As mile by mile is seen
No trespasser's reproach,   10
And love's best glasses reach
No fields but are his own.

QUESTIONS
1. Describe the sound relationships among the last words in the lines of each stanza.   **2.** What is the controlling metaphor in the poem? Is it appropriate for a love poem?   **3.** If it were suggested that the poem describes a homosexual relationship, would your response to the poem's figurative language change?

My Papa's Waltz   1948

THEODORE ROETHKE   [1908–1963]

The whiskey on your breath
Could make a small boy dizzy;
But I hung on like death:
Such waltzing was not easy.

We romped until the pans
Slid from the kitchen shelf;
My mother's countenance
Could not unfrown itself.

The hand that held my wrist
Was battered on one knuckle;   10
At every step you missed
My right ear scraped a buckle.

You beat time on my head
With a palm caked hard by dirt,
Then waltzed me off to bed
Still clinging to your shirt.

QUESTIONS

1. Why is iambic trimeter an appropriate meter for this poem?   **2.** Identify the details that reveal the kind of person the father is.   **3.** How would you characterize the boy's feelings about his father? The father's about the boy?

WRITING TOPIC

Robert Hayden's "Those Winter Sundays" (p. 751), Ted Hughes's "Crow's First Lesson" (pp. 760–761), and Sylvia Plath's "Daddy" (pp. 762–764) also deal with a child's feelings about a parent. Compare one of them with this poem.

I Knew a Woman   1958

THEODORE ROETHKE   [1908–1963]

I knew a woman, lovely in her bones,
When small birds sighed, she would sigh back at them;
Ah, when she moved, she moved more ways than one:
The shapes a bright container can contain!
Of her choice virtues only gods should speak,
Or English poets who grew up on Greek
(I'd have them sing in chorus, cheek to cheek).

How well her wishes went! She stroked my chin,
She taught me Turn, and Counter-turn, and Stand;
She taught me Touch, that undulant white skin;   10
I nibbled meekly from her proffered hand;
She was the sickle; I, poor I, the rake,
Coming behind her for her pretty sake
(But what prodigious mowing we did make).

Love likes a gander, and adores a goose:
Her full lips pursed, the errant note to seize;

She played it quick, she played it light and loose;
My eyes, they dazzled at her flowing knees;
Her several parts could keep a pure repose,
Or one hip quiver with a mobile nose   20
(She moved in circles, and those circles moved).

Let seed be grass, and grass turn into hay:
I'm martyr to a motion not my own;
What's freedom for? To know eternity.
I swear she cast a shadow white as stone.
But who would count eternity in days?
These old bones live to learn her wanton ways:
(I measure time by how a body sways).

One Art   1976

ELIZABETH BISHOP   [1911–1979]

The art of losing isn't hard to master;
so many things seem filled with the intent
to be lost that their loss is no disaster.

Lose something every day. Accept the fluster
of lost door keys, the hour badly spent.
The art of losing isn't hard to master.

Then practice losing farther, losing faster:
places, and names, and where it was you meant
to travel. None of these will bring disaster.

I lost my mother's watch. And look! my last, or   10
next-to-last, of three loved houses went.
The art of losing isn't hard to master.

I lost two cities, lovely ones. And, vaster,
some realms I owned, two rivers, a continent.
I miss them, but it wasn't a disaster.

—Even losing you (the joking voice, a gesture
I love) I shan't have lied. It's evident
the art of losing's not too hard to master
though it may look like (*Write* it!) like disaster.

Those Winter Sundays   1975

ROBERT HAYDEN   [1913–1980]

Sundays too my father got up early
and put his clothes on in the blueblack cold,
then with cracked hands that ached
from labor in the weekday weather made
banked fires blaze. No one ever thanked him.

I'd wake and hear the cold splintering, breaking.
When the rooms were warm, he'd call,
and slowly I would rise and dress,
fearing the chronic angers of that house,

Speaking indifferently to him,   10
who had driven out the cold
and polished my good shoes as well.
What did I know, what did I know
of love's austere and lonely offices?

Out in a Pasture   (1991)

DUANE LOCKE   [b. 1921]

Out in a pasture, pouring wine into glasses,
comparing the ruby reflection on grasses,
with the ruby coloring of sundews' globes,
we commented on the beauty of the sound *carnivorous*,
and how, remembering Alexander Pope,[1]
the sound did not fit the sense.
We speculated on what sounds make sense of a bird:
pájaro, vogel, oiseaux, uccèllo.[2]
We settled on the Italian for warblers,
the German for eagles, the French for swallows,
and dismissed the Spanish.

Out in a Pasture
    [1] English poet (1688–1744) who argued in his poem "An Essay on Criticism" that the sounds within a poem should seem an echo to the sense. See his passage on p. 1256.
    [2] The foreign word sequence is, in each case, Spanish, German, French, Italian.

We turned to the sounds for butterflies,
as a butterfly was flying over,
darkening our hands with fluttering shadows;
mariposa, Schmetterling, papillon, farfalla.
All sounds seemed appropriate, even the German.
We repeated the sounds for love:
amor, Liebe, amour, amore.
None seemed to fit, not even English.

QUESTIONS

1. What arguments would you use to defend the poet's assertion, in lines 9–11, that certain foreign words suggest particular birds, while the Spanish word seems utterly unbirdlike? What about the English word?   **2.** Extend your arguments to the words for butterfly. Does English work?

WRITING TOPIC

Make up some words that would sound like different kinds of love—young love, affection, brotherly love, passion, love of god. As best you can, explain why the sounds you select suggest certain emotions.

A Late Aubade   1968

RICHARD WILBUR   [b. 1921]

You could be sitting now in a carrel
Turning some liver-spotted page,
Or rising in an elevator-cage
Toward Ladies' Apparel.

You could be planting a raucous bed
Of salvia, in rubber gloves,
Or lunching through a screed of someone's loves
With pitying head,

Or making some unhappy setter
Heel, or listening to a bleak   10
Lecture on Schoenberg's serial technique.[1]
Isn't this better?

A Late Aubade
   [1] Arnold Schoenberg (1874–1951), Austrian born composer.

Think of all the time you are not
Wasting, and would not care to waste,
Such things, thank God, not being to your taste.
Think what a lot

Of time, by woman's reckoning,
You've saved, and so may spend on this,
You who had rather lie in bed and kiss
Than anything.   20

It's almost noon, you say? If so,
Time flies, and I need not rehearse
The rosebuds-theme of centuries of verse.[2]
If you *must* go,

Wait for a while, then slip downstairs
And bring us up some chilled white wine,
And some blue cheese, and crackers, and some fine
Ruddy-skinned pears.

QUESTIONS
1. Explain the title.   **2.** Is the speaker a sexist? Explain.   **3.** Explain lines 16–18.

Love Song: I and Thou   1961

ALAN DUGAN   [b. 1923]

Nothing is plumb, level or square:
    the studs are bowed, the joists
are shaky by nature, no piece fits
    any other piece without a gap
or pinch, and bent nails
    dance all over the surfacing
like maggots. By Christ
    I am no carpenter. I built
the roof for myself, the walls
    for myself, the floors
for myself, and got   10
    hung up in it myself. I
danced with a purple thumb

A Late Aubade
    [2] The *Carpe Diem* theme (see Glossary of Literary Terms).

at this house-warming, drunk
with my prime whiskey: rage.
    Oh I spat rage's nails
into the frame-up of my work:
    it held. It settled plumb,
level, solid, square and true
    for that great moment. Then   20
it screamed and went on through,
    skewing as wrong the other way.
God damned it. This is hell,
    but I planned it, I sawed it,
I nailed it, and I
    will live in it until it kills me.
I can nail my left palm
    to the left-hand cross-piece but
I can't do everything myself.
    I need a hand to nail the right,   30
a help, a love, a you, a wife.

The Dover Bitch   1968
A CRITICISM OF LIFE

ANTHONY HECHT   [b. 1923]

So there stood Matthew Arnold and this girl
With the cliffs of England crumbling away behind them,
And he said to her, "Try to be true to me,
And I'll do the same for you, for things are bad
All over, etc., etc."
Well now, I knew this girl. It's true she had read
Sophocles in a fairly good translation
And caught that bitter allusion to the sea,
But all the time he was talking she had in mind
The notion of what his whiskers would feel like   10
On the back of her neck. She told me later on
That after a while she got to looking out
At the lights across the channel, and really felt sad,
Thinking of all the wine and enormous beds
And blandishments in French and the perfumes.
And then she got really angry. To have been brought
All the way down from London, and then be addressed
As a sort of mournful cosmic last resort
Is really tough on a girl, and she was pretty.

Anyway, she watched him pace the room   20
And finger his watch-chain and seem to sweat a bit,
And then she said one or two unprintable things.
But you mustn't judge her by that. What I mean to say is,
She's really all right. I still see her once in a while
And she always treats me right. We have a drink
And I give her a good time, and perhaps it's a year
Before I see her again, but there she is,
Running to fat, but dependable as they come,
And sometimes I bring her a bottle of *Nuit d'Amour*.

QUESTIONS

1. This poem is a response to Matthew Arnold's "Dover Beach," which appears earlier in this section. Arnold's poem is often read as a pained response to the breakdown of religious tradition and social and political order in the mid-nineteenth century. Is this poem, in contrast, optimistic? Is the relationship between the speaker and the girl at the end of the poem admirable? Explain.   **2.** Do you suppose Hecht was moved to write this poem out of admiration for "Dover Beach"? Explain.

WRITING TOPIC

What is the fundamental difference between the speaker's conception of love in Arnold's poem and the "girl's" conception of love as reported in this poem?

The Mutes   1967

DENISE LEVERTOV   [b. 1923]

Those groans men use
passing a woman on the street
or on the steps of the subway

to tell her she is a female
and their flesh knows it,

are they a sort of tune,
an ugly enough song, sung
by a bird with a slit tongue

but meant for music?

Or are they the muffled roaring   10
of deafmutes trapped in a building that is
slowly filling with smoke?

Perhaps both.

Such men most often
look as if groan were all they could do,
yet a woman, in spite of herself,

knows it's a tribute:
if she were lacking all grace
they'd pass her in silence:

so it's not only to say she's   20
a warm hole. It's a word

in grief-language, nothing to do with
primitive, not an ur-language;[1]
language stricken, sickened, cast down

in decrepitude. She wants to
throw the tribute away, disgusted, and can't,

it goes on buzzing in her ear,
it changes the pace of her walk,
the torn posters in echoing corridors   30

spell it out, it
quakes and gnashes as the train comes in.
Her pulse sullenly

had picked up speed,
but the cars slow down and
jar to a stop while her understanding

keeps on translating:
'Life after life after life goes by

without poetry,
without seemliness,   40
without love.'

The Mutes
   [1] Primordial language.

QUESTIONS
1. Explain the title.   **2.** Why does the tribute go on "buzzing in her ear" (l. 28)?
3. Is this poem an attack on men? Explain.

Unwanted   1963

EDWARD FIELD   [b. 1924]

The poster with my picture on it
Is hanging on the bulletin board in the Post Office.

I stand by it hoping to be recognized
Posing first full face and then profile

But everybody passes by and I have to admit
The photograph was taken some years ago.

I was unwanted then and I'm unwanted now
Ah guess ah'll go up echo mountain and crah.

I wish someone would find my fingerprints somewhere
Maybe on a corpse and say, You're it.   10

Description: Male, or reasonably so
Complexion white, but not lily-white

Thirty-fivish, and looks it lately
Five-feet-nine and one-hundred-thirty pounds: no physique

Black hair going gray, hairline receding fast
What used to be curly, now fuzzy

Brown eyes starey under beetling brow
Mole on chin, probably will become a wen

It is perfectly obvious that he was not popular at school
No good at baseball, and wet his bed.   20

His aliases tell his history: Dumbell, Good-for-nothing,
Jewboy, Fieldinsky, Skinny, Fierce Face, Greaseball, Sissy.

Warning: This man is not dangerous, answers to any name
Responds to love, don't call him or he will come.

Bitch

1984

CAROLYN KIZER [b. 1925]

Now, when he and I meet, after all these years,
I say to the bitch inside me, don't start growling.
He isn't a trespasser anymore,
Just an old acquaintance tipping his hat.
My voice says, "Nice to see you,"
As the bitch starts to bark hysterically.
He isn't an enemy now,
Where are your manners, I say, as I say,
"How are the children? They must be growing up."
At a kind word from him, a look like the old days,   10
The bitch changes her tone: she begins to whimper.
She wants to snuggle up to him, to cringe.
Down, girl! Keep your distance
Or I'll give you a taste of the choke-chain.
"Fine, I'm just fine," I tell him.
She slobbers and grovels.
After all, I am her mistress. She is basically loyal.
It's just that she remembers how she came running
Each evening, when she heard his step;
How she lay at his feet and looked up adoringly   20
Though he was absorbed in his paper;
Or, bored with her devotion, ordered her to the kitchen
Until he was ready to play.
But the small careless kindnesses
When he'd had a good day, or a couple of drinks,
Come back to her now, seem more important
Than the casual cruelties, the ultimate dismissal.
"It's nice to know you are doing so well," I say.
He couldn't have taken you with him;
You were too demonstrative, too clumsy,   30
Not like the well-groomed pets of his new friends.
"Give my regards to your wife," I say. You gag
As I drag you off by the scruff,
Saying, "Goodbye! Goodbye! Nice to have seen you again."

QUESTIONS
1. Who is being addressed in lines 13 and 14? **2.** In what ways does the title suit
the poem? Consider the tone of "Bitch," as well as the many connotations of the

word, in answering this question.   **3.** What is "the ultimate dismissal" referred to in line 27?   **4.** How would you describe the speaker's present feelings about her former relationship?

The Farmer's Wife   1960

ANNE SEXTON   [1928–1974]

From the hodge porridge
of their country lust,
their local life in Illinois,
where all their acres look
like a sprouting broom factory,
they name just ten years now
that she has been his habit;
as again tonight he'll say
honey bunch let's go
and she will not say how there   10
must be more to living
than this brief bright bridge
of the raucous bed or even
the slow braille touch of him
like a heavy god grown light,
that old pantomime of love
that she wants although
it leaves her still alone,
built back again at last,
minds apart from him, living   20
her own self in her own words
and hating the sweat of the house
they keep when they finally lie
each in separate dreams
and then how she watches him,
still strong in the blowzy bag
of his usual sleep while
her young years bungle past
their same marriage bed
and she wishes him cripple, or poet,   30
or even lonely, or sometimes,
better, my lover, dead.

Living in Sin

1955

ADRIENNE RICH [b. 1929]

She had thought the studio would keep itself;
no dust upon the furniture of love.
Half heresy, to wish the taps less vocal,
the panes relieved of grime. A plate of pears,
a piano with a Persian shawl, a cat
stalking the picturesque amusing mouse
had risen at his urging.
Not that at five each separate stair would writhe
under the milkman's tramp; that morning light
so coldly would delineate the scraps   10
of last night's cheese and three sepulchral bottles;
that on the kitchen shelf among the saucers
a pair of beetle-eyes would fix her own—
Envoy from some village in the moldings . . .
Meanwhile, he, with a yawn,
sounded a dozen notes upon the keyboard,
declared it out of tune, shrugged at the mirror,
rubbed at his beard, went out for cigarettes;
while she, jeered by the minor demons,
pulled back the sheets and made the bed and found   20
a towel to dust the table-top,
and let the coffee-pot boil over on the stove.
By evening she was back in love again,
though not so wholly but throughout the night
she woke sometimes to feel the daylight coming
like a relentless milkman up the stairs.

Crow's First Lesson[1]

1970

TED HUGHES [b. 1930]

God tried to teach Crow how to talk.
"Love," said God. "Say, Love."

Crow's First Lesson
   [1] In Hughes's collection of poems about him, Crow seems to be a demigod, combining human and animal traits. His exploits form a kind of creation myth.

Crow gaped, and the white shark crashed into the sea
And went rolling downwards, discovering its own depth.

"No, no," said God, "Say Love, Now try it. LOVE."
Crow gaped, and a bluefly, a tsetse, a mosquito
Zoomed out and down
To their sundry flesh-pots.

"A final try," said God. "Now, LOVE."
Crow convulsed, gaped, retched and   10
Man's bodiless prodigious head
Bulbed out onto the earth, with swivelling eyes,
Jabbering protest—

And Crow retched again, before God could stop him.
And woman's vulva dropped over man's neck and tightened.
The two struggled together on the grass.
God struggled to part them, cursed, wept—

Crow flew guiltily off.

The ABC of Aerobics   1987

PETER MEINKE   [b. 1932]

Air seeps through alleys and our diaphragms
balloon blackly with this mix of
carbon monoxide and the thousand corrosives a city
doles out free to its constituents;
everyone's jogging through Edgemont Park,
frightened by death and fatty tissue,
gasping at the maximal heart rate,
hoping to outlive all the others streaming
in the lanes like lemmings lurching toward their last
jump. I join in despair   10
knowing my arteries jammed with
lint and tobacco, lard and bourbon—my
medical history a noxious marsh:
newts and moles slink through the sodden veins,
owls hoot in the lungs' dark branches;
probably I shall keel off the john like
queer Uncle George and lie on the bathroom floor
raging about Shirley Clark, my true love in
seventh grade, God bless her wherever she lives

tied to that turkey who hugely   20
undervalues the beauty of her tiny earlobes, one
view of which (either one: they are both perfect)
would add years to my life, and I could skip these
X-rays, turn in my insurance card, and trade
yoga and treadmills and jogging and zen and
zucchini for drinking and dreaming of her, breathing hard.

QUESTIONS
1. Who is "that turkey" (l. 20)?   **2.** What is the tone of the poem? Identify some devices the poet uses to achieve that tone.   **3.** Is this a poem about environmental pollution? Explain.

Daddy   1965

SYLVIA PLATH   [1932–1963]

You do not do, you do not do
Any more, black shoe
In which I have lived like a foot
For thirty years, poor and white,
Barely daring to breathe or Achoo.

Daddy, I have had to kill you,
You died before I had time—
Marble-heavy, a bag full of God,
Ghastly statue with one gray toe
Big as a Frisco seal   10

And a head in the freakish Atlantic
Where it pours bean green over blue
In the waters off beautiful Nauset.
I used to pray to recover you.
Ach, du.[1]

In the German tongue, in the Polish town
Scraped flat by the roller
Of wars, wars, wars.
But the name of the town is common.
My Polack friend   20

Daddy
   [1] German for "Ah, you."

Says there are a dozen or two.
So I never could tell where you
Put your foot, your root,
I never could talk to you.
The tongue stuck in my jaw.

It stuck in a barb wire snare.
Ich, ich, ich, ich,[2]
I could hardly speak.
I thought every German was you.
And the language obscene   30

An engine, an engine
Chuffing me off like a Jew.
A Jew to Dachau, Auschwitz, Belsen.
I began to talk like a Jew.
I think I may well be a Jew.

The snows of the Tyrol, the clear beer of Vienna
Are not very pure or true.
With my gypsy ancestress and my weird luck
And my Taroc pack and my Taroc pack
I may be a bit of a Jew.   40

I have always been scared of *you,*
With your Luftwaffe,[3] your gobbledygoo.
And your neat mustache
And your Aryan eye, bright blue.
Panzer-man,[4] panzer-man, O You—

Not God but a swastika
So black no sky could squeak through.
Every woman adores a Fascist,
The boot in the face, the brute
Brute heart of a brute like you.   50

You stand at the blackboard, daddy,
In the picture I have of you,
A cleft in your chin instead of your foot
But no less a devil for that, no not
Any less the black man who

---

[2] German for "I, I, I, I."
[3] Name of the German air force during World War II.
[4] Panzer refers to German armored divisions during World War II.

Bit my pretty red heart in two.
I was ten when they buried you.
At twenty I tried to die
And get back, back, back to you.   60
I thought even the bones would do

But they pulled me out of the sack,
And they stuck me together with glue.
And then I knew what to do.
I made a model of you,
A man in black with a Meinkampf⁵ look

And a love of the rack and the screw.
And I said I do, I do.
So daddy, I'm finally through.
The black telephone's off at the root,
The voices just can't worm through.   70

If I've killed one man, I've killed two—
The vampire who said he was you
And drank my blood for a year,
Seven years, if you want to know.
Daddy, you can lie back now.

There's a stake in your fat black heart
And the villagers never liked you.
They are dancing and stamping on you.
They always *knew* it was you.
Daddy, daddy, you bastard, I'm through.   80

QUESTIONS

1. How do the allusions to Nazism function in the poem? **2.** Does the poem exhibit the speaker's love for her father or her hatred for him? Explain. **3.** What sort of man does the speaker marry (see stanzas 13 and 14)? **4.** How does the speaker characterize her husband and her father in the last two stanzas? Might the "Daddy" of the last line of the poem refer to something more than the speaker's father? Explain.

WRITING TOPIC

What is the effect of the peculiar structure, idiosyncratic rhyme, unusual words (such as *achoo, gobbledygoo*), and repetitions in the poem? What emotional associations does the title "Daddy" possess? Are those associations reinforced or contradicted by the poem?

---

⁵ *My Battle*, the title of Adolf Hitler's political autobiography.

Power[1]   1978

AUDRE LORDE   [1934–1992]

The difference between poetry and rhetoric
is being
ready to kill
yourself
instead of your children.

I am trapped on a desert of raw gunshot wounds
and a dead child dragging his shattered black
face off the edge of my sleep
blood from his punctured cheeks and shoulders
is the only liquid for miles and my stomach   10
churns at the imagined taste while
my mouth splits into dry lips
without loyalty or reason
thirsting for the wetness of his blood
as it sinks into the whiteness
of the desert where I am lost
without imagery or magic
trying to make power out of hatred and destruction
trying to heal my dying son with kisses
only the sun will bleach his bones quicker.   20

The policeman who shot down a 10-year-old in Queens[2]
stood over the boy with his cop shoes in childish blood
and a voice said "Die you little motherfucker" and
there are tapes to prove that. At his trial
this policeman said in his own defense
"I didn't notice the size or nothing else

Power
  [1] "'Power' . . . is a poem written about Clifford Glover, the ten-year-old Black child shot by a
cop who was acquitted by a jury on which a Black woman sat. In fact, the day I heard on the radio
that O'Shea had been acquitted, I was going across town on Eighty-eighth Street and I had to pull
over. A kind of fury rose up in me; the sky turned red. I felt so sick. I felt as if I would drive this
car into a wall, into the next person I saw. So I pulled over. I took out my journal just to air some
of my fury, to get it out of my fingertips. Those expressed feelings are that poem" (Audre Lorde,
"My Words Will Be There," in *Black Women Writers* (1950–1980), ed. Mari Evans, New York,
1983, p. 266).
  [2] Queens is a borough in New York City.

only the color." and
there are tapes to prove that, too.

Today that 37-year-old white man with 13 years of police forcing
has been set free   30
by 11 white men who said they were satisfied
justice had been done
and one black woman who said
"They convinced me" meaning
they had dragged her 4' 10" black woman's frame
over the hot coals of four centuries of white male approval
until she let go the first real power she ever had
and lined her own womb with cement
to make a graveyard for our children.

I have not been able to touch the destruction within me.   40
But unless I learn to use
the difference between poetry and rhetoric
my power too will run corrupt as poisonous mold
or lie limp and useless as an unconnected wire
and one day I will take my teenaged plug
and connect it to the nearest socket
raping an 85-year-old white woman
who is somebody's mother
and as I beat her senseless and set a torch to her bed
a greek chorus will be singing in ¾ time[3]   50
"Poor thing. She never hurt a soul. What beasts they are."

There Is a Girl Inside   1977

LUCILLE CLIFTON   [b. 1936]

there is a girl inside.
she is randy as a wolf.
she will not walk away
and leave these bones
to an old woman.

she is a green tree
in a forest of kindling.

Power
[3] In classical Greek tragedy, a chorus chanted in response to the action in the play. Three-quarter time is waltz rhythm.

she is a green girl
in a used poet.

she has waited   10
patient as a nun
for the second coming,
when she can break through gray hairs
into blossom

and her lovers will harvest
honey and thyme
and the woods will be wild
with the damn wonder of it.

QUESTIONS

1. Who is the "girl" of this poem? What is she "inside" of? **2.** What are the "bones" of the first stanza? What does the speaker's statement that she will not defer to old women tell us about her? **3.** Describe the prevailing metaphor of the poem.

WRITING TOPIC

Compare this poem with Helen Sorrells's "From a Correct Address in a Suburb of a Major City." What do the two speakers share? In what ways are they different (p. 483).

Hard Mornings (1)   1973

KATHLEEN WIEGNER   [b. 1938]

You would take
everything
I had

and say
you'd earned it

with your
young body
and occasional
concern

as if it were hard.   10

At times
you stand
at the bedroom
window excited
by the girls' legs
flashing in the street

as if I had not
been with you
all night
long.

One time   20
you got excited
just talking
about them,

God, you said,
those short skirts
and I was lying
beside you
with nothing on.

The Trains   1984

WILLIAM HEYEN   [b. 1940]

Signed by Franz Paul Stangl, Commandant,
there is in Berlin a document,
an order of transmittal from Treblinka:[1]

248 freight cars of clothing,
400,000 gold watches,
25 freight cars of women's hair.

Some clothing was kept, some pulped for paper.
The finest watches were never melted down.
All the women's hair was used for mattresses, or dolls.

---

[1] A notorious Nazi concentration camp and extermination center located in Poland, northeast
of Warsaw.

Would these words like to use some of that same paper?   10
One of those watches may pulse in your own wrist.
Does someone you know collect dolls, or sleep on human hair?

He is dead at last, Commandant Stangl of Treblinka,
but the camp's three syllables still sound like freight cars
straining around a curve, Treblinka,

Treblinka. Clothing, time in gold watches,
women's hair for mattresses and dolls' heads.
Treblinka. The trains from Treblinka.

QUESTIONS

1. Show how the language of this poem (diction, imagery, sound pattern) evokes an emotional response.   **2.** How can such language, quietly celebrating the thrift and productivity of the Treblinka staff, generate such a response?   **3.** Discuss the poet's use of *Treblinka* as a pattern of sound.

WRITING TOPIC

Compare this poem with Anthony Hecht's "'More Light! More Light!'" and analyze the techniques each poet uses to move his readers.

Sex without Love   1984

SHARON OLDS   [b. 1942]

How do they do it, the ones who make love
without love? Beautiful as dancers,
gliding over each other like ice skaters
over the ice, fingers hooked
inside each other's bodies, faces
red as steak, wine, wet as the
children at birth whose mothers are going to
give them away. How do they come to the
come to the   come to the   God   come to the
still waters, and not love   10
the one who came there with them, light
rising slowly as steam off their joined
skin? These are the true religious,
the purists, the pros, the ones who will not
accept a false Messiah, love the
priest instead of the God. They do not

mistake the lover for their own pleasure,
they are like great runners: they know they are alone
with the road surface, the cold, the wind,
the fit of their shoes, their over-all cardio-   20
vascular health—just factors, like the partner
in the bed, and not the truth, which is the
single body alone in the universe
against its own best time.

QUESTIONS
1. Characterize the speaker's attitude toward "the ones who make love without love." **2.** Who are the "These" of line 13? **3.** What is the effect of the repetitions in lines 8 and 9? **4.** What does "factors" of line 21 refer to? **5.** Put into your own words the "truth" referred to in the final three lines. Is the speaker using the word straightforwardly or ironically? Explain.

The Victims   1984

SHARON OLDS   [b. 1942]

When Mother divorced you, we were glad. She took it and
took it, in silence, all those years and then
kicked you out, suddenly, and her
kids loved it. Then you were fired, and we
grinned inside, the way people grinned when
Nixon's helicopter lifted off the South
Lawn for the last time. We were tickled
to think of your office taken away,
your secretaries taken away,
your lunches with three double bourbons,   10
your pencils, your reams of paper. Would they take your
suits back, too, those dark
carcasses hung in your closet, and the black
noses of your shoes with their large pores?
She had taught us to take it, to hate you and take it
until we pricked with her for your
annihilation, Father. Now I
pass the bums in doorways, the white
slugs of their bodies gleaming through slits in their
suits of compressed silt, the stained   20
flippers of their hands, the underwater
fire of their eyes, ships gone down with the
lanterns lit, and I wonder who took it and

took it from them in silence until they had
given it all away and had nothing
left but this.

Say You Love Me   1989

MOLLY PEACOCK   [b. 1947]

What happened earlier I'm not sure of.
Of course he was drunk, but often he was.
His face looked like a ham on a hook above

me—I was pinned to the chair because
he'd hunkered over me with arms like jaws
pried open by the chair arms. "Do you love

me?" he began to sob. "Say you love me!"
I held out. I was probably fifteen.
What had happened? Had my mother—had she

said or done something? Or had he just been   10
drinking too long after work? "He'll get *mean*,"
my sister hissed, "just *tell* him." I brought my knee

up to kick him, but was too scared. Nothing
could have got the words out of me then. Rage
shut me up, yet "DO YOU?" was beginning

to peel, as of live layers of skin, age
from age from age from him until he gazed
through hysteria as a wet baby thing

repeating, "Do you love me? Say you do,"
in baby chokes, only loud, for they came   20
from a man. There wouldn't be a rescue

from my mother, still at work. The same
choking sobs said, "Love me, love me," and my game
was breaking down because I couldn't do

anything, not escape into my own
refusal, *I won't, I won't,* not fantasize
a kind, rich father, not fill the narrowed zone,

empty except for confusion until the size
of my fear ballooned as I saw his eyes,
blurred, taurean—my sister screamed—unknown,   30

unknown to me, a voice rose and leveled
off, "I love you," I said. *"Say 'I love you,*
Dad!'" "I love you, Dad," I whispered, leveled

by defeat into a cardboard image, untrue,
unbending. I was surprised I could move
as I did to get up, but he stayed, burled

onto the chair—my monstrous fear—she screamed,
my sister, "Dad, the phone! Go answer it!"
The phone wasn't ringing, yet he seemed

to move toward it, and I ran. He had a fit—   40
"It's not ringing!"—but I was at the edge of it
as he collapsed into the chair and blamed

both of us at a distance. No, the phone
was not ringing. There was no world out there,
so there we remained, completely alone.

QUESTIONS
1. Is the speaker a child or an adult? Explain.   **2.** How do the images of the sixth stanza capture the speaker's feelings?   **3.** When the speaker finally capitulates to her father's demand, she describes herself as "leveled / by defeat into a cardboard image, untrue, / unbending." What does she mean?   **4.** Explain what the speaker means by "my game" (l. 23).

WRITING TOPIC
What would motivate a parent, even a drunken one, to make the kind of demand the father makes on his daughter?

The Sunday News   1986

DANA GIOIA   [b. 1950]

Looking for something in the Sunday paper,
I flipped by accident through *Local Weddings*,
Yet missed the photograph until I saw
Your name among the headings.

And there you were, looking almost unchanged,
Your hair still long, though now long out of style,
And you still wore that stiff and serious look
You called a smile.

I felt as though we sat there face to face.
My stomach tightened. I read the item through.   10
It said too much about both families,
Too little about you.

Finished at last, I threw the paper down,
Stung by jealousy, my mind aflame,
Hating this man, this stranger whom you loved,
This printed name.

And yet I clipped it out to put away
Inside a book like something I might use,
A scrap I knew I wouldn't read again
But couldn't bear to lose.   20

WRITING TOPIC
Write an essay in which you analyze the feelings that might cause a rejected suitor
to do what the speaker describes doing in the final stanza.

Teodoro Luna's Two Kisses   1990

ALBERTO RÍOS   [b. 1952]

Mr. Teodoro Luna in his later years had taken to kissing
His wife
Not so much with his lips as with his brows.
This is not to say he put his forehead

Against her mouth—
Rather, he would lift his eyebrows, once, quickly:
Not so vigorously he might be confused with the villain
Famous in the theaters, but not so little as to be thought
A slight movement, one of accident. This way
He kissed her   10
Often and quietly, across tables and through doorways,
Sometimes in photographs, and so through the years themselves.
This was his passion, that only she might see. The chance
He might feel some movement on her lips
Toward laughter.

QUESTIONS
1. Characterize the tone of this poem.   **2.** What kind of person is Teodoro Luna?
What kind of person is his wife?   **3.** What is the purpose of Teodoro Luna's second
kind of kiss? Do we know whether he achieves his purpose? Explain.

WRITING TOPIC
Use your imagination to speculate on the nature of Teodoro Luna's marriage and
how it might have led him to devise his unusual way of kissing his wife.

Self-Portrait with Politics   1984

KATE DANIELS   [b. 1953]

At the dinner table, my brother says something
Republican he knows I will hate.
He has said it only for me, hoping
I will rise to the argument as I usually do
so he can call me "communist"
and accuse me of terrible things—not loving
the family, hating the country, unsatisfied
with my life. I feel my fingers tighten
on my fork and ask for more creamed potatoes
to give me time to think.   10

He's right: It's true I am not satisfied
with life. Each time I come home
my brother hates me more for the life
of the mind I have chosen to live.
He works in a factory and can never understand
why I am paid a salary for teaching poetry

just as I can never understand his factory job
where everyone loves or hates the boss like god.
He was so intelligent as a child
his teachers were scared of him.   20
He did everything well and fast
and then shot rubberbands at the girls' legs
and metal lunchboxes lined up neatly beneath the desks.
Since then, something happened I don't know about.
Now he drives a forklift every day.
He moves things in boxes from one place
to another place. I have never worked
in a factory and can only imagine
the tedium, the thousand escapes
the bright mind must make.   30

But tonight I will not fight again.
I just nod and swallow and in spite
of everything remember my brother as a child.
When I was six and he was five, I taught him everything
I learned in school each day while we waited for dinner.
I remember his face—smiling always,
the round, brown eyes, and how his lower lip
seemed always wet and ready to kiss.
I remember for a long time his goal in life
was to be a dog, how we were forced   40
to scratch his head, the pathetic sound
of his human bark. Now he glowers
and acts like a tyrant and cannot eat
and thinks I think
I am superior to him.

The others ignore him as they usually do:
My mother with her bristly hair.
My father just wanting to get back to the TV.
My husband rolling his eyes in a warning at me.

It has taken a long time to get a politics   50
I can live with in a world that gave me
poetry and my brother an assembly line.
I accept my brother for what he is
and believe in the beauty of work
but also know the reality of waste,
the good minds ground down through circumstance
and loss. I mourn the loss of all I think
he could have been, and this is what he feels,

I guess, and cannot face and hates me
for reminding him of what is gone and wasted   60
and won't come back.

For once, it's too sad to know all this.
So I give my brother back his responsibility
or blandly blame it all on sociology,
and imagine sadly how it could have been different,
how it will be different for the son I'll bear.
And how I hope in thirty years he'll touch
his sister as they touched as children
and let nothing come between the blood they share.

QUESTIONS

1. Characterize the speaker's feelings toward her brother. Does her brother have reason to think she feels superior to him? Explain.   **2.** The speaker says that her brother is right that she is not satisfied with her life. Is her brother satisfied with his life? Explain.   **3.** Explain the effect of the simile in line 18.   **4.** What do lines 39–42 add to the speaker's self-portrait?   **5.** Paraphrase lines 62–64.

WRITING TOPICS

1. Write an essay or a letter as if you were the speaker's brother responding to the poem.   **2.** If you have had an experience similar to the one described in this poem of becoming alienated from a brother or sister because your lives have taken different directions, describe how and when the estrangement occurred and how you have dealt with it.

Complaint   1985

GJERTRUD SCHNACKENBERG   [b. 1953]

I lean over the rail toward the dark town,
The rail a streak of cloud in piled snow,
The stairs cloud-piled around the balcony.
His house is lit below,

One light among the branches at my feet.
I look, and press my hands into the snow.
I think that I am inconsolable.
No path to him, I know

Of none but that I follow into sleep
To where he waits, I hurry through the snow   10

To where the man stands waiting in the dream.
He loves, he tells me so,

He kisses me until the ceiling dome
Parts overhead and snow is coming through,
Until heaven itself, empty of snow,
Opens above us too,

His hands melting the snow into my hair
Until I wake. Since he'll not have me, no,
I come out to the balcony and press
My hands into the snow,   20

And close my eyes, since he is blind to me.
Since he'll not hear me, then I'll be deaf too,
And draw my hair into a set of strings
I'll take a scissors to.

QUESTIONS
1. Characterize the speaker.   **2.** What is her problem?   **3.** What is her only path
to the man she loves? Characterize her "meeting" with him.   **4.** How does she
propose to deal with her inability to attract the man?

WRITING TOPIC
Describe the unusual metrical pattern and rhyme scheme in this poem. Defend the
proposition that the formal structure of the poem reinforces its sense.

LOVE
AND
HATE

Judith and Her Maidservant with the Head of Holofernes, ca. 1625 by Artemisia Gentileschi

DRAMA

Othello

WILLIAM SHAKESPEARE [1564–1616]

ca. 1604

CHARACTERS

Duke of Venice
Brabantio, a Senator
Senators
Gratiano, Brother to Brabantio
Lodovico, Kinsman to Brabantio
Othello, a noble Moor; in the service
  of the Venetian State
Cassio, his Lieutenant
Iago, his Ancient
Roderigo, a Venetian Gentleman

Montano, Othello's predecessor in
  the Government of Cyprus
Clown, Servant to Othello
Desdemona, Daughter to Brabantio,
  and Wife to Othello
Emilia, Wife to Iago
Bianca, Mistress to Cassio
**Sailor, Officers, Gentlemen,
  Messengers, Musicians, Heralds,
  Attendants**

SCENE

For the first Act, in Venice; during the rest of the Play, at a Sea-port in Cyprus

Act I

SCENE 1. Venice. A Street.

(Enter Roderigo and Iago.)

Roderigo.   Tush! Never tell me; I take it much unkindly
  That thou, Iago, who has had my purse
  As if the strings were thine, shouldst know of this.[1]

---

[1] I.e., Othello's successful courtship of Desdemona.

Iago. 'Sblood,[2] but you will not hear me:
   If ever I did dream of such a matter,
   Abhor me.
Roderigo.   Thou told'st me thou didst hold him[3] in thy hate.
Iago.   Despise me if I do not. Three great ones of the city,
   In personal suit to make me his lieutenant,
   Off-capp'd[4] to him; and, by the faith of man,   10
   I know my price, I am worth no worse a place;
   But he, as loving his own pride and purposes,
   Evades them, with a bombast circumstance[5]
   Horribly stuff'd with epithets of war;
   And, in conclusion,
   Nonsuits[6] my mediators;[7] for, 'Certes,'[8] says he,
   'I have already chosen my officer.'
   And what was he?
   Forsooth, a great arithmetician,
   One Michael Cassio, a Florentine,   20
   A fellow almost damn'd in a fair wife;[9]
   That never set a squadron in the field,
   Nor the division of a battle knows
   More than a spinster; unless[10] the bookish theoric,[11]
   Wherein the toged consuls can propose
   As masterly as he: mere prattle, without practice,
   Is all his soldiership. But he, sir, had the election;
   And I—of whom his eyes had seen the proof
   At Rhodes, at Cyprus, and on other grounds
   Christian and heathen—must be be-lee'd[12] and calm'd   30
   By debitor and creditor; this counter-caster,[13]
   He, in good time, must his lieutenant be,
   And I—God bless the mark!—his Moorship's ancient.[14]
Roderigo.   By heaven, I rather would have been his hangman.
Iago.   Why, there's no remedy: 'tis the curse of service,
   Preferment goes by letter and affection,
   Not by the old gradation,[15] where each second
   Stood heir to the first. Now, sir, be judge yourself,
   Whe'r[16] I in any just term am affin'd[17]
   To love the Moor.

---

2 By God's blood.   3 I.e., Othello.   4 Took off their caps.   5 Pompous wordiness, circumlocution.   6 Turns down.   7 Spokesmen.   8 In truth.   9 A much debated phrase. In the Italian source the Captain (i.e., Cassio) was married, and it may be that Shakespeare originally intended Bianca to be Cassio's wife but later changed his mind and failed to alter the phrase here accordingly. Or perhaps Iago simply sneers at Cassio as a notorious ladies' man.   10 Except.   11 Theory.   12 Left without wind for my sails.   13 Bookkeeper (*cf.* "arithmetician" above).   14 Ensign (but Iago's position in the play seems to be that of Othello's aide-de-camp).   15 Seniority.   16 Whether.   17 Obliged.

Roderigo.   I would not follow him then.   40
Iago.   O! sir, content you;
  I follow him to serve my turn upon him;
  We cannot all be masters, nor all masters
  Cannot be truly follow'd. You shall mark
  Many a duteous and knee-crooking knave,
  That, doting on his own obsequious bondage,
  Wears out his time, much like his master's ass,
  For nought but provender, and when he's old, cashier'd;
  Whip me such honest knaves. Others there are
  Who, trimm'd in forms and visages of duty,   50
  Keep yet their hearts attending on themselves,
  And, throwing but shows of service on their lords,
  Do well thrive by them, and when they have lin'd their coats
  Do themselves homage: these fellows have some soul;
  And such a one do I profess myself. For, sir,
  It is as sure as you are Roderigo,
  Were I the Moor, I would not be Iago:
  In following him, I follow but myself;
  Heaven is my judge, not I for love and duty,
  But seeming so, for my peculiar end: 60
  For when my outward action doth demonstrate
  The native act and figure of my heart
  In compliment extern,[18] 'tis not long after
  But I will wear my heart upon my sleeve
  For daws to peck at: I am not what I am.
Roderigo.   What a full fortune does the thick-lips owe,[19]
  If he can carry 't thus!
Iago.   Call up her father;
  Rouse him, make after him, poison his delight,
  Proclaim him in the streets, incense her kinsmen,
  And, though he in a fertile climate dwell,[20]   70
  Plague him with flies; though that his joy be joy,
  Yet throw such changes of vexation on 't
  As it may lose some colour.
Roderigo.   Here is her father's house; I'll call aloud.
Iago.   Do; with like timorous[21] accent and dire yell
  As when, by night and negligence, the fire
  Is spied in populous cities.
Roderigo.   What, ho! Brabantio: Signior Brabantio, ho!
Iago.   Awake! what, ho! Brabantio! thieves! thieves! thieves!
  Look to your house, your daughter, and your bags!   80
  Thieves! thieves!

---

[18] External show.   [19] Own.   [20] I.e., is fortunate.   [21] Frightening.

(Enter Brabantio, above, at a window.)

Brabantio.   What is the reason of this terrible summons?
    What is the matter there?
Roderigo.   Signior, is all your family within?
Iago.   Are your doors lock'd?
Brabantio.   Why? wherefore ask you this?
Iago.   'Zounds![22] sir, you're robb'd; for shame, put on your gown;
    Your heart is burst, you have lost half your soul;
    Even now, now, very now, an old black ram
    Is tupping[23] your white ewe. Arise, arise!
    Awake the snorting[24] citizens with the bell,   90
    Or else the devil will make a grandsire of you.
    Arise, I say.
Brabantio.   What! have you lost your wits?
Roderigo.   Most reverend signior, do you know my voice?
Brabantio.   Not I, what are you?
Roderigo.   My name is Roderigo.
Brabantio.   The worser welcome:
    I have charg'd thee not to haunt about my doors:
    In honest plainness thou hast heard me say
    My daughter is not for thee; and now, in madness,
    Being full of supper and distempering draughts,
    Upon malicious knavery dost thou come   100
    To start my quiet.
Roderigo.   Sir, sir, sir!
Brabantio.   But thou must needs be sure
    My spirit and my place[25] have in them power
    To make this bitter to thee.
Roderigo.   Patience, good sir.
Brabantio.   What tell'st thou me of robbing? this is Venice;
    My house is not a grange.[26]
Roderigo.   Most grave Brabantio,
    In simple and pure soul I come to you.
Iago.   'Zounds! sir, you are one of those that will not serve God if the devil
    bid you. Because we come to do you service and you think we are ruffians,
    you'll have your daughter covered with a Barbary horse; you'll have your
    nephews neigh to you; you'll have coursers for cousins and gennets[27] for
    germans.[28]
Brabantio.   What profane wretch art thou?
Iago.   I am one, sir, that comes to tell you, your daughter and the Moor are
    now making the beast with two backs.

---

[22] By God's wounds.   [23] Copulating.   [24] Snoring.   [25] Position.   [26] Isolated
farm house.   [27] Spanish horses.   [28] Blood relations.

Brabantio.   Thou art a villain.

Iago.   You are—a senator.

Brabantio.   This thou shalt answer; I know thee, Roderigo.

Roderigo.   Sir, I will answer any thing. But, I beseech you,   120
If 't be your pleasure and most wise consent,—
As partly, I find, it is,—that your fair daughter,
At this odd-even[29] and dull watch o' the night,
Transported with no worse nor better guard
But with a knave of common hire, a gondolier,
To the gross clasps of a lascivious Moor,—
If this be known to you, and your allowance,[30]
We then have done you bold and saucy wrongs;
But if you know not this, my manners tell me
We have your wrong rebuke. Do not believe   130
That, from[31] the sense of all civility,
I thus would play and trifle with your reverence:
Your daughter, if you have not given her leave,
I say again, hath made a gross revolt;
Tying her duty, beauty, wit and fortunes
In[32] an extravagant[33] and wheeling stranger
Of here and every where. Straight satisfy yourself:
If she be in her chamber or your house,
Let loose on me the justice of the state
For thus deluding you.

Brabantio.   Strike on the tinder, ho!   140
Give me a taper! call up all my people!
This accident[34] is not unlike my dream;
Belief of it oppresses me already.
Light, I say! light!   *(Exit, from above.)*

Iago.   Farewell, for I must leave you:
It seems not meet nor wholesome to my place
To be produc'd,[35] as, if I stay, I shall,
Against the Moor; for I do know the state,
However this may gall him with some check,[36]
Cannot with safety cast him; for he's embark'd
With such loud reason to the Cyprus wars,—   150
Which even now stand in act,—that, for their souls,
Another of his fathom[37] they have none,
To lead their business; in which regard,
Though I do hate him as I do hell-pains,
Yet, for necessity of present life,

---

[29] Between night and morning.   [30] By your approval.   [31] Away from.   [32] To.
[33] Expatriate.   [34] Happening.   [35] I.e., as a witness.   [36] Restraining adversity.
[37] Caliber, ability.

I must show out a flag and sign of love,
Which is indeed but sign. That you shall surely find him,
Lead to the Sagittary[38] the raised search;
And there will I be with him. So, farewell.   *(Exit.)*

(Enter below, Brabantio, and servants with torches.)

Brabantio.   It is too true an evil: gone she is,   160
  And what's to come of my despised time
  Is nought but bitterness. Now, Roderigo,
  Where didst thou see her? O, unhappy girl!
  With the Moor, sayst thou? Who would be a father!
  How didst thou know 'twas she? O, she deceives me
  Past thought. What said she to you? Get more tapers!
  Raise all my kindred! Are they married, think you?
Roderigo.   Truly, I think they are.
Brabantio.   O heaven! How got she out? O treason of the blood:
  Fathers, from hence trust not your daughters' minds   170
  By what you see them act. Are there not charms
  By which the property of youth and maidhood
  May be abus'd? Have you not read, Roderigo,
  Of some such thing?
Roderigo.   Yes, sir, I have indeed.
Brabantio.   Call up my brother. O! that you had had her.
  Some one way, some another! Do you know
  Where we may apprehend her and the Moor?
Roderigo.   I think I can discover him, if you please
  To get good guard and go along with me.   180
Brabantio.   Pray you, lead on. At every house I'll call;
  I may command at most. Get weapons, ho!
  And raise some special officers of night.
  On, good Roderigo; I'll deserve[39] your pains.   *(Exeunt.)*

SCENE 2.   Another street.

(Enter Othello, Iago, and Attendants, with torches.)

Iago.   Though in the trade of war I have slain men,
  Yet do I hold it very stuff o' the conscience
  To do no contriv'd murder: I lack iniquity
  Sometimes to do me service. Nine or ten times
  I had thought to have yerk'd[40] him here under the ribs.
Othello.   'Tis better as it is.

---

[38] The name of an inn (?).   [39] I.e., reward.   [40] Stabbed.

Iago.   Nay, but he prated,
And spoke such scurvy and provoking terms
Against your honour
That, with the little godliness I have,
I did full hard forbear him. But, I pray, sir,   10
Are you fast married? Be assur'd of this,
That the magnifico[41] is much belov'd,
And hath in his effect a voice potential
As double[42] as the duke's; he will divorce you,
Or put upon you what restraint and grievance
The law—with all his might to enforce it on—
Will give him cable.[43]
Othello.   Let him do his spite:
My services which I have done the signiory[44]
Shall out-tongue his complaints. 'Tis yet to know,[45]
Which when I know that boasting is an honour   20
I shall promulgate, I fetch my life and being
From men of royal siege, and my demerits[46]
May speak unbonneted[47] to as proud a fortune
As this[48] that I have reach'd; for know, Iago,
But that I love the gentle Desdemona,
I would not my unhoused[49] free condition
Put into circumscription and confine
For the sea's worth. But, look! what lights come yond?
Iago.   Those are the raised[50] father and his friends:
You were best[51] go in.
Othello.   Not I; I must be found: 30
My parts, my title, and my perfect[52] soul
Shall manifest me rightly. Is it they?
Iago.   By Janus,[53] I think no.

(Enter Cassio and certain Officers, with torches.)

Othello.   The servants of the duke, and my lieutenant.
The goodness of the night upon you, friends!
What is the news?
Cassio.   The duke does greet you, general,
And he requires your haste-post-haste appearance,
Even on the instant.

---

[41] One of the grandees, or rulers, of Venice; here, Brabantio.   [42] Iago means that Brabantio's influence equals that of the Doge's with his double vote.   [43] I.e., scope.   [44] The Venetian government.   [45] I.e., the signiory does not as yet know.   [46] Merits.   [47] I.e., as equals.   [48] I.e., that of Desdemona's family.   [49] Unconfined.   [50] Aroused.   [51] Had better.   [52] Untroubled by a bad conscience.   [53] The two-faced Roman god of portals and doors and (hence) of beginnings and ends.

Othello. What is the matter, think you?
Cassio. Something from Cyprus, as I may divine.
    It is a business of some heat;[54] the galleys   40
    Have sent a dozen sequent[55] messengers
    This very night at one another's heels,
    And many of the consuls,[56] rais'd and met,
    Are at the duke's already. You have been hotly call'd for;
    When, being not at your lodging to be found,
    The senate hath sent about three several[57] quests
    To search you out.
Othello. 'Tis well I am found by you.
    I will but spend a word here in the house,
    And go with you.   *(Exit.)*
Cassio. Ancient, what makes he here?
Iago. Faith, he to-night hath boarded a land carrack;[58]   50
    If it prove lawful prize, he's made for ever.
Cassio. I do not understand.
Iago. He's married.
Cassio. To who?

(Re-enter Othello.)

Iago. Marry,[59] to—Come, captain, will you go?
Othello. Have with you.
Cassio. Here comes another troop to seek for you.
Iago. It is Brabantio. General, be advis'd;
    He comes to bad intent.

(Enter Brabantio, Roderigo, and Officers, with torches and weapons.)

Othello. Holla! stand there!
Roderigo. Signior, it is the Moor.
Brabantio. Down with him, thief!

(They draw on both sides.)

Iago. You, Roderigo! Come, sir, I am for you.[60]
Othello. Keep up your bright swords, for the dew will rust them.
    Good signior, you shall more command with years   60
    Than with your weapons.
Brabantio. O thou foul thief! where hast thou stow'd my daughter?
    Damn'd as thou art, thou hast enchanted her;

---

[54] Urgency.   [55] Following one another.   [56] I.e., senators.   [57] Separate.   [58] Treasure ship.   [59] By the Virgin Mary.   [60] Let you and me fight.

For I'll refer me to all things of sense,
If she in chains of magic were not bound,
Whether a maid so tender, fair, and happy,
So opposite to marriage that she shunn'd
The wealthy curled darlings of our nation,
Would ever have, to incur a general mock,
Run from her guardage to the sooty bosom   70
Of such a thing as thou; to fear, not to delight.
Judge me the world, if 'tis not gross in sense[61]
That thou hast practis'd on her with foul charms,
Abus'd her delicate youth with drugs or minerals
That weaken motion:[62] I'll have 't disputed on;
'Tis probable, and palpable to thinking.
I therefore apprehend and do attach[63] thee
For an abuser of the world, a practiser
Of arts inhibited and out of warrant.[64]
Lay hold upon him: if he do resist,   80
Subdue him at his peril.
Othello.   Hold your hands,
Both you of my inclining,[65] and the rest:
Were it my cue to fight, I should have known it
Without a prompter. Where will you that I go
To answer this your charge?
Brabantio.   To prison; till fit time
Of law and course of direct session[66]
Call thee to answer.
Othello.   What if I do obey?
How may the duke be therewith satisfied,
Whose messengers are here about my side,
Upon some present[67] business of the state   90
To bring me to him?
Officer.   'Tis true, most worthy signior;
The duke's in council, and your noble self,
I am sure, is sent for.
Brabantio.   How! the duke in council!
In this time of the night! Bring him away.
Mine's not an idle cause: the duke himself,
Or any of my brothers of the state,[68]
Cannot but feel this wrong as 'twere their own;
For if such actions may have passage free,
Bond-slaves and pagans shall our statesmen be.   (*Exeunt.*)

---

[61] Obvious.   [62] Normal reactions.   [63] Arrest.   [64] Prohibited and illegal.   [65] Party.
[66] Normal process of law.   [67] Immediate, pressing.   [68] Fellow senators.

SCENE 3.   A Council Chamber.

(The Duke and Senators sitting at a table. Officers attending.)

Duke.   There is no composition[69] in these news
   That gives them credit.
First Senator.   Indeed, they are disproportion'd;
   My letters say a hundred and seven galleys.
Duke.   And mine, a hundred and forty.
Second Senator.   And mine, two hundred:
   But though they jump[70] not on a just[71] account,—
   As in these cases, where the aim[72] reports,
   'Tis oft with difference,—yet do they all confirm
   A Turkish fleet, and bearing up to Cyprus.
Duke.   Nay, it is possible enough to judgment:
   I do not so secure me in[73] the error,   10
   But the main article[74] I do approve[75]
   In fearful sense.
Sailor *(within)*.   What, ho! what, ho! what, ho!
Officer.   A messenger from the galleys.

(Enter a Sailor.)

Duke.   Now, what's the business?
Sailor.   The Turkish preparation makes for Rhodes;
   So was I bid report here to the state
   By Signior Angelo.
Duke.   How say you by this change?
First Senator.   This cannot be
   By no[76] assay[77] of reason; 'tis a pageant[78]
   To keep us in false gaze.[79] When we consider
   The importancy of Cyprus to the Turk,   20
   And let ourselves again but understand,
   That as it more concerns the Turk than Rhodes,
   So may he with more facile question bear[80] it,
   For that it stands not in such warlike brace,[81]
   But altogether lacks the abilities
   That Rhodes is dress'd in: if we make thought of this,
   We must not think the Turk is so unskilful
   To leave that latest which concerns him first,

---

[69] Consistency, agreement.   [70] Coincide.   [71] Exact.   [72] Conjecture.   [73] Draw comfort from.   [74] Substance.   [75] Believe.   [76] Any.   [77] Test.   [78] (Deceptive) show.   [79] Looking in the wrong direction.   [80] More easily capture.   [81] State of defense.

Neglecting an attempt of ease and gain,
To wake and wage a danger profitless.   30
Duke.   Nay, in all confidence, he's not for Rhodes.
Officer.   Here is more news.

(Enter a Messenger)

Messenger.   The Ottomites,[82] reverend and gracious,
Steering with due course toward the isle of Rhodes,
Have there injointed[83] them with an after fleet.[84]
First Senator.   Ay, so I thought. How many, as you guess?
Messenger.   Of thirty sail; and now they do re-stem[85]
Their backward course, bearing with frank appearance
Their purposes toward Cyprus. Signior Montano,
Your trusty and most valiant servitor,   40
With his free duty[86] recommends[87] you thus,
And prays you to believe him.
Duke.   'Tis certain then, for Cyprus.
Marcus Luccicos, is not he in town?
First Senator.   He's now in Florence.
Duke.   Write from us to him; post-post-haste dispatch.
First Senator.   Here comes Brabantio and the valiant Moor.

(Enter Brabantio, Othello, Iago, Roderigo, and Officers.)

Duke.   Valiant Othello, we must straight employ you
Against the general enemy Ottoman.
(To Brabantio) I did not see you; welcome, gentle signior;   50
We lack'd your counsel and your help to-night.
Brabantio.   So did I yours. Good your Grace, pardon me;
Neither my place nor aught I heard of business
Hath rais'd me from my bed, nor doth the general care
Take hold of me, for my particular grief
Is of so flood-gate[88] and o'erbearing nature
That it engluts and swallows other sorrows
And it is still itself.
Duke.   Why, what's the matter?
Brabantio.   My daughter! O! my daughter.
Duke.   ⎫
Senators. ⎬   Dead?
Brabantio.   Ay, to me;
She is abus'd, stol'n from me, and corrupted   60

---

[82] Turks.   [83] Joined.   [84] Fleet that followed after.   [85] Steer again.   [86] Unquali-
fied expressions of respect.   [87] Informs.   [88] Torrential.

By spells and medicines bought of mountebanks;
For nature so preposterously to err,
Being not deficient, blind, or lame of sense,
Sans[89] witchcraft could not.

Duke.   Whoe'er he be that in this foul proceeding
Hath thus beguil'd your daughter of herself
And you of her, the bloody book of law
You shall yourself read in the bitter letter
After your own sense; yea, though our proper[90] son
Stood[91] in your action.[92]

Brabantio.   Humbly I thank your Grace.   70
Here is the man, this Moor; whom now, it seems,
Your special mandate for the state affairs
Hath hither brought.

Duke.   ⎫
Senators.   ⎬   We are very sorry for it.

Duke *(to Othello).*   What, in your own part, can you say to this?
Brabantio.   Nothing, but this is so.
Othello.   Most potent, grave, and reverend signiors,
My very noble and approv'd[93] good masters,
That I have ta'en away this old man's daughter,
It is most true; true, I have married her:
The very head and front of my offending   80
Hath this extent, no more. Rude am I in my speech,
And little bless'd with the soft phrase of peace;
For since these arms of mine had seven years' pith,[94]
Till now some nine moons wasted,[95] they have us'd
Their dearest action in the tented field;
And little of this great world can I speak,
More than pertains to feats of broil and battle;
And therefore little shall I grace my cause
In speaking for myself. Yet, by your gracious patience,
I will a round[96] unvarnish'd tale deliver   90
Of my whole course of love; what drugs, what charms,
What conjuration, and what mighty magic,
For such proceeding I am charg'd withal,
I won his daughter.

Brabantio.   A maiden never bold;
Of spirit so still and quiet, that her motion
Blush'd at herself;[97] and she, in spite of nature,
Of years, of country, credit, every thing,

---

[89] Without.   [90] Own.   [91] Were accused.   [92] Suit.   [93] Tested (by past experience).   [94] Strength.   [95] Past.   [96] Blunt.   [97] I.e., (her modesty was such that) she blushed at her own emotions; or: could not move without blushing.

To fall in love with what she fear'd to look on!
It is a judgment maim'd and most imperfect
That will confess[98] perfection so could err   100
Against all rules of nature, and must be driven
To find out practices of cunning hell,
Why this should be. I therefore vouch again
That with some mixtures powerful o'er the blood,
Or with some dram conjur'd to this effect,
He wrought upon her.
Duke.   To vouch this, is no proof,
Without more certain and more overt test
Than these thin habits[99] and poor likelihoods
Of modern[100] seeming do prefer against him.
First Senator.   But, Othello, speak: 110
Did you by indirect and forced courses
Subdue and poison this young maid's affections;
Or came it by request and such fair question[101]
As soul to soul affordeth?
Othello.   I do beseech you;
Send for the lady to the Sagittary,
And let her speak of me before her father:
If you do find me foul in her report,
The trust, the office I do hold of you,
Not only take away, but let your sentence
Even fall upon my life.
Duke.   Fetch Desdemona hither.   120
Othello.   Ancient, conduct them; you best know the place.

(Exeunt Iago and Attendants.)

And, till she come, as truly as to heaven
I do confess the vices of my blood,
So justly to your grave ears I'll present
How I did thrive in this fair lady's love,
And she in mine.
Duke.   Say it, Othello.
Othello.   Her father lov'd me; oft invited me;
Still[102] question'd me the story of my life
From year to year, the battles, sieges, fortunes   130
That I have pass'd.
I ran it through, even from my boyish days
To the very moment that he bade me tell it;

---

[98] Assert.   [99] Weak appearances.   [100] Commonplace.   [101] Conversation.   [102] Always, regularly.

Wherein I spake of most disastrous chances,
Of moving accidents by flood and field,
Of hair-breadth 'scapes i' the imminent deadly breach,
Of being taken by the insolent foe
And sold to slavery, of my redemption thence
And portance[103] in my travel's history;
Wherein of antres[104] vast and deserts idle,[105]   140
Rough quarries, rocks, and hills whose heads touch heaven,
It was my hint[106] to speak, such was the process;
And of the Cannibals that each other eat,
The Anthropophagi,[107] and men whose heads
Do grow beneath their shoulders. This to hear
Would Desdemona seriously incline;
But still the house-affairs would draw her thence;
Which ever as she could with haste dispatch,
She'd come again, and with a greedy ear
Devour up my discourse. Which I observing,   150
Took once a pliant[108] hour, and found good means
To draw from her a prayer of earnest heart
That I would all my pilgrimage dilate,[109]
Whereof by parcels[110] she had something heard,
But not intentively:[111] I did consent;
And often did beguile her of her tears,
When I did speak of some distressful stroke
That my youth suffer'd. My story being done,
She gave me for my pains a world of sighs:
She swore, in faith, 'twas strange, 'twas passing[112] strange;   160
'Twas pitiful, 'twas wondrous pitiful:
She wish'd she had not heard it, yet she wish'd
That heaven had made her[113] such a man; she thank'd me,
And bade me, if I had a friend that lov'd her,
I should but teach him how to tell my story,
And that would woo her. Upon this hint I spake.
She lov'd me for the dangers I had pass'd,
And I lov'd her that she did pity them.
This only is the witchcraft I have us'd:
Here comes the lady; let her witness it.   170

(Enter Desdemona, Iago, and Attendants.)

Duke.   I think this tale would win my daughter too.
Good Brabantio,

---

[103] Behavior.   [104] Caves.   [105] Empty, sterile.   [106] Opportunity.   [107] Man-eaters.
[108] Suitable.   [109] Relate in full.   [110] Piecemeal.   [111] In sequence.   [112] Sur-
passing.   [113] Direct object; not "for her."

Take up this mangled matter at the best;
Men do their broken weapons rather use
Than their bare hands.

Brabantio.   I pray you, hear her speak:
If she confess that she was half the wooer,
Destruction on my head, if my bad blame
Light on the man! Come hither, gentle mistress:
Do you perceive in all this noble company
Where most you owe obedience?

Desdemona.   My noble father,   180
I do perceive here a divided duty:
To you I am bound for life and education;
My life and education both do learn[114] me
How to respect you; you are the lord of duty,
I am hitherto your daughter: but here's my husband;
And so much duty as my mother show'd
To you, preferring you before her father,
So much I challenge[115] that I may profess
Due to the Moor my lord.

Brabantio.   God be with you! I have done.
Please it your Grace, on to the state affairs;   190
I had rather to adopt a child than get it.
Come hither, Moor:
I here do give thee that with all my heart
Which, but thou hast[116] already, with all my heart
I would keep from thee. For your sake,[117] jewel,
I am glad at soul I have no other child;
For thy escape would teach me tyranny,
To hang clogs on them. I have done, my lord.

Duke.   Let me speak like yourself and lay a sentence,[118]
Which as a grize[119] or step, may help these lovers   200
Into your favour.
When remedies are past, the griefs are ended
By seeing the worst, which[120] late on hopes depended.
To mourn a mischief that is past and gone
Is the next way to draw new mischief on.
What cannot be preserv'd when Fortune takes,
Patience her injury a mockery makes.[121]
The robb'd that smiles steals something from the thief;
He robs himself that spends a bootless grief.

Brabantio.   So let the Turk of Cyprus us beguile;   210
We lose it not so long as we can smile.

---

[114] Teach.   [115] Claim as right.   [116] Didn't you have it.   [117] Because of you.   [118] Provide a maxim.   [119] Step.   [120] The antecedent is "griefs."   [121] To suffer an irreparable loss patiently is to make light of injury (i.e., to triumph over adversity).

He bears the sentence[122] well that nothing bears
But the free comfort which from thence he hears;
But he bears both the sentence and the sorrow
That, to pay grief, must of poor patience borrow.
These sentences, to sugar, or to gall,
Being strong on both sides, are equivocal:[123]
But words are words: I never yet did hear
That the bruis'd heart was pierced[124] through the ear.
I humbly beseech you, proceed to the affairs of state.   220

Duke.   The Turk with a most mighty preparation makes for Cyprus. Othello,
the fortitude[125] of the place is best known to you; and though we have there
a substitute of most allowed sufficiency,[126] yet opinion, a sovereign mistress
of effects, throws a more safer voice on you:[127] you must therefore be content
to slubber[128] the gloss of your new fortunes with this more stubborn[129] and
boisterous expedition.

Othello.   The tyrant custom, most grave senators,
Hath made the flinty and steel couch of war
My thrice-driven[130] bed of down: I do agnize[131]
A natural and prompt alacrity   230
I find in hardness, and do undertake
These present wars against the Ottomites.
Most humbly therefore bending to your state,[132]
I crave fit disposition[133] for my wife,
Due reference of place and exhibition,[134]
With such accommodation and besort[135]
As levels with[136] her breeding.

Duke.   If you please,
Be 't at her father's.

Brabantio.   I'll not have it so.

Othello.   Nor I.

Desdemona.   Nor I; I would not there reside,
To put my father in impatient thoughts   240
By being in his eye. Most gracious duke,
To my unfolding[137] lend your gracious ear;
And let me find a charter[138] in your voice
To assist my simpleness.

Duke.   What would you, Desdemona?

Desdemona.   That I did love the Moor to live with him,
My downright violence and storm of fortunes

---

[122] (1) Verdict, (2) Maxim.   [123] Sententious comfort (like the Duke's trite maxims) can hurt
as well as soothe.   [124] (1) Lanced (i.e., cured), (2) Wounded.   [125] Strength.   [126] Admitted competence.   [127] General opinion, which mainly determines action, thinks Cyprus
safer with you in command.   [128] Besmear.   [129] Rough.   [30] Made as soft as possible.
[131] Recognize.   [132] Submitting to your authority.   [133] Disposal.   [134] Provision.
[135] Fitness.   [136] Is proper to.   [137] Explanation.   [138] Permission.

May trumpet to the world; my heart's subdu'd
Even to the very quality of my lord;[139]   250
I saw Othello's visage in his mind,
And to his honours and his valiant parts
Did I my soul and fortunes consecrate.
So that, dear lords, if I be left behind,
A moth of peace, and he go to the war,
The rites[140] for which I love him are bereft me,
And I a heavy interim shall support[141]
By his dear[142] absence. Let me go with him.

Othello.   Let her have your voices.
Vouch with me, heaven, I therefore beg it not
To please the palate of my appetite,   260
Nor to comply with heat,—the young affects[143]
In me defunct,—and proper satisfaction,
But to be free and bounteous to her mind;
And heaven defend[144] your good souls that you think
I will your serious and great business scant
For[145] she is with me. No, when light-wing'd toys
Of feather'd Cupid seel[146] with wanton dulness
My speculative and offic'd instruments,[147]
That[148] my disports corrupt and taint my business,
Let housewives make a skillet of my helm,   270
And all indign[149] and base adversities
Make head against my estimation![150]

Duke.   Be it as you shall privately determine,
Either for her stay or going. The affair cries haste,
And speed must answer it.

First Senator.   You must away to-night.

Othello.   With all my heart.

Duke.   At nine i' the morning here we'll meet again.
Othello, leave some officer behind,
And he shall our commission bring to you;
With such things else of quality and respect   280
As doth import you.[151]

Othello.   So please your Grace, my ancient;
A man he is of honesty and trust:
To his conveyance I assign my wife,
With what else needful your good grace shall think
To be sent after me.

---

[139] I.e., I have become a soldier, like Othello.   [140] I.e., of marriage, or of war, or of both.
[141] Endure.   [142] Closely concerning (i.e., Desdemona).   [143] The passions of youth
(hence, here, *immoderate* sexual passion).   [144] Forbid.   [145] Because.   [146] Blind (v.)
by sewing up the eyelids (a term from falconry).   [147] Reflective and executive faculties and
organs.   [148] So that.   [149] Shameful.   [150] Reputation.   [151] Concern.

Duke.   Let it be so.
Good-night to every one. *(To Brabantio)* And, noble signior,
If virtue no delighted[152] beauty lack,
Your son-in-law is far more fair than black.
First Senator.   Adieu, brave Moor! use Desdemona well.
Brabantio.   Look to her, Moor, if thou hast eyes to see: 290
She has deceiv'd her father, and may thee.

                              (Exeunt Duke, Senators, Officers, &c.)

Othello.   My life upon her faith! Honest Iago,
My Desdemona must I leave to thee:
I prithee, let thy wife attend on her;
And bring them after in the best advantage.[153]
Come, Desdemona; I have but an hour
Of love, of worldly matters and direction,
To spend with thee: we must obey the time.

                              (Exeunt Othello and Desdemona.)

Roderigo.   Iago!
Iago.   What sayst thou, noble heart?   300
Roderigo.   What will I do, think'st thou?
Iago.   Why, go to bed, and sleep.
Roderigo.   I will incontinently[154] drown myself.
Iago.   Well, if thou dost, I shall never love thee after.
Why, thou silly gentleman!
Roderigo.   It is silliness to live when to live is torment; and then have we a
prescription to die when death is our physician.
Iago.   O! villanous; I have looked upon the world for four times seven years,
and since I could distinguish betwixt a benefit and an injury, I never found
man that knew how to love himself. Ere I would say, I would drown myself
for the love of a guinea-hen, I would change my humanity with a baboon.
Roderigo.   What should I do? I confess it is my shame to be so fond;[155] but it
is not in my virtue[156] to amend it.
Iago.   Virtue! a fig! 'tis in ourselves that we are thus, or thus. Our bodies are
our gardens, to the which our wills are gardeners; so that if we will plant
nettles or sow lettuce, set hyssop and weed up thyme, supply it with one
gender[157] of herbs or distract it with many, either to have it sterile with
idleness or manured with industry, why, the power and corrigible[158] authority
of this lies in our wills. If the balance of our lives had not one scale of reason

---

[152] Delightful.   [153] Opportunity.   [154] Forthwith.   [155] Infatuated.   [156] Strength.
[157] Kind.   [158] Corrective.

to poise another of sensuality, the blood and baseness of our natures would conduct us to most preposterous conclusions; but we have reason to cool our raging motions, our carnal stings, our unbitted[159] lusts, whereof I take this that you call love to be a sect or scion.[160]

Roderigo. It cannot be.

Iago. It is merely a lust of the blood and a permission of the will. Come, be a man. Drown thyself! drown cats and blind puppies. I have professed me thy friend, and I confess me knit to thy deserving with cables of perdurable toughness; I could never better stead thee than now. Put money in thy purse; follow these wars; defeat thy favour[161] with a usurped[162] beard; I say, put money in thy purse. It cannot be that Desdemona should long continue her love to the Moor,—put money in thy purse,—nor he his to her. It was a violent commencement in her, and thou shalt see an answerable sequestration;[163] put but money in thy purse. These Moors are changeable in their wills;—fill thy purse with money:—the food that to him now is as luscious as locusts,[164] shall be to him shortly as bitter as coloquintida.[165] She must change for youth: when she is sated with his body, she will find the error of her choice. She must have change, she must: therefore put money in thy purse. If thou wilt needs damn thyself, do it a more delicate way than drowning. Make all the money thou canst. If sanctimony and a frail vow betwixt an erring[166] barbarian and a supersubtle[167] Venetian be not too hard for my wits and all the tribe of hell, thou shalt enjoy her; therefore make money. A pox of drowning thyself! it is clean out of the way: seek thou rather to be hanged in compassing thy joy than to be drowned and go without her.

Roderigo. Wilt thou be fast to my hopes, if I depend on the issue?[168]

Iago. Thou art sure of me: go, make money. I have told thee often, and I retell thee again and again, I hate the Moor; my cause is hearted; thine hath no less reason. Let us be conjunctive[169] in our revenge against him; if thou canst cuckold him, thou dost thyself a pleasure, me a sport. There are many events in the womb of time which will be delivered. Traverse;[170] go: provide thy money. We will have more of this to-morrow. Adieu.

Roderigo. Where shall we meet i' the morning?

Iago. At my lodging.

Roderigo. I'll be with thee betimes.

Iago. Go to: farewell. Do you hear, Roderigo?

Roderigo. What say you?

Iago. No more of drowning, do you hear?

Roderigo. I am changed. I'll sell all my land.

Iago. Go to; farewell! put money enough in your purse. *(Exit Roderigo.)*
  Thus do I ever make my fool my purse;

---

[159] I.e., uncontrolled. [160] Offshoot. [161] Change thy appearance (for the worse?). [162] Assumed. [163] Estrangement. [164] Sweet-tasting fruits (perhaps the carob, the edible seed-pod of an evergreen tree in the Mediterranean area). [165] Purgative derived from a bitter apple. [166] Vagabond. [167] Exceedingly refined. [168] Rely on the outcome. [169] Allied. [170] March.

For I mine own gain'd knowledge should profane,   360
If I would time expend with such a snipe[171]
But for my sport and profit. I hate the Moor,
And it is thought abroad[172] that 'twixt my sheets
He has done my office: I know not if 't be true,
But I, for mere suspicion in that kind,
Will do as if for surety.[173] He holds me well;[174]
The better shall my purpose work on him.
Cassio's a proper[175] man; let me see now:
To get his place; and to plume up[176] my will
In double knavery; how, how? Let's see: 370
After some time to abuse Othello's ear
That he[177] is too familiar with his wife:
He hath a person and a smooth dispose[178]
To be suspected; framed[179] to make women false,
The Moor is of a free and open nature,
That thinks men honest that but seem to be so,
And will as tenderly be led by the nose
As asses are.
I have 't; it is engender'd: hell and night
Must bring this monstrous birth to the world's light.   (*Exit.*)

Act II

SCENE 1.   A Sea-port Town in Cyprus. An open place near the Quay.

(*Enter Montano and two Gentlemen.*)

Montano.   What from the cape can you discern at sea?
First Gentleman.   Nothing at all: it is a high-wrought flood;
   I cannot 'twixt the heaven and the main[180]
   Descry a sail.
Montano.   Methinks the wind hath spoke aloud at land;
   A fuller blast ne'er shook our battlements;
   If it hath ruffian'd so upon the sea,
   What ribs of oak, when mountains melt on them,
   Can hold the mortise?[181] What shall we hear of this?
Second Gentleman.   A segregation[182] of the Turkish fleet;   10
   For do but stand upon the foaming shore,

---

[171] Dupe.   [172] People think.   [173] As if it were certain.   [174] In high regard.   [175] Handsome.   [176] Make ready.   [177] I.e., Cassio.   [178] Bearing.   [179] Designed, apt.   [180] Ocean.   [181] Hold the joints together.   [182] Scattering.

The chidden billow seems to pelt the clouds;
The wind-shak'd surge, with high and monstrous mane,
Seems to cast water on the burning bear[183]
And quench the guards of the ever-fixed pole:[184]
I never did like[185] molestation view
On the enchafed[186] flood.
Montano.   If that[187] the Turkish fleet
Be not enshelter'd and embay'd, they are drown'd;
It is impossible they bear it out.

(Enter a Third Gentleman.)

Third Gentleman.   News, lad! our wars are done.   20
The desperate tempest hath so bang'd the Turks
That their designment halts;[188] a noble ship of Venice
Hath seen a grievous wrack and suffrance[189]
On most part of their fleet.
Montano.   How! is this true?
Third Gentleman.   The ship is here put in,
A Veronesa;[190] Michael Cassio,
Lieutenant to the warlike Moor Othello,
Is come on shore: the Moor himself's at sea,
And is in full commission here for Cyprus.
Montano.   I am glad on 't; 'tis a worthy governor.   30
Third Gentleman.   But this same Cassio, though he speak of comfort
Touching the Turkish loss, yet he looks sadly
And prays the Moor be safe; for they were parted
With foul and violent tempest.
Montano.   Pray heaven he be;
For I have serv'd him, and the man commands
Like a full soldier. Let's to the sea-side, ho!
As well to see the vessel that's come in
As to throw out our eyes for brave Othello,
Even till we make the main and the aerial blue
An indistinct regard.[191]
Third Gentleman.   Come, let's do so;   40
For every minute is expectancy
Of more arrivance.

---

[183] Ursa Minor (the Little Dipper).   [184] Polaris, the North Star, almost directly above the Earth's axis, is part of the constellation of the Little Bear, or Dipper.   [185] Similar.   [186] Agitated.   [187] If.   [188] Plan is stopped.   [189] Damage.   [190] Probably a *type* of ship, rather than a ship from Verona—not only because Verona is an inland city but also because of "a noble ship of Venice" above.   [191] Till our (straining) eyes can no longer distinguish sea and sky.

(Enter Cassio.)

Cassio.   Thanks, you the valiant of this warlike isle,
That so approve the Moor. O! let the heavens
Give him defence against the elements,
For I have lost him on a dangerous sea.
Montano.   Is he well shipp'd?
Cassio.   His bark is stoutly timber'd, and his pilot
Of very expert and approv'd allowance;[192]
Therefore my hopes, not surfeited to death,[193]   50
Stand in bold cure.[194]

(Within, 'A sail!—a sail!—a sail!' Enter a Messenger.)

Cassio.   What noise?
Messenger.   The town is empty; on the brow o' the sea
Stand ranks of people, and they cry 'A sail!'
Cassio.   My hopes do shape him for the governor.

(Guns heard.)

Second Gentleman.   They do discharge their shot of courtesy;
Our friends at least.
Cassio.   I pray you, sir, go forth.
And give us truth who 'tis that is arriv'd.
Second Gentleman.   I shall.   *(Exit.)*
Montano.   But, good lieutenant, is your general wiv'd?   60
Cassio.   Most fortunately: he hath achiev'd a maid
That paragons[195] description and wild fame;
One that excels the quirks[196] of blazoning pens,
And in th' essential vesture of creation[197]
Does tire the ingener.[198]

(Re-enter Second Gentleman.)

                    How now! who has put in?
Second Gentleman.   'Tis one Iago, ancient to the general.
Cassio.   He has had most favourable and happy speed:
Tempests themselves, high seas, and howling winds,
The gutter'd[199] rocks, and congregated sands,

---

[192] Admitted and proven to be expert.   [193] Overindulged.   [194] With good chance of being fulfilled.   [195] Exceeds, surpasses.   [196] Ingenuities.   [197] I.e., just as God made her; or: (even in) the (mere) essence of human nature.   [198] Inventor (i.e., of her praises?).
[199] Jagged; or: submerged.

Traitors ensteep'd[200] to clog the guiltless keel,   70
As having sense of beauty, do omit
Their mortal[201] natures, letting go safely by
The divine Desdemona.
Montano.   What is she?
Cassio.   She that I spake of, our great captain's captain,
Left in the conduct of the bold Iago,
Whose footing[202] here anticipates our thoughts
A se'nnight's[203] speed. Great Jove, Othello guard,
And swell his sail with thine own powerful breath,
That he may bless this bay with his tall[204] ship,
Make love's quick pants in Desdemona's arms,   80
Give renew'd fire to our extinct spirits,
And bring all Cyprus comfort!

(Enter Desdemona, Emilia, Iago, Roderigo, and Attendants.)

                            O! behold,
The riches of the ship is come on shore.
Ye men of Cyprus, let her have your knees.
Hail to thee, lady! and the grace of heaven,
Before, behind thee, and on every hand,
Enwheel thee round!
Desdemona.   I thank you, valiant Cassio.
What tidings can you tell me of my lord?
Cassio.   He is not yet arriv'd; nor know I aught
But that he's well, and will be shortly here.   90
Desdemona.   O! but I fear—How lost you company?
Cassio.   The great contention of the sea and skies
Parted our fellowship. But hark! a sail.

(Cry within, 'A sail—a sail!' Guns heard.)

Second Gentleman.   They give their greeting to the citadel:
This likewise is a friend.
Cassio.   See for the news!   *(Exit Gentleman.)*
Good ancient, you are welcome:—*(To Emilia)* welcome, mistress.
Let it not gall your patience, good Iago,
That I extend my manners; 'tis my breeding
That gives me this bold show of courtesy.   *(Kissing her.)*
Iago.   Sir, would she give you so much of her lips   100
As of her tongue she oft bestows on me,
You'd have enough.

---

[200] Submerged.   [201] Deadly.   [202] Landing.   [203] Week's.   [204] Brave.

Desdemona.   Alas! she has no speech.

Iago.   In faith, too much;
    I find it still when I have list[205] to sleep:
    Marry, before your ladyship, I grant,
    She puts her tongue a little in her heart,
    And chides with thinking.[206]

Emilia.   You have little cause to say so.

Iago.   Come on, come on; you are pictures[207] out of doors,
    Bells[208] in your parlours, wild cats in your kitchens,   110
    Saints in your injuries, devils being offended,
    Players[209] in your housewifery,[210] and housewives[211] in your beds.

Desdemona.   O! fie upon thee, slanderer.

Iago.   Nay, it is true, or else I am a Turk:
    You rise to play and go to bed to work.

Emilia.   You shall not write my praise.

Iago.   No, let me not.

Desdemona.   What wouldst thou write of me, if thou shouldst praise me?

Iago.   O gentle lady, do not put me to 't,
    For I am nothing if not critical.

Desdemona.   Come on; assay. There's one gone to the harbour?   120

Iago.   Ay, madam.

Desdemona *(aside).*   I am not merry, but I do beguile
    The thing I am by seeming otherwise.
    (To Iago.) Come, how wouldst thou praise me?

Iago.   I am about it; but indeed my invention
    Comes from my pate[212] as birdlime does from frize;[213]
    It plucks out brains and all: but my muse labours
    And thus she is deliver'd.
    If she be fair and wise, fairness and wit,
    The one's for use, the other useth it.   130

Desdemona.   Well prais'd! How if she be black and witty?

Iago.   If she be black,[214] and thereto have a wit,
    She'll find a white that shall her blackness fit.

Desdemona.   Worse and worse.

Emilia.   How if fair and foolish?

Iago.   She never yet was foolish that was fair,
    For even her folly[215] help'd to an heir.

Desdemona.   These are old fond[216] paradoxes to make fools laugh i' the ale-
house. What miserable praise has thou for her that's foul and foolish?

---

[205] Wish.   [206] I.e., without words.   [207] I.e., made up, "painted."   [208] I.e., jangly.
[209] Triflers, wastrels.   [210] Housekeeping.   [211] (1) Hussies, (2) (unduly) frugal with their
sexual favors, (3) businesslike, serious.   [212] Head.   [213] Coarse cloth.   [214] Brunette,
dark haired.   [215] Here also, wantonness.   [216] Foolish.

Iago.   There's none so foul and foolish thereunto,   140
  But does foul pranks which fair and wise ones do.

Desdemona.   O heavy ignorance! thou praisest the worst best. But what praise
  couldst thou bestow on a deserving woman indeed, one that, in the authority
  of her merit, did justly put on the vouch[217] of very malice itself?

Iago.   She that was ever fair and never proud,
  Had tongue at will and yet was never loud,
  Never lack'd gold and yet went never gay,
  Fled from her wish and yet said 'Now I may,'
  She that being anger'd, her revenge being nigh,
  Bade her wrong stay and her displeasure fly,   150
  She that in wisdom never was so frail
  To change the cod's head for the salmon's tail,[218]
  She that could think and ne'er disclose her mind,
  See suitors following and not look behind,
  She was a wight, if ever such wight were,—

Desdemona.   To do what?

Iago.   To suckle fools and chronicle small beer.[219]

Desdemona.   O most lame and impotent conclusion! Do not learn of him,
  Emilia, though he be thy husband. How say you, Cassio? Is he not a most
  profane and liberal[220] counsellor?

Cassio.   He speaks home,[221] madam; you may relish him more in the   160
  soldier than in[222] the scholar.

Iago (aside).   He takes her by the palm: ay, well said, whisper; with as little a
  web as this will I ensnare as great a fly as Cassio. Ay, smile upon her, do; I
  will gyve[223] thee in thine own courtship. You say true, 'tis so, indeed. If
  such tricks as these strip you out of your lieutenantry, it had been better you
  had not kissed your three fingers so oft, which now again you are most apt
  to play the sir[224] in. Very good; well kissed! an excellent courtesy! 'tis so,
  indeed. Yet again your fingers to your lips? would they were clyster-pipes[225]
  for your sake! (A trumpet heard.) The Moor! I know his trumpet.[226]

Cassio.   'Tis truly so.   170

Desdemona.   Let's meet him and receive him.

Cassio.   Lo! where he comes.

(Enter Othello and Attendants.)

Othello.   O my fair warrior!

Desdemona.   My dear Othello!

---

[217] Compel the approval.   [218] To make a foolish exchange (a bawdy secondary meaning is
probable).   [219] I.e., keep petty household accounts.   [220] Free-spoken, licentious.
[221] To the mark, aptly.   [222] As . . . as.   [223] Entangle.   [224] Gentleman.
[225] Syringes, enema pipes.   [226] I.e., Othello's distinctive trumpet call.

Othello.   It gives me wonder great as my content
  To see you here before me. O my soul's joy!
  If after every tempest come such calms,
  May the winds blow till they have waken'd death!
  And let the labouring bark climb hills of seas
  Olympus-high, and duck again as low
  As hell's from heaven! If it were now to die,
  'Twere now to be most happy, for I fear   180
  My soul hath her content so absolute
  That not another comfort like to this
  Succeeds in unknown fate.
Desdemona.   The heavens forbid
  But that our loves and comforts should increase
  Even as our days do grow!
Othello.   Amen to that, sweet powers!
  I cannot speak enough of this content;
  It stops me here; it is too much of joy:
  And this, and this, the greatest discords be   *(Kissing her.)*
  That e'er our hearts shall make!
Iago *(aside).*   O! you are well tun'd now,   190
  But I'll set down[227] the pegs that make this music,
  As honest as I am.
Othello.   Come, let us to the castle.
  News, friends; our wars are done, the Turks are drown'd.
  How does my old acquaintance of this isle?
  Honey, you shall be well desir'd[228] in Cyprus;
  I have found great love amongst them. O my sweet,
  I prattle out of fashion, and I dote
  In mine own comforts. I prithee, good Iago,
  Go to the bay and disembark my coffers.
  Bring thou the master to the citadel;   200
  He is a good one, and his worthiness
  Does challenge much respect. Come, Desdemona,
  Once more well met at Cyprus.

                             (Exeunt all except Iago and Roderigo.)

Iago.   Do thou meet me presently at the harbour. Come hither. If thou be'st valiant, as they say base men being in love have then a nobility in their natures more than is native to them, list[229] me. The lieutenant to-night watches on the court of guard:[230] first, I must tell thee this, Desdemona is directly in love with him.
Roderigo.   With him! Why, 'tis not possible.

---

[227] Loosen.   [228] Welcomed.   [229] Listen to.   [230] Guardhouse.

Iago.   Lay thy finger thus, and let thy soul be instructed. Mark me with what violence she first loved the Moor but for bragging and telling her fantastical lies; and will she love him still for prating? let not thy discreet heart think it. Her eye must be fed; and what delight shall she have to look on the devil? When the blood is made dull with the act of sport, there should be, again to inflame it, and to give satiety a fresh appetite, loveliness in favour, sympathy in years, manners, and beauties; all which the Moor is defective in. Now, for want of these required conveniences, her delicate tenderness will find itself abused, begin to heave the gorge,[231] disrelish and abhor the Moor; very nature will instruct her in it, and compel her to some second choice. Now, sir, this granted, as it is a most pregnant[232] and unforced position, who stands so eminently in the degree of this fortune as Cassio does? a knave very voluble, no further conscionable[233] than in putting on the mere form of civil and humane seeming, for the better compassing of his salt[234] and most hidden loose affection? why, none; why, none: a slipper[235] and subtle knave, a finder-out of occasions, that has an eye can stamp and counterfeit advantages, though true advantage never present itself; a devilish knave! Besides, the knave is handsome, young, and hath all those requisites in him that folly and green minds look after; a pestilent complete knave! and the woman hath found him already.

Roderigo.   I cannot believe that in her; she is full of most blessed condition.

Iago.   Blessed fig's end! the wine she drinks is made of grapes;[236] if she had been blessed she would never have loved the Moor; blessed pudding! Didst thou not see her paddle with the palm of his hand? didst not mark that?

Roderigo.   Yes, that I did; but that was but courtesy.

Iago.   Lechery, by this hand! an index[237] and obscure prologue to the history of lust and foul thoughts. They met so near with their lips, that their breaths embraced together. Villanous thoughts, Roderigo! when these mutualities so marshal the way, hard at hand comes the master and main exercise, the incorporate[238] conclusion. Pish![239] But, sir, be you ruled by me: I have brought you from Venice. Watch you to-night; for the command, I'll lay 't upon you: Cassio knows you not. I'll not be far from you: do you find some occasion to anger Cassio, either by speaking too loud, or tainting[240] his discipline; or from what other course you please, which the time shall more favourably minister.

Roderigo.   Well.

Iago.   Sir, he is rash and very sudden in choler, and haply may strike at you: provoke him, that he may; for even out of that will I cause these of Cyprus to mutiny, whose qualification[241] shall come into no true taste again but by the displanting of Cassio. So shall you have a shorter journey to your desires by the means I shall then have to prefer[242] them; and the impediment most

---

[231] Vomit.   [232] Obvious.   [233] Conscientious.   [234] Lecherous.   [235] Slippery.
[236] I.e., she is only flesh and blood.   [237] Pointer.   [238] Carnal.   [239] Exclamation of disgust.   [240] Disparaging.   [241] Appeasement.   [242] Advance.

profitably removed, without the which there were no expectation of our prosperity.

Roderigo. I will do this, if I can bring it to any opportunity.

Iago. I warrant thee. Meet me by and by at the citadel: I must fetch his necessaries ashore. Farewell.

Roderigo. Adieu. (*Exit.*)

Iago. That Cassio loves her, I do well believe it;
That she loves him, 'tis apt,[243] and of great credit:[244]
The Moor, howbeit that I endure him not,
Is of a constant, loving, noble nature;
And I dare think he'll prove to Desdemona
A most dear[245] husband. Now, I do love her too;
Not out of absolute lust,—though peradventure[246]
I stand accountant[247] for as great a sin,—
But partly led to diet my revenge,
For that I do suspect the lusty Moor
Hath leap'd into my seat; the thought whereof
Doth like a poisonous mineral gnaw my inwards;
And nothing can or shall content my soul
Till I am even'd with him, wife for wife;
Or failing so, yet that I put the Moor
At least into a jealousy so strong
That judgment cannot cure. Which thing to do,
If this poor trash[248] of Venice, whom I trash[249]
For his quick hunting, stand the putting-on,[250]
I'll have our Michael Cassio on the hip;
Abuse him to the Moor in the rank garb,[251]
For I fear Cassio with my night-cap too,
Make the Moor thank me, love me, and reward me
For making him egregiously an ass
And practising upon his peace and quiet
Even to madness. 'Tis here, but yet confus'd:
Knavery's plain face is never seen till us'd. (*Exit.*)

SCENE 2. A Street.

(*Enter a Herald with a proclamation; people following.*)

Herald. It is Othello's pleasure, our noble and valiant general, that, upon certain tidings now arrived, importing the mere[252] perdition of the Turkish

---

[243] Natural, probable. [244] Easily believable. [245] A pun on the word in the sense of expensive. [246] Perchance, perhaps. [247] Accountable. [248] I.e., Roderigo. [249] Check, control. [250] Inciting. [251] Gross manner. [252] Utter.

fleet, every man put himself into triumph; some to dance, some to make bonfires, each man to what sport and revels his addiction leads him; for, besides these beneficial news, it is the celebration of his nuptial. So much was his pleasure should be proclaimed. All offices[253] are open, and there is full liberty of feasting from this present hour of five till the bell have told eleven. Heaven bless the isle of Cyprus and our noble general Othello!

(Exeunt.)

SCENE 3.   A Hall in the Castle.

(Enter Othello, Desdemona, Cassio, and Attendants.)

Othello.   Good Michael, look you to the guard to-night:
Let's teach ourselves that honourable stop,[254]
Not to outsport discretion.
Cassio.   Iago hath direction what to do:
But, notwithstanding, with my personal[255] eye
Will I look to 't.
Othello.   Iago is most honest.
Michael, good-night; to-morrow with your earliest
Let me have speech with you. *(To Desdemona.)* Come, my dear love,
The purchase made, the fruits are to ensue;
That profit's yet to come 'twixt me and you.   10
Good-night.

(Exeunt Othello, Desdemona, and Attendants.)
(Enter Iago.)

Cassio.   Welcome, Iago; we must to the watch.
Iago.   Not this hour, lieutenant; 'tis not yet ten o' the clock. Our general casts us thus early for the love of his Desdemona, who let us not therefore blame; he hath not yet made wanton the night with her, and she is sport for Jove.
Cassio.   She's a most exquisite lady.
Iago.   And, I'll warrant her, full of game.
Cassio.   Indeed, she is a most fresh and delicate creature.
Iago.   What an eye she has! methinks it sounds a parley[256] of provocation.
Cassio.   An inviting eye: and yet methinks right modest.   20
Iago.   And when she speaks, is it not an alarum[257] to love?
Cassio.   She is indeed perfection.
Iago.   Well, happiness to their sheets! Come, lieutenant, I have a stoup of

---

[253] Kitchens and storehouses.   [254] Discipline.   [255] Own.   [256] Conference.
[257] Call-to-arms.

wine, and here without are a brace[258] of Cyprus gallants that would fain have a measure to the health of black Othello.

Cassio. Not to-night, good Iago: I have very poor and unhappy brains for drinking: I could well wish courtesy would invent some other custom of entertainment.

Iago. O! they are our friends; but one cup: I'll drink for you.

Cassio. I have drunk but one cup to-night, and that was craftily qualified[259] too, and, behold, what innovation[260] it makes here: I am unfortunate in the infirmity, and dare not task my weakness with any more.

Iago. What, man! 'tis a night of revels; the gallants desire it.

Cassio. Where are they?

Iago. Here at the door; I pray you, call them in.

Cassio. I'll do 't; but it dislikes me.   (*Exit.*)

Iago. If I can fasten but one cup upon him,
With that which he hath drunk to-night already,
He'll be as full of quarrel and offence
As my young mistress' dog. Now, my sick fool Roderigo,   40
Whom love has turn'd almost the wrong side out,
To Desdemona hath to-night carous'd
Potations pottle-deep;[261] and he's to watch.
Three lads of Cyprus, noble swelling spirits,
That hold their honours in a wary distance,[262]
The very elements[263] of this warlike isle,
Have I to-night fluster'd with flowing cups,
And they watch too. Now, 'mongst this flock of drunkards,
Am I to put our Cassio in some action
That may offend the isle. But here they come.   50
If consequence[264] do but approve my dream,
My boat sails freely, both with wind and stream.

(*Re-enter Cassio, with him Montano, and Gentlemen. Servant following with wine.*)

Cassio. 'Fore God, they have given me a rouse[265] already.

Montano. Good faith, a little one; not past a pint, as I am a soldier.

Iago. Some wine, ho!
(*Sings.*)   And let me the canakin[266] clink, clink;
                And let me the canakin clink:
                A soldier's a man;
                A life's but a span;
                Why then let a soldier drink.   60
Some wine, boys!

---

[258] Pair.   [259] Diluted.   [260] Change, revolution.   [261] Bottoms-up.   [262] Take offense easily.   [263] Types.   [264] Succeeding events.   [265] Drink.   [266] Small cup.

Cassio. 'Fore God, an excellent song.

Iago. I learned it in England, where indeed they are most potent in potting;
your Dane, your German, and your swag-bellied[267] Hollander,—drink ho!—
are nothing to your English.

Cassio. Is your Englishman so expert in his drinking?

Iago. Why, he drinks you[268] with facility your Dane dead drunk; he sweats
not to overthrow your Almain;[269] he gives your Hollander a vomit ere the
next pottle can be filled.

Cassio. To the health of our general!   70

Montano. I am for it, lieutenant; and I'll do you justice.

Iago. O sweet England!

(*Sings.*)   King Stephen was a worthy peer,
        His breeches cost him but a crown;
     He held them sixpence all too dear,
        With that he call'd the tailor lown.[270]
     He was a wight of high renown,
        And thou art but of low degree:
     'Tis pride that pulls the country down,
        Then take thine auld cloak about thee.   80

Some wine, ho!

Cassio. Why, this is a more exquisite song than the other.

Iago. Will you hear 't again?

Cassio. No; for I hold him to be unworthy of his place that does those things.
Well, God's above all; and there be souls must be saved, and there be souls
must not be saved.

Iago. It's true, good lieutenant.

Cassio. For mine own part,—no offence to the general, nor any man of
quality,—I hope to be saved.

Iago. And so do I too, lieutenant.   90

Cassio. Ay; but, by your leave, not before me; the lieutenant is to be saved
before the ancient. Let's have no more of this; let's to our affairs. God forgive
us our sins! Gentlemen, let's look to our business. Do not think, gentlemen,
I am drunk: this is my ancient; this is my right hand, and this is my left
hand. I am not drunk now; I can stand well enough, and speak well enough.

All. Excellent well.

Cassio. Why, very well, then; you must not think then that I am drunk.

                                                     (*Exit.*)

Montano. To the platform, masters; come, let's set the watch.

Iago. You see this fellow that is gone before;
He is a soldier fit to stand by Caesar   100
And give direction; and do but see his vice;
'Tis to his virtue a just equinox,[271]

---

[267] With a pendulous belly.   [268] The "ethical" dative, i.e., you'll see that he drinks.
[269] German.   [270] Lout, rascal.   [271] Equivalent.

The one as long as the other; 'tis pity of him.
I fear the trust Othello puts him in,
On some odd time of his infirmity,
Will shake this island.

Montano. But is he often thus?

Iago. 'Tis evermore the prologue to his sleep;
He'll watch the horologe a double set,[272]
If drink rock not his cradle.

Montano. It were well 110
The general were put in mind of it.
Perhaps he sees it not; or his good nature
Prizes the virtue that appears in Cassio,
And looks not on his evils. Is not this true?

(Enter Roderigo.)

Iago *(aside to him).* How now, Roderigo!
I pray you, after the lieutenant; go. *(Exit Roderigo.)*

Montano. And 'tis great pity that the noble Moor
Should hazard such a place as his own second
With one of an ingraft[273] infirmity;
It were an honest action to say 120
So to the Moor.

Iago. Not I, for this fair island:
I do love Cassio well, and would do much
To cure him of this evil. But hark! what noise?

(Cry within, 'Help! Help!' Re-enter Cassio, driving in Roderigo.)

Cassio. You rogue! you rascal!

Montano. What's the matter, lieutenant?

Cassio. A knave teach me my duty!
I'll beat the knave into a twiggen[274] bottle.

Roderigo. Beat me!

Cassio. Dost thou prate, rogue?

(Striking Roderigo.)

Montano *(staying him).* Nay, good lieutenant;
I pray you, sir, hold your hand.

Cassio. Let me go, sir,
Or I'll knock you o'er the mazzard.[275]

---

[272] Stand watch twice twelve hours.   [273] Ingrained.   [274] Wicker.   [275] Head.

Montano.   Come, come; you're drunk.   130
Cassio. Drunk!

(They fight.)

Iago *(aside to Roderigo).*   Away, I say! go out, and cry a mutiny.
                                    (Exit Roderigo.)
Nay, good lieutenant! God's will, gentlemen!
Help, ho! Lieutenant! sir! Montano! sir!
Help, masters! Here's a goodly watch indeed!

(Bell rings.)

Who's that that rings the bell? Diablo, ho!
The town will rise: God's will! lieutenant, hold!
You will be sham'd for ever.

(Re-enter Othello and Attendants.)

Othello.   What is the matter here?
Montano.   'Zounds! I bleed still; I am hurt to the death.

(He faints.)

Othello.   Hold, for your lives!
Iago.   Hold, ho, lieutenant! Sir! Montano! gentlemen!   140
Have you forgot all sense of place and duty?
Hold! the general speaks to you; hold for shame!
Othello.   Why, how now, ho! from whence ariseth this?
Are we turn'd Turks, and to ourselves do that
Which heaven hath forbid the Ottomites?
For Christian shame put by this barbarous brawl;
He that stirs next to carve for his own rage
Holds his soul light; he dies upon his motion.
Silence that dreadful bell! it frights the isle
From her propriety. What is the matter, masters?   150
Honest Iago, that look'st dead with grieving,
Speak, who began this? On thy love, I charge thee.
Iago.   I do not know; friends all but now, even now,
In quarter[276] and in terms like bride and groom
Devesting[277] them for bed; and then, but now,—
As if some planet had unwitted men,—
Swords out, and tilting one at other's breast,

---

[276] On duty.   [277] Undressing.

In opposition bloody. I cannot speak
Any beginning to this peevish odds,[278]
And would in action glorious I had lost   160
Those legs that brought me to a part of it!

Othello.   How comes it, Michael, you are thus forgot?

Cassio.   I pray you, pardon me; I cannot speak.

Othello.   Worthy Montano, you were wont be civil;
The gravity and stillness of your youth
The world hath noted, and your name is great
In mouths of wisest censure:[279] what's the matter,
That you unlace[280] your reputation thus
And spend your rich opinion[281] for the name
Of a night-brawler? give me answer to it.   170

Montano.   Worthy Othello, I am hurt to danger;
Your officer, Iago, can inform you,
While I spare speech, which something now offends[282] me,
Of all that I do know; nor know I aught
By me that 's said or done amiss this night,
Unless self-charity be sometimes a vice,
And to defend ourselves it be a sin
When violence assails us.

Othello.   Now, by heaven,
My blood begins my safer guides to rule,
And passion, having my best judgment collied,[283]   180
Assays to lead the way. If I once stir,
Or do but lift this arm, the best of you
Shall sink in my rebuke. Give me to know
How this foul rout began, who set it on;
And he that is approv'd[284] in this offence,
Though he had twinn'd with me—both at a birth—
Shall lose me. What! in a town of war,
Yet wild, the people's hearts brimful of fear,
To manage private and domestic quarrel,
In night, and on the court and guard of safety!   190
'Tis monstrous. Iago, who began 't?

Montano.   If partially affin'd,[285] or leagu'd in office,
Thou dost deliver more or less than truth,
Thou art not soldier.

Iago.   Touch me not so near;
I had rather[286] have this tongue cut from my mouth
Than it should do offence to Michael Cassio;

---

[278] Silly quarrel.   [279] Judgment.   [280] Undo.   [281] High reputation.   [282] Pains, harms.   [283] Clouded.   [284] Proved (i.e., guilty).   [285] Favorably biased (by ties of friendship, or as Cassio's fellow officer).   [286] More quickly.

Yet, I persuade myself, to speak the truth
Shall nothing wrong him. Thus it is, general.
Montano and myself being in speech,
There comes a fellow crying out for help,   200
And Cassio following with determin'd sword
To execute upon him. Sir, this gentleman
Steps in to Cassio, and entreats his pause;
Myself the crying fellow did pursue,
Lest by his clamour, as it so fell out,
The town might fall in fright; he, swift of foot,
Outran my purpose, and I return'd the rather
For that I heard the clink and fall of swords,
And Cassio high in oath, which till to-night
I ne'er might say before. When I came back,—   210
For this was brief,—I found them close together,
At blow and thrust, even as again they were
When you yourself did part them.
More of this matter can I not report:
But men are men; the best sometimes forget:
Though Cassio did some little wrong to him,
As men in rage strike those that wish them best,
Yet, surely Cassio, I believe, receiv'd
From him that fled some strange indignity,
Which patience could not pass.
Othello.   I know, Iago.   220
  Thy honesty and love doth mince[287] this matter,
  Making it light to Cassio. Cassio, I love thee;
  But never more be officer of mine.

(Enter Desdemona, attended.)

  Look! if my gentle love be not rais'd up;
  (To Cassio.) I'll make thee an example.
Desdemona.   What's the matter?
Othello.   All's well now, sweeting; come away to bed.
  Sir, for your hurts, myself will be your surgeon.
  Lead him off.   *(Montano is led off.)*
  Iago, look with care about the town,
  And silence those whom this vile brawl distracted.   230
  Come, Desdemona; 'tis the soldier's life,
  To have their balmy slumbers wak'd with strife.

                         (Exeunt all but Iago and Cassio.)

---

[287] Tone down.

Iago.   What! are you hurt, lieutenant?

Cassio.   Ay; past all surgery.

Iago.   Marry, heaven forbid!

Cassio.   Reputation, reputation, reputation! O! I have lost my reputation. I have lost the immortal part of myself, and what remains is bestial. My reputation, Iago, my reputation!

Iago.   As I am an honest man, I thought you had received some bodily wound; there is more offence in that than in reputation. Reputation is an idle and most false imposition;[288] oft got without merit, and lost without deserving: you have lost no reputation at all, unless you repute yourself such a loser. What! man; there are ways to recover the general again; you are but now cast in his mood,[289] a punishment more in policy[290] than in malice; even so as one would beat his offenceless dog to affright an imperious lion. Sue to him again, and he is yours.

Cassio.   I will rather sue to be despised than to deceive so good a commander with so slight, so drunken and so indiscreet an officer. Drunk! and speak parrot![291] and squabble, swagger, swear, and discourse fustian[292] with one's own shadow! O thou invisible spirit of wine! if thou hast no name to be known by, let us call thee devil!

Iago.   What was he that you followed with your sword? What hath he done to you?

Cassio.   I know not.

Iago.   Is 't possible?

Cassio.   I remember a mass of things, but nothing distinctly; a quarrel, but nothing wherefore. O God! that men should put an enemy in their mouths to steal away their brains; that we should, with joy, pleasance,[293] revel, and applause, transform ourselves into beasts.

Iago.   Why, but you are now well enough; how came you thus recovered?

Cassio.   It hath pleased the devil drunkenness to give place to the devil wrath; one unperfectness shows me another, to make me frankly despise myself.

Iago.   Come, you are too severe a moraler. As the time, the place, and the condition of this country stands, I could heartily wish this had not befallen, but since it is as it is, mend it for your own good.

Cassio.   I will ask him for my place again; he shall tell me I am a drunkard! Had I as many mouths as Hydra,[294] such an answer would stop them all. To be now a sensible man, by and by a fool, and presently a beast! O strange! Every inordinate cup is unblessed and the ingredient[295] is a devil.

Iago.   Come, come; good wine is a good familiar creature if it be well used; exclaim no more against it. And, good lieutenant, I think you think I love you.

Cassio.   I have well approved it, sir. I drunk!

---

[288] Something external.   [289] Dismissed because he is angry.   [290] I.e., more for the sake of the example, or to show his fairness.   [291] I.e., without thinking.   [292] I.e., nonsense. [293] Pleasure.   [294] Many-headed snake in Greek mythology.   [295] Contents.

Iago.   You or any man living may be drunk at some time, man. I'll tell you
what you shall do. Our general's wife is now the general; I may say so in
this respect, for that he hath devoted and given up himself to the contemplation, mark, and denotement of her parts and graces: confess yourself freely
to her; importune her; she'll help to put you in your place again. She is of
so free, so kind, so apt, so blessed a disposition, that she holds it a vice in
her goodness not to do more than she is requested. This broken joint between
you and her husband entreat her to splinter;[296] and, my fortunes against any
lay[297] worth naming, this crack of your love shall grow stronger than it was
before.

Cassio.   You advise me well.

Iago.   I protest, in the sincerity of love and honest kindness.

Cassio.   I think it freely; and betimes in the morning I will beseech the virtuous
Desdemona to undertake for me. I am desperate of my fortunes if they check
me here.

Iago.   You are in the right. Good-night, lieutenant; I must to the watch.

Cassio.   Good-night, honest Iago!   (*Exit.*)

Iago.   And what's he then that says I play the villain?   290
When this advice is free I give and honest,
Probal[298] to thinking and indeed the course
To win the Moor again? For 'tis most easy
The inclining Desdemona to subdue
In any honest suit; she's fram'd as fruitful[299]
As the free elements. And then for her
To win the Moor, were 't to renounce his baptism,
All seals and symbols of redeemed sin,
His soul is so enfetter'd to her love,
That she may make, unmake, do what she list,   300
Even as her appetite shall play the god
With his weak function.[300] How am I then a villain
To counsel Cassio to this parallel[301] course,
Directly to his good? Divinity of hell!
When devils will the blackest sins put on,
They do suggest at first with heavenly shows,
As I do now; for while this honest fool
Plies Desdemona to repair his fortunes,
And she for him pleads strongly to the Moor,
I'll pour this pestilence into his ear   310
That she repeals[302] him for her body's lust;
And, by how much she strives to do him good,
She shall undo her credit with the Moor.

---

[296] Bind up with splints.   [297] Wager.   [298] Provable.   [299] Generous.   [300] Faculties.   [301] Purposeful.   [302] I.e., seeks to recall.

So will I turn her virtue into pitch,
And out of her own goodness make the net
That shall enmesh them all.

(Re-enter Roderigo.)

How now, Roderigo!

Roderigo.   I do follow here in the chase, not like a hound that hunts, but one
that fills up the cry.[303] My money is almost spent; I have been to-night
exceedingly well cudgelled; and I think the issue will be, I shall have so
much experience for my pains; and so, with no money at all and a little
more wit, return again to Venice.

Iago.   How poor are they that have not patience!
What wound did ever heal but by degrees?
Thou know'st we work by wit and not by witchcraft,
And wit depends on dilatory time.
Does 't not go well? Cassio hath beaten thee,
And thou by that small hurt hast cashiered Cassio.
Though other things grow fair against the sun,
Yet fruits that blossom first will first be ripe:
Content thyself awhile. By the mass, 'tis morning;   330
Pleasure and action make the hours seem short.
Retire thee; go where thou art billeted:
Away, I say; thou shalt know more hereafter:
Nay, get thee gone. *(Exit Roderigo.)* Two things are to be done,
My wife must move for Cassio to her mistress;
I'll set her on;
Myself the while to draw the Moor apart,
And bring him jump[304] when he may Cassio find
Soliciting his wife: ay, that's the way:
Dull not device by coldness and delay.   *(Exit.)*

Act III

SCENE 1.   Cyprus. Before the Castle.

(Enter Cassio, and some Musicians.)

Cassio.   Masters, play here, I will content your pains;[305]
Something that's brief; and bid 'Good-morrow, general.'   *(Music.)*

(Enter Clown.)

---

[303] Pack (hunting term).   [304] At the exact moment.   [305] Reward your efforts.

Clown.   Why, masters, have your instruments been in Naples, that they speak
i' the nose[306] thus?

First Musician.   How, sir, how?

Clown.   Are these, I pray you, wind-instruments?

First Musician.   Ay, marry, are they, sir.

Clown.   O! thereby hangs a tale.

First Musician.   Whereby hangs a tale, sir?

Clown.   Marry, sir, by many a wind-instrument that I know. But, masters,
here's money for you; and the general so likes your music, that he desires
you, for love's sake, to make no more noise with it.

First Musician.   Well, sir, we will not.

Clown.   If you have any music that may not be heard, to 't again; but, as they
say, to hear music the general does not greatly care.

First Musician.   We have none such, sir.

Clown.   Then put up your pipes in your bag, for I'll away.
Go; vanish into air; away!   (*Exeunt Musicians.*)

Cassio.   Dost thou hear, mine honest friend?

Clown.   No, I hear not your honest friend; I hear you.

Cassio.   Prithee, keep up thy quillets.[307] There's a poor piece of gold for thee.
If the gentlewoman that attends the general's wife be stirring, tell her there's
one Cassio entreats her a little favour of speech: wilt thou do this?

Clown.   She is stirring, sir: if she will stir hither, I shall seem to notify unto
her.

Cassio.   Do, good my friend.   (*Exit Clown.*)

(*Enter Iago.*)

                         In happy time, Iago.

Iago.   You have not been a-bed, then?

Cassio.   Why, no; the day had broke
Before we parted. I have made bold, Iago,
To send in to your wife; my suit to her
Is, that she will to virtuous Desdemona   30
Procure me some access.

Iago.   I'll send her to you presently;
And I'll devise a mean to draw the Moor
Out of the way, that your converse and business
May be more free.

Cassio.   I humbly thank you for 't.   (*Exit Iago.*)
                         I never knew
A Florentine more kind and honest.[308]

---

[306] Naples was notorious for venereal disease, and syphilis was believed to affect the nose.
[307] Quibbles.   [308] Cassio means that not even a fellow Florentine could behave to him in a
friendlier fashion than does Iago.

(Enter Emilia.)

Emilia.   Good-morrow, good lieutenant: I am sorry
For your displeasure,[309] but all will soon be well.
The general and his wife are talking of it,
And she speaks for you stoutly: the Moor replies   40
That he you hurt is of great fame in Cyprus
And great affinity,[310] and that in wholesome wisdom
He might not but refuse you; but he protests he loves you,
And needs no other suitor but his likings
To take the safest occasion by the front[311]
To bring you in again.[312]
Cassio.   Yet, I beseech you,
If you think fit, or that it may be done,
Give me advantage of some brief discourse
With Desdemona alone.
Emilia.   Pray you, come in:
I will bestow you where you shall have time   50
To speak your bosom[313] freely.
Cassio.   I am much bound to you.   *(Exeunt.)*

SCENE 2.   A Room in the Castle.

(Enter Othello, Iago, and Gentlemen.)

Othello.   These letters give, Iago, to the pilot,
And by him do my duties to the senate;
That done, I will be walking on the works;
Repair there to me.
Iago.   Well, my good lord, I'll do 't.
Othello.   This fortification, gentlemen, shall we see 't?
Gentlemen.   We'll wait upon your lordship.   *(Exeunt.)*

SCENE 3.   Before the Castle.

(Enter Desdemona, Cassio, and Emilia.)

Desdemona.   Be thou assur'd, good Cassio, I will do
All my abilities in thy behalf.
Emilia.   Good madam, do: I warrant it grieves my husband,
As if the case were his.

---

[309] Disgrace.   [310] Family connection.   [311] Forelock.   [312] Restore you (to Othello's favor).   [313] Heart, inmost thoughts.

Desdemona.   O! that's an honest fellow. Do not doubt, Cassio,
   But I will have my lord and you again
   As friendly as you were.
Cassio.   Bounteous madam,
   Whatever shall become of Michael Cassio,
   He's never any thing but your true servant.
Desdemona.   I know 't; I thank you. You do love my lord;   10
   You have known him long; and be you well assur'd
   He shall in strangeness[314] stand no further off
   Than in a politic[315] distance.
Cassio.   Ay, but, lady,
   That policy may either last so long,
   Or feed upon such nice[316] and waterish diet,
   Or breed itself so out of circumstance,
   That, I being absent and my place supplied,
   My general will forget my love and service.
Desdemona.   Do not doubt[317] that; before Emilia here
   I give thee warrant of thy place. Assure thee,   20
   If I do vow a friendship, I'll perform it
   To the last article; my lord shall never rest;
   I'll watch him tame,[318] and talk him out of patience;
   His bed shall seem a school, his board a shrift;[319]
   I'll intermingle every thing he does
   With Cassio's suit. Therefore be merry, Cassio;
   For thy solicitor shall rather die
   Than give thy cause away.[320]

(Enter Othello, and Iago at a distance.)

Emilia.   Madam, here comes my lord.
Cassio.   Madam, I'll take my leave.   30
Desdemona.   Why, stay, and hear me speak.
Cassio.   Madam, not now; I am very ill at ease,
   Unfit for mine own purposes.
Desdemona.   Well, do your discretion.   *(Exit Cassio.)*
Iago.   Ha! I like not that.
Othello.   What dost thou say?
Iago.   Nothing, my lord: or if—I know not what.
Othello.   Was not that Cassio parted from my wife?
Iago.   Cassio, my lord? No, sure, I cannot think it,
   That he would steal away so guilty-like,
   Seeing you coming.

---

[314] Aloofness.   [315] I.e., dictated by policy.   [316] Slight, trivial.   [317] Fear.
[318] Outwatch him (i.e., keep him awake) till he submits.   [319] Confessional.   [320] Abandon
your cause.

Othello.   I do believe 'twas he.   40
Desdemona.   How now, my lord!
  I have been talking with a suitor here,
  A man that languishes in your displeasure.
Othello.   Who is 't you mean?
Desdemona.   Why, your lieutenant, Cassio. Good my lord,
  If I have any grace or power to move you,
  His present³²¹ reconciliation take;
  For if he be not one that truly loves you,
  That errs in ignorance and not in cunning,
  I have no judgment in an honest face.   50
  I prithee³²² call him back.
Othello.   Went he hence now?
Desdemona.   Ay, sooth; so humbled,
  That he hath left part of his grief with me,
  To suffer with him. Good love, call him back.
Othello.   Not now, sweet Desdemona; some other time.
Desdemona.   But shall 't be shortly?
Othello.   The sooner, sweet, for you.
Desdemona.   Shall 't be to-night at supper?
Othello.   No, not to-night.
Desdemona.   To-morrow dinner, then?
Othello.   I shall not dine at home;
  I meet the captains at the citadel.
Desdemona.   Why, then, to-morrow night; or Tuesday morn;
  Or Tuesday noon, or night; or Wednesday morn: 60
  I prithee name the time, but let it not
  Exceed three days: in faith, he's penitent;
  And yet his trespass, in our common reason,—
  Save that they say, the wars must make examples
  Out of their best,—is not almost³²³ a fault
  To incur a private check.³²⁴ When shall he come?
  Tell me, Othello: I wonder in my soul,
  What you could ask me, that I should deny,
  Or stand so mammering³²⁵ on. What! Michael Cassio,   70
  That came a wooing with you, and so many a time,
  When I have spoke of you dispraisingly,
  Hath ta'en your part; to have so much to do
  To bring him in! Trust me, I could do much,—
Othello.   Prithee, no more; let him come when he will;
  I deny thee nothing.
Desdemona.   Why, this is not a boon;

---

³²¹ Immediate.   ³²² Pray thee.   ³²³ Hardly.   ³²⁴ (Even) a private reprimand.
³²⁵ Shilly-shallying.

'Tis as I should entreat you wear your gloves,
Or feed on nourishing dishes, or keep you warm,
Or sue to you to do a peculiar profit
To your own person: nay, when I have a suit   80
Wherein I mean to touch your love indeed,
It shall be full of poise[326] and difficult weight,
And fearful to be granted.
Othello.   I will deny thee nothing:
Whereon, I do beseech thee, grant me this,
To leave me but a little to myself.
Desdemona.   Shall I deny you? no: farewell, my lord.
Othello.   Farewell, my Desdemona: I'll come to thee straight.
Desdemona.   Emilia, come. Be as your fancies teach you;
Whate'er you be, I am obedient.   *(Exit, with Emilia.)*
Othello.   Excellent wretch![327] Perdition catch my soul,   90
But I do love thee! and when I love thee not,
Chaos is[328] come again.
Iago.   My noble lord,—
Othello.   What dost thou say, Iago?
Iago.   Did Michael Cassio, when you woo'd my lady,
Know of your love?
Othello.   He did, from first to last: why dost thou ask?
Iago.   But for a satisfaction of my thought;
No further harm.
Othello.   Why of thy thought, Iago?
Iago.   I did not think he had been acquainted with her.
Othello.   O! yes; and went between us very oft.   100
Iago.   Indeed!
Othello.   Indeed! ay, indeed; discern'st thou aught in that?
Is he not honest?
Iago.   Honest, my lord?
Othello.   Honest! ay, honest.
Iago.   My lord, for aught I know.
Othello.   What dost thou think?
Iago.   Think, my lord!
Othello.   Think, my lord!
By heaven, he echoes me,
As if there were some monster in his thought
Too hideous to be shown. Thou dost mean something:
I heard thee say but now, thou lik'dst not that,
When Cassio left my wife; what didst not like?   110
And when I told thee he was of my counsel
In my whole course of wooing, thou criedst, 'Indeed!'

---

[326] Weight.   [327] Here, a term of endearment.   [328] Will have.

And didst contract and purse thy brow together,
As if thou then hadst shut up in thy brain
Some horrible conceit.[329] If thou dost love me,
Show me thy thought.

Iago.   My lord, you know I love you.

Othello.   I think thou dost;
And, for[330] I know thou art full of love and honesty,
And weigh'st thy words before thou givest them breath,
Therefore these stops[331] of thine fright me the more;   120
For such things in a false disloyal knave
Are tricks of custom, but in a man that's just
They are close dilations,[332] working from the heart
That passion cannot rule.

Iago.   For Michael Cassio,
I dare be sworn I think that he is honest.

Othello.   I think so too.

Iago.   Men should be what they seem;
Or those that be not, would they might seem none!

Othello.   Certain men should be what they seem.

Iago.   Why then, I think Cassio's an honest man.

Othello.   Nay, yet there's more in this.   130
I pray thee, speak to me as to thy thinkings,
As thou dost ruminate, and give thy worst of thoughts
The worst of words.

Iago.   Good my lord, pardon me;
Though I am bound to every act of duty,
I am not bound to[333] that all slaves are free to.
Utter my thoughts? Why, say they are vile and false;
As where's that palace whereinto foul things
Sometimes intrude not? who has a breast so pure
But some uncleanly apprehensions[334]
Keep leets and law-days,[335] and in session sit   140
With meditations lawful?

Othello.   Thou dost conspire against thy friend, Iago,
If thou but think'st him wrong'd, and mak'st his ear
A stranger to thy thoughts.

Iago.   I do beseech you,
Though I perchance am vicious in my guess,—
As, I confess, it is my nature's plague
To spy into abuses, and oft my jealousy[336]
Shapes faults that are not,—that your wisdom yet,

---

[329] Fancy.   [330] Because.   [331] Interruptions, hesitations.   [332] Secret (i.e., involuntary, unconscious) revelations.   [333] Bound with regard to.   [334] Conceptions.   [335] Sittings of the local courts.   [336] Suspicion.

From one that so imperfectly conceits,
Would take no notice, nor build yourself a trouble   150
Out of his scattering and unsure observance.
It were not for your quiet nor your good,
Nor for my manhood, honesty, or wisdom,
    To let you know my thoughts.
Othello.   What dost thou mean?
Iago.   Good name in man and woman, dear my lord,
    Is the immediate jewel of[337] their souls:
    Who steals my purse steals trash; 'tis something, nothing;
    'Twas mine, 'tis his, and has been slave to thousands;
    But he that filches from me my good name
    Robs me of that which not enriches him,   160
    And makes me poor indeed.
Othello.   By heaven, I'll know thy thoughts.
Iago.   You cannot, if my heart were in your hand;
    Nor shall not, whilst 'tis in my custody.
Othello.   Ha!
Iago.   O! beware, my lord, of jealousy;
    It is the green-ey'd monster which doth mock
    The meat it feeds on: that cuckold[338] lives in bliss
    Who, certain of his fate, loves not his wronger;
    But, O! what damned minutes tells[339] he o'er
    Who dotes, yet doubts; suspects, yet soundly loves!   170
Othello.   O misery!
Iago.   Poor and content is rich, and rich enough,
    But riches fineless[340] is as poor as winter
    To him that ever fears he shall be poor.
    Good heaven, the souls of all my tribe defend
    From jealousy!
Othello.   Why, why is this?
    Think'st thou I'd make a life of jealousy,
    To follow still the changes of the moon
    With fresh suspicions? No; to be once in doubt
    Is once to be resolved. Exchange me for a goat   180
    When I shall turn the business of my soul
    To such exsufflicate[341] and blown[342] surmises,
    Matching thy inference. 'Tis not to make me jealous
    To say my wife is fair, feeds well, loves company,
    Is free of speech, sings, plays, and dances well;
    Where virtue is, these are more virtuous:
    Nor from mine own weak merits will I draw

---

[337] Jewel closest to.   [338] Husband of an adulterous woman.   [339] Counts.   [340] Bound-less.   [341] Spat out (?).   [342] Fly-blown.

The smallest fear, or doubt of her revolt;
For she had eyes, and chose me. No, Iago;
I'll see before I doubt; when I doubt, prove;   190
And, on the proof, there is no more but this,
Away at once with love or jealousy!

Iago.   I am glad of it; for now I shall have reason
To show the love and duty that I bear you
With franker spirit; therefore, as I am bound,
Receive it from me; I speak not yet of proof.
Look to your wife; observe her well with Cassio;
Wear your eye thus, not jealous nor secure:
I would not have your free and noble nature
Out of self-bounty[343] be abus'd; look to 't: 200
I know our country disposition[344] well;
In Venice they do let heaven see the pranks
They dare not show their husbands; their best conscience
Is not to leave 't undone, but keep 't unknown.

Othello.   Dost thou say so?

Iago.   She did deceive her father, marrying you;
And when she seem'd to shake and fear your looks,
She lov'd them most.

Othello.   And so she did.

Iago.   Why, go to,[345] then;
She that so young could give out such a seeming,
To seel her father's eyes up close as oak,   210
He thought 'twas witchcraft; but I am much to blame;
I humbly do beseech you of your pardon
For too much loving you.

Othello.   I am bound to thee for ever.

Iago.   I see, this hath a little dash'd your spirits.

Othello.   Not a jot, not a jot.

Iago.   I' faith, I fear it has.
I hope you will consider what is spoke
Comes from my love. But I do see you're mov'd;
I am to pray you not to strain my speech
To grosser issues nor to larger reach
Than to suspicion.   220

Othello.   I will not.

Iago.   Should you do so, my lord,
My speech should fall into such vile success
As my thoughts aim not at. Cassio's my worthy friend—
My lord, I see you're mov'd.

---

[343] Innate generosity.   [344] I.e., that of Venice.   [345] Colloquialism; here, something like
"all right."

Othello.   No, not much mov'd:
  I do not think but Desdemona's honest.[346]
Iago.   Long live she so! and long live you to think so!
Othello.   And yet, how nature erring from itself,—
Iago.   Ay, there's the point: as, to be bold with you,
  Not to affect many proposed matches
  Of her own clime,[347] complexion, and degree,[348]   230
  Whereto, we see, in all things nature tends;
  Foh! one may smell in such, a will most rank,
  Foul disproportion, thoughts unnatural.
  But pardon me; I do not in position [349]
  Distinctly[350] speak of her, though I may fear
  Her will, recoiling[351] to her better judgment,
  May fall to match you with her country forms
  And happily[352] repent.
Othello.   Farewell, farewell:
  If more thou dost perceive, let me know more;
  Set on thy wife to observe. Leave me, Iago.   240
Iago.   My lord, I take my leave.   *(Going.)*
Othello.   Why did I marry? This honest creature, doubtless,
  Sees and knows more, much more, than he unfolds.
Iago *(returning).*   My lord, I would I might entreat your honour
  To scan this thing no further; leave it to time.
  Although 'tis fit that Cassio have his place,
  For, sure he fills it up with great ability,
  Yet, if you please to hold him off awhile,
  You shall by that perceive him and his means:
  Note if your lady strain his entertainment[353]   250
  With any strong or vehement importunity;
  Much will be seen in that. In the mean time,
  Let me be thought too busy[354] in my fears,
  As worthy cause I have to fear I am,
  And hold her free, I do beseech your honour.
Othello.   Fear not my government.
Iago.   I once more take my leave.   *(Exit.)*
Othello.   This fellow's of exceeding honesty,
  And knows all qualities, with a learned spirit,
  Of human dealings; if I do prove her haggard,[355]   260
  Though that her jesses[356] were my dear heart-strings,
  I'd whistle her off and let her down the wind,[357]

---

[346] Chaste.   [347] Country.   [348] Social rank.   [349] In definite assertion.   [350] Specifically.   [351] Reverting.   [352] Perhaps.   [353] Urge his re-welcome (i.e., to Othello's trust and favor).   [354] Meddlesome.   [355] Wild hawk.   [356] Leather thongs by which the hawk's legs were strapped to the trainer's wrist.   [357] I'd let her go and take care of herself.

To prey at fortune. Haply, for I am black,
And have not those soft parts of conversation
That chamberers[354] have, or, for I am declin'd
Into the vale of years—yet that's not much—
She's gone, I am abus'd;[359] and my relief
Must be to loathe her. O curse of marriage!
That we can call these delicate creatures ours,
And not their appetites. I had rather be a toad,　　　　　　270
And live upon the vapour of a dungeon,
Than keep a corner in the thing I love
For others' uses. Yet, 'tis the plague of great ones;
Prerogativ'd[360] are they less than the base;
'Tis destiny unshunnable, like death:
Even then this forked plague[361] is fated to us
When we do quicken.[362]
　　　　　　　　　Look! where she comes.
If she be false, O! then heaven mocks itself.
I'll not believe it.

(Re-enter Desdemona and Emilia.)

Desdemona.　　　How now, my dear Othello!
　Your dinner and the generous[363] islanders　　　　　　280
　By you invited, do attend your presence.
Othello.　I am to blame.
Desdemona.　　　　　Why do you speak so faintly?
　Are you not well?
Othello.　I have a pain upon my forehead here.[364]
Desdemona.　Faith, that's with watching; 'twill away again:
　Let me but bind it hard, within this hour
　It will be well.
Othello.　　　Your napkin[365] is too little:

(She drops her handkerchief.)

　Let it alone. Come, I'll go in with you.
Desdemona.　I am very sorry that you are not well.

(Exeunt Othello and Desdemona.)

Emilia.　I am glad I have found this napkin;　　　　　　290
　This was her first remembrance from the Moor;

---

[358] Courtiers; or (more specifically): gallants, frequenters of bed chambers.　　[359] Deceived.
[360] Privileged.　　[361] I.e., the cuckold's proverbial horns.　　[362] Are conceived, come alive.
[363] Noble.　　[364] Othello again refers to his cuckoldom.　　[365] Handkerchief.

My wayward husband hath a hundred times
Woo'd me to steal it, but she so loves the token,
For he conjur'd her she should ever keep it,
That she reserves it evermore about her
To kiss and talk to. I'll have the work ta'en out, [366]
And giv 't Iago:
What he will do with it heaven knows, not I;
I nothing but [367] to please his fantasy. [368]

(Enter Iago.)

Iago.   How now! what do you here alone?   300
Emilia.   Do not you chide; I have a thing for you.
Iago.   A thing for me? It is a common thing—
Emilia.   Ha!
Iago.   To have a foolish wife.
Emilia.   O! is that all? What will you give me now
  For that same handkerchief?
Iago.   What handkerchief?
Emilia.   What handkerchief!
  Why, that the Moor first gave to Desdemona:
  That which so often you did bid me steal.
Iago.   Hath stol'n it from her?   310
Emilia.   No, faith; she let it drop by negligence,
  And, to the advantage, I, being there, took 't up.
  Look, here it is.
Iago.   A good wench; give it me.
Emilia.   What will you do with 't, that you have been so earnest
  To have me filch it?
Iago.   Why, what's that to you?   *(Snatches it.)*
Emilia.   If it be not for some purpose of import
  Give 't me again; poor lady! she'll run mad
  When she shall lack it.
Iago.   Be not acknown on 't; [369] I have use for it.
  Go, leave me.   *(Exit Emilia.)*
  I will in Cassio's lodging lose this napkin,   321
  And let him find it; trifles light as air
  Are to the jealous confirmations strong
  As proofs of holy writ; this may do something.
  The Moor already changes with my poison:
  Dangerous conceits are in their natures poisons,
  Which at the first are scarce found to distaste, [370]

---

[366] Pattern copied.   [367] I.e., only want.   [368] Whim.   [369] You know nothing about
it.   [370] Scarce can be tasted.

But with a little act upon the blood,
Burn like the mines of sulphur. I did say so:
Look! where he comes!

(Enter Othello.)

                            Not poppy,[371] nor mandragora,[372]   330
Nor all the drowsy syrups[373] of the world,
  Shall ever medicine thee to that sweet sleep
  Which thou ow'dst yesterday.
Othello.   Ha! ha! false to me?
Iago. Why, how now, general! no more of that.
Othello. Avaunt! be gone! thou hast set me on the rack;
  I swear 'tis better to be much abus'd
  Than but to know 't a little.
Iago.   How now, my lord!
Othello. What sense had I of her stol'n hours of lust?
  I saw 't not, thought it not, it harm'd not me;
  I slept the next night well, was free and merry;   340
  I found not Cassio's kisses on her lips;
  He that is robb'd, not wanting what is stol'n,
  Let him not know 't, and he's not robb'd at all.
Iago. I am sorry to hear this.
Othello. I had been happy, if the general camp,[374]
  Pioners[375] and all, had tasted her sweet body,
  So[376] I had nothing known. O! now, for ever
  Farewell the tranquil mind; farewell content!
  Farewell the plumed troop and the big wars
  That make ambition virtue! O, farewell!   350
  Farewell the neighing steed, and the shrill trump,
  The spirit-stirring drum, the ear-piercing fife,
  The royal banner, and all quality,
  Pride, pomp, and circumstance[377] of glorious war!
  And, O you mortal engines,[378] whose rude throats
  The immortal Jove's dread clamours counterfeit,
  Farewell! Othello's occupation's gone!
Iago. Is it possible, my lord?
Othello. Villain, be sure thou prove my love a whore,
  Be sure of it; give me the ocular proof;   360
  Or, by the worth of mine eternal soul,
  Thou hadst been better have been born a dog
  Than answer my wak'd wrath.

---

[371] Opium.   [372] A soporific.   [373] I.e., soporifics.   [374] Whole army.   [375] Lowest rank of manual laborers in the army.   [376] As long as.   [377] Pageantry.   [378] Deadly artillery.

Iago.   Is 't come to this?

Othello.   Make me to see 't; or, at the least, so prove it,
    That the probation[379] bear no hinge nor loop
    To hang a doubt on; or woe upon thy life!

Iago.   My noble lord—

Othello.   If thou dost slander her and torture me,
    Never pray more; abandon all remorse;
    On horror's head horrors accumulate;   370
    Do deeds to make heaven weep, all earth amaz'd;
    For nothing canst thou to damnation add
    Greater than that.

Iago.   O grace! O heaven forgive me!
    Are you a man! have you a soul or sense?
    God be wi' you; take mine office. O wretched fool!
    That liv'st to make thine honesty a vice.
    O monstrous world! Take note, take note, O world!
    To be direct and honest is not safe.
    I thank you for this profit,[380] and, from hence
    I'll love no friend, sith[381] love breeds such offence.   380

Othello.   Nay, stay; thou shouldst be honest.

Iago.   I should be wise; for honesty's a fool,
    And loses that it works for.

Othello.   By the world,
    I think my wife be honest and think she is not;
    I think that thou art just and think thou art not.
    I'll have some proof. Her name, that was as fresh
    As Dian's[382] visage, is now begrim'd and black
    As mine own face. If there be cords or knives,
    Poison or fire or suffocating streams,
    I'll not endure it. Would I were satisfied!   390

Iago.   I see, sir, you are eaten up with passion.
    I do repent me that I put it to you.
    You would be satisfied?

Othello.   Would! nay, I will.

Iago.   And may; but how? how satisfied, my lord?
    Would you, the supervisor,[383] grossly gape on;
    Behold her tupp'd?

Othello.   Death and damnation! O!

Iago.   It were a tedious[384] difficulty, I think,
    To bring them to that prospect; damn them then,
    If ever mortal eyes do see them bolster[385]
    More[386] than their own! What then? how then?   400
    What shall I say? Where's satisfaction?

---

[379] Proof.   [380] Lesson.   [381] Since.   [382] Diana's, the goddess of the moon.
[383] Observer.   [384] Laborious.   [385] Lie together.   [386] Other.

It is impossible you should see this,
Were they as prime[387] as goats, as hot as monkeys,
As salt as wolves in pride,[388] and fools as gross
As ignorance made drunk; but yet, I say,
If imputation, and strong circumstances,
Which lead directly to the door of truth,
Will give you satisfaction, you may have it.
Othello.   Give me a living reason she's disloyal.
Iago.   I do not like the office;   410
But, sith I am enter'd in this cause so far,
Prick'd to 't by foolish honesty and love,
I will go on. I lay with Cassio lately;
And, being troubled with a raging tooth,
I could not sleep.
There are a kind of men so loose of soul
That in their sleeps will mutter their affairs;
One of this kind is Cassio.
In sleep I heard him say, 'Sweet Desdemona,
Let us be wary, let us hide our loves!'   420
And then, sir, would he gripe[389] and wring my hand,
Cry, 'O, sweet creature!' and then kiss me hard,
As if he pluck'd up kisses by the roots,
That grew upon my lips; then laid his leg
Over my thigh, and sigh'd, and kiss'd; and then
Cried, 'Cursed fate, that gave thee to the Moor!'
Othello.   O monstrous! monstrous!
Iago.   Nay, this was but his dream.
Othello.   But this denoted a foregone conclusion:[390]
'Tis a shrewd doubt,[391] though it be but a dream.
Iago.   And this may help to thicken other proofs   430
That do demonstrate thinly.
Othello.   I'll tear her all to pieces.
Iago.   Nay, but be wise; yet we see nothing done;
She may be honest yet. Tell me but this:
Have you not sometimes seen a handkerchief
Spotted with strawberries in your wife's hand?
Othello.   I gave her such a one; 'twas my first gift.
Iago.   I know not that; but such a handkerchief—
I am sure it was your wife's—did I to-day
See Cassio wipe his beard with.
Othello.   If it be that,—
Iago.   If it be that, or any that was hers,   440
It speaks against her with the other proofs.

---

[387] Lustful.   [388] Heat.   [389] Seize.   [390] Previous consummation.   [391] (1) Cursed,
(2) Acute, suspicion.

Othello.   O! that the slave had forty thousand lives;
    One is too poor, too weak for my revenge.
    Now do I see 'tis true. Look here, Iago;
    All my fond love thus do I blow to heaven:
    'Tis gone.
    Arise, black vengeance, from the hollow hell!
    Yield up, O love! thy crown and hearted throne
    To tyrannous hate. Swell, bosom, with thy fraught,[392]
    For 'tis of aspics'[393] tongues!
Iago.   Yet be content.[394]   450
Othello.   O! blood, blood, blood!
Iago.   Patience, I say; your mind, perhaps, may change.
Othello.   Never, Iago. Like to the Pontic sea,[395]
    Whose icy current and compulsive course
    Ne'er feels retiring ebb, but keeps due on
    To the Propontic and the Hellespont,[396]
    Even so my bloody thoughts, with violent pace,
    Shall ne'er look back, ne'er ebb to humble love,
    Till that a capable[397] and wide revenge
    Swallow them up.   *(Kneels.)*
                        Now, by yond marble heaven,   460
    In the due reverence of a sacred vow
    I here engage my words.
Iago.   Do not rise yet.   *(Kneels.)*
    Witness, you ever-burning lights above!
    You elements that clip[398] us round about!
    Witness, that here Iago doth give up
    The execution of his wit, hands, heart,
    To wrong'd Othello's service! Let him command,
    And to obey shall be in me remorse,[399]
    What bloody business ever.[400]   *(They rise.)*
Othello.   I greet thy love,
    Not with vain thanks, but with acceptance bounteous,   470
    And will upon the instant put thee to 't:
    Within these three days let me hear thee say
    That Cassio 's not alive.
Iago.   My friend is dead; 'tis done at your request:
    But let her live.
Othello.   Damn her, lewd minx! O, damn her!
    Come, go with me apart; I will withdraw.

---

[392] Burden.   [393] Poisonous snakes.   [394] Patient.   [395] The Black Sea.   [396] The
Sea of Marmara, the Dardanelles.   [397] Comprehensive.   [398] Encompass.
[399] Probably a corrupt line; the meaning appears to be: "to obey shall be my solemn
obligation."   [400] Soever.

To furnish me with some swift means of death
For the fair devil. Now art thou my lieutenant.
Iago.   I am your own for ever.   (*Exeunt.*)

SCENE 4.   Before the Castle.

(*Enter Desdemona, Emilia, and Clown.*)

Desdemona.   Do you know, sirrah,[401] where Lieutenant Cassio lies?[402]
Clown.   I dare not say he lies any where.
Desdemona.   Why, man?
Clown.   He is a soldier; and for one to say a soldier lies, is stabbing.[403]
Desdemona.   Go to;[404] where lodges he?
Clown.   To tell you where he lodges is to tell you where I lie.
Desdemona.   Can anything be made of this?
Clown.   I know not where he lodges, and for me to devise[405] a lodging, and
   say he lies here or he lies there, were to lie in mine own throat.
Desdemona.   Can you inquire him out, and be edified by report?
Clown.   I will catechize the world for him; that is, make questions, and by
   them answer.
Desdemona.   Seek him, bid him come hither; tell him I have moved my lord
   in his behalf, and hope all will be well.
Clown.   To do this is within the compass of man's wit, and therefore I will
   attempt the doing it.   (*Exit.*)
Desdemona.   Where should I lose that handkerchief, Emilia?
Emilia.   I know not, madam.
Desdemona.   Believe me, I had rather have lost my purse
   Full of cruzadoes;[406] and, but my noble Moor   20
   Is true of mind, and made of no such baseness
   As jealous creatures are, it were enough
   To put him to ill thinking.
Emilia.   Is he not jealous?
Desdemona.   Who! he? I think the sun where he was born
   Drew all such humours from him.
Emilia.   Look! where he comes.
Desdemona.   I will not leave him now till Cassio
   Be call'd to him.

(*Enter Othello.*)

          How is 't with you, my lord?

---

[401] Common form of address to inferiors.   [402] Lives.   [403] I.e., is cause for stabbing.
[404] Here apparently: "Come on!"   [405] Invent.   [406] Portuguese gold coins.

Othello. Well, my good lady. *(Aside)* O! hardness to dissemble.
  How do you, Desdemona?
Desdemona.   Well, my good lord.
Othello. Give me your hand. This hand is moist,[407] my lady.   30
Desdemona. It yet has felt no age nor known no sorrow.
Othello. This argues fruitfulness and liberal[408] heart;
  Hot, hot, and moist; this hand of yours requires
  A sequester[409] from liberty, fasting and prayer,
  Much castigation, exercise devout;
  For here 's a young and sweating devil here,
  That commonly rebels. 'Tis a good hand,
  A frank one.
Desdemona. You may, indeed, say so;
  For 'twas that hand that gave away my heart.
Othello. A liberal hand; the hearts of old gave hands,   40
  But our new heraldry[410] is hands not hearts.
Desdemona. I cannot speak of this. Come now, your promise.
Othello. What promise, chuck?[411]
Desdemona. I have sent to bid Cassio come speak with you.
Othello. I have a salt and sorry rheum offends me.
  Lend me thy handkerchief.
Desdemona.   Here, my lord.
Othello. That which I gave you.
Desdemona.   I have it not about me.
Othello. Not?
Desdemona. No, indeed, my lord.
Othello.   That is a fault.
  That handkerchief
  Did an Egyptian[412] to my mother give;   50
  She was a charmer,[413] and could almost read
  The thoughts of people; she told her, while she kept it,
  'Twould make her amiable[414] and subdue my father
  Entirely to her love, but if she lost it
  Or made a gift of it, my father's eye
  Should hold her loathed, and his spirits should hunt
  After new fancies.[415] She dying gave it me;
  And bid me, when my fate would have me wive,
  To give it her. I did so; and take heed on 't;
  Make it a darling like your precious eye;   60

---

[407] A supposed symptom of a lustful nature.   [408] With overtones of: too free, loose.
[409] Separation.   [410] I.e., new heraldic symbolism (Othello means that the new way is not to give the heart together with the hand).   [411] Common term of endearment.   [412] Gypsy.
[413] Sorceress.   [414] Lovable, desirable.   [415] Loves.

To lose 't or give 't away, were such perdition
As nothing else could match.
Desdemona.   Is 't possible?
Othello.   'Tis true; there 's magic in the web of it;
A sibyl,[416] that had number'd in the world
The sun to course two hundred compasses,
In her prophetic fury sew'd the work;
The worms were hallow'd that did breed the silk,
And it was dy'd in mummy[417] which the skilful
Conserv'd of maidens' hearts.
Desdemona.   Indeed! is 't true?
Othello.   Most veritable; therefore look to 't well.   70
Desdemona.   Then would to heaven that I had never seen it!
Othello.   Ha! wherefore?
Desdemona.   Why do you speak so startingly and rash?
Othello.   Is 't lost? is 't gone? speak, is it out o' the way?
Desdemona.   Heaven bless us!
Othello.   Say you?
Desdemona.   It is not lost; but what an if[418] it were?
Othello.   How!
Desdemona.   I say, it is not lost.
Othello.   Fetch 't, let me see 't!
Desdemona.   Why, so I can, sir, but I will not now.
This is a trick to put me from my suit: 80
Pray you let Cassio be receiv'd again.
Othello.   Fetch me the handkerchief; my mind misgives.
Desdemona.   Come, come;
You'll never meet a more sufficient[419] man.
Othello.   The handkerchief!
Desdemona.   I pray, talk[420] me of Cassio.
Othello.   The handkerchief!
Desdemona.   A man that all his time
Hath founded his good fortunes on your love,
Shar'd dangers with you,—
Othello.   The handkerchief!
Desdemona.   In sooth, you are to blame.   90
Othello.   Away!   (*Exit.*)
Emilia.   Is not this man jealous?
Desdemona.   I ne'er saw this before.
Sure, there's some wonder in this handkerchief;
I am most unhappy in the loss of it.

---

[416] Prophetess.   [417] Drug (medicinal or magic) derived from embalmed bodies.   [418] If.
[419] Adequate.   [420] Talk to.

Emilia.   'Tis not a year or two shows us a man;
 They are all but[421] stomachs, and we all but[421] food;
 They eat us hungerly, and when they are full
 They belch us. Look you! Cassio and my husband.

(Enter Iago and Cassio.)

Iago.   There is no other way; 'tis she must do 't:
 And, lo! the happiness;[422] go and importune her.   100
Desdemona.   How now, good Cassio! what 's the news with you?
Cassio.   Madam, my former suit: I do beseech you
 That by your virtuous means I may again
 Exist, and be a member of his love
 Whom I with all the office[423] of my heart
 Entirely honour; I would not be delay'd.
 If my offence be of such mortal kind
 That nor my service past, nor present sorrows,
 Nor purpos'd merit in futurity,
 Can ransom me into his love again,   110
 But to know so must be my benefit;
 So shall I clothe me in a forc'd content,
 And shut myself up in some other course
 To fortune's alms.
Desdemona.   Alas! thrice-gentle Cassio!
 My advocation is not now in tune;
 My lord is not my lord, nor should I know him,
 Were he in favour[424] as in humour alter'd.
 So help me every spirit sanctified,
 As I have spoken for you all my best
 And stood within the blank of[425] his displeasure   120
 For my free speech. You must awhile be patient;
 What I can do I will, and more I will
 Than for myself I dare: let that suffice you.
Iago.   Is my lord angry?
Emilia.   He went hence but now,
 And certainly in strange unquietness.
Iago.   Can he be angry? I have seen the cannon,
 When it hath blown his ranks[426] into the air,
 And, like the devil, from his very arm
 Puff'd his own brother; and can he be angry?

---

[421] Only . . . only.   [422] "What luck!"   [423] Duty.   [424] Appearance.   [425] As the target for.   [426] I.e., his soldiers.

Something of moment[427] then; I will go meet him;   130
There's matter in 't indeed, if he be angry.
Desdemona.   I prithee, do so. *(Exit Iago.)* Something, sure, of state,[428]
Either from Venice, or some unhatch'd[429] practice
Made demonstrable here in Cyprus to him,
Hath puddled[430] his clear spirit; and, in such cases
Men's natures wrangle with inferior things,
Though great ones are their object. 'Tis even so;
For let our finger ache, and it indues[431]
Our other healthful members even to that sense
Of pain. Nay, we must think men are not gods,   140
Nor of them look for such observancy[432]
As fits the bridal.[433] Beshrew me much, Emilia,
I was—unhandsome warrior as I am—
Arraigning his unkindness with[434] my soul;
But now I find I had suborn'd the witness,[435]
And he 's indicted falsely.
Emilia.   Pray heaven it be state matters, as you think,
And no conception,[436] nor no jealous toy[437]
Concerning you.
Desdemona.   Alas the day! I never gave him cause.   150
Emilia.   But jealous souls will not be answer'd so;
They are not ever jealous for the cause,
But jealous for they are jealous; 'tis a monster
Begot upon itself, born on itself.
Desdemona.   Heaven keep that monster from Othello's mind!
Emilia.   Lady, amen.
Desdemona.   I will go seek him. Cassio, walk hereabout;
If I do find him fit, I'll move your suit
And seek to effect it to my uttermost.
Cassio.   I humbly thank your ladyship.   160

                              (Exeunt Desdemona and Emilia.)
(Enter Bianca.)

Bianca.   Save you, friend Cassio!
Cassio.   What make you from home?
How is it with you, my most fair Bianca?
I' faith, sweet love, I was coming to your house.
Bianca.   And I was going to your lodging, Cassio.

---

[427] Important.   [428] Public affairs.   [429] Abortive or budding plot.   [430] Muddied.
[431] Brings, leads.   [432] Attention.   [433] Wedding.   [434] To.   [435] I.e., caused my soul to bring in wrong charges.   [436] Fancy, supposition.   [437] Fancy.

What! keep a week away? seven days and nights?
Eight score eight hours? and lovers' absent hours,
More tedious than the dial eight score times?
O weary reckoning!
Cassio.　　　　　Pardon me, Bianca,
I have this while with leaden thoughts been press'd;
But I shall, in a more continuate[438] time,　　　　　170
Strike off[439] this score of absence. Sweet Bianca,

(Giving her Desdemona's handkerchief.)

Take me this work out.
Bianca.　　　　　O Cassio! whence came this?
This is some token from a newer friend;
To the felt absence now I feel a cause;
Is 't come to this? Well, well.
Cassio.　　　　　Go to, woman!
Throw your vile guesses in the devil's teeth,
From whence you have them. You are jealous now
That this is from some mistress, some remembrance:
No, in good troth, Bianca.
Bianca.　　　　　Why, whose is it?　　　　　180
Cassio.　I know not, sweet; I found it in my chamber.
I like the work well; ere it be demanded,—[440]
As like enough it will,—I'd have it copied;
Take it and do 't; and leave me for this time.
Bianca.　Leave you! wherefore?
Cassio.　I do attend here on[441] the general,
And think it no addition,[442] nor my wish,
To have him see me woman'd.
Bianca.　　　　　Why, I pray you?
Cassio.　Not that I love you not.
Bianca.　　　　　But that you do not love me.
I pray you, bring me on the way a little　　　　　190
And say if I shall see you soon at night.
Cassio.　'Tis but a little way that I can bring you,
For I attend here; but I'll see you soon.
Bianca.　'Tis very good; I must be circumstanc'd.[443]　　　　　*(Exeunt.)*

---

[438] Uninterrupted.　　[439] Cancel (i.e., make up for).　　[440] Asked for.　　[441] Wait for.
[442] Advantage, credit.　　[443] Governed by circumstances.

Act IV

SCENE 1.   Cyprus. Before the Castle.

(Enter Othello and Iago.)

Iago.   Will you think so?
Othello.   Think so, Iago!
Iago.   What!
  To kiss in private?
Othello.   An unauthoriz'd kiss.
Iago.   Or to be naked with her friend a-bed
  An hour or more, not meaning any harm?
Othello.   Naked a-bed, Iago, and not mean harm?
  It is hypocrisy against the devil:[444]
  They that mean virtuously, and yet do so,
  The devil their virtue tempts, and they tempt heaven.
Iago.   If they do nothing, 'tis a venial slip;
  But if I give my wife a handkerchief,—   10
Othello.   What then?
Iago.   Why, then, 'tis hers, my lord; and, being hers,
  She may, I think, bestow 't on any man.
Othello.   She is protectress of her honour too;
  May she give that?
Iago.   Her honour is an essence that 's not seen;
  They have it very oft that have it not:[445]
  But for the handkerchief,—
Othello.   By heaven, I would most gladly have forgot it:—
  Thou said'st,—O! it comes o'er my memory,   20
  As doth the raven[446] o'er the infected house,
  Boding to all,—he had my handkerchief.
Iago.   Ay, what of that?
Othello.   That's not so good now.
Iago.   What,
  If I had said I had seen him do you wrong?
  Or heard him say, as knaves be such abroad,[447]
  Who having, by their own importunate suit,
  Or voluntary dotage[448] of some mistress,
  Convinced or supplied them,[449] cannot choose
  But they must blab.

---

[444] I.e., by not committing the sin which the situation invites.   [445] I.e., some unchaste women are thought chaste.   [446] (1) A bad omen, (2) A carrier of the plague.   [447] As there are some such in the world.   [448] Foolish affection.   [449] Overcome (their reluctance) or satisfied (their desires).

Othello.   Hath he said any thing?
Iago.   He hath, my lord; but be you well assur'd,   30
  No more than he'll unswear.
Othello.   What hath he said?
Iago.   Faith, that he did— I know not what he did.
Othello.   What? what?
Iago.   Lie—
Othello.   With her?
Iago.   With her, on her; what you will.
Othello.   Lie with her; lie on her! We say, lie on her, when they belie her.
  Lie with her! that's fulsome. Handkerchief,—confessions,—handkerchief!
  To confess, and be hanged for his labour. First, to be hanged, and then to
  confess: I tremble at it. Nature would not invest herself in such shadowing
  passion without some instruction.[450] It is not words that shake me thus. Pish!
  Noses, ears, and lips. It is possible?—Confess!—Handkerchief!—O devil!

(Falls in a trance.)

Iago.   Work on,
  My medicine, work! Thus credulous fools are caught;
  And many worthy and chaste dames even thus,
  All guiltless, meet reproach. What, ho! my lord!
  My lord, I say! Othello!

(Enter Cassio.)

                How now, Cassio!
Cassio.   What's the matter?
Iago.   My lord is fallen into an epilepsy;[451]
  This is his second fit; he had one yesterday.
Cassio.   Rub him about the temples.
Iago.   No, forbear;
  The lethargy[452] must have his quiet course,   50
  If not, he foams at mouth, and by and by
  Breaks out to savage madness. Look! he stirs;
  Do you withdraw yourself a little while,
  He will recover straight; when he is gone,
  I would on great occasion[453] speak with you.   *(Exit Cassio.)*
  How is it, general? have you not hurt your head?
Othello.   Dost thou mock me?[454]
Iago.   I mock you! no, by heaven.
  Would you would bear your fortune like a man!

---

[450] I would not fall into such passion unless there were some real grounds for it.   [451] Seizure,
fit.   [452] Coma.   [453] Important matter.   [454] Another allusion to the cuckold's horns.

Othello.   A horned man's a monster and a beast.

Iago.   There's many a beast then, in a populous city,   60
And many a civil[455] monster.

Othello.   Did he confess it?

Iago.   Good sir, be a man;
Think every bearded fellow that's but yok'd
May draw[456] with you; there's millions now alive
That nightly lie in those unproper[457] beds
Which they dare swear peculiar;[458] your case is better.
O! 'tis the spite of hell, the fiend's arch-mock,
To lip[459] a wanton in a secure[460] couch,
And to suppose her chaste. No, let me know;
And knowing what I am, I know what she shall be.   70

Othello.   O! thou art wise; 'tis certain.

Iago.   Stand you awhile apart;
Confine yourself but in a patient list.[461]
Whilst you were here o'erwhelmed with your grief,—
A passion most unsuiting such a man,—
Cassio came hither; I shifted him away,
And laid good 'scuse upon your ecstasy;[462]
Bade him anon return and here speak with me;
The which he promis'd. Do but encave yourself,
And mark the fleers, the gibes, and notable scorns,
That dwell in every region of his face;   80
For I will make him tell the tale anew,
Where, how, how oft, how long ago, and when
He hath, and is again to cope[463] your wife:
I say, but mark his gesture. Marry, patience;
Or I shall say you are all in all in spleen,[464]
And nothing of a man.

Othello.   Dost thou hear, Iago?
I will be found most cunning in my patience;
But—dost thou hear?—most bloody.

Iago.   That's not amiss:
But yet keep time[465] in all. Will you withdraw?   *(Othello goes apart.)*
Now will I question Cassio of Bianca,   90
A housewife[466] that by selling her desires
Buys herself bread and clothes; it is a creature
That dotes on Cassio; as 'tis the strumpet's plague

---

[455] Citizen.   [456] I.e., pull the burden of cuckoldom.   [457] Not exclusively their own.
[458] Exclusively their own.   [459] Kiss.   [460] I.e., without suspicion of having a rival.
[461] Bounds of patience.   [462] Derangement, trance.   [463] Close with.   [464] Completely
overcome by passion.   [465] Maintain control.   [466] Hussy.

To beguile many and be beguil'd by one.
He, when he hears of her, cannot refrain
From the excess of laughter. Here he comes:

(Re-enter Cassio.)

As he shall smile, Othello shall go mad;
And his unbookish[467] jealousy must construe
Poor Cassio's smiles, gestures, and light behaviour
Quite in the wrong. How do you now, lieutenant?   100
Cassio.   The worser that you give me the addition[468]
Whose want[469] even kills me.
Iago.   Ply Desdemona well, and you are sure on 't.
(Speaking lower.) Now, if this suit lay in Bianca's power,
How quickly should you speed!
Cassio.   Alas! poor caitiff![470]
Othello.   Look! how he laughs already!
Iago.   I never knew woman love man so.
Cassio.   Alas! poor rogue, I think i' faith, she loves me.
Othello.   Now he denies it faintly, and laughs it out.
Iago.   Do you hear, Cassio?
Othello.   Now he importunes him   110
To tell it o'er: go to; well said, well said.
Iago.   She gives it out that you shall marry her;
Do you intend it?
Cassio.   Ha, ha, ha!
Othello.   Do you triumph, Roman?[471] do you triumph?
Cassio.   I marry her! what? a customer?[472] I prithee, bear some charity to my
wit;[473] do not think it so unwholesome. Ha, ha, ha!
Othello.   So, so, so, so. They laugh that win.[474]
Iago.   Faith, the cry goes that you shall marry her.
Cassio.   Prithee, say true.   120
Iago.   I am a very villain else.
Othello.   Have you scored me?[475] Well.
Cassio.   This is the monkey's own giving out: she is persuaded I will marry
her, out of her own love and flattery, not out of my promise.
Othello.   Iago beckons me;[476] now he begins the story.
Cassio.   She was here even now; she haunts me in every place. I was the other
day talking on the sea-bank with certain Venetians, and thither comes this
bauble,[477] and, by this hand, she falls me thus about my neck;—

---

[467] Unpracticed, naive.   [468] Title.   [469] The want of which.   [470] Wretch.
[471] I.e., one who triumphs (?).   [472] Courtesan, prostitute.   [473] Give me credit for some
sense.   [474] "He who laughs last laughs longest" (?).   [475] Wounded, defaced (?); or: settled
my account (?).   [476] Signals.   [477] Plaything.

Othello.   Crying, 'O dear Cassio!' as it were; his gesture imports it.

Cassio.   So hangs and lolls and weeps upon me; so hales[478] and pulls me; ha, ha, ha!

Othello.   Now he tells how she plucked him to my chamber. O! I see that nose of yours, but not the dog I shall throw it to.

Cassio.   Well, I must leave her company.

Iago.   Before me![479] look, where she comes.

Cassio.   'Tis such another fitchew![480] marry, a perfumed one.

(Enter Bianca.)

What do you mean by this haunting of me?

Bianca.   Let the devil and his dam haunt you! What did you mean by that same handkerchief you gave me even now? I was a fine fool to take it. I must take out the work! A likely piece of work, that you should find it in your chamber, and not know who left it there! This is some minx's token, and I must take out the work! There, give it your hobby-horse;[481] wheresoever you had it I'll take out no work on 't.

Cassio.   How now, my sweet Bianca! how now, how now!

Othello.   By heaven, that should be[482] my handkerchief!

Bianca.   An you'll come to supper to-night, you may; an you will not, come when you are next prepared[483] for.   *(Exit.)*

Iago.   After her, after her.

Cassio.   Faith, I must; she'll rail in the street else.

Iago.   Will you sup there?

Cassio.   Faith, I intend so.

Iago.   Well, I may chance to see you, for I would very fain[484] speak with you.

Cassio.   Prithee come; will you?

Iago.   Go to; say no more.   *(Exit Cassio.)*

Othello *(advancing).*   How shall I murder him, Iago?

Iago.   Did you perceive how he laughed at his vice?

Othello.   O! Iago!

Iago.   And did you see the handkerchief?

Othello.   Was that mine?

Iago.   Yours, by this hand; and to see how he prizes the foolish woman your wife! she gave it him, and he hath given it his whore.

Othello.   I would have him nine years a-killing. A fine woman! a fair woman! a sweet woman!

Iago.   Nay, you must forget that.

Othello.   Ay, let her rot, and perish, and be damned to-night; for she shall

---

[478] Hauls.   [479] An exclamation of surprise.   [480] Polecat, noted both for its strong smell and for its lechery.   [481] Harlot.   [482] I.e., I think that is.   [483] Expected (Bianca means that if he does not come that night, she will never want to see him again).   [484] Gladly.

not live. No, my heart is turned to stone; I strike it, and it hurts my hand. O! the world hath not a sweeter creature; she might lie by an emperor's side and command him tasks.

Iago.   Nay, that's not your way.[485]

Othello.   Hang her! I do but say what she is. So delicate with her needle! An admirable musician! O, she will sing the savageness out of a bear. Of so high and plenteous wit and invention!

Iago.   She's the worse for all this.

Othello.   O! a thousand, a thousand times. And then, of so gentle a condition![486]

Iago.   Ay, too gentle.[487]

Othello.   Nay, that's certain;—but yet the pity of it, Iago!
O! Iago, the pity of it, Iago!

Iago.   If you are so fond over her iniquity, give her patent to offend; for, if it touch not you, it comes near nobody.

Othello.   I will chop her into messes.[488] Cuckold me!

Iago.   O! 'tis foul in her.

Othello.   With mine officer!

Iago.   That's fouler.

Othello.   Get me some poison, Iago; this night: I'll not expostulate with her, lest her body and beauty unprovide my mind again.[489] This night, Iago.

Iago.   Do it not with poison, strangle her in her bed, even the bed she hath contaminated.

Othello.   Good, good; the justice of it pleases; very good.

Iago.   And for Cassio, let me be his undertaker;[490] you shall hear more by midnight.

Othello.   Excellent good. (*A trumpet within.*) What trumpet is that same?

Iago.   Something from Venice, sure. 'Tis Lodovico,
Come from the duke; and see, your wife is with him.

(*Enter Lodovico, Desdemona, and Attendants.*)

Lodovico.   God save you, worthy general!

Othello.   With all my heart, sir.

Lodovico.   The duke and senators of Venice greet you.

(*Gives him a packet.*)

Othello.   I kiss the instrument of their pleasures.

(*Opens the packet, and reads.*)

---

[485] Proper course.   [486] So much the high-born lady.   [487] I.e., yielding.   [488] Bits.
[489] Unsettle my intention.   [490] Dispatcher.

Desdemona.   And what's the news, good cousin Lodovico?
Iago.   I am very glad to see you, signior;
  Welcome to Cyprus.
Lodovico.   I thank you. How does Lieutenant Cassio?
Iago.   Lives, sir.   200
Desdemona.   Cousin, there's fall'n between him and my lord
  An unkind[491] breach; but you shall make all well.
Othello.   Are you sure of that?
Desdemona.   My lord?
Othello *(reads).*   'This fail you not to do, as you will'—
Lodovico.   He did not call; he's busy in the paper.
  Is there division[492] twixt my lord and Cassio?
Desdemona.   A most unhappy one; I would do much
  To atone[493] them, for the love I bear to Cassio.
Othello.   Fire and brimstone!
Desdemona.   My lord?
Othello.   Are you wise?   210
Desdemona.   What! is he angry?
Lodovico.   May be the letter mov'd him;
  For, as I think, they do command him home,
  Deputing Cassio in his government.
Desdemona.   Trust me, I am glad on 't.
Othello.   Indeed!
Desdemona.   My lord?
Othello.   I am glad to see you mad.
Desdemona.   Why, sweet Othello?
Othello.   Devil!   *(Strikes her.)*
Desdemona.   I have not deserved this.
Lodovico.   My lord, this would not be believ'd in Venice,
  Though I should swear I saw 't; 'tis very much;
  Make her amends, she weeps.
Othello.   O devil, devil!
  If that the earth could teem with woman's tears,
  Each drop she falls[494] would prove a crocodile.[495]   220
  Out of my sight!
Desdemona.   I will not stay to offend you.   *(Going.)*
Lodovico.   Truly, an obedient lady;
  I do beseech your lordship, call her back.
Othello.   Mistress!
Desdemona.   My lord?
Othello.   What would you with her, sir?

---

[491] Unnatural.   [492] Estrangement.   [493] Reconcile.   [494] Lets fall.   [495] The
crocodile's tears were supposed to be hypocritical.

Lodovico.   Why, I, my lord?
Othello.   Ay; you did wish that I would make her turn:
   Sir, she can turn, and turn, and yet go on,
   And turn again; and she can weep, sir, weep;
   And she's obedient, as you say, obedient,   230
   Very obedient. Proceed you in your tears.
   Concerning this, sir—O well-painted passion!—
   I am commanded home. Get you away;
   I'll send for you anon. Sir, I obey the mandate,
   And will return to Venice. Hence! avaunt![496]   *(Exit Desdemona.)*
   Cassio shall have my place. And, sir, to-night,
   I do entreat that we may sup together;
   You are welcome, sir, to Cyprus. Goats and monkeys!   *(Exit.)*
Lodovico.   Is this the noble Moor whom our full senate
   Call all-in-all sufficient? is this the noble nature   240
   Whom passion could not shake? whose solid virtue
   The shot of accident nor dart of chance
   Could neither graze nor pierce?
Iago.   He is much chang'd.
Lodovico.   Are his wits safe? is he not light of brain?
Iago.   He's that he is; I may not breathe my censure.
   What he might be, if, what he might, he is not,
   I would to heaven he were![497]
Lodovico.   What! strike his wife!
Iago.   Faith, that was not so well; yet would I knew
   That stroke would prove the worst!
Lodovico.   Is it his use?
   Or did the letters work upon his blood,   250
   And new-create this fault?
Iago.   Alas, alas!
   It is not honesty in me to speak
   What I have seen and known. You shall observe him,
   And his own courses[498] will denote him so
   That I may save my speech. Do but go after
   And mark how he continues.
Lodovico.   I am sorry that I am deceiv'd in him.   *(Exeunt.)*

   SCENE 2.   A Room in the Castle.

(Enter Othello and Emilia.)

---

[496] Begone!   [497] Another of Iago's gnomic speeches; perhaps approximately: "If now he is not himself, I wish he would be what he could be!"   [498] Actions.

Othello.   You have seen nothing, then?
Emilia.   Nor ever heard, nor ever did suspect.
Othello.   Yes, you have seen Cassio and her together.
Emilia.   But then I saw no harm, and then I heard
  Each syllable that breath made up between them.
Othello.   What! did they never whisper?
Emilia.   Never, my lord.
Othello.   Nor send you out o' the way?
Emilia.   Never.
Othello.   To fetch her fan, her gloves, her mask, nor nothing?[499]
Emilia.   Never, my lord.   10
Othello.   That's strange.
Emilia.   I durst, my lord, to wager she is honest,
  Lay down my soul at stake: if you think other,
  Remove your thought; it doth abuse your bosom.
  If any wretch have put this in your head,
  Let heaven requite it with the serpent's curse!
  For, if she be not honest, chaste, and true,
  There's no man happy; the purest of their wives
  Is foul as slander.
Othello.   Bid her come hither; go.   *(Exit Emilia.)*
  She says enough; yet she 's a simple[500] bawd
  That cannot say as much. This is a subtle whore,   20
  A closet lock and key of villanous secrets;
  And yet she 'll kneel and pray; I have seen her do 't.

(Re-enter Emilia with Desdemona.)

Desdemona.   My lord, what is your will?
Othello.   Pray, chuck, come hither.
Desdemona.   What is your pleasure?
Othello.   Let me see your eyes;
  Look in my face.
Desdemona.   What horrible fancy 's this?
Othello *(to Emilia).*   Some of your function,[501] mistress;
  Leave procreants alone and shut the door;
  Cough or cry 'hem' if any body come;
  Your mystery,[502] your mystery; nay, dispatch.   *(Exit Emilia.)*
Desdemona.   Upon my knees, what doth your speech import?   31
  I understand a fury in your words.
  But not the words.
Othello.   Why, what art thou?

---

[499] Anything.   [500] Simpleminded.   [501] To your duty, business.   [502] Trade.

Desdemona.   Your wife, my lord; your true
  And loyal wife.
Othello.   Come, swear it, damn thyself;
  Lest, being like one of heaven, the devils themselves
  Should fear to seize thee; therefore be double-damn'd;
  Swear thou art honest.
Desdemona.   Heaven doth truly know it.
Othello.   Heaven truly knows that thou art false as hell.
Desdemona.   To whom, my lord? with whom? how am I false?   40
Othello.   Ah! Desdemona; away, away, away!
Desdemona.   Alas, the heavy day!—Why do you weep?
  Am I the motive of these tears, my lord?
  If haply you my father do suspect
  An instrument of this your calling back,
  Lay not your blame on me; if you have lost him,
  Why, I have lost him too.
Othello.   Had it pleas'd heaven
  To try me with affliction, had he rain'd
  All kinds of sores and shames on my bare head,
  Steep'd me in poverty to the very lips,   50
  Given to captivity me and my utmost hopes,
  I should have found in some part of my soul
  A drop of patience; but, alas! to make me
  The fixed figure for the time of scorn[503]
  To point his slow and moving finger at;
  Yet could I bear that too; well, very well:
  But there, where I have garner'd[504] up my heart,
  Where either I must live or bear no life,
  The fountain from the which my current runs
  Or else dries up; to be discarded thence!   60
  Or keep it as a cistern for foul toads
  To knot and gender in![505] Turn thy complexion there,[506]
  Patience, thou young and rose-lipp'd cherubin;
  Ay, there, look grim as hell!
Desdemona.   I hope my noble lord esteems me honest.
Othello.   O! ay; as summer flies are in the shambles,[507]
  That quicken even with blowing. O thou weed!
  Who art so lovely fair and smell'st so sweet
  That the sense aches at thee, would thou hadst ne'er been born.
Desdemona.   Alas! what ignorant sin have I committed?   70
Othello.   Was this fair paper, this most goodly book,

---

[503] I.e., the scornful world.   [504] Stored.   [505] Bunch up and procreate.   [506] I.e.,
change your color to suit the "cistern for foul toads."   [507] Slaughterhouse.

Made to write 'whore' upon? What committed!
Committed! O thou public commoner![508]
I should make very forges of my cheeks,
That would to cinders burn up modesty,
Did I but speak thy deeds. What committed!
Heaven stops the nose at it and the moon winks,[509]
The bawdy wind that kisses all it meets
Is hush'd within the hollow mine of earth,
And will not hear it. What committed!
Impudent strumpet!   80
Desdemona.   By heaven, you do me wrong.
Othello.   Are not you a strumpet?
Desdemona.   No, as I am a Christian.
If to preserve this vessel for my lord
From any other foul unlawful touch
Be not to be a strumpet, I am none.
Othello.   What! not a whore?
Desdemona.   No, as I shall be sav'd.
Othello.   Is it possible?
Desdemona.   O! heaven forgive us.
Othello.   I cry you mercy,[510] then;
I took you for that cunning whore of Venice
That married with Othello. You, mistress,   90
That have the office opposite to Saint Peter,
And keep the gate of hell!

(Re-enter Emilia.)

You, you, ay, you!
We have done our course; there's money for your pains.
I pray you, turn the key and keep our counsel.   *(Exit.)*
Emilia.   Alas! what does this gentleman conceive?[511]
How do you, madam? how do you, my good lady?
Desdemona.   Faith, half asleep.
Emilia.   Good madam, what 's the matter with my lord?
Desdemona.   With who?
Emilia.   Why, with my lord, madam.   100
Desdemona.   Who is thy lord?
Emilia.   He that is yours, sweet lady.
Desdemona.   I have none; do not talk to me, Emilia;
I cannot weep, nor answer have I none,
But what should go by water.[512] Prithee, to-night

---

[508] Harlot.   [509] Closes her eyes.   [510] Beg your pardon.   [511] Imagine.   [512] Be conveyed by means of tears.

Lay on my bed my wedding sheets: remember:
And call thy husband hither.
Emilia.   Here is a change indeed!   (*Exit.*)
Desdemona.   'Tis meet I should be us'd so, very meet.
How have I been behav'd, that he might stick
The small'st opinion on my least misuse?[513]

(*Re-enter Emilia, with Iago.*)

Iago.   What is your pleasure, madam? How is it with you?   110
Desdemona.   I cannot tell. Those that do teach young babes
Do it with gentle means and easy tasks;
He might have chid me so; for, in good faith,
I am a child to chiding.
Iago.   What 's the matter, lady?
Emilia.   Alas, Iago, my lord hath so bewhor'd her,
Thrown such despite[514] and heavy terms upon her,
As true hearts cannot bear.
Desdemona.   Am I that name, Iago?
Iago.   What name, fair lady?
Desdemona.   Such as she says my lord did say I was.
Emilia.   He call'd her whore; a beggar in his drink   120
Could not have laid such terms upon his callat.[515]
Iago.   Why did he so?
Desdemona.   I do not know; I am sure I am none such.
Iago.   Do not weep, do not weep. Alas the day!
Emilia.   Has she forsook so many noble matches,
Her father and her country and her friends,
To be call'd whore? would it not make one weep?
Desdemona.   It is my wretched fortune.
Iago.   Beshrew[516] him for it!
How comes this trick upon him?
Desdemona.   Nay, heaven doth know.
Emilia.   I will be hang'd, if some eternal villain,   130
Some busy and insinuating rogue,
Some cogging[517] cozening slave, to get some office,
Have not devis'd this slander; I'll be hang'd else.
Iago.   Fie! there is no such man; it is impossible.
Desdemona.   If any such there be, heaven pardon him!
Emilia.   A halter pardon him, and hell gnaw his bones!
Why should he call her whore? who keeps her company?

---

[513] The least suspicion on my slightest misconduct.   [514] Abuse.   [515] Slut.
[516] Curse.   [517] Cheating.

What place? what time? what form? what likelihood?
The Moor 's abus'd by some most villanous knave,
Some base notorious knave, some scurvy fellow.   140
O heaven! that such companions[518] thou'dst unfold,
And put in every honest hand a whip
To lash the rascals naked through the world,
Even from the east to west!

Iago.   Speak within door.

Emilia.   O! fie upon them. Some such squire he was
   That turn'd your wit the seamy side without,[519]
   And made you to suspect me with the Moor.

Iago.   You are a fool; go to.

Desdemona.   O good Iago,
   What shall I do to win my lord again?
   Good friend, go to him; for, by this light of heaven,   150
   I know not how I lost him. Here I kneel:
   If e'er my will did trespass 'gainst his love,
   Either in discourse of thought or actual deed,
   Or that mine eyes, mine ears, or any sense,
   Delighted them[520] in any other form;
   Or that I do not yet,[521] and ever did,
   And ever will, though he do shake me off
   To beggarly divorcement, love him dearly,
   Comfort forswear me! Unkindness may do much;
   And his unkindness may defeat[522] my life,   160
   But never taint my love. I cannot say 'whore':
   It does abhor me now I speak the word;
   To do the act that might the addition earn
   Not the world's mass of vanity could make me.

Iago.   I pray you be content, 'tis but his humour;
   The business of the state does him offence,
   And he does chide with you.

Desdemona.   If 'twere no other,—

Iago.   'Tis but so, I warrant.   (*Trumpets.*)
   Hark! how these instruments summon to supper;
   The messengers of Venice stay the meat: 170
   Go in, and weep not; all things shall be well.

                              (*Exeunt Desdemona and Emilia.*)

(*Enter Roderigo.*)

---

[518] Fellows (derogatory).   [519] Outward.   [520] Found delight.   [521] Still.
[522] Destroy.

How now, Roderigo!

Roderigo.   I do not find that thou dealest justly with me.

Iago.   What in the contrary?[523]

Roderigo.   Every day thou daffest me[524] with some device, Iago; and rather, as it seems to me now, keepest from me all conveniency,[525] than suppliest me with the least advantage of hope. I will indeed no longer endure it, nor am I yet persuaded to put up[526] in peace what already I have foolishly suffered.

Iago.   Will you hear me, Roderigo?

Roderigo.   Faith, I have heard too much, for your words and performances are no kin together.

Iago.   You charge me most unjustly.

Roderigo.   With nought but truth. I have wasted myself out of my means. The jewels you have had from me to deliver to Desdemona would half have corrupted a votarist;[527] you have told me she has received them, and returned me expectations and comforts of sudden respect[528] and acquaintance, but I find none.

Iago.   Well; go to; very well.

Roderigo.   Very well! go to! I cannot go to, man; nor 'tis not very well: by this hand, I say, it is very scurvy, and begin to find myself fobbed[529] in it.

Iago.   Very well.

Roderigo.   I tell you 'tis not very well. I will make myself known to Desdemona; if she will return me my jewels, I will give over my suit and repent my unlawful solicitation; if not, assure yourself I will seek satisfaction of you.

Iago.   You have said now.[530]

Roderigo.   Ay, and said nothing, but what I protest intendment of doing.

Iago.   Why, now I see there's mettle in thee, and even from this instant do build on thee a better opinion than ever before. Give me thy hand, Roderigo; thou hast taken against me a most just exception; but yet, I protest, I have dealt most directly in thy affair.

Roderigo.   It hath not appeared.

Iago.   I grant indeed it hath not appeared, and your suspicion is not without wit and judgment. But, Roderigo, if thou hast that in thee indeed, which I have greater reason to believe now than ever, I mean purpose, courage, and valour, this night show it: if thou the next night following enjoy not Desdemona, take me from this world with treachery and devise engines for[531] my life.

Roderigo.   Well, what is it? is it within reason and compass?

Iago.   Sir, there is especial commission come from Venice to depute Cassio in Othello's place.

---

[523] I.e., what reason do you have for saying that.   [524] You put me off.   [525] Favorable circumstances.   [526] Put up with.   [527] Nun.   [528] Immediate consideration.   [529] Cheated.   [530] I.e., "I suppose you're through?" (?); or: "Now you're talking" (?).   [531] Devices against.

Roderigo. Is that true? why, then Othello and Desdemona return again to
    Venice.
Iago. O, no! he goes into Mauritania, and takes away with him the fair
    Desdemona, unless his abode be lingered here by some accident; wherein
    none can be so determinate[532] as the removing of Cassio.
Roderigo. How do you mean, removing of him?
Iago. Why, by making him uncapable of Othello's place; knocking out his
    brains.
Roderigo. And that you would have me do?
Iago. Ay; if you dare do yourself a profit and a right. He sups to-night with a
    harlotry,[533] and thither will I go to him; he knows not yet of his honourable
    fortune. If you will watch his going thence,—which I will fashion to fall out
    between twelve and one,—you may take him at your pleasure; I will be near
    to second your attempt, and he shall fall between us. Come, stand not
    amazed at it, but go along with me; I will show you such a necessity in his
    death that you shall think yourself bound to put it on him. It is now high
    supper-time, and the night grows to waste; about it.
Roderigo. I will hear further reason for this.
Iago. And you shall be satisfied.   *(Exeunt.)*

SCENE 3. Another Room in the Castle.

(Enter Othello, Lodovico, Desdemona, Emilia, and Attendants.)

Lodovico. I do beseech you, sir, trouble yourself no further.
Othello. O! pardon me; 'twill do me good to walk.
Lodovico. Madam, good-night; I humbly thank your ladyship.
Desdemona. Your honour is most welcome.
Othello.   Will you walk, sir?
    O! Desdemona,—
Desdemona. My lord?
Othello. Get you to bed on the instant; I will be returned forthwith; dismiss
    your attendant there; look it be done.
Desdemona. I will, my lord.   *(Exeunt Othello, Lodovico, and Attendants.)*
Emilia. How goes it now? He looks gentler than he did.   10
Desdemona. He says he will return incontinent;[534]
    He hath commanded me to go to bed,
    And bade me to dismiss you.
Emilia.   Dismiss me!
Desdemona. It was his bidding; therefore, good Emilia,
    Give me my nightly wearing, and adieu:
    We must not now displease him.

---

[532] Effective.   [533] Harlot.   [534] At once.

Emilia.   I would you had never seen him.

Desdemona.   So would not I; my love doth so approve him,
That even his stubbornness,[535] his checks[536] and frowns,—
Prithee, unpin me,—have grace and favour in them.   20

Emilia.   I have laid those sheets you bade me on the bed.

Desdemona.   All's one.[537] Good faith! how foolish are our minds!
If I do die before thee, prithee, shroud me
In one of those same sheets.

Emilia.   Come, come, you talk.

Desdemona.   My mother had a maid call'd Barbara;
She was in love, and he she lov'd prov'd mad[538]
And did forsake her; she had a song of 'willow';
An old thing 'twas, but it express'd her fortune,
And she died singing it; that song to-night
Will not go from my mind; I have much to do   30
But to go hang my head all at one side,
And sing it like poor Barbara. Prithee, dispatch.

Emilia.   Shall I go fetch your night-gown?

Desdemona.   No, unpin me here.
This Lodovico is a proper man.

Emilia.   A very handsome man.

Desdemona.   He speaks well.

Emilia.   I know a lady in Venice would have walked barefoot to Palestine for
a touch of his nether lip.

Desdemona (*sings*).

The poor soul sat sighing by a sycamore tree,
    Sing all a green willow;   40
Her hand on her bosom, her head on her knee,
    Sing willow, willow, willow:
The fresh streams ran by her, and murmur'd her moans;
    Sing willow, willow, willow:
Her salt tears fell from her and soften'd the stones;—

Lay by these:—
    Sing willow, willow, willow:

Prithee, hie thee;[539] he 'll come anon.—

Sing all a green willow must be my garland.
    Let nobody blame him, his scorn I approve,—   50
Nay, that's not next. Hark! who is it that knocks?

---

[535] Roughness.   [536] Rebukes.   [537] I.e., it doesn't matter.   [538] Wild.
[539] Hurry.

Emilia.   It is the wind.

Desdemona.

I call'd my love false love; but what said he then?
  Sing willow, willow, willow:
If I court moe[540] women, you 'll couch with moe men.

So, get thee gone; good-night. Mine eyes do itch;
  Doth that bode weeping?

Emilia.   'Tis neither here nor there.

Desdemona.   I have heard it said so. O! these men, these men!
  Dost thou in conscience think, tell me, Emilia,
  That there be women do abuse their husbands   60
  In such gross kind?

Emilia.   There be some such, no question.

Desdemona.   Wouldst thou do such a deed for all the world?

Emilia.   Why, would not you?

Desdemona.   No, by this heavenly light!

Emilia.   Nor I neither by this heavenly light;
  I might do 't as well i' the dark.

Desdemona.   Wouldst thou do such a deed for all the world?

Emilia.   The world is a huge thing; 'tis a great price
  For a small vice.

Desdemona.   In troth, I think thou wouldst not.

Emilia.   In troth, I think I should, and undo 't when I had done. Marry, I
  would not do such a thing for a joint-ring,[541] nor measures of lawn,[542] nor
  for gowns, petticoats, nor caps, nor any petty exhibition;[543] but for the whole
  world, who would not make her husband a cuckold to make him a monarch?
  I should venture purgatory for 't.

Desdemona.   Beshrew me, if I would do such a wrong
  For the whole world.

Emilia.   Why, the wrong is but a wrong i' the world; and having the world for
  your labour, 'tis a wrong in your own world, and you might quickly make it
  right.

Desdemona.   I do not think there is any such woman.

Emilia.   Yes, a dozen; and as many to the vantage,[544] as   80
  Would store[545] the world they played for.
  But I do think it is their husbands' faults
  If wives do fall. Say that they slack their duties,
  And pour our treasures into foreign laps,
  Or else break out in peevish jealousies,
  Throwing restraint upon us; or say they strike us,

---

[540] More.   [541] Ring made in separable halves.   [542] Fine linen.   [543] Offer, gift.
[544] Over and above.   [545] Populate.

Or scant[546] our former having[547] in despite;
Why, we have galls;[548] and though we have some grace,
Yet have we some revenge. Let husbands know
Their wives have sense like them; they see and smell,   90
And have their palates both for sweet and sour,
As husbands have. What is it that they do
When they change us for others? Is it sport?[549]
I think it is; and doth affection breed it?
I think it doth; is 't frailty that thus errs?
It is so too; and have not we affections,
Desires for sport, and frailty, as men have?
Then, let them use us well; else let them know,
The ills we do, their ills instruct us so.
Desdemona.   Good-night, good night; heaven me such usage[550] send,   100
Not to pick bad from bad, but by bad mend!   (*Exeunt.*)

Act V

SCENE 1.   Cyprus. A Street.

(*Enter Iago and Roderigo.*)

Iago.   Here, stand behind this bulk,[551] straight will he come:
Wear thy good rapier bare, and put it home.
Quick, quick; fear nothing; I 'll be at thy elbow.
It makes us, or it mars us; think on that,
And fix most firm thy resolution.
Roderigo.   Be near at hand; I may miscarry in 't.
Iago.   Here, at thy hand: be bold, and take thy stand.   (*Retires.*)
Roderigo.   I have no great devotion to the deed;
And yet he has given me satisfying reasons:
'Tis but a man gone: forth, my sword; he dies.   10
Iago.   I have rubb'd this young quat[552] almost to the sense,[553]
And he grows angry. Now, whether he kill Cassio,
Or Cassio him, or each do kill the other,
Every way makes my gain: live Roderigo,
He calls me to a restitution large
Of gold and jewels that I bobb'd[554] from him,
As gifts to Desdemona;

---

[546] Reduce.   [547] Allowance.   [548] Spirits, temper.   [549] Lust, sexual enjoyment.
[550] Habits (?), treatment (?).   [551] Jutting part of a wall.   [552] Pimple.   [553] To the
quick.   [554] Swindled.

It must not be: if Cassio do remain,
He hath a daily beauty in his life
That makes me ugly: and, besides, the Moor   20
May unfold me to him; there stand I in much peril.
No, he must die. But so;[555] I hear him coming.

(Enter Cassio.)

Roderigo.   I know his gait; 'tis he. Villain, thou diest!

(Makes a pass at Cassio.)

Cassio.   That thrust had been mine enemy indeed
   But that my coat is better than thou know'st;
   I will make proof of thine.

(Draws, and wounds Roderigo.)

Roderigo.   O! I am slain.

(Iago from behind wounds Cassio in the leg, and exit.)

Cassio.   I am maim'd for ever. Help, ho! murder! murder!   *(Falls.)*

(Enter Othello, at a distance.)

Othello.   The voice of Cassio: Iago keeps his word.
Roderigo.   O! villain that I am!
Othello.   It is e'en so.
Cassio.   O, help, ho! light! a surgeon!   30
Othello.   'Tis he: O brave Iago, honest and just!
   That hast such noble sense of thy friend's wrong;
   Thou teachest me. Minion,[556] your dear lies dead,
   And your unblest fate hies; strumpet, I come!
   Forth of my heart those charms, thine eyes, are blotted;
   Thy bed lust-stain'd shall with lust's blood be spotted.   *(Exit.)*

(Enter Lodovico and Gratiano, at a distance.)

Cassio.   What ho! no watch? no passage?[557] murder! murder!
Gratiano.   'Tis some mischance; the cry is very direful.
Cassio.   O, help!

---

[555] I.e., that's the only way.   [556] (Cassio's) darling, i.e., Desdemona.   [557] Passer-by.

Lodovico.   Hark!   40
Roderigo.   O wretched villain!
Lodovico.   Two or three groans: it is a heavy[558] night;
   These may be counterfeits; let 's think 't unsafe
   To come in to the cry[559] without more help.
Roderigo.   Nobody come? then shall I bleed to death.
Lodovico.   Hark!

(Re-enter Iago, with a light.)

Gratiano.   Here 's one comes in his shirt, with light and weapons.
Iago.   Who 's there? whose noise is this that cries on murder?
Lodovico.   We do not know.
Iago.   Did not you hear a cry?
Cassio.   Here, here! for heaven's sake, help me.
Iago.   What's the matter?   50
Gratiano.   This is Othello's ancient, as I take it.
Lodovico.   The same indeed; a very valiant fellow.
Iago.   What are you here that cry so grievously?
Cassio.   Iago? O! I am spoil'd, undone by villains!
   Give me some help.
Iago.   O me, lieutenant! what villains have done this?
Cassio.   I think that one of them is hereabout,
   And cannot make away.
Iago.   O treacherous villains!
   (To Lodovico and Gratiano.) What are you there? come in, and
   give some help.
Roderigo.   O! help me here.   60
Cassio.   That's one of them.
Iago.   O murderous slave! O villain!

(Stabs Roderigo.)

Roderigo.   O damn'd Iago! O inhuman dog!
Iago.   Kill men i' the dark! Where be these bloody thieves?
   How silent is this town! Ho! murder! murder!
   What may you be? are you of good or evil?
Lodovico.   As you shall prove us, praise us.
Iago.   Signior Lodovico?
Lodovico.   He, sir.
Iago.   I cry you mercy. Here 's Cassio hurt by villains.
Gratiano.   Cassio!   70

---

[558] Dark.   [559] Where the cry comes from.

Iago.   How is it, brother?

Cassio.   My leg is cut in two.

Iago.   Marry, heaven forbid.

Light, gentlemen; I 'll bind it with my shirt.

(Enter Bianca.)

Bianca.   What is the matter, ho? who is 't that cried?

Iago.   Who is 't that cried!

Bianca.   O my dear Cassio! my sweet Cassio!

O Cassio, Cassio, Cassio!

Iago.   O notable strumpet! Cassio, may you suspect

Who they should be that have thus mangled you?

Cassio.   No.   80

Gratiano.   I am sorry to find you thus; I have been to seek you.

Iago.   Lend me a garter. So. O! for a chair,

To bear him easily hence!

Bianca.   Alas; he faints! O Cassio, Cassio, Cassio!

Iago.   Gentlemen all, I do suspect this trash[560]

To be a party in this injury.

Patience awhile, good Cassio. Come, come.

Lend me a light. Know we this face, or no?

Alas! my friend and my dear countryman,

Roderigo? no: yes, sure, O heaven! Roderigo.   90

Gratiano.   What! of Venice?

Iago.   Even he, sir, did you know him?

Gratiano.   Know him! ay.

Iago.   Signior Gratiano? I cry you gentle pardon;

These bloody accidents must excuse my manners,

That so neglected you.

Gratiano.   I am glad to see you.

Iago.   How do you, Cassio? O! a chair, a chair!

Gratiano.   Roderigo!

(A chair brought in.)

Iago.   He, he, 'tis he,—O! that 's well said; the chair:

Some good men bear him carefully from hence;

I 'll fetch the general's surgeon. *(To Bianca.)* For you, mistress,   100

Save you your labour. He that lies slain here, Cassio,

Was my dear friend. What malice was between you?

Cassio.   None in the world; nor do I know that man.

Iago *(to Bianca).*   What! look you pale? O! bear him out o' the air—

---

[560] I.e., Bianca.

(Cassio and Roderigo are borne off.)

Stay you, good gentlemen. Look you pale, mistress?—
Do you perceive the gastness[561] of her eye?
Nay, if you stare, we shall hear more anon.
Behold her well; I pray you, look upon her.
Do you see, gentlemen? nay, guiltiness will speak
Though tongues were out of use.   110

(Enter Emilia.)

Emilia. 'Las! what 's the matter? what 's the matter, husband?
Iago. Cassio hath here been set on in the dark
  By Roderigo and fellows that are 'scaped:
  He 's almost slain, and Roderigo dead.
Emilia. Alas! good gentleman; alas! good Cassio!
Iago. This is the fruit of whoring. Prithee, Emilia,
  Go know of Cassio where he supp'd to-night.
  (To Bianca.) What! do you shake at that?
Bianca. He supp'd at my house; but I therefore shake not.
Iago. O! did he so? I charge you, go with me.   120
Emilia. Fie, fie, upon thee, strumpet!
Bianca. I am no strumpet, but of life as honest
  As you that thus abuse me.
Emilia.   As I! foh! fie upon thee!
Iago. Kind gentlemen, let 's go see poor Cassio dress'd.[562]
  Come, mistress, you must tell 's another tale.
  Emilia, run you to the citadel,
  And tell my lord and lady what hath happ'd.
  Will you go on afore? *(Aside.)* This is the night
  That either makes me or fordoes[563] me quite.   *(Exeunt.)*

SCENE 2. A Bedchamber in the Castle. Desdemona in bed asleep. A light
burning.

(Enter Othello.)

Othello. It is the cause,[564] it is the cause, my soul;
  Let me not name it to you, you chaste stars!
  It is the cause. Yet I 'll not shed her blood,
  Nor scar that whiter skin of hers than snow,

---

[561] Terror.   [562] Bandaged.   [563] Ruins.   [564] I.e., Desdemona's unchastity (Othello
means that the severity of the punishment is required by the nature of her sin).

And smooth as monumental alabaster.
Yet she must die, else she 'll betray more men.
Put out the light, and then put out the light:
If I quench thee, thou flaming minister,[565]
I can again thy former light restore,
Should I repent me; but once put out thy light,   10
Thou cunning'st[566] pattern of excelling nature,
I know not where is that Promethean[567] heat
That can thy light relume.[568] When I have pluck'd the rose,
I cannot give it vital growth again,
It needs must wither: I 'll smell it on the tree. (*Kisses her.*)
O balmy breath, that dost almost persuade
Justice to break her sword! One more, one more.
Be thus when thou art dead, and I will kill thee,
And love thee after. One more, and this the last:
So sweet was ne'er so fatal. I must weep,   20
But they are cruel tears; this sorrow 's heavenly,
It strikes where it doth love. She wakes.
Desdemona.   Who 's there? Othello?
Othello.   Ay, Desdemona.
Desdemona.   Will you come to bed, my lord?
Othello.   Have you pray'd to-night, Desdemona?
Desdemona.   Ay, my lord.
Othello.   If you bethink yourself of any crime
Unreconcil'd as yet to heaven and grace,
Solicit for it straight.
Desdemona.   Alas! my lord, what may you mean by that?
Othello.   Well, do it, and be brief; I will walk by:[569]   30
I would not kill thy unprepared spirit;
No; heaven forfend![570] I would not kill thy soul.
Desdemona.   Talk you of killing?
Othello.   Ay, I do.
Desdemona.   Then heaven
Have mercy on me!
Othello.   Amen! with all my heart.
Desdemona.   If you say so, I hope you will not kill me.
Othello.   Hum!
Desdemona.   And yet I fear you; for you are fatal then
When your eyes roll so. Why I should fear I know not,
Since guiltiness I know not; but yet I feel I fear.

---

[565] I.e., the candle.   [566] Most intricately wrought.   [567] In Greek mythology the demigod Prometheus stole fire from the gods and gave it to man.   [568] Relight.   [569] Nearby.
[570] Forbid.

Othello.   Think on thy sins.
Desdemona.   They are loves I bear to you.   40
Othello.   Ay, and for that thou diest.
Desdemona.   That death's unnatural that kills for loving.
    Alas! why gnaw you so your nether lip?
    Some bloody passion shakes your very frame;
    These are portents,[571] but yet, I hope, I hope
    They do not point on me.
Othello.   Peace, and be still!
Desdemona.   I will so. What 's the matter?
Othello.   That handkerchief which I so lov'd and gave thee
    Thou gav'st to Cassio.
Desdemona.   No, by my life and soul!
    Send for the man and ask him.
Othello.   Sweet soul, take heed,   50
    Take heed of perjury; thou 'rt on thy death-bed.
Desdemona.   Ay, but not yet to die.
Othello.   Yes, presently;[572]
    Therefore confess thee freely of thy sin;
    For to deny each article with oath
    Cannot remove nor choke the strong conception[573]
    That I do groan withal. Thou art to die.
Desdemona.   Then Lord have mercy on me!
Othello.   I say, amen.
Desdemona.   And have you mercy too! I never did
    Offend you in my life; never lov'd Cassio
    But with such general warranty[574] of heaven   60
    As I might love; I never gave him token.
Othello.   By heaven, I saw my handkerchief in 's hand.
    O perjur'd woman! thou dost stone[575] my heart,
    And mak'st me call what I intend to do
    A murder, which I thought a sacrifice:
    I saw the handkerchief.
Desdemona.   He found it then;
    I never gave it him. Send for him hither;
    Let him confess a truth.
Othello.   He had confessed.
Desdemona.   What, my lord?
Othello.   That he hath us'd thee.
Desdemona.   How? Unlawfully?
Othello.   Ay.   70

---

[571] Omens.   [572] At once.   [573] Belief.   [574] Permission.   [575] Turn to stone.

Desdemona. He will not say so.
Othello. No; his mouth is stopp'd:
  Honest Iago hath ta'en order for 't.[576]
Desdemona. O! my fear interprets. What! is he dead?
Othello. Had all his hairs been lives, my great revenge
  Had stomach[577] for them all.
Desdemona. Alas! he is betray'd and I undone.
Othello. Out, strumpet! Weep'st thou for him to my face?
Desdemona. O! banish me, my lord, but kill me not!
Othello. Down, strumpet!
Desdemona. Kill me to-morrow; let me live to-night! 80
Othello. Nay, if you strive,—
Desdemona. But half an hour!
Othello. Being done, there is no pause.
Desdemona. But while I say one prayer!
Othello. It is too late. *(He smothers her.)*
Emilia *(within).* My lord, my lord! what, ho! my lord, my lord!
Othello. What noise is this? Not dead? Not yet quite dead?
  I that am cruel am yet merciful;
  I would not have thee linger in thy pain.
  So, so.
Emilia *(within).* What, ho! my lord, my lord!
Othello. Who's there?
Emilia *(within).* O! good my lord, I would speak a word with you! 90
Othello. Yes; 'tis Emilia: by and by.[578] She's dead.
  'Tis like[579] she comes to speak of Cassio's death;
  The noise was high. Ha! no more moving?
  Still as the grave. Shall she come in? were 't good?[580]
  I think she stirs again: no. What 's best to do?
  If she come in she'll sure speak to my wife:
  My wife! my wife! what wife? I have no wife;
  O, insupportable! O heavy hour!
  Methinks it should be now a huge eclipse
  Of sun and moon, and that the affrighted globe 100
  Should yawn[581] at alteration.
Emilia *(within).* I do beseech you
  That I may speak with you, O! good my lord.
Othello. I had forgot thee: O! come in, Emilia:
  Soft, by and by: let me the curtains draw.
  Where art thou? *(Unlocks the door.)*

---

[576] Taken steps.   [577] Appetite.   [578] I.e., "just a moment."   [579] Likely.
[580] Would that be wise.   [581] Open up (as in an earthquake).

(*Enter Emilia.*)

                   What 's the matter with thee now?
Emilia.   O! my good lord, yonder 's foul murder done.
Othello.   What! now?
Emilia.   But now, my lord.
Othello.   It is the very error[582] of the moon;
   She comes more near the earth than she was wont,   110
   And makes men mad.
Emilia.   Cassio, my lord, has kill'd a young Venetian
   Call'd Roderigo.
Othello.   Roderigo kill'd!
  And Cassio kill'd?
Emilia.   No, Cassio is not kill'd.
Othello.   Not Cassio kill'd! then murder 's out of tune,
   And sweet revenge grows harsh.
Desdemona.   O! falsely, falsely murder'd.
Emilia.   Alas! what cry is that?
Othello.   That! what?
Emilia.   Out, and alas! that was my lady's voice:
   Help! Help, ho! help! O lady, speak again!   120
   Sweet Desdemona! O! sweet mistress, speak.
Desdemona.   A guiltless death I die.
Emilia.   O! who hath done this deed?
Desdemona.   Nobody; I myself; farewell:
   Commend me to my kind lord. O! farewell!   (*Dies.*)
Othello.   Why, how should she be murder'd?
Emilia.   Alas! who knows?
Othello.   You heard her say herself it was not I.
Emilia.   She said so; I must needs report the truth.
Othello.   She 's like a liar gone to burning hell;
   'Twas I that kill'd her.
Emilia.   O! the more angel she,   130
   And you the blacker devil.
Othello.   She turn'd to folly, and she was a whore.
Emilia.   Thou dost belie her, and thou art a devil.
Othello.   She was false as water.
Emilia.   Thou art rash as fire to say
   That she was false! O! she was heavenly true.
Othello.   Cassio did tup her; ask thy husband else.
   O! I were damn'd beneath all depth in hell
   But that I did proceed[583] upon just grounds
   To this extremity. Thy husband knew it all.

---

[582] Straying.   [583] Had I not proceeded.

Emilia.   My husband!   140
Othello.   Thy husband.
Emilia.   That she was false to wedlock?
Othello.   Ay, with Cassio. Nay, had she been true,
If heaven would make me such another world
Of one entire and perfect chrysolite,[584]
I'd not have sold her for it.
Emilia.   My husband!
Othello.   Ay, 'twas he that told me first:
An honest man he is, and hates the slime
That sticks on filthy deeds.
Emilia.   My husband!
Othello.   What needs this iterance,[585] woman? I say thy husband.   150
Emilia.   O mistress! villany hath made mocks with love.
My husband say that she was false!
Othello.   He, woman;
I say, thy husband: dost understand the word?
My friend, thy husband, honest, honest Iago.
Emilia.   If he say so, may his pernicious soul
Rot half a grain a day! he lies to the heart:
She was too fond of her most filthy bargain.[586]
Othello.   Ha!
Emilia.   Do thy worst:
This deed of thine is no more worthy heaven   160
Than thou wast worthy her.
Othello.   Peace! you were best.[587]
Emilia.   Thou hast not half the power to do me harm
As I have to be hurt. O gull! O dolt!
As ignorant as dirt! thou hast done a deed,—
I care not for thy sword; I'll make thee known,
Though I lost twenty lives. Help! help, ho! help!
The Moor has kill'd my mistress! murder! murder!

(Enter Montano, Gratiano, Iago, and others.)

Montano.   What is the matter? How now, general!
Emilia.   O! are you come, Iago? you have done well,
That men must lay their murders on your neck.   170
Gratiano.   What is the matter?
Emilia.   Disprove this villain if thou be'st a man:
He says thou told'st him that his wife was false.

---

[584] Topaz.   [585] Repetition.   [586] I.e., Othello.   [587] You'd better be quiet.

I know thou didst not, thou 'rt not such a villain.
Speak, for my heart is full.
Iago. I told him what I thought, and told no more
Than what he found himself was apt and true.
Emilia. But did you ever tell him she was false?
Iago. I did.
Emilia. You told a lie, an odious damned lie;   180
Upon my soul, a lie, a wicked lie;
She false with Cassio! Did you say with Cassio?
Iago. With Cassio, mistress. Go to, charm[588] your tongue.
Emilia. I will not charm my tongue; I am bound to speak.
My mistress here lies murder'd in her bed.
All. O heavens forfend!
Emilia. And your reports have set the murder on.
Othello. Nay, stare not, masters; it is true, indeed.
Gratiano. 'Tis a strange truth.
Montano. O monstrous act!
Emilia.   Villany! villany! villany!   190
I think upon 't, I think, I smell 't; O villany!
I thought so then;[589] I'll kill myself for grief.
O! villany, villany!
Iago. What! are you mad? I charge you, get you home.
Emilia. Good gentlemen, let me have leave to speak:
'Tis proper I obey him, but not now.
Perchance, Iago, I will ne'er go home.
Othello. O! O! O!   *(Falls on the bed.)*
Emilia.   Nay, lay thee down and roar,
For thou hast kill'd the sweetest innocent
That e'er did lift up eye.
Othello.   O! she was foul.   *(Rises.)*
I scarce did know you, uncle. There lies your niece,   201
Whose breath, indeed, these hands have newly stopp'd:
I know this act shows terrible and grim.
Gratiano. Poor Desdemona! I am glad thy father 's dead.
Thy match was mortal to him, and pure grief
Shore[590] his old thread in twain: did he live now,
This sight would make him do a desperate turn,
Yea, curse his better angel from his side,
And fall to reprobation.[591]

---

[588] I.e., into silence.   [589] *Cf.* "I will be hang'd, if some eternal villain, / Some busy and insinuating rogue, / Some cogging cozening slave, to get some office, / Have not devis'd this slander; . . ." (IV, ii, 130 ff.). Emilia means, not that she guessed Iago's guilt, but that she rightly guessed the slanderer's motive.   [590] Cut.   [591] Damnation.

Othello. 'Tis pitiful; but yet Iago knows   210
    That she with Cassio hath the act of shame
    A thousand times committed; Cassio confess'd it:
    And she did gratify[592] his amorous works
    With that recognizance and pledge of love
    Which I first gave her. I saw it in his hand:
    It was a handkerchief, an antique token
    My father gave my mother.
Emilia. O heaven! O heavenly powers!
Iago.   Come, hold your peace.
Emilia. 'Twill out, 'twill out; I hold my peace, sir? no;
    No, I will speak as liberal as the north;[593]   220
    Let heaven and men and devils, let them all,
    All, all, cry shame against me, yet I'll speak.
Iago. Be wise, and get you home.
Emilia.   I will not.

(Iago threatens to stab Emilia.)

Gratiano.   Fie!
    Your sword upon a woman!
Emilia. O thou dull Moor! that handkerchief thou speak'st of
    I found by fortune and did give my husband;
    For often, with a solemn earnestness,
    More than, indeed, belong'd to such a trifle,
    He begg'd of me to steal it.
Iago.   Villainous whore!
Emilia. She give it Cassio! no, alas! I found it,   230
    And I did give 't my husband.
Iago.   Filth, thou liest!
Emilia. By heaven, I do not, I do not, gentlemen.
    O murderous coxcomb![594] what should such a fool
    Do with so good a wife?
Othello.   Are there no stones[595] in heaven
    But what serve for the thunder? Precious villain!

(He runs at Iago. Iago stabs Emilia.)

Gratiano. The woman falls; sure, he has kill'd his wife.   *(Exit Iago.)*
Emilia. Ay, ay; O! lay me by my mistress' side.
Gratiano. He 's gone; but his wife 's kill'd.
Montano. 'Tis a notorious[596] villain. Take you this weapon,

---

[592] Reward.   [593] I.e., the north wind (?), the supposedly free-spoken people of north
England (?).   [594] Idiot.   [595] I.e., thunderbolts (to strike Iago down).   [596] Notable.

Which I have here recover'd from the Moor.   240
Come, guard the door without; let him not pass,
But kill him rather. I'll after that same villain,
For 'tis a damned slave.   *(Exeunt Montano and Gratiano.)*
Othello.   I am not valiant neither,
But every puny whipster[597] gets my sword.
But why should honour outlive honesty?
Let it go all.
Emilia.   What did thy song bode, lady?
Hark, canst thou hear me? I will play the swan,
And die in music:—
(Sings.)   Willow, willow, willow.
Moor, she was chaste; she lov'd thee, cruel Moor;
So come my soul to bliss as I speak true;   250
So speaking as I think, I die, I die.   *(Dies.)*
Othello.   I have another weapon in this chamber;
It is a sword of Spain, the ice-brook's temper.[598]
O! here it is. Uncle, I must come forth.
Gratiano *(within).*   If thou attempt it, it will cost thee dear:
Thou hast no weapon, and perforce must suffer.
Othello.   Look in upon me then, and speak with me,
Or, naked[599] as I am, I will assault thee.

(Re-enter Gratiano.)

Gratiano.   What is the matter?
Othello.   Behold! I have a weapon;
A better never did itself sustain   260
Upon a soldier's thigh: I have seen the day,
That with this little arm, and this good sword,
I have made my way through more impediments
Than twenty times your stop: but, O vain boast!
Who can control his fate? 'tis not so now.
Be not afraid, though you do see me weapon'd;
Here is my journey's end, here is my butt,[600]
And very sea-mark of my utmost sail.[601]
Do you go back dismay'd? 'tis a lost fear;
Man but a rush[602] against Othello's breast,   270
And he retires. Where should Othello go?
Now how dost thou look now? O ill-starr'd wench!

---

[597] I.e., a small boy whipping a top.   [598] Tempered in icy water (or the reference may be to Innsbruck, famed for the quality of its steel, but this hardly fits "a sword of Spain"). [599] Unarmed.   [600] Goal, end, limit.   [601] Destination of my farthest journey. [602] Wield but a reed.

Pale as thy smock! when we shall meet at compt,[603]
This look of thine will hurl my soul from heaven,
And fiends will snatch at it. Cold, cold, my girl!
Even like thy chastity.
O! cursed, cursed slave. Whip me, ye devils,
From the possession of this heavenly sight!
Blow me about in winds! roast me in sulphur!
Wash me in steep-down gulfs of liquid fire!   280
O Desdemona! Desdemona! dead!
Oh! Oh! Oh!

(Enter Lodovico, Montano, Cassio carried in a chair, and Officers with Iago, prisoner.)

Lodovico.   Where is this rash and most unfortunate man?
Othello.   That's he that was Othello; here I am.
Lodovico.   Where is that viper? bring the villain forth.
Othello.   I look down towards his feet;[604] but that 's a fable.
   If that thou be'st a devil, I cannot kill thee.   *(Wounds Iago.)*
Lodovico.   Wrench his sword from him.   *(Othello is disarmed.)*
Iago.   I bleed, sir; but not kill'd.
Othello.   I am not sorry neither; I'd have thee live;
   For, in my sense,[605] 'tis happiness to die.   290
Lodovico.   O thou Othello! that wert once so good,
   Fall'n in the practice[606] of a damned slave,[607]
   What shall be said to thee?
Othello.   Why, any thing:
   An honourable murderer, if you will;
   For nought did I in hate, but all in honour.
Lodovico.   This wretch hath part confess'd his villany:
   Did you and he consent in Cassio's death?
Othello   Ay.
Cassio.   Dear general, I never gave you cause.
Othello.   I do believe it, and I ask your pardon.   300
   Will you, I pray, demand that demi-devil
   Why he hath thus ensnar'd my soul and body?
Iago.   Demand me nothing: what you know, you know:
   From this time forth I never will speak word.
Lodovico.   What! not to pray?
Gratiano.   Torments will ope[608] your lips.

---

[603] On the day of judgment.   [604] I.e., for the Devil's cloven hoof.   [605] The way I feel.
[606] Plot, machination.   [607] I.e., Iago.   [608] Open.

Othello. Well, thou dost best.

Lodovico. Sir, you shall understand what hath befall'n,
 Which, as I think, you know not. Here is a letter
 Found in the pocket of the slain Roderigo,
 And here another; the one of them imports   310
 The death of Cassio to be undertook
 By Roderigo.

Othello. O villain!

Cassio.   Most heathenish and most gross!

Lodovico. Now here's another discontented paper,
 Found in his pocket too; and this, it seems,
 Roderigo meant to have sent this damned villain,
 But that, belike,[609] Iago in the interim[610]
 Came in and satisfied him.

Othello.   O the pernicious caitiff!
 How came you, Cassio, by that handkerchief
 That was my wife's?

Cassio.   I found it in my chamber;   320
 And he himself confess'd but even now
 That there he dropp'd it for a special purpose
 Which wrought to his desire.

Othello.   O fool! fool! fool!

Cassio. There is besides in Roderigo's letter
 How he upbraids Iago that he made him
 Brave me upon the watch; whereon it came
 That I was cast:[611] and even but now he spake,
 After long seeming dead, Iago hurt him,
 Iago set him on.

Lodovico. You must forsake this room and go with us;   330
 Your power and your command is taken off,
 And Cassio rules in Cyprus. For this slave,
 If there be any cunning cruelty
 That can torment him much and hold him long,
 It shall be his. You shall close prisoner rest,
 Till that the nature of your fault be known
 To the Venetian state. Come, bring him away.

Othello. Soft you; a word or two before you go.
 I have done the state some service, and they know 't;
 No more of that. I pray you, in your letters,   340
 When you shall these unlucky deeds relate,
 Speak of me as I am; nothing extenuate,

---

[609] Most likely.   [610] In the meantime.   [611] Dismissed.

Nor set down aught[612] in malice: then, must you speak
Of one that lov'd not wisely but too well;
Of one not easily jealous, but, being wrought,
Perplex'd[613] in the extreme; of one whose hand
Like the base Indian,[614] threw a pearl away
Richer than all his tribe; of one whose subdu'd[615] eyes
Albeit unused to the melting mood,
Drop tears as fast as the Arabian trees   350
Their med'cinable gum. Set you down this;
And say besides, that in Aleppo once,
Where a malignant and a turban'd Turk
Beat a Venetian and traduc'd the state,
I took by the throat the circumcised dog,
And smote him, thus.   *(Stabs himself.)*
Lodovico. O bloody period![616]
Gratiano.   All that's spoke is marr'd.
Othello.   I kiss'd thee ere I killed thee; no way but this.
                                              (Falling upon Desdemona.)
    Killing myself to die upon a kiss.   *(Dies.)*
Cassio.   This did I fear, but thought he had no weapon;
    For he was great of heart.
Lodovico *(to Iago).*   O Spartan dog!
    More fell[617] than anguish, hunger, or the sea.
    Look on the tragic loading of this bed;
    This is thy work; the object poisons sight;
    Let it be hid. Gratiano, keep the house,
    And seize upon the fortunes of the Moor,
    For they succeed on you. To you, lord governor,
    Remains the censure of this hellish villain,
    The time, the place, the torture; O! enforce it.
    Myself will straight aboard, and to the state   370
    This heavy act with heavy heart relate.   *(Exeunt.)*

QUESTIONS

1. In what sense might it be said that Othello is responsible for his own downfall? **2.** Compare the speeches of Cassio and Iago in Act II, Scene 1. What does the difference in language and style reveal about their characters? **3.** Carefully determine how much time elapses between the arrival at Cyprus and the end of the action. Can you find narrated events that could not possibly have occurred within

---

[612] Anything.   [613] Distracted.   [614] The Folio reads "Iudean." Both readings denote the foolish infidel who fails to appreciate the treasure he possesses.   [615] Overcome (by grief).
[616] Ending.   [617] Grim, cruel.

that time? Do the chronological inconsistencies disturb you? Explain.   **4.** The first part of Act IV, Scene 2 (until Othello exits), is sometimes called the "brothel" scene. What features of Othello's language and behavior justify that designation? **5.** Discuss the relationship between love and hate in this play.

WRITING TOPICS

1. Examine the reasons Iago gives for his actions. Do you find them consistent and convincing? Explain.   **2.** Discuss the functions of the minor characters, such as Roderigo, Bianca, and Emilia, in the play.   **3.** Othello crumbles in Act III, Scene 3, as Iago creates the jealousy that destroys Othello's self-confidence and peace of mind. Is the rapidity of Othello's emotional collapse justified? Does his being black have anything to do with his emotional turmoil?

Loving Women

1984

PAM GEMS [b. 1925]

CHARACTERS

Frank
Susannah
Crystal

SYNOPSIS OF SCENES

ACT I

SCENE I: Bed-sitting room of a flat in Notting Hill Gate, London. The time is
1973.

SCENE II: The same, a year later

ACT II The same room, ten years later

THE SETTING The furnishings and style of the room reveal the inhabitants. As
they change, so the room changes, and from the physical alterations we deduce
their social, political and psychological history.

Act I

SCENE I

The interior of a flat, 1973. The bed is on the floor, a mattress with an old
eiderdown over. Furniture is sparse, but there is a hi-fi with large twin speakers.
Political or ethnic posters, including Ché and Mao.[1]

---

[1] Ernesto (Ché) Guevara (1928–1967), Argentine-born Cuban revolutionary who became a
martyr to many radicals. Mao Tse-Tung (1893–1976), Chinese Communist leader and chief theorist
of the Chinese Revolution.

A man sits up in bed, propped up with cushions. There is something worrying about him . . . something sharp, intense, melancholy, even dangerous. He looks ill—his face is pale under the beard. This is Frank.

The young woman sitting on the floor and leaning over him is thin and angular in tight, faded jeans. She is not particularly good-looking or noticeable until her face becomes alive with humour or feeling. She wears a battered old anorak, has an enormous cloth shoulder-bag weighed down with books and papers. This is Susannah. She leans over Frank, groping in her bag with a smile, then presents him with a record, looking at his face to record his pleasure. He takes it and looks at it neutrally.

Frank.   Oh . . . thanks.
Susannah.   I knew you'd want it.
Frank.   Yuh.
Susannah.   Quite a job to get it—sold out!

He nods, inspecting the sleeve.

   Well. So—how's it going?
Crystal [*enters*].   Hey you're not gonna talk about work, are you?

She is dazzling, young and fresh with long limbs and shining hair, her clothes bang on fashion.

Susannah.   No, no.
Crystal.   Only he's not supposed to.
Susannah.   Sure.
Crystal.   The doctor said no worry.
Susannah.   Sure—great. No . . . everything's OK. The department's coping all right . . . well enough for you not to worry . . . not so well that you aren't missed, of course. [*She puts her hand on her heart.*] 'It ain't the same, mate!'
Frank.   What are you doing?
Susannah.   Oh a fantastic new scheme . . . we're involving *all* the kids— music, design, dance . . . everybody involved, we're after total interdepend-ence. [*Hugs him.*] Natural follow-on from you, love.
Frank.   Sounds quite a big thing.
Crystal.   Come ON! He's not supposed to talk about it!
Susannah.   Oh . . . sorry! No . . . great . . . sorry, Crystal! How's she been as a nurse?
Frank.   Fine. Beautiful pair of knockers bending over me, I have to feel good.

He reaches for a cigarette, and Crystal quickly gets up and lights it for him. Susannah notices that he is smoking, and shakes her head, frowning slightly.

Frank draws gratefully on the cigarette and picks up the disc, examining the sleeve.

Susannah.   Do you want to hear it?
Frank.   Yeah.

She hands him the earphones, crosses, puts on the record. Frank, wearing the earphones, nods and smiles briefly. Susannah and Crystal move apart for a chat.

Susannah.   How is he?
Crystal.   Not too grand.
Susannah.   He looks terrible. Thanks a bundle, Crystal, it's really great of you, I'd no idea it was going to be such a chore.
Crystal.   Don't worry about it.
Susannah.   I feel awful—
Crystal.   No I enjoy it, honest. Gives me something to do at nights . . . least I don't go out spending money. Anyway, for God's sake, you done me a favour! Couldn't wait to get out of that squat.[2]
Susannah.   Squitty?[3]
Crystal.   I had to clean the whole place out so's me Mum could come and visit. Hey, she said . . . our Crystal . . . you're never living in here with all these fellers! Give her the thrill of her life.

They laugh.

She needn't have worried.
Susannah.   What do you mean?
Crystal.   We-ell . . .

Susannah continues to look puzzled.

. . . they're all your sort of lot, ain't they?
Susannah.   What do you mean?
Crystal.   They're all—liberated. Puts you off.
Susannah.   Oh . . . why?
Crystal.   You know Harry, the one with the beard?
Susannah.   Tall?
Crystal.   No, that's Pete, his is all scratchy, no, the silky one . . .

Susannah lifts her head in a nod.

---

[2] Vacant premises in which squatters have taken up illegal residence.
[3] Shitty.

—you don't know what you're getting, mate of mine didn't half get a shock when her old man shaved off, he had a hare lip . . . they were married and all. Anyway . . . this Harry . . . asks me out for a burger . . . nips in for a six-pack on the way home, I think iyiy . . . back to the squat, he sits me down on one of them big cushions you keep rolling off . . . starts pulling on his boots and I think we-ell, he smells all right . . . you know, clean— anyway, I get a bit of a cuddle, I'm just relaxing, fishing round for it when all of a sudden he puts his mush in me ear and whispers, 'What would you like me to do, Crystal?'

They both burst out laughing.

Susannah [*laughing*].   What did you say?
Crystal.   I thought of a thing or two, I can tell you. 'Look,' he says, 'I'm not one of those geezers that jumps a gal . . . I'm not the bam-bam, thank-you ma'am type.' I said, 'What?' Got out the bloody cigarettes.
Susannah.   It put you off?

There is an objective curiosity in Susannah's glance.

Crystal.   I thought he was going to bring out the manual—Christ, what are they after, good marks or something?
Susannah.   You like the man to take the lead?
Crystal.   Sure . . . within reason. Tell you one thing, your lot's never gonna be up for rape.

Susannah gives her another mild look, as at a specimen.

Susannah.   How long had you been there . . . at the squat?
Crystal.   I was only filling in, till I got somewhere. I couldn't find anything. It's ridiculous.
   I really love the room here, I'm ever so grateful . . . I mean, what with it being near the salon—
Susannah.   Sure . . . well, it's OK for now. I mean, when I get back, we'll have to—
Crystal.   Sssh. [*As Frank stirs, listening to the music*] Did you say something, Frank?

Frank lifts the bins[4] *inquiringly.*

Need anything?

---

[4] Earphones.

He smiles, shakes his head, puts back the earphones.

[*Lowering her voice*] He's been ever so rough.
Susannah.   Oh? Why didn't you let me know?
Crystal.   He didn't want to.
Susannah.   You should have told me.
Crystal.   He said not to worry you, what with the new job and everything. It
    was all in his eyes.
Susannah.   His eyes?
Crystal.   This rash . . . all up the side of his head! The ulcers got in his eyes,
    it was terrible! [*Her eyes glisten at the horror of it.*]
Susannah.   My God!
Crystal.   Oh, it's OK now.
Susannah.   You're sure? I must talk to the doctor—
Crystal.   Nah, honest. He says just to build him up . . . you know.
Susannah.   You should have told me. It's so bloody unfair! He's worked so
    hard!
Crystal.   Will he get his job back?
Susannah.   Oh yes, he's established—but he's missing this marvellous new
    project. It's a follow-on from what we were doing here at the Centre—d'you
    remember, we were telling you about it.
Crystal.   Oh. Yeah.
Susannah.   I wish you'd go down there, Crystal. The girls would love to hear
    about hairdressing . . . you know, just to tell them what it's like . . . nothing
    formal, just a gossip. I could give them a ring if you like—what nights are
    you free?
Crystal.   I work late quite a bit.
Susannah.   What about next Thursday . . . they all come for the disco.
Crystal.   No, not really.
Susannah.   'It's for the community' . . .
Crystal.   No, well . . .
Susannah.   I don't want to force you.
Crystal.   You know how it is.
Susannah.   Sure.
Crystal.   Only I'm on my feet all day.
Susannah.   No, I understand, really. It was just that—
Crystal.   Oh, sure. I'll get his dinner.

She exits. Susannah crosses to Frank, takes off his earphones.

Susannah.   OK, love?
Frank.   Come here.

They embrace.

Frank.   I've missed you.
Susannah.   How's it been?
Frank.   OK.
Susannah.   No, really—

He gives a funny little mirthless smile that doesn't convince her.

—God, I should be here!
Frank.   You're keeping things going.
Susannah.   Yes. Birmingham[5] needs you! How long do you think it will be before—
Frank [*quick*].   Hard to say.
Susannah.   But you're feeling better?
Frank.   Yuh. Well . . . more real.
Susannah.   Great. Wait till you see the new schedules . . . we have not been idle! [*She delves into her bag.*] I brought you some of that ginseng . . . Vitamin E . . . Clare made some sesame cakes but the dog with the complicated psyche ate them. God, my mother turned up. She's into haute classe[6] gardening now . . . peonies—are you feeling all right?
Frank.   Mmm.
Susannah.   No more panics?
Frank.   A bit. Coping. [*He gives her a darting, accusing look.*] I was bloody glad to get out, I can tell you that.
Susannah.   But I thought—I thought you liked it.

He looks up at the ceiling with a grimace of distaste. Slight pause.

Yes. Not funny. Still, we were lucky . . . getting you into Ian's group.

He nods briefly.

Look I know you hated jumping the queue. [*Slight pause*] What could I do—you were going up the wall! The only alternative was to—
Frank.   I couldn't have stood—
Susannah.   I know, we've seen it. [*With a little shudder*] Knowing too much makes it tough. Anyway, Ian's a marvellous guy.
Frank.   Yeah. [*Another darting look, unobserved by Susannah.*]
Susannah.   Human.
Frank.   Mmm.
Susannah.   There should be thousands of small units like that, places where you can work things out without hassle instead of awful great wards full of—
Frank.   Yup.

---

[5] An industrial center, the second-largest city in England.
[6] French, meaning "high class."

A silence

Susannah.   How goes it with Crystal?
Frank.   Crystal? Oh, fine.
Susannah.   Not too—she doesn't bug you?
Frank.   No, no . . . she really looks after me, she's great.
Susannah.   Good! Of course it works on a bilateral level—
Frank.   What?
Susannah.   It's not a patronizing situation . . . she's able to contribute. There's no question of tenure . . . I mean, when I get back—
Frank.   When are you coming?
Susannah.   Tomorrow! [*She hugs him fiercely.*] I wish it was tomorrow! Don't worry. I'm not about to abandon the fort. I know the last thing you need is some soppy, individualistic gesture . . . hang on, Snoopy! We'll sort Crystal out—for God's sake she can afford an economic rent, fair rent anyway, she pulls a fortune crimping.[7] I asked her to go down to the Centre, talk to the kids.
Frank.   What did she say?
Susannah.   Nothing in it for her. She's pretty single-minded really. After some upmarket guy in a sports car. You can understand it, her background's pretty deprived . . . still . . . I mean, they are her own sort.
Frank.   She's OK.
Susannah.   Oh, great. I was afraid she might be getting on your nerves, she comes on a bit. Still, fine for now. We're lucky really, it bridges the gap—

Crystal enters with a tray of food.

Crystal [*to Frank*].   I done you some supper and you got to eat it. [*To Susannah*] You didn't want nothing, did you, love?
Susannah [*with a swift appraisal of Frank's tray*].   No thanks. [*To Frank, in surprise*] Are you eating meat?
Crystal.   Oh I got him off that vegetarian—it's useless! You can get deficiencies, I read it. You have to eat pounds of chickpeas to get the protein, unless you're doing heavy labour you can't work off the starch, it's a load of rubbish. D'you want some sauce, Frank?
Frank.   Thanks!

He sloshes on the sauce and begins to eat heartily, to Susannah's astonishment.

Crystal.   I'll get the crumble.[8] Sure you don't want none, Susannah?

Susannah smiles, shakes her head. Crystal goes.

---

[7] Hairdressing.
[8] A hot baked fruit dessert.

Susannah.   Darling, I can shove it all in my *Evening Standard*, she'll never
  know.
Frank [*mouth full*].   It's fine, thanks.
Susannah.   You should be on a decent diet—that's dried potato!
Frank.   She puts butter and pepper in, it's good.

He offers her a forkful. She shakes her head, smiling.

Susannah.   Oh I don't care what it is, it's great to see you eating again.

*She grasps his hand. He is busy eating. Crystal enters. She puts down the
pudding, sets Frank's napkin straight. Frank looks up at her and grins.*

  Are you still on antibiotics?
Crystal.   His bum's[9] like a pincushion.

She gets a look from Frank. He bends to the plate, eating.

Susannah.   He ought to be on goat's milk yoghurt. It puts the flora back in
  the stomach.
Crystal.   I'll get him some cream. [*She goes out.*]
Susannah [*embraces him*].   Have you missed me?
Frank.   Mmm.
Susannah.   If it weren't for this bloody project! Oh! Your hands!
Frank.   What's the matter?
Susannah.   They're so thin!

She takes his dinner plate, fondles his hands. He lies back among the cushions.

  You're getting better. I can feel it. There's so much to do. If you could see
  the kids! I was in tears the other day . . . tears of rage—I had to talk to this
  pisser of a headmaster about this kid . . . he wants to be a doctor—he's
  bright, for God's sake, but a West Indian . . . not even a Paki,[10] well, I
  mean, Christ, no wonder we fragment. Oh, my love. But we grow! It's
  painful . . . the mould cracks all the time, it makes us invalids—but we do
  reshape, we do grow! Did I tell you, we've got twenty-five per cent coloureds
  in the group now!

*Crystal enters, bearing the cream. She is wearing the most beautiful, semi-see-
through kimono in fragile silk, with floating wisps and panels, making her look
like a creature from another world.*

---

⁹ Buttocks.
¹⁰ Pakistani.

Crystal. Here, Susannah, what d'you think of this?
Susannah. Wow . . . 'great, man'!
Crystal. Got it off a client.
Susannah. Fantastic. Is it . . . um . . . is it for anyone special?
Crystal. Nah, I'm breaking it in on Frank . . . bit of skin therapy.

She laughs loudly, and begins to walk about, showing off the kimono, doing a turn.

Susannah [*to Frank*]. You're not tired?
Frank. I'm fine.
Crystal. Guess who this is?
Susannah. Oh . . . ah . . . Racquel Welch?
Crystal. Nah.
Susannah. Marlene?
Crystal. No! Come on, Frank . . .
Frank. Marilyn Monroe.
Crystal. Right! Your favourite!
Susannah. Marilyn Monroe?[11]
Crystal. Right. He's been holding out on you, Susannah.

She puts on some music and begins to move to the music.

Susannah [*to Frank*]. Do you really go for her?
Frank. What, love?
Susannah. Marilyn Monroe.

He nods, watching Crystal.

Frank [*watching Crystal*]. Why not?
Susannah. No reason. You and a few million other guys.

Slight pause, they watch Crystal.

She was such a sad woman.
Frank. Oh, I don't know.

Slight pause, they watch Crystal.

---

[11] Racquel Welch (b. 1940), Marlene Dietrich (1901–1992), and Marilyn Monroe (1926–1962), movie actresses celebrated for their sex appeal.

Susannah.   What do you mean?
Frank.   What?
Susannah.   Nothing.

Crystal dances. She is beautiful. Frank watches, a dazed expression on his face. Susannah watches with a smile, wagging her head to the music.

The music ends.

Crystal throws herself down, legs in the air. Frank does a slow clap, then applauds.

Crystal.   Phew . . . wow! Rrrah! Hey! I nearly forgot . . . Frank—the surprise . . . we forgot! [*She trips off in her mod shoes to the kitchen . . . calls back*] . . . Susannah's present!
Susannah.   For me?
Crystal.   Hang on, won't be a sec!
Susannah.   She's great, isn't she?
Frank.   Yeah.
Crystal [*off*].   Oh sod it.
Susannah.   Never mind, Crystal, next time will do if you can't find it.
Crystal [*as she enters*].   I'm getting it all over me. Here. For you.
Susannah.   What is it?
Crystal.   Lemon curd. We made it. Frank said you liked it.
Susannah.   Oh—lovely! Oh . . . [*She smiles, happy, at Frank.*]
Crystal.   Here, have a taste. [*She takes back the jar, unscrews the lid, dips a finger in and tastes.*] Ooh it's great, here—no, go on . . .

They all dip in . . .

[*To Frank*] you twot, you've got it all over the bed . . . oh, fantastic, now he's got it in his hair . . . honest! You should of seen him in the kitchen, Susannah, Jesus! [*She laughs, leans over the bed, cleaning him off.*] Here, Susannah, want to lick it off?
Susannah.   Do you need a tissue?

Crystal takes the tissue from her, dabs at Frank. The tissue sticks to his hair.

Crystal [*giggling*].   Now he looks really pretty! Don't he look a pretty boy—you got to stay like that, eh Susannah?
Susannah.   It's very good, Crystal. Is it your own recipe?
Crystal.   Me Mum's. It would have been even better only someone was demanding onion soup at the time, so it tastes a bit of onions.
Susannah.   No, it's lovely.
Crystal.   All the real thing—

Frank.   Sugar, lemons—
Crystal.   Butter and eggs—see, we'll get him doing it yet!

Susannah tightens the lid carefully, wraps the jar in a scarf and puts it carefully into a shoulder bag.

Susannah.   Shit, I must go. [*She looks at Frank poignantly.*]
Crystal.   Oh. Right. I'll just go and . . . [*She makes herself scarce. Slight pause*]
Susannah.   I hate leaving you . . . I hate it, it doesn't feel right. Are you really OK?

He nods briefly.

You're sure? [*She bends and kisses him, and then hugs him urgently.*] This thing is really fantastic, love. If it works and it's bloody going to after all our struggle we'll stream the pilot and introduce a play-integrated growth scheme for every school-leaver in the UK—urban, rural, the lot. Believe it, love . . . just hang in there, hmm? [*She bends, kisses him on the mouth, squeezes his hand in a last affectionate gesture and rises, giving a clenched-fist salute in farewell.*] Up the revolution!

Frank looks up at her, nods.

Crystal [*off*].   Oh, you off?
Susannah [*going*].   I must go. Keep an eye on him for me, Crystal.
Crystal [*off*].   Sure.
Susannah [*off*].   Look, you will give me a call if . . . you know . . . if anything—
Crystal [*off*].   Yeah, course I will.
Susannah [*off*].   He's lost so much weight!
Crystal [*off*].   Don't worry, soon build him up.

Their voices become distant. The sound of a door, sonorous. Crystal returns. She crosses to the window, parts the curtains slightly to watch Susannah recede across the street. She turns, as Frank looks up. He looks away.

Feeling bad?
Frank.   No, I feel fine.
Crystal.   Good! [*She sits on the bed.*]

He stares ahead, his mind elsewhere. She slips a look at him, jumps up.

Ahh! I'm a nurd!

She runs over to the table, picks up a large envelope, returns, and showers travel brochures over the bed.

Right, what do you fancy? Club Méditerranée? It's a new idea, you get to meet people . . . nah, maybe not this time . . . [*She forages*] . . . what about Costa del Sol—warm there. Friend of mine works in a bar near Estepona, in the winter she goes skiing—yeah, in Spain, she's says it's only a two-hour drive, they're really going to open it up, bring in facilities.

He laughs briefly.

Good for yuh! Muscles! [*She looks at other brochures.*] What about the Canary Islands?

He looks at her. She smooths his hair back.

Think about nice things.

He nods.

Why not? You might as well. [*She sings, and rises and does a march to the song.*] 'What's the use of worrying, It never was worth while, So, pack up your troubles in your old kitbag, And smile, smile, smile!' [*She salutes at the end of the song.*] My Uncle Ted used to sing that to me when I was little. Course he really went for the Dorsey brothers and Glenn Miller[12] . . . you know, swing.
    Come on.
    My trouble is I talk too much.

She sits on the bed again, nestling close, whispers in his ear

Fancy a tongue sandwich?

Frank grabs her with a sudden, urgent savagery, and they embrace so fiercely that they roll on to the floor. She hooks her knees round him in a fierce, prolonged embrace. They break apart.

Frank. What's the matter?
Crystal. Nothing.
Frank. What are you thinking?
Crystal. Nothing. You got a bit of colour in your face, that's all.

---

[12] Tommy Dorsey (1905–1956), Jimmy Dorsey (1904–1967), and Glenn Miller (1904–1944), popular band leaders during the 1930s and 1940s.

The lights begin to go.
They stay on the floor, arms about each other.

Course there's always Jersey, that's nice in the summer. Or Capri—what about Capri?

SCENE II

The same. A few changes. The bed has gone. There is a sofa, some cane furniture, a mobile, bright cushions and a carrycot. The pictures have been changed. Mao and Ché have gone and are replaced by the Aristide Bruant and a Mucha[13] poster of a girl.

Susannah is onstage. She wears a coat, her bag over her shoulder. She prowls, inspecting the room, sees a wedding photograph on a bookcase, crosses, picks it up and looks at it intently.

Crystal [*off*].   Won't be a minute . . . I'll just turn the oven down. [*She enters, bright in a Laura Ashley dress and a Twiggy bandeau.*] Oh, don't look at that, we was all pissed out of our heads.

Susannah replaces the photograph carefully.

Susannah.   You look wonderful.
Crystal.   Yeah, not too bad. Cost a fortune that. I was thinking of having it dyed, so I could wear it round the clubs.
Susannah.   It's beautiful.
Crystal.   So . . . how've you been?

Susannah shrugs.

Sit yourself down, take your coat off—here, I'll hang it up for you.
Susannah.   Don't bother.
Crystal.   No, it's no trouble.
Susannah.   Thank you.
Crystal.   You look ever so well.
Susannah.   Thanks. [*She sits.*]
Crystal.   Frank's not back. Any minute. Would you like a drink? I don't know what we've got . . . [*It is all sitting there ready, on a tray.*] Whisky? Gin, vodka? Bacardi?

---

[13] Aristide Bruant (1851–1925), French songwriter and cabaret singer; Alfonse Mucha (1860–1925), Czech-born French designer and artist.

Susannah.   Oh . . . ah, I'll . . .
Crystal.   How about a sherry?
Susannah.   Fine.
Crystal.   Light or dark?
Susannah.   What? Oh, light.
Crystal.   It's more dry. The light.
Susannah.   Yes.

She watches as Crystal pours the sherry carefully into the correct glass, then pours herself a very generous whisky.

Crystal.   It's been ages. You didn't mind me ringing—
Susannah.   Of course not.
Crystal.   Only we met some of his friends and they said, like, you was back. It seemed silly not to . . . well, you know . . . you're all friends and we often have little do's—anyway, I said, listen, I'm going to ring Susannah—
Susannah.   What did he say?
Crystal.   Huh, don't listen to him, no, it's really nice. Cheers.

They drink. Slight pause

I'm glad you could come.
Susannah.   You're looking very well.
Crystal.   Put on a bit of weight.
Susannah.   It doesn't show.
Crystal.   I still have to suck in. [*She draws herself in.*] Come and see Nicole.

They go. We hear their voices.

[*Off*] There! What do you think of her . . . ah . . . she's asleep . . . ah! Who do you think she looks like? Look, a little bubble, did you see? Mum made the jacket, it's wool, most of the stuff I got's acrylic, it's better for washing, but wool's warmer really. Look at her little fist she always does that, d'you like the blue elephant? My sister-in-law give it me, I said it should have been pink—ooh now don't wake up, there's a good girl . . . perhaps we better . . .

They return.

Susannah.   Are you feeding her yourself?
Crystal.   I did at first—hey, it makes you ever so tired. Anyway, I'm back at work now so she's on the bottle. It's better really. You're more free.
Susannah.   You manage all right?

Crystal.   Oh yes. I drop her in at the nursery, I'm dead lucky, it's only down the road. Then, pick her up at four, do the shopping, get back in time for Frank's tea. It works very well really.

Silence

Susannah.   She's lovely.
Crystal.   Ah, she's no trouble. I like babies, well, they're cuddly, ain't they . . . even if you do have to clean up the shit! So . . . how have you been? Still working with the—what was it you were doing . . . with the kids?
Susannah.   Oh—no, that finished. There was a change of authority.
Crystal.   What a shame.
Susannah.   Yes.
Crystal.   Didn't you do that panto[14] thing, that show you was into?
Susannah.   No—well, actually we did a smaller piece—sort of goodbye thing.
Crystal.   Nice. What was it about?
Susannah.   We tried to improvise on things the kids brought themselves . . . we were anxious not to impose.

Crystal nods wisely.

Obviously the idea was to celebrate *their* feelings, *their* values.
Crystal.   Sort of do your own thing sort of thing?
Susannah [*delighted*].   Yes!
Crystal.   What did they choose, horror comics? [*With a laugh.*]
Susannah.   I know! Actually we did a thing on canals.
Crystal.   Canals?
Susannah.   We got them going round the libraries, researching the records . . . you know, old maps, books, songs . . . the singing was great . . . [*She sings*]

> If thou'll plod me,
> Then I'll plod thee,
> And the horse'll plod, the three o' we.
> The towpath's long,
> But my man is strong,
> And to Pluckett's Lock,
> We'll surely be.

She ends dashingly, looks to Crystal for response.

With a rock backing, of course.
Crystal.   Oh. Yeah. Sure.
Susannah.   I brought some pictures. I thought Frank might like to see them.

---

[14] Pantomime.

Silence

Crystal. I'm sorry you couldn't come to the wedding. We missed you.
Susannah. Yes.
Crystal. If it wasn't for you, we wouldn't have met. I mean, it's not as if you and Frank was serious.
Susannah. We weren't married, if that's what you mean.
Crystal. He said you didn't want to.
Susannah. Oh. Well, he certainly never asked.
Crystal. But you're not into it, your lot. You've jacked all that in. [*Pause*] It was his idea, you know, getting married.
Susannah. You didn't think about an abortion?
Crystal. No! I hate it, I wouldn't . . . anyway, I'd be too scared—you can get yourself knocked up for good doing that, happened to a friend of mine. Anyway . . .

Susannah looks at her. Crystal shrugs.

Look, he'd already asked me by then. We was going to get married . . . that's why I never bothered. We was well away when you came down to see us that time. It was a bit awkward really.
Susannah. I didn't know that.
Crystal. No, well, he should of said. Still, he was ill. I think he didn't want to upset you.
Susannah. Upset me!
Crystal. He was feeling bad about leaving all the work to you.
Susannah. Why didn't he tell me? He could have said something! For God's sake! We'd been together for five years!
Crystal. But you were never serious.
Susannah. Serious? What's that supposed to mean? I'm sorry but—look, this *was* my home! I *found* it! . . . God knows it took long enough. I even plastered the walls. When I found this flat—when I found this flat there was one cold tap sticking out of the wall over there . . . that was it! I can't believe it's the same place. I'm sorry, Crystal, I don't want to be rude. It's just that everything looks so different.
Crystal [*small*]. Well it's bound to, isn't it? [*Slight pause*] Frank's changed.
Susannah. Changed? What do you mean—he's all right?
Crystal. Oh yes. But he's given up all that—well, you know.
Susannah. All what?
Crystal. All that stuff.
Susannah. What do you mean? What stuff?
Crystal. You know—projects. What you were doing together. He's settling down, Susannah.
Susannah. Frank? Settling down? [*She gives a brief yok.*] He's vulnerable, he always has been . . . used to faint when we visited loony bins, it gets the men . . . no, not Frank. He's a fighter. Look . . . Crystal . . . I'm not trying

to . . . look, believe me . . . it's just that Frank's very special—not just to me—well, to me as well . . . after all, we were together for a . . . [*She falters*] . . . for a long time. Naturally it was a blow . . . it was a shock, you must have realized that, both of you. How could I have come down, I'm surprised you even thought of asking, couldn't believe it . . . to be honest I still can't. Then when I heard about the baby there wasn't much point . . . [*She sighs*] . . . was he hurt? That I didn't come . . . to the wedding?

Crystal.   I think he was relieved, really. You know what they're like.

Susannah.   Anyway, there it is. And after all, five years of me and he ends up in the bin.

Crystal.   Nah it wasn't that, it was overwork!

Susannah.   Yes. Yes, he did risk himself. We all did. A lot of it . . . OK, a bit half-assed but at least . . . some of it will stick! You have to try. It's not going to work any more, running for the same old burrows . . . we're rafting off into space—God! Frank sees it. He said to me one day, 'Suse . . . you know what's going to do for us all? Not the failure of intellect, moral, muscle—but the failure of imagination! They're all too busy with their snouts in the trough to smell the fire.'

Crystal.   Yeah, he says some really daft things.

Susannah.   He'll never give up. I know that. That is one thing I know. For certain. You're obviously what he needs. If it's working for him—just so long as he's on his base again, got his head back. I couldn't—but there's no danger of that. Not Frank. How is he, in himself?

Crystal.   He's fine. I mean, he's different—my mother says he's a changed man.

Susannah.   How?

Crystal.   Drop more?

Susannah shakes her head.

Sure? We've got plenty.

Susannah.   No thanks.

Crystal.   I'll just freshen mine up.

She crosses, helps herself liberally to more whisky.

He's settled down . . . [*She helps herself to ice.*] . . . well, you're bound to, I mean, with the kiddie and all.

Susannah.   Yes.

Crystal.   He's getting on ever so well at the school. He likes teaching—I mean, we don't go out much, we're saving up, I can't wait to get a place of me own—a proper house, you know, with a garden.

Susannah.   Does he see any of his friends?

Crystal.   Oh yes, now and then. We've joined the Labour Party . . . well, it was to please my Dad, really.

Susannah [*shocked*].   You what?
Crystal.   The Labour Party. We go down there for a drink every Friday.
Susannah.   Oh God.
Crystal.   What's the matter? Don't you approve?
Susannah.   Of Social Democracy? My God. Well, that's it.

She gets up, picks up her bag.

Crystal.   You off?
Susannah.   Yes, I'm sorry, there's no—
Crystal.   But I've got a steak and kidney in the oven . . . what's the matter?
 Susannah . . . [*A wail, as she bursts into tears.*]
Susannah.   Oh love . . . oh . . . tch! Sit down . . .

She cuddles Crystal, who weeps.

 Don't cry . . . oh my dear . . . all right, you cry—have a good cry.
Crystal.   I've been a bit tired lately, what with working and the baby . . . he's
 late!
Susannah.   Bastard was always late—hang on, I've got a hankie somewhere.
Crystal.   He promised he'd be back in time.
Susannah.   Would you like another drink?

There is a sound at the door. They both turn. Frank is standing there.

Crystal [*voice quivering*].   You're late!
Frank.   What's the matter?

Crystal runs out of the room, weeping.

 What's up?
Susannah.   I seem to have upset her.

He turns away, takes off his coat, puts down his stuff.

 I hear you've joined the Labour Party.

As he exits to see Crystal. He returns almost at once.

 Is she all right?
Frank.   Yes.
Susannah.   I shouldn't have come, of course.
Frank.   Why not?
Susannah.   Yes, it's probably more organic . . . or isn't that the in word any
 more?

Frank. I don't know.

Susannah. Well, since I am here, you might as well fill me in. Like, why you did it.

He doesn't answer.

Was it the breakdown?

He looks, nervous that Crystal might hear.

Well what? Some sort of gesture . . . direct-action consciousness raising? Or did you just fall for nursey?

Frank. Susannah . . . [*He gestures her to keep her voice down.*]

Susannah. I want to know!

Frank. Look, will you—

Susannah. I want to know, dammit! [*She walks about, angry.*] You didn't even get in touch! When I tried to ring, all I got was her on the line rabbiting on about a white wedding—she even asked me to be a bloody bridesmaid— did you know that?

Frank. No, of course not.

Susannah. I'm not talking about her, I'm talking about *you*. Why? Why didn't you ring . . . I mean, you must have . . . what did you think . . . didn't you think about me? You must have thought *something* . . . unless you were round the bloody twist. I'm sorry. But why? Just tell me why. You owe me. I want to know why.

Pause

Frank. I had to.

Susannah. What do you mean?

Frank. I had to, that's all.

Susannah. Because she was pregnant?

Frank [*after a pause*]. Ye-es.

Susannah. You bloody liar. She told me you asked her to marry you before that. You hateful sodding liar. [*Slight pause*] Christ.

Pause

Frank. I don't know. [*Pause*] She was there when I needed someone.

Susannah. You had me.

Frank. That was different. [*Slight pause*] Different world.

Susannah. Our world.

Frank [*frowns*]. Yes. [*Pause*] It wasn't real. It was all out there. Unreal.

Susannah. And she *was* . . . real?

Frank. Something like that.

Susannah. Oh come on! Look . . . I know it cracked for you, God knows you—but . . . Frank. [*She takes a turn.*] What do you mean? Aren't high-rises real? Aren't the kids we work with real? For God's sake . . . weren't WE real?

Frank. No. Not really. I don't think so.

Susannah. Not real? All that work? All that fucking we did—not real?

Frank. It was different.

Susannah [*after a pause*]. What you mean is, you've given up. Caved in.

Frank. I don't know. Perhaps.

Susannah. Well I do. I felt it coming, long before the breakdown.
  Manic! Social guilt! Idiotic! The rest of us couldn't even see a movie! Remember the night you found me reading Maigret?[15] Your face! I thought you were going to knife me. [*Slight pause*] Ian told me it would end in suicide or a crack-up—

Frank. He said that?

Crystal appears in the doorway, in an apron.

Susannah. He said it to you!

Crystal. Chicken soup?

Susannah. You wouldn't listen!

Crystal. It's ready.

They wave at her vaguely.

Susannah. We trusted you. Stuck our necks out—

Crystal. Where shall we—

Susannah. Serves us right. Nothing but bloody, bourgeois, individualist adventurism. [*To Crystal*]

Crystal. Eh?

Susannah. The guru! [*Waving a hand at him. Crystal gives him a blanched look and disappears.*] You should have gone for a Jesus cult, you'd be king of the ashram by now.

Frank. Oh stop it.

Susannah. Well what do you know? What have you ever known? You're privileged.

Frank. Me?

Susannah. Yes, you! You've never been off the tit. Eleven-plus,[16] scholarship, research fellowship, project grant. You're free . . . white—and male. And you've caved in.

Pause

---

¹⁵ The detective-hero in many of the novels of Georges Simenon (1903–1989).

¹⁶ A now-obsolete school examination taken by English children at age eleven years plus to determine scholastic aptitude and academic future.

Frank.   I'm sorry. I wish I could—[*He sighs deeply, rubs his head.*]—the fact is, I'm tired. I've been teaching all week . . . my brain's a mash.

Slight pause

Susannah.   And the rest of us don't work, I suppose.

Another slight pause

Frank.   What are you doing now?

Susannah.   I'm with Brian Mason. New set-up, kids in care. Not more than eight kids to a house . . . at least the numbers are possible.

Frank.   Sounds good.

Susannah.   Except that I've just been promoted. At the moment it's eight little pairs of accusing eyes—God, just when they were beginning to trust me! [*Slight pause*] Where are you teaching?

Frank.   Compton Beck.

Susannah.   What? My God. Middle class! My—God. Three years we worked to get that project off the ground . . . fighting the bloody government, the GLC, Nuffield, Arts Council, Rowntree . . . keep going till they crumble, remember? And then you cop out. And bring the rest of us down with you. A breakdown, yes. But you never came back!

Silence. He moves about the room. He pauses by the table, picks up a book and turns the pages idly.

Frank.   I read to her. In the evenings. [*He puts the book down. Pause*] It died on me. All of it. All the collaborative, collective crap of it. And the polemic—yes, the polemic we were peddling—

Susannah.   What's wrong with that? Group decision! Raise consciousness among the cases—fight submissiveness—

Frank.   So we indoctrinated . . . oh, we weren't into fascism, there weren't any slogans or uniforms, no giveaways—'Hi kids, I'm Frank, this is Susie, what say we all sit in a circle?' And straight into the knocking copy.

Susannah.   I don't recall you with a better suggestion. On the contrary—

Frank.   Banging away at the pit props with fraternal smiles . . . oh, we were going to clear the lot away—revolution . . . fresh start—

Susannah.   You believed it.

Frank [*smiles at her*].   The humanist dream.

Susannah.   Yes!

Frank.   Only without blood, of course. Messy stuff, that.

Susannah.   Right. Damn right. Our way. The possible way. Words . . . media . . . subversion.

Frank.   Subversion? Subversion . . . us? Susannah—we're the bloody props!

Susannah.   What!?

Frank. Destroy the system . . . our sort? We cultivate it. 'Inter-Related Structures of Third World Matrix Performances . . . foreword by Professor Schumberg, Cal. Tech.' Whatever it is we nourish, it isn't the oppressed. When we arrive, when we knock on all those doors, the tension goes UP!

Susannah. Balls. Who brought every resident on the Churchill estate out on the street—

Frank. Was anything done? [*Slight pause*] We're social workers. It's us and Valium instead of a housing policy. We got rid of the nuclear family all right—for you and bloody Brian Mason to go and play mothers and fathers with the debris. Till it's time to make the right career choice and move on.

Susannah. I can't believe this. Industrialized society got rid of the extended family. We, the robot consumers, exist to man the machines. I quote you.

Frank. Oh? So . . . leave us not impose ourselves—Gahd, we're not into hierarchy. Boss figures? As though we aren't imposing ourselves by just being there? What the hell are we doing, crashing into people's lives?

Susannah. I'm not listening to this, it's sick—

Frank [*shouting*]. We add to the pain! We're one more threat!

Crystal erupts into the room, indignant.

Crystal. Look, d'you mind? You'll wake the baby!

Susannah. Oh . . . God—sorry, love. No, don't go.

Frank. Stay, Crystal—don't go.

Crystal sits on the edge of the sofa. Silence.

Susannah [*mutters*]. I refuse to accept them and us, I never have. It's your problem. [*Direct*] I do not detach myself from the human race as you so consistently and fatally do—and please don't correct my grammar. Nobody's pretending it's easy. God knows there's little enough on offer for most people—

Crystal. Yeah.

Susannah. What?—but if we can break out a few choices . . . give them a chance to choose, make *some* sort of celebration—

Frank. Choose?

Crystal [*warning*]. Frank . . .

Frank. Choose what? Celebrate what? Fly-overs? No, stay! [*To Crystal*]

Susannah [*to Crystal*]. Don't go—

Frank. What was it? Yeah, sure . . . community theatre—the great civic venting operation . . . steel bands,[17] your actual black faces . . . way out, man. Only, when they got themselves a carnival together last year, you were

---

[17] A musical band of Trinidadian origin, composed of percussion instruments fashioned from oil drums.

all shitting yourselves. It was getting out of hand, right? Or was it that you felt that your delicate white faces weren't all that gratefully welcome. After all . . . [*He directs this at Crystal, who happens to be in front of him.*] . . . it is our backyard, right? Robert Ardrey[18] on territory, right?

Crystal grimaces at him for hush, goes quickly.

Susannah.   Frank, that's so unfair. OK . . . OK.
Frank.   There's no need to humour me. I'm perfectly all right.
Susannah.   I didn't suggest that you weren't. I think you're being unfair, that's all. But if that's what you believe—I'm not claiming to lay down lines. On anything.
Frank.   Sure. I know. The atom is random . . . we make ourselves up. The old order smasheth, decadence rules. So what do we have? Here we are, kids . . . come and get it—a great big, steaming basinful of fucking nothing at all. Not even a fart.
Susannah.   Frank, I don't know what you're talking about.
Frank.   No? No, of course you don't. You're bolted up the bloody middle like Frankenstein's monster, same as the rest of them. Listen . . . listen! Aren't *we* people, too? We've turned ourselves into fucking computerized case histories, along with the rest of them. My God! I'm telling you! The more we stepped backwards into that sour-faced vacuum, the more I—oh Christ, run for your life! Find it, quick . . . a world of green forest and wet pools—lakes of white water . . . leaves and violet skies . . . blue electric toads, hopping . . .
Susannah [*alarmed, she speaks in a careful, level voice*].   Frank . . . what are you talking about?
Frank.   The more 'real' we became, the more I . . .

Words fail him and he plays with a lamp fitting, unable for a moment to continue.

We're parasites.
Susannah.   Don't.
Frank.   We suck the life out. It makes us feel good. The pay's shitty, we say, who can afford a car? Never mind, it's the work that counts. That's what features.
Susannah.   Yes. It is. And what is more, some of us see it as more than bandages. A vehicle for change.
Frank.   Change?—oh, we change things. We're the Changemakers all right. We take the magic out of life, and what do we give them? Who needs books on cows and rabbits, are they real life? Let's celebrate reality, for fuck's sake,

---

[18] Author of *The Territorial Imperative* (1966).

pop-up sex manuals, Jenny and Kevin at the supermarket—who needs Hans Andersen, anyway wasn't he a pederast or was that Lewis Carroll? Dante . . . Titian—are they the revolution? Rembrandt . . . Tolstoy[19]—elitist garbage, man, culture's for the pooves![20] Remember your beauty contest? Eight-year-old girls in stuffed bras?

Susannah.   Yes, you did make your feelings known, may I remind you that as far as the kids were—

Frank.   'Kids'—

Susannah.   Yes, kids—what do you want me to call them, juveniles? They enjoyed themselves. What's wrong with tits, for God's sake . . . anyway, look, we agreed! Some diminution in quality—yes! If we were challenged— yes. For as long as it takes.

Frank.   We kill people.

Susannah.   You're mad.

Frank.   We suck the life out.

Susannah [*in a singing tone*].   I think I hear the cracked bell of revisionism.

Frank.   Remember going to Austria last year?

Susannah.   I asked you to come, you wouldn't take the time off.

Frank.   Once to ski, and again in the spring . . . to renew yourself. For the fight. You didn't even bring back pressed flowers. You took pictures, but you didn't show them to the kids—why not?

Susannah.   I don't know!

Frank.   Because it was nothing to do with them. That was *your* life . . . anyway, ours not to point up the gap. Bridge-building? Common ground? Skiing, for the likes of black kids in North Kensington . . . not on. And don't remind me that your father once worked for the Water Board. Not one act of imaginative love. Not one.

Susannah.   You seem, at least, to have your energy back.

Frank.   I've been trying to get it right. [*He sighs deeply.*] I don't even know what 'it' is any more.

Susannah.   Oh for God's—

Frank.   I don't know anything. Except her. [*Pause*] I read to her. In the evenings. We're reading *Lord Jim* at the moment. Remember the opening, where he goes on about Jim's job as a tout for a ships' chandler?

Susannah.   What?

Frank.   After a couple of pages describing the tattiness of a tout's life he ends up . . . 'a beautiful and humane occupation.' Irony. She liked that. She got it.

Pause

---

[19] Hans Christian Andersen (1805–1875), author of fairy tales. Lewis Carroll, pseudonym of Charles Dodgson (1832–1898), English mathematician and author of *Alice in Wonderland*. Dante Alighieri (1265–1321), Italian poet, author of *The Divine Comedy*. Rembrandt (1606–1669), Dutch painter. Leo Tolstoy (1828–1910), Russian novelist.

[20] British slang for a male homosexual or effeminate male.

Susannah. You pompous renegade. You bloody social-democrat do-gooder.

Frank. It's real. I feel real.

Susannah. Well good luck to you. [*She picks up her bag.*] What's she like in bed?

Frank. A goer. I have trouble keeping up.

Susannah. I notice she does all the cooking and shopping, all the work. What's in it for her?

Frank. She wants a husband, children. She's not after the world.

Susannah. She'd better be, or she'll end up like your Mum and mine . . . vicious. You bloody exploitative shit. I hope it rots off.

She leaves.

A short pause. Crystal enters in a dressing gown.

Crystal. She gone?

He nods.

Jesus. [*He doesn't reply. She contemplates him.*] I had a shower.

Frank. Oh?

Crystal. Smell me.

Frank [*grabbing her and burying his face*]. Mmmmm . . .

Crystal. Guess what it is . . . no, you got to guess . . .

Frank. It's called 'Expensive.'

Crystal [*laughing*]. You ain't seen nothing.

She drops the dressing gown. She is wearing very little, but it is sensational.

Frank. Christ!

Crystal. Thought I better do something.

Frank. No need.

Crystal. Really?

Frank. Look, it's old history.

Crystal. I started to feel like, you know, a fucking gooseberry in me own place.

Frank. Finished. Over.

Crystal. Right. Well . . . in that case . . . [*She sits on his lap, legs astride.*]

Frank. Here, what about my dinner?

Crystal. It'll keep. [*She kisses him.*]

Frank. I'm a hungry man.

Crystal. I know. [*Kisses him.*] I've made allowances. [*Kisses him.*] Last course first tonight . . .

They embrace as lights to black.

ACT II

The flat, ten years later. The decor is now a simple retro,[21] with Thirties' lamps, and some pictures of old movie stars in plastic frames. There are signs of children . . . a child's bicycle, toys brimming from a traditional washerwoman's basket. Apart, there is a large old trestle table with a typewriter, and piles of papers and books. Near the table is a bookcase brimming with books which have spread to nearby furniture. There is a large board, with leaflets tacked up . . . these, too, have spread to the wall. This is Frank's working area. It is in sharp contrast to the smart sofa, lamps, and the retro side table with the music centre.

Frank sits at the table, working. He is absorbed in what he is doing, writing an article straight on to the typewriter. He makes errors and curses under his breath. He reaches behind him, grabs a bottle of beer, has a drink and continues to work.

The telephone rings. He grabs it absently.

Frank.   Yup? Oh, hullo Ann—good . . . yeah, I brought them here, we managed to get some transport. Yeah. Right, look, don't bother, I'll drop you in a thousand copies in the morning, the sooner we move them—yeah. See you.

He puts down the telephone, and resumes working.
Crystal enters. She is now a successful West End hairdresser. She looks slender in highly fashionable clothes, with beautifully washed, simple hair and a model's modulated make-up. Her shoes and bag are expensive. She carries two bags, one an expensive-looking carrier, the other with food. During the next scene she takes the food to the kitchen . . . comes and goes, taking a shower, eating a slice of quiche, looking for a pair of shoes, changing her clothes. At one point she comes to the living room to do her eyes, where the light is best.

From time to time Frank watches her, in casual appreciation. Obviously a familiar ritual. She smiles and gives him a genial wink and wag of the head once in acknowledgment.

   That you?
Crystal.   Nah, Brooke Shields[22] . . . your lucky night. [*She unpacks the food, takes it out to the kitchen.*] What's the time?
Frank.   Half-past seven.

---

[21] Retrospective fashion or style.
[22] American actress (b. 1965).

She returns, takes an expensive-looking dress from the glossy carrier bag, holds it up against herself briefly, for his inspection, and goes, with the dress.

You going out again?

Crystal [*enters, throwing off her clothes rapidly but without fuss*].   What's it look like—aw, I'm bushed. [*She goes again. He gets up, picks up her clothes, takes them out.*]

Frank [*returning*].   Anything special for the kids? [*He picks up the food carrier, reads the label.*] Christ.

Crystal [*off*].   At least I know they're getting some decent nosh, tell them it's in the fridge. Where are they?

Frank.   Next door, watching the film with Inez.

Crystal [*re-enters, drying herself and throwing on clothes*].   That bloody water's not hot again. Did you ring the plumber?

Frank claps his hand to his head, he has forgotten.

Oh no! I need a bloody shower when I come in . . . I'm sweating like a navvy! [*She grabs the telephone and dials.*]

Frank.   What're you doing?

Crystal.   Ringing up for an emergency—

Frank.   Don't do that! It's thirty quid[23] before they come through the door— I've told you, I've got somebody—

Crystal [*dials*].   Hullo? All-Night Plumbers? Yeah, me again. Yeah, same problem. Could you—? Good. Right. Hey . . . hullo? Could you ring both bells? Yeah. [*She puts down the telephone.*] They'll be here in half an hour.

Frank.   I'm going out. I thought *you* were going to be in tonight.

Crystal.   It's all right, I've told them to ring Inez's bell.

She finishes getting ready. He watches her.

Frank.   You look good.

She blows him a kiss.

Where are you off to, anywhere special?

Crystal [*spitting into her eye make-up*].   Now, now.

Frank.   What?

Crystal [*turns*].   Listen, love. I don't ask about your things.

Frank.   Sure.

Crystal [*doing her mouth*].   Just a couple of beers with the mates. You doing a movie?

---

[23] British slang for a pound sterling.

Frank.   Yeah, thought I might.
Crystal.   Which one? [*She gives him a swift, speculative look behind his back.*]
Frank.   Alan Arkin.
Crystal.   Good, you like him. Tell you what, why don't you look in on Jean
   and Freddy after?
Frank.   I'll see how I feel.
Crystal [*en passant, as she finishes her toilette with rapid precision, gives him a
   hug*].   Yeah, go on . . .
Frank.   Why not?
Crystal.   You could eat at that Greek place.
Frank.   OK.
Crystal.   Be nice, that.
Frank.   Right. That's me sorted out.
Crystal.   Ah, you know what I'm like.

*She turns for him to do up the back of her dress, throws her coat over her
shoulders, remembers something, totters in her heels to the bag she has just
emptied when changing her bag, finds an envelope, thrusts it under his nose.*

Frank.   What's this?
Crystal.   Can't you read, it's the phone bill.
Frank [*reading the amount, whistles*].   Christ!
Crystal [*checking herself in the glass*].   Yeah. Down to you and your lot.
Frank.   Come on, you're never off the bloody thing.
Crystal.   Rubbish, you're here more than me, why don't you pass the hat
   round those mates of yours, ripping you off for free calls, I wouldn't stand
   for it—ahhh! [*Making him jump.*]
Frank.   Now what's wrong?
Crystal.   They keep sitting on it!
Frank.   Who?
Crystal.   All those limp dicks of yours—
Frank.   Why not, it's a sofa—
Crystal.   There you are! Cigarette burn. Ah . . . what a shame.
Frank.   Come off—
Crystal.   *And* this end's all squashed. Tch. [*She plumps up the sofa, muttering*]
   Bloody meetings . . . how can you ask anybody back, it's all crummy. [*She
   tidies swiftly.*] It's no wonder I want to get out of it.
Frank.   Do you?
Crystal.   What?
Frank.   Want to get out of it?
Crystal.   Oh don't be so daft.
Frank.   You brought it up.
Crystal.   I need some fun at the end of the day, that's all.
Frank.   So do the kids.
Crystal.   What's that supposed to mean?

Frank.   Crystal, we never see you.

Crystal.   Don't tell such lies.

Frank.   This last few weeks—

Crystal.   I've told you, we're under-staffed!

Frank.   They miss you.

Crystal.   Oh yes, go on, I'm a rotten mother now.

Frank.   I didn't say that.

Crystal.   You can't expect me to stick in every night. *I* want a bit of fun out of life, I won't have it for ever—

Frank.   I'm not trying to stop you . . .

Crystal.   I earn it, I gotta right to spend it . . . I'm the one that pays the bills—

Frank.   That's not true.

Crystal.   Most of them . . . more than half. Everything in this place is what I've bought—

Frank.   Rubbish.

Crystal.   I have!

Frank.   Balls.

Crystal.   Thank you. Lovely. Super language coming from a schoolteacher, no wonder they're all hooligans.

Frank.   Oh Christ, your tongue.

Crystal [*she flares, then changes her mind*].   Frank . . . don't be like that.

She cuddles him . . . he kisses her. The telephone rings.

Go on . . . it'll be for you.

Frank [*picks up telephone*].   Hang on, please . . .

He divests himself from Crystal, who picks up her things, ready to go out.

Crystal.   Which one is it . . . [*in an upper-class accent*] Lady Jane . . . or the little fat one? You know why she sits and reads all that stuff of yours, it's pathetic really. I'm off.

She crosses, for a perfunctory kiss.

Listen, that quiche and toffee pudding's for the kids so keep your thieving mitts off it. [*But it is said jokily. She kisses him again.*] Ciao, lover.

She is about to go, changes her mind, crosses, takes most of his cigarettes from the packet. Frank looks after her, then remembers the phone in his hand.

Frank.   Hullo . . . hullo . . . sorry to keep you . . . hullo, yes . . . speaking . . . why? No! I don't believe it! Where are you, where are you speaking from . . . haha . . . no, no, I'm just knocked out, that's all.

Pause. He listens, nodding

Oh fine . . . fine . . . good—you mean you—no . . . where are you now . . . no, sure, why not? Great! I thought you were in Bolivia . . . yeah, OK . . . no, just come straight up . . . hey, Susannah . . . hullo . . .

But she has gone.

He puts down the telephone, and throws himself down momentarily on the sofa, legs up . . . he is very affected. He looks around the room, galvanized . . . scrapes his papers together, takes the dirty coffee cups from his table, pushes odd books under the sofa. He looks around, moves the furniture slightly . . . takes a look at himself in the mirror . . . goes off. He returns, putting on another shirt . . . goes out at once after a quick glimpse in the mirror, comes in with another shirt, goes out, returns putting on his original shirt. Puts a record on the record player, low, finds glasses, and opens a bottle of wine.

[*To the bottle*] Chambrez, you devil.

He puts it on the radiator. He stands back, spins round for a look . . . has his back to Susannah when she appears . . . spins back to find her standing there.

Susannah.   The door was open.
Frank.   You were quick.
Susannah.   I was just round the corner.

For a second they regard each other across the room. Then they leap into each other's arms, he swings her round, and they hang on to each other as for dear life. She gives a little, sad, animal moan. Eventually they pull apart, and both become matter-of-fact in manner, bridging the moment.

You look older.
Frank.   I am older. You look just the same.
Susannah.   I don't, my skin's a terrible mess.
Frank.   You look fine to me.
Susannah.   How is everyone? Crystal?
Frank.   You've just missed her.
Susannah.   And the family?
Frank.   Fine. They're with the people next door, watching Alan Ladd.[24]
Susannah.   Alan Ladd?

---

[24] American film star (1913–1964).

They laugh.

    Have you had any more . . . children?
Frank.   No, just the two . . . Nicky and Pete.
Susannah.   How old are they now?
Frank.   Ten and nine . . . nearly.
Susannah.   My God, is it really that long? The last time we met was in Leeds
    . . . that awful symposium.
Frank [*together*].   The symposium! And once in the Fulham Road.
Susannah.   Coming out of the pictures.
Frank.   You were with some Chileans.
Susannah.   That's right.

A pause

Frank.   So you're back.
Susannah.   I'm back.
Frank.   Back in the oo-ld country.
Susannah.   As they say.
Frank.   Good. Good. How does it feel?
Susannah.   Pretty weird. I'm a bit disoriented.

She prowls, inspecting the room, calm, unsmiling, dignified in black.

    [*Bending to look at a picture, murmurs*] I'd no idea I was so chauvinistic.
Frank.   Land of hope and glory, eh? Bit of a change from the dark sub-
    continent.
Susannah.   Yes. So small! How on earth did we ever do it?
Frank.   Conquer the world, you mean? You're right. Distinctly puzzling.
Susannah [*sits*].   I got an aeroplane to Paris, then the boat train. Amazing. It
    was like coming back to a tiny old ghost-town . . . everything looks grey,
    even the people! Nothing seems to work any more . . . holes in the roads,
    the clocks tell the wrong time. I went to the Post Office. Four booths shut,
    two long queues, one not moving. When it was my turn I asked for the
    postal rate to Bolivia. He said he didn't know. I said, you must know. He
    went away and he didn't come back. What's happened?
Frank.   Oh, c'est la guerre.[25]
Susannah.   When I left there was confrontation, colour—
Frank.   Hah.
Susannah.   What happened? Where did it go?

---

[25] French, meaning "That's war."

Frank.   Very simple. The money ran out. It *was* happening. We were getting somewhere. Mrs down-the-road from the shop got on the Council. Real change. Movement. And then the Arabs upped the oil—[26]

Susannah.   And down fell Jack.

Frank.   Oh yes. And out of the thickets they came. The carrot-and-stick boys, the law-and-order analysts. The up-you bastards. [*Upper-class voice*] 'There you are, you see? Doesn't do, chaps. Back in the old cage.'

Susannah.   I'm so out of touch—you mean—?

Frank.   Yeah. Cold climate. When there's no wage packet or hope of employment—[*He shrugs.*] Fear works. Put your hand in the flame, you won't do it twice . . . ask any circus trainer.

Susannah.   What about North Sea Oil? I thought we were all going to float away on it.

Frank.   Sold off. Good capitalism—talk national, deal international. Sound Tory[27] dogma.

Susannah.   Depressing.

Frank.   Mmm. So much for the right to work.

Susannah.   Yes. I've been reading the figures. It's—[*She shakes her head, overcome with shock and indignation.*]

Frank [*slight pause*].   They fished a man out of the canal last week with his toolbox tied to his leg.

Susannah gasps.

They call it shake-out. [*Pause*] Same old story. Who are you governing FOR? [*Slight pause*] So . . . it's Jingo-shit movie time and Space Invaders.

Susannah.   Space Invaders? [*She smiles, shaking her head, baffled.*]

Frank.   Yup. Who knows? Perhaps we'll go to sleep for four hundred years, like Spain. Could happen.

Susannah.   Oh I doubt that! Not here . . . not without a fixed system.

Frank [*from the kitchen, getting glasses*].   We've always had that!

Susannah.   What?

Frank [*enters*].   We've always had that . . . the fucking shires.[28]

Susannah [*groans*].   Oh no, not all over again!

Frank.   Sure thing. Flat 'at, gun under the arm. They're all peddling heating systems during the week, but it's up the M1[29] and let's play squire at the weekends.

Susannah.   The old class nastiness? You mean it?

---

[26] A reference to the period in the early 1970s when actions taken by the Arab oil-producing countries led to a steep rise in the price of oil. North sea oil: The rich oil fields in the North Sea, off the coast of England.

[27] A political conservative.

[28] A shire is a territorial division of Great Britain roughly equivalent to a county.

[29] A major superhighway.

Frank.   And the new Puritanism.

Susannah.   Puritanism?

Frank.   'Victorian values' is the phrase. If you're poor, jobless, it's your own fault so—[*He makes a punching gesture.*]

Susannah.   A touch of the Puritans may see us through. A bit of sharing, inconspicuous consumption—[*She smiles.*]

Frank [*hugs her fondly*].   It's good to see you! [*He gives her a drink.*] Welcome home!

Susannah.   To your very best health.

Frank.   To you.

They drink.

Susannah.   How's the job?

Frank.   I'm supply teaching at the moment.

Susannah.   Are you? I had you all dug in as senior history master. You look pretty busy. [*She picks up a pamphlet.*]

Frank.   Socialist Combination. I've thrown my lot in, now that it's highly unfashionable.

They laugh.

Susannah.   And what about freedom from party dogma?

Frank.   Ah. Freedom. Plenty of that about. Freedom to sink. To go to hell. Opportunities for boys to train as butlers—I'm not kidding, there was a programme on television.

Susannah.   Jesus.

Susannah.   What about women?

Frank.   Unemployment hasn't helped. The scene's changed since you left.

Susannah.   Oh, how?

Frank.   More polarized, I think. I'll run you down to Greenham.

Susannah.   Already been. So, you're active?

Frank.   Full-time from next month.

Susannah [*surprised*].   You're giving up teaching? Completely?

Frank [*nods*].   I'll miss it.

Susannah.   Can you afford to?

Frank.   Just about. [*He shrugs.*] Crystal pulls a fortune.

Susannah.   I see. [*Pause*] Is it OK . . . you and Crystal?

Frank.   No. But there are the children.

Susannah.   Wouldn't they be better off?

Frank.   Possibly. I doubt it. They're still a bit young. Can I fill you up?

Susannah.   Mm, please. It's good . . . luxury—I'm used to something much rougher.

Frank.   Yes! What about you? What have you been doing?

Susannah.   Working in a mining town.

Frank.   Same place.

Susannah.   Most of the time. [*She drinks.*]

Frank.   Well? What's it like? [*He leans forward, eager.*]

Susannah.   Oh . . . very high up . . . very wet . . . very cold—not a bit picturesque.

Frank.   What were you doing there? Martin Raven said he'd heard from you but that was ages ago.

Susannah.   Not much point in writing. I was too tired most of the time. Nothing really, Frank. [*She looks at him bleakly.*] No quaint costumes worth a television team . . . [*shrugs*] just people, trying to stay alive.

Frank.   Sounds rough. What were you doing there?

Susannah.   Documentation. I was a field officer.

Frank.   Vital.

Susannah.   I had to change in '81 . . . there was a coup. I've been doing union work.

Frank.   Great!

She turns to look at him, seemingly puzzled. She looks about the room, seemingly absorbed in the decorations.

Susannah [*absently*].   They chew coca leaves. Stops the hunger pangs.

Frank.   You sound bitter.

Susannah [*lightly*].   Oh I am, I am. No one in their right mind would stay there for an hour if there were anywhere else on God's earth. For the last year I've been counting the days—and it rained for most of them.

Frank.   That bad?

Susannah [*short laugh*].   Goes for most people on this globe. I sat next to this shit of an American woman on the plane. She was telling me about her villa, near Malaga. All built in the traditional style—guitar-shaped swimming pool.

He laughs.

Only one 'problem' . . . the Spanish people . . . so 'dirdy'—

She falters.

Frank.   Suse?

Susannah [*recovers*].   I was talking to one of the miners' wives just before I left. She'd lost another baby. I tried to console her. No, she said, you don't understand. I said I thought I did but she said no, I couldn't. I was rich. I tried to tell her that I wasn't, that I didn't own a thing. And she looked me in the eyes, it's a thing they never do but she was a bit mad from losing the child, and she said, 'You're white. You're rich.'

A pause

Frank.   You're not going back?
Susannah.   I should. I'm experienced. I can just about balance my worth against what I eat. No. I'm not going back. Ever.

Pause

Frank.   What are you going to do?
Susannah [*lightly*].   Have a baby, I hope.
Frank.   What? [*Pointing to her stomach in smiling inquiry.*]
Susannah [*shaking her head*].   No, no. It's just that the only thing I really want to do right now is have a baby. The need to [*exaggerated drawl*] 'give birth' has been rather overwhelming lately. I seem to be somewhat . . . seething with it. [*She drops the number.*] I want a child before I start getting infertile.
Frank.   Is there anyone in mind? I mean—
Susannah.   No.

They look at each other. He laughs.

Frank.   It's fantastically good to see you. Well! Right. So. How are you going to go about it? You going solo?
Susannah.   Possibly. I shall have to find somewhere to live, acquire an income somehow—I thought teaching . . . could you help me with that?
Frank.   Sure.
Susannah.   Then there's the father. Have to find myself a feller.
Frank.   What kind of feller?
Susannah.   Oh, either a healthy and intelligent one-night stand with intent on my part and innocence on his . . . or I could try to set up a more permanent arrangement with a fatherly citizen, preferably with a roof over his head. God, I'd love my own patch . . . a few rooms, an apple tree to sit under with my children. You'd be amazed at the things I can do with a few spuds and an onion. Delicioso.[30]
Frank.   You want to settle down?
Susannah.   Probably. It sounds like it.
Frank.   You mean marriage?
Susannah.   Possibly.
Frank.   You've changed!

---

[30] Spanish, meaning "Delicious."

Susannah. Ye-es. No longer the heroine of the revolution.
Frank. I'm sorry to hear that.

She turns, surprised.

They're all on the run now. Following the action. I didn't think you would.
Susannah. It's funny, isn't it? The last time we were here—hah, I remember it—
Frank. So do I!
Susannah. You seemed to be—I thought you'd . . . I mean, I really did think you'd—
Frank. Sold out?
Susannah. I've gone over and over it in my mind. I should have been there. When you were ill. I realize that now.
Frank. I wasn't myself.
Susannah. I should have been there. That bloody project—God, we were so intense! We were going to change the world. Hah.
Frank. I know.
Susannah. I thought we were indissoluble. Mistake number one. We were so in step . . . at least, that's what I thought. That fucking Pill.
Frank. What?
Susannah. If it weren't for the Pill I'd have been pregnant three times over, the way we went at it. Remember the woman downstairs coming up with half the ceiling in her hair? And you offering to show her how it was done? We thought we were so clever. Beating nature. I've been done out of it.
Frank. Still time.
Susannah. God, the agony of choice! [*She groans.*] I mean! There's never a good time to have a baby, if you can afford it you're too old, and who needs Marmite[31] sandwiches and little morons for ten years when you're just getting your head together—God, how I envy Crystal!
Frank. Is that why you've come back? A touch of the domestics?
Susannah. There was a bad mine accident. We lost half the men in the village. Makes you think. About going it alone.
Frank. Very fashionable now, single parenting.
Susannah. Is that what they call it? Orphaning children? No.
Frank [*shrugs*]. The right to choose.
Susannah. Oh, rights! They need their father—there's a right if you like. I saw the loss, in the tribe. Imbalance. I've begun to have a silly respect for that rare constant in human psychology—the blood relation.
Frank. Hah! [*Laughs*] We spent half our time together fending off our bloody parents!

---

[31] A highly flavored yeast extract used as a sandwich spread.

Susannah.   Yer . . . well . . . they were squares . . . straights . . . 'don't show me up, man'!

He laughs and hugs her.

Still do anything in the world for us. Who else can you say that of? You couldn't say it of me. I pissed off when you were ill. Your mother didn't. They cashed in their life insurance to send you and Crystal on holiday.

She moves apart, walks about.

I want them. My family. Sisters, aunts, cousins . . . great-uncles once removed. Someone to go to . . . argue with . . . grumble about—at least they're there! I watched television last night. God, I couldn't believe it. Programme after programme . . . the Twenties . . . the Thirties . . . bath after bath of nostalgia, all created with such love, affection. What the hell have we done?

She walks, restless.

I'm tired of being on my own. It's an over-rated privilege.
Frank.   You have changed.

She laughs.

Susannah.   I still talk too much. What about you? What about you, Frank?
Frank.   Here and now? I don't know. Yes. Excited. Pretty excited.
Susannah [*turns to him, her face alight, just as he turns away*].   You mean . . . ?

She sees that he does not mean because she is back, and covers quickly.

Why? What about? About changing your work?
Frank.   Don't know. Can't say. Yes, I suppose it is that. Taking the risk. Only this time it's sane. No more shrieking about revolution, man the fucking barriers. Kids' talk. Murderers' talk. Our aims are as clear as we can make them. Precise. Practical. And modest.
Susannah.   Gradualist?
Frank.   Remember what you used to say? Not one hair of one baby's head?
Susannah.   You gave me shit for it.
Frank.   We have to be realistic. Select . . . win where possible, influence, subvert, create models, communicate—God knows the channels are open now. Anything's possible, d'you see? Because everything's collapsed. Politics . . . religion . . . imperialism. At least it makes for clarity.
Susannah.   Dangerous.

Frank. Do you think so? I wonder.

At least there's less shit. People won't stand for it . . . no, not any more. They're a lot more criminal, sure . . . or rather, they know where criminality lies, they see the con. I think we could be in with a chance. We're misty bloody Islanders, with a head full of words. Which is a problem.

Susannah. How, how d'you mean? [*She leans forward, loving the talk, not able to get enough of it.*]

Frank. Romantics, the lot of us. Shakespeare spawn. We could double the gross national product if we put turrets on the factories. I've even thought that maybe we should stick with titles . . . only not be so farting mean with it . . . spread them around the way they did in Russia before the Rev. Everyone in with a chance for a fur-collared overcoat.

Susannah. Don't tell me *you've* become a royalist?

Frank. Stranger things have happened.

I'm kidding. Under this string vest there beats a pure republican heart.

Susannah. I'm not convinced. You're an Englishman. Quite capable of being corrupted by a piece of twopenny ribbon.

Laughing, she prowls among his papers.

What's the party line?

Frank. Anarcho-syndicalist.

Susannah. De-centralization?

Frank. Community politics, fifty-fifty ownership, management and labour, government and people. Internationalist. Some ecology. We're eclectic. And pragmatic.

Susannah. Sounds like the new . . . what is it . . . the SDP.[32]

Frank [*throwing a cushion at her*]. Marxist hack!

Susannah. And you're happy?

Frank. Nothing's perfect. I have regular moments of pure fascism . . .

Susannah. Plus ça change[33] . . .

Frank. . . . and I wish I could make some money, like my brother.

Susannah. How is he?

Frank. Weighs fifteen stone and has five children, boxer dog, and a villa in Majorca, mit pool.

Susannah. Nice?

Frank. Very comfy.

Susannah. Ye-es. Yes . . . I want a baby. How about it?

Frank. You looking at me, squire?

---

[32] Social Democrat Party. Originally a faction of the middle-of-the-road Liberal Party, no longer in existence.

[33] *Plus ça change, plus c'est la même chose,* a French expression meaning "The more things change, the more they are the same."

Susannah.   You'd do. You'd do very well. In fact . . . in fact it's going to be difficult to find a substitute for you.
Frank.   Suse . . .

They kiss gently. He takes her hand again.

Susannah.   I saw your daughter. Just after she was born. When I came to see you and we had that flaming row. I remember it very clearly. I wasn't into babies at all and Crystal had her tricked out in pink with obscene rabbits in spats camping about all over the cot.
Frank.   I remember.
Susannah.   I really hated being forced in there, and I was determined not to make the usual noises. What I wasn't prepared for was this . . . person. She was fast asleep and frowning, as though she was concentrating on something as hard as she could, it was as though she was . . . growing. She had your long skull . . . I've never forgotten. Are you faithful, you and Crystal?
Frank.   I am. She isn't. She's very good with the children . . . natural mother. As they say. We-ell, at the moment it's not so hot, she's stopped feeding us.
Susannah [*drily*].   Oh dear. Poor old you.
Frank.   Figure of speech.
Susannah.   What's gone wrong?
Frank.   She's fed up.
Susannah.   With you?
Frank.   Mostly.
Susannah.   Why?
Frank.   I don't stand up to her. Not in the way that she wants.
Susannah.   Why not? If that's what she needs.
Frank.   Come on. You can't play a part in your own home. Home's where you leave off.
   She's restless. She doesn't know it but what she really wants is a child every other year. That's what her body wants. They're all breeders, the women in her family. Insatiable. She has such a body . . . breasts . . . contours . . . valleys . . . all—alive! It's a crime to clothe her . . . she should be decked with flowers and worshipped. I'm a mere mortal. I deprive her. So she takes it out of me.
Susannah.   It sounds disastrous.
Frank.   Yeah. But it's poetry. And the children. I live in a permanent daze of wonder at the beauty of them. The things they say! New! Fresh . . . another coinage. They don't see with our eyes. They come after us. They judge us. Of course at the moment I'm Dad . . . I can do no wrong. They'll find me out soon enough. Realize I'm not Superman.
Susannah [*slight pause*].   Frank . . . it's bad, isn't it?
Frank.   Yes.
Susannah.   Let go.
Frank.   I can't.

Susannah.   But surely—

Frank.   'My Kingdom.'

Susannah.   But if it's no good? I could put up a fight this time. I'm much tougher now.

Frank.   No. Not yet, anyway.

Susannah.   Oh for Christ's sake! If you think I'm going to stand back and watch you—have you any idea what I've—[*She catches herself up with difficulty.*] I'm sorry. It's your life. But oh, Frank, if you knew. How lucky we are. To waste any of it . . . !

Pause

It's self-indulgent to talk of bringing even one more mouth into the world. We're cannibals, the lot of us. Living off cash crops when we could . . . [*She pauses, then turns, speaks mildly.*] We should stop. Here. Right now. This minute. All of us. Most of the volume of pain in the world could be easily prevented. We have the means. [*She sighs.*]

I escaped. Because I could. Every night I'd crawl into my damp, sagging hammock and dream about clean dry clothes, about red meat . . . beef, chops, liver . . . about lights that switched on . . . warmth . . . about cars, buses, smooth roads . . . shops, theatres, libraries . . . all the things I could have again, and that they would never, ever have.

Frank.   Love . . . [*He puts an arm about her.*]

Susannah.   The woman on the plane showed me her new handbag. Crocodile. A thousand dollars—and she was proud of it. Enough to feed a village for a year.

Frank.   Yes. Yes, a bit of a joke.

Susannah.   Most of all our sort. The do-gooders.

Frank.   We're not arms dealers.

Susannah.   Sure. [*Pause*] I don't know what to do. Except, as I say . . .

Slight pause

Frank.   Join us. [*He indicates the poster on the wall.*]

Susannah.   Save the baby seals?

Frank.   That amongst other things. That as well. For all these kids you're about to have. The Greens[34] aren't wrong . . . we are the custodians . . . of the planet.

Susannah.   Hah! [*She laughs.*] When were you any good at maintenance?

They both laugh.

---

[34] A multinational, progressive political party (founded in West Germany in 1979) organized to protect the environment.

Frank.   You'll need something.
Susannah.   Perhaps. I don't know. [*She ruffles his papers.*] So much . . . paper.
Frank.   Recycled though.

She laughs.

You must belong to something. I mean, you have to. Otherwise it's just—

She nods.

Frank.   Give us a try. There is a space—we can't pay much, you'd need
something as well. Think about it.
Susannah.   Perhaps.
Frank.   Have a look round, of course.
Susannah.   Yes. Perhaps. [*Pause*] Frank. I need a child. You could give me a
child. You could give me a child here and now. If you like I'll go away and
never see you again. If you love her.

Frank gets up, walks away. He plays with things on the table. Silence

Frank.   It was fine at first. I was educated, a college boy, she thought she'd
gotten a real bargain. She liked showing me off, doing her friends in the
eye.
Susannah.   What about you?
Frank.   Oh, fantastic, just to be with her. It's a big aphrodisiac being with a
woman other men want. And I'd done it . . . married a straight-down-the-
line working-class girl. You'd have loved some of the confrontations with
our more bourgeois acquaintance . . .

She looks at him objectively.

It wasn't the reason I'd married her, but it was damned exhilarating. We
were both on a real high. And then the pregnancies. She was magnificent.
Brave. Like a lion. God, bloody painful—[*He catches Susannah's eye.*]—she
was fine. Eating steak and chips the minute Pete was out.

Pause

And then . . . I don't know. She went back to work . . . we needed the
bread. The hours are dodgy, it's a strain . . . it's not just that you're on your
feet all day, you're giving out to people. You've no idea what people tell
their hairdressers, Christ, she's heard the lot . . . little old ladies getting a
last hairdo before a major cancer operation . . . cheering up a woman who's
just had her nose broken by her old man and wants something to make him
fancy her on her birthday. The end of the day, we were both knackered and

with two young kids—one's all right, you can cope, but with two it's a family
. . . they need . . . [*He shrugs, pauses.*] And then . . .

I don't know. I began to relax. Stopped playing games. I let her get right
in—she has that contemptuous familiarity of people bred at close quarters
with no privacy, no respite for the mind. She's used to quarrelling, picking
fights . . . she gets off that way. I can't do that. I couldn't rise. God, she
can be vicious!

He walks about. Pause.

She got bored. Began to take me for granted. And there are all those randy
hairdressers, they're not all gay, believe me. She'd tell me about it . . .
getting a quick one between floors on the way down to the tinting . . . parties
. . . pick-ups . . . musicians after a gig . . . discos . . . receptions . . . you
make big money doing hair privately. There'd be dances, weddings—she'd
get it from the waiters . . . the best man . . . the bridegroom . . . even the
bloody bride . . .

Susannah.   She tells you?

Frank.   She's a blabbermouth. She doesn't like to feel uneasy.

Susannah.   Phew!

Frank.   She's settled down a bit. She has . . . boyfriends. There was a big
Irishman, then an actor, then some electronics wizard with a pocketful of
money. This one, the one she's got now, is really loaded . . . Formula One
racing driver, man about town, knows the score. And tough. She likes a
man who's tough. I talk soft. I don't come on all the time. I look for
tenderness and she wants invention. What I ought to do is take a strap to
her. She'd like that.

Susannah.   You're obsessed.

Frank.   Yes. She escapes me.

Susannah.   Oh my dear.

He sits beside her, smiles, caresses her face.

You've been in my thoughts for years.

He makes to kiss her.

Crystal [*from the door*].   Ahhh!

She enters, genial, puts down a bottle.

[*To Susannah*] God, where the hell have you been? What's happened to
your skin?

Susannah [*standing awkwardly*].   I've been working in Bolivia.

Crystal.   You didn't leave a day too soon.

Susannah.   You look wonderful.
Crystal.   Drink?

Susannah shakes her head.

   Well, carry on. Don't mind me. [*She sits, crossing her legs flamboyantly.*]
Frank.   Carry on what?

But Crystal jumps up with a clatter, making them both jump.

Crystal.   I know! Stereo! Whatcha fancy? [*Peering at Susannah's face en pas-
   sant*] Christ. [*She fumbles with the records.*]
Susannah.   How are the children?
Crystal.   Oh, I expect he's been filling you in. With the details.
Susannah.   No . . . as a matter of fact I've only just—
Crystal [*puts on a disc . . . to Frank*].   I thought you was going to the pictures?
Frank.   Changed my mind. So?
Crystal.   Well, it's a bit awkward.
Frank.   Why?
Crystal [*moves about, restless*].   Look . . . why don't we get sensible? I thought
   you was going to be out a couple of hours, I got a friend coming in. I mean,
   I don't mind . . . you've kept it very dark—
Frank.   What do you mean? There's nothing going on—

He looks to Susannah for support but she sits like a totem pole.

   —who's coming?
Crystal.   Nobody. Friend of mine.
Frank.   A girl?
Crystal.   No.
Frank.   Have you been making a habit of this?
Crystal.   Hark at him, you can tell he's a schoolmaster, can't you . . . that's
   how he goes on. Look, cock, this is my place.
Frank.   No it isn't.
Crystal.   It bloody is—
Susannah [*rising*].   I'd better go.
Frank [*irritable*].   No.
Crystal.   All I'm saying is, why don't we—
Frank.   No!
Crystal [*a whine*].   Frank . . . he'll be here in a minute!
Frank.   I've told you—no!
Crystal.   Come on! You might as well—
Frank.   What? Might as well what?

Crystal [*sullen*].   It's not as though you don't know about it. Look—
Frank.   Shut up!!

There is a long silence. Susannah makes to speak, thinks better of it.

Crystal.   Right. That's it, then. We know where we are.
Susannah.   Frank—
Crystal.   All right for some.
Frank.   What are you talking about?
Crystal.   I'm not having it.
Frank.   Having what?
Crystal.   You can make your mind up. What do you want to do . . . do you
  want to finish?

He looks at her, aghast.

Susannah [*seeing his face*].   Crystal, I've only just come back. Frank and I
  haven't seen each other for—

But, at the sound of a loud knock, Frank and Crystal make for the door.

Crystal.   Shit! [*As she makes for the door.*]
Frank [*pushing her out of the way*].   Get out of it—
Susannah.   Frank, don't! [*She moves to the door, trying to hear.*]
Frank [*off*].   You, push off.
Man [*upper class*].   What's the matter, what's going on?
Crystal.   Look love, it's off, Frank's got his girlfriend in—
Man.   Has he, now?
Crystal.   You better go.
Man.   I'm coming in—
Frank.   Go on, get out—out! [*The sound of a fight*]
Susannah [*runs off*].   Frank, don't!
Crystal.   Leave it off, you bloody fool—leave him alone, get out of it, you big
  prick—

Sounds of a further scuffle.

Susannah and Crystal enter, supporting Frank. He is bleeding.

Crystal exits. We hear her whispering urgently to the man.

Crystal [*off*].   Naow . . . don't! No, you done enough already! How can I . . .
  I can't, can I?
Man.   Listen, ducky, make your fucking mind up—
Crystal [*off*].   Oh shove off. [*Comes in.*] Now he's on the fucking turn.

Susannah [*mopping Frank's face*].   Was he hurt?
Crystal.   You kidding? [*She fetches water and Listerine.*] Keep still.
Susannah.   Is it deep?

They inspect the cut.

Crystal.   I don't know, what do you think . . . is it hurting, Frank?

He mumbles.

   God, he's really out of it.
Frank.   Ow! [*As she puts on the antiseptic and a Bandaid*]
Crystal.   Sorry, love.

Susannah lights up, offers Frank a cigarette, he shakes his head. Crystal takes the bowl out.

Susannah.   You all right?
Crystal [*returning*].   He'll be OK.
Frank [*to Crystal*].   So you were bringing him back here?
Crystal.   Yeah.
Frank.   Here, to our bed?
Crystal.   Yeah, why not?
Frank.   Sure, why not invite the kids in, make it a show.
Crystal.   There's no need to be filthy.
Susannah.   I think I'd better go.
Frank.   No, don't.
Crystal.   No, stay.
Frank.   It's not the first time, is it?
Crystal.   Forget it, you're upset.
Susannah.   I'd better go.
Frank.   No.
Crystal.   Sit down. Have a drink—I know, cup of tea.

She exits to kitchen, but he follows her off. We hear their voices, prolonged. Susannah is uncertain whether to go or stay. The voices are raised, she picks up her bag to go. There is a screech from Crystal, she decides to stay. Silence. Now she is really non-plussed. What are they doing? Could they be—? She goes to the kitchen door, to listen. Just manages to step back as Crystal enters regally with a tray of tea, a mod pot and matching set of retro cups and saucers.

   Sit down, Susannah, make yourself at home. Like me cups? Present from
   Boy George. Sugar?
Susannah.   Two, please.
Crystal.   Bad for the skin.

Susannah.   Where's Frank?

Crystal.   He's lying down.

Susannah.   In the kitchen?

Crystal [*bright*].   Mmm. Well? What d'you think?

Susannah.   I beg your pardon?

Crystal.   Of him . . . of me feller . . .

Susannah.   Sorry?

Crystal.   What did you think of him?

Susannah.   I didn't really get a good look.

Crystal.   Anyway, he's better with his clothes off.
    Ooh, that's better. [*She puts down her cup.*] You back for good?

Susannah.   Yes.

Crystal.   Not going abroad no more?

Susannah.   No.

Crystal.   Packed it in, eh?

Susannah.   Yes.

Crystal.   What you going to do?

Susannah.   I haven't made my mind up.

Crystal.   There's not a lot about.

Susannah.   So I gather.

Crystal.   Still, you'll be able to pull something, eh? With your qualifications.
    Always room for your sort of work, eh?

Susannah.   Is he all right?

Crystal.   Sure. You don't look as if you've been having a good time.

Susannah.   You could say that.

Crystal.   Make up for it! You're only young once, that's what my Mum says.
    Tell you what, come down to the salon. I'll give you a peel . . . a skin-peel.
    For nothing. Cost you over fifty, you know . . . they vacuum your wallet as
    soon as you come through the door. What about the Dance Studio? Be good
    for your neck, that.

Susannah.   What's wrong with my neck?

Crystal [*manipulates Susannah's neck*].   There . . . you see? Stiff! You're all
    rigid! There's a lot of stuff now, dance, exercise, body-shaping . . . look . . .
    [*She displays her body, does a flip and the splits.*] I used to be ever so thick
    here. And here. I do this every morning. [*She demonstrates a floor exercise.
    Frank enters, stands watching her. She sees him.*] Frank, how you feeling?

*He does not reply. He finds an old grip behind his table, begins to throw things
into it.*

What do you think you're doing?

He glares at her, continues to pack.

Don't be so silly.

Frank.   Get out. [*As she tries to stop him*] Leave it!

Crystal.   Frank . . .

Frank.   Will you get out of my way?

Crystal.   What are you looking for, there's nothing in that drawer—Frank! Look, don't be so stupid—

They scuffle.

Susannah.   Please, stop it . . . look, this is ridiculous . . . ow! [*She gets hit on the nose.*]

Crystal.   Now look what you've done, what do you think you're doing . . . [*She helps Susannah to her feet.*] . . . you shove Harry down the stairs . . . just as well he was legless, he'd have given you a right pasting . . . look at her nose, it'll be the size of a marrow in the morning . . . Susannah . . . [*she shouts as if Susannah is unconscious*] . . . Susannah—you all right?

Susannah.   Oof . . . ooergh . . .

Crystal.   Oh Christ. [*She exits swiftly, returns with bowl, flannel and the Listerine.*] Florence fucking Nightingale, I thought I was going to have a quiet night . . . [*She looks at Frank.*] . . . crumbs, your eye!

Frank [*to Susannah*].   I'm sorry, I didn't mean to hit you.

Susannah.   Ooh . . .

Crystal.   Oh look, she looks terrible! Ah! Talk about Karl Malden.[35] She hasn't set foot in the country five minutes, first thing you do—honest, I don't know. [*She ministers, with swift competence.*] Lie back.

Susannah.   I'm all right. No really, I'm OK.

Crystal.   It'll be a week before she can see straight. Well, are you going or stopping?

Frank [*glares at her, sits abruptly, clutching his bag. To Susannah*].   I'm sorry, love.

Susannah nods, tries to smile.

Crystal.   No thanks to you. [*She takes the bowl off for a refill.*]

Susannah.   I should go.

Frank.   Where are you staying?

Susannah.   At the YW.[36]

Crystal [*returns, hears this*].   You kidding? She can't stay there!

Frank.   Stay here. At least for the night. [*To Crystal*] OK?

Crystal.   Sure . . . up to you.

Frank [*sitting firmly*].   I'm going.

Crystal.   Leave it out.

---

[35] Karl Malden, American actor featured in a television commercial that claimed a traveller's best protection against theft and accident was an American Express credit card.

[36] Short for YWCA, Young Women's Christian Association.

Frank.   I'm going!

Crystal.   You're not. He's not, is he, Susannah?

Susannah [*speaking with difficulty, a tissue up her nose*].   Frank, you're upset— why not sleep on it?

Frank.   Fouling her own nest . . . I'm not having that.

Crystal.   Oh don't be so ridiculous, anyway where do you think you're going? You can't go anywhere, you can't afford it for a start, where's the bread coming from, you'd have to work!

Frank.   I do work.

Crystal.   Work?

Frank.   You try teaching kids—

Crystal.   I didn't mean that, I meant all your other stuff. [*Pause*] If it comes down to it, I'm the one to go. It's your place. Yours and hers. That's how it started. I'll go.

Frank.   Set you up, has he?

Crystal.   You kidding? If I get out of here, I'm finding something decent for me and the kids.

Frank.   You're not taking the kids.

Crystal.   I'm not leaving them.

Susannah.   Please. I'll go. Obviously I'm the one to go. I can't bear to see him unhappy!

Crystal.   Him?! He never even got me a decent house, all the girls I was at school with got a roof over their heads, one's living in Wimbledon! I should have gone in with Ray, I could of had me own salon by now, but no, dirty word, innit, business . . . no co-operation at all. It's all right for me to work me ass off seven days a week . . . we-ell, I'm rubbish, aren't I? I'm getting veins now. [*She displays an elegant leg.*]

Frank.   There's nothing wrong with your legs. You don't have to put in the hours. You do it because you want to.

Crystal [*to Susannah*].   You got any money?

Susannah.   Yes I have as a matter of fact. [*To Frank*] Dad died.

Frank.   Oh. I'm sorry.

Susannah.   It was quick. Mark said he got up from the breakfast table, said 'I think I'll just stroll over to the links' and was dead before he hit the floor.

Crystal stifles a giggle.

Crystal.   Leave a lot, did he?

Susannah.   Enough to put a roof over my head.

Crystal.   Yeah? [*Slight pause*] Tell you what . . .

Frank.   Shut up.

Crystal.   I was only thinking.

Pause

Susannah.   What? What were you thinking?

Crystal.   This girl I know. She's got a house. Some guy set her up—actually it's two houses knocked into one, so the garden's fantastic . . . you remember, Frank? I showed you.

He glares, and she pulls a resigned face.

It's a great house—she leaves dustbins and rubbish outside, you know, so's she don't get done over[37]—but inside she's spent a fortune, it's all pale blue deco with a studio out the back.

Susannah.   She wants to sell?

Crystal.   Yeah, she's marrying an Arab . . . I introduced them. [*Flicks a glance at Frank.*] We could get it for nothing, don't mean a thing to her and, like I say, she owes me a favour.

Susannah.   You mean I should buy it?

Crystal.   We could share. Frank, sit down.

Susannah.   Sit down, Frank. How do you mean, share, Crystal?

Crystal.   Well, the way I look at it . . . I mean, if Frank and you think it's a good idea. [*To Frank*] I mean, let's face it, love, it's OK in bed but I bore the tits off you when I open me mouth . . . I mean, sometimes I don't but that's because I act up and make you laugh. Only you don't always feel like playing Betty Boop[38] . . . know what I mean? [*to Susannah*] Have you seen the kids?

Susannah shakes her head.

Ah, you'll love them.

Susannah gazes at her, mesmerized.

Susannah.   Will I?

Crystal.   They both look like Frank. [*Pause*] I've always felt bad about it. Taking him off you. I was potty for a baby. Frank happened to turn up at the right moment.

Susannah.   That looks painful. [*As Frank favours his eye.*]

Crystal.   He'll be all right.

Susannah wrings out a cloth in the bowl. He applies it to his eye.

Susannah [*to Crystal*].   You were saying?

Crystal.   What?

---

[37] Burglarized.

[38] Betty Boop, a cartoon character who was portrayed as an airhead.

Susannah. About the house . . .
Frank. Forget it.

He tries to rise, they press him back.

Crystal. It's perfect for sharing, there's lots of rooms. She's got them all done simple, the bedrooms are like little nuns' cells, I mean little cells for nuns, not little nuns . . .

They giggle.

> . . . then there's this huge big kitchen, two sitting rooms, and another little room Frank could use as an office—it backs on to the cemetery so it's nice and quiet, for work.

The last flicked at Frank, who looks at her without expression.

> We've got *some* money, and we'll get something for the lease on this.

Susannah. Frank?
Frank. No.
Susannah. Frank . . .
Frank. Susannah!

She retires, defeated. Slight pause

Crystal. It could work, love.
Frank. Fuck off.
Crystal. Oh come on! What's all the sulking for? You know I've always had a bit on the side. Don't be so double-faced—what's the matter, are you afraid of being shown up in front of Susannah? Look, I'm not like you two. I don't want to get it out of books, I like living!

They look at her without response.

> I just think it could work, that's all. The three of us.

Frank looks from one girl to the other without reply.

> Look at him, he wants the best of both! What a face! No good looking like you want to wring my neck . . . you done me out of a bit of hey diddle diddle, mate. You know what your trouble is—you think too much. Look, tell you what, why don't you have a talk about it? I'll push off, go to bed . . . you two have a talk, sort it out . . . OK?

Frank [*low and furious*]. And you've got all the answers—what do you mean, sort it out? What's that supposed to mean? We're married! We are married.

We have two children. You know what my plans are . . . you agreed! You
agreed about chucking the teaching—

Crystal.   Sure . . . fine—

Frank.   I'm doing it off your back, and I know very well you've no idea, not
the faintest idea what I'm about . . . any more than you ever have—I'm not
blaming you, simply stating a fact, I take full responsibility for the marriage,
for . . . Just the same . . . just the same . . . [*He puts his head in his hands
momentarily.*] . . . it *is* a marriage. We have created a marriage. We are a
family. There are your parents, my parents . . . [*To Susannah*] . . . I know
you'll understand . . . there are facts and truths and values here . . . I'm not
prepared to overturn, not just *my* life, God knows that's worth little enough,
it's unimportant enough, not a swallow would be affected, oh, I'm well aware
of that, of what the world thinks . . . my mates . . . [*To Crystal*] . . . you
. . . nonetheless . . . nonetheless . . . [*He looks up at Crystal without
expression.*] . . . it is our marriage.

Pause

Crystal.   I know you've put a lot in. You don't want to waste it. Nobody wants
to think they've wasted their life. But I'm not a fucking ornament. And I
don't need you trying to tell me what to do. Why don't you work your own
patch for a change? For Christ's sakes, can't you see? She's bloody grieving
for you!

Susannah.   Crystal, please.

Crystal.   Right. Nothing to do with me, right? Only I'm not having my kids
messed about. There'll be no splitting off out of it. Might do for some, not
for me. We got a solution—[*To Frank*] if you can just get your fucking
jealousy out of it.

Pause

Frank [*low*].   I'll kill you.
    And myself. And the kids.

Silence

Crystal [*mutters*].   It's what it's all about. What it's always been about. Watch
it, Susannah. They're not going to change.

Silence

Frank.   I . . . I don't know what to do any more. I try. But I don't seem to
be able to—
    The women yell, and complain, and I see it . . . I accept the argument.
And I wash the nappies, and the kids' drawers. And I wait at the school gate.

And you don't respect me. If I were a bugger you'd respect me. But because
I try to respect you, you don't.

Crystal.   I'm not yours. You don't own me. [*Pause*] If you want me to go, I'll
go . . . but the kids come with me.

He gives her a dangerous look.

Susannah.   No. I'll go. This is all my fault, I should never have—[*But she
falters and begins to cry.*] It's just that I . . . I want . . . [*She cries.*]

Crystal [*full of sympathy*].   Ah!

Susannah.   I'm sorry—

Crystal.   No, go on—have a good cry. [*She cuddles Susannah.*] It's him, isn't
it?

Susannah.   Does it show?

Crystal.   When you're with him. Always did. I done you out of it. I'm the
one to go.

Susannah.   No—

Frank.   I'm bloody going.

Crystal.   We can't all go.

Pause

Crystal.   Stay then.

Pause

Susannah.   Frank?

Crystal.   Frank? Ah, look at his poor eye. Shall I see if Inez has got a steak?

Frank.   Stuff it. [*He rises, looms over her dangerously, then exits to the bedroom.*]

Susannah.   How big is the garden?

Crystal.   A hundred foot, *and* round the side.

Susannah.   Wow!

Crystal.   And there's a conker tree.

Frank returns. He is stuffing clothes into his bag.

I said I'd let her know.

Susannah.   Frank?

He looks from one to the other. And goes.

Damn.

Crystal.   Don't worry.

Susannah.   His poor eye.

Crystal.   He'll be all right.

Susannah.   Do you think he—I mean, has he—?

Crystal.   Nah. Don't think so. Do you?

Susannah.   I don't know. He does have a tendency to pop his cork.

Crystal.   He'll be back.

Susannah.   I wonder.

Crystal.   He's left his books.

Susannah [*doubtful*].   Mmm.

Crystal.   Oh well, soon find out. More tea—oh, it's cold. I know, drop of the ruin—be good for your nose.

Susannah.   I doubt it but thanks, yes I will.

Crystal.   Put your feet up. [*She crosses to record player, puts on* How Long Blues *by Jimmy Yancey.*]

Susannah.   D'you think he—

Crystal.   Relax. Don't worry about it.

She gives Susannah a drink, picks up her own drink, in a long glass, and sashays to the music, glass in hand.

Susannah drinks, lies back and relaxes. She looks around the room she has thought of so often, taking it all in again. She feels comfortable, and warm, and where she wants to be. She sighs aloud, a long sigh.

Crystal.   What?

Susannah.   I mean . . . is it too much to ask?

Crystal.   What?

Susannah.   You seem to manage.

Crystal [*with an eloquent gesture towards the door*].   You kidding?

Susannah [*giggles*].   He always was an old chauve[39]—well, they all are.

Crystal.   Yeah, and rapists.

Susannah [*getting a bit drunk*].   Oh no—not Frank! No!

Crystal [*rueful*].   No.

Susannah laughs.

What's he been telling you?

Susannah.   Nothing.

Crystal.   No, go on—[*She makes to sit by Susannah but jumps up*]—I'll bring the bottle.

Susannah.   Listen . . . was that the door?

Crystal [*shakes her head*].   He'll be down the pub, drowning his miseries. Look, forget it, let him do what he wants.

---

[39] Male chauvinist.

Susannah.   But we need to talk this over.

Crystal.   Sod him, who needs him! Here, what's he been telling you? [*She adds gin to Susannah's glass.*]

Susannah.   Nothing really—well . . .

She laughs and tilts slightly, then she and Crystal, heads together, begin to gossip and giggle, their voices inaudible under the music of the blues.

QUESTIONS

1. Show how the opening dialogue (up to the point where Crystal exits to get Frank's dinner) establishes the character of Susannah, Crystal, and Frank and the relationships among them.   **2.** Describe the changes each character undergoes in the course of the play.   **3.** In Act I, Scene ii, Frank explains to Susannah why he has rejected their earlier idealism. Summarize the major reasons for his disillusionment. At the end of the play, Susannah explains to Frank why she has returned from Bolivia disillusioned. Are the sources of her disillusionment similar to Frank's? Explain.   **4.** Among the three characters, whom do you find the strongest and most admirable? The weakest and least admirable? Explain.   **5.** Explain the meaning of the title.

WRITING TOPICS

1. Are we meant to admire Susannah for her decision to withdraw from political activism and have a baby?   **2.** To what extent does this play rely upon male/female stereotypes?

Widows and Children First! 1979

HARVEY FIERSTEIN [b. 1954]

CHARACTERS

Ed Reiss: Now forty, still handsome, still with a disarming boyish charm and innocence.
David: Fifteen going on thirty. A wonderfully bright and handsome boy.
Arnold: Thirty, as witty and personable as ever.
Mrs. Beckoff: Arnold's mother. Sixtyish. A real Jewish mother. A fighter.

SYNOPSIS OF SCENES

1) Arnold's apartment, 7 A.M. on a Thursday in June.
2) Same, 5 P.M. that day.
3) A bench in the park below, immediately following.
4) The apartment, 6 A.M. the next morning.

Scene One

The stage is a realistically represented living/dining room and kitchenette. There is an entrance door, a bathroom door, and a hallway that leads to two offstage bedrooms. It is the set of a conventional sit-com with a convertible sofa, windows overlooking Central Park, and assorted objects and props. There is also a miniset for Scene 3, which is described herein. As the lights come up, a radio is blaring Fanny Brice singing "I'm Cooking Breakfast for the One I Love." Ed is busily cooking. The song ends. . . .

Radio. It's seven-eighteen in the Big Apple and this is Hi Tide wishin' you a good, good Mornin'. *(A chorus of singers twitter, "Good Morning, Good Morning, Good Morning to you!")* And now for all you sleepyheads what just can't shake them nighttime blues, number one on our hot-pick chart and guaranteed to raise the dead . . . Edward O. Wilson's[1] "I Was Born This Way, What's Your Excuse." *(Music begins.)*

---

[1] An inside joke. Edward O. Wilson is not a musician, he is an eminent sociobiologist. His 1978 study *On Human Nature* argues that "Human diversity is to be treasured, not merely tolerated. . . . Discrimination against ethnic groups, homosexuals, and women is based on a complete misunderstanding of biological fact."

Ed (*Quickly changing to a mellower station*).   There's a thought to start the day.

David (*From within the bathroom*).   Arnold? You got anything I could put on my eye?

Ed (*Calling back*).   He's in the bedroom.

David.   What?

Ed.   Arnold's still in the bedroom.

David.   Never mind, I found somethin'.

Ed (*Hollering down the hall*).   Arnold, you up? Breakfast is on the table.

David.   What?

Ed.   I was talking to Arnold. (*An explosion in the kitchen*)

Arnold (*Offstage*).   What the hell was that?

Ed (*Running to kitchen*).   I think the coffee's ready.

Arnold (*Enters in bathrobe and bunny-shaped slippers*).   And a "Good Morning, Good Morning, Good Morning to you." You're making breakfast? Aren't you an angel. Smells terrible.

Ed.   My specialty: Eggs, onions, and kippered herring en casserole.

Arnold.   Toast for me, I'm on a diet.

Ed.   Since when?

Arnold.   Since I heard the specialty. (*Yelling down hall*) David, you up yet?

Ed.   He's in the throne room.

Arnold (*Knocks on door*).   Hurry up, Sugar-Puss, you'll be late for school.

Ed.   You look well-rested.

Arnold.   I feel like freeze-dried death. (*Sees mess*) Ed, since when do you make coffee in a pressure cooker?

Ed.   The water boils faster.

David (*Through crack in door*).   Everybody ready? Stand back from the door and hang onto your apron strings 'cause here I come. (*Enters modeling a three-piece suit*) Well? Whatcha think?

Arnold (*As Ed whistles approval*).   What's the occasion? Ms. Schnable isn't due till next week.

David.   But your mother is due today. Think she'll like me?

Arnold.   Who'd dare not like my baby?

David.   And look, I put some gook on. You can't even see the black eye.

Arnold (*Examining*).   When I think of that kid hitting you, I wanna tear down to that school and beat the shit outta him.

Ed (*Serving the food*).   Your maternal instincts are incredible.

David.   I can take care of myself.

Arnold.   I see.

David.   Would you stop.

Ed.   What'd the two of you fight about anyway?

David.   He called me something I didn't like, so I slugged him. (*Helping Arnold fold the couch*)

Ed.   So how'd you end up with the black eye?

David.   I didn't slug him fast enough.

Arnold.   That's my son, The Champ.

David *(Posing).*   That's me, Champ David.

Ed.   What was it he called you?

David.   A douche bag.

Arnold.   How fifties.

Ed.   Soup's on!

Arnold *(Exiting to bathroom).*   You stay away from that kid today. I ain't got no money to buy no new suit.

David.   He's somethin', ain't he? What's with this dentist music? *(Switches to rock station. It is the same song only discoed.)* Much better.

Ed *(Holding out chair).*   May I seat you, sir?

David.   Don't mind if you do. *(Sits)* What died in here?

Ed.   Breakfast. *(Holding plate over David's head)* I cooked it myself. Any complaints?

David.   From me? Are you kidding? You know me, always ready for a gastronomic adventure. *(Ed sets down plate.)* Looks wonderful. Could you pass the salt? How'd you sleep?

Ed.   The couch and I aren't speaking.

David.   It's only your fourth night. You'll get used to it. Could you pass the pepper? I slept on it for weeks while we worked on my room, and I'm still walking.

Ed.   I'll probably be able to find a place by the weekend.

David.   What's your rush? Can I have the ketchup? It's great having you here. Could you pass the mustard?

Ed.   Something wrong with the food?

David.   Not at all. Very tasty. Can I have the mayo, please? *(Ed shoots a look.)* Hold the mayo. *(Tastes it)* Mmmmmm. Delicious. Oh, I forgot, your wife called.

Ed.   When?

David.   Middle of the night. I tried to wake you but you were out of it. I told her you'd call back in the morning.

Ed.   What time did she call?

David.   Musta been around two. Somethin' about some papers for you to sign.

Ed.   Thanks. I'd better call. Help yourself to seconds, there's plenty.

David.   And I was worried. *(Ed goes to phone.)* You sure are a heavy sleeper. The phone rang five times.

Ed.   What were you doing up so late?

David.   Answering the phone.

Ed *(Into phone).*   Hello, Laurel? What's up? . . . Couldn't that have waited till morning? . . . I don't think it's fair to wake the whole house. . . .

Arnold *(Entering).*   Hey, Champ, remember to bring back your report card. I signed it.

David.   Where'd you put it?

Arnold.   By the door.

David.   Is Ms. Schnable really coming next week?

Arnold.   Every third Thursday for the next three months. So stay outta trouble and pray that eye heals. I wish this damned probation period was over already. Gives me the creeps havin' someone check up on us all the time.

David.   What's the rush? When the adoption papers come through we stop gettin' the foster-care checks and we need the money.

Arnold.   You may find this hard to believe, but I didn't take you in for the money.

David.   Then you're the first.

Arnold (*Seeing Ed*).   Who's on the phone?

David.   Ed.

Arnold.   I thought I recognized the voice.

Ed.   . . . Laurel, I wish you wouldn't. . . . Not on the phone!

Arnold.   There's nothing more frustrating than a one-sided conversation.

David.   There's another kind?

Ed.   . . . I really don't want to discuss this now. . . . Because, there are other people in the room.

David.   Don't mind us. (*Arnold swats him.*)

Ed.   . . . Can we please talk about this later? . . . Hello? . . . Laurel, are you there? . . . For God's sake, are you crying?

Arnold (*Under his breath*).   Animal.

Ed.   Laurel, please. I'll come over and we can talk. . . . I don't know when. This afternoon. I don't know. . . . All right, I'll see you then. . . . Bye-bye. (*Hangs up*)

David.   She gave you a hard time, huh? (*Arnold swats him again.*) Ow! That hurt.

Arnold (*Big smile*).   Want some coffee?

Ed.   No, I'm fine. After four days of those calls I think I'm getting used to them. I mean, I understand why she calls; she's confused, alone . . . What I can't understand is her damned crying.

Arnold.   Of course it's just a wild guess, but do you suppose it's because she's confused and alone?

Ed.   Well, I don't see why. This separation wasn't all my idea.

Arnold.   Look, Ed, I realize this is a trying time for you and I'll gladly supply a place to sleep, a home-thrown meal, and all the amoral support I can muster, but you've got to keep the gory details to yourself.

Ed (*Grandly*).   Ah, what price compassion?!!

Arnold.   Fifty bucks an hour and I don't take credit cards.

Ed.   Fifty?

Arnold.   Hey, talk's cheap, but listening'll cost ya. Buck up, Bronco, things are bound to get easier.

Ed.   Oh, I know. I just wish she wouldn't carry on like that. You wouldn't believe the crazy accusations she was making. . . .

Arnold.   Ed, I'm serious. I really don't want to hear about it.

Ed (*Mock pout*).   Some friend you are.

Arnold.   I'm your ex-lover, Ed, not your friend.

David.   Oooooh. The heavy stuff. And it ain't even eight o'clock.

Arnold *(Turning David's head back to his plate).*   Don't talk with your mouth full.

David.   But my mouth's . . . *(Arnold glares.)* Is full. Very full.

Arnold.   I didn't say that to be mean. Really. But I can't help remembering a phone call not unlike that one from someone in this very room, if you get my drift.

Ed.   Didn't think of that.

Arnold.   Well, do. Please do. And please don't ask for any advice, 'cause you don't want to hear what I have to say.

David.   Heartbreaker. *(Arnold glares.)* I'm eating. I'm eating.

Arnold.   All this and my mother too.

Ed.   Well, I'll see Laurel this afternoon and hopefully end these midnight calls.

Arnold.   That would be lovely. And while you're there could you see if she'd mind letting you stay with her Wednesday night? The Department of Child Welfare will be arriving early in the person of Our Ms. Schnable and I've got enough to explain without you on the couch.

Ed.   I'm good enough for your mother but not for David's social worker?

Arnold.   It has nothing to do with being good enough. Ms. Schnable frowns on casual cohabitation.

Ed.   Casual? We've known each other for six years.

Arnold.   Four of which you spent married to another woman. *(To David)* Take a glass of milk.

Ed *(Pouring David's milk).*   I get it, it's not me she'll object to but my bisexuality.

Arnold.   Could we please leave your perverted preferences unpurported this joyous morn?

Ed.   Bigot!

Arnold.   Reactionary Chickenshit!

David.   Please, not in front of the child.

Ed.   I could lie and tell her I'm gay.

Arnold.   Come on.

Ed.   Don't you think I could make a convincing homosexual?

David.   You could make this convincing homosexual.

Arnold.   David! Besides, if she thought you were gay, she'd never believe you slept on the couch.

Ed.   I could show you the scars.

Arnold.   I could show you the door.

David.   I could show you a good time.

Ed and Arnold.   David!

David.   Well, I'd love to sit and chat with you grown-up types, but we straight-C students pride ourselves on our punk-tuality.

Arnold.   Go brush your teeth.

David.   Oh, Maaaaaaaa!

Arnold.   Don't you "Oh, Ma" me. March. And don't call me Ma in front of my mother. *(David exits. Ed giggles.)* Having a good time?

Ed.   Sorry, but you do act like his mother.

Arnold.   Guess I do. But this parent act's still new to me. I can't quite get the hang of being mother, father, friend, and confessor all rolled into one.

Ed.   You're doin' great.

Arnold.   Think so?

Ed.   You're the best mother-father-friend-confessor I've ever seen. You've just got to let go a little more.

Arnold.   I will. Geez, I can't wait for my mother to get here; I can mother-smother David, she can mother-smother me . . .

Ed.   And I can mother-smother referee.

Arnold.   Laugh now, Leroy, but we're gonna need one. Y'know, this stuff smells awful, but it tastes much worse.

Ed.   Be nice or I'll tell people it's your recipe.

Arnold.   You don't have to threaten me twice.

Ed.   I'm enjoying being here with you and David enormously. I want you to know that.

Arnold.   Good.

Ed.   You ever wonder what things would be like if I'd never met Laurel?

Arnold.   That all depends, did I meet Alan?

Ed.   Of course not. If I didn't meet Laurel you wouldn't have met Alan.

Arnold.   Oh. So that's how it works. Well, did I adopt David?

Ed.   That's what I'm asking. Would we have stayed together and would we have adopted David?

Arnold.   How should I know?

Ed.   Well, didn't you ever wonder?

Arnold.   Ed, I have enough trouble with the "What nows" without starting in on the "What ifs."

Ed.   Yeah, but haven't you ever thought about what things would be like if we'd stayed together?

Arnold.   I guess so. When Alan died I thought about a lot of crazy things. I'm sure you were among them.

Ed.   And?

Arnold.   I don't know. Why, what do you think?

Ed.   I think we might've been very happy together. It's possible.

Arnold.   It's also possible that it could be me you just walked out on.

Ed.   I didn't just walk out. And who just said they didn't want to discuss this?

Arnold.   Who's discussing? I'm simply pointing out a certain pattern a certain person seems to have fallen into.

Ed.   People do make mistakes.

Arnold.   I wanna write that down.

Ed.   . . . and sometimes they are even forgiven for them.

Arnold.   Oh, don't be so melodramatic. I forgave you years ago. I don't think I could've been happy with Alan if I hadn't.

Ed.   Maybe you and your mother should spend some time alone. I can still find a hotel.

Arnold.   You're staying here and that's an order. You wouldn't leave me unprotected at a time like this, would you? Of course you would. But you ain't gonna. My mother isn't going to feature the idea of my becoming a father, and your professional opinion as an American educator will prove invaluable.

Ed.   She'll say I'm prejudiced.

Arnold.   She'll say a lot of things. You'll learn not to listen. More coffee?

Ed *(Hands his cup).*   Please.

Arnold *(Making coffee and cleaning up).*   My mother's all right. Basically. When I was a kid we had a healthy Mother/Son relationship. A delicate blend of love, concern, and guilt. We never talked much but when we did we kept things on an honest level. I mean, I told her I was gay when I was thirteen.

Ed.   You knew when you were thirteen?

Arnold.   When I was thirteen I knew everything. Senility set in sometime after. And look at me now: On the threshold of thirty I need a calculator to write a check, a cookbook to fry an egg, and Dial-a-Prayer to do the rest. *(To David)* Hurry up in there, you'll be late.

David *(Offstage).*   Don't rush an artist.

Arnold.   What was I saying?

Ed.   Something about your mother.

Arnold.   My mother: the Rita Hayworth of Brighton Beach. We always kept an open line of communication, that is, until my father died; then, I don't know, something happened, she clammed up. I mean, we saw each other more than ever, and we spoke daily on the phone, but somehow we managed to say less than ever. It became a contest to see who could talk most but say least.

Ed.   It's called Adult Conversation.

Arnold.   Thank you, Tom Snyder. Where was I?

Ed.   Your mother.

Arnold.   My mother: the Sylvia Sydney of Bay Twenty-fifth Street. I think the root of it was my father's death. She refused to talk about it, or about how she was coping alone. But Alan and I were living together then, so I always had a source of subject matter in him.

Ed.   She knew Alan?

Arnold.   Oh, yeah. And they got along as long as I didn't call him my lover. She preferred to call him my "Friend." Anyway, she retired, moved to Florida, which reduced our relationship to weekly phone calls and biannual visitations. And then Alan died and I was expected to observe the same vow of silence about him as she had about my father. So we've learned to make meaningful conversation from the weather, general health, and my brother's marital status. I never even told her how Alan was killed. She assumed it was a car accident and I didn't bother correcting her.

Ed. So now you don't know how to tell her about David.

Arnold. Oh, she knows about David. But she assumed he was my roommate and I . . .

Ed. . . . you didn't bother correcting her.

Arnold. It's not the telling that frightens me. But I shake when I think of the long-muzzled floodgates of motherly advice that will unleash when she gets wind of this.

Ed. How bad could it possibly be?

Arnold. Stick around, kid.

David *(Entering).* How's these? *(Big smile)* And look, I'm taking the brush with me so's I can give them a swipe before my big entrance. Think Granny'll be impressed?

Arnold. David, you can put your elbows on the table, use vile and abusive language, even pass gas loudly during conversation. But whatever you do . . . don't call her Granny!

David. You could save yourself a load of grief if you'd just let me break the good news to her.

Arnold. Thanks, but I've heard your subtle mouth at work.

David. Don't say I didn't offer. *(Phone rings)* I'll get it.

Ed *(To Arnold).* You want tea?

Arnold. Why not?

David *(Into phone).* Sister Arnold's House of Hope. You pay, we pray. Brother David speaking.

Arnold *(Grabs phone).* Give me that. Hello? . . . Oh, hi, Murray. . . . No, that was David's idea of discretion.

David. Think I have a future in the Diplomatic Corps?

Arnold. Hang on a sec. *(To David)* Don't you ever answer the phone like that again. What if this was Ms. Schnable? Have you got a comb? *(He produces one.)* A handkerchief? *(He moans.)* March!

Ed *(Handing tea to Arnold as David reads report card).* A handkerchief? Really, Arnold.

David. What the hell is this? *(Reads from card)* "I'm proud of his improvement and am sure he'll do even better on his finals."

Arnold. It said "Parent's Comments" and I had to write something.

David. No you didn't. *(Storms to bedroom)*

Arnold. Murray, can I call you back after I get my little men off to work? Okay, I'll call . . . David! Hang up that extension! . . . No, you can't have a divorce. We're not married. . . . Murray? I'll call you back. *(Hangs up)* All right, what'd I do wrong now?

Ed. The kids like to brag that they forged their parents' signatures. But if there's a sensible comment like that then everyone will know it's the real thing.

Arnold. How was I supposed to know? God, he makes me feel old.

Ed. Don't worry about it. What time is the Great Arrival?

Arnold. I don't know. I figure around noon.

David *(Enters with hankie)*.   I'm gettin' outta here before you think of something else.

Arnold.   Where are your schoolbooks?

David.   In school.

Arnold.   How'd you do your homework?

David.   Astral projection.

Arnold.   You forgetting something?

David.   What now?

Arnold.   Don't I get a kiss good-bye?

David *(Laughs)*.   You're unreal. *(Warm hug and kiss)* I love you.

Arnold.   Me too. Now, get outta here. You're late.

David *(Exiting)*.   Have a nice day, Ed. You too . . . Ma. *(Out)*

Ed.   Men kissing. What's this world coming to?

Arnold.   My father and brother and I all kissed. It's called affection. Aren't you going to work?

Ed.   It's Brooklyn Day. My school's closed.

Arnold.   Only the Brooklyn schools?

Ed.   And Queens.

Arnold.   Queens too? Sounds like Affirmative Action at work. *(Sees Ed clearing dishes)* That's all right. I'll do them.

Ed.   Then I'll go for the papers. Maybe I'll get a lead on an apartment.

Arnold.   Hurry back. I ain't facin' her alone. Do you and your mother get along?

Ed.   Sure. No problem. That is, as long as I remember to call her every now and then. And send her a card on her Birthday. And Mother's Day. And Christmas. Oh, and of course there's Valentine's Day, and St. Patrick's Day, Labor Day, Thanksgiving, Easter, Fourth of July, Election Day, and Christopher Columbus's Birthday.

Arnold.   You forgot Halloween.

Ed.   That's her Anniversary.

Arnold.   How romantic.

Ed.   Where's my blue jacket?

Arnold.   My room, left side. *(Ed exits.)* Ed? You ever tell your folks you were gay?

Ed *(Reentering)*.   But I'm not.

Arnold.   All right, bisexual. Don't be so technical. I ain't Kinsey.

Ed.   No.

Arnold.   Never?

Ed.   You need anything from the store?

Arnold.   Wait a minute. I mean, I know you were in the closet when we were together, but I figured once you got married you'd feel secure enough to tell them.

Ed.   Once I got married there was nothing to tell them. *(Defensive)* And I wasn't in the closet.

Arnold.   Ed, when the only people who know you're gay are the ones you're gaying with, that's called in the closet.

Ed.   Arnold, you may enjoy broadcasting your sexual preferences but I happen to believe that who I sleep with is my business and not the world's.

Arnold.   We'll discuss the world later, I'm asking about your mother.

Ed.   Why put them through that?

Arnold.   Through what?

Ed.   Making them feel that in some way they failed me or did something wrong. You know the trip.

Arnold.   But you could explain to them that they had nothing to do with it. Well, not that way, anyway.

Ed.   They'd still be miserable. Besides, I really don't think it's any of their business.

Arnold.   You told them about Laurel, didn't you?

Ed.   We were married.

Arnold.   You lived together for a year first. You sayin' they didn't know about her till after the wedding?

Ed.   Arnold, you told your parents, they accepted it, and I'm very happy for all of you. All right? Jesus. Your mother flies in for a visit and I get a Gay Consciousness-Raising lecture.

Arnold.   You have a Prim-Evil attitude about your sexuality, Mr. Reiss.

Ed.   Enough?

Arnold.   And they wonder why we broke up.

Ed.   Arnold, you have nothing to worry about. Believe me, your mother will see you and David together and will be pleased with both of you.

Arnold.   You really think I'm doing good with him?

Ed.   You've taken a punk kid who's spent the last three years on the streets and in juvenile court and turned him into a home-living, fun-loving, school-going teenager in all of six months. Yes, I think you're doing good with him.

Arnold.   I wish Alan was here. He woulda been great with the kid.

Ed.   I'll see you later.

Arnold.   Don't be too long.

Ed *(Exiting).*   Give me an hour.

Arnold.   See ya. *(Runs to door)* Ed? We need milk! Skimmed!! *(The phone rings. Arnold grunts and answers.)*

Arnold.   Hello? . . . Oh, hi, Murray. . . . Not much. The usual assortment of early-morning crises. What's up by you?

Ed *(Tears back into the room).*   Arnold, she's here!

Arnold.   Hang on, Murr. *(To Ed)* What?

Ed.   She's here. She's headed up the stairs.

Arnold.   Can't be. It's too early.

Ed.   There's a woman on the stairs checking all the apartment numbers.

Arnold.   What'd she look like?

Ed *(Indicating).*   This tall, this wide, carrying a suitcase and a shopping bag.

Arnold.   Mayday, Murray! I'll call you back.

Ed.   Calm down, Arnold. *(As Arnold runs around the room)*

Arnold.   She can't see the place looking like this. She'll walk through the door and head straight for the vacuum cleaner.

Ma *(In the open doorway)*.   Well, I might change my shoes first.

Arnold.   Ma. Hi. Come on in.

Ma *(Friendly to Ed)*.   Hello. You must be David.

Ed.   No, I'm Ed.

Ma *(Taking back her extended hand)*.   How do you do. I'm the mother.

Arnold *(Taking her bags)*.   I really didn't expect you this early.

Ma.   Obviously.

Ed *(Backing out)*.   Well, I've got to be off. Lovely meeting you, Mrs. Beckoff. I'll remember the milk. *(Out. Then back in.)* Skimmed. *(Out)*

Ma.   Nice-looking boy. Who is he?

Arnold.   That's Ed. . . .

Ma.   That's enough—for now. I'm sorry I snapped at him but that bus ride from the airport. . . . I had to stand the whole way. There wasn't a man on that bus would give me his seat. I'm telling you, Arnold, Women's Liberation is giving me varicose veins. So, let me look at you. How do you feel. You look good.

Arnold.   Good compared to the last time you saw me.

Ma.   The last time I saw you was at your friend's funeral. You're supposed to look lousy at funerals; it shows respect. You could stand a shave.

Arnold.   I just got up. Coffee?

Ma.   A glass of tea. And a can of Lysol. What's that stench?

Arnold.   Ed cooked breakfast.

Ma.   So I know he's not the cook. Pretty wallpaper.

Arnold.   It's not wallpaper. I stenciled the design.

Ma.   Next time use wallpaper. Covers a multitude of sins. Looks nice enough, but why you'd give up that lovely place in Brooklyn to move to Manhattan, God only knows.

Arnold.   The other place had one bedroom. We needed two.

Ma.   I thought your roommate's name was David.

Arnold.   It is. He isn't here right now.

Ma.   Three men, two bedrooms . . . I'll have my tea first.

Arnold.   Ed's transitory. The sofa's a convertible. Honey?

Ma.   Lemon. I brought my own Sweet 'n Low . . . from the plane. You don't get much light here.

Arnold.   We get what you call "indirect semishade." It's good for the plants.

Ma.   So's manure. Looks comfortable. How do you find the roaches?

Arnold.   I turn on the lights. *(A little laugh at his little joke)*

Ma.   Arnold, when a man's with his friends he makes wife jokes. When he's with his wife he makes mother jokes. And when he's with his mother . . . he lets her make the jokes. *(Arnold gets the message.)* You speak to your brother?

Arnold.   He was over for dinner last week.

Ma.   He brought a girl?

Arnold.   Andrea.

Ma.   He's still seeing her? Any talk of marriage?

Arnold.   You'll see him tomorrow, you can ask yourself.

Ma.   And be accused of meddling? Bite your tongue.

Arnold *(Entering with tea tray; Ma is seated on sofa).*   Are you getting shorter?

Ma.   No, I'm sitting down. So, who's this Ed?

Arnold.   A friend. Tell me about Florida. Anyone special in your life?

Ma.   Not particularly. You mean Ed's a friend-friend or a euphemism-friend?

Arnold.   He used to be a euphemism, now he's just a friend. Why aren't you seeing anyone?

Ma.   Because the only ones who ask me out are old men and the one thing I don't need is to become a nursemaid for some *alter kocker.*[2]

Arnold.   Don't you meet any men your own age?

Ma.   In Miami Beach? If he's not your friend why's he cooking your breakfast?

Arnold.   You never cook for your friends?

Ma.   Not breakfast. Didn't you used to have a friend named Ed who got married?

Arnold.   You've got a great tan.

Ma.   He's a teacher?

Arnold.   And a great memory.

Ma.   The girl was, too, right? They've got a house in the country.

Arnold.   Incredible.

Ma.   I remember thinking, "Now there's a man with his head on straight." What's he doing cooking your breakfast?

Arnold.   He and his wife have separated. He's staying here till he can find a place of his own.

Ma.   Separated? How come?

Arnold.   I don't know.

Ma.   Come on, the man's living with you. He must've said something.

Arnold.   I didn't ask and he didn't volunteer.

Ma.   You're involved?

Arnold.   No!

Ma.   Arnold?

Arnold.   Ma?

Ma.   So why's he staying here?

Arnold.   Because he asked if he could and I said yes.

Ma.   You must admit, it sounds a little queer: A man leaves his wife to move in with his old . . . . friend.

Arnold.   He's spending a few nights on my couch. What's the big deal?

---

[2] Derogatory Yiddish expression for an "old man."

Ma.   No big deal. But, you'd think he'd stay by friends that have more in common.

Arnold.   What does that mean?

Ma.   You know; someone he met after the marriage.

Arnold.   Maybe he needed to get away from all of that.

Ma.   You mean he's still? . . . *(Makes a motion with her hand)*

Arnold.   Can we talk about the weather now?

Ma.   I'm glad you reminded me. *(Heads for her shopping bag)* Your mother! If I didn't have my head screwed on . . . I baked you some cookies. *(Produces a tin)* Fresh from the Sunshiney State. Take a whiff; you can smell Miami.

Arnold.   David'll love these.

Ma.   I didn't know what to bring. I hadn't seen the place to know what you need.

Arnold *(Friendly and confident now).*   Oh, I didn't show you. . . . *(Takes out an afghan)* Look what I'm making. I took a class in weaving and crocheting at night school. Isn't it beautiful?

Ma.   I'm telling you! . . .

Arnold.   I made it for out here. Y'know, for taking a nap on the couch. I wanna make one for my bedroom too. You like it?

Ma *(Trying to look away).*   Nice.

Arnold.   Pretty design, huh?

Ma.   It's fairy nice.

Arnold *(The wind knocked out of him).*   Well, maybe you should unpack. You can put your things in my room.

Ma.   How are we arranging all of this?

Arnold.   You'll sleep in my room, David in his room, and Ed and I can share the couch.

Ma.   Wouldn't it be easier if I slept on the couch? That way you'll have your privacy.

Arnold.   We don't need privacy.

Ma.   How about if you shared David's room?

Arnold.   Did you see my cigarettes around?

Ma.   You still smoke? Shame on you. *(Arnold heaves a heavy sigh.)* What's the matter, *shayner boyalah?*[3] You didn't sleep good?

Arnold.   I'm fine. Just give me a minute to get myself together.

Ma.   Go on, get yourself together. I could use a get-together myself. *(Deep breath)* Arnold, where's the dog? He didn't come to say hello.

Arnold.   I had to give him away. He used to sit by the door and whine all day and night, waiting for Alan to come home. I couldn't take it so I gave him to Murray. *(Referring to stack of papers she has unpacked)* What's all that?

Ma.   Don't ask me why, they forwarded some of your mail to me.

Arnold.   Anything I should know about?

---

[3] Pretty little boy.

Ma.   Garbage. But there's a letter from Ernie the insurance man. You canceled your policy?

Arnold.   One of them.

Ma.   You need money? You know I'm always good for a loan.

Arnold.   Thanks but things are fine.

Ma.   Meanwhile you lost out on a very good deal. You wouldn't see a policy like that again.

Arnold.   What do I need with a twenty-five-thousand-dollar life insurance policy?

Ma.   Now you don't need it, but someday? . . . You never know; you might meet a nice girl . . .

Arnold.   Maaa!

Ma.   You never know. Look at your friend Ed.

Arnold.   I'm looking. He's separated.

Ma.   Separated, but not divorced. Believe me, you never know.

Arnold.   Believe me. I know.

Ma.   What's the matter; you don't want children?

Arnold.   Not the kind you mean.

Ma.   The kind I mean have two arms, two legs, a mother, a father, and Chicken Pox. How many kinds are there?

Arnold.   You'd be surprised.

Ma.   Arnold, you and your brother are the last of the Beckoffs.

Arnold.   So?

Ma.   Don't you feel you have a duty to continue the family name?

Arnold.   Not particularly. Anyway, there's always my brother. I'm sure there'll be lots of little Beckoffs running around.

Ma.   And what if he only has girls?

Arnold *(Thinks a moment)*.   I know a good surgeon.

Ma.   I don't get you.

Arnold.   Why don't you unpack while I take a shower and shave. And when I'm dressed we can sit and have a lonnng talk.

Ma.   A "lonnng" talk? I feel a gray hair growing in.

Arnold.   It's not that bad. Let me help with your bags.

Ma.   I can manage.

Arnold.   It's the room on the right. Shit, I didn't have time to make the bed.

Ma.   Take your shower. I'll do it.

Arnold.   There's fresh linen in the closet at the end of the hall.

Ma *(Waving him on)*.   Go. I'll get by.

Arnold.   I won't be long. *(Exits)*

Ma *(Gathering her things)*.   You see, Jack? They still need the old mama. *(Exiting)* Just think, if I wasn't here . . . who would make the beds?

(David enters through the front door, slowly, peeking in first. Seeing a deserted room, he enters fully and looks around. He spots the shopping bag.)

David. She has arrived. But where are she? (*Looks in kitchen, under table, goes to bathroom door, and listens*) We got us a live one. (*Arnold hums a bit of something.*) Wrong one. (*He is having fun. He tiptoes to the hall and exits. . . . A moment of silence, then a shriek. David runs out of the hall pursued by Ma, who is swinging at him with her purse.*) Mrs. Beckoff, please. I'm not a burglar!

Ma. Then what are you; some kind of weirdo who gets a kick watching middle-aged women strip beds?

David. I'm not a weirdo. Believe me.

Ma. Then you're a rapist. (*She screams again.*)

David. What would a rapist be doing in a three-piece suit?

Ma. How should I know? Maybe you got a wedding after.

Arnold (*Entering, dripping in a robe*). What the . . . David! What are you doing out of school?

Ma. This is your roommate?

David. Charmed, I'm sure.

Ma. You know that "lonnng" talk we're gonna have? It just got lonnnnnnnnnnger.

Arnold. What are you doing home?

David. I forgot, I had a double period of gym and no uniform. So I tole Mr. Kelley about your mother comin' and he said I could come home till after lunch.

Arnold. Just like that?

David. Well . . . you gotta call and say it's okay. Wasn't that nice of him?

Arnold (*Sees his mother's puzzled face*). We'll discuss this later. (*Trying to smile*) Ma, this is David.

Ma. So I gathered.

Arnold (*Long uncomfortable pause*). Okay. So, now we all know each other.

Ma. Arnold, you're dripping on my shoe.

Arnold. Oh. How about this: You go finish unpacking, I'll go finish my shower, and you go start lunch? . . .

David. It's only nine o'clock.

Arnold (*Parental order*). When I tell you to do something . . . (*Catches Ma staring*) Well, I'm going to dry off now.

Ma. You do that.

Arnold (*Slowly backing out*). So, you'll unpack, right? You'll make lunch, right? And I'll . . .

Ma. Dry up.

Arnold. Right. (*Takes a last look, crosses himself, and exits*)

David (*Pause*). Would you like a drink?

Ma. Maybe later. I'm sorry I hit you.

David. No sweat. I usually charge, but seein' how you're family . . . (*He laughs.*)

Ma. You have quite a little sense of humor. Shall we sit down?

David. Sure. (*They do.*)

Ma.   Tell me, David, you go to school?

David.   Yeah. *(Sees cookies)* You make these?

Ma.   Help yourself. *(He does, by the handful.)* So, you go to college.

David.   High school.

Ma *(Her heart!).*   High school. How nice. *(Hopeful)* Senior year?

David.   Freshman.

Ma.   That's very sweet. Tell me, David, just how old are you?

David.   Sixteen . . . in two months. *(Sees her dying)* Something wrong?

Ma.   Not at all. Sixteen . . . in two months . . . that's wonderful. You have your whole life ahead of you . . . while mine's flashing before my eyes.

David *(Chomping away).*   Good stuff.

Ma *(At first she thinks he referred to her life, then . . .).*   Thank you. David, it's none of my business, of course, but don't you think you're a little young to be out in the world all alone?

David.   No. But, the judge did, so here I am.

Arnold *(Sticking his head out).*   Everything all right out here?

Ma *(Choking).*   Fine, dear. Keep drying. *(Arnold withdraws.)*

David.   You like the place? We cleaned all week for you. Sorry I didn't get back to see your face when you got here.

Ma.   That face couldn't compare to this one.

David.   I woulda taken the whole morning off, but you know Arnold. . . . Hey, he better hurry up and call the school. Mr. Kelley'll think I was jivin' him.

Ma.   Does Arnold make all your excuses at school?

David *(Enjoying the game).*   Sure. Who else?

Ma.   Who else, indeed. I've got an idea. Why don't I call the school while you change your clothes?

David.   Hey, I wore this special for you.

Ma.   I've seen it, it's cute, now put it away.

David.   Yeah, but . . .

Ma *(Pointing).*   March.

David *(Exiting).*   Now I know where Arnold got his technique.

Ma.   Cute kid. *(Calling out)* David? Where do you keep the phone numbers?

David *(Off).*   In the phone book.

Ma.   A little too cute. *Oy*, Arnold, what have you got yourself into now? *(Finds book)* Here it is. Right on top. Must get used a lot. *(Starts to dial . . .)* David? What name shall I give them?

David.   What?

Ma.   Who shall I say is being excused? *(No response)* Your last name!

David *(Sticking his head in).*   Beckoff, of course.

Ma.   Really? That's quite a coincidence. Have you and Arnold ever compared notes to see if there's any family relation?

David.   I'm his son. What more relation could there be? *(Arnold steps out of the bathroom.)*

Ma.   You're his what?

David.   His son. (*Arnold goes right back into the bathroom.*) Would you like
that drink now?

(*The lights black out; music plays in the dark for a moment. It should be the
Hartz Mountain Canaries singing "The Blue Danube Waltz."*)[4]

Scene Two

*Later that afternoon. The stage is exactly as it was before (except deserted). Ed
lets himself in with his key. He enters carrying a small paper bag and newspaper.*

Ed.   Hello? Anybody home?

(*A platter flies across the room from the hallway and just misses his head,
smashing on the wall. It is followed by Arnold.*)

Arnold.   Deserter! Defector! Duty-dodger! Ditching your post at the first sign
of battle, you backstabbing, betraying, ball-breaking Buttercup! How could
you leave me unprotected? You Avoider! Abstainer! Abandoner! Absconderer!
Ed.   Absconderer?
Arnold.   If the shoe fits . . . Where have you been?
Ed.   Buying milk.
Arnold.   For nine hours?
Ed.   I was on the express line. What happened?
Arnold.   Happened? What could possibly have happened? My mother walked
through that door and within three minutes managed to insult the plane
ride, the bus ride, Women's Lib, the apartment, Manhattan, my personal
hygiene, sense of humor, afghan, smoking, stenciling, and cockroaches.
And, oh, you'll love this: She accused me of breaking up your marriage.
Ed.   You're kidding.
Arnold.   She practically called me a homewrecker. Okay, so far so good. We
finally sat down to chat when who should walk through the door, but the
Patron Saint of Truants himself: Champ David. My mother gets a gander at
him and goes, "What a sweet child. And whose little boy are you?" Giving
the long-awaited cue to my sweet little angel lamb to turncoat 'round and
point his every available finger at me.
Ed.   Oops.
Arnold.   Did you say "Oops"? No, Ed. "Oops" is when you fall down an
elevator shaft. "Oops" is when you skinny-dip in a school of piranha. "Oops"

---

[4] An allusion to a popular musical radio program sponsored by Hartz Mountain brand bird
food.

is for accidentally douching with Drāno. No, Ed, this was not an "Oops." This was a *(Strangled Scream)*!

Ed. Cut the dramatics and tell me what happened.

Arnold. I'm telling you, nothing happened.

Ed. Nothing?

Arnold. As in "Not a thing." Dear David went atwitter to his room, mother went to my room, and I sat in the bathroom making toilet-paper flowers and flushing them down the drain. Three hours I flowered and flushed, flowered and flushed, till, Thank God, I ran out of paper. Forced from my Autumn Beige Tiled retreat, I called a truce for lunch. It was eaten in silence. No one even chewed. (You ever gum down a hamburger?) After lunch David announced he was going back to school and my mother volunteered to walk him.

Ed. Where are they now?

Arnold. I haven't the smoggiest. Knowing David, he's probably fuming over some pinball machine. I was gonna look for him but it's better if he makes it home on his own.

Ed. That's very sensible.

Arnold. Not at all. But what would I say if I did find him. And the mother . . . I don't know where she could be.

Ed. "Leave them alone and they'll come home . . ."

Arnold. ". . . dragging a noose behind them." Help me with dinner.

Ed. A quick trip to the men's room and I'll set the table.

Arnold. You'll have to borrow a plunger from next door, first. A thousand sheets really do last longer. *(Picking up the broken china)* Look at this, you broke my favorite platter.

Ed. I broke?

Arnold. Come on, get going. And don't go disappearing on me again.

Ed. I'll be right back. *(Exits)*

(The phone rings. Arnold rushes to it.)

Arnold. Hello? . . . Oh, hi, Murray. . . . No, I've been home all day. . . . Because I was in the bathroom. . . . Yes, all day. You wanna sue me? . . . Look, Murr, I ain't got time to tear a herring with you now. You got somethin' to say? Say it. . . . Rocco who? Rocco DiGemma? The one with the Leatherette T-shirts? . . . Yeah, I know him. What about him? . . . You told him I'd do what?!!!? . . . Uh-huh. . . . Uh-huh. . . . Uh-huh. . . . Uh-huh. . . . and then? . . . Uh-huh. . . . Uh-huh. . . . Uh-huh. . . . Uh-huh. . . . Uh-huh. . . . Listen, Marie, *(At this point Ma and David enter happily)* you can call that poor excuse for a rubber creep back and tell him . . . *(He sees them)* . . . tell him I've got a previous engagement. Thanks for calling. Bye-bye. *(Hangs up)*

Ma *(Removing her jacket)*. Who was that, dear?

Arnold *(Puzzled)*. It was Murray. He wanted me to do a favor for a friend.

Ma. What did he want you to do?

Arnold. . . . Baby-sit. You were together?

David. I took your mother to school with me.

Ma. They were very nice. They let me sit in the back. He does very well; when he stays awake.

David. Then I took her to play pinball.

Ma. You weren't worried, were you?

Arnold. What, me worry?

David. Hey, Alfred E., what's for dinner? *(Heads to kitchen)*

Ma. Would you like to go out? My treat.

Arnold. I've started dinner here. But if you'd rather . . .

Ma. No, we'll go out tomorrow. Besides, my feet are screaming for my slippers.

Ed *(Enters with plunger).* Well, look who's here.

Ma. Hello, Ed. How was your day?

Ed. Fine . . . thank you, Mrs. Beckoff. And yours?

Ma. Surprisingly pleasant, once it was settled into. *(Exiting. To David)* After you do your homework I'll teach you how to play chess.

David *(With a can of soda).* Homework? Is she kidding? Hey, Arnold, we got a chess set?

Arnold. Top shelf of your closet.

David. Thanks. Hi, Ed. *(Exits)*

Ed. And you were worried. *(Goes toward bathroom)*

Arnold. I wasn't worried. I was concerned. *(Ed exits.)*

Ma *(Enters in bunny slippers like Arnold's).* Give me an apron and put me to work.

Arnold. That's all right, Ma. Ed's gonna help.

Ma. Oh, I wondered what the plunger was for. Listen, if I'm gonna die of ptomaine, it'll be from something I made myself. *(Holding up a potato)* What do you want done with these?

Arnold. I was going to bake them, but if I could twist your arm? . . .

Ma. You want my *Latkes?*[5]

Arnold. I'd love your *Latkes.*

Ma. Then you'll get my *Latkes.*

Ed *(Entering).* All fixed.

Arnold. Thanks, Ed.

David *(Off).* Hey, Arnold? I can't find the chessboard.

Arnold. Coming. *(Exits)* Be back.

Ma *(Trying to draw Ed in).* You like *Latkes,* Ed?

Ed. I don't know. I never had it.

Ma. Them. You're in for a treat.

---

[5] Potato pancakes.

Ed. I couldn't help noticing, you've got slippers like Arnold's. Mind if I ask who gave them to whom?

Ma *(Modeling them).* You like my slippers? Aren't they Chick? Arnold gave them to me. You know what they say; in matters of taste, there is none.

Ed. I see where Arnold gets his wit.

Ma. That and his appetite are from me. But the face? He's his father's son. He's got his heart too. Always a soft touch. Tell me, Ed, what do you think of Arnold taking in this boy?

Ed. I think it's wonderful.

Ma. You do? Frankly, I'm not wild for it. But look, it's only for a few more weeks, so what harm could it do?

Ed. Oops.

Ma *(Calling to Arnold).* Arnold? You have Matzo Meal?

Arnold *(Enters).* Yeah, I'll get it for you.

Ma *(Proud).* He has Matzo Meal. Did I bring him up right?

(David enters with a book, sits down on the couch, and begins to read.)

Arnold. Here you go, Ma. You need eggs?

Ma. Two, please. And an onion?

Ed *(Looking agog at David).* Are you doing homework?

David. Nah. I'm just readin' somethin' from school.

Ma. Arnold's father used to love my *Latkes*. But his favorite was my Potato Soup. You remember how he liked it, Arnold?

Arnold. I remember.

Ma. It wasn't potato soup like you think; made with vegetables and cream. What he liked was: You took a potato, boiled it in water, threw in a *bissel*[6] salt and pepper and that was Potato Soup. Arnold used to call it "Daddy's Potato Water." You remember?

Arnold. Yes, Ma.

Ma. We were Depression babies. You understand? Whether you have to or not, you carry that through your life. The tastes, the smells . . . they bring back a cozy feeling of a time you don't quite remember. You know what I'm talking?

Ed. I think so.

Ma. Good. 'Cause I don't. *(Arnold hugs her.)* What's that for?

Arnold. I'm glad you're here.

Ma. Me too, *Tatalah*.[7]

Ed *(To David).* I didn't know you could read.

David. I just look at the pictures.

Ed. What is it?

---

[6] Small amount.

[7] Term of endearment for a child.

David.   Some garbage for English.

Ed.   What?

David.   A poem. I don't know. *(Reading and mispronouncing the word "Gaol")* "The Ballad of Reading Gaol" by Oscar Wilde.[8]

Ed *(Correcting)*.   That's gaol, like in j-a-i-l.

David.   That ain't what it says.

Ed.   That's the British spelling.

Arnold *(From memory)*.

"Yet each man kills the thing he loves,
By each let this be heard,
Some do it with a bitter look, Some with a flattering word.
The coward does it with a kiss,
The brave man with a sword!"

Ed.   Very good.

Ma.   What? You think I raised a dope?

Arnold.   We had to learn it in high school. Y'know, I still get shivers when I think of that poor man going through all that pain and torment just to write a cliché.

David.   What's a cliché?

Arnold.   The sincerest form of flattery.

David *(To Ed)*.   Was that a joke?

Arnold *(Coming out of kitchen)*.   Did your teacher happen to mention how Oscar Wilde came to be imprisoned?

David.   Maybe. Who listens?

Arnold.   He was in jail for being gay.

David.   No, I think I woulda remembered that.

Ma *(Embarrassed)*.   Arnold, I can't find the oil.

Arnold.   In a minute, Ma. See, ten years earlier, the Parliament passed a law against homosexuality. And Oscar Wilde had this young lover named . . .

Ma.   Arnold, could you please give me a hand?

Arnold.   Just a second. His name was Lord Alfred.

David.   Royalty, huh?

Ed *(To Ma)*.   Anything I can help you with?

Ma.   No, thank you, Ed.

Arnold.   Now, Lord Alfred's father found out about them and started causing scenes in public; chasin' 'em outta hotels and stuff. But the straw that broke the dam was a note sent to Wilde's hotel. It said, "To Oscar Wilde, who poses as a Sodomite."

Ma.   For God's sake, Arnold. Could you change the subject?

Arnold *(Annoyed)*.   I'll finish later. *(Goes back to kitchen)*

Ed.   Here, we'll read the poem together and I'll explain anything you don't understand.

---

[8] Oscar Wilde (1854–1900) was an eminent Anglo-Irish poet, novelist, and playwright.

David. I want the rest of the dish. *(Ed kicks him.)* Ouch, that hurt.

(David and Ed read quietly and we hear the conversation from the kitchen.)

Arnold. I wish you wouldn't interfere like that; it's very embarrassing.

Ma. Excuse me, but listening to that is very embarrassing.

Arnold. I'm sorry you feel that way, but I have a responsibility to his education.

Ma. I am sure that the people who put him here did not have that kind of education in mind.

Arnold. The people who put him here had exactly that kind of education in mind. And I'll thank you not to interfere.

Ma. I am only suggesting that you should consider the huge responsibility you've taken on here.

Arnold. You think I'm unaware of it?

Ma. Then act like it. You should be setting an example for the boy.

Arnold. And I'm not?

Ma. Not when you talk like that, you're not. You've got to consider what you say to him for the remaining time. He's at an impressionable age. After all, it's only for a few more months.

Arnold *(Ed and David stop).*   What's for a few more months?

Ma. He's here on a nine-month program, right? And he's already been here six months, so . . .

Arnold. And what do you think happens then?

Ma. He leaves.

David. No, you misunderstoo— *(Ed kicks him again.)* Ow! This is getting serious.

Arnold. There seems to be a misinterpretation afoot. Yes, David is here on a nine-month program, but after that, if we agree and the Bureau of Child Welfare allows, I will legally adopt David. And believe me, Ma, if I have anything to say about it, he's not leaving.

(Ma tries to say something, she is angry, confused, frustrated. She throws down whatever is in her hands and storms out. We hear the door slam.)

Arnold. That was an "Oops."

Ed. I thought so.

Arnold *(To David).*   What'd you tell her?

David. I didn't say nothin'.

Arnold. You certainly got a way without words. Well, kids, wish me luck.

David. You goin' in there?

Arnold. Anybody got any suggestions?

David. Don't look at me.

Ed. Sorry, I'm just the baby-sitter.

Arnold. Somber times inspire your whimsicality. I'll remember that.

Ed. And don't forget to write.

David.   We'll be in the next room; so talk loud.

Arnold.   Thanks. *(Deep breath)* Well, here goes everything.

(He exits, we hear a knock on the door, then the door opens and closes. Ed and David jump up and rush to hallway.)

David.   You hear anything?

Ed.   Shhhhhhh.

David *(Going to kitchen).*   Ah, he stalled too long. They're gonna need time to warm up again. Let's eat.

Ed.   I can't hear a thing. This is ridiculous; a grown man listening at a hallway. I should go right up to the door. *(He exits.)*

David *(Shouting).*   You want a sandwich?

Ed *(Runs back in).*   Could you not yell like that?

David *(Whispers).*   Hear anything?

Ed.   No.

David.   Told ya. Have a sandwich. We'll know when they get goin'.

Ed.   You're taking this very calmly. I'm more curious than you, it seems.

David.   Looks that way, don't it?

Ed.   What'd you tell her, anyway?

David.   A little of this, a little of that. What's the difference? You know how it is with grown-ups: They only hear what they wanna. *(He listens.)* Hang on, we're about to get a bulletin.

(Ma enters as if she rushed away. She sits on couch. Arnold follows and stands staring at her.)

David.   Care to repose and repast?

Ed *(Grabs David).*   Come on, Kissinger. I'll teach you how to play chess.

David.   Wait, my sandwich.

Ed *(Pulling him off).*   You'll concentrate better on an empty stomach.

Arnold *(Sits next to her. Pause).*   Is this it? We gonna sit and stare into space?

Ma.   You want I should do a Bubble Dance?

Arnold.   I need a cigarette. *(He gets one.)*

Ma.   Frankly, Arnold, you've done a lot of crazy things, but this? . . .

Arnold.   Adopting David is not a crazy thing. It's a wonderful thing that I'm very proud of.

Ma.   If you're so proud how come you were too ashamed to tell your mother? Everything else you tell me. You shove your sex life down my throat like aspirin, every hour on the hour. But six months he's been here and not a word. Why?

Arnold.   I don't know.

Ma.   So what's new?

Arnold.   Ma . . . y'know, you're not the easiest person in the world to talk to.

Ma.   What did I say? Do I tell you how to run your life? Let me tell you something, my son: I learned long ago that no matter what I said or how I felt, you and your brother were going to do just as you pleased anyway. So, I wouldn't say a word. On purpose! You want to know why you didn't tell me about this? I'll tell you why: Because you knew it was wrong.

Arnold.   That's not true.

Ma.   No?

Arnold.   No!

Ma.   Why then?

Arnold.   . . . I don't know.

Ma.   You would if you'd listened.

Arnold.   This isn't something I decided to do overnight. We put in our application more than two years ago.

Ma.   Who "we"?

Arnold.   Alan and I.

Ma.   The two of you were going to do this together?

Arnold.   That was the idea.

Ma.   Now I've heard everything.

Arnold.   That's what I love about you; you're so open-minded.

Ma.   All right. So, Alan's not here. Why's the kid?

Arnold.   Because with everything else I forgot about the application. Then, one day, the phone rang. It was the foster parent program and they had David for us. I told them what happened to Alan and they said I could probably take David anyway.

Ma.   And you said, "Send him on over."

Arnold.   Not at first. But then I thought it all through, called them back, and said yes . . . on a trial basis.

Ma.   I'm glad you got a money-back guarantee, but you still haven't told me why you wanted him.

Arnold.   Because I was tired of widowing.

Ma.   Wida-whating?

Arnold.   Widowing. Widow-ing. It's a word of Murray's.

Ma.   And a nice one at that. What does it mean?

Arnold.   You know.

Ma.   No, I don't know.

Arnold.   Widowing . . . feeling sorry for myself, cursing every time I passed a couple walking hand in hand, watching Tearjerkers on TV, knowing they could only cheer me up. Christ, of all the things going down here, I was sure that was the one thing I wouldn't have to explain.

Ma.   How should I know about Whatchamacallit? Did you ever say a word to me?

Arnold.   I didn't think I had to. Christ, it's only been three years since Daddy died.

Ma.   Wait, wait, wait, wait, wait. Are you trying to compare my marriage with you and Alan? *(Haughty and incensed)* Your father and I were married for thirty-five years, had two children and a wonderful life together. You have the nerve to compare yourself to that?

Arnold *(Scared)*.   That's not what I mean, I'm talking about the loss.

Ma.   What loss did you have? You fooled around with some boy? . . . Where do you come to compare that to a marriage of thirty-five years?

Arnold.   You think it doesn't?

Ma.   Come on, Arnold. You think you're talking to one of your pals?

Arnold.   Ma, I lost someone that I loved very much . . .

Ma.   So you felt bad. Maybe you cried a little. But what would you know about what I went through? Thirty-five years I lived with that man. He got sick, I brought him to the hospital, and you know what they gave me back? I gave them a man . . . they gave me a paper bag with his watch, wallet, and wedding ring. How could you possibly know what that felt like. It took me two months until I could sleep in our bed alone, a year to learn to say "I" instead of "we." And you're going to tell me you were "widowing." How dare you!

Arnold.   You're right, Ma. How dare I. I couldn't possibly know how it feels to pack someone's clothes in plastic bags and watch the garbage-pickers carry them away. Or what it feels like to forget and set his place at the table. How about the food that rots in the refrigerator because you forgot how to shop for one? How dare I? Right, Ma? How dare I?

Ma *(Starting over his speech and continuing until her exit)*.   May God strike me dead! Whatever I did to my mother to deserve a child speaking to me this way. The disrespect! I only pray that one day you have a son and that he'll talk to you like this. The way you talk to me.

Arnold *(Over her speech)*.   Listen, Ma, you had it easy. You have thirty-five years to remember, I have five. You had your children and friends to comfort you, I had me! My friends didn't want to hear about it. They said, "What're you gripin' about? At least you had a lover." 'Cause everybody knows that queers don't feel nothin'. How dare I say I loved him? You had it easy, Ma. You lost your husband in a nice clean hospital, I lost mine out there. They killed him there on the street. Twenty-three years old, laying dead on the street. Killed by a bunch of kids with baseball bats. *(Ma has fled the room. Arnold continues to rant.)* Children. Children taught by people like you. 'Cause everybody knows that queers don't matter! Queers don't love! And those that do deserve what they get! *(He stops, catches his breath, sits down.)* Whatever happened to good ole American Momism and apple pie?

David *(Sticking his head out from the hall)*.   Could you keep it down? There's people tryin' to concentrate.

Arnold *(Laughing)*.   Sorry.

David.   Round one over?

Arnold.   I really lost control. I didn't mean to say any of that. But it came pouring out; I felt like I was fighting for my life.

David *(Coming close)*.   This is highly flattering. A duel to the death over li'l ole me.

Arnold.   Don't overdramatize. I do enough of that for both of us.

David *(Hug)*.   I think you're wonderful.

Arnold.   Where's Uncle Ed?

Ed *(Sticking his head out)*.   Present. Is round one over?

Arnold.   We've called a cease-fire to regroup.

David.   Can we eat now?

Arnold.   Why don't you two go out for something?

Ed.   How about you?

Arnold.   Don't know why, but I ain't hungry. Go on.

Ed.   You're not going back in there, are you?

Arnold.   I can't leave things like this.

Ed.   You're very brave.

Arnold.   I'm very stupid. None of this would've happened if I'd been honest all along.

Ed.   Or dishonest all along.

Arnold.   That's not for me. Get going.

Ed *(Intimate)*.   Let me stay. We can all talk together.

David.   You want us to bring something back for you?

Arnold *(To David)*.   No, thanks. *(To Ed)* No, thanks.

David *(His jacket on)*.   Put a candle in the window when it's clear to come home. We'll wait on the bench.

Arnold *(Hugging him)*.   I'll do that.

Ed *(At the door)*.   What'll it be; pizza?

David.   You paying?

Ed.   Sure.

David.   Then I know this intimate little French restaurant . . . *(Exit)*

Arnold *(Takes a deep breath)*.   Round two. *(Sits on couch, feet up)* Yoo-hoo, Mrs. Bloom! It's safe to come out. David and Ed went for a walk and we've got the whole place to fight in.

Ma *(Off)*.   Enjoy yourself. I'm going to bed.

Arnold.   Ma, I'm sorry I lost my temper.

Ma.   Ha! I'm glad you're sorry.

Arnold.   Please come out here. We can't talk like this.

Ma *(In doorway)*.   You don't want to talk, you want to fight. But I don't fight with my children. In your life did you ever hear your father and I fight? No. And do you know why? I'll tell you why: Because all my childhood I listened to fights. My father fought with my mother, my mother fought with my brother, my mother fought with me. . . . When I married your father I told him, "Jack, I'll talk, but I won't fight." And did you ever hear us fight? No. And now you know why.

Arnold.   You wanna sit down?

Ma *(Wandering over to the couch)*.   I'm sitting.

Arnold.   All right. . . .

Ma *(Warning)*.   And don't holler at me. People say things they don't mean when they holler and you've already said quite enough.

Arnold.   I won't holler. You just hit a raw nerve. We won't discuss Alan. Only David.

Ma.   So discuss.

Arnold.   Why don't you tell me what you already know, and we'll go on from there.

Ma *(Trying)*.   I don't know anything.

Arnold.   You spent the day with him. He must've said something.

Ma.   Let me think. He's an orphan . . .

Arnold.   He's not an orphan.

Ma.   He said he was an orphan.

Arnold.   Well, he's not. He was a battered child. They took him away from his parents. This is his third foster home. The first brought him back. The second he ran away from. So . . .

Ma.   So, he's a liar.

Arnold.   He's not a liar . . .

Ma.   This isn't going to work.

Arnold.   Come on, we're finally getting somewhere. . . .

Ma.   How do you expect me to sit here and discuss this insanity?

Arnold.   You're right, this isn't going to work.

Ma.   Arnold, Arnold, what do you know from raising a child?

Arnold.   What's to know? Whenever I have a problem I simply imagine how you would solve it, and do the opposite.

Ma *(Standing)*.   Is this what you invited me up here for? To insult me and spit on your father's grave?

Arnold.   For cryin' out . . . will you please sit down?

Ma *(Sitting)*.   Don't holler. I'm sitting. I don't know why, but I'm sitting.

Arnold.   All right. Now we're going to talk about David. Not Alan, not Daddy, just David. And we're going to stay calm.

Ma.   Ha!

Arnold.   I give up.

Ma.   Arnold, darling, open your eyes. Don't you see how ridiculous this is? I've been here less than a day, already I've seen you let him miss school, hang out on the street, go out without dinner . . .

Arnold.   This is hardly a typical day.

Ma.   You wanna talk or make excuses?

Arnold.   This isn't Little Lord Fauntleroy we're talking about here. If this kid decided I was coming down too hard on him, he'd pack and take off and I'd never get him back again. That sweet-looking little boy knows how to make more money in a night than you and I could make in a week.

Ma.   So you let him run wild?

Arnold.   No. But I don't beat him up either. I teach him. I advise him, I try to set an example for him . . .

Ma.   Some example. Arnold, look, you live the life you want. I put my fist in my mouth, I don't say a word. This is what you want. But think about the boy. He likes you. He told me he loves you. He sees you living like this . . . don't you think it's going to affect him?

Arnold.   Ma, David is gay.

Ma.   But he's only been here six months!

Arnold.   He came that way.

Ma.   No one comes that way.

Arnold.   What an opening.

Ma.   By you everything is a joke.

Arnold.   Don't you understand: The whole purpose of placing him here was for him to grow up with a positive attitude about his homosexuality.

Ma.   That's it. *(Stands)* I'm finished. The world has gone completely mad and I'm heading South for the summer.

Arnold.   You make it very difficult to have an intelligent conversation.

Ma.   You want an intelligent conversation? Do what I do: Talk to yourself. It's the only way.

Arnold.   You think this is easy for me? Look; my hands are shaking. I've been like this for days, knowing you'd be coming and we'd have to talk about this.

Ma.   Because you knew I'd show you how wrong you are.

Arnold.   I'm not wrong.

Ma.   No? Tell me something: How old was your friend Alan when you met him?

Arnold.   Seventeen.

Ma.   Seventeen. Seventeen and you were doing God knows what together. Now, tell me; how old is this "son" of yours?

Arnold.   I have no intention of sleeping with him if that's what you're driving at.

Ma.   I had no intention of having a homosexual for a son. So, look where intentions get you. Arnold, do what you want. You want to live like this? *Gay gezzintah hait.*[9] I don't care anymore. You're not going to make me sick like you did your father.

Arnold.   I made my father sick?

Ma.   No; he was thrilled to have a fairy for a son! You took a lifetime of dreams and threw them back in his face.

Arnold.   What lifetime of dreams? He knew I was gay for fourteen years.

Ma.   What? You think you walk into a room, say, "Hi, Dad, I'm queer," and that's that? You think that's what we brought you into the world for? Believe me, if I'd known I wouldn't have bothered. God should tear out my tongue, I should talk to my child this way. Arnold, you're my son, you're a good person, a sensitive person with a heart, *kennohorrah,*[10] like your father and I try to love you for that and forget this. But you won't let me. You've got

---

[9] Go in good health.

[10] Be safe from the evil eye—a Yiddish expression to deter demons when praising someone.

to throw me on the ground and rub my face in it. You haven't spoken a
sentence since I got here without the word "Gay" in it.

Arnold.   Because that's what I am.

Ma.   If that were all you could leave it in there *(Points to the bedroom)* where
it belongs; in private. No, you're obsessed by it. You're not happy unless
everyone is talking about it. I don't know why you don't just wear a big sign
and get it over with.

Arnold *(Bordering on hysteria)*.   I don't know what to say to you. I really don't.
I'm not trying to throw it in your face but it is what I am and it's not just a
matter of who I sleep with. *(Crosses to her)* Ma, try to imagine the world
the other way around. Imagine that every movie, book, magazine, TV show,
newspaper, commercial, billboard, told you that you should be homosexual.
But you know you're not and you know that for you this is right . . .

Ma.   Arnold, stop already. You're talking crazy.

Arnold.   You want to know what's crazy? That after all these years I'm still
here justifying my life. That's what's crazy.

Ma.   You call this a life? This is a sickness! But this is what you've chosen for
yourself.

Arnold *(Deep breath, one last try)*.   Ma, look: I'm gay. I don't know why. I
don't think anyone does. But that's what I am. For as far back as I can
remember. Back before I knew it was different or wrong . . .

Ma.   You have not heard a word I've said.

Arnold *(Losing control)*.   I know you'd rather I was straight but I am not!
Would you also rather I had lied to you? My friends all think I'm crazy for
telling you. They'd never dream of telling their parents. Instead they cut
their parents out of their lives. And the parents wonder, "Why are my
children so distant?" Is this what you'd rather?

Ma.   But it doesn't have to be our every conversation either.

Arnold.   You want a part in my life? I am not going to edit out the things you
don't like!

Ma *(Scared)*.   Can we end this conversation?

Arnold.   No. There's one more thing you've got to understand. You made fun
of my crocheting before. You think it's a cute little effeminate thing I do.
Let me tell you something; I have taught myself to sew, cook, fix plumbing,
do taxes, build furniture. . . . I can even pat myself on the back when
necessary. All so I don't have to ask anyone for anything. There is nothing
I need from anyone except love and respect. And anyone who can't give me
those two things has no place in my life. *(Breath)* You are my mother, and
I love you. I do. But if you can't respect me . . . then you've got no business
being here.

Ma.   You're throwing me out?

Arnold.   What I'm trying to . . .

Ma.   You're throwing me out! Isn't that nice? Listen, Mister, you get one
mother in this world. Only one. Wait. Just you wait.

(Ma exits to bedroom. Arnold is still as the next scene begins. The lights slowly crossfade.)

Scene Three

A bench in the park below. Immediately following. If possible the bench should be played on the couch. Through the use of gobos[11] and projections it is conceivable to create the nighttime park atmosphere on the apartment set. David and Ed enter talking, eating hot dogs.

David.   How's your hot dog, Big Spender?

Ed.   Been years since I bought one of these off the street. I just remembered why.

David.   Teach you to forget your wallet. *(David sits on bench.)*

Ed.   C'mon, lazy. I gotta walk this thing off.

David.   We're supposed to wait here. *(Pointing up)* Look. You can see our windows from here. Almost didn't take the apartment because of it.

Ed.   You lost me.

David.   Arnold never brung you here? This is where it happened.

Ed.   I didn't know.

David.   Yeah, here. They were walking back toward the street, Alan and the other guy, when the kids jumped out from behind these bushes. You can see; no way to run. Must've happened too quick anyway. Alan died right off, but the other guy crawled out to the street.

Ed.   I know.

David.   You can see a stain on the sidewalk in the daytime.

Ed.   Arnold showed you this?

David.   The day I moved in. At first I figured he was tryin' to scare me outta goin' into the park at night. I mean, I didn't know him from shit and here he takes me out, first day, and shows me some dried-up blood on the sidewalk. I figured him for a nut-case. Like maybe he had a case against the world or somethin'. I mean, havin' a bunch of piss-offs take out your lover for kicks. . . . I could understand him bein' crazy. So, I felt sorry for him, but just passed it off. Then about a week later we were watchin' the news on TV and there was this protest march; a bunch of Jews marchin' against Nazis. They had these signs that said "Never Again" and "We Remember." And I looked over at Arnold and he was like cryin' real soft, and just like that I connected. I knew why he showed me this.

Ed.   No candle in the window yet.

David.   Give 'em time, they got a lotta yellin' to catch up on.

---

[11] Black screens.

Ed. That's one thing I can do without hearing any more of today. I saw Laurel this afternoon.

David. Oh, yeah? What'd she want?

Ed *(Realizing to whom he's talking)*. Oh, nothing.

David. Sure.

Ed. Really.

David. You don't have to tell me.

Ed. It was nothing. Really.

David. Hey, it's cool. You don't have to tell me. It ain't like we're old friends or nothing. After all, what am I to you?

Ed. It was nothing. She just wanted to know if I was thinking of coming back.

David. And you told her no.

Ed. How do you know?

David. I know.

Ed. Frankly, I haven't made up my mind yet.

David. You won't go back.

Ed. Can we change the subject?

David. Sure. So, now that you and Laurel are washed up, you gonna start shoppin' around?

Ed. Well, since I haven't yet decided, then I haven't yet decided.

David. Don't think about it too long or you'll wind up like Arnold.

Ed. And that's bad?

David. Arnold goes out to work and shop. That's all and that ain't healthy.

Ed. You say that like you mean it.

David. Who knows more about sex and its effect on mental health than me? Got any idea how many couches I've been laid out on? *(Ed smirks.)* Psychiatrically speaking. Starting when they turned my folks in I've had Freudian Analysis, Primal Analysis, Gestalt Analysis, Handwriting Analysis, Scream Therapy, Dream Therapy, Aversion Therapy and est. When they finally ran outta cures to put me through, they stamped my file "Hopelessly Homo," shook my hand, wished me luck, and shipped me off to Arnold. So I picked up plenty of know-how on my journey down the "Leatherette Road."

Ed. Knowing and doing are two different things. You're only fifteen.

David. Guess you don't read *The New York Times*. Seems no matter how many petitions they sign, they just can't get God to raise the age of puberty to eighteen. Kids have sex. But that's another subject.

Ed. It certainly is.

David. Bottom line is, here's Arnold: Attractive, sensitive, intelligent, a great conversationalist, pretty good cook, and he's living like an old Italian widow.

Ed. So?

David. So it's time for a change. Don't you think?

Ed. Maybe.

David. Got any suggestions?

Ed. None I'd care to discuss with a fifteen-year-old.

David.   And you called him a bigot? Look, I ain't askin' for no miracles. (Though I must say I'd be proud to call you Daddy.) I'm simply suggestin' you could both use a little T.E.N.

Ed.   T.E.N.?

David.   Tension-Easing Nookie. Sex is very therapeutic.

Ed.   So you've said.

David.   What do you say?

(Arnold enters carrying two hot dogs like a wedding bouquet.)

Arnold *(à la Kate Hepburn).*   Hello, Mother. Hello, Father. The frankfurters are in bloom again. *(Examines them)* Such a strange flower. Suitable for any occasion. I wore one on my wedding day, and now I place them here in memory of something that has . . . I don't know when to stop, do I? I brought supplies.

Ed *(Holding his stomach).*   We had the same idea. They're poison.

David *(Grabbing two).*   And so unfilling.

Arnold.   Found your wallet on the table. Thought you might be hungry.

David.   Round two over?

Arnold.   Two, three, four, five . . .

David.   Who won?

Arnold.   When I left we both knew who won. Now only Robert Browning does. Ed, would you mind if I spoke to Champ alone?

Ed *(Embarrassed).*   Oh, sure.

David.   No, stay. I want witnesses.

Ed.   It's okay. Is it clear on the front?

Arnold.   Should be. Got your key?

Ed *(Checks).*   Yeah. I'll see you both later, then.

Arnold.   Thanks, Ed. *(He exits.)*

David.   That was lousy. He wanted to help.

Arnold.   I don't need his help, thank you. *(Pause)* Things got pretty "padded cell" up there.

David.   Yeah? *(Aloof)*

Arnold.   You had to sit here, didn't you? I'm sorry I didn't tell her about you before. But believe me, it's not 'cause I was ashamed.

David.   Glad to hear it.

Arnold.   My mother has a certain picture of what I should be doing with my life, and it's very hard for her to adjust to all the curves I throw in.

David.   Forge on.

Arnold.   All right. I knew that even if I told her about you, even before you came to live with me, that sooner or later we'd have this showdown. It has nothing to do with you. It's just her last go-for-broke campaign to straighten out my life.

David.   And?

Arnold.   I asked her to leave.

David.   You're good at that.

Arnold.   But you've got to understand that whatever happens between my mother and me has nothing to do with us.

David.   Come on, Arnold. This ain't Ed you're talking to. Whatever goes down with you two is exactly what will happen with us.

Arnold.   How do you figure that?

David.   'Cause you're just like her.

Arnold.   You wouldn't say that if you'd heard what went on up there.

David.   I know what goes on with mothers. Remember, you're my fourth. You think it's different 'cause we're both gay. But it's the same trip.

Arnold.   No offense, Angel-Puss, but you're mistaken.

David.   Think so? What would you do if I met a girl, came home, and told you I was straight?

Arnold.   If you were happy, I'd be happy.

David.   Bull-China! Here you are, workin' your butt off showin' me all the joys of gay life, givin' me the line of dignity and self-respect. . . . You tellin' me you wouldn't wonder where you went wrong?

Arnold.   Not if you were sure that that's what you wanted.

David.   Yeah, I see the way you treat Ed. The guy keeps tellin' you he's bi and all you keep doin' is callin' him a Closet Case.

Arnold.   See, you don't know what you're talking about. I'd be perfectly willing to believe he's bi if just once he thought about the person he was with before he considered what sex that person was.

David.   How could anybody do that? You ever meet someone and not know what sex they were?

Arnold.   That's not what I mean . . .

David.   I know what you mean and it's just as dumb. *(Arnold tries to speak.)* Shut up and let me finish. I stay with you because I want to. Dig? I really like living with you. I even like the way you try to mother me. But you can really be a shithead about things. But, you make me feel like I got a home. And a bunch of other assorted mushy stuff I don't want to get into here. But, Arnold, I'm tellin' you now: I'll walk if you try to use me as an excuse for sitting home alone, or to pick a fight with your mother or with Ed. Hey, you do what you gotta do. I ain't judgin'. Just don't blame anybody but yourself if you get my drift. *(Pause)* You get my drift? *(Arnold nods.)* I come down too heavy? *(Shakes his head)* Still want me to stay? *(Arnold nods.)* All right. Now we're dancin'.

Arnold.   I ever tell you, I think you're swell?

David *(Standing).*   Break this up. I got school tomorrow.

Arnold *(Standing).*   You go on ahead. I need an airing.

David.   Want company?

Arnold.   Go on. I'll be up.

David.   Okay. See you later.

Arnold.   David? You're not, are you?

David.   What?

Arnold *(Embarrassed).*   Straight?
David.   What would you do if I was?
Arnold.   Kill you.
David *(Laughs).*   Nice to know you care. *(Starts to leave)*
Arnold.   Watch how you cross the street.

(The lights fade down and out.)

Scene Four

Several hours later. The apartment. The lights are out, the couch unfolded, and Ed is asleep in it. Arnold enters in a robe from the bathroom, heading toward the kitchen, weaving, with an empty glass in his hand.

Ed *(Waking).*   Huh? What?
Arnold.   It's me. Go to sleep.
Ed.   Arnold? Oh. *(Trying to wake)* What time is it?
Arnold.   Almost six. Go to sleep.
Ed.   I waited up for you.
Arnold.   I see.
Ed.   You want to talk?
Arnold.   No. Go to sleep.
Ed.   I don't want to go to sleep.
Arnold.   So don't go to sleep.
Ed.   You just get home?
Arnold.   Awhile ago.
Ed.   I didn't hear you. Where'd you go? *(No response)* She said she's leaving.
Arnold.   I know. I tripped over her bags on my way in.
Ed.   She didn't want to stay the night, but she couldn't get a flight out until morning. When I came in she was walking out to spend the night in the airport. I got her calmed down a little. *(Pause)* She'd stay if you asked her.
Arnold.   Go to sleep.
Ed.   Stop telling me to go to sleep.
Arnold.   All right, go to hell! *(Sorry)* Want a drink?
Ed.   Sure, white wine. *(Arnold shoots a look.)* Juice. *(As Arnold makes the drinks)* You know, I saw Laurel today. That's where I went. I don't think she's overjoyed with the separation. She told me she's pregnant. She's not, but she said she was to see if I'd go back to her . . . if she was. God. The things that ran through my mind. Baby carriages, walks in the park, my folks playin' with it . . . Quite a sensation. I guess I would've gone back if she was. But then . . . I don't know.
Arnold.   I hope you didn't tell her that.

Ed. Of course I did. After five years of marriage, I'm not going to start lying to her now.

Arnold *(Numb)*. What'd she say?

Ed. She said she could be . . . if I came back. *(Pause)* She thinks we're sleeping together. Funny, huh? Laurel and your mother thinking the same thing. Maybe they know something we don't. *(Clears his throat)* I suppose it's her way of expressing anger. Laurel. Not your mother. Though I have seen happier women than her. Your mother, that is. *(Arnold is now sitting on the bed. He snickers.)* What's so funny?

Arnold. Seems like every time I turn around, here we are: Arnold and Ed in bed together.

Ed. Talking.

Arnold. Talking. Me with a lump in my throat and you with a foot in your mouth.

Ed. Why? What'd I say?

Arnold. Don't ask me. I stopped listening years ago.

Ed. I don't see what I said that's . . .

Arnold. It was nothing. Pay me no mind; I'm drunk.

Ed. Look, I know I'm not the most sensitive person in the world . . .

Arnold. Ed, take a note. Never fish for compliments in polluted waters.

Ed. Are you really drunk?

Arnold. I hold it well, don't I? A trick I learned in finishing school. It's done with mirrors. You think I'm here in bed next to you but actually I'm asleep under a table in a bar on Forty-third.

Ed *(Amused)*. This is the first time I've ever seen you drunk.

Arnold. Well, get a good look, Leon, 'cause I'm dryin' out in the morning.

Ed. Arnold Beckoff drunk.

Arnold. Blottoed, plastered, and plotzed . . . incorporated.

Ed. Why'd you get drunk?

Arnold *(Knocking on Ed's head)*. Hello? Anybody home? Sometimes you really frighten me.

Ed *(Offering his arms and shoulder)*. Care to talk about it?

Arnold. Sure. Why should the neighbors have all the fun? *(Lies back)* I had a genuinely superior motive for drinking this much. Don't tell anybody, but I'm a pushover when I'm drunk. And I thought that if I got good and looped I'd repent and ask my mother to stay. It worked too. Until I got a peek at her sitting in there on the bed with her "Holier-Than-Thou" attitude and her "Merry Martyr" smile. The way she acts you'd think she and God went to school together. She thinks I hate her. I know the way her mind works and she thinks I hate her.

Ed. I'm sure she knows you don't.

Arnold. Oh, no, she does. She thinks I hate her and everything she stands for. And I don't, for the life of me, know how to tell her that what I want more than anything is to have exactly the life she had. With a few minor alterations. My parents . . . They were something together. In all the years they were married the only time they were separated was for two days while my mother was in the hospital. And my father . . . He wouldn't even get into bed without her. He spent both nights on a chair in the living room. And the way they made my brother and me feel; like we were the smartest, handsomest, most talented, most important two people in the world. Didn't matter what we did, good or bad, it was the best. And she thinks she did something wrong.

Ed.   Are you really a pushover when you're drunk?

Arnold.   Earth to Ed. Earth to Ed. Come in, please. *(Ed giggles.)* You've got your own problems don'tcha? C'mon, spill your guts.

Ed.   David said you haven't gone out since Alan died.

Arnold.   We're talking about you now.

Ed.   I can understand you not wanting to at first, but still. You could at least go out for a few drinks, take a quick trip to the backroom. No harm in that.

Arnold.   You may not understand this, but I want more out of life than meeting a pretty face and sitting down on it. That answer your question?

Ed.   Graphically.

Arnold.   I do my best.

Ed.   If I made a pass at you now . . . Would you let me?

Arnold.   All right, who spiked the orange juice?

Ed.   Actually, it's David's idea. He thinks you're pushing chastity too far. He says it's unhealthy.

Arnold.   This is the first time I've been seduced in the guise of preventive medicine.

Ed.   I told him I'd consider it.

Arnold.   What a friend.

Ed.   I didn't mean it that way.

Arnold.   You never do.

Ed.   I mean, this is not exactly what I want.

Arnold.   I came to the same conclusion myself. I think it was the wedding that gave you away.

Ed.   I didn't want that either. I mean, I did, but it turned out not to be what I want. In fact, it made me less sure than ever about what it is I do want.

Arnold.   No problem. I've got a Sears catalog you can flip through. If you see it there give a primal scream and I'll get it for your birthday.

Ed.   You're not being fair.

Arnold.   I'm upset, uptight, and up to my nipples in Southern Comfort. I'm sorry.

Ed.   Never mind.

Arnold.   I said I'm sorry. You're trying to say something and I've got diarrhea of the mouth. Come on, I'll behave. I promise. *(No response)* Hey, this is Arnold here. You can tell me anything.

Ed.   I want another chance with you.

Arnold. Anything but that.

Ed. Wait. Just think about it for a minute. It makes a lot of sense. We know each other so well, there'd be no surprises. We know what to expect from each other. You said yourself we have no secrets.

Arnold. What'd that kid of mine say to you?

Ed. Just listen for a second. Laurel and I together . . . it wasn't enough. Obviously or I wouldn't be here. And that's the point: I am here. No matter what I do, I always end up back here, with you, in bed . . .

Arnold. Talking!

Ed. Talking. But here. Arnold, the time I've spent here with you and David . . . it's been the closest thing to whatever it is I want. I feel wonderful here. . . .

Arnold. "Don't care if the kid ain't mine, I wanna be the father of your baby." I saw that movie. I even read the book.

Ed. Are you finished?

Arnold. Ed, please.

Ed. Not five minutes ago it's what you said you wanted.

Arnold. I thought you weren't listening.

Ed. I know you're upset about your mother.

Arnold. That's not it . . .

Ed. Okay, so maybe it's too soon after Alan . . .

Arnold. Oh, Puh-lease!

Ed. I'm asking you to think about it. That's all. Just think.

Arnold. Don't you know that I have? How thick can you possibly be? Can't you see that since you called that's all I've thought about? Five days ago you walked through the door and from that moment I've been playing the dutiful wife and mother to your understanding if distant father. And David? He's been having the time of his life playing baby.

Ed. And it's been wonderful.

Arnold. It's been preposterous. It's a joke. Three grown men playing house!

Ed. You think this is playing house? You have no idea what playing house is. Arnold, I love Laurel. That may sound a little strange considering the circumstances, but my feelings for her are genuine and just as strong now as when we got married. It has, however, become apparent that what we have is a friendship, not a marriage.

Arnold. That's a hell of a lot more than most people have.

Ed. I'm almost forty, Arnold. Can you understand what that means? It means it's time for me to stop jerkin' around. I want more than a marriage which is at best purposeless, unfulfilling, but perfectly acceptable. Now, whatever you think of us, you could never describe us like that.

Arnold. Not the perfect part anyway.

Ed. Are you through making cracks?

Arnold. I just don't see what you think is here that you can't have with Laurel.

Ed. To tell you the truth I'm not sure either. But there's something that's kept me coming back. . . .

Arnold.   Are you forgetting why we broke up in the first place? You really think you could bring your friends here? You ready to introduce me to your parents as your lover and David as *our* son? Ed. Angel, I just threw my mother—my *mother*—out of my house and all she wanted was to not talk about it. You think I'll ask less from you?

Ed.   I think it's time to find out.

Arnold.   I don't know, Ed. Christ, I mean, I don't even know what this is supposed to be. I can't exactly buy a book or study some *Reader's Digest* article that's gonna tell me. All I know is whatever this is, it's not a Grade-B imitation of a heterosexual marriage. See, I thought that Alan and David and I could find out together . . . so now . . .

Ed.   Let me help you find out. You, me, and David.

Arnold.   I can't.

Ed.   Why? You scared I'll walk out again? Of course I can't guarantee anything . . .

Arnold.   That's not it.

Ed.   Then is it David? You afraid I'll hurt him?

Arnold.   I know how you feel about him, I know you wouldn't.

Ed.   Then what, Arnold?

Arnold *(Deep breath)*.   I am not Laurel.

Ed.   I'm counting on that.

Arnold.   Go home, Ed.

Ed.   Are you crying?

Arnold.   Leave me alone.

Ed.   I can't. Not with you like this. You need someone to talk to.

Arnold *(Striking out)*.   I don't need anyone. Thank you.

Ed.   Well, maybe I do.

Arnold.   Then go home. You've got a lovely wife who'd do anything for you. She can give you a home, a two-car garage, a child of your own, white picket fence . . . the whole shebang, double-dipped in chocolate and government-approved. Go home, Ed. I ain't got nothin' like that here.

Ed.   You really believe that? *(Arnold nods.)* Your mother did quite a job on you. *(Teasing)* Hello? Anybody home? You're gonna make me say it, aren't you? Undemonstrative soul that I am, you're gonna make me say it.

Arnold.   I don't want you to say anything.

Ed.   Oh no, I'll say it. I'm not ashamed, embarrassed maybe, but not ashamed. But I'll be damned if I say it to your back. *(Pulls Arnold over and pins him down.)*

Arnold.   Ed! For Chrissake!

Ed.   You ready? Now, you better listen good 'cause I don't know when I'll get the guts to say it again.

Arnold.   Ed, you're gonna wake my mother.

Ed.   So, let her hear. I hope they're both listening. Might as well let everyone know. Is everybody listening? Okay. Here goes. Arnold Beckoff . . . I love . . .

David (*Interrupting as he enters*).   What the hell's going on in here?

Ed.   Perfect timing.

David (*Throwing on the lights: We can now see his black-and-blue eye.*).   Oh, am I interrupting something? I hope, I hope, I hope.

Arnold (*Straightening up his appearance*).   You're not, you're not. What're you doing up at this hour?

David.   My alarm went off ten minutes ago. In case you lovebirds haven't noticed, it's morning.

Ed.   Jesus!

David.   Is this a closed marriage or can anybody join in?

Arnold (*As David climbs into bed between them*).   And baby makes three.

Ed.   My first pajama party.

David (*To Arnold*).   You look awful. Didn't you sleep?

Arnold.   Nary a wink, blink, or nod.

Ed.   . . . incorporated.

Arnold.   Thank you.

Ed.   Don't mention it.

Arnold.   Any news from the other camp?

David.   I heard shuffling. I think she's ready to leave.

Arnold.   I'd better splash my face and get ready for the grand exit.

Ed (*As Arnold struggles to rise*).   Need help?

Arnold.   I think my battery's dead. Gimme a boost. (*They shove from behind, Arnold flies to his feet. Then, à la Mae West*) Thanks, boys. (*Exits into bathroom*)

David (*Anxiously*).   Well?

Ed.   I struck out. He said no.

David.   You asked first? Don't you know anything? It don't mean nothin', anyway. Arnold always says no when you ask him a question. Then he thinks about it and . . . Watch. (*Calling out*) Hey, Arnold? You want breakfast?

Arnold (*Off*).   No, thanks.

David (*Counts to ten on his fingers*).   Now . . .

Arnold (*Off*).   David? Maybe I'll have an egg.

David.   Most contrary person I've ever met.

Ed (*Getting out of bed*).   We better get dressed. They should be alone for the final round.

David.   I am dressed.

Ed.   Show-off. Well, start the coffee while I catch up. (*Exits*)

David (*Heading to the kitchen*).   Do you like pancakes?

Ed (*Off*).   I love pancakes.

David.   Great. I'll make you some . . . when I learn to cook. (*He turns on the radio.*)

Radio.   Plaza 6-6654 with your requests. It's six fifty-four in the Big Apple on what looks to be a beautiful June day. And I'm here, with you, dedicated to the one you love. Now an oldie by request, from Beulah to Robert and

Michael. Guess she just can't make up her mind. Ha-ha. All right, Beulah, here it is with love. *(Music begins.)* Our number's Plaza 6-6654 and I'm waiting to play one for you. *(Music continues into the scene.)*

Arnold *(Entering).*   What're you listening to?

David.   One of those call-in shows, I think. Want me to change it?

Arnold.   No, leave it. I ever tell you about the time Alan phoned in a request to one of those shows? They read the dedication wrong. He announced, "From Ellen to Arnold." He musta thought it was a typo or somethin'.

you'd be talking to a woman with a size six Wedgie sticking out of her forehead. But I didn't raise my children like that. I wanted them to respect me because they wanted to. Not because I beat it in to them. Go know.

Arnold.   Ask her, not me. Has she shown her face yet?

David.   Nope.

Arnold.   Go on in and see if she needs any help.

David *(Dramatically).*   "Into the jaws of death, into the mouth of hell!" Any message?

Arnold.   No. *(David exits. Arnold folds the couch. Ma screams offstage.)* Not again.

Ma *(Enters with David).*   Arnold, did you see this eye? How could you let him walk around with a face like this? *(Drags him to the kitchen)* Come over here. I'm going to put some ice on it.

David.   Mrs. Beckoff, it's all right.

Ma.   All right? You look like an ad for "I'd rather fight than switch."

Arnold *(To David's rescue as Ed enters).*   Ma, leave him alone. Ice won't help. He's had it for two days.

Ma.   What're you talking? I saw him yesterday . . .

Arnold.   He covered it up with makeup so he'd look nice for you.

David.   I'm okay. Really. But thanks, anyway.

Ed.   C'mon, Champ. I'll buy you breakfast out.

David *(Surveying the scene).*   Great. But I gotta do somethin' first. *(Toward bedroom)* I'll be out in a minute.

Ed *(Putting on his jacket).*   I guess I'll see you later. *(To Ma)* It was a pleasure meeting you, Mrs. Beckoff.

Ma.   The pleasure was mine, Ed. I hope you and your wife come to your senses. Couples must learn to live with conflict. After all, a problem is never as permanent as a solution.

Ed.   Uh . . . thank you. *(Shouting)* David? Hurry up.

Arnold.   Aren't you going to wash up first?

Ed.   That's all right. I'm all right. *(Pause. Desperate.)* David!!!

David *(Off).*   I'm comin', already!

Arnold *(Taking Ed aside).*   Ed? What we were talking about before? Y'know, six years is a long time . . . I don't know. But we can talk.

Ed.   That's all I'm asking. *(Trying to control himself)* Good. Good.

David *(Enters with a big grin).*   Here I is.

Ma.   You take care of that eye.

David.   I will. It was nice meeting you. *(To Ed)* Remember your wallet this time? *(Ed checks.)* See you later, Arnold. *(Gives him a peck on the cheek)*

Arnold.   Have a nice day. And don't come home before school's over!

David *(To Ed)*.   You look like someone kicked you in the head. *(They exit. David sticks his head back in.)* And you two play like nice children. *(Out)*

Ed *(Off)*.   Yahoo!

Arnold *(Holding back a laugh)*.   He likes the wallpaper. Covers a multitude of sins.

Ma *(Bringing her bags to the door)*.   I'll be leaving myself, now.

Arnold.   You don't have to fly back to Florida. You could stay . . .

Ma.   With your brother? No. It's better if he doesn't know about this. I'll call him from Miami, tell him I changed my plans and couldn't make it up this week.

Arnold.   I'm going to tell him what happened.

Ma *(Angry)*.   Do what you want. I don't care.

Arnold.   Ma, it's important that he knows. He's part of this family too.

Ma.   What else do you want to do to me? What, Arnold, what? You want me to leave? I'm leaving. You want me to fight? I'm too tired. You want me to change? I'm too old and I can't. I can't, I can't, I can't. So you do what you have to do, and I'll do what I have to do and I hope you're satisfied. *(Arnold groans.)* If I had ever opened a mouth to my mother like you did to me, you'd be talking to a woman with a size six Wedgie sticking out of her forehead. But I didn't raise my children like that. I wanted them to respect me because they wanted to. Not because I beat it in to them. Go know.

Arnold.   Do we have to start this again?

Ma.   Yes. Because you can't put all the blame on me. It's not fair. Some of it was my fault, but not all. You think I didn't know about you, Arnold? Believe me, I knew. And not because you told me. I didn't need you to tell me. I knew but I said no. I hoped . . . What's the difference, I knew and I turned my back. But I wasn't the only one. There are other things you should have told me. You opened a mouth to me about your friend Alan. . . . How was I supposed to know?

Arnold.   Why? You would have understood?

Ma.   Maybe. Maybe not. You can't know for sure. But I flew up for the funeral and you never said a word.

Arnold.   So you could've done what? Tell me he's better off dead?

Ma.   Or maybe I could've comforted you. Told you what to expect. You and your "widowing." *(She turns to leave, stops, takes a breath. One last try.)* And about this Ed: You love him?

Arnold.   I don't know. I think so.

Ma.   Like you loved Alan?

Arnold.   No. They're very different. Alan loved all my faults: my temper, my bitchiness, my fat. . . . He looked for faults to love. And Ed? Ed loves the rest. And really, who needs to be loved for their virtues? Anyway, it's easier to love someone who's dead; they make so few mistakes.

Ma.   You've got an unusual way of looking at things, Arnold Beckoff.

Arnold.   Runs in the family. Ma, I miss him so much.

Ma.   Give yourself time, Arnold. It gets better. But, Arnold, it won't ever go away. You can work longer hours, adopt a son, fight with me . . . whatever, it'll still be there. But that's all right. It becomes part of you, like wearing a ring or a pair of glasses. You get used to it and it's good . . . because it makes sure you don't forget. You don't want to forget him, do you? (*Arnold shakes his head.*) So, it's good. (*Pause*) I guess that's what I would have said . . . (*The phone rings*) if I'd known. You'd better answer that. It may be something with that . . . son of yours.

(*Arnold goes to the phone. As soon as he's turned his back, Ma slips out the door with her bags. Arnold doesn't notice.*)

Arnold (*Answering*).   Hello. . . . Hi, Murray. . . . What? . . . The radio? It's on. . . . All right, hang on. (*He puts the phone down and goes to the radio, turning up the volume.*) It's Murray, something about the radio.

Radio (*Mid-sentence*).   . . . no, I've just checked with my producer, who took the call, and he's confirmed it. What a morning. Whatever is this world coming to? So, here it is, a dedication from David to Arnold with all his love . . .

(*Music begins to play. It is Big Maybelle singing "I Will Never Turn My Back on You."*)

Arnold.   How do you like that? That's some kid I got there, huh? (*Turning*) You hear that, Ma? (*Sees she's gone*) Ma? (*Goes to door*) Ma?

(*Runs to window and looks out as the music plays. He turns toward the audience and listens to the song calmly. As the music ends, the lights fade and the curtain falls.*)

QUESTIONS

1. Many people view homosexuality as an illness, while others do not. Is Arnold ill? Explain. How does Arnold's mother feel about his homosexuality?   **2.** What do you suppose led Arnold to apply to adopt a homosexual teenager?   **3.** What does Arnold want out of life? What does his mother want? What does David want?

WRITING TOPIC
Write an essay in which you describe what form the conflicts in this play might
take if all the characters were heterosexual. Would the conflicts be similar or
substantially different? Explain.

Love and Hate

QUESTIONS AND WRITING TOPICS

1. Almost every story in this section incorporates some sexual element. Distinguish among the functions served by the sexual aspects of the stories. **Writing Topic:** Contrast the function of sexuality in Moravia's "The Chase" and Faulkner's "A Rose for Emily."

2. Examine the works in this section in terms of the support they provide for the contention that love and hate are closely related emotions. **Writing Topic:** Discuss the relationship between love and hate in Gems's *Loving Women* and Shakespeare's *Othello*.

3. What images are characteristically associated with love in the prose and poetry of this section? What images are associated with hate? **Writing Topic:** Compare the image patterns in Shakespeare's sonnets 18 and 130 or the image patterns in Donne's "A Valediction: Forbidding Mourning" and Christopher Marlowe's "The Passionate Shepherd to His Love."

4. The Greeks have three words that can be translated by the English word *love: eros, agape,* and *philia.* Describe the differences among these three types of love. **Writing Topic:** Find a story or poem that you think is representative of each type of love. In analyzing each work, discuss the extent to which the primary notion of love being addressed or celebrated is tempered by the other two types.

5. Blake's "A Poison Tree," Dickinson's "Mine Enemy Is Growing Old," Dugan's "Love Song: I and Thou," and Plath's "Daddy" all seem to describe aspects of hate. How can one distinguish the different varieties of hatred being expressed? **Writing Topic:** Compare and contrast the source of the speaker's hatred in two of these poems.

6. Chopin's "The Storm" and Lessing's "To Room Nineteen" deal with infidelity. Distinguish between the attitudes toward infidelity developed by these stories. **Writing Topic:** Describe the effects of marital infidelity on the lives of the major characters in each story.

7. Gems's *Loving Women* and Lessing's "To Room Nineteen" deal with failed marriages. Why do they fail? **Writing Topic:** Compare and contrast the sources of the marital conflict in these works.

8. Moravia's "The Chase" and Shaw's "The Girls in Their Summer Dresses" deal with jealousy. Contrast both the sources of the jealousy and the resolution of the problems caused by jealousy in the stories. **Writing Topic:** Who in your opinion has the better reason for being jealous, the husband in "The Chase" or the wife in "The Girls in Their Summer Dresses"? Explain.

9. Which works in this section treat love or hate in a way that corresponds with your own experience or conception of those emotional states? Which contradict your experience? **Writing Topic:** Isolate, in each case, the elements in the work that provoke your response and discuss them in terms of their "truth" or "falsity."

The Presence of Death

Dream of a Sunday Afternoon in the Alameda, 1947–1948 by Diego Rivera.

The inevitability of death is not implied in the Biblical story of creation; it required an act of disobedience before an angry God passed sentence of hard labor and mortality on humankind: "In the sweat of your face you shall eat bread till you return to the ground, for out of it you were taken; you are dust and to dust you shall return." These words, written down some 2,800 years ago, preserve an ancient explanation for a condition of life that yet remains persistently enigmatic—the dissolution of the flesh and the personality as accident or age culminates in death, the "undiscovered country, from whose bourn / No traveller returns." Though we cannot know what death is like, from earliest times men and women have attempted to characterize death, to cultivate beliefs about it. The mystery of it and the certainty of it make death, in every age, an important theme for literary art.

Beliefs about the nature of death vary widely. The ancient Jews of the Pentateuch reveal no conception of immortality. Ancient Buddhist writings describe death as a mere translation from one painful life to another in an ongoing expiation that only the purest can avoid. The Christians came to conceive of a soul, separate from the body, which at the body's death is freed for a better (or worse) disembodied eternal life. More recently in the Western world, the history of the attitudes about death reflects the great intellectual revolutions that affected all thought—the Copernican revolution, which displaced the earth from the center of the solar system; the Darwinian revolution, which replaced humans, the greatest glory of God's creation, with upright primates with opposable thumbs whose days, like the dinosaur's, are likely to be numbered by the flux between the fire and ice of geological history; and the Freudian revolution, which robbed men and women of their proudest certainty, the conviction that they possessed a dependable and controlling rational mind. All these ideological changes serve to diminish us, to mock our self-importance, and, inevitably, to alter our conception of death.

But despite the impact of intellectual history, death remains invested with a special awe—perhaps because it infallibly mediates between all human differences. For the churchly, death, like birth and marriage, is the occasion for solemn ritual that reaffirms for the congregation its own communal life and the promise of a better life hereafter—though the belief in immortality does not eliminate sadness and regret. For those for whom there is no immortality, death is nonetheless a ceremonial affair, full of awe, for nothing human is so purely defined, so utterly important, as a life ended. Furthermore, both the religious and the secular see death in moral terms. For both, the killer is hateful. For both, there are some deaths that are deserved, some deaths that human weakness makes inevitable, some deaths that are outrageously unfair. For both, there are courageous deaths, which exalt the community, and cowardly deaths too embarrassing to recognize.

The speaker in Robert Frost's "Stopping by Woods on a Snowy Evening" gazes into the dark woods filling up with snow, momentarily drawn toward the peace it represents. But Frost's is a secular poem and the speaker turns back to life. In much religious poetry—John Donne's sonnet "Death, Be Not Proud" is an outstanding example—death is celebrated as a release from a burdensome existence into the eternal happiness of the afterlife. Another view that establishes death as the great leveler, bringing citizens and emperors to that selfsame dust, reassures the impoverished when they contrast their misery with the wealth of the mighty.

That leveling aspect of death, apparent in such poems as Nashe's "A Litany in Time of Plague" and Shakespeare's "Fear No More the Heat o' the Sun," leads easily and logically to the tradition wherein life itself is made absurd by the fact of death. You may remember that Macbeth finally declares that life is "a tale / Told by an idiot, full of sound and fury, / Signifying nothing." And the contemplation of suicide, which the pain and absurdity of life would seem to commend, provokes such diverse responses as Mishima's macabre story "Patriotism" and Edwin Arlington Robinson's ironic "Richard Cory." Some rage against death—Dylan Thomas in "Do Not Go Gentle into That Good Night"; others caution a quiet resignation—Frost in "After Apple-Picking" and Catherine Davis in her answer to Thomas, "After a Time." Much fine poetry on death is elegiac; it speaks the melancholy response of the living to the fact of death in such poems as Gray's "Elegy Written in a Country Churchyard," Housman's "To an Athlete Dying Young," Ransom's "Bells for John Whiteside's Daughter," and Roethke's "Elegy for Jane."

In short, literary treatments of death display immense diversity. In Tolstoy's *The Death of Iván Ilých*, dying leads to a redemptive awareness. In Malamud's tragicomic "Idiots First," the protagonist insists upon and wins fair treatment from death, and in Cummings's "nobody loses all the time" and in Woody Allen's "Death Knocks," the comic lightens the weight of death. The inevitability of death and the way one confronts it paradoxically lend to life its meaning and its value.

FOR THINKING AND WRITING

As you read the selections in this section, consider the following questions. You may want to write out your thoughts informally in a journal or notebook as a way of preparing to respond to the selections, or you may wish to make one of these questions the basis for a formal essay.

1. Have you had a close relative or friend who died? Was the person young or old, vigorous or feeble? How did you feel? How might the circumstances of death alter one's feelings toward death, or toward the person who died?

2. Do you believe that some essential part of you will survive the death of your body? On what do you base the belief? How does it alter your feelings about the death of people close to you? How does it alter your own behavior?

3. Are there any circumstances that justify suicide? Explain. If you feel that some suicides are justifiable, would it also be justifiable to help someone end his or her life? Explain.

4. Are there any circumstances that justify killing someone? Explain.

5. Imagine as best you can and describe the circumstances of your own death.

THE
PRESENCE
OF DEATH

The Dead Mother, by Edvard Munch.

FICTION

The Masque of the Red Death 1842

EDGAR ALLAN POE [1809–1849]

The "Red Death" had long devastated the country. No pestilence had ever been so fatal, or so hideous. Blood was its Avatar[1] and its seal—the redness and the horror of blood. There were sharp pains, and sudden dizziness, and then profuse bleeding at the pores, with dissolution. The scarlet stains upon the body and especially upon the face of the victim, were the pest ban which shut him out from the aid and from the sympathy of his fellow-men. And the whole seizure, progress and termination of the disease, were the incidents of half an hour.

But the Prince Prospero was happy and dauntless and sagacious. When his dominions were half depopulated, he summoned to his presence a thousand hale and light-hearted friends from among the knights and dames of his court, and with these retired to the deep seclusion of one of his castellated abbeys. This was an extensive and magnificent structure, the creation of the prince's own eccentric yet august taste. A strong and lofty wall girdled it in. This wall had gates of iron. The courtiers, having entered, brought furnaces and massy hammers and welded the bolts. They resolved to leave means neither of ingress or egress to the sudden impulses of despair or of frenzy from within. The abbey was amply provisioned. With such precautions the courtiers might bid defiance to contagion. The external world could take care of itself. In the meantime it was folly to grieve, or to think. The prince had provided all the appliances of pleasure. There were buffoons, there were improvisatori,[2] there were ballet-dancers, there were musicians, there was Beauty, there was wine. All these and security were within. Without was the "Red Death."

It was toward the close of the fifth or sixth month of his seclusion, and while the pestilence raged most furiously abroad, that the Prince Prospero entertained his thousand friends at a masked ball of the most unusual magnificence.

It was a voluptuous scene, that masquerade. But first let me tell of the rooms

---

[1] Manifestation.
[2] Musicians who improvise.

in which it was held. There were seven—an imperial suite. In many palaces, however, such suites form a long and straight vista, while the folding doors slide back nearly to the walls on either hand, so that the view of the whole extent is scarcely impeded. Here the case was very different; as might have been expected from the duke's love of the *bizarre*. The apartments were so irregularly disposed that the vision embraced but little more than one at a time. There was a sharp turn at every twenty or thirty yards, and at each turn a novel effect. To the right and left, in the middle of each wall, a tall and narrow Gothic window looked out upon a closed corridor which pursued the windings of the suite. These windows were of stained glass whose color varied in accordance with the prevailing hue of the decorations of the chamber into which it opened. That at the eastern extremity was hung, for example, in blue—and vividly blue were its windows. The second chamber was purple in its ornaments and tapestries, and here the panes were purple. The third was green throughout, and so were the casements. The fourth was furnished and lighted with orange—the fifth with white—the sixth with violet. The seventh apartment was closely shrouded in black velvet tapestries that hung all over the ceiling and down the walls, falling in heavy folds upon a carpet of the same material and hue. But in this chamber only, the color of the windows failed to correspond with the decorations. The panes here were scarlet—a deep blood color. Now in no one of the seven apartments was there any lamp or candelabrum, amid the profusion of golden ornaments that lay scattered to and fro or depended from the roof. There was no light of any kind emanating from lamp or candle within the suite of chambers. But in the corridors that followed the suite, there stood, opposite to each window, a heavy tripod, bearing a brazier of fire that projected its rays through the tinted glass and so glaringly illumined the room. And thus were produced a multitude of gaudy and fantastic appearances. But in the western or black chamber the effect of the fire-light that streamed upon the dark hangings through the blood-tinted panes, was ghastly in the extreme, and produced so wild a look upon the countenances of those who entered, that there were few of the company bold enough to set foot within its precincts at all.

It was in this apartment, also, that there stood against the western wall, a gigantic clock of ebony. Its pendulum swung to and fro with a dull, heavy, monotonous clang; and when the minute-hand made the circuit of the face, and the hour was to be stricken, there came from the brazen lungs of the clock a sound which was clear and loud and deep and exceedingly musical, but of so peculiar a note and emphasis that, at each lapse of an hour, the musicians of the orchestra were constrained to pause, momentarily, in their performance, to hearken to the sound; and thus the waltzers perforce ceased their evolutions; and there was a brief disconcert of the whole gay company; and, while the chimes of the clock yet rang, it was observed that the giddiest grew pale, and the more aged and sedate passed their hands over their brows as if in confused reverie or meditation. But when the echoes had fully ceased, a light laughter at once pervaded the assembly; the musicians looked at each other and smiled as if at their own nervousness and folly, and made whispering vows, each to the other, that the next chiming of the clock should produce in them no similar emotion; and then, after the lapse of sixty minutes, (which embrace three thousand and six hundred seconds of the Time that flies,) there came yet another chiming of the clock, and then were the same disconcert and tremulousness and meditation as before.

But, in spite of these things, it was a gay and magnificent revel. The tastes of the duke were peculiar. He had a fine eye for colors and effects. He disregarded the *decora*[3] of mere fashion. His plans were bold and fiery, and his conceptions glowed with barbaric lustre. There are some who would have thought him mad. His followers felt that he was not. It was necessary to hear and see and touch him to be *sure* that he was not.

He had directed, in great part, the moveable embellishments of the seven chambers, upon occasion of this great *fête*; and it was his own guiding taste which had given character to the masqueraders. Be sure they were grotesque. There were much glare and glitter and piquancy and phantasm—much of what has been since seen in "Hernani."[4] There were arabesque figures with unsuited limbs and appointments. There were delirious fancies such as the madman fashions. There was much of the beautiful, much of the wanton, much of the *bizarre*, something of the terrible, and not a little of that which might have excited disgust. To and fro in the seven chambers there stalked, in fact, a multitude of dreams. And these—the dreams—writhed in and about, taking hue from the rooms, and causing the wild music of the orchestra to seem as the echo of their steps. And, anon, there strikes the ebony clock which stands in the hall of the velvet. And then, for a moment, all is still, and all is silent save the voice of the clock. The dreams are stiff-frozen as they stand. But the echoes of the chime die away—they have endured but an instant—and a light, half-subdued laughter floats after them as they depart. And now again the music swells, and the dreams live, and writhe to and fro more merrily than ever, taking hue from the many-tinted windows through which stream the rays from the tripods. But to the chamber which lies most westwardly of the seven, there are now none of the maskers who venture; for the night is waning away; and there flows a ruddier light through the blood-colored panes; and the blackness of the sable drapery appals; and to him whose foot falls upon the sable carpet, there comes from the near clock of ebony a muffled peal more solemnly emphatic than any which reaches *their* ears who indulge in the more remote gaieties of the other apartments.

But these other apartments were densely crowded, and in them beat feverishly the heart of life. And the revel went whirlingly on, until at length there commenced the sounding of midnight upon the clock. And then the music ceased, as I have told; and the evolutions of the waltzers were quieted; and there was an uneasy cessation of all things as before. But now there were twelve

---

[3] Dictates.
[4] A play by Victor Hugo (1802–1885).

strokes to be sounded by the bell of the clock; and thus it happened, perhaps, that more of thought crept, with more of time, into the meditations of the thoughtful among those who revelled. And thus, too, it happened, perhaps, that before the last echoes of the last chime had utterly sunk into silence, there were many individuals in the crowd who had found leisure to become aware of the presence of a masked figure which had arrested the attention of no single individual before. And the rumor of this new presence having spread itself whisperingly around, there arose at length from the whole company a buzz, or murmur, expressive of disapprobation and surprise—then, finally, of terror, of horror, and of disgust.

In an assembly of phantasms such as I have painted, it may well be supposed that no ordinary appearance could have excited such sensation. In truth the masquerade license of the night was nearly unlimited; but the figure in question had out-Heroded Herod,[5] and gone beyond the bounds of even the prince's indefinite decorum. There are chords in the hearts of the most reckless which cannot be touched without emotion. Even with the utterly lost, to whom life and death are equally jests, there are matters of which no jest can be made. The whole company, indeed, seemed now deeply to feel that in the costume and bearing of the stranger neither wit nor propriety existed. The figure was tall and gaunt, and shrouded from head to foot in the habiliments of the grave. The mask which concealed the visage was made so nearly to resemble the countenance of a stiffened corpse that the closest scrutiny must have had difficulty in detecting the cheat. And yet all this might have been endured, if not approved, by the mad revellers around. But the mummer had gone so far as to assume the type of the Red Death. His vesture was dabbled in *blood*— and his broad brow, with all the features of the face, was besprinkled with the scarlet horror.

When the eyes of Prince Prospero fell upon this spectral image (which with a slow and solemn movement, as if more fully to sustain its *rôle*, stalked to and fro among the waltzers) he was seen to be convulsed, in the first moments with a strong shudder either of terror or distaste; but, in the next, his brow reddened with rage.

"Who dares?" he demanded hoarsely of the courtiers who stood near him— "who dares insult us with this blasphemous mockery? Seize him and unmask him—that we may know whom we have to hang at sunrise, from the battlements!"

It was in the eastern or blue chamber in which stood the Prince Prospero as he uttered these words. They rang throughout the seven rooms loudly and clearly—for the prince was a bold and robust man, and the music had become hushed at the waving of his hand.

It was in the blue room where stood the prince, with a group of pale courtiers

---

[5] I.e., ranted and raved (see Matthew 2).

by his side. At first, as he spoke, there was a slight rushing movement of this group in the direction of the intruder, who at the moment was also near at hand, and now, with deliberate and stately step, made closer approach to the speaker. But from a certain nameless awe with which the mad assumptions of the mummer had inspired the whole party, there were found none who put forth hand to seize him; so that, unimpeded, he passed within a yard of the prince's person; and, while the vast assembly, as if with one impulse, shrank from the centres of the rooms to the walls, he made his way uninterruptedly, but with the same solemn and measured step which had distinguished him from the first, through the blue chamber to the purple—through the purple to the green—through the green to the orange—through this again to the white—and even thence to the violet, ere a decided movement had been made to arrest him. It was then, however, that the Prince Prospero, maddening with rage and the shame of his own momentary cowardice, rushed hurriedly through the six chambers, while none followed him on account of a deadly terror that had seized upon all. He bore aloft a drawn dagger, and had approached, in rapid impetuosity, to within three or four feet of the retreating figure, when the latter, having attained the extremity of the velvet apartment, turned suddenly and confronted his pursuer. There was a sharp cry—and the dagger dropped gleaming upon the sable carpet, upon which, instantly afterwards, fell prostrate in death the Prince Prospero. Then, summoning the wild courage of despair, a throng of the revellers at once threw themselves into the black apartment, and, seizing the mummer, whose tall figure stood erect and motionless within the shadow of the ebony clock, gasped in unutterable horror at finding the grave-cerements and corpse-like mask which they handled with so violent a rudeness, untenanted by any tangible form.

And now was acknowledged the presence of the Red Death. He had come like a thief in the night. And one by one dropped the revellers in the blood-bedewed halls of their revel, and died each in the despairing posture of his fall. And the life of the ebony clock went out with that of the last of the gay. And the flames of the tripods expired. And Darkness and Decay and the Red Death held illimitable dominion over all.

QUESTIONS

1. Poe is celebrated for his ability to create stories that rely not on rounded and well-developed characters in a recognizable environment but haunted, mad, intense characters whose destinies unfold in a forbidding, ominous, isolated world. Did Poe succeed in drawing you into his world or were you put off by its lack of realism and developed character, as well as the thinness of plot? Explain. **2.** In a few sentences, state the theme of Poe's story. **3.** We are told that Prince Prospero gathers a thousand "friends from among the knights and dames of his court" to save them from the plague. Would you agree or disagree with the argument that the story dramatizes the futility of the rich and privileged attempting to cut themselves off from ordinary citizens? Explain.

WRITING TOPICS
1. Is this merely a horror story, meant to titillate the reader with foreboding and terror (like many horror movies), or does it advance a serious, moral statement? **2.** Based upon an analysis of diction, sentence structure, and imagery, characterize Poe's style in this story.

The Death of Iván Ilých*   1886

LEO TOLSTOY   [1828–1910]

CHAPTER I

During an interval in the Melvínski trial in the large building of the Law Courts the members and public prosecutor met in Iván Egórovich Shébek's private room, where the conversation turned on the celebrated Krasóvski case. Fëdor Vasílievich warmly maintained that it was not subject to their jurisdiction, Iván Egórovich maintained the contrary, while Peter Ivánovich, not having entered into the discussion at the start, took no part in it but looked through the *Gazette* which had just been handed in.

"Gentlemen," he said, "Iván Ilých has died!"

"You don't say so!"

"Here, read it yourself," replied Peter Ivánovich, handing Fëdor Vasílievich the paper still damp from the press. Surrounded by a black border were the words: "Praskóvya Fëdorovna Goloviná, with profound sorrow, informs relatives and friends of the demise of her beloved husband Iván Ilých Golovín, Member of the Court of Justice, which occurred on February the 4th of this year 1882. The funeral will take place on Friday at one o'clock in the afternoon."

Iván Ilých had been a colleague of the gentlemen present and was liked by them all. He had been ill for some weeks with an illness said to be incurable. His post had been kept open for him, but there had been conjectures that in case of his death Alexéev might receive his appointment, and that either Vínnikov or Shtábel would succeed Alexéev. So on receiving the news of Iván Ilých's death the first thought of each of the gentlemen in that private room was of the changes and promotions it might occasion among themselves or their acquaintances.

"I shall be sure to get Shtábel's place or Vínnikov's," thought Fëdor Vasílievich. "I was promised that long ago, and the promotion means an extra eight hundred rubles a year for me besides the allowance."

"Now I must apply for my brother-in-law's transfer from Kalúga," thought Peter Ivánovich. "My wife will be very glad, and then she won't be able to say that I never do anything for her relations."

"I thought he would never leave his bed again," said Peter Ivánovich aloud. "It's very sad."

"But what really was the matter with him?"

---

* Translated by Aylmer Maude.

"The doctors couldn't say—at least they could, but each of them said something different. When last I saw him I thought he was getting better."

"And I haven't been to see him since the holidays. I always meant to go."

"Had he any property?"

"I think his wife had a little—but something quite trifling."

"We shall have to go to see her, but they live so terribly far away."

"Far away from you, you mean. Everything's far away from your place."

"You see, he never can forgive my living on the other side of the river," said Peter Ivánovich, smiling at Shébek. Then, still talking of the distances between different parts of the city, they returned to the Court.

Besides considerations as to the possible transfers and promotions likely to result from Iván Ilých's death, the mere fact of the death of a near acquaintance aroused, as usual, in all who heard of it the complacent feeling that, "it is he who is dead and not I."

Each one thought or felt, "Well, he's dead but I'm alive!" But the more intimate of Iván Ilých's acquaintances, his so-called friends, could not help thinking also that they would now have to fulfill the very tiresome demands of propriety by attending the funeral service and paying a visit of condolence to the widow.

Fëdor Vasílievich and Peter Ivánovich had been his nearest acquaintances. Peter Ivánovich had studied law with Iván Ilých and had considered himself to be under obligations to him.

Having told his wife at dinner-time of Iván Ilých's death, and of his conjecture that it might be possible to get her brother transferred to their circuit, Peter Ivánovich sacrificed his usual nap, put on his evening clothes, and drove to Iván Ilých's house.

At the entrance stood a carriage and two cabs. Leaning against the wall in the hall downstairs near the cloak-stand was a coffin-lid covered with cloth of gold, ornamented with gold cord and tassels, that had been polished up with metal powder. Two ladies in black were taking off their fur cloaks. Peter Ivánovich recognized one of them as Iván Ilých's sister, but the other was a stranger to him. His colleague Schwartz was just coming downstairs, but on seeing Peter Ivánovich enter he stopped and winked at him, as if to say: "Iván Ilých has made a mess of things—not like you and me."

Schwartz's face with his Piccadilly whiskers, and his slim figure in evening dress, had as usual an air of elegant solemnity which contrasted with the playfulness of his character and had a special piquancy here, or so it seemed to Peter Ivánovich.

Peter Ivánovich allowed the ladies to precede him and slowly followed them upstairs. Schwartz did not come down but remained where he was, and Peter Ivánovich understood that he wanted to arrange where they should play bridge that evening. The ladies went upstairs to the widow's room, and Schwartz with seriously compressed lips but a playful look in his eyes, indicated by a twist of his eyebrows the room to the right where the body lay.

Peter Ivánovich, like everyone else on such occasions, entered feeling uncertain what he would have to do. All he knew was that at such times it is always safe to cross oneself. But he was not quite sure whether one should make obeisances while doing so. He therefore adopted a middle course. On entering the room he began crossing himself and made a slight movement resembling a bow. At the same time, as far as the motion of his head and arm allowed, he surveyed the room. Two young men—apparently nephews, one of whom was a high-school pupil—were leaving the room, crossing themselves as they did so. An old woman was standing motionless, and a lady with strangely arched eyebrows was saying something to her in a whisper. A vigorous, resolute Church Reader, in a frock-coat, was reading something in a loud voice with an expression that precluded any contradiction. The butler's assistant, Gerásim, stepping lightly in front of Peter Ivánovich, was strewing something on the floor. Noticing this, Peter Ivánovich was immediately aware of a faint odour of a decomposing body.

The last time he had called on Iván Ilých, Peter Ivánovich had seen Gerásim in the study. Iván Ilých had been particularly fond of him and he was performing the duty of a sick nurse.

Peter Ivánovich continued to make the sign of the cross slightly inclining his head in an intermediate direction between the coffin, the Reader, and the icons on the table in a corner of the room. Afterwards, when it seemed to him that this movement of his arm in crossing himself had gone on too long, he stopped and began to look at the corpse.

The dead man lay, as dead men always lie, in a specially heavy way, his rigid limbs sunk in the soft cushions of the coffin, with the head forever bowed on the pillow. His yellow waxen brow with bald patches over his sunken temples was thrust up in the way peculiar to the dead, the protruding nose seeming to press on the upper lip. He was much changed and had grown even thinner since Peter Ivánovich had last seen him, but, as is always the case with the dead, his face was handsomer and above all more dignified than when he was alive. The expression on the face said that what was necessary had been accomplished, and accomplished rightly. Besides this there was in that expression a reproach and a warning to the living. This warning seemed to Peter Ivánovich out of place, or at least not applicable to him. He felt a certain discomfort and so he hurriedly crossed himself once more and turned and went out of the door—too hurriedly and too regardless of propriety, as he himself was aware.

Schwartz was waiting for him in the adjoining room with legs spread wide apart and both hands toying with his top-hat behind his back. The mere sight of that playful, well-groomed, and elegant figure refreshed Peter Ivánovich. He felt that Schwartz was above all these happenings and would not surrender to any depressing influences. His very look said that this incident of a church service for Iván Ilých could not be a sufficient reason for infringing the order of the session—in other words, that it would certainly not prevent his unwrapping a new pack of cards and shuffling them that evening while a footman placed four fresh candles on the table: in fact, there was no reason for supposing that this incident would hinder their spending the evening agreeably.

Indeed he said this in a whisper as Peter Ivánovich passed him, proposing that they should meet for a game at Fëdor Vasílievich's. But apparently Peter Ivánovich was not destined to play bridge that evening. Praskóvya Fëdorovna (a short, fat woman who despite all efforts to the contrary had continued to broaden steadily from her shoulders downwards and who had the same extraordinarily arched eyebrows as the lady who had been standing by the coffin), dressed all in black, her head covered with lace, came out of her own room with some other ladies, conducted them to the room where the dead body lay, and said: "The service will begin immediately. Please go in."

Schwartz, making an indefinite bow, stood still, evidently neither accepting nor declining this invitation. Praskóvya Fëdorovna recognizing Peter Ivánovich, sighed, went close up to him, took his hand, and said: "I know you were a true friend to Iván Ilých . . ." and looked at him awaiting some suitable response. And Peter Ivánovich knew that, just as it had been the right thing to cross himself in that room, so what he had to do here was to press her hand, sigh, and say, "Believe me . . ." So he did all this and as he did it he felt that the desired result had been achieved: that both he and she were touched.

"Come with me. I want to speak to you before it begins," said the widow. "Give me your arm."

Peter Ivánovich gave her his arm and they went to the inner rooms, passing Schwartz who winked at Peter Ivánovich compassionately.

"That does for our bridge! Don't object if we find another player. Perhaps you can cut in when you do escape," said his playful look.

Peter Ivánovich sighed still more deeply and despondently, and Praskóvya Fëdorovna pressed his arm gratefully. When they reached the drawing-room, upholstered in pink cretonne and lighted by a dim lamp, they sat down at the table—she on a sofa and Peter Ivánovich on a low pouffe, the springs of which yielded spasmodically under his weight. Praskóvya Fëdorovna had been on the point of warning him to take another seat, but felt that such a warning was out of keeping with her present condition and so changed her mind. As he sat down on the pouffe Peter Ivánovich recalled how Iván Ilých had arranged this room and had consulted him regarding this pink cretonne with green leaves. The whole room was full of furniture and knick-knacks, and on her way to the sofa the lace of the widow's black shawl caught on the carved edge of the table. Peter Ivánovich rose to detach it, and the springs of the pouffe, relieved of his weight, rose also and gave him a push. The widow began detaching her shawl herself, and Peter Ivánovich again sat down, suppressing the rebellious springs of the pouffe under him. But the widow had not quite freed herself and Peter Ivánovich got up again, and again the pouffe rebelled and even creaked. When this was all over she took out a clean cambric handkerchief and began to weep. The episode with the shawl and the struggle with the pouffe had cooled Peter Ivánovich's emotions and he sat there with a sullen look on his face. This awkward situation was interrupted by Sokolóv, Iván Ilých's butler, who came to report that the plot in the cemetery that Praskóvya Fëdorovna had chosen would cost two hundred rubles. She stopped weeping and, looking at Peter Ivánovich with the air of a victim, remarked in French that it was very hard for her. Peter Ivánovich made a silent gesture signifying his full conviction that it must indeed be so.

"Please smoke," she said in a magnanimous yet crushed voice, and turned to discuss with Sokolóv the price of the plot for the grave.

Peter Ivánovich while lighting his cigarette heard her inquiring very circumstantially into the price of different plots in the cemetery and finally decide which she would take. When that was done she gave instructions about engaging the choir. Sokolóv then left the room.

"I look after everything myself," she told Peter Ivánovich, shifting the albums that lay on the table; and noticing that the table was endangered by his cigarette-ash, she immediately passed him an ashtray, saying as she did so: "I consider it an affectation to say that my grief prevents my attending to practical affairs. On the contrary, if anything can—I won't say console me, but—distract me, it is seeing to everything concerning him." She again took out her handkerchief as if preparing to cry, but suddenly, as if mastering her feeling, she shook herself and began to speak calmly. "But there is something I want to talk to you about."

Peter Ivánovich bowed, keeping control of the springs of the pouffe, which immediately began quivering under him.

"He suffered terribly the last few days."

"Did he?" said Peter Ivánovich.

"Oh, terribly! He screamed unceasingly, not for minutes but for hours. For the last three days he screamed incessantly. It was unendurable. I cannot understand how I bore it; you could hear him three rooms off. Oh, what I have suffered!"

"Is it possible that he was conscious all that time?" asked Peter Ivánovich.

"Yes," she whispered. "To the last moment. He took leave of us a quarter of an hour before he died, and asked us to take Volódya away."

The thought of the sufferings of this man he had known so intimately, first as a merry little boy, then as a school-mate, and later as a grown-up colleague, suddenly struck Peter Ivánovich with horror, despite an unpleasant consciousness of his own and this woman's dissimulation. He again saw that brow, and that nose pressing down on the lip, and felt afraid for himself.

"Three days of frightful suffering and then death! Why, that might suddenly, at any time, happen to me," he thought, and for a moment felt terrified. But—he did not himself know how—the customary reflection at once occurred to him that this had happened to Iván Ilých and not to him, and that it should not and could not happen to him, and that to think that it could would be yielding to depression which he ought not to do, as Schwartz's expression plainly showed. After which reflection Peter Ivánovich felt reassured, and began to ask with interest about the details of Iván Ilých's death, as though death was an accident natural to Iván Ilých but certainly not to himself.

After many details of the really dreadful physical sufferings Iván Ilých had

endured (which details he learnt only from the effect those sufferings had produced on Praskóvya Fëdorovna's nerves) the widow apparently found it necessary
to get to business.

"Oh, Peter Ivánovich, how hard it is! How terribly, terribly hard!" and she
again began to weep.

Peter Ivánovich sighed and waited for her to finish blowing her nose. When
she had done so he said, "Believe me . . ." and she again began talking and
brought out what was evidently her chief concern with him—namely, to question him as to how she could obtain a grant of money from the government on
the occasion of her husband's death. She made it appear that she was asking
Peter Ivánovich's advice about her pension, but he soon saw that she already
knew about that to the minutest detail, more even than he did himself. She
knew how much could be got out of the government in consequence of her
husband's death, but wanted to find out whether she could not possibly extract
something more. Peter Ivánovich tried to think of some means of doing so, but
after reflecting for a while and, out of propriety, condemning the government
for its niggardliness, he said he thought that nothing more could be got. Then
she sighed and evidently began to devise means of getting rid of her visitor.
Noticing this, he put out his cigarette, rose, pressed her hand, and went out
into the anteroom.

In the dining-room where the clock stood that Iván Ilých had liked so much
and had bought at an antique shop, Peter Ivánovich met a priest and a few
acquaintances who had come to attend the service, and he recognized Iván
Ilých's daughter, a handsome young woman. She was in black and her slim
figure appeared slimmer than ever. She had a gloomy, determined, almost angry
expression, and bowed to Peter Ivánovich as though he were in some way to
blame. Behind her, with the same offended look, stood a wealthy young man,
an examining magistrate, whom Peter Ivánovich also knew and who was her
fiancé, as he had heard. He bowed mournfullly to them and was about to pass
into the death-chamber, when from under the stairs appeared the figure of Iván
Ilých's schoolboy son, who was extremely like his father. He seemed a little
Iván Ilých, such as Peter Ivánovich remembered when they studied law together.
His tear-stained eyes had in them the look that is seen in the eyes of boys of
thirteen or fourteen who are not pure-minded. When he saw Peter Ivánovich
he scowled morosely and shamefacedly. Peter Ivánovich nodded to him and
entered the death-chamber. The service began: candles, groans, incense, tears,
and sobs. Peter Ivánovich stood looking gloomily down at his feet. He did not
look once at the dead man, did not yield to any depressing influence, and was
one of the first to leave the room. There was no one in the anteroom, but
Gerásim darted out of the dead man's room, rummaged with his strong hands
among the fur coats to find Peter Ivánovich's and helped him on with it.

"Well, friend Gerásim," said Peter Ivánovich, so as to say something. "It's a
sad affair, isn't it?"

"It's God's will. We shall all come to it some day," said Gerásim, displaying
his teeth—the even, white teeth of a healthy peasant—and, like a man in the

thick of urgent work, he briskly opened the front door, called the coachman, helped Peter Ivánovich into the sledge, and sprang back to the porch as if in readiness for what he had to do next.

Peter Ivánovich found the fresh air particularly pleasant after the smell of incense, the dead body, and carbolic acid.

"Where to, sir?" asked the coachman.

"It's not too late even now. . . . I'll call round on Fëdor Vasílievich."

He accordingly drove there and found them just finishing the first rubber, so that it was quite convenient for him to cut in.

CHAPTER II

Iván Ilých's life had been most simple and most ordinary and therefore most terrible.

He had been a member of the Court of Justice, and died at the age of forty-five. His father had been an official who after serving in various ministries and departments in Petersburg had made the sort of career which brings men to positions from which by reason of their long service they cannot be dismissed, though they are obviously unfit to hold any responsible position, and for whom therefore posts are specially created, which though fictitious carry salaries of from six to ten thousand rubles that are not fictitious, and in receipt of which they live on to a great age.

Such was the Privy Councillor and superfluous member of various superfluous institutions, Ilyá Epímovich Golovín.

He had three sons, of whom Iván Ilých was the second. The eldest son was following in his father's footsteps only in another department, and was already approaching that stage in the service at which a similar sinecure would be reached. The third son was a failure. He had ruined his prospects in a number of positions and was now serving in the railway department. His father and brothers, and still more their wives, not merely disliked meeting him, but avoided remembering his existence unless compelled to do so. His sister had married Baron Greff, a Petersburg official of her father's type. Iván Ilých was *le phénix de la famille*[1] as people said. He was neither as cold and formal as his elder brother nor as wild as the younger, but was a happy mean between them— an intelligent, polished, lively and agreeable man. He had studied with his younger brother at the School of Law, but the latter had failed to complete the course and was expelled when he was in the fifth class. Iván Ilých finished the course well. Even when he was at the School of Law he was just what he remained for the rest of his life: a capable, cheerful, good-natured, and sociable man, though strict in the fulfilment of what he considered to be his duty: and he considered his duty to be what was so considered by those in authority. Neither as a boy nor as a man was he a toady, but from early youth was by

---

[1] The phoenix of the family, here meaning "rare bird" or "prodigy."

nature attracted to people of high station as a fly is drawn to the light, assimilating their ways and views of life and establishing friendly relations with them. All the enthusiasms of childhood and youth passed without leaving much trace on him; he succumbed to sensuality, to vanity, and latterly among the highest classes to liberalism, but always within limits which his instinct unfailingly indicated to him as correct.

At school he had done things which had formerly seemed to him very horrid and made him feel disgusted with himself when he did them; but when later on he saw that such actions were done by people of good position and that they did not regard them as wrong, he was able not exactly to regard them as right, but to forget about them entirely or not be at all troubled at remembering them.

Having graduated from the School of Law and qualified for the tenth rank of the civil service, and having received money from his father for his equipment, Iván Ilých ordered himself clothes at Scharmer's, the fashionable tailor, hung a medallion inscribed *respice finem*[2] on his watch-chain, took leave of his professor and the prince who was patron of the school, had a farewell dinner with his comrades at Donon's first-class restaurant, and with his new and fashionable portmanteau, linen, clothes, shaving and other toilet appliances, and a travelling rug, all purchased at the best shops, he set off for one of the provinces where, through his father's influence, he had been attached to the Governor as an official for special service.

In the province Iván Ilých soon arranged as easy and agreeable a position for himself as he had had at the School of Law. He performed his official tasks, made his career, and at the same time amused himself pleasantly and decorously. Occasionally he paid official visits to country districts, where he behaved with dignity both to his superiors and inferiors, and performed the duties entrusted to him, which related chiefly to the sectarians,[3] with an exactness and incorruptible honesty of which he could not but feel proud.

In official matters, despite his youth and taste for frivolous gaiety, he was exceedingly reserved, punctilious, and even severe; but in society he was often amusing and witty, and always good-natured, correct in his manner, and *bon enfant*, as the governor and his wife—with whom he was like one of the family—used to say of him.

In the provinces he had an affair with a lady who made advances to the elegant young lawyer, and there was also a milliner; and there were carousals with aides-de-camp who visited the district, and after-supper visits to a certain outlying street of doubtful reputation; and there was too some obsequiousness to his chief and even to his chief's wife, but all this was done with such a tone of good breeding that no hard names could be applied to it. It all came under the heading of the French saying: "Il faut que jeunesse se passe."[4] It was all

---

[2] Regard the end.
[3] A large sect, whose members were placed under many legal restrictions, which broke away from the Orthodox Church in the seventeenth century.
[4] Youth must have its fling.

done with clean hands, in clean linen, with French phrases, and above all among people of the best society and consequently with the approval of people of rank.

So Iván Ilých served for five years and then came a change in his official life. The new and reformed judicial institutions were introduced, and new men were needed. Iván Ilých became such a new man. He was offered the post of Examining Magistrate, and he accepted it though the post was in another province and obliged him to give up the connections he had formed and to make new ones. His friends met to give him a send-off; they had a group-photograph taken and presented him with a silver cigarette-case, and he set off to his new post.

As examining magistrate Iván Ilých was just as *comme il faut*[5] and decorous a man, inspiring general respect and capable of separating his official duties from his private life, as he had been when acting as an official on special service. His duties now as examining magistrate were far more interesting and attractive than before. In his former position it had been pleasant to wear an undress uniform made by Scharmer, and to pass through the crowd of petitioners and officials who were timorously awaiting an audience with the governor, and who envied him as with free and easy gait he went straight into his chief's private room to have a cup of tea and a cigarette with him. But not many people had then been directly dependent on him—only police officials and the sectarians when he went on special missions—and he liked to treat them politely, almost as comrades, as if he were letting them feel that he who had the power to crush them was treating them in this simple, friendly way. There were then but few such people. But now, as an examining magistrate, Iván Ilých felt that everyone without exception, even the most important and self-satisfied, was in his power, and that he need only write a few words on a sheet of paper with a certain heading, and this or that important, self-satisfied person would be brought before him in the role of an accused person or a witness, and if he did not choose to allow him to sit down, would have to stand before him and answer his questions. Iván Ilých never abused his power; he tried on the contrary to soften its expression, but the consciousness of it and of the possibility of softening its effect, supplied the chief interest and attraction of his office. In his work itself, especially in his examinations, he very soon acquired a method of eliminating all considerations irrelevant to the legal aspect of the case, and reducing even the most complicated case to a form in which it would be presented on paper only in its externals, completely excluding his personal opinion of the matter, while above all observing every prescribed formality. The work was new and Iván Ilých was one of the first men to apply the new Code of 1864.[6]

On taking up the post of examining magistrate in a new town, he made new

---

[5] Proper.
[6] Judicial procedures were thoroughly reformed after the emancipation of the serfs in 1861.

acquaintances and connections, placed himself on a new footing, and assumed a somewhat different tone. He took up an attitude of rather dignified aloofness towards the provincial authorities, but picked out the best circle of legal gentlemen and wealthy gentry living in the town and assumed a tone of slight dissatisfaction with the government, of moderate liberalism, and of enlightened citizenship. At the same time, without at all altering the elegance of his toilet, he ceased shaving his chin and allowed his beard to grow as it pleased.

Iván Ilých settled down very pleasantly in this new town. The society there, which inclined towards opposition to the Governor, was friendly, his salary was larger, and he began to play *vint*,[7] which he found added not a little to the pleasure of life, for he had a capacity for cards, played good-humouredly, and calculated rapidly and astutely, so that he usually won.

After living there for two years he met his future wife, Praskóvya Fëdorovna Míkhel, who was the most attractive, clever, and brilliant girl of the set in which he moved, and among other amusements and relaxations from his labours as examining magistrate, Iván Ilých established light and playful relations with her.

While he had been an official on special service he had been accustomed to dance, but now as an examining magistrate it was exceptional for him to do so. If he danced now, he did it as if to show that though he served under the reformed order of things, and had reached the fifth official rank, yet when it came to dancing he could do it better than most people. So at the end of an evening he sometimes danced with Praskóvya Fëdorovna, and it was chiefly during these dances that he captivated her. She fell in love with him. Iván Ilých had at first no definite intention of marrying, but when the girl fell in love with him he said to himself: "Really, why shouldn't I marry?"

Praskóvya Fëdorovna came of a good family, was not bad looking and had some little property. Iván Ilých might have aspired to a more brilliant match, but even this was good. He had his salary, and she, he hoped, would have an equal income. She was well connected, and was a sweet, pretty, and thoroughly correct young woman. To say that Iván Ilých married because he fell in love with Praskóvya Fëdorovna and found that she sympathized with his views of life would be as incorrect as to say that he married because his social circle approved of the match. He was swayed by both these considerations: the marriage gave him personal satisfaction, and at the same time it was considered the right thing by the most highly placed of his associates.

So Iván Ilých got married.

The preparations for marriage and the beginning of married life, with its conjugal caresses, the new furniture, new crockery, and new linen, were very pleasant until his wife became pregnant—so that Iván Ilých had begun to think that marriage would not impair the easy, agreeable, gay and always decorous character of his life, approved of by society and regarded by himself as natural,

---

[7] A card game similar to bridge.

but would even improve it. But from the first months of his wife's pregnancy, something new, unpleasant, depressing, and unseemly, and from which there was no way of escape, unexpectedly showed itself.

His wife, without any reason—*de gaieté de coeur* as Iván Ilých expressed it to himself—began to disturb the pleasure and propriety of their life. She began to be jealous without any cause, expected him to devote his whole attention to her, found fault with everything, and made coarse and ill-mannered scenes.

At first Iván Ilých hoped to escape from the unpleasantness of this state of affairs by the same easy and decorous relation to life that had served him heretofore: he tried to ignore his wife's disagreeable moods, continued to live in his usual easy and pleasant way, invited friends to his house for a game of cards, and also tried going out to his club or spending his evenings with friends. But one day his wife began upbraiding him so vigorously, using such coarse words, and continued to abuse him every time he did not fulfil her demands, so resolutely and with such evident determination not to give way till he submitted—that is, till he stayed at home and was bored just as she was—that he became alarmed. He now realized that matrimony—at any rate with Praskóvya Fëdorovna—was not always conducive to the pleasures and amenities of life but on the contrary often infringed both comfort and propriety, and that he must therefore entrench himself against such infringement. And Iván Ilých began to seek for means of doing so. His official duties were the one thing that imposed upon Praskóvya Fëdorovna, and by means of his official work and the duties attached to it he began struggling with his wife to secure his own independence.

With the birth of their child, the attempts to feed it and the various failures in doing so, and with the real and imaginary illnesses of mother and child, in which Iván Ilých's sympathy was demanded but about which he understood nothing, the need of securing for himself an existence outside his family life became still more imperative.

As his wife grew more irritable and exacting and Iván Ilých transferred the centre of gravity of his life more and more to his official work, so did he grow to like his work better and became more ambitious than before.

Very soon, within a year of his wedding, Iván Ilých had realized that marriage, though it may add some comforts to life, is in fact a very intricate and difficult affair towards which in order to perform one's duty, that is, to lead a decorous life approved of by society, one must adopt a definite attitude just as towards one's official duties.

And Iván Ilých evolved such an attitude towards married life. He only required of it those conveniences—dinner at home, housewife, and bed—which it could give him, and above all that propriety of external forms required by public opinion. For the rest he looked for light-hearted pleasure and propriety, and was very thankful when he found them, but if he met with antagonism and querulousness he at once retired into his separate fenced-off world of official duties, where he found satisfaction.

Iván Ilých was esteemed a good official, and after three years was made

Assistant Public Prosecutor. His new duties, their importance, the possibility of indicting and imprisoning anyone he chose, the publicity his speeches received, and the success he had in all these things, made his work still more attractive.

More children came. His wife became more and more querulous and ill-tempered, but the attitude Iván Ilých had adopted towards his home life rendered him almost impervious to her grumbling.

After seven years' service in that town he was transferred to another province as Public Prosecutor. They moved, but were short of money and his wife did not like the place they moved to. Though the salary was higher the cost of living was greater, besides which two of their children died and family life became still more unpleasant for him.

Praskóvya Fëdorovna blamed her husband for every inconvenience they encountered in their new home. Most of the conversations between husband and wife, especially as to the children's education, led to topics which recalled former disputes, and those disputes were apt to flare up again at any moment. There remained only those rare periods of amorousness which still came to them at times but did not last long. These were islets at which they anchored for a while and then again set out upon that ocean of veiled hostility which showed itself in their aloofness from one another. This aloofness might have grieved Iván Ilých had he considered that it ought not to exist, but he now regarded the position as normal, and even made it the goal at which he aimed in family life. His aim was to free himself more and more from those unpleasantnesses and to give them a semblance of harmlessness and propriety. He attained this by spending less and less time with his family, and when obliged to be at home he tried to safeguard his position by the presence of outsiders. The chief thing however was that he had his official duties. The whole interest of his life now centered in the official world and that interest absorbed him. The consciousness of his power, being able to ruin anybody he wished to ruin, the importance, even the external dignity of his entry into court, or meetings with his subordinates, his success with superiors and inferiors, and above all his masterly handling of cases, of which he was conscious—all this gave him pleasure and filled his life, together with chats with his colleagues, dinners, and bridge. So that on the whole Iván Ilých's life continued to flow as he considered it should do—pleasantly and properly.

So things continued for another seven years. His eldest daughter was already sixteen, another child had died, and only one son was left, a schoolboy and a subject of dissension. Iván Ilých wanted to put him in the School of Law, but to spite him Praskóvya Fëdorovna entered him at the High School. The daughter had been educated at home and had turned out well: the boy did not learn badly either.

CHAPTER III

So Iván Ilých lived for seventeen years after his marriage. He was already a Public Prosecutor of long standing, and had declined several proposed transfers while awaiting a more desirable post, when an unanticipated and unpleasant occurrence quite upset the peaceful course of his life. He was expecting to be offered the post of presiding judge in a University town, but Happe somehow came to the front and obtained the appointment instead. Iván Ilých became irritable, reproached Happe, and quarreled both with him and with his immediate superiors—who became colder to him and again passed him over when other appointments were made.

This was in 1880, the hardest year of Iván Ilých's life. It was then that it became evident on the one hand that his salary was insufficient for them to live on, and on the other that he had been forgotten, and not only this, but that what was for him the greatest and most cruel injustice appeared to others a quite ordinary occurrence. Even his father did not consider it his duty to help him. Iván Ilých felt himself abandoned by everyone, and that they regarded his position with a salary of 3,500 rubles as quite normal and even fortunate. He alone knew that with the consciousness of the injustices done him, with his wife's incessant nagging, and with the debts he had contracted by living beyond his means, his position was far from normal.

In order to save money that summer he obtained leave of absence and went with his wife to live in the country at her brother's place.

In the country, without his work, he experienced *ennui* for the first time in his life, and not only *ennui* but intolerable depression, and he decided that it was impossible to go on living like that, and that it was necessary to take energetic measures.

Having passed a sleepless night pacing up and down the veranda, he decided to go to Petersburg and bestir himself, in order to punish those who had failed to appreciate him and to get transferred to another ministry.

Next day, despite many protests from his wife and her brother, he started for Petersburg with the sole object of obtaining a post with a salary of five thousand rubles a year. He was no longer bent on any particular department, or tendency, or kind of activity. All he now wanted was an appointment to another post with a salary of five thousand rubles, either in the administration, in the banks, with the railways, in one of the Empress Márya's Institutions,[8] or even in the customs—but it had to carry with it a salary of five thousand rubles and be in a ministry other than that in which they had failed to appreciate him.

And this quest of Iván Ilých's was crowned with remarkable and unexpected success. At Kursk an acquaintance of his, F. I. Ilyín, got into the first-class carriage, sat down beside Iván Ilých, and told him of a telegram just received by the Governor of Kursk announcing that a change was about to take place in the ministry: Peter Ivánovich was to be superseded by Iván Semënovich.

The proposed change, apart from its significance for Russia, had a special significance for Iván Ilých, because by bringing forward a new man, Peter Petróvich, and consequently his friend Zachár Ivánovich, it was highly favourable for Iván Ilých, since Zachár Ivánovich was a friend and colleague of his.

In Moscow this news was confirmed, and on reaching Petersburg Iván Ilých

---

[8] A charitable organization founded in the late eighteenth century by the Empress Márya.

found Zachár Ivánovich and received a definite promise of an appointment in his former Department of Justice.

A week later he telegraphed to his wife: "Zachár in Miller's place. I shall receive appointment on presentation of report."

Thanks to this change of personnel, Iván Ilých had unexpectedly obtained an appointment in his former ministry which placed him two stages above his former colleagues besides giving him five thousand rubles salary and three thousand five hundred rubles for expenses connected with his removal. All his ill humour towards his former enemies and the whole department vanished, and Iván Ilých was completely happy.

He returned to the country more cheerful and contented than he had been for a long time. Praskóvya Fëdorovna also cheered up and a truce was arranged between them. Iván Ilých told of how he had been fêted by everybody in Petersburg, how all those who had been his enemies were put to shame and now fawned on him, how envious they were of his appointment, and how much everybody in Petersburg had liked him.

Praskóvya Fëdorovna listened to all this and appeared to believe it. She did not contradict anything, but only made plans for their life in the town to which they were going. Iván Ilých saw with delight that these plans were his plans, that he and his wife agreed, and that, after a stumble, his life was regaining its due and natural character of pleasant lightheartedness and decorum.

Iván Ilých had come back for a short time only, for he had to take up his new duties on the 10th of September. Moreover, he needed time to settle into the new place, to move all his belongings from the province, and to buy and order many additional things: in a word, to make such arrangements as he had resolved on, which were almost exactly what Praskóvya Fëdorovna too had decided on.

Now that everything had happened so fortunately, and that he and his wife were at one in their aims and moreover saw so little of one another, they got on together better than they had done since the first years of marriage. Iván Ilých had thought of taking his family away with him at once, but the insistence of his wife's brother and her sister-in-law, who had suddenly become particularly amiable and friendly to him and his family, induced him to depart alone.

So he departed, and the cheerful state of mind induced by his success and by the harmony between his wife and himself, the one intensifying the other, did not leave him. He found a delightful house, just the thing both he and his wife had dreamt of. Spacious, lofty reception rooms in the old style, a convenient and dignified study, rooms for his wife and daughter, a study for his son— it might have been specially built for them. Iván Ilých himself superintended the arrangements, chose the wallpapers, supplemented the furniture (preferably with antiques which he considered particularly *comme it faut*), and supervised the upholstering. Everything progressed and progressed and approached the ideal he had set himself: even when things were only half completed they exceeded his expectations. He saw what a refined and elegant character, free from vulgarity, it would all have when it was ready. On falling asleep he pictured to himself how the reception-room would look. Looking at the yet unfinished drawing-room he could see the fireplace, the screen, the what-not, the little chairs dotted here and there, the dishes and plates on the walls, and the bronzes, as they would be when everything was in place. He was pleased by the thought of how his wife and daughter, who shared his taste in this matter, would be impressed by it. They were certainly not expecting as much. He had been particularly successful in finding, and buying cheaply, antiques which gave a particularly aristocratic character to the whole place. But in his letters he intentionally understated everything in order to be able to surprise them. All this so absorbed him that his new duties—though he liked his official work— interested him less than he had expected. Sometimes he even had moments of absent-mindedness during the Court Sessions, and would consider whether he should have straight or curved cornices for his curtains. He was so interested in it all that he often did things himself, rearranging the furniture, or rehanging the curtains. Once when mounting a step-ladder to show the upholsterer, who did not understand, how he wanted the hangings draped, he made a false step and slipped, but being a strong and agile man he clung on and only knocked his side against the knob of the window frame. The bruised place was painful but the pain soon passed, and he felt particularly bright and well just then. He wrote: "I feel fifteen years younger." He thought he would have everything ready by September, but it dragged on till mid-October. But the result was charming not only in his eyes but to everyone who saw it.

In reality it was just what is usually seen in the houses of people of moderate means who want to appear rich, and therefore succeed only in resembling others like themselves: there were damasks, dark wood, plants, rugs, and dull and polished bronzes—all the things people of a certain class have in order to resemble other people of that class. His house was so like the others that it would never have been noticed, but to him it all seemed to be quite exceptional. He was very happy when he met his family at the station and brought them to the newly furnished house all lit up, where a footman in a white tie opened the door into the hall decorated with plants, and when they went on into the drawing room and the study uttering exclamations of delight. He conducted them everywhere, drank in their praises eagerly, and beamed with pleasure. At tea that evening, when Praskóvya Fëdorovna among other things asked him about his fall, he laughed and showed them how he had gone flying and had frightened the upholsterer.

"It's a good thing I'm a bit of an athlete. Another man might have been killed, but I merely knocked myself, just here; it hurts when it's touched, but it's passing off already—it's only a bruise."

So they began living in their new home—in which, as always happens, when they got thoroughly settled in they found they were just one room short— and with the increased income, which as always was just a little (some five hundred rubles) too little, but it was all very nice.

Things went particularly well at first, before everything was finally arranged and while something had still to be done: this thing bought, that thing ordered, another thing moved, and something else adjusted. Though there were some disputes between husband and wife, they were both so well satisfied and had so much to do that it all passed off without any serious quarrels. When nothing was left to arrange it became rather dull and something seemed to be lacking, but they were then making acquaintances, forming habits, and life was growing fuller.

Iván Ilých spent his mornings at the law court and came home to dinner, and at first he was generally in a good humour, though he occasionally became irritable just on account of his house. (Every spot on the tablecloth or the upholstery, and every broken window-blind string, irritated him. He had devoted so much trouble to arranging it all that every disturbance of it distressed him.) But on the whole his life ran its course as he believed life should do: easily, pleasantly, and decorously.

He got up at nine, drank his coffee, read the paper, and then put on his undress uniform and went to the law courts. There the harness in which he worked had already been stretched to fit him and he donned it without a hitch: petitioners, inquiries at the chancery, the chancery itself, and the sittings public and administrative. In all this the thing was to exclude everything fresh and vital, which always disturbs the regular course of official business, and to admit only official relations with people, and then only on official grounds. A man would come, for instance, wanting some information. Iván Ilých, as one in whose sphere the matter did not lie, would have nothing to do with him: but if the man had some business with him in his official capacity, something that could be expressed on officially stamped paper, he would do everything, positively everything he could within the limits of such relations, and in doing so would maintain the semblance of friendly human relations, that is, would observe the courtesies of life. As soon as the official relations ended, so did everything else. Iván Ilých possessed this capacity to separate his real life from the offical side of affairs and not mix the two, in the highest degree, and by long practice and natural aptitude had brought it to such a pitch that sometimes, in the manner of a virtuoso, he would even allow himself to let the human and official relations mingle. He let himself do this just because he felt that he could at any time he chose resume the strictly official attitude again and drop the human relation. And he did it all easily, pleasantly, correctly, and even artistically. In the intervals between the sessions he smoked, drank tea, chatted a little about politics, a little about general topics, a little about cards, but most of all about official appointments. Tired, but with the feelings of a virtuoso— one of the first violins who has played his part in an orchestra with precision— he would return home to find that his wife and daughter had been out paying calls, or had a visitor, and that his son had been to school, had done his homework with his tutor, and was duly learning what is taught at High Schools. Everything was as it should be. After dinner, if they had no visitors, Iván Ilých sometimes read a book that was being much discussed at the time, and in the evening settled down to work, that is, read official papers, compared the depositions of witnesses, and noted paragraphs of the Code applying to them. This was neither dull nor amusing. It was dull when he might have been playing bridge, but if no bridge was available it was at any rate better than doing nothing or sitting with his wife. Iván Ilých's chief pleasure was giving little dinners to which he invited men and women of good social position, and just as his drawing-room resembled all other drawing-rooms so did his enjoyable little parties resemble all other such parties.

Once they even gave a dance. Iván Ilých enjoyed it and everything went off well, except that it led to a violent quarrel with his wife about the cakes and sweets. Praskóvya Fëdorovna had made her own plans, but Iván Ilých insisted on getting everything from an expensive confectioner and ordered too many cakes, and the quarrel occurred because some of those cakes were left over and the confectioner's bill came to forty-five rubles. It was a great and disagreeable quarrel. Praskóvya Fëdorovna called him "a fool and an imbecile," and he clutched at his head and made angry allusions to divorce.

But the dance itself had been enjoyable. The best people were there, and Iván Ilých had danced with Princess Trúfonova, a sister of the distinguished founder of the Society "Bear My Burden."

The pleasures connected with his work were pleasures of ambition; his social pleasures were those of vanity; but Iván Ilých's greatest pleasure was playing bridge. He acknowledged that whatever disagreeable incident happened in his life, the pleasure that beamed like a ray of light above everything else was to sit down to bridge with good players, not noisy partners, and of course to four-handed bridge (with five players it was annoying to have to stand out, though one pretended not to mind), to play a clever and serious game (when the cards allowed it) and then to have supper and drink a glass of wine. After a game of bridge, especially if he had won a little (to win a large sum was unpleasant), Iván Ilých went to bed in specially good humour.

So they lived. They formed a circle of acquaintances among the best people and were visited by people of importance and by young folk. In their views as to their acquaintances, husband, wife and daughter were entirely agreed, and tacitly and unanimously kept at arm's length and shook off the various shabby friends and relations who, with much show of affection, gushed into the drawing-room with its Japanese plates on the walls. Soon these shabby friends ceased to obtrude themselves and only the best people remained in the Golovíns' set.

Young men made up to Lisa, and Petríshchev, an examining magistrate and Dmítri Ivanovich Petríshchev's son and sole heir, began to be so attentive to her that Iván Ilých had already spoken to Praskóvya Fëdorovna about it, and considered whether they should not arrange a party for them or get up some private theatricals.

So they lived, and all went well, without change, and life flowed pleasantly.

CHAPTER IV

They were all in good health. It could not be called ill health if Iván Ilých sometimes said that he had a queer taste in his mouth and felt some discomfort in his left side.

But this discomfort increased and, though not exactly painful, grew into a sense of pressure in his side accompanied by ill humour. And his irritability became worse and worse and began to mar the agreeable, easy, and correct life that had established itself in the Golovín family. Quarrels between husband and wife became more and more frequent, and soon the ease and amenity disappeared and even the decorum was barely maintained. Scenes again became frequent, and very few of those islets remained on which husband and wife could meet without explosion. Praskóvya Fëdorovna now had good reason to say that her husband's temper was trying. With characteristic exaggeration she said he had always had a dreadful temper, and that it had needed all her good nature to put up with it for twenty years. It was true that now the quarrels were started by him. His bursts of temper always came just before dinner, often just as he began to eat his soup. Sometimes he noticed that a plate or dish was chipped, or the food was not right, or his son put his elbow on the table, or his daughter's hair was not done as he liked it, and for all this he blamed Praskóvya Fëdorovna. At first she retorted and said disagreeable things to him, but once or twice he fell into such a rage at the beginning of dinner that she realized it was due to some physical derangement brought on by taking food, and so she restrained herself and did not answer, but only hurried to get the dinner over. She regarded this self-restraint as highly praiseworthy. Having come to the conclusion that her husband had a dreadful temper and made her life miserable, she began to feel sorry for herself, and the more she pitied herself the more she hated her husband. She began to wish he would die; yet she did not want him to die because then his salary would cease. And this irritated her against him still more. She considered herself dreadfully unhappy just because not even his death could save her, and though she concealed her exasperation, that hidden exasperation of hers increased his irritation also.

After one scene in which Iván Ilých had been particularly unfair and after which he had said in explanation that he certainly was irritable but that it was due to his not being well, she said that if he was ill it should be attended to, and insisted on his going to see a celebrated doctor.

He went. Everything took place as he had expected and as it always does. There was the usual waiting and the important air assumed by the doctor, with which he was so familiar (resembling that which he himself assumed in court), and the sounding and listening, and the questions which called for answers that were foregone conclusions and were evidently unnecessary, and the look of importance which implied that "if only you put yourself in our hands we will arrange everything—we know indubitably how it has to be done, always in the same way for everybody alike." It was all just as it was in the law courts. The doctor put on just the same air towards him as he himself put on towards an accused person.

The doctor said that so-and-so indicated that there was so-and-so inside the patient, but if the investigation of so-and-so did not confirm this, then he must assume that and that. If he assumed that and that, then . . . and so on. To Iván Ilých only one question was important: was his case serious or not? But the doctor ignored that inappropriate question. From his point of view it was not the one under consideration, the real question was to decide between a floating kidney, chronic catarrh, or appendicitis. It was not a question of Iván Ilých's life or death, but one between a floating kidney and appendicitis. And that question the doctor solved brilliantly, as it seemed to Iván Ilých, in favour of the appendix, with the reservation that should an examination of the urine give fresh indications the matter would be reconsidered. All this was just what Iván Ilých had himself brilliantly accomplished a thousand times in dealing with men on trial. The doctor summed up just as brilliantly, looking over his spectacles triumphantly and even gaily at the accused. From the doctor's summing up Iván Ilých concluded that things were bad, but that for the doctor, and perhaps for everybody else, it was a matter of indifference, though for him it was bad. And this conclusion struck him painfully, arousing in him a great feeling of pity for himself and of bitterness towards the doctor's indifference to a matter of such importance.

He said nothing of this, but rose, placed the doctor's fee on the table, and remarked with a sigh: "We sick people probably often put inappropriate questions. But tell me, in general, is this complaint dangerous, or not? . . ."

The doctor looked at him sternly over his spectacles with one eye, as if to say: "Prisoner, if you will not keep to the questions put to you, I shall be obliged to have you removed from the court."

"I have already told you what I consider necessary and proper. The analysis may show something more." And the doctor bowed.

Iván Ilých went out slowly, seated himself disconsolately in his sledge, and drove home. All the way home he was going over what the doctor had said, trying to translate those complicated, obscure, scientific phrases into plain language and find in them an answer to the question: "Is my condition bad? Is it very bad? Or is there as yet nothing much wrong?" And it seemed to him that the meaning of what the doctor had said was that it was very bad. Everything in the streets seemed depressing. The cabmen, the houses, the passers-by, and the shops, were dismal. His ache, this dull gnawing ache that never ceased for a moment, seemed to have acquired a new and more serious significance from the doctor's dubious remarks. Iván Ilých now watched it with a new and oppressive feeling.

He reached home and began to tell his wife about it. She listened, but in the middle of his account his daughter came in with her hat on, ready to go out with her mother. She sat down reluctantly to listen to this tedious story, but could not stand it long, and her mother too did not hear him to the end.

"Well, I am very glad," she said. "Mind now to take your medicine regularly. Give me the prescription and I'll send Gerásim to the chemist's." And she went to get ready to go out.

While she was in the room Iván Ilých had hardly taken time to breathe, but he sighed deeply when she left it.

"Well," he thought, "perhaps it isn't so bad after all."

He began taking his medicine and following the doctor's directions, which had been altered after the examination of the urine. But then it happened that there was a contradiction between the indications drawn from the examination of the urine and the symptoms that showed themselves. It turned out that what was happening differed from what the doctor had told him, and that he had either forgotten, or blundered, or hidden something from him. He could not, however, be blamed for that, and Iván Ilých still obeyed his orders implicitly and at first derived some comfort from doing so.

From the time of his visit to the doctor, Iván Ilých's chief occupation was the exact fulfilment of the doctor's instructions regarding hygiene and the taking of medicine, and the observation of his pain and his excretions. His chief interests came to be people's ailments and people's health. When sickness, deaths, or recoveries were mentioned in his presence, especially when the illness resembled his own, he listened with agitation which he tried to hide, asked questions, and applied what he heard to his own case.

The pain did not grow less, but Iván Ilých made efforts to force himself to think that he was better. And he could do this so long as nothing agitated him. But as soon as he had any unpleasantness with his wife, any lack of success in his official work, or held bad cards at bridge, he was at once acutely sensible of his disease. He had formerly borne such mischances, hoping soon to adjust what was wrong, to master it and attain success, or make a grand slam. But now every mischance upset him and plunged him into despair. He would say to himself: "There now, just as I was beginning to get better and the medicine had begun to take effect, comes this accursed misfortune, or unpleasantness. . . ." And he was furious with the mishap, or with the people who were causing the unpleasantness and killing him, for he felt that this fury was killing him but could not restrain it. One would have thought that it should have been clear to him that this exasperation with circumstances and people aggravated his illness, and that he ought therefore to ignore unpleasant occurrences. But he drew the very opposite conclusion: he said that he needed peace, and he watched for everything that might disturb it and became irritable at the slightest infringement of it. His condition was rendered worse by the fact that he read medical books and consulted doctors. The progress of his disease was so gradual that he could deceive himself when comparing one day with another—the difference was so slight. But when he consulted the doctors it seemed to him that he was getting worse, and even very rapidly. Yet despite this he was continually consulting them.

That month he went to see another celebrity, who told him almost the same as the first had done but put his questions rather differently, and the interview with this celebrity only increased Iván Ilých's doubts and fears. A friend of a friend of his, a very good doctor, diagnosed his illness again quite differently from the others, and though he predicted recovery, his questions and suppositions bewildered Iván Ilých still more and increased his doubts. A homeopathist diagnosed the disease in yet another way, and prescribed medicine which Iván Ilých took secretly for a week. But after a week, not feeling any improvement and having lost confidence both in the former doctor's treatment and in this one's, he became still more despondent. One day a lady acquaintance mentioned a cure effected by a wonder-working icon. Iván Ilých caught himself listening attentively and beginning to believe that it had occurred. This incident alarmed him. "Has my mind really weakened to such an extent?" he asked himself. "Nonsense! It's all rubbish. I mustn't give way to nervous fears but having chosen a doctor must keep strictly to his treatment. That is what I will do. Now it's all settled. I won't think about it, but will follow the treatment seriously till summer, and then we shall see. From now there must be no more of this wavering!" This was easy to say but impossible to carry out. The pain in his side oppressed him and seemed to grow worse and more incessant, while the taste in his mouth grew stranger and stranger. It seemed to him that his breath had a disgusting smell, and he was conscious of a loss of appetite and strength. There was no deceiving himself: something terrible, new, and more important than anything before in his life, was taking place within him of which he alone was aware. Those about him did not understand or would not understand it, but thought everything in the world was going on as usual. That tormented Iván Ilých more than anything. He saw that his household, especially his wife and daughter who were in a perfect whirl of visiting, did not understand anything of it and were annoyed that he was so depressed and so exacting, as if he were to blame for it. Though they tried to disguise it he saw that he was an obstacle in their path, and that his wife had adopted a definite line in regard to his illness and kept to it regardless of anything he said or did. Her attitude was this: "You know," she would say to her friends, "Iván Ilých can't do as other people do, and keep to the treatment prescribed for him. One day he'll take his drops and keep strictly to his diet and go to bed in good time, but the next day unless I watch him he'll suddenly forget his medicine, eat sturgeon— which is forbidden—and sit up playing cards till one o'clock in the morning."

"Oh, come, when was that?" Iván Ilých would ask in vexation. "Only once at Peter Ivánovich's."

"And yesterday with Shébek."

"Well, even if I hadn't stayed up, this pain would have kept me awake."

"Be that as it may you'll never get well like that, but will always make us wretched."

Praskóvya Fëdorovna's attitude to Iván Ilých's illness, as she expressed it both to others and to him, was that it was his own fault and was another of the annoyances he caused her. Iván Ilých felt that this opinion escaped her involuntarily—but that did not make it easier for him.

At the law courts too, Iván Ilých noticed, or thought he noticed, a strange attitude towards himself. It sometimes seemed to him that people were watching him inquisitively as a man whose place might soon be vacant. Then again, his friends would suddenly begin to chaff him in a friendly way about his low spirits, as if the awful, horrible, and unheard-of thing that was going on within him, incessantly gnawing at him and irresistibly drawing him away, was a very agreeable subject for jests. Schwartz in particular irritated him by his jocularity, vivacity, and *savoir-faire*, which reminded him of what he himself had been ten years ago.

Friends came to make up a set and they sat down to cards. They dealt, bending the new cards to soften them, and he sorted the diamonds in his hand and found he had seven. His partner said "No trumps" and supported him with two diamonds. What more could be wished for? It ought to be jolly and lively. They would make a grand slam. But suddenly Iván Ilých was conscious of that gnawing pain, that taste in his mouth, and it seemed ridiculous that in such circumstances he should be pleased to make a grand slam.

He looked at his partner Mikháil Mikháylovich, who rapped the table with his strong hand and instead of snatching up the tricks pushed the cards courteously and indulgently towards Iván Ilých that he might have the pleasure of gathering them up without the trouble of stretching out his hand for them. "Does he think I am too weak to stretch out my arm?" thought Iván Ilých, and forgetting what he was doing he over-trumped his partner, missing the grand slam by three tricks. And what was most awful of all was that he saw how upset Mikháil Mikháylovich was about it but did not himself care. And it was dreadful to realize why he did not care.

They all saw that he was suffering and said: "We can stop if you are tired. Take a rest." Lie down? No, he was not at all tired, and he finished the rubber. All were gloomy and silent. Iván Ilých felt that he had diffused this gloom over them and could not dispel it. They had supper and went away, and Iván Ilých was left alone with the consciousness that his life was poisoned and was poisoning the lives of others, and that this poison did not weaken but penetrated more and more deeply into his whole being.

With this consciousness, and with physical pain besides the terror, he must go to bed, often to lie awake the greater part of the night. Next morning he had to get up again, dress, go to the law courts, speak, and write; or if he did not go out, spend at home those twenty-four hours a day each of which was a torture. And he had to live thus all alone on the brink of an abyss, with no one who understood or pitied him.

CHAPTER V

So one month passed and then another. Just before the New Year his brother-in-law came to town and stayed at their house. Iván Ilých was at the law courts and Praskóvya Fëdorovna had gone shopping. When Iván Ilých came home and entered his study he found his brother-in-law there—a healthy, florid man—unpacking his portmanteau himself. He raised his head on hearing Iván Ilých's footsteps and looked up at him for a moment without a word. That stare told Iván Ilých everything. His brother-in-law opened his mouth to utter an exclamation of surprise but checked himself, and that action confirmed it all.

"I have changed, eh?"

"Yes, there is a change."

And after that, try as he would to get his brother-in-law to return to the subject of his looks, the latter would say nothing about it. Praskóvya Fëdorovna came home and her brother went out to her. Iván Ilých locked the door and began to examine himself in the glass, first full face, then in profile. He took up a portrait of himself taken with his wife, and compared it with what he saw in the glass. The change in him was immense. Then he bared his arms to the elbow, looked at them, drew the sleeves down again, sat down on an ottoman, and grew blacker than night.

"No, no, this won't do!" he said to himself, and jumped up, went to the table, took up some law papers and began to read them, but could not continue. He unlocked the door and went into the reception-room. The door leading to the drawing room was shut. He approached it on tiptoe and listened.

"No, you are exaggerating!" Praskóvya Fëdorovna was saying.

"Exaggerating! Don't you see it? Why, he's a dead man! Look at his eyes—there's no light in them. But what is it that is wrong with him?"

"No one knows. Nikoláevich (that was another doctor) said something, but I don't know what. And Leshchetítsky (this was the celebrated specialist) said quite the contrary . . ."

Iván Ilých walked away, went to his own room, lay down, and began musing: "The kidney, a floating kidney." He recalled all the doctors had told him of how it detached itself and swayed about. And by an effort of imagination he tried to catch that kidney and arrest it and support it. So little was needed for this, it seemed to him. "No, I'll go to see Peter Ivánovich again." (That was the friend whose friend was a doctor.) He rang, ordered the carriage, and got ready to go.

"Where are you going, Jean?" asked his wife, with a specially sad and exceptionally kind look.

This exceptionally kind look irritated him. He looked morosely at her.

"I must go to see Peter Ivánovich."

He went to see Peter Ivánovich, and together they went to see his friend, the doctor. He was in, and Iván Ilých had a long talk with him.

Reviewing the anatomical and physiological details of what in the doctor's opinion was going on inside him, he understood it all.

There was something, a small thing, in the vermiform appendix. It might all come right. Only stimulate the energy of one organ and check the activity of another, then absorption would take place and everything would come right. He got home rather late for dinner, ate his dinner, and conversed cheerfully, but could not for a long time bring himself to go back to work in his room. At last, however, he went to his study and did what was necessary, but the consciousness that he had put something aside—an important, intimate matter which he would revert to when his work was done—never left him. When he had finished his work he remembered that this intimate matter was the thought of his vermiform appendix. But he did not give himself up to it, and went to the drawing-room for tea. There were callers there, including the examining magistrate who was a desirable match for his daughter, and they were conversing, playing the piano and singing. Iván Ilých, as Praskóvya Fëdorovna remarked, spent that evening more cheerfully than usual, but he never for a moment forgot that he had postponed the important matter of the appendix. At eleven o'clock he said good-night and went to his bedroom. Since his illness he had slept alone in a small room next to his study. He undressed and took up a novel by Zola, but instead of reading it he fell into thought, and in his imagination that desired improvement in the vermiform appendix occurred. There was the absorption and evacuation and the reestablishment of normal activity. "Yes, that's it!" he said to himself. "One need only assist nature, that's all." He remembered his medicine, rose, took it, and lay down on his back watching for the beneficent action of the medicine and for it to lessen the pain. "I need only take it regularly and avoid all injurious influences. I am already feeling better, much better." He began touching his side: it was not painful to the touch. "There, I really don't feel it. It's much better already." He put out the light and turned on his side . . . "The appendix is getting better, absorption is occurring." Suddenly he felt the old, familiar, dull, gnawing pain, stubborn and serious. There was the same familiar loathsome taste in his mouth. His heart sank and he felt dazed. "My God! My God!" he muttered. "Again, again! and it will never cease." And suddenly the matter presented itself in a quite different aspect. "Vermiform appendix! Kidney!" he said to himself. "It's not a question of appendix or kidney, but of life and . . . death. Yes, life was there and now it is going, going and I cannot stop it. Yes. Why deceive myself? Isn't it obvious to everyone but me that I'm dying, and that it's only a question of weeks, days . . . it may happen this moment. There was light and now there is darkness. I was here and now I'm going there! Where?" A chill came over him, his breathing ceased, and he felt only the throbbing of his heart.

"When I am not, what will there be? There will be nothing. Then where shall I be when I am no more? Can this be dying? No, I don't want to!" He jumped up and tried to light the candle, felt for it with trembling hands, dropped candle and candlestick on the floor, and fell back on his pillow.

"What's the use? It makes no difference," he said to himself, staring with wide-open eyes into the darkness. "Death. Yes, death. And none of them know or wish to know it, and they have no pity for me. Now they are playing." (He heard through the door the distant sound of a song and its accompaniment.) "It's all the same to them, but they will die too! Fools! I first, and they later, but it will be the same for them. And now they are merry . . . the beasts!"

Anger choked him and he was agonizingly, unbearably miserable. "It is impossible that all men have been doomed to suffer this awful horror!" He raised himself.

"Something must be wrong. I must calm myself—must think it all over from the beginning." And he again began thinking. "Yes, the beginning of my illness: I knocked my side, but I was still quite well that day and the next. It hurt a little, then rather more. I saw the doctors, then followed despondency and anguish, more doctors, and I drew nearer to the abyss. My strength grew less and I kept coming nearer and nearer, and now I have wasted away and there is no light in my eyes. I think of the appendix—but this is death! I think of mending the appendix, and all the while here is death! Can it really be death?" Again terror seized him and he gasped for breath. He leant down and began feeling for the matches, pressing with his elbow on the stand beside the bed. It was in his way and hurt him, he grew furious with it, pressed on it still harder, and upset it. Breathless and in despair he fell on his back, expecting death to come immediately.

Meanwhile the visitors were leaving. Praskóvya Fëdorovna was seeing them off. She heard something fall and came in.

"What has happened?"

"Nothing. I knocked it over accidentally."

She went out and returned with a candle. He lay there panting heavily, like a man who has run a thousand yards, and stared upwards at her with a fixed look.

"What is it, Jean?"

"No . . . o . . . thing. I upset it." ("Why speak of it? She won't understand," he thought.)

And in truth she did not understand. She picked up the stand, lit his candle, and hurried away to see another visitor off. When she came back he still lay on his back, looking upwards.

"What is it? Do you feel worse?"

"Yes."

She shook her head and sat down.

"Do you know, Jean, I think we must ask Leshchetítsky to come and see you here."

This meant calling in the famous specialist, regardless of expense. He smiled malignantly and said "No." She remained a little longer and then went up to him and kissed his forehead.

While she was kissing him he hated her from the bottom of his soul and with difficulty refrained from pushing her away.

"Good-night. Please God you'll sleep."

"Yes."

CHAPTER VI

Iván Ilých saw that he was dying, and he was in continual despair.

In the depth of his heart he knew he was dying, but not only was he not accustomed to the thought, he simply did not and could not grasp it.

The syllogism he had learnt from Kiezewetter's Logic:[9] "Caius is a man, men are mortal, therefore Caius is mortal," had always seemed to him correct as applied to Caius, but certainly not as applied to himself. That Caius—man in the abstract—was mortal, was perfectly correct, but he was not Caius, not an abstract man, but a creature quite, quite separate from all others. He had been little Ványa, with a mamma and a papa; with Mitya and Volódya, and

---

[9] Karl Kiezewetter (1766–1819), author of an outline of logic widely used in Russian schools at the time.

the toys, a coachman and a nurse, afterwards with Kátenka and with all the joys, griefs, and delights of childhood, boyhood, and youth. What did Caius know of the smell of that striped leather ball Ványa had been so fond of? Had Caius kissed his mother's hand like that, and did the silk of her dress rustle so for Caius? Had he rioted like that at school when the pastry was bad? Had Caius been in love like that? Could Caius preside at a session as he did? "Caius really was mortal, and it was right for him to die; but for me, little Ványa, Iván Ilých, with all my thoughts and emotions, it's altogether a different matter. It cannot be that I ought to die. That would be too terrible."

Such was his feeling.

"If I had to die like Caius I should have known it was so. An inner voice would have told me so, but there was nothing of the sort in me and I and all my friends felt that our case was quite different from that of Caius. And now here it is!" he said to himself. "It can't be. It's impossible! But here it is. How is this? How is one to understand it?"

He could not understand it, and tried to drive this false, incorrect, morbid thought away and to replace it by other proper and healthy thoughts. But that thought, and not the thought only but the reality itself, seemed to come and confront him.

And to replace that thought he called up a succession of others, hoping to find in them some support. He tried to get back into the former current of thoughts that had once screened the thought of death from him. But strange to say, all that had formerly shut off, hidden, and destroyed, his consciousness of death, no longer had that effect. Iván Ilých now spent most of his time in attempting to re-establish that old current. He would say to himself: "I will take up my duties again—after all I used to live by them." And banishing all doubts he would go to the law courts, enter into conversation with his colleagues, and sit carelessly as was his wont, scanning the crowd with a thoughtful look and leaning both his emaciated arms on the arms of his oak chair; bending over as usual to a colleague and drawing his papers nearer he would interchange whispers with him, and then suddenly raising his eyes and sitting erect would pronounce certain words and open the proceedings. But suddenly in the midst of those proceedings the pain in his side, regardless of the stage the proceedings had reached, would begin its own gnawing work. Iván Ilých would turn his attention to it and try to drive the thought of it away, but without success. *It* would come and stand before him and look at him, and he would be petrified and the light would die out of his eyes, and he would again begin asking himself whether *It* alone was true. And his colleagues and subordinates would see with surprise and distress that he, the brilliant and subtle judge, was becoming confused and making mistakes. He would shake himself, try to pull himself together, manage somehow to bring the sitting to a close, and return home with the sorrowful consciousness that his judicial labours could not as formerly hide from him what he wanted them to hide, and could not deliver him from *It*. And what was worst of all was that *It* drew his attention to itself not in order to make him take some action but only that he should look at *It*, look it straight in the face: look at it and without doing anything, suffer inexpressibly.

And to save himself from this condition Iván Ilých looked for consolations— new screens—and new screens were found and for a while seemed to save him, but then they immediately fell to pieces or rather became transparent, as if *It* penetrated them and nothing could veil *It*.

In these latter days he would go into the drawing-room he had arranged— that drawing-room where he had fallen and for the sake of which (how bitterly ridiculous it seemed) he had sacrificed his life—for he knew that his illness originated with that knock. He would enter and see that something had scratched the polished table. He would look for the cause of this and find that it was the bronze ornamentation of an album, that had got bent. He would take up the expensive album which he had lovingly arranged, and feel vexed with his daughter and her friends for their untidiness—for the album was torn here and there and some of the photographs turned upside down. He would put it carefully in order and bend the ornamentation back into position. Then it would occur to him to place all those things in another corner of the room, near the plants. He could call the footman, but his daughter or wife would come to help him. They would not agree, and his wife would contradict him, and he would dispute and grow angry. But that was all right, for then he did not think about *It*. *It* was invisible.

But then, when he was moving something himself, his wife would say: "Let the servants do it. You will hurt yourself again." And suddenly *It* would flash through the screen and he would see it. It was just a flash, and he hoped it would disappear, but he would involuntarily pay attention to his side. "It sits there as before, gnawing just the same!" And he could no longer forget *It*, but could distinctly see it looking at him from behind the flowers. "What is it all for?"

"It really is so! I lost my life over that curtain as I might have done when storming a fort. Is that possible? How terrible and how stupid. It can't be true! It can't, but it is."

He would go to his study, lie down, and again be alone with *It*: face to face with *It*. And nothing could be done with *It* except to look at it and shudder.

CHAPTER VII

How it happened it is impossible to say because it came about step by step, unnoticed, but in the third month of Iván Ilých's illness, his wife, his daughter, his son, his acquaintances, the doctors, the servants, and above all he himself, were aware that the whole interest he had for other people was whether he would soon vacate his place, and at last release the living from the discomfort caused by his presence and be himself released from his sufferings.

He slept less and less. He was given opium and hypodermic injections of morphine, but this did not relieve him. The dull depression he experienced in a somnolent condition at first gave him a little relief, but only as something new, afterwards it became as distressing as the pain itself or even more so.

Special foods were prepared for him by the doctors' orders, but all those foods became increasingly distasteful and disgusting to him.

For his excretions also special arrangements had to be made, and this was a torment to him every time—a torment from the uncleanliness, the unseemliness, and the smell, and from knowing that another person had to take part in it.

But just through this most unpleasant matter Iván Ilých obtained comfort. Gerásim, the butler's young assistant, always came in to carry the things out. Gerásim was a clean, fresh peasant lad, grown stout on town food and always cheerful and bright. At first the sight of him, in his clean Russian peasant costume, engaged on that disgusting task embarrassed Iván Ilých.

Once when he got up from the commode too weak to draw up his trousers, he dropped into a soft armchair and looked with horror at his bare, enfeebled thighs with the muscles so sharply marked on them.

Gerásim with a firm light tread, his heavy boots emitting a pleasant smell of tar and fresh winter air, came in wearing a clean Hessian apron, the sleeves of his print shirt tucked up over his strong bare young arms; and refraining from looking at his sick master out of consideration for his feelings, and restraining the joy of life that beamed from his face, he went up to the commode.

"Gerásim!" said Iván Ilých in a weak voice.

Gerásim started, evidently afraid he might have committed some blunder, and with a rapid movement turned his fresh, kind, simple young face which just showed the first downy signs of a beard.

"Yes, sir?"

"That must be very unpleasant for you. You must forgive me. I am helpless."

"Oh, why, sir," and Gerásim's eyes beamed and he showed his glistening white teeth, "what's a little trouble? It's a case of illness with you, sir."

And his deft strong hands did their accustomed task, and he went out of the room stepping lightly. Five minutes later he as lightly returned.

Iván Ilých was still sitting in the same position in the armchair.

"Gerásim," he said when the latter had replaced the freshly-washed utensil. "Please come here and help me." Gerásim went up to him. "Lift me up. It is hard for me to get up, and I have sent Dmítri away."

Gerásim went up to him, grasped his master with his strong arms deftly but gently, in the same way that he stepped—lifted him, supported him with one hand, and with the other drew up his trousers and would have set him down again, but Iván Ilých asked to be led to the sofa. Gerásim, without an effort and without apparent pressure, led him, almost lifting him, to the sofa and placed him on it.

"Thank you. How easily and well you do it all!"

Gerásim smiled again and turned to leave the room. But Iván Ilých felt his presence such a comfort that he did not want to let him go.

"One thing more, please move up that chair. No, the other one—under my feet. It is easier for me when my feet are raised."

Gerásim brought the chair, set it down gently in place, and raised Iván Ilých's legs on to it. It seemed to Iván Ilých that he felt better while Gerásim was holding up his legs.

"It's better when my legs are higher," he said. "Place that cushion under them."

Gerásim did so. He again lifted the legs and placed them, and again Iván Ilých felt better while Gerásim held his legs. When he set them down Iván Ilých fancied he felt worse.

"Gerásim," he said. "Are you busy now?"

"Not at all, sir," said Gerásim, who had learnt from the townsfolk how to speak to gentlefolk.

"What have you still to do?"

"What have I to do? I've done everything except chopping the logs for tomorrow."

"Then hold my legs up a bit higher, can you?"

"Of course I can. Why not?" And Gerásim raised his master's legs higher and Iván Ilých thought that in that position he did not feel any pain at all.

"And how about the logs?"

"Don't trouble about that, sir. There's plenty of time."

Iván Ilých told Gerásim to sit down and hold his legs, and began to talk to him. And strange to say it seemed to him that he felt better while Gerásim held his legs up.

After that Iván Ilých would sometimes call Gerásim and get him to hold his legs on his shoulders, and he liked talking to him. Gerásim did it all easily, willingly, simply, and with a good nature that touched Iván Ilých. Health, strength, and vitality in other people were offensive to him, but Gerásim's strength and vitality did not mortify but soothed him.

What tormented Iván Ilých most was the deception, the lie, which for some reason they all accepted, that he was not dying but was simply ill, and that he only need keep quiet and undergo a treatment and then something very good would result. He however knew that do what they would nothing would come of it, only still more agonizing suffering and death. This deception tortured him—their not wishing to admit what they all knew and what he knew, but wanting to lie to him concerning his terrible condition, and wishing and forcing him to participate in that lie. Those lies—lies enacted over him on the eve of his death and destined to degrade this awful, solemn act to the level of their visitings, their curtains, their sturgeon for dinner—were a terrible agony for Iván Ilých. And strangely enough, many times when they were going through their antics over him he had been within a hairbreadth of calling out to them: "Stop lying! You know and I know that I am dying. Then at least stop lying about it!" But he had never had the spirit to do it. The awful, terrible act of his dying was, he could see, reduced by those about him to the level of a casual, unpleasant, and almost indecorous incident (as if someone entered a drawing-room diffusing an unpleasant odour) and this was done by that very decorum which he had served all his life long. He saw that no one felt for him, because no one even wished to grasp his position. Only Gerásim recognized it and pitied him. And so Iván Ilých felt at ease only with him. He felt comforted when Gerásim supported his legs (sometimes all night long) and refused to go to bed, saying, "Don't you worry, Iván Ilých. I'll get sleep enough later on," or when he suddenly became familiar and exclaimed: "If you weren't sick it would be another matter, but as it is, why should I grudge a little trouble?" Gerásim alone did not lie; everything showed that he alone understood the facts of the case and did not consider it necessary to disguise them, but simply felt sorry for his emaciated and enfeebled master. Once when Iván Ilých was sending him away he even said straight out: "We shall all of us die, so why should I grudge a little trouble?"—expressing the fact that he did not think his work burdensome, because he was doing it for a dying man and hoped someone would do the same for him when his time came.

Apart from this lying, or because of it, what most tormented Iván Ilých was that no one pitied him as he wished to be pitied. At certain moments after prolonged suffering he wished most of all (though he would have been ashamed to confess it) for someone to pity him as a sick child is pitied. He longed to be petted and comforted. He knew he was an important functionary, that he had a beard turning grey, and that therefore what he longed for was impossible, but still he longed for it. And in Gerásim's attitude towards him there was something akin to what he wished for, and so that attitude comforted him. Iván Ilých wanted to weep, wanted to be petted and cried over, and then his colleague Shébek would come, and instead of weeping and being petted, Iván Ilých would assume a serious, severe, and profound air, and by force of habit would express his opinion on a decision of the Court of Cassation and would stubbornly insist on that view. This falsity around him and within him did more than anything else to poison his last days.

CHAPTER VIII

It was morning. He knew it was morning because Gerásim had gone, and Peter the footman had come and put out the candles, drawn back one of the curtains, and begun quietly to tidy up. Whether it was morning or evening, Friday or Sunday, made no difference, it was all just the same: the gnawing, unmitigated, agonizing pain, never ceasing for an instant, the consciousness of life inexorably waning but not yet extinguished, that approach of that ever dreaded and hateful Death which was the only reality, and always the same falsity. What were days, weeks, hours, in such a case?

"Will you have some tea, sir?"

"He wants things to be regular, and wishes the gentlefolk to drink tea in the morning," thought Iván Ilých, and only said "No."

"Wouldn't you like to move onto the sofa, sir?"

"He wants to tidy up the room, and I'm in the way. I am uncleanliness and disorder," he thought, and said only:

"No, leave me alone."

The man went on bustling about. Iván Ilých stretched out his hand. Peter came up, ready to help.

"What is it, sir?"

"My watch."

Peter took the watch which was close at hand and gave it to his master.

"Half-past eight. Are they up?"

"No, sir, except Vladímir Ivánich" (the son) "who has gone to school. Praskóvya Fëdorovna ordered me to wake her if you asked for her. Shall I do so?"

"No, there's no need to." "Perhaps I'd better have some tea," he thought, and added aloud: "Yes, bring me some tea."

Peter went to the door but Iván Ilých dreaded being left alone. "How can I keep him here? Oh yes, my medicine." "Peter, give me my medicine." "Why not? Perhaps it may still do me some good." He took a spoonful and swallowed it. "No, it won't help. It's all tomfoolery, all deception," he decided as soon as he became aware of the familiar, sickly, hopeless taste. "No, I can't believe in it any longer. But the pain, why this pain? If it would only cease just for a moment!" And he moaned. Peter turned towards him. "It's all right. Go and fetch me some tea."

Peter went out. Left alone Iván Ilých groaned not so much with pain, terrible though that was, as from mental anguish. Always and for ever the same, always these endless days and nights. If only it would come quicker! If only *what* would come quicker? Death, darkness? . . . No, no! Anything rather than death!

When Peter returned with the tea on a tray, Iván Ilých stared at him for a time in perplexity, not realizing who and what he was. Peter was disconcerted by that look and his embarrassment brought Iván Ilých to himself.

"Oh, tea! All right, put it down. Only help me to wash and put on a clean shirt."

And Iván Ilých began to wash. With pauses for rest, he washed his hands and then his face, cleaned his teeth, brushed his hair, and looked in the glass. He was terrified by what he saw, especially by the limp way in which his hair clung to his pallid forehead.

While his shirt was being changed he knew that he would be still more frightened at the sight of his body, so he avoided looking at it. Finally he was ready. He drew on a dressing-gown, wrapped himself in a plaid, and sat down in the armchair to take his tea. For a moment he felt refreshed, but as soon as he began to drink the tea he was again aware of the same taste, and the pain also returned. He finished it with an effort, and then lay down stretching out his legs, and dismissed Peter.

Always the same. Now a spark of hope flashes up, then a sea of despair rages, and always pain; always pain, always despair, and always the same. When alone he had a dreadful and distressing desire to call someone, but he knew beforehand that with others present it would be still worse. "Another dose of morphine—to lose consciousness. I will tell him, the doctor, that he must think of something else. It's impossible, impossible, to go on like this."

An hour and another pass like that. But now there is a ring at the door bell. Perhaps it's the doctor? It is. He comes in fresh, hearty, plump, and cheerful, with that look on his face that seems to say: "There now, you're in a panic about something, but we'll arrange it all for you directly!" The doctor knows this expression is out of place here, but he has put it on once for all and can't take it off—like a man who has put on a frock-coat in the morning to pay a round of calls.

The doctor rubs his hands vigorously and reassuringly.

"Brr! How cold it is! There's such a sharp frost; just let me warm myself!" he says, as if it were only a matter of waiting till he was warm, and then he would put everything right.

"Well now, how are you?"

Iván Ilých feels that the doctor would like to say: "Well, how are our affairs?" but that even he feels that this would not do, and says instead: "What sort of a night have you had?"

Iván Ilých looks at him as much as to say: "Are you really never ashamed of lying?" But the doctor does not wish to understand this question, and Iván Ilých says: "Just as terrible as ever. The pain never leaves me and never subsides. If only something . . ."

"Yes, you sick people are always like that. . . . There, now I think I am warm enough. Even Praskóvya Fëdorovna, who is so particular, could find no fault with my temperature. Well, now I can say good-morning," and the doctor presses his patient's hand.

Then, dropping his former playfulness, he begins with a most serious face to examine the patient, feeling his pulse and taking his temperature, and then begins the sounding and auscultation.

Iván Ilých knows quite well and definitely that all this is nonsense and pure deception, but when the doctor, getting down on his knee, leans over him, putting his ear first higher then lower, and performs various gymnastic movements over him with a significant expression on his face, Iván Ilých submits to it all as he used to submit to the speeches of the lawyers, though he knew very well that they were all lying and why they were lying.

The doctor, kneeling on the sofa, is still sounding him when Praskóvya Fëdorovna's silk dress rustles at the door and she is heard scolding Peter for not having let her know of the doctor's arrival.

She comes in, kisses her husband, and at once proceeds to prove that she has been up a long time already, and only owing to a misunderstanding failed to be there when the doctor arrived.

Iván Ilých looks at her, scans her all over, sets against her the whiteness and plumpness and cleanness of her hands and neck, the gloss of her hair, and the sparkle of her vivacious eyes. He hates her with his whole soul. And the thrill of hatred he feels for her makes him suffer from her touch.

Her attitude towards him and his disease is still the same. Just as the doctor had adopted a certain relation to his patient which he could not abandon, so had she formed one towards him—that he was not doing something he ought to do and was himself to blame, and that she reproached him lovingly for this— and she could not now change that attitude.

"You see he doesn't listen to me and doesn't take his medicine at the proper time. And above all he lies in a position that is no doubt bad for him—with his legs up."

She described how he made Gerásim hold his legs up.

The doctor smiled with a contemptuous affability that said: "What's to be done? These sick people do have foolish fancies of that kind, but we must forgive them."

When the examination was over the doctor looked at his watch, and then Praskóvya Fëdorovna announced to Iván Ilých that it was of course as he pleased, but she had sent to-day for a celebrated specialist who would examine him and have a consultation with Michael Danílovich (their regular doctor).

"Please don't raise any objections. I am doing this for my own sake," she said ironically, letting it be felt that she was doing it all for his sake and only said this to leave him no right to refuse. He remained silent, knitting his brows. He felt that he was so surrounded and involved in a mesh of falsity that it was hard to unravel anything.

Everything she did for him was entirely for her own sake, and she told him she was doing for herself what she actually was doing for herself, as if that was so incredible that he must understand the opposite.

At half-past eleven the celebrated specialist arrived. Again the sounding began and the significant conversations in his presence and in another room, about the kidneys and the appendix, and the questions and answers, with such an air of importance that again, instead of the real question of life and death which now alone confronted him, the question arose of the kidney and appendix which were not behaving as they ought to and would now be attacked by Michael Danílovich and the specialist and forced to amend their ways.

The celebrated specialist took leave of him with a serious though not hopeless look, and in reply to the timid question Iván Ilých, with eyes glistening with fear and hope, put to him as to whether there was a chance of recovery, said that he could not vouch for it but there was a possibility. The look of hope with which Iván Ilých watched the doctor out was so pathetic that Praskóvya Fëdorovna, seeing it, even wept as she left the room to hand the doctor his fee.

The gleam of hope kindled by the doctor's encouragement did not last long. The same room, the same pictures, curtains, wall-paper, medicine bottles, were all there, and the same aching suffering body, and Iván Ilých began to moan. They gave him a subcutaneous injection and he sank into oblivion.

It was twilight when he came to. They brought him his dinner and he swallowed some beef tea with difficulty, and then everything was the same again and night was coming on.

After dinner, at seven o'clock, Praskóvya Fëdorovna came into the room in evening dress, her full bosom pushed up by her corset, and with traces of powder on her face. She had reminded him in the morning that they were going to the theater. Sarah Bernhardt was visiting the town and they had a box, which he had insisted on their taking. Now he had forgotten about it and her toilet offended him, but he concealed his vexation when he remembered that he had himself insisted on their securing a box and going because it would be an instructive and aesthetic pleasure for the children.

Praskóvya Fëdorovna came in, self-satisfied but yet with a rather guilty air. She sat down and asked how he was, but, as he saw, only for the sake of asking and not in order to learn about it, knowing that there was nothing to learn—and then went on to what she really wanted to say: that she would not on any account have gone but that the box had been taken and Helen and their daughter were going, as well as Petríshchev (the examining magistrate, their daughter's fiancé) and that it was out of the question to let them go alone; but that she would have much preferred to sit with him for a while; and he must be sure to follow the doctor's orders while she was away.

"Oh, and Fëdor Petróvich" (the fiancé) "would like to come in. May he? And Lisa?"

"All right."

Their daughter came in in full evening dress, her fresh young flesh exposed (making a show of that very flesh which in his own case caused so much suffering), strong, healthy, evidently in love, and impatient with illness, suffering, and death, because they interfered with her happiness.

Fëdor Petróvich came in too, in evening dress, his hair curled *á la Capoul*, a tight stiff collar round his long sinewy neck, an enormous white shirt-front and narrow black trousers tightly stretched over his strong thighs. He had one white glove tightly drawn on, and was holding his opera hat in his hand.

Following him the schoolboy crept in unnoticed, in a new uniform, poor little fellow, and wearing gloves. Terribly dark shadows showed under his eyes, the meaning of which Iván Ilých knew well.

His son had always seemed pathetic to him, and now it was dreadful to see the boy's frightened look of pity. It seemed to Iván Ilých that Vásya was the only one besides Gerásim who understood and pitied him.

They all sat down and again asked how he was. A silence followed. Lisa asked her mother about the opera-glasses, and there was an altercation between mother and daughter as to who had taken them and where they had been put. This occasioned some unpleasantness.

Fëdor Petróvich inquired of Iván Ilých whether he had ever seen Sarah Bernhardt. Iván Ilých did not at first catch the question, but then replied: "No, have you seen her before?"

"Yes, in *Adrienne Lecouvreur*."[10]

Praskóvya Fëdorovna mentioned some roles in which Sarah Bernhardt was

---

[10] A play by the French dramatist Eugène Scribe (1791–1861).

particularly good. Her daughter disagreed. Conversation sprang up as to the elegance and realism of her acting—the sort of conversation that is always repeated and is always the same.

In the midst of the conversation Fëdor Petróvich glanced at Iván Ilých and became silent. The others also looked at him and grew silent. Iván Ilých was staring with glittering eyes straight before him, evidently indignant with them. This had to be rectified, but it was impossible to do so. The silence had to be broken, but for a time no one dared to break it and they all became afraid that the conventional deception would suddenly become obvious and the truth become plain to all. Lisa was the first to pluck up courage and break that silence, but by trying to hide what everybody was feeling, she betrayed it.

"Well, if we are going it's time to start," she said, looking at her watch, a present from her father, and with a faint and significant smile at Fëdor Petróvich relating to something known only to them. She got up with a rustle of her dress.

They all rose, said good-night, and went away.

When they had gone it seemed to Iván Ilých that he felt better; the falsity had gone with them. But the pain remained—that same pain and that same fear that made everything monotonously alike, nothing harder and nothing easier. Everything was worse.

Again minute followed minute and hour followed hour. Everything remained the same and there was no cessation. And the inevitable end of it all became more and more terrible.

"Yes, send Gerásim here," he replied to a question Peter asked.

CHAPTER IX

His wife returned late at night. She came in on tiptoe, but he heard her, opened his eyes, and made haste to close them again. She wished to send Gerásim away and to sit with him herself, but he opened his eyes and said: "No, go away."

"Are you in great pain?"

"Always the same."

"Take some opium."

He agreed and took some. She went away.

Till about three in the morning he was in a state of stupefied misery. It seemed to him that he and his pain were being thrust into a narrow, deep black sack, but though they were pushed further and further in they could not be pushed to the bottom. And this, terrible enough in itself, was accompanied by suffering. He was frightened yet wanted to fall through the sack, he struggled but yet co-operated. And suddenly he broke through, fell, and regained consciousness. Gerásim was sitting at the foot of the bed dozing quietly and patiently, while he himself lay with his emaciated stockinged legs resting on Gerásim's shoulders; the same shaded candle was there and the same unceasing pain.

"Go away, Gerásim," he whispered.

"It's all right, sir. I'll stay a while."

"No. Go away."

He removed his legs from Gerásim's shoulders, turned sideways onto his arm, and felt sorry for himself. He only waited till Gerásim had gone into the next room and then restrained himself no longer but wept like a child. He wept on account of his helplessness, his terrible loneliness, the cruelty of man, the cruelty of God, and the absence of God.

"Why hast Thou done all this? Why hast Thou brought me here? Why, why dost Thou torment me so terribly?"

He did not expect an answer and yet wept because there was no answer and could be none. The pain again grew more acute, but he did not stir and did not call. He said to himself: "Go on! Strike me! But what is it for? What have I done to Thee? What is it for?"

Then he grew quiet and not only ceased weeping but even held his breath and became all attention. It was as though he were listening not to an audible voice but to the voice of his soul, to the current of thoughts arising within him.

"What is it you want?" was the first clear conception capable of expression in words, that he heard.

"What do you want? What do you want?" he repeated to himself.

"What do I want? To live and not to suffer," he answered.

And again he listened with such concentrated attention that even his pain did not distract him.

"To live? How?" asked his inner voice.

"Why, to live as I used to—well and pleasantly."

"As you lived before, well and pleasantly?" the voice repeated.

And in imagination he began to recall the best moments of his pleasant life. But strange to say none of those best moments of his pleasant life now seemed at all what they had then seemed—none of them except the first recollections of childhood. There, in childhood, there had been something really pleasant with which it would be possible to live if it could return. But the child who had experienced that happiness existed no longer, it was like a reminiscence of somebody else.

As soon as the period began which had produced the present Iván Ilých, all that had then seemed joys now melted before his sight and turned into something trivial and often nasty.

And the further he departed from childhood and the nearer he came to the present the more worthless and doubtful were the joys. This began with the School of Law. A little that was really good was still found there—there was light-heartedness, friendship, and hope. But in the upper classes there had already been fewer of such good moments. Then during the first years of his official career, when he was in the service of the Governor, some pleasant moments again occurred: they were the memories of love for a woman. Then all became confused and there was still less of what was good; later on again there was still less that was good, and the further he went the less there was. His marriage, a mere accident, then the disenchantment that followed it, his wife's bad breath and the sensuality and hypocrisy: then that deadly official life and those preoccupations about money, a year of it, and two, and ten, and twenty, and always the same thing. And the longer it lasted the more deadly it became. "It is as if I had been going downhill while I imagined I was going up. And that is really what it was. I was going up in public opinion, but to the same extent life was ebbing away from me. And now it is all done and there is only death."

"Then what does it mean? Why? It can't be that life is so senseless and horrible. But if it really has been so horrible and senseless, why must I die and die in agony? There is something wrong!"

"Maybe I did not live as I ought to have done," it suddenly occurred to him. "But how could that be, when I did everything properly?" he replied, and immediately dismissed from his mind this, the sole solution of all the riddles of life and death, as something quite impossible.

"Then what do you want now? To live? Live how? Live as you lived in the law courts when the usher proclaimed 'The judge is coming!'" "The judge is coming, the judge!" he repeated to himself. "Here he is, the judge. But I am not guilty!" he exclaimed angrily. "What is it for?" And he ceased crying, but turning his face to the wall continued to ponder on the same question: Why, and for what purpose, is there all this horror? But however much he pondered he found no answer. And whenever the thought occurred to him, as it often did, that it all resulted from his not having lived as he ought to have done, he at once recalled the correctness of his whole life and dismissed so strange an idea.

CHAPTER X

Another fortnight passed. Iván Ilých now no longer left his sofa. He would not lie in bed but lay on the sofa, facing the wall nearly all the time. He suffered ever the same unceasing agonies and in his loneliness pondered always on the same insoluble question: "What is this? Can it be that it is Death?" And the inner voice answered: "Yes, it is Death."

"Why these sufferings?" And the voice answered, "For no reason—they just are so." Beyond and besides this there was nothing.

From the very beginning of his illness, ever since he had first been to see the doctor, Iván Ilých's life had been divided between two contrary and alternating moods: now it was despair and the expectation of this uncomprehended and terrible death, and now hope and an intently interested observation of the functioning of his organs. Now before his eyes there was only a kidney or an intestine that temporarily evaded its duty, and now only that incomprehensible and dreadful death from which it was impossible to escape.

These two states of mind had alternated from the very beginning of his illness, but the further it progressed the more doubtful and fantastic became the conception of the kidney, and the more real the sense of impending death.

He had but to call to mind what he had been three months before and what he was now, to call to mind with what regularity he had been going downhill, for every possibility of hope to be shattered.

Latterly during that loneliness in which he found himself as he lay facing the back of the sofa, a loneliness in the midst of a populous town and surrounded by numerous acquaintances and relations but that yet could not have been more complete anywhere—either at the bottom of the sea or under the earth—during that terrible loneliness Iván Ilých had lived only in memories of the past. Pictures of his past rose before him one after another. They always began with what was nearest in time and then went back to what was most remote—to his childhood—and rested there. If he thought of the stewed prunes that had been offered him that day, his mind went back to the raw shrivelled French plums of his childhood, their peculiar flavor and the flow of saliva when he sucked their stones, and along with the memory of that taste came a whole series of memories of those days: his nurse, his brother, and their toys. "No, I mustn't think of that. . . . It is too painful," Iván Ilých said to himself, and brought himself back to the present—to the button on the back of the sofa and the creases in its morocco. "Morocco is expensive, but it does not wear well: There had been a quarrel about it. It was a different kind of quarrel and a different kind of morocco that time when we tore father's portfolio and were punished, and mamma brought us some tarts. . . ." And again his thoughts dwelt on his childhood, and again it was painful and he tried to banish them and fix his mind on something else.

Then again together with that chain of memories another series passed through his mind—of how his illness had progressed and grown worse. There also the further back he looked the more life there had been. There had been more of what was good in life and more of life itself. The two merged together. "Just as the pain went on getting worse and worse so my life grew worse and worse," he thought. "There is one bright spot there at the back, at the beginning of life, and afterwards all becomes blacker and blacker and proceeds more and more rapidly—in inverse ratio to the square of the distance from death," thought Iván Ilých. And the example of a stone falling downwards with increasing velocity entered his mind. Life, a series of increasing sufferings, flies, further and further towards its end—the most terrible suffering. "I am flying. . . ." He shuddered, shifted himself, and tried to resist, but was already aware that resistance was impossible, and again with eyes weary of gazing but unable to cease seeing what was before them, he stared at the back of the sofa and waited—awaiting that dreadful fall and shock and destruction.

"Resistance is impossible!" he said to himself. "If I could only understand what it is all for! But that too is impossible. An explanation would be possible if it could be said that I have not lived as I ought to. But it is impossible to say that," and he remembered all the legality, correctitude, and propriety of his life. "That at any rate can certainly not be admitted," he thought, and his lips smiled ironically as if someone could see that smile and be taken in by it. "There is no explanation! Agony, death. . . . What for?"

CHAPTER XI

Another two weeks went by in this way and during that fortnight an event occurred that Iván Ilých and his wife had desired. Petríshchev formally proposed. It happened in the evening. The next day Praskóvya Fëdorovna came into her husband's room considering how best to inform him of it, but that very night there had been a fresh change for the worse in his condition. She found him still lying on the sofa but in a different position. He lay on his back, groaning and staring fixedly straight in front of him.

She began to remind him of his medicines, but he turned his eyes towards her with such a look that she did not finish what she was saying; so great an animosity, to her in particular, did that look express.

"For Christ's sake, let me die in peace!" he said.

She would have gone away, but just then their daughter came in and went up to say good morning. He looked at her as he had done at his wife, and in reply to her inquiry about his health said dryly that he would soon free them all of himself. They were both silent and after sitting with him for a while went away.

"Is it our fault?" Lisa said to her mother. "It's as if we were to blame! I am sorry for papa, but why should we be tortured?"

The doctor came at his usual time. Iván Ilých answered "Yes" and "No," never taking his angry eyes from him, and at last said: "You know you can do nothing for me, so leave me alone."

"We can ease your sufferings."

"You can't even do that. Let me be."

The doctor went into the drawing-room and told Praskóvya Fëdorovna that the case was very serious and that the only resource left was opium to allay her husband's sufferings, which must be terrible.

It was true, as the doctor said, that Iván Ilých's physical sufferings were terrible, but worse than the physical sufferings were his mental sufferings which were his chief torture.

His mental sufferings were due to the fact that that night, as he looked at Gerásim's sleepy, good-natured face with its prominent cheek-bones, the question suddenly occurred to him: "What if my whole life has really been wrong?"

It occurred to him that what had appeared perfectly impossible before, namely that he had not spent his life as he should have done, might after all be true. It occurred to him that his scarcely perceptible attempts to struggle against what was considered good by the most highly placed people, those scarcely noticeable impulses which he had immediately suppressed, might have been the real thing, and all the rest false. And his professional duties and the whole arrangement of his life and of his family, and all his social and official interests, might all have been false. He tried to defend all those things to himself and suddenly felt the weakness of what he was defending. There was nothing to defend.

"But if that is so," he said to himself, "and I am leaving this life with the consciousness that I have lost all that was given me and it is impossible to rectify it—what then?"

He lay on his back and began to pass his life in review in quite a new way. In the morning when he saw first his footman, then his wife, then his daughter, and then the doctor, their every word and movement confirmed to him the awful truth that had been revealed to him during the night. In them he saw himself—all that for which he had lived—and saw clearly that it was not real at all, but a terrible and huge deception which had hidden both life and death. This consciousness intensified his physical suffering tenfold. He groaned and tossed about, and pulled at his clothing which choked and stifled him. And he hated them on that account.

He was given a large dose of opium and became unconscious, but at noon his sufferings began again. He drove everybody away and tossed from side to side.

His wife came to him and said:

"Jean, my dear, do this for me. It can't do any harm and often helps. Healthy people often do it."

He opened his eyes wide.

"What? Take communion? Why? It's unnecessary! However. . . ."

She began to cry.

"Yes, do, my dear. I'll send for our priest. He is such a nice man."

"All right. Very well," he muttered.

When the priest came and heard his confession, Iván Ilých was softened and seemed to feel a relief from his doubts and consequently from his sufferings, and for a moment there came a ray of hope. He again began to think of the vermiform appendix and the possibility of correcting it. He received the sacrament with tears in his eyes.

When they laid him down again afterwards he felt a moment's ease, and the hope that he might live awoke in him again. He began to think of the operation that had been suggested to him. "To live! I want to live!" he said to himself.

His wife came in to congratulate him after his communion, and when uttering the usual conventional words she added:

"You feel better, don't you?"

Without looking at her he said "Yes."

Her dress, her figure, the expression of her face, the tone of her voice, all revealed the same thing. "This is wrong, it is not as it should be. All you have lived for and still live for is falsehood and deception, hiding life and death from you." And as soon as he admitted that thought, his hatred and his agonizing physical suffering again sprang up, and with that suffering a consciousness of the unavoidable, approaching end. And to this was added a new sensation of grinding shooting pain and a feeling of suffocation.

The expression of his face when he uttered that "yes" was dreadful. Having uttered it, he looked her straight in the eyes, turned on his face with a rapidity extraordinary in his weak state and shouted:

"Go away! Go away and leave me alone!"

CHAPTER XII

From that moment the screaming began that continued for three days, and was so terrible that one could not hear it through two closed doors without horror. At the moment he answered his wife he realized that he was lost, that there was no return, that the end had come, the very end, and his doubts were still unsolved and remained doubts.

"Oh! Oh! Oh!" he cried in various intonations. He had begun by screaming "I won't!" and continued screaming on the letter "o."

For three whole days, during which time did not exist for him, he struggled in that black sack into which he was being thrust by an invisible, resistless force. He struggled as a man condemned to death struggles in the hands of the executioner, knowing that he cannot save himself. And every moment he felt that despite all his efforts he was drawing nearer and nearer to what terrified him. He felt that his agony was due to his being thrust into that black hole and still more to his not being able to get right into it. He was hindered from getting into it by his conviction that his life had been a good one. That very justification of his life held him fast and prevented his moving forward, and it caused him most torment of all.

Suddenly some force struck him in the chest and side, making it still harder to breathe, and he fell through the hole and there at the bottom was a light. What had happened to him was like the sensation one sometimes experiences in a railway carriage when one thinks one is going backwards while one is really going forwards and suddenly becomes aware of the real direction.

"Yes, it was all not the right thing," he said to himself, "but that's no matter. It can be done. But what *is* the right thing?" he asked himself, and suddenly grew quiet.

This occurred at the end of the third day, two hours before his death. Just then his schoolboy son had crept softly in and gone up to the bedside. The dying man was still screaming desperately and waving his arms. His hand fell on the boy's head, and the boy caught it, pressed it to his lips, and began to cry.

At that very moment Iván Ilých fell through and caught sight of the light, and it was revealed to him that though his life had not been what it should have been, this could still be rectified. He asked himself, "What *is* the right thing?" and grew still, listening. Then he felt that someone was kissing his hand. He opened his eyes, looked at his son, and felt sorry for him. His wife came up to him and he glanced at her. She was gazing at him open-mouthed, with undried tears on her nose and cheek and a despairing look on her face. He felt sorry for her too.

"Yes, I am making them wretched," he thought. "They are sorry, but it will be better for them when I die." He wished to say this but had not the strength to utter it. "Besides, why speak? I must act," he thought. With a look at his wife he indicated his son and said: "Take him away . . . sorry for him . . . sorry for you too. . . ." He tried to add, "forgive me," but said "forego" and waved his hand, knowing that He whose understanding mattered would understand.

And suddenly it grew clear to him that what had been oppressing him and would not leave him was all dropping away at once from two sides, from ten sides, and from all sides. He was sorry for them, he must act so as not to hurt them: release them and free himself from these sufferings. "How good and how simple!" he thought. "And the pain?" he asked himself. "What has become of it? Where are you, pain?"

He turned his attention to it.

"Yes, here it is. Well, what of it? Let the pain be."

"And death . . . where is it?"

He sought his former accustomed fear of death and did not find it. "Where is it? What death?" There was no fear because there was no death.

In place of death there was light.

"So that's what it is!" he suddenly exclaimed aloud. "What joy!"

To him all this happened in a single instant, and the meaning of that instant did not change. For those present his agony continued for another two hours. Something rattled in his throat, his emaciated body twitched, then the gasping and rattle became less and less frequent.

"It is finished!" said someone near him.

He heard these words and repeated them in his soul.

"Death is finished," he said to himself. "It is no more!"

He drew in a breath, stopped in the midst of a sigh, stretched out, and died.

QUESTIONS

1. Why does Tolstoy begin the story immediately after Ilých's death and then move back to recount his life?   **2.** Is there any evidence that Ilých's death is a moral judgment—that is, a punishment for his life? Explain.   **3.** Why is Gerásim, Ilých's peasant servant, most sympathetic to his plight?

WRITING TOPIC

At the very end, Ilých achieves peace and understanding, and the questions that have been torturing him are resolved. He realizes that "though his life had not been what it should have been, this could still be rectified." What does this mean?

Odour of Chrysanthemums   1911

D. H. LAWRENCE   [1885–1930]

I

The small locomotive engine, Number 4, came clanking, stumbling down from Selston with seven full wagons. It appeared round the corner with loud threats of speed, but the colt that it startled from among the gorse, which still flickered indistinctly in the raw afternoon, out-distanced it at a canter. A woman, walking up the railway line to Underwood, drew back into the hedge, held her basket aside, and watched the footplate of the engine advancing. The trucks thumped heavily past, one by one, with slow inevitable movement, as she stood insignificantly trapped between the jolting black wagons and the hedge; then they curved away towards the coppice where the withered oak leaves dropped noiselessly, while the birds, pulling at the scarlet hips beside the track, made off into the dusk that had already crept into the spinney. In the open, the smoke from the engine sank and cleaved to the rough grass. The fields were dreary and forsaken, and in the marshy strip that led to the whimsey, a reedy pit-pond, the fowls had already abandoned their run among the alders, to roost in the tarred fowl-house. The pit-bank loomed up beyond the pond, flames like red sores licking its ashy sides, in the afternoon's stagnant light. Just beyond rose the tapering chimneys and the clumsy black headstocks of Brinsley Colliery. The two wheels were spinning fast up against the sky, and the winding engine rapped out its little spasms. The miners were being turned up.

The engine whistled as it came into the wide bay of railway lines beside the colliery, where rows of trucks stood in harbour.

Miners, single, trailing and in groups, passed like shadows diverging home. At the edge of the ribbed level of sidings squat a low cottage, three steps down from the cinder track. A large bony vine clutched at the house, as if to claw down the tiled roof. Round the bricked yard grew a few wintry primroses. Beyond, the long garden sloped down to a bush-covered brook course. There were some twiggy apple trees, winter-crack trees, and ragged cabbages. Beside the path hung dishevelled pink chrysanthemums, like pink cloths hung on bushes. A woman came stooping out of the felt-covered fowl-house, half-way down the garden. She closed and padlocked the door, then drew herself erect, having brushed some bits from her white apron.

She was a tall woman of imperious mien, handsome, with definite black eyebrows. Her smooth black hair was parted exactly. For a few moments she stood steadily watching the miners as they passed along the railway: then she turned towards the brook course. Her face was calm and set, her mouth was closed with disillusionment. After a moment she called:

"John!" There was no answer. She waited, and then said distinctly:

"Where are you?"

"Here!" replied a child's sulky voice from among the bushes. The woman looked piercingly through the dusk.

"Are you at that brook?" she asked sternly.

For answer the child showed himself before the raspberry-canes that rose like whips. He was a small, sturdy boy of five. He stood quite still, defiantly.

"Oh!" said the mother, conciliated. "I thought you were down at that wet brook—and you remember what I told you ———"

The boy did not move or answer.

"Come, come on in," she said more gently, "it's getting dark. There's your grandfather's engine coming down the line!"

The lad advanced slowly, with resentful, taciturn movement. He was dressed in trousers and waistcoat of cloth that was too thick and hard for the size of the garments. They were evidently cut down from a man's clothes.

As they went slowly towards the house he tore at the ragged wisps of chrysanthemums and dropped the petals in handfuls along the path.

"Don't do that—it does look nasty," said his mother. He refrained, and she, suddenly pitiful, broke off a twig with three or four wan flowers and held them against her face. When mother and son reached the yard her hand hesitated, and instead of laying the flower aside, she pushed it in her apron-band. The mother and son stood at the foot of the three steps looking across the bay of lines at the passing home of the miners. The trundle of the small train was imminent. Suddenly the engine loomed past the house and came to a stop opposite the gate.

The engine-driver, a short man with round grey beard, leaned out of the cab high above the woman.

"Have you got a cup of tea?" he said in a cheery, hearty fashion.

It was her father. She went in, saying she would mash.[1] Directly, she returned.

"I didn't come to see you on Sunday," began the little grey-bearded man.

"I didn't expect you," said his daughter.

The engine-driver winced; then, reassuming his cheery, airy manner, he said:

"Oh, have you heard then? Well, and what do you think ———?"

"I think it is soon enough," she replied.

At her brief censure the little man made an impatient gesture, and said coaxingly, yet with dangerous coldness:

"Well, what's a man to do? It's no sort of life for a man of my years, to sit at my own hearth like a stranger. And if I'm going to marry again it may as well be soon as late—what does it matter to anybody?"

The woman did not reply, but turned and went into the house. The man in

---

[1] Make tea.

the engine-cab stood assertive, till she returned with a cup of tea and a piece of bread and butter on a plate. She went up the steps and stood near the footplate of the hissing engine.

"You needn't 'a' brought me bread an' butter," said her father. "But a cup of tea"—he sipped appreciatively—"it's very nice." He sipped for a moment or two, then: "I hear as Walter's got another bout on," he said.

"When hasn't he?" said the woman bitterly.

"I heerd tell of him in the 'Lord Nelson' braggin' as he was going to spend that b—— afore he went: half a sovereign[2] that was."

"When?" asked the woman.

"A' Sat'day night—I know that's true."

"Very likely," she laughed bitterly. "He gives me twenty-three shillings."

"Aye, it's a nice thing, when a man can do nothing with his money but make a beast of himself!" said the grey-whiskered man. The woman turned her head away. Her father swallowed the last of his tea and handed her the cup.

"Aye," he sighed, wiping his mouth. "It's a settler,[3] it is ——"

He put his hand on the lever. The little engine strained and groaned, and the train rumbled towards the crossing. The woman again looked across the metals. Darkness was settling over the spaces of the railway and trucks: the miners, in grey sombre groups, were still passing home. The winding engine pulsed hurriedly, with brief pauses. Elizabeth Bates looked at the dreary flow of men, then she went indoors. Her husband did not come.

The kitchen was small and full of firelight; red coals piled glowing up the chimney mouth. All the life of the room seemed in the white, warm hearth and the steel fender reflecting the red fire. The cloth was laid for tea; cups glinted in the shadows. At the back, where the lowest stairs protruded into the room, the boy sat struggling with a knife and a piece of white wood. He was almost hidden in the shadow. It was half-past four. They had but to await the father's coming to begin tea. As the mother watched her son's sullen little struggle with the wood, she saw herself in his silence and pertinacity; she saw the father in her child's indifference to all but himself. She seemed to be occupied by her husband. He had probably gone past his home, slunk past his own door, to drink before he came in, while his dinner spoiled and wasted in waiting. She glanced at the clock, then took the potatoes to strain them in the yard. The garden and fields beyond the brook were closed in uncertain darkness. When she rose with the saucepan, leaving the drain steaming into the night behind her, she saw the yellow lamps were lit along the high road that went up the hill away beyond the space of the railway lines and the field.

Then again she watched the men trooping home, fewer now and fewer.

Indoors the fire was sinking and the room was dark red. The woman put her saucepan on the hob, and set a batter-pudding near the mouth of the oven.

---

[2] Ten shillings. A relatively large portion of a miner's weekly wage in 1911.
[3] The final blow.

Then she stood unmoving. Directly, gratefully, came quick young steps to the door. Someone hung on the latch a moment, then a little girl entered and began pulling off her outdoor things, dragging a mass of curls, just ripening from gold to brown, over her eyes with her hat.

Her mother chid her for coming late from school, and said she would have to keep her at home the dark winter days.

"Why, mother, it's hardly a bit dark yet. The lamp's not lighted, and my father's not home."

"No, he isn't. But it's a quarter to five! Did you see anything of him?"

The child became serious. She looked at her mother with large, wistful blue eyes.

"No, mother, I've never seen him. Why? Has he come up an' gone past, to Old Brinsley? He hasn't, mother, 'cos I never saw him."

"He'd watch that," said the mother bitterly, "he'd take care as you didn't see him. But you may depend upon it, he's seated in the 'Prince o' Wales.' He wouldn't be this late."

The girl looked at her mother piteously.

"Let's have our teas, mother, should we?" said she.

The mother called John to table. She opened the door once more and looked out across the darkness of the lines. All was deserted: she could not hear the winding-engines.

"Perhaps," she said to herself, "he's stopped to get some ripping[4] done."

They sat down to tea. John, at the end of the table near the door, was almost lost in the darkness. Their faces were hidden from each other. The girl crouched against the fender slowly moving a thick piece of bread before the fire. The lad, his face a dusky mark on the shadow, sat watching her who was transfigured in the red glow.

"I do think it's beautiful to look in the fire," said the child.

"Do you?" said her mother. "Why?"

"It's so red, and full of little caves—and it feels so nice, and you can fair smell it."

"It'll want mending directly," replied her mother, "and then if your father comes he'll carry on and say there never is a fire when a man comes home sweating from the pit. A public house is always warm enough."

There was silence till the boy said complainingly: "Make haste, our Annie."

"Well, I am doing! I can't make the fire do it no faster, can I?"

"She keeps wafflin' it about so's to make 'er slow," grumbled the boy.

"Don't have such an evil imagination, child," replied the mother.

Soon the room was busy in the darkness with the crisp sound of crunching. The mother ate very little. She drank her tea determinedly, and sat thinking. When she rose her anger was evident in the stern unbending of her head. She looked at the pudding in the fender and broke out:

---

[4] A mining term: cutting away coal or stone.

"It is a scandalous thing as a man can't even come home to his dinner! If it's crozzled up to a cinder I don't see why I should care. Past his very door he goes to get to a public-house, and here I sit with his dinner waiting for him ———"

She went out. As she dropped piece after piece of coal on the red fire, the shadows fell on the walls, till the room was almost in total darkness.

"I canna see," grumbled the invisible John. In spite of herself, the mother laughed.

"You know the way to your mouth," she said. She set the dustpan outside the door. When she came again like a shadow on the hearth, the lad repeated, complaining sulkily:

"I canna see."

"Good gracious!" cried the mother irritably, "you're as bad as your father if it's a bit dusk!"

Nevertheless, she took a paper spill from a sheaf on the mantelpiece and proceeded to light the lamp that hung from the ceiling in the middle of the room. As she reached up, her figure displayed itself just rounding with maternity.

"Oh, mother ——— !" exclaimed the girl.

"What?" said the woman, suspended in the act of putting the lamp-glass over the flame. The copper reflector shone handsomely on her, as she stood with uplifted arm, turning to face her daughter.

"You've got a flower in your apron!" said the child, in a little rapture at this unusual event.

"Goodness me!" exclaimed the woman, relieved. "One would think the house was afire." She replaced the glass and waited a moment before turning up the wick. A pale shadow was seen floating vaguely on the floor.

"Let me smell!" said the child, still rapturously, coming forward and putting her face to her mother's waist.

"Go along, silly!" said the mother, turning up the lamp. The light revealed their suspense so that the woman felt it almost unbearable. Annie was still bending at her waist. Irritably, the mother took the flowers out from her apron-band.

"Oh, mother—don't take them out!" Annie cried, catching her hand and trying to replace the sprig.

"Such nonsense!" said the mother, turning away. The child put the pale chrysanthemums to her lips, murmuring:

"Don't they smell beautiful!"

Her mother gave a short laugh.

"No," she said, "not to me. It was chrysanthemums when I married him, and chrysanthemums when you were born, and the first time they ever brought him home drunk, he'd got brown chrysanthemums in his buttonhole."

She looked at the children. Their eyes and their parted lips were wondering. The mother sat rocking in silence for some time. Then she looked at the clock.

"Twenty minutes to six!" In a tone of fine bitter carelessness she continued:

"Eh, he'll not come now till they bring him. There he'll stick! But he needn't come rolling in here in his pit-dirt, for *I* won't wash him. He can lie on the floor ——— Eh, what a fool I've been, what a fool! And this is what I came here for, to this dirty hole, rats and all, for him to slink past his very door. Twice last week—he's begun now ———"

She silenced herself, and rose to clear the table.

While for an hour or more the children played, subduedly intent, fertile of imagination, united in fear of the mother's wrath, and in dread of their father's home-coming, Mrs. Bates sat in her rocking-chair making a "singlet" of thick cream-coloured flannel, which gave a dull wounded sound as she tore off the grey edge. She worked at her sewing with energy, listening to the children, and her anger wearied itself, lay down to rest, opening its eyes from time to time and steadily watching, its ears raised to listen. Sometimes even her anger quailed and shrank, and the mother suspended her sewing, tracing the footsteps that thudded along the sleepers outside; she would lift her head sharply to bid the children "hush," but she recovered herself in time, and the footsteps went past the gate, and the children were not flung out of their play-world.

But at last Annie sighed, and gave in. She glanced at her wagon of slippers, and loathed the game. She turned plaintively to her mother.

"Mother!"—but she was inarticulate.

John crept out like a frog from under the sofa. His mother glanced up.

"Yes," she said, "just look at those shirt-sleeves!"

The boy held them out to survey them, saying nothing. Then somebody called in a hoarse voice away down the line, and suspense bristled in the room, till two people had gone by outside, talking.

"It is time for bed," said the mother.

"My father hasn't come," wailed Annie plaintively. But her mother was primed with courage.

"Never mind. They'll bring him when he does come—like a log." She meant there would be no scene. "And he may sleep on the floor till he wakes himself. I know he'll not go to work tomorrow after this!"

The children had their hands and faces wiped with a flannel. They were very quiet. When they had put on their night-dresses, they said their prayers, the boy mumbling. The mother looked down at them, at the brown silken bush of intertwining curls in the nape of the girl's neck, at the little black head of the lad, and her heart burst with anger at their father, who caused all three such distress. The children hid their faces in her skirts for comfort.

When Mrs. Bates came down, the room was strangely empty, with a tension of expectancy. She took up her sewing and stitched for some time without raising her head. Meantime her anger was tinged with fear.

II

The clock struck eight and she rose suddenly, dropping her sewing on her chair. She went to the stair-foot door, opened it, listening. Then she went out, locking the door behind her.

Something scuffled in the yard, and she started, though she knew it was only the rats with which the place was over-run. The night was very dark. In the great bay of railway lines, bulked with trucks, there was no trace of light, only away back she could see a few yellow lamps at the pit-top, and the red smear of the burning pit-bank on the night. She hurried along the edge of the track, then, crossing the converging lines, came to the stile by the white gates, whence she emerged on the road. Then the fear which had led her shrank. People were walking up to New Brinsley; she saw the lights in the houses; twenty yards farther on were the broad windows of the "Prince of Wales," very warm and bright, and the loud voices of men could be heard distinctly. What a fool she had been to imagine that anything had happened to him! He was merely drinking over there at the "Prince of Wales." She faltered. She had never yet been to fetch him, and she never would go. So she continued her walk towards the long straggling line of houses, standing back on the highway. She entered a passage between the dwellings.

"Mr. Rigley?—Yes! Did you want him? No, he's not in at this minute."

The raw-boned woman leaned forward from her dark scullery and peered at the other, upon whom fell a dim light through the blind of the kitchen window.

"Is it Mrs. Bates?" she asked in a tone tinged with respect.

"Yes. I wondered if your Master was at home. Mine hasn't come yet."

"'Asn't 'e! Oh, Jack's been 'ome an' 'ad 'is dinner an' gone out. 'E's just gone for 'alf an hour afore bed-time. Did you call at the 'Prince of Wales'?"

"No ———"

"No, you didn't like ——— ! It's not very nice." The other woman was indulgent. There was an awkward pause. "Jack never said nothink about—about your Master," she said.

"No!—I expect he's stuck in there!"

Elizabeth Bates said this bitterly, and with recklessness. She knew that the woman across the yard was standing at her door listening, but she did not care. As she turned:

"Stop a minute! I'll just go an' ask Jack if 'e knows anythink," said Mrs. Rigley.

"Oh no—I wouldn't like to put ——— !"

"Yes, I will, if you'll just step inside an' see as th' childer doesn't come downstairs and set theirselves afire."

Elizabeth Bates, murmuring a remonstrance, stepped inside. The other woman apologised for the state of the room.

The kitchen needed apology. There were little frocks and trousers and childish undergarments on the squab and on the floor, and a litter of playthings everywhere. On the black American cloth[5] of the table were pieces of bread and cake, crusts, slops, and a teapot with cold tea.

"Eh, ours is just as bad," said Elizabeth Bates, looking at the woman, not at the house. Mrs. Rigley put a shawl over her head and hurried out, saying:

---

[5] Oilcloth.

"I shanna be a minute."

The other sat, noting with faint disapproval the general untidiness of the room. Then she fell to counting the shoes of various sizes scattered over the floor. There were twelve. She sighed and said to herself: "No wonder!"— glancing at the litter. There came the scratching of two pairs of feet on the yard, and the Rigleys entered. Elizabeth Bates rose. Rigley was a big man, with very large bones. His head looked particularly bony. Across his temple was a blue scar, caused by a wound got in the pit, a wound in which the coal-dust remained blue like tattooing.

"'Asna 'e come whoam yit?" asked the man, without any form of greeting, but with deference and sympathy. "I couldna say wheer he is—'e's non ower theer!"—he jerked his head to signify the "Prince of Wales."

"'E's 'appen gone up to th' 'Yew,'" said Mrs. Rigley.

There was another pause. Rigley had evidently something to get off his mind: "Ah left 'im finishin' a stint," he began. "Loose-all[6] 'ad bin gone about ten minutes when we com'n away, an' I shouted: 'Are ter comin', Walt?' an' 'e said: 'Go on, Ah shanna be but a'ef a minnit,' so we com'n ter th' bottom, me an' Bowers, thinkin' as 'e wor just behint, an' 'ud come up i' th' next ban-tle[7] ———"

He stood perplexed, as if answering a charge of deserting his mate. Elizabeth Bates, now again certain of disaster, hastened to reassure him:

"I expect 'e's gone up to th' 'Yew Tree,' as you say. It's not the first time. I've fretted myself into a fever before now. He'll come home when they carry him."

"Ay, isn't it too bad!" deplored the other woman.

"I'll just step up to Dick's an' see if 'e *is* there," offered the man, afraid of appearing alarmed, afraid of taking liberties.

"Oh, I wouldn't think of bothering you that far," said Elizabeth Bates, with emphasis, but he knew she was glad of his offer.

As they stumbled up the entry, Elizabeth Bates heard Rigley's wife run across the yard and open her neighbour's door. At this, suddenly all the blood in her body seemed to switch away from her heart.

"Mind!" warned Rigley. "Ah've said many a time as Ah'd fill up them ruts in this entry, sumb'dy 'll be breakin' their legs yit."

She recovered herself and walked quickly along with the miner.

"I don't like leaving the children in bed, and nobody in the house," she said.

"No, you dunna!" he replied courteously. They were soon at the gate of the cottage.

"Well, I shanna be many minnits. Dunna you be frettin' now, 'e'll be all right," said the butty.[8]

---

[6] Signal to quit work.
[7] Group.
[8] Workmate.

"Thank you very much, Mr. Rigley," she replied.

"You're welcome!" he stammered, moving away. "I shanna be many minnits."

The house was quiet. Elizabeth Bates took off her hat and shawl, and rolled back the rug. When she had finished, she sat down. It was a few minutes past nine. She was startled by the rapid chuff of the winding-engine at the pit, and the sharp whirr of the brakes on the rope as it descended. Again she felt the painful sweep of her blood, and she put her hand to her side, saying aloud: "Good gracious!—it's only the nine o'clock deputy going down," rebuking herself.

She sat still listening. Half an hour of this, and she was wearied out.

"What am I working myself up like this for?" she said pitiably to herself, "I s'll only be doing myself some damage."

She took out her sewing again.

At a quarter to ten there were footsteps. One person! She watched for the door to open. It was an elderly woman, in a black bonnet and a black woollen shawl—his mother. She was about sixty years old, pale, with blue eyes, and her face all wrinkled and lamentable. She shut the door and turned to her daughter-in-law peevishly.

"Eh, Lizzie, whatever shall we do, whatever shall we do!" she cried.

Elizabeth drew back a little, sharply.

"What is it, mother?" she said.

The elder woman seated herself on the sofa.

"I don't know, child, I can't tell you!"—she shook her head slowly. Elizabeth sat watching her, anxious and vexed.

"I don't know," replied the grandmother, sighing very deeply. "There's no end to my troubles, there isn't. The things I've gone through, I'm sure it's enough —— !" She wept without wiping her eyes, the tears running.

"But, mother," interrupted Elizabeth, "what do you mean? What is it?"

The grandmother slowly wiped her eyes. The fountains of her tears were stopped by Elizabeth's directness. She wiped her eyes slowly.

"Poor child! Eh, you poor thing!" she moaned. "I don't know what we're going to do, I don't—and you as you are—it's a thing, it is indeed!"

Elizabeth waited.

"Is he dead?" she asked, and at the words her heart swung violently, though she felt a slight flush of shame at the ultimate extravagance of the question. Her words sufficiently frightened the old lady, almost brought her to herself.

"Don't say so, Elizabeth! We'll hope it's not as bad as that; no, may the Lord spare us that, Elizabeth. Jack Rigley came just as I was sittin' down to a glass afore going to bed, an' 'e said: ''Appen you'll go down th' line, Mrs. Bates. Walt's had an accident. 'Appen you'll go an' sit wi' 'er till we can get him home.' I hadn't time to ask him a word afore he was gone. An' I put my bonnet on an' come straight down, Lizzie. I thought to myself: 'Eh, that poor blessed child, if anybody should come an' tell her of a sudden, there's no knowing' what'll 'appen to 'er.' You mustn't let it upset you, Lizzie—or you know what to expect. How long is it, six months—or is it five, Lizzie? Ay!"—the old woman shook her head—"time slips on, it slips on! Ay!"

Elizabeth's thoughts were busy elsewhere. If he was killed—would she be able to manage on the little pension and what she could earn?—she counted up rapidly. If he was hurt—they wouldn't take him to the hospital—how tiresome he would be to nurse!—but perhaps she'd be able to get him away from the drink and his hateful ways. She would—while he was ill. The tears offered to come to her eyes at the picture. But what sentimental luxury was this she was beginning? She turned to consider the children. At any rate she was absolutely necessary for them. They were her business.

"Ay!" repeated the old woman, "it seems but a week or two since he brought me his first wages. Ay—he was a good lad, Elizabeth, he was, in his way. I don't know why he got to be such a trouble, I don't. He was a happy lad at home, only full of spirits. But there's no mistake he's been a handful of trouble, he has! I hope the Lord'll spare him to mend his ways. I hope so, I hope so. You've had a sight o' trouble with him, Elizabeth, you have indeed. But he was a jolly enough lad wi' me, he was, I can assure you. I don't know how it is . . ."

The old woman continued to muse aloud, a monotonous irritating sound, while Elizabeth thought concentratedly, startled once, when she heard the winding-engine chuff quickly, and the brakes skirr with a shriek. Then she heard the engine more slowly, and the brakes made no sound. The old woman did not notice. Elizabeth waited in suspense. The mother-in-law talked, with lapses into silence.

"But he wasn't your son, Lizzie, an' it makes a difference. Whatever he was, I remember him when he was little, an' I learned to understand him and to make allowances. You've got to make allowances for them ———"

It was half-past ten, and the old woman was saying: "But it's trouble from beginning to end; you're never too old for trouble, never too old for that ———" when the gate banged back, and there were heavy feet on the steps.

"I'll go, Lizzie, let me go," cried the old woman, rising. But Elizabeth was at the door. It was a man in pit-clothes.

"They're bringin' 'im, Misses," he said. Elizabeth's heart halted a moment. Then it surged on again, almost suffocating her.

"Is he—is it bad?" she asked.

The man turned away, looking at the darkness:

"The doctor says 'e'd been dead hours. 'E saw 'im i' th' lamp-cabin."

The old woman, who stood just behind Elizabeth, dropped into a chair, and folded her hands, crying: "Oh, my boy, my boy!"

"Hush!" said Elizabeth, with a sharp twitch of a frown. "Be still, mother, don't waken th' children: I wouldn't have them down for anything!"

The old woman moaned softly, rocking herself. The man was drawing away. Elizabeth took a step forward.

"How was it?" she asked.

"Well, I couldn't say for sure," the man replied, very ill at ease. "'E wor finishin' a stint an' th' butties 'ad gone, an' a lot o' stuff come down atop 'n 'im."

"And crushed him?" cried the widow, with a shudder.

"No," said the man, "it fell at th' back of 'im. 'E wor under th' face, an' it niver touched 'im. It shut 'im in. It seems 'e wor smothered."

Elizabeth shrank back. She heard the old woman behind her cry:

"What?—what did 'e say it was?"

The man replied, more loudly: "'E wor smothered!"

Then the old woman wailed aloud, and this relieved Elizabeth.

"Oh, mother," she said, putting her hand on the old woman, "don't waken th' children, don't waken th' children."

She wept a little, unknowing, while the old mother rocked herself and moaned. Elizabeth remembered that they were bringing him home, and she must be ready. "They'll lay him in the parlour," she said to herself, standing a moment pale and perplexed.

Then she lighted a candle and went into the tiny room. The air was cold and damp, but she could not make a fire, there was no fireplace. She set down the candle and looked round. The candlelight glittered on the lustre-glasses, on the two vases that held some of the pink chrysanthemums, and on the dark mahogany. There was a cold, deathly smell of chrysanthemums in the room. Elizabeth stood looking at the flowers. She turned away, and calculated whether there would be room to lay him on the floor, between the couch and the chiffonier. She pushed the chairs aside. There would be room to lay him down and to step round him. Then she fetched the old red tablecloth, and another old cloth, spreading them down to save her bit of carpet. She shivered on leaving the parlour; so, from the dresser drawer she took a clean shirt and put it at the fire to air. All the time her mother-in-law was rocking herself in the chair and moaning.

"You'll have to move from there, mother," said Elizabeth. "They'll be bringing him in. Come in the rocker."

The old mother rose mechanically, and seated herself by the fire, continuing to lament. Elizabeth went into the pantry for another candle, and there, in the little pent-house under the naked tiles, she heard them coming. She stood still in the pantry doorway, listening. She heard them pass the end of the house, and come awkwardly down the three steps, a jumble of shuffling footsteps and muttering voices. The old woman was silent. The men were in the yard.

Then Elizabeth heard Matthews, the manager of the pit, say: "You go in first, Jim. Mind!"

The door came open, and the two women saw a collier backing into the room, holding one end of a stretcher, on which they could see the nailed pit-boots of the dead man. The two carriers halted, the man at the head stooping to the lintel of the door.

"Wheer will you have him?" asked the manager, a short, white-bearded man.

Elizabeth roused herself and came from the pantry carrying the unlighted candle.

"In the parlour," she said.

"In there, Jim!" pointed the manager, and the carriers backed round into the tiny room. The coat with which they had covered the body fell off as they awkwardly turned through the two doorways, and the women saw their man, naked to the waist, lying stripped for work. The old woman began to moan in a low voice of horror.

"Lay th' stretcher at th' side," snapped the manager, "an' put 'im on th' cloths. Mind now, mind! Look you now ———— !"

One of the men had knocked off a vase of chrysanthemums. He stared awkwardly, then they set down the stretcher. Elizabeth did not look at her husband. As soon as she could get in the room, she went and picked up the broken vase and the flowers.

"Wait a minute!" she said.

The three men waited in silence while she mopped up the water with a duster.

"Eh, what a job, what a job, to be sure!" the manager was saying, rubbing his brow with trouble and perplexity. "Never knew such a thing in my life, never! He'd no business to ha' been left. I never knew such a thing in my life! Fell over him clean as a whistle, an' shut him in. Not four foot of space, there wasn't—yet it scarce bruised him."

He looked down at the dead man, lying prone, half naked, all grimed with coal-dust.

"''Sphyxiated,' the doctor said. It *is* the most terrible job I've ever known. Seems as if it was done o' purpose. Clean over him, an' shut 'im in, like a mouse-trap"—he made a sharp, descending gesture with his hand.

The colliers standing by jerked aside their heads in hopeless comment.

The horror of the thing bristled upon them all.

Then they heard the girl's voice upstairs calling shrilly: "Mother, mother— who is it? Mother, who is it?"

Elizabeth hurried to the foot of the stairs and opened the door:

"Go to sleep!" she commanded sharply. "What are you shouting about? Go to sleep at once—there's nothing ———— "

Then she began to mount the stairs. They could hear her on the boards, and on the plaster floor of the little bedroom. They could hear her distinctly:

"What's the matter now?—what's the matter with you, silly thing?"—her voice was much agitated, with an unreal gentleness.

"I thought it was some men come," said the plaintive voice of the child. "Has he come?"

"Yes, they've brought him. There's nothing to make a fuss about. Go to sleep now, like a good child."

They could hear her voice in the bedroom, they waited whilst she covered the children under the bedclothes.

"Is he drunk?" asked the girl, timidly, faintly.

"No! No—he's not! He—he's asleep."

"Is he asleep downstairs?"

"Yes—and don't make a noise."

There was silence for a moment, then the men heard the frightened child again:

"What's that noise?"

"It's nothing, I tell you, what are you bothering for?"

The noise was the grandmother moaning. She was oblivious of everything, sitting on her chair rocking and moaning. The manager put his hand on her arm and bade her "Sh—sh!!"

The old woman opened her eyes and looked at him. She was shocked by this interruption, and seemed to wonder.

"What time is it?" the plaintive thin voice of the child, sinking back unhappily into sleep, asked this last question.

"Ten o'clock," answered the mother more softly. Then she must have bent down and kissed the children.

Matthews beckoned to the men to come away. They put on their caps and took up the stretcher. Stepping over the body, they tiptoed out of the house. None of them spoke till they were far from the wakeful children.

When Elizabeth came down she found her mother alone on the parlour floor, leaning over the dead man, the tears dropping on him.

"We must lay him out," the wife said. She put on the kettle, then returning knelt at the feet, and began to unfasten the knotted leather laces. The room was clammy and dim with only one candle, so that she had to bend her face almost to the floor. At last she got off the heavy boots and put them away.

"You must help me now," she whispered to the old woman. Together they stripped the man.

When they arose, saw him lying in the naïve dignity of death, the women stood arrested in fear and respect. For a few moments they remained still, looking down, the old mother whimpering. Elizabeth felt countermanded. She saw him, how utterly inviolable he lay in himself. She had nothing to do with him. She could not accept it. Stooping, she laid her hand on him, in claim. He was still warm, for the mine was hot where he had died. His mother had his face between her hands, and was murmuring incoherently. The old tears fell in succession as drops from wet leaves; the mother was not weeping, merely her tears flowed. Elizabeth embraced the body of her husband, with cheek and lips. She seemed to be listening, inquiring, trying to get some connection. But she could not. She was driven away. He was impregnable.

She rose, went into the kitchen, where she poured warm water into a bowl, brought soap and flannel and a soft towel.

"I must wash him," she said.

Then the old mother rose stiffly, and watched Elizabeth as she carefully washed his face, carefully brushing the big blond moustache from his mouth with the flannel. She was afraid with a bottomless fear, so she ministered to him. The old woman, jealous, said:

"Let me wipe him!"—and she kneeled on the other side drying slowly as Elizabeth washed, her big black bonnet sometimes brushing the dark head of her daughter-in-law. They worked thus in silence for a long time. They never forgot it was death, and the touch of the man's dead body gave them strange emotions, different in each of the women; a great dread possessed them both, the mother felt the lie was given to her womb, she was denied; the wife felt the utter isolation of the human soul, the child within her was a weight apart from her.

At last it was finished. He was a man of handsome body, and his face showed no traces of drink. He was blond, full-fleshed, with fine limbs. But he was dead.

"Bless him," whispered his mother, looking always at his face, and speaking out of sheer terror. "Dear lad—bless him!" She spoke in a faint, sibilant ecstasy of fear and mother love.

Elizabeth sank down again to the floor, and put her face against his neck, and trembled and shuddered. But she had to draw away again. He was dead, and her living flesh had no place against his. A great dread and weariness held her: she was so unavailing. Her life was gone like this.

"White as milk he is, clear as a twelve-month baby, bless him, the darling!" the old mother murmured to herself. "Not a mark on him, clear and clean and white, beautiful as ever a child was made," she murmured with pride. Elizabeth kept her face hidden.

"He went peaceful, Lizzie—peaceful as sleep. Isn't he beautiful, the lamb? Ay—he must ha' made his peace, Lizzie. 'Appen he made it all right, Lizzie, shut in there. He'd have time. He wouldn't look like this if he hadn't made his peace. The lamb, the dear lamb. 'Eh, but he had a hearty laugh. I loved to hear it. He had the heartiest laugh, Lizzie, as a lad ———"

Elizabeth looked up. The man's mouth was fallen back, slightly open under the cover of the moustache. The eyes, half shut, did not show glazed in the obscurity. Life with its smoky burning gone from him, had left him apart and utterly alien to her. And she knew what a stranger he was to her. In her womb was ice of fear, because of this separate stranger with whom she had been living as one flesh. Was this what it all meant—utter, intact separateness, obscured by heat of living? In dread she turned her face away. The fact was too deadly. There had been nothing between them, and yet they had come together, exchanging their nakedness repeatedly. Each time he had taken her, they had been two isolated beings, far apart as now. He was no more responsible than she. The child was like ice in her womb. For as she looked at the dead man, her mind, cold and detached, said clearly: "Who am I? What have I been doing? I have been fighting a husband who did not exist. He existed all the time. What wrong have I done? What was that I have been living with? There lies the reality, this man." And her soul died in her for fear: she knew she had never seen him, he had never seen her, they had met in the dark and had fought in the dark, not knowing whom they met nor whom they fought. And now she saw, and turned silent in seeing. For she had been wrong. She had said he was something he was not; she had felt familiar with him. Whereas he was apart all the while, living as she never lived, feeling as she never felt.

In fear and shame she looked at his naked body, that she had known falsely. And he was the father of her children. Her soul was torn from her body and stood apart. She looked at his naked body and was ashamed, as if she had denied it. After all, it was itself. It seemed awful to her. She looked at his face, and she turned her own face to the wall. For his look was other than hers, his way was not her way. She had denied him what he was—she saw it now. She had refused him as himself. And this had been her life, and his life. She was grateful to death, which restored the truth. And she knew she was not dead.

And all the while her heart was bursting with grief and pity for him. What had he suffered? What stretch of horror for this helpless man! She was rigid with agony. She had not been able to help him. He had been cruelly injured, this naked man, this other being, and she could make no reparation. There were the children—but the children belonged to life. This dead man had nothing to do with them. He and she were only channels through which life had flowed to issue in the children. She was a mother—but how awful she knew it now to have been a wife. And he, dead now, how awful he must have felt it to be a husband. She felt that in the next world he would be a stranger to her. If they met there, in the beyond, they would only be ashamed of what had been before. The children had come, for some mysterious reason, out of both of them. But the children did not unite them. Now he was dead, she knew how eternally he was apart from her, how eternally he had nothing more to do with her. She saw this episode of her life closed. They had denied each other in life. Now he had withdrawn. An anguish came over her. It was finished then: it had become hopeless between them long before he died. Yet he had been her husband. But how little!

"Have you got his shirt, 'Lizabeth?"

Elizabeth turned without answering, though she strove to weep and behave as her mother-in-law expected. But she could not, she was silenced. She went into the kitchen and returned with the garment.

"It is aired," she said, grasping the cotton shirt here and there to try. She was almost ashamed to handle him; what right had she or anyone to lay hands on him; but her touch was humble on his body. It was hard work to clothe him. He was so heavy and inert. A terrible dread gripped her all the while: that he could be so heavy and utterly inert, unresponsive, apart. The horror of the distance between them was almost too much for her—it was so infinite a gap she must look across.

At last it was finished. They covered him with a sheet and left him lying, with his face bound. And she fastened the door of the little parlour, lest the children should see what was lying there. Then, with peace sunk heavy on her heart, she went about making tidy the kitchen. She knew she submitted to life, which was her immediate master. But from death, her ultimate master, she winced with fear and shame.

QUESTIONS

1. Explain the last sentence of part I: "Meantime her anger was tinged with fear." **2.** What does the encounter between Elizabeth Bates and the Rigleys reveal about Elizabeth Bates's character? **3.** Elizabeth "was grateful to death, which restored the truth." What was the truth of her marriage? How does her husband's death restore it?

WRITING TOPIC
Analyze the way in which Lawrence uses chrysanthemums symbolically in the story.

Idiots First

1963

BERNARD MALAMUD [1914–1986]

The thick ticking of the tin clock stopped. Mendel, dozing in the dark, awoke in fright. The pain returned as he listened. He drew on his cold embittered clothing, and wasted minutes sitting at the edge of the bed.

"Isaac," he ultimately sighed.

In the kitchen, Isaac, his astonished mouth open, held six peanuts in his palm. He placed each on the table. "One . . . two . . . nine."

He gathered each peanut and appeared in the doorway. Mendel, in loose hat and long overcoat, still sat on the bed. Isaac watched with small eyes and ears, thick hair graying the sides of his head.

"Schlaf," he nasally said.

"No," muttered Mendel. As if stifling he rose. "Come, Isaac."

He wound his old watch though the sight of the stopped clock nauseated him.

Isaac wanted to hold it to his ear.

"No, it's late." Mendel put the watch carefully away. In the drawer he found the little paper bag of crumpled ones and fives and slipped it into his overcoat pocket. He helped Isaac on with his coat.

Isaac looked at one dark window, then at the other. Mendel stared at both blank windows.

They went slowly down the darkly lit stairs, Mendel first, Isaac watching the moving shadows on the wall. To one long shadow he offered a peanut.

"Hungrig."

In the vestibule the old man gazed through the thin glass. The November night was cold and bleak. Opening the door he cautiously thrust his head out. Though he saw nothing he quickly shut the door.

"Ginzburg, that he came to see me yesterday," he whispered in Isaac's ear.

Isaac sucked air.

"You know who I mean?"

Isaac combed his chin with his fingers.

"That's the one, with the black whiskers. Don't talk to him or go with him if he asks you."

Isaac moaned.

"Young people he don't bother so much," Mendel said in afterthought.

It was suppertime and the street was empty but the store windows dimly lit their way to the corner. They crossed the deserted street and went on. Isaac, with a happy cry, pointed to the three golden balls. Mendel smiled but was exhausted when they got to the pawnshop.

The pawnbroker, a red-bearded man with black horn-rimmed glasses, was eating a whitefish at the rear of the store. He craned his head, saw them, and settled back to sip his tea.

In five minutes he came forward, patting his shapeless lips with a large white handkerchief.

Mendel, breathing heavily, handed him the worn gold watch. The pawnbroker, raising his glasses, screwed in his eyepiece. He turned the watch over once. "Eight dollars."

The dying man wet his cracked lips. "I must have thirty-five."

"So go to Rothschild."

"Cost me myself sixty."

"In 1905." The pawnbroker handed back the watch. It had stopped ticking. Mendel wound it slowly. It ticked hollowly.

"Isaac must go to my uncle that he lives in California."

"It's a free country," said the pawnbroker.

Isaac, watching a banjo, snickered.

"What's the matter with him?" the pawnbroker asked.

"So let be eight dollars," muttered Mendel, "but where will I get the rest till tonight?"

"How much for my hat and coat?" he asked.

"No sale." The pawnbroker went behind the cage and wrote out a ticket. He locked the watch in a small drawer but Mendel still heard it ticking.

In the street he slipped the eight dollars into the paper bag, then searched in his pockets for a scrap of writing. Finding it, he strained to read the address by the light of the street lamp.

As they trudged to the subway, Mendel pointed to the sprinkled sky.

"Isaac, look how many stars are tonight."

"Eggs," said Isaac.

"First we will go to Mr. Fishbein, after we will eat."

They got off the train in upper Manhattan and had to walk several blocks before they located Fishbein's house.

"A regular palace," Mendel murmured, looking forward to a moment's warmth.

Isaac stared uneasily at the heavy door of the house.

Mendel rang. The servant, a man with long sideburns, came to the door and said Mr. and Mrs. Fishbein were dining and could see no one.

"He should eat in peace but we will wait till he finishes."

"Come back tomorrow morning. Tomorrow morning Mr. Fishbein will talk to you. He don't do business or charity at this time of the night."

"Charity I am not interested—"

"Come back tomorrow."

"Tell him it's life or death—"

"Whose life or death?"

"So if not his, then mine."

"Don't be such a big smart aleck."

"Look me in my face," said Mendel, "and tell me if I got time till tomorrow morning?"

The servant stared at him, then at Isaac, and reluctantly let them in.

The foyer was a vast high-ceilinged room with many oil paintings on the walls, voluminous silken draperies, a thick flowered rug at foot, and a marbled staircase.

Mr. Fishbein, a paunchy bald-headed man with hairy nostrils and small patent leather feet, ran lightly down the stairs, a large napkin tucked under a tuxedo coat button. He stopped on the fifth step from the bottom and examined his visitors.

"Who comes on Friday night to a man that he has guests, to spoil him his supper?"

"Excuse me that I bother you, Mr. Fishbein," Mendel said. "If I didn't come now I couldn't come tomorrow."

"Without more preliminaries, please state your business. I'm a hungry man."

"Hungrig," wailed Isaac.

Fishbein adjusted his pince-nez. "What's the matter with him?"

"This is my son Isaac. He is like this all his life."

Isaac mewled.

"I am sending him to California."

"Mr. Fishbein don't contribute to personal pleasure trips."

"I am a sick man and he must go tonight on the train to my Uncle Leo."

"I never give to unorganized charity," Fishbein said, "but if you are hungry I will invite you downstairs in my kitchen. We having tonight chicken with stuffed derma."

"All I ask is thirty-five dollars for the train ticket to my uncle in California. I have already the rest."

"Who is your uncle? How old a man?"

"Eighty-one years, a long life to him."

Fishbein burst into laughter. "Eighty-one years and you are sending him this halfwit."

Mendel, flailing both arms, cried, "Please, without names."

Fishbein politely conceded.

"Where is open the door there we go in the house," the sick man said. "If you will kindly give me thirty-five dollars, God will bless you. What is thirty-five dollars to Mr. Fishbein? Nothing. To me, for my boy, is everything."

Fishbein drew himself up to his tallest height.

"Private contributions I don't make—only to institutions. This is my fixed policy."

Mendel sank to his creaking knees on the rug.

"Please, Mr. Fishbein, if not thirty-five, give maybe twenty."

"Levinson!" Fishbein angrily called.

The servant with the long sideburns appeared at the top of the stairs.

"Show this party where is the door—unless he wishes to partake food before leaving the premises."

"For what I got chicken won't cure it," Mendel said.

"This way if you please," said Levinson, descending.

Isaac assisted his father up.

"Take him to an institution," Fishbein advised over the marble balustrade. He ran quickly up the stairs and they were at once outside, buffeted by winds.

The walk to the subway was tedious. The wind blew mournfully. Mendel, breathless, glanced furtively at shadows. Isaac, clutching his peanuts in his frozen fist, clung to his father's side. They entered a small park to rest for a minute on a stone bench under a leafless two-branched tree. The thick right branch was raised, the thin left one hung down. A very pale moon rose slowly. So did a stranger as they approached the bench.

"Gut yuntif" [Happy holiday], he said hoarsely.

Mendel, drained of blood, waved his wasted arms. Isaac yowled sickly. Then a bell chimed and it was only ten. Mendel let out a piercing anguished cry as the bearded stranger disappeared into the bushes. A policeman came running, and though he beat the bushes with his nightstick, could turn up nothing. Mendel and Isaac hurried out of the little park. When Mendel glanced back the dead tree had its thin arm raised, the thick one down. He moaned.

They boarded a trolley, stopping at the home of a former friend, but he had died years ago. On the same block they went into a cafeteria and ordered two fried eggs for Isaac. The tables were crowded except where a heavy-set man sat eating soup with kasha. After one look at him they left in haste, although Isaac wept.

Mendel had another address on a slip of paper but the house was too far away, in Queens, so they stood in a doorway shivering.

What can I do, he frantically thought, in one short hour?

He remembered the furniture in the house. It was junk but might bring a few dollars. "Come, Isaac." They went once more to the pawnbroker's to talk to him, but the shop was dark and an iron gate—rings and gold watches glinting through it—was drawn tight across his place of business.

They huddled behind a telephone pole, both freezing. Isaac whimpered.

"See the big moon, Isaac. The whole sky is white."

He pointed but Isaac wouldn't look.

Mendel dreamed for a minute of the sky lit up, long sheets of light in all directions. Under the sky, in California, sat Uncle Leo drinking tea with lemon. Mendel felt warm but woke up cold.

Across the street stood an ancient brick synagogue.

He pounded on the huge door but no one appeared. He waited till he had breath and desperately knocked again. At last there were footsteps within, and the synagogue door creaked open on its massive brass hinges.

A darkly dressed sexton, holding a dripping candle, glared at them.

"Who knocks this time of night with so much noise on the synagogue door?"

Mendel told the sexton his troubles. "Please, I would like to speak to the rabbi."

"The rabbi is an old man. He sleeps now. His wife won't let you see him. Go home and come back tomorrow."

"To tomorrow I said goodbye already. I am a dying man."

Though the sexton seemed doubtful he pointed to an old wooden house next door. "In there he lives." He disappeared into the synagogue with his lit candle casting shadows around him.

Mendel, with Isaac clutching his sleeve, went up the wooden steps and rang the bell. After five minutes a big-faced, gray-haired bulky woman came out on the porch with a torn robe thrown over her nightdress. She emphatically said the rabbi was sleeping and could not be waked.

But as she was insisting, the rabbi himself tottered to the door. He listened a minute and said, "Who wants to see me let them come in."

They entered a cluttered room. The rabbi was an old skinny man with bent shoulders and a wisp of white beard. He wore a flannel nightgown and black skullcap; his feet were bare.

"Vey is mir" [Woe is me], his wife muttered. "Put on shoes or tomorrow comes sure pneumonia." She was a woman with a big belly, years younger than her husband. Staring at Isaac, she turned away.

Mendel apologetically related his errand. "All I need more is thirty-five dollars."

"Thirty-five?" said the rabbi's wife. "Why not thirty-five thousand? Who has so much money? My husband is a poor rabbi. The doctors take away every penny."

"Dear friend," said the rabbi, "if I had I would give you."

"I got already seventy," Mendel said, heavy-hearted. "All I need more is thirty-five."

"God will give you," said the rabbi.

"In the grave," said Mendel. "I need tonight. Come, Isaac."

"Wait," called the rabbi.

He hurried inside, came out with a fur-lined caftan, and handed it to Mendel.

"Yascha," shrieked his wife, "not your new coat!"

"I got my old one. Who needs two coats for one body?"

"Yascha, I am screaming—"

"Who can go among poor people, tell me, in a new coat?"

"Yascha," she cried, "what can this man do with your coat? He needs tonight the money. The pawnbrokers are asleep."

"So let him wake them up."

"No." She grabbed the coat from Mendel.

He held on to a sleeve, wrestling her for the coat. Her I know, Mendel thought. "Shylock," he muttered. Her eyes glittered.

The rabbi groaned and tottered dizzily. His wife cried out as Mendel yanked the coat from her hands.

"Run," cried the rabbi.

"Run, Isaac."

They ran out of the house and down the steps.

"Stop, you thief," called the rabbi's wife.

The rabbi pressed both hands to his temples and fell to the floor.

"Help!" his wife wept. "Heart attack! Help!"

But Mendel and Isaac ran through the streets with the rabbi's new fur-lined caftan. After them noiselessly ran Ginzburg.

It was very late when Mendel bought the train ticket in the only booth open.

There was no time to stop for a sandwich so Isaac ate his peanuts and they hurried to the train in the vast deserted station.

"So in the morning," Mendel gasped as they ran, "there comes a man that he sells sandwiches and coffee. Eat but get change. When reaches California the train, will be waiting for you on the station Uncle Leo. If you don't recognize him he will recognize you. Tell him I send best regards."

But when they arrived at the gate to the platform it was shut, the light out.

Mendel, groaning, beat on the gate with his fists.

"Too late," said the uniformed ticket collector, a bulky, bearded man with hairy nostrils and a fishy smell.

He pointed to the station clock. "Already past twelve."

"But I see standing there still the train," Mendel said, hopping in his grief.

"It just left—in one more minute."

"A minute is enough. Just open the gate."

"Too late I told you."

Mendel socked his bony chest with both hands. "With my whole heart I beg you this little favor."

"Favors you had enough already. For you the train is gone. You shoulda been dead already at midnight. I told you that yesterday. This is the best I can do."

"Ginzburg!" Mendel shrank from him.

"Who else?" The voice was metallic, eyes glittered, the expression amused.

"For myself," the old man begged, "I don't ask a thing. But what will happen to my boy?"

Ginzburg shrugged slightly. "What will happen happens. This isn't my responsibility. I got enough to think about without worrying about somebody on one cylinder."

"What then is your responsibility?"

"To create conditions. To make happen what happens. I ain't in the anthropomorphic business."

"Whatever business you in, where is your pity?"

"This ain't my commodity. The law is the law."

"Which law is this?"

"The cosmic universal law, goddamit, the one I got to follow myself."

"What kind of a law is it?" cried Mendel. "For God's sake, don't you understand what I went through in my life with this poor boy? Look at him. For thirty-nine years, since the day he was born, I wait for him to grow up, but he don't. Do you understand what this means in a father's heart? Why don't you let him go to his uncle?" His voice had risen and he was shouting.

Isaac mewled loudly.

"Better calm down or you'll hurt somebody's feelings," Ginzburg said with a wink toward Isaac.

"All my life," Mendel cried, his body trembling, "what did I have? I was poor. I suffered from my health. When I worked I worked too hard. When I didn't work was worse. My wife died a young woman. But I didn't ask from anybody nothing. Now I ask a small favor. Be so kind, Mr. Ginzburg."

The ticket collector was picking his teeth with a match stick.

"You ain't the only one, my friend, some got it worse than you. That's how it goes in this country."

"You dog you." Mendel lunged at Ginzburg's throat and began to choke. "You bastard, don't you understand what it means human?"

They struggled nose to nose, Ginzburg, though his astonished eyes bulged, began to laugh. "You pipsqueak nothing. I'll freeze you to pieces."

His eyes lit in rage and Mendel felt an unbearable cold like an icy dagger invading his body, all of his parts shriveling.

Now I die without helping Isaac.

A crowd gathered. Isaac yelped in fright.

Clinging to Ginzburg in his last agony, Mendel saw reflected in the ticket collector's eyes the depth of his terror. But he saw that Ginzburg, staring at himself in Mendel's eyes, saw mirrored in them the extent of his own awful wrath. He beheld a shimmering, starry, blinding light that produced darkness.

Ginzburg looked astounded. "Who me?"

His grip on the squirming old man slowly loosened, and Mendel, his heart barely beating, slumped to the ground.

"Go." Ginzburg muttered, "take him to the train."

"Let pass," he commanded a guard.

The crowd parted. Isaac helped his father up and they tottered down the steps to the platform where the train waited, lit and ready to go.

Mendel found Isaac a coach seat and hastily embraced him. "Help Uncle Leo, Isaakil. Also remember your father and mother."

"Be nice to him," he said to the conductor. "Show him where everything is."

He waited on the platform until the train began slowly to move. Isaac sat at the edge of his seat, his face strained in the direction of his journey. When the train was gone, Mendel ascended the stairs to see what had become of Ginzburg.

QUESTIONS

1. Can this story be read as a religious drama? In this connection, consider the rabbi, the only person who helps Mendel. His compassion and his indifference to material things reveal him as a man of God. What does the supernatural Ginzburg represent? **2.** What is the significance of the fact that Isaac, for whom Mendel is determined to provide before death claims him, is an idiot? **3.** Mendel wins his battle with Ginzburg. What does that victory signify?

WRITING TOPIC
How do the various episodes in this story establish Mendel's character and prepare the reader for the final, climactic confrontation between Mendel and Ginzburg?

Patriotism*

1966

YUKIO MISHIMA   [1925–1970]

In the twenty-eighth of February, 1936 (on the third day, that is, of the February Incident[1]), Lieutenant Shinji Takeyama of the Konoe Transport Battalion—profoundly disturbed by the knowledge that his closest colleagues had been with the mutineers from the beginning, and indignant at the imminent prospect of Imperial troops attacking Imperial troops—took his officer's sword and ceremonially disemboweled himself in the eight-mat room of his private residence in the sixth block of Aoba-chō, in Yotsuya Ward. His wife, Reiko, followed him, stabbing herself to death. The lieutenant's farewell note consisted of one sentence: "Long live the Imperial Forces." His wife's, after apologies for her unfilial conduct in thus preceding her parents to the grave, concluded: "The day which, for a soldier's wife, had to come, has come. . . ." The last moments of this heroic and dedicated couple were such as to make the gods themselves weep. The lieutenant's age, it should be noted, was thirty-one, his wife's twenty-three; and it was not half a year since the celebration of their marriage.

2

Those who saw the bride and bridegroom in the commemorative photograph—perhaps no less than those actually present at the lieutenant's wedding—had exclaimed in wonder at the bearing of this handsome couple. The lieutenant, majestic in military uniform, stood protectively beside his bride, his right hand resting upon his sword, his officer's cap held at his left side. His expression was severe, and his dark brows and wide-gazing eyes well conveyed the clear integrity of youth. For the beauty of the bride in her white over-robe no comparisons were adequate. In the eyes, round beneath soft brows, in the slender, finely shaped nose, and in the full lips, there was both sensuousness and refinement. One hand, emerging shyly from a sleeve of the over-robe, held a fan, and the tips of the fingers, clustering delicately, were like the bud of a moonflower.

After the suicide, people would take out this photograph and examine it, and sadly reflect that too often there was a curse on these seemingly flawless unions. Perhaps it was no more than imagination, but looking at the picture

---

* Translated by Geoffrey W. Sargeant.
[1] On February 26, 1936, a long period of political turmoil culminated in an attempted coup led by young officers. Units commanded by the rebels seized and held central Tokyo for a number of days, and numerous high-ranking government officials, including Lord Privy Seal Saitō, were assassinated. The mutiny was crushed by loyal troops, and the leaders were executed.

after the tragedy it almost seemed as if the two young people before the gold-lacquered screen were gazing, each with equal clarity, at the deaths which lay before them.

Thanks to the good offices of their go-between, Lieutenant General Ozeki, they had been able to set themselves up in a new home at Aoba-chō in Yotsuya. "New home" is perhaps misleading. It was an old three-room rented house backing onto a small garden. As neither the six- nor the four-and-a-half-mat room downstairs was favored by the sun, they used the upstairs eight-mat room as both bedroom and guest room. There was no maid, so Reiko was left alone to guard the house in her husband's absence.

The honeymoon trip was dispensed with on the grounds that these were times of national emergency. The two of them had spent the first night of their marriage at this house. Before going to bed, Shinji, sitting erect on the floor with his sword laid before him, had bestowed upon his wife a soldierly lecture. A woman who had become the wife of a soldier should know and resolutely accept that her husband's death might come at any moment. It could be tomorrow. It could be the day after. But, no matter when it came—he asked—was she steadfast in her resolve to accept it? Reiko rose to her feet, pulled open a drawer of the cabinet, and took out what was the most prized of her new possessions, the dagger her mother had given her. Returning to her place, she laid the dagger without a word on the mat before her, just as her husband had laid his sword. A silent understanding was achieved at once and the lieutenant never again sought to test his wife's resolve.

In the first few months of her marriage Reiko's beauty grew daily more radiant, shining serene like the moon after rain.

As both were possessed of young, vigorous bodies, their relationship was passionate. Nor was this merely a matter of the night. On more than one occasion, returning home straight from maneuvers, and begrudging even the time it took to remove his mud-splashed uniform, the lieutenant had pushed his wife to the floor almost as soon as he had entered the house. Reiko was equally ardent in her response. For a little more or a little less than a month, from the first night of their marriage Reiko knew happiness, and the lieutenant, seeing this, was happy too.

Reiko's body was white and pure, and her swelling breasts conveyed a firm and chaste refusal; but, upon consent, those breasts were lavish with their intimate, welcoming warmth. Even in bed these two were frighteningly and awesomely serious. In the very midst of wild, intoxicating passions, their hearts were sober and serious.

By day the lieutenant would think of his wife in the brief rest periods between training; and all day long, at home, Reiko would recall the image of her husband. Even when apart, however, they had only to look at the wedding photograph for their happiness to be once more confirmed. Reiko felt not the slightest surprise that a man who had been a complete stranger until a few months ago should now have become the sun about which her whole world revolved.

All these things had a moral basis, and were in accordance with the Education Rescript's[2] injunction that "husband and wife should be harmonious." Not once did Reiko contradict her husband, nor did the lieutenant ever find reason to scold his wife. On the god shelf below the stairway, alongside the tablet from the Great Ise Shrine,[3] were set photographs of their Imperial Majesties, and regularly every morning, before leaving for duty, the lieutenant would stand with his wife at this hallowed place and together they would bow their heads low. The offering water was renewed each morning, and the sacred sprig of *sasaki* was always green and fresh. Their lives were lived beneath the solemn protection of the gods and were filled with an intense happiness which set every fiber in their bodies trembling.

3

Although Lord Privy Seal Saitō's house was in their neighborhood, neither of them heard any noise of gunfire on the morning of February 26. It was a bugle, sounding muster in the dim, snowy dawn, when the ten-minute tragedy had already ended, which first disrupted the lieutenant's slumbers. Leaping at once from his bed, and without speaking a word, the lieutenant donned his uniform, buckled on the sword held ready for him by his wife, and hurried swiftly out into the snow-covered streets of the still darkened morning. He did not return until the evening of the twenty-eighth.

Later, from the radio news, Reiko learned the full extent of this sudden eruption of violence. Her life throughout the subsequent two days was lived alone, in complete tranquility, and behind locked doors.

In the lieutenant's face, as he hurried silently out into the snowy morning, Reiko had read the determination to die. If her husband did not return, her own decision was made: she too would die. Quietly she attended to the disposition of her personal possessions. She chose her sets of visiting kimonos as keepsakes for friends of her schooldays, and she wrote a name and address on the stiff paper wrapping in which each was folded. Constantly admonished by her husband never to think of the morrow, Reiko had not even kept a diary and was now denied the pleasure of assiduously rereading her record of the happiness of the past few months and consigning each page to the fire as she did so. Ranged across the top of the radio were a small china dog, a rabbit, a squirrel, a bear, and a fox. There were also a small vase and a water pitcher. These comprised Reiko's one and only collection. But it would hardly do, she imagined, to give such things as keepsakes. Nor again would it be quite proper to ask specifically for them to be included in the coffin. It seemed to Reiko, as

---

[2] The Education Rescript was a code promulgated during the Meiji, the reign of Emperor Mutsuhito which lasted from 1867 to 1912. The period is regarded as a historic era in the development of modern Japan.

[3] The Great Ise Shrine is the highest ranking shrine in Japan. The emperor's ancestors were buried there.

these thoughts passed through her mind, that the expressions on the small animals' faces grew even more lost and forlorn.

Reiko took the squirrel in her hand and looked at it. And then, her thoughts turning to a realm far beyond these childlike affections, she gazed up into the distance at the great sunlike principle which her husband embodied. She was ready, and happy, to be hurtled along to her destruction in that gleaming sun chariot—but now, for these few moments of solitude, she allowed herself to luxuriate in this innocent attachment to trifles. The time when she had genuinely loved these things, however, was long past. Now she merely loved the memory of having once loved them, and their place in her heart had been filled by more intense passions, by a more frenzied happiness. . . . For Reiko had never, even to herself, thought of those soaring joys of the flesh as a mere pleasure. The February cold, and the icy touch of the china squirrel, had numbed Reiko's slender fingers; yet, even so, in her lower limbs, beneath the ordered repetition of the pattern which crossed the skirt of her trim *meisen* kimono, she could feel now, as she thought of the lieutenant's powerful arms reaching out toward her, a hot moistness of the flesh which defied the snows.

She was not in the least afraid of the death hovering in her mind. Waiting alone at home, Reiko firmly believed that everything her husband was feeling or thinking now, his anguish and distress, was leading her—just as surely as the power in his flesh—to a welcome death. She felt as if her body could melt away with ease and be transformed to the merest fraction of her husband's thought.

Listening to the frequent announcements on the radio, she heard the names of several of her husband's colleagues mentioned among those of the insurgents. This was news of death. She followed the developments closely, wondering anxiously, as the situation became daily more irrevocable, why no Imperial ordinance was sent down, and watching what had at first been taken as a movement to restore the nation's honor came gradually to be branded with the infamous name of mutiny. There was no communication from the regiment. At any moment, it seemed, fighting might commence in the city streets where the remains of the snow still lay.

Toward sundown on the twenty-eighth Reiko was startled by a furious pounding on the front door. She hurried downstairs. As she pulled with fumbling fingers at the bolt, the shape dimly outlined beyond the frosted-glass panel made no sound, but she knew it was her husband. Reiko had never known the bolt on the sliding door to be so stiff. Still it resisted. The door just would not open.

In a moment, almost before she knew she had succeeded, the lieutenant was standing before her on the cement floor inside the porch, muffled in a khaki greatcoat, his top boots heavy with slush from the street. Closing the door behind him, he returned the bolt once more to its socket. With what significance, Reiko did not understand.

"Welcome home."

Reiko bowed deeply, but her husband made no response. As he had already unfastened his sword and was about to remove his greatcoat, Reiko moved around behind to assist. The coat, which was cold and damp and had lost the odor of horse dung it normally exuded when exposed to the sun, weighed heavily upon her arm. Draping it across a hanger, and cradling the sword and leather belt in her sleeves, she waited while her husband removed his top boots and then followed behind him into the "living room." This was the six-mat room downstairs.

Seen in the clear light from the lamp, her husband's face, covered with a heavy growth of bristle, was almost unrecognizably wasted and thin. The cheeks were hollow, their luster and resilience gone. In his normal good spirits he would have changed into old clothes as soon as he was home and have pressed her to get supper at once, but now he sat before the table still in his uniform, his head dropping dejectedly. Reiko refrained from asking whether she should prepare the supper.

After an interval the lieutenant spoke.

"I knew nothing. They hadn't asked me to join. Perhaps out of consideration, because I was newly married. Kano, and Homma too, and Yamaguchi."

Reiko recalled momentarily the faces of high-spirited young officers, friends of her husband, who had come to the house occasionally as guests.

"There may be an Imperial ordinance sent down tomorrow. They'll be posted as rebels, I imagine. I shall be in command of a unit with orders to attack them. . . . I can't do it. It's impossible to do a thing like that."

He spoke again.

"They've taken me off guard duty, and I have permission to return home for one night. Tomorrow morning, without question, I must leave to join the attack. I can't do it, Reiko."

Reiko sat erect with lowered eyes. She understood clearly that her husband had spoken of his death. The lieutenant was resolved. Each word, being rooted in death, emerged sharply and with powerful significance against this dark, unmovable background. Although the lieutenant was speaking of his dilemma, already there was no room in his mind for vacillation.

However, there was a clarity, like the clarity of a stream fed from melting snows, in the silence which rested between them. Sitting in his own home after the long two-day ordeal, and looking across at the face of his beautiful wife, the lieutenant was for the first time experiencing true peace of mind. For he had at once known, though she said nothing, that his wife divined the resolve which lay beneath his words.

"Well, then . . ." The lieutenant's eyes opened wide. Despite his exhaustion they were strong and clear, and now for the first time they looked straight into the eyes of his wife. "Tonight I shall cut my stomach."

Reiko did not flinch.

Her round eyes showed tension, as taut as the clang of a bell.

"I am ready," she said. "I ask permission to accompany you."

The lieutenant felt almost mesmerized by the strength in those eyes. His words flowed swiftly and easily, like the utterances of a man in delirium, and it was beyond his understanding how permission in a matter of such weight could be expressed so casually.

"Good. We'll go together. But I want you as a witness, first, for my own suicide. Agreed?"

When this was said a sudden release of abundant happiness welled up in both their hearts. Reiko was deeply affected by the greatness of her husband's trust in her. It was vital for the lieutenant, whatever else might happen, that there should be no irregularity in his death. For that reason there had to be a witness. The fact that he had chosen his wife for this was the first mark of his trust. The second, and even greater mark, was that though he had pledged that they should die together he did not intend to kill his wife first—he had deferred her death to a time when he would no longer be there to verify it. If the lieutenant had been a suspicious husband, he would doubtless, as in the usual suicide pact, have chosen to kill his wife first.

When Reiko said, "I ask permission to accompany you," the lieutenant felt these words to be the final fruit of the education which he had himself given his wife, starting on the first night of their marriage, and which had schooled her, when the moment came, to say what had to be said without a shadow of hesitation. This flattered the lieutenant's opinion of himself as a self-reliant man. He was not so romantic or conceited as to imagine that the words were spoken spontaneously, out of love for her husband.

With happiness welling almost too abundantly in their hearts, they could not help smiling at each other. Reiko felt as if she had returned to her wedding night.

Before her eyes was neither pain nor death. She seemed to see only a free and limitless expanse opening out into vast distances.

"The water is hot. Will you take your bath now?"

"Ah yes, of course."

"And supper . . . ?"

The words were delivered in such level, domestic tones that the lieutenant came near to thinking, for the fraction of a second, that everything had been a hallucination.

"I don't think we'll need supper. But perhaps you could warm some sake?"

"As you wish."

As Reiko rose and took a *tanzen* gown from the cabinet for after the bath, she purposely directed her husband's attention to the opened drawer. The lieutenant rose, crossed to the cabinet, and looked inside. From the ordered array of paper wrappings he read, one by one, the addresses of the keepsakes. There was no grief in the lieutenant's response to this demonstration of heroic resolve. His heart was filled with tenderness. Like a husband who is proudly shown the childish purchases of a young wife, the lieutenant, overwhelmed by affection, lovingly embraced his wife from behind and implanted a kiss upon her neck.

Reiko felt the roughness of the lieutenant's unshaven skin against her neck. This sensation, more than being just a thing of this world, was for Reiko almost the world itself, but now—with the feeling that it was soon to be lost forever—it had freshness beyond all her experience. Each moment had its own vital strength, and the senses in every corner of her body were reawakened. Accepting her husband's caresses from behind, Reiko raised herself on the tips of her toes, letting the vitality seep through her entire body.

"First the bath, and then, after some sake . . . lay out the bedding upstairs, will you?"

The lieutenant whispered the words into his wife's ear. Reiko silently nodded.

Flinging off his uniform, the lieutenant went to the bath. To faint background noises of slopping water Reiko tended the charcoal brazier in the living room and began the preparations for warming the sake.

Taking the *tanzen*, a sash, and some underclothes, she went to the bathroom to ask how the water was. In the midst of a coiling cloud of steam the lieutenant was sitting cross-legged on the floor, shaving, and she could dimly discern the rippling movements of the muscles on his damp, powerful back as they responded to the movement of his arms.

There was nothing to suggest a time of any special significance. Reiko, going busily about her tasks, was preparing side dishes from odds and ends in stock. Her hands did not tremble. If anything, she managed even more efficiently and smoothly than usual. From time to time, it is true, there was strange throbbing deep within her breast. Like distant lightning, it had a moment of sharp intensity and then vanished without trace. Apart from that, nothing was in any way out of the ordinary.

The lieutenant, shaving in the bathroom, felt his warmed body miraculously healed at last of the desperate tiredness of the days of indecision and filled—in spite of the death which lay ahead—with pleasurable anticipation. The sound of his wife going about her work came to him faintly. A healthy physical craving, submerged for two days, reasserted itself.

The lieutenant was confident there had been no impurity in that joy they had experienced when resolving upon death. They had both sensed at that moment—though not, of course, in any clear and conscious way—that those permissible pleasures which they shared in private were once more beneath the protection of Righteousness and Divine Power, and of a complete and unassailable morality. On looking into each other's eyes and discovering there an honorable death, they had felt themselves safe once more behind steel walls which none could destroy, encased in an impenetrable armor of Beauty and Truth. Thus, so far from seeing any inconsistency or conflict between the urges of his flesh and the sincerity of his patriotism, the lieutenant was even able to regard the two as parts of the same thing.

Thrusting his face close to the dark, cracked, misted wall mirror, the lieutenant shaved himself with great care. This would be his death face. There must be no unsightly blemishes. The clean-shaven face gleamed once more with a youthful luster, seeming to brighten the darkness of the mirror. There was a certain elegance, he even felt, in the association of death with this radiantly healthy face.

Just as it looked now, this would become his death face! Already, in fact, it had half departed from the lieutenant's personal possession and had become the bust above a dead soldier's memorial. As an experiment he closed his eyes tight. Everything was wrapped in blackness, and he was no longer a living, seeing creature.

Returning from the bath, the traces of the shave glowing faintly blue beneath his smooth cheeks, he seated himself beside the now well-kindled charcoal brazier. Busy though Reiko was, he noticed, she had found time lightly to touch up her face. Her cheeks were gay and her lips moist. There was no shadow of sadness to be seen. Truly, the lieutenant felt, as he saw this mark of his young wife's passionate nature, he had chosen the wife he ought to have chosen.

As soon as the lieutenant had drained his sake cup he offered it to Reiko. Reiko had never before tasted sake, but she accepted without hesitation and sipped timidly.

"Come here," the lieutenant said.

Reiko moved to her husband's side and was embraced as she leaned backward across his lap. Her breast was in violent commotion, as if sadness, joy, and the potent sake were mingling and reacting within her. The lieutenant looked down into his wife's face. It was the last face he would see in this world, the last face he would see of his wife. The lieutenant scrutinized the face minutely, with the eyes of a traveler bidding farewell to splendid vistas which he will never revisit. It was a face he could not tire of looking at—the features regular yet not cold, the lips lightly closed with a soft strength. The lieutenant kissed those lips, unthinkingly. And suddenly, though there was not the slightest distortion of the face into the unsightliness of sobbing, he noticed that tears were welling slowly from beneath the long lashes of the closed eyes and brimming over into a glistening stream.

When, a little later, the lieutenant urged that they should move to the upstairs bedroom, his wife replied that she would follow after taking a bath. Climbing the stairs alone to the bedroom, where the air was already warmed by the gas heater, the lieutenant lay down on the bedding with arms outstretched and legs apart. Even the time at which he lay waiting for his wife to join him was no later and no earlier than usual.

He folded his hands beneath his head and gazed at the dark boards of the ceiling in the dimness beyond the range of the standard lamp. Was it death he was now waiting for? Or a wild ecstasy of the senses? The two seemed to overlap, almost as if the object of this bodily desire was death itself. But, however that might be, it was certain that never before had the lieutenant tasted such total freedom.

There was the sound of a car outside the window. He could hear the screech of its tires skidding in the snow piled at the side of the street. The sound of its horn re-echoed from near-by walls. . . . Listening to these noises he had the feeling that this house rose like a solitary island in the ocean of a society going as restlessly about its business as ever. All around, vastly and untidily, stretched the country for which he grieved. He was to give his life for it. But would that great country, with which he was prepared to remonstrate to the extent of destroying himself, take the slightest heed of his death? He did not know; and it did not matter. His was a battlefield without glory, a battlefield where none could display deeds of valor: it was the front line of the spirit.

Reiko's footsteps sounded on the stairway. The steep stairs in this old house creaked badly. There were fond memories in that creaking, and many a time, while waiting in bed, the lieutenant had listened to its welcome sound. At the thought that he would hear it no more he listened with intense concentration, striving for every corner of every moment of this precious time to be filled with the sound of those soft footfalls on the creaking stairway. The moments seemed transformed to jewels, sparkling with inner light.

Reiko wore a Nagoya sash about the waist of her *yukata*, but as the lieutenant reached toward it, its redness sobered by the dimness of the light, Reiko's hand moved to his assistance and the sash fell away, slithering swiftly to the floor. As she stood before him, still in her *yukata*, the lieutenant inserted his hands through the side slits beneath each sleeve, intending to embrace her as she was; but at the touch of his finger tips upon the warm naked flesh, and as the armpits closed gently about his hands, his whole body was suddenly aflame.

In a few moments the two lay naked before the glowing gas heater.

Neither spoke the thought, but their hearts, their bodies, and their pounding breasts blazed with the knowledge that this was the very last time. It was as if the words "The Last Time" were spelled out, in invisible brushstrokes, across every inch of their bodies.

The lieutenant drew his wife close and kissed her vehemently. As their tongues explored each other's mouths, reaching out into the smooth, moist interior, they felt as if the still unknown agonies of death had tempered their senses to the keenness of red-hot steel. The agonies they could not yet feel, the distant pains of death, had refined their awareness of pleasure.

"This is the last time I shall see your body," said the lieutenant. "Let me look at it closely." And, tilting the shade on the lampstand to one side, he directed the rays along the full length of Reiko's outstretched form.

Reiko lay still with her eyes closed. The light from the low lamp clearly revealed the majestic sweep of her white flesh. The lieutenant, not without a touch of egocentricity, rejoiced that he would never see this beauty crumble in death.

At his leisure, the lieutenant allowed the unforgettable spectacle to engrave itself upon his mind. With one hand he fondled the hair, with the other he softly stroked the magnificent face, implanting kisses here and there where his eyes lingered. The quiet coldness of the high, tapering forehead, the closed eyes with their long lashes beneath faintly etched brows, the set of the finely shaped nose, the gleam of teeth glimpsed between full, regular lips, the soft cheeks and the small, wise chin . . . these things conjured up in the lieutenant's mind the vision of a truly radiant death face, and again and again he pressed his lips tight against the white throat—where Reiko's own hand was soon to strike—and the throat reddened faintly beneath his kisses. Returning to the mouth he laid his lips against it with the gentlest of pressures, and moved them rhythmically over Reiko's with the light rolling motion of a small boat. If he closed his eyes, the world became a rocking cradle.

Wherever the lieutenant's eyes moved his lips faithfully followed. The high, swelling breasts, surmounted by nipples like the buds of a wild cherry, hardened as the lieutenant's lips closed about them. The arms flowed smoothly downward from each side of the breast, tapering toward the wrists, yet losing nothing of their roundness or symmetry, and at their tips were those delicate fingers which had held the fan at the wedding ceremony. One by one, as the lieutenant kissed them, the fingers withdrew behind their neighbor as if in shame. . . . The natural hollow curving between the bosom and the stomach carried in its lines a suggestion not only of softness but of resilient strength, and while it gave forewarning of the rich curves spreading outward from here to the hips it had, in itself, an appearance only of restraint and proper discipline. The whiteness and richness of the stomach and hips was like milk brimming in a great bowl, and the sharply shadowed dip of the navel could have been the fresh impress of a raindrop, fallen there that very moment. Where the shadows gathered more thickly, hair clustered, gentle and sensitive, and as the agitation mounted in the now no longer passive body there hung over this region a scent like the smoldering of fragrant blossoms, growing steadily more pervasive.

At length, in a tremulous voice, Reiko spoke.

"Show me. . . . Let me look too, for the last time."

Never before had he heard from his wife's lips so strong and unequivocal a request. It was as if something which her modesty had wished to keep hidden to the end had suddenly burst its bonds of constraint. The lieutenant obediently lay back and surrendered himself to his wife. Lithely she raised her white, trembling body, and—burning with an innocent desire to return to her husband what he had done for her—placed two white fingers on the lieutenant's eyes, which gazed fixedly up at her, and gently stroked them shut.

Suddenly overwhelmed by tenderness, her cheeks flushed by a dizzying uprush of emotion, Reiko threw her arms about the lieutenant's close-cropped head. The bristly hairs rubbed painfully against her breast, the prominent nose was cold as it dug into her flesh, and his breath was hot. Relaxing her embrace, she gazed down at her husband's masculine face. The severe brows, the closed eyes, the splendid bridge of the nose, the shapely lips drawn firmly together . . . the blue, cleanshaven cheeks reflecting the light and gleaming smoothly. Reiko kissed each of these. She kissed the broad nape of the neck, the strong, erect shoulders, the powerful chest with its twin circles like shields and its russet nipples. In the armpits, deeply shadowed by the ample flesh of the shoulders and chest, a sweet and melancholy odor emanated from the growth of hair, and in the sweetness of this odor was contained, somehow, the essence of young death. The lieutenant's naked skin glowed like a field of barley, and everywhere the muscles showed in sharp relief, converging on the lower abdomen about the small, unassuming navel. Gazing at the youthful, firm stomach, modestly covered by a vigorous growth of hair, Reiko thought of it as it was soon to be, cruelly cut by the sword, and she laid her head upon it, sobbing in pity, and bathed it with kisses.

At the touch of his wife's tears upon his stomach the lieutenant felt ready to endure with courage the cruelest agonies of his suicide.

What ecstasies they experienced after these tender exchanges may well be imagined. The lieutenant raised himself and enfolded his wife in a powerful embrace, her body now limp with exhaustion after her grief and tears. Passionately they held their faces close, rubbing cheek against cheek. Reiko's body was trembling. Their breasts, moist with sweat, were tightly joined, and every inch of the young and beautiful bodies had become so much one with the other that it seemed impossible there should ever again be a separation. Reiko cried out. From the heights they plunged into the abyss, and from the abyss they took wing and soared once more to dizzying heights. The lieutenant panted like the regimental standard-bearer on a route march. . . . As one cycle ended, almost immediately a new wave of passion would be generated, and together—with no trace of fatigue—they would climb again in a single breathless movement to the very summit.

4

When the lieutenant at last turned away, it was not from weariness. For one thing, he was anxious not to undermine the considerable strength he would need in carrying out his suicide. For another, he would have been sorry to mar the sweetness of these last memories by overindulgence.

Since the lieutenant had clearly desisted, Reiko too, with her usual compliance, followed his example. The two lay naked on their backs, with fingers interlaced, staring fixedly at the dark ceiling. The room was warm from the heater, and even when the sweat had ceased to pour from their bodies they felt no cold. Outside, in the hushed night, the sounds of passing traffic had ceased. Even the noises of the trains and streetcars around Yotsuya station did not penetrate this far. After echoing through the region bounded by the moat, they were lost in the heavily wooded park fronting the broad driveway before Akasaka Palace. It was hard to believe in the tension gripping this whole quarter, where the two factions of the bitterly divided Imperial Army now confronted each other, poised for battle.

Savoring the warmth glowing within themselves, they lay still and recalled the ecstasies they had just known. Each moment of the experience was relived. They remembered the taste of kisses which had never wearied, the touch of naked flesh, episode after episode of dizzying bliss. But already, from the dark boards of the ceiling, the face of death was peering down. These joys had been final, and their bodies would never know them again. Not that joy of this intensity—and the same thought had occurred to them both—was ever likely to be reexperienced, even if they should live on to old age.

The feel of their fingers intertwined—this too would soon be lost. Even the wood-grain patterns they now gazed at on the dark ceiling boards would be taken from them. They could feel death edging in, nearer and nearer. There could be no hesitation now. They must have the courage to reach out to death themselves, and to seize it.

"Well, let's make our preparations," said the lieutenant. The note of determination in the words was unmistakable, but at the same time Reiko had never heard her husband's voice so warm and tender.

After they had risen, a variety of tasks awaited them.

The lieutenant, who had never once before helped with the bedding, now cheerfully slid back the door of the closet, lifted the mattress across the room by himself, and stowed it away inside.

Reiko turned off the gas heater and put away the lamp standard. During the lieutenant's absence she had arranged this room carefully, sweeping and dusting it to a fresh cleanness, and now—if one overlooked the rosewood table drawn into one corner—the eight-mat room gave all the appearance of a reception room ready to welcome an important guest.

"We've seen some drinking here, haven't we? With Kanō and Homma and Noguchi. . . ."

"Yes, they were great drinkers, all of them."

"We'll be meeting them before long, in the other world. They'll tease us, I imagine, when they find I've brought you with me."

Descending the stairs, the lieutenant turned to look back into this calm clean room, now brightly illuminated by the ceiling lamp. There floated across his mind the faces of the young officers who had drunk there, and laughed, and innocently bragged. He had never dreamed then that he would one day cut open his stomach in this room.

In the two rooms downstairs husband and wife busied themselves smoothly and serenely with their respective preparations. The lieutenant went to the toilet, and then to the bathroom to wash. Meanwhile Reiko folded away her husband's padded robe, placed his uniform tunic, his trousers, and a newly cut bleached loincloth in the bathroom, and set out sheets of paper on the living-room table for the farewell notes. Then she removed the lid from the writing box and began rubbing ink from the ink tablet. She had already decided upon the wording of her own note.

Reiko's fingers pressed hard upon the cold gilt letters of the ink tablet, and the water in the shallow well at once darkened, as if a black cloud had spread across it. She stopped thinking that this repeated action, this pressure from her fingers, this rise and fall of faint sound, was all and solely for death. It was a routine domestic task, a simple paring away of time until death should finally stand before her. But somehow, in the increasingly smooth motion of the tablet rubbing on the stone, and in the scent from the thickening ink, there was unspeakable darkness.

Neat in his uniform, which he now wore next to his skin, the lieutenant emerged from the bathroom. Without a word he seated himself at the table, bolt upright, took a brush in his hand, and stared undecidedly at the paper before him.

Reiko took a white silk kimono with her and entered the bathroom. When she reappeared in the living room, clad in the white kimono and with her face lightly made up, the farewell note lay completed on the table beneath the lamp. The thick black brushstrokes said simply:

"Long Live the Imperial Forces—Army Lieutenant Takeyama Shinji."

While Reiko sat opposite him writing her own note, the lieutenant gazed in silence, intensely serious, at the controlled movement of his wife's pale fingers as they manipulated the brush.

With their respective notes in their hands—the lieutenant's sword strapped to his side, Reiko's small dagger thrust into the sash of her white kimono—the two of them stood before the god shelf and silently prayed. Then they put out all the downstairs lights. As he mounted the stairs the lieutenant turned his head and gazed back at the striking, white-clad figure of his wife, climbing behind him, with lowered eyes, from the darkness beneath.

The farewell notes were laid side by side in the alcove of the upstairs room. They wondered whether they ought not to remove the hanging scroll, but since it had been written by their go-between, Lieutenant General Ozeki, and consisted, moreover, of two Chinese characters signifying "Sincerity," they left it where it was. Even if it were to become stained with splashes of blood, they felt that the lieutenant general would understand.

The lieutenant sitting erect with his back to the alcove, laid his sword on the floor before him.

Reiko sat facing him, a mat's width away. With the rest of her so severely white the touch of rouge on her lips seemed remarkably seductive.

Across the dividing mat they gazed intently into each other's eyes. The lieutenant's sword lay before his knees. Seeing it, Reiko recalled their first night and was overwhelmed with sadness. The lieutenant spoke, in a hoarse voice:

"As I have no second to help me I shall cut deep. It may look unpleasant, but please do not panic. Death of any sort is a fearful thing to watch. You must not be discouraged by what you see. Is that all right?"

"Yes."

Reiko nodded deeply.

Looking at the slender white figure of his wife the lieutenant experienced a bizarre excitement. What he was about to perform was an act in his public capacity as a soldier, something he had never previously shown his wife. It called for a resolution equal to the courage to enter battle; it was a death of no less degree and quality than death in the front line. It was his conduct on the battlefield that he was now to display.

Momentarily the thought led the lieutenant to a strange fantasy. A lonely death on the battlefield, a death beneath the eyes of his beautiful wife . . . in the sensation that he was now to die in these two dimensions, realizing an impossible union of them both, there was sweetness beyond words. This must be the very pinnacle of good fortune, he thought. To have every moment of his death observed by those beautiful eyes—it was like being borne to death on a gentle, fragrant breeze. There was some special favor here. He did not understand precisely what it was, but it was a domain unknown to others: a dispensation granted to no one else had been permitted to himself. In the radiant, bridelike figure of his white-robed wife the lieutenant seemed to see a vision of all those things he had loved and for which he was to lay down his life—the Imperial Household, the Nation, the Army Flag. All these, no less than the wife who sat before him, were presences observing him closely with clear and never-faltering eyes.

Reiko too was gazing intently at her husband, so soon to die, and she thought that never in this world had she seen anything so beautiful. The lieutenant always looked well in uniform, but now, as he contemplated death with severe brows and firmly closed lips, he revealed what was perhaps masculine beauty at its most superb.

"It's time to go," the lieutenant said at last.

Reiko bent her body low to the mat in a deep bow. She could not raise her face. She did not wish to spoil her make-up with tears, but the tears could not be held back.

When at length she looked up she saw hazily through the tears that her husband had wound a white bandage around the blade of his now unsheathed sword, leaving five or six inches of naked steel showing at the point.

Resting the sword in its cloth wrapping on the mat before him, the lieutenant rose from his knees, resettled himself cross-legged, and unfastened the hooks of his uniform collar. His eyes no longer saw his wife. Slowly, one by one, he undid the flat brass buttons. The dusky brown chest was revealed, and then the stomach. He unclasped his belt and undid the buttons of his trousers. The pure whiteness of the thickly coiled loincloth showed itself. The lieutenant pushed the cloth down with both hands, further to ease his stomach, and then reached for the white-bandaged blade of his sword. With his left hand he massaged his abdomen, glancing downward as he did so.

To reassure himself on the sharpness of his sword's cutting edge the lieutenant folded back the left trouser flap, exposing a little of his thigh, and lightly drew the blade across the skin. Blood welled up in the wound at once, and several streaks of red trickled downward, glistening in the strong light.

It was the first time Reiko had ever seen her husband's blood, and she felt a violent throbbing in her chest. She looked at her husband's face. The lieutenant was looking at the blood with calm appraisal. For a moment—though thinking at the same time that it was hollow comfort—Reiko experienced a sense of relief.

The lieutenant's eyes fixed his wife with an intense, hawk-like stare. Moving the sword around to his front, he raised himself slightly on his hips and let the upper half of his body lean over the sword point. That he was mustering his whole strength was apparent from the angry tension of the uniform at his shoulders. The lieutenant aimed to strike deep into the left of his stomach. His sharp cry pierced the silence of the room.

Despite the effort he had himself put into the blow, the lieutenant had the impression that someone else had struck the side of his stomach agonizingly with a thick rod of iron. For a second or so his head reeled and he had no idea what had happened. The five or six inches of naked point had vanished completely into his flesh, and the white bandage, gripped in his clenched fist, pressed directly against his stomach.

He returned to consciousness. The blade had certainly pierced the wall of the stomach, he thought. His breathing was difficult, his chest thumped violently, and in some far deep region, which he could hardly believe was a part of himself, a fearful and excruciating pain came welling up as if the ground had split open to disgorge a boiling stream of molten rock. The pain came suddenly nearer, with terrifying speed. The lieutenant bit his lower lip and stifled an instinctive moan.

Was this *seppuku*?—he was thinking. It was a sensation of utter chaos, as if the sky had fallen on his head and the world was reeling drunkenly. His will power and courage, which had seemed so robust before he made the incision, had now dwindled to something like a single hairlike thread of steel, and he was assailed by the uneasy feeling that he must advance along this thread, clinging to it with desperation. His clenched fist had grown moist. Looking down, he saw that both his hand and the cloth were drenched in blood. His loincloth too was dyed a deep red. It struck him as incredible that, amidst this terrible agony, things which could be seen could still be seen, and existing things existed still.

The moment the lieutenant thrust the sword into his left side and she saw the deathly pallor fall across his face, like an abruptly lowered curtain, Reiko had to struggle to prevent herself from rushing to his side. Whatever happened, she must watch. She must be a witness. That was the duty her husband had lain upon her. Opposite her, a mat's space away, she could clearly see her husband biting his lip to stifle the pain. The pain was there, with absolute certainty, before her eyes. And Reiko had no means of rescuing him from it.

The sweat glistened on her husband's forehead. The lieutenant closed his eyes, and then opened them again, as if experimenting. The eyes had lost their luster, and seemed innocent and empty like the eyes of a small animal.

The agony before Reiko's eyes burned as strong as the summer sun, utterly remote from the grief which seemed to be tearing herself apart within. The pain grew steadily in stature, stretching upward. Reiko felt that her husband had already become a man in a separate world, a man whose whole being had been resolved into pain, a prisoner in a cage of pain where no hand could reach out to him. But Reiko felt no pain at all. Her grief was not pain. As she thought about this, Reiko began to feel as if someone had raised a cruel wall of glass high between herself and her husband.

Ever since her marriage her husband's existence had been her own existence, and every breath of his had been a breath drawn by herself. But now, while her husband's existence in pain was a vivid reality, Reiko could find in this grief of hers no certain proof at all of her own existence.

With only his right hand on the sword the lieutenant began to cut sideways across his stomach. But as the blade became entangled with the entrails it was pushed constantly outward by their soft resilience; and the lieutenant realized that it would be necessary, as he cut, to use both hands to keep the point pressed deep into his stomach. He pulled the blade across. It did not cut as easily as he had expected. He directed the strength of his whole body into his right hand and pulled again. There was a cut of three or four inches.

The pain spread slowly outward from the inner depths until the whole stomach reverberated. It was like the wild clanging of a bell. Or like a thousand bells which jangled simultaneously at every breath he breathed and every throb of his pulse, rocking his whole being. The lieutenant could no longer stop himself from moaning. But by now the blade had cut its way through to below the navel, and when he noticed this he felt a sense of satisfaction, and a renewal of courage.

The volume of blood had steadily increased, and now it spurted from the wound as if propelled by the beat of the pulse. The mat before the lieutenant was drenched red with splattered blood, and more blood overflowed onto it from pools which gathered in folds of the lieutenant's khaki trousers. A spot, like a bird, came flying across to Reiko and settled on the lap of her white silk kimono.

By the time the lieutenant had at last drawn the sword across to the right side of his stomach, the blade was already cutting shallow and had revealed its naked tip, slippery with blood and grease. But, suddenly stricken by a fit of vomiting, the lieutenant cried out hoarsely. The vomiting made the fierce pain fiercer still, and the stomach, which had thus far remained firm and compact, now abruptly heaved, opening wide its wound, and the entrails burst through, as if the wound too were vomiting. Seemingly ignorant of their master's suffering, the entrails gave an impression of robust health and almost disagreeable vitality as they slipped smoothly out and spilled over into the crotch. The lieutenant's head dropped, his shoulders heaved, his eyes opened to narrow slits, and a thin trickle of saliva dribbled from his mouth. The gold markings on his epaulettes caught the light and glinted.

Blood was scattered everywhere. The lieutenant was soaked in it to his knees, and he sat now in a crumpled and listless posture, one hand on the floor. A raw smell filled the room. The lieutenant, his head drooping, retched repeatedly, and the movement showed vividly in his shoulders. The blade of the sword, now pushed back by the entrails and exposed to its tip, was still in the lieutenant's right hand.

It would be difficult to imagine a more heroic sight than that of the lieutenant at this moment, as he mustered his strength and flung back his head. The movement was performed with sudden violence, and the back of his head struck with a sharp crack against the alcove pillar. Reiko had been sitting until now with her face lowered, gazing in fascination at the tide of blood advancing toward her knees, but the sound took her by surprise and she looked up.

The lieutenant's face was not the face of a living man. The eyes were hollow, the skin parched, the once so lustrous cheeks and lips the color of dried mud. The right hand alone was moving. Laboriously gripping the sword, it hovered shakily in the air like the hand of a marionette and strove to direct the point at the base of the lieutenant's throat. Reiko watched her husband make this last, most heart-rending, futile exertion. Glistening with blood and grease, the point was thrust at the throat again and again. And each time it missed its aim. The strength to guide it was no longer there. The straying point struck the collar and the collar badges. Although its hooks had been unfastened, the stiff military collar had closed together again and was protecting the throat.

Reiko could bear the sight no longer. She tried to go to her husband's help, but she could not stand. She moved through the blood on her knees, and her white skirts grew deep red. Moving to the rear of her husband, she helped no more than by loosening the collar. The quivering blade at last contacted the naked flesh of the throat. At that moment Reiko's impression was that she herself had propelled her husband forward; but that was not the case. It was movement planned by the lieutenant himself, his last exertion of strength. Abruptly he threw his body at the blade, and the blade pierced his neck, emerging at the nape. There was a tremendous spurt of blood and the lieutenant lay still, cold blue-tinged steel protruding from his neck at the back.

5

Slowly, her socks slippery with blood, Reiko descended the stairway. The upstairs room was now completely still.

Switching on the ground-floor lights, she checked the gas jet and the main gas plug and poured water over the smoldering, half-buried charcoal in the brazier. She stood before the upright mirror in the four-and-a-half-mat room and held up her skirts. The bloodstains made it seem as if a bold, vivid pattern was printed across the lower half of her white kimono. When she sat down before the mirror, she was conscious of the dampness and coldness of her husband's blood in the region of her thighs, and she shivered. Then, for a long while, she lingered over her toilet preparations. She applied the rouge generously to her cheeks, and her lips too she painted heavily. This was no longer make-up to please her husband. It was make-up for the world which she would leave behind, and there was a touch of the magnificent and the spectacular in her brushwork. When she rose, the mat before the mirror was wet with blood. Reiko was not concerned about this.

Returning from the toilet, Reiko stood finally on the cement floor of the porchway. When her husband had bolted the door here last night it had been in preparation for death. For a while she stood immersed in the consideration of a simple problem. Should she now leave the bolt drawn? If she were to lock the door, it could be that the neighbors might not notice their suicide for several days. Reiko did not relish the thought of their two corpses putrifying before discovery. After all, it seemed, it would be best to leave it open. . . . She released the bolt, and also drew open the frosted-glass door a fraction. . . . At once a chill wind blew in. There was no sign of anyone in the midnight streets and stars glittered ice-cold through the trees in the large house opposite.

Leaving the door as it was, Reiko mounted the stairs. She had walked here and there for some time and her socks were no longer slippery. About halfway up, her nostrils were already assailed by a peculiar smell.

The lieutenant was lying on his face in a sea of blood. The point protruding from his neck seemed to have grown even more prominent than before. Reiko walked heedlessly across the blood. Sitting beside the lieutenant's corpse, she stared intently at the face, which lay on one cheek on the mat. The eyes were opened wide, as if the lieutenant's attention had been attracted by something. She raised the head, folding it in her sleeve, wiped the blood from the lips, and bestowed a last kiss.

Then she rose and took from the closet a new white blanket and a waist cord. To prevent any derangement of her skirts, she wrapped the blanket about her waist and bound it firmly with the cord.

Reiko sat herself on a spot about one foot distant from the lieutenant's body. Drawing the dagger from her sash, she examined its dully gleaming blade intently, and held it to her tongue. The taste of the polished steel was slightly sweet.

Reiko did not linger. When she thought how the pain which had previously opened such a gulf between herself and her dying husband was now to become a part of her own experience, she saw before her only the joy of herself entering a realm her husband had already made his own. In her husband's agonized face there had been something inexplicable which she was seeing for the first time. Now she would solve that riddle. Reiko sensed that at last she too would be able to taste the true bitterness and sweetness of that great moral principle in which her husband believed. What had until now been tasted only faintly through her husband's example she was about to savor directly with her own tongue.

Reiko rested the point of the blade against the base of her throat. She thrust hard. The wound was only shallow. Her head blazed, and her hands shook uncontrollably. She gave the blade a strong pull sideways. A warm substance flooded into her mouth, and everything before her eyes reddened, in a vision of spouting blood. She gathered her strength and plunged the point of the blade deep into her throat.

QUESTIONS

1. Despite the title and the political event that sets the plot in motion, this story focuses almost exclusively on the relationship between the hero and heroine, their lovemaking, and their ritual suicides. In what ways do the intensely psychological explorations of the story define and clarify the meaning of patriotism for Lieutenant

Takeyama?   **2.** In the West, we tend to view the family—the relationship between husband and wife—as a private and personal matter that has little to do with public, political life. How do Lieutenant Takeyama and his wife view their relationship?   **3.** Lieutenant Takeyama views "the urges of his flesh and the sincerity of his patriotism" as "two parts of the same thing." What does he mean by this?   **4.** What does Mishima achieve by the opening paragraph? Why does he sacrifice suspense by recounting at the outset the major events and the story's outcome?   **5.** What is the significance of Reiko's deliberations as to whether or not she should leave the door bolt drawn?

WRITING TOPIC

What connections does the story establish between love, marriage, and death?

Rough Translations   1985

MOLLY GILES [b. 1942]

There was so much to do that Ramona felt dizzy, and when Ramona felt dizzy,
Ramona lay down; once down she stayed for the count and then some. Shadow
and sun took their turns on her ceiling, the phone rang unanswered, a Mozart
sonata spun silently on the turntable by the window. Ramona dozed, and
dreamed she was dancing. When she awoke she found her own hands clinging
to her own ribs as if for dear life. It's the funeral, she decided. It's the funeral
that's killing me.

She must have spoken out loud because her son Potter stared from the
doorway. He was balancing a bag of groceries in one arm and his pet cat and
violin case in the other. In his slipped-down glasses and long brown ponytail
he looked as careworn as any young housewife, and Ramona felt the familiar
urge to apologize, an urge she stifled with a shamed little laugh and a wave
from the pillows. If my timing had been better, she thought, Potter could be
touring Europe right now, playing music with his friends, having some fun
. . . can Potter have fun? Potter frowned and said, "What is it? You okay?"

"Alive," Ramona cried gaily, "and kicking." She lifted one moccasined foot
to demonstrate and knocked the phone book off the bedspread. Potter's frown
deepened. He had never smiled at Ramona's jokes, nor had his sister Nora;
finding their mother unamusing was the one trait they shared. Sometimes
Ramona thought: It's because they can't forgive me. Other times she thought:
It's because they have no sense of humor. She watched as Potter, frowning, put
down his burdens and moved into her room. He snapped the record player off,
drew the curtains closed, turned the lamp on, plumped her pillows, and pressed
his lips gingerly to her forehead to feel her temperature. Ramona, tucked under
his chin like a violin being tuned, tried to sound the right note. "I had the
funniest dream," she said, but even as she began to tell the dream she saw
Potter didn't think it was funny; his face was so pained she started to lie. One
lie, as always, led to another, and down she went, deeper and deeper. "So there
I was," she finished, breathless, "tap-dancing among the gravestones like Ginger
Rogers in a horror film. Isn't that a scream?"

"It might make a good drawing for *The Beacon*," Potter said. Ramona bowed
her head, contrite. She knew what Potter thought of her drawings. She had
heard him describe the cartoons she did for the village weekly as "illustrated
idioms, the kind you find on cocktail napkins," which she supposed was a fair
description—not kind, but fair. A few days before, propped up in bed, she had
finished her last assignment: a pen and ink sketch of a little ark floating on a
sea of question marks with a caption that read "Flooded by Doubts." Her very

favorite submission, "Tour de Force," had showed a docent dragging a group
of tourists through the Louvre at gunpoint, and it was true she had seen a
cartoon much like it etched onto a highball glass at the church rummage sale;
she had bought the glass, of course, and pitched it into a garbage bin at once.
She tried now to imagine how she would draw her dancing dream. She'd sketch
herself as she was: a small, wide-eyed old woman with bad posture and a frizz
of gray bangs. She'd dress herself in a straw hat and tux and set herself among
the headstones at Valley View . . . Valley View? Was that right? Was that the
cemetery she had finally decided on? Or was that the one where Hale had been
buried? Should she be buried by Hale after all? Would he want her there?
Would he let her stay? Her fingers started to clutch at her ribs again, and again
she sighed and said, "So much to do. So many decisions. I hope you never
have to go through this, Potter."

"Right," said Potter. He replaced the phone book on the bed, gave Ramona
another of his shy hard stares, and left with the cat meowing at his heels to
start cooking their dinner.

Ramona reached for her glasses, picked up the phone book, and turned
again to the back. She had memorized the five listings for Funerals, but she
had not yet found the nerve to dial. She stared at the ads again, narrowing in
on the Manis Funeral Home, which said, "Call at Any Time," and The
Evergreens, which advertised air-conditioned chapels. The air-conditioning
tempted her, for the summer afternoons had been growing warm, but when
she finally started to dial and her finger slipped, she took it as an omen. She
did not think the Manis Home, despite its insistence, should receive calls at
dinner time; she'd call them tomorrow too.

She fell into her old habit of reading the phone book, leafing through the
classifieds for Mourners, then for Paid Professional Mourners, then finally for
Mummers. She still wondered where Hale had found that little blonde who
wept so competently at his graveside—a waitress Ramona had not been told
about? an extra secretary? How delicious it would be, she thought, if I could
hire the equivalent of that little blonde—some good-looking young boy, an
acting student down on his luck . . . someone who would be willing to fling
himself down on the coffin . . . She shivered happily, thinking how that would
shock Nora, and then, penitent, she reached for the phone again and dialed
Nora's number, the words "I hate to bother you" already forming on her lips.
She knew Nora would be busy. Nora was always busy. Right now, Ramona
feared, Nora would be kneading a loaf of whole wheat bran bread, knitting a
sweater, cutting the baby's hair, balancing her husband's business accounts,
checking the twins' homework, and drafting a proposal for a new gymnasium
while her old mother, with nothing better to do, lay slumped in a filthy bathrobe
on an unmade bed covered with overdue library books, wanting a chat. Oh
Lord, Ramona thought, gazing around her cluttered room, but Potter and I
live like two French whores, underwear everywhere, and jars full of dead roses.
I can never have the funeral here. The best thing to do is go to Nora's at once
and get buried in Nora's backyard like a pet hamster in a shoe box.

"I can't decide between the Manis or The Evergreens," she said, when Nora picked up the phone. "How can I find out which one is the best?"

"I'll find out for you," Nora said. "Next?"

Nora's knitting needles clicked like static on the other end of the line while Ramona tried to think of something else to ask for. "Medication?" Nora suggested. "Has Potter been giving you the right medication?"

"I think so." Ramona glanced at the bottle by the bed, rechecked it to be sure it was labeled for her and not the cat, and leaned back. "It's just planning this funeral."

"Do you know what I'd do about that funeral if I were you?" Nora said.

Ramona waited, grateful.

"I'd forget it," Nora said. "I'd file it away in my Not-to-Worry drawer."

"Not-to-Worry drawer?"

"That's right. I'd file it away and swallow the key. Do you understand?"

"I'm not a child," Ramona began, but Nora, her voice flat, sweet, and dangerous, said, "Have Potter cook you some real food for once. I'll come by and see you in the morning. I don't like the idea of you thinking about your funeral all day. It's not healthy."

Not healthy? thought Ramona. That's a good one. She said good-bye to Nora and lay back. Her heart began to race and her fingers raced too, drumming and tapping on top of the phone book. What should she do, what should she do? Perhaps there was still enough time to go crazy? She had always meant to spend her last days tiptoeing around in a flowered hat with a fingertip pressed to her lips, but no luck. These were her last days and she felt no crazier than usual. She felt as she always had when there were decisions to be made: harassed and dreamy, wildly anxious and unable to move. She reached up to twist one earring off, realizing, with dismay, that one was all she was wearing; in her haste to prove she could still dress herself she had forgotten to put on the other. Her bathrobe buttons—were they closed? They were. She wished she could push a button and make herself disappear, right now, before her body became a burden to them all, before they learned how complicated, dull, and expensive it was to dispose of even a small person's final remains.

"You know who I admire?" she said to Potter as she joined him in the kitchen for dinner. "Junie Poole. Junie sat down in the hall outside the coroner's office one night and tried to kill herself by drinking a thermos of gin mixed with pills. When they arrested her she was too drunk to talk, but they found this note pinned to her mink coat saying she hoped her children would appreciate the fact that she had at least taken herself to the morgue. Of course, no one's appreciated anything Junie's ever done, before or since, but that's not the point. The point is that she did try to make things easy for her family. I want to make things easy too." She picked up her fork and looked down at her plate. "Liver? Won't Nora be impressed." She tried to eat a little. But when she saw the cat, in the corner, licking from an identical plate, she put the fork down and regarded Potter, who had done this to her before, once with canned salmon and once with pickled herring. He was either trying to be very economical or his values were more confused than she suspected. "Potter," she said, watching the old gray cat huddled murmurously over its plate, "do you think I should just crawl off to the woods?"

"There aren't any woods within crawling distance," said Potter. Ramona smiled; Potter did not. "I think . . ." Potter began. He stopped. Ramona folded her hands and waited. Potter, born when she was over forty, had been a talkative child, full of ideas and advice and so original that even Hale had paid attention, but Potter had stopped talking years ago, at least to her. "I think," Potter repeated, one thin hand fluttering before his downcast face, "that you are using this funeral to mask your real feelings."

Ramona waited, her own head bent. "And what are my real feelings?" she asked at last.

"Rage," Potter said, his shy eyes severe behind his smudged glasses. "Terror. Awe. Grief. Self-pity."

"Heavens," said Ramona. She was impressed. Once again she wished she were the mother her children deserved, and once again she found herself having to tell them she was not. "I'm afraid, Potter," she said, "you give me credit. I don't feel any more of those 'real' feelings now than I ever have. What I feel now is a sort of social panic, the same old panic I used to feel when Hale wanted me to give a dinner party for his clients and the guests would arrive and I'd still be in my slip clutching a bucket of live lobsters. I'm sorry, dear, I can't eat this. I'm too nervous. I'm going to have to make a list."

She sat at her drawing desk, staring at a piece of paper, wondering where to start after printing "To File in the Worry Drawer" across the top of the page. In the next room Potter talked to Nora on the telephone, his voice reluctant and slow. If only my children liked each other, Ramona thought. She sighed and pressed her palm to a few of the places that hurt. Sometimes the pains were gone for hours altogether and sometimes they felt like ripping cloth; sometimes they widened and sometimes they narrowed and sometimes they overwhelmed her completely. Right now she was being treated to a new pain, a persistent jabbing in her chest that tapped back and forth like an admonishing finger. It feels like I'm being lectured by a bully, she thought. Lectured on my failures. If I had been lovable, Hale would have loved me, and if Hale had loved me, I would have loved myself, and if I'd loved myself, Nora would have loved me, and if Nora had loved me, Potter would have loved her, and then Potter wouldn't have had to grow up loving nothing but his music and his wretched cat. Hale and I, she thought, set a bad example for the children as far as loving went . . . the children! she thought. She pushed her chair back and stood up. "Tell Nora," she called out to Potter, "tell Nora I'm sorry but this is going to be an adults-only funeral, X-rated, no grandchildren allowed. Maybe the boys, but by no means the twins. By no means the baby. I've seen little children at funerals before," she added, when Potter finally returned from the phone, "and it's no picnic, believe me."

"Nora said to give you this." He handed Ramona a mug of warm milk and his eyes were so sad that she drank it all down even though there was a cat whisker floating on top.

That night Ramona dreamed her funeral was held outdoors on the slope of a mountain; it was a bright summer afternoon and everyone she'd ever cared about was there: her parents, her grandparents, Hale, all her friends from childhood on. She was there herself, hovering in the sky like a Chagall[1] bride, her pretty shroud rippling around her crossed ankles. She had never felt so happy. Tables set up under flowering trees were laden with cakes and roasts and sparkling wines; music came from somewhere; there were rainbows, fountains. The conversations she overheard made her laugh with pleasure; people were saying kind, affectionate, funny things to each other, some of them so wonderful, so insightful, that Ramona could scarcely wait to wake up and write them down.

Half-asleep, she groped for pencil and pad and quickly, in the dark, jotted down every scrap of conversation she could remember. In the morning, unsurprised, she studied her notes. They were illegible, as frail and choppy as an EKG. Lost, she thought. Like everything else. Lost like all the words I've tried to string together throughout my life. For a brief, bitter second she thought of all the poems, stories, prayers, and revelations that had evaporated like breath in cold air when she tried to express them. I have never said anything right, she decided. Even my jokes, even the drawings I do for *The Beacon* are wrong— rough translations of a foreign language I hear but cannot master.

She took her pen and quickly tied all the choppy lines on the paper together, making a scrawl across the top, and then she drew herself at the bottom of the page, an anxious old lady staring straight up, and then she wrote "Over My Dead Body" and tore the paper up.

She took the day's second dose of Percodan into her palm and thought again of Junie Poole passed out in front of the coroner's office. It was then she saw how her own funeral truly would be: a small gathering of silent relatives sitting in uncomfortable pews in a little Consolation Chapel somewhere. Pink and yellow light would fall through the stained-glass window over the casket where she lay. The air would smell unwholesomely floral. Muzak would be piped in. She would be wearing an evening gown that Nora, at the last minute, would have had to alter to fit, a terrible dress, mauve, with long sleeves and net at the neck. Her nails would be painted mauve to match, and her lips. Her five grandchildren would be wild with horror and boredom. The boys would be thinking about basketball and sex, basketball and sex. The twins would be cracking their knuckles, glancing cross-eyed at each other, giggling. The baby, whose damp quick hands were never still, would be digging a design into the plush seat with a thumbnail, a design no one but the baby would know was a

---

[1] Marc Chagall (1889–1985) was a Russian-born French painter who often depicted people floating in the sky.

skull and red flames. Nora would be shushing and clucking the children as she counted the heads in the chapel, trying to decide if she had made enough potato salad. A minister chosen by Nora's husband would give a speech. The minister would say that Ramona was in a far better place than she had been before. Potter, picking cat hair off his pressed blue jeans, would think about this. He would regret he had not gone to Europe with his friends when he had the chance; he could be in a better place, too, he would think, if it weren't for his mother. After the ceremony the mourners would bunch on the sidewalk in the sun, ill-at-ease and restless . . . and I'll still be lying beneath the pink and yellow lights, Ramona thought, reeking of hairspray and formaldehyde—and the garnet necklace I want Nora to save for the baby will still be around my neck, forgotten in that damn mauve net.

She eased herself out of bed, walked unsteadily toward her closet, opened the door, and peered in. The darkness surprised her. At first she could not see the mauve dress and she even had a wild hope she had thrown it out, years ago, but then she saw it, hanging in its plastic bag like a hideous orchid. As she reached up to strike it off the clothes rod, she lost her balance and fainted forward. It was so strange to fall face forward into soft dark clothes that when she came to she was not even frightened. She tried to tell Potter how strange it had been, how comfortable, how sexy really, like falling into outheld arms, like dancing. Oh but that time Hale twirled her at the Christmas party and she was feeling almost beautiful that night and so deeply in love and as she came out of the twirl Hale turned to another woman, neglecting to catch her, and she lost her balance and spun across the dance floor, all the colored lights a blur, and she was completely alone and she was laughing, even before she fell and cracked her coccyx she was laughing, prepared for the laughter of others, prepared to say, "It's all right, I'm not hurt a bit," even though it wasn't all right, even though she *was* hurt a bit. Quite a bit. Always after that she saw herself as Hale saw her: a clumsy woman with breasts that were too big and lips that were too wide and little awkward hands that couldn't hold a man. She saw herself as someone who could be dropped. "Oh Ramona bounces back," Hale drawled and didn't she though, bouncing back like any old kickball. Well, the secret was not to take yourself too seriously. No matter where they kicked you it couldn't hurt if you didn't let it, if you got right down there with the dancing shoes and laughed—if you could do that, you could rise like a rose in the air when they toed you.

"I have something to say," she said to Potter. "I have a statement to make. Are you ready? You should write this down. It's very important. Listen, Potter. Words of wisdom: Lie low. Move fast. Bounce."

"Don't try to talk," Potter said. He knelt beside her, stroking her forehead with the same light scratchy touch he used on the cat. "Don't keep making jokes. You don't have to be funny any more. Just breathe slow. Relax."

Ramona flushed with temper and turned her head away. She could not relax. She was angry at Potter and at Hale and at Nora and at herself too, angry at everything that wasn't funny any more, angry at everyone who had let her down, down, so far down that when young Dr. Seton stood up from the chair by her bed it was as if he were stretching up toward the ceiling and she was sinking down through the floor, sinking faster and faster, and only the thought of her funeral made her stop: the last straw, she thought, and wouldn't you know it's the one straw I reach for. "Good girl," Dr. Seton said. "You're coming back to us."

Coming back? Of course she was coming back. How could she leave? There was so much to do. There was her life to understand and Hale to forgive and Nora to charm and Potter to cheer up. There was the novel. Where was the novel? Lying in a cardboard box somewhere, half-alive, unfinished, unformed. There were all the paintings, the little canvasses of pastel flower arrangements that Hale had called "stillborns" instead of "still lifes"—where were those? Facing the walls of the garage? She didn't want anyone seeing those paintings; she didn't want anyone reading the journal she had kept in the first years after Hale's death, or playing the tapes she had made of her own voice, singing her own songs to her own accompaniment on an old guitar. She was not ready to be judged; her work wasn't done yet; it wasn't begun; she didn't even know what her work was, for God's sake. "You seem to have developed a faintly comedic point of view," her last art teacher had told her. "Have you thought of doing cartoons?" And he had dismissed her, turning his head, stifling his yawn; he had dropped her, not bothering to watch the direction of his kick, nor the way it hooked, nor the way she bounced, landing on both flat, splayed, calloused feet before the editor of *The Beacon* with a sheaf of drawings in one shaking hand. She had an occupation now. But was that her work?

"Those cartoons," she said, looking up into Nora's puzzled face, "those cartoons were the hardest things I ever did and they were never what I meant to do. I meant to do something quite important and beautiful with my life, you see—something that would astonish and delight and make you all proud."

"Still trying to talk," Nora said. "Half-alive and she's still trying to talk. She's probably worried we're going to take her to the hospital. Well, don't worry, Mother. Dr. Seton said you might as well stay here—although why you'd want to, I'm sure I don't know. The house is a mess. It's filthy dirty and there's nothing in the cupboards but cat food. I've sent the boys out to rake the yard and the twins are making cocoa, and the baby, here's the baby, the baby will keep you company while I discuss a few things with Potter. And his cat."

After Nora left the room, the baby—a lanky, curt, fast-moving four-year-old whose given name, Hope, was so unsuitable that Ramona had never been able to use it—sidled close and peered down into Ramona's face. "Ba?" said Ramona. It was all she could say. "Ba? Ah wa pa."

"You. Want. Paper," the child repeated.

Ramona pointed toward her desk and Hope tugged at the drawers until she found the drawing supplies. She gave Ramona one pad and one pencil and then, engrossed, she chose a thicker pad, a sharper pencil, for herself. Ramona struggled upright in her bed. For a long time she and Hope sat quietly, thinking. Then Hope ducked over her pad and started to draw a city. Ramona sat immobile. Even if I try, she thought, I won't succeed. I've never been able to organize my life; how dare I attempt to order my death? My funeral will be as disastrous a failure as my childhood, my marriage, my motherhood, my dotage. There will be the same dry coughs, the same scraping of chairs, the same artificial smiles I've seen all my life. I'll be put to rest like all the rest, and no one will ever know how much I had to give the world, or how I longed to give it. She glanced at her granddaughter's page. Hope had finished the city and was peopling it quickly with vampires and werewolves. It's enough to make the old blood stagger, Ramona thought. In the next room Potter and Nora were arguing. The smell of burnt cocoa drifted in from the kitchen. Ramona dozed. She dreamt Hale was in bed with her, asleep, his back turned to her, his weight warm, familiar, a great comfort, and she snuggled close, glad to have him there but afraid to wake him, afraid he might awaken saying some other woman's name.

When she opened her eyes it was dark in the house. She turned on her light, picked up the pad and pencil, and began to write. She had just had the one idea that would make her funeral the successful occasion she knew it could be. She knew the music, the foods, the psalm, the location. She wrote quickly, covering the page. She wrote until she had said everything she had to say, and then, content, she slipped the paper into the top drawer of her nightstand, lay back, and slept.

It was a restless, busy, broken sleep and it seemed to go on for a long long time. Dreams came and went, some of them nightmares, some so full of light she fought to stay in them. Nora nursed her with unsmiling vigilance, bathing and dressing her with swift cool hands. Nora's children took over the house, the boys mowing and trimming the lawn, the twins scrubbing the kitchen and bathrooms. Only the baby refused to pitch in. She sat at the desk beside Ramona's bed, covering page after page with intricate, disordered drawings. Potter too ignored Nora's orders; he locked himself in his room with the cat and tuned and retuned his violin. Ramona, listening to him play over the sound of the vacuum and the dishwasher, felt a robot was playing to her from the moon, so strange and cold and simple the music. Sometimes one of the children would drag a chair to the bureau and bring her the photos she asked for— portraits of Hale, his smile lean, gleaming, and enticing as ever, group pictures of old school friends standing arm in arm in sunny gardens, photos of her own children as children and herself as child, girl, and mother. When Ramona looked from these pictures to the face in the mirror Nora held up, she was pleased. She finally had a face she liked, sharp-boned, flushed, with enormous eyes—a stylish face, at last. She still could not speak clearly enough to be understood and when visitors told her she looked beautiful she could only tip her head, a queen accepting homage. There's a price tag to all this glamour, she wanted to tell them. Nothing big. A pay-later plan.

One afternoon Nora said, "Come on, Potter, help me for once. I want to carry Mother outside." The two of them linked hands and carried Ramona out into the garden, pausing to point out the bright banks of amaryllis and filling her bathrobe skirts with Japanese plums from the unpruned trees against the fence. Ramona looked into their pale distracted faces and said, "If you two would just like each other a little, I think I could go to heaven this second," and Nora said, "Still trying to talk? I wish she'd give up," and Potter said, "She can't give up; she's tough; she's not like us," and Nora said, "Speak for yourself; I don't slop around feeling sorry for myself all day," and Potter said, "That's because you don't know how to feel anything, period," and they carried Ramona into the house and dropped her on the bed a little too roughly. That night Potter announced that since Nora had taken over so well, he was leaving. He was moving in with another unemployed musician who had a house by the sea. "I'd like to move to a house by the sea," Ramona said suddenly, and this first clear sentence after weeks of gibberish made Potter turn and Nora stop in mid-sentence. "I'd like to go there right now," Ramona said, "and never come back."

"Don't make me cry," Nora said sharply.

"She means she wants to die," Potter said.

"I know what she means," Nora said.

Potter picked up the cat and held it close to his heart, then laid it by Ramona's side like a bouquet of gray flowers. Nora came and stood beside them. "She's asleep again," Nora said. "No I'm not," Ramona said. "There's so much I've wanted to tell her," Nora said. "But I don't have her gift. I've never known how to put things."

"Well," Ramona answered, pleased, "I thank you and I think I finally have put things in place myself. I've taken care of everything at last." But nobody heard her. It was dark in her room and she was alone. Why look at me, she thought. I've gone and died with my big mouth wide open. She started to laugh and in that same second she started to spin, which made her laugh harder, for she knew that with this last breath she would fall, fall and break herself and bounce, bounce far beyond laughter forever.

The cat leapt off the bed and meowed for Potter, but Potter and Nora were sitting in the kitchen drinking coffee together and talking about a time when they had both thought their mother the gayest and most beautiful woman in the world, their father the richest and kindest man. The only one who heard the cat cry was the baby. The baby had slipped from her sleeping bag and was prowling through the house, searching for paper. She let herself into Ramona's room and went to the desk, but the drawers were depleted, all paper gone. In the top drawer of the nightstand by the bed she found some paper, one side ruined by her grandmother's writing, but the other side fresh and clean. She turned to the clean side and went to the window. Squatting in the moonlight with the cat winding around her, the baby drew the dream that had awakened her: a woman shooting off the edge of the planet, her lips like two red wings, flapping up toward the stars. She studied the drawing, shook her head, and tore it up.

Nora made the arrangements for the funeral. It didn't take long. She was pretty sure she knew what her mother wanted. She found a long purplish evening dress in the closet that looked brand new, and she gave it with instructions for matching nail polish to the cosmetician at The Evergreens. Her husband knew a minister who agreed to say a few words. After the service, which was mercifully short for such a warm afternoon, the mourners were asked to return to the house for refreshments. Most of the mourners seemed to be truly mourning; some of them were weeping. Ramona had been so brave, they said, so uncomplaining. She had kept her sense of humor to the end, they said, and they paused to study the display of drawings from *The Beacon*, their faces long and somber. The cat wandered companionably through the crowd. Potter sat in the garden with his violin, playing a song that everyone knew but no one could place. The notes seemed to come together in little rushes, rise, fade off, rush in again. "My Mother's Voice," Potter said, when the minister asked the name of the piece. The baby, swaying to the music, pushed open the door of Ramona's room, climbed the chair by the bureau, brought down all the photographs, and dropped them out the window, chanting "Bury Bury" as they fluttered down. She was about to throw a garnet necklace out too when her father caught her and gave her a spanking. Nora, handsome in black, was too busy to pay attention to her daughter's screams; she was telling everyone how childlike Ramona had seemed toward the end, how dependent and docile. "It was as if I were the mother . . ." Nora began, but she was interrupted by a large lady named Junie Poole who hugged her impulsively, spilling gin down her dress. "This is the best funeral I've ever been to," Junie declared, and although the others turned away to hide their smiles, they all said later they agreed. It was a good funeral. The weather was fine and sunny, the house was welcoming. The only thing missing was Ramona herself.

QUESTIONS
1. Do Potter's and Nora's attitudes toward their mother's dying differ? Explain. **2.** What do Ramona's dreams tell us about her state of mind? **3.** What does Ramona mean when she characterizes her work as a "rough translation of a foreign language I hear but cannot master"? **4.** What role does Junie Poole play in the story?

WRITING TOPIC
Is the reader meant to accept as accurate Ramona's evaluation of her life as a failure?

Preparation

ROBERT OLEN BUTLER [b. 1945]

Though Thủy's dead body was naked under the sheet, I had not seen it since we were girls together and our families took us to the beaches of Nha Trang. This was so even though she and I were best friends for all our lives and she became the wife of Lê Văn Lý, the man I once loved. Thủy had a beautiful figure and breasts that were so tempting in the tight bodice of our aó dàis[1] that Lý could not resist her. But the last time I saw Thủy's naked body, she had no breasts yet at all, just the little brown nubs that I also had at seven years old, and we ran in the white foam of the breakers and we watched the sampans out beyond the coral reefs.

We were not common girls, the ones who worked the fields and seemed so casual about their bodies. And more than that, we were Catholics, and Mother Mary was very modest, covered from her throat to her ankles, and we made up our toes beautifully, like the statue of Mary in the church, and we were very modest about all the rest. Except Thủy could seem naked when she was clothed. We both ran in the same surf, but somehow her flesh learned something there that mine did not. She could move like the sea, her body filled her clothes like the living sea, fluid and beckoning. Her mother was always worried about her because the boys grew quiet at her approach and noisy at her departure, and no one was worried about me. I was an expert pair of hands, to bring together the herbs for the lemon grass chicken or to serve the tea with the delicacy of a wind chime or to scratch the eucalyptus oil into the back of a sick child.

And this won for me a good husband, though he was not Lê Văn Lý, nor could ever have been. But he was a good man and a surprised man to learn that my hands could also make him very happy even if my breasts did not seem so delightful in the tight bodice of my aó dài. That man died in the war which came to our country, a war we were about to lose, and I took my sons to America and I settled in this place in New Orleans called Versailles that has only Vietnamese. Soon my best friend Thủy also came to this place, with her husband Lê Văn Lý and her children. They left shortly for California, but after three years they returned, and we all lived another decade together and we expected much longer than that, for Thủy and I would have become fifty years old within a week of each other next month.

Except that Thủy was dead now and lying before me in this place that Mr.

---

[1] The national dress of Vietnamese women. It consists of an ankle length dress with a tight bodice, slit to the hip on both sides. It is worn over loose black slacks.

Hoa, the mortician for our community, called the "preparation room," and she was waiting for me to put the makeup on her face and comb her hair for the last time. She died very quickly, but she knew enough to ask for the work of my hands to make her beautiful in the casket. She let on to no one—probably not even herself—when the signs of the cancer growing in her ovaries caused no pain. She was a fearful person over foolish little things, and such a one as that will sometimes ignore the big things until it is too late. But thank God that when the pain did come and the truth was known, the end came quickly afterward.

She clutched my hand in the hospital room, the curtain drawn around us, and my own grip is very strong, but on that morning she hurt me with the power of her hand. This was a great surprise to me. I looked at our locked hands, and her lovely, slender fingers were white with the strength in them and yet the nails were still perfect, each one a meticulously curved echo of the others, each one carefully stroked with the red paint the color of her favorite Winesap apples. This was a very sad moment for me. It made me sadder even than the sounds of her pain, this hand with its sudden fearful strength and yet the signs of her lovely vanity still there.

But I could not see her hands as I stood beside her in the preparation room. They were somewhere under the sheet and I had work to do, so I looked at her face. Her closed eyes showed the mostly Western lids, passed down by more than one Frenchman among her ancestors. This was a very attractive thing about her, I always knew, though Lý never mentioned her eyes, even though they were something he might well have complimented in public. He could have said to people, "My wife has such beautiful eyes," but he did not. And his certain regard for her breasts, of course, was kept very private. Except with his glance.

We three were young, only sixteen, and Thūy and I were at the Cirque Sportif in Saigon. This was where we met Lý for the first time. We were told that if Mother Mary had known the game of tennis, she would have allowed her spiritual children to wear the costume for the game, even if our legs did show. We loved showing our legs. I have very nice legs, really. Not as nice as Thūy's but I was happy to have my legs bare when I met Lê Văn Lý for the first time. He was a ball boy at the tennis court, and when Thūy and I played, he would run before us and pick up the balls and return them to us. I was a more skillful player than Thūy and it wasn't until too late that I realized how much better it was to hit the ball into the net and have Lý dart before me on this side and then pick up my tennis ball and return it to me. Thūy, of course, knew this right away and her game was never worse than when we played with Lê Văn Lý poised at the end of the net waiting for us to make a mistake.

And it was even on that first meeting that I saw his eyes move to Thūy's breasts. It was the slightest of glances but full of meaning. I knew this because I was very attuned to his eyes from the start. They were more like mine, with nothing of the West but everything of our ancestors back to the Kindly Dragon, whose hundred children began Vietnam. But I had let myself forget that the

Kindly Dragon married a fairy princess, not a solid homemaker, so my hopes were still real at age sixteen. He glanced at Thūy's breasts, but he smiled at me when I did miss a shot and he said, very low so only I could hear it, "You're a very good player." It sounded to me at sixteen that this was something he would begin to build his love on. I was a foolish girl.

But now she lay before me on a stainless-steel table, her head cranked up on a chrome support, her hair scattered behind her and her face almost plain. The room had a faint smell, a little itch in the nose of something strong, like the smell when my sons killed insects for their science classes in school. But over this was a faint aroma of flowers, though not real flowers, I knew. I did not like this place and I tried to think about what I'd come for. I was standing before Thūy and I had not moved since Mr. Hoa left me. He tied the smock I was wearing at the back and he told me how he had washed Thūy's hair already. He turned up the air conditioner in the window, which had its glass panes painted a chalky white, and he bowed himself out of the room and closed the door tight.

I opened the bag I'd placed on the high metal chair and I took out Thūy's pearl-handled brush and I bent near her. We had combed each other's hair all our lives. She had always worn her hair down, even as she got older. Even to the day of her death, with her hair laid carefully out on her pillow, something she must have done herself, very near the end, for when Lý and their oldest son and I came into the room that evening and found her, she was dead and her hair was beautiful.

So now I reached out to Thūy and I stroked her hair for the first time since her death and her hair resisted the brush and the resistance sent a chill through me. Her hair was still alive. The body was fixed and cold and absolutely passive, but the hair defied the brush, and though Thūy did not cry out at this first brush stroke as she always did, the hair insisted that she was still alive and I felt something very surprising at that. From the quick fisting of my mind at the image of Thūy, I knew I was angry. From the image of her hair worn long even after she was middle aged instead of worn in a bun at the nape of the neck like all the Vietnamese women our age. I was angry and then I realized that I was angry because she was not completely dead, and this immediately filled me with a shame so hot that it seemed as if I would break into a sweat.

The shame did not last very long. I straightened and turned my face to the flow of cool air from the air conditioner and I looked at all the instruments hanging behind the glass doors of the cabinet in the far wall, all the glinting clamps and tubes and scissors and knives. This was not the place of the living. I looked at Thūy's face and her pale lips were tugged down into a faint frown and I lifted the brush and stroked her hair again and once again, and though it felt just the way it always had felt when I combed it, I continued to brush.

And I spoke a few words to Thūy. Perhaps her spirit was in the room and could hear me. "It's all right, Thūy. The things I never blamed you for in life I won't blame you for now." She had been a good friend. She had always appreciated me. When we brushed each other's hair, she would always say how beautiful mine was and she would invite me also to leave it long, even though I am nearly fifty and I am no beauty at all. And she would tell me how wonderful my talents were. She would urge me to date some man or other in Versailles. I would make such and such a man a wonderful wife, she said. These men were successful men that she recommended, very well off. But they were always older men, in their sixties or seventies. One man was eighty-one, and this one she did not suggest to me directly but by saying casually how she had seen him last week and he was such a vigorous man, such a fine and vigorous man.

And her own husband, Lê Văn Lý, was of course more successful than any of them. And he is still the finest-looking man in Versailles. How fine he is. The face of a warrior. I have seen the high cheeks and full lips of Lê Văn Lý in the statues of warriors in the Saigon Museum, the men who threw the Chinese out of our country many centuries ago. And I lifted Thūy's hair and brushed it out in narrow columns and laid the hair carefully on the bright silver surface behind the support, letting the ends dangle off the table. The hair was very soft and it was yielding to my hands now and I could see this hair hanging perfectly against the back of her pale blue aó dài as she and Lý strolled away across the square near the Continental Palace Hotel.

I wish there had been some clear moment, a little scene; I would even have been prepared not to seem so solid and level-headed; I would have been prepared to weep and even to speak in a loud voice. But they were very disarming in the way they let me know how things were. We had lemonades on the veranda of the Continental Palace Hotel, and I thought it would be like all the other times, the three of us together in the city, strolling along the river or through the flower markets at Nguyễn Huệ or the bookstalls on Lê Lợi. We had been three friends together for nearly two years, ever since we'd met at the club. There had been no clear choosing, in my mind. Lý was a very traditional boy, a courteous boy, and he never forced the issue of romance, and so I still had some hopes.

Except that I had unconsciously noticed things, so when Thūy spoke to me and then, soon after, the two of them walked away from the hotel together on the eve of Lý's induction into the Army, I realized something with a shock that I actually had come to understand slowly all along. Like suddenly noticing that you are old. The little things gather for a long time, but one morning you look in the mirror and you understand them in a flash. At the flower market on Nguyễn Huệ I would talk with great spirit of how to arrange the flowers, which ones to put together, how a home would be filled with this or that sort of flower on this or that occasion. But Thūy would be bending into the flowers, her hair falling through the petals, and she would breathe very deeply and rise up and she would be inflated with the smell of flowers and of course her breasts would seem to have grown even larger and more beautiful and Lý would look at them and then he would close his eyes softly in appreciation. And at the bookstalls— I would be the one who asked for the bookstalls—I would be lost in what I thought was the miracle of all these little worlds inviting me in, and I was unaware of the little world near my elbow, Thūy looking at the postcards and talking to Lý about trips to faraway places.

I suppose my two friends were as nice to me as possible at the Continental Palace Hotel, considering what they had to do. Thūy asked me to go to the rest room with her and we were laughing together at something Lý had said. We went to the big double mirror and our two faces were side by side, two girls eighteen years old, and yet beside her I looked much older. Already old. I could see that. And she said, "I am so happy."

We were certainly having fun on this day, but I couldn't quite understand her attitude. After all, Lý was going off to fight our long war. But I replied, "I am, too."

Then she leaned near me and put her hand on my shoulder and she said, "I have a wonderful secret for you. I couldn't wait to tell it to my dear friend."

She meant these words without sarcasm. I'm sure of it. And I still did not understand what was coming.

She said, "I am in love."

I almost asked who it was that she loved. But this was only the briefest final pulse of naïveté. I knew who she loved. And after laying her head on the point of my shoulder and smiling at me in the mirror with such tenderness for her dear friend, she said, "And Lý loves me, too."

How had this subject not come up before? The answer is that the two of us had always spoken together of what a wonderful boy Lý was. But my own declarations were as vivid and enthusiastic as Thūy's—rather more vivid, in fact. So if I was to assume that she loved Lý from all that she'd said, then my own declaration of love should have been just as clear. But obviously it wasn't, and that was just as I should have expected it. Thūy never for a moment had considered me a rival for Lý. In fact, it was unthinkable to her that I should even love him in vain.

She lifted her head from my shoulder and smiled at me as if she expected me to be happy. When I kept silent, she prompted me. "Isn't it wonderful?"

I had never spoken of my love for Lý and I knew that this was the last chance I would have. But what was there to say? I could look back at all the little signs now and read them clearly. And Thūy was who she was and I was different from that and the feeling between Lý and her was already decided upon. So I said the only reasonable thing that I could. "It is very wonderful."

This made Thūy even happier. She hugged me. And then she asked me to comb her hair. We had been outside for an hour before coming to the hotel and her long, straight hair was slightly ruffled and she handed me the pearl-handled brush that her mother had given her and she turned her back to me. And I began to brush. The first stroke caught a tangle and Thūy cried out in a pretty, piping voice. I paused briefly and almost threw the brush against the wall and walked out of this place. But then I brushed once again and again, and she was turned away from the mirror so she could not see the terrible pinch of my face when I suggested that she and Lý spend their last hours now alone together. She nearly wept in joy and appreciation at this gesture from her dear friend, and I kept on brushing until her hair was perfect.

And her hair was perfect now beneath my hands in the preparation room. And I had a strange thought. She was doing this once more to me. She was having me make her hair beautiful so she could go off to the spirit world and seduce the one man there who could love me. This would be Thūy's final triumph over me. My hands trembled at this thought and it persisted. I saw this clearly: Thūy arriving in heaven and her hair lying long and soft down her back and her breasts are clearly beautiful even in the white robe of the angels, and the spirit of some great warrior who fought at the side of the Tru'ng sisters[2] comes to her, and though he has waited nineteen centuries for me, he sees Thūy and decides to wait no more. It has been only the work of my hands that he has awaited and he lifts Thūy's hair and kisses it.

I drew back from Thūy and I stared at her face. I saw it in the mirror at the Continental Palace Hotel and it was very beautiful, but this face before me now was rubbery in death, the beauty was hidden, waiting for my hands. Thūy waited for me to make her beautiful. I had always made her more beautiful. Just by being near her. I was tempted once more to turn away. But that would only let her have her condescending smile at me. Someone else would do this job if I did not, and Thūy would fly off to heaven with her beautiful face and I would be alone in my own shame.

I turned to the sheet now, and the body I had never looked upon in its womanly nakedness was hiding there and this was what Lý had given his love for. The hair and the face had invited him, but it was this hidden body, her secret flesh, that he had longed for. I had seen him less than half an hour ago. He was in Mr. Hoa's office when I arrived. He got up and shook my hand with both of his, holding my hand for a long moment as he said how glad he was that I was here. His eyes were full of tears and I felt very sorry for Lê Văn Lý. A warrior should never cry, even for the death of a beautiful woman. He handed me the bag with Thūy's brush and makeup and he said, "You always know what to do."

What did he mean by this? Simply that I knew how to brush Thūy's hair and paint her face? Or was this something he had seen about me in all things, just as he had once seen that I was a very good tennis player? Did it mean he understood that he had never been with a woman like that, a woman who would always know what to do for him as a wife? When he stood before me in Mr. Hoa's office, I felt like a foolish teenage girl again, with that rush of hope. But perhaps it wasn't foolish; Thūy's breasts were no longer there for his eyes to slide away to.

Her breasts. What were these things that had always defined my place in the world of women? They were beneath the sheet and my hand went out and

---

[2] In 43 A.D., the Tru'ng sisters led a revolt against the Chinese masters of the region.

grasped it at the edge, but I stopped. I told myself it was of no matter now. She was dead. I let go of the sheet and turned to her face of rubber and I took out her eye shadow and her lipstick and her mascara and I bent near and painted the life back into this dead thing.

And as I painted, I thought of where she would lie, in the cemetery behind the Catholic church, in a stone tomb above the ground. It was often necessary in New Orleans, the placing of the dead above the ground, because the water table was so high. If we laid Thūy in the earth, one day she would float to the surface and I could see that day clearly, her rising from the earth and awaking and finding her way back to the main street of Versailles in the heat of the day, and I would be talking with Lý, he would be bending near me and listening as I said all the things of my heart, and suddenly his eyes would slide away and there she would be, her face made up and her hair brushed and her breasts would be as beautiful as ever. But the thought of her lying above the ground made me anxious, as well. As if she wasn't quite gone. And she never would be. Lý would sense her out there behind the church, suspended in the air, and he would never forget her and would take all the consolation he needed from his children and grandchildren.

My hand trembled now as I touched her eyes with the brush, and when I held the lipstick, I pressed it hard against her mouth and I cast aside the shame at my anger and I watched this mouth in my mind, the quick smile of it that never changed in all the years, that never sensed any mood in me but loyal, subordinate friendship. Then the paint was all in place and I pulled back and I angled my face once more into the flow of cool air and I tried to just listen to the grinding of the air conditioner and forget all of these feelings, these terrible feelings about the dead woman who had always been my friend, who I had never once challenged in life over any of these things. I thought, What a coward I am.

But instead of hearing this righteous charge against me, I looked at Thūy and I took her hair in my hands and I smoothed it all together and wound it into a bun and I pinned it at the nape of her neck. She was a fifty-year-old woman, after all. She was as much a fifty-year-old woman as I was. Surely she was. And at this I looked to the sheet.

It lay lower across the chest than I thought it might. But her breasts were also fifty years old, and they were spread flat as she lay on her back. She had never let her dear friend see them, these two secrets that had enchanted the man I loved. I could bear to look at them now, vulnerable and weary as they were. I stepped down and I grasped the edge of the sheet at her throat, and with the whisper of the cloth I pulled it back.

And one of her breasts was gone. The right breast was lovely even now, even in death, the nipple large and the color of cinnamon, but the left breast was gone and a large crescent scar began there in its place and curved out of sight under her arm. I could not draw a breath at this, as if the scar was in my own chest where my lungs had been yanked out, and I could see that her scar was old, years old, and I thought of her three years in California and how she had never spoken at all about this, how her smile had hidden all that she must have suffered.

I could not move for a long moment, and then at last my hands acted as if on their own. They pulled the sheet up and gently spread it at her throat. I suppose this should have brought back my shame at the anger I'd had at my friend Thūy, but it did not. That seemed a childish feeling now, much too simple. It was not necessary to explain any of this. I simply leaned forward and kissed Thūy on her brow and I undid the bun at the back of her neck, happy to make her beautiful once more, happy to send her off to a whole body in heaven where she would catch the eye of the finest warrior. And I knew she would understand if I did all I could to make Lê Văn Lý happy.

Prisoner on the Hell Planet   1986

A CASE HISTORY

ART SPIEGELMAN   [b. 1948]

This self-contained story is imbedded in the relentlessly unsentimental *Maus: A Survivor's Tale*. That work describes, in comic book format, Spiegelman's parents' suffering under the Nazi persecution of the Jews during World War II. The Jews in *Maus* are represented as mice; the Nazis are cats. The book deals, as well, with the author's attempt (as a child of Holocaust survivors) to understand and relate to parents whose lives have been warped by the unspeakable horrors they witnessed and endured. In 1968, Anja, Spiegelman's mother, committed suicide. Spiegelman published "Prisoner on the Hell Planet: A Case History" in Short Order Comix, #1 in 1973—and in 1986 included it in *Maus*—the only segment of the book with human rather than animal characters.

The Hebrew passages on page 1089 are the opening lines of the Kaddish—the prayer for the dead: "Extolled and hallowed be the name of God throughout the world which he has created and which he governs according to his righteous will. . . ."

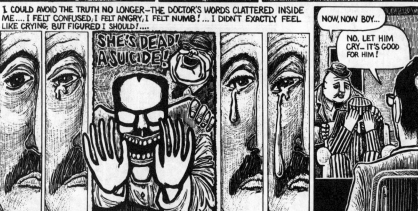

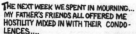

THE
PRESENCE
OF DEATH

Knight, Death, and the Devil, 1513, by Albrect Durer.

POETRY

The Ruin

ca. 900

ANONYMOUS

Well-wrought this wall: Wierds° broke it.   Fates
The stronghold burst. . . .[1]

Snapped rooftrees, towers fallen,
the work of the Giants, the stonesmiths,
mouldereth.
          Rime scoureth gatetowers
          rime on mortar.

Shattered the showershields, roofs ruined,
age under-ate them.
          And the wielders & wrights?   10
Earthgrip holds them—gone, long gone,
fast in gravesgrasp while fifty fathers
and sons have passed.
          Wall stood,
grey lichen, red stone, kings fell often,
stood under storms, high arch crashed—
stands yet the wallstone, hacked by weapons,
by files grim-ground . . .
. . . shone the old skilled work
. . . sank to loam-crust.

Mood quickened mind, and a man of wit,
cunning in rings, bound bravely the wallbase   20
with iron, a wonder.

---

[1] This poem is a fragment; the ellipses indicate missing words and lines.

Bright were the buildings, halls where springs ran,
high, horngabled, much throng-noise;
these many meadhalls men filled
with loud cheerfulness: Wierd° changed that.   Fate

Came days of pestilence, on all sides men fell dead,
death fetched off the flower of the people;
where they stood to fight, waste places
and on the acropolis, ruins.

                        Hosts who would build again
shrank to the earth. Therefore are these courts dreary   30
and that red arch twisteth tiles,
wryeth from roof-ridge, reacheth groundwards. . . .
Broken blocks. . . .

                 There once many a man
mood-glad, goldbright, of gleams garnished,
flushed with wine-pride, flashing war-gear,
gazed on wrought gemstones, on gold, on silver,
on wealth held and hoarded, on light-filled amber,
on this bright burg of broad dominion.

Stood stone houses; wide streams welled   40
hot from source, and a wall all caught
in its bright bosom, that the baths were
hot at hall's hearth; that was fitting . . .
. . . .

Thence hot streams, loosed, ran over hoar stone
unto the ring-tank. . . .
    . . . It is a kingly thing
    . . . city. . . .

Edward

ANONYMOUS

1

"Why does your brand° sae° drap wi' bluid,   sword/so
        Edward, Edward,
Why does your brand sae drap wi' bluid,
  And why sae sad gang° ye, O?"   go

"O I ha'e killed my hawk sae guid,
    Mither, mither,
O I ha'e killed my hawk sae guid,
  And I had nae mair but he, O."

2

"Your hawke's bluid was never sae reid,°   red
    Edward, Edward,   10
Your hawke's bluid was never sae reid,
  My dear son I tell thee, O."
"O I ha'e killed my reid-roan steed,
    Mither, mither,
O I ha'e killed my reid-roan steed,
  That erst was sae fair and free, O."

3

"Your steed was auld, and ye ha'e gat mair,
    Edward, Edward,
Your steed was auld, and ye ha'e gat mair,
  Some other dule° ye drie,° O."   grief/suffer
"O I ha'e killed my fader dear,   21
    Mither, mither,
O I ha'e killed my fader dear,
  Alas, and wae° is me, O!"   woe

4

"And whatten penance wul ye drie for that,
    Edward, Edward?
And whatten penance wul ye drie for that,
  My dear son, now tell me, O?"
"I'll set my feet in yonder boat,
    Mither, mither,   30
I'll set my feet in yonder boat,
  And I'll fare over the sea, O."

5

"And what wul ye do wi' your towers and your ha',
    Edward, Edward?
And what wul ye do wi' your towers and your ha',
  That were sae fair to see, O?"
"I'll let them stand tul they down fa',

Mither, mither,
I'll let them stand tul they down fa',   39
 For here never mair maun° I be, O."   must

6

"And what wul ye leave to your bairns° and your wife,   children
  Edward, Edward?
And what wul ye leave to your bairns and your wife,
 Whan ye gang over the sea, O?"
"The warlde's° room, let them beg thrae° life,   world's/through
  Mither, mither,
The warlde's room, let them beg thrae life,
 For them never mair wul I see, O."

7

"And what wul ye leave to your ain mither dear,
  Edward, Edward?   50
And what wul ye leave to your ain mither dear,
 My dear son, now tell me, O?"
"The curse of hell frae° me sall° ye bear,   from/shall
  Mither, mither,
The curse of hell frae me sall ye bear,
 Sic° counsels ye gave to me, O."   such

QUESTIONS
1. Why does the mother reject Edward's answers to her first two questions? **2.** Does the poem provide any clues as to the motive of the murder? **3.** Edward has murdered his father and then bitterly turns away from his mother, wife, and children. What basis is there in the poem for nevertheless sympathizing with Edward?

WRITING TOPIC
What effects are achieved through the question-and-answer technique and the repetition of lines?

Sonnet   1609

WILLIAM SHAKESPEARE   [1564–1616]

73

That time of year thou mayst in me behold
When yellow leaves, or none, or few, do hang
Upon those boughs which shake against the cold,
Bare ruined choirs, where late the sweet birds sang.
In me thou see'st the twilight of such day
As after sunset fadeth in the west;
Which by and by black night doth take away,
Death's second self, that seals up all in rest.
In me thou see'st the glowing of such fire,
That on the ashes of his youth doth lie,   10
As the deathbed whereon it must expire,
Consumed with that which it was nourished by.
This thou perceiv'st, which makes thy love more strong,
To love that well which thou must leave ere long.

Fear No More
the Heat o' the Sun   1623

WILLIAM SHAKESPEARE   [1564–1616]

Fear no more the heat o' the sun,[1]
  Nor the furious winter's rages;
Thou thy worldly task hast done,
  Home art gone, and ta'en thy wages:
Golden lads and girls all must,
As chimney-sweepers, come to dust.

Fear no more the frown o' the great;
  Thou art past the tyrant's stroke;
Care no more to clothe and eat;
  To thee the reed is as the oak: 10

Fear No More the Heat o' the Sun
  [1] From *Cymbeline*, Act IV, Scene 2.

The scepter, learning, physic,° must[2]   medicine
All follow this, and come to dust.

Fear no more the lightning flash,
    Nor the all-dreaded thunder stone;[3]
Fear not slander, censure rash;
    Thou hast finished joy and moan:
All lovers young, all lovers must
Consign to° thee, and come to dust.   agree with

No exorciser harm thee!
Nor no witchcraft charm thee!   20
Ghost unlaid forbear thee!
Nothing ill come near thee!
Quiet consummation have;
And renownéd be thy grave!

A Litany in Time of Plague   1600

THOMAS NASHE   [1567–1601]

Adieu, farewell, earth's bliss;
This world uncertain is;
Fond° are life's lustful joys;   foolish
Death proves them all but toys;
None from his darts can fly;
I am sick, I must die.
    Lord, have mercy on us!

Rich men, trust not in wealth,
Gold cannot buy you health;
Physic himself must fade.   10
All things to end are made,
The plague full swift goes by;
I am sick, I must die.
    Lord, have mercy on us!

Beauty is but a flower
Which wrinkles will devour;
Brightness falls from the air;

---

[2] I.e., kings, scholars, and physicians.
[3] It was believed that thunder was caused by falling meteorites.

Queens have died young and fair;
Dust hath closed Helen's[1] eye.
I am sick, I must die.   20
    Lord, have mercy on us!

Strength stoops unto the grave,
Worms feed on Hector[2] brave;
Swords may not fight with fate,
Earth still holds ope her gate.
"Come, come!" the bells do cry.
I am sick, I must die.
    Lord, have mercy on us.

Wit with his wantonness
Tasteth death's bitterness;   30
Hell's executioner
Hath no ears for to hear
What vain art can reply.
I am sick, I must die.
    Lord, have mercy on us.

Haste, therefore, each degree,
To welcome destiny;
Heaven is our heritage,
Earth but a player's stage;
Mount we unto the sky.   40
I am sick, I must die.
    Lord, have mercy on us.

Death, Be Not Proud   1633

JOHN DONNE [1572–1631]

Death be not proud, though some have call éd thee
Mighty and dreadful, for thou art not so;
For those whom thou think'st thou dost overthrow
Die not, poor Death, nor yet canst thou kill me.
From rest and sleep, which but thy pictures be,
Much pleasure; then from thee much more must flow,

A Litany in Time of Plague
    [1] Helen of Troy, a fabled beauty.
    [2] Commander of the Trojan forces in the Trojan War.

And soonest our best men with thee do go,
Rest of their bones, and soul's delivery.
Thou art slave to fate, chance, kings, and desperate men,
And dost with poison, war, and sickness dwell,   10
And poppy or charms can make us sleep as well
And better than thy stroke; why swell'st thou then?
One short sleep past, we wake eternally
And death shall be no more; Death, thou shalt die.

Elegy Written in a
Country Churchyard   1753

THOMAS GRAY   [1716–1771]

The curfew tolls the knell of parting day,
    The lowing herd wind slowly o'er the lea,
The plowman homeward plods his weary way,
    And leaves the world to darkness and to me.

Now fades the glimmering landscape on the sight,
    And all the air a solemn stillness holds,
Save where the beetle wheels his droning flight,
    And drowsy tinklings lull the distant folds;

Save that from yonder ivy-mantled tower
    The moping owl does to the moon complain   10
Of such, as wandering near her secret bower,
    Molest her ancient solitary reign.

Beneath those rugged elms, that yew tree's shade,
    Where heaves the turf in many a moldering heap,
Each in his narrow cell forever laid,
    The rude° forefathers of the hamlet sleep.   untaught

The breezy call of incense-breathing Morn,
    The swallow twittering from the straw-built shed,
The cock's shrill clarion, or the echoing horn,°   hunter's horn
    No more shall rouse them from their lowly bed.   20

For them no more the blazing hearth shall burn,
    Or busy housewife ply her evening care;

No children run to lisp their sire's return,
  Or climb his knees the envied kiss to share.

Oft did the harvest to their sickle yield,
  Their furrow oft the stubborn glebe° has broke;   field
How jocund did they drive their team afield!
  How bowed the woods beneath their sturdy stroke!

Let not Ambition mock their useful toil,
  Their homely joys, and destiny obscure;   30
Nor Grandeur hear with a disdainful smile
  The short and simple annals of the poor.

The boast of heraldry,° the pomp of power,   noble birth
  And all that beauty, all that wealth e'er gave,
Awaits alike the inevitable hour.
  The paths of glory lead but to the grave.

Nor you, ye proud, impute to these the fault,
  If Memory o'er their tomb no trophies° raise,   memorial
Where through the long-drawn aisle and fretted° vault   decorated
  The pealing anthem swells the note of praise.   40

Can storied° urn or animated bust   inscribed
  Back to its mansion call the fleeting breath?
Can Honor's voice provoke the silent dust,
  Or Flattery soothe the full cold ear of Death?

Perhaps in this neglected spot is laid
  Some heart once pregnant with celestial fire;
Hands that the rod of empire might have swayed,
  Or waked to ecstasy the living lyre.

But Knowledge to their eyes her ample page
  Rich with the spoils of time did ne'er unroll;   50
Chill Penury repressed their noble rage,
  And froze the genial current of the soul.

Full many a gem of purest ray serene,
  The dark unfathomed caves of ocean bear:
Full many a flower is born to blush unseen,
  And waste its sweetness on the desert air.

Some village Hampden,[1] that with dauntless breast
   The little tyrant of his fields withstood;
Some mute inglorious Milton here may rest,
   Some Cromwell guiltless of his country's blood.   60

The applause of listening senates to command,
   The threats of pain and ruin to despise,
To scatter plenty o'er a smiling land,
   And read their history in a nation's eyes,

Their lot forbade: nor circumscribed alone
   Their growing virtues, but their crimes confined;
Forbade to wade through slaughter to a throne,
   And shut the gates of mercy on mankind,

The struggling pangs of conscious truth to hide,
   To quench the blushes of ingenuous shame,   70
Or heap the shrine of Luxury and Pride
   With incense kindled at the Muse's flame.

Far from the madding crowd's ignoble strife,
   Their sober wishes never learned to stray;
Along the cool sequestered vale of life
   They kept the noiseless tenor of their way.

Yet even these bones from insult to protect
   Some frail memorial still erected nigh,
With uncouth rhymes and shapeless sculpture decked,
   Implores the passing tribute of a sigh.   80

Their name, their years, spelt by the unlettered Muse,
   The place of fame and elegy supply:
And many a holy text around she strews,
   That teach the rustic moralist to die.

For who to dumb Forgetfulness a prey,
   This pleasing anxious being e'er resigned,
Left the warm precincts of the cheerful day,
   Nor cast one longing lingering look behind?

Elegy Written in a Country Churchyard
  [1] John Hampden (1594–1643) championed the people against the autocratic policies of Charles I.

On some fond breast the parting soul relies,
    Some pious drops the closing eye requires;   90
Even from the tomb the voice of Nature cries,
    Even in our ashes live their wonted fires.

For thee, who mindful of the unhonored dead
    Dost in these lines their artless tale relate;
If chance, by lonely contemplation led,
    Some kindred spirit shall inquire thy fate,

Haply some hoary-headed swain may say,
    "Oft have we seen him at the peep of dawn
Brushing with hasty steps the dews away
    To meet the sun upon the upland lawn.   100

"There at the foot of yonder nodding beech
    That wreathes its old fantastic roots so high,
His listless length at noontide would he stretch,
    And pore upon the brook that babbles by.

"Hard by yon wood, now smiling as in scorn,
    Muttering his wayward fancies he would rove,
Now drooping, woeful wan, like one forlorn,
    Or crazed with care, or crossed in hopeless love.

"One morn I missed him on the customed hill,
    Along the heath and near his favorite tree;   110
Another came; nor yet beside the rill,
    Nor up the lawn, nor at the wood was he;

"The next with dirges due in sad array
    Slow through the churchway path we saw him borne.
Approach and read (for thou canst read) the lay,
    Graved on the stone beneath yon aged thorn."

THE EPITAPH

Here rests his head upon the lap of Earth
    A youth to Fortune and to Fame unknown
Fair Science° frowned not on his humble birth,   learning
    And Melancholy marked him for her own.   120

Large was his bounty, and his soul sincere,
    Heaven did a recompense as largely send:
He gave to Misery all he had, a tear,
    He gained from Heaven ('twas all he wished) a friend.

No farther seek his merits to disclose,
  Or draw his frailties from their dread abode
(There they alike in trembling hope repose),
  The bosom of his Father and his God.

QUESTIONS
1. Why have the people Gray honors in this poem lived and died in obscurity?
Does the poet offer any suggestions for change? Explain.   **2.** Why would "Ambition
mock their useful toil" (l. 29)?

WRITING TOPIC
Does this poem celebrate the advantages of obscurity and ignorance over fame,
wealth, and knowledge?

Lines Inscribed upon a Cup
Formed from a Skull   1814

GEORGE GORDON, LORD BYRON   [1788–1824]

Start not—nor deem my spirit fled;
  In me behold the only skull,
From which, unlike a living head,
  Whatever flows is never dull.

I lived, I loved, I quaff'd, like thee:
  I died: let earth my bones resign;
Fill up—thou canst not injure me;
  The worm hath fouler lips than thine.

Better to hold the sparkling grape,
  Than nurse the earth-worm's slimy brood;   10
And circle in the goblet's shape
  The drink of gods, than reptile's food.

Where once my wit, perchance, hath shone,
  In aid of others' let me shine;
And when, alas! our brains are gone,
  What nobler substitute than wine?

Quaff while thou canst: another race,
  When thou and thine, like me, are sped,
May rescue thee from earth's embrace,
  And rhyme and revel with the dead.   20

Why not? since through life's little day
  Our heads such sad effects produce;
Redeem'd from worms and wasting clay,
  This chance is theirs, to be of use.

The Destruction of Sennacherib[1]

1815

GEORGE GORDON, LORD BYRON   [1788–1824]

The Assyrian came down like the wolf on the fold,
And his cohorts were gleaming in purple and gold;
And the sheen of their spears was like stars on the sea,
When the blue wave rolls nightly on deep Galilee.

Like the leaves of the forest when summer is green,
That host with their banners at sunset were seen:
Like the leaves of the forest when autumn hath blown,
That host on the morrow lay withered and strown.

For the Angel of Death spread his wings on the blast,
And breathed in the face of the foe as he passed;   10
And the eyes of the sleepers waxed deadly and chill,
And their hearts but once heaved—and for ever grew still!

And there lay the steed with his nostril all wide,
But through it there rolled not the breath of his pride;
And the foam of his gasping lay white on the turf,
And cold as the spray of the rock-beating surf.

And there lay the rider distorted and pale,
With the dew on his brow, and the rust on his mail;
And the tents were all silent, the banners alone,
The lances unlifted, the trumpet unblown.   20

The Destruction of Sennacherib
  [1] Byron retells the account of the Assyrian siege of Jerusalem, found in II Kings 19, which culminates in the death of 185,000 Assyrian troops at the hand of the angel of the Lord.

And the widows of Ashur[2] are loud in their wail,
And the idols are broke in the temple of Baal;[3]
And the might of the Gentile,[4] unsmote by the sword,
Hath melted like snow in the glance of the Lord!

Ozymandias[1] 1818

PERCY BYSSHE SHELLEY   [1792–1822]

I met a traveller from an antique land
Who said: Two vast and trunkless legs of stone
Stand in the desert . . . Near them, on the sand,
Half sunk, a shattered visage lies, whose frown,
And wrinkled lip, and sneer of cold command,
Tell that its sculptor well those passions read
Which yet survive, stamped on these lifeless things,
The hand that mocked them, and the heart that fed:
And on the pedestal these words appear:
"My name is Ozymandias, king of kings: 10
Look on my works, ye Mighty, and despair!"
Nothing beside remains. Round the decay
Of that colossal wreck, boundless and bare
The lone and level sands stretch far away.

Ode to a Nightingale 1819

JOHN KEATS   [1795–1821]

1

My heart aches, and a drowsy numbness pains
   My sense, as though of hemlock I had drunk,
Or emptied some dull opiate to the drains
   One minute past, and Lethe-wards[1] had sunk:
'Tis not through envy of thy happy lot,
   But being too happy in thine happiness—

The Destruction of Sennacherib
   [2] Another name for Assyria.
   [3] A Canaanite deity.
   [4] A non-Hebrew, in this case Sennacherib, the King of Assyria.
Ozymandias
   [1] Egyptian monarch of the thirteenth century B.C., said to have erected a huge statue of himself.
Ode to a Nightingale
   [1] Towards Lethe, in Greek mythology the river in Hades which caused forgetfulness.

That thou, light-wingéd Dryad of the trees,
  In some melodious plot
Of beechen green, and shadows numberless,
  Singest of summer in full-throated ease.   10

2

O, for a draught of vintage! that hath been
  Cooled a long age in the deep-delvéd earth,
Tasting of Flora² and the country green,
  Dance, and Provencal song,³ and sunburnt mirth!
O for a beaker full of the warm South,
  Full of the true, the blushful Hippocrene,⁴
    With beaded bubbles winking at the brim,
      And purple-stainéd mouth;
  That I might drink, and leave the world unseen,
    And with thee fade away into the forest dim: 20

3

Fade far away, dissolve, and quite forget
  What thou among the leaves hast never known,
The weariness, the fever, and the fret
  Here, where men sit and hear each other groan;
Where palsy shakes a few, sad, last gray hairs,
  Where youth grows pale, and specter-thin, and dies;
    Where but to think is to be full of sorrow
      And leaden-eyed despairs,
  Where Beauty cannot keep her lustrous eyes,
    Or new Love pine at them beyond tomorrow.   30

4

Away! away! for I will fly to thee,
  Not charioted by Bacchus⁵ and his pards,
But on the viewless wings of Poesy,
  Though the dull brain perplexes and retards:
Already with thee! tender is the night,
  And haply the Queen-Moon is on her throne,
    Clustered around by all her starry Fays;°   fairies

---

² Roman goddess of flowers
³ Provence, in southern France, renowned for its medieval troubadors.
⁴ In Greek mythology, the fountain of the Muses whose waters gave poetic inspiration.
⁵ The god of wine, often represented in a chariot drawn by leopards ("pards").

But here there is no light,
Save what from heaven is with the breezes blown
  Through verdurous glooms and winding mossy ways.   40

5

I cannot see what flowers are at my feet,
  Nor what soft incense hangs upon the boughs,
But, in embalmèd darkness, guess each sweet
  Wherewith the seasonable month endows
The grass, the thicket, and the fruit tree wild;
  White hawthorn, and the pastoral eglantine;
    Fast fading violets covered up in leaves;
      And mid-May's eldest child,
The coming musk-rose, full of dewy wine,
  The murmurous haunt of flies on summer eves.   50

6

Darkling° I listen; and for many a time   *in darkness*
  I have been half in love with easeful Death,
Called him soft names in many a musèd rhyme,
  To take into the air my quiet breath;
Now more than ever seems it rich to die,
  To cease upon the midnight with no pain,
    While thou art pouring forth thy soul abroad
      In such an ecstasy!
  Still wouldst thou sing, and I have ears in vain—
    To thy high requiem become a sod.   60

7

Thou wast not born for death, immortal Bird!
  No hungry generations tread thee down;
The voice I hear this passing night was heard
  In ancient days by emperor and clown:
Perhaps the selfsame song that found a path
  Through the sad heart of Ruth,[6] when, sick for home,
    She stood in tears amid the alien corn;
      The same that ofttimes hath

---

[6] The young widow in the Old Testament (Ruth 2) who left her own people to live in a strange land, where she gleaned in the barley fields ("alien corn").

Charmed magic casements, opening on the foam
   Of perilous seas, in faery lands forlorn.   70

8

Forlorn! the very word is like a bell
   To toll me back from thee to my sole self!
Adieu! the fancy cannot cheat so well
   As she is famed to do, deceiving elf.
Adieu! adieu! thy plaintive anthem fades
   Past the near meadows, over the still stream,
      Up the hill side; and now 'tis buried deep
         In the next valley-glades:
   Was it a vision, or a waking dream?
      Fled is that music:—Do I wake or sleep?   80

QUESTIONS

1. What does the nightingale represent?   **2.** In stanza 6, Keats declares that the very moment at which the nightingale's song is most ecstatic would be the right moment to die; yet the realization that the nightingale's song would continue after his death jars him. Why?   **3.** In what sense is the nightingale "not born for death" (l. 61)? Does this line imply that all men are born for death? Explain.

WRITING TOPIC

In stanza 4, Keats says that he will reach the nightingale "on the viewless wings of Poesy." Why are the wings of poetry "viewless," and what is the connection between the nightingale and poetry?

Ode on a Grecian Urn   1820

JOHN KEATS   [1795–1821]

I

Thou still unravished bride of quietness,
   Thou foster child of silence and slow time,
Sylvan historian, who canst thus express
   A flowery tale more sweetly than our rhyme:
What leaf-fringed legend haunts about thy shape
   Of deities or mortals, or of both,

In Tempe or the dales of Arcady?[1]
What men or gods are these? What maidens loath?
What mad pursuit? What struggle to escape?
    What pipes and timbrels? What wild ecstasy?   10

II

Heard melodies are sweet, but those unheard
    Are sweeter; therefore, ye soft pipes, play on;
Not to the sensual ear, but, more endeared,
    Pipe to the spirit ditties of no tone:
Fair youth, beneath the trees, thou canst not leave
    Thy song, nor ever can those trees be bare;
        Bold Lover, never, never canst thou kiss,
Though winning near the goal—yet, do not grieve;
    She cannot fade, though thou hast not thy bliss,
    Forever wilt thou love, and she be fair!   20

III

Ah, happy, happy boughs! that cannot shed
    Your leaves, nor ever bid the Spring adieu;
And, happy melodist, unweariéd,
    Forever piping songs forever new;
More happy love! more happy, happy love!
    Forever warm and still to be enjoyed,
        Forever panting, and forever young;
All breathing human passion far above,[2]
    That leaves a heart high-sorrowful and cloyed,
    A burning forehead, and a parching tongue.   30

IV

Who are these coming to the sacrifice?
    To what green altar, O mysterious priest,
Lead'st thou that heifer lowing at the skies,
    And all her silken flanks with garlands dressed?
What little town by river or sea shore,
    Or mountain-built with peaceful citadel,
        Is emptied of this folk, this pious morn?

Ode on a Grecian Urn
    [1] Tempe and Arcady are valleys in Greece famous for their beauty. In ancient times, Tempe
was regarded as sacred to Apollo.
    [2] I.e., far above all breathing human passion.

And, little town, thy streets forevermore
   Will silent be; and not a soul to tell
      Why thou art desolate, can e'er return.   40

      V

O Attic[3] shape! Fair attitude! with brede
   Of marble men and maidens overwrought,
With forest branches and the trodden weed;
   Thou, silent form, dost tease us out of thought
As doth eternity: Cold Pastoral!
   When old age shall this generation waste,
      Thou shalt remain, in midst of other woe
Than ours, a friend to man, to whom thou say'st,
"Beauty is truth, truth beauty,—that is all
   Ye know on earth, and all ye need to know."   50

QUESTIONS

1. Describe the scene the poet sees depicted on the urn. Describe the scene the poet imagines as a consequence of the scene on the urn.   **2.** Why are the boughs, the piper, and the lovers happy in stanza 3?   **3.** Explain the assertion of stanza 2 that "Heard melodies are sweet, but those unheard / Are sweeter."   **4.** Does the poem support the assertion of the last two lines? What does that assertion mean?

WRITING TOPIC

In what sense might it be argued that this poem is about mortality and immortality? In this connection, consider the meaning of the phrase "Cold Pastoral!" (l. 45).

The Conqueror Worm   1838

EDGAR ALLAN POE   [1809–1849]

Lo! 'tis a gala night
   Within the lonesome latter years!
An angel throng, bewinged, bedight
   In veils, and drowned in tears,
Sit in a theatre, to see
   A play of hopes and fears,
While the orchestra breathes fitfully
   The music of the spheres.

Ode on a Grecian Urn
   [3] Athenian, thus simple and graceful.

Mimes, in the form of God on high,
　Mutter and mumble low,
And hither and thither fly—
　Mere puppets they, who come and go
At bidding of vast formless things
　That shift the scenery to and fro,
Flapping from out their Condor wings
　Invisible Woe! 10

That motley drama!—oh, be sure
　It shall not be forgot!
With its Phantom chased forever more,
　By a crowd that seize it not,
Through a circle that ever returneth in
　To the self-same spot, 20
And much of Madness and more of Sin
　And Horror the soul of the plot.

But see, amid the mimic rout,
　A crawling shape intrude!
A blood-red thing that writhes from out
　The scenic solitude!
It writhes!—it writhes!—with mortal pangs
　The mimes become its food,
And the seraphs sob at vermin fangs 30
　In human gore imbued.

Out—out are the lights—out all!
　And over each quivering form,
The curtain, a funeral pall,
　Comes down with the rush of a storm,
And the angels, all pallid and wan,
　Uprising, unveiling, affirm
That the play is the tragedy, "Man,"
　And its hero the Conqueror Worm. 40

from

In Memoriam A. H. H. 1850

ALFRED, LORD TENNYSON [1809–1892]

54

O, yet we trust that somehow good
  Will be the final goal of ill.
  To pangs of nature, sins of will,
Defects of doubt, and taints of blood;

That nothing walks with aimless feet;
  That not one life shall be destroyed,
  Or cast as rubbish to the void,
When God hath made the pile complete;

That not a worm is cloven in vain;
  That not a moth with vain desire   10
  Is shriveled in a fruitless fire,
Or but subserves another's gain.

Behold, we know not anything;
  I can but trust that good shall fall
  At last—far off—at last, to all,
And every winter change to spring.

So runs my dream; but what am I?
  An infant crying in the night;
  An infant crying for the light,
And with no language but a cry.   20

55

The wish, that of the living whole
  No life may fail beyond the grave,
  Derives it not from what we have
The likest God within the soul?

Are God and Nature then at strife,
  That Nature lends such evil dreams?
  So careful of the type° she seems,   species
So careless of the single life,

That I, considering everywhere
  Her secret meaning in her deeds,
  And finding that of fifty seeds   10
She often brings but one to bear,

I falter where I firmly trod,
  And falling with my weight of cares
  Upon the great world's altar-stairs
That slope through darkness up to God,

I stretch lame hands of faith, and grope,
  And gather dust and chaff, and call
  To what I feel is Lord of all,
And faintly trust the larger hope.[1]   20

56

"So careful of the type?" but no.
  From scarpéd[2] cliff and quarried stone
  She[3] cries, "A thousand types are gone;
I care for nothing, all shall go.

"Thou makest thine appeal to me:
  I bring to life, I bring to death;
  The spirit does but mean the breath:
I know no more." And he, shall he,

Man, her last work, who seemed so fair,
  Such splendid purpose in his eyes,   10
  Who rolled the psalm to wintry skies,
Who built him fanes° of fruitless prayer,   temples

Who trusted God was love indeed
  And love Creation's final law—
  Though Nature, red in tooth and claw
With ravine, shrieked against his creed—

In Memoriam A. H. H.
  [1] The hope expressed in the first two lines of this section.
  [2] Cut away (so that fossil remains can be seen).
  [3] Nature.

Who loved, who suffered countless ills,
  Who battled for the True, the Just,
  Be blown about the desert dust,
Or sealed within the iron hills?[4]   20

No more? A monster then, a dream,
  A discord. Dragons of the prime,
  That tare° each other in their slime,   tore
Were mellow music matched with him.

O life as futile, then, as frail!
  O for thy voice to soothe and bless!
  What hope of answer, or redress?
Behind the veil, behind the veil.

QUESTIONS
1. In these self-contained sections from Tennyson's long elegy to a friend who died at 22, the poet raises some anguished questions about God, humanity, and nature. What conviction is embodied in the first verses of sections 54 and 55? What issues does the poet raise that threaten that conviction?   **2.** How is nature characterized in section 55? In section 56?   **3.** In section 56, how does the poet characterize humanity's notions about God? Are those notions justified by the remainder of the section?

WRITING TOPIC
Do these verses culminate in positive affirmation of the human condition and the relationship of individuals to God and nature? Explain.

Growing Old   1867

MATTHEW ARNOLD   [1822–1888]

What is it to grow old?
Is it to lose the glory of the form,
The luster of the eye?
Is it for beauty to forego her wreath?
—Yes, but not this alone

In Memoriam A. H. H.
    [4] Entombed in rock.

Is it to feel our strength—
Not our bloom only, but our strength—decay?
Is it to feel each limb
Grow stiffer, every function less exact,
Each nerve more loosely strung?   10

Yes, this, and more; but not
Ah, 'tis not what in youth we dreamed 'twould be!
'Tis not to have our life
Mellowed and softened as with sunset glow,
A golden day's decline.

'Tis not to see the world
As from a height, with rapt prophetic eyes,
And heart profoundly stirred;
And weep, and feel the fullness of the past,
The years that are no more.   20

It is to spend long days
And not once feel that we were ever young;
It is to add, immured
In the hot prison of the present, month
To month with weary pain.

It is to suffer this,
And feel but half, and feebly, what we feel.
Deep in our hidden heart
Festers the dull remembrance of a change,
But no emotion—none.   30

It is—last stage of all—
When we are frozen up within, and quite
The phantom of ourselves,
To hear the world applaud the hollow ghost
Which blamed the living man.

After Great Pain, a Formal Feeling Comes   (ca. 1862)

EMILY DICKINSON   [1830–1886]

After great pain, a formal feeling comes—
The Nerves sit ceremonious, like Tombs—

The stiff Heart questions was it He, that bore,
And Yesterday, or Centuries before?

The Feet, mechanical, go round—
Of Ground, or Air, or Ought—
A Wooden way
Regardless grown,
A Quartz contentment, like a stone—

This is the Hour of Lead—   10
Remembered, if outlived,
As Freezing persons, recollect the Snow—
First—Chill—then Stupor—then the letting go—

QUESTION
1. Is this poem about physical or psychic pain? Explain.

WRITING TOPIC
What is the meaning of "stiff Heart" (l. 3) and "Quartz contentment" (l. 9)? What
part do they play in the larger pattern of images?

I Heard a Fly Buzz—
When I Died   (ca. 1862)

EMILY DICKINSON   [1830–1886]

I heard a Fly buzz—when I died—
The Stillness in the Room
Was like the Stillness in the Air—
Between the Heaves of Storm—

The Eyes around—had wrung them dry—
And Breaths were gathering firm
For that last Onset—when the King
Be witnessed—in the Room—

I willed my Keepsakes—Signed away
What portion of me be   10
Assignable—and then it was
There interposed a Fly—

With Blue—uncertain stumbling Buzz—
Between the light—and me—
And then the Windows failed—and then
I could not see to see—

Apparently with No Surprise   ca. 1884

EMILY DICKINSON [1830–1886]

Apparently with no surprise
To any happy Flower,
The Frost beheads it at its play
In accidental power.
The blond Assassin passes on,
The Sun proceeds unmoved
To measure off another Day
For an Approving God.

To an Athlete Dying Young   1896

A. E. HOUSMAN [1859–1936]

The time you won your town the race
We chaired you through the market place;
Man and boy stood cheering by,
And home we brought you shoulder-high.

Today, the road all runners come,
Shoulder-high we bring you home,
And set you at your threshold down,
Townsman of a stiller town.

Smart lad, to slip betimes away
From fields where glory does not stay,   10
And early though the laurel grows
It withers quicker than the rose.

Eyes the shady night has shut
Cannot see the record cut,
And silence sounds no worse than cheers
After earth has stopped the ears:

Now you will not swell the rout
Of lads that wore their honors out,
Runners whom renown outran
And the name died before the man.   20

So set, before its echoes fade,
The fleet foot on the sill of shade,
And hold to the low lintel up
The still-defended challenge cup.

And round that early-laureled head
Will flock to gaze the strengthless dead
And find unwithered on its curls
The garland briefer than a girl's.

Sailing to Byzantium[1]   1927

WILLIAM BUTLER YEATS   [1865–1939]

1

That is no country for old men. The young
In one another's arms, birds in the trees
—Those dying generations—at their song,
The salmon-falls, the mackerel-crowded seas,
Fish, flesh, or fowl, commend all summer long
Whatever is begotten, born, and dies.
Caught in that sensual music all neglect
Monuments of unaging intellect.

2

An aged man is but a paltry thing,
A tattered coat upon a stick, unless   10
Soul clap its hands and sing, and louder sing
For every tatter in its mortal dress,
Nor is there singing school but studying
Monuments of its own magnificence;

Sailing to Byzantium
  [1] Capital of the ancient Eastern Roman Empire, Byzantium (modern Istanbul) is celebrated for
its great art, including mosaics (in ll. 17–18, Yeats addresses the figures in one of these mosaics).
In *A Vision*, Yeats cites Byzantium as possibly the only civilization which had achieved what he
called "Unity of Being," a state where "religious, aesthetic and practical life were one. . . ."

And therefore I have sailed the seas and come
To the holy city of Byzantium.

3

O sages standing in God's holy fire
As in the gold mosaic of a wall,
Come from the holy fire, perne in a gyre,[2]
And be the singing-masters of my soul.   20
Consume my heart away; sick with desire
And fastened to a dying animal
It knows not what it is; and gather me
Into the artifice of eternity.

4

Once out of nature I shall never take
My bodily form from any natural thing,
But such a form as Grecian goldsmiths make
Of hammered gold and gold enameling
To keep a drowsy Emperor awake;[3]
Or set upon a golden bough to sing   30
To lords and ladies of Byzantium
Of what is past, or passing, or to come.

QUESTIONS

1. This poem incorporates a series of contrasts, among them "That" country and Byzantium, the real birds of the first stanza and the artificial bird of the final stanza. What others do you find? **2.** What are the meanings of "generations" (l. 3)? **3.** For what is the poet "sick with desire" (l. 21)? **4.** In what sense is eternity an "artifice" (l. 24)?

WRITING TOPIC

In what ways are the images of bird and song used throughout this poem?

---

[2] I.e., whirl in a spiral motion. Yeats associated this motion with the cycles of history and the fate of the individual. Here he entreats the sages represented in the mosaic to take him out of the natural world described in the first stanza and into the eternal world of art.

[3] "I have read somewhere," Yeats wrote, "that in the Emperor's palace at Byzantium was a tree made of gold and silver, and artificial birds that sang." The poet wishes to become an artificial bird (a work of art) in contrast to the real birds of the first stanza.

Richard Cory   1897

EDWIN ARLINGTON ROBINSON   [1869–1935]

Whenever Richard Cory went down town,
We people on the pavement looked at him:
He was a gentleman from sole to crown,
Clean favored, and imperially slim.

And he was always quietly arrayed,
And he was always human when he talked;
But still he fluttered pulses when he said,
"Good-morning," and he glittered when he walked.

And he was rich—yes, richer than a king—
And admirably schooled in every grace: 10
In fine, we thought that he was everything
To make us wish that we were in his place.

So on we worked, and waited for the light,
And went without the meat, and cursed the bread;
And Richard Cory, one calm summer night,
Went home and put a bullet through his head.

Mr. Flood's Party   1921

EDWIN ARLINGTON ROBINSON   [1869–1935]

Old Eben Flood, climbing alone one night
Over the hill between the town below
And the forsaken upland hermitage
That held as much as he should ever know
On earth again of home, paused warily.
The road was his with not a native near;
And Eben, having leisure, said aloud,
For no man else in Tilbury Town to hear:

"Well, Mr. Flood, we have the harvest moon
Again, and we may not have many more;   10
The bird is on the wing, the poet says,
And you and I have said it here before.
Drink to the bird." He raised up to the light

The jug that he had gone so far to fill,
And answered huskily: "Well, Mr. Flood,
Since you propose it, I believe I will."

Alone, as if enduring to the end
A valiant armor of scarred hopes outworn,
He stood there in the middle of the road
Like Roland's ghost winding a silent horn.   20
Below him, in the town among the trees,
Where friends of other days had honored him,
A phantom salutation of the dead
Rang thinly till old Eben's eyes were dim.

Then, as a mother lays her sleeping child
Down tenderly, fearing it may awake,
He set the jug down slowly at his feet
With trembling care, knowing that most things break;
And only when assured that on firm earth
It stood, as the uncertain lives of men   30
Assuredly did not, he paced away,
And with his hand extended paused again:

"Well, Mr. Flood, we have not met like this
In a long time; and many a change has come
To both of us, I fear, since last it was
We had a drop together. Welcome home!"
Convivially returning with himself,
Again he raised the jug up to the light;
And with an acquiescent quaver said:
"Well, Mr. Flood, if you insist, I might.   40

"Only a very little, Mr. Flood—
For auld lang syne. No more, sir; that will do."
So, for the time, apparently it did,
And Eben evidently thought so too;
For soon amid the silver loneliness
Of night he lifted up his voice and sang,
Secure, with only two moons listening,
Until the whole harmonious landscape rang—

"For auld lang syne." The weary throat gave out,
The last word wavered, and the song being done,   50
He raised again the jug regretfully
And shook his head, and was again alone.
There was not much that was ahead of him,

And there was nothing in the town below—
Where strangers would have shut the many doors
That many friends had opened long ago.

After Apple-Picking   1914

ROBERT FROST   [1874–1963]

My long two-pointed ladder's sticking through a tree
Toward heaven still,
And there's a barrel that I didn't fill
Beside it, and there may be two or three
Apples I didn't pick upon some bough.
But I am done with apple-picking now.
Essence of winter sleep is on the night,
The scent of apples: I am drowsing off.
I cannot rub the strangeness from my sight
I got from looking through a pane of glass   10
I skimmed this morning from the drinking trough
And held against the world of hoary grass.
It melted, and I let it fall and break.
But I was well
Upon my way to sleep before it fell,
And I could tell
What form my dreaming was about to take.
Magnified apples appear and disappear,
Stem end and blossom end,
And every fleck of russet showing clear.   20
My instep arch not only keeps the ache,
It keeps the pressure of a ladder-round.
I feel the ladder sway as the boughs bend.
And I keep hearing from the cellar bin
The rumbling sound
Of load on load of apples coming in.
For I have had too much
Of apple-picking: I am overtired
Of the great harvest I myself desired.
There were ten thousand thousand fruit to touch,   30
Cherish in hand, lift down, and not let fall.
For all
That struck the earth,
No matter if not bruised or spiked with stubble,
Went surely to the cider-apple heap
As of no worth.

One can see what will trouble
This sleep of mine, whatever sleep it is.
Were he not gone,
The woodchuck could say whether it's like his   40
Long sleep, as I describe its coming on,
Or just some human sleep.

QUESTIONS
1. What does apple-picking symbolize?   **2.** At the end of the poem, why is the speaker uncertain about what kind of sleep is coming on him?

Nothing Gold Can Stay   1923

ROBERT FROST   [1874–1963]

Nature's first green is gold,
Her hardest hue to hold.
Her early leaf's a flower;
But only so an hour.
Then leaf subsides to leaf.
So Eden sank to grief,
So dawn goes down to day.
Nothing gold can stay.

QUESTIONS
1. Does this poem protest or accept the transitoriness of things?   **2.** Why does Frost use the word "subsides" in line 5 rather than a word like "expands" or "grows"?   **3.** How are "Nature's first green" (l. 1), "Eden" (l. 6), and "dawn" (l. 7) linked together?

'Out, Out—'[1]   1916

ROBERT FROST   [1874–1963]

The buzz-saw snarled and rattled in the yard
And made dust and dropped stove-length sticks of wood,

'Out, Out—'
 [1] The title is taken from the famous speech of Macbeth upon hearing that his wife has died (*Macbeth*, Act V, Scene 5).

Sweet-scented stuff when the breeze drew across it.
And from there those that lifted eyes could count
Five mountain ranges one behind the other
Under the sunset far into Vermont.
And the saw snarled and rattled, snarled and rattled,
As it ran light, or had to bear a load.
And nothing happened: day was all but done.
Call it a day, I wish they might have said   10
To please the boy by giving him the half hour
That a boy counts so much when saved from work.
His sister stood beside them in her apron
To tell them 'Supper.' At the word, the saw,
As if to prove saws knew what supper meant,
Leaped out at the boy's hand, or seemed to leap—
He must have given the hand. However it was,
Neither refused the meeting. But the hand!
The boy's first outcry was a rueful laugh,
As he swung toward them holding up the hand   20
Half in appeal, but half as if to keep
The life from spilling. Then the boy saw all—
Since he was old enough to know, big boy
Doing a man's work, though a child at heart—
He saw all spoiled. 'Don't let him cut my hand off—
The doctor, when he comes. Don't let him, sister!'
So. But the hand was gone already.
The doctor put him in the dark of ether.
He lay and puffed his lips out with his breath.
And then—the watcher at his pulse took fright.   30
No one believed. They listened at his heart.
Little—less—nothing!—and that ended it.
No more to build on there. And they, since they
Were not the one dead, turned to their affairs.

Stopping by Woods on a Snowy Evening

1923

ROBERT FROST   [1874–1963]

Whose woods these are I think I know.
His house is in the village though;
He will not see me stopping here
To watch his woods fill up with snow.

My little horse must think it queer
To stop without a farmhouse near
Between the woods and frozen lake
The darkest evening of the year.

He gives his harness bells a shake
To ask if there is some mistake.   10
The only other sound's the sweep
Of easy wind and downy flake.

The woods are lovely, dark and deep,
But I have promises to keep,
And miles to go before I sleep,
And miles to go before I sleep.

QUESTIONS

1. What does the description of the horse tell us about the speaker?   **2.** What function does the repetition in the last two lines of the poem serve?   **3.** Why does the speaker refer to the owner of the woods in the opening stanza?

Design   1936

ROBERT FROST   [1874–1963]

I found a dimpled spider, fat and white,
On a white heal-all, holding up a moth
Like a white piece of rigid satin cloth—
Assorted characters of death and blight
Mixed ready to begin the morning right,
Like the ingredients of a witches' broth—
A snow-drop spider, a flower like a froth,
And dead wings carried like a paper kite.

What had that flower to do with being white,
The wayside blue and innocent heal-all?   10
What brought the kindred spider to that height,
Then steered the white moth thither in the night?
What but design of darkness to appall?—
If design govern in a thing so small.

WRITING TOPIC

Compare this poem with Emily Dickinson's "Apparently with No Surprise."

Tract   1917

WILLIAM CARLOS WILLIAMS   [1883–1963]

I will teach you my townspeople
how to perform a funeral—
for you have it over a troop
of artists—
unless one should scour the world—
you have the ground sense necessary.
See! the hearse leads.
I begin with a design for a hearse.
For Christ's sake not black—
nor white either—and not polished!   10
Let it be weathered—like a farm wagon—
with gilt wheels (this could be
applied fresh at small expense)
or no wheels at all:
a rough dray to drag over the ground.

Knock the glass out!
My God—glass, my townspeople!
For what purpose? Is it for the dead
to look out or for us to see
how well he is housed or to see   20
the flowers or the lack of them—
or what?
To keep the rain and snow from him?
He will have a heavier rain soon:
pebbles and dirt and what not.
Let there be no glass—
and no upholstery! phew!
and no little brass rollers
and small easy wheels on the bottom—
my townspeople what are you thinking of!   30

A rough plain hearse then
with gilt wheels and no top at all.
On this the coffin lies
by its own weight.
                No wreaths please—
especially no hot-house flowers.

Some common memento is better,
something he prized and is known by:
his old clothes—a few books perhaps—
God knows what! You realize   40
how we are about these things,
my townspeople—
something will be found—anything—
even flowers if he had come to that.
So much for the hearse.

For heaven's sake though see to the driver!
Take off the silk hat! In fact
that's no place at all for him
up there unceremoniously
dragging our friend out of his own dignity!   50
Bring him down—bring him down!
Low and inconspicuous! I'd not have him ride
on the wagon at all—damn him—
the undertaker's understrapper!
Let him hold the reins
and walk at the side
and inconspicuously too!

Then briefly as to yourselves:
Walk behind—as they do in France,
seventh class, or if you ride   60
Hell take curtains! Go with some show
of inconvenience; sit openly—
to the weather as to grief.
Or do you think you can shut grief in?
What—from us? We who have perhaps
nothing to lose? Share with us
share with us—it will be money
in your pockets.
               Go now
I think you are ready.   70

Bells for John Whiteside's Daughter

1924

JOHN CROWE RANSOM   [1888–1974]

There was such speed in her little body,
And such lightness in her footfall,

It is no wonder that her brown study°   reverie
Astonishes us all.

Her wars were bruited in our high window.
We looked among orchard trees and beyond,
Where she took arms against her shadow,
Or harried unto the pond

The lazy geese, like a snow cloud
Dripping their snow on the green grass,   10
Tricking and stopping, sleepy and proud,
Who cried in goose, Alas,

For the tireless heart within the little
Lady with rod that made them rise
From their noon apple-dreams, and scuttle
Goose-fashion under the skies!

But now go the bells, and we are ready;
In one house we are sternly stopped
To say we are vexed at her brown study,
Lying so primly propped.   20

Dulce et Decorum Est   1920

WILFRED OWEN   [1893–1918]

Bent double, like old beggars under sacks,
Knock-kneed, coughing like hags, we cursed through sludge,
Till on the haunting flares we turned our backs,
And towards our distant rest began to trudge.
Men marched asleep. Many had lost their boots,
But limped on, blood-shod. All went lame, all blind;
Drunk with fatigue; deaf even to the hoots
Of gas-shells dropping softly behind.

Gas! GAS! Quick, boys!—An ecstasy of fumbling,
Fitting the clumsy helmets just in time,   10
But someone still was yelling out and stumbling
And flound'ring like a man in fire or lime.—
Dim through the misty panes and thick green light,
As under a green sea, I saw him drowning.
In all my dreams before my helpless sight
He plunges at me, guttering, choking, drowning.

If in some smothering dreams, you too could pace
Behind the wagon that we flung him in,
And watch the white eyes writhing in his face,
His hanging face, like a devil's sick of sin,   20
If you could hear, at every jolt, the blood
Come gargling from the froth-corrupted lungs
Bitter as the cud
Of vile, incurable sores on innocent tongues,—
My friend, you would not tell with such high zest
To children ardent for some desperate glory,
The old lie: *Dulce et decorum est*
Pro patria mori.[1]

nobody loses all the time   1926

E. E. CUMMINGS   [1894–1962]

nobody loses all the time

i had an uncle named
Sol who was a born failure and
nearly everybody said he should have gone
into vaudeville perhaps because my Uncle Sol could
sing McCann He Was A Diver on Xmas Eve like Hell Itself which
may or may not account for the fact that my Uncle

Sol indulged in that possibly most inexcusable
of all to use a highfalootin phrase
luxuries that is or to   10
wit farming and be
it needlessly
added

my Uncle Sol's farm
failed because the chickens
ate the vegetables so
my Uncle Sol had a
chicken farm till the
skunks ate the chickens when

Dulce et Decorum Est
   [1] A quotation from the Latin poet Horace, "It is sweet and fitting to die for one's country."

my Uncle Sol   20
had a skunk farm but
the skunks caught cold and
died and so
my Uncle Sol imitated the
skunks in a subtle manner

or by drowning himself in the watertank
but somebody who'd given my Uncle Sol a Victor
Victrola and records while he lived presented to
him upon the auspicious occasion of his decease a
scrumptious not to mention splendiferous funeral with   30
tall boys in black gloves and flowers and everything and

i remember we all cried like the Missouri
when my Uncle Sol's coffin lurched because
somebody pressed a button
(and down went
my Uncle
Sol

and started a worm farm)

QUESTIONS
1. Explain the title.   **2.** What is the speaker's attitude toward Uncle Sol?

O sweet spontaneous   1923

E. E. CUMMINGS   [1894–1962]

O sweet spontaneous
earth how often have
the
doting

        fingers of
prurient philosophers pinched
and
poked

thee
, has the naughty thumb   10
of science prodded
thy

        beauty   .how
often have religions taken
thee upon their scraggy knees
squeezing and

buffeting thee that thou mightest conceive
gods
        (but
true   20

to the incomparable
couch of death thy
rhythmic
lover

        thou answerest

them only with

                spring)

QUESTIONS
1. Analyze the erotic imagery in this poem. What does it tell us about the speaker's attitude toward philosophy, science, and religion?   **2.** What does the speaker mean by calling death earth's "lover" (l. 24)? And why "rhythmic" lover (l. 23)?   **3.** In what sense is "spring" (l. 27) an answer?

In Memory of W. B. Yeats   1940
(D. JAN. 1939)

W. H. AUDEN   [1907–1973]

1

He disappeared in the dead of winter:
The brooks were frozen, the airports almost deserted,
And snow disfigured the public statues;
The mercury sank in the mouth of the dying day.
O all the instruments agree
The day of his death was a dark cold day.

Far from his illness
The wolves ran on through the evergreen forests,
The peasant river was untempted by the fashionable quays;
By mourning tongues   10
The death of the poet was kept from his poems.

But for him it was his last afternoon as himself,
An afternoon of nurses and rumors;
The provinces of his body revolted,
The squares of his mind were empty,
Silence invaded the suburbs,
The current of his feeling failed: he became his admirers.

Now he is scattered among a hundred cities
And wholly given over to unfamiliar affections;
To find his happiness in another kind of wood   20
And be punished under a foreign code of conscience.
The words of a dead man
Are modified in the guts of the living.

But in the importance and noise of tomorrow
When the brokers are roaring like beasts on the floor of the Bourse,[1]
And the poor have the sufferings to which they are fairly accustomed,
And each in the cell of himself is almost convinced of his freedom;
A few thousand will think of this day
As one thinks of a day when one did something slightly unusual.
O all the instruments agree   30
The day of his death was a dark cold day.

2

You were silly like us: your gift survived it all;
The parish of rich women, physical decay,
Yourself; mad Ireland hurt you into poetry.
Now Ireland has her madness and her weather still,
For poetry makes nothing happen: it survives
In the valley of its saying where executives
Would never want to tamper; it flows south
From ranches of isolation and the busy griefs,
Raw towns that we believe and die in; it survives,   40
A way of happening, a mouth.

In Memory of W. B. Yeats
  [1] A European stock exchange, especially that in Paris.

3

Earth, receive an honored guest;
William Yeats is laid to rest:
Let the Irish vessel lie
Emptied of its poetry.

In the nightmare of the dark
All the dogs of Europe bark,
And the living nations wait,
Each sequestered in its hate;

Intellectual disgrace   50
Stares from every human face,
And the seas of pity lie
Locked and frozen in each eye.

Follow, poet, follow right
To the bottom of the night,
With your unconstraining voice
Still persuade us to rejoice;

With the farming of a verse
Make a vineyard of the curse,
Sing of human unsuccess   60
In a rapture of distress;

In the deserts of the heart
Let the healing fountain start,
In the prison of his days
Teach the free man how to praise.

QUESTIONS
1. In what sense does a dead poet become "his admirers" (l. 17)?   **2.** Is Auden's statement that "poetry makes nothing happen" (l. 36) consistent with the attitudes expressed in the final three stanzas?

WRITING TOPIC
Why does Auden view the death of Yeats as a significant event?

Landscape with the Fall of Icarus, ca. 1560 by Pieter Brueghel the Elder

Musée des Beaux Arts   1940

W. H. AUDEN   [1907–1973]

About suffering they were never wrong,
The Old Masters: how well they understood
Its human position; how it takes place
While someone else is eating or opening a window or just walking dully
    along;
How, when the aged are reverently, passionately waiting
For the miraculous birth, there always must be
Children who did not specially want it to happen, skating
On a pond at the edge of the wood:
They never forgot
That even the dreadful martyrdom must run its course   10
Anyhow in a corner, some untidy spot
Where the dogs go on with their doggy life and the torturer's horse
Scratches its innocent behind on a tree.

In Brueghel's *Icarus*,[1] for instance: how everything turns away
Quite leisurely from the disaster; the plowman may
Have heard the splash, the forsaken cry,
But for him it was not an important failure; the sun shone
As it had to on the white legs disappearing into the green
Water; and the expensive delicate ship that must have seen
Something amazing, a boy falling out of the sky,   20
Had somewhere to get to and sailed calmly on.

Elegy for Jane   1958
MY STUDENT, THROWN BY A HORSE

THEODORE ROETHKE [1908–1963]

I remember the neckcurls, limp and damp as tendrils;
And her quick look, a sidelong pickerel smile;
And how, once startled into talk, the light syllables leaped for her,
And she balanced in the delight of her thought,
A wren, happy, tail into the wind,
Her song trembling the twigs and small branches.
The shade sang with her;
The leaves, their whispers turned to kissing;
And the mold sang in the bleached valleys under the rose.

Oh, when she was sad, she cast herself down into such a pure depth,   10
Even a father could not find her:
Scraping her cheek against straw;
Stirring the clearest water.

My sparrow, you are not here,
Waiting like a fern, making a spiny shadow.
The sides of wet stones cannot console me,
Nor the moss, wound with the last light.

If only I could nudge you from this sleep,
My maimed darling, my skittery pigeon.
Over this damp grave I speak the words of my love: 20
I, with no rights in this matter,
Neither father nor lover.

Musée des Beaux Arts
  [1] This poem describes and comments on Pieter Brueghel's painting *Landscape with the Fall of Icarus*. (See p. 1135.) According to myth, Daedalus and his son Icarus made wings, whose feathers they attached with wax, to escape Crete. Icarus flew so near the sun that the wax melted and he fell into the sea.

Between the World and Me   1935

RICHARD WRIGHT   [1908–1960]

And one morning while in the woods I stumbled suddenly upon the
  thing,
Stumbled upon it in a grassy clearing guarded by scaly oaks and elms.
And the sooty details of the scene rose, thrusting themselves between the
  world and me. . . .
There was a design of white bones slumbering forgottenly upon a cushion
  of ashes.
There was a charred stump of a sapling pointing a blunt finger accusingly
  at the sky.
There were torn tree limbs, tiny veins of burnt leaves, and a scorched coil
  of greasy hemp;
A vacant shoe, an empty tie, a ripped shirt, a lonely hat, and a pair of
  trousers stiff with black blood.
And upon the trampled grass were buttons, dead matches, butt-ends of
  cigars and cigarettes, peanut shells, a drained gin-flask, and a whore's
  lipstick;
Scattered traces of tar, restless arrays of feathers, and the lingering smell of
  gasoline.
And through the morning air the sun poured yellow surprise into the eye
  sockets of a stony skull. . . .   10
And while I stood my mind was frozen with a cold pity for the life that
  was gone.
The ground gripped my feet and my heart was circled by icy walls of
  fear—
The sun died in the sky; a night wind muttered in the grass and fumbled
  the leaves in the trees; the woods poured forth the hungry yelping of
  hounds; the darkness screamed with thirsty voices; and the witnesses
  rose and lived: The dry bones stirred, rattled, lifted, melting themselves
  into my bones.
The grey ashes formed flesh firm and black, entering into my flesh.
The gin-flask passed from mouth to mouth; cigars and cigarettes glowed,
  the whore smeared the lipstick red upon her lips,
And a thousand faces swirled around me, clamoring that my life be
  burned. . . .
And then they had me, stripped me, battering my teeth into my throat till
  I swallowed my own blood.
My voice was drowned in the roar of their voices, and my black wet body
  slipped and rolled in their hands as they bound me to the sapling.
And my skin clung to the bubbling hot tar, falling from me in limp
  patches.   20
And the down and quills of the white feathers sank into my raw flesh, and
  I moaned in my agony.

Then my blood was cooled mercifully, cooled by a baptism of gasoline.
And in a blaze of red I leaped to the sky as pain rose like water, boiling
    my limbs.
Panting, begging I clutched childlike, clutched to the hot sides of death.
Now I am dry bones and my face a stony skull staring in my yellow
    surprise at the sun. . . .

Do Not Go Gentle
into That Good Night

1952

DYLAN THOMAS   [1914–1953]

Do not go gentle into that good night,
Old age should burn and rave at close of day;
Rage, rage against the dying of the light.

Though wise men at their end know dark is right,
Because their words had forked no lightning they
Do not go gentle into that good night.

Good men, the last wave by, crying how bright
Their frail deeds might have danced in a green bay,
Rage, rage against the dying of the light.

Wild men who caught and sang the sun in flight,   10
And learn, too late, they grieved it on its way,
Do not go gentle into that good night.

Grave men, near death, who see with blinding sight
Blind eyes could blaze like meteors and be gay,
Rage, rage against the dying of the light.

And you, my father, there on the sad height,
Curse, bless, me now with your fierce tears, I pray.
Do not go gentle into that good night.
Rage, rage against the dying of the light.

QUESTIONS
1. What do wise, good, wild, and grave men have in common?   **2.** Why does the
poet use the adjective "gentle" rather than the adverb "gently"?   **3.** What is the
"sad height" (l. 16)?

The Death of the
Ball Turret Gunner   1945

RANDALL JARRELL   [1914–1965]

From my mother's sleep I fell into the State,
And I hunched in its belly till my wet fur froze.
Six miles from earth, loosed from its dream of life,
I woke to black flak and the nightmare fighters.
When I died they washed me out of the turret with a hose.

QUESTIONS
1. To what do "its" (ll. 2 and 3) and "they" (l. 5) refer? **2.** Why is the mother
described as asleep?

Aubade¹   1977

PHILIP LARKIN   [1922–1985]

I work all day, and get half drunk at night.
Waking at four to soundless dark, I stare.
In time the curtain-edges will grow light.
Till then I see what's really always there:
Unresting death, a whole day nearer now;
Making all thought impossible but how
And where and when I shall myself die.
Arid interrogation: yet the dread
Of dying, and being dead,
Flashes afresh to hold and horrify.   10

The mind blanks at the glare. Not in remorse
—The good not done, the love not given, time
Torn off unused—nor wretchedly because
An only life can take so long to climb
Clear of its wrong beginnings, and may never;
But at the total emptiness for ever,

Aubade.
    ¹ An aubade is a morning song.

The sure extinction that we travel to
And shall be lost in always. Not to be here,
Not to be anywhere,
And soon; nothing more terrible, nothing more true.   20

This is a special way of being afraid
No trick dispels. Religion used to try,
That vast moth-eaten musical brocade
Created to pretend we never die,
And specious stuff that says *No rational being*
Can fear a thing it will not feel, not seeing
That this is what we fear—no sight, no sound.
No touch or taste to smell, nothing to think with.
Nothing to love or link with,
The anaesthetic from which none come round.   30

And so it stays just on the edge of vision,
A small unfocused blur, a standing chill
That slows each impulse down to indecision.
Most things may never happen: this one will.
And realisation of it rages out
In furnace-fear when we are caught without
People or drink. Courage is no good:
It means not scaring others. Being brave
Lets no one off the grave.
Death is no different whined at than withstood.   40

Slowly light strengthens, and the room takes shape.
It stands plain as a wardrobe, what we know,
Have always known, know that we can't escape,
Yet can't accept. One side will have to go.
Meanwhile telephones crouch, getting ready to ring
In locked-up offices, and all the uncaring
Intricate rented world begins to rouse.
The sky is white as clay, with no sun.
Work has to be done.
Postmen like doctors go from house to house.   50

After a Time   (1961?)

CATHERINE DAVIS [b. 1924]

After a time, all losses are the same.
One more thing lost is one thing less to lose;
And we go stripped at last the way we came.

Though we shall probe, time and again, our shame,
Who lack the wit to keep or to refuse,
After a time, all losses are the same.

No wit, no luck can beat a losing game;
Good fortune is a reassuring ruse:
And we go stripped at last the way we came.

Rage as we will for what we think to claim,   10
Nothing so much as this bare thought subdues:
After a time, all losses are the same.

The sense of treachery—the want, the blame—
Goes in the end, whether or not we choose,
And we go stripped at last the way we came.

So we, who would go raging, will go tame
When what we have we can no longer use:
After a time, all losses are the same;
And we go stripped at last the way we came.

QUESTIONS
1. What difference in effect would occur if the refrain "After a time" were changed to "When life is done"? **2.** What are the various meanings of "stripped" in line 3 and line 19? **3.** Explain the meaning of "The sense of treachery" (l. 13). **4.** Does this poem say that life is meaningless? Explain.

WRITING TOPIC
Compare this poem with Dylan Thomas's "Do Not Go Gentle into That Good Night."

Woodchucks   1972

MAXINE KUMIN   [b. 1925]

Gassing the woodchucks didn't turn out right.
The knockout bomb from the Feed and Grain Exchange
was featured as merciful, quick at the bone
and the case we had against them was airtight
both exits shoehorned shut with puddingstone,
but they had a sub-sub-basement out of range.

Next morning they turned up again, no worse
for the cyanide than we for our cigarettes
and state-store Scotch, all of us up to scratch.
They brought down the marigolds as a matter of course   10
and then took over the vegetable patch
nipping the broccoli shoots, beheading the carrots.

The food from our mouths, I said, righteously thrilling
to the feel of the .22, the bullets' neat noses.
I, a lapsed pacifist fallen from grace
puffed with Darwinian pieties for killing,
now drew a bead on the littlest woodchuck's face.
He died down in the everbearing roses.

Ten minutes later I dropped the mother. She
flipflopped in the air and fell, her needle teeth   20
still hooked in a leaf of early Swiss chard.
Another baby next. O one-two-three
the murderer inside me rose up hard,
the hawkeye killer came on stage forthwith.

There's one chuck left. Old wily fellow, he keeps
me cocked and ready day after day after day.
All night I hunt his humped-up form. I dream
I sight along the barrel in my sleep.
If only they'd all consented to die unseen
gassed underground the quiet Nazi way.   30

To Aunt Rose   1961

ALLEN GINSBERG [b. 1926]

Aunt Rose—now—might I see you
with your thin face and buck tooth smile and pain
            of rheumatism—and a long black heavy shoe
                for your bony left leg
    limping down the long hall in Newark on the running carpet
                past the black grand piano
                    in the day room
                        where the parties were

and I sang Spanish loyalist songs[1]
            in a high squeaky voice   10
                    (hysterical) the committee listening
            while you limped around the room
                collected the money—
Aunt Honey, Uncle Sam, a stranger with a cloth arm
            in his pocket
                and huge young bald head
                    of Abraham Lincoln Brigade

—your long sad face
            your tears of sexual frustration
                    (what smothered sobs and bony hips   20
                        under the pillows of Osborne Terrace)
    —the time I stood on the toilet seat naked
            and you powdered my thighs with Calomine
                against the poison ivy—my tender
                    and shamed first black curled hairs
    what were you thinking in secret heart then
                knowing me a man already—
    and I an ignorant girl of family silence on the thin pedestal
                of my legs in the bathroom—Museum of Newark.

                        Aunt Rose   30
        Hitler is dead, Hitler is in Eternity; Hitler is with
                Tamburlane and Emily Brontë[2]

Though I see you walking still, a ghost on Osborne Terrace
            down the long dark hall to the front door
            limping a little with a pinched smile
                in what must have been a silken
                    flower dress
    welcoming my father, the Poet, on his visit to Newark
            —see you arriving in the living room
                dancing on your crippled leg   40

To Aunt Rose
    [1] Between 1936 and 1939, a civil war occurred in Spain in which rebel forces under General
Francisco Franco defeated the Loyalist forces supporting the politically liberal monarchy. In some
ways a foreshadowing of World War II, the Spanish Civil War attracted the attention of the great
powers, with Russia supporting the Loyalist forces and Germany and Italy supporting the rebel
forces. Many American writers and intellectuals saw the war as a struggle between fascism and
democracy and supported the Loyalist cause energetically; the Abraham Lincoln Brigade (line 17)
was a volunteer unit of Americans that fought on the Loyalist side.
    [2] Tamburlane (1336?–1405), Mongol conqueror; Emily Brontë (1818–1848), English novelist.

and clapping hands his book
had been accepted by Liveright[3]

Hitler is dead and Liveright's gone out of business
The Attic of the Past and *Everlasting Minute* are out of print
Uncle Harry sold his last silk stocking
Claire quit interpretive dancing school
Buba sits a wrinkled monument in Old
Ladies Home blinking at new babies

last time I saw you was the hospital
pale skull protruding under ashen skin   50
blue veined unconscious girl
in an oxygen tent
the war in Spain has ended long ago
Aunt Rose

Casual Wear   1984

JAMES MERRILL   [b. 1926]

Your average tourist: Fifty. 2.3
Times married. Dressed, this year, in Ferdi Plinthbower
Originals. Odds 1 to 9[10]
Against her strolling past the Embassy

Today at noon. Your average terrorist:
Twenty-five. Celibate. No use for trends,
At least in clothing. Mark, though, where it ends.
People have come forth made of colored mist

Unsmiling on one hundred million screens
To tell of his prompt phone call to the station,   10
"Claiming responsibility"—devastation
Signed with a flourish, like the dead wife's jeans.

To Aunt Rose
[3] A publishing firm.

Five Ways to Kill a Man   1963

EDWIN BROCK   [b. 1927]

There are many cumbersome ways to kill a man:
you can make him carry a plank of wood
to the top of a hill and nail him to it. To do this
properly you require a crowd of people
wearing sandals, a cock that crows, a cloak
to dissect, a sponge, some vinegar and one
man to hammer the nails home.

Or you can take a length of steel,
shaped and chased° in a traditional way,   ornamented
and attempt to pierce the metal cage he wears.   10
But for this you need white horses,
English trees, men with bows and arrows,
at least two flags, a prince and a
castle to hold your banquet in.

Dispensing with nobility, you may, if the wind
allows, blow gas at him. But then you need
a mile of mud sliced through with ditches,
not to mention black boots, bomb craters,
more mud, a plague of rats, a dozen songs
and some round hats made of steel.   20

In an age of aeroplanes, you may fly
miles above your victim and dispose of him by
pressing one small switch. All you then
require is an ocean to separate you, two
systems of government, a nation's scientists,
several factories, a psychopath and
land that no one needs for several years.

These are, as I began, cumbersome ways
to kill a man. Simpler, direct, and much more neat
is to see that he is living somewhere in the middle   30
of the twentieth century, and leave him there.

For the Anniversary of My Death

1967

W. S. MERWIN   [b. 1927]

Every year without knowing it I have passed the day
When the last fires will wave to me
And the silence will set out
Tireless traveller
Like the beam of a lightless star

Then I will no longer
Find myself in life as in a strange garment
Surprised at the earth
And the love of a woman
And the shamelessness of men   10
As today writing after three days of rain
Hearing the wren sing and the falling cease
And bowing not knowing to what

People*

(trans. 1962)

YEVGENY YEVTUSHENKO   [b. 1933]

No people are uninteresting.
Their fate is like the chronicle of planets.

Nothing in them is not particular,
and planet is dissimilar from planet.

And if a man lived in obscurity
making his friends in that obscurity
obscurity is not uninteresting.

To each his world is private,
and in that world one excellent minute.

People
  * Translated by Robin Milner-Gulland and Peter Levi.

And in that world one tragic minute.   10
These are private.

In any man who dies there dies with him
his first snow and kiss and fight.
It goes with him.

They are left books and bridges
and painted canvas and machinery.

Whose fate is to survive.
But what has gone is also not nothing:

by the rule of the game something has gone.
Not people die but worlds die in them.   20

Whom we knew as faulty, the earth's creatures.
Of whom, essentially, what did we know?

Brother of a brother? Friend of friends?
Lover of lover?

We who knew our fathers
in everything, in nothing.

They perish. They cannot be brought back.
The secret worlds are not regenerated.

And every time again and again
I make my lament against destruction.   30

The Ignominy of the Living   1989

KATHLEEN NORRIS   [b. 1947]

The undertaker had placed pink netting
around your face. I removed it
and gave you a small bouquet, encumbering you
into eternity. "Impedimenta," I hear you say,
scornfully, the way you said it at Penn Station
when we struggled to put your bag onto a contraption

of cords and wheels. "Laurel and Hardy[1] got paid for this,"
I said the third time it fell off,
narrowly missing my foot.

You would have laughed   10
at the place we brought you to, the hush of carpet,
violins sliding through "The Way We Were."
"Please turn the music off," I said, civilly,
to the undertaker's assistant.
We had an open grave—no artificial turf—
and your friends lowered you into the ground.

Once you dreamed your mother sweeping
an earthen floor
in a dark, low-ceilinged room.
I see her now: I, too, want to run.   20
And the "ignominy of the living,"
words you nearly spat out
when one of your beloved dead
was ill-remembered; I thought of that
as I removed the netting.

Today I passed St. Mary's
as the Angelus[2] sounded.
You would have liked that, the ancient practice
in the prairie town not a hundred years old,
the world careering disastrously toward the twenty-first century.   30
I stopped and prayed for you.
Then a recording of "My Way" came scratching out
on the electronic carillon.
"Oh, hell," I said,
and prayed for Frank Sinatra, too.

QUESTIONS
1. Explain the title.   **2.** Why does the speaker ask the assistant undertaker to turn
off the music? In this connection, why does she say, "Oh, hell" at the end when
she hears the electronic carillon playing "My Way"?   **3.** Explicate lines 17–19.

---

[1] Stan Laurel (1890–1965) and Oliver Hardy (1892–1957) were a celebrated comedy team who
made many popular movies during the 1920s, 1930s, and 1940s.
[2] In the Roman Catholic Church, a bell rung as a call to prayer.

WRITING TOPIC
If you have ever attended the funeral of someone you knew well, describe your
feelings and reactions to the service. Did it seem appropriate and tasteful? Did it
leave you satisfied that the tribute was sincere and honest, that the person being
eulogized was the person you knew?

God, A Poem   1984

JAMES FENTON   [b. 1949]

A nasty surprise in a sandwich,
A drawing-pin caught in your sock,
The limpest of shakes from a hand which
You'd thought would be firm as a rock,

A serious mistake in a nightie,
A grave disappointment all round
Is all that you'll get from th'Almighty,
Is all that you'll get underground.

Oh he *said*: "If you lay off the crumpet
I'll see you alright in the end.   10
Just hang on until the last trumpet.
Have faith in me, chum—I'm your friend."

But if you remind him, he'll tell you:
"I'm sorry, I must have been pissed—
Though your name rings a sort of a bell. You
Should have guessed that I do not exist.

"I didn't exist at Creation,
I didn't exist at the Flood,
And I won't be around for Salvation
To sort out the sheep from the cud—   20

"Or whatever the phrase is. The fact is
In soteriological terms
I'm a crude existential malpractice
And you are a diet of worms.

"You're a nasty surprise in a sandwich.
You're a drawing-pin caught in my sock.
You're the limpest of shakes from a hand which
I'd have thought would be firm as a rock,

"You're a serious mistake in a nightie,
You're a grave disappointment all round—   30
That's all that you are," says th'Almighty,
"And that's all that you'll be underground."

Fast Break   1985

In memory of Dennis Turner, 1946–1984

EDWARD HIRSCH   [b. 1950]

A hook shot kisses the rim and
hangs there, helplessly, but doesn't drop,

and for once our gangly starting center
boxes out his man and times his jump

perfectly, gathering the orange leather
from the air like a cherished possession

and spinning around to throw a strike
to the outlet who is already shoveling

an underhand pass toward the other guard
scissoring past a flat-footed defender   10

who looks stunned and nailed to the floor
in the wrong direction, trying to catch sight

of a high, gliding dribble and a man
letting the play develop in front of him

in slow motion, almost exactly
like a coach's drawing on the blackboard,

both forwards racing down the court
the way that forwards should, fanning out

and filling the lanes in tandem, moving
together as brothers passing the ball   20

between them without a dribble, without
a single bounce hitting the hardwood

until the guard finally lunges out
and commits to the wrong man

while the power-forward explodes past them
in a fury, taking the ball into the air

by himself now and laying it gently
against the glass for a lay-up,

but losing his balance in the process,
inexplicably falling, hitting the floor   30

with a wild, headlong motion
for the game he loved like a country

and swiveling back to see an orange blur
floating perfectly through the net.

QUESTIONS
1. What clues suggest that this poem is about more than a basketball game maneuver?   **2.** The last three stanzas describe an event on the basketball court; what
might that event suggest about the life of Dennis Turner, to whom the poem is
dedicated?

WRITING TOPIC
In an essay, use the rules and language of some sport as an extended metaphor for
an event in your life. (You might get some ideas from Robert Francis's poem,
"Pitcher" [p. 1234].)

Funeral Home   1991

MARIANNE BURKE   [b. 1957]

Let us think of you spared, carried gently
in the arms of the ocean that's piped
through speakers, spreading a hush in Parmele's[1]
where we sit, adrift, on the parlor couch
between time, in death's caesura.

Funeral Home
    [1] The name of the funeral home.

The funeral director ticks off a list
of questions. He wants the facts, reduces you
to an abstract—mother with a capital "M."
Nowhere will it say how petite you were,
that your wedding ring fits my pinkie finger,   10

or that, tucked into your coffin, you will look
like a doll we will never outgrow.
Downstairs, he shows us his fleet
of caskets, satin-lined, open-lidded—
music boxes whose strains are too fine

for us to hear, like your voice,
utterless, our names dead on your tongue.
Even here the ocean's cold hush.

You are lost at sea.
To think we must choose a vessel,   20
one that will not float but sink.
Mahogany is what we set you in—
our mother of pearl, our buried treasure.

QUESTIONS
1. Trace the sea and ship imagery within the poem. Do you find it appropriate?
Explain.   **2.** How is the funeral director characterized? How does the speaker
respond to his behavior?

THE
PRESENCE
OF DEATH

Tombstones, 1942 by Jacob Lawrence

DRAMA

No Exit

1944

JEAN-PAUL SARTRE [1905–1980]

CHARACTERS

Valet
Garcin
Estelle
Inez

Huis Clos (No Exit) was presented for the first time at the Théâtre du Vieux-Colombier, Paris, in May 1944.

> **SCENE:** *A drawing-room in Second Empire style. A massive bronze ornament stands on the mantelpiece.*

Garcin (*enters, accompanied by the room-valet, and glances around him*).   Hm! So here we are?
Valet.   Yes, Mr. Garcin.
Garcin.   And this is what it looks like?
Valet.   Yes.
Garcin.   Second Empire furniture, I observe. . . . Well, well, I dare say one gets used to it in time.
Valet.   Some do. Some don't.
Garcin.   Are all the other rooms like this one?
Valet.   How could they be? We cater for all sorts: Chinamen and Indians, for instance. What use would they have for a Second Empire chair?
Garcin.   And what use do you suppose *I* have for one? Do you know who I was? . . . Oh, well, it's no great matter. And, to tell the truth, I had quite a habit of living among furniture that I didn't relish, and in false positions. I'd even come to like it. A false position in a Louis-Philippe dining-room—you know the style?—well, that had its points, you know. Bogus in bogus, so to speak.

Valet.   And you'll find that living in a Second Empire drawing-room has its points.

Garcin.   Really? . . . Yes, yes, I dare say. . . . *(He takes another look around.)* Still, I certainly didn't expect—this! You know what they tell us down there?

Valet.   What about?

Garcin.   About *(makes a sweeping gesture)* this—er—residence.

Valet.   Really, sir, how could you believe such cock-and-bull stories? Told by people who'd never set foot here. For, of course, if they had—

Garcin.   Quite so. *(Both laugh. Abruptly the laugh dies from Garcin's face.)* But, I say, where are the instruments of torture?

Valet.   The what?

Garcin.   The racks and red-hot pincers and all the other paraphernalia?

Valet.   Ah, you must have your little joke, sir!

Garcin.   My little joke? Oh, I see. No, I wasn't joking. *(A short silence. He strolls around the room.)* No mirrors, I notice. No windows. Only to be expected. And nothing breakable. *(Bursts out angrily.)* But, damn it all, they might have left me my toothbrush!

Valet.   That's good! So you haven't yet got over your—what-do-you-call-it?— sense of human dignity? Excuse me smiling.

Garcin *(thumping ragefully the arm of an armchair)*.   I'll ask you to be more polite. I quite realize the position I'm in, but I won't tolerate . . .

Valet.   Sorry, sir. No offense meant. But all our guests ask me the same questions. Silly questions, if you'll pardon me saying so. Where's the torture-chamber? That's the first thing they ask, all of them. They don't bother their heads about the bathroom requisites, that I can assure you. But after a bit, when they've got their nerve back, they start in about their toothbrushes and what-not. Good heavens, Mr. Garcin, can't you use your brains? What, I ask you, would be the point of brushing your teeth?

Garcin *(more calmly)*.   Yes, of course you're right. *(He looks around again.)* And why should one want to see oneself in a looking-glass? But that bronze contraption on the mantelpiece, that's another story. I suppose there will be times when I stare my eyes out at it. Stare my eyes out—see what I mean? . . . All right, let's put our cards on the table. I assure you I'm quite conscious of my position. Shall I tell you what it feels like? A man's drowning, choking, sinking by inches, till only his eyes are just above water. And what does he see? A bronze atrocity by—what's the fellow's name?—Barbedienne. A collector's piece. As in a nightmare. That's their idea, isn't it? . . . No, I suppose you're under orders not to answer questions; and I won't insist. But don't forget, my man, I've a good notion of what's coming to me, so don't you boast you've caught me off my guard. I'm facing the situation, facing it. *(He starts pacing the room again.)* So that's that; no toothbrush. And no bed, either. One never sleeps, I take it?

Valet.   That's so.

Garcin.   Just as I expected. *Why* should one sleep? A sort of drowsiness steals on you, tickles you behind the ears, and you feel your eyes closing—but why sleep? You lie down on the sofa and—in a flash, sleep flies away. Miles and miles away. So you rub your eyes, get up, and it starts all over again.

Valet.   Romantic, that's what you are.

Garcin.   Will you keep quiet, please! . . . I won't make a scene, I shan't be sorry for myself, I'll face the situation, as I said just now. Face it fairly and squarely. I won't have it springing at me from behind, before I've time to size it up. And you call that being "romantic"! . . . So it comes to this; one doesn't need rest. Why bother about sleep if one isn't sleepy? That stands to reason, doesn't it? Wait a minute, there's a snag somewhere; something disagreeable. Why, now, should it be disagreeable? . . . Ah, I see; it's life without a break.

Valet.   What do you mean by that?

Garcin.   What do I mean? *(Eyes the Valet suspiciously.)* I thought as much. That's why there's something so beastly, so damn bad-mannered, in the way you stare at me. They're paralyzed.

Valet.   What are you talking about?

Garcin.   Your eyelids. We move ours up and down. Blinking, we call it. It's like a small black shutter that clicks down and makes a break. Everything goes black; one's eyes are moistened. You can't imagine how restful, refreshing, it is. Four thousand little rests per hour. Four thousand little respites— just think! . . . So that's the idea. I'm to live without eyelids. Don't act the fool, you know what I mean. No eyelids, no sleep; it follows, doesn't it? I shall never sleep again. But then—how shall I endure my own company? Try to understand. You see, I'm fond of teasing, it's a second nature with me—and I'm used to teasing myself. Plaguing myself, if you prefer; I don't tease nicely. But I can't go on doing that without a break. Down there I had my nights. I slept. I always had good nights. By way of compensation, I suppose. And happy little dreams. There was a green field. Just an ordinary field. I used to stroll in it. . . . Is it daytime now?

Valet.   Can't you see? The lights are on.

Garcin.   Ah yes, I've got it. It's *your* daytime. And outside?

Valet.   Outside?

Garcin.   Damn it, you know what I mean. Beyond that wall.

Valet.   There's a passage.

Garcin.   And at the end of the passage?

Valet.   There's more rooms, more passages, and stairs.

Garcin.   And what lies beyond them?

Valet.   That's all.

Garcin.   But surely you have a day off sometimes. Where do you go?

Valet.   To my uncle's place. He's the head valet here. He has a room on the third floor.

Garcin.   I should have guessed as much. Where's the light-switch?

Valet.   There isn't any.

Garcin.   What? Can't one turn off the light?

Valet. Oh, the management can cut off the current if they want to. But I can't remember their having done so on this floor. We have all the electricity we want.

Garcin. So one has to live with one's eyes open all the time?

Valet. To *live*, did you say?

Garcin. Don't let's quibble over words. With one's eyes open. Forever. Always broad daylight in my eyes—and in my head. (*Short silence.*) And suppose I took that contraption on the mantelpiece and dropped it on the lamp—wouldn't it go out?

Valet. You can't move it. It's too heavy.

Garcin (*seizing the bronze ornament and trying to lift it*). You're right. It's too heavy.

(*A short silence follows.*)

Valet. Very well, sir, if you don't need me any more, I'll be off.

Garcin. What? You're going? (*The Valet goes up to the door.*) Wait. (*Valet looks around.*) That's a bell, isn't it? (*Valet nods.*) And if I ring, you're bound to come?

Valet. Well, yes, that's so—in a way. But you can never be sure about that bell. There's something wrong with the wiring, and it doesn't always work. (*Garcin goes to the bell-push and presses the button. A bell purrs outside.*)

Garcin. It's working all right.

Valet (*looking surprised*). So it is. (*He, too, presses the button.*) But I shouldn't count on it too much if I were you. It's—capricious. Well, I really must go now. (*Garcin makes a gesture to detain him.*) Yes, sir?

Garcin. No, never mind. (*He goes to the mantelpiece and picks up a paper-knife.*) What's this?

Valet. Can't you see? An ordinary paper-knife.

Garcin. Are there books here?

Valet. No.

Garcin. Then what's the use of this? (*Valet shrugs his shoulders.*) Very well. You can go. (*Valet goes out.*)

(*Garcin is by himself. He goes to the bronze ornament and strokes it reflectively. He sits down; then gets up, goes to the bell-push, and presses the button. The bell remains silent. He tries two or three times, without success. Then he tries to open the door, also without success. He calls the Valet several times, but gets no result. He beats the door with his fists, still calling. Suddenly he grows calm and sits down again. At the same moment the door opens and Inez enters, followed by the Valet.*)

Valet. Did you call, sir?

Garcin (*on the point of answering "Yes"—but then his eyes fall on Inez*). No.

Valet (*turning to Inez*).   This is your room, madam. (*Inez says nothing.*) If there's any information you require—? (*Inez still keeps silent, and the Valet looks slightly huffed.*) Most of our guests have quite a lot to ask me. But I won't insist. Anyhow, as regards the toothbrush, and the electric bell, and that thing on the mantelshelf, this gentleman can tell you anything you want to know as well as I could. We've had a little chat, him and me. (*Valet goes out.*) (*Garcin refrains from looking at Inez, who is inspecting the room. Abruptly she turns to Garcin.*)

Inez.   Where's Florence? (*Garcin does not reply.*) Didn't you hear? I asked you about Florence. Where is she?

Garcin.   I haven't an idea.

Inez.   Ah, that's the way it works, is it? Torture by separation. Well, as far as I'm concerned, you won't get anywhere. Florence was a tiresome little fool, and I shan't miss her in the least.

Garcin.   I beg your pardon. Who do you suppose I am?

Inez.   You? Why, the torturer, of course.

Garcin (*looks startled, then bursts out laughing*).   Well, that's a good one! Too comic for words. I the torturer! So you came in, had a look at me, and thought I was—er—one of the staff. Of course, it's that silly fellow's fault; he should have introduced us. A torturer indeed! I'm Joseph Garcin, journalist and man of letters by profession. And as we're both in the same boat, so to speak, might I ask you, Mrs.—?

Inez (*testily*).   Not "Mrs." I'm unmarried.

Garcin.   Right. That's a start, anyway. Well, now that we've broken the ice, do you *really* think I look like a torturer? And, by the way, how does one recognize torturers when one sees them? Evidently you've ideas on the subject.

Inez.   They look frightened.

Garcin.   Frightened! But how ridiculous! Of whom should they be frightened? Of their victims?

Inez.   Laugh away, but I know what I'm talking about. I've often watched my face in the glass.

Garcin.   In the glass? (*He looks around him.*) How beastly of them! They've removed everything in the least resembling a glass. (*Short silence.*) Anyhow, I can assure you I'm not frightened. Not that I take my position lightly; I realize its gravity only too well. But I'm not afraid.

Inez (*shrugging her shoulders*).   That's your affair. (*Silence.*) Must you be here all the time, or do you take a stroll outside, now and then?

Garcin.   The door's locked.

Inez.   Oh! . . . That's too bad.

Garcin.   I can quite understand that it bores you having me here. And I, too— well, quite frankly, I'd rather be alone. I want to think things out, you know; to set my life in order, and one does that better by oneself. But I'm sure we'll manage to pull along together somehow. I'm no talker, I don't move much; in fact I'm a peaceful sort of fellow. Only, if I may venture on a suggestion, we should make a point of being extremely courteous to each other. That will ease the situation for us both.

Inez.   I'm not polite.

Garcin.   Then I must be polite for two.

(*A longish silence. Garcin is sitting on a sofa, while Inez paces up and down the room.*)

Inez (*fixing her eyes on him*).   Your mouth!

Garcin (*as if waking from a dream*).   I beg your pardon.

Inez.   Can't you keep your mouth still? You keep twisting it about all the time. It's grotesque.

Garcin.   So sorry. I wasn't aware of it.

Inez.   That's just what I reproach you with. (*Garcin's mouth twitches.*) There you are! You talk about politeness, and you don't even try to control your face. Remember you're not alone; you've no right to inflict the sight of your fear on me.

Garcin (*getting up and going towards her*).   How about you? Aren't you afraid?

Inez.   What would be the use? There was some point in being afraid *before*; while one still had hope.

Garcin (*in a low voice*).   There's no more hope—but it's still "before." We haven't yet begun to suffer.

Inez.   That's so. (*A short silence.*) Well? What's going to happen?

Garcin.   I don't know. I'm waiting.

(*Silence again. Garcin sits down and Inez resumes her pacing up and down the room. Garcin's mouth twitches; after a glance at Inez he buries his face in his hands. Enter Estelle with the Valet. Estelle looks at Garcin, whose face is still hidden by his hands.*)

Estelle (*to Garcin*).   No! Don't look up. I know what you're hiding with your hands. I know you've no face left. (*Garcin removes his hands.*) What! (*A short pause. Then, in a tone of surprise*) But I don't know you!

Garcin.   I'm not the torturer, madam.

Estelle.   I never thought you were. I—I thought someone was trying to play a rather nasty trick on me. (*To the Valet*) Is anyone else coming?

Valet.   No, madam. No one else is coming.

Estelle.   Oh! Then we're to stay by ourselves, the three of us, this gentleman, this lady, and myself. (*She starts laughing.*)

Garcin (*angrily*).   There's nothing to laugh about.

Estelle (*still laughing*).   It's those sofas. They're so hideous. And just look how they've been arranged. It makes me think of New Year's Day—when I used to visit that boring old aunt of mine, Aunt Mary. Her house is full of horrors like that. . . . I suppose each of us has a sofa of his own. Is that one mine?

(To the Valet) But you can't expect me to sit on that one. It would be too horrible for words. I'm in pale blue and it's vivid green.

Inez.   Would you prefer mine?

Estelle.   That claret-colored one, you mean? That's very sweet of you, but really—no, I don't think it'd be so much better. What's the good of worrying, anyhow? We've got to take what comes to us, and I'll stick to the green one. *(Pauses.)* The only one which might do, at a pinch, is that gentleman's. *(Another pause.)*

Inez.   Did you hear, Mr. Garcin?

Garcin *(with a slight start)*.   Oh—the sofa, you mean. So sorry. *(He rises.)* Please take it, madam.

Estelle.   Thanks. *(She takes off her coat and drops it on the sofa. A short silence.)* Well, as we're to live together, I suppose we'd better introduce ourselves. My name's Rigault. Estelle Rigault. *(Garcin bows and is going to announce his name, but Inez steps in front of him.)*

Inez.   And I'm Inez Serrano. Very pleased to meet you.

Garcin *(bowing again)*.   Joseph Garcin.

Valet.   Do you require me any longer?

Estelle.   No, you can go. I'll ring when I want you. *(Exit Valet, with polite bows to everyone.)*

Inez.   You're very pretty. I wish we'd had some flowers to welcome you with.

Estelle.   Flowers? Yes, I loved flowers. Only they'd fade so quickly here, wouldn't they? It's so stuffy. Oh, well, the great thing is to keep as cheerful as we can, don't you agree? Of course, you, too, are—

Inez.   Yes. Last week. What about you?

Estelle.   I'm—quite recent. Yesterday. As a matter of fact, the ceremony's not quite over. *(Her tone is natural enough, but she seems to be seeing what she describes.)* The wind's blowing my sister's veil all over the place. She's trying her best to cry. Come dear! Make another effort. That's better. Two tears, two little tears are twinkling under the black veil. Oh dear! What a sight Olga looks this morning! She's holding my sister's arm, helping her along. She's not crying, and I don't blame her; tears always mess one's face up, don't they? Olga was my bosom friend, you know.

Inez.   Did you suffer much?

Estelle.   No. I was only half conscious, mostly.

Inez.   What was it?

Estelle.   Pneumonia. *(In the same tone as before)* It's over now, they're leaving the cemetery. Good-by. Good-by. Quite a crowd they are. My husband's stayed at home. Prostrated with grief, poor man. *(To Inez)* How about you?

Inez.   The gas stove.

Estelle.   And you, Mr. Garcin?

Garcin.   Twelve bullets through my chest. *(Estelle makes a horrified gesture.)* Sorry! I fear I'm not good company among the dead.

Estelle.   Please, please don't use that word. It's so—so crude. In terribly bad taste, really. It doesn't mean much, anyhow. Somehow I feel we've never been so much alive as now. If we've absolutely got to mention this—this state of things, I suggest we call ourselves—wait!—absentees. Have you been—been absent for long?

Garcin.   About a month.

Estelle.   Where do you come from?

Garcin.   From Rio.

Estelle.   I'm from Paris. Have you anyone left down there?

Garcin.   Yes, my wife. *(In the same tone as Estelle has been using)* She's waiting at the entrance of the barracks. She comes there every day. But they won't let her in. Now she's trying to peep between the bars. She doesn't yet know I'm—absent, but she suspects it. Now she's going away. She's wearing her black dress. So much the better, she won't need to change. She isn't crying, but she never did cry, anyhow. It's a bright sunny day and she's like a black shadow creeping down the empty street. Those big tragic eyes of hers—with that martyred look they always had. Oh, how she got on my nerves!

(A short silence. Garcin sits on the central sofa and buries his head in his hands.)

Inez.   Estelle!

Estelle.   Please, Mr. Garcin!

Garcin.   What is it?

Estelle.   You're sitting on my sofa.

Garcin.   I beg your pardon. *(He gets up.)*

Estelle.   You looked so—so far away. Sorry I disturbed you.

Garcin.   I was setting my life in order. *(Inez starts laughing.)* You may laugh, but you'd do better to follow my example.

Inez.   No need. My life's in perfect order. It tidied itself up nicely of its own accord. So I needn't bother about it now.

Garcin.   Really? You imagine it's so simple as that. *(He runs his hand over his forehead.)* Whew! How hot it is here! Do you mind if—? *(He begins taking off his coat.)*

Estelle.   How dare you! *(More gently)* No, please don't. I loathe men in their shirt-sleeves.

Garcin *(putting on his coat again)*.   All right. *(A short pause.)* Of course, I used to spend my nights in the newspaper office, and it was a regular Black Hole, so we never kept our coats on. Stiflingly hot it could be. *(Short pause. In the same tone as previously)* Stifling, that it *is*. It's night now.

Estelle.   That's so. Olga's undressing; it must be after midnight. How quickly the time passes, on earth!

Inez.   Yes, after midnight. They've sealed up my room. It's dark, pitch-dark, and empty.

Garcin.   They've slung their coats on the backs of the chairs and rolled up their shirt-sleeves above the elbow. The air stinks of men and cigar-smoke. *(A short silence.)* I used to like living among men in their shirt-sleeves.

Estelle *(aggressively).*   Well, in that case our tastes differ. That's all it proves. *(Turning to Inez)* What about you? Do you like men in their shirt-sleeves?

Inez.   Oh, I don't care much for men any way.

Estelle *(looking at the other two with a puzzled air).*   Really I can't imagine why they put us three together. It doesn't make sense.

Inez *(stifling a laugh).*   What's that you said?

Estelle.   I'm looking at you two and thinking that we're going to live together. . . . It's so absurd. I expected to meet old friends, or relatives.

Inez.   Yes, a charming old friend—with a hole in the middle of his face.

Estelle.   Yes, him too. He danced the tango so divinely. Like a professional. . . . But why, why should we of all people be put together?

Garcin.   A pure fluke, I should say. They lodge folks as they can, in the order of their coming. *(To Inez)* Why are you laughing?

Inez.   Because you amuse me, with your "flukes." As if they left anything to chance! But I suppose you've got to reassure yourself somehow.

Estelle *(hesitantly).*   I wonder, now. Don't you think we may have met each other at some time in our lives?

Inez.   Never. I shouldn't have forgotten you.

Estelle.   Or perhaps we have friends in common. I wonder if you know the Dubois-Seymours?

Inez.   Not likely.

Estelle.   But *everyone* went to their parties.

Inez.   What's their job?

Estelle.   Oh, they don't do anything. But they have a lovely house in the country, and hosts of people visit them.

Inez.   I didn't. I was a post-office clerk.

Estelle *(recoiling a little).*   Ah, yes. . . . Of course, in that case—(A *pause.*) And you, Mr. Garcin?

Garcin.   We've never met. I always lived in Rio.

Estelle.   Then you must be right. It's mere chance that has brought us together.

Inez.   Mere chance? Then it's by chance this room is furnished as we see it. It's an accident that the sofa on the right is a livid green, and that one on the left's wine-red. Mere chance? Well, just try to shift the sofas and you'll see the difference quick enough. And that statue on the mantelpiece, do you think it's there by accident? And what about the heat here? How about that? *(A short silence.)* I tell you they've thought it all out. Down to the last detail. Nothing was left to chance. This room was all set for us.

Estelle.   But really! Everything here's so hideous; all in angles, so uncomfortable. I always loathed angles.

Inez *(shrugging her shoulders).*   And do you think *I* lived in a Second Empire drawing-room?

Estelle.   So it was all fixed up beforehand?

Inez.   Yes. And they've put us together deliberately.

Estelle.   Then it's not mere chance that *you* precisely are sitting opposite *me?* But what can be the idea behind it?

Inez. Ask me another! I only know they're waiting.

Estelle. I never could bear the idea of anyone's expecting something from me. It always made me want to do just the opposite.

Inez. Well, do it. Do it if you can. You don't even know what they expect.

Estelle (*stamping her foot*). It's outrageous! So something's coming to me from you two? (*She eyes each in turn.*) Something nasty, I suppose. There are some faces that tell me everything at once. Yours don't convey anything.

Garcin (*turning abruptly towards Inez*). Look here! Why are we together? You've given us quite enough hints, you may as well come out with it.

Inez (*in a surprised tone*). But I know nothing, absolutely nothing about it. I'm as much in the dark as you are.

Garcin. We've *got* to know. (*Ponders for a while.*)

Inez. If only each of us had the guts to tell—

Garcin. Tell what?

Inez. Estelle!

Estelle. Yes?

Inez. What have you done? I mean, why have they sent you here?

Estelle (*quickly*). That's just it. I haven't a notion, not the foggiest. In fact, I'm wondering if there hasn't been some ghastly mistake. (*To Inez*) Don't smile. Just think of the number of people who—who become absentees every day. There must be thousands and thousands, and probably they're sorted out by—by understrappers, you know what I mean. Stupid employees who don't know their job. So they're bound to make mistakes sometimes. . . . Do stop smiling. (*To Garcin*) Why don't you speak? If they made a mistake in my case, they may have done the same about you. (*To Inez*) And you, too. Anyhow, isn't it better to think we've got here by mistake?

Inez. Is that all you have to tell us?

Estelle. What else should I tell? I've nothing to hide. I lost my parents when I was a kid, and I had my young brother to bring up. We were terribly poor and when an old friend of my people asked me to marry him I said yes. He was very well off, and quite nice. My brother was a very delicate child and needed all sorts of attention, so really that was the right thing for me to do, don't you agree? My husband was old enough to be my father, but for six years we had a happy married life. Then two years ago I met the man I was fated to love. We knew it the moment we set eyes on each other. He asked me to run away with him, and I refused. Then I got pneumonia and it finished me. That's the whole story. No doubt, by certain standards, I did wrong to sacrifice my youth to a man nearly three times my age. (*To Garcin*) Do *you* think that could be called a sin?

Garcin. Certainly not. (*A short silence.*) And now, tell me, do you think it's a crime to stand by one's principles?

Estelle. Of course not. Surely no one could blame a man for that!

Garcin. Wait a bit! I ran a pacifist newspaper. Then war broke out. What was I to do? Everyone was watching me, wondering: "Will he dare?" Well, I dared. I folded my arms and they shot me. Had I done anything wrong?

Estelle *(laying her hand on his arm)*. Wrong? On the contrary. You were—

Inez *(breaks in ironically)*. —a hero! And how about your wife, Mr. Garcin?

Garcin. That's simple. I'd rescued her from—from the gutter.

Estelle *(to Inez)*. You see! You see!

Inez. Yes, I see. *(A pause.)* Look here! What's the point of play-acting, trying to throw dust in each other's eyes? We're all tarred with the same brush.

Estelle *(indignantly)*. How dare you!

Inez. Yes, we are criminals—murderers—all three of us. We're in hell, my pets; they never make mistakes, and people aren't damned for nothing.

Estelle. Stop! For heaven's sake—

Inez. In hell! Damned souls—that's us, all three!

Estelle. Keep quiet! I forbid you to use such disgusting words.

Inez. A damned soul—that's you, my little plaster saint. And ditto our friend there, the noble pacifist. We've had our hour of pleasure, haven't we? There have been people who burned their lives out for our sakes—and we chuckled over it. So now we have to pay the reckoning.

Garcin *(raising his fist)*. Will you keep your mouth shut, damn it!

Inez *(confronting him fearlessly, but with a look of vast surprise)*. Well, well! *(A pause.)* Ah, I understand now. I know why they've put us three together.

Garcin. I advise you to—to think twice before you say any more.

Inez. Wait! You'll see how simple it is. Childishly simple. Obviously there aren't any physical torments—you agree, don't you? And yet we're in hell. And no one else will come here. We'll stay in this room together, the three of us, for ever and ever. . . . In short, there's someone absent here, the official torturer.

Garcin *(sotto voce)*. I'd noticed that.

Inez. It's obvious what they're after—an economy of man-power—or devil-power, if you prefer. The same idea as in the cafeteria, where customers serve themselves.

Estelle. What ever do you mean?

Inez. I mean that each of us will act as torturer of the two others.

(There is a short silence while they digest this information.)

Garcin *(gently)*. No, I shall never be your torturer. I wish neither of you any harm, and I've no concern with you. None at all. So the solution's easy enough; each of us stays put in his or her corner and takes no notice of the others. You here, you here, and I there. Like soldiers at our posts. Also, we mustn't speak. Not one word. That won't be difficult; each of us has plenty of material for self-communings. I think I could stay ten thousand years with only my thoughts for company.

Estelle. Have *I* got to keep silent, too?

Garcin. Yes. And that way we—we'll work out our salvation. Looking into ourselves, never raising our heads. Agreed?

Inez. Agreed.

Estelle *(after some hesitation).* I agree.
Garcin. Then—good-by.

(He goes to his sofa and buries his head in his hands. There is a long silence; then Inez begins singing to herself.)

Inez *(singing).*

> What a crowd in Whitefriars Lane!
> They've set trestles in a row,
> With a scaffold and the knife,
> And a pail of bran below.
> Come, good folks, to Whitefriars lane,
> Come to see the merry show!
>
> The headsman rose at crack of dawn,
> He'd a long day's work in hand,
> Chopping heads off generals,
> Priests and peers and admirals,
> All the highest in the land.
> What a crowd in Whitefriars Lane!
>
> See them standing in a line,
> Ladies all dressed up so fine.
> But their heads have got to go,
> Heads and hats roll down below.
> Come, good folks, to Whitefriars Lane,
> Come to see the merry show!

(Meanwhile Estelle has been plying her powder-puff and lipstick. She looks round for a mirror, fumbles in her bag, then turns towards Garcin.)

Estelle. Excuse me, have you a glass? *(Garcin does not answer.)* Any sort of glass, a pocket-mirror will do. *(Garcin remains silent.)* Even if you won't speak to me, you might lend me a glass. *(His head still buried in his hands, Garcin ignores her.)*
Inez *(eagerly).* Don't worry. I've a glass in my bag. *(She opens her bag. Angrily)* It's gone! They must have taken it from me at the entrance.
Estelle. How tiresome!

(A short silence. Estelle shuts her eyes and sways, as if about to faint. Inez runs forward and holds her up.)

Inez. What's the matter?
Estelle *(opens her eyes and smiles).* I feel so queer. *(She pats herself.)* Don't you ever get taken that way? When I can't see myself I begin to wonder if I

really and truly exist. I pat myself just to make sure, but it doesn't help much.

Inez.   You're lucky. I'm always conscious of myself—in my mind. Painfully conscious.

Estelle.   Ah yes, in your mind. But everything that goes on in one's head is so vague, isn't it? It makes one want to sleep. (*She is silent for a while.*) I've six big mirrors in my bedroom. There they are. I can see them. But they don't see me. They're reflecting the carpet, the settee, the window—but how empty it is, a glass in which I'm absent! When I talked to people I always made sure there was one near by in which I could see myself. I watched myself talking. And somehow it kept me alert, seeing myself as the others saw me. . . . Oh dear! My lipstick! I'm sure I've put it on all crooked. No, I can't do without a looking-glass for ever and ever, I simply can't.

Inez.   Suppose I try to be your glass? Come and pay me a visit, dear. Here's a place for you on my sofa.

Estelle.   But—(*Points to Garcin.*)

Inez.   Oh, he doesn't count.

Estelle.   But we're going to—to hurt each other. You said it yourself.

Inez.   Do I look as if I wanted to hurt you?

Estelle.   One never can tell.

Inez.   Much more likely *you'll* hurt *me.* Still, what does it matter? If I've got to suffer, it may as well be at your hands, your pretty hands. Sit down. Come closer. Closer. Look into my eyes. What do you see?

Estelle.   Oh, I'm there! But so tiny I can't see myself properly.

Inez.   But *I* can. Every inch of you. Now ask me questions. I'll be as candid as any looking-glass.

(*Estelle seems rather embarrassed and turns to Garcin, as if appealing to him for help.*)

Estelle.   Please, Mr. Garcin. Sure our chatter isn't boring you?

(*Garcin makes no reply.*)

Inez.   Don't worry about him. As I said, he doesn't count. We're by ourselves. . . . Ask away.

Estelle.   Are my lips all right?

Inez.   Show! No, they're a bit smudgy.

Estelle.   I thought as much. Luckily (*throws a quick glance at Garcin*) no one's seen me. I'll try again.

Inez.   That's better. No. Follow the line of your lips. Wait! I'll guide your hand. There. That's quite good.

Estelle.   As good as when I came in?

Inez.   Far better. Crueler. Your mouth looks quite diabolical that way.

Estelle. Good gracious! And you say you like it! How maddening, not being able to see for myself! You're quite sure, Miss Serrano, that it's all right now?

Inez. Won't you call me Inez?

Estelle. Are you sure it looks all right?

Inez. You're lovely, Estelle.

Estelle. But how can I rely upon your taste? Is it the same as *my* taste? Oh, how sickening it all is, enough to drive one crazy!

Inez. I *have* your taste, my dear, because I like you so much. Look at me. No, straight. Now smile. I'm not so ugly, either. Am I not nicer than your glass?

Estelle. Oh, I don't know. You scare me rather. My reflection in the glass never did that; of course, I knew it so well. Like something I had tamed. . . . I'm going to smile, and my smile will sink down into your pupils, and heaven knows what it will become.

Inez. And why shouldn't you "tame" *me*? *(The women gaze at each other, Estelle with a sort of fearful fascination.)* Listen! I want you to call me Inez. We must be great friends.

Estelle. I don't make friends with women very easily.

Inez. Not with postal clerks, you mean? Hullo, what's that—that nasty red spot at the bottom of your cheek? A pimple?

Estelle. A pimple? Oh, how simply foul! Where?

Inez. There. . . . You know the way they catch larks—with a mirror? I'm your lark-mirror, my dear, and you can't escape me. . . . There isn't any pimple, not a trace of one. So what about it? Suppose the mirror started telling lies? Or suppose I covered my eyes—as he is doing—and refused to look at you, all that loveliness of yours would be wasted on the desert air. No, don't be afraid, I can't help looking at you, I shan't turn my eyes away. And I'll be nice to you, ever so nice. Only you must be nice to me, too.

(A short silence.)

Estelle. Are you really—attracted by me?

Inez. Very much indeed.

(Another short silence.)

Estelle *(indicating Garcin by a slight movement of her head).* But I wish he'd notice me, too.

Inez. Of course! Because he's a Man! *(To Garcin)* You've won. *(Garcin says nothing.)* But look at her, damn it! *(Still no reply from Garcin.)* Don't pretend. You haven't missed a word of what we've said.

Garcin. Quite so; not a word. I stuck my fingers in my ears, but your voices thudded in my brain. Silly chatter. Now will you leave me in peace, you two? I'm not interested in you.

Inez.   Not in me, perhaps—but how about this child? Aren't you interested in her? Oh, I saw through your game; you got on your high horse just to impress her.

Garcin.   I asked you to leave me in peace. There's someone talking about me in the newspaper office and I want to listen. And, if it'll make you any happier, let me tell you that I've no use for the "child," as you call her.

Estelle.   Thanks.

Garcin.   Oh, I didn't mean it rudely.

Estelle.   You cad!

(They confront each other in silence for some moments.)

Garcin.   So that's that. *(Pause.)* You know I begged you not to speak.

Estelle.   It's *her* fault; she started. I didn't ask anything of her and she came and offered me her—her glass.

Inez.   So you say. But all the time you were making up to him, trying every trick to catch his attention.

Estelle.   Well, why shouldn't I?

Garcin.   You're crazy, both of you. Don't you see where this is leading us? For pity's sake, keep your mouths shut. *(Pause.)* Now let's all sit down again quite quietly; we'll look at the floor and each must try to forget the others are there.

(A longish silence. Garcin sits down. The women return hesitantly to their places. Suddenly Inez swings round on him.)

Inez.   To forget about the others? How utterly absurd! I *feel* you there, in every pore. Your silence clamors in my ears. You can nail up your mouth, cut your tongue out—but you can't prevent your *being there*. Can you stop your thoughts? I hear them ticking away like a clock, tick-tock, tick-tock, and I'm certain you hear mine. It's all very well skulking on your sofa, but you're everywhere, and every sound comes to me soiled, because you've intercepted it on its way. Why, you've even stolen my face; you know it and I don't! And what about her, about Estelle? You've stolen her from me, too; if she and I were alone do you suppose she'd treat me as she does? No, take your hands from your face, I won't leave you in peace—that would suit your book too well. You'd go on sitting there, in a sort of trance, like a yogi, and even if I didn't see her I'd feel it in my bones—that she was making every sound, even the rustle of her dress, for your benefit, throwing you smiles you don't see. . . . Well, I won't stand for that, I prefer to choose my hell; I prefer to look you in the eyes and fight it out face to face.

Garcin.   Have it your own way. I suppose we were bound to come to this; they knew what they were about, and we're easy game. If they'd put me in a room with men—men can keep their mouths shut. But it's no use wanting the impossible. *(He goes to Estelle and lightly fondles her neck.)* So I attract you, little girl? It seems you were making eyes at me?

Estelle.   Don't touch me.

Garcin.   Why not? We might, anyhow, be natural. . . . Do you know, I used to be mad about women? And some were fond of me. So we may as well stop posing, we've nothing to lose. Why trouble about politeness, and decorum, and the rest of it? We're between ourselves. And presently we shall be naked as—as new-born babes.

Estelle.   Oh, let me be!

Garcin.   As new-born babes. Well, I'd warned you, anyhow. I asked so little of you, nothing but peace and a little silence. I'd put my fingers in my ears. Gomez was spouting away as usual, standing in the center of the room, with all the pressmen listening. In their shirt-sleeves. I tried to hear, but it wasn't too easy. Things on earth move so quickly, you know. Couldn't you have held your tongues? Now it's over, he's stopped talking, and what he thinks of me has gone back into his head. Well, we've got to see it through somehow. . . . Naked as we were born. So much the better; I want to know whom I have to deal with.

Inez.   You know already. There's nothing more to learn.

Garcin.   You're wrong. So long as each of us hasn't made a clean breast of it—why they've damned him or her—we know nothing. Nothing that counts. You, young lady, you shall begin. Why? Tell us why. If you are frank, if we bring our specters into the open, it may save us from disaster. So—out with it! Why?

Estelle.   I tell you I haven't a notion. They wouldn't tell me why.

Garcin.   That's so. They wouldn't tell me, either. But I've a pretty good idea. . . . Perhaps you're shy of speaking first? Right. I'll lead off. *(A short silence.)* I'm not a very estimable person.

Inez.   No need to tell us that. We know you were a deserter.

Garcin.   Let that be. It's only a side-issue. I'm here because I treated my wife abominably. That's all. For five years. Naturally, she's suffering still. There she is: the moment I mention her, I see her. It's Gomez who interests me, and it's she I see. Where's Gomez got to? For five years. There! They've given her back my things; she's sitting by the window, with my coat on her knees. The coat with the twelve bullet-holes. The blood's like rust; a brown ring round each hole. It's quite a museum-piece, that coat; scarred with history. And I used to wear it, fancy! . . . Now, can't you shed a tear, my love? Surely you'll squeeze one out—at last? No? You can't manage it? . . . Night after night I came home blind drunk, stinking of wine and women. She'd sat up for me, of course. But she never cried, never uttered a word of reproach. Only her eyes spoke. Big, tragic eyes. I don't regret anything. I must pay the price, but I shan't whine. . . . It's snowing in the street. Won't you cry, confound you? That woman was a born martyr, you know; a victim by vocation.

Inez *(almost tenderly)*.   Why did you hurt her like that?

Garcin.   It was so easy. A word was enough to make her flinch. Like a sensitive plant. But never, never a reproach. I'm fond of teasing. I watched and waited. But no, not a tear, not a protest. I'd picked her up out of the gutter, you understand. . . . Now she's stroking the coat. Her eyes are shut and she's feeling with her fingers for the bullet-holes. What are you after? What do you expect? I tell you I regret nothing. The truth is, she admired me too much. Does that mean anything to you?

Inez.   No. Nobody admired *me*.

Garcin.   So much the better. So much the better for you. I suppose all this strikes you as very vague. Well, here's something you can get your teeth into. I brought a half-caste girl to stay in our house. My wife slept upstairs; she must have heard—everything. She was an early riser and, as I and the girl stayed in bed late, she served us our morning coffee.

Inez.   You brute!

Garcin.   Yes, a brute, if you like. But a well-beloved brute. (*A far-away look comes to his eyes.*) No, it's nothing. Only Gomez, and he's not talking about *me*. . . . What were you saying? Yes, a brute. Certainly. Else why should I be here? (*To Inez*) Your turn.

Inez.   Well, I was what some people down there called "a damned bitch." Damned already. So it's no surprise, being here.

Garcin.   Is that all you have to say?

Inez.   No. There was that affair with Florence. A dead man's tale. With three corpses to it. He to start with; then she and I. So there's no one left, I've nothing to worry about; it was a clean sweep. Only that room. I see it now and then. Empty, with the doors locked. . . . No, they've just unlocked them. "To Let." It's to let; there's a notice on the door. That's—too ridiculous.

Garcin.   Three. Three deaths, you said?

Inez.   Three.

Garcin.   One man and two women?

Inez.   Yes.

Garcin.   Well, well. (*A pause.*) Did he kill himself?

Inez.   He? No, he hadn't the guts for that. Still, he'd every reason; we led him a dog's life. As a matter of fact, he was run over by a tram. A silly sort of end. . . . I was living with them; he was my cousin.

Garcin.   Was Florence fair?

Inez.   Fair? (*Glances at Estelle.*) You know, I don't regret a thing; still, I'm not so very keen on telling you the story.

Garcin.   That's all right. . . . So you got sick of him?

Inez.   Quite gradually. All sorts of little things got on my nerves. For instance, he made a noise when he was drinking—a sort of gurgle. Trifles like that. He was rather pathetic really. Vulnerable. Why are you smiling?

Garcin.   Because I, anyhow, am *not* vulnerable.

Inez.   Don't be too sure. . . . I crept inside her skin, she saw the world through my eyes. When she left him, I had her on my hands. We shared a bed-sitting-room at the other end of the town.

Garcin. And then?

Inez. Then that tram did its job. I used to remind her every day: "Yes, my pet, we killed him between us." (A *pause.*) I'm rather cruel, really.

Garcin. So am I.

Inez. No, you're not cruel. It's something else.

Garcin. What?

Inez. I'll tell you later. When I say I'm cruel, I mean I can't get on without making people suffer. Like a live coal. A live coal in others' hearts. When I'm alone I flicker out. For six months I flamed away in her heart, till there was nothing but a cinder. One night she got up and turned on the gas while I was asleep. Then she crept back into bed. So now you know.

Garcin. Well! Well!

Inez. Yes? What's on your mind?

Garcin. Nothing. Only that it's not a pretty story.

Inez. Obviously. But what matter?

Garcin. As you say, what matter? (*To Estelle*) Your turn. What have you done?

Estelle. As I told you, I haven't a notion. I rack my brain, but it's no use.

Garcin. Right. Then we'll give you a hand. That fellow with the smashed face, who was he?

Estelle. Who—who do you mean?

Inez. You know quite well. The man you were so scared of seeing when you came in.

Estelle. Oh, him! A friend of mine.

Garcin. Why were you afraid of him?

Estelle. That's my business, Mr. Garcin.

Inez. Did he shoot himself on your account?

Estelle. Of course not. How absurd you are!

Garcin. Then why should you have been so scared? He blew his brains out, didn't he? That's how his face got smashed.

Estelle. Don't! Please don't go on.

Garcin. Because of you. Because of you.

Inez. He shot himself because of you.

Estelle. Leave me alone! It's—it's not fair, bullying me like that. I want to go! I want to go! (*She runs to the door and shakes it.*)

Garcin. Go if you can. Personally, I ask for nothing better. Unfortunately, the door's locked.

(*Estelle presses the bell-push, but the bell does not ring. Inez and Garcin laugh. Estelle swings round on them, her back to the door.*)

Estelle (*in a muffled voice*). You're hateful, both of you.

Inez. Hateful? Yes, that's the word. Now get on with it. That fellow who killed himself on your account—you were his mistress, eh?

Garcin. Of course she was. And he wanted to have her to himself alone. That's so, isn't it?

Inez. He danced the tango like a professional, but he was poor as a church mouse—that's right, isn't it? *(A short silence.)*

Garcin. Was he poor or not? Give a straight answer.

Estelle. Yes, he was poor.

Garcin. And then you had your reputation to keep up. One day he came and implored you to run away with him, and you laughed in his face.

Inez. That's it. You laughed at him. And so he killed himself.

Estelle. Did you use to look at Florence in that way?

Inez. Yes. *(A short pause, then Estelle bursts out laughing.)*

Estelle. You've got it all wrong, you two. *(She stiffens her shoulders, still leaning against the door, and faces them. Her voice grows shrill, truculent.)* He wanted me to have a baby. So there!

Garcin. And you didn't want one?

Estelle. I certainly didn't. But the baby came, worse luck. I went to Switzerland for five months. No one knew anything. It was a girl. Roger was with me when she was born. It pleased him no end, having a daughter. It didn't please *me!*

Garcin. And then?

Estelle. There was a balcony overlooking the lake. I brought a big stone. He could see what I was up to and he kept on shouting: "Estelle, for God's sake, don't!" I hated him then. He saw it all. He was leaning over the balcony and he saw the rings spreading on the water—

Garcin. Yes? And then?

Estelle. That's all. I came back to Paris—and he did as he wished.

Garcin. You mean he blew his brains out?

Estelle. It was absurd of him, really; my husband never suspected anything. *(A pause.)* Oh, how I loathe you! *(She sobs tearlessly.)*

Garcin. Nothing doing. Tears don't flow in this place.

Estelle. I'm a coward. A coward! *(Pause.)* If you knew how I hate you!

Inez *(taking her in her arms).* Poor child! *(To Garcin)* So the hearing's over. But there's no need to look like a hanging judge.

Garcin. A hanging judge? *(He glances around him.)* I'd give a lot to be able to see myself in a glass. *(Pause.)* How hot it is! *(Unthinkingly he takes off his coat.)* Oh, sorry! *(He starts putting it on again.)*

Estelle. Don't bother. You can stay in your shirt-sleeves. As things are—

Garcin. Just so. *(He drops his coat on the sofa.)* You mustn't be angry with me, Estelle.

Estelle. I'm not angry with you.

Inez. And what about me? Are you angry with me?

Estelle. Yes.

(A short silence.)

Inez.   Well, Mr. Garcin, now you have us in the nude all right. Do you understand things any better for that?

Garcin.   I wonder. Yes, perhaps a trifle better. *(Timidly)* And now suppose we start trying to help each other.

Inez.   I don't need help.

Garcin.   Inez, they've laid their snare damned cunningly—like a cobweb. If you make any movement, if you raise your hand to fan yourself, Estelle and I feel a little tug. Alone, none of us can save himself or herself; we're linked together inextricably. So you can take your choice. *(A pause.)* Hullo? What's happening?

Inez.   They've let it. The windows are wide open, a man is sitting on my bed. *My* bed, if you please! They've let it, let it! Step in, step in, make yourself at home, you brute! Ah, there's a woman, too. She's going up to him, putting her hands on his shoulders. . . . Damn it, why don't they turn the lights on? It's getting dark. Now he's going to kiss her. But that's my room, *my* room! Pitch-dark now. I can't see anything, but I hear them whispering, whispering. Is he going to make love to her on *my* bed? What's that she said? That it's noon and the sun is shining? I must be going blind. *(A pause.)* Blacked out. I can't see or hear a thing. So I'm done with the earth, it seems. No more alibis for me! *(She shudders.)* I feel so empty, desiccated—really dead at last. All of me's here, in this room. *(A pause.)* What were you saying? Something about helping me, wasn't it?

Garcin.   Yes.

Inez.   Helping me to do what?

Garcin.   To defeat their devilish tricks.

Inez.   And what do you expect me to do, in return?

Garcin.   To help *me*. It only needs a little effort, Inez; just a spark of human feeling.

Inez.   Human feeling. That's beyond my range. I'm rotten to the core.

Garcin.   And how about me? *(A pause.)* All the same, suppose we try?

Inez.   It's no use. I'm all dried up. I can't give and I can't receive. How could *I* help you? A dead twig, ready for the burning. *(She falls silent, gazing at Estelle, who has buried her head in her hands.)* Florence was fair, a natural blonde.

Garcin.   Do you realize that this young woman's fated to be your torturer?

Inez.   Perhaps I've guessed it.

Garcin.   It's through her they'll get you. I, of course, I'm different—aloof. I take no notice of her. Suppose you had a try—

Inez.   Yes?

Garcin.   It's a trap. They're watching you, to see if you'll fall into it.

Inez.   I know. And you're another trap. Do you think they haven't foreknown every word you say? And of course there's a whole nest of pitfalls that we can't see. Everything here's a booby-trap. But what do I care? I'm a pitfall, too. For her, obviously. And perhaps I'll catch her.

Garcin.   You won't catch anything. We're chasing after each other, round and round in a vicious circle, like the horses on a roundabout. That's part of their plan, of course. . . . Drop it, Inez. Open your hands and let go of everything. Or else you'll bring disaster on all three of us.

Inez.   Do I look the sort of person who lets go? I know what's coming to me. I'm going to burn, and it's to last forever. Yes, I *know* everything. But do you think I'll let go? I'll catch her, she'll see you through my eyes, as Florence saw that other man. What's the good of trying to enlist my sympathy? I assure you I know everything, and I can't feel sorry even for myself. A trap! Don't I know it, and that I'm in a trap myself, up to the neck, and there's nothing to be done about it? And if it suits their book, so much the better!

Garcin (*gripping her shoulders*).   Well, I, anyhow, can feel sorry for you, too. Look at me, we're naked, naked right through, and I can see into your heart. That's one link between us. Do you think I'd want to hurt you? I don't regret anything, I'm dried up, too. But for you I can still feel pity.

Inez (*who has let him keep his hands on her shoulders until now, shakes herself loose*).   Don't. I hate being pawed about. And keep your pity for yourself. Don't forget, Garcin, that there are traps for you, too, in this room. All nicely set for you. You'd do better to watch your own interests. (*A pause.*) But, if you will leave us in peace, this child and me, I'll see I don't do you any harm.

Garcin (*gazes at her for a moment, then shrugs his shoulders*).   Very well.

Estelle (*raising her head*).   Please, Garcin.

Garcin.   What do you want of me?

Estelle (*rises and goes up to him*).   You can help *me*, anyhow.

Garcin.   If you want help, apply to her.

(*Inez has come up and is standing behind Estelle, but without touching her. During the dialogue that follows she speaks almost in her ear. But Estelle keeps her eyes on Garcin, who observes her without speaking, and she addresses her answers to him, as if it were he who is questioning her.*)

Estelle.   I implore you, Garcin—you gave me your promise, didn't you? Help me quick. I don't want to be left alone. Olga's taken him to a cabaret.

Inez.   Taken whom?

Estelle.   Peter. . . . Oh, now they're dancing together.

Inez.   Who's Peter?

Estelle.   Such a silly boy. He called me his glancing stream—just fancy! He was terribly in love with me. . . . She's persuaded him to come out with her tonight.

Inez.   Do you love him?

Estelle.   They're sitting down now. She's puffing like a grampus. What a fool the girl is to insist on dancing! But I dare say she does it to reduce. . . . No, of course I don't love him; he's only eighteen, and I'm not a baby-snatcher.

Inez.   Then why bother about them? What difference can it make?

Estelle.   He belonged to me.

Inez.   Nothing on earth belongs to you any more.

Estelle.   I tell you he was mine. All mine.

Inez.   Yes, he *was* yours—once. But now—Try to make him hear, try to touch him. Olga can touch him, talk to him as much as she likes. That's so, isn't it? She can squeeze his hands, rub herself against him—

Estelle.   Yes, look! She's pressing her great fat chest against him, puffing and blowing in his face. But, my poor little lamb, can't you see how ridiculous she is? Why don't you laugh at her? Oh, once I'd have only had to glance at them and she'd have slunk away. Is there really nothing, nothing left of me?

Inez.   Nothing whatever. Nothing of you's left on earth—not even a shadow. All you own is here. Would you like that paper-knife? Or that ornament on the mantelpiece? That blue sofa's yours. And I, my dear, am yours forever.

Estelle.   You mine! That's good! Well, which of you two would dare to call me his glancing stream, his crystal girl? You know too much about me, you know I'm rotten through and through. . . . Peter dear, think of me, fix your thoughts on me, and save me. All the time you're thinking "my glancing stream, my crystal girl," I'm only half here, I'm only half wicked, and half of me is down there with you, clean and bright and crystal-clear as running water. . . . Oh, just look at her face, all scarlet, like a tomato! No, it's absurd, we've laughed at her together, you and I, often and often. . . . What's that tune?—I always loved it. Yes, the *St. Louis Blues*. . . . All right, dance away, dance away. Garcin, I wish you could see her, you'd die of laughing. Only—she'll never know I *see* her. Yes, I see you Olga, with your hair all anyhow, and you do look a dope, my dear. Oh, now you're treading on his toes. It's a scream! Hurry up! Quicker! Quicker! He's dragging her along, bundling her round and round—it's too ghastly! He always said I was so light, he loved to dance with me. *(She is dancing as she speaks.)* I tell you, Olga, I can see you. No, she doesn't care, she's dancing through my gaze. What's that? What's that you said? "Our poor dear Estelle"? Oh, don't be such a humbug! You didn't even shed a tear at the funeral. . . . And she has the nerve to talk to him about her poor dear friend Estelle! How dare she discuss me with Peter? Now then, keep time. She never could dance and talk at once. Oh, what's that? No, no. Don't tell him. Please, please don't tell him. You can keep him, do what you like with him, but please don't tell him about—that! *(She has stopped dancing.)* All right. You can have him now. Isn't it *foul*, Garcin? She told him everything, about Roger, my trip to Switzerland, the baby. "Poor Estelle wasn't exactly—" No, I wasn't exactly—True enough. He's looking grave, shaking his head, but he doesn't seem so very much surprised, not what one would expect. Keep him, then—

I won't haggle with you over his long eyelashes, his pretty girlish face. They're yours for the asking. His glancing stream, his crystal. Well, the crystal's shattered into bits. "Poor Estelle!" Dance, dance, dance. On with it. But do keep time. One, two. One, two. How I'd love to go down to earth for just a moment, and dance with him again. (She dances again for some moments.) The music's growing fainter. They've turned down the lights, as they do for a tango. Why are they playing so softly? Louder, please. I can't hear. It's so far away, so far away. I—I can't hear a sound. (She stops dancing.) All over. It's the end. The earth has left me. (To Garcin) Don't turn from me—please. Take me in your arms.

(Behind Estelle's back, Inez signs to Garcin to move away.)

Inez (commandingly).   Now then, Garcin!

(Garcin moves back a step, and, glancing at Estelle, points to Inez.)

Garcin.   It's to her you should say that.

Estelle (clinging to him).   Don't turn away. You're a man, aren't you, and surely I'm not such a fright as all that! Everyone says I've lovely hair and, after all, a man killed himself on my account. You have to look at something, and there's nothing here to see except the sofas and that awful ornament and the table. Surely I'm better to look at than a lot of stupid furniture. Listen! I've dropped out of their hearts like a little sparrow fallen from its nest. So gather me up, dear, fold me to your heart—and you'll see how nice I can be.

Garcin (freeing himself from her, after a short struggle).   I tell you it's to that lady you should speak.

Estelle.   To her? But she doesn't count, she's a woman.

Inez.   Oh, I don't count? Is that what you think? But, my poor little fallen nestling, you've been sheltering in my heart for ages, though you didn't realize it. Don't be afraid; I'll keep looking at you for ever and ever, without a flutter of my eyelids, and you'll live in my gaze like a mote in a sunbeam.

Estelle.   A sunbeam indeed! Don't talk such rubbish! You've tried that trick already, and you should know it doesn't work.

Inez.   Estelle! My glancing stream! My crystal!

Estelle.   Your crystal? It's grotesque. Do you think you can fool me with that sort of talk? Everyone knows by now what I did to my baby. The crystal's shattered, but I don't care. I'm just a hollow dummy, all that's left of me is the outside—but it's not for you.

Inez.   Come to me, Estelle. You shall be whatever you like: a glancing stream, a muddy stream. And deep down in my eyes you'll see yourself just as you want to be.

Estelle. Oh, leave me in peace. You haven't any eyes. Oh, damn it, isn't there anything I can do to get rid of you? I've an idea. *(She spits in Inez's face.)* There!

Inez. Garcin, you shall pay for this.

(A pause. Garcin shrugs his shoulders and goes to Estelle.)

Garcin. So it's a man you need?

Estelle. Not *any* man. You.

Garcin. No humbug now. Any man would do your business. As I happen to be here, you want me. Right! *(He grips her shoulders.)* Mind, I'm not your sort at all, really; I'm not a young nincompoop and I don't dance the tango.

Estelle. I'll take you as you are. And perhaps I shall change you.

Garcin. I doubt it. I shan't pay much attention; I've other things to think about.

Estelle. What things?

Garcin. They wouldn't interest you.

Estelle. I'll sit on your sofa and wait for you to take some notice of me. I promise not to bother you at all.

Inez *(with a shrill laugh).* That's right, fawn on him, like the silly bitch you are. Grovel and cringe! And he hasn't even good looks to commend him!

Estelle *(to Garcin).* Don't listen to her. She has no eyes, no ears. She's—nothing.

Garcin. I'll give you what I can. It doesn't amount to much. I shan't love you; I know you too well.

Estelle. Do you want me, anyhow?

Garcin. Yes.

Estelle. I ask no more.

Garcin. In that case—*(He bends over her.)*

Inez. Estelle! Garcin! You must be going crazy. You're not alone. I'm here too.

Garcin. Of course—but what does it matter?

Inez. Under my eyes? You couldn't—couldn't do it.

Estelle. Why not? I often undressed with my maid looking on.

Inez *(gripping Garcin's arm).* Let her alone. Don't paw her with your dirty man's hands.

Garcin *(thrusting her away roughly).* Take care. I'm no gentleman, and I'd have no compunction about striking a woman.

Inez. But you promised me; you promised. I'm only asking you to keep your word.

Garcin. Why should I, considering you were the first to break our agreement?

(Inez turns her back on him and retreats to the far end of the room.)

Inez. Very well, have it your own way. I'm the weaker party, one against two. But don't forget I'm here, and watching. I shan't take my eyes off you, Garcin; when you're kissing her, you'll feel them boring into you. Yes, have it your own way, make love and get it over. We're in hell; my turn will come.

(During the following scene she watches them without speaking.)

Garcin *(coming back to Estelle and grasping her shoulders).* Now then. Your lips. Give me your lips. *(A pause. He bends to kiss her, then abruptly straightens up.)*
Estelle *(indignantly).* Really! *(A pause.)* Didn't I tell you not to pay any attention to her?
Garcin. You've got it wrong. *(Short silence.)* It's Gomez; he's back in the pressroom. They've shut the windows; it must be winter down there. Six months since I—Well, I warned you I'd be absent-minded sometimes, didn't I? They're shivering, they've kept their coats on. Funny they should feel the cold like that, when I'm feeling so hot. Ah, this time he's talking about me.
Estelle. Is it going to last long? *(Short silence.)* You might at least tell me what he's saying.
Garcin. Nothing. Nothing worth repeating. He's a swine, that's all. *(He listens attentively.)* A god-damned bloody swine. *(He turns to Estelle.)* Let's come back to—to ourselves. Are you going to love me?
Estelle *(smiling).* I wonder now!
Garcin. Will you trust me?
Estelle. What a quaint thing to ask! Considering you'll be under my eyes all the time, and I don't think I've much to fear from Inez, so far as you're concerned.
Garcin. Obviously. *(A pause. He takes his hands off Estelle's shoulders.)* I was thinking of another kind of trust. *(Listens.)* Talk away, talk away, you swine. I'm not there to defend myself. *(To Estelle)* Estelle, you *must* give me your trust.
Estelle. Oh, what a nuisance you are! I'm giving you my mouth, my arms, my whole body—and everything could be so simple. . . . My trust! I haven't any to give, I'm afraid, and you're making me terribly embarrassed. You must have something pretty ghastly on your conscience to make such a fuss about my trusting you.
Garcin. They shot me.
Estelle. I know. Because you refused to fight. Well, why shouldn't you?
Garcin. I—I didn't exactly refuse. *(In a far-away voice)* I must say he talks well, he makes out a good case against me, but he never says what I should have done instead. Should I have gone to the general and said: "General, I decline to fight"? A mug's game; they'd have promptly locked me up. But I wanted to show my colors, my true colors, do you understand? I wasn't going

to be silenced. *(To Estelle)* So I—I took the train. . . . They caught me at the frontier.

Estelle. Where were you trying to go?

Garcin. To Mexico. I meant to launch a pacifist newspaper down there. *(A short silence.)* Well, why don't you speak?

Estelle. What could I say? You acted quite rightly, as you didn't want to fight. *(Garcin makes a fretful gesture.)* But, darling, how on earth can I guess what you want me to answer?

Inez. Can't you guess? Well, *I* can. He wants you to tell him that he bolted like a lion. For "bolt" he did, and that's what's biting him.

Garcin. "Bolted," "went away"—we won't quarrel over words.

Estelle. But you *had* to run away. If you'd stayed they'd have sent you to jail, wouldn't they?

Garcin. Of course. *(A pause.)* Well, Estelle, am I a coward?

Estelle. How can I say? Don't be so unreasonable, darling. I can't put myself in your skin. You must decide that for yourself.

Garcin *(wearily)*. I can't decide.

Estelle. Anyhow, you must remember. You must have had reasons for acting as you did.

Garcin. I had.

Estelle. Well?

Garcin. But were they the real reasons?

Estelle. You've a twisted mind, that's your trouble. Plaguing yourself over such trifles!

Garcin. I'd thought it all out, and I wanted to make a stand. But was that my real motive?

Inez. Exactly. That's the question. Was that your real motive? No doubt you argued it out with yourself, you weighed the pros and cons, you found good reasons for what you did. But fear and hatred and all the dirty little instincts one keeps dark—they're motives too. So carry on, Mr. Garcin, and try to be honest with yourself—for once.

Garcin. Do I need you to tell me that? Day and night I paced my cell, from the window to the door, from the door to the window. I pried into my heart, I sleuthed myself like a detective. By the end of it I felt as if I'd given my whole life to introspection. But always I harked back to the one thing certain—that I had acted as I did, I'd taken that train to the frontier. But why? Why? Finally I thought: My death will settle it. If I face death courageously, I'll prove I am no coward.

Inez. And how did you face death?

Garcin. Miserably. Rottenly. *(Inez laughs.)* Oh, it was only a physical lapse—that might happen to anyone; I'm not ashamed of it. Only everything's been left in suspense, forever. *(To Estelle)* Come here, Estelle. Look at me. I want to feel someone looking at me while they're talking about me on earth. . . . I like green eyes.

Inez. Green eyes! Just hark to him! And you, Estelle, do you like cowards?

Estelle.   If you knew how little I care! Coward or hero, it's all one—provided he kisses well.

Garcin.   There they are, slumped in their chairs, sucking at their cigars. Bored they look. Half-asleep. They're thinking: "Garcin's a coward." But only vaguely, dreamily. One's got to think of something. "That chap Garcin was a coward." That's what they've decided, those dear friends of mine. In six months' time they'll be saying: "Cowardly as that skunk Garcin." You're lucky, you two; no one on earth is giving you another thought. But I—I'm long in dying.

Inez.   What about your wife, Garcin?

Garcin.   Oh, didn't I tell you? She's dead.

Inez.   Dead?

Garcin.   Yes, she died just now. About two months ago.

Inez.   Of grief?

Garcin.   What else should she die of? So all is for the best, you see; the war's over, my wife's dead, and I've carved out my place in history.

(He gives a choking sob and passes his hand over his face. Estelle catches his arm.)

Estelle.   My poor darling! Look at me. Please look. Touch me. Touch me. *(She takes his hand and puts it on her neck.)* There! Keep your hand there. *(Garcin makes a fretful movement.)* No, don't move. Why trouble what those men are thinking? They'll die off one by one. Forget them. There's only me, now.

Garcin.   But *they* won't forget *me*, not they! They'll die, but others will come after them to carry on the legend. I've left my fate in their hands.

Estelle.   You think too much, that's your trouble.

Garcin.   What else is there to do now? I was a man of action once. . . . Oh, if only I could be with them again, for just one day—I'd fling their lie in their teeth. But I'm locked out; they're passing judgment on my life without troubling about me, and they're right, because I'm dead. Dead and done with. *(Laughs.)* A back number.

(A short pause.)

Estelle *(gently).*   Garcin.

Garcin.   Still there? Now listen! I want you to do me a service. No, don't shrink away. I know it must seem strange to you, having someone asking you for help; you're not used to that. But if you'll make the effort, if you'll only *will* it hard enough, I dare say we can really love each other. Look at it this way. A thousand of them are proclaiming I'm a coward; but what do numbers matter? If there's someone, just one person, to say quite positively I did not run away, that I'm not the sort who runs away, that I'm brave and decent and the rest of it—well, that one person's faith would save me. Will you have that faith in me? Then I shall love you and cherish you for ever. Estelle—will you?

Estelle *(laughing).*   Oh, you dear silly man, do you think I could love a coward?

Garcin.   But just now you said—

Estelle.   I was only teasing you. I like men, my dear, who're real men, with tough skin and strong hands. You haven't a coward's chin, or a coward's mouth, or a coward's voice, or a coward's hair. And it's for your mouth, your hair, your voice, I love you.

Garcin.   Do you mean this? *Really* mean it?

Estelle.   Shall I swear it?

Garcin.   Then I snap my fingers at them all, those below and those in here. Estelle, we shall climb out of hell. *(Inez gives a shrill laugh. He breaks off and stares at her.)* What's that?

Inez *(still laughing).*   But she doesn't mean a word of what she says. How can you be such a simpleton? "Estelle, am I a coward?" As if she cared a damn either way.

Estelle.   Inez, how dare you? *(To Garcin)* Don't listen to her. If you want me to have faith in you, you must begin by trusting me.

Inez.   That's right! That's right! Trust away! She wants a man—that far you can trust her—she wants a man's arm round her waist, a man's smell, a man's eyes glowing with desire. And that's all she wants. She'd assure you you were God Almighty if she thought it would give you pleasure.

Garcin.   Estelle, is this true? Answer me. Is it true?

Estelle.   What do you expect me to say? Don't you realize how maddening it is to have to answer questions one can't make head or tail of? *(She stamps her foot.)* You do make things difficult. . . . Anyhow, I'd love you just the same, even if you were a coward. Isn't that enough?

(A short pause.)

Garcin *(to the two women).*   You disgust me, both of you. *(He goes towards the door.)*

Estelle.   What are you up to?

Garcin.   I'm going.

Inez *(quickly).*   You won't get far. The door is locked.

Garcin.   I'll *make* them open it. *(He presses the bell-push. The bell does not ring.)*

Estelle.   Please! Please!

Inez *(to Estelle).*   Don't worry, my pet. The bell doesn't work.

Garcin.   I tell you they shall open. *(Drums on the door.)* I can't endure it any longer, I'm through with you both. *(Estelle runs to him; he pushes her away.)* Go away. You're even fouler than she. I won't let myself get bogged in your eyes. You're soft and slimy. Ugh! *(Bangs on the door again.)* Like an octopus. Like a quagmire.

Estelle. I beg you, oh, I beg you not to leave me. I'll promise not to speak again, I won't trouble you in any way—but don't go. I daren't be left alone with Inez, now she's shown her claws.

Garcin. Look after yourself. I never asked you to come here.

Estelle. Oh, how mean you are! Yes, it's quite true you're a coward.

Inez *(going up to Estelle)*. Well, my little sparrow fallen from the nest, I hope you're satisfied now. You spat in my face—playing up to him, of course—and we had a tiff on his account. But he's going, and a good riddance it will be. We two women will have the place to ourselves.

Estelle. You won't gain anything. If that door opens, I'm going, too.

Inez. Where?

Estelle. I don't care where. As far from you as I can.

(Garcin has been drumming on the door while they talk.)

Garcin. Open the door! Open, blast you! I'll endure anything, your red-hot tongs and molten lead, your racks and prongs and garrotes—all your fiendish gadgets, everything that burns and flays and tears—I'll put up with any torture you impose. Anything, anything would be better than this agony of mind, this creeping pain that gnaws and fumbles and caresses one and never hurts quite enough. *(He grips the door-knob and rattles it.)* Now will you open? *(The door flies open with a jerk, and he just avoids falling.)* Ah! *(A long silence.)*

Inez. Well, Garcin? You're free to go.

Garcin *(meditatively)*. Now I wonder why that door opened.

Inez. What are you waiting for? Hurry up and go.

Garcin. I shall not go.

Inez. And you, Estelle? *(Estelle does not move. Inez bursts out laughing.)* So what? Which shall it be? Which of the three of us will leave? The barrier's down, why are we waiting? . . . But what a situation! It's a scream! We're inseparables!

(Estelle springs at her from behind.)

Estelle. Inseparables? Garcin, come and lend a hand. Quickly. We'll push her out and slam the door on her. That'll teach her a lesson.

Inez *(struggling with Estelle)*. Estelle! I beg you, let me stay. I won't go, I won't go! Not into the passage.

Garcin. Let go of her.

Estelle. You're crazy. She hates you.

Garcin. It's because of her I'm staying here.

(Estelle releases Inez and stares dumbfoundedly at Garcin.)

Inez. Because of me? (*Pause.*) All right, shut the door. It's ten times hotter here since it opened. (*Garcin goes to the door and shuts it.*) Because of me, you said?

Garcin. Yes. *You*, anyhow, know what it means to be a coward.

Inez. Yes, I know.

Garcin. And you know what wickedness is, and shame, and fear. There were days when you peered into yourself, into the secret places of your heart, and what you saw there made you faint with horror. And then, next day, you didn't know what to make of it, you couldn't interpret the horror you had glimpsed the day before. Yes, you know what evil *costs*. And when you say I'm a coward, you know from experience what that means. Is that so?

Inez. Yes.

Garcin. So it's you whom I have to convince; you are of my kind. Did you suppose I meant to go? No, I couldn't leave you here, gloating over my defeat, with all those thoughts about me running in your head.

Inez. Do you really wish to convince me?

Garcin. That's the one and only thing I wish for now. I can't hear them any longer, you know. Probably that means they're through with me. For good and all. The curtain's down, nothing of me is left on earth—not even the name of coward. So, Inez, we're alone. Only you two remain to give a thought to me. She—she doesn't count. It's you who matter; you who hate me. If you'll have faith in me I'm saved.

Inez. It won't be easy. Have a look at me. I'm a hard-headed woman.

Garcin. I'll give you all the time that's needed.

Inez. Yes, we've lots of time in hand. *All* time.

Garcin (*putting his hands on her shoulders*). Listen! Each man has an aim in life, a leading motive; that's so, isn't it? Well, I didn't give a damn for wealth, or for love. I aimed at being a real man. A tough, as they say. I staked everything on the same horse. . . . Can one possibly be a coward when one's deliberately courted danger at every turn? And can one judge a life by a single action?

Inez. Why not? For thirty years you dreamt you were a hero, and condoned a thousand petty lapses—because a hero, of course, can do no wrong. An easy method, obviously. Then a day came when you were up against it, the red light of real danger—and you took the train to Mexico.

Garcin. I "dreamt," you say. It was no dream. When I chose the hardest path, I made my choice deliberately. A man is what he wills himself to be.

Inez. Prove it. Prove it was no dream. It's what one does, and nothing else, that shows the stuff one's made of.

Garcin. I died too soon. I wasn't allowed time to—to do my deeds.

Inez. One always dies too soon—or too late. And yet one's whole life is complete at that moment, with a line drawn neatly under it, ready for the summing up. You are—your life, and nothing else.

Garcin. What a poisonous woman you are! With an answer for everything.

Inez. Now then! Don't lose heart. It shouldn't be so hard, convincing me. Pull yourself together, man, rake up some arguments. (*Garcin shrugs his shoulders.*) Ah, wasn't I right when I said you were vulnerable? Now you're going to pay the price, and what a price! You're a coward, Garcin, because I wish it. I wish it—do you hear?—I wish it. And yet, just look at me, see how weak I am, a mere breath on the air, a gaze observing you, a formless thought that thinks you. (*He walks towards her, opening his hands.*) Ah, they're open now, those big hands, those coarse, man's hands! But what do you hope to do? You can't throttle thoughts with hands. So you've no choice, you must convince me, and you're at my mercy.

Estelle. Garcin!

Garcin. What?

Estelle. Revenge yourself.

Garcin. How?

Estelle. Kiss me, darling—then you'll hear her squeal.

Garcin. That's true, Inez. I'm at your mercy, but you're at mine as well.

(*He bends over Estelle. Inez gives a little cry.*)

Inez. Oh, you coward, you weakling, running to women to console you!

Estelle. That's right, Inez. Squeal away.

Inez. What a lovely pair you make! If you could see his big paw splayed out on your back, rucking up your skin and creasing the silk. Be careful, though! He's perspiring, his hand will leave a blue stain on your dress.

Estelle. Squeal away, Inez, squeal away! . . . Hug me tight, darling; tighter still—that'll finish her off, and a good thing too!

Inez. Yes, Garcin, she's right. Carry on with it, press her to you till you feel your bodies melting into each other; a lump of warm, throbbing flesh. . . . Love's a grand solace, isn't it, my friend? Deep and dark as sleep. But I'll see you don't sleep.

(*Garcin makes a slight movement.*)

Estelle. Don't listen to her. Press your lips to my mouth. Oh, I'm yours, yours, yours.

Inez. Well, what are you waiting for? Do as you're told. What a lovely scene: coward Garcin holding baby-killer Estelle in his manly arms! Make your stakes, everyone. Will coward Garcin kiss the lady, or won't he dare? What's the betting? I'm watching you, everybody's watching. I'm a crowd all by myself. Do you hear the crowd? Do you hear them muttering, Garcin? Mumbling and muttering. "Coward! Coward! Coward! Coward!"—that's what they're saying. . . . It's no use trying to escape, I'll never let you go. What do you hope to get from her silly lips? Forgetfulness? But I shan't forget you, not I! "It's I you must convince." So come to me. I'm waiting.

Come along, now. . . . Look how obedient he is, like a well-trained dog who comes when his mistress calls. You can't hold him, and you never will.

Garcin. Will night never come?

Inez. Never.

Garcin. You will always see me?

Inez. Always.

(Garcin moves away from Estelle and takes some steps across the room. He goes to the bronze ornament.)

Garcin. This bronze. *(Strokes it thoughtfully.)* Yes, now's the moment; I'm looking at this thing on the mantelpiece, and I understand that I'm in hell. I tell you, everything's been thought out beforehand. They knew I'd stand at the fireplace stroking this thing of bronze, with all those eyes intent on me. Devouring me. *(He swings round abruptly.)* What? Only two of you? I thought there were more; many more. *(Laughs.)* So this is hell. I'd never have believed it. You remember all we were told about the torture-chambers, the fire and brimstone, the "burning marl." Old wives' tales! There's no need for redhot pokers. Hell is—other people!

Estelle. My darling! Please—

Garcin *(thrusting her away).* No, let me be. She is between us. I cannot love you when she's watching.

Estelle. Right! In that case, I'll stop her watching.

(She picks up the paper-knife from the table, rushes at Inez, and stabs her several times.)

Inez *(struggling and laughing).* But, you crazy creature, what do you think you're doing? You know quite well I'm dead.

Estelle. Dead?

(She drops the knife. A pause. Inez picks up the knife and jabs herself with it regretfully.)

Inez. Dead! Dead! Dead! Knives, poison, ropes—all useless. It has happened *already,* do you understand? Once and for all. So here we are, forever. *(Laughs.)*

Estelle *(with a peal of laughter).* Forever. My God, how funny! Forever.

Garcin *(looks at the two women, and joins in the laughter).* For ever, and ever, and ever.

(They slump onto their respective sofas. A long silence. Their laughter dies away and they gaze at each other.)

Garcin. Well, well, let's get on with it. . . .

Curtain

QUESTIONS

1. Characterize Garcin, Inez, and Estelle as they first appear. What sort of person does each *appear* to be?   **2.** Why was Garcin damned? Inez? Estelle?   **3.** Why are there no mirrors in the room?   **4.** Find out what Second Empire furniture and interior decoration are like. Why is such a room made the private hell of these three characters?   **5.** When the door suddenly opens late in the play, why does Estelle want to expel Inez? Why does Garcin refuse? Why do the three of them choose to remain in the room?   **6.** What is the significance of Estelle's knife attack on Inez?   **7.** Which character do you sympathize with most? Least? Explain.

WRITING TOPIC

This play was first performed in Paris in 1944, during World War II, while the city was occupied by the army of Nazi Germany. Consider the play in its historical context, and in an essay, discuss *No Exit* as an attack on Sartre's own countrymen. Your argument might include a discussion of France under the Second Empire, the social and political positions of the three damned characters, the reasons for their damnation, the absence of mirrors, the unwillingness of any of them to leave the room when they have the opportunity, and the knife attack.

Steambath*   1970

BRUCE JAY FRIEDMAN   [b. 1930]

> **SETTING:**   A Steambath
> **TIME:**   The Present

Act One

*A steamroom. Benches or slabs and a single overhead shower. Effect of steam is
achieved by either steam or light or both. People speak, disappear in the haze,
reappear. Characters are costumed in sheets or cloths or something in between.
At the beginning of the action, a young man (thirty-five to forty-five) enters and
sits down next to an Oldtimer. He is ever so slightly puzzled by his surroundings
but does his best to conceal this mild concern. He has a great deal of trouble
when he makes contact with the hot seat.*

Oldtimer.   That's really something, isn't it, when you sit down?
Tandy.   It's a bitch.
Oldtimer.   It don't bother me. When you're a young fellow, it bothers you,
   but then you develop a tough ass.
Tandy.   I knew your beard got tough, but I didn't realize the other thing . . .
Oldtimer.   It's true.

(They sit awhile)

   I've had some wonderful sweats in my time.
Tandy.   That right?
Oldtimer.   Oh yeah. When the Polish came in, the union gave them a
   steambath down on Fulton Street . . . Nobody sweats like the Polish . . .
   What you're doing now . . .
Tandy *(Feeling himself)*.   Yes?
Oldtimer.   That's garbage. You're not sweatin' . . . I never exercised much,
   though. You see this area here. *(Pulls flesh in his lower back region)* I always
   wanted to keep that nice and soft in case I got some spinal trouble. So the
   needle could go right in. I know guys, athletes, they're so hard you can't
   stick a needle into them . . . I figure it's a good idea to keep it soft back
   there.

---

* Edited for television version.

(They sit awhile longer)

How do you feel about heart attacks?

Tandy.   I'm against them.

Oldtimer.   Lot of people are. I'll say this for them, though. They don't mark you on the outside. They leave you clean as a whistle. That's more than you can say for a gall bladder.

Tandy.   I agree with you there.

Oldtimer.   I seen guys get cut up for ulcers they got bellies look like the map of downtown Newark, New Jersey . . . People have always been a little too rough on heart attacks. The heart attack's always gotten a raw deal.

(Bieberman, an unattractive fellow, concealed behind a pillar, clears his throat and then spits on the floor)

Hey, I saw that.

Bieberman.   What?

Oldtimer.   You know what. What you did. Expectorating like that. It's disgusting.

Bieberman.   What's wrong? It's a natural fluid.

Oldtimer.   You're a disgrace. *(To Tandy)* You got to watch him like a hawk. Probably farting back there, too. Who the hell would ever know in a steambath.

Bieberman *(Still concealed).*   I heard that. I'm not farting.

Oldtimer.   Congratulations . . .

Bieberman.   My generation doesn't do that.

Oldtimer.   Your generation can kiss my tail. *(To Tandy)* What's your line, young fella?

Tandy.   I just quit my job. I was teaching art appreciation over at the Police Academy.

Oldtimer.   That right. What the hell . . . I guess you got to do something. Police, eh? Ever notice how you never get any trouble from the good people?

Tandy.   Well, that's for sure.

Oldtimer.   It's the bad ones you got to watch. You run the bad ones off the street that'll be the end of your crime. You got a son?

Tandy.   No, I've got a little girl.

Oldtimer.   You got a son, I hope he's a drunk. That'll keep him off drugs. He starts in on that dope stuff you can bid him a fond farewell. *(In reference to Bieberman)* What's that guy doing now?

Tandy *(Checking behind pillar).*   Looks like he's eating an orange.

Oldtimer.   Yeah, but what's he *doing?*

Tandy *(Checks again, gets hit by a shower of seeds).*   He's spitting out the pits.

Oldtimer.   Stupid mother. *(Shouting to Bieberman)* Hey, knock it off, will you?

Bieberman.   Well, what am I supposed to do with them?

Oldtimer. Hold them in your hand. Swallow them. Stick 'em up your nose, what do I care. Just don't spit them out. Didn't you ever hear of a person tripping on pits? *(To Tandy)* They get some crowd in here. He's probably a fag, too.

Two Young Men *(Invisible, speaking in unison).* No, we're the fags.

Oldtimer. I beg your pardon. *(More or less to himself)* I knew there were fags in here. *(To Tandy)* You broke a sweat yet, son?

Tandy. I can feel one coming.

Oldtimer. You know what would go down really well now? A nice cool brew.

(A Bar Boy enters with two cold beers and glasses. In later appearances, he is referred to as Gottlieb. Tandy and the Oldtimer each take a beer and begin to sip at it.)

I drank a lot of beer in my time. One thing I'll say for myself is that I never gained weight. I gained bloat. The trouble is—bloat weighs a lot too. Most people don't realize that. Bloat can kill you.

Tandy. What do you do?

Oldtimer. I done a lot of things. In my late years I took to hackin' a cab. I was terrific once I got my daily icebreaker. But until then I wasn't fit to live with. That's how I had my crash—worried sick about getting my icebreaker. I come on the job at eight in the morning, it's twelve o'clock noon I still hadn't nailed a fare. I'm so upset I drive right through a furrier's window. Into the beaver pelts, I wound up with a car radio in my stomach. And I mean in my stomach, too. I had folk music coming out of my butt. So that was it.

Tandy. That was it?

Oldtimer. That was it.

(A beautiful young girl comes forth, wearing a sheet, humming a tune. She is very blonde. Matter-of-factly She drops the sheet, steps beneath the shower and pulls the shower chain. Little cry of alarm when the water hits her, but She enjoys it. She puts the sheet back on and disappears in the haze.)

Tandy. She come in here often?

Oldtimer. Can't say. Nice set of maracas on her, though.

Tandy. Damn right.

Oldtimer. You know, a lot of guys let the little old frankfurter rule their heads. I always say, let your head rule the little old frankfurter. You go along with that?

Tandy *(After thinking it over).* Yeah! Well . . .

Oldtimer. I never forget this rich bitch on Long Island had her eye on me. I said, madame, that little old weenie you're so interested in don't run the show. I'm the one that runs the show. She didn't like that.

Tandy *(Distracted).* That was unusual.

Oldtimer.   What's that?

Tandy.   That girl. Taking a shower that way.

Oldtimer.   Nah, they got everything today.

(*The Two Young Men come down and do a dancing and singing musical number from a popular Broadway musical comedy, complete with intricate steps, high kicks—in perfect unison. They have a little Panasonic-type player, of the cheap 42nd Street variety. This is the source of the music. They are quite good, semi-professional. They finish up big and then go back to their seats*)

Tandy.   This is some place.

Oldtimer.   Lucky they didn't slip on the pits.

(*Hoarse, guttural sounds in the back, suspiciously from Bieberman's direction*)

Oldtimer.   What are you doing now?

Bieberman.   Gargling. I have a rough throat.

Oldtimer.   That's what I was afraid of. You watch your step, meathead. (*To Tandy*) He starts blowing his nose, I'm going after him . . .

Tandy.   They were very good. The dancers.

Oldtimer.   They do some good work. I never could enjoy a show much. I was always more interested in what was going on in the wings. I figured the real show, the good stuff, was going on back there. I'd rather sit and watch the wings than your top show on Broadway.

Tandy.   I'd rather watch a show. I've never been that interested in the wings. But I see what you mean.

(*Blonde Girl approaches*)

Meredith.   Are you all right?

Tandy.   I'm fine. How was your shower?

Meredith.   It was wonderful. Some day I'd like to meet the man who invented the needle-point showerhead and thank him for all the pleasure he's given me.

Tandy.   Do you come here often?

Meredith.   I don't know. All I can remember is that I was buying this little skirt at Bloomingdale's . . . it couldn't have been this big and they were . . .

Bieberman (*Appearing for the first time, on a ledge above Tandy and Meredith. He speaks with a certain stopped-up anger*).   You have no idea what those skirts have meant to members of my generation. What a skirt like that means to a fellow who could sit through the same movie seven times, willing to sell himself into bondage on a farm in Mississippi if he could see just an eighth of an inch of Ann Rutherford's inner thigh. And then there they are, out of the blue, those pitzel cocker skirts. And the girls wearing them, more beautiful than Ann Rutherford herself, are handing out massive looks at their thighs and crotches. No one has properly realized the effect of all that exposed and quivering flesh on the national character. And my generation is condemned to watch this country, representing one of the greatest social experiments in Western civilization, choke itself to death on an easy diet of boobs and tushes.

Tandy.   Look, do you mind? We were having a private conversation . . .

Bieberman.   As you wish.

(He drops his sheet, and, in his jockey shorts, begins to do a vigorous exercise, disgustingly close to Tandy and Meredith)

Tandy.   Do you have to do that here?

Oldtimer.   He's just getting warmed up.

Bieberman.   It's just till I work up a good healthy sweat.

Tandy.   Do it somewhere else, will you.

Bieberman *(Under his breath, as he moves off)*.   Putz.[1]

Tandy *(Starting to chase Bieberman)*.   Hey! *(To Oldtimer)* He *is* disgusting. I never saw it until just now.

Meredith.   You were a little hard on him.

Tandy.   Was I? I didn't realize it. I was with the cops for a while. In the cultural section. I still have a little of the cop style left.

Meredith.   Listen, if you were with the cops, could you tell me exactly where to kick someone so that he's temporarily paralyzed and can't rape you—yet at the same time doesn't feel you're an insensitive person . . .

Tandy.   We stayed away from that stuff in the art department. . . .

Meredith.   Well, I have to move out of the city anyway. All the men you meet here insist on dressing you up in something before they make love to you—garter belts, stiletto heels *(Demonstrates)*, earmuffs, Luftwaffe[2] costumes. Right in the middle of this cultural wonderland, I spend all my time dressing up for weirdos, I don't need that. I could've gotten that in St. Louis. . . .

Tandy.   What really puzzles me is that I am able to talk to you so easily.

Meredith.   What do you mean?

Tandy.   Well, until recently, I had a great deal of trouble talking to yellow-haired girls. I felt I had to talk to them in verse or something . . . maybe wear special gloves. But apparently I've gotten over that.

Meredith.   You're so nice. I love meeting a nice new person like you. But look, I don't want to get involved.

Tandy.   Involved?

Meredith.   I just can't go through with that again . . . I've had that this year . . . the phone calls . . . My skin . . . For what it does to my skin alone,

---

[1] Yiddish, a slang expression for the male organ.
[2] The German air force during World War II.

it's not worth it . . . Look, I just don't have the strength for another affair . . . Maybe around Labor Day . . . If it's worth anything, it'll be good then, too . . . Will you call me then?

Tandy *(Thinks awhile).*   I'll give you a ring.

Meredith.   You're not angry, are you?

Tandy.   I'm not angry.

Meredith.   It's got nothing to do with you personally . . . you seem like a very sensual person.

Oldtimer.   There is a terrible stink in here. And I got a pretty good idea who's responsible for it.

Bieberman.   I haven't done a thing recently.

Oldtimer.   You'll never convince me of that. Whatever you're doing, cut it out—for my sake, for the sake of this steambath, and for the sake of America.

Bieberman.   I'm just sitting here, being natural, being myself . . .

Oldtimer.   That's what it is? Natural? . . . That's what you've got to stop.

Tandy *(To Meredith).*   Listen, what do you think of this place?

Meredith.   I like it.

Tandy.   Notice anything peculiar about it?

Meredith.   It smells a little funny.

Oldtimer.   It sure as hell does.

Bieberman.   I haven't done a thing. I've been doing a crossword puzzle. *(To Tandy)* What's a six-letter word that means little red spikes of corn?

Oldtimer.   How about "giggie"? Used in a sentence, it goes: "Up your giggie."

Bieberman.   Lovely.

(Lights darken. A screen drops. Stock quotations flash across the screen as they do in a brokerage office. A fellow appears with a chair, sits down opposite the screen, and watches the quotations)

Broker *(Taking notes).*   They put that in for me.

Tandy.   How's the market?

Broker.   Lousy. If you own good stocks. When I went into this business, I had one piece of advice for every one of my customers: "Put your money in good stuff. Stay away from garbage. That's what you want, find yourself another broker. I don't touch it." So what happens in the last five years? The good stuff lays there, garbage goes right through the roof. Some of my customers, they went to other brokers, they bought garbage, they made fortunes . . .

Meredith *(Very trusting).*   Maybe the good stuff will improve. If it's really and truly good.

Broker.   Nah . . . It's too late for that . . .

(Screen disappears. He picks up chair, recedes into the haze)

Tandy.   That's the kind of thing I was talking about . . .

Meredith.   What do you mean?

Tandy.   A guy like that . . . in here . . . watching stocks . . . it's strange.

Meredith.   I just wish the numbers wouldn't go by so fast. You hardly have any time to enjoy them. Am I wrong or have you been doing pretty well lately?

Tandy.   I'm doing fine. I got a divorce. I quit the Police Academy. I'm writing a novel about Charlemagne.[3] And I just got involved in a charity. Helping brain-damaged welders. I was looking for a charity and that's the one I picked. They send out a terrific brochure. There are an awful lot of them . . . welders . . . with brain damage . . . and they're really grateful when you help them. You should see the looks on some of those welders' faces. Could break your heart . . . I've been doing pretty well . . . I'm real close to my ten-year-old daughter.

Meredith.   You have a ten-year-old daughter?

Tandy.   Oh yeah, we just got back from Vegas.

Meredith.   How did she like it?

Tandy.   We got very close on that trip. So I've been doing pretty well lately . . .

Meredith.   Listen, you don't think . . .

Tandy.   What? What?

Meredith.   All I can remember is that Sheila and I were buying skirts at Bloomingdale's. Then we went back to our high-rise apartment on 84th Street and, oh, yes, the supermarket delivery boy was waiting behind the drapes, with a crazy look on his face, holding a blunt instrument . . .

Tandy.   I was in my favorite restaurant, eating some Chinese food. I was just about to knock off a double order of won shih pancakes . . .

Meredith.   You don't think?

Tandy.   . . . We're dead? Is that what you were going to say? That's what I was going to say. That's what we are. The second I said it, I knew it. Bam! Dead! Just like that! Christ!

Meredith.   I had it pictured an entirely different way.

Tandy.   What's that?

Meredith.   Being dead. I thought dying meant that you'd have to spend every day of your life at a different Holiday Inn. Then I decided it was seeing *So Proudly We Hail* with Veronica Lake[4] over and over for the rest of time. In a place where there were no Mounds bars.

(*Voice is heard:* "Cold drinks, popcorn, Raisinettes, Goobers. And no Mounds bars")

Tandy.   Don't pay any attention. Somebody's kidding around.

Meredith (*With real loss*).   No Mounds bars . . .

---

[3] A king who ruled the European kingdom of the Franks (768–814).
[4] A Hollywood actress popular in films of the 1940s.

Tandy.   I don't know about you, but I'm not accepting this.

Meredith.   What do you mean?

Tandy.   I don't like the whole way it was done. Bam. Dead. Just like that. Just like you're a schmuck[5] or something.

Meredith.   What are you going to do?

Tandy.   I'll do something. Don't worry. I'm a doer. If you had any idea of the agony I went through to change my life around you'd see why I'm so roped off. To be picked off like this when I haven't even started to enjoy the good stuff.

Meredith.   Well, how about me? I just had my first orgasm.

Tandy.   Just now?

Meredith.   No. While I was watching the Dick Cavett Show. I was all alone, eating some peach yogurt and I got this funny feeling.

Tandy.   I'll tell you right now, I'm not going along with it. Not now. Not when I'm just getting off the ground. Another time, later on, they want me to be dead, fine. Not now. Uh-uh.

Meredith.   I feel exactly the same way. How can I die? I haven't even bought any of those chunky platform shoes. And I've got to get my thighs down. Everything I eat has a little sign on it that says, "Do not pass go. Move directly to thighs." No, I absolutely can't die. Is there something you can do?

Tandy.   I'll check around, see if I can find out something.

(Disappears in haze)

Oldtimer *(Reading newspaper)*.   Says here they got a new gas, one gallon of it'll wipe out an entire enemy country . . .

Broker.   They got more than that. They got another one—just one drop in the water supply and the whole continent starts vomiting.

Oldtimer *(Sniffing)*.   They could bottle the smell around here, they don't need any gas. You hear that back there?

Bieberman.   I'm not doing anything. I'm working on my toes.

Oldtimer.   I knew it, the sonofabitch. What are you doing to them?

Bieberman.   Trimming down the nails.

Oldtimer.   In here? This is where you picked? Cut it out will you, you slob, you're trying my patience.

Tandy *(Taking aside Oldtimer)*.   Can I see you a second, Oldtimer?

Oldtimer.   What's on your mind, fella? Havin' trouble breathin'? *(Demonstrating)* Suck it in through your mouth awhile.

Tandy.   I was sitting over there with this girl . . .

Oldtimer *(Lasciviously)*.   The one with them chitty-chitty bang-bangs?

Tandy.   That's the one.

---

⁵ Yiddish, a slang expression for the male organ.

Oldtimer.   Don't let her get hold of your liverwurst. They get an armlock on that they never let go.

Tandy.   I got the idea that we were dead. And she agrees with me. Now I can take the dead part. That doesn't scare me. I get older, a little tired, fine. I even thought maybe later on, things go smoothly, maybe I'll knock myself off. Make it simple. But the timing's all wrong now. I'm just getting off the ground. I'm in the middle of writing an historical novel. Right in the goddamn middle. (I don't talk this way in the book.) It's about Charlemagne. I've got a great new girl friend cooks me shish kebab. Bryn Mawr[6] girl. And she still cooks shish kebab. Doesn't bother her a bit. And I never think about Wendy.

Oldtimer.   Wendy?

Tandy.   My ex-wife. Wendy Tandy. Jesus, I just realized, she was Wendy Hilton, I turned her into Wendy Tandy. I probably blew the whole marriage right there. She never went for that name. Can't say that I blame her. Anyway, I don't think about her anymore. Weeks at a time. She could be out balling the whole Royal Canadian Mounties I don't give it a thought. I forgive her. She's a little weak. It's got nothing to do with me. So, you see, I'm really just starting a wonderful new chapter of my life. And along comes this death number—I thought maybe you could help me . . .

Oldtimer.   I hardly know what to say to you, fella. You come at me like a ten-foot wave.

Tandy.   Is there a guy in charge? Somebody I can talk to. E. G. Marshall? Raymond Burr?

Oldtimer.   There's a guy comes around. I see him I'll point him out.

Tandy.   Thanks. You're a good guy. When we get out of this, maybe we can pal around together.

Oldtimer.   You probably smell the sea on me. Before I took up hackin' I worked the China coast for seventeen years. Me and my friend Ollie were the most widely respected duo west of Macao. We'd get ourselves a couple of juki-juki girls, take 'em up on deck and do a little missionary work with 'em anchored in front of Bruce Wong's Monkey Meat Shop in Hong Kong Harbor. They arrested Ollie for abusing himself into the holy water fountain at the Merchant Seaman's Chapel. He died in irons and I lost the best friend I ever had . . .

(Fades off, a bit overcome with emotion)

Meredith.   What did that old man say?

Tandy.   He said there's a fellow around who seems to be in charge. That he'd point him out to me. Listen, how do you feel?

---

[6] A women's college in Pennsylvania.

Meredith.   I don't mind being nude, if that's what you mean. I just don't attribute that much importance to it.

Tandy.   I know that. I can tell.

Meredith.   I wouldn't want to get out there and do splits or anything.

Tandy.   Who asked you to do splits? Is that what you think I want—splits?

Meredith.   I just like to be nude sometimes. It's very tranquil.

(*A Puerto Rican Attendant has been mopping up the steambath for awhile. He comes clearly into view now. He sings "Sorrento." Lah lah lah lah sentimento . . . lah lah lah lah sentirinco . . . lah lah lah lah ladimento . . . lah lah lah lah lah lah lah. Stops mopping to do the bridge, really performing now . . . lah lah lah lah lah lah . . . etc. After a big finish, He says, "Thank you, music lovers" as though to a nightclub audience . . .*)

Oldtimer (*Signaling to Tandy*).   Psssst.

Tandy (*Gesturing toward Attendant*).   Him?

(*Oldtimer acknowledges correctness with a wink*)

You sure?

Oldtimer.   Yup . . .

Tandy (*To Meredith*).   He says that's the fellow in charge.

Meredith.   He's cute.

Attendant.   Hiya, baby.

(*Attendant now wheels out what appears to be a console with a screen. It is a very tacky-looking affair. The screen is visible to the attendant but not to the audience. The console, from time to time, answers the Attendant with little blipping noises as though taking note of his instructions. In between sections of his monologue, the Puerto Rican does little snatches of "Sorrento" again*)

(*Leaning over console*) San Diego Freeway . . . All right, first thing, I want that Pontiac moving south past Hermosa Beach to crash into the light blue Eldorado coming the other way. Make it a head-on collision . . . the guy in the Chevy—his wife's got her behind out the window—it's the only way they get their kicks—they're going to jump the rail into the oncoming lane, and screw up a liquor salesman in a tan Cougar. No survivors . . .

All right, what's-his-name, Perez, the Puerto Rican schmuck from the Bronx. The one who says, "My wife and I—we are married forty years. We are born on the same hill. There can be no trouble." He comes home tonight, I want her in bed with her brother. Perez walks in, goes crazy, starts foaming at the mouth, the other tenants in the building have to tie him to a radiator . . .

All right, the guy from St. Louis . . . bedspread salesman . . . adopted all those Korean kids. Him they pick up in the men's room of the Greyhound

Bus Terminal, grabbing some truckdriver's schvontz.[7] They ask around, find out he's been doing it for years . . . The kids get shipped back to Korea.

Now, here's one I like . . . The screenwriter flying out to Beverly Hills. Coming on with the broads. Here's what happens. Over Denver, a stewardess throws a dart in his eye. No doctor on board. He has to go all the way to Los Angeles like that. Give Debbie Reynolds an ear infection.

Now, the producer up in New Haven. Never had a hit. Doing a $750,000 musical . . . the whole show depends on the female star. All right. A police dog gets loose in the theatre and bites her tits off. The understudy is scared to death, but she goes on anyway. Bombsville. Next day, the guy gets out of the business . . .

(Starts to leave, returns)

Wait a minute, I got an idea. Back to the Freeway. That guy whose radiator boiled over . . . on the side of the road, saw the whole thing. Thought he got away clean. He gets knocked unconscious by the broad with her behind out the window. Never knew what hit him. That's all for now.

(He picks up mop and continues to mop the steambath floor. He sings "Sorrento." And he disappears for the moment in the haze)

Tandy. You sure that's the fellow in charge?
Oldtimer. That's him all right. He runs the show.
Tandy. What's his name?
Oldtimer. Morty.
Tandy. A Puerto Rican guy? Morty?
Oldtimer. It's Spanish. *(Pronouncing name with Spanish inflection)* Mawwrrrteee.
Tandy *(To Meredith)*. He's sure that's the fellow in charge.
Meredith. Well if he isn't, he certainly has a rich imagination.
Tandy. You say he hangs around here.
Oldtimer. All the time. He comes and goes.

(Attendant returns, singing softly, sweeping, goes to console again. His voice is much softer now)

Attendant. Okay, the other side of the coin. The kid in a hospital in Trenton, beautiful kid, works for Kentucky Fried Chicken. Got his foot shot off in a stick-up. The night nurse comes in, jerks him off under the covers. Lovely broad, little old, but she really knows what she's doing . . .
   Give Canada a little more rain . . .

---

[7] Yiddish, a slang expression for the male organ.

That Indian tribe outside of Caracas. Sick little guys, they ain't got a hundred bucks between 'em . . . Government doesn't give a damn. CBS moves in, shoots a jungle series there, throws a lot of money around . . .

The old lady with the parakeet, flies out the window, flies back in . . .

Wellesley[8] girl, parents got a lot of dough—she's sitting on a ledge—35th floor of the Edison Hotel. A cop crawls out after her, tells her she's full of hot air. They go back in, watch a hockey game on TV . . . And clean up that garbage in the lobby . . . It's disgusting . . . All right, that's enough good stuff.

Voice.   You need one more.

Attendant.   Christ, I'm exhausted. Uhh . . . Put bigger bath towels in all the rooms at the Tel Aviv Hilton Hotel.

Voice.   Terrific!

Attendant.   You kidding, buddy . . .

(*Exits*)

Meredith.   I liked him much more the second time.

Tandy.   He's got some style. Who's he think he is?

Oldtimer.   God.

Tandy.   You believe that?

Oldtimer.   I'm not saying yes and I'm not saying no. I been around and I seen a lot of strange things in my time. I once stood in an Algerian pissoir urinal and watched the head of a good friend of mine come rolling up against my size 12 moccasins like a bowling ball. Cut right off at the neck. He'd gotten into a little scuffle with some Gurkhas. May have called one of them a fag. Didn't know there aren't any fag Gurkhas.

Two Young Men.   That's what you think.

Tandy.   Well, what the hell are we supposed to do, just stay here?

Broker.   There's nothing that great out there. The market stinks. You don't make a quarter unless you're in pork bellies. That ain't investing.

Tandy.   I'm not going along with this. For Christ's sakes, I'm in the middle of writing an historical novel. About Charlemagne. I got all that research to do. So far I've been going on instinct. What the hell do I know about Charlemagne. But the book feels good . . .

Meredith.   And I've got an appointment at the beauty parlor. To get a Joan of Arc haircut. And my roommate Sheila and I are going to make little plastic surrealistic doodads and sell them to boutiques.

Tandy.   I'll get us out of this. Did you try the door?

Meredith.   No, why?

---

[8] A women's college in Massachusetts.

Tandy.   Don't try it. I'm pretty sure it doesn't open. If I find out for sure I'll get claustrophobia . . . Is there another way out? What's this door? *(Referring to second door at opposite side of the stage)*

Oldtimer.   You go through there.

Tandy.   When's that?

Oldtimer.   Hard to say . . . We had a guy, a baker, he put him in there.

Tandy.   What did he do?

Oldtimer.   Not much. Beat the Puerto Rican in arm-wrestling.

Broker.   Had a little trouble with his baking though. Everything used to burn up on him. Pastries, cupcakes . . . meat pies . . .

Tandy.   Don't tell me about cupcakes now . . . no cupcakes. When he puts you in there, does he let you out?

(Oldtimer chuckles, as if to say, "Are you kidding?")

And that's it, the two doors?

Oldtimer.   That's it. That's the whole cheesecake.

(Tandy very casually sidles up to entrance door, tries it. It doesn't open. Tries a little harder. Still won't)

Tandy.   About the way I figured. I'll get us out of here, don't worry. You with me?

Meredith.   Are you serious? Of course. But you haven't said how.

Tandy.   I'll get us out. You'll find I do most things well. Of course, I have never been able to get out to Kennedy Airport. On my own. I can get near it, but never really in it. The Van Wyck Expressway scene really throws me.

Meredith.   You're sort of inconsistent, aren't you?

Tandy.   You noticed that, eh. I admit it. I've got wonderful qualities, but getting out to airports is not one of them. Don't worry, though, I'll get us out of here. By sheer strength of will and determination. I believe I can do anything if I really put my mind to it. I've always felt that even if I had a fatal illness, with an army of diseased phagocytes coursing through my body in triumph, if I really decided to, I could reverse the course of those phagocytes and push them the hell back where they belong . . .

Meredith.   The world admires that kind of determination.

Tandy.   You're damned right.

Meredith.   What if we really are dead, though?

Tandy.   I know. I've been trying not to think about it. No more toast. No more clams. Clams oregano . . . *Newsweek* . . . Jesus, no more *Newsweek*. Wait a minute, I'll get this straightened out right now . . . *(He approaches Attendant, who has come mopping into view)* Say, fella . . .

Attendant.   You addressing I?

Tandy.   That's right. What's the deal around here? The Oldtimer says you're God.

Attendant. Some people call me that.

Tandy. But that's ridiculous . . . a Puerto Rican . . .

Attendant. The Puerto Ricans go back hundreds of years. Millions. There were Puerto Ricans in Greece, Rome. Diogenes—very big, very strong Puerto Rican. Too many people make fun of the Puerto Ricans. Very fine people. Lots of class. We got Herman Badillo[9], Mario Puzo.[10]

Tandy. All right, I'll go along with you for a second. You're God. Why would you be sweeping up, a lowly job like that?

Attendant. It's therapeutic. I like it. It's easy on the nerves.

Tandy. God . . . A Puerto Rican steambath attendant. That'll be the day.

Attendant. Look, I'll tell you what, fella. You say I'm not God. All right. You got it. I'm not God. Fabulous. You got what you want. *(Pointing to Bieberman)* He's God.

Oldtimer. He ain't God. He's a slob.

Bieberman. Everything doesn't pay off in cleanliness. There are other virtues.

Oldtimer. You stink to the high heavens.

Two Young Men. We've reached the conclusion that you're being much too tough on him.

Oldtimer. Don't you two ever split up?

Two Young Men *(Seductively)*. Make us an offer.

Attendant. Mister, just don't bug me. All right? I got a lot on my mind.

Tandy. There's another one. God talking slang. How can I go along with that?

Attendant. I talk any way I want, man. The Lord speaks in funny ways. Remember that. You want to discuss the relativity of mass, the Lorentz Transformation, galactic intelligence, I'll give you that, too. Just don't bug me. All right? Don't be no wise ass.

Tandy. That was more like it. You had me going there for a second. I respect anyone who really knows something, my work being as transitory as it is. It's when you talk dirty . . .

Attendant. The way I talk, the way I talk . . . Don't you see that's just a little blink of an eye in terms of the universe, the job I got to do? The diameter of an electron is one ten-trillionth of an inch. And you're telling me I shouldn't talk dirty. Let me talk the way I want. Let me relax a little.

(Approaches console screen again)

All right, give that girl on the bus a run on her body stocking. I want to close up that branch of Schrafft's . . . And send up a bacon-and-lettuce-and-tomato sandwich, hold the mayo. You burn the toast, I'll smite you down with my terrible swift sword.

---

[9] A Puerto Rican novelist and politician.

[10] American novelist and screenwriter.

(Leaves the console)

Tandy. I still don't buy it. That could be an ordinary TV screen. You could have been watching *All in the Family.*

Attendant. *All in the Family? (Goes over to console)* Cancel *All in the Family.* You still want to fool around?

Tandy. I don't watch *All in the Family.* Only thing I watch on TV is pro football. Gets better every year. Look, you're asking me to buy a whole helluva lot. You're challenging every one of my beliefs.

Attendant. You think I care about your beliefs? With the job I got on my mind?

Tandy. You care. I may be one man, but there exists within me the seed of all mankind.

Attendant. Very good. I'm going to give you a ninety on that.

Tandy. I used to tell that to my art-appreciation students over at the Police Academy.

Attendant. Nice bunch of boys.

Tandy. You mean to tell me that you control every action on earth by means of that monitor over there? Every sneeze, every headache, every time a guy cuts himself? How can you possibly do so much?

Attendant. I go very fast. You got to move like crazy. You can't stop and talk to every schmuck who comes along . . .

(Gottlieb, Attendant's assistant, comes in with a tray)

Gottlieb. Your BLT down, sir.

Attendant. Thank you. What do I owe you for that?

Gottlieb. Are you kidding, sire?

Attendant. Just thought I'd ask. You don't have to get snotty about it.

(Gottlieb goes off. Attendant eats)

Tandy. I don't know. It's awfully hard to accept. I've heard of having your faith tested, but this is ridiculous.

Attendant *(Chewing BLT).* And who said you could speak while I was eating?

Tandy. All right. I'm sorry. I beg your pardon. One minute you're casual, the next you're formal. How can I keep up with you?

Attendant. Changeable, mysterious, infinite, unfathomable. That's my style . . .

Tandy. Yeah—except that you're not God.

Attendant. That's the conclusion you reached after all the time I spent with you? I'll tell you right now you're getting me roped off. I get roped off, watch out. Then you're really in trouble. *(Pulling himself together)* All right. I'll tell you what. You say I'm not God, right?

Tandy. Right.

Attendant (*Pulling out deck of cards, and spreading them, like fan*).   All right.
Pick a card, any card.
Tandy.   What's that gonna prove?
Attendant.   Go ahead, just do what I'm tellin' you. You'll see.

(*Tandy picks card*)

You look at it?
Tandy.   Yes.
Attendant (*Squinting eyes*).   Okay . . . you got the . . . King of Hearts . . .
Right?

(*Broker, most nervous of all characters, applauds*)

Tandy.   All right. You did it. So what?
Attendant.   So there y'are.
Tandy.   There I am what? You do a simple card trick that any kid can do—a
retarded kid can do—and I'm supposed to think you're God.
Attendant.   Can you do it?
Tandy.   No, I can't do it. I can't even deal a hand of blackjack. But there are
hundreds of guys who can do that trick. In every village and hamlet in the
country. What the hell does that prove?
Attendant.   Not in the hamlets. It's not that easy. In the villages, maybe, but
not in the hamlets. All right, I show you a trick that's not as easy as it seems,
you won't buy it. Fair enough. You're pushing me to the wall. I'm not
saying a word. Now, check my pants. And easy on the corporeal contact.

(*Tandy begrudgingly does so*)

Anything in there?
Tandy.   There's nothing in there.
Attendant (*With a flourish*).   Now . . . (*Pulls out a long multi-colored scarf*)
How's that? (*Drapes it over Meredith as a shawl*)
Tandy.   I've seen it about a dozen times.
Attendant.   Where?
Tandy.   On the Sullivan Show.[11] These Slavic guys come over here and do
that trick. On a bicycle. Look, I'm sorry. I don't know quite how to say this,
but you are not even putting a *dent* in me. What kind of second-rate crap
is this?
Attendant (*Gesturing as though he is pulling a knife out of his chest*).   Madre
de Dios. You hurt my feelings just now, you know that, don't you?
Tandy.   There's a perfect example. God with his feelings hurt. Ridiculous.

---

[11] A popular television show, hosted by Ed Sullivan, that aired from 1955 to 1971.

Attendant.   My feelings are not supposed to get hurt? Once in a while? All right. Now I'm really going to give you one. *(Calling into the wings)* Gottlieb.

(Assistant runs out with a footlocker kept shut by a huge padlock. Sets it down)

Thanks, Gottlieb, I won't forget this. *(To Tandy)* All right. Check the lock.
Tandy *(Following instructions)*.   I checked it.
Attendant.   Is it strong?
Tandy.   Very strong, very powerful. Big deal.
Attendant.   All right. Observez-vous.

(Gottlieb ties his hands behind him. He kneels down and, with his teeth, sawing away like a bulldog, chews and chews and finally springs the lock. Gottlieb has been doing an accompanying song-and-dance routine, neatly timed, as though they have been through this many times before. With lock in his teeth, arms upraised, like a trapeze man, Attendant acknowledges applause. Gottlieb throws a few ribbons of confetti over his head)

Voilà!
Tandy.   It was okay, I admit. It was a little better than the others. At least you're showing me a little something. Look, I don't know how to get this across to you, but you are not reaching me with this stuff. Maybe I'm crazy. If you had made one interesting intellectual assault on my mind, maybe that would do it.
Attendant.   De gustibus non est disputandum.[12]
Tandy.   That's it? That's the intellectual assault? Freshman English?
Attendant.   Have you ever really pondered it? Savored it? Rolled it around on your tongue and really tasted of its fruit?
Tandy.   That's right. I have. And it's nothing. It's garbage. It's not the kind of insight to make the senses reel.
Attendant *(Gathering others about him)*.   Consider the mind, an independent substance implanted within the soul and incapable of being destroyed . . . The City of Satan, whatever its artifices in art, war, or philosophy, was essentially corrupt and impious, its joy but a comic mask and its beauty the whitening of a sepulchre. It stood condemned before man's better conscience by its vanity, cruelty, and secret misery, by its ignorance of all that it truly behooved a man to know who was destined to immortality . . . Or how about this one: "A little philosophy inclineth man's mind to atheism, but depth in philosophy bringeth men's minds about to religion."
Tandy.   Much better. Maybe I could even chew on some of that. But you still haven't got me. All I can see is a fairly interesting guy. For a Puerto Rican.

---

[12] Latin, meaning "There is no disputing about taste."

If I ran into you at a bar—a Puerto Rican bar—maybe we could kick around a few ideas. All I'm saying is I don't see God yet. Where's God?

Attendant.   You don't see God, huh? Boy, you're some pistol. All right, here comes a little number that is going to make your head swim. You happen to be in luck, fella, because you caught me at cocktail time and I'm dry as a bone. Gottlieb . . . Now you watch this carefully . . .

(*Gottlieb emerges with tray of drinks*)

How many drinks you estimate are on that tray?

Tandy.   Ten . . .

(*Attendant begins to knock them off, one at a time*)

. . . and you don't even have to bother drinking them, because I can name you two lushes out there on Eighth Avenue who can do the same thing . . . I mean, what is this . . . it's not even as good as the trunk. You might have snapped off a few teeth on that one . . . but this cheap, trivial, broken-down, ninth-rate . . .

(*As He speaks, Gottlieb returns, struggling to bring in an enormous whiskey sour, one that towers above Tandy's head. Tandy is thunderstruck*)

Are you mad?

Attendant.   Un momento.

(*He leaps to top tier of column, sits opposite rim of glass, pulls out a straw and takes a sip*)

Delicious. That sonofabitch makes some drink.

(*Attendant finishes up with a flourish, leaps down*)

All right, what have you got to say to that, baby? Incidentally, you like the cherry, go ahead, don't be embarrassed . . .

Tandy.   It was pretty good. All right. I take that back. Fair is fair. It was great. My hat goes off to you. It was really remarkable. I figure the odds were about fifty to one against. I hardly know how to say this next thing, but I'm still not buying it. The God routine.

Attendant.   You're still not buying it?

Tandy.   No sir. The fact that I just said "sir" will give you an indication that I'm really impressed. You got a lot going for you. But I'm not really there yet. If I said I bought the whole thing you'd know I wasn't being straight. It would be an injustice of a kind. A real sell-out.

Attendant.   So then you still don't buy it.

Tandy.   No, sir.
Attendant.   You really making me work, boy. All right. I have but one choice,
my son. *(Gestures)* Shazam . . .

*(Stage, theatre, suddenly fill with deafening organ music, churchlike, ancient,
soaring, almost unbearable. Theatre then fills with angels or other miraculous
and heavenly effects. Attendant stands majestically, his head crowned with
celestial light. He ascends to highest tier in steambath. Music is deafening in its
churchlike call to the divinity. Voice of Attendant, magnified a hundred-fold,
booms out)*

Attendant's Voice.   ASCRIBE UNTO THE LORD YE KINDREDS OF THE PEOPLES . . .
ASCRIBE UNTO THE LORD
GLORY AND STRENGTH . . .
ASCRIBE UNTO THE LORD
THE GLORY DUE UNTO HIS NAME
BRING AN OFFERING
AND COME UNTO HIS COURTS
OH, WORSHIP THE LORD
IN THE BEAUTY OF HOLINESS
TREMBLE BEFORE HIM
ALL THE EARTH . . .

*(One by one, the Steambath People drop to their knees. Tandy looks around,
observes that He is the only one standing. He shrugs, goes to one knee)*

Curtain

Act Two

*People are all lying around, exhausted, as though after a heavy night-long
bacchanal*

(Broker comes skipping in with a rope)

Broker *(To Tandy).*   You ought to try this . . . Really gets the weight off you
. . . Look in the mirror sometime while you're doing it. Everything moves.
The stuff way inside—where you have the real weight—that's moving too
. . . *(Stops jumping)* How much do you weigh? . . .
Tandy.   Me? Around 190 . . . 195 . . . somewhere in there . . .

Broker. I'm 179 myself. I'd like to lose around ten, twelve pounds. Twelve pounds I'd feel like a tiger . . . *(Grabbing some flesh about his waist)* I got to lose it around here—that's where it's rough . . . 'specially when you get around my age . . .

Tandy. That's right . . .

Broker. One hundred sixty-eight. That's my perfect weight. You should see me at 168. Never seen anything like it . . .

Tandy. I bet you look great . . .

Broker. I do. I get up in the middle, high seventies, forget it. It's all gone . . . You want to hear something else . . .

Tandy. Shoot.

Broker. When I'm 168, I get a beautiful bowel movement . . . How about you. You pretty regular?

Tandy. I don't want to hurt your feelings or anything, but I'm really not that interested in your bowel movements . . .

Broker. I can see that . . . Sorry if I was presumptuous . . .

Tandy. Perfectly all right . . .

Broker. I once bought a stock at 168—my exact weight . . . Fellow who recommended it said this is a stock you don't worry about. It goes off, for argument's sake, ten, twenty, fifty points, I don't care if it goes off a hundred points . . . you don't worry about this stock. So I hold it. And it *does* go off ten, twenty, over a hundred points. The stock is now selling at a fast ten points. So I call the guy. It's down to ten, I say. When do I start worrying? "Never," he says. He just wasn't a worrier. I lost every penny . . . Shows you . . . go trust people . . . I should've stuck to ferns . . .

Tandy. Ferns?

Broker. That's right. I was in the fern game for a while. A lot of people go in for ferns, you'd be surprised. I was cleaning up. But I couldn't take the social pressure . . . Guy at a party'd ask me what do you do, I'd say I'm in ferns . . . How do you think that made me feel?

Oldtimer. Turn off that TV set . . .

Broker. I had to get out . . .

Bieberman. I'm watching a wonderful forties' movie. And it's down very low.

Oldtimer. Turn it off, I tell you. I'm trying to catch a quick snooze. Turn it off or I'll come up there and kick you in the bazanzas . . .

Bieberman. What are they?

Oldtimer. Never mind. You'll find out fast enough if I kick you there.

Bieberman. Anti-Semite.

Oldtimer. I'm an anti-stinkite. That's what *you* got to worry about. Now turn it off, I tell you . . .

Bieberman *(Always a little bitter, angry when He speaks, spitting the words out deliberately).* I suppose it never occurred to you that every smile, every whisper, every puff of a cigarette taken by my generation was inspired by the forties' movie. That my generation wouldn't know how to mix a drink, drive a car, kiss a girl, straighten a tie—if it weren't for Linda Darnell[13] And George Brent . . . That the sole reason for my generation's awkward floundering in the darkness is that Zachary Scott is gone . . . and I assure you that Mick Jagger is no substitute . . .

Oldtimer.   I'll tell you what your generation needs. A movie that instructs you on how to smell like a human being. You can star in it. *(To Tandy)* How can he even see the screen with all this steam . . .

Bieberman.   When it gets too dense I smear it off with a corner of my jockey shorts . . .

Oldtimer.   I spent four years in the Philippines I never ran into a slob like that. *(Suddenly clutches at his chest, as though having a heart attack, then realizes this is impossible and gestures as if to say "The hell with it")*

Tandy.   C'mon, you guys, knock it off. You're supposed to be dead. Act like it.

Meredith.   It's wonderful the way they listen to you.

Tandy.   It's probably that time I spent with the cops. It really changes you. Even when you're in the art department.

Meredith.   Oh, my God . . .

Tandy.   What's wrong?

Meredith.   I just remembered. I haven't paid my Bloomingdale's bill.

Tandy.   When was it due?

Meredith.   Last Monday . . . now they'll probably send me one of those thin gray envelopes . . . You have no idea how much I hate those envelopes . . .

Tandy.   But it's ridiculous. You can't pay your bills now. The store will understand.

Meredith.   Bloomingdale's!

Tandy.   Look, obviously none of this has sunk in. We're in big trouble. We could be stuck in this lousy steambath forever. You're sitting around talking Bloomingdale's. You saw that Puerto Rican guy . . . He wasn't kidding around . . .

Meredith.   That was fun.

Tandy.   What do you mean?

Meredith.   The part where we got down on our knees. We used to do that at Marymount every morning, first thing, and it was freezing. It was fun getting down on a nice warm floor for a change . . .

Tandy.   It wasn't any fun for me. I got to get out of here. I got all this Charlemagne research to do. There's going to be a whole Charlemagne revival, I can tell. Books, movies, musical comedies. Dolls—that's right. Little Charlemagne dolls. And I'll be left out of it. Where is that guy? I'm going to take another shot at him.

---

[13] Hollywood actress popular in films of the 1940s. George Brent and Zachary Scott were actors during the same era.

(Disappears for the moment in haze)

Bieberman.   Anyone have some pimple lotion?

Oldtimer.   There he goes again, the meathead.

Bieberman.   Well, can I control my complexion, can I?

Oldtimer.   Of course you can. Ever hear of cutting down on malteds?

Bieberman.   I'll never cut down on malteds, never.

Oldtimer.   Well, then, don't come to me with your pimples, you stupid bastard.

Bieberman.   Malteds are the marijuana of my generation.

Oldtimer.   Your generation . . . what the hell generation is that?

Bieberman.   It went by very quickly . . . It was Dolf Camilli, Dane Clark, Uncle Don, Ducky Medwick and out . . .

Oldtimer.   Sounds like a bunch of winners.

Bieberman.   We produced Norman Podhoretz.

Oldtimer.   Congratulations . . . *(To the Broker)* Who the hell is Norman Podhoretz?

Broker.   Probably some wealthy guy who made it when you could keep it.

Tandy *(Entering)*.   We're all set.

Meredith.   What's up?

Tandy.   I've got a whole bunch of carpet tacks.

Meredith.   Wow. Where did you get them?

Tandy.   They got an old carpet rolled up back there.

Meredith.   What good'll they do?

Tandy.   Plenty. Don't undersell them. I once saw a guy with only a handful of carpet tacks get the best of two armed cops.

Meredith.   That's remarkable, overpowering two policemen that way.

Tandy.   That's right. Where is that guy. Listen, we get out, I'd like you to see my apartment. I've got big steel bars on the windows—I had a few robberies— but I've got the bars painted in psychedelic colors. I've got huge double security locks—they're painted in psychedelic colors, too. Burglar alarm— same deal.

Meredith.   I'd love to see your apartment.

Tandy.   I'd like you to see it. It's not a horny thing. I won't jump on you or anything.

Meredith.   Oh, I know that.

Tandy.   Well, as a matter of fact, it *is* a partially horny thing. You're a very good-looking girl . . . but I'm also proud of the apartment.

Meredith.   Don't you have a girl friend?

Tandy.   Oh yes, I've got an ex-wife, a mistress, a mother . . . I'm covered on all sides. Now I just need a girl . . .

Meredith.   I understand. You just want someone totally uncomplicated.

Tandy.   That's right.

Meredith.   It's only fair to tell you that I can only sleep with one man at a time. If I slept with you I might reach across in the middle of the night and think I was stroking Raymondo.

Tandy.   Raymondo? Listen, don't worry about it. I just want you to see my place sometime . . . Listen, you and your roommate don't . . . I mean . . . together.

Meredith.   Make scenes? . . . Oh no . . . we don't do that.

Tandy.   I hope you don't take offense . . . I was just checking.

Meredith.   We don't any more, that is. We did take a mescaline trip recently with one of my stockbroker friends. It didn't work out. It turned into a sort of business trip.

Tandy.   Well, look, I don't need that right now. I got my hands full the way it is . . . It's just that when you work with the cops you see a lot of crazy things, you get ideas. You should go out on a few homicides. You should see what incensed Mexicans do to their common-law wives when they step out of line. Believe me, you'd never want to be a Mexican common-law wife.

Meredith.   Oh, I don't know. I hear Cuernavaca's beautiful.

Oldtimer *(To Broker)*.   Toughest sonofabitch I ever knew used to dress up like Carmen Miranda.[14] They found him floating five kilometers outside Hamburg Harbor . . . all those bananas bobbing in the water.

(Attendant enters, Gottlieb along with him)

Attendant.   All right, everybody, campfire time. Gottlieb, give out the Mounds bars.

(Gottlieb distributes candy bars to Steambath Inhabitants, who gather round an improvised campfire site)

Meredith *(Accepting a candy bar)*.   Oh, I love these . . .

Tandy *(Calling Attendant aside)*.   Listen, I want to talk to you about getting out of here. I got a lot of deals going on the outside, a lot of things to clear up. I don't know if you know anything about Charlemagne . . .

Attendant.   The Puerto Rican?

Tandy.   Cute. Listen, I haven't mentioned it yet, but I want you to know that was very impressive stuff you did, drinking all that stuff, those lights . . . very good . . .

Attendant.   I saw you on your knees.

Tandy.   One knee. I just went down on one knee . . . Maybe that's half-assed, I don't know. Maybe a straight solid guy—a Henry Kissinger—would have

---

[14] Portuguese-born actress who appeared in popular Hollywood films of the 1940s set in Latin America. In these films, she often danced in elaborate costumes.

either given you both knees or said the hell with it . . . I don't know. I figured you run the place I'll throw you one knee. A little respect. Meanwhile, I got to talk to you about getting out of here. I don't belong here, I don't need this.

Attendant.   You know what I don't need? Right now? Aggravation.

Tandy.   God, aggravated. There's another hot one.

Attendant.   Listen, if you're God, the name of the game is aggravation. Anyway, I don't want to hear anymore. You say another word, baby, I'll become wrathful and vengeance-seeking.

(Gestures to Broker to begin)

Broker.   For twenty years I was mad at my partner.

Attendant.   Once upon a time . . .

Broker.   Excuse me . . . Once upon a time for twenty years I was mad at my partner.

Attendant.   Hold it a second. Any broads in this story?

Broker.   No.

Attendant.   Gottlieb, you want to stay?

(Gottlieb shrugs)

He likes serious stuff, too, otherwise I wouldn't keep him around. But once in a while he likes to hear about broads. Go ahead . . .

Broker.   We were partners for twenty years. Somehow he had everything—a glass house, schnauzer dogs, cuff links you should have seen the size of them . . . And I'm living in three rooms in Washington Heights. It was eating at me. I figure we're partners. How come I don't have a glass house and schnauzer dogs. So one day I went to visit him in his house and I put it to him. He listens to my complaints, goes inside, and comes out with a check for eight hundred dollars. Well, I couldn't figure out that check. How did he come up with that figure? But amazingly, I wasn't angry. After all, eight hundred was eight hundred. So I went outside and sat on the golf course. I never liked to play, but I do like to sit on a golf course. And that's how they found me, sitting on a director's chair, right near the fourth hole, with the eight-hundred dollar check in my lap and my head thrown back like this *(He demonstrates, throwing back his head, opening his mouth wide and baring his teeth grotesquely)* They all came back and when they saw me, they all made that face too, that same face. They threw back their heads and opened their mouths and made the same dead face I had. *(He demonstrates again)*

Attendant.   It's going to be hard to give you a ninety on that one.

Meredith.   I thought it was fascinating. I wonder why they wanted to make that face. *(She tries it)*

Oldtimer.   That's easy. They wanted to taste a little death without really being dead.

Meredith.   Oh, I see. Gee, this is good. It's just like Camp Aurora. Who's next?

Two Young Men.   We both hung ourselves for love of the same boy—a swing dancer in the national company of *Zorba*.[15]

We never realized we could love someone that . . . indifferent . . . we loved the way he moved . . . the rough carving of his arms . . . the way the veins were printed on them.

We'd go to the all-night skating rinks . . . And then, unaccountably, he simply left the show—and went back to school in North Carolina.

Totally unmarked by us—as though we'd been a slight change in the direction of the wind.

Neither of us meant a thing to him . . .

. . . We were no more than a pair of cats that crossed his path in a strange village and slowed his walk for a moment.

He was beautiful.

Attendant.   To tell you the truth, I never went in very much for fag stories.

Meredith.   I thought it was very touching.

Attendant.   I'm a sympathizer . . . but they don't really satisfy me.

Two Young Men.   Well, you wrote it.

Attendant.   That's true. But you know how it is when you're a writer. You write some stuff you don't like. Who's got a good one?

Tandy.   This is very unjust. You've obviously set this thing up for your own amusement.

Attendant.   And you don't like that. I'm not allowed to have a few laughs. Listen, you been giving me a hard time ever since you come in here . . . You show up . . . you don't like it . . . you hand me this Charlemagne routine . . . I'm going to do a bad thing to you now.

Tandy (*Alarmed*).   What's that? I admit I'm frightened. What are you going to do? (*Looks at second door*) You're not going to put me in there, are you?

Attendant.   No. (*Points to Oldtimer*) I'm putting him in there. (*To Tandy*) You come in here . . . you're looking for fair, reasonable . . . Where'd you get that from? Old man . . .

Oldtimer (*Rising*).   My time, eh?

Attendant.   That's right, baby.

Oldtimer.   Well, that's okay. I done everything. I once had a pair of perfectly matched wooden-legged frauleins powder me up from head to toe and dress me up in silk drawers. I run up against a Greek sailor walking around for thirty years with a lump on his chest he took to be a natural growth. Turned out to be the unborn fetus of a twin brother he'd spent all his life hankering for. I seen most everything. I dipped my beak in Madrid, Spain; Calcutta,

---

[15] A musical based on Greek writer Nikos Kazantzakis's novel *Zorba the Greek*.

India; Leningrad, Russia, and I never once worried about them poisoning the water. I had myself the fifth-richest woman in Sydney, Australia, genuine duchess she was, all dressed up in a tiger suit; by the time I finished with her I had them stripes going the wrong way. I played a pretty good trumpet. I had to face the fact that I was no Harry James, but then again, Sir Harry couldn't go in there and break up a Polish wedding the way I could. I talked back to the biggest guys. Didn't bother me. I didn't care if it was me way down in the valley, hollering up at Mount Zion. I'd holler up some terrific retorts. You're not going to show me anything I haven't seen. I paid my dues. *(Starts to go)* And I'll tell you something else. If there's anything in there kicks me, you watch and see if I don't bite.

(He hitches himself up with great dignity and does a sailor's dance, then a proud oldman's walk into the grated room)

Attendant.   Old man had a lot of balls.

Tandy.   Damn right. *(To Attendant)* Listen, I was the wise guy. Why didn't you send me in there?

Attendant.   That's direct. I don't work that way. I always put a little spin on the ball. Okay. This is the last one. I want live actors this time.

(A cheap lower-class bar is set up—or at least the skeletal representation of one. Two Men stand on opposite sides of the bar. One is a Longshoreman; the other is Gottlieb, who plays the part of a bartender for this scene)

Longshoreman *(setting the scene for the Attendant)*.   A longshoreman's bar in Astoria, Queens.

(Attendant gestures for him to proceed)

Longshoreman.   We ought to take our six toughest guys—and the Russians— they take their six toughest guys. Send 'em into a forest—they can have it over there if they want. And the guys that walk out of that forest—that's it.

Gottlieb *(Tending bar)*.   Those Commies would have to shut up.

Longshoreman.   Oh, the Russians are all right. If you ask me, they can build a machine as good as America. But fortunately for us, they lack the human people to operate that machine.

Gottlieb.   You better believe it.

(A couple enters the bar. The Man is in a wheelchair; his legs, braced, are apparently useless. He wears steel-rimmed glasses and his neck, too, is coiled in a brace, as though he has been in a whiplash accident. Very eerie. He is with a young pretty girl in a short skirt. The Girl puts a quarter in the jukebox—some rock music begins. The Girl starts to dance—in the modern style—quite seduc-

tively, in front of the wheelchaired fellow. The Fellow in the chair snaps his fingers and responds to the music to the best of his abilities)

Gottlieb *(Referring to couple).*   Hey . . .
Longshoreman.   Yeah . . .
Gottlieb.   Ever seen anything like that?
Longshoreman.   No, I never have.

(They watch the couple awhile)

Longshoreman.   Watch this. *(He approaches Couple, speaks to Girl)* Say, miss . . .
Girl Dancer.   Yes . . .
Longshoreman *(Referring to fellow in chair).*   All systems are not go . . .
Girl Dancer *(Still dancing).*   I don't follow you . . .
Longshoreman.   You know . . . astronauts . . . all systems are not go. Wouldn't you rather move around with a guy whose systems are all à go-go?
Wheelchaired Man *(Talking through a throat box, as though the victim of a laryngectomy).*   Why are you harassing us? We were behaving peaceably.
Longshoreman.   I hadn't noticed. *(He grabs Girl)* C'mon, baby, let's move around a little . . . *(Girl moves halfheartedly)*
Wheelchaired Man.   You just made a serious mistake, fella.
Longshoreman.   That right?
Wheelchaired Man.   That's right. First of all . . . *(He switches off throat box and speaks in a normal tone)* I don't really speak that way. *(Twirls off whiplash collar)* Second of all, I don't wear this . . . Third of all . . . *(Getting to his feet and kicking off braces)* I don't need these. Last but not least . . . *(Whipping off his shirt to show a well-muscled frame and huge championship belt)* . . . silver-belt karate, the highest karate level of all . . . *(With three quick moves, He wipes out Longshoreman, who falls to the floor. At a certain point in the Wheelchaired Man's metamorphosis, it has become apparent that He is Bieberman)*
Bieberman.   That's right.
Attendant.   How many times you get away with that stunt?
Bieberman.   Twenty-five times. Sarah and I started to do it every Friday night, as a form of social involvement, a means of smoking out society's predators . . .
Attendant.   But you kept getting away with it. I forget, what are you doing here?
Bieberman.   An Arab at the 92nd Street YMHA[16] dropped a 200-pound barbell on my neck.

---

[16] Young Men's Hebrew Association.

Attendant.   That's right. And don't you forget it. . . . All right, everybody, that does it . . . You told some pretty good stuff, but we got to make room for the next crowd. (*Gesturing toward second door*) . . . Everybody in there . . . We enjoyed having you, sincerely.

Broker.   All this exercise—the steam—what good did it do?

Attendant.   What are you complaining about—you're in the best shape of your life . . .

Broker.   That's true. Well, I'll go first. I been finished for a long time. (*Hesitates*) Years ago, when you wound up your steambath, there'd be a man outside selling pumpernickel and pickled fish . . .

Attendant.   I'll send some in . . . don't worry . . . Now let's go . . . chop-chop . . .

(*Broker goes through the door*)

1st Young Man.   Do I look all right?

2nd Young Man.   You look great. It'll be a relief to get out of all that steam.

1st Young Man.   It's destroyed your hair. Maybe Ralph will be in there.

2nd Young Man.   Ralph? From Amagansett?

1st Young Man.   He *was* tacky.

(*They go through the door*)

Bieberman (*To Meredith*).   Goodbye. My generation's out of style—I know that—but you'll never know the thrill of having belonged to it. (*Starting through grated door*) John Hodiak[17]—hold on, I'll be right with you . . .

(*He goes through*)

Attendant (*Hollering after departed group*).   And if I find any candy wrappers I'll send Gottlieb in there to kick your ass.

(*Only Tandy and Meredith remain*)

Tandy.   Kick your ass, kick your ass . . . I'm supposed to respect that? . . . Where's the grandeur? . . . the majesty? . . .

Attendant.   I'm saving that for the next group that's coming in. I hear they got some terrific broads. They're single. Bunch of nurses. They fell from a cable car . . . I'm going to hit them with all this grandeur and majesty . . .

---

[17] An actor popular in films of the 1940s.

(Goes over to console, which appears in the mist)

Start a new rock and roll group called Grandeur and Majesty . . .

(Console blips back its response. To Meredith)

You goin', lady?

Meredith *(Hesitating).* Well, as I was telling Mr. Tandy, I've only recently had my first orgasm . . . and I haven't paid my Bloomingdale's bill. I've never been to Nassau in the Bahamas . . .

Attendant. First orgasm . . . good-looking girl like you . . . Must have been a slip-up. Maybe you been having them all along and didn't realize it . . . All right, let's go, you two . . . I got a lot of cleaning up to do . . .

Tandy. I told you I'm not accepting this.

Attendant. You want me to get rough?

Tandy. How would you like it if you were in the middle of a great Chinese restaurant . . . you've had your spare-ribs, a little soup—you're working up a terrific appetite and bam! You're thrown out of the restaurant. You never get to enjoy the won shih pancakes.

Attendant. I can get any kind of food I want up here . . . except lox. The lox is lousy, pre-sliced . . . the kind you get in those German delicatessens . . . I can't get any fresh lox . . . I don't know why that is . . .

Tandy. It's like a guy about to have some terrific operation. The odds against him surviving are ridiculous, Newton High School against the Miami Dolphins. They're working on his eyes, ears, nose, throat, and brains. A whole squadron of doctors is flown in from the Caucasus where they have all these new Caucasus techniques. He's hanging by a hair—and miracle of miracles, he makes it. Gets back on his feet, says goodbye to the doctors, goes home, and gets killed by a junkie in front of the Automat . . . That's the kind of thing you want me to accept.

Attendant. That's a pretty good one. *(Takes a note on it)* I'm gonna use that . . . Yes, come to think of it, that is the kind of thing I want you to accept.

Tandy. Well, I can't. I worked too hard to get where I am . . . You know about Wendy Tandy, my ex-wife . . .

Attendant. Good-looking broad, I know about her . . .

Tandy. That stunt she pulled?

Attendant. That was a good one . . . Gottlieb, you got to hear this . . .

(Gottlieb comes over)

Tandy *(More to Meredith than anyone).* She's an unfaithful wife. Fine. You put up with it, you don't. I did. Fair and square. So then we meet a retired hairdresser who has become an underground film-maker. He shoots his film through those filters of teased hair . . . it's a new technique. This is the guy Wendy falls madly in love with. And she moves out—to live with him. Fair and square. She prefers him, she's got him. Swingin'. I'm getting along fine—got a few deals of my own cooking—and all of a sudden I get an invitation to go see a film that this hairdresser has put Wendy in—down on Charles Street. And I find out—in one of the Village papers—that what he's done is make a huge blow-up—in one of the scenes—I don't know how to say this—of her private parts. It's very artistic, don't get me wrong . . . The audience thinks it's a Soviet train station . . .

Meredith.   God, I'd never do that. How did he get her to do that. She must have really loved him.

Attendant.   Hey, Gottlieb, what did I tell you?

(Gottlieb hangs his head. He's shy)

Tandy.   Well, that makes me the supreme schmuck, cuckold, whatever you want to call it, everybody agreed? Half the city sitting in a theater, looking at my wife's gazoo for Christ's sakes . . .

Meredith.   For heaven's sake, what did you do?

Tandy.   That's what I'm getting at. The old me would have come in with guns. I'm a very good shot—at under seven feet. There's a technique I learned over at the academy. You run into a little room after this cornered guy and as you shoot you're supposed to start screaming *(Demonstrates)* YI, YI, YI, YI, YI, YI. That's in case you miss, you scare the hell out of him. But I finally figured, what the hell, it's nothing to do with me. She's that kind of a girl. I knock off this guy, the next one'll be Xeroxing her ass all over Times Square. So I said the hell with it and I went to the movie.

Meredith.   How was it?

Tandy.   Not bad. As a director, the guy had some pretty good moves. It fell apart in the middle, but it was worth seeing. I sat in the balcony . . . But you see, I got past all that baloney. Out in the clear, after ten years . . . and I started getting straight in other areas, too. I got a wonderful, calm girl friend . . . We could be sitting at McGinnis' restaurant and Fidel Castro could walk in, she'd stay calm, low, even, maybe give him a little smile. I love that. I never had it . . . And then I forgave my mother . . .

Meredith.   For what?

Tandy.   I never liked the work she was doing. She ran a chain of dancing schools in Appalachia. She'd talk these starving families into taking mambo lessons . . . very bitter woman. Anyway, I took her out of Appalachia, got her an apartment in White Plains, and I like her now. She's seventy, and all that iron has dropped out of her.

Gottlieb *(To Attendant)*.   Any more sex parts?

Attendant.   Shut up, Gottlieb. I think that's wonderful the boy's nice to his mother. I didn't know that . . . *(To Tandy)*. What else you got?. . .

Tandy.   I just kept ironing out all the wrinkles in my life. The toughest thing, believe it or not, was leaving my art-appreciation job over at the Police Academy. I really thought those cops would kill me if I left. They didn't.

They gave me a wonderful send-off party. They hired a little combo—four convicted forgers—and they ran some Danish art films they'd confiscated at a Bar Mitzvah in Great Neck.[18] And then at the end my art students gave me a replica of Michelangelo's *David*—seventy-five bucks over at Brentano's . . . Only one fellow gave me any trouble, detective named Flanders, said if I left he'd trail me all over the world, any place I tried to hide—and hunt me down like a dog.

(*Detective Flanders appears, gun in hand*)

Flanders.   Tandy . . .
Tandy (*Running*).   Jesus . . .
Attendant.   You kidding? Don't worry about this guy.

(*Gestures and Flanders' gun turns to a milkshake*)

All right now, get in there.

(*Flanders goes through the door*)

Tandy.   That was close.
Meredith.   I'm glad he's on our side.
Attendant.   You see, I told you. And you said nasty things about me. You called me a bad guy . . .
Tandy.   Anyway, you get the idea. I've gotten my whole life on the right track for the first time. I don't hate Wendy. I'm doing this wonderful work for brain-damaged welders. You ask the welders what they think of me. And I've got a marvelous new girl who's got this surprising body. You look at her face you just don't expect all that voluptuousness. You say to yourself, she's a little girl, a quiet little girl, comes from a nice family, where did these tits come from . . .
Attendant.   Hey, hey, there's a lady . . .
Meredith.   Oh, that's all right. I don't mind tits. Knockers is the one I don't care for.
Tandy.   All right, excuse me, but do you get the idea? I got everything bad swept out of the room. I'm closer than ever to my daughter. That trip to Vegas really brought us together. I'm doing work that I love. Warner Brothers saw the first hundred pages of my Charlemagne book and I understood they like it for Steve McQueen . . .
Attendant.   Twentieth is going to buy it . . . for Charlton Heston . . .
Tandy.   Then you admit . . . you admit I'm getting out of here.
Attendant.   They're going to buy it from your estate . . .

---

[18] A town on Long Island, New York.

Tandy.   I'm at the goddamned starting line. I'm ready to breathe clean air. I tore myself inside out to get where I am—and I'm not taking up anybody's space. I'm ready to cook a little. Swing. What kind of fellow is that to snuff out?

Attendant.   A good fellow. But I'm snuffing him out anyway.

Tandy.   Where's your compassion?

Attendant.   I do plenty of good things. Half the things I do are good, maybe even a little more, that's right, maybe even a little more. Nobody notices them. I never get any credit, but I do plenty of good things. I make trees, forests, soccer fields. I let hernias get better . . .

Tandy.   But you'll wipe out a guy like me . . . and a lovely blonde girl like that . . .

Meredith.   Oh, listen, the blonde part shouldn't enter into it, I can see that.

Attendant.   I let you go, I got to let the next guy go. Pretty soon nobody's dead. You'd have people coming out of your ears. Have you seen Istanbul lately? Downtown Istanbul? Los Angeles?

Meredith.   I'd never live in L.A. I don't think there's one sincere person in the whole city.

Attendant.   Let me ask you something. While you were doing all those things, unloading your old lady, you know, straightening out your head, how did you feel?

Tandy.   Good. Excited . . . it was like being in a whirlpool bath. An emotional whirlpool bath. It even made my body feel good; it got springy and toughened up . . .

Attendant.   There y'are. You felt good, you had a whirlpool bath . . . a springy body . . . Need I say more?

Tandy.   You don't understand something. I probably never made it clear. This is very important to me. We're talking about my life. I'm not asking you for seats to a hockey game.

Attendant *(Mocking)*.   It's very important to him. Nobody else is alive.

Tandy.   Is there anything I can do for you?

Attendant.   You got to be kidding. *You* do something for *me*? What in the world would God want?

Tandy.   A sacrifice? . . . burnt offering?[19]

Attendant *(As though He is finished with Tandy)*.   I got no time to fool around. I got a whole new crowd coming in.

Tandy.   That's it. You're going through with this? Well, I'll tell you right now, if you're capable of wiping out a once-confused fellow who's now a completely straight and sweet guy, then I got no choice but to call you a putz. *(To Meredith)* I'm sorry.

Meredith.   Oh, that's all right. You can say putz. Schvontz is the one I don't care for.

---

[19] An animal, food, or other substance burned upon an altar as a sacrifice or offering to a god.

Attendant *(Astonished).*   God? . . . Did I hear you correctly? . . . Can I
  believe my ears? . . . Blasphemy?. . .
Tandy.   That's right. If you're capable of doing something like that. Taking a
  fellow to the very threshold of marvelous things, teasing him along and then
  aceing him out just when he's ready to scoop up one lousy drop of gravy—
  that is bad news, I'm sorry . . .
Attendant.   I'll tell you right now nobody ever called me that. That's bad,
  boy, that *is* low. Wowee . . . That's what I call sinning, baby. You're in real
  trouble now. You have put your foot in it this time, fella . . . You going to
  stick to what you called me? . . . that dirty name? . . . talking that way to
  God?
Tandy.   Yeah, I'm going to stick to it . . . and you know why . . . because
  when I was in that Chinese restaurant . . . and I lost my breath, and I had
  no feelings, and I was numb and white, as white as a piece of typing paper,
  and I said over and over and over I don't want to die, I don't want to die, I
  don't want to die . . . and told you, in my way, how much I treasured every
  drop of life—you weren't impressed, you didn't hear a whisper of it . . .
Attendant.   That right, Gottlieb? Did he do that?

(Gottlieb nods)

Tandy.   I thought you knew everything.
Attendant.   Almost everything. Once in a while there's an administrative error.
  Anyway, I did hear you. You came over a little weak, a little static thrown
  in there, but I heard you. That's why you're here. Otherwise . . . *(Pointing
  to grated door)* . . . you'd have gone straight in there . . .
Tandy.   Then not everybody comes here . . .
Attendant.   Neurotics, freaks . . . *(contemptuously)* . . . those with stories to
  tell.
Tandy.   How was mine?
Attendant.   Not bad. I heard worse.
Tandy.   You were touched . . . You just won't admit it. *(He advances,
  threateningly)* Now let me out of here.
Attendant.   You come near me, I'll send you back with cancer, then you'll
  know real trouble.

*(Tandy grabs Gottlieb, wrestles him to the floor, holding him around the neck,
threatening him with his other hand)*

Tandy.   All right, talk, and be quick about it. Otherwise, you get these carpet
  tacks right in your face. How do we get out of here?
Attendant.   You talk, Gottlieb, and I'll see to it that you never work again.
  What can he do with a lousy bunch of carpet tacks?
Gottlieb.   I don't know. But I'm not taking any chances . . . Get a mirror.
Meredith *(Reaching into a purse).*   I've got one here.

Gottlieb.   Shine it in his face. He can't stand that.

(*She hesitates, then does*)

Attendant (*Cringing, trying to hide*).   Take that away. I don't want to see
   myself. A homely guy, with pockmarks.
Tandy (*Releasing Gottlieb, deflecting Meredith's mirror*).   All right, wait a
   minute, I can't go through with this . . . Leave him alone . . .
Attendant (*Gets himself together—then, as though feelings are really hurt*).   Et
   tu,[20] Gottlieb . . . (*Makes a move to Meredith, indicating it is her turn*)
Meredith.   Au revoir, Mr. Tandy. Did I do all right with the mirror?
Tandy.   You did fine, kid.

(*Meredith goes through the door*)

Attendant (*To Tandy*).   You couldn't stand that, right, to see God get wiped
   out . . . It gave you a funny feeling.
Tandy.   I don't like to see anybody get wiped out . . . I'm notorious for
   breaking up fights . . . I once threw a guy through the window of a furniture
   store because somebody was picking on him and I didn't want him to get
   hurt.
Attendant.   You got a lot of nice qualities . . . Too bad I'm filled up. I'd let
   you work around here for a while . . . Listen, what are you giving yourself
   such a hard time for . . . Suppose, for a second, I let you out of here . . .
   What would you do? . . .
Tandy.   What would I do? . . . Are you kidding? . . . What is this, a put-on?
   . . . You didn't hear me go on about my new life? My new style? The
   exciting world that's out there waiting for me? . . . This terrific new quiet
   girl friend who practically brings me the newspaper in her teeth—who
   watches me like a hawk for the slightest sign of sexual tension—and then
   whop—she's in there like a shot to drain it off and make me feel comfortable
   again . . . And if I feel like going out at four in the morning to get some
   eggs—she's right there at my side—because she comes from a tradition where
   the man is like a gypsy king and the woman is someone who drags mutton
   to him on her back, all the way up a hill. And all she ever hopes for is that
   he'll throw her a lousy mutton bone while she's sleeping in the dirt at his
   feet . . . And this is an intelligent girl, too . . . a Bryn Mawr girl . . . When
   I'm alone with her . . .
Attendant.   You like this girl . . .
Tandy.   Like her? . . . Oh, I see what you mean . . . Yeah . . . if I'm so
   crazy about her, how come I'm constantly chasing chicks all over the place

---

[20] Latin, meaning "Thou also." The famous line from Shakespeare's *Julius Caesar* is uttered
by Julius Caesar on seeing his friend Brutus among his assassins.

. . . All right, I'll admit to you that she's a little on the quiet side—that sometimes all that quiet drives me nuts . . . All right, let's face it, she's basically a dull girl. Terrific kid, loyal, faithful, brings you mutton, but the sparks don't fly . . . And it did cross my mind that maybe I'll find another girl who's got a little more pizazz . . . I'll give you that . . .

Attendant.   Another girl. . . .

Tandy.   Yeah. Another girl. Oh, I got ya', I got ya'—a new one isn't going to be the answer either . . . As delicious as she looks now, in two months I'm a little restless again . . . And that's the way it's got to be if I live to be a hundred . . . *(Trails off)* . . . I got friends, terrific friends. We hang around this bar called The Quonset Hut, run by a dyke, a rich retired dyke. We hang around there, sometimes till five in the morning, talking about Milton[21] and the Brontë sisters.[22] These friends of mine are terrific people—they're a little screwed up in their personal lives—most of them have been divorced three or four times—but very often those are the best people, the ones who get divorced over and over . . . Anyway, I want to do a lot more of that, hanging around this dyke bar till five in the morning with my divorced friends, talking about Milton and the Brontë sisters . . .

And I have to get back to my book. Now I know what you're going to say and I'm way ahead of you—that I have no real visceral interest in Charlemagne—that I just picked that subject because it has a prestige sound to it. Well, you're wrong. To me it's just a loosening-up process, a way of warming up the writing muscles so I can be ready for the real book I want to write on—Vasco da Gama and the Straits of Magellan. *(Weak little laugh as though aware He's told a joke. No response from Attendant)* No, seriously . . . you have to get the muscles limber . . . What you're saying is if I really wanted to write I'd stop crapping around with Charlemagne . . . I see what you mean . . . You get more prestige from a truly observed book about . . . cheeseburgers than you can from a schlock Charlemagne book . . . Boy, you really nailed that one down . . .

I'll tell you what, let me smoke a cigar, all right?

(Takes one out; Attendant has sat down and begun to arrange the cards for a game of solitaire)

I get these from Switzerland from a guy who brings them in from Cuba. It costs you a little extra, but it's really worth it. They say you're supposed to stop smoking these when you get about half way down, but I don't know. Sometimes I think the last half of the cigar is the best part.

I can tell a Havana cigar in one puff. It's not the tobacco so much as the rolling process they use. They have a secret rolling process that nobody's

---

[21] John Milton (1608–1674), an English poet.
[22] Charlotte (1816–1855), Emily (1818–1848), and Anne (1820–1849) Brontë, English novelists.

ever been able to pry away from the Cubans . . .

If it kills me I got to get back and have some more weekends with my daughter. Those weekends are the most beautiful part of my life now. I mean there's no more hassle . . . no more crazy marriage in the background . . . It all gets telescoped down to just me and her, hanging around together.

(*Looks at Attendant for response, doesn't get one*)

. . . So you're asking me how come I'm always going crazy thinking up places to take her . . . How come I'm always dragging her to puppet shows . . . Well, all I can say is that it's the city's fault . . . Where the hell are you supposed to take a kid in the city . . . If we were out on a farm, it'd be a different story . . .

But I do see what you mean—Jesus, you really know how to zing it in there . . . what you're driving at is that I have to keep taking her places because I actually have nothing to say to her . . . Maybe I don't even like kids . . . She'd be better off staying home and hanging around with a pack of little girls . . . (*Handling cigar*) A guy once told me the reason for the special flavor of these Havana cigars is that the tobacco is supposed to be rolled on the thighs of Cuban women . . . Jesus, wouldn't that be something . . .

I got to get out of here . . . I got to get out of here . . . I got things to do . . .

(*Attendant continues his game of solitaire—the last sound heard is the flicking of the cards . . .*)

Curtain

QUESTIONS

1. Why is Tandy outraged by his situation? Are his reasons convincing? Do you admire him? **2.** Does the play ridicule homosexuals? Explain. **3.** What is Meredith's role in the play? Are we meant to respect her? Explain. **4.** Compare the Oldtimer's justification for his life just before he passes through the door with Tandy's final monologue. How do the passages define the characters? Which character, if either, do you find admirable? Explain.

WRITING TOPICS

1. What effect does the author achieve by making God a Puerto Rican steambath attendant? Do you find the God in this play believable? **2.** Discuss the theme of the play, particularly with respect to what the playwright is saying about the values we should cultivate.

Death Knocks

1968

WOODY ALLEN   [b. 1935]

The play takes place in the bedroom of the Nat Ackerman's two-story house, somewhere in Kew Gardens. The carpeting is wall-to-wall. There is a big double bed and a large vanity. The room is elaborately furnished and curtained, and on the walls there are several paintings and a not really attractive barometer. Soft theme music as the curtain rises. Nat Ackerman, a bald, paunchy fifty-seven-year-old dress manufacturer, is lying on the bed finishing off tomorrow's Daily News. He wears a bathrobe and slippers, and reads by a bed light clipped to the white headboard of the bed. The time is near midnight. Suddenly we hear a noise, and Nat sits up and looks at the window.

Nat.   What the hell is that?

(Climbing awkwardly through the window is a sombre, caped figure. The intruder wears a black hood and skintight black clothes. The hood covers his head but not his face, which is middle-aged and stark white. He is something like Nat in appearance. He huffs audibly and then trips over the windowsill and falls into the room.)

Death *(for it is no one else).*   Jesus Christ. I nearly broke my neck.
Nat *(watching with bewilderment).*   Who are you?
Death.   Death.
Nat.   Who?
Death.   Death. Listen—can I sit down? I nearly broke my neck. I'm shaking like a leaf.
Nat.   Who *are* you?
Death.   *Death.* You got a glass of water?
Nat.   Death? What do you mean, Death?
Death.   What is wrong with you? You see the black costume and the whitened face?
Nat.   Yeah.
Death.   Is it Halloween?
Nat.   No.
Death.   Then I'm Death. Now can I get a glass of water—or a Fresca?
Nat.   If this is some joke—

Death. What kind of joke? You're fifty-seven? Nat Ackerman? One eighteen Pacific Street? Unless I blew it—where's that call sheet? *(He fumbles through pocket, finally producing a card with an address on it. It seems to check.)*

Nat. What do you want with me?

Death. What do I want? What do you think I want?

Nat. You must be kidding. I'm in perfect health.

Death *(unimpressed).* Uh-huh. *(Looking around)* This is a nice place. You do it yourself?

Nat. We had a decorator, but we worked with her.

Death *(looking at picture on the wall).* I love those kids with the big eyes.

Nat. I don't want to go yet.

Death. *You* don't want to go? Please don't start in. As it is, I'm nauseous from the climb.

Nat. What climb?

Death. I climbed up the drainpipe. I was trying to make a dramatic entrance. I see the big windows and you're awake reading. I figure it's worth a shot. I'll climb up and enter with a little—you know . . . *(Snaps fingers)* Meanwhile, I get my heel caught on some vines, the drainpipe breaks, and I'm hanging by a thread. Then my cape begins to tear. Look, let's just go. It's been a rough night.

Nat. You broke my drainpipe?

Death. Broke. It didn't break. It's a little bent. Didn't you hear anything? I slammed into the ground.

Nat. I was reading.

Death. You must have really been engrossed. *(Lifting newspaper Nat was reading)* "NAB COEDS IN POT ORGY." Can I borrow this?

Nat. I'm not finished.

Death. Er—I don't know how to put this to you, pal. . . .

Nat. Why didn't you just ring downstairs?

Death. I'm telling you, I could have, but how does it look? This way I get a little drama going. Something. Did you read "Faust"?

Nat. What?

Death. And what if you had company? You're sitting there with important people. I'm Death—I should ring the bell and traipse right in the front? Where's your thinking?

Nat. Listen, Mister, it's very late.

Death. Yeah. Well, you want to go?

Nat. Go where?

Death. Death. It. The Thing. The Happy Hunting Grounds. *(Looking at his own knee)* Y'know, that's a pretty bad cut. My first job, I'm liable to get gangrene yet.

Nat. Now, wait a minute. I need time. I'm not ready to go.

Death. I'm sorry. I can't help you. I'd like to, but it's the moment.

Nat. How can it be the moment? I just merged with Modiste Originals.

Death. What's the difference, a couple of bucks more or less.

Nat. Sure, what do you care? You guys probably have all your expenses paid.

Death. You want to come along now?

Nat *(studying him).* I'm sorry, but I cannot believe you're Death.

Death. Why? What'd you expect—Rock Hudson?

Nat. No, it's not that.

Death. I'm sorry if I disappointed you.

Nat. Don't get upset. I don't know, I always thought you'd be . . . uh . . . taller.

Death. I'm five seven. It's average for my weight.

Nat. You look a little like me.

Death. Who should I look like? I'm your death.

Nat. Give me some time. Another day.

Death. I can't. What do you want me to say?

Nat. One more day. Twenty-four hours.

Death. What do you need it for? The radio said rain tomorrow.

Nat. Can't we work out something?

Death. Like what?

Nat. You play chess?

Death. No, I don't.

Nat. I once saw a picture of you playing chess.

Death. Couldn't be me, because I don't play chess. Gin rummy, maybe.

Nat. You play gin rummy?

Death. Do I play gin rummy? Is Paris a city?

Nat. You're good, huh?

Death. Very good.

Nat. I'll tell you what I'll do—

Death. Don't make any deals with me.

Nat. I'll play you gin rummy. If you win, I'll go immediately. If I win, give me some more time. A little bit—one more day.

Death. Who's got time to play gin rummy?

Nat. Come on. If you're so good.

Death. Although I feel like a game . . .

Nat. Come on. Be a sport. We'll shoot for a half hour.

Death. I really shouldn't.

Nat. I got the cards right here. Don't make a production.

Death. All right, come on. We'll play a little. It'll relax me.

Nat *(getting cards, pad, and pencil).* You won't regret this.

Death. Don't give me a sales talk. Get the cards and give me a Fresca and put out something. For God's sake, a stranger drops in, you don't have potato chips or pretzels.

Nat. There's M&M's downstairs in a dish.

Death. M&M's. What if the President came? He'd get M&M's too?

Nat. You're not the President.

Death. Deal.

(*Nat deals, turns up a five.*)

Nat.   You want to play a tenth of a cent a point to make it interesting?
Death.   It's not interesting enough for you?
Nat.   I play better when money's at stake.
Death.   Whatever you say, Newt.
Nat.   Nat, Nat Ackerman. You don't know my name?
Death.   Newt, Nat—I got such a headache.
Nat.   You want that five?
Death.   No.
Nat.   So pick.
Death (*surveying his hand as he picks*).   Jesus, I got nothing here.
Nat.   What's it like?
Death.   What's what like?

(*Throughout the following, they pick and discard.*)

Nat.   Death.
Death.   What should it be like? You lay there.
Nat.   Is there anything after?
Death.   Aha, you're saving twos.
Nat.   I'm asking. Is there anything after?
Death (*absently*).   You'll see.
Nat.   Oh, then I will actually see something?
Death.   Well, maybe I shouldn't have put it that way. Throw.
Nat.   To get an answer from you is a big deal.
Death.   I'm playing cards.
Nat.   All right, play, play.
Death.   Meanwhile, I'm giving you one card after another.
Nat.   Don't look through the discards.
Death.   I'm not looking. I'm straightening them up. What was the knock card?
Nat.   Four. You ready to knock already?
Death.   Who said I'm ready to knock. All I asked was what was the knock card.
Nat.   And all I asked was is there anything for me to look forward to.
Death.   Play.
Nat.   Can't you tell me anything? Where do we go?
Death.   We? To tell you the truth, *you* fall in a crumpled heap on the floor.
Nat.   Oh, I can't wait for that! Is it going to hurt?
Death.   Be over in a second.
Nat.   Terrific. (*Sighs*) I needed this. A man merges with Modiste Originals
    . . .
Death.   How's four points?
Nat.   You're knocking?

Death.   Four points is good?

Nat.   No, I got two.

Death.   You're kidding.

Nat.   No, you lose.

Death.   Holy Christ, and I thought you were saving sixes.

Nat.   No. Your deal. Twenty points and two boxes. Shoot. *(Death deals.)* I must fall on the floor, eh? I can't be standing over the sofa when it happens?

Death.   No. Play.

Nat.   Why not?

Death.   Because you fall on the floor! Leave me alone. I'm trying to concentrate.

Nat.   Why must it be on the floor? That's all I'm saying! Why can't the whole thing happen and I'll stand next to the sofa?

Death.   I'll try my best. Now can we play?

Nat.   That's all I'm saying. You remind me of Moe Lefkowitz. He's also stubborn.

Death.   I remind you of Moe Lefkowitz. I'm one of the most terrifying figures you could possibly imagine, and him I remind of Moe Lefkowitz. What is he, a furrier?

Nat.   You should be such a furrier. He's good for eighty thousand a year. Passementeries. He's got his own factory. Two points.

Death.   What?

Nat.   Two points. I'm knocking. What have you got?

Death.   My hand is like a basketball score.

Nat.   And it's spades.

Death.   If you didn't talk so much.

(They redeal and play on.)

Nat.   What'd you mean before when you said this was your first job?

Death.   What does it sound like?

Nat.   What are you telling me—that nobody ever went before?

Death.   Sure they went. But I didn't take them.

Nat.   So who did?

Death.   Others.

Nat.   There's others?

Death.   Sure. Each one has his own personal way of going.

Nat.   I never knew that.

Death.   Why should you know? Who are you?

Nat.   What do you mean who am I? Why—I'm nothing?

Death.   Not nothing. You're a dress manufacturer. Where do you come to knowledge of the eternal mysteries?

Nat.   What are you talking about? I make a beautiful dollar. I sent two kids through college. One is in advertising, the other's married. I got my own home. I drive a Chrysler. My wife has whatever she wants. Maids, mink

coat, vacations. Right now she's at the Eden Roc. Fifty dollars a day because she wants to be near her sister. I'm supposed to join her next week, so what do you think I am—some guy off the street?
Death.   All right. Don't be so touchy.
Nat.   Who's touchy?
Death.   How would you like it if I got insulted quickly?
Nat.   Did I insult you?
Death.   You didn't say you were disappointed in me?
Nat.   What do you expect? You want me to throw you a block party?
Death.   I'm not talking about that. I mean me personally. I'm too short, I'm this, I'm that.
Nat.   I said you looked like me. It's like a reflection.
Death.   All right, deal, deal.

(*They continue to play as music steals in and the lights dim until all is in total darkness. The lights slowly come up again, and now it is later and their game is over. Nat tallies.*)

Nat.   Sixty-eight . . . one-fifty . . . Well, you lose.
Death (*dejectedly looking through the deck*).   I knew I shouldn't have thrown that nine. Damn it.
Nat.   So I'll see you tomorrow.
Death.   What do you mean you'll see me tomorrow?
Nat.   I won the extra day. Leave me alone.
Death.   You were serious?
Nat.   We made a deal.
Death.   Yeah, but—
Nat.   Don't "but" me. I won twenty-four hours. Come back tomorrow.
Death.   I didn't know we were actually playing for time.
Nat.   That's too bad about you. You should pay attention.
Death.   Where am I going to go for twenty-four hours?
Nat.   What's the difference? The main thing is I won an extra day.
Death.   What do you want me to do—walk the streets?
Nat.   Check into a hotel and go to a movie. Take a *schvitz*.[1] Don't make a federal case.
Death.   Add the score again.
Nat.   Plus you owe me twenty-eight dollars.
Death.   *What?*
Nat.   That's right, Buster. Here it is—read it.
Death (*going through pockets*).   I have a few singles—not twenty-eight dollars.
Nat.   I'll take a check.
Death.   From what account?

---

[1] Steam bath.

Nat.   Look who I'm dealing with.

Death.   Sue me. Where do I keep my checking account?

Nat.   All right, gimme what you got and we'll call it square.

Death.   Listen, I need that money.

Nat.   Why should you need money?

Death.   What are you talking about? You're going to the Beyond.

Nat.   So?

Death.   So—you know how far that is?

Nat.   So?

Death.   So where's gas? Where's tolls?

Nat.   We're going by car!

Death.   You'll find out. *(Agitatedly)* Look—I'll be back tomorrow, and you'll give me a chance to win the money back. Otherwise I'm in definite trouble.

Nat.   Anything you want. Double or nothing we'll play. I'm liable to win an extra week or a month. The way you play, maybe years.

Death.   Meantime I'm stranded.

Nat.   See you tomorrow.

Death *(being edged to the doorway).*   Where's a good hotel? What am I talking about hotel, I got no money. I'll go sit in Bickford's[2] *(He picks up the* News.*)*

Nat.   Out. Out. That's my paper. *(He takes it back.)*

Death *(exiting).*   I couldn't just take him and go. I had to get involved in rummy.

Nat *(calling after him).*   And be careful going downstairs. On one of the steps the rug is loose.

(And, on cue, we hear a terrific crash. Nat sighs, then crosses to the bedside table and makes a phone call.)

Nat.   Hello, Moe? Me. Listen, I don't know if somebody's playing a joke, or what, but Death was just here. We played a little gin . . . No, *Death.* In person. Or somebody who claims to be Death. But, Moe, he's such a *schlep!*[3]

Curtain

QUESTIONS

1. Upon what allusions does this play depend for its humor?   **2.** Characterize the speech patterns of the characters. How do they contribute to the play's effect?

---

[2] Bickford's was a chain of inexpensive all-night cafeterias in New York City.
[3] Boring jerk.

The Presence of Death

QUESTIONS AND WRITING TOPICS

1. Although Gray's "Elegy Written in a Country Churchyard," Housman's "To an Athlete Dying Young," Ransom's "Bells for John Whiteside's Daughter," Auden's "In Memory of W. B. Yeats," and Roethke's "Elegy for Jane" employ different poetic forms, they all embody a poetic mode called *elegy*. Define *elegy* in terms of the characteristic tone of these poems. Compare the elegiac tone of these poems. **Writing Topic:** Compare the elegiac tone of one of these poems with the tone of Poe's "The Conqueror Worm" or Owen's "Dulce et Decorum Est" or Thomas's "Do Not Go Gentle into That Good Night."

2. What figurative language in the prose and poetry of this section is commonly associated with death itself? With dying? Contrast the characteristic imagery of this section with the characteristic imagery of love poetry. **Writing Topic:** Compare the imagery in Shakespeare's sonnet 18 with the imagery in sonnet 73.

3. In Tolstoy's "The Death of Iván Ilých," Friedman's *Steambath*, and Donne's sonnet "Death, Be Not Proud," death and dying are considered from a religious viewpoint. **Writing Topic:** Discuss whether these works develop a similar attitude toward death, or whether the attitudes they develop differ crucially.

4. State the argument against resignation to death made in Thomas's "Do Not Go Gentle into That Good Night." State the argument of Catherine Davis's reply, "After a Time." **Writing Topic:** Using these positions as the basis of your discussion, select for analysis two works that support Thomas's argument and two works that support Davis's.

5. Discuss the attitude toward death developed in Mishima's "Patriotism." **Writing Topic:** Contrast the treatment of death in Mishima's "Patriotism" with the treatment of death developed in any other story in this section.

6. Malamud's "Idiots First" and Friedman's *Steambath* both present a grim picture of the human condition, yet they are often funny. What function does humor serve in each work? **Writing Topic:** Which work embodies a more hopeful vision of the human condition? Explain.

7. Which works in this section treat death and dying in a way that corresponds most closely with your own attitudes toward mortality? Which contradict your attitudes? **Writing Topic:** Choose two works, each of which affects you differently, and isolate and discuss the elements responsible for your response.

APPENDICES

The Librarian, 1566 by G. Arcimboldo.

APPENDICES

Poems about Poetry

Most of us would probably define poetry as a form of writing that employs rhyme and metrical regularity and deals with serious and "heavy" subjects (unless, of course, it's light verse). But you don't have to go further than the poems in this anthology to see that many poems do not use rhyme, have no metrical regularity, and deal with ordinary subjects in prosaic language. Maybe we can best define poetry (someone once did) as the kind of writing where the lines don't end at the same place on the right-hand side of the page. Here are a few poems about poetry, in which poets attempt to describe what it is, how it works, what it does, and why it does it.

Ars Poetica   1926

ARCHIBALD MacLEISH   [1892–1982]

A poem should be palpable and mute
As a globed fruit,

Dumb
As old medallions to the thumb,

Silent as the sleeve-worn stone
Of casement ledges where the moss has grown—

A poem should be wordless
As the flight of birds.

A poem should be motionless in time
As the moon climbs,   10

Leaving, as the moon releases
Twig by twig the night-entangled trees,

Leaving, as the moon behind the winter leaves,
Memory by memory the mind—

A poem should be motionless in time
As the moon climbs.

A poem should be equal to:
Not true.

For all the history of grief
An empty doorway and a maple leaf.   20

For love
The leaning grasses and two lights above the sea—

A poem should not mean
But be.

Pitcher   1960

ROBERT FRANCIS [1901–1987]

His art is eccentricity, his aim
How not to hit the mark he seems to aim at,

His passion how to avoid the obvious,
His technique how to vary the avoidance.

The others throw to be comprehended. He
Throws to be a moment misunderstood.

Yet not too much. Not errant, arrant, wild,
But every seeming aberration willed.

Not to, yet still, still to communicate
Making the batter understand too late.   10

QUESTIONS
1. The poem describes the art of the baseball pitcher. But the description is an
extended metaphor for the art of the poet. Is the pitcher described accurately?   **2.** Is
the analogy between pitcher and poet apt? Explain.

Very Like a Whale   1945

OGDEN NASH   [1902–1971]

One thing that literature would be greatly the better for
Would be a more restricted employment by authors of simile and metaphor.
Authors of all races, be they Greeks, Romans, Teutons or Celts,
Can't seem just to say that anything is the thing it is but have to go out of
   their way to say that it is like something else.
What does it mean when we are told
That the Assyrian came down like a wolf on the fold?[1]
In the first place, George Gordon Byron had had enough experience
To know that it probably wasn't just one Assyrian, it was a lot of Assyrians.
However, as too many arguments are apt to induce apoplexy and thus
   hinder longevity,
We'll let it pass as one Assyrian for the sake of brevity.   10
Now then, this particular Assyrian, the one whose cohorts were gleam-
   ing in purple and gold,
Just what does the poet mean when he says he came down like a wolf on
   the fold?
In heaven and earth more than is dreamed of in our philosophy there are
   a great many things,
But I don't imagine that among them there is a wolf with purple and gold
   cohorts or purple and gold anythings.

No, no, Lord Byron, before I'll believe that this Assyrian was actually
   like a wolf I must have some kind of proof;
Did he run on all fours and did he have a hairy tail and a big red mouth
   and big white teeth and did he say Woof woof?
Frankly I think it very unlikely, and all you were entitled to say, at the
   very most,
Was that the Assyrian cohorts came down like a lot of Assyrian cohorts
   about to destroy the Hebrew host.
But that wasn't fancy enough for Lord Byron, oh dear me no, he had to
   invent a lot of figures of speech and then interpolate them,
With the result that whenever you mention Old Testament soldiers to
   people they say Oh yes, they're the ones that a lot of wolves dressed
   up in gold and purple ate them.   20

---

[1] Nash is responding to Lord Byron's "The Destruction of Sennacherib," a poetic account of the events in 2 Kings 19. Byron's poem appears on p. 1105.

That's the kind of thing that's being done all the time by poets, from
   Homer to Tennyson;
They're always comparing ladies to lilies and veal to venison,
And they always say things like that the snow is a white blanket after a
   winter storm.
Oh it is, is it, all right then, you sleep under a six-inch blanket of snow
   and I'll sleep under a half-inch blanket of unpoetical blanket material
   and we'll see which one keeps warm,
And after that maybe you'll begin to comprehend dimly
What I mean by too much metaphor and simile.

Constantly Risking Absurdity   1958

LAWRENCE FERLINGHETTI [b. 1919]

   Constantly risking absurdity
                     and death
        whenever he performs
                 above the heads
                       of his audience
  the poet like an acrobat
            climbs on rime
                to a high wire of his own making
and balancing on eyebeams
                above a sea of faces   10
     paces his way
            to the other side of day
  performing entrechats
           and sleight-of-foot tricks
and other high theatrics
          and all without mistaking
     any thing
       for what it may not be

   For he's the super realist
               who must perforce perceive   20
      taut truth
          before the taking of each stance or step
  in his supposed advance
          toward that still higher perch
where Beauty stands and waits
        with gravity
          to start her death-defying leap

And he
          a little charleychaplin man
                who may or may not catch   30
       her fair eternal form
              spreadeagled in the empty air
       of existence

A Poet's Progress   1950

MICHAEL HAMBURGER [b. 1924]

Like snooker balls thrown on the table's faded green,
Rare ivory and weighted with his best ambitions,
At first his words are launched: not certain what they mean,
He loves to see them roll, rebound, assume positions
Which—since not he—some power beyond him has assigned.

But now the game begins: dead players, living critics
Are watching him—and suddenly one eye goes blind,
The hand that holds the cue shakes like a paralytic's,
Till every thudding, every clinking sound portends
New failure, new defeat. Amazed, he finds that still   10
It is not he who guides his missiles to their ends
But an unkind geometry that mocks his will.

If he persists, for years he'll practise patiently,
Lock all the doors, learn all the tricks, keep noises out,
Though he may pick a ghost or two for company
Or pierce the room's inhuman silence with a shout.
More often silence wins; then soon the green felt seems
An evil playground, lawless, lost to time, forsaken,
And he a fool caught in the water weeds of dreams
Whom only death or frantic effort can awaken.   20

At last, a master player, he can face applause,
Looks for a fit opponent, former friends, emerges;
But no one knows him now. He questions his own cause,
And has forgotten why he yielded to those urges,
Took up a wooden cue to strike a coloured ball.
Wise now, he goes on playing; both his house and heart
Unguarded solitudes, hospitable to all
Who can endure the cold intensity of art.

For Saundra   1968

NIKKI GIOVANNI   [b. 1943]

i wanted to write
a poem
that rhymes
but revolution doesn't lend
itself to be-bopping

then my neighbor
who thinks i hate
asked—do you ever write
tree poems—i like trees
so i thought   10

i'll write a beautiful green tree poem
peeked from my window
to check the image
noticed the school yard was covered
with asphalt
no green—no trees grow
in manhattan

then, well, i thought the sky
i'll do a big blue sky poem

but all the clouds have winged   20
low since no-Dick[1] was elected

so i thought again
and it occurred to me
maybe i shouldn't write
at all
but clean my gun
and check my kerosene supply

---

[1] A derogatory reference to Richard Nixon.

perhaps these are not poetic
times
at all   30

Today Is a Day of Great Joy   1968

VICTOR HERNÁNDEZ CRUZ   [b. 1949]

when they stop poems
in the mail & clap
their hands & dance to
them
when women become pregnant
by the side of poems
the strongest sounds making
the river go along

it is a great day

as poems fall down to   10

movie crowds in restaurants
in bars

when poems start to
knock down walls to
choke politicians
when poems scream &
begin to break the air

that is the time of
true poets that is
the time of greatness   20

a true poet aiming
poems & watching things
fall to the ground

it is a great day.

Reading Fiction

An author is a god, creator of the world he or she describes. That world has a limited and very special landscape. It is peopled with men and women of a particular complexion, of particular gifts and failings. Its history, almost always, is determined by the interaction of its people within its narrow geography. Everything that occurs in a work of fiction—every figure, every tree, every furnished room and crescent moon and dreary fog—has been *purposely* put there by its creator. When a story pleases, when it moves its reader, he or she has responded to that carefully created world. The pleasure, the emotional commitment, the human response are not results of analysis. The reader has not registered in some mental adding machine the several details that establish character, the particular appropriateness of the weather to the events in the story, the marvelous rightness of the furnishings, the manipulation of the point of view, the plot, the theme, the style. The reader has recognized and accepted the world of the author and has been delighted (or saddened or angered) by what happens in it.

But how does it come about that readers recognize the artificial worlds, often quite different from their own, that authors create? And why is it that readers who recognize some fictional worlds effortlessly are bewildered and lost in other fictional worlds? Is it possible to extend the boundaries of readers' recognition? Can more and more of the landscapes and societies of fiction be made available to that onlooking audience?

The answer to the first of these questions is easy. Readers are comfortable in literary worlds that, however exotic the landscapes and the personalities that people them, incorporate moral imperatives that reflect the value system in the readers' world. Put another way, much fiction ends with its virtuous characters rewarded and its villains punished. This we speak of as poetic justice, and *poetic* seems to suggest that somehow such endings are ideal rather than "real." Not much experience of life is required to recognize that injustice, pain, frustration, and downright villainy often prevail, that the beautiful young heroine and the strong, handsome hero do not always overcome all obstacles, marry, and live happily ever after, that not every man is strong and handsome nor every woman beautiful. But readers, knowing that, respond to tragic fiction as well—where virtue is defeated, where obstacles prove too much for the men and women, where ponderous forces result in defeat, even death. Unhappy outcomes are painful to contemplate, but it is not difficult to recognize the world in which they occur. That world is much like our own. And unhappy outcomes serve to emphasize the very ideals that we have established as the aims and targets of human activity. Consequently, both the "romantic" comedies that gladden with justice and success and the "realistic" stories that end in defeat provide readers with recognizable and available emotional worlds, however exotic the settings and the characters in those stories might be.

If we look at fiction this way, the answer to the question "Why is it that some readers are bewildered and lost in some fictional worlds?" is clearly implied. Some fictional worlds *seem* to incorporate a strange set of moral imperatives. Readers are not altogether certain who are the virtuous characters and who are the villains or even what constitutes virtue and evil. Sometimes tragic oppositions in a fictional world that brooks no compromise puzzle readers who live in a world where compromise has become almost a virtue. Sometimes, particularly in more recent fiction that reflects the ever-widening influence of psychoanalytic theory, the landscape and the behavior of characters is designed to represent deep interiors, the less-than-rational hearts and minds of characters. Those weird interiors are not part of the common awareness of readers; the moral questions raised there are not the same moral questions that occupy most of our waking hours. Such fictional worlds are difficult to map, and bewildered readers may well reject these underworlds for the sunshine of the surfaces they know more immediately.

Fiction and Reality

Why do people read fiction (or watch TV narratives or go to movies)? The question is not so easy to answer as one might suppose. The first response is likely to have something to do with "amusement" or "entertainment." But you have doubtless read stories and novels (or seen movies) that end tragically. Is it accurate to say that they were amusing or entertaining? Is it entertaining to be saddened or to be angered by the defeat of "good" people? Or does the emotional impact of such stories somehow enlarge our own humanity? Fiction teaches its readers by providing them a vast range of experience that they could not acquire otherwise. Especially for the relatively young, conceptions of love, of success in life, of war, of malignant evil and cleansing virtue are learned from fiction, including movies and TV—not from life. And herein lies a great danger, for literary artists are notorious liars, and their lies frequently become the source of people's convictions about human nature and human society.

To illustrate, a huge number of television series based on the exploits of the FBI, or the Miami police force, or the dedicated surgeons at the general hospital, or the young lawyers always end with a capture, with a successful (though dangerous) operation, with justice triumphant. But, in the real world, police are able to resolve only about 10 percent of reported crime, disease ravages, and economic and political power often extends into the courtroom. The very existence of such television drama bespeaks a yearning that things should be different; its heroes are heroic in that they regularly overcome those obstacles that we all experience, but that, alas, we do not overcome.

Some writers, beginning about the middle of the nineteenth century, were particularly incensed at the real damage that a lying literature promotes, and they devoted their energies to exposing and counteracting the lies of the novelists, particularly those lies that formed attitudes about what constituted human success and happiness. Yet that popular fiction, loosely called *escapist*, is still most widely read for reasons that would probably fill several studies in social psychology. It needs no advocate. The fiction in this book, on the other hand, has been chosen largely because it does not lie about life—at least it does not lie about life in the ordinary way. And the various authors employ a large variety of literary methods and modes in an effort to illuminate the deepest wells of human experience. Consequently, many of these stories do not retail high adventure (though some do), since an adventurous inner life does not depend on an incident-filled outer life. Some stories, like Toomer's "Theater," might almost be said to be about what does *not* happen rather than what does—not-happening being as much incident, after all, as happening.

All fiction attempts to be interesting, to involve readers in situations, to force some aesthetic response from them—most simply put, in the widest sense of the word, to entertain. Some fiction aspires to nothing more. Other fiction seeks, as well, to establish some truth about the nature of humankind—Hemingway's "A Clean, Well-Lighted Place" and Lessing's "To Room Nineteen" ask readers to perceive the inner life of central figures. Some fiction seeks to explore the relationships among people—Faulkner's "A Rose for Emily," Toomer's "Theater," and Lawrence's "Odour of Chrysanthemums" depend for their force on the powerful interaction of one character with another. Still other fiction seeks to explore the connection between people and society—Ellison's "'Repent, Harlequin!' Said the Ticktockman" and Wright's "The Man Who Lived Underground" acquire their force from the implied struggle between people seeking a free and rich emotional life and the tyrannically ordering society that would sacrifice their humanity to some ideal of social efficiency.

We have been talking about that aspect of fiction that literary theorists identify as *theme*. Theorists also talk about plot, characterization, setting, point of view, and conflict—all terms naming aspects of fiction that generally have to do with the author's technique. Let us here deal with one story—James Joyce's "Araby" (p. 27). Read it. Then compare your private responses to the story with what we hope will be helpful and suggestive remarks about the methods of fiction.

The Methods of Fiction

One can perceive only a few things simultaneously and can hardly respond to everything contained in a well-wrought story all at once. After reading the story, the reader likely thinks back, makes adjustments, and reflects on the significance of things before reaching that set of emotional and intellectual experiences that we refer to as *response*. Most readers of short stories respond first to what may be called the *tone* of the opening lines. Now tone is an aspect of literature about which it is particularly difficult to talk, because it is an aura—a shimmering and shifting atmosphere that depends for its substance on rather delicate emotional responses to language and situation. Surely, before readers know anything at all about the plot of "Araby," they have experienced the tone.

> North Richmond Street, being blind, was a quiet street except at the hour when the Christian Brothers' School set the boys free. An uninhabited house of two storeys stood at the blind end, detached from its neighbors in a square ground. The other houses of the street, conscious of decent lives within them, gazed at one another with brown imperturbable faces.

Is the scene cheerful? Vital and active? Is this opening appropriate for a story that goes on to celebrate joyous affirmations about life and living? You will probably answer these questions negatively. Why? Because the dead-end street is described as "blind," because the Christian Brothers' School sounds much like a prison (it "sets the boys free"), because a vacant house fronts the dead end, because the other houses, personified, are "conscious of decent lives within" (a mildly ironic description—*decent* suggesting ordinary, thin-lipped respectability rather than passion or heroism), because those houses gaze at one another with "brown imperturbable faces"—*brown* being nondescript, as opposed, say, to scarlet, gold, bright blue, and *imperturbable faces* reinforcing the priggish decency within.

   Short stories, of course, are short, but this fact implies some serious considerations. In some ways, a large class of good short fiction deals with events that may be compared to the tip of the proverbial iceberg. The events animating the story represent only a tiny fraction of the characters' lives and experiences; yet, that fraction is terribly important because it provides the basis for wide understanding both to the characters within the story and to its readers.

   In "Araby," the *plot*—the connected sequence of events—may be simply stated. A young boy who lives in a rather drab, respectable neighborhood develops a crush on the sister of one of his playmates. She asks him if he intends to go to a charity fair that she cannot attend. He resolves to go and purchase a gift for her. He is tormented by the late and drunken arrival of his uncle who has promised him the money he needs. When the boy finally arrives at the bazaar, he is disappointed by the difference between his expectation and the actuality of the almost deserted fair. He perceives some minor events, overhears some minor conversation, and finally sees himself "as a creature driven and derided by vanity." Yet this tiny stretch of experience out of the life of the boy introduces him to an awareness about the differences between imagination and reality, between his romantic infatuation and the vulgar reality all about him. We are talking now about what is called the *theme* of the story. Emerging from the mundane events that constitute the story's plot is a general statement about intensely idealized childish "love," the shattering recognition of the false sentimentality that occasions it, and the enveloping vulgarity of adult life. The few pages of the story, by detailing a few events out of a short period of the protagonist's life, illuminate one aspect of the loss of innocence that we all endure and that is always painful. In much of the literature in the section on innocence and experience, the protagonists learn painfully the moral complexities of a world that had once seemed uncomplicated and predictable. That education does not always occur, as in "Araby," at an early age, either in literature or life.

Certainly theme is a centrally important aspect of prose fiction, but "good" themes do not necessarily ensure good stories. One may write a wretched story with the same theme as "Araby." What, then, independent of theme, is the difference between good stories and bad stories? Instinctively you know how to answer this question. Good stories, to begin with, are interesting; they present characters you care about; however fantastic, they are yet somehow plausible; they project a moral world you recognize. One of the obvious differences between short stories and novels is that story writers develop characters rapidly and limit the number of developed characters. Many stories have only one fleshed character; the other characters are frequently two-dimensional projections or even stereotypes. We see their surface only, not their souls. Rarely does a short story have more than three developed characters. Again, unlike novels, short stories usually work themselves out in a restricted geographical setting, in a single place, and within a rather short period of time.

We often speak of character, setting, plot, theme, and style as separate aspects of a story in order to break down a complex narrative into more manageable parts. But it is important to understand that this analytic process of separating various elements is something we have done to the story—the story (if it is a good one) is an integrated whole. The more closely we examine the separate elements, the clearer it becomes that each is integrally related to the others.

It is part of the boy's character that he lives in a brown imperturbable house in North Richmond Street, that he does the things he does (which is, after all, the plot), that he learns what he does (which is the theme), and that all of this characterization emerges from Joyce's rich and suggestive style. Consider this paragraph:

> Her image accompanied me even in places the most hostile to romance. On Saturday evenings when my aunt went marketing I had to go to carry some of the parcels. We walked through the flaring streets, jostled by drunken men and bargaining women, amid the curses of labourers, the shrill litanies of shop-boys who stood on guard by the barrels of pigs' cheeks, the nasal chanting of street-singers, who sang a *come-all-you* about O'Donovan Rossa, or a ballad about the troubles in our native land. These noises converged in a single sensation of life for me: I imagined that I bore my chalice safely through a throng of foes. Her name sprang to my lips at moments in strange prayers and praises which I myself did not understand. My eyes were often full of tears (I could not tell why) and at times a flood from my heart seemed to pour itself out into my bosom. I thought little of the future. I did not know whether I would ever speak to her or not or, if I spoke to her, how I could tell her of my confused adoration. But my body

was like a harp and her words and gestures were like fingers running upon the wires.

This paragraph furthers the plot. But it suggests much more. The boy thinks of his friend's sister even when he carries parcels for his aunt during the shopping trips through a crowded and coarse part of town. In those coarse market streets the shop-boys cry shrill "litanies," the girl's name springs to his lips in strange "prayers and praises," and the boy confesses a confused "adoration." Further, he bears his "chalice safely through a throng of foes." Now the words *litanies, prayers, praises, adoration* all come from a special vocabulary that is easy to identify. It is the vocabulary of the Roman Catholic Church. The *chalice* and the *throng of foes* come from the vocabulary of chivalric romance, which is alluded to in the first line of the quoted paragraph. Joyce's diction evokes a sort of holy chivalry that characterizes the boy on this otherwise altogether ordinary shopping trip. This paragraph suggests to the careful reader that the boy has cast his awakening sexuality in a mold that mixes the disparate shapes of the heroic knight, winning his lady by force of arms, and the ascetic penitent, adoring the Blessed Virgin, Mother of God.

Playing the word game, of course, can be dangerous. But from the beginning of this story to its end, a certain religious quality shimmers. That now-dead priest of the story's second paragraph had three books (at least). One is a romantic chivalric novel by Sir Walter Scott; one is a sensational account of the adventures of a famous criminal-turned-detective; one is what a priest might be expected to have at hand—an Easter week devotional guide. That priest who read Scott novels might have understood the boy's response—that mixture of religious devotion and romance.

Shortly after the shopping trip, the boy finally speaks to the girl, and it is instructive to see her as he does. He stands at the *railings* and looks up (presumably) at her, she bowing her head towards him. "The light from the lamp opposite our door caught the white curve of her neck, lit up her hair that rested there and, falling, lit up the hand upon the railing. It fell over one side of her dress and caught the white border of a petticoat, just visible as she stood at ease." Skip the petticoat, for a moment. Might the description of Mangan's sister remind the careful reader of quite common sculptured representations of the Virgin Mary? But the petticoat! And the white curve of her neck! This erotic overlay characterizes the boy's response. The sexuality is his own; the chivalry, the religious adoration, come from the culture in which he is immersed—come from Scott, the ballads sung in the market place, the "Arab's Farewell to his Steed" that the boy's uncle threatens to recite, and from his Catholic background. And it is the culture that so romanticizes and elevates the boy's yearning.

He finally gets to Araby—"the syllables of the word . . . were called to [him] through the silence in which [his] soul luxuriated and cast an Eastern enchantment over [him]." His purpose is to serve his lady—to bring her something from that exotic place. What he finds is a weary-looking man guarding a turnstile, the silence that pervades a church after a service, and two men counting money on a salver (that tray is called a *salver* by design). And in this setting he overhears a young woman flirting with two gentlemen:

> "O, I never said such a thing!"
> "O, but you did!"
> "O, but I didn't!"
> "Didn't she say that?"
> "Yes, I heard her."
> "O, there's a . . . fib!"

This is Araby, this is love in a darkened hall where money is counted. Is it any wonder that the boy, in the moment of personal illumination that Joyce calls an epiphany, sees himself as a creature driven and derided by vanity?

"Araby" is a careful, even a delicate story. Nothing much happens—what does occurs largely in the boy's perception and imagination. The story focuses on the boy's confusion of sexual attraction and the lofty sentiments of chivalry and religion. The climax occurs when he confronts the darkened, money-grubbing fair and the banal expression of the sexual attraction between the gentlemen and the young woman. The result is a sudden deflation of the boy's ego, his sense of self, as he recognizes his own delusions about the nature of love and the relationship between men, women, heroism, God, and money.

We would like to conclude with a discussion of one feature of fiction that sometimes proves troublesome to many readers. Often the events of a story, upon which much depends, puzzle or annoy readers. Why does that fool do that? Why doesn't X simply tell Y the way he or she feels and then the tragedy would be averted? In a sense, such responses reflect the intrusion of a reader into the world of the story. The reader, a sensible and sensitive person, under-stands some things about life after all and is oppressed by the characters' inability to understand at least as much. Characters choose to die when they might with a slight adjustment live. They risk danger when with a slight adjustment they might proceed safely. They suffer the pain of an unfortunate marriage when with a little trouble they might be free to live joyously. If the "whys" issuing from the reader are too insistent, too sensible, then the story must fail, at least for that reader. But many "whys" are not legitimate. Many are intrusions of the reader's hindsight, the reader's altogether different cultural and emotional fix. Henry James urged that the author must be allowed his or her *donnée*, his or her "given." The author creates the society and the rules by which it operates within his or her own fictional world. Sometimes this creation is so close to the reader's own world that it is hardly possible to object. African American readers will recognize the inner life of Wright's man who lived underground even if the events are bizarre. Those who have grown up in a southern town will recognize the atmosphere of Faulkner's "A Rose for Emily." But few readers of this book know 1895 Dublin and Irish middle-class society, which play a brooding role in "Araby" (as it does in almost all of Joyce's work). None know the futuristic world of Harlan Ellison's Harlequin. In every case, we must finally imagine those worlds, even where setting is familiar. If we cannot, the events that take place in them will be of no consequence. If those worlds are unimaginable, then the stories must fail. If they too much strain belief or remain too foreign to the reader's heart, they must likewise fail. But all response to fiction depends on the reader's acquiescence to the world of the author and the reader's perceptions of the moral consequences of acts and attitudes in that world. At best, that acquiescence will provide much pleasure as well as emotional insight into his or her own existence.

Reading Poetry

When I Heard the Learn'd Astronomer   1865

WALT WHITMAN   [1819–1892]

When I heard the learn'd astronomer,
When the proofs, the figures, were ranged in columns before me,
When I was shown the charts and diagrams, to add, divide, and measure
    them,
When I sitting heard the astronomer where he lectured with much applause
    in the lecture-room,
How soon unaccountable I became tired and sick,
Till rising and gliding out I wander'd off by myself,
In the mystical moist night-air, and from time to time,
Look'd up in perfect silence at the stars.

    The distinction implicit in Walt Whitman's poem between the mind (intel-
lectual knowledge) and the heart (emotion and feelings) is very old, but still a
useful one. All of us have no doubt felt at some time that the overexercise of
the mind interfered with our capacity to feel. Compelled to analyze, dissect,
categorize, and classify, we finally yearn for the simple and "mindless" pleasure
of unanalytical enjoyment. But the distinction between the mind and the heart
cannot be pushed too far before it breaks down. You may very well enjoy Dylan
Thomas's poem "Fern Hill" without recognizing its patterns of imagery or the
intricate way Thomas weaves together the past and the present. But understanding these elements will certainly deepen the pleasure the poem can give you.

    We don't mean to suggest by this that every poem needs to be studied long
and hard. Some poems are straightforward, requiring little analysis; others,
dense and complex, seem to yield little without some study. To test this out,
you might want to read right now two short poems (both twelve lines long),
Emily Dickinson's "After Great Pain, a Formal Feeling Comes" (p. 1116) and
Countee Cullen's "Incident" (p. 109). You will probably read straight through
the Cullen poem and understand what the poet is saying. If the Dickinson
poem doesn't stump you in the first line, it certainly will in the next three lines.

Yet you will surely understand (whatever "understand" might mean) the somber, serious tone and the image with which the poem ends.

Knowing a little about what poetry is and about its history can also enhance your appreciation. If your instructor asked you to define poetry, you would probably say it's the kind of writing that uses rhyme, a regular rhythm, unusual word order, and vivid, even unusual language and images. This kind of formal definition describes a good deal of poetry although by no means all, as a glance at any anthology (including this one) will quickly show. Up until about a century ago, poetry was governed by precise and often elaborate rules and conventions. Further, there existed a long tradition of poetic types (epic, elegy, ode, etc.), each with specific rules and characteristics. While these traditions still retain some force, the old notion that these forms are part of the natural scheme of things has been largely abandoned. Under the influence of Walt Whitman (the nineteenth-century poet who virtually invented "free verse") and the explosion of experimentalism beginning in the twentieth century, no one nowadays insists that what we call poetry must exhibit a combination of fixed characteristics (demonstrating once again that theory usually follows practice).

If the old formal criteria are no longer adequate, neither can we say that poetry deals only with certain subjects. Dylan Thomas's "Fern Hill" deals with death and the lost innocence of childhood in an elevated and formal language and an extremely complex stanzaic pattern. These formal characteristics along with the "lofty" subject matter mark it clearly as a poem. Anthony Hecht's "The Dover Bitch" uses a flat, conversational language and lines that have no apparent formal pattern. There is nothing lofty or noble about the woman who is the subject of the poem. But it *looks* like a poem—the lines end at different places on the right-hand side of the page! Carolyn Forché's "The Colonel" doesn't even *look* like a poem. The point is, like the formal characteristics, no hard and fast rules can be laid down about the subjects of poetry. The seventeenth-century poet John Milton declared that he had written his great epic *Paradise Lost* "to justify the ways of God to men." Archibald MacLeish tells us in "Ars Poetica" that "A poem should not mean / But be." They are both poems.

However we may define poetry, no culture we know about has been without it. We know that in ancient societies, the arts were not divided by types or differentiated from science. Poetry, dance, sculpture, and painting might all be parts of a tribal ceremony designed to propitiate the gods and so ensure a full harvest or a successful hunt. Poetry, then, was part of a primitive "science" that defined and helped control the natural world. Nature and the gods who controlled it might be harsh and unpredictable; the function of ritual was to control and appease these gods (to ensure rain, for example). But ritual also nurtured and strengthened the individual's communal spirit. The works in this anthology closest to this primitive world are the two tragedies written by Sophocles, *Oedipus Rex* and *Antigonê*, highly ritualized works that combine poetry (they are written in verse), dance (the Chorus moves in a choreographed fashion throughout) and painting and sculpture (the masks worn by the actors).

We in the West, of course, live very different lives. We inhabit an enormous industrialized society that over centuries abandoned primitive explanations and sought others. That development was marked by a differentiation and specialization of human endeavors, as science broke away from art and both divided into separate if related disciplines. Science became astronomy, biology, physics, and the like, while art branched into various types of aesthetic creation. And it was modern science, not poetry or the other arts, that produced profound and measurable changes in people's lives. Poetry might movingly and memorably remind us of the sorrow of unrequited love or the ravages of growing old, but the technology that science made possible produced undreamed-of material wealth and power.

It would be misleading to suggest that the scientist and the poet exist in separate worlds. But there are important differences. Science seeks the truth of physical reality. Social sciences such as psychology, sociology, and economics have tried to demonstrate that human behavior can be understood in terms of a set of definite and quantifiable mechanisms. Science can explain to us the physical phenomenon of death and explain its role in the ceaseless evolutionary struggle. But to understand the terror or emotional meaning of death, we turn to the poet. To return to the head/heart metaphor, we can say that the poet does speak to our heart while the scientist speaks to our head. But we should remember that the metaphor is not meant to suggest that one is superior to the other. We cannot exist without either the head or the heart. And at a deeper level, we might even say that the realm of science deals as much with beauty and mystery as the realm of poetry.

But poetry does speak more immediately, obviously, and powerfully to us about our inner lives. It helps us to learn who we are and to articulate what we feel. You may wonder what such an assertion means. What we feel, we feel. We don't need a poem to tell us. Not so. Often we don't know what we feel except in a vague way. A powerful poem articulates and thereby clarifies. Although the literary historian might observe that it is an academic exercise in wit, Andrew Marvell's poem "To His Coy Mistress" may well help readers understand their own feelings about the connection between physical love and mortality. The outrageous absurdity of death cutting down a person whose life has barely begun is articulated in Robert Frost's "'Out, Out—'" and John Crowe Ransom's "Bells for John Whiteside's Daughter."

Poetry at its highest and most general level is a form of communication, a means of defining, affirming, and deepening our humanity. This is not to say that we should approach poetry solemnly, expecting always to be loftily enlightened. We may, for instance, look upon a poem as a kind of game in which the poet skillfully works within a set of self-imposed rules—patterns of rhymes, rhythms, stanzas—while at the same time playing with language to achieve surprise, wit, and freshness. We delight in the comic effect Lord Byron achieves when he rhymes "intellectual" with "henpecked you all" or "maxim" with "tax 'em." In E. E. Cummings's "if everything happens that can't be done," the telescoping of two syntactic units in the lines "and buds know better / than books / don't grow" ("books" is both the object of the preposition "than" and the subject of "don't grow") is surprising, clever, and thematically appropriate.

Anyone familiar with Plato's theory that everything in our world is an imperfect replica of an ideal heavenly form will appreciate the beauty and condensed brilliance of William Butler Yeats's lines from "Among School Children":

> Plato thought nature but a spume that plays
> Upon a ghostly paradigm of things.

Some will discover, as children often do in nursery rhymes, the pleasure of rhythm, meter, and sound—the musical aspects of poetry. The pleasures of poetry range from the loftiest insights and discoveries to memorable lines and clever rhymes.

What follows are brief discussions about the major techniques and devices of poetry that will give you the tools for discussing and analyzing poems.

The Words of Poetry

It is not unusual to hear an original philosopher, sociologist, or economist referred to as a mediocre writer. Even while judging the writing poor, one may at the same time honor the originality and significance of the writer's ideas. Such a distinction cannot be made in poetry. If a poem is written poorly, it is a poor poem. "In reading prose," Ralph Waldo Emerson said, "I am sensitive as soon as a sentence drags; but in poetry as soon as one word drags." *Where* a poem arrives is inseparable from *how* it arrives. Everything must be right in a poem, every word. "The correction of prose," said William Butler Yeats, "is endless; a poem comes right with a click like a closing box."

Critics often describe poetry as "heightened language," meaning that the poet strives for precision and richness in the words he or she uses. For the poet, "precision" and "richness" are not contradictory. Words have dictionary or denotative meanings as well as associative or connotative meanings; they also have histories and relationships with other words. The English language is rich in synonyms, words whose denotative meanings are roughly the same but whose connotations vary widely *(excite, stimulate, titillate, inflame; poor, impoverished, indigent, destitute)*. Many words are identical in sound and often in spelling but different in meaning *(forepaws, four paws; lie [recline], lie [fib])*. The meanings of words have changed over time, and the poet may deliberately select a word whose older meaning adds a dimension to the poem. There are, of course, no hard and fast rules for judging a poet's effectiveness and skill in the handling of words (or anything else, for that matter). All we can do is look at particular works for examples of how a good poet uses words.

In a moving and passionate poem on his dying father, "Do Not Go Gentle into That Good Night," Dylan Thomas pleads with his father not to accept death passively but rather to "Rage, rage against the dying of the light." He declares that neither "wise men" nor "good men" nor "wild men" accept death quietly. And neither, Thomas adds, do "grave men," punning on *grave* in its meaning of both "serious" and "burial place." William Blake's poem about the inhumane jobs children were forced into in eighteenth-century England, "The Chimney Sweeper," begins:

> When my mother died I was very young,
> And my Father sold me while yet my tongue
> Could scarcely cry "'weep! 'weep! 'weep! 'weep!"
> So your chimneys I sweep, and in soot I sleep.

"'Weep," a clipped form of "sweep," is what the boy cries as he walks a street looking for work, but *weep* clearly evokes the tears and sorrow of his mother's death and the sadness of the small boy's cruel life. "Cry" is also an effective pun, the precise word to describe how the boy seeks work while simultaneously reinforcing the emotional meaning of *weep*.

Henry Reed's "Naming of Parts" develops a contrast between the instructions a group of soldiers are receiving on how to operate a rifle (in order to cause death) and the lovely world of nature (representing life and beauty). In the fourth stanza, bees are described as "assaulting and fumbling the flowers." "Fumbling," with its meaning of awkwardness and nervous uncertainty, may at first strike us as a puzzling word. Yet anyone who has watched a bee pollinating a flower will find the word denotatively effective. In addition, *fumbling* describes the actions of human beings caught up in sexual passion—a connotation appropriate to the poet's purposes, since pollination is a kind of sexual process. Furthermore, the meanings of *fumbling* contrast powerfully with the cold, mechanical precision of the death-dealing instruments the recruits are learning to use. The next line of the poem exhibits yet another resource of words: "They call it easing the Spring." The line is an exact repetition of a phrase used two lines earlier except *Spring* is now capitalized. While *Spring* retains its first meaning as part of the bolt action of the rifle, the capitalization makes it the season of the year when flowers are pollinated and the world of nature is reborn. With a typographical change, Reed is able to evoke in a single word the contrast (the cold steel of a rifle and the fecund beauty of nature) that gives the poem its structure and meaning.

Figurative Language

Figurative language is the general phrase we use to describe the many devices of language that allow us to speak nonliterally in order to achieve some special effect. When we wish to communicate a subjective state with more precision than the words of English give us, we reach for figurative language. When Robert Burns compares his love to a red rose in his poem "A Red, Red, Rose," it's not because he can't find the literal language he needs but because what he wants to say can only be expressed in figurative language. The interior world of emotions, feelings, and attitudes remains shadowy and insubstantial until figurative language gives it form and substance.

Figurative language allows us—and the poet—to transcend the confinement of the literal and the vagueness of the abstract through the use of *imagery*. The world is revealed to us through our senses—sight, sound, taste, touch, and smell. And while some philosophers and psychologists might disagree, it seems pretty clear that much, if not all, of our knowledge is linked to sensory experience. Through imagery, the poet creates a recognizable world by drawing on a fund of common experiences. Bad poetry is often bad because the imagery is stale ("golden sunset," "the smiling sun," "the rolling sea") or so skimpy that the poem dissolves into vague and meaningless abstraction.

A good poet never loses touch with the sensory world. The invisible, the intangible, the abstract, are anchored to the visible, the tangible, the concrete. Andrew Marvell begins his poem "To His Coy Mistress" with an elaborate statement of how he would court his beloved if their lives were measured in centuries rather than in years. He then describes the reality:

> But at my back I always hear
> Time's wingéd chariot hurrying near.
> And yonder all before us lie
> Deserts of vast eternity.
> Thy beauty shall no more be found,
> Nor, in thy marble vault, shall sound
> My echoing song; then worms shall try
> That long-preserved virginity,
> And your quaint honor turn to dust,
> And into ashes all my lust:
> The grave's a fine and private place,
> But none, I think, do there embrace.

Time, eternity, honor, and *lust* are all abstractions, vague and diffuse as abstractions always are. To overcome his mistress's coyness, Marvell needs to impart a sense of passionate urgency, to make her (and the reader) *see* these abstractions by linking them to the concrete. He does this by making time a *chariot*, eternity endless *deserts*, having honor turn to *dust*, and lust dwindle into *ashes*.

The difference between good and bad poetry often turns on the skill with which imagery (or other figurative language) is used. When Robert Frost in his poem "Birches" compares life to "a pathless wood" (line 44), the image strikes us as natural and appropriate (the comparison of life to a path or road is a common one, as is a wood or forest to a state of moral bewilderment).

However, when John Donne in "A Valediction: Forbidding Mourning" describes the relationship between him and his beloved in terms of a drawing compass, the image may seem jarring or even ludicrous. How can such a prosaic object help the poet define the nature of love, especially a love based upon spiritual affinities? In using such a conceit (see "Glossary of Literary

Terms"), Donne startles the reader into attention, maybe even hoping to create resistance or doubt that such an image is appropriate for a love poem. But as Donne elaborates the comparison through various stages, concluding it with the brilliantly appropriate image of the completed circle, our resistance and doubt give way to admiration for what Donne has done.

Words and phrases may take on figurative meaning over a period of time. Consider, for example, these familiar old sayings: "The grass is always greener on the other side of the fence"; "A rolling stone gathers no moss"; "A bird in the hand is worth two in the bush"; "The early bird catches the worm." While these sayings make literal sense (the grass you see from a distance *does* look greener than the grass under your feet), their meaning to a native speaker of English is clearly nonliteral. When we use them, we are making general and highly abstract observations about human attitudes and behavior. Yet strangely, these generalizations and abstractions are embodied in concrete and sensuous imagery. Try to explain what any of these expressions mean and you will quickly discover that you are using many more words and much vaguer language than the expression itself. This is precisely what happens when you try to put into your own words (paraphrase) a poem. Like poetry, these sayings rely on the figurative use of language.

Since poetry is an intense and heightened use of language that explores the worlds of feeling, it relies upon more frequent and original use of figurative language than does ordinary speech. One of the most common figurative devices, *metaphor*, where one thing is called something else, occurs frequently in ordinary speech. "School is a rat race," we say, or "He is a tower of strength," and the meaning is perfectly clear—too clear, perhaps, because these metaphors are so common and unoriginal they have lost what vividness they once had. But when John Donne says, "I am a little world made cunningly" or Henry David Thoreau declares, "I am a bundle of vain strivings," we have metaphors that are original and arresting (and provide the vehicle by which both authors define themselves). When W. H. Auden, commenting on the death of William Butler Yeats, says, "Let the Irish vessel lie / Emptied of his poetry," he pays a complex tribute to the great Irish poet.

Simile is closely related to metaphor. But where metaphor says that one thing is another, simile says that one thing is like another, as in Burns's "O My Luve's like a red, red rose" and Frost's "life is too much like a pathless wood." The distinction between simile and metaphor, while easy enough to make technically, is often difficult to distinguish in terms of effect. Frost establishes a comparison between life and a pathless wood and keeps the two even more fully separated by adding the qualifier "too much." Burns's simile maintains the same separation and, in addition, because it occurs in the opening line of the poem, eliminates any possible confusion the reader might experience if the line were, "O My Luve is a red, red rose." You can test the difference in effect by changing a metaphor into a simile or a simile into a metaphor to see if the meaning is in any way altered.

Another important use of figurative language is the *symbol*. In its broadest sense, a symbol is anything that stands for something else. In this sense, most words are symbolic: the word *tree* stands for an object in the real world. When we speak of a symbol in a literary work, however, we usually mean something more precise. In poetry, a symbol is an object or event that suggests more than itself. It is one of the most common and powerful devices available to the poet, for it allows him or her to convey economically and simply a wide range of meanings.

It is useful to distinguish between two kinds of symbols, *public symbols* and *contextual symbols*. Public symbols are those objects or events that history has invested with rich meanings and associations, for example, national flags or religious objects such as the cross. William Butler Yeats uses such a symbol in his poem "Sailing to Byzantium," drawing upon the celebrated and enduring art of the ancient Byzantine Empire as a symbol of timelessness. In "Curiosity," Alastair Reid uses cats and their proverbial curiosity to symbolize the kind of human beings who live the best and truest lives.

In contrast to public symbols, contextual symbols are objects or events that are symbolic by virtue of the poet's handling of them in a particular work— that is, by virtue of the context. Consider, for example, the opening lines of Robert Frost's "After Apple-Picking":

> My long two-pointed ladder's sticking through a tree
> Toward heaven still,
> And there's a barrel that I didn't fill
> Beside it, and there may be two or three
> Apples I didn't pick upon some bough.

The apple tree is a literal tree, but as one reads through the poem, it becomes clear that the apple tree symbolizes the speaker's life, with a wide range of possible meanings (do the few apples he hasn't picked symbolize the hopes, dreams, aspirations that even the fullest life cannot satisfy?).

Amy Lowell's "Patterns" is rich in symbols. The aristocratic speaker describes herself as walking down garden paths laid out in precise patterns. Her elegant gown is real; the path is a real path. But it quickly becomes apparent that her gown and the paths symbolize the narrowly restricted and oppressive life she is fighting against.

The paths in Amy Lowell's poem are clear and easily recognizable examples of contextual symbols. However, contextual symbols by their very nature tend to present more difficulties than public symbols, because recognizing them depends on a sensitivity to everything else in the poem. In T. S. Eliot's dense and difficult "The Love Song of J. Alfred Prufrock," the speaker twice says, "In the room the women come and go / Talking of Michelangelo," a baffling couplet because it seems to have no connection with what precedes and follows it. But once we see the pattern of religious imagery in the poem and recall that Michelangelo, one of the great Renaissance artists, created some of the greatest religious art of all time, including the *Pietà* of the Vatican and the paintings in the Sistine Chapel, we can at least begin to connect the couplet to the rest of the poem.

The reader who fails to recognize a symbol misses an important part of a poem's meaning. On the other hand, you want to avoid becoming so intent on finding symbolic meanings that you lose sight of the fact that an object must first have a literal meaning before it can function as a symbol. Or, to put it in terms of our earlier definition, an object or event must be itself before it can be something else. Finally, even careful readers may very well disagree on whether something should be taken as a symbol. When this occurs, the best criterion for judgment is probably, Does the symbolic interpretation add meanings to the poem that are consistent with other elements in the poem? As you will see in the "Glossary of Critical Approaches" (p. 1269), disagreement on virtually every matter of literary interpretation is a hallmark of modern theories of literature.

Music

The *music* of poetry, by which we mean the poetic use of all the devices of sound and rhythm inherent in language, is at once central to the poetic effect and yet the most difficult to account for. We can discuss the ways in which figurative language works with some clarity because we are using words to explain words. Any listener who has ever tried to explain the effect of a piece of music (or who has read music criticism) will be familiar with the problem of describing a nonverbal medium with words.

The possible musical effects of language are complex. The terms we have to describe various musical devices deal only with the most obvious and easily recognizable patterns. *Alliteration, assonance, consonance, caesura, meter, onomatopoeia, rhythm,* and *rhyme* (all of them defined in the Glossary of Literary Terms) are the key traditional terms for discussing the music of poetry. Along with the other terms already introduced, they are an indispensable part of the vocabulary one needs to discuss poetry. But the relationship between sound and sense is illustrated nicely in a celebrated passage from Alexander Pope's "An Essay on Criticism," in which his definitions of bad verse and then of well-managed verse are ingeniously supported by the music of the lines:

> These[1] equal syllables alone require,
> Though oft the ear the open vowels tire;
> While expletives their feeble aid do join;
> And ten low words oft creep in one dull line;
> While they ring round the same unvaried chimes,
> With sure returns of still expected rhymes;

---

[1] Bad poets.

Where 'er you find "the cooling western breeze,"
In the next line, it "whispers through the trees";
If crystal streams "with pleasing murmurs creep,"
The reader's threatened (not in vain) with "sleep";
Then, at the last and only couplet fraught
With some unmeaning thing they call a thought,
A needless Alexandrine[2] ends the song
That, like a wounded snake, drags its slow length along.

. . . . .

True ease in writing comes from art, not chance,
As those move easiest who have learned to dance.
'Tis not enough no harshness gives offense,
The sound must seem an echo to the sense:
Soft is the strain when Zephyr gently blows,
And the smooth stream in smoother numbers flows;
But when loud surges lash the sounding shore,
The hoarse, rough verse should like the torrent roar:
When Ajax[3] strives some rock's vast weight to throw,
The line too labors, and the words move slow;
Not so, when swift Camilla[4] scours the plain,
Flies o'er the unbending corn, and skims along the main.

When Pope speaks of open vowels, the line is loaded with open vowels. When Pope condemns the use of ten monosyllables, the line contains ten monosyllables. When Pope urges that the sound should echo the sense and speaks of the wind, the line is rich in sibilants that hiss, like the wind. When he speaks of Ajax striving, the combination of final consonants and initial sounds slow the line; when he speaks of Camilla's swiftness, the final consonants and initial sounds form liaisons that are swiftly pronounceable.

Or, consider the opening lines of Wilfred Owen's poem "Dulce et Decorum Est," describing a company of battle-weary World War I soldiers trudging toward their camp and rest:

Bent double, like old beggars under sacks,
Knock-kneed, coughing like hags, we cursed through sludge.

These lines are dominated by a series of harsh, explosive consonant sounds (*b, d, k, g*) that reinforce the meaning of the lines. More specifically, the first two syllables of each line are heavily stressed, which serves to slow the reading. And, finally, while the poem ultimately develops a prevailing meter, the meter is only faintly suggested in these opening lines, through the irregular rhythms used to describe a weary, stumbling march.

Let us remember, then, that analysis of musical (or for that matter any other)

---

[2] Twelve-syllable line.
[3] A Greek warrior celebrated for his strength.
[4] A swift-footed queen in Virgil's *Aeneid*.

devices can illuminate and enrich our understanding of poetry. But let us also remember that analysis has its limitations. Dylan Thomas once remarked:

> You can tear a poem apart to see what makes it technically tick and say to yourself when the works are laid out before you—the vowels, the consonants, the rhymes, and rhythms—"Yes, this is it. This is why the poem moves me so. It is because of the craftsmanship." But you're back where you began. The best craftsmanship always leaves holes and gaps in the works of the poem so that something that is not in the poem can creep, crawl, flash, or thunder in.

Another writer, X. J. Kennedy, puts the same idea with less reverence:

ARS POETICA   1985

The goose that laid the golden egg
Died looking up its crotch
To find out how its sphincter worked.
Would you lay well? Don't watch.

Reading Drama

Plays are fundamentally different from other literary forms. Unlike stories and poems, almost all plays are designed to be performed, not to be read. Thus, the reader (with the aid of some meager stage directions) must imagine the aural and the visual aspects of the drama, which should be at least as important as its dialogue. Great effort is invested in such matters as costuming, set design, lighting effects, and stage movement by the director and his or her staff; all of that effort is lost to the reader who must somehow contrive to supply imaginatively some of those dramatic features not contained on the printed page.

As much as possible, the way to read a play is to imagine that you are its director. Hence you will concern yourself with creating the set and the lighting. You will see people dressed so that their clothes give support to their words. You will think about timing—how long between events and speeches—and blocking—how the characters move as they interact on stage. Perhaps the best way to confront the literature of the stage, to respond most fully to what is there, is to attempt to produce some scenes in class or after class. If possible, attend the rehearsals of plays in production on the campus. Nothing will provide better insight into the complexities of the theater than attending a rehearsal where the problems are encountered and solved.

As an exercise, read the opening speeches of any of the plays here and make decisions. How should the lines be spoken (quietly, angrily, haltingly)? What should the characters do as they speak (remain stationary, look in some direction, traverse the stage)? How should the stage be lit (partially, brightly, in some color that contributes to the mood of the dialogue and action)? What should the characters who are not speaking do? What possibilities exist for conveying appropriate signals solely through gesture and facial expression—signals not contained in the words you read?

Staging

Since plays are written to be staged, the particular kind of theater available to the dramatist is often crucial to the structure of the play. The Greek theater of Dionysius in Athens, for which Sophocles wrote, was an open-air amphitheater seating about 14,000 people. (See p. 1262.) The skene, or stage house, from which actors entered, was fixed, though it might have had painted panels to suggest the scene. Consequently, there is no scene shifting in *Antigonê*. All the dialogue and action take place in the same location before the skene building, which represents the Palace of Creon. Important things happen elsewhere, but the audience is informed of these events by messenger. Three deaths occur, but none in sight of the audience, partly as a matter of taste and partly because the conditions of the Greek stage prevented the playwright from moving the action inside the palace or to that terrifying mausoleum where both Antigonê and her betrothed choose death before submission. Later dramatists, writing for a more flexible stage and a more intimate theater, were able to profit from the intensely dramatic nature of murder and suicide, but the Greeks, almost invariably, chose to tell, rather than show, the most gripping physical events in their stories.

Further, an outdoor theater of vast dimensions implies obvious restrictions on acting style. Facial expression can play no important role in such a theater, and, in fact, the actors of Sophoclean tragedy wore masks, larger than life and probably equipped with some sort of megaphone device to aid in voice projection. Those voices were denied the possibility of subtle variety in tone and expression, and the speeches were probably delivered in rather formal declamatory style. The characters wore special built-up footwear that made them larger than life. In addition to these limitations, Sophocles had as well to write within the formal limitations imposed by the Athenian government, which made available only three principal actors, all male, as the cast (exclusive of the chorus) for each play. Consequently, there are never more than three players on stage at once, and the roles are designed so that each actor takes several parts—signified by different masks. Yet, despite the austerity of production values, the unavoidable clumsiness of fortuitous messengers appearing at all the right moments, and the sharply restricted dramatis personae, among the few Greek plays that have survived are some still universally regarded as superlatively fine dramatic representations of tragic humanity.

Until recently we thought we had a clear conception of what Shakespeare's stage looked like. Scholarship has raised some doubts about this conception, but though we no longer accept the accuracy of the reconstruction shown here, we still have a good enough understanding of the shape of the playing area to recreate roughly the staging of a Shakespearean play. (See pp. 1262–1263.) That staging was altogether different from the Greek. Though both theaters were open air, the enclosure around the Elizabethan stage was much smaller and the audience capacity limited to something between 2,000 and 3,000. As in classical drama, men played all the roles, but they no longer wore masks, and a stage that protruded into the audience made for great intimacy. Hence the actors' art expanded to matters of facial expression, and the style of speech and movement was certainly closer than was Greek style to what we might loosely call realism. Shakespeare has Hamlet caution the actors: "Suit the action to the word, the word to the action, with this special observance, that you o'erstep not the modesty of nature: for anything so overdone is from the purpose of playing, whose end, both at first and now, was and is, to hold as 't were, the mirror up to nature. . . ." But the characteristic matter of Shakespearean tragedy certainly did not lend itself to a modern realistic style. Those great speeches are written in verse; they frequently are meant to augment the rather meager set design by providing verbal pictures to set the stage; they are much denser in texture, image, and import than is ordinary speech. These characteristics all serve to distinguish the Shakespearean stage from the familiar realism of most recent theater.

The Elizabethan stage made possible a tremendous versatility for the dramatist and the acting company. Most of the important action was played out on the uncurtained main platform, jutting into the audience and surrounded on three sides by spectators. The swiftly moving scenes followed each other without interruption, doubtless using different areas of the stage to signify different locations. There was some sort of terrace or balcony one story above the main stage, and there was an area at the back of the main protruding stage that could be curtained off when not in use. Although Shakespeare's plays are usually divided into five separate acts in printed versions, they were played straight through, without intermission, much like a modern motion picture.

Though more versatile and intimate than the Greek stage, the Elizabethan stage had limitations that clearly influenced the playwright. Those critical imperatives of time, place, and action (i.e., the time represented should not exceed one day, the location should be fixed in one place, and the action should be limited to one cohesive story line—one plot), the so-called unities that Aristotle discovered in the drama of Sophocles, may well reflect the physical conditions of the Greek theater. Elizabethan dramatists largely ignored them, and in *Othello* we move from Venice to Cyprus, from the fortifications of the island to the city streets to Desdemona's bedchamber. Certainly some props were used to suggest these locations, but nothing comparable to the furniture of Ibsen's nineteenth-century stage. Instead, the playwright often wove a sort of literary scenery into the speeches of the characters. For example, in *Othello*, Roderigo has occasion to say to Iago, "Here is her father's house; I'll call aloud." The second act of *Othello* opens with some gentlemen at "an open place near the Quay." Notice the dialogue:

> **Montano.** What from the cape can you discern at sea?
> **First Gentleman.** Nothing at all: it is a high-wrought flood;
>   I cannot 'twixt the heaven and the main
>   Descry a sail.
> **Montano.** Methinks the wind hath spoke aloud at land;
>   A fuller blast ne'er shook our battlements;
>   If it hath ruffian'd so upon the sea,
>   What ribs of oak, when mountains melt on them,
>   Can hold the mortise?

There is no sea, of course, and Elizabethan technology was not up to a wind machine. The men are, doubtless, looking offstage and creating the stormy setting through language. An open-air theater that played in daylight had few techniques for controlling lighting, and speeches had to be written to supply the effect:

> But look, the morn, in russet mantle clad,
> Walks o'er the dew of yon high eastern hill.

The ancient theater at Epidaurus, Greece

The Globe Theatre

Interior of the Swan Theatre, London, 1596

Hypothetical reconstruction of the interior of the Globe Theatre in the days of Shakespeare

A seventeenth-century French box stage

.her, the company had not the resources to place armies on the stage; hence,
.peaker in *King Henry V* boldly invites the audience to profit from imagination:

> Piece out our imperfections with your thoughts;
> Into a thousand parts divide one man,
> And make imaginary puissance;
> Think, when we talk of horses, that you see them
> Printing their proud hoofs i' the receiving earth.
> For 'tis your thoughts that now must deck our kings.

The theater in the Petit-Bourbon Palace, built about twenty-five years after
Shakespeare's death, was a forerunner of the common "box stage" on which so
much recent drama is acted. Essentially, this stage is a box with one wall
removed so that the audience can see into the playing area. (See p. 1263.) Such
a stage lends itself to realistic settings. Since the stage is essentially a room, it
can easily be furnished to look like one. If street scenes are required, painted
backdrops provide perspective and an accompanying sense of distance. Sets at
an angle to the edge of the stage might be constructed. The possibilities for
scenic design allowed by such a stage soon produced great set designers, and
the structure of such a stage led to the development of increasingly sophisticated
stage machinery, which in turn freed the dramatist from the physical limitations
imposed by earlier stages. By Ibsen's time the versatility of the box stage enabled
him to write elaborately detailed stage settings for the various locations in which
the drama unfolds. Further, the furnishing of the stage in Ibsen's plays sometimes functions symbolically to convey visually the choking quality of certain
bourgeois life-styles.

None of the historical stages has passed into mere history. The modern
theater still uses Greek amphitheaters such as that at Epidaurus, constructs
approximations of the Elizabethan stage for Shakespeare festivals, and employs
the box stage with ever-increasing inventiveness. Early in the twentieth century,
some plays were produced in the "round," the action taking place on a stage in
the center of the theater with the audience on all sides. A number of theaters
were built that incorporated a permanent in-the-round arrangement. But versatility has become so important to the modern production designer that some
feel the very best theater is simply a large empty room (with provisions for
technical flexibility in the matter of lighting) that can be rearranged to suit the
requirements of specific productions. This ideal of a "theater space" that can
be freely manipulated has become increasingly attractive—some have been
constructed—since it frees the dramatist and the performance from limitations
built into permanent stage design.

Drama and Society

The history of dramatic literature (like the history of literature in general)
provides evidence for another kind of history as well—the history of changing

attitudes, changing values, and even changing taste. In ancient Greece, in Elizabethan England when Shakespeare wrote his enduring tragedies, right up to the end of the eighteenth century, certain expectations controlled the nature of tragedy. Those expectations were discussed by Aristotle as early as 335 B.C.; they involved the fall of a noble figure from a high place. Such tragedy reflects important cultural attitudes. It flourished in conjunction with a certain sort of politics and certain notions about human nature. The largest part of an audience of several thousand Athenians in the fifth century B.C. was certainly not itself noble. Neither was Shakespeare's audience at the Globe Theatre in London. That audience, much as a modern audience, was composed of tradespeople, artisans, and petty officials. In Greece, even slaves attended the tragedy festivals. Why then were there no tragedies in which the central figure was a storekeeper, a baker, or a butcher?

There have been many attempts to answer this difficult question, and those answers tend to make assumptions about the way individuals see themselves and their society. If the butcher down the street dies, well, that is sad, but after all rather unimportant to society. If the king falls, however, society itself is touched, and a general grief prevails that makes possible sweeping observations about the chancy conditions of life. A culture always elevates some of its members to the status of heroes—often by virtue of the office they hold. Even now, societies are collectively moved, and moved profoundly, by the death of a president, a prime minister—a Kennedy, a de Gaulle, a Churchill—when they are not nearly so moved by immense disasters such as killing storms or earthquakes or civil wars. But things have changed.

New cultural values and new attitudes about human nature developed in the West during the nineteenth century, especially since the advent of industrialism and the publication of Freud's systematic observations about the way people's minds interact with their bodies. The result has been an increasing humanization of those who used to be heroes and an increasing realization of the capacity for heroism in those who are merely bakers and butchers. Thus Henrik Ibsen, frequently referred to as "the father of modern drama," can compel a serious emotional response from his audience over the tribulations of middle-class families. Such plays succeed in spite of their commonplace heroes because Western society can now accept the experiences of ordinary people as emblems of its own. Perhaps it can because modern political institutions have, at least theoretically, exalted the common person and rejected political aristocracy. Certainly the reasons for the change are complex. But it remains true that neither Sophocles nor Shakespeare could have written *An Enemy of the People*.

Dramatic Irony

Dramatic irony allows the audience to know more than the characters do about their own circumstances. Consequently, that audience *hears more* (the ironic component) than do the characters who speak. Shakespeare's *Othello* provides an excellent illustration of the uses of dramatic irony. At the end of Act II, Cassio, who has lost his position as Othello's lieutenant, asks Iago for advice on how to regain favor. Iago, who, unknown to Cassio, had engineered Cassio's disgrace, advises him to ask Desdemona, Othello's adored wife, to intervene. Actually this is good advice; ordinarily the tactic would succeed, so much does Othello love his wife and wish to please her. But Iago explains, in a soliloquy to the audience, that he is laying groundwork for the ruin of all the objects of his envy and hatred—Cassio, Desdemona, and Othello:

> . . . for while this honest fool
> Plies Desdemona to repair his fortunes,
> And she for him pleads strongly to the Moor,
> I'll pour this pestilence into his ear
> That she repeals him for her body's lust;
> And, by how much she strives to do him good,
> She shall undo her credit with the Moor.
> So will I turn her virtue into pitch,
> And out of her own goodness make the net
> That shall enmesh them all.

Of course Desdemona, Cassio, and Othello are ignorant of Iago's enmity. Worse, all of them consider Iago a loyal friend. But the audience knows Iago's design, and that knowledge provides the chilling dramatic irony of Act III, scene 3.

When Cassio asks for Desdemona's help, she immediately consents, declaring, "I'll intermingle every thing he does / With Cassio's suit." At this, the audience, knowing what it does, grows a little uneasy—that audience, after all, rather likes Desdemona and doesn't want her injured. As Iago and Othello come on stage, Cassio, understandably ill at ease, leaves at the approach of the commander who has stripped him of his rank, thus providing Iago with a magnificent tactical advantage. And as Cassio leaves, Iago utters an exclamation and four simple words that may rank among the most electrifying in all of English drama:

> Ha! I like not that.

They are certainly not very poetic words; they do not conjure up any telling images; they do not mean much either to Othello or Desdemona. But they are for the audience the intensely anticipated first drop of poison. Othello hasn't heard clearly:

> What dost thou say?

Maybe it all will pass, and Iago's clever design will fail. But what a hiss of held breath the audience expels when Iago replies:

> Nothing, my lord: or if—I know not what.

And Othello is hooked:

Was not that Cassio parted from my wife?

The bait taken, Iago begins to play his line:

Cassio, my lord? No, sure, I cannot think it,
That he would steal away, so guilty-like,
Seeing you coming.

And from this point on in the scene, Iago cleverly and cautiously leads Othello. He assumes the role of Cassio's great friend—reluctant to say anything that might cast suspicion on him. But he is also the "friend" of Othello and cannot keep silent his suspicions. So honest Iago (he is often called "honest" by the others in the play), apparently full of sympathy and kindness, skillfully brings the trusting Othello to emotional chaos. And every word they exchange is doubly meaningful to the audience, which perceives Othello led on the descent into a horrible jealousy by his "friend." The scene ends with Othello visibly shaken and convinced of Desdemona's faithlessness and Cassio's perfidy:

Damn her, lewd minx! O, damn her!
Come, go with me apart; I will withdraw,
To furnish me with some swift means of death
For the fair devil. Now art thou my lieutenant.

To which Iago replies:

I am your own for ever.

Now, all of Iago's speeches in this scene operate on the audience through dramatic irony. The tension, the horror, the urge to cry out, to save Cassio, Desdemona, and Othello from the devilish Iago—all the emotional tautness in the audience results from irony, from knowing what the victims do not know. The play would have much less force if the audience did not know Iago's intentions from the outset and did not anticipate as he bends so many innocent events to his own increasingly evil ends. Note that dramatic irony is not limited to the drama; poetry, sometimes (as in William Blake's "The Chimney Sweeper"), and fiction, often (as in Frank O'Connor's "My Oedipus Complex"), make use of this technique. But dramatic irony is the special tool of the dramatist, well suited to produce an electric tension in a live audience that overhears the interaction of people on stage.

Drama and Its Audience

Scholarly ordering that identifies the parts of drama and discusses the perceptive distinctions made by Aristotle among its parts can help you confront a play and understand how your responses were triggered by the playwright, the designers of the play, and the performers. But such analysis cannot substitute for the emotional experience produced by successful drama. Plays, perhaps more than other art forms, address the complex mélange of belief, attitude, intellect, and awareness that constitutes a human psyche. As in *Antigonê*, sometimes the play torments its audience by imposing on a courageous central character a duty that must be performed and must end in tragic death. Sometimes, as in Susan Glaspell's *Trifles*, the play mocks widely held cultural values—the notion that women are less rational than men—and compels the audience to reexamine some of its fundamental values. If, in our humanity, we did not share the capacity for possessive love as well as jealousy, with all its terror, all its threat to self-esteem, then the tragedy of *Othello* would be incomprehensible.

A lyric poem may simply meditate on the transience of life or express the pain of love unrequited. Plays, however, set characters within demanding social and cultural settings. Those cultural imperatives create dissatisfaction and conflict that may lead to a heightened awareness of or an insight into one's own limitations. What happens when the viewer's (or reader's) assumptions and beliefs conflict with those embodied in the play? If we do not believe that the world is ruled by the gods or a God, can we appreciate *Oedipus Rex* or *No Exit*? Such questions cannot be answered easily. We can say, however, that one of the functions of art is to force us to reexamine our most cherished abstract beliefs in the revealing light of the artist's work. Thus Bernard Shaw's *Major Barbara* forces us to reassess simplistic attitudes about the "goodness" of charitable works and the "badness" of munitions manufacturers and enables us to recognize the complex nature of evil, morality, and compassion.

Glossary of Critical Approaches

Introduction

This alphabetically arranged glossary attempts to define, briefly and in general terms, some major critical approaches to literature. Because literary criticism has to do with the *value* of literature, not with its history, judgments tend to be subjective and disagreements frequent and even acrimonious. The truth of a work of art is, obviously, very different from the truth of a mathematical formula. Certainly one's attitudes toward war, religion, sex, and politics are irrelevant to the truth of a formula but quite relevant to one's judgment of a literary work.

Yet any examination of the broad range of literary criticism reveals that groups of critics (and all readers, ultimately, are critics) share certain assumptions about literature. These shared assumptions govern the way critics approach a work, the elements they tend to look for and emphasize, the details they find significant or insignificant, and, finally, the overall value they place on the work.

We do not suggest that one approach is more valid than another or that the lines dividing the various approaches are always clear and distinct. Readers will, perhaps, discover one approach more congenial to their temperament, more "true" to their sense of the world, than another. More likely, they will find themselves utilizing more than one approach in dealing with a single work. Many of the diverse approaches described here actually overlap, and even those critics who champion a single abstract theory often draw on a variety of useful approaches when they write about a particular work.

Formalist critics assume that a literary text remains independent of the writer who created it. The function of the critic, then, is to discover how the author has deployed language to create (or perhaps failed to create) a formal and aesthetically satisfying structure. The influential American formalists of the 1940s and 1950s (the New Critics) were fond of describing literary texts as "autonomous," meaning that political, historical, biographical, and other considerations were always secondary if not irrelevant to any discussion of the work's merits.

Further, formalist critics argue, the various elements of a "great" work interweave to create a seamless whole that embodies "universal" values. Unsurprisingly, the "universal" values formalist critics praise, upon close analysis, tend to parallel the moral, political, and cultural ideals of the critics' social class.

But the formalist point of view, cherishing the artwork's structure, spawned its own antithesis—a group of theorists called *deconstructionists*. These writers argued that language itself was too shifty to support the expectations of formalist criticism. One reader might read a sentence literally, while another might read it ironically. Hence, their "understanding" of the text would be diametrically opposed.

The deconstructionists believe that intelligent, well-educated readers cannot be expected to ignore those responses that interfere with some "correct" or "desirable" reading of the piece. Given what they see as the notoriously ambiguous and unstable nature of language, deconstructionist critics argue that a literary text can never really be absolutely known. They, unlike the formalists, who search for coherence in texts, almost playfully insist on a (sometimes quite significant) incoherence in texts that, by their very nature, can have no fixed meaning.

While the formalists and deconstructionists wrestle over the philosophy of language and its implications for the nature of literary texts, other critics pursue quite different primary interests. The literary critic Wayne Booth, in his book *The Company We Keep: An Ethics of Fiction* (1988), examines the meaning and relevance of "ethical criticism," which he characterizes as "this most important of all forms of criticism." The term *ethical criticism* describes a variety of approaches, all of which argue that literature, like any other human activity, connects to the real world and, consequently, influences real people.

Ethical criticism may range from a casual appraisal of a work's moral content to the more rigorous and systematic analysis driven by a coherent set of stated beliefs and assumptions. A religious critic (committed to certain moral positions) might attack a work—regardless of its artfulness or brilliance—because it does not condemn adultery. A *feminist* critic might focus on the way literary works devalue women, a *black* critic on the way they stereotype blacks, a *Marxist* critic on the way they support class divisions, a new historicist critic on the way a dominant class interprets history to protect its own interests. But all of them agree that literary works invite ethical judgments. Most of them also agree that literary works must be judged as another means by which a society both defines and perpetuates its political institutions and cultural values. The feminist, the black, and the Marxist critics would also agree that the political institutions and cultural values of most Western societies have been carefully designed to serve the interests of a dominant class: male, white, and wealthy.

Other critical approaches analyze literary works from yet other perspectives. *Reader-response* critics assert that a work of art is created as much by its audience as by the artist. For these critics, art has no significant abstract existence—a reader's experience of the work gives birth to it and contributes crucially to its power and value. Further, since each reader embodies a unique set of experiences and values, each reader's response to the work will give birth to a unique, personal artwork. Beauty is in the eye of the beholder. *Psychoanalytic* criticism, similar to reader-response, is nevertheless distinctive in its application of psychoanalytic principles to works of art. Those principles, originally, were derived from the work of Sigmund Freud (1856–1939), but now often reflect the views of more recent theorists such as Jacques Lacan and others. There is, finally, the recently emergent approach called *new historical* criticism, which brings historical knowledge to bear on the analysis of literary works in new and sophisticated ways. The result is a sometimes dizzying proliferation of analyses that argue for the relationship between literature and life.

The glossary that follows, along with the quotations, reveals the widely diverse and often contradictory views expressed by professional theorists and critics.

There is, first, the literature of knowledge; and, secondly, the literature of power. The function of the first is—to teach; the function of the second is—to move: the first is a rudder; the second an oar or a sail. The first speaks to mere discursive understanding; the second speaks, ultimately, it may happen, to the higher understanding or reason, but always through affections of pleasure and sympathy. . . . It is in relation to [the] great moral capacities of man that the literature of power, as contradistinguished from that of knowledge, lives and has its field of action.

THOMAS DE QUINCEY, "THE LITERATURE OF KNOWLEDGE AND THE LITERATURE OF POWER" (1848)

The Affective Fallacy is a confusion between the poem and its results (what it is and what it does). . . . It begins by trying to derive the standard of criticism from the psychological effect of the poem and ends in impressionism and relativism.

W. K. WIMSATT, JR., "THE AFFECTIVE FALLACY," IN *THE VERBAL ICON* (1954)

There is no such thing as a literary work or tradition which is valuable in itself, regardless of what anyone might have said or come to say about it. "Value" is a transitive term: it means whatever is valued by certain people in specific situations, according to particular criteria and in light of given purposes. . . . There is no such thing as literature which is "really" great or "really" anything, independently of the ways in which that writing is treated within specific forms of social or institutional life.

TERRY EAGLETON, *LITERARY THEORY: AN INTRODUCTION* (1983)

Deconstructionism This approach grew out of the work of certain twentieth-century European philosophers, notably the Frenchman Jacques Derrida, whose study of language led to the conclusion that since we could only know through the medium of language and language is unstable and ambiguous, it is impossible to talk about truth and knowledge and meaning in any absolute sense. Verbal structures, these critics maintained, inevitably contained within themselves oppositions. Derrida asserted that in the Western world, language leads us to think in terms of opposites (soul/body, man/woman, master/slave, etc.) that imply what he called "a violent hierarchy" with one of the terms (the first) always being superior to the other (the second). The aim of deconstruction is to show that this hier-archy of values cannot be permanent and absolute.

Intelligent and well-educated readers therefore cannot be expected to ignore the oppositions and contradictions in a text just because they do not contribute to some "correct" or "desirable" reading of the piece which might uphold a particular political, social, or cultural view.

Formalism assures us that the successful artist is the master of language and that he or she consciously deploys all its resources to achieve a rich and unified work. Sensitive and intelligent readers can aspire to a complete understanding of a work undistorted by their own idiosyncrasies, subjective states, or ideological biases.

Rejecting the formalist assumption about authorial control and conscious design, deconstruction attempts to show that by its very nature, language is constantly "saying" more than the writer can control or even know. Thus, a close study of any text (literary or otherwise) will reveal contradictory and irreconcilable elements.

Deconstructionist critics do not necessarily reject the validity of feminist, Marxist, formalist, and other critical approaches. In fact, they often draw upon the insights furnished by them. But the deconstructionist critic says that any discourse or critical approach that fails to recognize the inherently shifting and unstable nature of language is bound to produce only a partial if not misleading interpretation. For example, in his study *America the Scrivener: Deconstruction and the Subject of Literary Studies* (1990), Gregory S. Jay finds Emily Grierson, the protagonist of William Faulkner's story "A Rose for Emily," a "puzzle" and warns against simplistic interpretations:

As feminist subject, her story speaks of a revolutionary subversion of patriarchy; as herself, a figure of racial and class power, Emily also enacts the love affair of patriarchy with its own past, despite all the signs of decline and degradation. She is a split subject, crossed by rival discourses. What the text forces us to think, then, is the complex and ironic alliances between modes of possession and subjection, desire and ownership, identity and position.

Like Marxism and feminism, deconstruction defines itself both as a critical theory of literature and as a philosophy of human values. Hence, it is applicable, not only to literature, but also to an understanding of the power relations among humans and the societies they create. In insisting that we recognize the way language embodies and supports class, gender, and other biases, deconstruction challenges both the ethnocentrism of political structures and the idea of "universal values" in literary works.

Deconstruction is not synonymous with destruction. . . . It is in fact much closer to the original meaning of the word analysis, which etymologically means "to undo"—a virtual synonym for "to de-construct." The de-construction of a text does not proceed by random doubt or arbitrary subversion, but by the careful teasing out of warring forces of signification within the text itself. If anything is destroyed in reading, it is not the text, but the claim to unequivocal domination of one mode of signifying over another.

BARBARA JOHNSON, *THE CRITICAL DIFFERENCE* (1980)

Deconstructive criticism does not present itself as a novel enterprise. There is, perhaps, more of a relentless focus on certain questions, and a new rigor when it comes to the discipline of close reading. Yet to suggest that meaning and language do not coincide, and to draw from that a peculiar strength, is merely to restate what literature has always revealed. There is the difference, for instance, between sound and sense, which both stimulates and defeats writers. Or the difference which remains when we try to reduce metaphorical expressions to the proper terms they have displaced. Or the difference between a text and the commentaries that elucidate it, and which accumulate as a variorum of readings that cannot all be reconciled.

GEOFFREY HARTMAN, *DECONSTRUCTION AND CRITICISM* (1984)

Feminist Criticism   Feminist critics hold that literature is merely one of many expressions of a patriarchal society whose purpose is to keep women subordinate to men. Thus literature, in the way it portrays gender roles, helps to condition women to accept as normal a society that directs them to become nurses rather than doctors, secretaries rather than attorneys or corporate executives, sex symbols rather than thinkers, elementary school teachers rather than university professors. Beyond this general critique of patriarchy, feminists differ in their detailed analyses. Some have reexamined history to show that a literary canon created by males has slighted and ignored female authors. Others, studying canonical works from a feminist perspective, have come up with fresh readings that challenge conventional interpretations, focusing on how women are empowered *in* literary texts or *through* writing literary texts. Some, believing that language itself allows men to impose their power, use literary analyses to expose the gender bias of language. Why, they ask, is the English language so rich in words to describe a quarrelsome, abusive woman ("shrew," "harridan," "termagant") but so lacking in comparable terms for men? Some feminists believe that the male bias of language, far deeper than mere words, is actually structural. The constellation of qualities connoted by "masculine" and "feminine," they say, reveals how deeply the positive (male) and negative (female) values are embedded in the language.

While a psychoanalytic critic might use Freud's Oedipal theories to explain Emily's relationship to Homer Barron in William Faulkner's "A Rose for Emily," the feminist critic Judith Fetterley maintains that the explanation is to be found in the fact that a patriarchal culture instills in us the notion "that men and women are made for each other" and that "'masculinity' and 'femininity' are the natural reflection of that divinely ordained complement." In a society where there is "a massive differentiation of everything according to sex," one sees that in reality a sexist culture is one in which men and women are not simply incompatible but murderously so. . . . Emily murders Homer Barron because she must at any cost get a man" (*The Resisting Reader: A Feminist Approach to American Fiction,* 1978).

The objection to their voting is the same as is urged, in the lobbies of legislatures against clergymen who take an active part in politics;—that if they are good clergymen they are unacquainted with the expediencies of politics, and if they become good politicians they are worse clergymen. So of women, that they cannot enter this arena without being contaminated and unsexed.

> RALPH WALDO EMERSON, "WOMAN"
> (A LECTURE READ BEFORE THE
> WOMAN'S RIGHTS CONVENTION,
> BOSTON, SEPTEMBER 20, 1855)

Feminine work has always been ahistorical by the definition of male historians: raising children and keeping house have customarily been viewed as timeless routines capable of only minor variations.

> ANN DOUGLAS, *THE FEMINIZATION*
> *OF AMERICAN CULTURE* (1977)

She [Emily Dickinson] was neither a professional poet nor an amateur; she was a private poet who wrote indefatigably as some women cook or knit. Her gift for words and the cultural predicament of her time drove her to poetry instead of antimacassars.

> R. P. BLACKMUR, "EMILY
> DICKINSON" (1937)

Literature is political. It is painful to have to insist on this fact, but the necessity of such insistence indicates the dimensions of the problem. John Keats once objected to poetry "that has a palpable design upon us." The major works of American fiction constitute a series of designs on the female reader, all the more potent in their effect because they are "impalpable." One of the main things that keeps the design of our literature unavailable to the consciousness of the woman reader, and hence impalpable, is the very posture of the apolitical, the pretense that literature speaks universal truths through forms from which all the merely personal, the purely subjective, has been burned away or at least transformed through the medium of art into the representative. . . .

JUDITH FETTERLEY, *THE RESISTING READER: A FEMINIST APPROACH TO AMERICAN FICTION* (1978)

The intellectual trajectory of feminist criticism has taken us from a concentration on women's literary subordination, mistreatment, and exclusion, to the study of women's separate literary traditions, to an analysis of the symbolic construction of gender and sexuality within literary discourse. It is now clear that what we are demanding is a new universal literary history and criticism that combines the literary experiences of both women and men, a complete revolution in the understanding of our literary heritage.

ELAINE SHOWALTER, *THE NEW FEMINIST CRITICISM* (1985)

Formalist Criticism Like deconstruction, formalism focuses on the ambiguous and multilayered nature of language but does so in order to achieve the precisely opposite effect. Formalism assures us that the successful artist is the master of language and consciously deploys all its resources to achieve a rich and unified work. Sensitive and intelligent readers can aspire to a complete understanding of a work undistorted by their own idiosyncrasies or subjective states or ideological biases. The formalist rejects the central tenet of the reader-response critic, that a work comes into existence, so to speak, through the interaction of the reader with the work. For the formalist, the work exists independent of any particular reader. The work is a structured and formal aesthetic object comprising such elements as symbol, image, and sound patterns. Political, biographical, or historical considerations not embodied in the work itself are irrelevant.

The formalist sees literature as a sort of Platonic ideal form—immutable and objective. Works close to that ideal are praised for their aesthetic energy and their "universality" (a characteristic of the greatest literature). Works that do not exhibit this prized formal coherence are dispraised, and often dismissed as neither "universal" nor important. Because formalism focuses on the internal structure of literature above all else, it rejects didactic works. During the 1940s and 1950s, when the New Critics (as the formalists were called) dominated academic literary criticism, social protest writing was generally dismissed as subliterary because it lacked the "universality" of great literature. What was important in a work of art was not that it might change people's behavior, but that its parts coalesced into a beautiful whole. Consider the following comment by two formalist critics on Nathaniel Hawthorne's "Young Goodman Brown":

The dramatic impact [of "Young Goodman Brown"] would have been stronger if Hawthorne had let the incidents tell their own story: Goodman Brown's behavior to his neighbors and finally to his wife show us that he is a changed man. Since fiction is a kind of shorthand of human behavior and one moment may represent years in a man's life, we would have concluded that the change was to last his entire life. But Hawthorne's weakness for moralizing and his insufficient technical equipment betray him into the anticlimax of the last paragraph.

CAROLINE GORDON AND ALLEN TATE, *THE HOUSE OF FICTION* (1950)

Black writers and critics, for example, especially complained that the criterion of universality was merely a way of protecting "white," conservative social and political dominance. The New Critics dismissed black literature that sought to deal with racism and the struggle for equality as mere didacticism or agitprop, not to be compared with the great "white" literary productions that achieved "universal" import. In a seminal work of New Criticism published in 1952, the influential critic R. P. Blackmur dismissed *Native Son*, a powerful and now classic novel about white racism, as "one of those books in which everything is undertaken with seriousness except the writing."

All art constantly aspires towards the condition of music.

WALTER PATER, *STUDIES IN THE*
HISTORY OF THE RENAISSANCE
(1873)

Poetry is not a turning loose of emotion, but an escape from emotion; it is not the expression of personality, but an escape from personality.

T. S. ELIOT, "TRADITION AND THE
INDIVIDUAL TALENT," FROM *THE*
SACRED WOOD (1920)

Modern criticism, through its exacting scrutiny of literary texts, has demonstrated with finality that in art beauty and truth are indivisible and one. The Keatsian overtones of these terms are mitigated and an old dilemma solved if for beauty we substitute form, and for truth, content. We may, without risk of loss, narrow them even more, and speak of technique and subject matter. Modern criticism has shown us that to speak of content as such is not to speak of art at all, but of experience; and that it is only when we speak of the achieved content, the form, the work of art as a work of art, that we speak as critics. The difference between content, or experience, and achieved content, or art, is technique.

MARK SCHORER, "TECHNIQUE AS
DISCOVERY" (1948)

*A poem should not mean
But be.*

ARCHIBALD MACLEISH, FROM
"ARS POETICA" (1926)

Marxist Criticism The Marxist critic sees literature as one activity among many to be studied and judged in terms of a larger and all-encompassing ideology derived from the economic, political, and social doctrines of Karl Marx (1818–1883). Marxism offers a comprehensive theory about the nature of humans and the way in which a few of them manage to seize control of the means of production and thereby exploit the masses of working people. But Marxism is about more than analysis. As Karl Marx himself said, "It is not enough to analyze society; we must also change it."

The Marxist critic analyzes literary works to show how, wittingly or unwittingly, they support the dominant social class, or how they, in some way, contribute to the struggle against oppression and exploitation. And since the Marxist critic views literature as just one among the variety of human activities that reflect power relations and class divisions, he or she is likely to be more interested in what a work says than in its formal structure.

The Marxist argues that one cannot properly understand a literary work unless one understands how it reflects the relationship between economic production and social class. Further, this relationship cannot be explored adequately without examining a range of questions that other critical approaches, notably formalism, deem irrelevant. How does the work relate to the profit-driven enterprise of publishing? What does the author's biography reveal about his or her class biases? Does the work accurately portray the class divisions of society? Does the work expose the economic bases of oppression and advance the cause of liberation?

And since Marxist critics see their duty—indeed, the duty of all responsible and humane people—as not merely to describe the world but to change it, they will judge literature by the contribution it makes to bringing about revolution or in some way enlightening its readers about oppression and the necessity for class struggle.

For example, a Marxist critic's analysis of Matthew Arnold's poem "Dover Beach" might see it not as a brilliantly structured pattern of images and sounds but as the predictable end product of a dehumanizing capitalist economy in which a small class of oligarchs is willing, at whatever cost, to protect its wealth and power. The Marxist critic, as a materialist who believes that humans make their own history, would find Arnold's reference to "the eternal note of sadness" (line 14) a mystic evasion of the real sources of his alienation and pain: Arnold's misery can be clearly and unmystically explained by his fearful responses to the socioeconomic conditions of his time.

Arnold's refusal to face this fact leads him to the conclusion typical of a bourgeois artist-intellectual who cannot discern the truth. But the cure for Arnold's pain, the Marxist would argue, cannot be found in a love relationship, because relations between people are determined crucially by socioeconomic conditions. The cure for the pain he describes so well will be found in the world of action, in the struggle to create a society that is just and humane. "Dover Beach," the Marxist critic would conclude, is both a brilliant evocation of the alienation and misery caused by a capitalist economy and a testimony to the inability of a bourgeois intellectual to understand what is responsible for his feelings.

The methods of formal analysis are necessary, but insufficient. You may count up the alliterations in popular proverbs, classify metaphors, count up the number of vowels and consonants in a wedding song. It will undoubtedly enrich our knowledge of folk art, in one way or anther; but if you don't know the peasant system of sowing, and the life that is based on it, if you don't know the part the scythe plays, and

if you have not mastered the meaning of the church calendar to the peasant, or the time when the peasant marries, or when the peasant women give birth, you will have only understood the outer shell of folk art, but the kernel will not have been reached.

> LEON TROTSKY, *LITERATURE AND REVOLUTION* (1925)

When we say that the relationship between literature and reality is important for the Marxist critic, we do not mean that one goes to literature for illustration of knowledge that can be derived just as well from other sources, from the sciences or Marxist theory, for example. On the contrary, one looks to the arts as an independent way of discovering and knowing the truth about man and society; the knowledge that comes from this source is unique and indispensable, not simply a substitute for some other kind of knowledge.

> GAYLOR C. LE ROY AND URSULA BEITZ, *PRESERVE AND CREATE: ESSAYS ON MARXIST LITERARY CRITICISM* (1973)

Marxist criticism is part of a larger body of theoretical analysis which aims to understand ideologies—the ideas, values and feelings by which men experience their societies at various times. And certain of those ideas, values and feelings are available to us only in literature. To understand ideologies is to understand both the past and the present more deeply; and such understanding contributes to our liberation.

> TERRY EAGLETON, *MARXISM AND LITERARY CRITICISM* (1976)

My present judgment is that it [Marxist literary theory] can be made to work and that, together with feminism (a problematic "together"), it is the only body of thought capable of giving theoretical guidance to socialist practice (and this includes guidance in the struggle against the repressive regimes of state capitalism and authoritarian party structures). In particular, it is a compelling alternative to the various forms of liberal humanism which in their indefinite deferral of political positioning have been able to offer no serious resistance to the depredations of a power which is neither liberal nor humane.

JOHN FROW, *MARXISM AND LITERARY HISTORY* (1986)

New Historical Criticism   There is nothing "new" about historians drawing upon literary works as significant documents to support and illuminate historical analysis; nor is there anything "new" about literary critics drawing upon history to illuminate literary works. For the historian, Sophocles' *Oedipus Rex* and *Antigonê* tell us much about the conflict between the old-time religion and the new secularism in fifth-century B.C. Athens. The literary critic of *Othello* goes to the historian to understand the way in which Shakespeare and his contemporaries viewed black Africans. But until recently, the provinces of the historian and of the literary critics were pretty much mutually exclusive.

The new historians (influenced by modern theories of language and literature) began to question the very idea of history as it had been practiced. The historians of the past tended, for the most part, to think of history in terms of overarching themes and theses, and attempted to understand it in terms of some perceived "Geist" or "spirit" of the time. This kind of history was often linked to nationalism. Hence (for one example), nineteenth-century Americans created the idea of Manifest Destiny, and then used it to explain and justify the Western movement and its attendant atrocities. When the Nazis came to power in Germany, they developed the idea that "true" Germans were descended from a superior Aryan race,

and then used that idea to deprive "inferior races" of civil rights, of property, and, finally, of life.

More abstractly, the purpose of writing history was to articulate and reinforce the values and beliefs that gave a culture unity. By that means, some new historians note, history became the story (and the ideas and beliefs and culture) of the rich, the powerful, the privileged, the victorious. The new historians see history not as the search for some grand, unifying thesis but as the articulation of the various kinds of "discourse" that compete with, contradict, overlap, and modify one another in the constant struggle for dominance. Indeed, the new historians, influenced by deconstructionist views of language, came to question the very idea of historical "truth."

The new historians also reject the traditional division between history and other disciplines, appropriating to historical studies many kinds of texts—including literary texts—that traditional historians left to others. These critics assert that without an understanding of the historical context that produced it, no work of literature could really be understood and, therefore, literature "belongs" as much to the historian as to the literary critic. Such critics aim at what they call a "thick" description of a literary work, one that brings to bear on a text as much information as can be gathered about every aspect of the author, his work, and his times. For example, Thomas McGann in *The Beauty of Inflections* (1985) shows how the literary journal in which Keats published his "Ode on a Grecian Urn" tells us something important about the meaning of the poem.

Finally, it should be noted that new historicism has developed only recently and cannot be defined in detail. While its practitioners generally share the fundamental ideas outlined above, they can differ widely in the tools and methodologies they bring to bear on a literary text. That is to say, a new historian may also be a Marxist, feminist, or deconstructionist.

The burden of the past that weighs like a nightmare on the brain of the West is an imperial burden, the anxiety that it might not all be of one piece, that secret histories, forgotten facts, other imaginations operate in all that we do and make, and that our massive ignorance of Othernesses is working to undermine what we do. Like Napoleon moving inexorably towards the capture of Moscow, Great Traditions follow their difficult and equivocal victories of imagination to an ultimate destruction.

JEROME MCGANN, "THE THIRD
WORLD OF CRITICISM" (1989)

. . . What is at stake in today's cultural debates is whether or not it is appropriate to raise questions of power, domination, exclusion, and emancipation in conjunction with the study of literature.

BROOK THOMAS, *THE NEW HISTORI-
CISM AND OTHER OLD-FASHIONED
TOPICS* (1991)

Psychoanalytic Criticism Psychoanalytic criticism always proceeds from a set of principles that describes the inner life of all men and women. Though differing psychological theorists argue for diverse views, all analysts and all psychoanalytic critics assume that the development of the psyche is analogous to the development of the body. Doctors can provide charts indicating physical growth stages; analysts can supply similar charts indicating stages in the growth of the psyche. Sigmund Freud, for all practical purposes, invented psychoanalysis by creating a theoretical model for the human (mostly male) psyche.

The Oedipus complex is a significant element in that model. Freud contends that everyone moves through a childhood stage of erotic attachment to the parent of the opposite sex, and an accompanying hostility and aggression against the parent of the same sex, who is seen as a rival. Such feelings, part of the natural biography of the psyche, pass or are effectively controlled in most cases. But sometimes, the child grown to adulthood is still strongly gripped by the Oedipal mode, which then may result in neurotic or even psychotic behavior.

A famous analysis of Shakespeare's *Hamlet* argues that he is best understood as gripped by Oedipal feelings—Hamlet hates Claudius not as the murderer of his father but as the interloper between Hamlet and his mother. But how could Shakespeare create an Oedipal Hamlet when Freud was not to be born for some two and a half centuries? The answer is that Freud did not invent the Oedipus complex—he simply described it. It was always there, especially noticeable in the work of great literary artists who, in every era, demonstrate a special insight into the human condition.

Along with Oedipal feelings, the psyche inevitably embodies aggressive feelings—the urge to attack those who exercise authority, who deny us our primal desires. For the young, the authority figure is frequently a parent. Adults must deal with police, government officials, the boss at the office. As far back as the Hebrew Bible story of the Tower of Babel and the old Greek myths in which the giant Titans, led by Cronus, overthrow their father, Uranus, and Zeus and the Olympians subsequently overthrow Cronus, there appears evidence of the rebellion against the parent-authority figure. Freud views that aggressive hostility as another component of the developing psyche. But, in the interest of civilization, society has developed ways to control that aggressiveness.

Freud saw us as divided selves. An unconscious *id* struggles to gratify aggressive and erotic primal urges, while a *superego* (roughly what society calls "conscience"), by producing guilt feelings, struggles to control the id. The *ego* (the self) is defined by the struggle. Thus the Freudian psychoanalytic critic is constantly aware that authors and their characters suffer and resuffer a primal tension that results from the conflict between psychic aggressions and social obligations.

Freud has been succeeded by a number of psychological theorists who present quite different models of the psyche—and recent literary theory has responded to these post-Freudian views. Among the most important are Carl Gustav Jung (1875–1961), who argued that there exists a collective (as well as a racial and individual) unconscious. Residing there are archetypes—original patterns—that emerge into our consciousness in the form of shadowy images that persistently appear and reappear in literature (for example, the search for the father, death and resurrection, the quest, and the double).

The psychoanalytic critic understands literature in terms of the psychic models that Freud and others defined. Originally, such critics tended to analyze literature in an attempt to identify the author's neuroses. More recently, psychoanalytic critics have argued that the symptoms they discover in works allow us to tap into and, perhaps, resolve our own neuroses.

. . . *"Cinderella" cannot fail to activate in us those emotions and unconscious ideals which, in our inner experience, are connected with our feelings of sibling rivalry. From his own experience with it, the child might well understand—without "knowing" anything about it—the welter of inner experiences connected with Cinderella. Recalling, if she is a girl, her repressed wishes to get rid of Mother and have Father all to herself, and now feeling guilty about such "dirty" desires, a girl may well "understand" why a mother would send her daughter out of sight to reside among cinders, and prefer her other children. Where is the child who has not wished to be able to banish a parent at*

some time, and who does not feel that in retaliation he merits the same fate? And where is the child who has not wanted to wallow to his heart's desire in dirt or mud; and, being made to feel dirty by parental criticism in consequence, become convinced that he deserves nothing better than to be relegated to a dirty corner?

> BRUNO BETTELHEIM, *THE USES OF*
> *ENCHANTMENT: THE MEANING AND*
> *IMPORTANCE OF FAIRY TALES* (1977)

. . . *Modern culture has become increasingly differentiated from traditional societies by the enormous enlargement of fictions through the fiction-producing qualities of the media. Newspapers, popular magazines, movies, and, most of all, television have so flooded modern culture with fictions that many people have difficulty distinguishing between social relations that are real and those that are fantasized. "Fictive culture" more accurately describes contemporary social life than do such phrases as "narcissistic," "minimalist," or "post-modern" culture; for the profusion of fictions is central to the creativity—and the crisis—of our modern condition.*

> JAY MARTIN, *WHO AM I THIS TIME?*
> *UNCOVERING THE FICTIVE*
> *PERSONALITY* (1988)

Reader-response Criticism   Reader-response criticism (also called transactional theory) emerged in the 1970s as one of the many challenges to formalist principles. Reader-response critics focus on the interaction between the work and the reader, holding that, in a sense, a work exists only when it is experienced by the reader. If the work exists only in the mind of the reader, the reader becomes an active participant in the creative process rather than a passive receptacle for an "autonomous" work. The creation of a work thus becomes a dynamic enterprise between the reader and the text, each acting on the other. The study of the affective power of a work becomes not a "fallacy," as formalism holds, but the central focus of criticism. The task of the critic is to investigate this dynamic relationship between reader and text in order to discover how it works.

We know that various readers respond differently to the same text. In fact, the same reader might respond to the text quite differently at a different time. The reader-response critic wants to know why. In what ways do such conditions as age, gender, upbringing, and race account for differing responses? Does the reader's mood at the time of reading make a difference? If you accept the principles of reader-response criticism, the inevitable conclusion—*reductio ad absurdum*, its critics would say—is that there is no limit to the possible readings of any text. Consequently, many reader-response critics qualify the intense subjectivity of their approach by admitting that an "informed" or "educated" reader is likely to produce a more "valid" reading than an "uninformed" or "uneducated" one.

"Gaps" or "blanks" in literary texts provide particular opportunities to readers. Every narrative work omits, for example, periods of time that the reader must fill in. In Nathaniel Hawthorne's "Young Goodman Brown" the author omits all the years of Brown's life between his emergence from the forest and his death. The reader is free to imagine that history. In Sophocles' *Antigonê* we never see Antigonê and her betrothed, Haimon, together. The reader will supply the energy of that courtship. The filling in of these blanks enables readers to participate in "creating" a text, and reinforces the arguments of reader-response theorists.

Nothing, no power, will keep a book steady and motionless before us, so that we may have time to examine its shape and design. As quickly as we read, it melts and shifts in memory; even at the moment when the last page is turned, a great part of the book, its finer detail, is already vague and doubtful. A little later, after a few days or months, how much is really left? A cluster of impressions, some clear points, emerging from a mist of uncertainty, this is all we can hope to possess, generally speaking, in the name of a book. The experience of reading it has left something behind, and these relics we call by the book's name; but how can they be considered to give us the material for judging and appraising the book?

PERCY LUBBOCK, *THE CRAFT OF FICTION* (1921)

All readings originate in the reader's personality—all are "subjective" in that sense. Some readings take a close account of the words-on-the-page and some do not, but no matter how much textual, "objective" evidence a reader brings into his own reading, he structures and adapts it according to his own inner needs.

NORMAN N. HOLLAND, *5 READERS READING* (1975)

. . . The text as an entity independent of interpretation and (ideally) responsible for its career [as formalism maintains] drops out and is replaced by the texts that emerge as a consequence of our interpretive activities. There are still formal patterns, but they do not lie innocently in the world; rather, they are themselves constituted by the interpretive act.

STANLEY FISH, *IS THERE A TEXT IN THE CLASS? THE AUTHORITY OF INTERPRETIVE COMMUNITIES* (1980)

You may well ask, if a range of responses is recognized as probable and acceptable, how can one response be more "valid" than another? How can validity be measured? Within the context of the transactional theory of the literary work, validity of a reading is identified in relation to a consistent set of criteria, implicit or explicit. Adequacy of interpretation can be mea-

sured against the constraints of the text: to what degree does the individual response include the various features of the text and the nuances of language; to what degree does it include aspects that do not reflect the text; to what degree has the reading evoked a consistent work? Thus, the out-of-context response—a memory or experience triggered by something in the text— takes the reader far afield or the strongly skewed response leads to the neglect of features of the text. These may be valuable responses for the reader but, given the criteria, invalid or less valid transactions with the text.

NICHOLAS J. KAROLIDES, *READER RESPONSE IN THE CLASSROOM: EVOKING AND INTERPRETING MEANING IN LITERATURE* (1992)

Writing about Literature*

Writing about literature compels the student to discover and come to terms with his or her response to an author's work. Every element in a literary work has been deliberately incorporated by the author—the description of the setting, the events that constitute the plot, the dialogue, the imagery. A rather mysterious intellectual and emotional event occurs within the reader as a result of the writer's purposeful manipulation of language. An essay about literature inevitably attempts some description of the author's purposes and techniques and some discussion of the reader's response.

As an illustration of the relationship between author's purpose and reader's response, consider these opening lines of a poem by W. H. Auden (the poem appears on p. 748):

> That night when joy began
> Our narrowest veins to flush,
> We waited for the flash
> Of morning's levelled gun.

The stanza tells of a new joy, probably erotic, that the speaker and his companion experience one night. But the reader must see that the speaker is apprehensive about that joy. The writer has created that mood of apprehension by using a violent image—the flash of morning's gun—to characterize the speaker's fears about the consequences of possible discovery. The images in the subsequent stanzas of the poem suggest that the lovers are trespassers and that the leveled gun they fear belongs to the keeper of the forbidden fields they enjoyed. Thus, the reader responds to the poem with an awareness that the lovers have risked danger for the sake of joy.

Though the correspondence between "writer's purpose" and "reader's response" is by no means exact, any attempt to write about literature is, in one way or another, an attempt to discover and describe that correspondence. In other words, whatever the assignment, your fundamental task is to provide the answers to two questions: "How do I respond to this piece? How has the author brought about my response?"

---

* See, as well, the appendices "Reading Fiction," "Reading Poetry," "Reading Drama," and the "Glossary of Critical Approaches." Those discussions may well suggest useful approaches to writing assignments.

The Journal

Many instructors will require you to keep a journal, a day-by-day account of your reactions to and reflections about what you've been reading. Even if a journal is not required, you might want to keep one for a variety of reasons. From a purely practical perspective, a journal provides valuable mental exercise: forcing yourself to write in a journal regularly is an excellent way to limber up your writing abilities and overcome the fear of facing a blank page. Because journals are like diaries in the sense that they are not meant to be seen by anyone else, you need not worry about whether you are constructing grammatical sentences, whether you are writing cohesive paragraphs and developing your ideas, or even whether you are always making sense. You are free to comment on some aspect of a work or set down a highly personal recollection that something in the work triggered. What is important is that you are recording your reactions, ideas, feelings, questions. If you are conscientious about keeping your journal, you may come to find the act of writing a challenging and—who knows?—even a pleasant activity.

A journal's usefulness extends beyond personal pleasure. When the time comes to write a formal essay for your class, the journal can provide you with a large range of possible topics. Suppose while you were reading Alastair Reid's poem "Curiosity" you confided to your journal your own curiosity about the reasons the poet selected cats and dogs to carry the theme. You might write an interesting essay on this topic, based on the thesis that, although both are domestic animals, the cat is a far wilder creature than the more docile and domestic dog.

You can also use a journal to record unfamiliar words that you encounter in your reading and plan to look up later. In reading Stevie Smith's "To Carry the Child," for example, you might wonder what *carapace* means. You enter the word in your journal, and when you look it up, you find that *carapace* means a bony shell, such as a turtle's. With this knowledge you can return to the poem and appreciate the image, which might suggest a topic for an essay.

Some of your journal entries will probably be confessions of bafflement and confusion. Why does Tolstoy begin "The Death of Iván Ilých" at the end? Why does Crane in "The Bride Comes to Yellow Sky" open Part III with a reference to a character's shirt and the place where it was made as well as the ethnic origin of the people who made it? Working out an answer to either of these questions could lead to an interesting essay.

Anything you want to enter in your journal is relevant, including the most personal feelings and recollections triggered by a work. Dylan Thomas's "Fern Hill" might remind you of feelings you experienced during a particular period of your childhood. Exploring your own childhood feelings and comparing them with those expressed in Thomas's poem could lead in any number of ways to a fascinating essay (for example, how poets give memorable and vivid expression to experiences we've all had). Or you might jot down, after reading Kate Chopin's "The Storm," your moral disapproval of the story's central event—

marital infidelity. You might then reread the story to discover whether it seems to disapprove of infidelity or whether you have imposed on it your own personal moral values. Sorting out such feelings could result in an essay on the interaction between the moral values of a reader and those embodied in a particular work.

Finally, remember that (unless your instructor has specific guidelines for your journal keeping) your journal will be the one place where you can write as much or as little as you please, as often or infrequently as you wish, with care and deliberation or careless speed. Its only purpose is to serve your needs. But if you write fairly regularly, you will probably be surprised not only at how much easier the act of writing becomes but also at how many ideas suddenly pop into your head in the act of writing. Henry Adams was surely right when he observed, "The habit of expression leads to the search for something to express."

Essays

Your journal will allow you to struggle privately with your reading. It may produce wonders of understanding; it should, as well, reveal to you lapses in understanding. The journal, while a useful tool for recording thoughts, responses, and impressions, remains, after all, a set of rough notes. Most instructors will demand some organization of those notes—they will ask you to write formal essays that provide evidence of your talent for critical response. Formal essays in introduction-to-literature courses characteristically fall into one of three modes: explication, analysis, and comparison and contrast.

Explication

In explication, you examine a work in as much detail as possible, line by line, stanza by stanza, scene by scene, explaining each part as fully as you can and showing how the author's techniques produce your response. An explication is essentially a demonstration of your thorough understanding of the poem, the story, or the play.

Here is a sample essay that explicates a relatively difficult poem, Dylan Thomas's "Do Not Go Gentle into That Good Night." (The poem appears on p. 1138.)

> Dylan Thomas's villanelle "Do Not Go Gentle into That
> Good Night" is addressed to his aged father. The poem is re-
> markable in a number of ways, most notably in that contrary
> to the most common poetic treatments of the inevitability of
> death, which argue for serenity or celebrate the peace that
> death provides, this poem urges resistance and rage in the
> face of death. It justifies that unusual attitude by describ-

ing the rage and resistance to death of four kinds of men, all of whom can summon up the image of a complete and satisfying life that is denied to them by death.

The first tercet of the intricately rhymed villanelle opens with an arresting line. The adjective <u>gentle</u> appears where we would expect the adverb <u>gently</u>. The strange diction suggests that <u>gentle</u> may describe both the going (i.e., gently dying) and the person (i.e., gentleman) who confronts death. Further, the speaker characterizes "night," here clearly a figure for death, as "good." Yet in the next line, the speaker urges that the aged should violently resist death, characterized as the "close of day" and "the dying of the light." In effect, the first three lines argue that however good death may be, the aged should refuse to die gently, should passionately rave and rage against death.

In the second tercet, the speaker turns to a description of the way the first of four types of men confronts death (which is figuratively defined throughout the poem as "that good night" and "the dying of the light"). These are the "wise men," the scholars, the philosophers, those who understand the inevitability of death, men who "know dark is right." But they do not acquiesce in death "because their words had forked no lightning," because their published wisdom failed to bring them to that sense of completeness and fulfillment that can accept death. Therefore, wise as they are, they reject the theoretical "rightness" of death and refuse to "go gentle."

The second sort of men—"good men," the moralists, the social reformers, those who attempt to better the world through action as the wise men attempt to better it through "words"—also rage against death. Their deeds are, after all, "frail." With sea imagery, the speaker suggests that these men might have accomplished fine and fertile things—their deeds "might have danced in a green bay." But with the "last wave" gone, they see only the frailty, the impermanence of their acts, and so they, too, rage against the death that deprives them of the opportunity to leave a meaningful legacy.

So, too, the "wild men," the poets who "sang" the loveliness and vitality of nature, learn, as they approach death, that the sensuous joys of human existence wane. As the life-giving sun moves toward dusk, as death approaches, their

singing turns to grieving, and they refuse to surrender
gently, to leave willingly the warmth and pleasure and beauty
that life can give.

 And finally, with a pun suggestive of death, the "grave
men," those who go through life with such high seriousness as
never to experience gaiety and pleasure, see, as death approaches, all the joyous possibilities that they were blind
to in life. And they, too, rage against the dying of a light
that they had never properly seen before.

 The speaker then calls upon his aged father to join
these men raging against death. Only in this final stanza do
we discover that the entire poem is addressed to the speaker's father and that, despite the generalized statements
about old age and the focus upon types of men, the poem is a
personal lyric. The edge of death becomes a "sad height," the
summit of wisdom and experience old age attains includes the
sad knowledge of life's failure to satisfy the vision we all
pursue. The depth and complexity of the speaker's sadness is
startlingly given in the second line when he calls upon his
father to both curse and bless him. These opposites richly
suggest several related possibilities. Curse me for not living up to your expectations. Curse me for remaining alive as
you die. Bless me with forgiveness for my failings. Bless me
for teaching you to rage against death. And the curses and
blessings are contained in the "fierce tears"—fierce because
you will burn and rave and rage against death. As the poem
closes by bringing together the two powerful refrains, we may
reasonably feel that the speaker himself, while not facing
imminent death, rages because his father's death will cut off
a relationship that is incomplete.

The explication, as you can see, deals with the entire poem by coming to grips
with each element in it. This same mode can be used to write about the drama
as well, but the length of plays will probably require that you focus on a single
segment—a scene, for example—rather than the entire play.

 You can learn a great deal about the technique of drama by selecting a short
self-contained scene and writing a careful description of it. This method, a
variety of explication, will force you to confront every speech and stage direction
and to come to some conclusion regarding its function. Why is the set furnished
as it is? Why does a character speak the words he or she does or remain silent?
What do we learn of characters from the interchanges among them? Assume
that everything that occurs in the play, whether on the printed page or on the

stage, is put there for a purpose. Seek to discover the purpose, and you will, at the same time, discover the peculiar nature of dramatic art.

Fiction, too, can be treated effectively in a formal explication. As with drama, it will be necessary to limit the text—you will not be able to explicate a 10-page story in a 1,000-word essay. Choose a key passage—a half page that reflects the form and content of the overall story, if possible. Often the first half page of a story, where the author, like the playwright, must supply information to the reader, will make a fine text for an explication. Although the explication will deal principally with only an excerpt, feel free to range across the story and show how the introductory material foreshadows what is to come. Or, perhaps, you can explicate the climax of the story—the half page that most pointedly establishes the story's theme—and subject it to a close line-by-line reading that illuminates the whole story.

Analysis

Analyzing literature is not the same kind of exercise as analyzing a chemical compound: breaking a literary work down into its elements is only the first step in literary analysis. When you are assigned an analysis essay, you are expected to focus on one of the elements that contribute to the complex compound that is the substance of any work of literary merit. This process requires that you extricate the element you plan to explore from the other elements that you can identify, study this element—not only in isolation but also in relation to the other elements and the work as a whole—and, using the insights you have gained from your special perspective, make an informed statement about it.

This process may sound complicated, but if you approach it methodically, each stage follows naturally from the stage that precedes it. If, for example, an instructor assigns an analysis essay on some aspect of characterization in *Othello*, you would begin by thinking about each character in the play. You would then select the character whose development you would like to explore and reread carefully those speeches that help to establish his or her substance. Exploring a character's development in this way involves a good deal of explication: in order to identify the "building blocks" that Shakespeare uses to create a three-dimensional role, you must comb very carefully through that character's speeches and actions. You must also be sensitive to the ways in which other characters respond to these speeches and actions. When you have completed this investigation, you will probably have a good understanding of why you intuitively responded to the character as you did when you first read the play. You will also probably be prepared to make a statement about the character's development: "From a realistic perspective, it is hard to believe that a man of Othello's position could be so gullible; however, Shakespeare develops the role with such craft that we accept the Moor as flesh and blood." At this point, you have moved from the broad *subject* "characterization in *Othello*" to a *thesis*, a statement that you must prove. As you formulate your thesis, think of it as a position that you intend to *argue* for with a reader who is not easy to persuade.

This approach is useful in any essay that requires a thesis—in other words, in any essay in which you move beyond simple explication and commit yourself to a stand. Note that "From a realistic perspective, it is hard to believe that a man of Othello's position could be so gullible; however, Shakespeare develops the role with such craft that we accept him as flesh and blood" is *argumentative* on two counts. "Characterization in *Othello*" is not remotely argumentative. Further, you have more than enough material to write a well-documented essay of 1,000 words supporting your proposition; you cannot write a well-documented 1,000-word essay on the general subject of characterization in *Othello* without being superficial.

You may be one among the many students who find it difficult to find a starting point. For example, you have been assigned an analysis essay on a very broad subject, such as "imagery in love poetry." A few poems come to mind, but you don't know where to begin. You read these poems and underline all the images that you can find. You look at these images over and over, finding no relation among them. You read some more poems, again underlining the images, but you still do not have even the germ of a thesis.

The technique of freewriting might help to overcome your block. You have read and reread the works you intend to write about. Now, put the assignment temporarily out of your mind and start writing about one or two of the poems without organizing your ideas, without trying to reach a point. Write down what you like about a poem, what you dislike about it, what sort of person the speaker is, which images seemed striking to you—anything at all about the work. If you do this for perhaps ten minutes, you will probably discover that you are voicing opinions. Pick one that interests you or seems the most promising to explore.

There are a few variations on the basic form of the analysis assignment. Occasionally, an instructor will narrow the subject to a specific assignment: analyze the development of Othello's character in Act I. This sort of assignment saves you the trouble of selecting a character on whom to focus and also limits the amount of text that you will have to study. However, the process from this point on is no different from the process that you would employ addressing a broader subject. Sometimes instructors will supply you with a thesis, and you will have to work backward from the thesis to find supporting material. Again, careful analysis of the text is required.

The problem you will have to address when writing an analytical essay remains the same regardless of the literary genre you are asked to discuss. You still must find an arguable thesis that deals with the literary sources of your response to the work. For instance, an analysis of a poem might show how a particular pattern of imagery contributes to the meaning of the poem. Or it might argue, from clues within the poem, that the speaker of the poem is a certain kind of character. Or it might demonstrate how the connotations of certain words in a poem help to create a particular mood. An analysis may also go outside the poem to throw light on it. For instance, a poem might be analyzed as an embodiment of (or departure from) a particular religious, social, political, or scientific doctrine; as an example of traditional poetic form such as the ballad or the pastoral elegy; or as a new expression of an ancient myth. These are but a few examples; the possibilities are almost endless.

Though plays can be analyzed, like stories and poems, in terms of theme, image patterns, and the like, the playwright must solve problems that are unique to drama as a literary form meant to be acted on a stage before an audience. For example, the mechanics of staging a play limit the extent to which the playwright can shift the locations and times of the action, whereas the writer of fiction can make such shifts readily. Similarly, the writer of fiction can, if he or she wishes, tell the story through a narrator who not only can comment on the meaning of events but can describe the thoughts and motives of the characters. In a play, on the other hand, the curtain rises and the characters must convey information through their own words or behavior. The audience does not generally know what the characters think unless they speak their thoughts aloud. As *readers* of a play, we may read the stage directions and any other information the author has provided for the director and actors (and perhaps for readers). We must bear in mind that the audience viewing the play can only know such things as the time of year, the location of the setting, the relationships among characters, or the events that have led up to the action with which the play begins if they are stated in the program or if someone or something on the stage conveys that information.

Playwrights have developed many techniques for solving their special problems, and you may wish to focus on one of these in your analysis of some aspect of a play. For example, you might explain the role of the chorus or the dramatic function of the messenger in Sophocles' *Oedipus Rex*. Or you might argue that the passage of time is distorted for dramatic purposes in Shakespeare's *Othello*. All of these subjects would involve the consideration of problems that are peculiar to the drama as a literary form that is meant to be acted on a stage.

When you confront the assignment to write about a play, ask yourself some fundamental questions. For instance, what sort of person is the protagonist? Is he or she admirable? If so, in what respects? Generous? Wise? Courageous? Fair-minded? What evidence do you find to support your judgment? Does it come from his or her own speeches and behavior or from what other characters say about him or her? If the latter, are we meant to take the opinions of those characters as the truth? Is the tragic conclusion of the play brought about by some flaw or weakness in the character or merely by the malice of others?

Of course, these questions represent only a very few of those you might ask as you think about a play and search for a thesis. If you do choose to deal with some aspect of characterization, you may find that a minor character interests you more as a subject than a major one. And, as we have suggested, you can also ask questions about imagery, about theme, or about various formal or structural aspects of a play. If you ask yourself enough questions, you will discover some thesis that you can argue.

Suppose your instructor has made the following assignment: write an analysis of Harlan Ellison's story, "'Repent, Harlequin!' Said the Ticktockman" (p. 436), in which you discuss the theme of the story in terms of the characters and the setting. Now consider the following opening (taken from a student paper):

> "'Repent, Harlequin!' Said the Ticktockman" is a story depicting a society in which time governs one's life. The setting is the United States, the time approximately A.D. 2400 somewhere in the heart of the country. Business deals, work shifts, and school lessons are started and finished with exacting precision. Tardiness is intolerable as this would hinder the system. In a society of order, precision, and punctuality, there is no room for likes, dislikes, scruples, or morals. Thus, personalities in people no longer exist. As these "personless" people know no good or bad, they very happily follow in the course of activities which their society has dictated.

At the outset, can you locate a thesis statement? The only sentences that would seem to qualify are the last three in the paragraph. But notice that, although those sentences are not unreasonable responses to the story, they do not establish a thesis that is *responsive to the assignment*. Because the assignment calls for a discussion of theme in terms of character and setting, there should be a thesis statement about the way in which character and setting embody the theme. Here is another opening paragraph on the same assignment (also taken from a student paper):

> Harlan Ellison's "'Repent, Harlequin!' Said the Ticktockman" opens with a quotation from Thoreau's essay "Civil Disobedience," which establishes the story's theme. Thoreau's observations about three varieties of men, those who serve the state as machines, those who serve it with their heads, and those who serve it with their consciences, are dramatized in Ellison's story, which takes place about 400 years in the future in a setting characterized by machinelike order. The interaction among the three characters, each of whom represents one of Thoreau's types, results in a telling restatement of his observation that "heroes, patriots, martyrs, reformers in the great sense, and men . . . necessarily resist [the state] and . . . are commonly treated as enemies by it."

Compare the two opening paragraphs sentence by sentence for their responsiveness to the assignment. The first sentence of the first opening does not refer to the theme of the story (or to its setting or characterization). In the second sentence, the discussion of the setting ignores the most important aspect—that the story is set in a machine- and time-dominated future. The last three sentences deal obliquely with character, but they are imprecise and do not establish a thesis. The second opening, on the other hand, immediately states the theme of the story. It goes on to emphasize the relevant aspects of the futuristic setting and then refers to the three characters that animate the story in terms of their reactions to the setting. The last sentence addresses the assignment directly and also serves as a thesis statement for the paper. It states the proposition that will be developed and supported in the rest of the paper. The reader of the second opening will expect the next paragraph of the paper to discuss the setting of the story and subsequent paragraphs to discuss the response to the setting of the three principal characters.

The middles of essays are largely determined by their opening paragraphs. However long the middle of any essay may be, each of its paragraphs ought to be responsive to some explicit statement made at the beginning of the essay. Note that it is practically impossible to predict what the paragraph following the first opening will address. Here is the first half of that next paragraph as the first student wrote it.

> The Harlequin is a man in the society with no sense of time. His having a personality enables him to have a sense of moral values and a mind of his own. The Harlequin thinks that it is obscene and wrong to let time totally govern the lives of people. So, he sets out to disrupt the time schedule with ridiculous antics such as showering people with jelly beans in order to try to break up the military fashion in which they are used to doing things.

The paragraph then goes on to discuss the Ticktockman, the capture and brainwashing of the Harlequin, and the resulting lateness of the Ticktockman.

Note that nothing in the opening of this student's paper prepared readers for the introduction of the Harlequin. In fact, the opening concluded rather inaccurately that the people within the story "happily follow in the course of activities which their society has dictated." Hence, the description of the Harlequin in the second paragraph is wholly unexpected. Further, because the student has not dealt with the theme of the story (remember the assignment explicitly asked for a discussion of *theme* in terms of character and setting), the comments about the Harlequin's antics remain disconnected from any clear purpose. They are essentially devoted to what teachers constantly warn against: a mere plot summary. The student has obviously begun to write before she has analyzed the story sufficiently to understand its theme. With further thought, the student would have perceived that the central thematic issue is resistance to an oppressive state—the issue stated in the epigraph from Thoreau. On the other hand, because the second opening makes that thematic point clearly, we can expect it to be followed by a discussion of the environment (that is, the setting) in which the action occurs. Here is such a paragraph taken from the second student's paper:

> Ellison creates a society that reflects one possible fu-
> ture development of the modern American passion for produc-
> tivity and efficiency. The setting is in perfect keeping with
> the time-conscious people who inhabit the city. It is pic-
> tured as a neat, colorless, and mechanized city. No mention
> is made of nature: grass, flowers, trees, and birds do not
> appear. The buildings are in a "Mondrian arrangement," stark
> and geometrical. The cold steel slidewalks, slowstrips, and
> expresstrips move with precision. Like a chorus line, people
> move in unison to board the movers without a wasted motion.
> Doors close silently and lock themselves automatically. An
> ideal efficiency so dominates the social system that any
> "wasted time" is deducted from the life of an inefficient
> citizen.

Once the setting has been established, as in the paragraph just quoted, writers attentive to the assignment will turn to the characters. But they will insistently link those characters to thematic considerations. It might be well to proceed with a short transitional paragraph that shapes the remainder of the middle of the essay:

> Into this smoothly functioning but coldly mechanized so-
> ciety, Ellison introduces three characters: Pretty Alice, one
> of Thoreau's machinelike creatures; the Ticktockman, one of
> those who "serve the state chiefly with their heads, and, as
> they rarely make any moral distinctions, they are as likely
> to serve the Devil without intending it, as God"; and Everett
> C. Marm, the Harlequin, whose conscience forces him to resist
> the oppressive state.

The reader will now expect a paragraph devoted to each of the three characters:

> Pretty Alice is, probably, very pretty. (Everett didn't
> fall in love with her brains.) In the brief section in which
> we meet her, we find her hopelessly ordinary in her atti-
> tudes. She is upset that Marm finds it necessary to go about
> "annoying people." She finds him ridiculous and wishes only
> that he would stay home, as other people do. Clearly, she has
> no understanding of what Everett is struggling against.
> Though her anger finally leads her to betray him, Everett

himself can't believe that she has done so. His own loyal and understanding nature colors his view of her so thoroughly that he cannot imagine the treachery that must have been so simple and satisfying for Pretty Alice, whose only desire is to be like everybody else.

The Ticktockman is more complex. He sees himself as a servant of the state, and he performs his duties with resolution and competence. He skillfully supports a System he has never questioned. The System exists; it must be good. His conscience is simply not involved in the performance of his duty. He is one of those who follows orders and expects others to follow orders. As a result, the behavior of the Harlequin is more than just an irritant or a rebellion against authority. It is unnerving. The Ticktockman wishes to understand that behavior, and with Everett's time-card in his hand, he muses that he has the name of "what he is . . . not who he is. . . . Before I can exercise proper revocation, I have to know who this what is." And when he confronts Everett, he does not just liquidate him. He insists that Everett repent. He tries to convince Everett that the System is sound, and when he cannot win the argument, he dutifully reconditions Everett, since he is, after all, more interested in justifying the System than in destroying its enemies. It is easy to see this man as a competent servant of the devil who thinks he is serving God.

But only Everett C. Marm truly serves the state, because his conscience requires him to resist. He is certainly not physically heroic. His very name suggests weak conformity. Though he loves his Pretty Alice, he cannot resign from the rebellious campaign on which his conscience insists. So, without violence, and mainly with the weapon of laughter, he attacks the mechanical precision of the System and succeeds in breaking it down simply by making people late. He is himself, as Pretty Alice points out, always late, and the delays that his antics produce seriously threaten the well-being of the smooth but mindless System he hates. He is, of course, captured. He refuses, even then, to submit and has his personality destroyed by the authorities that fear him. The Ticktockman is too strong for him.

An appropriate ending emerges naturally from this student's treatment of the assignment. Having established that the story presents characters who deal in different ways with the oppressive quality of life in a time- and machine-obsessed society, the student concludes with a comment on the author's criticisms of such a society:

> Harlequin is defeated, but Ellison, finally, leaves us with an optimistic note. The idea of rebellion against the System will linger in the minds of others. There will be more Harlequins and more disruption of this System. Many rebels will be defeated, but any System that suppresses individual- ism will give birth to resistance. And Harlequin's defeat is by no means total. The story ends with the Ticktockman him- self arriving for work three minutes late.

Comparison and Contrast

An essay in comparison and contrast, showing how two works are similar to and different from one another, almost always starts with a recognition of similarities, most likely similarities of subject matter. While it is possible to compare *any* two works, the best comparison and contrast essays emerge from the analysis of two works similar enough to illuminate each other (most com- parison and contrast assignments involve two works of the same genre). Two works about love, or death, or conformity, or innocence, or discovery give you something to begin with. But these are very large categories; two random poems about the same subject may be so dissimilar that a comparison and contrast essay about them would be very difficult. Both Shelley's "Ozymandias" and Randall Jarrell's "The Death of the Ball Turret Gunner" are about death; but they deal with the subject so differently that they would probably not yield a very interesting essay. On the other hand, not only are Dickinson's "Apparently with No Surprise" and Frost's "Design" both about death, but they both use remarkably similar events as the occasion for the poem. And starting with these similarities, you would soon find yourself noting the contrasts (in tone, for example, and theme) between nineteenth-century and twentieth-century views of the nature of God.

Before you begin writing your paper, you ought to have clearly in mind the points of comparison and contrast you wish to discuss and the order in which you can most effectively discuss them. You will need to give careful thought to the best way to organize your paper. As a general rule, it is best to avoid dividing the paper into separate discussions of each work. That methods tends to produce two separate, loosely joined analysis essays. The successful comparison and contrast essay treats some point of similarity or contrast between the two works, then moves on to succeeding points, and ends with an evaluation of the comparative merits of the works.

Like analysis essays—indeed like any essay that goes beyond simple expli- cation—comparison and contrast essays require theses. However, a comparison and contrast thesis is generally not difficult to formulate: you must identify the works under consideration and summarize briefly your reasons for making the comparison.

Here is a student paper that compares and contrasts a Dylan Thomas poem ("Do Not Go Gentle into That Good Night," explicated earlier in this discussion) with the poetic response it triggered from a poet with different views.

> Dylan Thomas's "Do Not Go Gentle into That Good Night" and Catherine Davis's "After a Time" demand comparison: Davis's poem was written in deliberate response to Thomas's. Davis assumes the reader's familiarity with "Do Not Go Gentle," which she uses to articulate her contrasting ideas. "After a Time," although it is a literary work in its own right, might even be thought of as serious parody—perhaps the greatest compliment one writer can pay another.

> "Do Not Go Gentle into That Good Night" was written by a young man of thirty-eight who addresses it to his old and ailing father. It's interesting to note that the author himself had very little of his own self-destructive life left as he was composing this piece. Perhaps that is why he seems to have more insight into the subject of death than most people of his age. He advocates raging and fighting against it, not giving in and accepting it.

> "After a Time" was written by a woman of about the same age and is addressed to no one in particular. Davis has a different philosophy about death. She "answers" Thomas's poem and presents her differing views using the same poetic form—a villanelle. Evidently, she felt it necessary to present a contrasting point of view eight years after Thomas's death.

> While "Do Not Go Gentle" protests and rages against death, Davis's poem suggests a quiet resignation and acquiescence. She seems to feel that raging against death is useless and profitless. She argues that we will eventually become tame, anyway, after the raging is done. At the risk of sounding sexist, I think it interesting that the man rages and the woman submits, as if the traditionally perceived differences between the behavior of men and women are reflected in the poems.

> Thomas talks about different types of men and why they rage against death. "Wise men" desire immortality. They rage against death occurring before they've made their mark on history. "Good men" lament the frailty of their deeds. Given

more time, they might have accomplished great things. "Wild men" regret their constant hedonistic pursuits. With more time they could prove their worth. "Grave men" are quite the opposite and regret they never took time for the pleasures in life. Now it is too late. They rage against death because they are not ready for it.

His father's death is painful to Thomas because he sees himself lying in that bed; his father's dying reminds him of his own inevitable death. The passion of the last stanza, in which the poet asks his father to bless and curse him, suggests that he has doubts about his relationship with his father. He may feel that he has not been enough of a son. He put off doing things with and for his father because he always felt there would be time later. Now time has run out and he feels cheated. He's raging for his father now. He'll rage for himself later.

Catherine Davis advocates a calm submission, a peaceful acquiescence. She feels raging is useless and says that those of us who rage will finally "go tame / When what we have we can no longer use." When she says "One more thing lost is one thing less to lose," the reader can understand and come to terms with the loss of different aspects of the mind and body, such as strength, eyesight, hearing, and intellect. Once we've lost one of these, it's one thing less to worry about losing. After a time, everything will be lost, and we'll accept that, too, because we'll be ready for it.

In a contest of imagery, Thomas would certainly win the day. His various men not only rage and rave, they <u>burn</u>. Their words "forked no lightning," their deeds might have "danced in a green bay," they "sang the sun in flight," and they see that "blind eyes could blaze like meteors." Davis's images are quiet—generally abstract and without much sensory suggestiveness. She gives us "things lost," a "reassuring ruse," and "all losses are the same." Her most powerful image—"And we go stripped at last the way we came"—makes its point with none of the excitement of Thomas's rage. And yet, I prefer the quiet intelligence of Davis to the high energy of Thomas.

"And we go stripped at last the way we came" can give strange comfort and solace to those of us who always envied those in high places. Death is a great leveler. People are not all created equal at birth, not by a long shot. But we

> will bloody well all be equal when we make our final exit.
> Kings, popes, and heads of state will go just as "stripped"
> as the rest of us. They won't get to take anything with them.
> All wealth, power, and trappings will be left behind. We will
> all finally and ultimately be equal. So why rage? It won't do
> us any good.

Writing the Essay

If you have thought about an assignment sufficiently and reread the work you intend to write about with enough care to formulate a thesis, then you have already accomplished a major part of the task. You have, however loosely, constructed an argument and marshaled some of the evidence to support it. Now you must begin to be rigorous. Take notes. The most efficient method is to use three-by-five-inch index cards. Take one note per card, and use some key words at the top to identify the subject of the note. This procedure allows you to arrange your note cards in the most workable order when you are drafting your paper.

As you take your notes and then arrange the cards, you will begin to get some sense of the number of paragraphs you will need to support the thesis you have announced in the opening paragraph. Generally, each paragraph will focus on one major point (perhaps with its own mini-thesis), and bring together the evidence necessary to support that point.

As you write and rewrite, you should make sure that the progression of ideas from paragraph to paragraph is clear. To accomplish this, link each paragraph to the preceding one with a transitional word or phrase. Even the most carefully organized essay may seem abrupt or disjointed to the reader if you neglect to provide bridges between the paragraphs. A simple *however, nevertheless, furthermore,* or *on the other hand* will often be adequate. Sometimes the entire opening sentence of a paragraph may provide the transition (and avoid the monotony of the standard words and phrases). Let us assume, for example, that you are writing an essay in which you argue that in Dylan Thomas's poem "Fern Hill" the mature speaker, now keenly aware of mortality, perceives the innocence of his childhood as a state of religious grace. In one or more paragraphs, you have analyzed the religious imagery of the poem, and you now begin a new paragraph with the sentence, "While the religious imagery dominates the poem, it is supported by a well-developed pattern of color imagery." Such a transitional sentence signals the reader that you will now consider another pattern of imagery that provides further evidence to support the thesis, because, as you will show, the color imagery is in fact a subpattern of the religious imagery.

Simply stated, in a tightly organized essay there ought to be a reason why one paragraph follows rather than precedes another. In fact, you can test the organization of your essay by asking yourself whether the paragraphs can be rearranged without significant effect. If they can be, chances are that your organization is weak, your ideas unclarified.

Having worked out an opening paragraph with a thesis and worked through the body of your essay to support the thesis, you now must confront the problem of how to conclude. Your conclusion should be brief, rarely more than three or four sentences. Ideally, it should leave the reader with a sense of both completeness and significance. For a short paper, it is unnecessary to restate or summarize your main points, because your reader will not have trouble remembering them. If your essay has been primarily appreciative and impressionistic, a general statement about the value of the work to you might bring the essay nicely to rest. Or you might conclude with a statement about the relevance of the work to the world in which we live. When you have said all you have to say, you have finished. Avoid the common error of turning the conclusion into a beginning by taking up new evidence or ideas in the final paragraph.

Exploring Fiction, Poetry, and Drama

Here are some questions you might ask yourself when you are faced with the task of writing about literature. Your answers to these questions can help you overcome the awful whiteness of the empty page.

Fiction

1. From what point of view is the story told? Can you speculate on the appropriateness of that point of view? If a story is told from the point of view of a first-person narrator who participates in the action, what significant changes would occur if it were told from the point of view of an omniscient author? And, of course, *vice versa*. Note that first-person narrators do not know what other characters think. On the other hand, omniscient narrators know everything about the lives of the characters. How would the story you are writing about be changed if the viewpoint were changed?

2. Who are the principal characters in the story? (There will rarely be more than three in a short story—the other characters will often be portrayed sketchily; sometimes they are even stereotypes.) What functions do the minor characters serve? Do any of the characters change during the course of the story? How, and why?

3. What is the plot of the story? Do the events that constitute the plot emerge logically from the nature of the characters and circumstances, or are the plot elements coincidental and arbitrary?

4. What is the setting of the story? Does the setting play an important role in the story, or is it simply the place where things happen? You might ask

yourself what the consequences of some other setting might be for the effectiveness of the story.

5. What is the tone of the story? The first several paragraphs of the story establish that tone. Does the tone change with events, or remain fixed? How does the tone contribute to the effect of the story?

6. Do you find ambiguities in the story? That is, can you interpret some element of the story in more than one way? Does that ambiguity result in confusion, or does it add to the complexity of the story?

7. Does the story seem to support or attack your own political and moral positions?

8. Bring your knowledge of history and contemporary events to bear on your reading of the story. Does the story clarify, enhance, or contradict your understanding of history?

9. What is the theme of the story? This, finally, is the most significant question to answer. All of the elements of fiction—point of view, tone, character, plot, setting—have been marshaled to project a theme—the moral proposition the author wishes to advance. When you write about fiction, or any literary form, you must resist the tendency to do the easiest thing—retell the plot, incident by incident. You must, instead, come to understand the devices the author uses to convey his or her theme, and, in your paper, reveal that understanding.

Poetry

1. Who is the speaker? What does the poem reveal about the speaker's character? In some poems the speaker may be nothing more than a voice meditating on a theme, while in others the speaker takes on a specific personality. For example, the speaker in Shelley's "Ozymandias" is a voice meditating on the transitoriness of all things; except for the views expressed in the poem, we know nothing about the speaker's character. The same might be said of the speaker in Hopkins's "Spring and Fall" but with this important exception: we know that he is older than Margaret and therefore has a wisdom she does not.

2. Is the speaker addressing a particular person? If so, who is that person, and why is the speaker interested in him or her? Many poems, like "Ozymandias," are addressed to no one in particular and therefore to anyone, any reader. Others, such as Donne's "A Valediction: Forbidding Mourning," while addressed to a specific person, reveal nothing about that person because the focus of the poem is on the speaker's feelings and attitudes. In a dramatic monologue (see "Glossary of Literary Terms"), the speaker usually addresses a silent auditor. The identity of the auditor will be important to the poem.

3. Does the poem have a setting? Is the poem occasioned by a particular event? The answer to these questions will often be "no" for lyric poems, such as Frost's "Fire and Ice." It will always be "yes" if the poem is a dramatic monologue or a poem that tells or implies a story, such as Tennyson's "Ulysses" and Lowell's "Patterns."

4. Is the theme of the poem stated directly or indirectly? Some poems, such as Frost's "Provide, Provide" and Owen's "Dulce et Decorum Est," use language in a fairly straightforward and literal way and state the theme, often in the final lines. Others may conclude with a statement of the theme that is more difficult to apprehend because it is made with figurative language and symbols. This difference will be readily apparent if you compare the final lines of the Frost and Owen poems mentioned above with, say, the final stanzas of Stevens's "Sunday Morning."

5. If the speaker is describing specific events, from what perspective (roughly similar to point of view in fiction) is he or she doing so? Is the speaker recounting events of the past or events that are occurring in the present? If past events are being recalled, what present meaning do they have for the speaker? These questions are particularly appropriate to the works in the section "Innocence and Experience," many of which contrast an early innocence with adult experience.

6. Does a close examination of the figurative language (see "Glossary of Literary Terms") of the poem reveal any patterns? Yeats's "Sailing to Byzantium" may begin to open up to you once you recognize the pattern of bird imagery. Likewise, Thomas's attitude toward his childhood in "Fern Hill" will be clearer if you detect the pattern of Biblical imagery that associates childhood with Adam and Eve before the fall.

7. What is the structure of the poem? Since narrative poems, those that tell stories, reveal a high degree of selectivity, it is useful to ask why the poet has focused on particular details and left out others. Analyzing the structure of a nonnarrative or lyric poem can be more difficult because it does not contain an obvious series of chronologically related events. The structure of Thomas's "Fern Hill," for example, is based in part on a description of perhaps a day and a half in the speaker's life as a child. But more significant in terms of its structure is the speaker's realization that the immortality he felt as a child was merely a stage in the inexorable movement of life toward death. The structure of the poem, therefore, will be revealed through an analysis of patterns of images (Biblical, color, day and night, dark and light) that embody the theme. To take another example, Marvell's "To His Coy Mistress" is divided into three verse paragraphs, the opening words of each ("Had we . . . ," "But . . . ," "Now therefore . . . ,") suggesting a logically constructed argument.

8. What do sound and meter (see "Glossary of Literary Terms") contribute to

the poem? Alexander Pope said that in good poetry "the sound must seem an echo to the sense," a statement that is sometimes easier to agree with than to demonstrate. For sample analyses of the music of poetry, see the section on music in the appendix "Reading Poetry" (p. 1248).

9. What was your response to the poem on first reading? Did your response change after study of the poem or class discussions about it?

Drama

1. How does the play begin? Is the exposition presented dramatically through the interaction among characters, or novelistically through long, unrealistic, and unwieldy speeches that convey a lot of information, or through some device such as the reading of long letters or lengthy reports delivered by a messenger?

2. How does the information conveyed in exposition (which may occur at various moments throughout the play) establish the basis for dramatic irony—that is, the ironic response generated in an audience when it knows more than do the characters? For example, because we know that Iago is a villain in Shakespeare's *Othello*, we hear an ironic dimension in his speeches that the characters do not hear, and that irony is the source of much tension in the audience. An assessment of dramatic irony in a play makes an interesting and instructive writing assignment.

3. Who are the principal characters, and how are the distinctive qualities of each dramatically conveyed? Inevitably, there will be minor characters in a play. What function do they serve? A paper that thoughtfully assesses the role of minor characters can often succeed better than the attempt to analyze the major figures who may embody too much complexity to deal with in 1,000 words.

4. Where is the play set? Does it matter that it is set there? Why? Does the setting play some significant role in the drama, or is it merely a place, any place?

5. What is the central conflict in the play? How is it resolved? Do you need to know something of the historical circumstances out of which the play emerged, or something of the life of the author in order to appreciate the play fully? If so, how does the information enhance your understanding?

6. Since plays are usually written to be performed rather than read, what visual and auditory elements of the play are significant to your response? Obviously, if you are writing from a reading text, you will have to place yourself in the position of the director and the actors in order to respond to this aspect of drama.

7. What is the play's theme? How does the dramatic action embody that theme?

Note that any one of these questions might provoke an effective paper—one could do a thousand words on the settings of *Othello,* or the minor characters of *An Enemy of the People,* or the methods of exposition in *Oedipus Rex.* But each of those papers, to be successful, needs to relate the issues it deals with to the thematic force of the play. Plot summaries (except as a variety of note taking) are unsatisfactory.

A Final Word

Many questions may be asked about literature. Your assignment may require you to compare and contrast literary works, to analyze the language of a work, to discuss the interaction of parts of a work, to discuss the theme of a work, to articulate your own responses to the work. Sometimes the instructor may give you free choice and ask simply that you write an essay on one of the pieces you read. This liberty will require you to create your own feasible boundaries—you will have to find a specific focus that suits the piece you choose and is manageable within a paper of the assigned length. But be sure that you do create boundaries—that, as we urged at the outset, you have a clear thesis.

Give yourself time. If you attempt to write your paper the night before it is due, you are unlikely to write a paper that is worth reading. Even professional writers rarely accomplish serious and thoughtful writing overnight. You must give yourself time to think before you write a draft. Let the draft age a bit before rewriting a final draft. If you do not allow yourself a reasonable time period, you will convert an assignment that has the potential to enlarge your understanding and to produce real pleasure into an obstacle that you will surely trip over.

Consider also that finally you have to feel something, know something, bring something of yourself to the assignment. We can discuss formal methods for dealing with the problem of writing essays—but if you bring neither awareness, nor information, nor genuine interest to the task, the essay will remain an empty form.

Suggestions for Writing

Fiction

1. Explicate the opening paragraph or page of a story in order to demonstrate how it sets the tone and anticipates what is to follow.

2. Select a story that uses a central symbol or symbolic event and analyze its function. Some suggestions:
   A. The tree in White's "The Second Tree from the Corner."
   B. Iván's fall from the ladder in Tolstoy's "The Death of Iván Ilých."

    C. The pink ribbon in Hawthorne's "Young Goodman Brown."

    D. The underground in Wright's "The Man Who Lived Underground."

    E. The mysterious stranger in Lessing's "To Room Nineteen."

3. Select a story in which the narrative does not unfold chronologically and explain why.

4. Here are some suggestions for essays in comparison and contrast:

    A. Compare and contrast the nature and function of the dream sequences in Hawthorne's "Young Goodman Brown" and Wright's "The Man Who Lived Underground."

    B. Compare and contrast the function of art as revealed in Mann's "*Gladius Dei*" and Paley's "A Conversation with My Father."

    C. Compare and contrast the idea of "the hero" in Crane's "The Bride Comes to Yellow Sky" and Thurber's "The Greatest Man in the World."

    D. Compare and contrast the attitude toward sexuality in Chopin's "The Storm" and Shaw's "The Girls in Their Summer Dresses."

    E. Compare and contrast the marriages in Shaw's "The Girls in Their Summer Dresses" and Carver's "What We Talk about When We Talk about Love."

5. Write an essay on an interesting story title.

6. Did the ending of any story you read violate your expectations? What led you to those expectations? Do you find the author's ending more satisfactory than the one you had anticipated?

7. Select a story you feel is weak, and explain why you feel so. You might consider the credibility of the plot or of a character's behavior.

Poetry

1. Select a short lyric poem you found difficult, and explicate it line by line. Conclude with a paragraph or two describing how the process of explication helped you to clarify the meaning of the poem.

2. Here is a list of poems about poets and poetry. Select two and compare and contrast their treatment of the subject.
    Auden, "In Memory of W. B. Yeats"
    Housman, "Terence, This Is Stupid Stuff"
    MacLeish, "Ars Poetica"
    Kennedy, "Ars Poetica"
    Francis, "Pitcher"
    Hamburger, "A Poet's Progress"

Wallace, "In a Spring Still Not Written Of"
Giovanni, "For Saundra"
Cruz, "Today Is a Day of Great Joy"

3. The poems listed below tell or imply a story. Select one, and write out the story in your own words. Use your imagination to fill in details.
Anonymous, "Bonny Barbara Allen"
Anonymous, "Edward"
Tennyson, "Ulysses"
Browning, "My Last Duchess"
Hardy, "The Ruined Maid"
Lowell, "Patterns"
Eliot, "The Love Song of J. Alfred Prufrock"
Owen, "Dulce et Decorum Est"
Wright, "Between the World and Me"

4. Analyze a poem in which the author uses a particular kind of diction. Identify the pattern, and explain how it functions in the poem. Some suggestions:

A. The language of bureaucracy in Auden's "The Unknown Citizen" or Frost's "Departmental."

B. Contrasting patterns of diction in Reed's "Naming of Parts."

C. Colloquial and formal diction in Hughes's "Same in Blues."

D. Prosaic diction in Forché's "The Colonel" or Mezey's "My Mother."

E. Colloquial diction in Kizer's "Bitch."

5. As an exercise to illuminate the importance of connotation, select a poem that you like, identify some of its key words, and then consult a dictionary or thesaurus for synonyms of those key words. Reread the poem, substituting the synonyms for the words the poet used (for purposes of this exercise, ignore the fact that the synonyms may have more or fewer syllables and thus alter the rhythm). Write an essay analyzing the effects of your substitutions. Provide a sample of the rewritten poem.

6. Select one of the following titles for an essay in comparison and contrast.

A. The Cost of Conformity: Dickinson's "What Soft—Cherubic Creatures" and Cummings's "the Cambridge ladies who live in furnished souls."

B. The Psychology of Hate: Blake's "A Poison Tree" and Dickinson's "Mine Enemy Is Growing Old."

C. The Meaning of Love: Marvell's "To His Coy Mistress" and Donne's "A Valediction: Forbidding Mourning."

D. The Logic of Love: Donne's "The Flea" and Marvell's "To His Coy Mistress."

E. The Images of Love: Shakespeare's Sonnet 130 and Millay's "Love Is Not All."

F. In Praise of a Beloved: Frost's "The Silken Tent" and Roethke's "I Knew a Woman."

G. The Death of Love: Sexton's "The Farmer's Wife" and from Meredith's "Modern Love."

H. Remembering Childhood: Frost's "Birches" and Thomas's "Fern Hill."

I. What the Young Can Never Understand: Housman's "When I Was One-and-Twenty" and Wallace's "In a Spring Still Not Written Of."

J. The Woman's Role: Rich's "Living in Sin" and Sexton's "Cinderella."

K. The Meaning of Nature: Dickinson's "Apparently with No Surprise" and Frost's "Design."

L. The Meaning of Old Age: Arnold's "Growing Old" and Yeats's "Sailing to Byzantium."

M. Untimely Death: Frost's "'Out, Out—'" and Housman's "To an Athlete Dying Young" or Ransom's "Bells for John Whiteside's Daughter" and Roethke's "Elegy for Jane."

N. The Attitude toward Death: Stevens's "Sunday Morning" and Thomas's "Do Not Go Gentle into That Good Night."

7. Analyze the allusions in a poem. Include in your discussion an explanation of the allusion and what it contributes to the poem. Some suggestions:
   Eliot's "The Love Song of J. Alfred Prufrock"
   Auden's "The Unknown Citizen"
   Frost's "Provide, Provide"
   Reid's "Curiosity"
   Milton's Sonnet XVII
   Wordsworth's "The World Is Too Much with Us"
   Cummings's "the Cambridge ladies who live in furnished souls"
   Arnold's "Dover Beach"
   Plath's "Daddy"
   Yeats's "Sailing to Byzantium"
   Frost's "'Out, Out—'"
   Baker's "Formal Application"

8. Analyze the use of irony in a poem. Some suggestions:
   Blake's "The Chimney Sweeper"
   Browning's "My Last Duchess"
   Arnold's "Growing Old"

Hardy's "The Ruined Maid"
Robinson's "Richard Cory"
Frost's "'Out, Out—'"
Bishop's "One Art"

9. Analyze the use of one form of figurative language in a poem. Some suggestions:

   A. Hyperbole in Burns's "A Red, Red Rose" or Marvell's "To His Coy Mistress."

   B. Simile and metaphor in Donne's "A Valediction: Forbidding Mourning," Marvell's "To His Coy Mistress," Frost's "The Silken Tent," Burns's "A Red, Red Rose," Keats's "On First Looking into Chapman's Homer," Shakespeare's sonnets 18 and 130, MacLeish's "Ars Poetica," or Cummings's "O sweet spontaneous."

   C. Symbols in Waller's "Go, Lovely Rose!" Blake's "The Tyger," Frost's "Fire and Ice," Lowell's "Patterns," Reid's "Curiosity," or Meinke's "Advice to My Son."

   D. Paradox in Wallace's "In a Spring Still Not Written Of," Meinke's "Advice to My Son," Yeats's "Easter 1916," Blake's "The Tyger," Stevens's "Peter Quince at the Clavier," Stevens's "Sunday Morning," or Donne's "Death, Be Not Proud."

10. Look carefully at the reproduction of Brueghel's painting *The Fall of Icarus* (p. 1135), and jot down your impressions of it. Include a sentence or two on the "statement" you think Brueghel is making. Now read Auden's poem "Musée des Beaux Arts." In an essay, compare your impressions of the painting with those of the poet. If the poem taught you something about the painting, include that in your essay.

Drama

1. Explicate the opening scene of a play in order to demonstrate how the dramatist lays the groundwork for what is to follow. Some questions you might consider: What information necessary to understanding the action are we given? What do we learn about the characters and their relationships? Do settings and costumes contribute to the exposition?

2. Analyze a play in order to show how nonverbal elements, such as costumes and stage sets, contribute to the theme.

3. Select a minor character in a play, and analyze that character's function. Some possibilities: Roderigo in *Othello*; Marc in *M. Butterfly*; the Valet in *No Exit*.

4. Analyze the language of a play for patterns of imagery that contribute to the development of character, mood, or theme. Some suggestions: images of bestial sexuality in Shakespeare's *Othello*; images of blindness and seeing in Sophocles' *Oedipus Rex*; images of furniture in Sartre's *No Exit*.

5. Assume you are the director of one of the plays in this anthology. For one of the major characters, write a set of director's notes intended for the actor playing the role, in which you describe your conception of how the role should be played.

6. In an essay, describe the playwright's method for achieving dramatic irony in one of the plays you have read.

7. When you attend a performance of a play, you are usually given a program indicating, among other things, the number of acts, the elapsed time between acts, the time and place of the action. It will not include the stage directions of the printed version of the play. Examine the stage directions of a play, and suggest how a director might convey in a performance what the dramatist describes in the stage directions.

And one final general question: One of the commonly accepted notions of art is that it helps us to clarify our own feelings, to give us in vivid and memorable form what we had perhaps felt or thought only vaguely. Select a work (one that you found especially relevant to your own life), and describe how it clarified your own feelings.

Some Matters of Form

Titles

The first word and all main words of titles are capitalized. Ordinarily (unless, of course, they are the first or last word), articles (*a, an,* and *the*), prepositions (*in, on, of, with, about,* etc.), and conjunctions (*and, but, or,* etc.) are not capitalized.

The titles of parts of larger collections, short stories, poems, articles, essays, and songs are enclosed in quotation marks.

The titles of plays, books, movies, periodicals, operas, paintings, and newspapers are italicized. In typed and handwritten manuscripts, italics are represented by underlining.

The title you give your own essay is neither placed in quotation marks nor underlined. However, a quotation used as a part of your title would be enclosed in quotation marks (see the following section on quotations). Similarly, the title of a literary work used as a part of your title would be either placed in quotation marks or underlined depending on the type of work it is.

Quotations

Quotation marks indicate you are transcribing someone else's words; those words must, therefore, be *exactly* as they appear in your source.

As a general rule, quotations of not more than four lines of prose or two lines of poetry are placed between quotation marks and incorporated in your own text:

> At the climactic moment, Robin observes "an uncovered cart.
> There the torches blazed the brightest, there the moon shone
> out like day, and there, in tar-and-feather dignity, sat his
> kinsman, Major Molineux!"

If you are quoting two lines of verse in your text, indicate the division between lines with a slash. Leave a space before and after the slash:

> Prufrock hears the dilettantish talk in a room where "the
> women come and go / Talking of Michelangelo."

Longer quotations are indented ten typewriter spaces and are double-spaced. They are not enclosed in quotation marks, since the indentation signals a quotation.

As noted above, anything quoted, whether enclosed in quotation marks or indented, must be reproduced exactly. If you insert anything—even a word—the inserted material must be placed within brackets. If you wish to omit some material from a passage in quotation marks, the omission (ellipsis) must be indicated by three spaced periods: . . . (an ellipsis mark). When an ellipsis occurs between complete sentences or at the end of a sentence, a fourth period, indicating the end of the sentence, should be inserted. No space precedes the first period.

Full quotation from original:

> As one critic puts it, "Richard Wright, like Dostoevsky be-
> fore him, sends his hero underground to discover the truth
> about the upper world, a world that has forced him to confess
> to a crime he has not committed."

With insertion and omissions:

> As one critic puts it, "Richard Wright . . . sends his hero
> [Fred Daniels] underground to discover the truth about the
> upper world. . . ."

Use a full line of spaced periods to indicate the omission of a line or more of poetry (or of a whole paragraph or more of prose):

```
For I have known them all already, known them all--
Have known the evenings, mornings, afternoons,
I have measured out my life with coffee spoons;

. . . . . . . . . . . . . . . . . . . . . . . . .

And I have known the eyes already, known them all--
The eyes that fix you in a formulated phrase.
```

Periods and commas are placed *inside* quotation marks:

```
In "My Oedipus Complex," the narrator says, "The war was the
most peaceful period of my life."
```

Other punctuation marks go outside the quotation marks unless they are part of the material being quoted.

For poetry quotations, provide the line number or numbers in parentheses immediately following the quotation:

```
With ironic detachment, Prufrock declares that he is "no
prophet" (l. 83).
```

Documentation

You must acknowledge the source of ideas you paraphrase and material you quote. Such acknowledgments are extremely important, for even an unintentional failure to give formal credit to others for their words or ideas can leave you open to an accusation of plagiarism—that is, the presentation of someone else's ideas as your own.

If you use published works as you prepare your paper, you should list those sources as the last page of your essay. Then, in the body of your essay, you will use parenthetical citations that refer to the works you quote or paraphrase. Here is a sample list of works cited that illustrates the mechanical form for different kinds of sources. These samples will probably satisfy your needs, but if you use kinds of sources not listed here, you should consult Joseph Gibaldi and Walter S. Achtert, *MLA Handbook for Writers of Research Papers*, 3rd ed. (New York: Modern Language Association, 1988). That handbook provides sample entries for every imaginable source.

Works Cited

Abcarian, Richard, and Marvin Klotz, eds. Literature: The Human Experience. 6th ed. New York: St. Martin's, 1994.

Cooper, Wendy. Hair, Sex, Society, Symbolism. New York: Stein, 1971.

Fiedler, Leslie. "Come Back to the Raft Ag'in, Huck Honey." Partisan Review 15 (1948): 664–71.

Joyce, James. "Araby." Literature: The Human Experience. 6th ed. Eds. Richard Abcarian and Marvin Klotz. New York: St. Martin's, 1994. 27–31.

———. Dubliners. Eds. Robert Scholes and A. Walton Litz. New York: Penguin, 1976.

The first of these citations is this book. You would use it if you used materials from the editors' introduction or critical appendices. The entry illustrates the form for citing a book with two editors. Note that the first editor's name is presented surname first, but the second is presented with the surname last.

The second entry illustrates the form for citing a book with one author. The third gives the form for an article published in a periodical (note that the title of the article is in quotes and the title of the journal is underlined). The fourth entry shows how to cite a work included in an anthology. The fifth citation, because it is by the same author as the fourth, begins with three hyphens in place of the author's name.

The following paragraph demonstrates the use of parenthetical citations.

> Leslie Fiedler's controversial view of the relationship between Jim and Huck (669–70) uses a method often discussed by other critics (Abcarian and Klotz 1278–79). Cooper's 1971 study (180) raises similar issues, but such methods are not useful when one deals with such a line as "North Richmond Street, being blind, was a quiet street except at the hour when the Christian Brothers' School set the boys free" (Joyce, "Araby" 27). But when Joyce refers to the weather (Dubliners 224), the issue becomes clouded.

This rather whimsical paragraph illustrates the form your parenthetical citations should take. The first citation gives only the page reference, which is all that is necessary because the author's name is given in the text and only one work by that author appears in the list of works cited.

The second citation gives the editors' names and thus identifies the work being cited. It then indicates the appropriate pages.

The third citation, because the author's name is mentioned in the text, gives only a page reference.

The fourth citation must provide the author's name *and* the work cited, because two works by the same author appear in the bibliography.

The last citation, because it refers to an author with two works in the list of works cited, gives the name of the work and the page where the reference can be found.

In short, your parenthetical acknowledgment should contain (1) the *minimum* information required to lead the reader to the appropriate work in the list of works cited and (2) the location within the work to which you refer.

Rather than parenthetical references, some instructors may prefer footnotes (or endnotes). Here is the same paragraph documented with footnotes.

> Leslie Fiedler's controversial view of the relationship between Jim and Huck[1] uses a method often discussed by other critics.[2] Cooper's 1971 study[3] raises similar issues, but such methods are not useful when one deals with such a line as "North Richmond Street, being blind, was a quiet street except at the hour when the Christian Brothers' School set the boys free."[4] But when Joyce refers to the weather,[5] the issue becomes clouded.

> [1]"Come Back to the Raft Ag'in, Huck Honey." Partisan Review 15 (1948): 664–71.
> [2]Richard Abcarian and Marvin Klotz, eds., Literature: The Human Experience, 6th ed. (New York: St. Martin's, 1994) 1278–1279.
> [3]Hair, Sex, Society, Symbolism (New York: Stein, 1971) 180.
> [4]James Joyce, "Araby," Literature: The Human Experience, 6th ed., eds. Richard Abcarian and Marvin Klotz (New York: St. Martin's, 1994) 27.
> [5]Dubliners, eds. Robert Scholes and A. Walton Litz (New York: Penguin, 1976) 224.

Note that when the author's name is given in the text, you do not have to repeat it in the footnote. Subsequent references to a work generally require only the surname of the author (or authors, editor, or editors) and the page number; thus:

> [4]Cooper 175.

If you need to find a model for a different kind of source, don't despair. Simply refer to the *MLA Handbook* (1988).

The main thing to remember about footnoting, and about citations in general, is that the object is to give credit to others wherever it is due and to enable your reader to go directly to your sources, if he or she wishes to do so, as quickly and easily as possible.

Summing Up: A Checklist

1. Start early. You're going to need time for thinking, time for reading and taking notes, time for writing, and (very important) time for breaks between steps.

2. Read the work carefully, and more than once.

3. If you are allowed to choose a topic, choose one that interests you and that you can explore in some depth in a paper of the assigned length. If you have trouble finding a topic, ask yourself as many questions as you can about the work: *What* is it about? *Who* is it about? *Why* do I respond to it as I do? And so forth. Many kinds of questions have been suggested in the preceding pages, and there are numerous questions following the selections and at the ends of the four main sections in this anthology.

4. Convert your topic into a clearly defined thesis: a proposition you intend to argue for and support with evidence from the work. If you have trouble shaping a thesis, try the technique of freewriting—forget about form and just scribble down all your thoughts and opinions: what you like, what you don't like, anything at all. Then ask yourself what made you think or feel as you do.

5. Once you have a thesis, reread the work and take careful notes on three-by-five-inch cards, one note to a card, with a page (or, for poetry, line) reference and a short descriptive heading to remind you of the note's significance. Then arrange the cards in the order that seems appropriate to follow in your essay. If you have access to a word processor, you might type notes on various aspects of your problem and use page breaks to separate materials so that you can arrange hard copy in appropriate order before writing your first draft. Or you can type your notes into a file and use a split screen that will allow you to scan your notes as you write your draft.

6. Start writing, and keep going. This is a rough draft—essentially a blueprint—and is for your eyes only, so don't worry about formalities and polishing. The point is to get your ideas down on paper in approximately the right order. If making a rough outline first will help you, do it. If spontaneous writing works better, do that. But do get a clear statement of your thesis into your first paragraph; it will guide you as you write, since everything you write will (or should) be related to it.

7. Take a break. Let the rough draft cool for at least a few hours, preferably overnight. When you come back to it, you'll be refreshed and you'll think more clearly. You may find that you want to do some reorganizing or add or delete material. You may also want to go back and reread or at least take another look at the work you're writing about.

8. Now, more carefully, working from your rough draft, write a second draft. This will be fuller, clearer, more polished. You'll have a chance to revise (assuming you followed step 1, above), so don't get unnecessarily bogged down; but write this version *as if* it were the version your reader will see. This version, when finished, should be logically and clearly organized. The point of each paragraph should be clear—well expressed and well supported by details or examples—and its relationship to the thesis should be apparent. Transitions between paragraphs should be supplied wherever necessary to make the argument progress smoothly. Quotations should be in place and accurately transcribed.

9. Take a break. This time allow the draft to age for two or three days. At the moment, you're too close to the draft to read it objectively.

10. Pick up the draft as if you were the reader and had never seen it before. Now you will make your final revisions. More than polishing is involved here. This is the time to cut out, mercilessly, things that are not pertinent to your discussion, no matter how interesting or well written they may be. Putting yourself in your reader's place, clarify anything that is vague or ambiguous. Make sure each word is the most precise one you could have chosen for your purpose. Watch, too, for overkill—points that are driven into the ground by too much discussion or detail. Finally, no matter how careful you think you have been, check all your quotations and citations for accuracy. Instructors—rightly—take these things seriously.

11. Here are some tips that will improve the quality of your writing. Search your penultimate draft for sentences that begin "There is," "There are," "It is." Often, a few words later, a "that," "which," or "who" will appear. Reword the sentence to eliminate these insignificant words—have the *subject* of the sentence govern an *active* verb. For example, change: "*There is* a destiny *that* controls the fate *of* man" to "Destiny controls man's fate."

    Generally, replace copulative verbs (forms of the verb *to be*) and passive constructions (the ball *was thrown*) with active verbs and active constructions. Change "To be a student is to know oppression" to "Students know oppression." Change "The essay was read by the class" to "The class read the essay."

    Look for lengthy sequences of prepositional phrases: "The book *with* a red cover *on* the table *in* the living room *of* Bob's house should be read *by* all" might be nicely tightened to "Everyone should read the red-covered book *on* Bob's living room table." We have eliminated four of the first sentence's five prepositions and reduced its twenty-one words to twelve.

Remember that in American English, periods and commas always go inside the concluding quotation mark: His nickname was "Yogi." Despite his peculiar nickname, "Yogi," he was an all-star catcher in the American League.

Colons and semicolons go outside the concluding quotation mark: He was nicknamed "Yogi"; he was a great catcher for the Yankees.

12. Type or neatly write out in ink the final copy for submission to your instructor, taking care to follow any special instructions about format that you have been given. Don't rush; be meticulous. When you have finished, proofread the final copy very carefully, keeping an eye out for errors in spelling or punctuation, omitted words, disagreement between subjects and verbs or between pronouns and antecedents, and other flaws (such as typographical errors) that will detract from what you have worked so hard to write.

Biographical Notes on the Authors

Samuel Allen (b. 1917)   Born in Columbus, Ohio, the son of a member of the clergy, Allen attended Fisk University and graduated from Harvard Law School in 1941. He spent a year as deputy assistant district attorney in New York City, had his own private law practice, and held an assortment of posts including assistant deputy counsel for the U.S. Information Agency (1961–1964). Previously a professor of law (Texas Southern University) and humanities (Tuskegee Institute), Allen joined the English department of Boston University in 1971, the same year he won the National Endowment for the Arts award for poetry. He published *Every Round* and *Other Poems* in 1987. Allen's translations, essays, and poems have appeared in scores of anthologies and journals, including *Presence Africaine* and *Journal of Afro-American Studies*, often under the pen name Paul Vesey.

Woody Allen (b. 1935)   After being dismissed from both City College of New York and New York University, this precocious and prototypical New Yorker became a television comedy writer at the age of eighteen. He wrote two successful Broadway plays; his first screenplay, *What's New Pussycat?*, appeared in 1965. A dozen years in show business gave him the confidence to set out on his own, and he began performing as a standup comic. Soon after, he embarked on the filmmaking—writing, performing, directing, and producing—career for which he is famous. His talents, and those of the actors and technical group he has brought together as a kind of filmmaking repertory company, account for his reputation as an innovative contributor to cinema history. (His 1977 film, *Annie Hall*, won four Academy Awards.) In his spare time, he plays the clarinet in a Dixieland jazz group at a New York nightspot, and continues to write occasional pieces like *Death Knocks*.

Matthew Arnold (1822–1888)   Born in Middlesex, England, Arnold attended Rugby School (where his father was headmaster) and studied classics at Oxford. Following his graduation in 1844, he became a fellow at Oxford, and a master at Rugby School. In 1851, he was appointed inspector of schools in England and was sent by the government to observe educational systems in Europe. He remained in that post for some thirty-five years. As a poet, Arnold took inspiration from Greek tragedies, Keats, and Wordsworth. His collections include *Empedocles on Etna and Other Poems* (1852). An eminent social and literary critic in his later years, Arnold lectured in America in 1883 and 1886. His essay "The Function of Criticism" sheds light on his transition from poet to critic.

Much of his work is collected in *Complete Prose Works* (11 volumes, 1960–1977).

W. H. Auden (1907–1973)   A poet, playwright, translator, librettist, critic, and editor, Wystan Hugh Auden was born in York, son of a medical officer and a nurse. He attended Oxford from 1925 to 1928, then taught, traveled, and moved from faculty to faculty of several universities in the United States (where he became a naturalized citizen in 1946). He won the Pulitzer Prize in 1948 for his collection *The Age of Anxiety*, an expression he coined to describe the 1930s. While his early writing exhibited Marxist sympathies and reflected the excitement of new Freudian psychoanalytic thought, he later embraced Christianity and produced sharply honed verse in the rhyme and meter of traditional forms.

Donald W. Baker (b. 1923)   Born in Boston, son of a cabdriver, Baker earned a Ph.D. in 1955 from Brown University, where he taught English from 1948 to 1953. He joined the faculty of Wabash College in Crawfordsville, Indiana, in 1953, served six years as the director of drama, and was named poet-in-residence in 1964. Married in 1945 and the father of two, Baker has enjoyed giving readings and workshops. However, he is no stranger to writer's block and wryly admits: "I'm not prolific and have a lot of trouble producing anything at all."

Toni Cade Bambara (b. 1939)   Born in New York City, Bambara was educated there and in Italy and Paris. Early in her career she worked as an investigator for the New York State Department of Social Welfare but has devoted herself for many years to teaching and writing. One of the best representatives of a group of African American writers who emerged in the 1960s, Bambara has been a consistent civil rights activist, both politically and culturally involved in African American life. Much of her writing focuses on African American women, particularly as they confront experiences that force them to new awareness. She is the author of three collections of short stories, *Gorilla, My Love* (1972), *Tales and Stories for Black Folks* (1971), and *The Sea Birds Are Still Alive: Collected Stories* (1977), and two novels, *The Salt Eaters* (1980) and *If Blessing Comes* (1987). She is also editor of *The Black Woman: An Anthology* (1970).

Imamu Amiri Baraka (LeRoi Jones) (b. 1934)   Born in Newark, New Jersey, Baraka spent a year at Rutgers, then moved to and graduated from Howard University in 1954. He then spent three years in the U.S. Air Force. As a civilian again, he studied at the New School for Social Research and Columbia. Between 1961 and 1967, he taught at the New School for Social Research, the University of Buffalo, Columbia, and San Francisco State University, and wrote three violent, antiwhite one-act plays, *Dutchman* (1963), *The Slave* (1964), and *The Toilet* (1964). In 1965 (the same year he divorced his white wife) he changed his name to emphasize his African American identity. During those years he was arrested a number of times for his radical political activities. One arrest culminated in his conviction and unusually harsh three-year prison sentence for illegal possession of weapons during the Newark riots of 1967. That conviction was overturned on appeal. He has published essays, stories, poems, and plays. As well, he wrote a history of black Americans through their music, *Blues People: Negro Music in America* (1963). In collaboration with his wife Amina, he continued those studies with *The Music: Reflections on Jazz and Blues* (1987). Determined to discover and nourish the talents within the African American community, he founded the Black Arts Repertory Theater and, later, Spirit House, an African American community theater in Newark. Baraka is currently at work on an epic poem tentatively titled *Why's/Wise.*

Donald Barthelme (1931–1989)   Born in Philadelphia and raised in Texas, Barthelme wrote poetry, essays, and reviews for his high school and college papers before turning to short fiction. His first stories appeared in the *New Yorker*, where he continued to publish. His first collection of stories, *Come Back, Doctor Caligari* (1964), brought him immediate critical fame; popular fame followed with his novel *Snow White* (1967). Barthelme's early reputation as an experimentalist and technical innovator was enhanced by *City Life* (1970), a collection of short stories. Although some Barthelme detractors have called his fiction "nonsensical," "absurd," and "deranged," the publication of *Sixty Stories* (1981) led to a surge of critical interest that secured his reputation as a major writer. He was the recipient of a Guggenheim Fellowship (1966), and *The Slightly Irregular Fire Engine* won the 1971 National Book Award for Children's Literature.

Elizabeth Bishop (1911–1979)   Bishop was born in Worcester, Massachusetts. Her father died before she was a year old; four years later, when her mother suffered a mental breakdown, Bishop was taken to live with her grandmother in Nova Scotia. Although her mother lived until 1934, Bishop saw her for the last time in 1916, a visit recalled in one of her rare autobiographical stories, "In the Village." Bishop planned to enter Cornell Medical School after graduating from Vassar, but was persuaded by Marianne Moore to become a writer. For the next fifteen years, she was a virtual nomad, traveling in Canada, Europe, and North and South America. In 1951, she finally settled in Rio de Janeiro, where she lived for almost twenty years. During the final decade of her life, Bishop continued to travel, but she resumed living in the United States and taught frequently at Harvard. She was an austere writer, publishing only four slim volumes of poetry: *North and South* (1946); *A Cold Spring* (1955), which won the Pulitzer Prize; *Questions of Travel* (1965); and *Geography III* (1976), which won the National Book Critics' Circle Award. *The Complete Poems (1927–1979)* was published after her death, as was a collection of her prose. Despite her modest output, she has earned an enduring place of respect among twentieth-century poets.

William Blake (1757–1827)   Born in London to an obscure family, Blake was educated at home until he was ten, then enrolled in a drawing school, advancing ultimately to a formal apprenticeship as an engraver. At an early age, Blake exhibited talent as both an artist and a poet, and throughout his life read widely among modern philosophers and poets. Throughout his life, he experienced mystical visions that provided him with the inspiration for many of his poems. Blake devised a process he called illuminated printing, which involved the preparation of drawings and decorative frames to complement his poems. He published *Songs of Innocence* (1789) and *Songs of Experience* (1794) in this fashion. These books, as well as the many subsequent works he wrote and illustrated, earned him a reputation as one of the most important artists of his day. Many of Blake's works assert his conviction that the established church and state hinder rather than nurture human freedom and the sense of divine love.

Louise Bogan (1879–1970)   Bogan was born in Livermore Falls, Maine, attended Girls' Latin School in Boston (1910–1915), and spent one year at Boston University. After her husband's death in 1920, she spent time in Vienna and published her first collection of poems, *Body of This Death* (1923). She was visiting professor at the University of Washington (1948) and Brandeis University (1964–1965), as well as a frequent contributor to the *New Yorker* (1931–1968). Bogan's concise and emotionally restrained poems, reminiscent of Emily Dickinson's, are collected in *The Blue Estuaries* (1968). Her sharp wit is revealed in a 1973 collection of correspondence, *What the Woman Lived: Selected Letters 1920–1970*, and in her collection of critical essays, *A Poet's Alphabet: Reflections on the Literary Art and Vocation* (1970). Bogan's honors include two Guggenheim Fellowships and the 1955 Bollingen Prize.

Jorge Luis Borges (1899–1986)   Borges was born in Buenos Aires, Argentina, to a middle-class family that spoke both Spanish and English at home. His love of literature began early, encouraged by a father who had himself aspired to a writing career. As a young man, he traveled and studied in Europe, where he published reviews, essays, and poetry. When he returned to Buenos Aires in 1921, he became a well-known exponent of experimental writing. However, he remained relatively unknown outside Argentina until he received an important international literary prize in 1961, the Prix Formentor. The fame that came with the prize led to the simultaneous publication in six countries of a collection of short stories, *Fictions* (1945), and to the first of his many lecture tours in the United States. Borges created much of his best-known fiction during his later years, when failing eyesight (eventually resulting in blindness) and poor health made him a semi-invalid. By the time of his death, his prolific and innovative writing had earned him a reputation and influence that extended far beyond his native Argentina.

Elizabeth Brewster (b. 1922)   Born in Chipman, New Brunswick, Canada, Elizabeth Brewster earned a B.A. (1946) from the University of New Brunswick, and an A.M. (1947) from Radcliffe College. She completed a degree in library science in 1953 at the University of Toronto, and worked as a library cataloger at Carleton University, Ottawa, for several years thereafter. She moved to the University of Indiana library in 1957, and completed her Ph.D. there in 1962. Her first book of poems, *East Coast*, was published in 1951, and she has produced, over the years, a half dozen volumes of poetry as well as a novel (*The Sisters* [1974]). She has been twice recognized by the Canada Council with Senior Artist Awards (1971, 1976). Her professional career shifted from the library to the classroom in 1971, when she became a professor at the University of Saskatchewan.

Edwin Brock (b. 1927)   Born in London, Brock served two years in the Royal Navy. He was a police officer when he completed his first poetry collection, *An Attempt at Exorcism* (1959). Influenced by American confessional poets, Brock writes about family relationships, childhood memories, and sometimes shifts into the linguistic mode of an advertising copywriter (which he became in 1959). Suggesting that all poetry is to some extent autobiographical, Brock argues "that most activity is an attempt to define oneself in one way or another: for me poetry, and only poetry, has provided this self-defining act." His works include over a dozen poetry collections; a novel, *The Little White God* (1962); and an autobiography, *Here. Now. Always.* (1977).

Gwendolyn Brooks (b. 1917)   Brooks was born in Topeka, Kansas, attended public schools in Chicago, and graduated from Wilson Junior College in 1936. Her poetic talent was recognized when she attended a poetry workshop at Chicago's Southside Community Art Center. Shortly after, she published her first book of poems, *A Street in Bronzeville* (1945). She soon established her reputation as a major poet and won many honors, including the Pulitzer Prize for poetry in 1950. No African American woman before her had ever achieved such critical acclaim as a poet. While her poetry has always focused on the hardships and joys of being poor and black in America, she steadily moved away from the apolitical integrationist views of her early years until, by the 1960s, she had become a passionate advocate of African American consciousness and activism. Besides reworking traditional forms such as the ballad and sonnet, Brooks achieves great power in many of her poems by juxtaposing formal speech with black vernacular. Among her other works are *Annie Allen* (1949), *The Bean Eaters* (1960), *In the Mecca* (1968), and *To Disembark* (1981).

Robert Browning (1812–1889)   Born in London, Browning attended a private school and was later tutored at home. After one year as a student of Greek at the University of London, he moved with his family to Hatcham, where he studied, wrote poetry, and practiced writing for the theater. In 1845, he began exchanging poems and letters with the already famous poet Elizabeth Barrett;

they eloped in 1846. They moved to Italy, where Browning completed most of his work. When Elizabeth died in 1861, he returned to England and began to establish his own reputation. He is noted especially for his fine dramatic monologues in which a wide range of characters reveals the complexity of human belief and passion. His many volumes of poetry include *Dramatis Personae* (1864) and *The Ring and the Book* (1868–1869).

Marianne Burke (b. 1957)   Born in Poughkeepsie, New York, Marianne Burke started writing poetry in her sophomore year at Vassar. She went on to Stanford University, where she earned an M.A. She won writing fellowships to both Yaddo (1991) and McDowell (1992), and has published her poems in various magazines, including the *Southern Poetry Review*, the *Threepenny Review*, and the *New Yorker*. Until recently she worked in the *New Yorker*'s editorial department. She lives in New York City. When asked to comment about her work she pointed out that "one of my earliest teachers, the poet William Heyen, used to say that it was possible to write too much. I'm just beginning to understand what he means. For instance, my poem 'Funeral Home' took two years to write. I needed that much time to write both feelingly and impersonally about my mother's death. Having lost both my parents at too early an age, death is one of my favorite subjects. I don't write poems to merely record my losses or to open old wounds, but to recover some of life's sweetness and mystery."

Robert Burns (1759–1796)   Born in Scotland to a family of poor tenant farmers, Burns was working in the fields with his father by age twelve. During these early years, the family moved often in fruitless attempts to improve its lot. Although Burns received formal education only intermittently, he read widely on his own. After the death of his father, Burns and his brother worked vainly to make their farm pay, an effort Burns was able to abandon when his first volume of poetry, *Poems, Chiefly in the Scottish Dialect* (1786) brought him overnight fame. One result of this fame was his appointment as an excise officer, a position that gave him some financial security while he continued to write poetry. Burns's humble origins instilled in him a lifelong sympathy for the poor and downtrodden, the rebels and iconoclasts, as well as a disdain for religion, particularly Calvinism and what he considered the hypocrisy of its "devout" ministers.

Robert Olen Butler, Jr. (b. 1945)   Born in Granite City, Illinois, Butler attended Northwestern University as a theater major (B.S., 1967) and then switched to playwriting at the University of Iowa (M.A., 1969). He rose to the rank of sergeant in the Army Military Intelligence while serving in Vietnam (1969–1972). There he became a fluent speaker of the language and came to understand and honor Vietnamese culture. In 1972 he married the poet Marylin Geller—they have one child. After the usual collection of odd jobs, including steel mill labor, taxi driving, and substitute teaching in high schools, Butler joined Fairfield Publications and worked on such trade publications as *Electronic News*. He became editor-in-chief of *Energy User News* in 1975. Although his first published novel, *The Alleys of Eden* (1981), was rejected twenty-one times before it was finally published, it was well received and even nominated for a number of literary prizes. *Sun Dogs* (1982), as did his first novel, makes use of Butler's Vietnam experiences, and his collection of short stories, *A Good Scent from a Strange Mountain* (1992), reveals his remarkable ability to identify with the Vietnamese refugees trying to remake their lives in the United States. In a review of Butler's first novel, the writer praised Butler's "ability to catch tiny shifts of feeling, momentary estrangements, sudden dislocations of mood—a tool as valuable to the novelist as a scalpel to the surgeon." *A Good Scent from a Strange Mountain* was awarded the 1993 Pulitzer Prize for fiction.

George Gordon, Lord Byron (1788–1824)   Born in London of an aristocratic family, Byron was educated at the best grammar schools and at Cambridge. He early became a public figure, as much for the notoriety of his personal life as for the popularity of his irreverent, satiric poetry. Among his scandalous affairs, the one he was rumored to have had with his half-sister forced him into European exile in 1816. His political life was equally flamboyant: he began his career in the House of Lords with a speech defending the working classes and he met his death in Greece as the result of a fever he contracted while fighting for Greek independence. Byron published a volume of poetry while at Cambridge, but fame and popularity came with later volumes of poems, notably *Childe Harold's Pilgrimage* (1812–1818) and *Don Juan* (1819–1824). Despite Byron's acknowledged literary greatness and popularity, he was deemed morally unfit for burial in Westminster Abbey.

Thomas Campion (1567–1620)   Campion spent his early childhood in London, studied at Cambridge, then returned to London in 1586 to study law. It appears that Campion served, for a short time, as a soldier in France. In 1595, he published a collection of Latin poems, *Poemata*. After the publication of this volume, he apparently went abroad to study medicine and, later, music (though it is not known when or where). His first volume of English poems, *A Book of Ayres*, appeared in 1601; the other three volumes appeared between 1601 and 1617. Campion also wrote masques for presentation at court, often composing the music for his own lyrics. Toward the end of his life, he wrote a treatise on music that became a standard text.

Raymond Carver (1938–1989)   Carver was born in Clatskanie, Oregon, the son of a sawmill worker and a mother who did odd jobs. He graduated from high school at eighteen and was married and the father of two children before he was twenty. The following years were difficult as he struggled to develop a writing career while supporting a family. While at Chico State College (now California State University, Chico), Carver took a creative writing course that profoundly affected him. He went on to earn a B.A. degree (1963) from Humboldt State College in Eureka; he spent the following year studying writing at the University of Iowa. As he became known, he began to lecture on English and creative writing at various universities, including the University of Iowa Writer's Workshop. He taught at Goddard College in Vermont and was from 1980 to 1983 professor of English at Syracuse University. In 1983, he received the Mildred and Harold Straus living award, which allowed him for the next five years to devote himself full-time to writing. His first collection of short stories, *Will You Please Be Quiet, Please* (1976), was nominated for the National Book Award. Other short story collections include *What We Talk about When We Talk about Love* (1981) and *Cathedral* (1984). He also published five volumes of poems, among them *Near Klamath* (1968), *Ultramarine* (1986), and *A New Path to the Waterfall* (1989), his last book. During the last years of his life, Carver lived with the poet and short story writer Tess Gallagher, whom he married shortly before his death.

Kate Chopin (1851–1904)   Born Kate O'Flaherty in St. Louis, Missouri, Chopin was raised by her mother, grandmother, and great-grandmother, all widows, after her father's death when she was four. In 1870, following her graduation from Sacred Heart Convent, she married Oscar Chopin and moved to New Orleans, where she became a housewife and mother (she had six children). Upon her husband's death in 1882, she returned to her mother's home in St. Louis and began her career as a writer. Her first novel, *At Fault* (1890), and her stories, collected in *Bayou Folk* (1894) and *A Night in Acadie* (1897), gained her a reputation as a vivid chronicler of the lives of Creoles and Acadians ("Cajuns") in Louisiana. Many of these stories explore a female protagonist's attempts to achieve self-fulfillment. Her novel *The Awakening* (1899) is probably her most ambitious exploration of this theme. It is the story of a woman whose awakening to her passion and inner self leads her to adultery and suicide. The storm of controversy with which this work was met virtually ended Chopin's literary career.

Lucille Clifton (b. 1936)   Born in Depew, New York, Clifton attended Howard University (1953–1955) and Fredonia State Teachers College. She worked as a claims clerk in the New York State Division of Employment, Buffalo (1958–1960), and as literature assistant in the Office of Education in Washington, D.C. (1960–1971). In 1969, she received the YM-YWHA Poetry Center Discovery Award, and her first collection, *Good Times*, was selected as one of the ten best books of 1969 by the *New York Times*. From 1971 to 1974 she was poet-in-residence at Coppin State College in Baltimore, and in 1979 she was named poet laureate of the state of Maryland. She has written many collections for children and a free-verse chronicle of five generations of her family, *Generations: A Memoir* (1976). Her most recent volume of poetry is *Quilting: Poems 1987–1990* (1991). Noted for celebrating ordinary people and everyday things, Clifton has said "I am a black woman poet, and I sound like one."

Stephen Crane (1871–1900)   Born in Newark, New Jersey, the fourteenth and youngest child of a Methodist minister who died when Stephen was nine years old, Crane was raised by his strong-minded mother. His brief college career, first at Lafayette College and then at Syracuse University, was dominated by his interest in baseball; he left college after two semesters, and moved on to a bohemian life in New York City. There he wandered through the slums, observing and developing a strong sympathy for the underclass of boozers and prostitutes that inhabited the Bowery. His first novel, *Maggie: A Girl of the Streets* (1893), described the inevitable consequences of grinding poverty—but no publisher would take a chance on Crane's bleak and biting vision. He published it at his own expense, but it found no audience. Without any military experience, and at the age of twenty-four, Crane produced *The Red Badge of Courage* (1895), a novel that made him famous and became an American classic. For the remainder of his life, he traveled about the world as a writer and war correspondent. He died of a tubercular infection in Badenweiler, Germany. Despite the brevity of his writing career, Crane left behind a substantial volume of work that includes a number of brilliant short stories and innovative poems.

Victor Hernández Cruz (b. 1949)   Cruz was born in Aguas Buenas, Puerto Rico, and came with his family to New York City in 1954. He recalls, "My family life was full of music, guitars and conga drums, maracas and songs. . . . Even when it was five below zero in New York [my mother] sang warm tropical ballads." By 1966, he had already completed a collection of verse, *Papo Got His Gun*, and in 1969 published *Snaps*. He has edited *Umbra* magazine in New York, lectured at the University of California, Berkeley, and taught at San Francisco State University. Cruz says he writes in three languages: Spanish, English, and Bilingual. "From the mixture a totally new language emerges, an intense collision, not just of words, but of attitudes." His other works include *Mainland* (1973), *Tropicalizations* (1976), and *Rhythm, Content, and Flavor: New Selected Poems* (1989).

Countee Cullen (1903–1946)   Born Countee L. Porter in New York City, Cullen was adopted by the Reverend and Mrs. Cullen in 1918 and raised in Harlem. He was extraordinarily precocious, and by 1920 his poems had been published in *Poetry*, the *Nation*, and *Harper's*. He published his famous poem "Heritage" in 1925, the year he graduated from New York University. After earning an M.A. in English from Harvard in 1926, he taught French in a junior high school and was assistant editor of the National Urban League's *Opportunity: Journal of Negro Life*. Cullen, along with Langston Hughes and Jean Toomer, was a central figure in the Harlem Renaissance of the 1920s. He received a Guggenheim Fellowship in 1929. In addition to five volumes of poetry, he published a novel, *One Way to Heaven* (1932), which deals with the interaction between upper- and lower-class African Americans in Harlem in the 1920s.

E. E. Cummings (1894–1962)   Born in Cambridge, Massachusetts, Edward Estlin Cummings attended Harvard (B.A., 1915; M.A., 1916), served as a volunteer ambulance driver in France during World War I, was imprisoned for three months in a French detention camp, served in the United States Army (1918–1919), then studied art and painting in Paris (1920–1924). His prose narrative *The Enormous Room* (1922), a recollection of his imprisonment, brought instant acclaim. Several volumes of poetry followed. His experiments with punctuation, line division, and capitalization make his work immediately recognizable. In a letter to young poets published in a high school newspaper, Cummings said, "[N]othing is quite so easy as using words like somebody else. We all of us do exactly this nearly all the time—and whenever we do it, we're not poets."

Kate Daniels (b. 1953)   Born in Richmond, Virginia, Daniels was educated at the University of Virginia (B.A., 1975) and Columbia University (M.A., 1975). She has taught at the University of Virginia and at the University of Massachusetts and is presently an instructor in creative writing at Louisiana State University. Since 1979, she has been coeditor of *Poetry East*. Her first collection of poems, *The White Wave* (1984), won the Agnes Lynch Starrett Poetry Prize of the University of Pittsburgh in 1983. In 1985 she was awarded a fellowship from the Mary Ingraham Bunting Institute of Harvard University for her literary biography of the poet Muriel Rukeyser (1984). Her works have been published by many journals, among them the *Virginia Quarterly Review*, the *Massachusetts Review*, and the *New England Review*.

Emily Dickinson (1830–1886)   Dickinson, one of three children, was born in Amherst, Massachusetts. Her father was a prominent lawyer. Except for one year away at a nearby college and a trip with her sister to Washington, D.C., to visit her father when he was serving in Congress, she lived out her life, unmarried, in her parents' home. During her trip to Washington, she met the Reverend Charles Wadsworth, a married man, whom she came to characterize as her "dearest earthly friend." Little is known of this relationship except that Dickinson's feelings for Wadsworth were strong. In 1862 Wadsworth moved to San Francisco, an event that coincided with a period of Dickinson's intense poetic creativity. Also in that year, she initiated a literary correspondence with the critic T. W. Higginson, to whom she sent some of her poems for his reactions. Higginson, although he recognized her talent, was puzzled by her startling originality and urged her to write more conventionally. Unable to do so, she concluded, we may surmise, that she would never see her poems through the press. In fact, only seven of her poems were published while she was alive, none of them with her consent. After her death, the extraordinary richness of her imaginative life came to light with the discovery of her more than one thousand lyrics.

John Donne (1572–1631)   Born in London into a prosperous Roman Catholic family of tradespeople, at a time when England was staunchly anti-Catholic, Donne was forced to leave Oxford without a degree because of his religion. He studied law and, at the same time, read widely in theology in an attempt to decide whether the Roman or the Anglican Church was the true Catholic Church, a decision he was not able to make for many years. In the meantime, he became known as a witty man of the world and the author of original, often dense, erotic poems. Donne left his law studies, participated in two naval expeditions, and then became secretary to a powerful noble, a job he lost when he was briefly sent to prison for secretly marrying his patron's niece. In 1615, at the age of forty-two, Donne accepted ordination in the Anglican Church. He quickly earned a reputation as one of the greatest preachers of his time. He was Dean of St. Paul's from 1621 until his death. In his later years, Donne rejected the poetry of his youth.

Michael Drayton (1563–1631)   Born in Warwickshire, England, Drayton was ten years old when he asked his tutor to make him a poet. He was presumably trained to follow rigid rules and drilled in the art of imitation. Because Drayton failed to mention the late Queen Elizabeth in his congratulatory verse when King James I was crowned, he was denied any reward or appointment by the new king. During a long career, he was the first to write English odes in the style of Horace. He also wrote *England's Heroicall Epistles* (1597), a series of imagined letters exchanged between renowned lovers in English history, as well as pastorals, plays, and a 30,000-line historical-geographical poem called *Poly-Olbion*. A friend of both William Shakespeare and Ben Jonson, he was devoted to Anne Goodere, Lady Rainsford, and revealed his devotion in a sonnet cycle, *Ideas Mirrour*, first published in 1594.

Alan Dugan (b. 1923)   Dugan was born in Brooklyn, New York, attended Queens College and Olivet College, served in the Air Force during World War II, and received a B.A. in English from Mexico City College in 1951. He taught at Sarah Lawrence College from 1967 to 1971, then joined the faculty of the Fine Arts Work Center in Provincetown, Massachusetts. Winner of the Pulitzer Prize (1962) for his first published collection, *Poems* (1961), Dugan has been admired for his prosaic, unsentimental language, and his ironic treatment of humorously mundane subjects.

Paul Laurence Dunbar (1872–1906)   The son of former slaves, Dunbar was born in Dayton, Ohio, where he graduated from Dayton High School (1891) and worked for two years as an elevator operator. In 1894, he worked in Chicago at the World's Columbian Exhibition. His first verse collection, *Oak and Ivy*, was published in 1893. William Dean Howells, an eminent editor, author, and critic, encouraged him to write and had him join a Lecture Bureau in 1896. Dunbar read his own works in the United States and traveled to England in 1897. While Dunbar maintained that African American poetry was not much different from white (and wrote many poems in standard English), he often wrote poems in black dialect that seemed to cater to the racial stereotypes of his white audience. He died of tuberculosis in 1906. His complete works appear in *The Dunbar Reader* (1975).

T. S. Eliot (1888–1965)   Thomas Stearns Eliot was born in St. Louis, Missouri. His father was president of the Hydraulic Press Brick Company, his mother a teacher, social worker, and writer. Educated in private academies, Eliot earned two philosophy degrees at Harvard (B.A., 1909; M.A., 1910). After graduate study in Paris and England, he worked for eight years as a clerk in Lloyd's Bank in London, and became a naturalized British citizen in 1927. He was editor, then director of Faber & Gwyer Publishers (later Faber & Faber) from 1925 to 1965, and spent time in the United States as a visiting lecturer and scholar. Admirers and detractors agree that Eliot was the most imposing and influential poet writing between the world wars. His poems "The Love Song of J. Alfred Prufrock" (1917) and *The Waste Land* (1922) are among his earliest and most famous. Acknowledging his dependence on a preexisting cultural tradition, Eliot explained: "The existing order is complete before the new work arrives; for order to persist after the supervention of novelty, the whole existing order must be altered." Eliot also wrote plays, including *Murder in the Cathedral* (1935) and *The Cocktail Party* (1950). The long-running Broadway musical *Cats* is based on his 1939 verse collection, *Old Possum's Book of Practical Cats*. He won the Nobel Prize for literature in 1948.

Harlan Ellison (b. 1934)   Born in Cleveland, Ohio, Ellison published his first story when he was thirteen. He left Ohio State University after two years and worked at a variety of odd jobs while establishing himself as a writer. In a career spanning over thirty-seven years, he has written or edited fifty-eight books, more than twelve hundred stories, essays, reviews, articles, motion picture scripts, and teleplays. He has won the Hugo award eight and a half times, the Nebula three times, the Edgar Allan Poe award of the Mystery Writers of America twice, the Bram Stoker award of Horror Writers of America twice, the World Fantasy Award, the British Fantasy Award, and the Silver Pen award for journalism from P.E.N. He is the only scenarist in Hollywood ever to have won the Writers Guild of America award for Most Outstanding Teleplay four times for solo work. His latest books are *The Harlan Ellison Hornbook*, a thirty-five-year retrospective of his work; *The Essential Ellison*; and *The City on the Edge of Forever*, the first book publication of his *Star Trek* script in its original (not aired) version. He lives with his wife, Susan, in the Lost Aztec Temple of Mars somewhere in the Los Angeles area.

Louise Erdrich (b. 1954)   Born in Little Falls, Minnesota, Erdrich grew up in Wahepton, North Dakota, a member of the Turtle Mountain Band of Chippewa. Her grandfather was for many years tribal chair of the reservation where her parents taught in the Bureau of Indian Affairs School. She attended Dartmouth College, earning a degree in anthropology (1976) as well as prizes for fiction and poetry, including the American Academy of Poets Prize. She returned to North Dakota for a brief period of teaching before going on to study creative writing at Johns Hopkins University (M.A., 1979). The following year, she returned to Dartmouth as a writer-in-residence. Her works have appeared in the *New England Review* and *Redbook* as well as such anthologies of Native American writing as *Earth Power Coming* and *That's What She Said: Contemporary Poetry and Fiction by Native American Women*. She has published two collections of poems, *Jacklight* (1984) and *Baptism of Desire* (1989). Her novel *Love Medicine* (1984) won the National Book Critics Circle Award. *Beet Queen* (1986) and *Tracks* (1988) extend the histories of families dealt with in *Love Medicine*. In 1991, Erdrich and her husband, Michael Dorris, a professor of Native American Studies at Dartmouth, published *The Crown of Columbus*, a collaborative novel about Christopher Columbus's discovery of America. They have pledged to donate a part of their royalties to American Indian charities.

William Faulkner (1897–1962)   Faulkner was born in New Albany, Mississippi, and lived most of his life in Oxford, the seat of the University of Mississippi. Although he did not graduate from high school, he did attend the university as a special student from 1919 to 1921. During this period, he also worked as a janitor, a bank clerk, and a postmaster. His southern forebears had held slaves, served during the Civil War, endured the indignities of Reconstruction, fought duels, even wrote the occasional romance of the old South. Faulkner mined these generous layers of history in his work. He created the mythical Yoknapatawpha County in northern Mississippi, and traced the destinies of its inhabitants from the colonial era to the middle of the twentieth century in such novels as *The Sound and the Fury* (1929), *Light in August* (1932), and *Absalom, Absalom!* (1936). Further, Faulkner described the decline of the pre–Civil War aristocratic families and the rise of mean-spirited money grubbers in a trilogy: *The Hamlet* (1940), *The Town* (1957), *The Mansion* (1959). Recognition came late, and Faulkner fought a constant battle to keep afloat financially. During the 1940s, he wrote screenplays in Hollywood. But, finally, his achievement brought him the Nobel Prize in 1950.

James Fenton (b. 1949)   Born in Lincoln, England, Fenton earned a B.A. (1970) from Magdalen College, Oxford University. His earliest volumes of verse appeared during his undergraduate years: *Our Western Furniture* (1968) and *Put Thou Thy Tears Into My Bottle* (1969). He wrote for the *New Statesman and Nation* and continued to publish relatively few but always finely crafted poems. Almost half of his collection *Children in Exile: Poems 1968–1984* is light verse, but often those poems move from whimsy to horror. He won the 1984 Geoffrey Faber Memorial Prize for his poetry. He translated the lyrics of Verdi's opera *Rigoletto*, controversially setting the action in the 1950s New York Mafia world. He accompanied Redmond O'Hanlon on a remarkable trip to

Borneo that served as the source for O'Hanlon's comic travel book *Into the Heart of Borneo* (1984). *Children in Exile*'s appearance in the United States (1985) generated an enthusiastic response to the relatively unknown British poet. More recently, Fenton has published a collection of essays, *The Snap Revolution* (1986) and a travel book with political overtones, *All the Wrong Places: Adrift in the Politics of the Pacific Rim* (1988).

Lawrence Ferlinghetti (b. 1919)   Born Lawrence Ferling, this irreverent writer restored his original family name in 1954. He earned a B.A. in journalism from the University of North Carolina in 1941, became lieutenant commander in the U.S. Naval Reserve during World War II, then received graduate degrees from Columbia and the Sorbonne. He worked as a translator of French before rising to prominence in the "beat" poetry movement of the 1950s, which sought to rejuvenate and popularize poetry. His controversial work drew raves from many critics, even though one critic called it "real jivy, real groovy, all that— but ultimately kind of stupid." Known chiefly for his poetry, he has written a novel, *Her* (1960), and some unsympathetically reviewed plays. As a successful publisher (he cofounded the San Francisco bookstore, City Lights, and the two publishing enterprises, City Lights Books and the Pocket Poets Series), Ferlinghetti appreciates the irony of his ascendance in a system he has repudiated. His early work, *A Coney Island of the Mind* (1958), remains a best-selling poetry collection.

Edward Field (b. 1924)   Born in Brooklyn, New York, Field attended New York University and served in the U.S. Air Force during World War II. His confessional, often humorous poetry grew out of an unhappy, repressed childhood. One critic calls him a "Jewish Walt Whitman" who writes "to encourage the heart." His honors include the Lamont Award (1962), a Guggenheim Fellowship (1963), and the Shelley Memorial Award (1975). His collections include *Stand Up, Friend, with Me* (1963), *A Full Heart* (1977), and *Sweet Gwendolyn and the Countess* (1977). *New and Selected Poems from The Book of My Life* appeared in 1987, and, with Gerald Locklin and Charles Stetler, he compiled *A New Geography of Poetry* in 1992.

Harvey Fierstein (b. 1954)   Fierstein was born in Brooklyn, New York. His father was a handkerchief manufacturer and his mother, a school librarian. He began his career in the theater at the age of eleven as a founding actor in the Gallery Players Community Theater in Brooklyn. Aware of his sexual orientation as a teenager, he performed in nightclubs as a female impersonator. He earned a B.F.A. from Pratt Institute in 1973, and added writing and producing to his early acting skills as he embarked on a remarkable career. He wrote the three one-act plays that constitute *Torch Song Trilogy* between 1976 and 1979— all were produced in small theaters. But when he starred in the production that opened in an off-off-Broadway house (1981), and later moved to Broadway, his considerable talents were widely recognized. In fact, he is the first person to win a Tony award for best actor and best play for the same production. Fierstein has characterized himself as the first "real live, out-of-the-closet queer on Broadway." He pointed out to one critic that Arnold, the homosexual central figure in the *Torch Song Trilogy*, is much like us all. "Everyone wants what Arnold wants—an apartment they can afford, a job they don't hate too much, a chance to go to the store once in a while and someone to share it all with." Fierstein wrote the book for the musical version of *La Cage aux Folles*, and a number of one-act and full-length plays and television dramas. His work has been recognized with numerous awards in addition to his Tonys. The original producer of *Torch Song Trilogy* illuminated the source of Fierstein's success when he pointed out that "what Harvey proved was that you could use a gay context and a gay experience and speak in universal truths."

Carolyn Forché (b. 1950)   Born in Detroit, Forché earned a B.A. in international relations and creative writing at Michigan State University in 1972. After graduate study at Bowling Green State University in 1975, she taught at the University of Virginia, the University of Arkansas, New York University, Vassar, and Columbia. She won the Yale Series of Younger Poets Award in 1976 for her first collection, *Gathering the Tribes*. Other honors include a Guggenheim Fellowship and the Lamont Award (1981). Forché was a journalist for Amnesty International in El Salvador in 1983 and Beirut correspondent for the National Public Radio program "All Things Considered." Her collection *The Country between Us* (1981) embodies an unusual combination of political passion and technical proficiency.

Robert Francis (1901–1987)   Born in Upland, Pennsylvania, Francis studied at Harvard (A.B., 1923; Ed.M., 1926). He taught at summer workshops and conferences and lectured at universities across the United States. His works include *Stand with Me Here* (1936); *Like Ghosts of Eagles: Poems 1966–1974* (1974); a novel, *We Fly Away* (1948); and an autobiography, *The Trouble with Francis* (1971). He won the Shelley Memorial Award in 1939.

Bruce Jay Friedman (b. 1930)   Friedman began writing while in high school in the Bronx, New York, where he was born. He attended the University of Missouri, earning a degree in journalism in 1951. Friedman's novels, stories, and plays have earned him critical acclaim for his mordantly comic portrayal of (mostly) Jewish protagonists who, alienated from both their Jewish heritage and the wasteland of urban America, are unable to live authentic lives. Friedman is usually labeled a black humorist, a term he himself used to describe his writings, which include four novels, *Stern* (1962), *A Mother's Kisses* (1964), *The Dick* (1970), and *About Harry Towns* (1974); two plays, *Scuba Duba: A Tense Comedy* (1968) and *Steambath* (1971); and two collections of short stories, *Far from the City of Class* (1963) and *Black Angels* (1966).

Robert Frost (1874–1963)   Frost was born in San Francisco but from the age of ten lived in New England. He attended Dartmouth College briefly, then became a teacher, but soon decided to resume his formal training and enrolled at Harvard. He left Harvard after two years without a degree, and for several years supported himself and his growing family by tending a farm his grandfather bought for him. When he was not farming, he read and wrote intensively, though he received little recognition. Discouraged by his lack of success, he sold the farm and moved his family to England, where he published his first volumes of poetry, *A Boy's Will* (1913) and *North of Boston* (1914). After three years in England, Frost returned to America a recognized poet. Later volumes, notably *Mountain Interval* (1916), *New Hampshire* (1923), *West-Running Brook* (1928), and *A Further Range* (1936), won Frost numerous awards, including two Pulitzer Prizes, and a wide popularity. By the time he delivered his poem, "The Gift Outright," at the inauguration of President John F. Kennedy in 1962, Frost had achieved the status of unofficial poet laureate of America, widely revered and beloved for his folksy manner and seemingly artless, accessible poems.

Tess Gallagher (b. 1943)   Born in Port Angeles, Washington, to a mother and father who were both loggers, Gallagher was educated at the University of Washington, where she earned a B.A. (1963) and an M.A. (1970). She received an M.F.A. (1974) from the University of Iowa. She has taught creative writing at various universities, including the University of Montana, Missoula; the University of Arizona, Tucson; and Syracuse University in New York. Her 1976 volume of poetry, *Instructions to the Double*, won the Elliston Award for the "best book of poetry published by a small press" in 1977. Among other honors, she received the *American Poetry Review* award for best poem of 1980. Gallagher has been a prolific writer in all genres. Beginning with *Outside* (1974), she has published some half dozen volumes of poems, the most recent being *Amplitude: New and Selected Poems* (1987) and *Moon Crossing Bride* (1992). *A Concert of Tenses* (1986) is a collection of her essays on poetry. She has written a teleplay, *The Wheel* (1970), and a screenplay, *The Night Belongs to the Police* (1982). She has also been a columnist for the *American Poetry Review* and a contributor of stories, poems, and essays to many periodicals. Gallagher lived with the writer Raymond Carver during the last decade of his life and married him shortly before his death.

Pam Gems (b. 1925)   Born in Bransgore, Hampshire, England, Gems graduated from the University of Manchester with first-class honors. She worked variously as a chambermaid, metal worker, hatcheck girl, and cashier. From 1944 to 1946, she served in the Women's Royal Navy. She was employed from 1950 to 1953 as a research assistant for the British Broadcasting Corporation. While Gems began writing plays at an early age, she was in her forties before her plays began to be produced. Her first successes were in little theaters, whose production schedules were flexible enough so as not to interfere with her responsibilities as the mother of four children. Since then, her plays have been produced frequently, a number of them by the Royal Shakespeare Company. Among her many plays are *Betty's Wonderful Christmas* (1972), *Go West, Young Woman* (1974), *Dusa, Fish, Stas and Vi* (1976), *Piaf* (1978), *Camille* (1984), and *Pasionaria* (1985). Gems serves on the steering committee of the Women's Playhouse Trust, which supports women in the theater.

Molly Giles (b. 1942)   Giles was born and educated in California. She married in 1961, divorced in 1974, and is the mother of two children. She attended the University of California, Berkeley, and San Francisco State University, where she received a B.A. (1978) and an M.A. (1980). From 1980 to 1986, she taught creative writing at San Francisco State University. Her works have been published in the *North American Review*, the *New England Review*, *Redbook*, and *Playgirl*. *Rough Translations* (1985) is a collection of her short stories told mostly from a woman's point of view.

Allen Ginsberg (b. 1926)   Ginsberg was born in Newark, New Jersey, earned an A.B. from Columbia in 1948, and became one of the most influential writers of the 1950s as the preeminent "beat" poet. His long poem *Howl* (1956), formally influenced by Walt Whitman's work, cried out against a brutal, stifling society. Because of graphic, sexual language in *Howl*, San Francisco police declared it obscene and arrested its publisher, Lawrence Ferlinghetti. In a well-publicized trial, Judge Clayton W. Horn ruled the work not obscene. A lifelong consciousness-raiser, Ginsberg helped create the "flower power" movement of the 1960s, cultivated meditation and mantra-chanting, and converted to Buddhism in 1972. While Ginsberg was largely ignored or attacked by the mainstream literary establishment in the 1950s and 1960s, in 1974 he won a National Book Award for *The Fall of America: Poems of These States 1965–1971* (1972). For all his literary ground breaking, Ginsberg considers himself a follower of Thoreau, Emerson, and Whitman, carrying "old-time American transcendentalist individualism . . . into the 20th century."

Dana Gioia (b. 1950)   Born in Los Angeles, Gioia (pronounced *Joy-uh*) grew up in a working-class family, his father a cab driver and his mother a telephone operator. He received a B.A. with high honors and an M.B.A. from Stanford University (1973; 1977) and an M.A. from Harvard University (1975). He went to work for General Foods Corporation in 1977, first as manager of new business development and, since 1988, as marketing manager. In addition to contributing poems and reviews to many magazines, he has served since 1985 on the board of directors of Wesleyan University Writers Conference. His publications include three volumes of poetry, *Summer* (1983), *Daily Horoscope* (1986), and *The Gods of Winter* (1991).

Nikki Giovanni (b. 1943)   Born Yolande Cornelia Giovanni, Jr., in Knoxville, Tennessee, daughter of a probation officer and a social worker, Giovanni graduated with honors from Fisk University in 1967. She attended the University of Pennsylvania School of Social Work and Columbia School of the Arts, was assistant professor of black studies at Queens College (1968), associate professor of English at Rutgers University (1968–1970), and founded a publishing firm, Niktom, in 1970. Giovanni's early work reflected her social activism as an African American college student in the 1960s. Later, she fell outside the mainstream of African American poetry, concentrating on the individual struggle for fulfillment rather than the collective struggle for black empowerment. Her books include *Black Feeling, Black Talk* (1970), *My House* (1972), and *The Women and the Men* (1975). A collection of essays, *Sacred Cows . . . and Other Edibles*, appeared in 1988.

Susan Glaspell (1882–1948) Born and raised in Davenport, Iowa, Glaspell began her career as a novelist and author of sentimental short stories for popular magazines. By 1915, she had turned her energies to the theater, becoming one of the founders of the Provincetown Players, a group devoted to experimental drama. In 1916, Glaspell moved with the company, now called the Playwright's Theatre, to Greenwich Village in New York, where for two seasons—as writer, director, and actor—she played an important role in a group that came to have a major influence on the development of American drama. *Trifles* was written to be performed with a group of one-act plays by Eugene O'Neill at the company's summer playhouse on Cape Cod. Also among her longer plays that embody a feminist perspective are *The Verge* (1921) and *Allison's House* (1931), a Pulitzer Prize–winning drama based upon the life of Emily Dickinson. Among more than forty short stories, some twenty plays, and ten novels, Glaspell's best works deal with the theme of the "new woman," presenting a protagonist who embodies the American pioneer spirit of independence and freedom.

Nadine Gordimer (b. 1923) Gordimer was born and spent her childhood in the gold-mining town of Springs, Transvaal, South Africa. Her father, a Jew who had emigrated to Africa at thirteen, was a jeweler; her mother was born in England. Educated privately at the University of Witwatersrand, Johannesburg, Gordimer was a rebellious child, both as student and daughter. She disliked the convent school her parents sent her to and refused to follow the conventional path—school, low-level job, marriage—expected of white, middle-class women. She was an early reader and writer, winning her first writing prize at fourteen. By this time, she had begun to take a keen interest in politics and the oppression of black South Africans. She ultimately came to reject the system of apartheid, and despite her frequent travels, has continued to make Johannesburg her home. She has made writing her career (she is a wife and mother as well) and has lectured at many American universities, including Harvard, Princeton, Northwestern, Columbia, and Tulane. She has received many prizes and honors, among them honorary degrees from Harvard and Yale (both 1987) and the New School for Social Research (1988). In 1991, she was awarded the Nobel Prize for literature. Among her many novels are *The Lying Days* (1953), *A World of*

Strangers (1958), *Burger's Daughter* (1979), and *A Sport of Nature* (1987). Her collections of short stories include *Face to Face* (1949), *The Soft Voice of the Serpent* (1952), *Not for Publication* (1965), *Selected Stories* (1975), and *Something Out There* (1984). Her nonfiction works include *South African Writing Today* (1967; coeditor), *The Black Interpreters: Notes on African Writing* (1973), *Lifetimes under Apartheid* (1986), and *The Essential Gesture: Politics and Places* (1988). Her most recent publications are *My Son's Story* (1990), about apartheid and politics in South Africa; and *Jump: And Other Stories* (1991).

Robert Graves (1895–1985)   Graves was born in London, son of an Irish poet. He served in the Royal Welsh Fusiliers during World War I and rose to the rank of captain. He studied at Oxford, and in 1926 was professor of English literature at Cairo University. In 1929, he left his wife and four children to live in Mallorca, Spain, with Laura Riding, an American poet. Controversial in both his personal life and his work, Graves aroused indignation with his translation of *The Rubáiyát of Omar Khayyám*, which departed markedly from the popular Edward Fitzgerald translation (1859). During the late 1950s and 1960s, he taught at Oxford and lectured in the United States. *Goodbye to All That* (1929), his early autobiography, provides a nice insight into the culture that nourished him. Among his numerous works are the influential "historical grammar of poetic myth," *The White Goddess* (1948, 1952), and the historical novels, *I, Claudius* (1934) and *Claudius the God* (1934).

Thomas Gray (1716–1771)   Born in London, Gray was educated at Eton. He interrupted his stay at Cambridge with a two-year tour of Italy and France with Horace Walpole. He returned to Cambridge in 1742, but, before graduating, dropped out again and lived with his mother while he studied and wrote. During this period, he composed some of his most important poems, including his famous "Elegy Written in a Country Churchyard" (revised over many years and finally published in 1751). He received his degree from Cambridge in 1744. By 1757, Gray was recognized as the foremost poet of his day and offered the poet laureateship, which he refused. In 1768, he was appointed professor of history and modern languages at Cambridge.

Michael Hamburger (b. 1924)   Hamburger was born in Berlin. His father, a physician and professor, took the family to England in 1933 at Hitler's rise to power. After serving four years in the British Army, Hamburger graduated from Oxford (B.A., M.A., 1948), then worked as a free-lance writer until 1952. From 1952 to 1964 he lectured in German at the Universities of London and Reading. Hamburger has held visiting professorships at many universities in the United States. He is most renowned for his superb translation of the German poet Friedrich Hölderlin. Translator of over thirty-five works, he won the Institute of Linguists' Gold Medal in 1977. His poems are compiled in *Collected Poems 1941–1983* (1984).

Barry Hannah (b. 1942)   Born in Clinton, Mississippi, Hannah earned a B.A. from Mississippi College and went on to the University of Arkansas, where he earned M.A. and M.F.A. degrees. His first novel, *Geronimo Rex* (1972), won the William Faulkner prize—appropriately, since his "gothic sense of humor" and the "lyricism of his prose," in the words of one critic, make him the logical heir to William Faulkner. In addition to the Faulkner prize, he won awards from the American Academy and Institute of Arts and Letters, the Bellaman Foundation (1970), a Breadloaf Fellowship (1971), and the first Arnold Gingrich Short Fiction Award (1978). His second novel, *Nightwatchman* (1973), is a sort of campus murder mystery, and was followed by a collection of short stories, *Airships* (1978). *Never Die* appeared in 1991. Hannah has held a number of teaching positions around the country and is presently on the faculty at the University of Mississippi. "Much of Hannah's fiction," wrote one critic, "is experimental and belongs in the category of dark comedy. All of it composes a highly original portrait of American life, both past and present, particularly American life in the South. It is a fiction that is consistently poetic, with a language and style both dazzling and believable."

Thomas Hardy (1840–1928)   Hardy was born near Dorchester, in southeastern England (on which he based the "Wessex" of many of his novels and poems). Hardy worked for the ecclesiastical architect John Hicks from 1856 to 1861. He then moved to London to practice architecture, and took evening classes at King's College for six years. In 1867, he gave up architecture to become a full-time writer, and after writing short stories and poems found success as a novelist. *The Mayor of Casterbridge* (1886) and *Tess of the d'Urbervilles* (1891) reveal Hardy's concern for victims of circumstance and his appeal to humanitarian sympathy in readers. After his novel *Jude the Obscure* (1896) was strongly criticized, Hardy set aside prose fiction and returned to poetry—a genre in which he was most prolific and successful after he reached the age of seventy.

Nathaniel Hawthorne (1804–1864)   The son of a merchant sea-captain who died in a distant port when Nathaniel was four, Hawthorne grew up in genteel poverty in Massachusetts and Maine. His earliest American ancestor, the magistrate William Hathorne, ordered the whipping of a Quaker woman in Salem. William's son John was one of the three judges at the Salem witch trials of 1692. Aware of his family's role in colonial America, Hawthorne returned to Salem after graduating from Bowdoin College (where future president Franklin Pierce was a friend and classmate), determined to be a writer. He recalled and destroyed copies of his first novel, the mediocre *Fanshawe* (1828). His short stories, often set in Puritan America, revealed a moral complexity that had not troubled his righteous ancestors William and John. His success as an author allowed him to marry Sophia Peabody in 1842 (after a four-year engagement). Though his stories were critically praised, they did not earn much money, and, in 1846, he used his political connections with the Democratic party to obtain a job at the Salem custom house. His dismissal in 1849 (when the Democrats lost) produced both anger and resolve. The result was a great American novel, *The Scarlet Letter* (1850), which made him famous and improved his fortune. Although he was friendly with Emerson and his circle of optimistic transcendentalists (some of whom established the utopian socialist community at Brook Farm), Hawthorne's vision of the human condition was considerably darker. Herman Melville dedicated *Moby Dick* to Hawthorne, and characterized him as a man who could say "No" in thunder.

Robert Hayden (1913–1980)   Born in Detroit, Hayden studied at Wayne State University and the University of Michigan (M.A., 1944). In 1946, he joined the faculty of Fisk University. He left Fisk in 1968 for a professorship at the University of Michigan, where he remained until his death. He produced some ten volumes of poetry but did not receive the acclaim many thought he deserved until late in life, with the publication of *Words in the Mourning Time: Poems* (1971). In the 1960s, he aroused some hostility from African Americans who wanted him to express more militancy. But Hayden did not want to be part of what he called a "kind of literary ghetto." He considered his own work "a form of prayer—a prayer for illumination, perfection."

Anthony Hecht (b. 1923)   Born in New York City, Hecht attended Bard College (B.A., 1944). After three years in the U.S. Army, serving in Europe and Japan, he continued his education at Columbia University (M.A., 1950). Hecht has taught at several universities, including the University of Rochester, where he was professor of poetry and rhetoric in 1967. He is presently a professor in the graduate school of Georgetown University. His awards include a 1951 Prix de Rome, and Guggenheim, Rockefeller, and Ford Foundation Fellowships, as well as the Bollingen Prize in Poetry. His first book of poetry, *A Summer of Stones* (1954), was followed by *Hard Hours* (1968), which won a Pulitzer Prize for poetry, *Millions of Strange Shadows* (1977), and *Venetian Vespers* (1979). His most recent collection of poems is *The Transparent Man* (1990). Hecht is also the author of a collection of critical essays, *Obbligati* (1986). Acclaimed for his technical expertise, Hecht was first devoted to traditional poetic forms, and his work was sometimes described as "baroque" and "courtly." More recently, his work has become less decorative.

Ernest Hemingway (1899–1961)   Born in Oak Park, Illinois, Hemingway became a cub reporter after high school. He was seriously wounded while serving as an ambulance driver in World War I. After the war, he lived in Paris, a member of a lively and productive expatriate community characterized by Gertrude Stein as "a lost generation." He lived an active life, not only as a writer, but as a war correspondent, big game hunter, and fisherman. In such novels as *The Sun Also Rises* (1926), *A Farewell to Arms* (1929), and *For Whom the Bell Tolls* (1940), his fictional characters exhibit a passion for courage and integrity, for grace under pressure. Hemingway's spare, unembellished style reinforced his central theme that one must confront danger and live honorably.

He won the Nobel Prize in 1954. In 1961, unable to write because treatment for mental instability affected his memory, he killed himself with the shotgun he had so often used as a hunter.

Amy Hempel (b. 1951)   Hempel was born in Chicago and spent her early years in California, where she attended Whittier College and San Francisco State College—"your basic non-linear education," she called it. She moved to New York to pursue a career in writing and was for a time a contributing editor at *Vanity Fair* magazine. Some of her unhappy experiences as a struggling writer in New York as well as the deaths of family members provide much of the material for *Reasons to Live* (1985), a collection of stories set in California, which grew out of a fiction workshop she attended at Columbia University in 1982. In many of these stories, her protagonists struggle against the alienating culture of California. Her most recent collection of stories is *At the Gates of the Animal Kingdom* (1990). "I am really interested in resilience," Hempel recently told an interviewer. "Dr. Christian Barnard said, 'Suffering isn't ennobling, recovery is.' If I have a motto for this particular bunch of stories, that's what it is."

Robert Herrick (1591–1674)   Born in London, Herrick was apprenticed to his uncle, a goldsmith, for ten years until, at age twenty-two, he was sent to Cambridge in recognition of his academic talents. Little is known of the decade following his graduation from Cambridge, although it seems certain that he associated with a circle of literary artists. In 1629, Herrick was appointed vicar at Dean Prior, Devonshire, a rural parish that the sophisticated and cosmopolitan Herrick looked upon as a kind of exile. Yet, Herrick was fascinated by the pagan elements of local songs and dances and often drew upon pre-Christian writers for inspiration. His chief work, *Hesperides* (1648), is a collection of some twelve hundred poems, mostly written in Devonshire, about local scenery, customs, and people.

William Heyen (b. 1940)   William Heyen's father immigrated from Germany in 1928 and made a living as a bartender and carpenter. Heyen was born in Brooklyn, but grew up on suburban Long Island. He attended the State University of New York at Brockport (B.S.Ed., 1961), where, at six feet, four inches, he played basketball and twice earned All-American recognition in soccer. He received a Ph.D. from Ohio University in 1967 and joined the faculty of his alma mater at Brockport the same year. He won a Fulbright grant to Germany (1971–1972). Heyen married in 1962 and has two children. His father's two brothers remained in Germany, fought on the Nazi side, and were killed during World War II. His family history clearly marked Heyen powerfully—three of the dozen books of poems he has produced (*The Swastika Poems* [1977], *Erika: Poems of the Holocaust* [1984], and, with Daniel Brodsky, *Falling from Heaven: Holocaust Poems of a Jew and a Gentile* [1991]) deal with Nazi Germany and the Holocaust. As well, Heyen's passion for nature is manifested in *Pterodactyl*

Rose: Poems of Ecology (1991). The work of this prolific poet has been repeatedly honored with prizes: among others, he won the Borestone Mountain poetry award in 1966, the annual *Ontario Review* poetry prize in 1978, and a Guggenheim Fellowship in 1977–1978. In addition to his poetry, which has appeared in over one hundred periodicals, Heyen has edited three anthologies of American poets and produced a novel, *Vic Holyfield and the Class of 1957* (1986).

Edward Hirsch (b. 1950) Hirsch was born in Chicago and earned a B.A. from Grinnell College in Iowa (1972). In 1977 he married the assistant curator of an art museum. With a Ph.D. from the University of Pennsylvania (1979), he joined the English department at Wayne State University in Detroit. He has won prizes for poetry from several bodies including the Academy of American Poets and the Ingram Merrill Foundation. He is a Fellow of the American Council of Learned Societies. In addition to poems, Hirsch has published articles and stories in such journals as the *New Yorker*, the *North American Review*, the *Partisan Review*, the *Nation*, and the *New Republic*. His first book of poetry, *For the Sleepwalkers*, appeared in 1981. Later books include *Wild Gratitude* (1986) and *The Night Parade* (1989). Asked about his work, Hirsch replied: "My goal is to write a few poems that are unforgettable. I love enchanted stories, magical realism, secret signs, and the great modern artists of childhood— Archille Gorky and Paul Klee. Jean Cocteau once said that the goal of every artist should be his own extremity. I want to write poems that are imaginative, astonishing, playful, mysterious, and extreme."

Linda Hogan (b. 1947) Hogan was born in Denver, Colorado, and educated at the University of Colorado, where she received her M.A. in 1978. For a time, she supported herself with odd jobs and free-lance writing. By 1980, her success as a writer led to her appointment as writer-in-residence for the states of Colorado and Oklahoma. In 1982 she became an assistant professor in the TRIBES program at Colorado College, Colorado Springs. She is now associate professor of American Indian studies at the University of Minnesota. In 1980, her play, *A Piece of Moon*, won the Five Civilized Tribes Playwriting Award. In 1983, she received the *Stand* magazine fiction award. Her writings include five volumes of poetry, *Calling Myself Home* (1979), *Daughters, I Love You* (1981), *Eclipse* (1983), *Seeing Through the Sun* (1985), and *Savings* (1991), and two collections of stories, *That Horse* (1985) and *The Big Woman* (1987).

Gerard Manley Hopkins (1844–1889) Raised in London, Hopkins won a scholarship to Balliol College, Oxford, where he studied classical literature. He converted to Roman Catholicism in 1866 and two years later entered the Jesuit Novitiate. In 1877, he was ordained as a Jesuit priest and served in missions in London, Liverpool, Oxford, and Glasgow until 1882. From 1884 to his death in 1889, he was professor of Greek at University College, Dublin. A technically innovative poet, Hopkins saw only three of his poems published during his lifetime, but gained posthumous recognition in 1918 when a friend (the Poet Laureate Robert Bridges) published his complete works. His early poems celebrate the beauty of God's world, but later works reflect his poor health and depression.

A. E. Housman (1859–1936)   Born in Fockbury, England, and an outstanding student, Alfred Edward Housman nonetheless failed his final examinations at Oxford in 1881 (possibly as a result of emotional chaos caused by his love for a male classmate). Working as a clerk in the Patent Office in London, he pursued classical studies on his own, earned an M.A., and was appointed to the Chair of Latin at University College, London. In 1910, he became professor of Latin at Cambridge, where he remained until his death in 1936. As a poet, Housman was concerned primarily with the fleetingness of love and the decay of youth. After his first collection, *A Shropshire Lad*, was rejected by several publishers, Housman published it at his own expense in 1896. It gained popularity during World War I, and his 1922 collection, *Last Poems*, was well received. In his lecture "The Name and Nature of Poetry" (1933), Housman argued that poetry should appeal to emotions rather than intellect. *More Poems* (1936) was published posthumously.

Pam Houston (b. 1962)   Houston grew up in New Jersey, the only child of an actress and an unsuccessful businessman. After graduating in English from Denison University in Ohio, she rode across Canada on a bicycle and then down to Colorado, where she worked at various odd jobs, among them bartender and flagwoman on a highway crew. Eventually, she entered a doctoral program at the University of Utah but is presently taking time off from her studies to teach creative writing at her alma mater in Ohio. Her first collection of short stories, *Cowboys Are My Weakness*, was published in 1992. Her stories have also appeared in *Crazyhorse, Cimarron, Puerto del Sol*, the *Apalachee Quarterly*, and *Mademoiselle* and her nonfiction has appeared in *Mirabella*. She and her husband, a safari guide from South Africa, live in Utah, where she occasionally works as a licensed river guide. In explaining her pursuit of outdoor and often dangerous activities during her early twenties, she says: "You think I spent three summers leading hunters through Alaska because I like watching guys like David Duke shoot sheep? No. It was because if I didn't go with my boyfriend, somebody else would. I wanted to win."

Langston Hughes (1902–1967)   Hughes was born in Joplin, Missouri. His father was a businessperson and lawyer, his mother a teacher. Hughes attended Columbia, graduated from Lincoln University in 1929, traveled throughout the world, and held many odd jobs as a young man. While Hughes had a long and prolific career as a writer in all genres, he is still remembered as the central figure of the Harlem Renaissance of the 1920s, a movement which committed itself to the examination and celebration of black life in America and its African heritage. He was the Madrid correspondent for the Baltimore *Afro-American*

(1937) and a columnist for the Chicago *Defender* (1943–1967) and the New York *Post* (1962–1967). His poems of racial affirmation and protest are often infused with the rhythms of blues and jazz music. He wrote over two dozen plays (many musicalized) and founded the Suitcase Theater (Harlem, 1938), the New Negro Theater (Los Angeles, 1939), and the Skyloft Players (Chicago, 1941). His works include *The Weary Blues* (1926), *Montage of a Dream Deferred* (1951), and *The Panther and the Lash: Poems of Our Times* (1969).

Ted Hughes (b. 1930)   Born in Yorkshire, Hughes served two years in the Royal Air Force and attended Pembroke College, Cambridge (B.A. in archeology and anthropology, 1954; M.A., 1959). His first wife was poet Sylvia Plath, who committed suicide in 1963. A full-time writer of plays, essays, children's verse, and editor of many anthologies, Hughes created a poetry of animals, full of primitive passion and violence. The most famous of these is the title character of his 1970 volume, *Crow*. One critic calls Hughes a "20th-century Aesop whose fables lack an explicit moral." Many have found in his animal subjects a telling portrayal of the human condition.

David Henry Hwang (b. 1957)   Born in Los Angeles to immigrants, his father a banker and his mother a professor of piano, Hwang graduated from Stanford University in 1979. But by 1978 he had already written his first play, *FOB* [Fresh Off the Boat], which won the 1981 Obie Award as the best new play of the season when Joseph Papp brought it to Off-Broadway in New York. Hwang attended the famous Yale School of Drama during 1980 and 1981. Two more promising plays, *The Dance and the Railroad* and *Family Devotions*, based on the problems of immigrants—trying, sometimes, to assimilate and sometimes to avoid assimilation in a new culture—appeared in 1981. His 1985 marriage to Ophelia Y. M. Chong, an artist, ended in divorce. Hwang continued to write and direct during the 1980s, moving from the relatively narrow early material to "wider concerns of race, gender, and culture." His 1988 Broadway hit, *M. Butterfly*, won the Tony Award for best play, and established him as a major modern American playwright. A critic writing in *Time* argued that "the final scene of *M. Butterfly*, when the agony of one soul finally takes precedence over broad-ranging commentary, is among the most forceful in the history of the American theater. . . . If Hwang can again fuse politics and humanity, he has the potential to become the first important dramatist of American public life since Arthur Miller, and maybe the best of them all."

Henrik Ibsen (1828–1906)   Ibsen was born in Skien, Norway (a seaport about a hundred miles south of Oslo), the son of a wealthy merchant. When Ibsen was eight, his father's business failed, and at fifteen he was apprenticed to an apothecary in the tiny town of Grimstad. He hated this profession. To solace himself, he read poetry and theology and began to write. When he was twenty-two, he became a student in Christiania and published his first play. In 1851, his diligent, though unremarkable, writing earned him an appointment as "theater-poet" to a new theater in Bergen, where he remained until 1857, learning both the business and the art of drama. He wrote several plays based on Scandinavian folklore, held positions at two theaters in Christiania, and married. When he was thirty-six, he applied to the government for a poet's pension—a stipend that would have permitted him to devote himself to writing. The stipend was refused. Enraged, he left Norway, and, though he was granted the stipend two years later, spent the next twenty-seven years in Italy and Germany, where he wrote the realistic social dramas that established his repu-tation as the founder of modern theater. Such plays as *Ghosts* (1881), *An Enemy of the People* (1882), and *A Doll's House* (1878) inevitably generated controversy as Ibsen explored venereal disease, the stupidity and greed of the "compact majority," and the position of women in society. In 1891, he returned to live in Christiania, where he was recognized and honored as one of Norway's (and Europe's) finest writers.

Randall Jarrell (1914–1965)   Called by Robert Lowell "the most heartbreaking English poet of his generation," Jarrell was born in Nashville, Tennessee, and studied at Vanderbilt University (B.S. in psychology, 1936; M.A. in English, 1939). During World War II, he served as a navigation tower operator in the Air Corps. He taught at Sarah Lawrence College, Kenyon College, and was visiting fellow, lecturer, and professor at other colleges and universities across the country. In 1947, he joined the faculty at the Women's College of the University of North Carolina (now U.N.C. at Greensboro), where he remained until his death. In his poetry, Jarrell explored loneliness and lost childhood; in his influential criticism, he encouraged other writers and helped determine the course of contemporary poetry. His works include the volumes of poetry, *Little Friend, Little Friend* (1945), *Losses* (1948), and *The Lost World* (1965), and a novel, *Pictures from an Institution* (1954). Jarrell was struck and killed by an automobile in 1965.

June Jordan (b. 1936)   Jordan was born in Harlem, New York, and educated at Barnard College (1953–1955) and the University of Chicago (1955–1956). A poet, novelist, and writer of children's books, she has taught widely at university campuses, including the City College of the City University of New York (1966–1968) and Connecticut College (1969–1974), where she both taught English and served as director of Search for Education, Elevation and Knowledge (SEEK). She is currently Professor of English at the State University of New York, Stonybrook. In addition to many appointments as visiting professor, she has served as Chancellor's Distinguished Lecturer, University of California, Berkeley (1986). Her numerous honors include the Prix de Rome in Environ-mental Design (1970–1971) and the Nancy Bloch Award (1971) for her reader *The Voice of the Children*, and the achievement award from the National Association of Black Journalists (1984). Her many books include *His Own Where* (1971), *Dry Victories* (1972), and *Kimako's Story* (1981), all for juvenile and young adult readers. Her collections of poetry include *Things That I Do in the*

Dark (1977), *Living Room: New Poems, 1980–1984* (1985), *Naming Our Destiny: New and Selected Poems* (1989), and *Poetic Justice* (1991). Jordan is also the author of *On Call: New Political Essays, 1981–1985* (1985).

James Joyce (1882–1941)   Though educated in Jesuit schools, Joyce came to reject Catholicism; though an expatriate living in Paris, Trieste, and Zurich for most of his adult life, he wrote almost exclusively about his native Dublin. Joyce's rebelliousness, which surfaced during his university career, generated a revolution in modern literature. His novels *Ulysses* (1922) and *Finnegans Wake* (1939) introduced radically new narrative techniques. "Araby," from his first collection of short stories, *Dubliners* (1914), is one of a series of sharply realized vignettes based on Joyce's experience in Ireland, the homeland he later characterized as "a sow that eats its own farrow." Joyce lived precariously on earnings as a language teacher and modest contributions from wealthy patrons. That support Joyce justified—he is certainly one of the most influential novelists of the twentieth century. Because *Ulysses* dealt frankly with sexuality and used coarse language, the U.S. Post Office charged that the novel was obscene, and forbade its importation. A celebrated 1933 court decision lifted the ban in the United States.

John Keats (1795–1821)   Keats was born in London, the eldest son of a stablekeeper who died in an accident in 1804. His mother died of tuberculosis shortly after remarrying, and the grandmother who raised Keats and his siblings died in 1814. At eighteen, Keats wrote his first poem, "Imitation of Spenser," inspired by Edmund Spenser's long narrative poem *The Faerie Queene.* The thirty-three poems he wrote while training to be a surgeon were published in 1817, and Keats then gave up medicine for writing. After more traumatic losses in 1818, including the departure of one brother for America and the death of his other brother of tuberculosis, Keats wrote his second collection, *Lamia, Isabella, The Eve of St. Agnes, and Other Poems* (1820). Ill with tuberculosis himself, Keats was sent to Rome to recover. He died at twenty-six, but despite his short career, he is a major figure of the romantic period.

X. J. Kennedy (b. 1929)   Born Joseph Charles Kennedy in Dover, New Jersey, Kennedy published his own science fiction magazine, *Terrifying Test-Tube Tales,* at age 12. He honed his writing skills at Seton Hall University and earned an M.A. degree from Columbia in 1951. From 1951 to 1955, he served in the U.S. Navy, at one time publishing a daily newssheet for the entertainment-starved crew of a destroyer at sea. Kennedy notes: "Nothing I have ever written since has been received so avidly." After further study, at the Sorbonne in Paris and the University of Michigan, Kennedy taught English at the University of North Carolina and moved to Tufts University in Massachusetts in 1963. His first poetry collection, *Nude Descending a Staircase* (1961), won the Lamont Award for that year. A free-lance writer since 1979, Kennedy prefers writing within the constraints of rhyme and metrical patterns. His most recent volume, with Dorothy M. Kennedy, is *Talking Like the Rain: A First Book of Poems* (1992).

Carolyn Kizer (b. 1925)   Kizer was born in Spokane, Washington. Her father was a lawyer, her mother a biologist and professor. After graduating from Sarah Lawrence College in 1945, Kizer pursued graduate study at Columbia and the University of Washington. From 1959 to 1965, she was editor of *Poetry Northwest* (which she founded in 1959 in Seattle), and spent 1964 and 1965 as a State Department specialist in Pakistan, where she taught at a women's college and translated poems from Urdu into English. She chose to leave early after the U.S. decision to bomb North Vietnam in 1965. Later, she joined archaeological tours in Afghanistan and Iran. She has worked as director of literary programs for the National Endowment for the Arts in Washington, D.C., has taught at several universities, and was poet-in-residence at the University of North Carolina and Ohio University. Her works include *Poems* (1959) and *Mermaids in the Basement: Poems for Women* (1984).

Etheridge Knight (1933–1991)   Knight was born in Corinth, Mississippi, attended two years of public high school in Kentucky, and served in the U.S. Army from 1948 to 1951. Convicted on a robbery charge and sentenced in 1960 to twenty years in Indiana State Prison, he discovered poetry; his first collection is entitled *Poems from Prison* (1968). Knight was paroled after eight years. From 1968 to 1971 he was poet-in-residence at several universities. An important African American voice in the 1960s and 1970s, Knight rejected the American and European esthetic tradition, arguing that "the red of this esthetic rose got its color from the blood of black slaves, exterminated Indians, napalmed Vietnamese children." His collection *Belly Song and Other Poems* was nominated for the National Book Award and the Pulitzer Prize in 1973. His awards include National Endowment for the Arts and Guggenheim grants, and the 1987 American Book Award for *The Essential Etheridge Knight* (1986).

Maxine Kumin (b. 1925)   Born Maxine Winokur, Kumin attended Radcliffe College (B.A., 1946; M.A., 1948), and has lectured at many universities, including Princeton, Tufts, and Brandeis. She is the author of several collections of poetry, including *Up Country* (1972), for which she won a Pulitzer Prize, and, most recently, *Nurture* (1989) and *Looking for Luck: Poems* (1992). She has also published several novels, a collection of short stories, and more than twenty children's books, three of them in collaboration with the poet Anne Sexton.

Philip Larkin (1922–1985)   Born in Coventry, Larkin attended St. John's College, Oxford (B.A., 1943; M.A., 1947). He was appointed librarian at the University of Hull in 1955, wrote jazz feature articles for the London *Daily Telegraph* from 1961 to 1971, and won numerous poetry awards, including the Queen's Gold Medal (1965) and the Benson Medal (1975). His first collection,

The North Ship (1945), was not well received, but he gained recognition after publication of *The Less Deceived* (1960). Larkin once said "Form holds little interest for me. Content is everything."

D. H. Lawrence (1885–1930)   David Herbert Lawrence grew up amidst the strife between his genteel and educated mother, and his coarse miner father. As a youth in the Nottinghamshire mining village of Eastwood, Lawrence resented the rough ways of his drunken father, and adopted his mother's refined values as his own. Diligence brought him a scholarship to the local high school. Upon graduation, he worked as a clerk and as an elementary school teacher, and, in 1908, earned a teaching certificate from Nottingham University. He published a group of poems in 1909 and *The White Peacock*, his first novel, in 1911. He resigned his teaching position to devote himself to writing in 1912. That same year he ran away with Frieda von Richthofen Weekley (the sister of the World War I German ace fighter pilot), who left behind a husband and three children. They were married following her divorce in 1914. In 1915, his novel *The Rainbow* was declared indecent and suppressed in England. Angered by this event and by continual harassment for his outspoken opposition to World War I and his marriage to a prominent German, the Lawrences left England after the war. They traveled widely—in Europe, Australia, Mexico, and the American Southwest—seeking a community receptive to Lawrence's ideas and a climate to restore his failing health. His output was prodigious and included novels, short stories, poems, nonfiction, travel books, and letters. As a mature writer, Lawrence rejected the gentility his mother represented, and began to see his father's earthiness as a virtue. He died of tuberculosis in the south of France.

David Leavitt (b. 1961)   Born in Pittsburgh, Leavitt, the son of a professor, attended Yale University (B.A., 1983). He enrolled in a number of creative writing courses, some of which he found nourishing, others destructive. An undergraduate story, "Territory," won him a prize for fiction at Yale, and was published in the *New Yorker*. That early success was no fluke, and Leavitt, while working as a reader and editorial assistant at Viking-Penguin in New York, published several short stories and essays in such periodicals as *Harper's*, *Esquire*, and the *New York Times Book Review*. His first short-story collection, *Family Dancing* (1984), includes several stories that explore the "trauma of homosexual life," as does his novel *The Lost Language of Cranes* (1986). The latter has been made into a TV motion picture. Leavitt left his editorial job in 1984 when he found that his own work was balefully influenced by the bad manuscripts he had to read. A later story collection, *A Place I've Never Been*, appeared in 1990. Leavitt won the O'Henry Award in 1984, and was nominated for the National Book Critics Circle and the P.E.N.-Faulkner Awards in 1985 for *Family Dancing*.

Ursula K. LeGuin (b. 1929)   The daughter of distinguished University of California, Berkeley, anthropologists, LeGuin graduated from Radcliffe and earned an M.A. from Columbia. She enjoyed early success writing for science fiction and fantasy magazines (a genre often stigmatized as subliterary popular fiction). But she quickly established a reputation that places her alongside such modern writers as Kurt Vonnegut, Jr., and in the tradition of older writers who used fantastic circumstances to shape their understanding of the human condition, such as Jonathan Swift, Edgar Allan Poe, and H. G. Wells. In addition to speculative fiction, she has written poetry and children's books.

John Lennon (1940–1980) **and Paul McCartney** (b. 1942)   Lennon and McCartney met at a church fete in 1957 where they were both performing. Later that year, they formed a duo called The Nurk Twins. By 1962, after various incarnations and personnel changes, Lennon, McCartney, George Harrison, and Ringo Starr emerged as The Beatles, and were launched on their successful career by their new manager, Brian Epstein. Lennon and McCartney wrote most of The Beatles' songs. "Love Me Do," their first recording with E.M.I., sold 100,000 copies in 1962. Exhausted by obsessed fans at sold-out concerts around the world, the foursome became a studio band in 1966. Epstein's death in 1967 and Lennon's marriage to Yoko Ono in 1969 contributed to the group's demise. Ego problems plagued their 1971 movie *Let It Be*, and the group officially disbanded a month after its release. Lennon and McCartney continued their songwriting careers separately. Lennon died of gunshot wounds on December 8, 1980.

Doris Lessing (b. 1919)   Born in Iran of British parents, at the age of five Lessing was taken by her family to Southern Rhodesia (now Zimbabwe), where she spent her early years. At age fifteen, she left school and worked in Salisbury as a typist and telephone operator. After the failure of her first marriage, which produced two children, Lessing became active in radical politics, married a Communist, and in 1949 moved to England with her husband and new son, carrying the manuscript of her first book, *The Grass Is Singing* (1950), a novel about the horrors of apartheid. After divorcing her husband in 1949, she supported herself and her son by writing. Her second novel, *Martha Quest* (1952), was the first in what became a five-volume chronicle, titled *The Children of Violence*, tracing the life of a protagonist often regarded as Lessing's fictional double. Her best known work and generally acknowledged masterpiece is *The Golden Notebook* (1962), a landmark of modern feminist writing. Lessing's prolific writings, both fiction and nonfiction, reveal an intense interest in politics as well as women's liberation. Between 1979 and 1983, Lessing published a five-volume science fiction sequence under the collective title *Canopus in Argus Archives*. Her novel *The Good Terrorist* (1985) satirizes left-wing groups in London. *Particularly Cats . . . and Rufus* (1991) is a series of vignettes about her favorite pets. In 1979, when Zimbabwe became an independent state ruled by a black majority, Lessing was able to visit her native land from which she had been banned for twenty-five years. *African Lands* (1992) includes reflections based upon her recent visits to Zimbabwe, including the problem of AIDS, political corruption, and the deterioration of the environment.

Denise Levertov (b. 1923)   Born in Ilford, England, Levertov was raised in a literary household (her father was an Anglican priest) and educated privately. She was a nurse at a British Hospital in Paris during World War II; after the war, she worked in an antique store and bookstore in London. Married to an American writer, she came to the United States in 1948, became a naturalized citizen in 1956, and taught at several universities, including M.I.T. and Tufts. Levertov began as what she called a "British romantic with almost Victorian background" and has become more politically active and feminist with time. She protested U.S. involvement in the Vietnam War and has also been involved in the antinuclear movement. Regarding angst-filled confessional poetry, Levertov once said, "I do not believe that a violent imitation of the horrors of our times is the concern of poetry. . . . I long for poems of an inner harmony in utter contrast to the chaos in which they exist." Her works include *The Double Image* (1946), *Relearning the Alphabet* (1970), and *A Door in the Hive* (1989).

C. Day Lewis (1904–1972)   Born in Ireland, son of a minister, Cecil Day Lewis began writing poetry at age six. He attended Oxford, taught for seven years, served as editor for the Ministry of Information (1941–1946), was professor of poetry at Oxford (1951–1956), and visiting professor at Harvard (1964–1965). His early works *From Feathers to Iron* (1931) and *The Magnetic Mountain* (1933) reflect a politically radical ideology, but Lewis mellowed enough to be named poet laureate in 1968. From 1935 to 1964 he wrote nearly two dozen detective novels under the pseudonym Nicholas Blake. He commented, "In my young days, words were my antennae, my touch-stones, my causeway over a quaking bog of mistrust."

Duane Locke (b. 1921)   Locke was born on a farm near Plains, Georgia, but because of the poverty of Depression years farm life, his parents brought their only child to Tampa, Florida, where he has lived ever since, except for stays in Europe. He attended the University of Tampa and earned a Ph.D. from the University of Florida. He spent his entire teaching career at the University of Tampa, and retired in 1989. He has published over a thousand pieces, mostly poetry, in over four hundred different magazines, and produced fourteen small press books of poems. By his own account, he now lives "unemployed with eight cats . . . and one wife in the slums of Tampa, Florida, where daily I experience the lower depths, although it has been about six weeks since I have seen a bleeding man dying in the streets."

Barry Holstun Lopez (b. 1945)   Born in Port Chester, New York, Lopez graduated from the University of Notre Dame in 1966, married, and earned an M.A.T. there in 1968. He went on to further graduate study at the University of Oregon (1969–1970). He envisioned his earliest fiction, *Desert Notes: Re-*

flections in the Eye of a Raven (1976), as the first of a trilogy which, ultimately, would include *River Notes: The Dance of Herons* (1979) and *Animal Notes*. Keenly interested in the traditions of the Northwest Indians, as well as natural history, he published a collection of Indian legends, *Giving Birth to Thunder, Sleeping with His Daughter* (1977). The nonfiction study *Of Wolves and Men* followed in 1978. A collection of short stories, *Winter Count* (1981), reveals how deeply Lopez feels about the American Indian experience, and in 1990 he published a children's book based on Indian traditions, *Crow and Weasel*. *Arctic Dreams: Imagination and Desire in a Northern Landscape* appeared in 1986. Lopez's skill as a photographer is evident in the illustrations included in several of his works. A collection of essays, *The Rediscovery of North America*, appeared in 1991.

Audre Lorde (1934–1992)   Born to middle-class, West Indian immigrant parents in New York City, Lorde grew up in Harlem and attended the National University of Mexico (1954), Hunter College (B.A., 1959) and Columbia (M.L.S., 1961). Her marriage in 1962, which produced two children, ended in divorce in 1970. During these early years, she worked as a librarian, but in 1968 her growing reputation as a writer led to her appointment as lecturer in creative writing at City College in New York and, in the following year, lecturer in the education department at Herbert H. Lehman College. In 1970, she joined the English department at John Jay College of Criminal Justice and in 1980 returned to Hunter College as professor of English. Besides teaching, Lorde combined raising a son and a daughter in an interracial lesbian relationship with political organizing of other Black feminists and lesbians, and in the early 1980s, helping to start Kitchen Table: Women of Color Press. In 1991, she was named New York State Poet. Lorde is probably best known for her prose writings, among them two collections of essays, *Sister Outsider* (1984) and *Burst of Light* (1988), and the autobiographical *Zami: The Cancer Journals* (1980), a chronicle of her struggle with the breast cancer that ultimately claimed her life. Her poetry publications include *The First Cities* (1968), *The Black Unicorn* (1978), and *Undersong: Chosen Poems Old and New* (1993). Near the end of her life, Lorde made her home on St. Croix, U.S. Virgin Islands, and adopted the African name Gamba Adisa ("Warrior—She Who Makes Her Meaning Known").

Amy Lowell (1874–1925)   Born to a prominent family in Brookline, Massachusetts, Lowell was privately educated. After the death of her parents, she inherited the family's ten-acre estate, including a staff of servants and a well-stocked library. Lowell wrote a great deal of undistinguished poetry that, unfortunately, prejudiced critics and readers against her better work. While traveling abroad, she became associated with the Imagists, a group of English and American poets in London who felt that sharply realized images gave poetry its power, and she gained recognition promoting their work in America after 1913. Her first collection of poems, *A Dome of Many-Coloured Glass*, appeared in

1912. Though her poetry never reached a wide audience, her criticism helped shape American poetic tastes of the time.

Archibald MacLeish (1892–1982)   Born in Glencoe, Illinois, MacLeish earned a B.A. from Yale (1915), then went on to Harvard, where he earned a law degree (1919) and taught constitutional and international law for one year. After three years with a law firm, MacLeish gave up law in 1923, moved to France, and began his career as a writer. The works of this expatriate period, many of them verse dramas, express the despair and alienation found in many post–World War I writings. The works following MacLeish's return in 1928 to the Depression-era United States reflect his growing interest in his national and cultural heritage. *Frescoes for Mr. Rockefeller's City* (1933) celebrates the American dream, while his Pulitzer Prize–winning epic poem *Conquistador* (1932) tells the story of the conquest of Mexico. MacLeish's later works include *Collected Poems, 1917–1952* (which won the Pulitzer Prize, Bollingen Prize, Shelley Memorial Award, and National Book Award; 1952); *New and Collected Poems* (1976); as well as verse dramas and essays. His distinguished career as a person of letters was recognized by his appointments as Librarian of Congress (1939–1944), assistant secretary of state (1944–1945), and Boylston Professor of Rhetoric and Oratory at Harvard (1948–1962).

Bernard Malamud (1914–1986)   Born in Brooklyn, New York, and educated at the City College of New York and Columbia, Malamud is one of a number of post–World War II writers whose works drew heavily on their urban New York, Jewish backgrounds. Malamud's works often dramatize the tension arising out of the clash between Jewish conscience and American energy and materialism or the difficulty of keeping alive the Jewish sense of community and humanism in American society. *A New Life* (1961); *The Fixer* (1966; winner of both a National Book Award and a Pulitzer Prize); and *Pictures of Fidelman* (1969) all have protagonists who struggle with these problems. Some of his other novels are *The Natural* (1952), *The Assistant* (1957), *The Tenants* (1971), and *God's Grace* (1982). His short stories are collected in *The Magic Barrel* (1958; winner of the National Book Award in 1959), *Idiots First* (1963), and *Rembrandt's Hat* (1973).

Thomas Mann (1875–1955)   Son of a merchant and senator in the north of Germany, Mann moved to Munich at nineteen and worked in an insurance office while he learned the craft of writing. After some time at the university and a sojourn in Italy, Mann published his first novel, *Buddenbrooks, Decline of a Family* (1901). In this chronicle, Mann explored themes he would return to throughout his literary career—civilization in decay and the conflict between art and life. This theme appears in his classic short novel, *Death in Venice* (1925). His masterpiece, *The Magic Mountain* (1924), explored the forces that disrupted European society. He was awarded the Noble Prize in 1929. His political liberalism made life in Hitler's Germany impossible, and Mann left in

1933. Deprived of his citizenship in 1936, he became an American citizen in 1944, and in 1954 moved to Zurich, Switzerland, where he died the following year.

Christopher Marlowe (1564–1593) Born in Canterbury, Marlowe was educated at Cambridge, where he embarked on a career of writing and political activity, eventually giving up his original intention of entering the priesthood. He was arrested in 1593 on a charge of atheism, but before he could be brought to trial he was murdered in a brawl apparently involving a wealthy family that had reason to want him silenced. Marlowe's literary reputation rests primarily on his plays, powerful in their own right and the most significant precursors of Shakespeare's poetic dramas. The most important are *Tamburlaine, Parts I and II* (ca. 1587–1588; published 1590), *The Jew of Malta* (1589; published 1633), and *The Tragical History of the Life and Death of Dr. Faustus* (1592; published 1604).

Andrew Marvell (1621–1678) Born in Yorkshire and educated at Cambridge, Marvell received an inheritance upon his father's death that allowed him to spend four years traveling the Continent. Though not a Puritan himself, Marvell supported the Puritans' cause during the civil war and held a number of posts during the Puritan regime, including that of assistant to the blind John Milton, Cromwell's Latin Secretary. In 1659, a year before the Restoration, Marvell was elected to Parliament, where he served until his death. Soon after the Restoration, Marvell expressed strong disagreements with the government in a series of outspoken and anonymously printed satires. It was for these satires, rather than for his many love poems, that he was primarily known in his own day.

Claude McKay (1890–1948) Born in Sunny Ville, Jamaica, McKay had already completed two volumes of poetry before coming to the United States in 1912 at the age of twenty-three (the two volumes earned him awards, which paid his way). The racism he encountered as a black immigrant brought a militant tone to his writing. His popular poem "If We Must Die" (1919) helped to initiate the Harlem Renaissance of the 1920s. Between 1922 and 1934 he lived in Great Britain, Russia, Germany, France, Spain, and Morocco. His writings include four volumes of poems, many essays, an autobiography (*A Long Way from Home* [1937]), a novel (*Home to Harlem* [1928]), and a sociological study of Harlem. His conversion to Roman Catholicism in the 1940s struck his audience as an ideological retreat. McKay wrote in a letter to a friend: "[T]o have a religion is very much like falling in love with a woman. You love her for her . . . beauty, which cannot be defined."

Peter Meinke (b. 1932) Born in Brooklyn, New York, son of a salesman, Meinke served in the U.S. Army from 1955 to 1957, attended Hamilton College (B.A., 1955), the University of Michigan (M.A., 1961), and earned his Ph.D. at the University of Minnesota (1965). He taught English at a New Jersey high school, Hamline University, and Presbyterian College (now Eckerd College) in Florida, where he began directing the writing workshop in 1972. His reviews, poems, and stories have appeared in periodicals such as the *Atlantic*, the *New Yorker*, and the *New Republic*. The latest of his three books in the Pitt Poetry Series is *Nightwatch on the Chesapeake* (1987). His collection of stories, *The Piano Tuner*, won the 1986 Flannery O'Connor Award. Also, he has been the recipient of an NEA Fellowship in Poetry.

Herman Melville (1819–1891)   The death of his merchant father when Melville was twelve shattered the economic security of his family. The financial panic of 1837 reduced the Melvilles to the edge of poverty, and, at age nineteen, Melville went to sea. Economic conditions upon his return were still grim, and after a frustrating stint as a country school teacher, he again went to sea—this time on a four-year whaling voyage. He deserted the whaler in the South Pacific, lived some time with cannibals, made his way to Tahiti and Hawaii, and finally joined the navy for a return voyage. He mined his experiences for two successful South Sea adventure books, *Typee* (1846) and *Omoo* (1847). On the strength of these successes he married, but his next novel, *Mardi* (1849), was too heavy-handed an allegory to succeed. Driven by the obligation to support his growing family, Melville returned to sea adventure stories, with moderate success. But neither his masterpiece, *Moby Dick* (1851), nor his subsequent short stories and novels found much of an audience, and, in 1886, he accepted an appointment as customs inspector in Manhattan, a job he held until retirement. He continued to write, mostly poetry, and lived to see himself forgotten as an author. *Billy Budd*, found among his papers after his death and published in 1924, led to a revival of interest in Melville, now recognized as one of America's greatest writers.

George Meredith (1828–1909)   Born in Portsmouth, England, Meredith was apprenticed to a lawyer in London in 1845 after spending two years in Germany. He gave up law for journalism, and in 1866 worked as special foreign correspondent in Italy for the London *Morning Post* during the Austro-Italian War. He worked as contributing editor for several journals, including *Fortnightly Review*, and condemned the self-destructive hypocrisy of Victorian society in his novel *The Ordeal of Richard Feverel: A History of Father and Son* (1859). His reputation as a free-thinker was enhanced by *The Egoist* (1879), a comedy of manners, and his candid treatment of his own disintegrating marriage in a cycle of "extended" (i.e., 16-line) sonnets, *Modern Love* (1862).

James Merrill (b. 1926)   Born into a wealthy New York family (his father cofounded the Merrill Lynch stockbrokerage firm), Merrill was privately educated at home and then at Amherst College, where he received a B.A. degree in 1947. His first volume of poems, *First Poems* (1951), established his reputation as a writer of technical virtuosity, urbane eloquence, and wit. With the more personal and passionate poems of *Nights and Days* (1966) and *Mirabell*:

Books of Number (1979), both recipients of the National Book Award, Merrill gained a wider and more enthusiastic audience. Merrill is probably most widely known as "the Ouija poet" for his narrative poems that record the Ouija board sessions he and a friend conducted with "spirits from another world." Merrill has also written plays (*The Immortal Husband* [1956] and *The Bait* [1960]) and novels (*The Seraglio* [1957] and *The (Diblos) Notebook* [1965]). In 1990, Merrill won the Bobbitt Prize from the Library of Congress.

W. S. Merwin (b. 1927)   Born in New York City and raised in New Jersey and Pennsylvania, Merwin graduated from Princeton in 1947. His first poetry collection, *A Mask for Janus* (1952), completed while he tutored in Europe, won the Yale Series of Younger Poets Award. Associated with contemporary oracular poets, Merwin has offered a unique vision of solitude and nothingness. His collection *A Carrier of Ladders* (1970) won the Pulitzer Prize in 1971. He has published several other collections, four plays, and a number of translations. His latest work, *The Lost Upland* (1992), is a collection of stories set in France.

Robert Mezey (b. 1935)   Born in Philadelphia, Mezey attended Kenyon College and served a troubled hitch in the U.S. Army before earning his B.A. from the University of Iowa in 1959. He worked as a probation officer, advertising copywriter, and social worker, did graduate study at Stanford, and began teaching English at Case Western Reserve University in 1963. After a year as poet-in-residence at Franklin and Marshall College, he joined the English department of California State University, Fresno, spent three years at the University of Utah, and settled in 1976 at Pomona College in Claremont, California. Winner in 1960 of the Lamont Award for *The Lovemaker*, he has published many poetry collections, coedited *Naked Poetry* (1969), and was one of several translators for *Poems from the Hebrew* (1973). *Evening Wind*, a book of poems, appeared in 1987.

Edna St. Vincent Millay (1892–1950)   Millay was born in Maine and educated at Vassar. By the time she graduated in 1917, she had already achieved considerable fame as a poet; in the same year, she moved to Greenwich Village in New York and published her first volume of poetry, *Renascence and Other Poems*. In Greenwich Village, she established her reputation as a poet and became notorious for her bohemian life and passionate love affairs. In 1923 she received a Pulitzer Prize for a collection of sonnets, *The Harp-Weaver*, that dealt wittily and flippantly with love. Her later works exhibit a more subdued and contemplative tone as well as a growing preoccupation with social and political affairs. Nevertheless, her best and most memorable verse deals with the bittersweet emotions of love and the brevity of life.

John Milton (1608–1674)   Born in London to an affluent and artistic family, Milton was educated privately as a child and later attended Cambridge, where he wrote both Latin and English poems. After leaving Cambridge, he was supported for five years by his family while he read the classics, wrote, and traveled. When civil war broke out in 1642, Milton actively supported the Puritans against the crown. The Puritan victory in 1649 led to his appointment as Latin Secretary to Oliver Cromwell, his main duty being to translate foreign diplomatic correspondence. He voluntarily wrote many pamphlets defending the new regime, including a justification of the execution of Charles I in 1649. Doctors warned him that continued writing would damage his eyesight, but Milton ignored their advice and at age forty-three he became totally blind. Thereafter, Andrew Marvell assisted him in his secretarial duties. With the Restoration of Charles II in 1660, Milton went into retirement and was able to devote himself to composing the epic work he had long contemplated. This project reached fruition in 1667 with the publication of *Paradise Lost*, a blank verse epic in which Milton announced that he would "justify the ways of God to men." One of Milton's last works, often seen as autobiographical, is *Samson Agonistes* (1671), a poetic drama about the blind Samson triumphing over the treachery of those around him.

Yukio Mishima (1925–1970)   Born Kimitake Hiroaka in Tokyo, Japan, Mishima (his pen name) established his reputation in 1949 with the publication of his first novel, *Confessions of a Mask*, a fictional account of the author's own awareness that he would have to conceal his homosexuality. Mishima's life, and much of his writings, were devoted to extolling the virtues of the *Samurai* tradition—honor, obedience to the emperor, and military discipline. The clash between Japanese traditional values and the modern world is explored in his novel *The Temple of the Golden Pavilion* (1959). Mishima's career ended with his dramatic suicide—a ritual act of *seppuku*—following his failed attempt to spark a military revolt that he hoped would be the first step in rescuing Japan from what he saw as the corruptions of Western industrialism. It appears that Mishima recognized, long before his suicide, that his efforts to revive the old values were doomed to failure; one critic reports, "Mishima said that he worked so hard on body building because he intended to die before he was fifty and wanted to have a good-looking corpse."

Felix Mnthali (b. 1933)   Mnthali was born and grew up in Malawi in south central Africa. He was educated at Malawi University and Cambridge University in England. He returned to Africa, and as a visitor at the University of Ibadan in Nigeria, he wrote and privately published *Echoes from Ibadan* (1961). Back in his homeland he became the head of the department of English at Malawi University. He recently left Malawi to reside in Botswana.

Alberto Moravia (1907–1990)   Born in Rome, Moravia contracted tuberculosis as a child and was educated privately at home. Following the publication of his first novel, *A Time of Indifference* (1929), he traveled widely in Europe and America, supporting himself by writing articles for Italian newspapers. Moravia's writings brought him into conflict with the Fascist regime, and he was forced to flee Italy when the Germans occupied Rome. Moravia's international fame was established in the postwar period with the publication of such novels as *The Woman of Rome* (1947), *Conjugal Love* (1949), and *The Conformist* (1951). Many of his short stories appear in *Roman Tales* (translated in 1956) and *More Roman Tales* (translated in 1963).

Bharati Mukherjee (b. 1940)   Mukherjee was born in Calcutta, India. Her father was a chemist. She attended the University of Calcutta (B.A., 1959), the University of Baroda (M.A., 1961), and the University of Iowa, where she took an M.F.A. in 1963 and a Ph.D. in 1969. In 1963 she married Clark Blaise, a Canadian writer and professor, and joined the faculty at McGill University in Montreal. In 1973, Mukherjee and her husband visited India together and kept separate diaries of the trip, published as *Days and Nights in Calcutta* (1977). The diaries reveal marked differences in their responses: Mukherjee found her home environs, especially the status of women, worse than she remembered, while Blaise, after an initial revulsion at the squalor and poverty, found India a fascinating and attractive culture compared to the West. Mukherjee "left Canada after fifteen years due to the persistent effects of racial prejudice against people of my national origin," and joined the faculty at Skidmore College, Saratoga Springs, New York. Later she moved to Queens College of the City University of New York. Her fiction frequently explores the tensions inevitable in intercultural relationships. Her first novel, *The Tiger's Daughter* (1972), deals with the disappointment of an expatriate's return to India. In her second novel, *Wife* (1975), a psychologically abused woman finally kills her husband. *The Middleman and Other Stories* appeared in 1988.

Ogden Nash (1902–1971)   Frederick Ogden Nash was born in Rye, New York, and attended Harvard. He worked as a teacher, a bond salesperson, and then in the editorial and publicity departments of Doubleday Doran, Publishers, in New York City. For a time he moved to a rival publishing house, but soon joined the editorial staff of the *New Yorker*. Nash enjoyed immense popularity as a writer of light verse, choosing simple subjects and relying heavily on rhyme. His poems are collected in *I Wouldn't Have Missed It* (1975). Author of many children's books, Nash also cowrote the 1943 Broadway Musical *One Touch of Venus* (music by Kurt Weill).

Thomas Nashe (1567–1601)   Born in Lowestoft, England, the son of a minister, Nashe graduated from Cambridge, made a tour of France and Italy, and by 1588 was establishing himself in London as a professional writer. His hatred of Puritanism led him to join a group of pamphleteers who were defending the Anglican Church and its bishops against Puritan attacks. Nashe also wrote several plays and a picaresque prose narrative, *The Unfortunate Traveler* (1594), that inaugurated the novel of adventure in English literature.

Kathleen Norris (b. 1947) Norris was born in Washington, D.C., and educated at Bennington College in Vermont (B.A., 1969). From 1969 to 1973, she worked for the Academy of American Poets in New York and was later affiliated with Leaves of Grass, Inc., in Lemmon, South Dakota, where she lives. Her awards include a Provincetown Fine Arts Center Fellowship (1972) and a Creative Artists Public Service Grant from the state of New York (1972–1973). Her works have appeared in many periodicals, including *Dragonfly, Lillabulero,* and the *New Yorker*. She is the author of two collections of poems, *Falling Off* (1971) and *The Middle of the World* (1981).

Frank O'Connor (1903–1966) Born Michael O'Donovan in Cork, Ireland, O'Connor later adopted his pen name to separate his civil-service career from his writing career. His family's poverty forced him to leave school at age fourteen. During the Irish struggle for independence, O'Connor served in the Irish Republican Army, and after the establishment of the Irish Free State, he worked as a librarian. Despite his lack of formal education, he became director of the Abbey Theatre in Dublin. He moved to America in the 1950s and taught at Harvard and Northwestern. A storyteller in the great Gaelic oral tradition, he appeared for a time on Sunday morning television. A perfectionist, O'Connor constantly polished and reworked his stories. He added to his stature with fine critical studies of the novel (*The Mirror in the Roadway* [1956]) and the short story (*The Lonely Voice* [1963]), and introduced Gaelic poetry to a wide audience through his English translations.

Sharon Olds (b. 1942) Born in San Francisco, Olds attended Stanford (B.A., 1964) and Columbia (Ph.D., 1972). She joined the faculty of Theodor Herzl Institute in 1976 and has given readings at many colleges. She won the Madeline Sadin Award from the *New York Quarterly* in 1978 for "The Death of Marilyn Monroe." Often compared to confessional poets Sylvia Plath and Anne Sexton, Olds published her first collection, *Satan Says*, in 1980, and won both the National Book Critics' Circle Award and the Lamont Award for *The Dead and the Living* in 1983. *The Gold Cell* was published in 1987, and her most recent book of poems, *The Father*, appeared in 1992.

Wilfred Owen (1893–1918) Born in the Shropshire countryside of England, Owen had begun writing verse before he matriculated at London University, where he was known as a quiet and contemplative student. After some years of teaching English in France, Owen returned to England and joined the army. He was wounded in 1917 and killed in action leading an attack a few days before the armistice was declared in 1918. Owen's poems, published only after his death, along with his letters from the front to his mother, are perhaps the most powerful and vivid accounts of the horror of war to emerge from the First World War.

Grace Paley (b. 1922) The child of Russian immigrants, Grace Paley read so voraciously and spent so much time writing that she never completed college. Her achievements as a writer, however, brought her invitations to teach at Columbia and at Syracuse University, and an appointment to the literature faculty at Sarah Lawrence College. She is a committed feminist and an active pacifist. In her work, Paley relies on conversation rather than action, and reproduces the ethnic dialects of the people she writes about. She prefers to create the voices of characters dealing with fragments of everyday life, rather than tightly plotted, eventful stories. Her short stories are collected in *The Little Disturbances of Man: Stories of Women and Men at Love* (1959), *Enormous Changes at the Last Minute* (1974), and *Later the Same Day* (1985). *New and Collected Poems* appeared in 1992.

Molly Peacock (b. 1947) Born in Buffalo, New York, Peacock was educated at the State University of New York at Binghamton and at Johns Hopkins University, where she received an M.A. with honors in 1977. From 1970 to 1973, she was the director of academic advising at her alma mater in Binghamton. She was appointed honorary fellow at Johns Hopkins in 1977 and, in the following year, poet-in-residence at the Delaware State Arts Council in Wilmington. Since 1979, she has directed the Wilmington Writing Workshops. She has published in many magazines, including the *Southern Review,* the *Ohio Review,* and the *Massachusetts Review.* She has published three books of poems, *And Live Apart* (1980), *Raw Heaven* (1984), and *Take Heart* (1989), the latter dealing with her father's alcoholism and the mental and physical abuse she endured while growing up.

Luigi Pirandello (1867–1936) Pirandello was born in Sicily, but moved to Rome when he was nineteen. He earned a degree in philosophy from the University of Bonn, and returned to Rome in 1897 to teach at a girl's high school. There he remained until 1923. He wrote poetry in his youth, but soon enjoyed considerable success for his novels and short stories. In 1912, a friend persuaded him to dramatize one of his own short stories, and that experience led to distinguished achievement in the theater. Pirandello's plays, particularly *Six Characters in Search of an Author* (1921), were performed and critically acclaimed throughout Europe and the United States. In 1920, he said: "My art is full of bitter compassion for all those who deceive themselves; but this compassion cannot fail to be followed by the ferocious derision of destiny which condemns man to deception." He won the Nobel Prize for literature in 1934.

Sylvia Plath (1932–1963) Plath was born in Boston, Massachusetts, where her parents taught at Boston University. She graduated summa cum laude in English from Smith College (1955), earned an M.A. as a Fulbright scholar at Newnham College, Cambridge (1955–1957), and married British poet Ted Hughes (1956). Plath's poetry reveals the anger and anxiety that would eventually lead to her suicide. Her view that all relationships were in some way destructive and predatory surely darkened her life. Yet in 1963, during the month between the publication of her only novel, *The Bell Jar* (about a suicidal college student), and her death, Plath was extraordinarily productive; she produced finished poems every day. One critic suggests that for her, suicide was a positive act, a "refusal to collaborate" in a world she could not accept. Her *Collected Poems* was published in 1981.

Edgar Allan Poe (1809–1849)   Poe, the son of traveling actors, was born in Boston, Massachusetts. Within a year, his alcoholic father deserted his mother and three infant children. When his mother died of tuberculosis in Richmond, Virginia, three-year-old Edgar was adopted by John Allan and his wife. Allan, a prosperous businessperson, spent time in England, where Poe began his education at private schools. Back in the United States, Allan forced Poe to leave the University of Virginia in 1826, when Poe incurred gambling debts he could not pay. He served in the U.S. Army from 1827 to 1829, eventually attaining the rank of sergeant-major. Poe next attended West Point hoping for further military advancement. Shortly thereafter, Mrs. Allan died of tuberculosis. Poe angrily confronted his foster father about his extramarital affairs; for this candor he was disowned. Believing that Allan would never reinstate him as heir, Poe deliberately violated rules to provoke his dismissal from the Academy. In 1835, Poe began his career as editor, columnist, and reviewer, earning a living he could not make as a writer of stories and poems. He married his thirteen-year-old cousin, Virginia Clemm, in 1836, and lived with her and her mother during a period marked by illness and poverty. Virginia died of tuberculosis in 1847. Poe died, delirious, under mysterious circumstances, in 1849. He perfected the gothic horror story ("Fall of the House of Usher") and originated the modern detective story ("The Gold Bug," "The Murders in the Rue Morgue"). Poe's work fascinated the French poet Baudelaire, who translated it into French.

Alexander Pope (1688–1744)   Born in London to a prosperous merchant family, Pope was educated mostly by tutors because schools and universities were closed to Roman Catholics. Despite this situation and an illness that left him hunchbacked and stunted, his brilliance as a wit and poet early gained him entry into the most sophisticated circles of London society. By age thirty, he was acknowledged as the premier poet of England. He came to typify an age known for its sense of order, balance, and decorum, as well as its concern for the relation of the individual to society. Pope's poetry reflects these concerns in the polished and balanced heroic couplets he uses to write about the social, religious, and philosophical issues of his age. His *Essay on Criticism* (1711) and *Essay on Man* (1733–1734) are heavily didactic, while his satires, such as *The Rape of the Lock* (1712–1714), *The Dunciad* (1728), and *Epistle to Dr. Arbuthnot* (1735) try to instill reasonableness and proportion by ridiculing the follies and absurdities of humankind.

Sir Walter Ralegh (1552?–1618)   Born in Devonshire, England, into the landed gentry, Ralegh attended Oxford but dropped out after a year in order to fight for the Huguenot cause in France. He returned to England, began the study of law, but again was drawn to a life of adventure and exploration. Through the influence of friends he came to the attention of Queen Elizabeth, and thenceforth his career flourished: he was knighted, given a number of lucrative commercial monopolies, made a member of Parliament and, in 1587, named captain of the Yeoman of the Guard. During these years, he invested in various colonies in North America, but all his settlements failed. He was briefly imprisoned in the Tower of London for offending the Queen but was soon back in favor and in command of an unsuccessful expedition to Guiana (now Venezuela) in 1595. In 1603, he was again imprisoned in the Tower, this time on a probably trumped-up charge of treason, where he remained until 1616, spending part of his time writing A *History of the World* (1614). After his release, he undertook still another expedition to Guiana but again returned empty-handed. As a consequence of more political intrigue, James I ordered him executed. Although Ralegh epitomized the great merchant adventurers of Elizabethan England, he was also a gifted poet.

Dudley Randall (b. 1914)   Born in Washington, D.C., Randall worked during the Depression in the foundry of the Ford Motor Company in Dearborn, Michigan, and then as a carrier and clerk for the U.S. Post Office in Detroit. He served in the U.S. Army Signal Corps (1942–1946), graduated from Wayne State University (B.A., 1949) and the University of Michigan (M.A.L.S., 1951). He was a librarian at several universities, and founded the Broadside Press in 1965 "so black people could speak to and for their people." Randall told *Negro Digest*, "Precision and accuracy are necessary for both white and black writers. . . . 'A black aesthetic' should not be an excuse for sloppy writing." He urges African American writers to reject what was false in "white" poetry but not to forsake universal concerns in favor of a racial agenda. His works include *On Getting a Natural* (1969) and A *Litany of Friends: New and Selected Poems* (1981).

John Crowe Ransom (1888–1974)   Born in Pulaski, Tennessee, Ransom graduated from Vanderbilt University in 1909 and was a Rhodes Scholar at Oxford from 1910 to 1913. He joined the faculty of Vanderbilt in 1914 and soon led a group of teachers and students (known as the Fugitives) in a movement against contemporary trends in writing and politics. The Fugitives spawned what became known as the New Criticism. Ransom served in the U.S. Army from 1917 to 1919, returned to Vanderbilt, then joined the faculty of Kenyon College in 1937, where he remained until 1974. While there, he founded and edited the *Kenyon Review*, a literary review that is still being published. His early influential work is collected in *Chills and Fever* (1924) and *Two Gentlemen in Bonds* (1927). Winner of the Bollingen Prize (1951) and the National Book

Award (1964), Ransom argued that good poetry should "induce the mode of thought that is imaginative rather than logical."

Henry Reed (b. 1914)   Reed was born in Birmingham, England, earned a B.A. from the University of Birmingham (1937), worked as a teacher and free-lance writer (1937–1941), and served in the British Army (1941–1942). His early poetry dealt with political events before and during World War II. "Naming of Parts" and "Judging Distances" were based on his frustrating experience in cadet training. His only collection of poetry, *A Map of Verona* (1946), revealed a formal, reverent, but also humorous and ironic voice. Reed began writing radio plays in 1947 and has generated as many as four scripts a year. His best-known satirical work is the "Hilda Tablet" series, a 1960s BBC-Radio production that parodied British society of the 1930s.

Alastair Reid (b. 1926)   Born in Scotland, son of a minister, Reid graduated with honors from St. Andrews University after serving in the Royal Navy. He taught at Sarah Lawrence College (1951–1955) and, after his appointment as staff writer at the *New Yorker* in 1959, occasionally enjoyed visiting professor-ships across the United States and in England, teaching Latin American studies and literature. Acclaimed for his light, engaging style, Reid has been enthusi-astically received as a poet, translator, essayist, and author of children's books, moving between genres as easily as he has moved between countries. Reid has lived in Spain, Latin America, Greece, and Morocco (to name a few places) and rejects the label "Scottish" writer. His deliberate rootlessness shows in his poetry, which is characterized by, in one critic's words, "natural irregularity."

Adrienne Rich (b. 1929)   Born to a middle-class family, Rich was educated by her parents until she entered public school in the fourth grade. She graduated Phi Beta Kappa from Radcliffe College in 1951, the same year her first book of poems, *A Change of World*, appeared. That volume, chosen by W. H. Auden for the Yale Series of Younger Poets Award, and her next, *The Diamond Cutters and Other Poems* (1955), earned her a reputation as an elegant, controlled stylist. In the 1960s, however, Rich began a dramatic shift away from her earlier mode as she took up political and feminist themes and stylistic experimentation in such works as *Snapshots of a Daughter-in-Law* (1963), *The Necessities of Life* (1966), *Leaflets* (1969), and *The Will to Change* (1971). In *Diving into the Wreck* (1973) and *The Dream of a Common Language* (1978), she continued to experiment with form and to deal with the experiences and aspirations of women from a feminist perspective. In addition to her poetry, Rich has pub-lished many essays on poetry, feminism, motherhood, and lesbianism. Her most recent collection of poems, *An Atlas of the Difficult World*, appeared in 1991.

Alberto Ríos (b. 1952)   Born in Nogales, Arizona, to a Mexican father and an English mother, Ríos was educated at the University of Arizona, where he received a B.A. in English and creative writing (1974) and an M.F.A. (1975).

He began teaching at Arizona State University in 1983 and is presently professor of English there. Ríos has served on various state and national boards and commissions devoted to the arts. His awards include a first place in the Academy of American Arts poetry contest (1977) and the Chicanos Por La Causa Community Appreciation Award (1988). Ríos's publications include three poetry chapbooks, *Elk Heads on the Wall* (1979), *Sleeping on Fists* (1981), and *Whispering to Fool the Wind* (1982), as well as a collection of stories, *The Iguana Killer: Twelve Stories of the Heart* (1984). His most recent volume of poetry is *Teodoro Luna's Two Kisses* (1990). Ríos's poetry has been set to music in a cantata called "Tito's Story" on an EMI release, "Away from Home." He is also featured in the documentary *Birthwrite: Growing Up Hispanic.*

Edwin Arlington Robinson (1869–1935)   Robinson grew up in Gardiner, Maine, attended Harvard, returned to Gardiner as a free-lance writer, then settled in New York City in 1896. His various odd jobs included a one-year stint as subway-construction inspector. President Theodore Roosevelt, a fan of his poetry, had him appointed to the United States Customs House in New York, where he worked from 1905 to 1909. Robinson wrote about people, rather than nature, particularly New England characters remembered from his early years. Describing his first volume of poems, *The Torrent and the Night Before* (1896), he told a friend there was not "a single red-breasted robin in the whole collection." Popular throughout his career, Robinson won three Pulitzer Prizes (1921, 1924, 1927).

Theodore Roethke (1908–1963)   Born in Saginaw, Michigan, Roethke was the son of a greenhouse owner; greenhouses figure prominently in the imagery of his poems. He graduated magna cum laude from the University of Michigan in 1929, where he also earned an M.A. in 1936 after graduate study at Harvard. He taught at several universities, coached two varsity tennis teams, and settled at the University of Washington in 1947. Intensely introspective and demanding of himself, Roethke was renowned as a great teacher, though sometimes incapacitated by an ongoing manic-depressive condition. His collection *The Waking: Poems 1933–1953*, won the Pulitzer Prize in 1954. Other awards include Guggenheim Fellowships in 1945 and 1950, and a National Book Award and the Bollingen Prize in 1959 for *Words for the Wind* (1958).

Muriel Rukeyser (1913–1980)   Born in New York City, Rukeyser attended Vassar and Columbia, then spent a short time at Roosevelt Aviation School, which no doubt helped shape her first published volume of poetry, *Theory of Flight* (1935). In the early 1930s, she joined Elizabeth Bishop, Mary McCarthy, and Eleanor Clark in founding a literary magazine that challenged the policies of the *Vassar Review*. (The two magazines later merged.) A social activist, Rukeyser witnessed the Scottsboro trials (where she was one of the reporters arrested by authorities) in 1933. She visited suffering tunnel workers in West Virginia (1936) and went to Hanoi to protest U.S. involvement in the Vietnam

War. She gave poetry readings across the United States and received several awards, including a Guggenheim Fellowship and the Copernicus Award. *Waterlily Fire: Poems 1935–1962* appeared in 1962, and later work was collected in *29 Poems* (1970). *The Collected Poems of Muriel Rukeyser* appeared in 1978. Her only novel, *The Orgy*, appeared in 1965.

Sappho (ca. 610–ca. 580 B.C.)   Almost nothing certain is known of the finest woman lyric poet of the ancient world. She was born to an aristocratic family, had three brothers, one of whom was a court cupbearer (a position limited to the sons of good families). She is associated with the island of Lesbos, set in the Aegean Sea. She married and had a daughter. Until recently, her reputation depended on fragments of her work quoted by other ancient authors. However, in the late nineteenth century a cache of papyrus and vellum codices (dating from the second to the sixth centuries A.D.) containing authentic transcriptions of a few of her lyrical poems was discovered in Egypt. Unlike other ancient Greek poets, she wrote in ordinary Greek rather than an exalted literary dialect; her lyrics, despite their simple language, conveyed women's concerns with intense emotion.

Jean-Paul Sartre (1905–1980)   Sartre was born in Paris, the son of a naval officer who died when Sartre was a child. He graduated from the prestigious École Normale Supérieure (1930), and spent his early career as a philosophy professor. During World War II, he was imprisoned in Germany for nine months, and, when released, joined the French Resistance (1941–1944). At the conclusion of the war, Sartre devoted himself to his extraordinary writing career. His philosophical writings, dating from as early as 1936, gave shape to existentialism. His first novel, *Nausea* (1938), won the first of many prizes awarded for his work. Some of these, including the Nobel Prize for Literature (1964), Sartre refused. In addition to his copious output as a technical philosopher and fiction writer, Sartre became a distinguished playwright, a discerning literary critic, and a prolific apologist for leftist political theory. Although they never married, Sartre maintained a durable relationship with Simone de Beauvoir, the eminent French writer and feminist. In 1956, the *New Statesman and Nation* wrote: "The Vatican has placed his works on the Index; yet Gabriel Marcel, himself a militant Catholic, regarded him as the greatest of French thinkers. The State Department found his novels subversive; but *Les Mains Sale* [Dirty Hands] was the most effective counter-revolutionary play of the entire cold war. Sartre has been vilified by the Communists in Paris and feted by them in Vienna. No great philosopher ever had fewer disciples, but no other could claim the intellectual conquest of an entire generation."

Gjertrud Schnackenberg (b. 1953)   Born in Tacoma, Washington, Schnackenberg graduated from Mount Holyoke College in 1975 and was honored by her alma mater with an honorary doctorate in 1985. She has published three volumes of poetry: *Portraits and Elegies* (1982), *The Lamplit Answer* (1985), and *A Gilded Lapse of Time* (1992). She has received numerous awards, including the Rome Prize in literature from the American Academy and Institute of Arts and Letters, which provided a year at the American Academy in Rome (1983), and fellowships from the National Endowment for the Arts and the Guggenheim Foundation.

Anne Sexton (1928–1974)   Born in Newton, Massachusetts, Sexton attended Garland Junior College and Boston University, where she studied under Robert Lowell. She worked for a year as a fashion model in Boston and later wrote her first poetry collection, *To Bedlam and Part Way Back* (1960), while recovering from a nervous breakdown. Writing a poem almost every day was successful therapy for her. From 1961 to 1963, Sexton was a scholar at the Radcliffe Institute for Independent Study. A confessional poet, Sexton acknowledged her debt to W. D. Snodgrass, whose collection of poetry, *Heart's Needle* (1959), influenced her profoundly. Her second collection, *All My Pretty Ones* (1962), includes a quote from a letter by Franz Kafka that expresses her own literary philosophy: "A book should serve as the axe for the frozen sea within us." *Live or Die* (1967), her third collection of poems, won a Pulitzer Prize. She committed suicide in 1974.

William Shakespeare (1564–1616)   Shakespeare was born at Stratford-on-Avon in April 1564. His father became an important public figure, rising to the position of high bailiff (equivalent to mayor) of Stratford. Although we know practically nothing of his personal life, we may assume that Shakespeare received a decent grammar school education in literature, logic, and Latin (though not in mathematics or natural science). When he was eighteen, he married Anne Hathaway, eight years his senior; six months later their son was born. Two years later, Anne bore twins. We do not know how the young Shakespeare supported his family, and we do not hear of him again until 1592, when a rival London playwright sarcastically refers to him as an "upstart crow." Shakespeare seems to have prospered in the London theater world. He probably began as an actor, and earned enough as author and part owner of his company's theaters to acquire property. His sonnets, which were written during the 1590s, reveal rich and varied interests. Some are addressed to an attractive young man (whom the poet urges to marry); others to the mysterious dark lady; still others suggest a love triangle of two men and a woman. His dramas include historical plays based on English dynastic struggles; comedies, both festive and dark; romances such as *Pericles* (1608) and *Cymbeline* (1611) that cover decades in the lives of their characters; and the great tragedies: *Hamlet* (1602), *Othello* (1604), *King Lear* (1605), and *Macbeth* (1606). About 1611 (at age forty-seven), he retired to the second largest house in Stratford. He died in 1616, leaving behind a body of work that still stands as a pinnacle in world literature.

George Bernard Shaw (1856–1950)   Born in Dublin, Ireland, to an English family, Shaw left school at the age of fourteen. After five years' employment in a land agent's office, Shaw left Ireland to rejoin his music teacher mother in London. His unpromising early literary ambitions took the form of unsuccessful novels, but Shaw found employment with London newspapers as a witty and intellectually stimulating critic of music and drama. He was appalled by the intractable poverty and misery that seemed to him an inevitable consequence of English economic and social systems, and, in 1884, joined with others to found the Fabian Society. This organization promoted a gradual introduction of socialism. As a drama critic Shaw admired and praised for its concern with social problems the work of the Norwegian playwright Henrik Ibsen. Shaw's critical study of Ibsen's work, *The Quintessence of Ibsenism*, appeared in 1891. Shaw was thirty-six when his first play, *Widowers' Houses*, was produced in 1891; the play deals with the problem of slum landlordism. His second play, *Mrs. Warren's Profession* (1893), dealt with prostitution, and so offended official sensibilities that it was promptly banned. From the very outset, Shaw confronted the dark side of modern life and forced his audience to reevaluate its pious certainties and recognize its pervasive hypocrisy. Among his greatest works, almost all of which confound the audience's expectations with unheroic heroes and interesting villains, are *Man and Superman* (1904), *Major Barbara* (1907), *Pygmalion* (1912), *Heartbreak House* (1919), and *Saint Joan* (1923). Shaw developed an intense distaste for the peculiarities of English spelling and punctuation rules (particularly the use of apostrophes), and, characteristically, insisted on reforming those usages in his own published work.

Irwin Shaw (1913–1984)   Born and educated in New York City, where he received a B.A. from Brooklyn College in 1934, Shaw began his career as a scriptwriter for popular radio programs of the 1930s, then went to Hollywood to write for the movies. Disillusioned with the film industry, Shaw returned to New York. His first piece of serious writing, an antiwar play entitled *Bury the Dead*, was produced on Broadway in 1936. About this time, Shaw began contributing short stories to such magazines as the *New Yorker* and *Esquire*. His first collection of stories, *Sailor off the Bremen and Other Stories* (1939), earned him an immediate and lasting reputation as a writer of fiction. While continuing to write plays and stories, Shaw turned to the novel and published in 1948 *The Young Lions*, which won high critical praise as one of the most important novels to come out of World War II. The commercial success of the book and the movie adaptation brought Shaw financial independence and allowed him to devote the rest of his career to writing novels, among them *The Troubled Air* (1951), *Lucy Crown* (1956), *Rich Man, Poor Man* (1970), and *Acceptable Losses* (1982). Shaw's stories are collected in *Short Stories: Five Decades* (1978).

Percy Bysshe Shelley (1792–1822)   Born near Horsham, England, Shelley was the son of a wealthy landowner who sat in Parliament. At University College, Oxford, he befriended Thomas Jefferson Hogg. Both became interested in radical philosophy and quickly became inseparable. After one year at Oxford they were expelled together for writing and circulating a pamphlet entitled "The

Necessity of Atheism." Shelley married Harriet Westbrook soon after leaving Oxford. Though they had two children, the marriage was unsuccessful, and in 1814, Shelley left Harriet for Mary Wollstonecraft Godwin (author of *Franken-stein* [1818]). After Harriet's death (an apparent suicide), Shelley and Godwin were married. Escaping legal problems in England, he settled in Pisa, Italy, in 1820, and died in a sailing accident before his thirtieth birthday. A playwright and essayist as well as a romantic poet, Shelley is admired for his dramatic poem "Prometheus Unbound" (1820).

Stevie Smith (1902–1971)   Born Florence Margaret Smith in Hull, England, Stevie Smith was a secretary at Newnes Publishing Company in London from 1923 to 1953, and occasionally worked as a writer and broadcaster for the BBC. Though she began publishing verse, which she often illustrated herself, in the 1930s, Smith did not reach a wide audience until 1962—with the publication of *Selected Poems* and her appearance in the Penguin Modern Poets Series. She is noted for her eccentricity and mischievous humor, often involving an acerbic twist on nursery rhymes, common songs, or hymns. Force-fed with what she considered lifeless language in the New English Bible, she often aimed satirical barbs at religion. Smith won the Queen's Gold Medal for poetry in 1969, two years before her death. She published three novels in addition to her eight volumes of poetry.

W. D. Snodgrass (b. 1926)   Born in Pennsylvania, son of an accountant, William Dewitt Snodgrass attended Geneva College, earned three degrees from the University of Iowa (B.A., 1949; M.A., 1951; M.F.A., 1953), then taught at Cornell University, the University of Rochester, and Wayne State University. Acknowledged as one of the original confessional poets, he won the Pulitzer Prize in 1960 for his first collection, *Heart's Needle* (1959). His poems are deeply personal and often involve references to the wives and children from his three marriages. Surprising critics who had grown tired of his self-analytical style, Snodgrass distinguished himself again with his third collection, *The Führer Bunker: A Cycle of Poems in Progress* (1977), in which he explores the psyches of Hitler's senior officials during the month they shared his bunker in 1945. *Selected Poems, 1957–1987* appeared in 1987.

Sophocles (496?–406 B.C.)   Born into a wealthy family at Colonus, a village just outside Athens, Sophocles distinguished himself early in life as a performer, musician, and athlete. Our knowledge of him is based on a very few ancient laudatory notices, but he certainly had a brilliant career as one of the three great Greek classical tragedians (the other two are Aeschylus, an older contemporary, and Euripides, a younger contemporary). He won the drama competition associated with the Dionysian festival (entries consisted of a tragic trilogy and a farce) at least twenty times (far more often than his two principal rivals). However, *Oedipus Rex*, his most famous tragedy, and the three other plays it was grouped with, took second place (ca. 429 B.C.). He lived during the golden age of Athens, when architecture, philosophy, and the arts flourished under Pericles. In 440 B.C., Sophocles was elected as one of the ten *strategoi* (military commanders), an indication of his stature in Athens. But his long life ended in sadder times—when the Peloponnesian War (431–404 B.C.), between the Athenian empire and an alliance led by Sparta, darkened the region. Though Sophocles wrote some 123 plays, only 7 have survived; nonetheless, these few works establish him as the greatest of the ancient Western tragedians.

Helen Sorrells (b. 1908)   Born in Stafford, Kansas, the daughter of farmers, Sorrells earned a B.S. from Kansas State University in 1931. She married a technical writer, had two children and was approaching her seventh decade when she won the Borestone Award for her poem "Cry Summer." In 1968, she won the *Arizona Quarterly* Award for poetry and in 1973 received a creative writing grant from the National Endowment for the Arts, as well as the Poetry Society of America's Cecil Hemley Award for the poem "Tunnels." She has contributed to *Esquire* and *Reporter*, among others, and published a collection of poems, *Seeds as They Fall* (1971).

Art Spiegelman (b. 1948)   Spiegelman's parents, Anja and Vladek, were Polish Jews who survived imprisonment in the Nazi concentration camp at Auschwitz. Spiegelman was born in Stockholm, Sweden, and his family immigrated to the United States. He attended Harpur College (now State University of New York at Binghamton) from 1965 to 1968. His mother, Anja, committed suicide in 1968. In 1977 he married Francoise Mouly, a publisher. As a student, Spiegelman developed his talent for drawing and writing and became a creative consultant, designer, and writer for Topps Chewing Gum, Inc., where he produced novelty packaging and bubble gum cards. But he was fascinated by the provocative underground comics of the sixties, and began to create original and powerful comic book work addressed to an adult audience. *The Complete Mr. Infinity* appeared in 1970, succeeded by numerous other productions that culminated in *Maus: A Survivor's Tale* (1986). *Maus*, based on his father's experience as a Nazi concentration camp survivor, was nominated for a National Book Critics Circle Award, and won the Joel M. Cavior Award for Jewish Writing. In his "comic book," Spiegelman portrays the Nazis as cats and the Jews as their victim mice. He published the second volume of *Maus—And Here My Troubles Began (From Mauschwitz to the Catskills and Beyond)* in 1991. In 1980, Spiegelman and his wife founded *Raw*—an annual magazine that showcases the talents of avant-garde artist-writers of adult comics.

Wallace Stevens (1879–1955)   Born in Reading, Pennsylvania, Stevens graduated from Harvard in 1900, worked for a year as a reporter for the New York *Herald Tribune*, graduated from New York University Law School in 1903, and practiced law in New York for twelve years. From 1916 to 1955, Stevens worked for the Hartford Accident and Indemnity Company, where he was appointed vice-president in 1934. He was in his forties when he published his first book of poetry, *Harmonium, Ideas of Order* (1923). Stevens argued that poetry is a "supreme fiction" that shapes chaos and provides order to both nature and human relationships. He illuminates his philosophy in *Ideas of Order* (1935) and *Notes toward a Supreme Fiction* (1942). His *Collected Poems* (1954) won the Pulitzer Prize and established him as a major American poet.

Alfred, Lord Tennyson (1809–1892)   Tennyson was born in Lincolnshire and attended Trinity College, Cambridge (1828–1831), where he won the Chancellor's Medal for Poetry in 1829. His 1842 collection, *Poems*, was not well received, but he gained prominence and the Queen's favor with the 1850 publication of *In Memoriam*, an elegy written over seventeen years and inspired by the untimely death of his friend Arthur Hallam in 1833. That same year he finally married Emily Sellwood, after a fourteen-year engagement. In 1850, he was named poet laureate of England after Wordsworth's death. His works include *Maud and Other Poems* (1855) and *Idylls of the King* (1859), based on the legendary exploits of King Arthur and the knights of the Round Table.

Dylan Thomas (1914–1953)   Born in Swansea, Wales, Thomas decided to pursue a writing career directly after grammar school. At age twenty, he published his first collection, *Eighteen Poems* (1934), but his lack of a university degree deprived him of most opportunities to earn a living as a writer in England. Consequently, his early life (as well as the lives of his wife and children) was darkened by a poverty compounded by his free spending and heavy drinking. A self-proclaimed romanticist, Thomas called his poetry a "record of [his] struggle from darkness towards some measure of light." *The Map of Love* appeared in 1939 and *Deaths and Entrances* in 1946. Later, as a radio playwright and screenwriter, Thomas delighted in the sounds of words, sometimes at the expense of sense. *Under Milk Wood* (produced in 1953) is filled with his private, onomatopoetic language. He suffered from alcoholism and lung ailments, and died in a New York hospital in 1953. Earlier that year, he noted in his *Collected Poems:* "These poems, with all their crudities, doubts and confusions are written for the love of man and in Praise of God, and I'd be a damn fool if they weren't."

James Thurber (1894–1961)   Born in Columbus, Ohio, Thurber went through the local public schools and graduated from Ohio State University. He began his writing career as a reporter, first for an Ohio newspaper, and later in Paris and New York City, before he became a staff member of the *New Yorker*. There he wrote the humorous satirical essays and fables (often illustrated with his whimsical drawings of people and animals) upon which his reputation rests— the most famous being "The Secret Life of Walter Mitty." In 1929, he and another *New Yorker* staffer, E. B. White, wrote *Is Sex Necessary? or, Why You Feel the Way You Do*, a spoof of the increasingly popular new psychological theories. In 1933, he published his humorous autobiography, *My Life and Hard Times*. With Elliott Nugent, he wrote *The Male Animal* (1940), a comic play that pleads for academic freedom, and, in 1959, he memorialized his associates at the *New Yorker* in *The Years with Ross.*

Leo Tolstoy (1828–1910)   Born in Russia into a family of aristocratic land-owners, Tolstoy cut short his university education and joined the army, serving among the primitive Cossacks, who became the subject of his first novel, *The Cossacks* (1863). Tolstoy left the army and traveled abroad but was disappointed by Western materialism and returned home. After a brief period in St. Peters-burg, he became bored with the life of literary celebrity and returned to his family estate. There he wrote his two greatest novels, *War and Peace* (1869) and *Anna Karenina* (1877). Around 1876, Tolstoy experienced a kind of spir-itual crisis that ultimately led him to reject his former beliefs, way of life, and literary works. Henceforth, he adopted the simple life of the Russian peasants, rejecting orthodoxy in favor of a rational Christianity that disavowed private property, class divisions, secular and institutional religious authority, as well as all art (including his own) that failed to teach the simple principles he espoused.

Jean Toomer (1894–1967)   Descended from Pinckney Benton Stewart Pinch-back, a Reconstruction governor of Louisiana whose mother had been a slave, Jean Toomer became one of the leaders in the literary world of the Harlem Renaissance and produced one of that movement's most distinguished works, *Cane* (1923). He also worked in the mainstream white New York literary scene. Although his best work illuminates the African American experience of the Georgia sugar cane fields, he once wrote "I would consider it libelous for anyone to refer to me as a colored man, for I have not lived as one." Born in Wash-ington, D.C., he graduated from public school and, aiming for a law degree, enrolled briefly at the University of Wisconsin and the City College of New York. But college life proved ungratifying, and he wandered, living among a variety of social and racial groups. He married twice—first a novelist, who died in childbirth, then the daughter of a wealthy New York broker. Both his wives were white. He said of himself: "I am of no particular race, I am of the human race, a man at large in the human world, preparing a new race."

Alice Walker (b. 1944)   Born in Eatonton, Georgia, the eighth child of share-croppers, Walker was educated at Spelman College and Sarah Lawrence Col-lege. She has been deeply involved in the civil rights movement, working to register voters in Georgia and on behalf of welfare rights and Head Start in Mississippi. She also worked for the New York City Department of Welfare. She has taught at Wellesley and Yale and been an editor of *Ms.* Her nonfiction works include a biography for children, *Langston Hughes: American Poet* (1973); numerous contributions to anthologies about African American writers; and a collection of essays, *In Search of Our Mothers' Gardens: Womanist Prose* (1983). She has published several novels dealing with the African American experience: *The Third Life of Grange Copeland* (1973), *Meridian* (1976), *The Color Purple* (1982), which won the Pulitzer Prize and established her as a major writer, and

The Temple of My Familiar (1989). Her short stories are collected in two volumes, *In Love and Trouble: Stories of Black Women* (1973) and *You Can't Keep a Good Woman Down* (1981). Among her collections of poetry are *Good Night, Willie Lee, I'll See You in the Morning* (1979) and *Horses Make a Landscape Look More Beautiful* (1984). Her most recent novel, *Possessing the Secrets of Joy,* appeared in 1992.

Robert Wallace (b. 1932)   Born in Springfield, Missouri, Wallace graduated summa cum laude from Harvard in 1953. After serving in the U.S. Army, he earned an M.A. (with honors) from Cambridge in 1959. He taught English at Bryn Mawr, Sweet Briar College, and Vassar, and in 1965 joined the English department of Case Western Reserve University in Cleveland. There Wallace directs Bits Press, which publishes the work of contemporary poets. An award-winning poet himself, Wallace has contributed poems to many periodicals, including the *New Yorker,* the *Atlantic, Harper's,* and the *New Republic.* In addition to his several collections of poems, he has published a book of children's poems, *Critters* (1978) and a textbook, *Writing Poems* (1982).

Edmund Waller (1606–1687)   Born in Hertfordshire, England, Waller was privately instructed as a young child, then sent to Eton and Cambridge. He served for several years as a member of Parliament, first as an opponent of the crown and later, as a Royalist. His advocacy of the Royalist cause and his attempts to moderate between the crown and the Puritans in an increasingly revolutionary period led to his imprisonment and exile. He made his peace with Cromwell and returned to England in 1651. When the monarchy was restored in 1660, Waller regained his seat in Parliament. Waller was one of the earliest poets to use the heroic couplet, a form that was to dominate English poetry for over a century.

E. B. White (1899–1985)   Born in Mount Vernon, New York, Elwyn Brooks White was educated at Cornell and began his career as a journalist, but he soon abandoned journalism in favor of essay writing. His graceful and witty style led to his appointment to the staff of the *New Yorker,* where over the years his personal, informal essays earned him a reputation as one of America's finest writers. From 1938 to 1943 he wrote a regular column for *Harper's,* pieces that were collected in *One Man's Meat* (1944). Other essays, as well as short stories, are collected in *The Second Tree from the Corner* (1954). If, as one critic has observed, White is known among writers as "an essayist's essayist," he is more widely known to the general public as the author of two classic works of children's literature, *Stuart Little* (1945) and *Charlotte's Web* (1952). Among his many other works, White wrote, with James Thurber, *Is Sex Necessary? or, Why You Feel the Way You Do* (1929).

Walt Whitman (1819–1892)   One of nine children, Whitman was born in Huntington, Long Island, in New York, and grew up in Brooklyn, where his father worked as a carpenter. At age eleven, after five years of public school, Whitman took a job as a printer's assistant. He learned the printing trade and, before his twentieth birthday, became editor of the *Long Islander*, a Huntington newspaper. He edited several newspapers in the New York area and one in New Orleans before leaving the newspaper business in 1848. He then lived with his parents, worked as a part-time carpenter, and began writing *Leaves of Grass*, which he first published at his own expense in 1855. After the Civil War (during which he was a devoted volunteer, ministering to the wounded), Whitman was fired from his job in the Department of the Interior by Secretary James Harlan, who considered *Leaves of Grass* obscene. Soon, however, he was rehired in the attorney general's office, where he remained until 1874. In 1881, after many editions, *Leaves of Grass* finally found a publisher willing to print it uncensored. Translations were enthusiastically received in Europe, but Whitman remained relatively unappreciated in America, where it was only after his death that a large audience would come to admire his original and innovative expression of American individualism.

Kathleen Wiegner (b. 1938)   Wiegner was born in Milwaukee, Wisconsin, to parents who were both educators. She earned three degrees including a Ph.D. (1967) from the University of Wisconsin–Madison. Thereafter, she joined the faculty at the University of Wisconsin at Milwaukee, where she remained until 1973. She has a daughter, but her 1960 marriage ended in divorce in 1970. In 1974 she moved to California and became an associate editor at the West Coast Bureau of *Forbes* magazine. She received the poetry prize from the Wisconsin Writers Council for *Country Western Breakdown* (1974) and has published several volumes of verse. She once remarked that "My secret ambition would be to live in a world where poems were performed in Las Vegas, where the poet sat on a piano like Ruth Etting and 'sang' poems to an audience that clapped and wept."

Richard Wilbur (b. 1921)   Son of a portrait artist, Wilbur was born in New York City, graduated from Amherst College in 1942, became staff sergeant in the U.S. Army during World War II, then earned an M.A. from Harvard in 1947. He taught English at Harvard, Wellesley, and Wesleyan University, and was named writer-in-residence at Smith College in 1977. Winner of the Pulitzer Prize, National Book Award, and the Bollingen Prize, Wilbur has distinguished himself, in his several volumes of poetry, by using established poetic forms and meters, mining new insights from common, tangible images. A translator of French plays by Molière and Racine, Wilbur was colyricist (with Lillian Hellman) of *Candide*, the 1957 Broadway musical based on Voltaire's satirical novel. *New and Collected Poems* appeared in 1988 and *More Opposites* in 1991.

William Carlos Williams (1883–1963)   Born in Rutherford, New Jersey, Williams graduated from the University of Pennsylvania (M.D., 1906), interned at hospitals in New York City for two years, studied pediatrics in Leipzig, then returned to practice medicine in his hometown. As a general practitioner, Williams found ample poetic inspiration in his patients, and scribbled down lines between appointments and on the way to house calls. His early collections include *The Tempers* (1913), *Kora in Hell: Improvisations* (1920), and *Sour Grapes* (1921). A stroke in the mid-1950s forced him to retire from his medical practice, but gave him more time to write. His many honors include the National Book Award (1950) and the Pulitzer Prize (1963). *The Williams Reader* was published in 1966.

William Wordsworth (1770–1850)   Born in Cockermouth, in the Lake District of England, Wordsworth was educated at Cambridge. During a summer tour in France in 1790, Wordsworth had an affair with Annette Vallon that resulted in the birth of a daughter. The tour also made of Wordsworth an ardent defender of the French Revolution of 1789 and kindled his sympathies for the plight of the common person. Wordsworth's acquaintance with Samuel Taylor Coleridge in 1795 began a close friendship that led to the collaborative publication of *Lyrical Ballads* in 1798. Wordsworth supplied a celebrated preface to the second edition in 1800, in which he announced himself a nature poet of pantheistic leanings, committed to democratic equality and the language of common people. He finished *The Prelude* in 1805, but it was not published until after his death. As he grew older, Wordsworth grew increasingly conservative and, while he continued to write prolifically, little that he wrote during the last decades of his life attained the heights of his earlier work. In 1843, he was appointed poet laureate.

Richard Wright (1908–1960)   Wright grew up in Memphis, Tennessee, where his sharecropper father moved the family after he was forced off the farm near Natchez, Mississippi, where Wright was born. When Wright was six, his father abandoned the family, leaving his mother to support Wright and his younger brother with whatever jobs she could find. While their mother worked, the boys shifted for themselves. When he was eight, Wright's mother enrolled him in grammar school, but she fell ill and was unable to work. Consequently, Wright and his brother were placed in an orphanage; reunited, the family lived with relatives, and Wright was able to resume his education, graduating from high school as valedictorian in 1925. Wright left the South for Chicago in 1927, hoping, as he said, that "gradually and slowly I might learn who I was, what I might be." After working at odd jobs, his efforts at writing paid off when he received a job as publicity agent for the Federal Negro Theater. Wright joined the Communist party in 1932 and was a member of the Federal Writers' Project from 1935 to 1937. He published his first collection, *Uncle Tom's Children*, in 1938. About the same time, he began a novel about a poor and angry ghetto youth who accidentally murders the daughter of his white, millionaire employer. The novel, *Native Son* (1940), was published to much critical and popular acclaim and remains his best-known work. Unable to accept party discipline, Wright quit the Communist party in 1944, and in the following year published *Black Boy,* an autobiography of his early years. Discouraged with the racism of America, Wright soon moved his family to France, where he spent the remainder of his life writing and supporting the cause of African independence. His later works include the novels *The Outsider* (1953) and *The Long Dream* (1958), the nonfiction works *Black Power* (1954) and *White Man, Listen!* (1957).

Sir Thomas Wyatt (1503?–1542)   Born to a noble family and educated at Cambridge, Wyatt, like many of his peers, wrote poems of great wit and charm while pursuing a career as a politician and diplomat. As a young man, he was sent by the crown on a mission to France and, later, to Italy, where he fell under the influence of the works of the great Italian poet Petrarch (1304–1374). Wyatt held many important diplomatic posts during his distinguished career, including the ambassadorship to Spain. He was briefly imprisoned in 1536, probably because of a quarrel with a powerful noble, though there has been some speculation it was because of his involvement with Queen Anne Boleyn. In the year before his death, he was charged with treason but, after speaking in his own defense, received a full pardon. His poems were first published in a number of anthologies that appeared about fifteen years after his death.

William Butler Yeats (1865–1939)   Yeats was born in Ireland and educated in both Ireland and London. Much of his poetry and many of his plays reflect his fascination with the history of Ireland, particularly the myths and legends of its ancient, pagan past, as well as his interest in the occult. As Yeats matured, he turned increasingly to contemporary subjects, expressing his nationalism in poems about the Irish struggle for independence from England. In 1891, he became one of the founders of an Irish literary society in London (the Rhymers' Club) and of another in Dublin the following year. Already a recognized poet, Yeats helped to establish the Irish National Theater in 1899; its first production was his play *The Countess Cathleen* (written in 1892). His contribution to Irish cultural and political nationalism led to his appointment as a senator when the Irish Free State was formed in 1922. Yeats's preeminence as a poet was recognized in 1923, when he received the Nobel Prize for Literature. Among his works are *The Wanderings of Oisin and Other Poems* (1889), *The Wind among the Reeds* (1899), *The Green Helmet and Other Poems* (1910), *Responsibilities: Poems and a Play* (1914), *The Tower* (1928), and *Last Poems and Two Plays* (1939).

Yevgeney Yevtushenko (b. 1933)   Son of two geologists, Yevtushenko was born in Siberia. He attended Gorky Literary Institute from 1951 to 1954, and worked on a geological expedition, at the same time establishing himself as an influential Soviet poet. During the 1950s, his books were published regularly and he was allowed to travel abroad. In 1960, he gave readings in Europe and the United States, but was criticized by Russians for linking them with anti-Semitism in his poem "Babi Yar," the name of a ravine near Kiev where 96,000 Jews were killed by Nazis during World War II. Although considering himself a "loyal revolutionary Soviet citizen," he elicited official disapproval by opposing the 1968 occupation of Czechoslovakia (a performance of his play *Bratsk Power Station* [1967] was cancelled as a result) and for sending a telegram to then-Premier Brezhnev expressing concern for Aleksandr Solzhenitsyn after his arrest in 1974. His works include *A Precocious Autobiography* (1963) and *From Desire to Desire* (1976). His analysis of recent Russian history, *Fatal Half Measures: The Culture of Democracy in the Soviet Union*, appeared in 1991.

Glossary of Literary Terms

Abstract Language Language that describes ideas, concepts, or qualities, rather than particular or specific persons, places, or things. *Beauty, courage, love* are abstract terms, as opposed to such concrete terms as *man, stone, woman.* George Washington, the Rosetta Stone, and Helen of Troy are particular concrete terms. Characteristically, literature uses *concrete* language to animate *abstract* ideas and principles. When Robert Frost, in "Provide, Provide" (p. 101), describes the pain of impoverished and lonely old age, he doesn't speak of an old, no longer beautiful female. He writes:

> The witch that came (the withered hag)
> To wash the steps with pail and rag,
> Was once the beauty Abishag.

Alexandrine In poetry, a line containing six iambic feet (iambic hexameter). Alexander Pope, in "An Essay on Criticism" (p. 1256), reveals his distaste for the form in a couplet: "A needless Alexandrine ends the song, / That like a wounded snake, drags its slow length along." *See* Meter.

Allegory A narrative in verse or prose, in which abstract qualities (*death, pride, greed,* for example) are personified as characters. In Bernard Malamud's story "Idiots First" (p. 1041), Ginzburg is the personification of death.

Alliteration The repetition of the same initial consonant (or any initial vowel) sounds in close proximity. The "w" sounds in these lines from Robert Frost's "Provide, Provide" (p. 101) alliterate: "The witch that came (the withered hag) / To wash the steps with pail and rag, / Was once the beauty Abishag."

Allusion A reference in a literary work to something outside the work. The reference is usually to some famous person, event, or other literary work.

Ambiguity A phrase, statement, or situation that may be understood in two or more ways. In literature, ambiguity is used to enrich meaning or achieve irony by forcing readers to consider alternative possibilities. When the duke in Robert Browning's "My Last Duchess" (p. 90) says that he "gave commands; / Then all smiles stopped together. There she stands / As if alive," the reader cannot know exactly what those commands were or whether the last words refer to the commands (as a result of which she is no longer alive) or merely refer to the skill of the painter (the painting is extraordinarily lifelike).

Anapest A three-syllable metrical foot consisting of two unaccented syllables followed by an accented syllable. *See* Meter.

Antagonist A character in a story, play, or narrative poem who stands in opposition to the hero (*see* Protagonist). The conflict between antagonist and protagonist often generates the action or plot of the story.

Antistrophe *See* Strophe.

Apostrophe A direct address to a person who is absent, or to an abstract or inanimate entity. In one of his Holy Sonnets (p. 1099), John Donne admonishes: "Death, be not proud!" And Wordsworth speaks to a river in Wales: "How oft, in spirit, have I turned to thee, / O sylvan Wye! thou wanderer through the woods."

Archaism   The literary use of obsolete language. When Keats, in "Ode on a Grecian Urn" (p. 1109), writes: "with brede / Of marble men and maidens overwrought," he uses an archaic word for *braid* and intends an obsolete definition, "worked all over" (that is, "ornamented"), for *overwrought*.

Archetype   Themes, images, and narrative patterns that are universal and thus embody some enduring aspects of human experience. Some of these themes are the death and rebirth of the hero, the underground journey, and the search for the father.

Assonance   The repetition of vowel sounds in a line, stanza, or sentence. For example, Gwendolyn Brooks, in "The Children of the Poor" (p. 486), describes a character whose "lesions are legion." By using assonance that occurs at the end of words—*my, pie*—or a combination of assonance and consonance (that is, the repetition of final consonant sounds)—*fish, wish*—poets creates rhyme. But some poets, particularly modern poets, often use assonantial and consonantial off rhymes (*see* Near Rhyme). W. H. Auden, in "Five Songs" (p. 748), writes:

> That night when joy began
> Our narrowest veins to flush,
> We waited for the flash
> Of morning's levelled gun.

Flush and *gun* are assonantial, *flush* and *flash* are consonantial (and, of course, alliterative).

Atmosphere   *See* Tone.

Aubade   A love song or lyric to be performed at sunrise. Richard Wilbur's comic "A Late Aubade" (p. 752) is a modern example. Philip Larkin's "Aubade" (p. 1139) uses the form ironically in a somber contemplation of mortality.

Ballad   A narrative poem, originally of folk origin, usually focusing upon a climactic episode and told without comment. The most common ballad form consists of quatrains of alternating four- and three-stress iambic lines, with the second and fourth lines rhyming. Often, the ballad will employ a *refrain*—that is, the last line of each stanza will be identical or similar. "Edward" (p. 1094) and "Bonny Barbara Allan" (p. 717) are traditional ballads. Dudley Randall's "Ballad of Birmingham" (p. 484) is a twentieth-century example of the ballad tradition.

Blank Verse   Lines of unrhymed iambic pentameter. Shakespeare's dramatic poetry and Milton's *Paradise Lost* (p. 459) are written principally in blank verse. *See* Meter.

Cacophony   Language that sounds harsh and discordant, sometimes used to reinforce the sense of the words. Consider the plosive *b, p,* and *t* sounds in the following lines from Shakespeare's Sonnet 129 (p. 723): "and till action, lust / Is perjured, murderous, bloody, full of blame, / Savage, extreme, rude, cruel, not to trust." *Compare* Euphony.

Caesura   A strong pause within a line of poetry. Note the caesuras in these lines from Robert Browning's "My Last Duchess" (p. 90):

> That's my last Duchess painted on the wall,
> Looking as if she were alive. ‖ I call
> That piece a wonder, now: ‖ Frà Pandolf's hands
> Worked busily a day, ‖ and there she stands.

Carpe Diem   Latin, meaning "seize the day." A work, usually a lyric poem, in which the speaker calls the attention of the auditor (often a young woman) to the shortness of youth, and life, and then urges the auditor to enjoy life while there is time. Andrew Marvell's "To His Coy Mistress" (p. 729) is among the best of the carpe diem tradition in English. The opening stanza of a famous Robert Herrick poem nicely illustrates carpe diem principles.

> Gather ye rosebuds while ye may,
> Old Time is still a-flying
> And this same flower that smiles today,
> Tomorrow will be dying.

Catharsis   A key concept in the *Poetics* of Aristotle that attempts to explain why representations of suffering and death in drama paradoxically leave the audience feeling relieved rather than depressed. According to Aristotle, the fall of a tragic hero arouses in the viewer feelings of "pity" and "terror"—pity because the hero is an individual of great moral worth, and terror because the viewer identifies with and, consequently, feels vulnerable to the hero's tragic fate. Ideally, the circumstances within the drama allow viewers to experience a catharsis that purges those feelings of pity and terror and leaves them emotionally purified.

Central Intelligence   *See* Point of View.

Chorus   Originally, a group of masked dancers who chanted lyric hymns at religious festivals in ancient Greece. In the plays of Sophocles, the chorus, while circling around the altar to Dionysius, chants the odes that separate the episodes. These odes, in some respects, represented an audience's reaction to, and comment on, the action in the episodes. In Elizabethan drama, and even, on occasion, in modern drama, the chorus appears, usually as a single person who comments on the action.

Comedy   In drama, the representation of situations that are designed to delight and amuse, and which end happily. Comedy often deals with ordinary people in their human condition, while tragedy deals with the ideal and heroic and, until recently, embodied only the high born as tragic heroes. *Compare* Tragedy.

Conceit   A figure of speech that establishes an elaborate parallel between unlike things. The *Petrarchan conceit* (named for the fourteenth-century Italian writer of love lyrics) was often imitated by Elizabethan sonneteers until the device became so hackneyed that Shakespeare mocked the tendency in Sonnet 130 (p. 724):

> My mistress' eyes are nothing like the sun;
> Coral is far more red than her lips' red;
> If snow be white, why then her breasts are dun;
> If hairs be wires, black wires grow on her head.

The *metaphysical conceit*, as used by John Donne for example, employs strange, even bizarre, comparisons to heighten the wit of the poem. Perhaps the most famous metaphysical conceit is Donne's elaborate and extended parallel of a drawing compass to the souls of the couple in "A Valediction: Forbidding Mourning" (p. 726).

Concrete Language   *See* Abstract Language.

Conflict   The struggle of a protagonist, or main character, with forces that threaten to destroy him or her. The struggle creates suspense and is usually resolved at the end of the narrative. The force opposing the main character may be either another person—the antagonist—(as in Frank O'Connor's "My Oedipus Complex," p. 36), or society (as in Harlan Ellison's "'Repent, Harlequin!' Said the Ticktockman," (p. 436), or natural forces (as in Bernard Malamud's "Idiots First," p. 1041). A fourth type of conflict reflects the struggle of opposing tendencies within an individual (as in Tolstoy's "The Death of Iván Ilých," p. 983).

Connotation   The associative and suggestive meanings of a word, in contrast to its literal or *denotative* meaning. One might speak of an *elected official*, a relatively neutral term without connotative implications. Others might call the same person a *politician*, a more negative term; still others might call him or her a *statesman*, a more laudatory term. *Compare* Denotation.

Consonance   Repetition of the final consonant sounds in stressed syllables. In the following verse from W. H. Auden's "Five Songs" (p. 748), lines one and four illustrate consonance, as do lines two and three.

> That night when joy began
> Our narrowest veins to flush,
> We waited for the flash
> Of morning's levelled gun.

Couplet   A pair of rhymed lines—for example, these from A. E. Housman's "Terence, This is Stupid Stuff" (p. 95).

> Why, if 'tis dancing you would be,
> There's brisker pipes than poetry.

Dactyl   A three-syllable metrical foot consisting of an accented syllable followed by two unaccented syllables. *See* Meter.

Denotation   The literal dictionary definition of a word, without associative and suggestive meanings. *See* Connotation.

Denouement   The final revelations that occur after the main conflict is resolved; literally, the "untying" of the plot following the climax.

Deus ex Machina   Latin for "god from a machine." Difficulties were sometimes resolved in ancient Greek and Roman plays by a god, who was lowered to the stage by means of machinery. The term is now used to indicate the use of unconvincing or improbable coincidences to advance or resolve a plot.

Diction   The choice of words in a work of literature, and hence, an element of style crucial to the work's effectiveness. The diction of a story told from the point of view of an inner-city child (as in Toni Cade Bambara's "The Lesson," p. 49) will differ markedly from a similar story told from the point of view of a jaded professional (as in E. B. White's "The Second Tree from the Corner," p. 372).

Didactic   A term applied to works with the primary and avowed purpose of persuading the reader that some philosophical, religious, or moral doctrine is true. Hence, although some didactic works are nonetheless successful works of art, the emphasis on moral purposes usually occurs at the expense of aesthetic considerations and produces preachy narratives.

Dimeter   A line of poetry consisting of two metrical feet. *See* Meter.

Distance   The property that separates an author or a narrator from the actions of the characters he or she creates, thus allowing a disinterested, or aloof, narration of events. Similarly, distance allows the reader or audience to view the characters and events in a narrative dispassionately.

Dramatic Irony   *See* Irony.

Dramatic Monologue   A type of poem in which the speaker addresses another person (or persons) whose presence is known only from the speaker's words. During the course of the monologue, the speaker (often unintentionally) reveals his or her own character. Such poems are dramatic because the speaker interacts with another character at a specific time and place; they are monologues because the entire poem is uttered by the speaker. Robert Browning's "My Last Duchess" (p. 90), Matthew

Arnold's "Dover Beach" (p. 735), and T. S. Eliot's "The Love Song of J. Alfred Prufrock" (p. 740) are dramatic monologues.

Elegy   Usually, a poem lamenting the death of a particular person, but often used to describe meditative poems on the subject of human mortality. A. E. Housman's "To an Athlete Dying Young" (p. 1118) and W. H. Auden's "In Memory of W. B. Yeats" (p. 1132) are elegies.

End-rhyme   *See* Rhyme.

End-stopped Line   A line of verse that embodies a complete logical and grammatical unit. A line of verse that does not constitute a complete syntactic unit is called *run-on*. For example, in the opening lines of Robert Browning's "My Last Duchess" (p. 90): "That's my last Duchess painted on the wall, / Looking as if she were alive. I call / That piece a wonder, now: . . .," The opening line is end-stopped, while the second line is run-on because the direct object of *call* runs on to the third line.

English Sonnet   Also called *Shakespearean sonnet. See* Sonnet.

Enjambment   The use of run-on lines. *See* End-stopped Line.

Epigraph   In literature, a short quotation or observation related to the theme and placed at the head of the work. T. S. Eliot's "The Love Song of J. Alfred Prufrock" (p. 740) has an epigraph, as does Donald W. Baker's "Formal Application" (p. 489).

Epiphany   In literature, a showing forth, or sudden manifestation. James Joyce used the term to indicate a sudden illumination that enables a character (and, presumably, the reader) to understand his situation. The narrator of Joyce's "Araby" (p. 27) experiences an epiphany toward the end of the story, as does Iván Ilých in Tolstoy's "The Death of Iván Ilých" (p. 983).

Epode   *See* Strophe.

Euphony   Language embodying sounds pleasing to the ear. *Compare* Cacophony.

Exposition   Information supplied to readers and audiences that enables them to understand narrative action. Often, exposition establishes what has occurred before the narrative begins or informs the audience about relationships among principal characters. The absence of exposition from some modern literature, particularly modern drama, contributes to the unsettling feelings sometimes experienced by the audience.

Farce   A type of comedy, usually satiric, that relies on exaggerated character types, ridiculous situations, and, often, horseplay.

Feminine Rhyme   A two-syllable rhyme in which the second syllable is unstressed, as in the second and fourth lines of these verses from Edward Arlington Robinson's "Miniver Cheevy" (p. 469):

> Miniver Cheevy, child of scorn,
> Grew lean while he assailed the seasons;
> He wept that he was ever born,
> And he had reasons.

Figurative Language   A general term covering the many ways in which language is used nonliterally. *See* Hyperbole, Irony, Metaphor, Metonymy, Paradox, Simile, Symbol, Synecdoche, Understatement.

First-person Narrator   *See* Point of View.

Foot   *See* Meter.

Free Verse   Poetry, usually unrhymed, that does not adhere to the metrical regularity of traditional verse. Although free verse is not metrically regular, it is nonetheless clearly more rhythmic than prose and makes use of other aspects of poetic discourse to achieve its effects.

Heroic Couplet   Iambic pentameter lines that rhyme *aa, bb, cc,* and so on. Usually, heroic couplets are *closed*—that is, the couplet's end coincides with a major syntactic unit so that the line is end-stopped. These lines from Alexander Pope's "Essay on Man" illustrate the form: "And, spite of pride, in erring reason's spite, / One truth is clear; Whatever IS, is RIGHT."

Hexameter   A line of verse consisting of six metrical feet. *See* Meter.

Hubris   In Greek tragedy, arrogance resulting from excessive pride. Oedipus, in Sophocles' *Oedipus Rex* (p. 131), is guilty of hubris.

Hyperbole   Figurative language that embodies overstatement or exaggeration. The boast of the speaker in Robert Burns's "A Red, Red Rose" (p. 731) is hyperbolic: "And I will luve thee still, my dear, / Till a' the seas gang dry."

Iamb   A metrical foot consisting of an unstressed syllable followed by a stressed syllable. *See* Meter.

Imagery   Language that embodies an appeal to a physical sense, usually sight, although the words may invoke sound, smell, taste, and touch as well. The term is often applied to all figurative language.

Internal Rhyme   *See* Rhyme.

Irony   Figurative language in which the intended meaning differs from the literal meaning. *Verbal irony* includes overstatement (hyperbole), understatement, and opposite statement. The following lines from Robert Burns's "A Red, Red Rose" (p. 731) embody overstatement:

> As fair as thou, my bonnie lass,
> So deep in luve am I;
> And I will luve thee still, my dear,
> Till a' the seas gang dry.

These lines from Andrew Marvell's "To His Coy Mistress" (p. 729) understate: "The grave's a fine and private place, / but none, I think, do there embrace." W. H. Auden's ironic conclusion to "The Unknown Citizen" (p. 482) reveals opposite statement: "Was he free? Was he happy? The question is absurd: / Had anything been wrong, we should certainly have heard." *Dramatic irony* occurs when a reader or audience knows things a character does not and, consequently, hears things differently. For example, in Shakespeare's *Othello* (p. 779), the audience knows that Iago is Othello's enemy, but Othello doesn't. Hence, the audience's understanding of Iago's speeches to Othello differs markedly from Othello's.

Italian Sonnet   Also called *Petrarchan sonnet. See* Sonnet.

Lyric   Originally, a song accompanied by lyre music. Now, a relatively short poem expressing the thought or feeling of a single speaker. Almost all the nondramatic poetry in this anthology is lyric poetry.

Metaphor   A figurative expression consisting of two elements in which one element is provided with special attributes by being equated with a second, unlike element. In Theodore Roethke's "Elegy for Jane" (p. 1136), for example, the speaker addresses his dead student: "If only I could nudge you from this sleep, / My maimed darling, my skittery pigeon." Here, Jane is characterized metaphorically as a "skittery pigeon," and all the reader's experience of a nervous pigeon's movement becomes attached to Jane. *See* Simile.

Meter   Refers to recurrent patterns of accented and unaccented syllables in verse. A metrical unit is called a *foot*, and there are four basic accented patterns. An *iamb*, or *iambic foot*, consists of an unaccented syllable followed by an accented syllable (bĕfóre, tŏdáy). A *trochee*, or *trochaic foot*, consists of an accented syllable followed by an unaccented syllable (fúnňy, phántŏm). An *anapest*, or *anapestic foot*, consists of two unaccented syllables followed by an accented syllable (in the line "Ĭf eṽ ‖ erȳthĭng háp ‖ pňs thăt cán't ‖ bĕ dóne," the second and third metrical feet are anapests). A *dactyl*, or *dactyllic foot*, consists of a stressed syllable followed by two unstressed syllables (sýllăblĕ, métrĭcăl). One common variant, consisting of two stressed syllables, is called a *spondee*, or *spondaic foot* (dáybřeak, moónshíne).

Lines are classified according to the number of metrical feet they contain.

one foot	monometer
two feet	dimeter
three feet	trimeter
four feet	tetrameter
five feet	pentameter
six feet	hexameter (An iambic hexameter line is an *Alexandrine*.)

Here are some examples of various metrical patterns:

Tŏ eách ‖ hĭs súff ‖ erĭngs: áll ‖ aře mén,	*iambic tetrameter*
Cŏndemńed ‖ ălíké ‖ tŏ groán;	*iambic trimeter*
Ońce ūp ‖ oń ă ‖ mídnĭght ‖ dréarȳ, ‖ whíle Ĭ ‖ póndeřed ‖	
wéak ănd ‖ wéarȳ	*trochaic octameter*
Thĕ Ăssýr ‖ iăn cam̌e doẃn ‖ lĭkĕ ă wólf ‖ ŏn ťhe fóld	*anapestic tetrameter*
Ĭs thís ‖ thĕ rég ‖ iŏn, thís ‖ thĕ soíl, ‖ thĕ clíme,	*iambic pentameter*
Fóllŏw ĭt ‖ úttĕrlȳ,	*dactyllic dimeter*
Hópe bĕ ‖ yońd hópe:	*dimeter line—trochee and spondee*

Metonymy   A figure of speech in which a word stands for a closely related idea. In the expression "The pen is mightier than the sword," *pen* and *sword* are metonyms for written ideas and physical force.

Muses   Nine goddesses, the daughters of Zeus and Mnemosyne (memory), who preside over various humanities. Although there are some variations, generally they may be assigned as follows: Calliope, epic poetry; Clio, history; Erato, lyric poetry; Euterpe, music; Melpomene, tragedy; Polyhymnia, sacred poetry; Terpsichore, dance; Thalia, comedy; and Urania, astronomy.

Near Rhyme   Also called *off rhyme, slant rhyme,* or *oblique rhyme.* Usually the occurrence of consonance where rhyme is expected, as in *pearl, alcohol* or *heaven, given.* *See* Rhyme.

Octave   An eight-line stanza. More often, the opening eight-line section of an Italian sonnet, rhymed *abbaabba,* followed by the sestet that concludes the poem. *See* Sonnet.

Ode   Usually, a long, serious poem on exalted subjects, often in the form of an address. Keats's "Ode on a Grecian Urn" (p. 1109) is representative. In Greek dramatic poetry, odes consisting of three parts, the *strophe,* the *antistrophe,* and the *epode,* were sung by the chorus between the episodes of the play. *See* Strophe.

Off Rhyme *See* Near Rhyme.

Omniscient Point of View *See* Point of View.

Onomatopoeia Language that sounds like what it means. Words like *buzz, bark,* and *hiss* are onomatopoetic. Also, sound patterns that reinforce the meaning may be designated onomatopoetic. Alexander Pope illustrates such onomatopoeia in a passage from "An Essay on Criticism" (p. 1256):

'Tis not enough no harshness gives offense,
The sound must seem an echo to the sense:
Soft is the strain when Zephyr gently blows,
And the smooth stream in smoother numbers flows;
But when loud surges lash the sounding shore,
The hoarse, rough verse should like the torrent roar:
When Ajax strives some rock's vast weight to throw,
The line too labors, and the words move slow;
Not so, when swift Camilla scours the plain,
Flies o'er th'unbending corn, and skims along the main.

Opposite Statement *See* Irony.

Ottava Rima An eight-line, iambic pentameter stanza rhymed *abababcc.* Originating with the Italian poet Boccaccio, the form was made popular in English poetry by Milton, Keats, and Byron, among others.

Oxymoron Literary, "acutely silly." A figure of speech in which contradictory ideas are combined to create a condensed paradox: *thunderous silence, sweet sorrow, wise fool.*

Paean In classical Greek drama, a hymn of praise, usually honoring Apollo. Now, any lyric that joyously celebrates its subject.

Paradox A statement that seems self-contradictory or absurd but is, somehow, valid. The conclusion of Donne's "Death, Be Not Proud" (p. 1099) illustrates: "One short sleep past, we wake eternally / And death shall be no more; Death, thou shalt die." In Holy Sonnet 14, Donne, speaking of his relationship with God, writes: "Take me to You, imprison me, for I, / Except You enthrall me, never shall be free, / Nor ever chaste, except You ravish me."

Pastoral *Pastor* is Latin for "shepherd," and the pastoral is a poetic form invented by ancient Roman writers that deals with the complexities of the human condition as if they exist in a world peopled by idealized rustic shepherds. Pastoral poetry suggests that country life is superior to urban life. In the hands of such English poets as Marlowe and Milton, the pastoral embodies highly conventionalized and artificial language and situations. Christopher Marlowe's "The Passionate Shepherd to His Love" (p. 720) is a famous example, as is Sir Walter Ralegh's mocking response, "The Nymph's Reply to the Shepherd" (p. 721).

Pentameter A line containing five metrical feet. *See* Meter.

Persona Literally, "actor's mask." The term is applied to a first-person narrator in fiction or poetry. The persona's views may differ from the author's.

Personification The attribution of human qualities to nonhuman things, such as animals, aspects of nature, or even ideas and processes. When Donne exclaims in "Death, Be Not Proud" (p. 1099), "Death, thou shalt die," he uses personification, as does Edmund Waller when the speaker of "Go, Lovely Rose!" (p. 729) says:

Go, lovely rose!
Tell her that wastes her time and me
That now she knows,

When I resemble her to thee,
How sweet and fair she seems to be.

Petrarchan Sonnet   Also called *Italian Sonnet*. See Sonnet.

Plot   A series of actions in a story or drama that bear a significant relationship to each other. E. M. Forster illuminates the definition: "'The King died, and then the Queen died,' is a story. 'The King died, and then the Queen died of grief,' is a plot."

Poetic License   Variation from standard word order to satisfy the demands of rhyme and meter.

Point of View   The person or intelligence a writer of fiction creates to tell the story to the reader. The major techniques are:

First person, where the story is told by someone, often, though not necessarily, the principal character, who identifies himself or herself as "I" (as in James Joyce's "Araby") (p. 27).

Third person, where the story is told by someone (not identified as "I") who is not a participant in the action and who refers to the characters by name or as "he," "she," and "they" (as in Harlan Ellison's "'Repent, Harlequin!' Said the Ticktockman") (p. 436).

Omniscient, a variation on the third person, where the narrator knows everything about the characters and events, can move about in time and place as well as from character to character at will, and can, whenever he or she wishes, enter the mind of any character, (as in Tolstoy's "The Death of Iván Ilých") (p. 983).

Central intelligence, another variation on the third person, where narrative elements are limited to what a single character sees, thinks, and hears.

Prosody   The study of the elements of versification, such as *rhyme, meter, stanzaic patterns*, and so on.

Protagonist   Originally, the first actor in a Greek drama. In Greek, *agon* means "contest." Hence, the protagonist is the hero, the main character in a narrative, in conflict either with his or her situation or with another character. *See* Antagonist.

Quatrain   A four-line stanza.

Refrain   The repetition within a poem of a group of words, often at the end of ballad stanzas.

Rhyme   The repetition of the final stressed vowel sound and any sounds following (*cat, rat; debate, relate; pelican, belly can*) produces perfect rhyme. When the last stressed syllable rhymes, the rhyme is called masculine (*cat, rat*). Two-syllable rhymes with unstressed last syllables are called feminine (*ending, bending*). When rhyming words appear at the end of lines, the poem is *end-rhymed*. When rhyming words appear within one line, the line contains *internal rhyme*. When the correspondence in sounds is imperfect (*heaven, given; began, gun*) *off rhyme, slant rhyme*, or *near rhyme* is produced.

Rhythm   The quality created by the relationship between stressed and unstressed syllables. A regular pattern of alternation between stressed and unstressed syllables produces *meter*. Irregular alternation of stressed and unstressed syllables produces *free verse*. Compare the rhythm of the following verses from Robert Frost's "Stopping by Woods on a Snowy Evening" (p. 1125) and Walt Whitman's "Out of the Cradle Endlessly Rocking":

Whose woods these are I think I know.
His house is in the village though;

He will not see me stopping here
To watch his woods fill up with snow.

Out of the cradle endlessly rocking,
Out of the mocking-bird's throat, the musical shuttle,
Out of the Ninth-month midnight,
Over the sterile sands and the fields beyond, where the child leaving his bed
  wander'd alone, bareheaded, barefoot,
Down from the shower'd halo,

Run-on Line   *See* End-stopped Line.

Satire   Writing in a comic mode that holds a subject up to scorn and ridicule, often with the purpose of correcting human vice and folly. Harlan Ellison's "'Repent, Harlequin!' Said the Ticktockman" (p. 436) satirizes a society obsessed with time and order.

Scansion   The analysis of patterns of stressed and unstressed syllables in order to establish the metrical or rhythmical pattern of a poem.

Sestet   The six-line resolution of a Petrarchan sonnet. *See* Sonnet.

Setting   The place where a story occurs. Often the setting contributes significantly to the story; for example, the radiance of Munich in Thomas Mann's "Gladius Dei" (p. 356) highlights the gloom of the religious zealot Hieronymus.

Shakespearean Sonnet   Also called *English sonnet*. *See* Sonnet.

Simile   Similar to metaphor, the simile is a comparison of unlike things introduced by the words *like* or *as*. Robert Burns, in "A Red, Red Rose" (p. 731), for example, exclaims, "O My Luve's like a red, red rose," and Shakespeare mocks extravagant similes when he admits in Sonnet 130, "My mistress' eyes are nothing like the sun" (p. 724).

Slant Rhyme   *See* Rhyme.

Soliloquy   A dramatic convention in which an actor, alone on the stage, speaks his or her thoughts aloud. Iago's speech that closes Act I of Shakespeare's *Othello* (p. 779) is a soliloquy, as is Othello's speech in Act III, Scene 3, lines 258–78.

Sonnet   A lyric poem of fourteen lines, usually of iambic pentameter. The two major types are the Petrarchan (or Italian) and Shakespearean (or English). The Petrarchan sonnet is divided into an octave (the first eight lines, rhymed *abbaabba*) and sestet (the final six lines, usually rhymed *cdecde* or *cdcdcd*). The Shakespearean sonnet consists of three quatrains and a concluding couplet, rhymed *abab cdcd efef gg*. In general, the sonnet establishes some issue in the octave or three quatrains and then resolves it in the sestet or final couplet. Robert Frost's "Design" (p. 1126) is an Italian sonnet; several Shakespearean sonnets appear in the text.

Spondee   A metrical foot consisting of two stressed syllables, usually a variation within a metrical line. *See* Meter.

Stanza   The grouping of a fixed number of verse lines in a recurring metrical and rhyme pattern. Keats's "Ode on a Grecian Urn" (p. 1109), for example, employs ten-line stanzas rhymed *ababcdecde*.

Stream-of-Consciousness   The narrative technique that attempts to reproduce the full and uninterrupted flow of a character's mental process, in which ideas, memories, and sense impressions may intermingle without logical transitions. Writers using this technique sometimes abandon conventional rules of syntax and punctuation.

Strophe   In Greek tragedy, the unit of verse the chorus chanted as it moved to the left in a dance rhythm. The chorus sang the *antistrophe* as it moved to the right and the *epode* while standing still.

Style   The way an author expresses his or her matter. Style embodies, and depends upon, all the choices an author makes—the diction, syntax, figurative language, and sound patterns of the piece.

Subplot   A second plot, usually involving minor characters. The subplot is subordinate to the principal plot, but often is resolved by events that figure in the main plot. For example, Iago's manipulation of Roderigo in Shakespeare's *Othello* (p. 779) is a subplot that enters the main plot and figures prominently in the play's climax.

Symbol   An object, an action, or a person that represents more than itself. In Stephen Crane's "The Bride Comes to Yellow Sky" (p. 18), Scratchy represents the old mythic West made obsolete by the encroachment of Eastern values. The urn in Keats's "Ode on a Grecian Urn" (p. 1109) symbolizes the cold immortality of art. In both of these, the symbolism arises from the *context*. *Public* symbols, in contrast to these *contextual* *symbols*, are objects, actions, or persons that history, myth, or legend has invested with meaning—the cross, Helen of Troy, a national flag.

Synecdoche   A figure of speech in which a part is used to signify the whole. In "Elegy Written in a Country Churchyard," Gray writes of "Some heart once pregnant with celestial fire; / Hands that the rod of empire might have swayed." That heart, and those hands, of course, refer to whole persons who are figuratively represented by significant parts.

Synesthesia   An image that uses a second sensory impression to modify the primary sense impression. When one speaks of a "cool green," for example, the primary *visual* evocation of green is combined with the *tactile* sensation of coolness. Keats, in "Ode to a Nightingale," asks for a drink of wine "Tasting of Flora and the country green, / Dance, and Provençal song, and sunburnt mirth!" Here, the *taste* of wine is synesthetically extended to the sight of flowers and meadows, the movement of dance, the sound of song, and the heat of the sun.

Tetrameter   A verse line containing four metrical feet. *See* Meter.

Theme   The abstract moral proposition that a literary work advances through the concrete elements of character, action, and setting. The theme of Harlan Ellison's "'Repent, Harlequin!' Said the Ticktockman" (p. 436), in which an ordinary person defies an oppressive system, might be that to struggle against dehumanizing authority is obligatory.

Third-person Narrator   A voice telling a story that refers to characters by name or as "he," "she," or "they." *See* Point of View.

Tone   The attitude embodied in the language a writer chooses. The tone of a work might be sad, joyful, ironic, solemn, playful. Compare, for example, the somber tone of Matthew Arnold's "Dover Beach" (p. 735) with the comic tone of Anthony Hecht's "The Dover Bitch" (p. 754).

Tragedy   The dramatic representation of serious and important actions that culminate in catastrophe for the protagonist, or chief actor, in the play. Aristotle saw tragedy as the fall of a noble figure from a high position and happiness to defeat and misery as a result of *hamartia*, some misjudgment or frailty of character. *Compare* Comedy.

Trimeter   A verse line consisting of three metrical feet. *See* Meter.

Triplet   A sequence of three verse lines that rhyme.

Trochee   A metrical foot consisting of a stressed syllable followed by an unstressed syllable. *See* Meter.

Understatement   A figure of speech that represents something as less important than it really is, hence, a form of irony. When in Robert Browning's "My Last Duchess" (p. 90) the duke asserts ". . . This grew; I gave commands; / Then all smiles stopped together . . .," the words ironically understate what was likely an order for his wife's execution.

Villanelle   A French verse form of nineteen lines (of any length) divided into six stanzas—five tercets and a final quatrain—employing two rhymes and two refrains. The refrains consist of lines one (repeated as lines six, twelve, and eighteen) and three (repeated as lines nine, fifteen, and nineteen). Dylan Thomas's "Do Not Go Gentle into That Good Night" (p. 1138) and Catherine Davis's response "After a Time" (p. 1140) are villanelles.

Acknowledgments (continued from copyright page)

Jorge Luis Borges, "The Intruder." From *The Aleph and Other Stories* by Jorge Luis Borges, translated by Norman Thomas di Giovanni. Translation copyright © 1968, 1969, 1970 by Emece Editores, S.A. and Norman Thomas di Giovanni. Used by permission of the publisher, Dutton, an imprint of New American Library, a division of Penguin Books USA Inc.

Elizabeth Brewster, "Disqualification." Reprinted by permission of the author.

Edwin Brock, "Five Ways to Kill a Man." Copyright Edwin Brock. Reprinted by permission of author.

Gwendolyn Brooks, "From Children of the Poor #4 (First fight, then fiddle . . .)" and "#11 (Life for My Child is Simple)." Copyright © 1991. From *Blacks* published by Third World Press, Chicago, 1991. Reprinted by permission of Gwendolyn Brooks.

Marianne Burke, "Funeral Home." Reprinted by permission of *The New Yorker*.

Robert Olen Butler, "Preparation." From *A Good Scent from a Strange Mountain* by Robert Olen Butler. First published in *The Sewanee Review*. Copyright © 1992 by Robert Olen Butler. Reprinted by permission of Henry Holt and Co., Inc.

Raymond Carver, "What We Talk About When We Talk About Love." From *What We Talk About When We Talk About Love* by Raymond Carver. Copyright © 1981 by Raymond Carver. Reprinted by permission of Alfred A. Knopf, Inc.

Kate Chopin, "The Storm." From *The Complete Works of Kate Chopin*, ed. by Per Seyersted. Reprinted by permission of Louisiana State University Press. Copyright © 1969 by Louisiana State University Press.

Lucille Clifton, "There is a Girl Inside." From *Two-Headed Woman* by Lucille Clifton. Copyright © 1980 by University of Massachusetts Press. Reprinted by permission of Curtis Brown, Ltd.

Victor Hernandez Cruz, "Today is a Day of Great Joy." From *Snaps* by Victor Hernandez Cruz. Copyright © 1968, 1969 by Victor Hernandez Cruz. Reprinted by permission of Random House, Inc.

Countee Cullen, "Incident." Reprinted by permission of GRM Associates, Inc., Agents for the Estate of Ida M. Cullen. From the book *Color* by Countee Cullen. Copyright © 1925 by Harper & Brothers; copyright renewed 1953 by Ida M. Cullen.

E. E. Cummings, "the Cambridge ladies who live in furnished souls" and "O sweet spontaneous." Reprinted from *Tulips and Chimneys* by E. E. Cummings, edited by George James Firmage. Reprinted by permission of Liveright Publishing Corporation. Copyright © 1923, 1925, and renewed 1951, 1953 by E. E. Cummings. Copyright © 1973, 1976 by the Trustees for the E. E. Cummings Trust. Copyright © 1973, 1976 by George James Firmage.

E. E. Cummings, "if everything happens that can't be done." Reprinted from *Complete Poems, 1913–1962,* by E. E. Cummings, by permission of Liveright Publishing Corporation. Copyright © 1923, 1925, 1931, 1935, 1938, 1939, 1940, 1944, 1945, 1946, 1947, 1948, 1949, 1950, 1951, 1952, 1953, 1954, 1955, 1956, 1957, 1958, 1959, 1960, 1961, 1962 by the Trustees for the E. E. Cummings Trust. Copyright © 1961, 1963, 1968 by Marion Morehouse Cummings.

E. E. Cummings, "nobody loses all the time." Reprinted from *IS 5* poems by E. E. Cummings, edited by George James Firmage, by permission of Liveright Publishing Corporation. Copyright © 1985 by E. E. Cummings Trust. Copyright 1926 by Horace Liveright. Copyright © 1954 by E. E. Cummings. Copyright © 1985 by George James Firmage.

Kate Daniels, "Self Portrait with Politics." From *The White Wave* by Kate Daniels. Reprinted by permission of the University of Pittsburgh Press. Copyright © by Kate Daniels.

Catherine Davis, "After a Time." Reprinted by permission of the author.

Emily Dickinson, "Apparently, With No Surprise," "I Felt a Funeral in my Brain," "Much Madness is Divinest Sense," "What Soft—Cherubic Creature," "She Rose to His Requirement," "Mine Enemy is Growing Old," "I Heard a Fly Buzz When I Died." Reprinted by permission of the publishers and the Trustees of Amherst College from *The Poems of Emily Dickinson*, Thomas H. Johnson, ed., Cambridge, Mass.: The Belknap Press of Harvard University Press, Copyright © 1951, 1955, 1979, 1983 by the President and Fellows of Harvard College.

Emily Dickinson, "After Great Pain, a Formal Feeling Comes." From *The Complete Poems of Emily Dickinson* edited by Thomas H. Johnson. Copyright 1929 by Martha Dickinson Bianchi; Copyright © renewed 1957 by Mary L. Hampson. By permission of Little, Brown & Co.

Alan Dugan, "Love Song, I and Thou." Copyright © 1961 by Alan Dugan. Originally published in *Poems, 1961* by Yale University Press. Reprinted by permission of the author.

1383

Harlan Ellison, "'Repent, Harlequin!' Said the Ticktockman." Copyright © 1966 by Harlan Ellison. Reprinted by arrangement with, and permission of, the Author and the Author's agent, Richard Curtis Associates, Inc., New York. All rights reserved.

T. S. Eliot, "The Lovesong of J. Alfred Prufrock." From *Collected Poems 1909–1962* by T.S. Eliot. Copyright 1936 by Harcourt Brace Jovanovich, Inc., copyright © 1964, 1963 by T.S. Eliot. Reprinted by permission of the publisher and by permission of Faber & Faber Ltd.

Louise Erdrich, "The Red Convertible." From *Love Medicine* by Louise Erdrich. Copyright © 1984 by Louise Erdrich. Reprinted by permission of Henry Holt and Co., Inc.

William Faulkner, "A Rose for Emily." From *Collected Stories of William Faulkner.* Copyright 1930 and renewed 1958 by William Faulkner. Reprinted by permission of Random House, Inc.

James Fenton, "God, A Poem." From *Children in Exile* by James Fenton. Published in *Poems 1968–1984.* Published by Vintage Books. Copyright 1972 by James Fenton. Reprinted by permission of Sterling Lord Literistic, Inc.

Lawrence Ferlinghetti, "Constantly Risking Absurdity" and "In Goya's Greatest Scenes." From *A Coney Island of the Mind.* Copyright © 1958 by Lawrence Ferlinghetti. Reprinted by permission of New Directions Publishing Corporation.

Edward Field, "Unwanted." From *Counting Myself Lucky: Selected Poems 1963–1992.* Published by Black Sparrow Press. Reprinted by permission of the author.

Harvey Fierstein, "Widows and Children First!" From *Torch Song Trilogy* by Harvey Fierstein. Copyright © 1978, 1979 by Harvey Fierstein. Reprinted by permission of Villard Books, a division of Random House, Inc.

Carolyn Forche, "The Colonel." From *The Country Between Us* by Carolyn Forche. Copyright © 1980 by Carolyn Forche. Reprinted by permission of HarperCollins Publishers Inc.

Robert Francis, "Pitcher." From *The Orb Weaver* by Robert Francis. Copyright 1960 by Robert Francis. Reprinted by permission of the University Press of New England.

Bruce Jay Friedman, *Steambath.* Copyright © 1971 by Bruce Jay Friedman. Reprinted by permission of Alfred A. Knopf, Inc.

Robert Frost, "After Apple-Picking," "Birches," "Departmental," "Design," "Fire and Ice," "Nothing Gold Can Stay," "Out,Out—" "Provide, Provide," "The Silken Tent," "Stopping by Woods on a Snowy Evening." From *The Poetry of Robert Frost* edited by Edward Connery Lathem. Copyright 1916, 1923, 1930, 1939, © 1969 by Holt, Rinehart and Winston. Copyright 1936, 1942, 1944, 1951, © 1958 by Robert Frost. Copyright © 1964, © 1967, © 1970 by Lesley Frost Ballantine. Reprinted by permission of Henry Holt and Co., Inc.

Tess Gallagher, "Conversation with a Fireman from Brooklyn." From *Amplitude* by Tess Gallagher. Copyright 1987 by Tess Gallagher. Reprinted with permission of Graywolf Press, Saint Paul, Minnesota.

Pam Gems, "Loving Women." From *Three Plays* by Pam Gems. Published by Penguin Books, 1985. Copyright © Pam Gems, 1985. Reprinted by permission of Penguin Books Ltd.

Molly Giles, "Rough Translations." From *Rough Translations* by Molly Giles. Reprinted by permission of The University of Georgia Press.

Allen Ginsberg, "To Aunt Rose." From *Collected Poems 1947–1980* by Allen Ginsberg. Copyright © 1958 by Allen Ginsberg. Reprinted by permission of HarperCollins Publishers Inc.

Dana Gioia, "Sunday News." From *Daily Horoscope* by Dana Gioia. Reprinted by permission of Graywolf Press, Saint Paul, Minnesota.

Nikki Giovanni, "Dreams." From *The Women and the Men* by Nikki Giovanni. Copyright © 1970, 1974, 1975, by Nikki Giovanni. Reprinted by permission of William Morrow & Company, Inc.

Nikki Giovanni, "For Saundra." From *Black Feeling, Black Talk, Black Judgment* by Nikki Giovanni. Copyright © 1968, 1970 by Nikki Giovanni. Reprinted by permission of William Morrow & Company, Inc.

Susan Glaspell, *Trifles.* This edition published by arrangement with Baker's Plays, 100 Chauncy Street, Boston, Massachusetts 02111. Copyright 1951 by Walter H. Baker Company. *Trifles* is the sole property of the author and is fully protected under the copyright laws of the United States, the British Empire including the Dominion of Canada, and all other countries of the Copyright Union, and are subject to royalty. The play may not be acted by professionals or amateurs without formal permission in writing and the payment of royalty. All rights, including professional, amateur, stock, radio and television broadcasting, motion picture, recitation, lecturing, public reading and the rights of translation in foreign languages are reserved. All inquiries should be directed to Baker's Plays, 100 Chauncy Street, Boston, Massachusetts 02111.

Nadine Gordimer, "Something for the Time Being." Copyright © 1960, renewed © 1988 by

Nadine Gordimer, from *Selected Stories* by Nadine Gordimer. Used by permission of Viking Penguin, a division of Penguin Books USA Inc.

Robert Graves, "Tilth." From *Collected Poems 1975* by Robert Graves. Copyright © 1975 by Robert Graves. Reprint by permission of Oxford University Press, Inc. and by permission of A.P. Watt Ltd. on behalf of the Trustees of the Robert Graves Copyright Trust.

Michael Hamburger, "A Poet's Progress." From *Collected Poems 1985.* Reprinted by permission of the author.

Barry Hannah, "Water Liars." From *Airships* by Barry Hannah. Copyright © 1978 by Barry Hannah. Reprinted by permission of Alfred A. Knopf, Inc.

Robert Hayden, "Those Winter Sundays." Reprinted from *Angle of Ascent, New and Selected Poems,* by Robert Hayden, by permission of Liveright Publishing Corporation. Copyright © 1975, 1972, 1970, 1966 by Robert Hayden.

Anthony Hecht, "More Light! More Light!" and "The Dover Bitch." From *Collected Earlier Poems* by Anthony Hecht. Copyright © 1990 by Anthony E. Hecht. Reprinted by permission of Alfred A. Knopf, Inc.

Ernest Hemingway, "A Clean, Well-Lighted Place." Reprinted with permission of Charles Scribner's Sons, an imprint of Macmillan Publishing Company, from *Winner Take Nothing* by Ernest Hemingway. Copyright 1933 by Charles Scribner's Sons; renewal copyright © 1961 by Mary Hemingway.

Amy Hempel, "Today Will Be a Quiet Day." From *Reasons to Live* by Amy Hempel. Copyright © 1985 by Amy Hempel. Reprinted by permission of Alfred A. Knopf, Inc.

William Heyen, "The Trains." From *Falling from Heaven: Holocaust Poems of a Jew and a Gentile* by Louis Daniel Brodsky and William Heyen. Reprinted by permission of Time Being Books. Copyright © 1991 by Timeless Press, Inc. All rights reserved.

Edward Hirsch, "Fast Break." From *Wild Gratitude* by Edward Hirsch. Copyright © 1985 by Edward Hirsch. Reprinted by permission of Alfred A. Knopf, Inc.

Linda Hogan, "First Light." "First Light" first appeared in *Savings* by Linda Hogan, Coffee House Press, 1988. Reprinted by permission of the publisher. Copyright © 1988 by Linda Hogan.

Langston Hughes, "Harlem." From *The Panther and the Lash* by Langston Hughes. Copyright 1951 by Langston Hughes. Reprinted by permission of Alfred A. Knopf, Inc.

Langston Hughes, "Same in Blues." From *Montage of a Dream Deferred.* Reprinted by permission of Harold Ober Associates Incorporated. Copyright 1951 by Langston Hughes. Copyright renewed 1979 by George Houston Bass. Reprinted by permission of Harold Ober Associates Incorporated.

Ted Hughes, "Crow's First Lesson." From *New Selected Poems* by Ted Hughes. Copyright © 1971 by Ted Hughes. Reprinted by permission of Harper Collins Publishers Inc. and Faber and Faber Ltd.

Pam Houston, "How to Talk to a Hunter." From *Cowboys Are My Weakness* by Pam Houston. Reprinted by permission of author and W. W. Norton & Company, Inc. Copyright © 1992 by Pam Houston.

David Henry Hwang, *M. Butterfly.* From *M. Butterfly* by David Henry Hwang. Copyright © 1989 by David Henry Hwang. Used by permission of New American Library, a division of Penguin Books USA Inc.

Henrik Ibsen, *An Enemy of the People.* Translated by R. Farquharson Sharp. Printed from the Everyman's Library edition, 1910. © David Campbell Publishers Ltd., London.

Randall Jarrell, "The Death of the Ball Turret Gunner." From *The Complete Poems* by Randall Jarrell. Copyright © 1945 and renewal copyright © 1972 by Mrs. Randall Jarrell. Reprinted by permission of Farrar, Straus & Giroux, Inc.

June Jordan, "Memo:" From *Passion: New Poems.* Copyright © 1990 by June Jordan. Reprinted by permission of the author.

X. J. Kennedy, "Ars Poetica" and "First Confession." From *Cross Ties: Selected Poems* by X. J. Kennedy. Reprinted by permission of The University of Georgia Press.

Lawrence Kearney, "Father Answers His Adversaries." From *Kingdom Come* by Lawrence Kearney. Copyright 1980 by Lawrence Kearney. Reprinted by permission of University Press of New England.

Carolyn Kizer, "Bitch." From *Mermaids in the Basement* by Carolyn Kizer. Copyright © 1984 by Carolyn Kizer. Reprinted by permission of Copper Canyon Press.

Etheridge Knight, "Hard Rock Returns to Prison from the Hospital for the Criminal Insane." From *Poems from Prison.* Reprint permission granted by Broadside Press, Hilda Ulet/Publisher.

Vincent Millay and Norma Millay Ellis. Reprinted by permission of Elizabeth Barnett, literary executor.

Yukio Mishima, "Patriotism." From *Death in Midsummer* by Yukio Mishima. Copyright © 1966 by New Directions Publishing Corporation. Reprinted by permission of New Directions Publishing Corporation.

Alberto Moravia, "The Chase." From *Una Cosa e Una Cosa* by Alberto Moravia. Copyright © 1967 Gruppo Editoriale Fabbri, Bompiani, Sonzogno, Etas SpA. Reprinted by permission of Gruppo Editoriale Fabbri, Bompiani, Sonzogno, Etas SpA.

Bharati Mukherjee, "Orbiting." From *The Middleman and Other Stories* by Bharati Mukherjee. Copyright © 1988 by Bharati Mukherjee. Used by permission of Grove Press, Inc. Reprinted by permission of Penguin Books Canada Limited.

Ogden Nash, "Very Like a Whale." From *Verses From 1929 On* by Ogden Nash. Copyright 1934 by The Curtis Publishing Company. Reprinted by permission of Little, Brown and Company.

Kathleen Norris, "The Ignominy of the Living." Reprinted by permission of *The New Yorker.*

Frank O'Connor, "My Oedipus Complex." From *Collected Stories* by Frank O'Connor. Copyright 1950 by Frank O'Connor. Reprinted by permission of Alfred A. Knopf, Inc. and Joan Daves Agency.

Sharon Olds, "Sex Without Love" and "The Victims." From *The Dead and the Living* by Sharon Olds. Copyright © 1983 by Sharon Olds. Reprinted by permission of Alfred A. Knopf, Inc.

Wilfred Owen, "Dulce et Decorum est." From *The Collected Poems of Wilfred Owen*, by Wilfred Owen. Copyright © 1963 by Chatto & Windus Ltd. Reprinted by permission of New Directions Publishing Corp.

Grace Paley, "A Conversation With My Father." From *Enormous Changes at the Last Minute* by Grace Paley. Copyright © 1972, 1974 by Grace Paley. Reprinted by permission of Alfred A. Knopf, Inc.

Molly Peacock, "Our Room." From *Raw Heaven* by Molly Peacock. Reprinted by permission of the author.

Molly Peacock, "Say You Love Me." From *Take Heart* by Molly Peacock. Copyright © 1989 by Molly Peacock. Reprinted by permission of Random House, Inc.

Luigi Pirandello, "War." From *The Medal and Other Stories* by Luigi Pirandello. Reprinted by permission of the Pirandello Estate and Toby Cole, agent © E.P. Dutton, NY 1932, 1967.

Sylvia Plath, "Daddy." From the *Collected Poems of Sylvia Plath*, edited by Ted Hughes. Copyright © 1963. Reprinted by permission of Harper Collins Publishers, Inc.

Dudley Randall, "Ballad of Birmingham." Reprint permission granted by Broadside Press. Hilda Ulet/Publisher.

John Crowe Ransom, "Bells for John Whiteside's Daughter." From *Selected Poems* by John Crowe Ransom. Copyright 1924 by Alfred A. Knopf, Inc. and renewed 1952 by John Crowe Ransom. Reprinted by permission of the publisher.

Henry Reed, "Naming of Parts." From *Collected Poems*, ed. by Jon Stallworthy (1991). Reprint permission granted by © The Executor of Henry Reed's Estate 1991. Reprinted by permission of Oxford University Press.

Alastair Reid, "Curiosity." From *Weathering* (Dutton) © 1959 Alastair Reid. Originally published in *The New Yorker.*

Otto Reinert, Notes on Shakespeare's *Othello.* Copyright 1964. Reprinted by permission of the author.

Adrienne Rich, "Living in Sin." From *The Fact of a Doorframe* by **Adrienne Rich.** Reprinted by permission of W. W. Norton & Company, Inc. Copyright © 1984 by Adrienne Rich. Copyright © 1975, 1978 by W. W. Norton & Company Inc. Copyright © 1981 by Adrienne Rich.

Alberto Rios, "Teodoro Luna's Two Kisses." From *Teodoro Luna's Two Kisses* by Alberto Rios. Reprinted by permission of W. W. Norton & Company, Inc. Copyright © 1990 by Alberto Rios.

Theodore Roethke, "My Papa's Waltz," "Elegy for Jane," "I Knew a Woman." From *The Collected Poems of Theodore Roethke* by Theodore Roethke. "My Papa's Waltz," copyright 1942 by Hearst Magazines, Inc. "Elegy for Jane," copyright 1950 by Theodore Roethke. "I Knew a Woman," copyright 1954 by Theodore Roethke. Used by permission of Doubleday, a division of Bantam Doubleday Dell Publishing Group, Inc.

Muriel Rukeyser, "Myth." From *Out of Silence*, copyright, William L. Rukeyser, 1992, Triquarterly Books, Evanston, IL. Reprinted by permission of William L. Rukeyser.

Sappho, "With his Venom." *Sappho: A New Translation* by Mary Barnard. Copyright © 1958

The Regents of the University of California; © renewed 1984 Mary Barnard. Reprinted by permission of the University of California Press.

Jean-Paul Sartre, "No Exit." From *No Exit and The Flies* by Jean-**Paul Sartre,** trans. S. Gilbert. Copyright 1946 by Stuart Gilbert. Copyright renewed 1974, 1975 by Maris Agnes Mathilde Gilbert. Reprinted by permission of Alfred A. Knopf, Inc. Canadian rights: "In Camera" from *Huis Clos* by Jean-Paul Sartre. Translated by Stuart Gilbert (Hamish Hamilton, 1946). Translation Copyright © Stuart Gilbert, 1946. Reprinted by permission of Hamish Hamilton Ltd.

Gjertrud Schnackenberg, "Complaint." From *The Lamplit Answer* by Gjertrud Schnackenberg. Copyright © 1982, 1985 by Gjertrud Schnackenberg. Reprinted by permission of Farrar, Straus & Giroux, Inc.

Anne Sexton, "Cinderella." From *Transformations* by Anne Sexton. Copyright © 1971 by Anne Sexton. Reprinted by permission of Houghton Mifflin Company. All rights reserved.

Anne Sexton, "The Farmer's Wife." From *To Bedlam and Part Way Back* by Anne Sexton. Copyright © 1960 by Anne Sexton. Reprinted by permission of Houghton Mifflin Company. All rights reserved.

Bernard Shaw, *Major Barbara.* Reprinted by permission of The Society of Authors on behalf of the Estate of Bernard Shaw.

Irwin Shaw, "The Girls in Their Summer Dresses." Reprinted by permission of the Irwin Shaw Literary Estate.

Stevie Smith, "Not Waving but Drowning" and "To Carry the Child." From *The Collected Poems of Stevie Smith* by Stevie Smith. Copyright © 1972 by Stevie Smith. Reprinted by permission of New Directions Publishing Company.

W. D. Snodgrass, "April Inventory." From *Heart's Needle* by W. D. Snodgrass. Copyright © 1959 by William D. Snodgrass. Reprinted by permission of Alfred A. Knopf, Inc.

Sophocles, *The Antigone of Sophocles: An English Version* translated by Dudley Fitts and Robert Fitzgerald. Copyright 1939 by Harcourt Brace Jovanovich, Inc. and renewed 1967 by Dudley Fitts and Robert Fitzgerald. Reprinted by permission of the publisher.

CAUTION: All rights, including professional, amateur, motion picture, recitation, lecturing, performance, public reading, radio broadcasting, and television are strictly reserved. Inquiries on all rights should be addressed to Harcourt Brace Jovanovich, Inc., Permissions Department, Orlando, FL 32887.

Sophocles, *Oedipus Rex.* From *The Oedipus Rex of Sophocles: An English Version* by Dudley Fitts and Robert Fitzgerald, copyright 1949 by Harcourt, Brace, Jovanovich, Inc. and renewed by Cornelia Fitts and Robert Fitzgerald, reprinted by permission of the publisher.

CAUTION: All rights, including professional, amateur, motion picture, recitation, lecturing, public reading, radio broadcasting, and television are strictly reserved. Inquiries on all rights should be addressed to Harcourt Brace Jovanovich, Inc., Permissions Department, Orlando, FL 32887.

Helen Sorrells, "From a Correct Address in a Suburb of a Major City." From *Seeds as They Fall* by Helen Sorrells. Published by Vanderbilt University Press, 1971. Reprinted by permission of Vanderbilt University Press.

Art Spiegelman, "Prisoner on the Hell Planet." From *Maus: A Survivor's Tale* by Art Spiegelman. Copyright © 1973, 1980, 1981, 1982, 1983, 1984, 1985, 1986 by Art Spiegelman. Reprinted by permission of Pantheon Books, a division of Random House, Inc.

Wallace Stevens, "Peter Quince at the Clavier," "Sunday Morning," and "Thirteen Ways of Looking at a Blackbird." From *Collected Poems* by Wallace Stevens. Copyright 1923 and renewed 1951 by Wallace Stevens. Reprinted by permission of Alfred A. Knopf, Inc.

Dylan Thomas, "Do Not Go Gentle Into That Good Night," "Fern Hill." From *The Poems of Dylan Thomas,* copyright 1945 by The Trustees for the Copyrights of Dylan Thomas, 1952 by Dylan Thomas. Reprinted by permission of New Directions Publishing Corporation and David Hingham Associates.

James Thurber, "The Greatest Man in the World." Copyright 1935 James Thurber. Copyright 1963 Helen W. Thurber and Rosemary A. Thurber. From *The Middle-Aged Man on the Flying Trapeze,* published by Harper & Row.

Jean Toomer, "Theater." Reprinted from *Cane* by Jean Toomer, by permission of Liveright Publishing Corporation. Copyright © 1923 by Boni & Liveright. Copyright renewed 1951 by Jean Toomer.

Alice Walker, "Everyday Use." From *In Love & Trouble: Stories of Black Women* copyright © 1973 by Alice Walker. Reprinted by permission of Harcourt Brace Jovanovich, Inc.

Robert Wallace, "In a Spring Still Not Written of." Copyright © 1965 by Robert Wallace. Reprinted by permission of the author.

Kathleen K. Wiegner, "At Times." From *Country Western Breakdown* by Kathleen K. Wiegner. Published by Crossing Press 1974 under the title "Hard Mornings (1). Copyright 1974 by Kathleen Wiegner.

E. B. White, "The Second Tree from the Corner." From *The Second Tree from the Corner* by E.B. White. Copyright 1947 by E. B. White. Reprinted by permission of HarperCollins Publishers Inc.

Richard Wilbur, "A Late Aubade." From *Walking to Sleep: New Poems and Translations*, by Richard Wilbur. Copyright © 1968 by Richard Wilbur. Reprinted by permission of Harcourt Brace Jovanovich, Inc.

William Carlos Williams, "Tract." From *The Collected Poems of William Carlos Williams, 1909–1939, vol. I.* Copyright 1938 by New Directions Publishing Corporation. Reprinted by permission of New Directions Publishing Corporation.

Richard Wright, "Between the World and Me" by Richard Wright. Reprinted by permission of Ellen Wright.

Richard Wright, "The Man Who Lived Underground." From the book *Eight Men* by Richard Wright. Copyright © 1987 by the Estate of Richard Wright. Used by permission of the publisher, Thunder's Mouth Press, and of John Hawkins & Associates.

Yevgeny Yevtushenko, "I Would Like." From *Selected Poems* of Yevgeny Yevtushenko edited by Albert C. Todd. Copyright © 1991 by Henry Holt and Co., Inc. Reprinted by permission of Henry Holt and Co., Inc.

Yevgeny Yevtushenko, "People." From *Selected Poems* by Yevgeny Yevtushenko. Translated by Robin Milner-Gulland and Peter Levi, (Penguin Books, 1962). Copyright © Robin Milner-Gulland and Peter Levi, 1962. Reprinted by permission of Penguin Books Ltd.

PICTURE CREDITS

Innocence and Experience

Part Opener, p. 2–3: *The Garden of Peaceful Arts* (Allegory of the Court of Isabelle d'Este), ca. 1530 by Lorenzo Costa. The Louvre, Paris. Photograph, Bridgeman/Art Resource.

Fiction, p. 6: *Woman and Child on a Beach,* ca. 1901 by Pablo Picasso. Private collection. Photograph, Bridgeman/Art Resource. © 1989 ARS NY / SPADEM.

Poetry, p. 80: *Il castello di carte* (The House of Cards) by Zinaida Serebriakova. Scala/Art Resource, NY.

Drama, p. 130: *Belisarius and the Boy,* 1802 by Benjamin West. Oil on canvas, 67 × 48 cm. © The Detroit Institute of Arts, Gift of A. Leonard Nicholson.

Conformity and Rebellion

Part Opener, p. 320–321: *Le Ventre Legislatif,* 1834 by Honore Daumier. Lithograph. Art Resource, NY.

Fiction, p. 324: *The Trial,* 1950 by Keith Vaughan. Worthing Museum and Art Gallery, England.

Poetry, p. 458: *Adam and Eve,* Sistine Chapel (photograph of restored figures). © Nippon Television Network Corporation, Tokyo, 1991.

Drama, p. 502: *Self Portrait,* ca. 1900–1905 by Gwen John. National Portrait Gallery, London.

Love and Hate

Part Opener, p. 622: *Mr. and Mrs. Clark and Percy,* 1970–1971 by David Hockney. The Tate Gallery, London/Art Resource, NY.

Fiction, p. 626: *A Husband Parting From His Wife and Child.* 1799 by William Blake. Pen and watercolor on paper, 11⅞ × 8⅞". '64-110-3, Philadelphia Museum of Art: Given by Mrs. William T. Tonner.

Poetry, p. 716: *La fontana della giovinezza, Eroe e Eroina,* (partial), 15th century by Giacomo Jaquerio. Scala/Art Resource, NY.

Drama, p. 778: *Judith and Her Maidservant with the Head of Holofernes*, ca. 1625 by Artemisia Gentileschi. Oil on canvas, 72½ × 55¾" (185.2 × 141.6 cm). © The Detroit Institute of the Arts. Gift of Mr. Leslie H. Green.

The Presence of Death

Part opener, pp. 970–971: *Dream of a Sunday Afternoon in the Alameda*, (detail), 1947–1948 by Diego Rivera. Schalkwijk/AMI/Art Resource, NY.
Fiction, p. 976: *The Dead Mother* by Edvard Munch. Marburg/Art Resource, NY.
Poetry, p. 1092: *Knight, Death, and the Devil*, 1513 by Albrect Durer. Engraving. Art Resource, NY.
P. 1135: *Landscape with the Fall of Icarus*, c. 1560 by Pieter Brueghel the Elder. Museum of Fine Arts, Brussels. Photograph, Art Resource, New York.
Drama, p. 1154: *Tombstones*, 1942 by Jacob Lawrence. Gouache, 29 × 20¾". Collection of Whitney Museum of American Art.

Appendices

Opening, p. 1232: *The Librarian*, 1566 by G. Arcimboldo. Skoklosters Slott, Stockholm.
Pp. 1262–1263: *The Globe Theatre; Interior of the Globe Theatre in the days of Shakespeare;* and *A French theater during Molier's management:* Courtesy of the Bettmann Archive, Inc. *Interior of the Swan Theatre*, London: Courtesy of Culver Pictures. *The Greek theater at Epidaurus:* Courtesy of the Greek National Tourist Office.

INDEX OF AUTHORS AND TITLES